APPLY SOCIOLOGICAL CONCEPTS TO EVERYDAY LIFE!

George Ritzer, one of Sociology's best-known thinkers, explains traditional sociological concepts and theories and some of the most compelling contemporary social phenomena, including globalization, consumer culture, the internet, and the "McDonaldization" of society.

KEEP YOUR COURSE CURRENT!

- **The most up-to-date** events, examples, research findings, and sociological data available

- *Trending* boxes highlight influential sociology books that have become a part of public conversation about important issues, such as Michelle Alexander's *The New Jim Crow* and Arlie Hochschild's *Strangers in Their Own Land*

- *Globalization* boxes expose students to cultures and communities beyond the United States, providing insight into the increasingly interconnected world that we live in

- *Digital Living* boxes help students recognize how their everyday lives are influenced by mass media, the internet, and social media

- The *Ask Yourself* marginal feature invites students to apply sociological concepts to their everyday life

- *Checkpoints* throughout the chapters offer a recap of major topics in each section

TRENDING

Pray the Gay Away: The Extraordinary Lives of Bible Belt Gays (New York University Press, 2012)

Bernadette Barton (Professor of Sociology and Women's Studies at Morehead State University; PhD, University of Kentucky, 2000)

In *Pray the Gay Away*, Bernadette Barton describes how homophobic attitudes of fundamentalist Christians are entrenched not just in religious institutions, but in families, workplaces, schools, politics, and social networks in the Bible Belt. Evangelical fundamentalists consider the Bible to be a source of authority and practice "witnessing," or spreading the word of Christ at every opportunity they can find, such as while standing in line at a grocery store or by placing religious flyers on a neighbor's doormat (2012, 2, 10). Bible Belt Christians often begin a conversation with what might seem like a relatively benign question: "What church do you belong to?" But Barton discovers that the answer to this question reinforces a form of "compulsory Christianity" that positions a person's Christian identity at the center of daily social interactions (2012, 4). Political and cultural ideologies are conveyed through identifying as a Bible Belt Christian, especially when it comes to sexual orientation. Regardless of denomination, Bible Belt Christians believe that homosexuality is sinful and contrary to the teachings of Jesus.

As a lesbian living (but not raised) in the Bible Belt of eastern Kentucky, Barton's encounters with Bible Belt Christians made her curious about the experiences of gay men and lesbians who grew up there. Using a variety of qualitative methodological techniques, including participant observations and interviews with 59 gay men and lesbians in Kentucky and Texas, Barton learned that most were forced to live in a "toxic closet" and hide their homosexuality or "risk rejection and ostracism" from their families and friends (2012, 5). Because they were taught that same-sex attraction is a sin, many literally tried to pray their gay away at their churches. The shame that many feel living in their toxic closets is amplified by having to confront compulsory Christianity on a daily basis. Barton likens this to living in a prison where gay men and lesbians are forced to monitor their daily lives for signs of Christian identity, such as a person wearing a fish belt buckle or a scripture printed on a store receipt. Such objects signify their social exclusion and alert them as to whether they should disclose their sexual identity (2012, 23).

Supplementary Resources
- You can watch a short clip of Bernadette Barton describing her book *Pray the Gay Away* at www.youtube.com/watch?v=sb4D62KQKoI.
- Learn more about the controversy surrounding praying away homosexuality in this episode of Dr. Drew's show that aired on HLN: www.youtube.com/watch?v=ES5OnnB5KCk.

SAGE PREMIUM VIDEO

Men 2.1 hours per day

Women 2.6 hours per day

Boost comprehension. Bolster analysis.

SAGE premium video helps your students do both. Easy access with an **Interactive eBook!**

Introduction to Sociology, **Fourth Edition, by George Ritzer** offers premium video, curated specifically for the text, to make learning more effective for all types of students. Access the videos through an Interactive eBook (when purchased with a new copy of the text) and go way beyond highlighting and note-taking.

UP-TO-DATE COVERAGE!

WHAT'S NEW

- Apply sociological thinking to **the latest developments on contemporary issues,** such as

  - the 2016 U.S. presidential election

  - Brexit

  - climate change

  - fourth-wave feminism

  - further segmentation of wealthy Americans in the "super rich" category

  - the global growth of the so-called Islamic State

  - the legalization of marijuana

  - transgender people in the U.S. armed forces

DIGITAL LIVING

Stratification in the New Sharing Economy

In the sharing economy, instead of buying or renting in the usual ways, we share goods and services—at low cost or free of charge—with others (Gansky 2010; Stein 2015). Instead of renting a hotel room, we can get a room in a private home, or even an entire home, through the online site Airbnb. Instead of hailing a taxi, we can use Uber's smartphone app and get a prepaid ride in a private automobile. Instead of waiting for a table at a "hot" restaurant, we can hire someone online to do so through TaskRabbit.

The sharing economy is clearly the wave of the future. But while some sharing is free of profit making and the exchange of money (Atsushi 2014), big businesses have become deeply engaged, and the sharing economy is growing highly stratified.

At the top are the founders, executives, and financiers of the most successful companies. Uber is now valued at about $68 billion (Austin, Canipe, and Slobin 2015), and its founders are likely to be millionaires or even billionaires. But for most of the drivers, the job is part-time and the pay low. Drivers use their own cars, pay their own expenses, and lack benefits and job security. As a result, they are likely to land in or near the lower class. Worse, their success is costing traditional taxi drivers their jobs. Uber cars now outnumber yellow taxis in New York City by more than three to one (Hu 2017; Pramuk 2015).

Airbnb, valued at about $25 billion, has created a similar stratification system, with founders and executives on top and many who list their apartments and homes nearer the bottom. However,

few of those participants are actually individuals sharing space with others. While New York City is attempting to crack down on this, commercial operators there supply more than one-third of Airbnb rental units and earn more than one-third of the profits; 6 percent of the hosts earned 37 percent of the revenue, and one had 272 units, earning revenue of $6.8 million. Some critics argue that, at least in this case, "the very term 'sharing economy' is ridiculous" (Austin, Canipe, and Slboin 2015; Streitfeld 2014, A1).

Belk (2014) argues that in all these cases and many others, sharing is being transformed into "pseudo-sharing" by, among others, profit-making organizations that have found this to be a way

to grow rich. As Ritzer (2017) puts it, there is "woefully little sharing" in the sharing economy. The sharing economy is creating a new stratification system, or at least new positions in the current system. Many people will be at or near the bottom.

Engaging the Digital World
Do you think that the stratification taking place in the sharing economy is inevitable? Why or why not? Should consumers avoid participating in this economy, even if the services offered are desirable and affordable? Why or why not? If you participate in the sharing economy, explain what types of services you use (or provide) most often and what the alternatives would be to each of them.

Smartphone apps, such as those of Uber and Airbnb, create a divide between those who control the sharing economy and those who work in it. Is such increased stratification inevitable?

SOCIALIZATION AND INTERACTION

⑤

Socialization and Variance

Mack Beggs won his weight class in the Texas state wrestling championships in February 2017—in the girls' league. Mack is a 17-year-old transgender boy, but state rules bar him from competing in the boys' league. The rules say that boys cannot compete against girls, and that students are required to compete as the gender noted on their birth certificate. After Beggs' final competition in an undefeated season, the crowd erupted in both cheers and boos.

Beggs, who began transitioning a year and a half prior to the championship, has been taking testosterone as part of that process. Some felt that he shouldn't have been competing against girls, because the added testosterone gave him an unfair advantage. A few parents even attempted legal injunctions to prevent Beggs from competing. Ignoring the controversy, Beggs credited his success to his teammates, noting that they all worked hard together. While the public, schools, and politicians debate the fluidity of gender, transgender students like Beggs face pressure to fit in with the social expectations of their peers, their families, and the wider world—and the repercussions when they don't.

The majority of transgender students from kindergarten through twelfth grade who are out or perceived as transgender while in school experience some form of mistreatment. In 2015, 54 percent acknowledged being verbally harassed, 24 percent said they had been physically attacked, and 13 percent were sexually assaulted because they were transgender. Some (17 percent) experienced such severe treatment that they left school (James et al. 2016). Such mistreatment due to gender identity or expression is not restricted to peers and schools, but may also pervade family and work life. Transgender people have an attempted suicide rate nine times that of the general U.S. population.

LEARNING OBJECTIVES

5.1 Describe the development of the self.

5.2 Discuss the concept of the individual as performer.

5.3 Explain the significance of socialization in childhood and adulthood.

5.4 Describe the key aspects of interaction with others.

5.5 Identify micro-level social structures.

edge.sagepub.com/ritzerintro4e
- Take the chapter quiz.
- Review key terms with eFlashcards
- Explore multimedia links and SAGE readings.

⊜SAGE edge™

113

- **Updated *Digital Living*** boxes provide new coverage of bitcoin, cyberactivism, digital privacy, net neutrality, Uber, WikiLeaks, and more.

INTERACT WITH SOCIOLOGY THROUGH DIGITAL RESOURCES!

CAPTURE YOUR STUDENTS' ATTENTION WITH COMPELLING ACTIVITIES

- Engage your students with carefully selected, **peer-reviewed teaching resources from ASA's TRAILS**

- Access the **Interactive eBook** through a bundle with a new print book to open up these resources and more:

  - Read the book **ANYWHERE, ANYTIME** with easy access across most devices

  - **SHARE** notes and highlights

  - **WATCH SAGE ORIGINAL CONCEPT VIDEOS** to bring clarity to difficult concepts

  - **CONNECT** to real-life events with curated AP News clips

  - **LISTEN** to engaging **AUDIO** resources

- Through **SAGE coursepacks**, it's easy to import our quality instructor and student resource content into your school's learning management system (LMS). Learn more at **sagepub.com/coursepacks**.

$SAGE coursepacks

Our Content Tailored to Your LMS

Instructors! **SAGE coursepacks** makes it easy to import our quality instructor and student resource content into your school's learning management system (LMS). Intuitive and simple to use, SAGE coursepacks allows you to customize course content to meet your students' needs. Learn more at **sagepub.com/coursepacks**.

Introduction to Sociology

Fourth Edition

Introduction to Sociology
Fourth Edition

George Ritzer
University of Maryland

Los Angeles | London | New Delhi
Singapore | Washington DC | Melbourne

FOR INFORMATION:

SAGE Publications, Inc.
2455 Teller Road
Thousand Oaks, California 91320
E-mail: order@sagepub.com

SAGE Publications Ltd.
1 Oliver's Yard
55 City Road
London EC1Y 1SP
United Kingdom

SAGE Publications India Pvt. Ltd.
B 1/I 1 Mohan Cooperative Industrial Area
Mathura Road, New Delhi 110 044
India

SAGE Publications Asia-Pacific Pte. Ltd.
3 Church Street
#10-04 Samsung Hub
Singapore 049483

Printed in Canada

Library of Congress Cataloging-in-Publication Data

Names: Ritzer, George, author.

Title: Introduction to sociology / George Ritzer, University of Maryland.

Description: Fourth edition. | Thousand Oaks, California : Sage, [2018] | Includes bibliographical references and index.

Identifiers: LCCN 2017014666 | ISBN 9781506362670 (pbk. : alk. paper)

Subjects: LCSH: Sociology.

Classification: LCC HM585 .R568 2018 | DDC 301—dc23
LC record available at https://lccn.loc.gov/2017014666

Acquisitions Editor: Jeff Lasser
Content Development Manager: Nancy Matuszak
Editorial Assistant: Adeline Wilson
Marketing Manager: Kara Kindstrom
Production Editor: Veronica Stapleton Hooper
Copy Editor: Laureen Gleason
Typesetter: C&M Digitals (P) Ltd.
Proofreader: Alison Syring
Indexer: Jean Casalegno
Cover Designer: Scott Van Atta

BRIEF CONTENTS

DETAILED CONTENTS

ORGANIZATIONS, SOCIETIES, AND GLOBAL RELATIONSHIPS   141

7   DEVIANCE AND CRIME   171

 **GENDER AND SEXUALITY   291**

 FAMILIES   323

17 POPULATION, URBANIZATION, AND THE ENVIRONMENT   471

18 SOCIAL CHANGE, SOCIAL MOVEMENTS, AND COLLECTIVE ACTION   505

LETTER FROM THE AUTHOR

To me, the social world, as well as the field of sociology that studies that world, is always interesting, exciting, and ever-changing. My goal in this newly revised fourth edition of *Introduction to Sociology* is not only to introduce *you*, the student, to sociology, but also to discuss what has made sociology my lifelong passion. My hope is that readers of this text learn a good deal about the social world from the perspective of sociology, as well as get at least a sense of why I am so passionate about it. Please let me explain how this book is, in many ways, an expression of that passion as well as of my personal sociological journey.

My initial interests in the field were the sociology of work and of organizations, but I was quickly drawn to sociological theory and how even the most classical theories were relevant to, and at play in, my everyday life—and yours. This interest came to fruition in the publication of *The McDonaldization of Society* in 1993 (the eighth edition of that book was published in 2015, and a ninth edition will be published in 2018). In that book, I apply and expand upon the famous classic theoretical ideas of Max Weber on rationality. I saw those ideas at work in my local fast-food restaurant, as well as in many other contemporary settings. The major themes addressed in *The McDonaldization of Society* are prominent in this textbook.

After the publication of *The McDonaldization of Society*, my thinking and research moved in many related and interesting directions, and these interests are manifest throughout this text. I grew very interested in the sociology of consumption and, more specifically, was drawn to the study of credit cards, which inspired *Expressing America: A Critique of the Global Credit Card Society*. I was surprised by the number of my undergraduate students who carried one or more credit cards. I was also distressed by their fears of growing indebtedness (in hindsight perhaps a harbinger of the Great Recession). Also in the area of consumption, I authored *Enchanting a Disenchanted World: Continuity and Change in the Cathedrals of Consumption*. Shopping malls, theme parks such as Disney World, Las Vegas–style casinos, and cruise ships are all "cathedrals of consumption," which lure consumers and lead them to overspend and to go deeply into debt.

Later, as I reflected on my research on fast-food restaurants, credit cards, and cathedrals of consumption, I was drawn to a fascinating newly emerging area of sociology—globalization. This led me to write *The Globalization of Nothing* and *Globalization: A Basic Text*. I realized that all of the phenomena of interest to me had been pioneered in the United States but had spread rapidly throughout much of the world. Accordingly, this book includes a strong emphasis on globalization, with the hope that students will better understand that process and better appreciate their roles within our increasingly globalized world.

Most recently, my sociological journey has led me to the internet, especially social networking sites such as Facebook, Twitter, and Pinterest. Internet sites are highly rationalized (or "McDonaldized"), are often places to consume (e.g., eBay, Amazon), and are all globalized (Facebook alone has almost 2 billion users throughout the world). Throughout this book—in boxes headed "Digital Living" and in the narrative—the sociological implications of the internet are discussed and explained; there is much in this topic for students to contemplate. Most of my work over the last decade has been on "prosumption," the process that combines production and consumption. This is especially prominent on the internet where, for example, we consume others' comments on Facebook and in tweets and produce our own comments.

The above describes much of my personal sociological journey. I hope that this book will provide *you* with a starting point to begin your own personal sociological journey, to examine your social world critically, and to develop your own sociological ideas and opinions. It is my hope that this book better equips you to see the social world in a different way and, more important, to use the ideas discussed here to help create a better world.

George Ritzer
University of Maryland
September 2017

To Sue: With much love for enduring, mostly with her usual good humor intact,
all the years I was often unavailable while writing this book

Sara Miller McCune founded SAGE Publishing in 1965 to support the dissemination of usable knowledge and educate a global community. SAGE publishes more than 1000 journals and over 800 new books each year, spanning a wide range of subject areas. Our growing selection of library products includes archives, data, case studies and video. SAGE remains majority owned by our founder and after her lifetime will become owned by a charitable trust that secures the company's continued independence.

Los Angeles | London | New Delhi | Singapore | Washington DC | Melbourne

ACKNOWLEDGMENTS

I need to begin with my friends for decades, and coauthors of a previous introductory textbook, Kenneth C. W. Kammeyer and Norman R. Yetman. That book went through seven editions, the last of which was published in 1997. It was most useful to me in this text in helping define various sociological concepts that have changed little over the years. I have also been able to build on discussions of many issues covered in that text. However, because of the passage of almost two decades in sociology and in the social world (an eternity in both), as well as the innumerable changes in them, this text has comparatively little in common with the earlier one. Nonetheless, my perspective on sociology was strongly shaped by that book and the many insights and ideas provided by my friends and coauthors before, during, and in the many years after the writing of that book.

Professor Rebecca Plante played a key role in the third edition of this book. She offered useful comments and suggestions throughout, and she was especially central in the revision of Chapter 11, on gender and sexuality. These are her areas of expertise, and the chapter is much improved because of her contributions to it. I would also like to thank Professor Paul Dean, coauthor of the second edition of my book *Globalization: A Basic Text,* for his numerous and important contributions to Chapter 8, on social stratification in the United States, and especially to Chapter 9, on global stratification.

Wendy Wiedenhoft Murphy took on huge responsibility for this, the fourth edition, and her contributions are to be found throughout this edition. Especially notable is her work reviewing and revising all boxes, as well as pedagogical features, end-of-chapter material, and data. Wendy played a key role in the creation of new content for boxes, particularly the "Trending" feature that makes its debut in this edition. I have been so impressed with her work that she will be brought on a coauthor of the forthcoming third edition of *Essentials of Sociology.*

Thanks also to P. J. Rey, William Yagatich, Jillet Sam, Zeynep Tufekci, and Margaret Austin Smith for their contributions. Also to be thanked for writing first drafts of parts of earlier versions of chapters are Professors William Carbonaro (Chapter 13, on education), Deric Shannon (Chapter 15, on politics), and Lester Kurtz (Chapter 14, on religion). Professor Peter Kivisto made particularly important and numerous contributions to the second edition of this book. I'm especially thankful for his work on the religion and education chapters.

At SAGE Publications, I am especially grateful for Senior Vice President Michele Sordi's confidence in, and support for, the project. She agreed from the beginning to do and spend whatever was necessary to make this a first-class introductory sociology text. As you can see from the finished project, she was true to her word. Michele also worked closely with me in an editorial capacity on the first edition to help get the project through some of its most difficult periods. Michele was a positive force and upbeat presence throughout the writing of this book, and I am deeply grateful for who she is and what she has done. Brenda Carter took over Michele's role for the second edition and performed it with the same level of expertise, good humor, and good sense (plus she got me prime seats to a game in New York involving my beloved Yankees). Jeff Lasser came on board at SAGE as sociology publisher during production of the second edition. He played a key role in it and has played a much more important role in the third and fourth editions. Jeff has proven to be not only easy to work with but a sage (pun intended) adviser on many aspects of the book and its publication. Unfortunately, he is a Boston Red Sox fan, but nobody is perfect.

I also need to thank Nathan Davidson at SAGE. The production of the first edition of this book really took off when he took over its day-to-day management. We worked together closely for about a year on virtually every aspect of the final project. Before Nathan came on board, I was in danger of being overwhelmed by the demands of finishing this book, but he provided the hard work, great organizational abilities, and good sense that helped me complete it—and on time. Nathan continued to manage the second and third editions of this book and, if possible, he has done an even better job with each one. While his imprint is found throughout this book, it is especially notable in the selection of an excellent set of photographs.

Nancy Matuszak took over from Nathan as the developmental editor for the fourth edition of this book. She has been amazing, demonstrating great competence, good sense, and a great sense of humor (much needed in dealing with me). She has managed the myriad details associated with a revision of a book of this magnitude with great aplomb. I would like to see her named "Developmental Editor for Life," but I suspect she has bigger plans and wider horizons.

To be thanked for her work on the second and third editions is Elisa Adams, who, first as a consultant and later as developmental editor, was instrumental in editing the entire book as well as helping create various features of the book. Sheri Gilbert is to be thanked for her work on the many permissions needed for material included in this edition, as well as the last. Scott Van Atta did great work on the cover for the fourth edition of this book. Thanks to Gabrielle Piccininni, digital content editor, for her work on the ancillary materials and e-book resources. Many thanks also to Adeline Wilson, editorial assistant, who held steady oversight over all of the small details needed to get this book into production. Thanks also to Veronica Stapleton Hooper, who amiably and capably managed the production of this book, as well as to Laureen Gleason, who capably handled the copyediting. Laureen also proved to be quite an expert on popular culture and contributed insights on that topic throughout the book.

I am particularly grateful to the following reviewers, who provided enormously helpful feedback for this edition:

Miguel Centellas, University of Mississicppi

James A. Curiel, Norfolk State University

Barry D. Kass, S.U.N.Y. Orange

Gary Maynard, University of Michigan at Flint

Lori Park-Smith, Ridgewater College

I'm also grateful to the following reviewers, advisory board members, and class testers who provided feedback for the previous editions. For the third edition: Paul Almeida, University of California, Merced; Cari Beecham-Bautista, Columbia College Chicago; Lynn G. Chin, Washington and Lee University; Jessica L. Collett, University of Notre Dame; Linda S. Cook, Houston Community College; Denise N. Cook, University of Nevada, Las Vegas; Irene J. Dabrowski, St. John's University; Regina Davis-Sowers, Santa Clara University; Michaela DeSoucey, North Carolina State University; Colleen P. Eren, City University of New York; Kimberly E. Fox, Bridgewater State University; Paul S. Gray, Boston College; Geoff Harkness, Morningside College; Aimee E. Huard, Nashua Community College; Joy Inouye, College of DuPage; Gary Jones, University of Winchester; Joachim S. Kibirige, Missouri Western State University; Heather Mooney, Eastern Michigan University; Kaitlyne A. Motl, University of Kentucky; Jennifer J. Reed, University of Nevada, Las Vegas; Michael A. Robinson, East Carolina University; Eric Tranby, University of Delaware; Catherine

Turcotte, Colby-Sawyer College; Okori Uneke, Winston Salem State University; Dennis L. Veleber, University of Great Falls; Heidi M. Williams, University of Louisville.

For the second edition: Augustine Aryee, Fitchburg State College; William Danaher, College of Charleston; Colleen Eren, Hunter College; Tammie Foltz, Des Moines Area Community College; Laura Gibson, Brescia University; Edward Glick, Des Moines Area Community College; Colin Goff, University of Winnipeg; Kristi Hagen, Coconino Community College; Marta Henrikson, Central New Mexico Community College; Hanna Jokinen-Gordon, Florida State University; Alan Kemp, Pierce College; Lloyd Klein, CUNY York College; Ke Liang, Baruch College; Wade Luquet, Gwynedd-Mercy College; Kim MacInnis, Bridgewater State College; Mahgoub Mahmoud, Tennessee State University–Nashville; Setsuko Matsuzawa, College of Wooster; Christine McClure, Cape Cod Community College; Hosik Min, Norwich University; Gail Mosby, West Virginia State University; Megan Nielsen, Midland Lutheran College; Nirmal Niroula, Franklin University; David O'Donnell, Vermilion Community College; Godpower Okereke, Texas A&M University–Texarkana; Dan Poole, Salt Lake Community College; Teresa Roach, Florida State University; Desireé Robertson, Mid South Community College; Amy Ruedisueli, Tidewater Community College; Luceal Simon, Wayne State University; Nicolas Simon, Eastern Connecticut State University; Rhianan Smith, Carroll College; Jennifer Solomon, Winthrop University; Paul Sturgis, Truman State University; Daniel Suh, Orange Coast College; Mary Texeira, California State University–San Bernardino; Miriam Thompson, Northwest Vista College; Okori Uneke, Winston-Salem State University; Paul Van Auken, University of Wisconsin–Oshkosh; Jonathan Van Wieren, Grand Valley State University; John Vlot, Lehigh Carbon Community College; Russell Ward, Maysville Community Tech College; Matthew Vox, Covenant College; Bernadette White, Ohlone College; Matthew Wilkinson, Coastal Carolina University; George Wilson, University of Miami; Melisa Wingfield, Wichita Area Tech College; Elizabeth Wissinger, Borough Manhattan Community College; Robert Wonser, College of the Canyons; Susan Wortmann, Nebraska Wesleyan University.

For the first edition: Sophia Krzys Acord, University of Florida; Kristian Alexander, University of Utah; Lori J. Anderson, Tarleton State University; Lester Andrist, University of Maryland; Meg Austin Smith, University of Maryland; Denise Bielby, University of California, Santa Barbara; Donna Bird, University of Southern Maine; David Daniel Bogumil, California State University, Northridge; Craig Boylstein, Coastal Carolina University; Yvonne Braun, University of Oregon; Robert Brenneman, Saint Michael's College; Rebecca Brooks, Ohio Northern University; Bradley Campbell, California State University,

Los Angeles; Brenda Chaney, Ohio State University, Marion; Langdon Clough, Community College of Rhode Island, Flan; Jessica Collett, University of Notre Dame; Keri Diggins, Scottsdale Community College; Scott Dolan, University at Albany–SUNY; Brenda Donelan, Northern State University; Gili Drori, Stanford University; Kathy Edwards, Ashland Community and Technical College; Pam Folk, North Hennepin Community College; Tammie Foltz, Des Moines Area Community College; Douglas Forbes, University of Wisconsin–Stevens Point; Sarah Michele Ford, Buffalo State College; S. Michael Gaddis, University of North Carolina, Chapel Hill; Deborah Gambs, Borough Manhattan, Community College–CUNY; Gilbert Geis, University of California, Irvine; Bethany Gizzi, Monroe Community College; Barry Goetz, Western Michigan University; Roberta Goldberg, Trinity Washington University; Elizabeth Grant, Chabot College; Kristi Hagen, Chippewa Valley Technical College; James Harris, Mountain View College; Cedric Herring, University of Illinois, Chicago; Joy Honea, Montana State University Billings; John C. Horgan, Concordia University–Wisconsin; Gabe Ignatow, University of North Texas; Mike Itashiki, Collin County Community College & University of North Texas; Wesley Jennings, University of South Florida; James R. Johnson, Southwest Indian Polytechnical Institute; Faye Jones, Mississippi Community College; Carolyn Kapinus, Ball State University; Mary Karpos, Vanderbilt University; Zeynep Kilic, University of Alaska, Anchorage; Jeanne Kimpel, Fordham University; Chuck Kusselow, River Valley Community College; Richard Lachmann, University at Albany–SUNY; Barbara LaPilusa, Montgomery College; Erin Leahey, University of Arizona; Maria Licuanan, Kent State University; John Lie, University of California, Berkeley; Cameron D. Lippard, Appalachian State University; David Lopez, California State University, Northridge; Jeanne M. Lorentzen, Northern Michigan University; Garvey Lundy, Montgomery County Community College; Aaron Major, University at Albany–SUNY; Vanessa Martinez, Holyoke Community College; Suzanne L. Maughan, University of Nebraska at Kearney; Patrick McGrady, Florida State University; Paul McLean, Rutgers University; Jeff Mullis, Emory University; Megan Nielsen, Midland University; Charles Norman, Indiana State University; Donna Philips, Bluegrass Community and Technical College; Alex Piquero, University of Texas, Dallas; Dwaine Plaza, Oregon State University; Winnie Poster, Washington University, Saint Louis; Malcolm Potter, Los Angeles Pierce College; Ekaterin Ralston, Concordia University, St. Paul; Rashawn Ray, University of California, Berkeley; P. J. Rey, University of Maryland; Adrienne Riegle, Iowa State University; David N. Sanders, Angelo State University; Mary Satian, Northern Virginia Community College; Dave Schall, Milwaukee Area Technical College; Elizabeth D. Scheel, St. Cloud State University; Jerald Schrimsher, Southern Illinois University, Carbondale; Sandra Schroer, Muskingum University; Howard Schuman, University of Michigan; Frank Scruggs, National-Louis University; Megan Seely, Sierra College; Vincent Serravallo, Rochester Institute of Technology; Mark Sherry, University of Toledo; Amber Shimel, Liberty University; Kristen Shorette, University of California, Irvine; Julia Spence, Johnson County Community College; Steven Stack, Wayne State University; Richard Sweeney, Modesto Junior College; Joyce Tang, CUNY Queens College; Rae Taylor, Loyola University New Orleans; Ha Thao, MiraCosta College; Santos Torres, California State University, Sacramento; Richard Tweksbury, University of Louisville; Mark Vermillion, Wichita State University; Russell Ward, Maysville Community and Technical College; Jeff Wilhelms, Rutgers University; Elizabeth Wissinger, Borough of Manhattan Community College; Rowan Wolf, Portland Community College; Susan Wortmann, Nebraska Wesleyan University; Kassia Wosick, New Mexico State University; Yuping Zhang, Lehigh University; Grace Auyang, University of Cincinnati, Raymond Walters College; Libby Barland, Lynn University; John Batsie, Parkland College; Cari Beecham, Columbia College, Chicago; Berch Berberoglu, University of Nevada, Reno; Miriam Boeri, Kennesaw State University; Ann Bullis, College of Southern Nevada; Josh Carreiro, University of Massachusetts; Susan Claxton, Georgia Highlands College; Evan Cooper, Farmingdale State College; Julie Cowgill, Oklahoma City University; David Embrick, Loyola University, Chicago; Heather Feldhaus, Bloomsburg University; Rosalind Fisher, University of West Florida; Karie Francis, University of Las Vegas, Nevada; Joshua Gamson, University of San Francisco; Robert Garot, John Jay College of Criminal Justice; Matthew Green, College of Dupage; Gary Heidinger, Roane State Community College; Marta Henriksen, Central New Mexico Community College; Anthony Hickey, Western Carolina University; Jeanne Humble, Bluegrass Community Technical College; Dai Ito, Georgia State University; Mike F. Jessup, Taylor University; Ellis Jones, Holy Cross University; Lloyd Klein, York College; Steve Lang, Laguardia Community College; Dongxiao Liu, Texas A&M University; Tara McKay, University of California, Los Angeles; Rohald Meneses, University of California, Pembroke; Eric Mielants, Fairfield University; Ami Moore, University of Northern Texas; Amanda Moras, Sacred Heart University; Brigitte Neary, University of South Carolina, Spartanburg; Michael O'Connor, Hawkeye Community College; Aurea Osgood, Winona State; Johanna Pabst, Boston College; Frank Roberts, Mount San Antonio College; Lauren Ross, Temple University; Janet Ruane, Montclair State University; Matthew Sargent, Madison Area Technical College; Lynn Schlesinger, SUNY College, Plattsburgh; Sarah Scruggs, Oklahoma City University; Meena Sharma,

Henry Ford Community College; Nicole Shortt, Florida Atlantic University, Boca; Chris Solario, Chemeketa Community College; William Staudenmeier, Eureka College; Kevin Sullivan, Bergen Community College; Donna Sullivan, Marshall University; Jaita Talukdar, Loyola University, New Orleans; Linda Treiber, Kennesaw State University; PJ Verrecchia, York College; Debra Welkley, California State University, Sacramento; Beau Weston, Centre College; George Wilson, University of Miami; Julie Withers, Butte College; Kassia Wosick-Correa, New Mexico State University; James Wright, Chattanooga Technical Community College; Paul Calarco, Hudson Valley Community College; Joyce Clapp, University of North Carolina, Greensboro; Tina Granger, Nicholls State University; Dan Gurash, Fairmont State University; Lee Hamilton, New Mexico State University; AJ Jacobs, East Carolina University; Barry Kass, Orange County Community College; Stacy Keogh, University of Montana; Crystal Lupo, Auburn University; Tiffany Parsons, University of West Georgia; Lindsey Prowell Myers, Ohio State University; Michael Steinhour, Purdue University; Sheryl Switaj, Schoolcraft College; Ruth Thompson-Miller, University of Dayton; Deanna Trella, Northern Michigan University; Kristie Vise, Northern Kentucky University; Wendy Wiedenhoft Murphy, John Carroll University; Jane Young, Luzerne County Community College.

ABOUT THE AUTHOR

George Ritzer is Distinguished University Professor at the University of Maryland. Among his awards are Honorary Doctorate from La Trobe University, Melbourne, Australia; Honorary Patron, University Philosophical Society, Trinity College, Dublin; American Sociological Association's Distinguished Contribution to Teaching Award; and being named the Eastern Sociological Society's Robin Williams Lecturer. He has chaired four sections of the American Sociological Association: Theoretical Sociology, Organizations and Occupations, Global and Transnational Sociology, and the History of Sociology. All of his theory texts, now coauthored with Jeff Stepnisky, have been, or soon will be, published by SAGE Publications. They are *Sociological Theory* (10th ed., 2018); *Modern Sociological Theory* (8th ed., 2018), and *Classical Sociological Theory* (7th ed., 2018); the 5th edition of *Contemporary Sociological Theory and Its Classical Roots: The Basics* is currently being revised for publication in 2019. In the application of social theory to the social world, Ritzer's books include *The McDonaldization of Society* (8th ed., 2015; 9th ed., forthcoming), *Enchanting a Disenchanted World* (3rd ed., 2010), and *The Globalization of Nothing* (2nd ed., 2007). He is the author of *Globalization: A Basic Text* (Blackwell, 2010; 2nd ed., 2015, with Paul Dean). He edited the *Wiley-Blackwell Companion to Sociology* (2012), *The Blackwell Companion to Globalization* (2008) and co-edited (with Jeff Stepnisky) the *Wiley-Blackwell Companions to Classical and Contemporary Major Social Theorists* (2012) and the *Handbook of Social Theory* (2001). He was founding editor of the *Journal of Consumer Culture.* He also edited the eleven-volume *Encyclopedia of Sociology* (2007; 2nd ed., forthcoming, with Chris Rojek), the two-volume *Encyclopedia of Social Theory* (2005), and the five-volume *Encyclopedia of Globalization* (2012). He co-edited a special double issue (2012) of the *American Behavioral Scientist* on prosumption. His books have been translated into more than twenty languages, with more than a dozen translations of *The McDonaldization of Society* alone.

1

AN INTRODUCTION TO SOCIOLOGY IN THE GLOBAL AGE

A Sociology of Revolutions and Counterrevolutions

In December 2010, street demonstrations, labor strikes, and other acts of civil resistance swept through the small North African nation of Tunisia. The demonstrators met strong resistance from the Tunisian government. Nevertheless, their protests eventually resulted in the overthrow of autocratic President Ben Ali after 23 years in power.

The trigger for the Tunisian protests was the self-immolation of Mohamed Bouazizi, a 26-year-old street vendor who claimed he had been harassed and humiliated by authorities. Bouazizi died in a burn and trauma center 18 days after setting himself on fire.

The Tunisian revolution was at the root of the "Arab Spring"— the wave of social unrest and social revolution that Tunisia's uprising inspired throughout the Middle East. Such events are not only important in themselves; so too are the counterreactions to them by other individuals as well as by larger organizations. Those responses have since undermined the revolutions that occurred during the Arab Spring (Worth 2016). In some cases, such as in Egypt, counterreaction by the military led to a return to the kind of autocratic government that was a cause of the protests in the first place. In the Persian Gulf states (Saudi Arabia, the United Arab Emirates, Kuwait, and Bahrain), monarchs have suppressed dissidents and thwarted efforts aimed at greater democratization (Fahim 2016). In the aftermath of the 2011 overthrow of dictator Muammar Qaddafi, Libya (and Yemen) have descended into civil wars, vicious fights for power, and, at least at the moment,

LEARNING OBJECTIVES

1.1 Identify major social changes since the 1880s studied by sociologists.

1.2 Explain why sociologists today focus on globalization, consumption, and the digital world.

1.3 Describe how sociologists understand continuity and change, particularly in the context of the sociological imagination and the social construction of reality.

1.4 Differentiate between sociology's two possible purposes, science and social reform.

1.5 Evaluate how sociology relates to other social sciences and how sociological knowledge differs from common sense.

large-scale anarchy. In Libya, but, more important, in Syria and Iraq, a radical Islamic group—the Islamic State (IS, also known as the Islamic State of Iraq and the Levant [ISIL], the Islamic State of Iraq and Syria [ISIS], or Da'ish, from an acronym for a name of the group in Arabic)—has swept through large portions of those countries and succeeded in dismembering them in its effort to form an independent state that spans much of the Middle East. That new state is envisioned to be a caliphate, dominated by a leader—a caliph—devoted to a strict interpretation of Islam. The success of IS led, in turn, to other counterreactions, both locally (especially by the Kurds and Iranians) and globally (with the United States helping the Iraqi government and Russia aiding the Syrian government), designed to limit IS's gains, if not to defeat it. By mid-2016 IS had been pushed back on a variety of fronts, but still controlled large parts of both Syria and Iraq and remained a force in Libya (and elsewhere).

By drawing on modern sociology's 200-year history while looking to the future, sociologists today can find the tools and resources to gain a better understanding of where we have been, where we are, and, perhaps most important, where we are going. Sociology has traditionally tried to understand the place of the individual—even a Tunisian street vendor—within society and society's effect on the individual. In today's global age, however, we need to look beyond given individuals and societies to global realities and processes. For example, IS has grown in strength through the influx of individual supporters and fighters from other parts of the world, including the United States and Great Britain. To take a more general example of globalization—one that is more directly relevant to most readers of this book—online networks that transcend national boundaries, such as Facebook and Twitter, have forever altered the ways in which we interact with each other as well as the societies that we shape and that shape us. As the world has become increasingly globalized, sociology has developed an increasingly global perspective. ●

One of the most important lessons that you will learn in your study of sociology is that what you think and do as an individual is affected by what is happening in groups, organizations, cultures, societies, and the world. This is especially true of social changes, even those that are global in scope and seem at first glance to be remote from you, such as Mohamed Bouazizi's public suicide and the revolution throughout much of the Middle East that it helped set in motion. The roots of that dramatic act of protest lay in poverty, high unemployment, an authoritarian government, and political corruption that affected Bouazizi personally. Before his actions, most Tunisians would never have risked their lives to protest against their country's repressive regime. Yet Bouazizi and tens of thousands of others in countries across the region did just that. While you may or may not be motivated to engage in revolutionary activities, you are continually affected by the social changes taking place around you.

A second important lesson in sociology is that you are not only affected by larger events, but also capable to some degree of having an impact on large-scale structures and processes. This is an example of the **butterfly effect** (Lorenz 1995). While this concept is generally applied to physical phenomena, it also applies to social phenomena (Daipha 2012). The idea is that a relatively small change in a specific location can have far-ranging, even global, effects over both time and distance. For example, Bouazizi's actions helped lead to the Tunisian revolution and, more generally, to street demonstrations and civil war, as well as counterreactions elsewhere in the Arab world that continue to reverberate throughout the region and many other parts of the world. Perhaps the arc of your life and career will be affected by the upheavals that began with the Arab Spring. More important, it is very possible that actions you take in your lifetime will have wide-ranging, perhaps global, effects.

For a very different example of the butterfly effect, consider the likely widespread use, perhaps as early 2021, of largely self-driving cars (Boudette and Isaac 2016). Wide use of these cars will lead, among other things, to the presence of many more cars on existing highways. Thanks to sophisticated sensors that will all but eliminate collisions, as many as eight times as many cars will be packed onto highways as can currently be accommodated safely. Among the far-reaching effects of this change will be a decline in the numbers of doctors, personal injury attorneys, and people admitted to hospital emergency rooms because of the great reduction in deaths (projected to be about 35,000 in 2016) and injuries resulting from automobile accidents. On an individual level, people are likely to live longer because of the sophisticated accident prevention systems built into driverless cars (Manjoo 2014; Mui 2013). Many urban parking lots will also be eliminated because driverless cars will be in something approaching perpetual motion. On the negative side, the ability to accommodate many more cars on our highways will lead to even more air pollution and to an acceleration of global climate change. This, in turn, could make people *more likely* to become ill, visit hospital emergency rooms, and perhaps have a shorter life span.

These examples of the relationships between people and larger social realities and changes set the stage for the definition of **sociology** as the systematic study of the ways in which people are affected by and affect the social structures

Will our highways be safer and injury rates lower because of the sensors in self-driving cars, like this one developed by Google's car project (which is now operating as Waymo)? Or will we have more air pollution and therefore more illness because there will be so many self-driving cars on the road? Sociologists assess the so-called butterfly effects of changes such as driverless cars.

and social processes associated with the groups, organizations, cultures, societies, and world in which they exist.

THE CHANGING NATURE OF THE SOCIAL WORLD—AND SOCIOLOGY

Sociology deals with contemporary phenomena, as you have seen, but its deep historical roots have led to many longer-term interests. In the fourteenth century, for instance, the Muslim scholar Abdel Rahman Ibn Khaldun studied various social relationships, including those between politics and economics. Of special importance to the founding of sociology was the eighteenth- and nineteenth-century Industrial Revolution. During this industrial age, many early sociologists concentrated on factories, the production that took place in those settings, and those who worked there, especially blue-collar, manual-labor workers. Sociologists also came to focus on the relationship between industry and the rest of society, including, for example, the state and the family.

By the middle of the twentieth century, manufacturing in the United States was in the early stages of a long decline that continues to this day. (However, manufacturing in other parts of the world, most notably in China, is booming.) The United States had moved from the industrial age to the "postindustrial age" (Bell 1973; Leicht and Fitzgerald 2006). In the United States, as well as in the Western world more generally, the center of the economy and the attention of many sociologists shifted from the factory to the office. That is, the focus moved from blue-collar, manual-labor work to white-collar office work (Mills 1951) as well as to the bureaucracies in which many people worked (Clegg and Lounsbury 2009; Weber [1921] 1968). Another change in the postindustrial age was the growth of the service sector of the economy, involving everyone from high-status service providers such as physicians and lawyers to lower-status workers behind the counters of fast-food restaurants and now those who drive for Uber.

The more recent rise of the "information age" (Castells 2010; David and Millwood 2012) can be seen as a part, or an extension, of the postindustrial age. Knowledge and information are critical in today's world. So, too, are the technologies—computers, smartphones, the world wide web—that have greatly increased the productivity of individual workers and altered the nature of their work. Rather than designers drawing designs by hand, computer-assisted technologies are now used to create designs for everything from electric power grids to patterned fabrics. The widespread use of smartphones has enabled, among many other things, the rise of companies such as Uber and Lyft, the success of which is threatening the rental car industry and especially the taxicab industry and the livelihoods of many taxi drivers (who are also threatened by driverless cars). A passenger uses an app to indicate that he or she needs a ride, and one is provided by an independent car owner for a set fee, which is automatically charged to the passenger's credit card (no tipping allowed). Some of the drivers work a few hours a day for these services in search of a little extra money, while others work full-time for the services. Their willingness to do this work has had the result of reducing the need for taxicabs and full-time taxi drivers.

However, it is not just work that has been affected by new technologies; virtually everyone and everything is being affected by them. Uber is part of the growing "sharing economy" (Sundarajan 2016), in which people share (for a fee) many things; most notably, some share their homes through websites such as Airbnb.com (Pogue 2014). One key component of this new technological world, Google (see the previous mention of Google's driverless car project, Waymo), is so powerful that a 2011 book is entitled *The Googlization of Everything* (Vaidhyanathan 2011). Thus, much sociological attention has shifted to computers and the internet, as well as those who work with them (Lynch 2016; Scholz 2013).

The transition from the industrial to the postindustrial and now to the information age has important personal implications. Had you been a man who lived in the industrial age, you would have worked (if you could find a job) for money (pay). You would have done so to be able to buy what you needed and wanted. Women working in the private sphere were largely uncompensated or compensated at a lower rate, as is often still the case. However, in the postindustrial age, it is increasingly likely that men and women will be willing, or forced, to work for free (Anderson 2009; Ritzer 2015b; Ritzer and Jurgenson 2010; Terranova 2013), as in the case of interns, bloggers, and contributors to YouTube and Wikipedia.

You may be willing to perform free labor because you enjoy it and because much of what is important in your life is, in any case, available for free on the internet. There is no need for you to buy newspapers when blogs are free or to buy CDs or DVDs when music and movies can be streamed by, for example, Spotify or downloaded at no cost or inexpensively from the internet. A whole range of software is also downloadable at no cost. However, while all of this, and much else, is available free of charge, the problem is that the essentials of life—food, shelter, clothing—still cost money, lots of money.

Many hope that the labor they currently perform for free will eventually have an economic payoff. One person (known as PewDiePie) played video games on YouTube,

garnered about 24 million subscribers, and reputedly earned millions of dollars per year (Jacobs 2014). Playing video games has become big business—one tournament drew 11,000 fans to a stadium and offered $11 million in prize money. Many hope that their work as bloggers or on YouTube will lead to full-time jobs.

These are but a few of the many social changes to be discussed in this book. The essential point is that the social world (people, groups, organizations, and so on)—*your* social world—is continually changing. Sociology is a field that is, and must be, constantly attuned to and involved in studying those changes.

CHECKPOINT 1.1: MAJOR SOCIAL CHANGES STUDIED BY SOCIOLOGISTS

TIME PERIOD	MAJOR SOCIAL CHANGES	RELATED ISSUES OF INTEREST TO SOCIOLOGISTS
Eighteenth and nineteenth centuries	Industrial Revolution	Rise of factories and blue-collar work
Mid-twentieth century	Postindustrial age	Growth of the service sector and white-collar work
Twenty-first century	Information age	Growth of the sharing economy and unpaid labor

CENTRAL CONCERNS FOR A TWENTY-FIRST-CENTURY SOCIOLOGY

While the social world has been changing dramatically over the last two centuries or so and sociology has adapted to those changes, sociology has continued to focus on many of its traditional concerns. We have already mentioned industry, production, and work as long-term sociological interests; others include deviance and crime (see Chapter 7), the family (see Chapter 12), and the city (see Chapter 17). Of particular concern to many sociologists has been, and continues to be, the issue of inequality as it affects the poor, particular racial and ethnic groups, women, and gays and lesbians (see Chapter 8). The bulk of this book will be devoted to these basic sociological topics and concerns, but the discussion will also encompass the nontraditional and very contemporary issues of consumption, the digital world, and especially globalization.

Blogging and Tweeting about Sociology

Blogging and tweeting are two popular ways to transmit and acquire information today. Current events are often posted in real time, sometimes by individuals who are witnessing them. For example, the Arab Spring was referred to as the Twitter Revolution because people around the world were able to follow these political uprisings through tweets posted by protestors. Sports fans can follow their favorite teams and on game day receive instantaneous alerts when their team scores a touchdown or scores a run. Individuals who want to find alternative perspectives on social issues from the mainstream press can follow a variety of alternate online sites (e.g., the far right-wing Breitbart News) and blogs (e.g., the left-leaning Mother Jones). Blogging and tweeting encourage individual agency. They offer the opportunity for all of us to participate in the social construction of reality and can be used as platforms to promote social reforms, such as #BlackLivesMatter. But there are a few structural constraints attached to these methods of communication. Twitter limits tweets to only 140 characters. Many popular blogs and Twitter accounts are written and maintained by celebrities, professional experts, and representatives of formal organizations (some of which are highly politicized), who have more power to shape reality than the average person does.

Sociologists and organizations devoted to sociological theory and research use blogs and tweets to expose others to the sociological imagination, helping individuals at the micro level realize that their private troubles are connected to larger public issues. Popular sociologists who blog include myself, George Ritzer (http://georgeritzer.wordpress.com)—I discuss the themes addressed in this book, such as McDonaldization, globalization, and consumption—and Philip Cohen, who writes about family inequality (http://familyinequality.wordpress.com). The Society Pages blog ring (http://thesocietypages.org) provides a set of sociology blogs such as The Color Line (http://thesocietypages.org/colorline) and Sociology Lens (http://thesocietypages.org/sociologylens) that keep readers current on issues pertaining to inequality, race, gender, crime, and health. The American Sociology Association's blog (http://speak4sociology.org) offers a forum for its followers to debate sociological issues. A variety of Twitter accounts regularly post comments about and links to relevant sociological topics, including @Soc_Imagination, @SociologyLens, @DiscoverSoc, @SocWomen, and @SocImages. In addition, professional sociologists, such as Michael Burawoy (@burawoy), Matthew Desmond (@just_shelter), Zeynep Tufekci (@zeynep), and Sudhir Venkatesh (@avsudhir), tweet to promote awareness about social problems and publicize their research and social activism.

Engaging the Digital World

Select one of the sociology blogs or Twitter accounts listed previously. Check this digital source periodically throughout the semester, keeping track of issues that you find most interesting or problematic. You can create your own blog to do this, or, if you have a Twitter account, you can tweet about the issues. At the end of the semester, write a summary of what you have learned, which you can include in your blog or a posted link to your Twitter account.

GLOBALIZATION

No social change is as important today as globalization, because it is continually affecting all aspects of the social world everywhere on the globe. A date marking the beginning of globalization cannot be given with any precision, and in fact is in great dispute (Ritzer 2012b; Ritzer and Dean 2015). However, the concept of globalization first began to appear in the popular and academic literature around 1990. Today, globalization is a central issue in the social world as a whole as well as in sociology; globalization and talk about it are all around us. In fact, we can be said to be living in the "global age" (Albrow 1996). However, this fact as well as the advantages of globalization for the United States were questioned by Donald Trump in the 2016 presidential campaign. In 2017, in the early days of his presidency, Trump adopted a slightly more balanced position by, for example, coming to see the merit in the North Atlantic Treaty Organization (NATO). Such questioning has led to talk of "deglobalization" (however, see my blog post "Deglobalization? Not a Chance" [Ritzer 2016]). Deglobalization was also behind the decision of the United Kingdom to exit the European Union (called Brexit), as well as actions taken by other European nations to create border restrictions. However, none of these actions are going to impact globalization as a whole or in such areas as the internet, the media, and culture.

A major component of any past or present definition of sociology is society. There are about 200 societies in the world, including those that encompass the United States, China, and South Africa. **Society** is a complex pattern of social relationships that is bounded in space and persists over time. The society has traditionally been the largest unit of analysis in sociology. However, in the global age, societies are seen as declining in importance (Holton 2011; Meyer, Boli, and Ramirez 1997). This is the case, in part, because larger transnational and global social structures are growing in importance. These include the United Nations (UN); the European Union (EU); the Organization of the Petroleum Exporting Countries (OPEC); multinational corporations (MNCs), such as Google and ExxonMobil; and multinational nongovernmental organizations (NGOs), such as Amnesty International. In at least some cases, these transnational structures are becoming more important than individual societies. OPEC, for example, is more important to the rest of the world's well-being than are the organization's key member societies, such as Abu Dhabi or even Saudi Arabia.

Social processes, like social structures, exist not only at the societal level but also at the global level, and these global processes are increasing in importance. Consider migration (see Chapter 17). People move about, or migrate, within and between societies. For example, many people have moved from the northeastern United States to the West and the South. However, in the global age, people are increasingly moving between societies, some halfway around the world. The United States now has a higher percentage of immigrants than it has had in almost a century (see Figure 1.1). Many have migrated from and through Mexico to the United

States (Massey 2003; Ortmeyer and Quinn 2012). More generally, large numbers of people are migrating from a number of predominantly Islamic societies in the Middle East and Africa to the West (Caldwell 2009; Voas and Fleischmann 2012). In many cases, they are fleeing from war-torn countries such as Syria, Iraq, and Libya (Yeginsu and Hartocollis 2015). In addition, the movement of thousands of people from the West to join radical Islamist organizations (such as the Islamic State), especially in Syria and Iraq, has been of major concern to Western governments. Some fear that at least some of those involved in radical Islamist activities there will migrate back to the West and engage in terrorist acts.

There have always been large-scale population movements. However, in the global age, and even with recent restrictions, people generally move around the world far more freely and travel much greater distances than ever before. Another way of saying this is that people—and much else—are more "fluid." That is, they move farther, more easily, and more quickly than ever before. Younger people, especially millennials (or Generation Y, those born from the early 1980s through the late 1990s), are likely to be especially mobile, including globally. Their greater fluidity is reflected in, among many other things, the fact that they are more likely to book airline tickets and to check in for flights online, and to use boarding passes sent directly to their smartphones (Lee 2013).

The movement of products of all types is also more fluid as a result of the existence of massive container ships, jet cargo planes, and package delivery services such as FedEx and UPS. Even more fluid is the digital "stuff" you buy on the internet when you download music, videos, movies, and so on. And in the realm of the family, tasks once confined to the home, such as caregiving and housework, have become increasingly fluid, as those who can afford to do so often outsource domestic labor (van der Lippe, Frey, and Tsvetkova 2012; Yeates 2009). More generally, that greater fluidity is manifested in the information that flows throughout the world in the blink of an eye as a result of the internet, texting, e-mail, and social networking sites such as Facebook, Instagram, Snapchat, and Twitter.

FIGURE 1.1 • Number of Immigrants and Their Share of the Total U.S. Population, 1850–2015

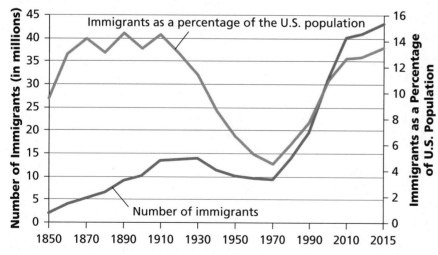

Migration Policy Institute tabulation of data from the U.S. Census Bureau's 2012, 2011, and 2010 American Community Surveys and 1970, 1990, and 2000 decennial Census data. All other data are from Campbell J. Gibson and Emily Lennon, U.S. Census Bureau, Working Paper No. 29, Historical Census Statistics on the Foreign-Born Population of the United States: 1850 to 1990, U.S. Government Printing Office, Washington, DC, 1999.

ASK YOURSELF

Have you ever thought of your posts on Facebook, Instagram, Snapchat, or Twitter as part of a global flow of information? In what ways do they actually fit this description? What does your position in this global flow of information reveal about you?

These flows can be expedited by structures of various types. For example:

- Air cargo delivery will increasingly be facilitated by the development of the "aerotropolis" (Kasarda and Lindsay 2011), a preplanned "city of the future" that is developed because of proximity and access to a large, modern airport (Kasarda 2016). For example, New Songdo, South Korea, is being built (it is over 50 percent completed) because such an airport (Incheon) is nearby and easily reached via a 12-mile-long bridge. This is in contrast to the usual situation where the airport (e.g., Reagan National in Washington, D.C.; LAX in Los Angeles; Heathrow in London) is built within or very close to a city center. Traditional airports are typically too small and too difficult to reach, create too much noise for city residents, and cannot expand much beyond their current confines.

- The European Union (EU), founded in 1993, is an example of a social structure that serves to ease the flow of citizens among member nations (but not of people living outside the EU). Although border restrictions have been increasing in recent years because of the flow of undocumented immigrants, they were reduced or eliminated completely among the 27 EU member nations. Similarly, the creation of the euro in 1975 greatly simplified economic transactions among the 18 EU countries that accept it as their currency.

- The continuing free flow of information on the internet is made possible by an organization called ICANN (Internet Corporation for Assigned Names and Numbers). It handles the net's underlying infrastructure.

There are also structures that impede various kinds of global flows. National borders, passports and passport controls (Robertson 2010; Torpey 2000, 2012), security checks, and customs controls limit the movement of people throughout the world. Such restrictions were greatly increased in many parts of the world after the terrorist attacks on New York City and Washington, D.C., on September 11, 2001. This made global travel and border crossing more difficult and time-consuming. Then there are the even more obvious structures designed to limit the movement of people across borders. Examples include the fences between Israel and the West Bank, as well as one between Israel and Egypt, which was completed in 2013. Even more recent are border fences under construction or completed in several European countries (e.g., Hungary, Slovenia), which are designed to limit, direct, or stop the flow of migrants from Syria and elsewhere (Surk 2015). During his presidential campaign, Donald Trump promised to turn the fence between the United States and Mexico into a wall, at least for part of the length of the distance required. In the early days of his presidency, Trump encountered opposition to the expanded wall because of its high cost and environmental concerns. It remains to be seen how much of the extended wall will actually be built. The existing fences across the Mexican border, and increased border police and patrols, have led unauthorized migrants to take longer and more risky routes into the United States. There are more than 200 immigration detention centers in the United States (see Figure 1.2), and Human Rights Watch found that 18 immigrants died in them between 2012 and 2015 due to negligent medical care (Jula and Preston 2016). A crisis arose at the Mexican border in mid-2014 when tens of thousands of children from Central America flooded the area and overwhelmed detention centers (Archibold 2014). There are, of course, many other structural barriers in the world,

FIGURE 1.2 • U.S. Immigration Detention Facilities, 2017

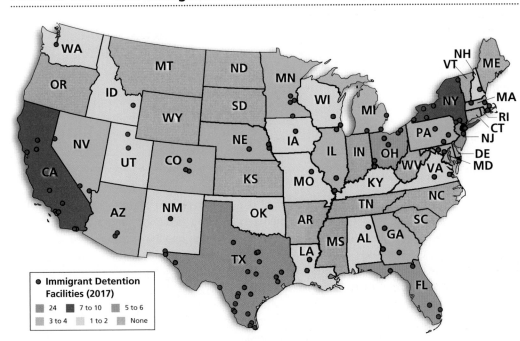

• Immigrant Detention Facilities (2017)

| 24 | 7 to 10 | 5 to 6 |
| 3 to 4 | 1 to 2 | None |

SOURCE: U.S. Customs and Immigration Enforcement, Detention Facility Locator, March 2017 (https://www.ice.gov/detention-facilities).

Sex Trafficking

Human trafficking is one aspect of the increased flow of people associated with globalization (Rao and Presenti 2012; Weitzer 2014). Human trafficking is illegal worldwide, but it is widely practiced. It is characterized by the use of coercion or deception to force human beings into providing such services as forced labor, commercial sex, and organ donation. Sex trafficking involves victims who are transported for the purpose of commercial sex, including prostitution, stripping, or pornography (Hodge 2008). Not all commercial sex involves those who have been trafficked, so consumers of commercial sexual services and performances may not always be associating with sex workers who have been trafficked.

One researcher estimates that 1.4 million women and girls are currently trafficked for sexual purposes each year (S. Lee 2012). Predictably, organized criminal networks have come to dominate transnational sex trafficking. Over the last few decades, many countries in the Global South (particularly in Southeast Asia), as well as countries of the former Soviet Union and Eastern Europe, have become major sources of sex workers, especially prostitutes.

The flow of people in the global sex industry involves both those who provide sexual services and those who consume those services. The providers of sexual services generally move within less developed countries, such as those in Southeast Asia, as well as to developed countries. Figure 1.3 shows the flow of providers of sexual services within Southeast Asia, especially in and around Thailand and Cambodia—major destinations for those in search of such services. Those interested in purchasing sexual services tend to flow from more to less developed areas of the world in order to avail themselves of the often cheaper and more exotic sexual services available at their destinations (Flynn 2011). In the

FIGURE 1.3 • Major Sex Trafficking Routes in Southeastern Asia

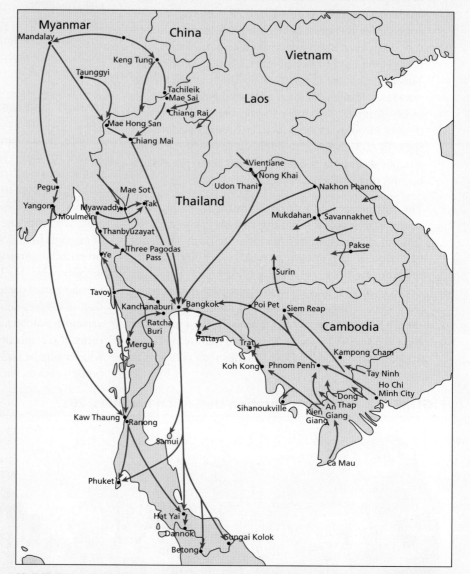

SOURCE: Transnational Organized Crime in East Asia and the Pacific: A Threat Assessment. Copyright © 2013, United Nations Office on Drugs and Crime (UNODC).

past the vast majority of buyers of sex have been men, but today women also travel the globe (for instance, from the United States to Costa Rica) in search of sexual services (Frohlick 2013).

Sex trafficking has far more negative consequences for the women who are trafficked than do other forms of human trafficking, such as for domestic work. Not only is sex work far more demeaning; it also exposes victims to sexually transmitted diseases such as HIV/AIDS, drug addiction, and a wide variety of other health risks. Trafficked individuals are frequently beaten, raped, stabbed, and strangled—sometimes to death— by traffickers, who are essentially their pimps. Pimps may threaten victims' family members and hold their children hostage to prevent the women from escaping.

Using the internet, customers can find sex workers almost anywhere in the world instantly, read reviews about their services, exchange information about location and price, and so on. Websites offer package tours, quote prices, and advertise sex workers and their services to the men of the developed world. In Cambodia, a U.S. resident started a "rape camp" that offered "Asian sex slaves" who were gagged, bound, and forced against their will into performing a variety of sex acts (Hughes 2000). Internet viewers could request and pay for specific rape acts to watch online, while traffickers could avoid prosecution by using encryption technologies. This rape camp was ultimately shut down, but other creative methods of exploiting women and children continue to exist on the internet.

Think About It

Do you think it was inevitable that the Global South would become a source from which women and children are exploited sexually? Was it inevitable that the internet would play such a large role in that exploitation? Why or why not? What effects have globalization and technology had on sex trafficking? Could they also be used to help limit it?

most notably trade barriers and tariffs, which limit the free movement of goods and services of many kinds.

In sum, **globalization** is defined by increasingly fluid global flows and the structures that expedite and impede those flows. Globalization is certainly increasing, and it brings with it a variety of both positive and negative developments (Ritzer and Dean 2015). On one side, most people throughout the world now have far greater access to goods, services, and information from around the globe than did people during the industrial age. On the other side, a variety of highly undesirable things also flow more easily around the world, including diseases such as Zika, HIV/AIDS, and Ebola and pollution released by industrialized countries that worsens the adverse effects of climate change (including global warming). Also on the negative side are the flows of such forms of "deviant globalization" as terrorism, sex trafficking, and the black markets for human organs and drugs (Gilman, Goldhammer, and Weber 2011).

CONSUMPTION

While consumption has been a central feature of societies for centuries, it is only in recent years that we can think in terms of a "world of consumers" (Trentmann 2016). Beginning in the 1950s, the center of many capitalist economies began to shift from production and work to **consumption**, or the process by which people obtain and utilize goods and services. During that period, the center of the U.S. economy shifted from the factory and the office to the shopping mall (Baudrillard [1970] 1998; Lipovetsky 2005). For many, work and production became less important than consumption.

ASK YOURSELF

Have your consumption habits or credit card use changed over the last six months? The last three years? Do you anticipate that your habits will change in the next three years? If so, how and why? Will you consume more or less?

The dramatic rise in consumption was made possible by, among other things, the growing affluence of the population. A more specific factor was the introduction (in the 1950s and 1960s) and increasing availability of credit cards. The use of credit cards has now become widespread at shopping malls, on the internet, and in many other settings. One indicator of the increase in consumption in the United States is the increase in credit card debt. As you can see in Figure 1.4, credit card debt per household grew astronomically in the early years of credit card use (the figure begins with $37 in 1969). Credit card debt reached its high point, $8,729, in 2008 and has been steadily declining since the Great Recession to an average of $5,946 per household. However, households that are classified as indebted, or carry a balance, have an average credit card debt of $16,060.

Consumption is certainly significant economically, but it is significant in other ways as well. For

FIGURE 1.4 • U.S. Credit Card Debt, 1969–2015

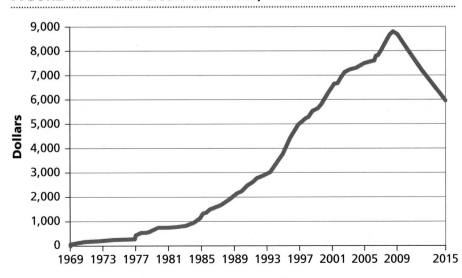

SOURCES: Data from the U.S. Federal Reserve and U.S. Census Bureau.

New consumption sites and products are often a hot cultural phenomenon. Many people will line up for hours, even camp out overnight, just to be among the first to be at such an event or to get such a product. This is clear in the crowd at the opening of a Kanye West pop-up store.

example, culture is very much shaped by consumption, and various aspects of consumption become cultural phenomena. A good example is the iPhone, which is used in many ways to consume, but more generally has revolutionized culture in innumerable ways. Millions of people have bought iPhones and similar smartphones as well as the ever-increasing number of apps associated with them. These phones have altered how and where people meet to socialize and the ways in which they socialize. In addition, the media and people in general spend so much time discussing the implications of the latest iPhone and similar products that these devices have become central to the larger culture in which we live. Rumors about the characteristics and release date of the next version of the iPhone continually add to the excitement.

Consumption and globalization are also deeply intertwined. Much of what we consume in the developed world comes from other countries. In 2015 alone, the United States imported more than $480 billion worth of goods from China; the comparable figure in 1985 was only $4 million in goods (www.census.gov/foreign-trade/balance/c5700.html; U.S. Census Bureau 2013). Furthermore, the speed and convenience of internet commerce tend to make global realities and distances irrelevant to consumers. Finally, travel to other parts of the world—a form of consumption itself—is increasingly affordable and common. A major objective of tourists is often the sampling of the foods of foreign lands, as well as the purchase of souvenirs (Chambers 2010; Gmelch 2010; Mak, Lumbers, and Eves 2012). Medical tourism is less common, but it is estimated that globally it is a $100-billion-per-year industry (Fetscherin and Stephano 2016). Large numbers of Americans—and many others—travel great distances for

such services as cosmetic procedures and even open-heart surgery. They do so largely because the costs are much lower elsewhere in the world. Many U.S. women who have difficulty conceiving travel to developing countries such as India in order to hire surrogates, "rent" their uteruses and ovaries, and exploit their eggs (Pfeffer 2011).

Sociologists are understandably interested in these developments in the realm of consumption. Early sociologists completed many studies of work, production, factories, and factory workers. Today's sociologists continue to study work-related issues, but they are devoting increasing attention to consumption in general (Sassatelli 2007) and more specifically to such phenomena as online shopping, done increasingly through the use of smartphones (Horrigan 2008; Morris 2013), the behavior of shoppers in more material locales such as department stores (Miller 1998; Zukin 2004), and the development of more recent consumption sites, such as fast-food restaurants (Ritzer, forthcoming) and shopping malls (Ritzer 2010b). All these have become increasingly global phenomena. The most popular destination for visitors to Barcelona is *not* one of Antoni Gaudí's amazing architectural creations, but rather a new outlet mall on the outskirts of the city (Mount 2014). Online shopping is increasingly popular in many places, including India and especially China (Bearak 2014; Wang and Pfanner 2013). The growth of online shopping in developed countries, and even more in less developed countries, has been made possible by the massive expansion and growing popularity of smartphones.

CHECKPOINT 1.2:
CHARACTERISTICS OF GLOBALIZATION, CONSUMPTION, AND THE DIGITAL WORLD

GLOBALIZATION IS CHARACTERIZED BY . . .	CONSUMPTION IS CHARACTERIZED BY . . .	THE DIGITAL WORLD IS CHARACTERIZED BY . . .
Increasingly fluid flows of people, goods, information, and ideas across national boundaries	Increasing affluence, readily available credit, and McDonaldization	Increasing use of digital technology to mediate social interactions, shop online, and review products and services

McDonaldization

My study of fast-food restaurants led to the development of the concept of **McDonaldization**, or the process by which the rational principles of the fast-food restaurant are coming to dominate more and more sectors of society and more societies throughout the world (Ritzer, forthcoming; for a number of critical essays on this perspective, see Ritzer 2010c: 275–357). This process leads to the creation of rational systems—like fast-food restaurants—that have four defining characteristics:

- *Efficiency.* The emphasis is on the use of the quickest and least costly means to whatever end is desired. It is clear that employees of fast-food restaurants work efficiently: Burgers are cooked and assembled as if on an assembly line, with no wasted movements or ingredients. Similarly, customers are expected to spend as little time as possible in the fast-food restaurant. Perhaps the best example of efficiency is the drive-through window, a highly organized means for employees to dole out meals in a matter of seconds.

- *Calculability.* You hear a lot at McDonald's about quantities: how large the food portions are—the Big Mac—and how low the prices are—the dollar breakfast. You don't hear as much, however, about the quality of the restaurant's ingredients or its products. Similarly, you may hear about how many burgers are served per hour or how quickly they are served, but you don't hear much about the skill of employees. A focus on quantity also means that tasks are often done under great pressure. This means that they are often done in a slipshod manner.

- *Predictability.* McDonaldization ensures that the entire experience of patronizing a fast-food chain is nearly identical from one geographic setting to another—even globally—and from one time to another. For example, when customers enter a McDonald's restaurant, employees ask what they wish to order, following scripts created by the corporation. For their part, customers can expect to find most of the usual menu items. Employees, following another script, can be counted on to thank customers for their order. Thus, a highly predictable ritual is played out in the fast-food restaurant.

- *Control.* In McDonaldized systems, technology exerts a good deal of control over people, processes, and products. French fry machines limit what employees can do and control any remaining tasks. They buzz when the fries are done and even automatically lift them out of the hot oil when they've reached just the right amount of crispiness. Workers must load fry baskets with uncooked fries and unload them when the baskets emerge from the oil. The automatic fry machine may save time and prevent accidents, but it limits and dictates employee actions and leaves them with little

meaningful work. Similarly, the drive-through window can be seen as a technology that ensures that customers dispose of their own garbage, if only by dumping it in the backseats of their cars or on the roadside.

Paradoxically, rationality often seems to lead to its exact opposite—irrationality. Just consider the problems of meaningless work, roadside litter due to drive-through services at fast-food restaurants, or the societal problems associated with childhood obesity, which has been blamed, in part, on the ubiquity of fast food. Another of the irrationalities of rationality is dehumanization. Fast-food employees are forced to work in dehumanizing jobs, which can lead to job dissatisfaction, alienation, and high turnover rates. Fast-food customers are forced to eat in dehumanizing settings, such as in the cold and impersonal atmosphere of the fast-food restaurant, in their cars, or on the move as they walk down the street. As more of the world succumbs to McDonaldization, dehumanization becomes increasingly pervasive.

Critiquing Consumption

The sociological study of consumption sites involves, among many other things, a critical look at the ways in which they are structured. (The previous discussion of the irrationalities associated with McDonaldized settings is one example of such a critical perspective.) These sites may be set up to lead people to consume certain things and not others, to consume more than they might have intended, and to go into debt (Brubaker, Lawless, and Tabb 2012; Manning 2001; Marron 2009; Ritzer 1995). Take, for example, the website Shoedazzle (www.shoedazzle.com), a site that uses commercials and "style quizzes" to recruit new members. Shoedazzle highlights an "exclusive" VIP membership status on its webpage, which anyone can join. Making its members feel special through seemingly personalized style quizzes and VIP memberships lures consumers into buying more shoes than they really need.

Sociologists are also interested in how consumers use shopping malls and e-tailers in ways that were not anticipated by their designers. For example, people often wander through shopping malls and their many shops, which have been designed to spur consumption, without buying anything. Defunct malls are serving as impromptu skate parks. Students are using Amazon.com as a source for term-paper bibliographies rather than buying the books. Travelers are using internet sites such as Expedia and KAYAK to compare prices but then buying airplane tickets on the airlines' own websites.

Social change continues. The Great Recession and its ongoing aftermath altered many things, including the degree to which society is dominated by consumption. Even today, long after the onset of the recession in 2007 and its supposed end, many U.S. consumers remain reluctant to spend money, or at least as much as they did in the

The McDonaldization of Society (SAGE, 2015)

George Ritzer (Distinguished University Professor at the University of Maryland; PhD, Cornell University, 1968)

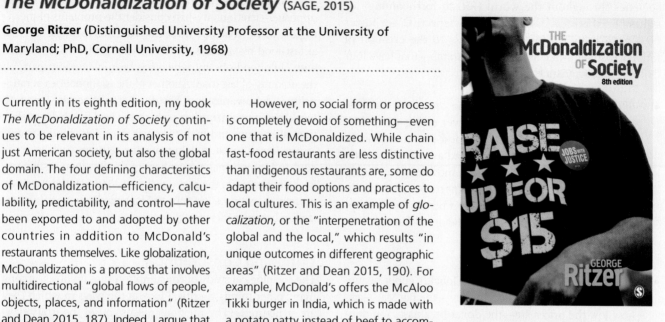

Currently in its eighth edition, my book *The McDonaldization of Society* continues to be relevant in its analysis of not just American society, but also the global domain. The four defining characteristics of McDonaldization—efficiency, calculability, predictability, and control—have been exported to and adopted by other countries in addition to McDonald's restaurants themselves. Like globalization, McDonaldization is a process that involves multidirectional "global flows of people, objects, places, and information" (Ritzer and Dean 2015, 187). Indeed, I argue that McDonaldization is a type of globalization, what I call the "globalization of nothing" (2015, 185). McDonaldization is a type of "nothing" because it and its offerings are centrally conceived and controlled, and lacking in distinctive content. In contrast, "something" (say, a home-cooked meal) is locally conceived and controlled, and rich in content (2015, 188–189). McDonald's, like other chain fast-food restaurants, is created and controlled by a central office. Most of its franchised restaurants look identical, offer similar food options, and treat their workers and customers in the same way. The global ambitions of the McDonald's corporation to impose its norms and values on other geographic regions is an example of *grobalization*. I argue that we are witnessing the grobalization of nothing because nothing is usually less expensive than something, appeals to a wider range of consumer tastes, and seamlessly fits into other cultures.

However, no social form or process is completely devoid of something—even one that is McDonaldized. While chain fast-food restaurants are less distinctive than indigenous restaurants are, some do adapt their food options and practices to local cultures. This is an example of *glocalization,* or the "interpenetration of the global and the local," which results "in unique outcomes in different geographic areas" (Ritzer and Dean 2015, 190). For example, McDonald's offers the McAloo Tikki burger in India, which is made with a potato patty instead of beef to accommodate Hindus who do not eat beef. Offering different food options to satisfy the cultural and religious preferences of consumers in different countries is a weak form of glocalization because it does not necessarily challenge McDonaldization—the McAloo Tikki burger in India is just as efficiently mass-produced, calculable, and predictable as the Big Mac in the United States is. Efforts of *DeMcDonaldization* face a similar dilemma. Starbucks might appear to be the antithesis of McDonald's, with its supposedly caring corporate image and its inviting cafes that encourage customers to linger for hours. However, the vast majority of Starbucks' customers do not even enter the stores; they use the drive-through windows. Like McDonald's, Starbucks cafes and products are standardized and predictable, and workers are controlled by technologies, such as automated espresso machines (2015, 198–199).

Supplementary Resources

- Watch an interview with me about my book *The McDonaldization of Society* at http://georgeritzer .wordpress.com/interviews.
- Examine photographs and learn more about what *Smithsonian* magazine has identified as the most unique McDonald's restaurants in the world at www.smithsonianmag.com/ travel/most-unique-mcdonalds -around-world-180955090. You can also look at menu items from different McDonald's restaurants on BuzzFeed at www.buzzfeed.com/gavon/ 45-mcdonalds-items-not -available-in-the-us-that? utm_term=.ljPKeMDK9W# .tbpJqb3JlV.

past, on consumption (Kurtz 2014). As a result, consumption sites have experienced great difficulties. Many outdoor strip malls and some indoor malls have emptied; they have become "dead malls" (as documented on the site http://deadmalls.com). Many of the malls that continue to exist have numerous vacant stores, including abandoned large department stores. Las Vegas, which has long been a capital for the consumption of entertainment and high-end goods and services, has been hurting (Nagourney 2013). Casinos in Atlantic City, New Jersey, are being shuttered, and there are those who want to see the city become more like the simpler beach community it once was (Hurdle 2014). Dubai, aspiring to be the consumption capital of the East, hit a financial rough spot in 2009 and has yet to recover completely from it. It seems possible, although highly unlikely, that even though we entered the consumption age only about half a century ago, we now may be on the verge of what could be called the "postconsumption age." While excessive consumption and the related high level of debt were key factors in causing the Great Recession, a postconsumption age would bring with it problems of its own, such as fewer jobs and a declining standard of living for many.

ASK YOURSELF

What would your life be like in a postconsumption age? In what ways might it be better? Worse? Why?

THE DIGITAL WORLD

Sociology has always concerned itself with the social aspects and implications of **technology**, or the interplay of machines, tools, skills, and procedures for the accomplishment of tasks. One example is the assembly line, a defining feature of early twentieth-century factories. Later, sociologists became interested in the automated technologies that came to define factories. However, technologies have continued to evolve considerably since then. Sociologists are now devoting an increasing amount of attention to the digital world that has emerged as a result of new technologies already mentioned in this chapter, such as computers, smartphones, the internet, and social networking sites such as Facebook and Twitter (Clough 2013).

While we will discuss life in the digital world throughout this book, living digitally is not separate from living in the social world. In fact, the two forms of living are increasingly intersecting and, in the process, creating an augmented world (Jurgenson 2012). For example, the wide-scale use of smartphones allows people to text many others to let them know they are going to be at a local club. This can lead to a spontaneous social gathering at the club that would not have occurred were it not for this new technology. However, the most dramatic examples of the effect of smartphones on the social world are seen in their use in mobilizing, especially through Twitter, large numbers of people to become involved, and stay involved, in social movements such as the revolutions in Egypt (2011) and Ukraine (2014).

The networking sites on the internet that involve social interaction are the most obviously sociological in character (Aleman and Wartman 2008; Patchin and Hinduja 2010). For example, Hodkinson (2015) has recently pointed out the similarities between teenagers' bedrooms and their social networking sites in terms of privacy issues. Both are intimate personal spaces where teenagers socialize and individualize in ways that express their identities. Social networking sites are especially important in North America, where the percentage of those with access to the internet is highest (see Figure 1.5). However, their importance is increasing elsewhere, especially in the Middle East and North Africa, as reflected in the role they played there in recent social revolutions. Protesters used cell phones and the internet to inform each other, and the world, about the evolving scene. To take another example, Facebook.com/yalaYL has become a key site where Israelis, Palestinians, and other Arabs communicate with each other about both everyday concerns and big issues such as the prospect for peace in the Middle East. This social networking takes place online, while peaceful face-to-face interaction between such people, and between their leaders, is difficult or nonexistent, especially in light of the 2014 war in and around Gaza, as well as

FIGURE 1.5 • Internet Access by Geographic Region, 2016

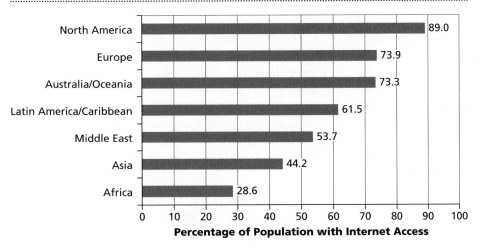

Region	Percentage
North America	89.0
Europe	73.9
Australia/Oceania	73.3
Latin America/Caribbean	61.5
Middle East	53.7
Asia	44.2
Africa	28.6

Percentage of Population with Internet Access

SOURCE: Data from Internet World Stats, Miniwatts Marketing Group.

Social changes brought about by the thorough integration of the internet in most areas of our lives have been enormously influential—and the changes are far from over. Teenagers and even very young children take our constant connectivity for granted, suggesting that most of the changes we are witnessing will become ever more pervasive.

the continuing violence there and elsewhere in and around Israel (Bronner 2011).

While social networking sites can bring about greater interaction, they also come between people and affect the nature of interaction. For example, Twitter limits each message to 140 characters, but face-to-face communication has no such limits. On the other hand, face-to-face communication is limited to a shared physical space, whereas communication via Twitter travels anywhere there is a device connected to the internet. Sociologists are interested in getting a better handle on the nature of the differences, as well as the similarities, between mediated and nonmediated (e.g., face-to-face) interaction. In technologically **mediated interaction**, technology such as the internet and the smartphone comes between the people who are communicating, while there is no such interference in nonmediated interaction. People who are shy and insecure when it comes to dating or sex, for example, may be much more comfortable relating to others on mediated websites such as Match.com or OkCupid.

Another sociological issue related to the internet is the impact on our lives of spending so much time interacting on social networking sites. For example, are you more likely to write term papers for your college classes using shorter sentences and more abbreviations because of your experience on Twitter or with texting? Consider also the impact of the 9 hours per day that young people between the ages of 13 and 18 spend on entertainment or screen media (Common Sense Media 2015). In some cases, little time remains for other activities (schoolwork, face-to-face interaction). Increasing the ability of children

to spend time on screen media is the growing availability of mobile devices such as smartphones, tablets, and iPads. In 2013, about 75 percent of children in the United States under 8 years of age lived in homes with mobile devices, compared to 52 percent just two years earlier. They were also more than twice as likely in 2013 to use such devices than they were in 2011 (Common Sense Media 2013). A study of parents and children in fast-food restaurants found that a significant majority of the parents were more absorbed in their mobile devices than they were in relating to their children (Radesky et al. 2014).

We may also multitask among several online and offline interactions simultaneously, such as in class or while doing homework. You may think you do a great job of multitasking, but dividing focus in this way can actually reduce your ability to comprehend and remember and thus lower your performance on tests and other assignments (PBS 2010).

Internet technology also affects the nature of consumption. More of it is taking place on such sites as eBay and Amazon.com, and that trend is expected to continue to grow. In 2010, a Pew study found that, during an average day, 21 percent of internet users in the United States look for information about a service or product they are thinking about buying (Jansen 2010). It is also easier for people to spend money on consumption on internet sites than it is in the material world. It is worth noting that these sites, as well as the internet in general, are global in their scope. The ease with which global interactions and transactions occur on the internet is a powerful indicator of, and spur to, the process of globalization.

Smartphones are also having a variety of effects on consumption. For example, on the one hand, they are making it easier for people to find particular kinds of restaurants and to get to them quickly and efficiently. On the other hand, when people are eating in those restaurants, smartphones tend to slow down service because diners take time photographing the meal, taking selfies, and asking wait staff to take photos of them (Griswold 2014).

GLOBALIZATION, CONSUMPTION, THE DIGITAL WORLD, AND YOU

The three main issues discussed previously, taken singly and collectively, are of great concern not only to society in general and to sociologists but also to you as a college student. You live a good part of your life in these three interrelated domains.

As a college student, you live a truly global existence in a college or university. A significant number of your classmates may come from elsewhere in the world. Your classes are increasingly being taught by teaching assistants and professors from other parts of the globe. The ideas you are learning are the most global of all, flowing freely from virtually everywhere in the world to become part of lectures and textbooks.

As consumers, you and your classmates are likely well acquainted with the college bookstore and the nearby shopping mall. In addition, on the internet you are able to find a nearly infinite variety of goods (including this textbook) and services, the majority of which are likely to come from the far reaches of the world.

Finally, an increasing portion of your education is obtained through the inherently global internet—for example, through e-learning on web-based courses and online degree programs. In 2013, the number of students taking at least one online course nearly doubled, to 45 percent, from 23 percent five years before (Bolkan 2013). With the emergence of massive open online courses (MOOCs), you, and perhaps hundreds of thousands of students from around the globe, are increasingly likely to participate in global classes (including courses in sociology; Behbehanian and Burawoy 2014) and other programs available on the internet (see Chapter 13 for more on MOOCs; see also Heller 2013; Lewin 2012).

Globalization, consumption, and the internet are of great importance on their own. However, perhaps more important are the ways in which they interact with one another and interpenetrate with your life as a college student—and the lives of virtually everyone else.

SOCIOLOGY: CONTINUITY AND CHANGE

This chapter has emphasized recent social changes and their impact on society and on sociology, but there is also much continuity in society, as well as in the field of sociology. This section deals with a number of traditional approaches and concerns in sociology that are of continuing relevance to even the most recent sociological issues.

THE SOCIOLOGICAL IMAGINATION

The systematic study of the social world has always required imagination on the part of sociologists. There are various ways to look at the social world. For example, instead of looking at the world from the point of view of an insider, one can, at least psychologically, place oneself

C. Wright Mills (1916–1962) was a prominent post–World War II sociologist who urged the use of the "sociological imagination" to study such as issues as the power elite and the military-industrial complex.

outside that world. The U.S. "War on Terror" might look defensible from the perspective of an American, especially one who lived through 9/11, but it would look quite different if you imagined yourself in the place of an innocent Muslim caught in the middle of that war (Philips 2016). The phenomenon of being able to look at the social world from different, imaginative perspectives attracted the attention of the famous sociologist C. Wright Mills, who in 1959 wrote a very important book entitled *The Sociological Imagination.* He argued that sociologists have a unique perspective—the **sociological imagination**—that gives them a distinctive way of looking at data or reflecting on the world around them (Scott and Nilsen 2013).

In his 1956 book *The Power Elite,* Mills demonstrated the application of the sociological imagination to the political world of his day. It was dominated by the Cold War between the United States and the Soviet Union and by the likelihood of nuclear war between the two nations. Mills argued that a "military-industrial complex" consisting of the military and many defense industries had come into existence in the United States. These entities favored war, or at least preparedness for war, and therefore the expenditure of huge sums of taxpayer money on armaments of all types. A few years after *The Power Elite* was published, President Dwight D. Eisenhower, a former five-star general, warned the nation of the threats to liberty and democracy posed by the military-industrial complex and its role in elevating the risk of war:

We must guard against the acquisition of unwarranted influence, whether sought or unsought, by the military-industrial complex. The potential for the disastrous rise of misplaced power exists and will persist.

We must never let the weight of this combination endanger our liberties or democratic processes. . . . Only an alert and knowledgeable citizenry can compel the proper meshing of the huge industrial and military machinery of defense with our peaceful methods and goals, so that security and liberty may prosper together. (Eisenhower 1961)

ASK YOURSELF

From what perspective do you view the 9/11 attacks on the United States? Could you ever consider them from a different angle? Why or why not? How does your answer to this question reflect your views about the military-industrial complex?

Sociology requires at least as much imagination today as it did in Mills's day, and probably more, to deal with new and emerging realities. For example, the risk of global warfare, especially nuclear war, has declined with the end of the Cold War and the demise of the Soviet Union. But a military-industrial complex remains in place in the United States and may be more powerful than ever. Consider the seemingly open-ended and perhaps never-ending War on Terror. Some sociologists would point out that the military and defense industries want, indeed need, hundreds of billions of dollars to be spent each year on armaments of all types. The new threats that arise regularly, real or imagined, lead to ever-greater expenditures and further expansion of the military-industrial complex. As Figure 1.6 illustrates, U.S. military expenditures increased dramatically after the terrorist attacks of September 11, 2001—reflecting overlapping wars with Iraq and Afghanistan. Given the economic problems facing the United States, there is talk of cutting the defense budget in future years. Whatever happens, we can be sure that a military-industrial complex will survive and fight hard against any reductions.

Of recent concern, and relevant to our interest in the internet, is the possibility of "information war" (Tumber and Webster 2006). Instead of relying on armaments, an information war might involve barrages of propaganda, increasingly online, by the warring parties—for example, Russia and Ukraine (Higgins 2016), Israel and the Palestinians, or the United States and the Islamic State. Videos of the beheading of American captives can be seen as an example of information war being waged by IS to frighten the American public as well as the group's local opponents. An information war might also involve cyber war, in which hackers engage in stealthy cyberattacks on an enemy nation's computer systems (Kaplan 2016). For example, in 2010 the Stuxnet worm attacked a number of computers around the world, but it was especially aimed at Iranian nuclear facilities, which were apparently badly hurt by the attack, at least in the short term. (See *Zero Days*, an excellent documentary on Stuxnet.) Most observers speculate that the attack was a joint U.S.–Israeli operation. It is likely that in future years the American military-industrial complex will claim, not without some justification, that large sums of money need to be spent on the development of expensive new technologies that will enable the United States to ward off, or engage in, cyberattacks as well as to make war on IS and other enemies.

A very different example of the utility of a sociological imagination begins with the ideas of one of the classic thinkers in the history of sociology, Georg Simmel, who was writing at the beginning of the twentieth century. Among many other things, Simmel ([1907] 1978) argued that money is crucial to a modern economy. For example, cash money allows people to be paid easily for their work and makes it just as easy for them to buy goods and services. However, money not only speeds up consumption but also allows people to consume more than they otherwise would. While a money economy creates its own problems, it is the credit economy that nearly wrecked the American, and much of the global, economy during the Great Recession. The availability of "money" had dramatically increased with the expansion of credit for individuals in the form of mortgage loans, auto loans, and credit card debt. People not only tended to spend all the cash (including savings) they had on hand; they were going into more and more debt because loans were easy to obtain. Simmel's imaginative thinking on money allows us to better understand the problems created by easy credit.

Private Troubles and Public Issues

The sociological imagination may be most useful in helping sociologists see the linkage between private troubles and public issues. For example, prior to the onset of the Great Recession, the sociological imagination would have been useful in alerting society to the fact that the increasing levels of individual consumption and debt, seen at the time as private issues, would soon morph into a public issue—the near collapse of the global economy. Credit cards can create both private troubles and public issues. A person going so deeply into debt that there is no way out other than declaring bankruptcy is experiencing a private trouble. However, private troubles become public issues when high levels of personal debt and bankruptcy lead to bank failures and even default on debts by various nations. Today, the sociological imagination could also be used to reflect on, for example, the fleeting nature of private social

FIGURE 1.6 • U.S. Defense Budget, 1949–2015

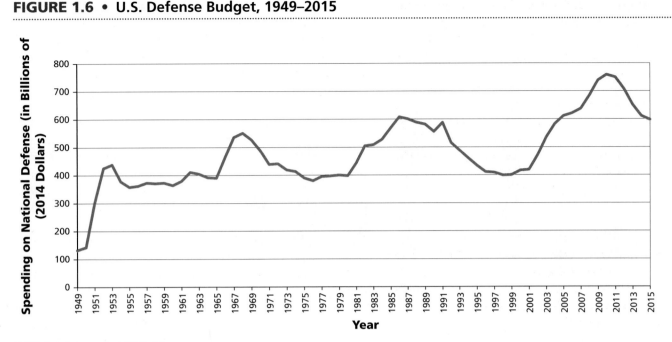

NOTE: Data is in constant 2014 dollars.

SOURCE: Data from Mackenzie Eaglen, "U.S. Defense Spending: The Mismatch Between Plans and Resources." Used by permission of The Heritage Foundation.

relationships on Facebook, Twitter, and Snapchat and whether this trend will lead all types of social relationships in the future in the same direction.

Many other examples of the link between private troubles and public issues relate to young people and students. For example, ADHD—attention-deficit/hyperactivity disorder—can easily be seen as a private trouble. For years there was little public awareness of ADHD, and those who had it were likely to suffer alone. But since the 1980s, it has become clear that ADHD is also a public issue, and it is becoming an increasingly important one not only in the United States but globally (Ellison 2015). The number of children in the United States ages 3 to 17 diagnosed with ADHD increased from 6 percent in 1997 to 1999 to 9 percent in 2014 (Bloom, Jones, and Freeman 2013; Goodwin 2011; Centers for Disease Control and Prevention 2014). It is clear that many people suffer from ADHD, which creates a number of larger problems for schools, employers, and society as a whole. The fact that it has become a public issue may make ADHD less of a private trouble for some, as there is now greater public understanding of the problem, and many more support groups are available.

In another example, a 2011 White House report details the fact that women are more likely than men to be concentrated in lower-paying jobs (see Figure 1.7; U.S. Department of Commerce 2011). For example, women are much more likely to be comparatively poorly paid dental hygienists than dentists, or legal assistants rather than lawyers. Being limited occupationally creates personal troubles for many

women, such as inadequate income and job dissatisfaction. This is also a public issue, not only because the discrepancy between the sexes is unfair to women as a whole but also because society is not benefiting from the many contributions women could be making.

ASK YOURSELF

Do you agree that private choices sometimes lead to, or are part of, public issues? Can you think of an example from your own life or the life of a family member?

The decision to pursue one college major or career path over another could become a private trouble if a student makes a poor choice or has one forced on him or her. Sociologists have also shown that such choices are very much related to larger public issues. If many people make poor choices, or are forced into them—as women and other minorities often are—this will lead to public issues such as wide-scale job dissatisfaction and poor performance on the job. Culturally based ideas about gender often shape personal preferences in choosing a college major (Charles and Bradley 2009), and gendered beliefs about career competence steer women and men toward different types of jobs and away from others (Correll 2001, 2004; Ridgeway and Correll 2004). Being in a poorly paid and unsatisfying job is a personal trouble for an individual woman, but it is a public issue when large numbers of women find themselves in this situation.

FIGURE 1.7 • Percentages of Women in Selected Occupations, 2014

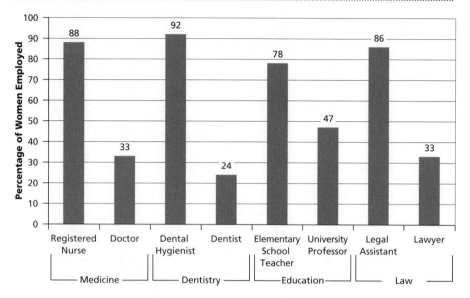

SOURCE: U.S. Census Bureau, 2014.

The Micro–Macro Relationship

The interest in personal troubles and public issues is a specific example of a larger and more basic sociological concern with the relationship between microscopic (**micro**, or small-scale) social phenomena, such as individuals and their thoughts and actions, and macroscopic (**macro**, or large-scale) social phenomena, such as groups, organizations, cultures, society, and the world, as well as the relationships

As they watch in real time the locating—and killing—of Osama bin Laden in 2011, the tension shows on the faces and the body language of the highest officials of the United States—including President Obama.

among them (Turner 2005). For example, Karl Marx, often considered one of the earliest and most important sociologists, was interested in the relationship between what workers do and think (micro issues) and the capitalist economic system in which the workers exist (a macro issue). To take a more contemporary example, Randall Collins (2009) has sought to develop a theory of violence that deals with everything from individuals skilled in violent interactions, such as attacking those who are weak, to the material resources needed by violent organizations to cause the destruction of other violent organizations. An example of the former type of violent organization is the well-equipped U.S. Navy SEALs team that killed Osama bin Laden in 2011 and through that act helped hasten the decline of al-Qaeda. However, the decline of al-Qaeda helped lead to the rise of a new, even more violent, organization, the Islamic State.

In fact, there is a continuum that runs from the most microscopic to the most macroscopic of social realities, with phenomena at roughly the midpoint of this continuum best thought of as meso (middle or intermediate) realities. The definition of sociology presented at the beginning of this chapter fits this continuum quite well. Individual actions and thoughts lie on the micro end of the continuum; groups, organizations, cultures, and societies fall more toward the macro end; and worldwide structures and processes are at the end point on the macro side of the continuum. Although in their own work the vast majority of individual sociologists focus on only very limited segments of this continuum, the field as a whole is concerned with the continuum in its entirety, as well as with the interrelationships among its various components.

The Agency–Structure Relationship

American sociologists tend to think in terms of the micro–macro relationship. In other parts of the world, especially in Europe, sociologists are more oriented to the agency–structure relationship. The agency–structure continuum is complex, but for our purposes we can think of agency as resembling the micro level and structure as resembling the macro level.

The utility of the agency–structure terminology is that it highlights several important social realities and aspects of the field of sociology. Of greatest significance is the fact that the term **agency** gives great importance to the individual—the "agent"— as having power and a capacity for creativity (Giddens 1984). In sociological work on agency, great emphasis is placed on the individual's mental abilities and the ways in which these abilities are used to create important, if not decisive, actions.

However, individual agents are seen as enmeshed in macro-level social and cultural structures that they create and by which they are constrained (King 2004). For example, as a student, you help create the universities you attend, but you are also constrained by them and the power they have over you. Your university can require you to do certain things (such as take specific courses in order to earn your degree) and prevent you from doing other things (such as taking courses that might be of greater interest, or even taking no courses at all). On the other hand, you as a student can act to change or overthrow those structures. You might organize student-run groups on topics of interest, such as religious rights or manga cartoons, attract many participants to the groups, and eventually prompt the university to add courses on those topics. Or perhaps you might organize students to stop enrolling in an elective course that seems irrelevant to their lives, causing that elective to be dropped from the course catalog.

Agents (you as a student, in this case) have great power. In the words of another important sociologist, Erving Goffman (1961b, 81), individuals are **dangerous giants**. That is, they have the potential to disrupt and destroy the structures in which they find themselves. Yet often agents do not realize the power they possess. As a result, social structures such as the university and the class you are currently taking function for long periods of time with little or no disruption by individual agents.

However, there are times, such as during the anti–Vietnam War protests of the late 1960s and early 1970s, when students come to realize that they are dangerous giants and act to change not only the university but also the

Students at many universities, including the elite Stanford University, have organized to protest rape on campus and the failure of school administrators to deal with the problem and to punish the rapists sufficiently, if at all.

larger society (Gitlin 1993). For example, students at some universities are protesting against the possible deportation of undocumented immigrants by pressuring school administrators to create "sanctuary campuses" that protect faculty, students, and staff from federal immigration authorities.

There are far more minor, everyday actions that reflect the fact that people can be dangerous giants. Examples involving students include questioning a professor's argument or going to the dean to protest the excessive absences of an instructor. However, most people most of the time do not realize that they are dangerous giants—that they have the capacity to greatly alter the social structures that surround them and in which they are enmeshed.

THE SOCIAL CONSTRUCTION OF REALITY

The discussion of agency and structure leads to another basic concept in sociology: the **social construction of reality** (Berger and Luckmann 1967; Knoblauch and Wilke 2016). People at the agency end of the continuum are seen as creating social reality, basically macro-level phenomena, through their thoughts and actions. That reality then comes to have a life of its own. That is, it becomes a structure that is partly or wholly separate from the people who created it and exist in it. Once macro phenomena have lives of their own, they constrain and even control what people do. Of course, people can refuse to accept these constraints and controls and create new social realities. This process of individual creation of structural realities, constraints, and coercion then begins anew, in a continuing loop. It is this continuous loop that is the heart of agency–structure and micro–macro relationships, the social world, and the field of sociology.

For example, in the realm of consumption, it is people—as designers, manufacturers, consumers, and bloggers—who create the world of fashion (Entwhistle 2015). However, once the fashion world comes into existence, that world has a great deal of influence over the social constructions, especially the tastes, of individuals who purchase the fashions it produces. Famous fashion houses such as Dior and Givenchy dominate the industry and perpetuate their existence through continual fashion changes. These companies—and, more important, the "fast-fashion" companies that copy and mass-produce their products, such as H&M, Forever 21, and Zara—control people's tastes in fashion and thereby the nature of the clothing they buy and wear. Changing fashions are highly profitable for the companies involved. Consumers are led to be eager to buy the latest fashions, although most often in the form of relatively inexpensive fast-fashion knockoffs.

The power of the fashion industry to affect consumers' social constructions and the products they buy has been analyzed by a number of sociologists (Lipovetsky [1987] 2002; Simmel [1904] 1971). Most notable is the work of another of the early giants in the field, Thorstein Veblen, who criticized the focus on the high heel and especially the skirt. He argued that women have been led to construct the skirt as desirable even though "it is expensive and hampers the wearer at every turn and incapacitates her for all useful exertion" (Veblen [1899] 1994, 171). Feminist theorists have extended this critique, arguing that the fashion industry's emphasis on beauty devices such as high heels helps maintain gender inequality by serving to limit women physically (Dworkin 1974; Jeffreys 2005). More subtly, these devices encourage women to construct as desirable a never-ending project of bodily discipline, especially an obsession with being thin. This project has been critiqued for creating an unreachable beauty ideal for most women (Bartky 1990; Wolf [1991] 2002). Unfortunately, as the recent documentary *The Illusionists* portrays, unrealistic Western beauty ideals of thin bodies and white skin are being exported across the globe.

Of course, many people do not accept such social constructions; they do not go along with the constraints of the fashion industry. They do not wear what the industry wants them to wear, and they do not change the way they dress because of changes in fashion induced by the fashion industry. Many people have their own sense of fashion and create their own way of dressing. Others ignore fashion altogether. Of greatest importance from this perspective is the fact that the idea of what is in fashion often comes not from the fashion industry but rather from the ways of dressing that people put together themselves. These people, in a real sense, construct their own social reality. In fact, in a process

known as "cool hunting" (Gloor and Cooper 2007), scouts for the fashion industry seek out new and interesting ways of dressing, often focusing on what young people in the suburbs and the inner cities are wearing. They bring those innovative ideas back to the fashion industry, and some of them are turned into next year's fashions.

Once this happens, however, we are back to a situation where the fashion industry is controlling, or at least attempting to control, people's social constructions of what they should wear. Many will accept the new fashion, but others, especially the "cool" kids who are sought out by the cool hunters, will not. They may well have moved on to some entirely new construction of what they want to wear. They will again attract the attention of cool hunters, and the process will begin anew. The development of fashion bloggers offers hope against the power of the fashion industry, although some bloggers work, overtly or covertly, for that industry, which also seeks to influence or control them.

SOCIAL STRUCTURES AND PROCESSES

Another nineteenth-century sociologist, Auguste Comte, was important not only for inventing the term *sociology* in 1839 but also for being the originator of sociology as a field. Crucial for our purposes here is his early distinction between what he called "social statics" and "social dynamics." In his social statics, Comte looked at the various "parts" (structures) of society, such as the manufacturers

Auguste Comte (1798–1857) invented the term "sociology," argued that the discipline should be a science, and created a general theory of the social world.

and retailers of clothing fashions, and the ways in which they relate to one another as well as to the whole of society. In examining such relationships, Comte investigated social processes among and between parts of society as well as in society as a whole. However, under the heading of social dynamics, his main focus was on a specific social process—social change—and how the various parts of society change.

It is important to emphasize here that **social structures** are enduring and regular social arrangements, such as the family and the state. While social structures do change, they are generally not very dynamic; they change very slowly. **Social processes** are the dynamic and ever-changing aspects of the social world.

The elements of globalization can be divided between structures (e.g., the United Nations) and a variety of more specific social processes (e.g., the migration of people across national borders). In terms of consumption, we can think of the shopping mall (or Amazon.com) as a structure and the shopping (or consumption) that takes place in it as a process. Finally, the internet as a whole and social networking sites in particular are structures, while the communication and the social interaction that take place in them can be viewed as processes.

Needless to say, neither the shopping mall nor the internet existed in Comte's day. Once again, we see that the social world is constantly changing and that sociologists, as well as students of sociology, must be sensitive to those changes. However, some of sociology's earliest concepts continue to be applicable, and usefully applied, to the social world.

CHECKPOINT 1.3:
UNDERSTANDING SOCIAL CONTINUITY AND CHANGE

Private troubles and public issues	Understanding how personal experiences are influenced by society
Micro–macro relationship	Understanding how small- and large-scale social phenomena are shaped by one another
Agency–structure relationship	Understanding how individual action is enabled and constrained by social structures
Social construction	Understanding how individuals create social reality through their thoughts and actions

SOCIOLOGY'S PURPOSE: SCIENCE OR SOCIAL REFORM?

Comte was famous not only for examining the relationship between structure and process but also for arguing that such study ought to be scientific. He believed that the social world was dominated by laws and that sociology's task was to uncover those laws. As those laws were uncovered, the science of sociology would develop. But Comte was also concerned about the problems of his day and interested in solving them through social reform. In fact, to Comte, science and reform should not be separated from one another. A number of classical sociologists—Karl Marx, Émile Durkheim, Jane Addams, and others—shared this view. Marx and Engels's *Communist Manifesto* (1848) was not only a commentary on the social ills of the capitalist economy but also a rallying cry to workers to organize and abolish capitalism.

Many of today's sociologists study social problems of all sorts, such as poverty and crime. They use a variety of scientific methods to collect large amounts of data on such problems (see Chapter 3). They also seek to use what they learn about those problems to suggest ways of reforming society. They believe that these two activities—scientific research and social reform—are not necessarily distinct; they can and should be mutually enriching. While many contemporary sociologists accept this position, a division has developed over time, with some sociologists focusing more on scientific research and others more engaged in activities designed to reform society and address social problems.

The sociologists who engage in "pure science" operate with the conviction that we need to have a better understanding of how the social world operates before we can change it, if that's what we want to do. The knowledge gained through social research may ultimately be used by those who want to change society, or to keep it as it is, but that is not the immediate concern of these researchers. For example, sociologists known as "ethnomethodologists" (see Chapter 2) argue that the task of the sociologist is to better understand common forms of social behavior (Rawls 2011). They research the details of everyday life, such as how we know when a laugh is expected in a conversation, or when to applaud or boo during a speech. For them, the goal is purely knowledge and understanding. Such sociologists argue that using that knowledge to reform society might adversely affect or distort social behaviors.

Other sociologists take the opposite position. C. Wright Mills, for example, was little interested in doing scientific research. He was mostly interested in such social reforms as limiting or eliminating the unwholesome and worrisome ties between the military and industry in the United States. He was also critical of many of the most prominent sociologists of his day for their orientation toward being pure scientists, their lack of concern for the pressing problems of the day, and their unwillingness to do anything about those problems. Feminist sociologists have extended the argument, pointing out that the topics and methods of objective, scientific sociology themselves sometimes reflect, and ultimately reinforce, social inequality along the lines of race, gender, and class because they are based on the assumptions of society's elite.

What do you believe is the best purpose of sociology: pure science or social reform? Why? Make a note to ask yourself this question again at the end of your course. Did you answer it differently?

For example, feminist scholar Cynthia Fuchs Epstein has argued that supposedly scientific distinctions between males and females have often been based on social biases. These social biases can be explained by the "prejudices against women and cultural notions emphasizing differences between the sexes" (Epstein 1988, 17). Until recently, scientific researchers have almost always been men. The questions about what problems were worthy of study reflected male interests rather than female interests. For example, issues more relevant to women, such as housework, pay inequality, and rape, were deemed trivial and were overshadowed by issues such as achievement and power (Riger 1992). Researchers' assumptions about and interpretations of the people they studied represented a male perspective. Most research subjects were male, and male behaviors and attitudes were treated as universal. Researchers did not consider how societies treat men and women differently and socialize them to feel and act in distinct ways. As a result, these seemingly "scientific" views of women reinforced false assumptions about male–female differences, held both men and women to supposedly universal male norms, and reproduced gender inequality (Rutherford, Vaughn-Blount, and Ball 2010).

CHECKPOINT 1.4: SCIENCE VERSUS SOCIAL REFORM

SOCIOLOGY AS PURE SCIENCE	SOCIOLOGY AS A MEANS OF SOCIAL REFORM
• Scientific methods are used to collect large quantities of data on the social world. • Using knowledge to effect social change might distort social behaviors.	• Social reform should address itself to and work on behalf of many diverse publics, especially society's marginalized groups. • Some "scientific" work has been distorted by social biases.

SOCIOLOGY, THE OTHER SOCIAL SCIENCES, AND COMMON SENSE

Sociology is one of the social sciences—that is, it is one of the fields that studies various aspects of the social world.

Among the others are anthropology, communication studies, economics, geography, political science, and psychology. Generally speaking, sociology is the broadest of these fields; social scientists in other fields are more likely than sociologists to delve into specific aspects of the social world in much greater depth. Sociological study touches on the culture of concern to anthropologists, the nation-state of interest to political scientists, and the mental processes that are the focus of psychologists. However, that does not mean that sociology is in any sense "better" than—or, conversely, not as good as—the other social sciences.

Rather than comparing and contrasting these fields in general terms, this concluding section will focus on the different ways in which these fields approach one of this book's signature concerns—globalization.

- *Anthropology:* Focuses on cultural aspects of societies around the world, such as the foods people eat and how they eat them, as well as the differences among cultures around the globe (Inda and Rosaldo 2008).

- *Communication studies:* Examines communications across the globe, with the internet obviously of focal concern in the contemporary world.

- *Economics:* Investigates the production, distribution, and consumption of resources through markets and other structures that span much of the globe, especially those based on and involving money.

- *Geography:* Studies spatial relationships on a global scale and maps those spaces (Herod 2009).

- *Political science:* Studies nation-states, especially the ways in which they relate to one another around the world as well as how they have grown increasingly unable to control global flows of migrants, viruses, recreational drugs, internet scams, and the like.

- *Psychology:* Examines the ways in which individual identities are shaped by increased awareness of the rest of the world and tensions associated with globalization (e.g., job loss), which may lead to individual psychological problems such as depression (Lemert and Elliott 2006).

Sociology encompasses all these concerns, and many others, in its approach to globalization. It studies globe-straddling cultures (such as consumer or fast-food culture), relationships between political systems (the European Union and its member nations, for example), communication networks (such as CNN and Al Jazeera or Twitter and Facebook), and markets (for labor or stocks and bonds, for example) that cover vast expanses of the globe. Sociology maps all of these, and even their impacts (both good and bad) on individuals. You might want to study the other fields to get a sense of the depth of what they have to offer on specific aspects of globalization. However, if you are looking for the field that gives you the broadest possible view of all of these things as well as the ways in which they interrelate, that field is sociology.

While sociology and the other social sciences differ from one another in important ways, they are all quite different from common-sense understandings of the social world. Everyone participates in globalization in one way or another. However, few if any people research these phenomena in the same rigorous way and to the same degree that social scientists examine them. That research leads, among other things, to a greater understanding of the nature of globalization. For example, you probably have a sense that globalization has changed society—perhaps even an impression that it is changing your life. What you are unlikely to know are globalization's causes, effects, and linkages to other social phenomena, or its largely invisible effects on society and the world. Research on the topic is also likely to yield much more insight into the pros and cons of globalization on personal, societal, and global levels. Such detailed knowledge and insight will help you, and others, more successfully navigate the accompanying changes in social processes and structures.

One example of the gap between common sense and social scientific knowledge relates to perceptions of the gap between the rich and the poor. A study of more than 5,000 Americans showed that people believe that the top fifth of the population in the United States possesses about 59 percent of the country's wealth. In fact, however, the top fifth actually holds almost 84 percent of the wealth (Norton and Ariely 2011). Figure 1.8 shows the results of this study. The commonsense view, then, is that wealth is far more evenly distributed than the scientific data reveal. This study also refuted the commonsense idea that the United States is a fair

FIGURE 1.8 • Wealth of the Top 20 Percent of U.S. Residents: Popular Views versus Reality

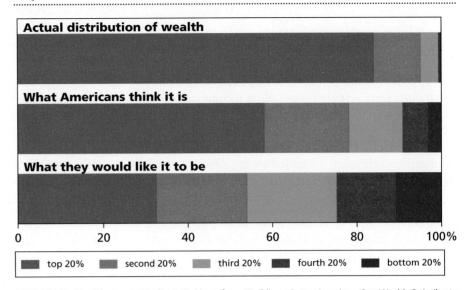

SOURCE: Wealth of the top 20% of U.S. Residents from "Building a Better America—One Wealth Quintile at a Time," by Michael I. Norton and Dan Ariely in *Perspectives on Psychological Science*, 2011, 6:1, pp. 9–12.

and equal society. When respondents were asked what the ideal wealth distribution would be, the average response was that the top fifth of the population should own only 32 percent of the wealth, not the 59 percent they guessed and certainly not the 84 percent that the upper fifth actually possesses.

While common sense is important, even to sociologists, there is no substitute for the systematic study of the social world in both its minutest detail and its broadest manifestations.

CHECKPOINT 1.5: SOCIOLOGY VERSUS COMMON SENSE

SOCIOLOGY	COMMON SENSE
• Developing theories to explain social phenomena	• Relying on one's opinion to explain social phenomena
• Conducting research to prove or disprove a theory	• Basing "facts" on informal observations

SUMMARY

Sociology is the systematic examination of the ways in which people are affected by and affect the social structures and social processes associated with the groups, organizations, cultures, societies, and world in which they exist. Social changes in the last few centuries, including the Industrial Revolution, the growth of the service sector, and the arrival of the information age, have strongly influenced the field of sociology. This book deals with innumerable social issues, but it focuses especially on three powerful structural forces in the social world that have drawn the attention of contemporary sociologists: globalization, consumption, and digital technology.

As the world has become more globalized, it has become more fluid as people, products, and information flow more quickly and easily across national borders. The role of consumption in our daily lives over the past few decades has resulted in the increasing use of credit cards and the growing popularity of online shopping. Digital technology is changing how and when we interact with others, including the near ubiquitous use of smartphones and social media. The process of McDonaldization, or an emphasis on efficiency, calculability, predictability, and technological control, characterizes many aspects of globalization, consumption, and digital technology.

Social changes such as globalization, consumption, and digital technology can be understood using C. Wright Mills's "sociological imagination," which calls on us to look at social phenomena not just from a personal perspective but also from the outside, from a distinctively sociological perspective. In addition, recognizing that much of our reality is socially constructed can

help us comprehend how the agency of individuals can bring about social change; at the same time, these changes become structures that both enable and constrain social action. These social structures become enduring and slow to change, while social processes represent the more dynamic aspects of society.

Sociologists study many issues, sometimes to understand them through scientific research and sometimes to help generate change and reform. The goal of sociology as a pure science is to collect large quantities of data about the social world to build knowledge, while the goal of sociology as a means of social reform aims to use this knowledge for social change.

Sociology, like other social sciences, distinguishes itself from commonsense opinions about the social world by developing rigorous theories and engaging in systematic research to study social phenomena. Sociology, the least specialized of the social sciences, encompasses aspects of anthropology, political science, psychology, economics, and communications.

KEY TERMS

agency, 19
butterfly effect, 2
consumption, 9
dangerous giant, 19
globalization, 9

macro, 18
McDonaldization, 11
mediated interaction, 14
micro, 18

social construction of
 reality, 19
social processes, 21
social structures, 21
society, 6

sociological
 imagination, 15
sociology, 2
technology, 13

REVIEW QUESTIONS

1. How is the projected impact of Waymo's driverless car an example of the butterfly effect? Use your sociological imagination to think of ways in which your individual choices and actions will be influenced by this development.
2. Your social world is continually changing. What are some examples of new technologies that have been developed during your lifetime? How have they changed the way you interact with and relate to others?
3. How do shopping malls reflect increasing globalization? Do you think shopping malls lead to a sameness of culture around the world, or do they allow local areas to retain their differences?

4. What items are you most likely to buy using the internet? How do social networking sites (e.g., Facebook, Twitter, Instagram) influence what you consume?
5. WikiLeaks has released thousands of confidential documents obtained from government, military, and corporate sources. Is this an example of an information war? Why or why not? What social structures have impeded the flow of this kind of information in the past? How have the internet and social networking sites made it easier to get around these structural barriers?
6. According to C. Wright Mills, how are private troubles different from public issues? How can we use the micro/

macro distinction to show how private troubles are related to public issues?

7. What is the difference between structure and agency? Within your classroom, could you be a "dangerous giant"? In what ways does your school prevent you from becoming a dangerous giant?

8. What do sociologists mean by the social construction of reality? How can you apply this perspective to better understand trends in the fashion industry?

9. Can you think of ways in which we can use "pure science" to better understand the process of McDonaldization? What do you believe should be the goal of research?

10. How is sociology's approach to globalization different from that of other social sciences? What are the advantages of using a sociological approach to understand globalization?

$SAGE edge™ Want a better grade?

Get the tools you need to sharpen your study skills. Access practice quizzes, eFlashcards, video and multimedia at **http://edge.sagepub.com/ritzerintro4e**.

THINKING SOCIOLOGICALLY

How Do Theories Help Us Understand Politics and Other Social Institutions?

The 2016 presidential election campaign was fraught with political maneuvering, fiery rhetoric, and intense partisanship. The supporters of Donald Trump and Hillary Clinton held radically different views on the state of American society and its future direction. While Trump was elected, the debate between those views has not ended. In fact, as President Trump sought to implement his largely conservative agenda, liberals ramped up their rhetoric and their opposition to it, including demonstrations and protests.

How would a sociologist explain such fierce political antagonism? The answer depends to a large extent on which sociologist you ask. Like other scientists, sociologists use theories to make sense of the phenomena they study. A sociologist's perspective on any given issue is therefore framed by the particular explanatory theories to which he or she subscribes.

Some sociologists suggest that political jockeying and debate, even if impassioned, are a normal function of stable government, necessary to resolve issues and move forward. Others believe that factions fighting to promote their own interests are enacting a simple, if large-scale, power struggle. Still others might explain the partisan actions as a reflection of the deep ideological divide that exists within the U.S. population as a whole. In this view, politicians' actions represent nothing more than the dominant ideas, beliefs, and feelings of their constituents.

In this chapter, we will identify the particular sociological theories that frame each of these perspectives—and many more. Each is the product of decades (and sometimes centuries) of development, and each has undergone testing, modification, and critique by some of sociology's greatest minds. As you learn about the notable sociological

LEARNING OBJECTIVES

2.1 Identify the most important classical sociologists and their major contributions to the field.

2.2 Identify other influential early figures in classical sociology.

2.3 Compare and contrast structural/functional, conflict/critical, and inter/actionist theories.

© AP Photo/Julio Cortez

thinkers—both classical and contemporary—and the theories they developed, consider the sociopolitical events that shaped them during their lives. Consider too the events that have shaped, and are shaping, you and your own perspectives on the world. ●

This chapter is devoted to the ways in which sociologists think, or theorize. All sociologists theorize. While some stay very close to their data, others feel free to depart from the data and offer very broad and general theories—"grand theories"—of the social world (Hoffman 2013; Skinner 1985; Vidal, Adler, and Delbridge 2015). Most of this chapter will be devoted to grand theories and to the people who produced them.

Theories are sets of interrelated ideas that have a wide range of applications, deal with centrally important issues, and have stood the test of time (Ritzer and Stepnisky 2017). Theories have stood the test of time when they continue to be applicable to the changing social world and have withstood challenges from those who accept other theories. Sociological theories are necessary to make sense of both the innumerable social phenomena and the many highly detailed findings of sociological research. Without such theories, we would have little more than knowledge of isolated bits of the social world. However, once those theories have been created, they can be applied broadly to such areas as the economy, organizations, religion, society as a whole, and even the globe. The theories to be discussed in this chapter deal with very important social issues that have affected the social world for centuries and will likely continue to affect it. Among these issues are violence, suicide, alienation and exploitation in the work world, and revolution.

Consider, for example, a recent theory of violence developed by Randall Collins (2008, 2009, 2012, 2013), which was mentioned briefly in Chapter 1. In line with the definition of theory offered previously, violence is clearly an important social issue, and Collins's theory promises to stand the test of time. Collins seeks to contradict the idea that violence is inherent in people and emphasizes the social contexts and causes of violence instead. He is developing a broad theory of violence that encompasses everything from a slap in the face to war, a quarrel to mass murder in gas chambers, drunken carousing to serial killing, a rape to systematic rape as a war crime, and the murder of someone with a different ethnicity to ethnic cleansing. Beyond being a very wide-ranging social phenomenon, violence usually generates powerful reactions among those who commit it, its victims, and those who witness it or read about it. As Collins puts it, violence is "horrible and heroic, disgusting and exciting, the most condemned and glorified of human

acts" (2008, 1). But the details of Collins's theory are not the concern here. Rather, it is the fact that he is seeking to develop a perspective that meets our definition of theory. In the coming years we will need to see whether Collins's specific theory actually stands the test of time. However, it is clear that violence is an important social phenomenon worth theorizing about (and studying). Collins has taken an important step in developing such a theory.

Violence is not only important in itself as a social phenomenon; it also raises important issues for other aspects of the social world. For example, the mass media are constantly confronted with decisions about how much violence—and the resulting carnage—they should show to the public. This dilemma came to the fore with the Islamic State's (IS's) 2014 mass murder of Iraqi soldiers and members of various ethnic groups and the beheading of others, including two U.S. journalists. Similar media problems have arisen in the case of mass deaths associated with IS-inspired terrorism in Paris, France, in late 2015, and the case of a truck being driven into the Christmas market in Berlin in late 2016, which killed at least a dozen people and injured many more. Near the end of 2016, the BBC showed a graphic clip of the murder of the Russian ambassador to Turkey by an opponent to Russia's involvement in the war in Syria. We have undoubtedly not seen the last of such individual and mass killings and the wrenching choices their depiction poses for the mass media (depictions that are readily available on internet sites such as You Tube and Twitter), to say nothing for the family and friends of the victims.

ASK YOURSELF

What social causes drive actors to carry out public violence? Does understanding those causes make the violence any more "acceptable"? Should the media lift all bans on showing such forms of violence? Or should they be even more restrictive about showing violent acts?

Theorizing about the social world is not restricted to sociologists such as Randall Collins; everyone theorizes. What, then, distinguishes the theorizing of sociologists from your own? One difference is that whereas you might theorize casually, sociologists go about their theorizing systematically by, among other things, making the social world their laboratory. For example, you might notice two people together. Drawing on your observations of how those people are interacting (including what they are wearing and their nonverbal communication) and your ideas of romantic relationships and behaviors, you may conclude that they are dating (Weigel 2016). You have a (perhaps unconscious) theory about dating, and you use it to interpret

YAVUZ ALATAN/AFP/Getty Images

YAVUZ ALATAN/AFP/Getty Images

At an art museum in Ankara, an off-duty Turkish policeman assassinated the Russian ambassador to Turkey in a protest over Russia's military involvement on behalf of Syrian President Bashir Assad's government. The BBC first showed the photo on the left with the dead ambassador's body, but later showed the one on the right with the body cropped out. Most media outlets in the United States would not show the photo with the dead body.

their actions and predict how they might interact next. In contrast, sociologists are likely to be conscious of their theory of dating. With that theory as background, they might study behaviors among many pairs of people, carefully analyze the similarities and differences among them, compare those behaviors to those of people in other societies, and then conclude that a particular style of interaction characterizes dating couples. More concretely, one recent study of 144 college students used a classical theory of deviance to demonstrate that academic and interpersonal stress increased dating violence (Mason and Smithey 2012). Using another (social learning) theory, Giordano and colleagues (2015) interviewed nearly 1,000 students in 32 different schools and found that the level of violence in a school was a significant predictor of whether a student would perpetrate a violent act. To some degree, perpetrators "learn" to commit violent acts in the context of schools characterized by violence. At some level, we are all theorists, but professional sociologists consciously use theories to analyze scientific data systematically in order to make better sense of their results, and of the social world.

Another difference between you and trained sociologists is that you are pretty much on your own in your theorizing, although the material in this book will help. In contrast, sociologists not only work directly with, and read the work of, other contemporary sociologists but also base their theories on the work of many important thinkers in the field who have come before them. As the great physicist Sir Isaac Newton ([1687] 2005) put it, "If I have seen further, it is only by standing on the shoulders of giants." Many of today's sociologists theorize because they are able to build on the thoughts of the classical "grand theorists" to be discussed in this chapter. To put it another way, many sociologists have, or can easily acquire, the "intellectual

capital" of the discipline: the knowledge of past theories. Such knowledge would be much more difficult for you as a student to acquire on your own. However, all of today's sociologists were once students like you. This book will begin to give you the intellectual capital you need to start thinking like a sociologist.

THE GIANTS OF CLASSICAL SOCIOLOGICAL THEORY

The roots of sociology lie primarily in early nineteenth-century Europe. However, there were much earlier thinkers whose ideas are relevant to sociology. Examples from the third and fourth centuries BCE are Plato and Aristotle. Centuries later, Ibn Khaldun (1332–1406) developed sociological theories that dealt with such issues as the scientific study of society, the interrelationship between politics and the economy, and the relationship between primitive societies and the medieval societies of his time (Alatas 2011, 2013). Such topics were also of interest to nineteenth-century theorists and continue to be of interest today. For example, Alatas (2014) has applied Khaldun's thinking to such modern Arab states as Syria and its prospects in light of the war currently raging there.

The emergence of sociological theory was closely related to intellectual and social developments throughout the nineteenth century in Europe. It is important to recognize that sociological theory did not develop in isolation or come of age in a social vacuum. In Chapter 1, we briefly mentioned the impact of the Industrial Revolution. Other changes that profoundly affected sociological theorizing were the political revolutions that wracked European

Though Herbert Spencer never earned an academic degree, his work contributed greatly to the field of scientific sociology, especially in the study of evolutionary change.

society (especially the French Revolution, 1789–1799), the rise of socialism, the women's rights movement, the urbanization occurring throughout Europe, ferment in the religious realm, and the growth of science.

Among the most important early sociological theorists are Auguste Comte, Harriet Martineau, and Herbert Spencer:

- *Auguste Comte* (1798–1857) is noted, as pointed out in Chapter 1, for the invention of the term *sociology*, development of a general theory of the social world, and interest in developing a science of sociology (Pickering 2011).

- *Harriet Martineau* (1802–1876), like Comte, developed a scientific and general theory, although she is best known today for her feminist, women-centered sociology (Hoecker-Drysdale 2011).

- *Herbert Spencer* (1820–1903) also developed a general, scientific theory of society, but his overriding theoretical interest was in social change, specifically evolution in not only the physical domain but also the intellectual and social domains (Francis 2011).

Although Comte, Martineau, and Spencer were important predecessors, the three theorists to be discussed in this section—Karl Marx, Max Weber, and Émile

Durkheim—are the most significant of the classical era's social theorists and of the greatest continuing contemporary relevance to sociology (and other fields). Their relevance to you lies in the fact that, among many other points, they analyzed the negative effects of too much (Marx and Weber) and too little (Durkheim) social control on people. Their analyses were connected to their major fears about the modern world—that capitalist systems alienate and exploit us (Marx), that rational systems trap and limit us (Weber), and that a weak shared culture exerts too little external control and leads us to run wild in the endless pursuit of that which ultimately proves unsatisfying, if not disastrous (Durkheim).

ASK YOURSELF

In what ways do you feel that too much social control is exercised over you? In what ways is there too little social control over you? Would you like to be controlled more or less? What would be the impact on you of more control? Of less control?

KARL MARX

Marx (1818–1883) is often dismissed as an ideologue. In recent years, he has been disparaged because of the failure of a social system—communism—that is generally considered to be his brainchild. In fact, the communism that came to be practiced in the Soviet Union and other countries had little relationship to Marx's abstract sense of communism. He would have been as critical of it as he was of capitalism. However, there is an important sociological theory in Marx's work (Antonio 2011; Holt 2015). Its importance is reflected in the fact that many theorists have built on it and many others have created theories in opposition to Marx's perspective (Sitton 2010).

Marx was mainly a macro theorist who focused most of his attention on the structure of capitalist society, a relatively new phenomenon in his day. Marx defined **capitalism** as an economic system based on the fact that one group of people—the **capitalists**—owns what is needed for production, including factories, machines, and tools. A second group—the **proletariat**, or workers—owns little or nothing except their capacity for work and labor. In order to work and survive, the workers must sell their labor time, primarily their working hours, to the capitalists in exchange for wages. In Marx's view, the capitalist system is marked by **exploitation**. The proletariat produces virtually everything but gets only a small portion of the income derived from the sale of the products. The capitalists, who do little productive work, reap the vast majority of the rewards. In other words, the capitalists *exploit* the workers. Furthermore, driven by the need to compete in the marketplace, the capitalists are forced to keep costs, including wages, as low as possible. Then, as competition with other capitalists intensifies, the pressure is on to reduce wages further. As a result, the proletariat barely subsists, living a miserable, animal-like existence.

In addition, the workers experience **alienation** on the job and in the workplace (Mészáros 2006). They are alienated because

- The work they do—for example, repetitively and mechanically inserting wicks into candles or attaching hubcaps to cars—is not a natural expression of human skills, abilities, and creativity.

- They have little or no connection to the finished product.

- Instead of working harmoniously with their fellow workers, they may have little or no contact with them. In fact, they are likely to be in competition or outright conflict with them over, for example, who keeps and who loses their jobs.

Thus, what defines people as human beings—their ability to think, to act on the basis of that thought, to be creative, to interact with other human beings—is denied to the workers in capitalism. As capitalists adopt new technologies to make their companies more competitive, alienation among the workers increases. For example, faster, more mechanized assembly lines make it even more difficult for coworkers to relate to one another.

Over time, Marx believed, the workers' situation would grow much worse as the capitalists increased the level of exploitation and restructured the work so that the proletariat became even more alienated. The gap between these two social classes would grow wider and increasingly visible in terms of the two groups' economic position and the nature of their work. Once workers understood how capitalism "really" worked, especially the ways in which it worked to their detriment, they would rise up and overthrow that system in what Marx called a proletarian revolution.

According to Marx, the outcome of the proletarian revolution would be the creation of a communist society. Interestingly, Marx had very little to say explicitly about what a communist society would look like. In fact, he was highly critical of utopian thinkers who wasted their time drawing beautiful portraits of an imaginary future state. Marx was too much the sociologist and concentrated instead on trying to better understand the structures of capitalist society. He was particularly interested in the ways in which they operated, especially to the advantage of the capitalists and to the disadvantage of the proletariat.

Marx believed that his work was needed because the capitalist class tried hard to make sure that the proletariat did not truly understand the nature of capitalism. One of the ways in which the capitalists did this was to produce a set of ideas, an **ideology**, that distorted the reality of capitalism and concealed the ways in which it really operated. As a result, the proletariat suffered from **false consciousness**—the workers did not truly understand capitalism and may have even believed, erroneously, that the system operated fairly and perhaps even to their benefit. Marx's work was devoted to providing the members of the proletariat with the knowledge they needed to see through these false ideas and achieve a truer understanding of the workings of capitalism.

Marx hypothesized that the workers could develop **class consciousness**, and such a collective consciousness would lead them to truly understand capitalism, their role in it, and their relationship to one another as well as to the capitalists. Class consciousness was a prerequisite of the revolutionary actions to be undertaken by the proletariat. In contrast, the capitalists could never achieve class consciousness because, in Marx's view, they were too deeply involved in capitalism to be able to see how it truly operated.

ASK YOURSELF

Do you agree with Marx's characterizations of false consciousness and class consciousness? Why or why not? Give some examples from your own experience to support your answer.

Marx's theories about capitalism are relevant to contemporary society. For example, in the United States, a capitalist country, the income gap that Marx predicted between those at the top of the economic system and the rest of the population is huge and growing. In 2014, the top 20 percent of the population in terms of household income had a greater average income than the rest of the population combined. Furthermore, as you can see in Figure 2.1, those at the top have greatly increased their average income since 1967; this is especially true of the top 5 percent of the population. In contrast, the lowest fifth has a lower average income than it had in 1967 (DeNavas-Walt, Proctor, and Smith 2012).

Marx also theorized that capitalism would force the capitalists to find the cheapest sources of labor and resources wherever they existed in the world (Panitch 2009). As Marx predicted, corporations continue to scour the globe for workers willing to work for lower wages, driving down pay closer to home and reaping as much profit as possible from lower labor costs.

However, history has failed to bear out much of Marx's thinking about the demise of capitalism. For example, there has been no proletarian revolution, and one seems less likely than ever. This is the case, if for no other reason, because the members of the proletariat of greatest interest to Marx—manufacturing workers—are rapidly declining in

FIGURE 2.1 • Mean Household Income Received by Each Fifth and Top 5 Percent, All Races: 1967–2014

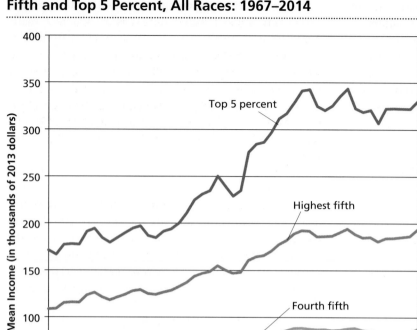

SOURCE: Data from U.S. Census Bureau, Current Population Survey, Annual Social and Economic Supplements.

number and importance, at least in developed countries like the United States (Rifkin 1995; Schwartz 2016a). Despite the threats to the proletariat, capitalism continues to exist, and Marx's ways of thinking about it, and the concepts he developed for that analysis, continue to be useful.

MAX WEBER

Although Karl Marx was a very important social theorist, he developed his ideas outside the academic world. It took time for those radical ideas to gain recognition from scholars. In contrast, Max Weber (1864–1920; pronounced VAY-ber) was a leading academician of his day (Kalberg 2011, 2017). Weber, like Marx, devoted great attention to the economy. Many of Marx's ideas informed Weber's thinking, in large part because those ideas were finding a wide public audience at the time that Weber was active. Furthermore, Weber understood the dramatic changes, inspired at least in part by Marx's ideas, taking place in Europe and elsewhere. After all, Weber lived during, and analyzed, the Russian Revolution in 1917 and the rise of communism there. Nevertheless, Weber rarely discussed Marx's theories explicitly. Thus, observers have characterized much of Weber's work as a debate with Marx's "ghost."

Weber's best-known work—*The Protestant Ethic and the Spirit of Capitalism* ([1904–1905] 1958)—is part of his historical-comparative study of religion in various societies throughout the world (see Chapter 3). One of his main objectives was to analyze the relationship between the economy and religion. This is a good example of his debate with Marx. Marx had argued that religion is a relatively minor force that serves to distract the masses from the problems caused by capitalism. In Marx's ([1843] 1970) famous words, religion "is the opium of the people." In contrast, Weber focused on the central role religion had played in the Western world's economic development.

Beginning in the seventeenth century, it was Protestantism in general, and especially Calvinism, that led to the rise of capitalism in the West and not in other areas of the world. Calvinists believed that people were predestined to go to heaven or hell; that is, they would end up in heaven or hell no matter what they did or did not do. While they could not affect their destiny, they could uncover "signs" that indicated whether or not they were "saved" and going to heaven. Economic success was a particularly important sign that one was saved. However, isolated successful economic successes were not sufficient. Calvinists had to devote their lives to hard work and economic success, as well as to other "good works." At the same time, the Calvinists were quite frugal. All of this was central to the distinctive ethical system of the Calvinists, and more generally Protestants, that Weber referred to as the **Protestant ethic**.

Weber was interested not only in the Protestant ethic but also in the "spirit of capitalism" that it helped spawn. The Protestant ethic was a system of ideas closely associated with religion, while the spirit of capitalism involved a transformation of those ideas into a perspective linked directly to the economy. As the economy came to be infused with the spirit of capitalism, it was transformed into a capitalist economic system. Eventually, however, the spirit of capitalism, and later capitalism itself, grew apart from its roots in Calvinism and the Protestant ethic. Capitalist thinking eventually could not accommodate such irrational forms of thought as ethics and religion.

Despite his attention to it, Weber was *not* interested in capitalism per se. He was more interested in the broader phenomenon of **rationalization**, or the process by which social structures are increasingly characterized by the most direct and efficient means to their ends. In Weber's view, this process was becoming more and more common in many sectors of society, including the economy, especially in bureaucracies and in the most rational economic system—capitalism. Capitalism is rational because of, for example, its continual efforts to find ways to produce more profitable products efficiently, with fewer inputs and simpler processes. A specific and early example of rationalization in capitalism is the assembly line, in which raw materials enter the line and finished products emerge at the end. Fewer workers performed very simple tasks in order to allow the assembly line to function efficiently. More recently, manufacturers have added more rational, "lean" production methods, such as the just-in-time inventory system (Janoski 2015). Instead of storing extra components in case they are needed, the just-in-time system relies on the delivery of materials when they are needed in the production process. This makes for highly efficient use of storage space and the funds needed to purchase materials.

Weber saw rationalization as leading to an "iron cage" of rationalized systems. Such a cage makes it increasingly difficult for people to escape the process. This gives a clear sense of his negative opinion of rationalization. In this light, consider what he has to say about the cagelike character of capitalism:

> Capitalism is today an immense cosmos into which the individual is born, and which presents itself to him, at least as an individual, as an unalterable order of things in which he must live. It forces the individual, in so far as he is involved in the system of market relationships, to conform to capitalist rules of action. (Weber [1904–1905] 1958, 54)

Such a negative view of rationalization and its constraints and socially harmful effects has persisted. It is frequently portrayed in popular entertainment, including George Orwell's novel, and later movie, *Nineteen Eighty-Four* (1949), as well as movies such as *Brazil* (1985), *V for Vendetta* (2005), and the *Hunger Games* series (2012–2015).

ASK YOURSELF

Efforts to exploit, alienate, and control us continue to this day. Is only capitalism to blame for this? Are there causes to be found in even larger systems in the modern world? Or are more microscopic sources, such as the nature of human beings, responsible for these efforts?

In sum, while for Marx the key problems in the modern world were the exploitation and alienation that are part of the capitalist economy, for Weber the central problem was the control that rationalized structures such as capitalism exercise over us in virtually all aspects of our lives. Furthermore, while Marx was optimistic and had great hope for socialism and communism, Weber was a pessimist about most things. Socialism and communism, he felt, would not eliminate or prevent the iron cage from enveloping us: "Not summer's bloom lies ahead of us, but rather a polar night of icy darkness and hardness, no matter which group may triumph externally now" (Weber [1919] 1958, 128).

Karl Marx, Émile Durkheim, and Max Weber were three of the most significant social theorists of their era. Though their theories were very different in many ways, all three were interested in the effect of social control on people.

ÉMILE DURKHEIM

Émile Durkheim (1858–1917) developed a theoretical orientation that was very different from those of his peers (Fournier 2013; Milibrandt and Pearce 2011). Like Marx and Weber, Durkheim focused on the macro end of the social continuum. However, while Marx and Weber were critical of the macro structures of prime concern to them—capitalism (Marx) and rationalized structures (Weber)—Durkheim generally had a positive view of macro structures.

For Durkheim, the major concern of the science of sociology was **social facts**. These are macro-level phenomena, such as social structures and cultural norms and values, that stand apart from people and, more important, impose themselves on people. Examples of social facts that impose themselves on you include the structures of your university and the U.S. government. They are Durkheimian social facts because they have an independent existence and are able to force people to do things. Durkheim felt that such structures and their constraints were not only necessary but also highly desirable.

The differences among Marx, Weber, and Durkheim can be traced to each theorist's sense of the essential character of human beings. Both Marx and Weber had a generally positive sense of people as thoughtful, creative, and naturally social. They criticized social structures for stifling and distorting people's innate characteristics. In contrast, Durkheim had a largely negative view of people as being slaves to their passions, such as lust, gluttony, and other deadly sins. Left to their own devices, he believed, people would seek to satisfy those passions. However, the satisfaction of one passion would simply lead to the need to satisfy other passions. This endless succession of passions could never be satisfied. In Durkheim's view, passions should be limited, but people are unable to exercise this control themselves. They need social facts that are capable of limiting and controlling their passions.

The most important of these social facts is the **collective conscience**, or the set of beliefs shared by people throughout society (Bowring 2016). In Durkheim's view, the collective conscience is highly desirable not only for society but also for individuals. For example, it is good for both society and individuals that we share the belief that we are not supposed to kill one another. Without a collective conscience, murderous passions would be left to run wild. Individuals would be destroyed, of course, and eventually so would society.

This leads us to Durkheim's *Suicide* ([1897] 1951), one of the most famous research studies in the history of sociology. Because he was a sociologist, Durkheim did not focus on why any given individual committed suicide. Rather, he dealt with the more collective issue of suicide rates and why one group of people had a higher rate of suicide than another. The study was in many ways an ideal example of the power of sociological research. Using publicly available data, Durkheim found, for example, that suicide rates were not related to psychological and biological factors such as alcoholism or race and heredity. The causes of differences in suicide rates were *not* to be found within individuals. Rather, suicide rates were related to social factors that exert negative pressure on the individual. These include collective feelings of rootlessness and normlessness. Suicide literally destroys individuals. It also constitutes a threat to society, because those who commit suicide are rejecting a key aspect of the collective conscience—that one should not kill oneself.

Suicide has at least two important characteristics. First, the study was designed, like much sociological research today, to contribute to the public understanding of an important sociological problem or issue. Second, and more important for the purposes of this introduction to sociology, it demonstrated the power of sociology to explain one of the most private and personal of acts. Suicide had previously been seen as the province of the field of psychology, and responsibility for the act was most often accorded to the individual. Durkheim believed that if sociology could be shown to be applicable to suicide, it could deal with any and all social phenomena.

ASK YOURSELF

What do you think led Durkheim to believe that if sociology could explain suicide, it could explain all social phenomena? Do you agree with him? Why or why not?

Durkheim differentiated among four different types of suicide. The most important one for our purposes is *anomic suicide*. **Anomie** is defined as people's feeling that they do not know what is expected of them in society—the feeling of being adrift in society without any clear or secure moorings. According to Durkheim, the risk of anomic suicide increases when people do not know what is expected of them, when society's regulation over them is low, and when their passions are allowed to run wild.

More generally, Durkheim believed that anomie is the defining problem of the modern world. In contrast to Marx and Weber, who worried about too much external control over people, Durkheim, at least in his thinking on anomie, worried about too little control, especially over passions. This broad view appeared in another famous work by Durkheim, *The Division of Labor in Society* ([1893] 1964). He began by describing an early form of society with little division of labor. People there were held together by a type of solidarity—**mechanical solidarity**—stemming from the fact that they all did pretty much the same kinds of work, including hunting, gathering, and cooking.

More important, people in this type of society had a strong collective conscience.

However, as Durkheim demonstrated, an increasing division of labor took place over time. Instead of continuing to do the same sorts of things, people began to specialize. Some became hunters, others farmers, and still others cooks. What held them together was not their similarities but their differences. That is, they had become more dependent on one another; people needed what others did and produced in order to survive. Durkheim called this later form of social organization **organic solidarity**. This can be a powerful form of solidarity, but it is accompanied by a decline in the power of the collective conscience. Because people were doing such different things, they no longer necessarily believed as strongly in the same set of ideas. This weakened collective conscience was a problem, Durkheim argued, because it progressively lost the power to control people's passions. Further, because of the weakened collective conscience, people were more likely to feel anomic and, among other things, were more likely to commit anomic suicide.

CHECKPOINT 2.1: LEADING EARLY THEORISTS IN SOCIOLOGY

THEORIST	MAJOR CONTRIBUTION TO SOCIOLOGY
Karl Marx	Examined the structure of capitalist society and its exploitation of the proletariat class
Max Weber	Focused on the role of religion in the economic development of the West and rationalization
Émile Durkheim	Studied how social facts, like collective conscience, constrain individual agency

OTHER IMPORTANT EARLY THEORISTS

Although Marx, Weber, and Durkheim are the classical sociologists whose theories have most shaped contemporary sociology, several others made important contributions as well. Georg Simmel, W. E. B. Du Bois, and Thorstein Veblen all had grand theories of society, and you will see references to their ideas throughout this book.

GEORG SIMMEL

Georg Simmel (1858–1918), whose economic theories were mentioned in Chapter 1, offered an important grand theory that parallels those of the thinkers discussed previously (Helle 2015), but his major importance in contemporary sociology lies in his contributions to micro theory.

Simmel believed that sociologists should focus on the way in which conscious individuals interact and associate with one another (Scaff 2011).

Simmel was interested in the *forms* taken by social interaction. One such form involves the interaction between superiors and subordinates. An example would be the interaction between the manager at Whole Foods and those who stock the shelves at that supermarket. Simmel was also interested in the *types* of people who engage in interaction. For example, one type is the poor person and another is the rich person. For Simmel, it was the nature of the interaction between these two types of people and not the nature of the people themselves that was of greatest importance. Therefore, poverty is not about the nature of the poor person but about the kind of interaction that takes place between the poor and the rich. A poor person is defined, then, not as someone who lacks money but rather as someone who receives aid from a rich person.

There is great detail in Simmel's analyses of forms of interaction and types of interactants, as there is in his larger macro theory. But for our purposes here, the main point is that Simmel was of greatest importance to the micro-interactionist theories to be discussed in this chapter and at other points in this book.

INTERFOTO/Alamy Stock Photo

Georg Simmel's interest in the forms taken by social interaction contributed to his influential theory that it is the interaction between people that defines them and society.

W. E. B. DU BOIS

Just as Harriet Martineau was a pioneer in bringing gender to the forefront in sociology, W. E. B. Du Bois (1868–1963) was crucial to the later focus of sociology on race. While Du Bois lived long into the modern era, his most important theoretical work was completed in the early twentieth century (Taylor 2011).

Du Bois is best known in sociology for his theoretical ideas but was also, like Durkheim and Weber, a pioneering researcher. In *The Philadelphia Negro* ([1899] 1996), Du Bois reported on his studies of the residents of the Seventh Ward in Philadelphia. He used a variety of social scientific methods, including field research, observation, and interviews. He dealt with such basic concerns in sociology as marriage and the family, education, work, the church, housing, and politics, as well as such social problems as illiteracy and crime. Du Bois placed most of the blame for the problems experienced by black Philadelphians on whites, racism, and discrimination. However, he did not ignore the role played by African Americans in these problems. One example was their tendency to visit white physicians, thereby adversely affecting the livelihood of black physicians.

As for his theoretical contributions, Du Bois saw what he called the "race idea" as central. He saw a "color line" existing between whites and blacks in the United States. (He ultimately came to recognize that such a divide existed globally.) This barrier was physical in the sense that African Americans could be distinguished visually, through their darker skin color, from white Americans. The barrier was also political in that much of the white population did not see African Americans as "true" Americans. As a result, they denied African Americans many political rights, such as the right to vote. And the barrier was psychological because, among other things, African Americans found it difficult to see themselves in ways other than the ways in which white society saw them.

One of Du Bois's goals, especially in *The Souls of Black Folk* ([1903] 1966), was to lift the veil of race and give whites a glimpse of "Negroes" in America. He also wanted to show blacks that they could see themselves in a different

Harriet Martineau, left, and W.E.B. Du Bois, right, were essential to efforts to bring a focus on gender and race, respectively, to the field of sociology.

The Scholar Denied: W. E. B. Du Bois and the Birth of Modern Sociology (University of California Press, 2015)

Aldon D. Morris (Leon Forrest Professor of Sociology and African American Studies at Northwestern University; PhD, State University of New York, Stony Brook, 1980)

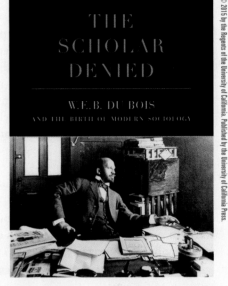

According to Morris, Du Bois has not been given the credit he deserves in establishing scientific sociology in the United States. In fact, Morris argues that the work of Du Bois was intentionally ignored by the white founders of American sociology, such as Albion Small, who defended Social Darwinism, or the idea that society is guided by natural laws (Morris 2015, 22). Instead of trying to empirically prove that these natural laws existed, these early sociologists developed speculative grand theories. Their belief in the existence of natural laws also led them to minimize the role of human agency in society and prevented them from developing a comparative perspective. Du Bois attempted to challenge Social Darwinism by using empirical methodology to demonstrate that racial inferiority was not a result of biology or natural law, but a product of society. Two decades before the Chicago School of sociology started using scientific methodology to investigate urban ethnic and immigrant communities, Du Bois conducted an empirical study of the black community in Philadelphia. His findings were published in his book *The Philadelphia Negro* ([1899] 1996), which

Morris hails as "the first major empirical sociological study" (2015, 45). However, the early Chicago School sociologists failed to acknowledge Du Bois's contributions in their work.

Even though Du Bois received his doctorate from Harvard, he was denied an academic position at a prestigious American university because of his race. He pursued his scholarly career at Atlanta University, a historically black college, where he established a sociology department with a strong empirical research program. Even though most American sociologists ignored Du Bois's work, he gained a famous advocate in Germany—Max Weber. Weber invited Du Bois to write an article on caste relations for his journal (*Archiv für Sozialwissensachaft and Sozialpolitik*) and tried to have a translation of Du Bois's *The Souls of Black Folk* published in Germany. Weber shared Du Bois's position that race was a social construct shaped by socioeconomic conditions, not biology. Like Du Bois, Weber was interested in the intersections between class and race relations and agreed that the color line was a critical problem of their era. Morris suggests that Weber's

theory of caste and status groups, as well as his embrace of cultural pluralism later in his career, was influenced by the work of Du Bois.

Supplementary Resources

- You can listen to Morris deliver a lecture on the relevance of Du Bois in science, the civil rights movement, and the Black Lives Matter movement at https://youtu.be/ji8JdUl38nE.
- An article about Morris and his book *A Scholar Denied* appeared in the Chicago Tribune: www.chicagotribune.com/news/columnists/ct-sociology-dubois-dawn-turner-20150916-column.html.

way, especially outside the view that white society had prescribed for them. Politically, he hoped for the day when the veil would be lifted forever, thereby freeing blacks. However, he did understand that destroying the veil of race would require a great deal of time and effort.

Another of Du Bois's important ideas is **double consciousness**. By this he meant that black Americans have a sense of "two-ness," of being American and of being African American. Black Americans want to tear down the barriers that confront them but do not want to give up their identity, traditions, knowledge, and experience. That is, black Americans, including former President Barack Obama (Terrill 2015), are both inside and outside dominant, white American society. Double consciousness results in a sense among black Americans that they are characterized by "two souls, two thoughts, two unreconciled strivings; two warring ideals" (Du Bois [1903] 1966, 5).

Double consciousness obviously produces great tension for black Americans, much greater than the tensions felt by white Americans in regard to their race. However, it also gives black Americans unusual insights into themselves, white Americans, and American society in general. Du Bois urged black Americans to reach full maturity as a social group by reconciling and integrating these two conflicting aspects of their selves.

ASK YOURSELF

How many "consciousnesses" do you have? What are they? In what ways are they sources of satisfaction for you? In what ways do they stress you?

The idea of double consciousness has much broader applicability than just to black Americans. Other racial and ethnic minorities can be seen as having such a double consciousness—for example, of being Hispanic and American. Similarly, women likely see themselves as both females and Americans. This leads us to wonder: Who does *not* have double consciousness? It also leads to the view that Du Bois did not go nearly far enough with this idea. There may be more, perhaps many more, than two consciousnesses. Consider, for example, the quadruple consciousness of a *female* immigrant from *Guatemala* who is *Hispanic* and has become an *American* citizen.

THORSTEIN VEBLEN

Like many of the other figures discussed in this chapter, Thorstein Veblen (1857–1929) had a broader theory (McCormick 2011), but given our focus in this book on consumption, we will address here only the ideas associated with his most famous book, *The Theory of the Leisure Class* (Veblen [1899] 1994). One of Veblen's main concerns involved the ways in which the upper classes demonstrate their wealth.

One way to show off wealth is through *conspicuous leisure,* or doing things that demonstrate quite publicly that one does not need to do what most people consider to be work. Veblen believed that the wealthy want to demonstrate to all that they can afford to waste time, often a great deal of time. Sitting on one's porch sipping margaritas, perhaps in "Margaritaville," having workers tend to one's lawn, and frequently playing golf at expensive golf clubs would be

examples of conspicuous leisure. However, the problem with conspicuous leisure is that it is often difficult for very many others to witness these displays.

Thus, over time the focus for the wealthy shifts from publicly demonstrating a waste of time to publicly demonstrating a waste of money. (Compare this set of values to the frugality of the Calvinists studied by Weber.) The waste of money is central to Veblen's most famous idea, **conspicuous consumption**. It is much easier for others to see conspicuous consumption than it is for them to see conspicuous leisure. Examples include building extravagant homes, such as David and Jackie Siegel's planned (but troubled) 90,000-square-foot mansion (named Versailles) in Orlando, Florida (Greenfield 2012); driving around one's neighborhood in a Porsche; and wearing Dolce & Gabbana clothing with the D&G logo visible to all. The well-to-do, Veblen's "leisure class," stand at the top of a society's social class system. Many in the social classes below the wealthy, the middle and lower classes, copy the leisure class. For example, people in lower social classes might build relatively inexpensive McMansions or buy cheap knockoffs of D&G clothing.

Veblen is important because he focused on consumption at a time when it was largely ignored by other social theorists. Furthermore, his specific ideas, especially conspicuous consumption, continue to be applied to the social world.

Thorstein Veblen studied the ways in which the upper classes demonstrate their wealth. He theorized that conspicuous consumption is a way for the wealthy to show off their wealth by purchasing expensive, highly visible houses, cars, jewelry, and clothing, among many other things.

CHECKPOINT 2.2: OTHER IMPORTANT EARLY THEORISTS IN SOCIOLOGY

THEORIST	MAJOR CONTRIBUTION TO SOCIOLOGY
Georg Simmel	Developed a micro-level theory of social interaction
W. E. B. Du Bois	Developed a sociology of race and the idea of double consciousness
Harriet Martineau	Conceptualized a feminist, women-centered sociology
Thorstein Veblen	Studied consumption, and in particular conspicuous consumption by the wealthy

CONTEMPORARY SOCIOLOGICAL THEORY

As sociology has developed and grown as a discipline, the grand theories of earlier sociologists have evolved and branched out into at least a dozen newer theories. The work of the classical theorists has influenced each of these theories. For example, Marx's thinking on the relationship between capitalists and the proletariat strongly affected conflict/critical theory, and Simmel's micro-sociological ideas on forms and types of interaction helped shape inter/actionist theories. As Table 2.1 shows, these contemporary theories and the others reviewed in the rest of this chapter can be categorized under three broad headings: structural/functional, conflict/critical, and inter/actionist theories.

STRUCTURAL/FUNCTIONAL THEORIES

Structural/functional theories have evolved out of the observation and analysis of large-scale social phenomena. These phenomena include the state and the culture, the latter encompassing the ideas and objects that allow people to carry out their collective lives (see Chapter 4 for more on culture). The two major theories under the broad heading of structural/functional theories are *structural-functionalism,* which looks at both social structures and their functions, and *structuralism,* which concerns itself solely with social structures, without concern for their functions. Note that while the names sound the same, structural-functionalism is one theory under the broader heading of structural/functional theories.

Structural-Functionalism

As the name suggests, **structural-functionalism** focuses on social structures as well as the functions that such structures perform. Structural-functionalists are influenced by the work of, among others, Émile Durkheim, who discussed, for example, the functions of and structural limits placed on deviance. Structural-functional theorists start out with a positive view of social structures. For example, in the case of the sociology of deviance (see Chapter 7), those structures might include the military, the police, and the Department of Homeland Security. Structural-functional theorists also assert that those structures are desirable, necessary, and even impossible to do without. However, as you will see later, not all sociologists view social structures as completely positive.

Structural-functionalism tends to be a "conservative" theory. The dominant view is that if given structures exist and are functional—and it is often assumed that if they exist, they are functional—they ought to be retained and conserved.

A series of well-known and useful concepts have been developed by structural-functionalists, especially Robert Merton ([1949] 1968; Crothers 2011). These concepts are easily explained in the context of one of this book's signature concerns, globalization. Specifically, they can be applied to issues such as border controls and the passports needed to pass through them (Torpey 2012), customs charges such as tariffs, and even the physical barriers at borders, such as the walls between the United States and Mexico.

TABLE 2.1 • Major Sociological Theories

STRUCTURAL/ FUNCTIONAL THEORIES	CONFLICT/ CRITICAL THEORIES	INTER/ ACTIONIST THEORIES
Structural-functionalism	Conflict theory	Symbolic interactionism
Structuralism	Critical theory	Ethnomethodology
	Feminist theory	Exchange theory
	Queer theory	Rational choice theory
	Critical theories of race and racism	
	Postmodern theory	

One central concept in Merton's version of structural-functionalism is function. **Functions** are the observable, positive consequences of a structure that help it survive, adapt, and adjust. National borders are functional in various ways. For example, the passport controls at borders allow a country to monitor who is entering the country and to refuse entry to those it considers undesirable or dangerous. This function has become increasingly important in the era of global terrorism. Some of the individuals who perpetrated the 9/11 attacks on the United States entered the country by passing without notice through passport controls. Obviously, those controls were deficient. Now, however, more stringent passport and border controls serve the function of keeping out most other potential foreign terrorists (although they are of no help with domestic terrorists, such as the one who killed 49 people in a nightclub in Orlando, Florida, in mid-2016).

Structural-functionalism is greatly enriched when we add the concept of **dysfunctions**, which are observable consequences that negatively affect the ability of a given system to survive, adapt, or adjust. While border and passport controls clearly have functions, they also have dysfunctions. For example, after 9/11, Congress passed many immigration-related acts. As a result, it has become much more difficult for everyone to enter the United States (Kurzban 2006). This is true not only for potential terrorists but also for legitimate workers and businesspeople. As a result, many talented workers and businesspeople from other countries have decided to go elsewhere in the world, where there are fewer restrictions on their ability to come and go. However, large numbers of students continue to flock to the United States. Table 2.2 lists the top 10 countries of origin of international students attending school in the United States. Note the dominance of students from China.

The fact that both functions and dysfunctions are associated with structures raises the issue of the relative weight of the functions and the dysfunctions. How can we determine whether a given structure is predominantly functional or dysfunctional? In terms of the tightening of border controls, we would need to weigh the benefits of keeping out potential terrorists against the losses in international business transactions and university enrollments by overseas students. Such weightings are never easy.

Merton further elaborated on his basic theory by differentiating between two types of functions. The first encompasses **manifest functions**, or positive consequences that are brought about consciously and purposely. For example, taxes (tariffs) are imposed on goods imported into the United States from elsewhere in the world in order to make the prices of those goods higher compared with American-made goods and thus protect U.S.-based producers. That is a manifest function of tariffs. However, such actions

TABLE 2.2 • Top 10 Countries of Origin of International Students in the United States, 2014–2015

RANK	COUNTRY OF ORIGIN	NUMBER OF STUDENTS	PERCENTAGE OF TOTAL
1	China	304,040	31.2
2	India	132,888	13.6
3	South Korea	63,710	6.5
4	Saudi Arabia	59,945	6.1
5	Canada	27,240	2.8
6	Brazil	23,675	2.4
7	Chinese Taipei	20,993	2.2
8	Japan	19,064	2.0
9	Vietnam	18,722	1.9
10	Mexico	17,052	1.7

SOURCE: Data from International Students in the United States, 2014–2015: Top 10 sending places of origin and percentage of total international student enrollment, Project Atlas, Atlas of Student Mobility; Institute of International Education, Inc.

often have **latent functions**, or unintended positive consequences. For example, when foreign products become more expensive and therefore less desirable, U.S. manufacturers may produce more and perhaps better goods in the United States. In addition, more jobs for Americans may be created. Note that in these examples, both manifest and latent functions, like all functions within the structural-functionalist perspective, are positive.

One more concept of note is the idea of **unanticipated consequences**, or consequences that are unexpected and can be either positive or, more important, negative. A negative unanticipated consequence of tariffs is the possibility of a trade war. China, for example, might respond to an increase in U.S. tariffs by raising its own tariffs on U.S. imports. If the United States were to retaliate with new and still higher tariffs, we could quickly be in the midst of an unanticipated, and probably undesirable, trade war involving the United States, China, and perhaps other nations.

Structuralism

A second structural/functional theory, **structuralism**, focuses on structures but is not concerned with their functions. In addition, while structural-functionalism focuses on quite visible structures, such as border fences, structuralism is more interested in the social impacts of hidden or underlying structures, such as the global economic order or gender relations. It adopts the view that these

The Contentious India–China Border

While the border between India and Pakistan is highly volatile (Kumar 2015), no border in the world has the potential to be more explosive—in structural-functionalist terms, more dysfunctional for the global political structure—than the 2,521-mile boundary between India and China (Harris and Wong 2013). Both countries, the two most populous in the world, will play increasingly decisive roles on the world stage in the years to come (Suroor 2011). Much will hinge on their stability and their relationship with each other.

Antagonism over the land between China and India stretches back to the 1841 Sino-Sikh War, in which premodern Indian forces invaded western Tibet (Lal 2008). Although the Chinese and Sikhs signed a treaty, the stage was set for further conflict. When in 1959 the Dalai Lama and thousands of his followers sought refuge from the Chinese government in India, China accused India of imperialism and seized almost 65,000 square miles of Indian land. Three years later, a major border dispute led to the short but bloody Sino-Indian War, which the Chinese won, but that conflict did not truly settle the ongoing border dispute (Polgreen 2010).

Today, India and China both have nuclear arsenals. Control over Kashmir, which lies between them, is still disputed, and much of the border is poorly marked. Because relations are still so tense, each country has tens of thousands of troops along the border (Bhaumik 2010).

China has built up the infrastructure on its side of the border to prepare for what could be the next war with India. It has built new highways, airports, and railroads, including a railway to Tibet (Polgreen 2010). India has not developed its own infrastructure anywhere near as much (Malik 2011). Part of the reason

FIGURE 2.2 • Disputed India–China Borders

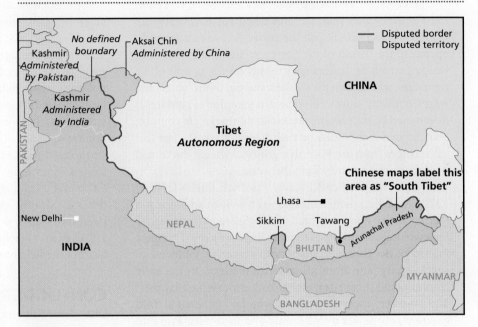

SOURCE: India, China Disputed Borders from The China Challenge: A Strategic Vision for U.S.–India Relations By Lisa Curtis and Dean Cheng, July 18, 2011 is reprinted by permission of The Heritage Foundation.

for India's comparative backwardness is the high cost of such development. China also has a larger middle class than India does and functions as a market for exports from around the world (Nayyer 2010). In 2010, China's gross domestic product ranked second in the world; India's ranked tenth (International Monetary Fund 2011). China has invested more than India has in improving living standards as well (Sen 2011).

India fears that an invading Chinese army could use India's own infrastructure to penetrate deeply into the Indian subcontinent. Nevertheless, in 2014 it completed the construction of a five-mile tunnel through the Pir Panjal mountain range, part of the Himalayas (Munford 2010). In the past, to move troops and supplies into contested areas, India has had to rely on the Rohtang Pass, highly

dangerous at best and snow covered for six months of the year.

The new tunnel greatly improves India's ability to resupply troops in the disputed territories. However, in case of war, an unintended consequence could be hundreds of thousands of invading Chinese troops marching right through the pass and into India. India might then be tempted to use its nuclear weapons, which could lead to nuclear retaliation by China and an all-out nuclear war.

Think About It

What are the intended manifest and latent consequences of the building of the Pir Panjal mountain tunnel? Can you think of any other recent political events that have had, or might have, unintended consequences?

hidden structures determine what transpires on the surface of the social world. This perspective comes from the field of linguistics, which has largely adopted the view that the surface, the way we speak and express ourselves, is determined by an underlying grammatical system (Saussure [1916] 1966). A sociological example would be that behind-the-scenes actions of capitalists and the capitalist system determine the public positions taken by political leaders.

Marx can be seen as a structuralist because he was interested in the hidden structures that determine how capitalism works. So, for example, on the surface capitalism seems to operate to the benefit of all. However, hidden below the surface is a structure that operates mostly for the benefit of the capitalists, who exploit the workers and pay them subsistence wages. Similarly, capitalists argue that the value of products is determined by supply and demand in the market. In contrast, Marx argued that hidden beneath the surface is the fact that value comes from the labor that goes into the products, and this labor comes entirely from the workers.

Marx's frequent collaborator Friedrich Engels ([1884] 1970) looked at relationships between women and men and theorized that the structures of capitalism and patriarchy kept women subordinated to men. Engels assumed, as most writers of his time did, that family structure followed an evolutionary path from primitive to modern. In the early communistic society, members had multiple sexual pairings, and the uncertainty about who had fathered a child gave women power in the family and in society. Property passed from mother to child, and women were held in high esteem. However, as wealth began to accumulate and men gained control of agricultural production, men claimed more status. To guarantee the fidelity of the wife and therefore the paternity of the children, the social system evolved so that the wife was subjugated to male power and men sought to claim women as their own property. Monogamy eventually led to the even more restrictive marriage bond. Engels believed that with the advent of "marriage begins the abduction and purchase of women" ([1884] 1970, 735).

Engels believed that female oppression was rooted in the hidden and underlying structure of private property rights in capitalism. As a result, he thought that the key to ending that oppression was to abolish private property. Engels was mistaken, however, in his conception of history. The period he describes as "primitive communism" never really existed. Nevertheless, the connections he drew between gender inequality and the underlying structure of society have proved to be enduring, and many contemporary feminist theorists have built more sophisticated analyses on them (Chae 2014).

A structuralist approach is useful because it leads sociologists to look beyond the surface for underlying structures and realities, which determine what transpires on the surface. Thus, for example, military threats made by North Korea, and its test firing of missiles, may not really be about military matters at all but instead about that country's failing economic system. North Korea may hope that the symbolic expression of military power will distract its citizens, strengthen its global prestige, frighten others, and perhaps coerce other countries, especially the United States, into providing economic aid.

A very useful sociological idea in this context is debunking (Berger 1963). **Debunking** plays off the idea that visible social structures such as the state are mere facades. It is the task of the sociologist to debunk, or to look beneath and beyond, such facades. This is very similar to the approach taken by many structuralists, although there is an important difference. The goal of many structuralists is merely to understand the underlying structure of, for example, the state, language, or family systems. In contrast, debunking not only seeks such understanding but also critically analyzes the underlying reality and its impact on visible social structures. Sociologists accomplish debunking by questioning societally accepted goals and the accounts provided by those in positions of authority. For example, while the United States seems to emphasize peace, as we have seen in Chapter 1, sociologists have pointed out that it has a hidden and powerful military-industrial complex with a vested interest in war, or at least in preparations for war (Ledbetter 2011). Many sociologists see debunking as going to the very heart of the field of sociology (Baehr and Gordon 2012).

CONFLICT/CRITICAL THEORIES

The idea of debunking is clearly critical in nature and therefore a perfect lead-in to a discussion of conflict/critical theories. Several different theories are discussed under this heading: conflict theory, critical theory, feminist theory, queer theory, critical theories of race and racism, and postmodern theory. They all tend to emphasize stresses, strains, and conflicts in society. They are critical of society in a variety of different ways, especially of the power that is exercised over less powerful members of society.

Conflict Theory

The best known of these theories, at least in American sociology, is **conflict theory** (R. Collins 2012). It has roots in Marx's theory, and much of it can be seen as an inversion of structural-functionalism, which conflict theory was designed to compete with and to counteract. While structural-functionalism emphasizes what is positive about society, conflict theory focuses on its negative aspects. To the structural-functionalist, society is held together by consensus; virtually everyone accepts the social structure, its legitimacy, and its benefits. To the conflict theorist, in contrast, society is held together by coercion. Those who are adversely affected by society, especially economically, would rebel were it not for coercive forces such as the police, the courts, and the military.

A good example of conflict theory is to be found in the work of Ralf Dahrendorf (1959). Although he was strongly influenced by Marx, he was more strongly motivated

The high pay and decision-making power of McDonald's executives contrasts sharply with the relative powerlessness of the company's low-paid employees. Some of those employees and their supporters are shown here demonstrating for higher pay. Structural conflicts like this one are the focus of conflict theory.

by a desire to develop a viable alternative to structural-functionalism. For example, while structural-functionalists tend to see society as static, conflict theorists like Dahrendorf emphasize the ever-present possibility of change. Where structural-functionalists see the orderliness of society, conflict theorists see dissension and conflict everywhere. Finally, structural-functionalists focus on the sources of cohesion internal to society, while conflict theorists stress the coercion and power that holds together an otherwise fractious society.

Overall, conflict theorists like Dahrendorf see two basic sides to society—consensus and conflict—and believe that both are needed. Sociology therefore needs, at least in this view, two different theories: conflict theory and "consensus" (or structural-functional) theory.

Dahrendorf offered a very sociological view of authority, arguing that it resides not in individuals (e.g., Donald J. Trump) but in positions (e.g., the presidency of the United States) and in various associations of people. In his view, those associations are controlled by a hierarchy of authority positions and the people who occupy them. However, there are many such associations in any society. Thus, a person may be in authority in one type of association but be subordinate in many others.

What most interested Dahrendorf was the potential for conflict between those in positions of authority and those who are subordinate. They usually have very different interests. Like authority, those interests are not characteristics of individuals but rather are linked to the positions they hold. Thus, the top management of a retail or fast-food corporation such as Walmart or McDonald's is interested in making the corporation more profitable by keeping wages low. In contrast, those who hold such low-level jobs as cashier or stock clerk are interested in increasing their wages to meet basic needs. Because of this inherent tension and conflict, authority within associations is always tenuous.

In general, the interests of those involved in associations are unconscious, but at times they become conscious and therefore more likely to lead to overt conflict. *Conflict groups* may form, as when a group of greeters goes on strike against Walmart. The coalitions formed out of resistance efforts often increase cohesion among group members, further uniting them and bolstering the strength of the movement (Coser 1956). The actions of conflict groups can change society, as well as elements of society such as the Walmart corporation, sometimes quite radically.

Critical Theory

While Marx's work was critical of the capitalist economy, **critical theory** shifts the focus to culture. Marx believed that culture is shaped by the economic system. In contrast, the critical school has argued that by the early twentieth century, and at an ever-accelerating rate to this day, culture has succeeded in becoming important in its own right. Furthermore, in many ways it has come to be more important than the economic system. Instead of being controlled by the capitalist economy, more of us are controlled—and controlled more often—by culture in general, specifically by the culture industry.

The **culture industry**, in Weber's sense, consists of the rationalized and bureaucratized structures that control modern culture. In their early years, the 1920s and 1930s, critical theorists focused on radio, magazines, and movies. Today, the movies remain important, but the focus has shifted to television and various aspects of the internet. These are critiqued for producing, or serving as an outlet for, **mass culture**, or cultural elements that are administered by organizations, lack spontaneity, and are phony. Two features of mass culture and its dissemination by the culture industry are of particular concern to critical theorists:

- *Falseness.* True culture should emanate from the people, but mass culture involves prepackaged sets of ideas that falsify reality. The so-called reality shows (e.g., *Survivor*) that dominate television today are a contemporary example of mass culture. These programs are also highly formulaic. They are presented as if they are authentic, but in fact they are scripted, highly controlled, and selectively edited—although in a different way than fictional dramas, comedies, and soap operas are. They are also false in the sense that they give consumers of mass culture the sense that there is a quick and easy route to fame and fortune.

- *Repressiveness.* Like Marx, the critical theorists feel that the masses need to be informed about things such as the falseness of culture so that they can develop a clear sense of society's failings and the need to rebel against them.

However, the effect of mass culture is to pacify, stupefy, and repress the masses so that they are far less likely to demand social change. Those who rush home nightly to catch up on their favorite reality TV shows are unlikely to have much interest in, or time for, revolutionary activities, or even civic activities and reforms. Additionally, according to some theorists, the culture industry has succeeded in creating a class of corporate brands that are globally recognized and sought after as cultural symbols (Arvidsson 2012; Lash and Lury 2007). Instead of engaging in revolutionary activities, many people are striving to keep up with and acquire the latest and hottest brands.

Critical theory can be applied to some of the newest media forms, such as YouTube, Facebook, Twitter, Snapchat, and Instagram (Denegri-Knott and Zwick 2012). Despite there being plenty of false and stupefying content on these sites, along with all the edifying material, the sites are not controlled by large rationalized bureaucracies—at least not yet. Almost all the content that appears on sites such as YouTube, Facebook, and eBay is provided by those who also consume material on the sites. The sites exercise little control over original content; they are arguably spontaneous and authentic. It's tempting to conclude that these new aspects of the culture industry are not assailable from a traditional critical theory perspective.

ASK YOURSELF

Do you see evidence of critical theory's ideas of falseness and repressiveness in the elements of mass culture to which you are exposed? If so, what form do they take?

Yet it could be argued that while the content is not produced by the culture industry, the content is disseminated by it. So although many websites have yet to become profitable, they have come to be worth many billions of dollars each because of investors' belief in their future profitability. More important, the masses are pacified, repressed, and stupefied by spending endless hours buying and selling on eBay, watching YouTube videos, updating their Facebook pages, and following day-to-day, even minute-by-minute, developments in the lives of others. Similar things could be said about Twitter's tweets, which inform us instantaneously that, among other things, one of our friends has gotten a haircut or a manicure. While people do find friends, learn useful things, and perhaps even foment revolutions on Twitter (as in the case of the Arab Spring uprisings in 2011 and, briefly, in the quickly aborted *coup d'etat* in Turkey in mid-2016), they also may spend, and likely waste, endless amounts of time on it. Not infrequently, they also may find that corporations are using increasingly sophisticated online techniques to target them and to get them to consume their products.

Feminist Theory

Historically, male social theorists have received the most attention (one exception, mentioned previously, is Harriet Martineau), and to a large extent that is still the case today. Not surprisingly, then, social theories in the main have downplayed or ignored women and the distinctive problems they face (one exception is the work of Engels discussed previously). Social theories have also tended to ignore gender more generally. Specifically, they have neglected to critically examine how femininity (and masculinity) are part of everything from social structures and institutions to everyday interactions. Feminist theorists point up and attempt to rectify the masculine bias built into most social theories. Similar to the broad range of sociological theories you have already encountered is a large and growing number of feminist theories that deal with a wide range of social issues (Lengermann and Niebrugge-Brantley 2014; Tong 2009; see also the journal *Feminist Theory*). A central aspect of **feminist theory** in general is the critique of patriarchy (male dominance) and the problems it poses not only for women but also for men. Feminist theory also offers ideas on how everyone's (women's *and* men's) situation can be bettered, if not revolutionized.

One fundamental debate within feminist theory is whether or not gender inequality causes or results from gender differences. A few feminist theorists (e.g., Rossi 1983) believe that there are *essential* (or biologically determined) differences between men's and women's behavior, and that gender inequality is a result of the social devaluing of female characteristics (such as nurturing). But the majority of feminist scholars argue that gender differences are *socially constructed*. In other words, the differences we see in behavior between men and women are not biologically determined but rather created socially.

Even feminist theorists who agree that gender differences are socially constructed disagree on the underlying causes. One view is that men, as the dominant group in society, have defined gender in such a way as to purposely restrain and subordinate women. Another view holds that social structures such as capitalist organizations and patriarchal families have evolved to favor men and traditionally male roles. Both structures benefit from the uncompensated labor of women, so there is little incentive for men as a dominant group to change the status quo. Clearly these perspectives all involve a critical orientation.

Despite the many global and individual changes in women's lives over the almost two centuries since sociology came into existence, there is also a broad consensus among feminist theorists that women continue to face extraordinary problems related directly to gender inequality. As you will learn about more in Chapter 11, these problems include, among innumerable others, a persistent wage gap between men and women in the United States and systematic and widespread rape by invading forces in wartime. These extraordinary problems require extraordinary solutions. However, feminist theories vary in the degree to which they support dramatic, even revolutionary, changes in women's situation. Some feminist theories suggest that the solution to gender inequality is to change social structures and institutions so that they are more inclusive of women and allow more gender diversity. Other feminist theories argue that because those very structures and institutions create gender difference and inequality, we must first deconstruct and then rebuild them in a wholly different way.

Women of color have sometimes been dissatisfied with feminist theory for not representing their interests very well. Several scholars argue that feminist theory generally reflects the perspective of white women while ignoring the unique experiences and viewpoints of women of color (Collins 2000; hooks 2000; Moraga and Anzaldua 2015; Zinn 2012). Similarly, studies related to race tend to focus largely (or wholly) on the position of men. Thus, many contemporary feminists have advocated for scholarship that takes into account not just gender but also how it intersects with race and ethnicity, social class, and sexuality. The upcoming discussion of critical theories of race and racism provides more detail on this view.

Queer Theory

The term *queer* was originally used as a negative term for gay men. Contemporary gay men, lesbians, bisexuals, and transgender and intersexed people have reclaimed the label *queer,* but now with a positive connotation. However, queer theory is *not* a theory of queer folks. In fact, it contrasts with *gay and lesbian studies,* which focuses on homosexualities. **Queer theory** is based on the argument that there are no fixed and stable identities that determine who we are (Plummer 2012). The theory also unsettles identities that have long been thought to be fixed, stable, or natural. Among others, it unsettles *queers* as a noun, as well as gender identities in general (Butler 1990). It is difficult to characterize queer theory as only one outlook or argument about the social world. It is really a diverse group of ideas about how cultures develop gender and sexuality norms, notions of conformity, and power relations.

While queer theory does not focus exclusively on homosexuality, it does examine the dynamics of the relationship between heterosexuals and homosexuals. It is especially concerned with the historic, systematic exercise of power by heterosexuals over homosexuals. In this sense, queer theory is clearly a form of conflict/critical theory. More generally, queer theorists are primarily interested in questions of gender, the concept of the gender binary, and redefinitions of sexual behaviors, norms, and practices.

Queer theory is in the early phases of its development. It promises to play a central role in the development of general theories about those who stand on the margins of society, to deepen our understanding of the full spectrum of sexuality, and to dispel a variety of myths. In addition, it could disrupt hierarchies of power. At the least, queer theory promises to broaden acceptance of sexual and other minorities and to promote greater inclusion for all.

Critical Theories of Race and Racism

As we saw earlier, W. E. B. Du Bois was a pioneer in the study of race and racism. In recent years this perspective has blossomed in sociology under the heading of **critical theories of race and racism** (Outlaw 2010; Slatton and Feagin 2012). Theorists who adopt this perspective argue that race continues to matter globally and that racism continues to

The Voluntariat

A new term that builds on Karl Marx's concept of the proletariat (see p. 30) has recently been coined—*voluntariat*. While the proletariat works for low pay, the voluntariat works for *no pay*. Like the proletariat, the voluntariat does work that requires little skill, such as posting a product review on Amazon.com or tweeting a comment on Twitter. However, some members of the voluntariat engage in free labor that otherwise would likely be carried out by highly paid skilled workers. For example, individuals who possess advanced university degrees perform free labor for massive open online courses, or MOOCs (Shullenberger 2014; see Chapter 1 and especially Chapter 13). Other highly skilled voluntarians translate courses taught in English into other languages at no charge, doing the work for its intrinsic reward. They are seen as "voluntarian scabs" because they threaten the livelihood of professional translators who do such work for a living. Regardless of work skills, the free labor of the voluntariat contributes to a corporation's profitability, just as does the poorly paid labor of the proletariat.

In the broader context of free, value-creating activity on social media, we are all voluntarians now, because we are increasingly engaged, usually unknowingly, in advancing the interests of profit-making organizations. When we post on Facebook or buy products on Amazon.com, we are voluntarily providing lots of invaluable and free information, or "big data," about ourselves that these organizations could not otherwise obtain, and that is the major source of their market

The free labor of the "voluntariat" has replaced the paid labor of innumerable workers in, for example, self-checkouts in supermarkets and gas stations. What are corporations giving you as a member of the voluntariat in return for your free labor?

value. Amazon's chairman and CEO Jeff Bezos believes that Amazon.com can earn far more money exploiting the data provided by voluntarians than it can by selling products. It is arguable whether or not many popular internet sites, such as Facebook, YouTube, or Flickr, could even exist without the free labor of thousands of people around the world.

We are also increasingly voluntarians when we act as "working consumers" (Dujarier 2014) in using ATMs, scanning and bagging our own groceries in the supermarket, and putting our own IKEA furniture together. These are all jobs that required wage workers not long ago. The fact that many consumers do this work without

protest, and often happily, saves corporations millions of dollars because they can reduce the number of workers they hire. The point is that "voluntarianism" is a widespread phenomenon that increasingly pervades our lives on- and offline.

Engaging the Digital World

Keep a record of how much unpaid labor you engage in for one week. You should list the type of activity you performed and how much time you spent doing it. If you were to be paid the minimum wage for this labor, how much would you receive? Do you feel like you are being exploited by corporations that are taking advantage of your free labor? Why or why not?

have adverse effects on people of color. Given its history of slavery and racism, the United States has often been singled out for analysis using this theory.

Some commentators have argued that racism today is of little more than historical interest because white Americans have become "color-blind." Those who adopt

this point of view argue that we have come to ignore skin color when discussing social groups and that skin color is no longer being used in hiring or admissions policies. However, critical theorists of race and racism disagree. They argue that while skin color has nothing to do with a person's physical or intellectual abilities, color blindness ignores the past and present realities facing racial minorities, including the social consequences of years of racial discrimination. As a result, critics of the claim of color blindness argue that it is little more than a "new racism," a smoke screen that allows whites to practice and perpetuate racial discrimination (Bonilla-Silva 2009, 2015). See the differing perceptions about employment opportunities illustrated in Figure 2.3, for example. The vast majority of white Americans believe that there is equal employment opportunity, but only a minority of black Americans subscribe to that view. The white belief in the smoke screen of equal opportunity serves to rationalize continued discrimination against blacks.

ASK YOURSELF

Think about the various ways in which you meet the definition of voluntariat, on- and offline. Are people like Jeff Bezos (Amazon.com) and Mark Zuckerberg (Facebook) multibillionaires largely because of your free labor and that of millions of other voluntarians? How do you feel about that?

The idea that racism continues was very much in the news in 2016 as Donald Trump emerged victorious in the presidential campaign to replace a black president, Barack Obama. During the campaign, Trump was accused of using "dog whistles" to appeal to white racists and others opposed to Obama and his designated successor, Hillary Clinton. *Dog whistles* are old-fashioned biased statements repackaged to make them more acceptable and to hide the true message from all but those with such biases. For example, at least initially, Trump refused to disavow the Ku Klux Klan and one of its most public figures, David Duke. That refusal was a dog whistle to white racists and other white supporters of his candidacy.

Of particular importance to recent work in this area is the idea of **intersectionality** (Collins 1990; Collins and Bilge 2016), which points to the fact that people are affected, often adversely, not only by their race but also by their gender, sexual orientation, class, age, and global location. The confluence, or intersection, of these various statuses and the inequality and oppression associated with combinations of them are what matter most. Not only are we unable to deal with race, gender, class, and so on separately; we also cannot gain an understanding of oppression by simply adding them together. For example, a poor black female lesbian faces a complex of problems different from the problems faced by a poor person or a black person or a woman or a lesbian.

ASK YOURSELF

Is your life affected by intersectionality? How many different statuses do you hold, and to which social and cultural groups do you belong?

Phenomena that were once associated almost exclusively with majority–minority relations in the United States are increasingly found elsewhere in the world. Europe, for example, has a long history of racism that includes centuries of colonialism, the African slave trade, anti-Semitism, and the Holocaust. Racial turmoil abated there after World War II, but it is again on the rise—at least in part because of the large influx of immigrants in the early twenty-first century. Racist propaganda, hate speech, and incitement to violence have become much more common in recent years, notably in France, Austria, Germany, Sweden, and the United Kingdom. The main victims have been Muslims, Jews, people of North African or Arab origin, and Roma people from Central and Eastern Europe, who are among the largest immigrant groups in these countries. In France in late 2014, a Roma family was refused burial space in a local cemetery when their two-month-old infant died, although the uproar that followed led to the child's burial there in early 2015 (Breeden 2015). The Roma (and others) are largely powerless because Europe has not experienced

FIGURE 2.3 • Do Black Americans Have the Same Chances as White Americans to Obtain the Same Level of Employment? (1963–2012, responses divided by race)

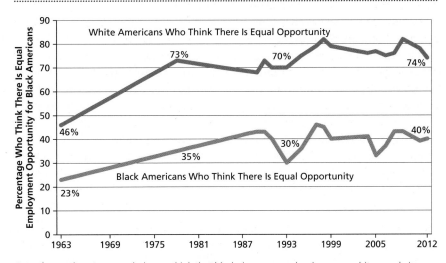

Actual question: In general, do you think that blacks have as good a chance as white people in your community to get any kind of job for which they are qualified, or do you think they don't have as good a chance?

SOURCE: Gallup (2014). Gallup Review: Black and White Differences in Views on Race (2014).

anything like the U.S. civil rights movement, which served to mobilize and organize black Americans.

Postmodern Theory

Postmodern theory has many elements that fit well under the heading of critical theory, although there is more to it than critique (Lipovetsky 2005). The term *postmodern* is used in various ways in relation to social theory. **Postmodernity**, for instance, is the state of society beyond the "modern era," which was the era analyzed by the classical social theorists. Among the characteristics of the modern world is rationality, as discussed in Weber's work. The postmodern world is less rational, nonrational, or even irrational. For example, while in the modern world groups such as the proletariat can plan in a rational manner to overthrow capitalism, in the postmodern world such changes come about accidentally or are simply fated to occur (Baudrillard [1983] 1990; Kellner 2011). Although modernity is characterized by a highly consistent lifestyle, postmodernity is characterized by eclecticism in what we eat, how we dress, and what sorts of music we listen to (Lyotard [1979] 1984).

Postmodernism refers to the emergence of new and different cultural forms in music, movies, art, architecture, and the like. One characteristic of these new cultural forms is pastiche. "Modern" movies, for example, are told in a linear fashion, and "modern" art is made up of internally consistent elements. But postmodern cultural forms are pastiches that combine very different elements. From a modern perspective, those elements often seem incompatible with one another. Thus, postmodern buildings combine classic and modern styles. Postmodern movies deal with historical realities but also include very modern elements, such as songs from the present day. *Her* (2013) takes place in futuristic Los Angeles, where a man develops a romantic relationship with a "female" computer operating system. The popular TV series *Sleepy Hollow* portrays historical characters, such as Ichabod Crane and Betsy Ross, in modern-day situations. **Postmodern theory** is a theoretical orientation that is a reaction against modern theory. Postmodern theory tends to be expressed in nonrational ways. For example, it might take the form of a series of terse, often unrelated statements rather than a logical, well-argued volume or series of volumes (like the work of modern thinkers such as Marx and Weber). Postmodernists are opposed to the grand narratives—the broad depictions of history and society—offered by modern theorists. An example of such a narrative is Weber's theory of the increasing rationalization of the world and the rise of an "iron cage" constraining our thoughts and activities. Instead, postmodernists tend to offer more limited, often unrelated, snapshots of the social world. In fact, postmodernists often deconstruct, or take apart, modern grand narratives. Postmodernists are also opposed to the scientific pretensions of much modern social theory. They adopt instead a nonscientific or even antiscientific approach to the social world. Feminist postmodernists reject the very language used by modern feminist scholars, because words like *lesbian* have been constructed out of modern, male-centered thought (Tong 2009). To some observers, the sociological study of deviance has all but disappeared because of postmodern conclusions that deviance is a purely relative phenomenon, dependent strictly on the definitions of those who have the power to define what is deviant (Sumner 1994).

In spite of, or perhaps because of, these differences, postmodern theory offers a new and important way of theorizing. Postmodern social theorists look at familiar social phenomena in different ways or adopt very different focuses for their work. For example, in his study of the history of prisons, Michel Foucault ([1975] 1979) was critical of the modernist view that criminal justice had grown progressively liberal. He contended that prisons had, in fact, grown increasingly oppressive through the use of techniques such as constant, enhanced surveillance of prisoners. Similarly, he argued against the traditional view that in the Victorian era people were sexually repressed; he found instead an explosion of sexuality in the Victorian era (Foucault 1978).

The most important postmodernist, Jean Baudrillard, argued that we are now living in a consumer society where much of our lives is defined not by our productive work but by what we consume and how we consume it. The postmodern world is in fact characterized by **hyperconsumption**, which involves consuming more than we need, more than we really want, and more than we can afford. The generally rising level of credit card debt in the United States in the past decade is a sign of the hyperconsumption Baudrillard noted (see Chapter 1). A more recent sign is found in "haul videos" posted online, mainly by young women, showing their "hauls" from given shopping trips accompanied by commentary on the products obtained.

Another of Baudrillard's critical ideas that demonstrates the nature of postmodern social theory is simulation. A **simulation** is an inauthentic or fake version of something. Baudrillard saw the world as increasingly dominated by simulations. For example, when we eat at McDonald's, we consume Chicken McNuggets, or simulated chicken. It is fake in the sense that it is often not meat from one chicken, but bits of meat that come from many different chickens. When we go to Disney World, we enter via Main Street, a simulation of early America that is really a shopping mall. We also go on simulated submarine rides to see simulated sea life rather than going to a nearby aquarium to see "real" sea life. When we go to Las Vegas, we stay in hotel-casinos that are simulations of New York of the early to mid-twentieth century (New York–New York), Venice (the Venetian), and ancient Egypt (the Luxor). The idea that we increasingly consume simulations and live a simulated life is a powerful critique of consumer society and, more generally, of the contemporary world. That is, not only are we consuming more; also, much of what we consume is fake.

ASK YOURSELF

Does a life devoted to hyperconsumption, especially online, cause you to become disconnected from others? Are new kinds of human connections created by a common investment in a life devoted to excessive consumption?

INTER/ACTIONIST THEORIES

The slash between *inter* and *action(ist)* in the heading to this section is meant to communicate the fact that we will deal with two closely related sets of theories here. The first consists of those theories that deal mainly with the interaction of two or more people (symbolic interactionism, ethnomethodology, and exchange theory). The second comprises those that focus more on the actions of individuals (rational choice theory). A common factor among these theories is that they focus on the micro level of individuals and groups. This is in contrast to the theories discussed previously that focus on the macro structures of society.

Symbolic Interactionism

As the name suggests, **symbolic interactionism** is concerned with the interaction of two or more people through the use of symbols (Kotarba, Salvini, and Merrill 2012). Interaction is clear enough. We all engage in mutual action with many others on a daily basis, whether it be face-to-face or more indirectly via cell phone, e-mail, or social media. But interaction could not take place without symbols: words, gestures, and even objects that stand for things. Symbols allow the communication of meaning among a group of people.

Although we can interact with one another without words, such as through physical gestures like the shrug of a shoulder, in the vast majority of cases we need and use words to interact. And words make many other symbols possible. For example, the Harley-Davidson brand has meaning because it symbolizes a particular type of motorcycle. Both the brand name and the motorcycle are further symbolized by nicknames such as "Harley" and "hog" (Holt 2004).

Symbolic interactionism has several basic principles:

- Human beings have a great capacity for thought, which differentiates them from lower animals. That innate capacity for thought is greatly shaped by social interaction. It is during social interaction that people acquire the symbolic meanings that allow them to exercise their distinctive ability to think. Those symbolic meanings in turn allow people to act and interact in ways that lower animals cannot.

- Symbolic meanings are not set in stone. People are able to modify them based on a given situation and their interpretation of it. The Christian cross, for example, is a symbol whose meaning can vary. Christians throughout the world define it in positive religious ways, but many in the Islamic world view it as a negative symbol. Muslims associate the cross with the medieval Crusades waged against their world by the Christian West.

- People are able to modify symbolic meanings because of their unique ability to think. Symbolic interactionists frame *thinking* as people's ability to interact with themselves. In that interaction with themselves, people are able to alter symbolic meanings. They are also able to examine various courses of action open to them in given situations, to assess the relative advantages and disadvantages of each, and then to choose among them.

- It is the pattern of those choices, of individual action and interaction, that is the basis of groups, larger structures such as bureaucracies, and society as a whole. Most generally, in this theoretical perspective, symbolic interaction is the basis of everything else in the social world.

This is not New York City but the hotel-casino called New York–New York in Las Vegas, Nevada. One hypothesis of postmodern theory is that we live in a world characterized by an increasing number of simulations of reality. How many others can you think of?

DESIGN PICS INC/National Geographic Creative

Symbolic interactionists are interested in how various aspects of identity are created and sustained in social interaction. For example, symbolic interactionists argue that gender (like ethnicity or career identity) is something that we "do" or perform (West and Zimmerman 1987). *Gender* is a means of identifying ourselves with a particular sex category. Thus, a male may take pains to act in a masculine way so that he will be seen as male by both himself and others. In some respects, his behavior (which is socially determined) can be considered symbolic of the male sex (which is largely biologically determined). People who see his behavior can then simply relate to him as male, according to the meaning of the symbolic behavior that has developed over time through innumerable interactions. Gender (i.e., masculinity and femininity) is thus both a result and a cause of social interaction.

Ethnomethodology

While symbolic interactionism deals primarily with people's interactions, it is also concerned with the mental processes, such as mind and self, that are deeply implicated in these interactions. **Ethnomethodology** is another inter/actionist theory, but it focuses on what people *do* rather than on what they think (Liu 2012). The Greek root of the term *ethnomethodology* refers to people (*ethno*) and the everyday methods through which they accomplish their daily lives. In other words, ethnomethodologists study the ways in which people organize everyday life.

Ethnomethodologists regard people's lives and social worlds as practical accomplishments that are really quite extraordinary. For example, one ethnomethodological study of coffee drinkers attempted to understand their participation in a subculture of coffee connoisseurship (Manzo 2010). Learning to enjoy coffee is something of an accomplishment itself; taking that enjoyment to the next level and becoming a connoisseur requires even more doing.

Ethnomethodologists take a different view of large-scale social structures than do structural-functionalists, who tend to see people and their actions as being highly constrained by those structures. Ethnomethodologists argue that this view tells us very little about what really goes on within structures such as courtrooms, hospitals, and police departments. Rather than being constrained, people act within these structures and go about much of their business using common sense rather than official procedures. They may even adapt those structures and rules to accomplish their goals. For example, an employee at Nordstrom might violate the rules about handling returns in order to please a customer and make the process easier or less stressful. Police departments have rules about categorizing a death as a homicide or manslaughter. However, police officers often apply their own commonsense rules rather than organizational rules when interpreting the evidence.

Many ethnomethodologists study conversations (Arminen 2012). In that study, they focus on three basic issues (Zimmerman 1988):

- *Vocal cues as an element of conversation.* Conversation involves not only words but also vocal cues, such as pauses, throat clearings, and silences. These nonverbal vocal behaviors can be important methods in making conversation. For example, one person may sit silently in order to force the other to speak. Or clearing one's throat may be meant to express disapproval of what the other person is saying.

- *Stable and orderly properties of conversations.* The people in conversation generally take turns speaking and know when it is their turn to talk. Ethnomethodologists might examine how those properties change when two strangers converse rather than two friends. One of their findings has been that a higher-status person is more likely to interrupt a lower-status person.

- *Actions necessary to maintain conversations.* The properties of conversation are not carved in stone. Those involved in a conversation can observe them, enforce them, or upset them. For example, turn taking is a stable and orderly property of a conversation, but in an actual conversation you need to act in order to get your turn to speak. Turn taking does not occur automatically.

The best-known example of an ethnomethodological approach relates to gender (Stokoe 2006; O'Brien 2016). Ethnomethodologists point out that people often erroneously think of gender as being biologically based. It is generally assumed that we do not have to do or say anything in order to be considered masculine or feminine; we are born that way. But, in fact, there are things we all do (e.g., the way we walk) and say (e.g., the tone of our voice) that allow us to accomplish being masculine or feminine. That is, being masculine or feminine is based on what people do on a regular basis. This is clearest in the case of those who are defined as being male or female at birth (based on biological characteristics) but then later do and say things that lead others to see them as belonging to the other gender (based on social characteristics). For example, the Dutch painter Einar Wegener enjoyed wearing feminine attire, which his wife, also a painter, discovered after he filled in for one of her models. With his wife's support he became the first man to undergo a sex change operation, becoming the female Lili Elbe. While such cases are extreme, we all say and do things that allow us to accomplish our gender (and, in certain ways, the opposite gender). If this is the case for gender, a great many other facts of our everyday lives can be analyzed as accomplishments.

Exchange Theory

Like ethnomethodologists, exchange theorists are not concerned with what goes on in people's minds and how that affects behavior. Instead, they are interested in the behavior itself and the rewards and costs associated with it (Molm, Whithama, and Melameda 2012). The key figure in **exchange theory**, George Homans (1910–1989), argued that instead of studying large-scale structures, sociologists should study the "elementary forms of social life" (Homans 1961, 13).

Exchange theorists are particularly interested in social behavior that usually involves two or more people and a variety of tangible and intangible exchanges. For example, you can reward someone who does you a favor with a tangible gift or with more intangible words of praise. Those exchanges are not always rewarding; they also can be punitive. You could, for example, punish someone who wrongs you by slapping him or complaining about him to mutual acquaintances.

In their actions and interactions, people are seen as rational profit seekers. Basically, people will continue on courses of action, or in interactions, in which the rewards are greater than the costs. Conversely, they will discontinue those in which the costs exceed the rewards. For example, people in search of a mate, especially a marriage partner, often choose to live in the city, even though the cost of living is higher, because there are more potential partners there. However, once they are married, they are more likely to move out of the city to where the costs are lower (Gautier, Svarer, and Teulings 2010). While exchange theory retains an interest in the elementary forms of social behavior, over the years it has grown more concerned with how those forms lead to more complex social situations. That is, individual exchanges can become stable over time and develop into persistent **exchange relationships**. One particular type of exchange relationship is "hooking up," or forming sexual relationships that are also sometimes called "friends with benefits." For example, because you and another person find your initial sexual interactions rewarding, you may develop a pattern of repeat interactions (also known as "hookups" or "booty calls").

Exchange relationships, including hookups, rarely develop in isolation from other exchange relationships. Sociologists study how hooking up is not an isolated occurrence—it happens within the context of college campuses, for example, where it has been normalized (Kuperberg and Padgett 2015). You may well form some of those relationships. All these exchange relationships may become so highly interconnected that they become a single network structure (Cook et al. 1983).

Key issues in such network structures, and in exchange relationships more generally, are the power that some members have over others and the dependency of some members (Molm 2007; Molm and Cook 1995). Exchange theorists are interested in studying the causes and effects of these status differences within exchange relationships and networks. For example, variations in the wealth, status, and power of individuals and their families affect the position they come to occupy in a social network and influence their ability to succeed educationally, financially, and occupationally (Lin 1999).

Rational Choice Theory

In **rational choice theory**, as in exchange theory, people are regarded as rational, but the focus is not on exchange, rewards, and costs. Rather, the basic principle in rational choice theory is that people act intentionally in order to achieve goals. People are seen as having purposes, as intending to do certain things. To achieve their goals, people have a variety of means available to them and choose among the available means on a rational basis. They choose the means that are likely to best satisfy their needs and wants; in other words, they choose on the basis of "utility" (Kroneberg and Kalter 2012). In the case of hookups, for example, we can easily imagine a series of potential purposes for hooking up, such as engaging in sexual exploration, having fun, and doing something sexual without the risk of getting deeply involved emotionally or getting hurt.

There are two important constraints on the ability to act rationally (Friedman and Hechter 1988):

- *Access to scarce resources.* It is relatively easy for those with access to lots of resources to act rationally and reach their goals. Those who lack access to such resources are less likely to be able to act rationally in order to achieve their goals. A simple example: If you have access to money, you can rationally pursue the goal of purchasing food for dinner. However, without access to money, you will have a much harder time taking rational actions that will lead to the acquisition of food. Those with ample resources may be able to pursue two or more goals simultaneously (obtaining the money needed for dinner and for club hopping afterward with friends). However, those with few resources may have to forgo one goal (socializing with friends) in order to attain the other (getting enough money to eat).

- *Requirements of social structures.* The structures in which people find themselves—businesses, schools, hospitals—often have rules that restrict the actions available to those within the structures. For example, the need to work overtime or on weekends may restrict a person's ability to socialize. Similarly, being a full-time student may limit one's ability to earn enough money to always be able to obtain the kind of food one prefers to eat.

Rational choice theorists understand that people do not always act rationally. They argue, however, that their predictions will generally hold despite these occasional deviations (Coleman 1990; Zafirovski 2013). The degree to which people act rationally is one of the many topics that can be, and has been, researched by sociologists. It is to the general topic of sociological research that we turn in the next chapter.

CHECKPOINT 2.3: MAJOR TYPES OF THEORIES IN CONTEMPORARY SOCIOLOGY

TYPES OF THEORIES	MAJOR POINTS
Structural/functional theories (macro level)	These theories examine social structures and the functions they perform, emphasizing their positive consequences. They posit that society is held together by consensus.
Conflict/critical theories (macro level)	These theories criticize how those in power control social structures and culture. They posit that society is held together by coercion.
Inter/actionist theories (micro level)	These theories focus on individual behavior, identity formation, social interactions between two or more people, and their meaning. They posit that society is held together through social interactions.

SUMMARY

The main theorists of classical sociology are Karl Marx, Max Weber, and Émile Durkheim.

Marx focused the majority of his attention on macro issues, particularly the structure of capitalist society. Unlike Marx, Weber did not focus exclusively on the economy but considered the importance of other social structures, particularly religion. Durkheim believed that social structures and cultural norms and values exert control over individuals that is not only necessary but also desirable.

Among other early sociological theorists, Georg Simmel focused on micro-level issues, specifically interactions among individuals. W. E. B. Du Bois was a pioneering researcher of race in America at the beginning of the twentieth century. Thorstein Veblen studied consumption, particularly the ways in which the rich show off their wealth through conspicuous consumption.

Three main schools of theory inform contemporary sociological theory: structural/functional, conflict/critical, and inter/actionist theories. Structural-functionalists such as Robert Merton are concerned with both social structures and the functions and dysfunctions the structures perform. They believe that society is held together by consensus. In contrast, structuralism studies the social impact of hidden or underlying structures.

Conflict/critical theories tend to emphasize societal struggles and inequality.

Conflict theorists believe that society is held together by power and coercion. Critical theorists critically analyze culture and how it is used to pacify opposition. Feminist theory critiques the social situation confronting women and offers ideas on how women's situation can be bettered, if not revolutionized. Queer theory addresses the relationship between heterosexuals and homosexuals but stresses the broader idea that there are no fixed and stable identities. Critical theories of race and racism argue that race continues to matter and raise the issue of oppression at the intersection of gender, race, sexual orientation, and other social statuses. Postmodern theory is similarly critical of society for, among other things, coming to be dominated by simulations.

Inter/actionist theories deal with micro-level interactions among people. Symbolic interactionism, for instance, studies the effect of symbols, including words, on the interaction between two or more people. Ethnomethodology focuses on what people do rather than on what they think and often analyzes conversations. Exchange theory looks not at what people think but at their behavior. Rational choice theory considers behavior to be based on rational evaluations of goals and the means to achieve them.

KEY TERMS

alienation, 31
anomie, 34
capitalism, 30
capitalists, 30
class consciousness, 31
collective conscience, 34
conflict theory, 42
conspicuous
    consumption, 38
critical theories of race
    and racism, 45
critical theory, 44

culture industry, 44
debunking, 42
double consciousness, 37
dysfunctions, 40
ethnomethodology, 50
exchange relationships, 51
exchange theory, 51
exploitation, 30
false consciousness, 31
feminist theory, 45
functions, 40
hyperconsumption, 48

ideology, 31
intersectionality, 47
latent functions, 40
manifest functions, 40
mass culture, 44
mechanical solidarity, 34
organic solidarity, 35
postmodernism, 48
postmodernity, 48
postmodern theory, 48
proletariat, 30
Protestant ethic, 32

queer theory, 45
rational choice theory, 51
rationalization, 32
simulation, 48
social facts, 34
structural-
    functionalism, 39
structuralism, 40
symbolic interactionism, 49
theories, 28
unanticipated
    consequences, 40

REVIEW QUESTIONS

1. What are theories, and how do sociologists use theories to make sense of the social world? In what ways are theories developed by sociologists better than your own theorizing?

2. According to Karl Marx, what are the differences between capitalists and the proletariat? How are workers alienated on the job and in the workplace? Do you think workers in the United States are alienated today? Why or why not?

3. Max Weber said that the world is becoming increasingly rationalized. What are the benefits and disadvantages of rationality? In what ways is McDonaldization the same as, or different from, rationalization?

4. Why has our collective conscience weakened over time, according to Émile Durkheim? Do you think that globalization continues to weaken our collective conscience? Why or why not?

5. You live in a world that is increasingly dominated by consumption. How are the items that you consume reflective of Thorstein Veblen's concept of "conspicuous consumption"?

6. What are the functions and dysfunctions of using the internet to consume goods and services? On balance, do you think that consumption through the internet is positive or negative?

7. What is mass culture, and why are critical theorists concerned about the dissemination of mass culture? Do you think the internet and social networking sites are elements of mass culture and part of the traditional "culture industry"?

8. Why is feminist theory considered to be a critical theory?

9. What would proponents of the critical theories of race and racism outlined in this chapter think of the racial "dog whistles" used by Donald Trump in the 2016 presidential campaign? Would they see this as an advance over the more overt racism evident in the past?

10. According to symbolic interactionist theory, why are symbols so important to our interactions? In what ways has language changed because of the development of the internet?

RESEARCHING THE SOCIAL WORLD

Sociology as a Science

Humankind has made amazing advances during its short existence on Earth. From the development of agriculture to the Industrial Revolution to the advent of the digital and the global ages, each generation has pushed further into an unknown future. Many, especially in the developed world, enjoy longer lives, improved standards of living, a plethora of inexpensive manufactured goods, affordable and readily available food, quick and effortless communication, and the ability to travel, even around the world. But this advancement, especially of those in the developed world, has come at a significant ecological price.

Climate change, marked by long-term fluctuations in Earth's intricate and interwoven weather patterns, has occurred since the formation of the planet. Some fluctuations affect only specific regions, while others affect the entire world. Some span decades; others occur over millions of years. Although gradual climate change is a natural process, a growing body of careful research suggests that significant recent changes, including fossil fuel combustion and deforestation, are directly attributable to human activities, especially in the developed world.

Despite this scientific consensus, our impact on climate change remains a hotly debated issue. If the available geological, atmospheric, and oceanographic evidence is solid enough to convince the scientific community, why do so many people remain fiercely unconvinced? Who is opposed to the notion that human actions are a major cause of climate change, and how have institutional forces influenced their personal beliefs over time?

Physical science can help us understand and explain climate change, but to understand the motivations, beliefs, and actions that affect our response to it, we need sociologists and their research methods. There are many types of social research; each can uncover unknown or even

LEARNING OBJECTIVES

3.1 Describe the scientific method.

3.2 Explain how scientific knowledge develops over time.

3.3 Identify the various methods of sociological research.

3.4 Explain how sociologists engage in secondary data analysis.

3.5 Discuss five key issues in social research.

edge.sagepub.com/ritzerintro4e

- Take the chapter quiz
- Review key terms with eFlashcards
- Explore multimedia links and SAGE readings

$SAGE edge™

unsuspected truths about the relationship between people and climate change, as well as many other social issues. Thus, sociology is a science, like—but also unlike—any other.

Like all scientists, passionate sociologists may unintentionally let their personal feelings or their drive to succeed affect their research. Although all sociologists—indeed all scientists—make occasional errors, the research methods that they use must be ethical, reliable, and valid for the results they yield to have a chance of being widely accepted. This is especially important because contemporary sociological research often deals with controversial, red-hot issues, such as the role of people and society in climate change.

As you learn about the major types and purposes of sociological research, consider the issues and phenomena that you yourself might like to research. You may someday have an opportunity to do so. ●

Sociology is a science of the social world, and research is absolutely central to such a science. All sociologists study others' research, and most do research of their own. Sociologists may theorize, speculate, and even rely on their imaginations for answers to questions about society. However, they almost always do so on the basis of data or information derived from research. Put another way, sociologists practice **empiricism**, which means that they gather information and evidence using their senses, especially their eyes and ears. Because we all do that in order to experience the world, what makes sociology different? In addition to using their senses, sociologists adopt the scientific method, or a similarly *systematic* approach, in search of a thorough understanding of the social world. They have a variety of methods at their disposal in researching and analyzing society, but they also experience a few significant constraints on their ability to conduct such research.

THE SCIENTIFIC METHOD

The **scientific method** is a structured way of finding answers to questions about the world (Carey 2011). The scientific method employed by sociologists is much the same as that used in other sciences. Although in practice creative sociological research often does not slavishly adhere to the following steps, they constitute the basic scientific method:

1. A sociologist uncovers *questions in need of answers.* These questions can be inspired by key issues in the larger society, personal experiences, or topics of concern specifically in sociology. The best and most durable research and findings often stem from issues that the researcher connects with personally. Karl Marx, for example, detested the exploitation of workers that characterized capitalism; Max Weber feared the depersonalizing impact of bureaucracies (see Chapter 2). Thus, powerful motivations spurred both Marx and Weber to do research on, and eventually to come up with key insights into, these monumentally important aspects of social life.

2. Sociologists review the *relevant literature* on the questions of interest to them. This is because others have likely done similar or related research in the past. After more than a century of doing scientific research, sociologists have learned a great deal about many things. It would make no sense to start over from the beginning. For example, my work on McDonaldization (Ritzer, forthcoming) is based on the study of the work on rationalization by Max Weber ([1921] 1968), his successors (such as Kalberg 1980), and contemporary researchers (Ram 2007). I concluded that the fast-food restaurant is an apt, current example of the rationalization process. Other scholars have since reviewed my work and that of other scholars of McDonaldization (for a collection of this work, see Ritzer 2010c). They have amplified the concept, and they have applied it to domains such as religion (Drane 2008, 2012), higher education (Hayes 2017; Hayes and Wynyard 2002), social work (Dustin 2007), psychotherapy (Goodman 2016), and Disney World (Bryman 2004; Huddleston, Garlen, and Sandlin 2016).

3. Researchers often develop *hypotheses,* or educated guesses, about how social phenomena can be expected to relate to one another. For example, Uri Ram (2007) hypothesized that Israeli society would grow increasingly McDonaldized, and he found evidence to support that idea. As another example, Marx hypothesized that the conflict between capitalists and workers would ultimately lead to the collapse of capitalism. Over the years, conflict between capitalists and workers has increased in some areas of the world, but it has decreased in others. Capitalism has not collapsed, although it came close in 1929 at the beginning of the Great Depression and maybe in 2008 at the onset of the Great Recession. This makes it clear that hypotheses are simply hypotheses. They may not be confirmed by research or borne out by social developments, but such speculation is important to the scientific method.

4. Researchers must choose *research methods* that will help them answer their research questions. Sociology

offers diverse methodological tools; some are better than others for answering certain kinds of questions. For example, some sociologists are interested in how a person's social class shapes his or her opinions about social issues. Surveys and other quantitative tools may be best to evaluate the relationship between *class* and *attitudes*. Other sociologists want to know how people interpret and make sense of their social world, and how this meaning-making shapes social action. Qualitative methods, such as observations and interviews, may be helpful for studying these issues. The researcher might observe two individuals flirting at a party. The researcher may interview the individuals to see how each of them interprets gestures, body language, clothing, and other nonverbal cues that might suggest romantic or sexual interest. Sociologists select from among these and other methods to best answer their research questions.

5. Researchers use their chosen methods to *collect data* that can confirm—or fail to confirm—their hypotheses. Many classical sociologists conducted their research in libraries, and some contemporary sociologists do as well, analyzing secondary sources, such as reports based on data collected by others. But many contemporary sociologists venture into the field to collect original data through observations, interviews, questionnaires, and other means.

6. Researchers *analyze the data* collected, assessing their meaning in light of the hypotheses that guided the research. For example, as you learned in Chapter 2, Émile Durkheim hypothesized that those who were involved with other people would be less likely to commit suicide than those who lived more isolated existences and were experiencing what he called *anomie*. (For a more recent study showing the relationship between isolation—and other social breakdowns—and the risk of dying in an extreme heat wave, see Klinenberg 2015.) That is, being integrated with other people would, in a way, "protect" an individual from suicide. Analyzing data from several nineteenth-century European countries, Durkheim ([1897] 1951) found that the suicide rates were, in fact, higher for widowed or divorced people than for those who were married and therefore presumably better integrated socially.

The research process may begin again if a researcher discovers additional questions when analyzing the existing data. For example, Robert Putnam, in his famous book *Bowling Alone* (2001), addresses the applicability of Durkheim's concept of anomie in the contemporary world. As the title of his book suggests, he found

A study of the social world concluded that people today are increasingly likely to undertake many activities—including bowling—alone. Does this conclusion apply to you and your life?

that people are now less likely to bowl in leagues and more likely to bowl alone. More generally, people are increasingly doing many things alone (for example, shopping online) that in the past they did with other people. Further analysis of Durkheim's work—or a new application of it—might lead to the hypothesis that people who "bowl alone" are more likely to commit suicide.

Here's an even more current example. Imagine that you are wondering how relying on social networks like Facebook might affect a person's susceptibility to suicide. Having read this far in the book, you already know something about Durkheim's work on suicide. However, as a professional sociologist, you would, of course, conduct a much more thorough review of the relevant theory and research on this issue. You would find some work that argues that social networking can prevent suicide (Luxton, June, and Kinn 2011). From this, and from what you now know about Durkheim's thinking, you might hypothesize that those who have many Facebook friends are more socially integrated and therefore less likely to commit suicide than those who have few Facebook friends or are not on Facebook at all. An alternative hypothesis would be that no matter how many friends one has on Facebook, those who have few, if any, friends in the "real world" are more likely to commit suicide.

How would you collect data to test your hypotheses? You'd probably need to get some data about a group's Facebook friends, their friends in the real world, and their suicide rates. You would then analyze the patterns in these data. And then, if all went well, you could determine whether either of these hypotheses is supported by the evidence. That would be a scientific approach to answering your questions.

Does the publicity associated with the suicide of a famous person, such as that of comedian Robin Williams in 2014, lead other people to commit suicide? What would be your hypothesis? How would you go about collecting data to test your hypothesis?

CHECKPOINT 3.1: THE SCIENTIFIC METHOD

STEPS IN THE RESEARCH PROCESS

1 Uncover a question in need of an answer.

2 Review the relevant literature.

3 Develop hypotheses.

4 Identify an appropriate method for answering the research question.

5 Collect data.

6 Analyze the data.

THE DEVELOPMENT OF SCIENTIFIC KNOWLEDGE

Scientific knowledge develops gradually and cumulatively as one set of empirical findings builds on another. Some studies fail to confirm earlier findings and come to be seen as dead ends. Other studies confirm previous findings. Confidence in those findings grows as they are confirmed by additional research, and eventually some of them begin to be treated as scientific facts. All sciences are built on such facts. Over time and with additional research, however, some widely accepted facts may be found to be erroneous. For example, early scientists who studied the brain believed that women's relatively smaller brain size in comparison to men's was evidence of mental inferiority. Later research demonstrated that brain size does not determine intelligence, so those earlier ideas are no longer accepted (Gould 1981; Van Valen 1974). But some facts do survive empirical tests; these facts come to form the basis of what we think of as a science. For example, as you learned in this chapter's opening vignette, an accumulation of data from research on climate patterns leads most scientists to treat the idea of climate change as a scientific fact. The National Aeronautics and Space Agency reports that 97 percent, or more, of climate scientists actively working in the field believe that the accumulated evidence is that the global warming we have witnessed over the last century is traceable to human actions (see Figure 3.1). The Intergovernmental Panel on Climate Change (IPCC 2007), the most authoritative group of global scientists studying climate change, reviewed past research findings and confirmed both that global warming is a scientific fact *and* that human activity is its main cause. This gradual and orderly pattern of scientific development is what we would expect from the systematic use of the scientific method and the evolution of a science.

Thomas Kuhn ([1962] 1970), a philosopher of science, proposed a different model of scientific development that focuses on the role of abrupt and dramatic scientific breakthroughs. According to Kuhn, what defines a science is the existence of a **paradigm**, a general model of the world that is accepted by most practitioners in the field. One such paradigm today is that humans are the main cause of climate change. Other long-held examples include the idea in astronomy that Earth and the other planets revolve around the sun and in biology that "germs" cause most infectious diseases. With a generally agreed-upon paradigm, scientists need not squabble among themselves over their general orientation and their most basic premises. They are free to do research within the confines and safety of that paradigm. As research expands upon the paradigm, it is "fleshed out" in a series of tiny steps. Its fundamentals remain unaltered, at least for a time.

But some research does not support the dominant paradigm, and serious questions arise. If those questions are not answered and new ones continue to be raised, the old paradigm eventually collapses and is replaced by a new paradigm; a scientific revolution occurs. Kuhn argues that it is in those revolutions—the death of an old paradigm and the birth of a new one—that science takes great leaps forward. For centuries scientists believed that Earth was at the center of the universe, with the sun orbiting it (a geocentric model). It was not until the sixteenth century, when better research methods became available, that the geocentric paradigm began to be supplanted by a paradigm that saw Earth as orbiting the sun (a heliocentric model). This was a revolution in astronomical thought. In the centuries that followed, other astronomers built upon that knowledge and came to the consensus that Earth and the sun are in fact parts of one solar system within one galaxy of many in the universe. Heliocentrism remains the dominant paradigm for explaining the relationship between Earth and the sun. However, the nature of paradigms means that new ones are always developing, leading to new explanations of the role of both bodies in the universe as it is currently understood.

Kuhn's single-paradigm approach fits very well with the history of the physical sciences, such as astronomy and physics, but sociology and the other social sciences (for example, geography; see Malik 2014) can perhaps

FIGURE 3.1 • Effects of Global Warming

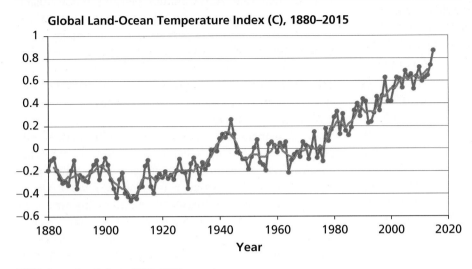

Global Land-Ocean Temperature Index (C), 1880–2015

NOTE: Anomaly with base: 1951–1980.

SOURCE: NASA/GISS.

Rising Sea Levels, 1870–2000

SOURCE: CSIRO Marine and Atmospheric Research, coastal tide gauge records, www.cmar.csiro.au, via NASA Global Climate Change, http://climate.nasa.gov.

and conflicts, the development of sociology as a whole tends to be slower and more sporadic than the development of the physical sciences. And because there has never been a single dominant paradigm in sociology, the field has never experienced any dramatic paradigm revolutions. Rather, the fortunes of various paradigms have risen and fallen over time.

In a multiple-paradigm science, it is more difficult to accumulate knowledge that is accepted by practically everyone in the field. Sociologists do not operate safely within the confines of a single dominant, broadly agreed-upon paradigm. The most basic assumptions of a given sociologist or group of sociologists are constantly open to question and attack by those who operate on the basis of other paradigms. There is a much less settled, universally agreed-upon knowledge base in sociology than there is in, say, biology or astronomy. Nonetheless, there *is* a substantial body of knowledge in sociology, some of which is summarized throughout this book. The lack of a dominant paradigm means that there are also many more controversies in sociology than there are in some other fields. As a result, you will find sociology to be characterized by many interesting, stimulating, and exciting debates, as well as many facts.

better be seen as "multiple-paradigm sciences" (Friedrichs 1970; Ritzer 1975; Bills 2013). The social world, social phenomena, and individuals—to say nothing of the interrelationships among them—are highly complex. No single paradigm is powerful enough to deal with all of them and able to unify the discipline. So research tends to occur *within* each sociological paradigm, expanding each over time but not contributing to a consensus in the discipline as a whole. Furthermore, some of the research stemming from one paradigm may be in conflict with research stemming from other paradigms. Because of these differences

CHECKPOINT 3.2: **THE DEVELOPMENT OF SCIENTIFIC KNOWLEDGE**

Empirical findings → studies confirm findings → most practitioners agree on a general paradigm → questions about the paradigm proliferate→ new paradigm develops

SOCIOLOGICAL RESEARCH

Sociological knowledge is derived from research that may use a variety of different methods. Typically, the method chosen is and should be driven by the nature of the research question. Imagine that you are a sociologist interested in studying differences in the behavior of people who visit Las Vegas. You might start by observing, perhaps by watching people gamble. You might look for variations: Are men and women equally represented at the slot machines? Are they equally likely to play craps or blackjack? Are there age differences in who plays which games? You could do much the same thing in looking for differences among those who attend the shows and musical events at the casinos. Are there gender differences between the audiences of, say, Cirque du Soleil's *Mystere* or *Ka* and the audience of a Penn & Teller magic show? Are there age differences between the audience members at a Carrot Top show and those at a Mariah Carey concert? In order to better understand such differences, you might be inspired to participate, to become a *participant-observer,* gambling or being entertained alongside those you are studying.

You may realize that your specific research questions are better answered through use of the interview method. You might interview those who have come to Las Vegas to gamble, asking about their expectations for having fun or winning a lot of money. This could be a more efficient use of your time because it would not entail waiting around for gamblers to do or say something relevant to your research question. But in interviews, people might not be willing to talk to you about their gambling experiences, especially if they have been losing money—and most gamblers lose most of the time! Furthermore, even if they are willing to talk to you, they might not give you totally honest answers.

In this case, perhaps administering an anonymous questionnaire or survey would be better. You could hand the questionnaires out to people leaving the casino, and the respondents might feel protected by the anonymity of the process. Unfortunately, survey questions are not easy to word in just the right way. And many people might not be willing to take your survey, especially if they have stayed up late gambling or have lost money. Even if they do take a questionnaire from you, they might not answer the questions or mail the questionnaire back to you. You could also develop an anonymous online survey and provide people with the link; this would be perhaps the most efficient way to administer a survey, but the response rate may still remain low.

Instead of randomly distributing questionnaires or an online survey link, you could be more systematic and scientific by obtaining a list of guests at a given hotel-casino. However, it is highly unlikely that you would be given such private information. You could use a random number table to generate a random sample of people drawn from the phone book in your hometown and mail each person in the sample your questionnaire or survey link, but it is unlikely that many of them would have visited Las Vegas recently. Among the relatively few who have, it is likely that only a very small number would return the completed questionnaires to you. And your phone book would not include the many people who have abandoned landlines and have only cell phones. In the age of the cell phone, phone books are declining in importance—in many areas they're disappearing altogether.

Observation is a primary method in sociological research. Do you think people behave differently when they know they are being observed?

You could also create an experiment. Using a social science lab at your university, you could set up a Las Vegas–style poker table and recruit students as participants. You could tell them that the typical player loses 90 percent of the time and that previous research has shown that *most* players lose *most of the time*. You could then ask whether, in spite of that information, they still want to gamble at your poker table. Of greatest interest would be those who say yes. You could interview them before they start "gambling" at your table, observe them as they gamble, and interview them again after they finish gambling. Did they start out believing, despite all the evidence to the contrary, that they would win? How could they have retained such a belief in spite of all the counterevidence? What are their feelings after gambling at your table? Did those feelings seem to be related to whether they won or lost? How likely are they to gamble again? Are there important differences between women and men in terms of their answers to these questions?

Observation, interviews, surveys, experiments, and other research methods are all useful and important to sociologists. All have strengths but also limitations. Before we examine these methods and their strengths and limitations in more detail, there is an important distinction between two basic types of research methods that should be clarified.

QUALITATIVE AND QUANTITATIVE RESEARCH

Each of the research methods in the wide variety available to sociologists can be classified as either qualitative or quantitative.

Qualitative research consists of studies done in natural settings that produce in-depth, descriptive information (e.g., in respondents' own words) about the social world (Denzin and Lincoln 2011; Silverman 2016). Such research does not necessarily require statistical methods for collecting and reporting data (Marshall and Rossman 2010). Observation—watching, listening, and taking detailed notes—and open-ended interviews are just two of the qualitative methods used by sociologists. These methods are used to capture descriptive information about an incredibly wide range of social phenomena, ranging from social movements to cultural practices, to people's lived experiences and feelings, to the ways in which organizations function, to interactions between nations. By gathering information from often small numbers of groups and individuals, studies employing qualitative methods produce rich data about the social world and in-depth understanding of particular social processes. Sometimes they help provide insights about new areas where little research has been done. However, because qualitative methods usually rely on small sample sizes, the findings cannot be generalized to the broader population; for this, we use quantitative methods.

Quantitative research involves the analysis of numerical data, usually derived from surveys and experiments

(Creswell 2008). The analysis of quantitative data on or from groups of people can help us describe and better understand important observable (empirical) social realities. In his analysis of social mobility in the United States, Gilbert (2015) analyzed previously collected General Social Survey (GSS) data on the relationship between the occupational status of fathers and the occupations achieved by their sons. (GSS data come from surveys that use random, representative samples drawn from the adult population of the United States.) Among Gilbert's findings is the fact that 42 percent of the sons of fathers who held upper-level white-collar occupations ultimately attained similarly high-level jobs, while only 15 percent of these sons went into lower-level manual work. At the other end of the occupational hierarchy, 36 percent of the sons of fathers who held lower-level manual occupations came to hold same-level occupations, while 20 percent moved up the ladder into upper-white-collar occupations. It is clear that if your father has a higher-level position in the occupational structure, you are more likely to reach a similar level in your lifetime. Such survey data provide great insights into the process of social mobility in the United States—and much else.

The mathematical method used to analyze numerical data is **statistics**. It is a powerful tool, and most sociological researchers learn statistical methods. Statistics can aid researchers in two ways:

- When researchers want to see trends over time or compare differences between groups, they use **descriptive statistics**. The purpose of such statistics is to *describe* some particular body of data that is based on a phenomenon in the real world (Salkind 2004, 8–10). For example, researchers can use survey data to track trends in occupational mobility over time and then use statistical analysis to describe how occupational mobility varies by race, gender, and age.

- To test hypotheses, researchers use **inferential statistics**. Such statistics allow researchers to use data from a relatively small group to speculate with some level of certainty about a larger group. For example, researchers might conduct research on racial discrimination in higher education by examining the acceptance rate of black and Latino students at a sample of select schools. They can draw generalizations about broader population of applicants based on their findings from this sample. Each method has its own set of strengths and limitations in terms of what it can do to help a researcher answer a specific question. Sociologists often debate the relative merits of quantitative versus qualitative methods, but they generally recognize that each method has value. There is a broad consensus that quantitative and qualitative research methods can complement one another (Ragin 2014; Riis 2012; Rueschemeyer, Stephens, and Stephens 1992). In practice, sociologists (and other social scientists) may combine both quantitative and qualitative research methods in a single study (*mixed-method research;* Guetterman, Fetters, and Creswell 2015).

OBSERVATIONAL RESEARCH

As mentioned earlier, one of the primary qualitative methods is **observation**. It consists of systematically watching, listening to, and recording what takes place in a natural social setting over some, usually extended, period of time (Hammersley 2007). Though the observational techniques of sociologists are similar to those used by investigative journalists, sociological techniques may be much more systematic and in-depth. The two primary observational methods are participant and nonparticipant observation.

There are several key dimensions to any type of observation in sociology:

- *The degree to which those being observed are aware that they are being observed.* This dimension can vary, from everyone involved being fully informed about the research to participants being observed from afar or through hidden cameras, one-way mirrors, and the like. Sexual behavior is one of many areas studied by sociologists using covert observational techniques (Frank 2015), but such covert observation is not limited to sociologists and academics more generally. In 2014 the National Geographic Channel produced a documentary film titled *Inside: Undercover in North Korea.* The film's camera crew was ostensibly in North Korea to document a medical team helping the blind. However, its real purpose was to observe and record what life is like in this secretive and difficult-to-penetrate country. The reality TV series *Undercover Boss* also employs covert observational research. Top-level executives work incognito at lower levels in their own firms to learn more about the work and the workers. While the boss might have ulterior motives, such as uncovering and firing incompetent employees, sociologists who do this kind of research are not supposed to have such motives. A desire to understand the complex facets of a setting or environment is their main motivation.

- *The degree to which the presence of the observer affects the actions of those being observed.* When people are aware that they are being observed, they often present themselves in the way they think the observer expects or will accept. For instance, North Koreans might behave differently toward outsiders if they notice they are being observed. Similarly, gang members might not engage in illegal activities in the presence of a researcher.

- *The degree to which the process is structured.* Highly structured observational research might use preset categories, codes, or a checklist to guide observations, but some observation studies are intended to seek the widest possible range of data. Researchers thus attempt to take note of as much as possible in the field setting; their method is totally open and unstructured.

Some of the most famous pieces of sociological research have used the observational method. Examples include studies of the social and economic contexts of people's lives, such as *The Philadelphia Negro: A Social Study* (Du Bois [1899] 1996), *Street Corner Society: The Social Structure of an Italian Slum* (Whyte 1943), *Tally's Corner: A Study of Negro Streetcorner Men* (Liebow 1967), *Floating City: A Rogue Sociologist Lost and Found in New York's Underground Economy* (Venkatesh 2014), and *On the Run: Fugitive Life in an American City* (Goffman 2014; see the Trending box in this chapter, page 78), as well as observations of African American families in *All Our Kin: Strategies for Survival in a Black Community* (Stack 1974) and of criminal behavior in *Code of the Street: Decency, Violence, and the Moral Life of the Inner City* (Anderson 1999). Most of the studies discussed in the Trending boxes throughout this book use observational methods.

Participant and Nonparticipant Observation

There are two major types of observational methods. One is **participant observation**, in which the researcher actually plays a role, even a minor one, in the group or setting being observed. A participant observer might become a hostess or bartender to study the sex industry in Ho Chi Minh City, Vietnam (Hoang 2015; see the Trending box in Chapter 9, page 244), sell books on the sidewalk to watch what happens on a busy city street (Duneier 1999), or live in a trailer park to witness how individuals cope with poverty (Desmond 2016; see the Trending box in Chapter 8, page 226). In one classic example of participant observation, a sociologist with tuberculosis methodically studied the hospital he was in, as well as the actions of doctors, nurses, and other patients (Roth 1963). In another, a sociologist researched gender segregation in the corporate world of the 1970s by, among other things, participating in group discussions and meetings at a major U.S. company (Kanter 1993). Barbara Ehrenreich (2001) worked in low-wage jobs (including as a waitress, hotel maid, housecleaner, nursing home aide, and Walmart associate) to study the experiences of low-wage workers. She found that many of the women she studied, despite working extra hours, were unable to meet the basic living expenses of housing, transportation, and food.

Like its predecessor *Dirty Jobs*, CNN's *Somebody's Gotta Do It* is essentially an informal exercise in the participant observation of work. The host, Mike Rowe, is *not* a trained sociologist and he is *not* trying, at least consciously, to uncover the sociological aspects of the jobs he was studying, but he *is* a participant observer. In each episode, he actually does the job being examined—he is a participant—and he observes the workers as well as their dirty jobs. Among the jobs Rowe has performed and observed on the show are "turd burner," owl vomit collector, baby chicken sexer, sheep castrator, rat exterminator, maggot farmer, diaper cleaner, and high-rise building window washer.

ASK YOURSELF

Do you think participant observers risk losing their objectivity when they grow too close to the subjects under study? Why or why not? What about nonparticipant observers? How can sociologists conducting observational research avoid becoming too involved with subjects?

Ethnographers generally spend a great deal of time, sometimes years, studying groups of people. Those being studied will likely be observed systematically and interviewed either formally or informally. Here an ethnographer visits members of an indigenous tribe in Papua New Guinea.

The second observational method is **nonparticipant observation**, where the sociologist plays little or no role in what is being observed. For example, sociologists Clare L. Stacey and Lindsay L. Ayers (2012) spent six months observing (and interviewing) 16 people who provide home care for the elderly or the disabled, as well as nurses and social workers who visit the elderly or disabled in their homes. The home care workers are paid (although poorly, $9 to $11 per hour) for their work. However, the care work that they do is normally provided free of charge by family members or friends of those in need of care. How do the care workers rationalize receiving pay for their work? For one thing, they emphasize the technical and emotional skills required to do the work. For another, they see themselves as providing a service that is of help to the larger society by, for example, saving taxpayers money. Because the recipients are poor, the state would have to pay a great deal more money to keep them in institutions than the sums paid to home care workers. One of sociology's most prolific observational researchers, Gary Fine, has done nonparticipant observation research on Little League baseball (Fine 1987), restaurant kitchens (Fine 2008), meteorologists (Fine 2010), and chess players involved in a chess tournament (Fine 2015).

Big Brother, a reality show that began on Dutch TV in 1999 and is now franchised in many television markets around the world, can be seen as another example of nonparticipant observation. Of course, sociologists are not involved in this show, and the observation is not as systematic as it would be if it were a sociological study. The show's premise is simple: Select a group of young people who have never met, have them live together in a "house" (stage set) that is cut off from the outside world, and see what happens. Although

cameras record much of the group's activities (including in the bathroom), no outsiders are present in the house to participate in those activities. The "observers" are the viewing audience, who can be seen as amateur nonparticipant observers in the sense that they "study" interaction patterns and other sociological aspects of what goes on among the residents.

In reality, there are no firm dividing lines between participant and nonparticipant observation, and at times the two blend imperceptibly into one another. The participant often becomes simply an observer. An example is the sociologist who begins with participant observation of a gang, hanging out with members in casual settings, but becomes a nonparticipant when illegal activities such as drug deals take place. And the nonparticipant observer sometimes becomes a participant. An example is the sociologist who is unable to avoid being asked to take sides or share opinions in squabbles among members of a Little League team or, more likely, among their parents.

Ethnography

At times sociologists pose research questions that require an observational method traditionally associated with anthropology. **Ethnography** is the creation of a detailed account of what a group of people do and the way they live (Adler and Adler 2012; Hammersley 2007), usually entailing much more intensive, immersive, and lengthy periods of observation (sometimes participant) than traditional sociological observation requires. Researchers may live for years with the groups, tribes, or subcultures (such as gamblers) being studied.

Netnography

The basic concerns of sociology—communications, relationships, and groups—are key elements of the internet, especially social media sites such as Facebook, Twitter, and Instagram. Online discussions, digital networking, and posting photos and videos are how many of us connect virtually with each other every day. Not surprisingly, **netnography**, or an account of what transpires online, has become an important method of sociological research (Kozinets 2015). Netnographers are digital ethnographers who are able to observe thousands of phenomena online. For example, they might follow the Twitter account of a celebrity or sports star to learn about their fans or play an online video game such as World of Warcraft to understand how individuals engage in virtual role playing and collaboration. One recent study used netnography to examine the blogs of female Chinese tourists in Macao, discovering how crossing the border influenced perceptions of their self-identity and enhanced their personal relationships (Zhang and Hitchcock 2014). Outside of academia, netnography is used by web designers, marketers, and advertisers to observe, record, and analyze our digital behaviors. The virtual data we create when shopping on Zappos or streaming music on Spotify offer these professionals valuable information that they can use to entice us to buy more products or visit new websites.

Netnography, like other social research, raises ethical questions. Researchers who join an internet community to observe its ongoing communications might not inform other members that they have joined with the objective of studying the group. The issue of informed consent is especially ambiguous when conducting online research because so much of what transpires in virtual reality is public. While we can take steps to protect our privacy online, many of us do not. For some internet users, the whole point of posting a video on YouTube or writing a blog is to attract as many views and followers as possible. Revealing personal information about ourselves, family, and friends is common on popular social media sites. This makes it easy for anyone, including social researchers, to investigate our relationships and our identities.

Engaging the Digital World
Select one student in your class or your course instructor and conduct a netnography to learn more about him or her. Write a report about what you were able to find on the internet, such as work histories, hobbies, family ties, or membership in student or professional organizations. Is there anything you found that is embarrassing or that you think should be hidden or deleted? State what search engines you used and social media sites you visited. Conclude your report with an introspective analysis of this exercise. Did you feel like you were "creeping" when conducting your netnography? Did you feel like you were violating this person's privacy? Share your report with the person you studied and ask him or her if the findings in your report are accurate, and whether he or she found them disturbing.

Sociologists interested in a variety of topics advocate the use of ethnographic methods. This is especially true of those interested in studying women (see Chapter 11), because such methods can reveal much about the experiences of traditionally understudied and marginalized groups of women—for example, Latina girls (Garcia 2012), lap dancers (Colosi 2010), and ex-convicts (Opsal 2011). Some suggest that the personal relationships that develop between researchers and subjects in ethnographic studies make it less likely that the power researchers exert over subjects will distort the results (Bourdieu 1992). Researchers who employ feminist methods are especially intent on ensuring that study participants are not coerced or exploited in the research process.

Normally ethnographies are small in scale, micro, and local. Researchers observe people, talk to them, hang out with them, sometimes live with them, and conduct formal and informal interviews with them over an extended period of time. Nevertheless, the ethnographic method has now been extended to the global level. Michael Burawoy (2000; see also Tsuda, Tapias, and Escandell 2014) argues that a **global ethnography** is the best way to understand globalization. This is a type of ethnography that is grounded in various parts of the world and seeks to understand globalization as it exists in people's social lives. Burawoy and his colleagues "set out from real experiences . . . of welfare clients, homeless recyclers, mobilized feminists, migrant nurses, union organizers, software engineers, poisoned villagers, redundant boilermakers, and breast cancer activists in order to explore *their* global contexts" (Burawoy 2000, 341).

Three interconnected phenomena are central to the global ethnographies undertaken by Burawoy and others:

- Do people experience globalization as an external force? If so, is it a force to be combated or accepted?

- In what ways, if at all, do people participate in creating and furthering global connections?

- Do people work for or against processes that are global in scope?

Burawoy and his colleagues have sought to answer these questions wherever in the world they have undertaken their studies.

One example of a global ethnography is a study of Vietnamese immigrants in the United States and their monetary relationships with their families in Vietnam (Thai 2014). Many of the homeless are out of work, often because of the global economic changes that have led many jobs to be outsourced to other countries. There are other linkages to globalization: For instance, at least some of the objects the homeless recycle may have been produced outside the United States; once they are recycled, those objects may once again find their way into new commodities that come to be distributed globally.

One of Burawoy's colleagues looked at nurses in Chicago who were originally from India and examined their place in the transnational community of nurses (George 2000). Concerns here might be American-born nurses who have lost their jobs as a result of the availability of qualified nurses from all over the world or who are unable to find jobs because the positions are being occupied by Indian nurses. There is also the issue of the communication linkages between Indian nurses in the United States and those back home in India, as well as the degree to which those linkages are used to bring still more Indian nurses to the United States.

INTERVIEWS

While observers often interview those they are studying, they usually do so very informally and on the spur of the moment. Other sociologists rely mainly, or exclusively, on **interviews** in which they seek information from participants (respondents) by asking a series of questions that have been spelled out, at least to some degree, before the research is conducted (Gubrium et al. 2012). Interviews are usually conducted face-to-face, although they can be done by phone and are increasingly being done via the internet (Farrell and Peterson 2010; Fontana 2007; James 2016). In addition, large-scale national surveys are increasingly including interviews. For example, the Centers for Disease Control and Prevention is known for its national surveys, but it also uses interviews in its National Health Interview Survey, which has been conducted continuously since 1957 (Sirkin et al. 2011; www.cdc.gov/nchs/nhis/about_nhis.htm).

The use of interviews has a long history in sociology. One very early example is W. E. B. Du Bois's ([1899] 1996) study of the "Philadelphia Negro." A watershed in the history of interviewing in sociology was reached during World War II, when large-scale interview studies of members of the American military were conducted. Some of the data from those studies were reported in a landmark study, *The American Soldier* (Stouffer et al. 1949). Allison Pugh (2009) interviewed and observed children and their families over a three-year period. Among other things, she found that parents tend to buy things for their children to help them be better integrated into groups at school and in their neighborhood, and they continue to do so even when declining economic circumstances make it more difficult for them to afford such purchases. Through these purchases, parents contribute directly to consumer culture; they help ensure that their children will become ever more deeply involved in that culture.

Types of Interviews

The questions asked in an interview may be preselected and prestructured so that respondents must choose from sets of preselected answers such as *agree* and *disagree*. Or an interview may be more spontaneous, unstructured, and completely open-ended. The latter form is used by those who do observational research. An unstructured interview offers no preset answers; respondents are free to say anything they want to say.

Prestructured interviews are attractive when the researcher wants to avoid any unanticipated reactions or responses from those being studied. In a prestructured interview, the interviewer attempts to

- Behave in the same way in each interview

- Ask the same questions, using the same exact words, and in the same sequence

- Ask closed-ended questions that the participant must answer by choosing from a set of preselected responses

- Offer the same explanations when they are requested by respondents

Interviews can take many forms and be more or less structured depending on the researcher's needs. Here an interviewer stops passersby.

- Not show any kind of reaction to the answers, no matter what they might be

Interviews conducted in this way often yield information that, like data obtained from questionnaires, can be coded numerically and then analyzed statistically.

There are problems associated with prestructured interviews. First, interviewers often find it difficult to live up to the guidelines for such interviews:

- They are frequently unable to avoid reacting to answers (especially unexpected or outrageous ones).

- They may use different intonation from one interview to another.

- They may change the wording, and even the order, of the questions asked (which can affect respondents' answers).

Second, respondents may not respond accurately or truthfully. For example, they may want to conceal things or give answers that they believe the interviewer wants to hear. Third, and most important, closed-ended questions limit the responses, possibly cutting off useful unanticipated information that might be provided in a more free-flowing interview.

The last problem is solved by the use of open-ended or *unstructured interviews*. The interviewer begins with only a general idea of the topics to be covered and the direction to be taken in the interview. The answers in unstructured interviews offer a good understanding of the respondents and what the issues under study mean to them. Such understandings and meanings are generally not obtained through structured interviews. However, unstructured interviews create problems of their own. For example, they may yield so much diverse information that it is hard to offer a coherent summary and interpretation of the results.

The Interview Process

Conducting interviews, especially those that are prestructured, usually involves several steps. The researcher does not simply make a list of questions and start asking them. Rather:

1. The interviewer must *gain access* to the setting being studied. This is relatively easy in some cases, such as when interviewing one's friends in the student union or at a local bar. However, access would likely be much more difficult if one wanted to interview one's friends in a sorority house or on the job. People might be less eager to talk to a researcher—to any outsider—in such settings. Some groups, such as the top executives of major corporations or the extremely wealthy, have the resources to insulate, or even isolate, themselves.

They can be quite difficult for researchers to gain access to and thus may be underrepresented in sociological research.

2. The interviewer must often seek to *locate a key informant* (Brown, Bankston, and Forsyth 2013; Rieger 2007). This is a person who has intimate knowledge of the group being studied and is willing to talk openly to the researcher about the group. A key informant can help the researcher gain access to the larger group of respondents and verify information being provided by them. The latter is useful because interviewees may well provide erroneous, perhaps purposely erroneous, information. For example, in William F. Whyte's (1943) famous study of "street corner society," a leader of the group, "Doc," served as Whyte's key informant. In Sudhir Venkatesh's (2008) study of a Chicago housing project and its gangs, his key informant was the gang leader "J. T." Of this relationship, Venkatesh said, "In the course of my fieldwork I became dependent on the continual support of J. T." (1994, 322). J. T. not only corrected Venkatesh's misinformation and misinterpretations but also retained the right to delete information from published reports on the study that might disclose his identity or that of his gang.

3. The interviewer must seek to *understand the language and culture* of the people being interviewed. In some cases this is very easy. For example, it is not a great problem for an academic interviewer to understand the language and culture of college students. However, it is more difficult if the academician interviews people with their own, very different language and culture. Examples might include interviews with members of motorcycle gangs or prostitutes. In these kinds of cases, it is all too easy for the researcher to misunderstand or to impose incorrect meanings on the words of respondents.

4. The researcher must *gain the trust of the respondents and develop a rapport* with them. Establishing trust and rapport can be easy or difficult, depending on the characteristics of the researcher. Well-educated and relatively powerful male researchers may intimidate less privileged female respondents. Older researchers may have trouble interviewing traditional-age college students. Depending on the field site, a researcher's point of view and (perceived) similarities with the respondents may ease rapport.

ASK YOURSELF

Have you ever conducted or participated in an interview, perhaps for a job or as part of a study? How closely did it adhere to the guidelines mentioned here?

In a few cases, trust and rapport need to be earned only once, but in many cases they need to be earned over and over. And trust can easily be lost. Venkatesh had to work constantly on his rapport with J. T., gang members, and many others who lived in the urban areas that he studied. In fact, J. T. thought at first that Venkatesh might be a cop, and he later confessed that he was never 100 percent sure that Venkatesh was not a police officer. Venkatesh was also in constant danger of losing the very tenuous trust his participants had in him and what he was doing. There was ever-present fear on the part of those he studied that he was in league with a rival gang or would inform on them to the police.

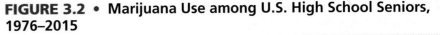

FIGURE 3.2 • Marijuana Use among U.S. High School Seniors, 1976–2015

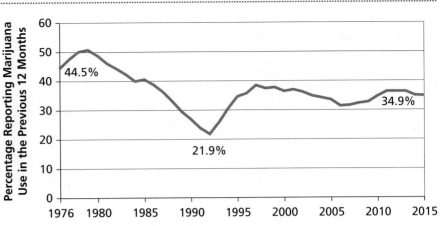

SOURCE: Data from Lloyd D. Johnston, Patrick O'Malley, Richard A. Miech, Jerald G. Bachman, and John E. Schulenberg. *Monitoring the Future: National Survey Results on Drug Use, 1975–2015: Overview, Key Findings on Adolescent Drug Use*, Table 6 (Ann Arbor: Institute for Social Research, University of Michigan, 2015).

SURVEY RESEARCH

Survey research involves the collection of information from a population, or more usually a representative portion of a population, through the use of interviews and, most important, questionnaires. While some sociologists do their own surveys, most rely on data derived from surveys done by others, such as the U.S. government (the U.S. census, for example) and the National Opinion Research Center, which conducts various opinion polls.

Interviews, as we know, involve questions asked by the researcher in person, on the telephone, or via the internet. Every two years the General Social Survey conducts face-to-face interviews with a large sample of Americans. In contrast, **questionnaires** are self-administered, written sets of questions. While the questions can be presented to respondents on a face-to-face basis, they are more often delivered to them by mail, asked over the telephone, or presented in a web-based format. Questionnaires are now increasingly being filled out on personal computers and over the phone (Snyder 2007).

Types of Surveys

There are two broad types of surveys. The first is the **descriptive survey**, which is designed to gather accurate information about, for example, members of a certain group, people in a given geographic area, or people in a particular organization. A descriptive survey might gather data on the level of sexual activity among college students, the employment status of Americans, or the way in which former manufacturing employees are coping with job loss. The best-known descriptive surveys are those conducted by organizations such as Gallup to gather information on the preferences, beliefs, and attitudes of given samples of people.

ASK YOURSELF

Has the increasing legalization of marijuana throughout the United States altered the data on marijuana use among high school seniors? Why or why not? How might any change affect data on the use of other drugs?

In one example of descriptive survey research using the internet, a survey was placed on a website designed to allow married people to find extramarital sexual partners. Based on a sample of more than 5,000 respondents, the data showed that females were more likely than males to engage in "sexting" (see Chapter 11) and that males and females involved in serious real-life relationships were about equally likely to engage in cheating on their partners, both online and in real life (Wysocki and Childers 2011).

For many years, the Institute for Social Research at the University of Michigan has conducted a descriptive survey of high school seniors in the United States. One of the subjects has been marijuana use. As you can see in Figure 3.2, the prevalence of marijuana use among high school seniors has risen and fallen, as if in waves. Marijuana use in this group peaked in 1979 (with more than half of students admitting use of the drug), reached a low of 22 percent in 1992, and has generally been rising since then, although it has never again approached the 1979 level. In 2015, slightly less than 35 percent of twelfth graders reported having used marijuana in the previous 12 months.

The data in Figure 3.2 are derived from descriptive surveys, but what if we wanted to explain, and not just statistically

FIGURE 3.3 • Random Samples and Stratified Samples

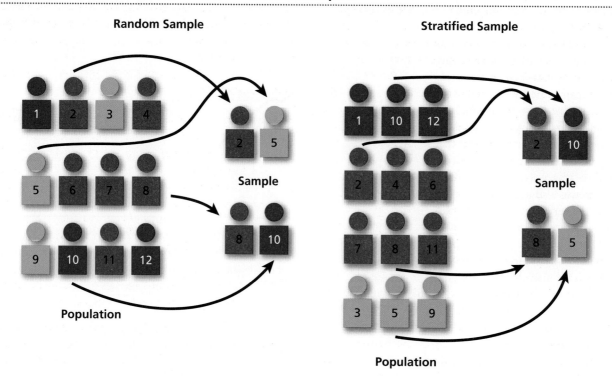

SOURCE: Random Samples and Stratified Samples is reprinted with permission of Dan Kernler, Associate Professor of Mathematics, Elgin Community College, Elgin, IL.

describe, changes in marijuana use among high school seniors? To get at this, we would need to do an **explanatory survey**, which seeks to uncover potential causes of, in this case, changes in marijuana use (e.g., the legalization of marijuana in states such as Colorado, California, and Maine [Monte, Zane, and Heard 2015]). For example, having discovered variations in marijuana use by high school students over the years, we might hypothesize that the variation is linked to students' (and perhaps the general public's) changing perceptions about the riskiness of marijuana use. Specifically, we might hypothesize that as students (and the public) increasingly come to see marijuana as less risky, marijuana use among students will go up. In this case, we would use the survey to learn more about respondents' attitudes toward and beliefs about the riskiness of marijuana use and not simply measure student use of marijuana.

Sampling

It is almost never possible to survey an entire population, such as all Americans, all students at your college or university, or even all sorority members at that university. Thus, survey researchers usually need to construct a **sample**, or a representative portion of the overall population. The more careful the researcher is in avoiding biases in selecting the sample, the more likely the findings are to be representative of the whole group.

The most common way to avoid bias is to create a **random sample**, a sample in which every member of the group

has an equal chance of being included. One way of obtaining a random sample is by using a list—for example, a list of the names of all the professors at your university. A coin is tossed for each name on the list, and those professors for whom the toss results in heads are included in the sample. More typical and efficient is the use of random number tables, found in most statistics textbooks, to select those in the sample (Kirk 2007). In our example, each professor is assigned a number, and those whose numbers come up in the random number table are included in the sample. More recently, use is being made of computer-generated random numbers. Other sampling techniques are used in survey research as well. For example, the researcher might create a **stratified sample** in which a larger group is divided into a series of subgroups (e.g., assistant, associate, and full professors) and then random samples are taken within each of these groups. This ensures representation from each group in the final sample, something that might not occur if one simply does a random sample of the larger group. Thus, random and stratified sampling are the safest ways of drawing accurate conclusions about a population as a whole. However, there is an element of chance in all sampling, especially random sampling, with the result that findings can vary from one sample to another. Even though sampling is the safest way to reach conclusions about a population, errors are possible. Random and stratified sampling are depicted in Figure 3.3.

Sometimes researchers use **convenience samples**, which avoid systematic sampling and simply include those who are conveniently available to participate in a research project. An example of a convenience sample might involve researchers passing out surveys to the students in their classes (Lunneborg 2007). These nonrandom samples are rarely ever representative of the larger population whose opinions the researcher is interested in knowing. Nonrandom samples therefore may create a substantial bias in researchers' results (Popham and Sirotnik 1973, 44). Many surveys that pop up on the internet are suspect because the respondents are the people who happened to be at a certain website (which is likely to reflect their interests) and who felt strongly enough about the topic of the survey to answer the questions.

Research using convenience samples is usually only exploratory. It is almost impossible to draw any definitive conclusions from such research. There are, however, some cases in which convenience sampling is not only justified but also useful. For researchers trying to study elite social networks (such as political leaders or the wealthy), simply gaining access to the group can be a difficult task in itself. Convenience sampling—surveying anyone in the group to whom one is introduced—may be the only way to proceed (Tansey 2006). Convenience sampling also sometimes leads to larger, more scientific projects that rely on random or stratified samples.

EXPERIMENTS

Sociologists do not do nearly as many experiments as do researchers in hard sciences such as chemistry, or even researchers in other social sciences such as psychology. However, some sociologists do perform experiments, and experimentation is one of the fundamental methods in the field (Jackson and Cox 2013). An **experiment** involves the manipulation of one or more characteristics in order to examine the effect of that manipulation (Kirk 2007).

A study by Devah Pager (2009) provides a good example of a sociological experiment. Pager was interested in how the background of a job applicant affects the likelihood of that individual's being called back for an interview. Pager randomly assigned fake criminal records to pairs of similar young men, one in each pair black and one white. Thus, in each pair, one person had a criminal record and one did not, and one was white and one was not. These young men then sent résumés to companies in Milwaukee, seeking entry-level jobs. One major finding of this experiment was that the young men believed to have criminal records received callbacks less than half as often as did those of the same race believed not to have criminal records. A second was that black men without criminal records received callbacks at about the same rate as white men with criminal records.

In this experiment, we can clearly see the relationship between two important elements of an experiment: independent and dependent variables. In Pager's experiment, the **independent variable**, the condition that was manipulated by the researcher, was the job applicant's combination of race and criminal background. The **dependent variable**, the characteristic or measurement that resulted from the manipulation, was whether or not the applicant was called in for an interview.

There are several different types of experiments (Walker and Willer 2007):

- *Laboratory experiments.* **Laboratory experiments** take place in controlled settings. The "laboratory" may be, for example, a classroom or a simulated environment. The setting offers the researcher great control over the selection of the participants as well as the independent variables—the conditions to which the participants are exposed (Lucas, Graif, and Lovaglia 2008). The famous experiments by Solomon Asch on conformity (see Chapter 5) were laboratory experiments. This type of experiment can be difficult to organize and sometimes yields artificial results. However, it allows for more accurate tests of research hypotheses.

- *Natural experiments.* **Natural experiments** are those in which researchers take advantage of a naturally occurring event to study its effect on one or more dependent variables. Such experiments offer the experimenter little or no control over independent variables (De Silva et al. 2010). For example, a recent natural experiment at Harvard University assigned first-year students from different races as roommates. Among the findings was that breakups among the roommates were more likely when an East Asian student lived with two white students (Chakravarti, Menon, and Winship 2014).

- *Field experiments.* In some natural situations, researchers are able to exert at least some control over who participates and what happens during experiments (Bertrand and Mullainathan 2004; Pager and Western 2012). These are called **field experiments**. One of the most famous studies in the history of sociology is the "Robbers Cave" field experiment (Sherif et al. [1954] 1961), so called because it took place in Robbers Cave State Park in Oklahoma. The researchers controlled important aspects of what took place at the site. For example, they were able to assign the 22 boys in the study into two groups, called the Rattlers and the Eagles. The researchers were also able to create various situations that led to rivalry, bickering, and hostility between the groups. At the end of the experiment, they had each group rate the other: 53 percent of ratings of the Eagles were unfavorable, while nearly 77 percent of ratings of the Rattlers were unfavorable. Later, the researchers introduced conditions that they hoped would reduce bad feelings and friction between the groups. In fact, greater harmony between the groups was created by having them work together on tasks such as securing needed water and paying collectively and equitably for a movie that everyone wanted to see. By the end of the latter part of the experiment, just 5 percent of the ratings of the Eagles were unfavorable, and unfavorable ratings of the Rattlers had dropped to 23 percent. A more recent field experiment in Sweden dealt, in part, with hiring discrimination against ethnic groups (Bursell 2014). Pairs of equally qualified applicants were sent to interview for open jobs. Those with Arabic or North African names were less likely to be called back for additional consideration.

Some observers see a bright future for experimentation in sociology, in part because of its growth in neighboring fields such as psychology and especially in fields such as economics and political science, which in the past did not do much experimentation. Another reason is the potential for using the internet as a site for sociological experiments (Hanson and Hawley 2010). In one internet-based experiment, male respondents were asked to evaluate the attractiveness of digitally altered pictures of females on the basis of their perception of the women's body mass index (BMI)—in other words, on how overweight the women appeared to be. One finding was that respondents who were overweight were less likely to report differences in the attractiveness of the women on the basis of the women's BMI (Conley and McCabe 2011). In another internet study in the Netherlands, similar to the field study discussed previously using résumés with white- and black-sounding names, fictitious résumés with Arabic and Dutch names were posted on online résumé databases. The résumés of those with Arabic names were requested less often than were those with Dutch names (Blommaert and Coenders 2014).

CHECKPOINT 3.3: RESEARCH METHODS IN SOCIOLOGY

METHOD	DESCRIPTION
Observation	Systematically watching, listening to, and recording what takes place in a natural setting over time
Ethnography	Creation of an account of what a group of people do and how they live over a long time period
Interview	Collection of data via a series of questions
Survey	Collection of information from a sample of the population through interviews and questionnaires
Experiment	Manipulation of one or more variables to examine their effect

SECONDARY DATA ANALYSIS

All of the methods discussed thus far involve the collection of new and original data, but many sociologists engage in **secondary data analysis**, in which they reanalyze data collected by others. Secondary analysis can involve a wide variety of different types of data, from censuses and other surveys to historical records and old transcripts of interviews and focus groups. Until recently, obtaining and using some of these secondary data sets was laborious and time-consuming. Today, however, thousands of data sets are available online, and they can be accessed with a few keystrokes. A number of websites provide both the data sets and statistical software for looking at them in different ways (Schutt 2007).

Secondary data analysis very often involves statistical analysis of government surveys and census data. The technique has a long history in sociology, extending back to Karl Marx's analyzing government statistics at the British Library. U.S. census data, which are collected every 10 years (last collected in 2010), are a gold mine for sociologists both in the United States and abroad. For example, researchers studying multi-racial identity used data from the 2000 and 2010 censuses and found that individuals who identified as two or more races increased from 6.8 million in 2000 to 9 million in 2010 (Jones and Bullock 2013). It is not unusual for one body of data to lead to hundreds of secondary analyses. For example, the World Values Survey (WVS; www.worldvaluessurvey.org/wvs.jsp; see also the "Globalization" box on page 72) is conducted in nearly 100 countries containing almost 90 percent of the world's population. Its six waves—a seventh wave is planned for 2017 to 2018—has been used to produce more than 1,000 research publications in more than 20 different languages. Some of this research has used the WVS to examine what social, cultural, and economic factors contribute to an individual's happiness. Figure 3.4 shows a "happiness map" depicting levels of happiness among the citizens of various countries included in the surveys from 2010 to 2014. Another study examined data from 1981 to 2007 and found that perceptions of freedom of choice are more likely to lead to higher levels of happiness (Inglehart et al. 2008). However, subsequent research may look differently at the data and describe new parts of the puzzle. Using similar data from the WVS, another study looking at individual cases within countries demonstrated that inequalities in health quality, among other factors, also shape happiness (Ovaska and Takashima 2010). A study focusing on migration found that emigration rates were high in countries with both high and low levels of happiness, but the rates were low for countries in the middle (Polgreen and Simpson 2011). Yet another study that looked at the impact of different welfare systems

FIGURE 3.4 • World Happiness: Rankings of 158 Countries

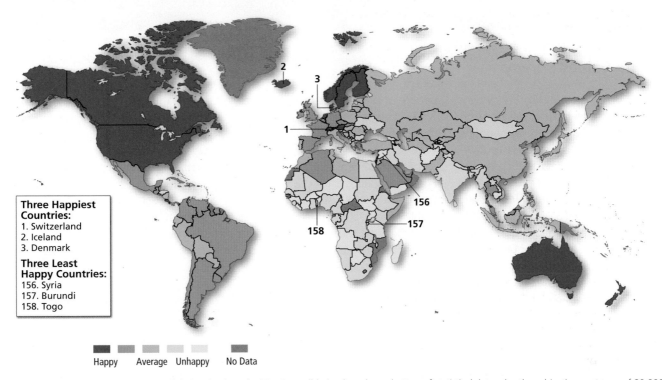

Three Happiest Countries:
1. Switzerland
2. Iceland
3. Denmark

Three Least Happy Countries:
156. Syria
157. Burundi
158. Togo

Happy   Average   Unhappy   No Data

NOTE: The World Happiness map is a global projection of subjective well-being based on a battery of statistical data, plus the subjective responses of 80,000 people worldwide, to map out well-being across 157 countries.

SOURCE: Helliwell, John F., Richard Layard, and Jeffrey Sachs, eds. 2015. *World Happiness Report 2015*. New York: Sustainable Development Solutions Network.

concluded that people who live in liberal and conservative countries are at least twice as likely to be unhappy as people living in social democratic welfare states (Deeming and Hayes 2012).

While secondary analysis is far easier and far less expensive to carry out than collecting one's own data is, especially for large amounts of data, it has distinct problems. For one thing, secondary researchers cannot refine their methods on the basis of preliminary research. For another, because others have chosen the methods of data collection, the data may not be ideal for the secondary researcher's needs. It is possible that the research may have to be abandoned until an appropriate data set is available or created. In some cases, researchers who find the data set inadequate for a study of their original interest may find that other relevant issues are covered better by the data. Another type of problem with using government data sets is political: Certain types of sensitive data may not have been collected. Or social or political changes may end the collection of certain types of data or change the ways in which the data are reported or categorized. For instance, the collection and reporting of U.S. census data on race have changed over the years to accommodate changing demographics and sensitivities. The resulting inconsistencies in the data set over time can pose great difficulties for the secondary researcher.

HISTORICAL-COMPARATIVE METHOD

The goal of **historical-comparative research** is to contrast how different historical events and conditions in various societies have led to different societal outcomes. The hyphenation of *historical-comparative* makes it clear that two separable methods are being combined. The historical component involves the study of the history of societies as well as of the major components of society, such as the state, religious system, and economy. The addition of the comparative element, comparing the histories of two or more societies, or of components of societies, makes this method more distinctively sociological.

One of the things that differentiates the discipline of history from historical-comparative sociology is the level of historical detail. Historians go into much more detail, and collect far more original historical data, than do sociologists. In contrast, sociologists are much more interested in generalizing about society than are historians. Perhaps the best way to exemplify the difference between a historical-comparative sociologist and a historian is in the concept of the ideal type (Clegg 2007; Weber [1921] 1968). An **ideal type**, as defined by Max Weber ([1903–1917] 1949, 90), is a "one-sided *accentuation*" of social reality. Unlike the goal of the historian, an ideal type is not meant

World Values Survey

The World Values Survey (WVS) is a source of cross-cultural data on the impact of globalization on people's worldviews, values, and basic motivations. The WVS collects demographic data and asks people in each surveyed country roughly 250 questions about personal values and beliefs. For example, respondents are asked to prioritize various aspects of their lives, including family, politics, work, religion, and service to others. They are also asked whether they would be comfortable having some of the following live near them: criminals, people of a different race, Muslims, Jews, immigrants or foreign workers, those with AIDS, homosexuals, and drug addicts.

The WVS emerged out of the European Values Study, which, in its first wave in 1981, was limited to 20 highly developed European countries. Since then, the survey has expanded to 97 countries, covering nearly 90 percent of the population of the world. Because changes in values and preferences appear to be linked to level of economic and technological development, it was important to include societies across the entire range of development, from less developed (or industrial) to highly developed societies. This expansion also enabled the WVS to hire native social scientists from many different countries. The result was more culturally conscious research design, analysis of data, and interpretation of results. The expansion of the project has also permitted the dissemination of advanced methods of social analysis to developing societies in which such research is just emerging.

FIGURE 3.5 • World Values Survey

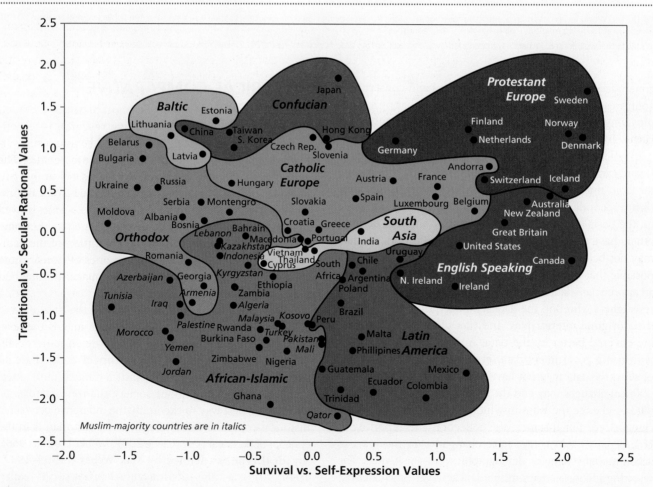

SOURCE: World Values Survey, "Survival vs. Self-Expression Values," WVS6 2015.

Sociologists have used data collected through the WVS for a wide variety of studies related to globalization. For instance, one study based on more than 20 years of WVS data found that people in almost all industrial societies have generally shifted from being religious and traditional toward being more secular and rational (at least in terms of the way in which being rational is defined in the developed Western world; Inglehart and Baker 2000). Respondents who identify with religion emphasize family values and tend to be more conservative on such issues as gender roles, childbearing and child rearing, divorce, abortion, sexual norms, euthanasia, and suicide. They also have high levels of national pride; they tend to be nationalistic. Respondents with secular values exhibit contrary preferences on each of these topics. They are also often more tolerant and accepting of nontraditional social roles.

The other major dimension of global variation is the distinction between survival and self-expression values. Respondents in industrialized and developed countries have tended to have fewer worries about survival or about meeting their basic needs for food and shelter. As a result, their priorities have shifted from an emphasis on economic and physical security (survival) to an interest in well-being and personal happiness. With this greater self-expressiveness comes a greater tolerance of minorities—including foreigners, gays, and various ethnic groups—who might otherwise be found threatening. This increase in trust and tolerance creates the type of social environment that is most conducive to the development of democracy.

The WVS has been used to define *cultural zones* based on this spectrum of values. As you can see in Figure 3.5, the English-speaking world generally embraces values that fall between traditional and secular-rational, but it ranks high on self-expression values, reflecting the relative well-being of its populace.

Think About It

What other kinds of diversity among WVS social scientists would you recommend to the WVS, if any? Your country of origin aside, where would you place yourself on Figure 3.5? Do you believe that there really are such things as "world values"?

to be an accurate depiction of reality. Rather, it is designed to help us better understand social reality. It is a sort of measuring rod. Thus, for example, Weber developed an ideal type of bureaucracy that accentuated its rational elements. He then used that ideal type to compare organizations in different societies and time periods in terms of their degree of rationality. Not surprisingly, he concluded that organizations of the modern West are the most rational and thus best approximate the ideal type of the bureaucracy.

Weber is the preeminent historical-comparative sociologist (Mahoney and Rueschemeyer 2003; Mahoney and Thelen 2015; Ragin 2014; Varcoe 2007). Consider his comparison of the world's major religions and their impact on the economy. Weber did comparative analyses of the histories of Protestantism in the West, Confucianism in China, and Hinduism in India. He sought to determine which religions fostered the development of capitalism and which served to impede its development. Of course, Weber knew that capitalism had developed in the West and not in China and India. The issue, then, was what about these religions (and many other social factors) did or did not foster the emergence of capitalism. A key factor was that in contrast to Protestantism, Confucianism, and Hinduism did not foster rationality and efficiency and a striving for material success. Sometimes they even served to inhibit rationality and efficiency, thus preventing the development of capitalism.

More recent instances of historical-comparative research have covered a wide range of issues. One researcher used historical-comparative research to examine whether internal wars could lead to state formation. Using the ability to collect taxes as a key factor, internal wars were found to strengthen states if solidarity existed among the elite (Rodriguez-Franco 2016; for a review of work on the relationship between the state and war, see Kestnbaum 2012).

Some scholars have combined the use of other methods with historical-comparative analysis to generate important theoretical insights about more contemporary issues. Although we typically imagine the field of economics to be a uniform science throughout the world, Marion Fourcade (2009) shows us otherwise in her study of how the economics profession differs in France, Britain, and the United States. Fourcade used in-depth interviews with economists to supplement existing historical evidence in order to show how the profession has taken on distinctly different shapes in the three countries. Overall, she found that in France economics is more closely aligned with the state, in Britain it is more moral and oriented toward the welfare of all, and in the United States it is more oriented toward science.

CONTENT ANALYSIS

Another type of secondary analysis, called **content analysis**, relies on the systematic and objective analysis of the content of cultural artifacts in print, visual, audio, and digital media, including photographs, movies, advertisements, speeches, and newspaper articles (Wolff 2007). The goal is to use qualitative and especially quantitative methods to understand the content of messages. In one well-known study, Herbert Gans (1979) did a quantitative and qualitative content analysis of news on television and in newsmagazines to identify patterns in the reporting of news. For example, he found that well-known people were dealt with much more frequently than were unknowns. Among non-war-related stories, government conflicts and disagreements were more likely to be dealt with than were government decisions. Gans supplemented the powerful insights that derived from his content analysis with additional participant observation research among journalists working at NBC and CBS News and *Time* and *Newsweek* magazines. This additional work enabled him to produce an incredibly rich and detailed account of the various political, commercial, and other forces that produce the values and informal rules that guide journalism.

Gans's content analysis took as its focus the overt content of the news, but it is also possible to use content analysis to analyze other issues, such as gender inequality. Some researchers did a content analysis of the number of times women appeared on the cover of *Sports Illustrated* from 2000 through 2011 (Weber and Carini 2012). They found that despite women's increasing participation in sports, they appeared on only 5 percent of the covers; the numbers did not change significantly over the period covered by the study, and, in fact, women were depicted on *more* covers between 1954 and 1965.

Marleen Klaasen and Jochen Peter (2015) did a content analysis of 400 popular pornographic videos derived from the most frequently visited pornographic websites. They were focally interested in the issue of gender inequality in pornography. One of their findings was that women were more frequently depicted as being submissive and men as dominant during sexual activities. Another finding was that there was more gender inequality in amateur pornography as far as women are concerned than in professional pornography.

CHECKPOINT 3.4: METHODS OF SECONDARY DATA ANALYSIS

METHOD	DESCRIPTION
Historical-comparative	Examines the way in which different historical events and conditions lead to different societal outcomes
Content analysis	Analyzes the content of cultural artifacts to identify meanings and patterns

ISSUES IN SOCIAL RESEARCH

The research conducted by sociologists raises a number of issues of great importance. Some of these issues concern how we should interpret the data that sociologists collect. Some involve the obligations that sociologists have to research participants and to society as a whole. Other issues are raised by sociologists themselves. As mentioned earlier, sociology is a multiple-paradigm science—with a full range of debates not only on various sociological perspectives but also on whether or not sociology can truly be as objective as a science is presumed to be.

RELIABILITY AND VALIDITY

A key issue with sociological data relates to one's ability to trust the findings. As a sociologist, you would want to be reassured that the data that you might use to further your own research, to formulate hypotheses, or to tell colleagues and the public about your research represent the social world as accurately as possible. As a consumer of sociological research, you would do well to evaluate the methods used in order to assess their trustworthiness. This issue is frequently raised in regard to reports of political and social surveys, but it affects every form of sociological research.

Scientists talk about two dimensions of trustworthiness: reliability and validity. **Reliability** involves the degree to which a given question, or another kind of measure, produces the same results time after time. In other words, would the same question asked one day get the same response from the participants or the same measurement on the scale the following day, or week, or month? For instance, do those involved in your hypothetical study of Las Vegas gamblers give the same answers at various points in time to questions about whether or not they routinely lose money when gambling?

The other dimension of trustworthiness is **validity**, or the degree to which a question, or another kind of measure, gets an accurate response. In other words, does the question measure what it is supposed to measure? For example, suppose you asked gamblers, "When you leave Las Vegas, do you consider yourself a 'winner'?" You may be asking this question to find out whether they left Las Vegas with more money than the amount they had when they arrived there. However, they may interpret the question more broadly as asking about the total experience of being in Las Vegas. Thus, even though they have lost money, they might answer yes to the question because they had a great time and consider their losses as part of the price for having such an experience. A more valid question might be, "On balance, do you win more money than you lose while gambling in Las Vegas?"

RESEARCH ETHICS

Ethics is concerned with issues of right and wrong, the choices that people make, and how they justify them (Hedgecoe 2016; Zeni 2007). World War II and the behavior of the Nazis helped make ethics a central issue in research. The Nazis engaged in horrendous medical experiments on

inmates in concentration camps. They used them as human guinea pigs to study such things as the effects of hypothermia, high altitudes, low altitudes, hemorrhages, and the drinking of saltwater. In some studies, inmates were infected with such diseases as typhus, malaria, and hepatitis to test various vaccines and drugs. Acting on the pseudoscience of Nazi race ideology, yet other doctors tried to develop efficient methods of mass sterilization of what the regime defined as inferior races (Korda 2006; Spitz 2005). This is the most outrageous example of a violation of the ethical code in the conduct of research, but it is certainly not the only one. Another well-known example is the research conducted between 1932 and 1972 at Tuskegee Institute in Alabama on 399 poor black American men suffering from syphilis. The researchers were interested in studying the natural progression of the disease over time, but they never told the participants that they were suffering from syphilis. Despite regular visits to collect data from and about the participants, the researchers did not treat them for the disease and allowed them to suffer over long periods of time before they died painfully (Reverby 2009).

A more recent example of questionable research ethics is the case of Henrietta Lacks (Skloot 2011; see also the 2017 HBO movie *The Immortal Life of Henrietta Lacks*). Lacks was a poor African American woman who died of cervical cancer in 1951. Without her knowledge or consent, some of her tumor was removed. Cancer cells from that tumor live on today and have spawned much research and even highly successful industries. While those cells have led to a variety of medical advances, a number of ethical issues are

Henrietta Lacks was responsible for major advances in medical science, all without her knowledge or consent. Cells taken during testing while she was undergoing treatment for cervical cancer in 1951 are still used today. Lacks's cells continue to be invaluable to researchers, but should the manner in which they were obtained affect how they are used?

raised by what happened to Lacks and subsequently to her family. For example, should the tumor have been removed and its cancer cells reproduced without Lacks and her family knowing about, and approving of, what was intended? Would the same procedures have taken place if Lacks were a well-to-do white woman? Finally, should Lacks's descendants get a portion of the earnings of the industries that have developed on the basis of her cancer cells?

No research undertaken by sociologists has caused the kind of suffering and death experienced by the people studied in Nazi Germany or at Tuskegee Institute, or even generated an ethical firestorm like the one raging around the Lacks case. Nonetheless, such research is the context and background for ethical concerns about the harmful or negative effects of research on participants in sociological research (the code of ethics of the American Sociological Association can be found online at www.asanet.org/about/ethics.cfm). There are three main areas of concern: physical and psychological harm to participants, illegal acts by researchers, and deception and violation of participants' trust. A final issue discussed here is the structure established to safeguard participants from these kinds of negative actions.

Physical and Psychological Harm

The first issue, following from the Nazi experiments and Tuskegee studies, is concern over whether research can actually cause participants physical harm. Most sociological research is not likely to cause such harm. However, physical harm may be an unintended consequence. In the Robbers Cave research, discussed earlier as an example of a natural experiment, competition and conflict were engendered between two groups of 12-year-old boys. The hostility reached such a peak that the boys engaged in apple-throwing fights and in raids on one another's compounds.

A much greater issue in sociological research is the possibility of psychological harm to those being studied. Even questionnaire or interview studies can cause psychological harm merely by asking people about sensitive issues such as sexual orientation, drug use, and experience with abortion. This risk is greatly increased when, unbeknownst to the researcher, a participant is hypersensitive to these issues because of a difficult or traumatic personal experience.

Some of the more extreme risks of psychological harm have occurred in experiments. The most famous example is Stanley Milgram's (1974) laboratory study of how far people will go when they are given orders by those in authority (the 2015 movie *Experimenter* deals in a fictionalized way with Milgram and his research). This study was inspired by the discovery after World War II that Nazi subordinates went so far as to torture and kill innocent citizens if ordered to do so by their superiors. In the Milgram experiment, one group, the "learners," were secretly paid to pretend that painful

FIGURE 3.6 • The Teacher (T), Learner (L), and Experimenter (E) in the Milgram Experiment

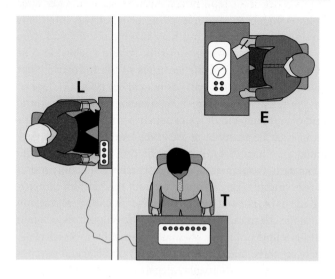

shocks were being applied to them by the other group of participants, the "teachers," who were led to believe that the shocks they thought they were applying were very real. The researcher, dressed officially in a white coat and projecting an aura of scientific respectability, ordered the teachers to apply shocks that appeared to be potentially lethal. The teachers did so even though the learners, who were in another room and not visible, were screaming with increasing intensity. The research clearly showed that if they were ordered to do so

by authority figures, people would violate the social norms against inflicting pain on, and even possibly endangering the lives of, others.

Compliance is a 2012 movie based explicitly on Milgram's work. It deals with a real-life case in which a caller spoke to a McDonald's restaurant manager and identified himself as a police officer investigating a theft. The caller was able to convince the manager of the restaurant that a young girl working there was a suspect in the theft. The caller eventually persuaded the manager to, among other things, allow the girl to be taken to a back room, where she was strip-searched and left with nothing on but an apron. The manager needed to return to her work in the busy front of the store, but the caller insisted that others be brought in to watch the girl. Eventually, the manager's fiancé was brought in and, under pressure from the caller, had the girl do nude jumping jacks, spanked her for not following directions, and eventually coerced her into performing oral sex on him. When the fiancé left, he was replaced by a male custodian who saw through the caller's requests. The police were called and discovered that similar incidents had occurred elsewhere (the movie claims that more than 70 such incidents had occurred throughout the United States). The real case on which *Compliance* was based took place in a small town in Kentucky in 2004; the caller, a telemarketer and family man, was apprehended, but he was acquitted of all charges in 2006 ("Acquittal in Hoax" 2006). Like the Milgram experiment, *Compliance* shows how far people are willing to go, even to the extent of committing a crime, when ordered to do so by someone they believe to be in an authority position.

The results of the Milgram experiment (as well as events depicted in the movie) are important in many senses. We are concerned here with what the study did to the psyches of the people involved. For one thing, the "teachers" came to know that they were very responsive to the dictates of authority figures, even if they were ordered to commit immoral acts. Some of them certainly realized that their behavior indicated that they were perfectly capable in such circumstances of harming, if not killing, other human beings. Such realizations had the possibility of adversely affecting the way participants viewed, and felt about, themselves. But the research has had several benefits as well, for both participants and others who have read about the Milgram studies. For example, those in powerful

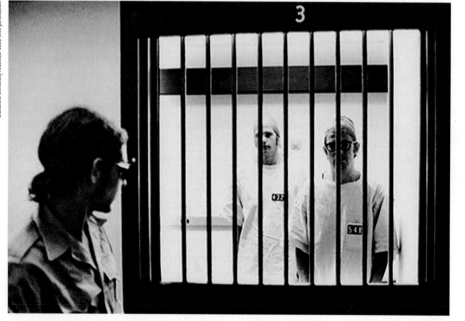

Philip Zimbardo's experimental re-creation of prison conditions was so realistic, and the participants were so severely affected by their involvement in it, that the experiment had to be cut short by several weeks. Could this early cutoff have invalidated the research?

positions can better understand, and therefore limit, the potential impact of their orders to subordinates, and subordinates can more successfully limit how far they are willing to go in carrying out the orders of their superiors.

Another famous study that raises similar ethical issues was conducted by Philip Zimbardo (1973). (The 2010 movie *The Experiment* is a fictionalized depiction of this experiment.) Zimbardo set up a prisonlike structure called "Stanford County Prison" as a setting in which to conduct his experiment. Participants were recruited to serve as either prisoners or guards. The "prison" was very realistic, with windowless cells, minimal toilet facilities, and strict regulations imposed on the inmates. The guards had uniforms, badges, keys, and clubs. They were also trained in the methods of managing prisoners.

The experiment was supposed to last six weeks, but it was ended after only six days when the researchers grew fearful about the health and sanity of the prisoners, whom some of the guards insulted, degraded, and dehumanized. Only a few guards were helpful and supportive. However, even the helpful guards refused to intervene when prisoners were being abused. The prisoners could have left, but they tended to go along with the situation, accepting both the authority of the guards and their own lowly and abused position. The ethical issues in this case are similar to those raised by the Milgram research. Some of the guards experienced psychological distress, but it was worse for the prisoners when they realized how much they had contributed to their own difficulties. Social researchers learned that a real or perceived imbalance of power between researcher and participant may lead the participant to comply with a researcher's demands even though they cause distress. However, like Milgram's research, the Zimbardo experiment yielded positive by-products, such as a greater understanding of how those put in guard positions may lose their humanity and how submissive prisoners can become.

ASK YOURSELF

Are there any other ways to answer the questions Milgram and Zimbardo explored? How would you tackle these questions as a social scientist?

Illegal Acts

In the course of ethnographic fieldwork, a researcher might witness or even become entangled in illegal acts. This problem confronted Randol Contreras in his research on a group of Dominican men who robbed upper-level drug dealers in the South Bronx (Contreras 2017). These "stickup kids" engaged in brutal acts of violence and possessed illegal drugs and cash. Contreras, himself a former—though admittedly unsuccessful—drug dealer, had to be careful to avoid participating in illegal activities that the stickup kids were describing to him, particularly because some of them were childhood friends.

In other cases, researchers must weigh sticky legal and ethical ramifications for participants. In one study of children in a nursery, the researchers witnessed an illegal act (Anspach and Mizrachi 2006). They had to decide whether or not to report it. They had to juggle concerns about the criminality of the act with a desire to protect their research participants and the trust they had extended. Other concerns lingered in the background. Publishing an account of such a dramatic act might help the researchers' careers, but it might also send the perpetrator of the illegal act to jail. It was also possible that not informing the police, or refusing to turn over field notes, could lead to imprisonment for the researchers (Emerson 2001; Van Maanen 1983).

The Violation of Trust

There are several ways in which researchers can betray participants' trust in the research enterprise. For instance, the researcher might inadvertently divulge the identity of respondents even though they were promised anonymity. There is also the possibility of exploitative relationships, especially with key informants. Exploitation is of special concern in cases where there is a real or perceived imbalance of power—often related to race, class, or gender—between researcher and participant. In the Tuskegee case, for example, African American men suffered the adverse effects of the research even though syphilis is distributed throughout the larger population. Although this research should not have occurred under any circumstances, a more equitable research design would have meant that most of the participants were white males.

It is also a betrayal of trust for the researcher to develop inappropriate relationships with participants. One noteworthy example of this is a study conducted by Erich Goode (2002) to better understand the stigma of obesity. Goode has publicly acknowledged that he had sexual relations with some of his female informants. He argues that because of this, he was able to obtain information that may not have been obtainable by any other means. However, one must ask about the cost to participants of his obtaining the knowledge in this way. One can only imagine how his participants felt when some of them discovered that Goode had an ulterior motive in having intimate relations with them. Many of his participants were already very sensitive about their body image and their relationships with men. Because Goode's participants did not have full knowledge of his motives, they were unable to make informed choices about engaging in sexual relations with him. In this case, the power imbalance between researcher and participant led to exploitation.

TRENDING

On the Run: Fugitive Life in an American City

(University of Chicago Press, 2014)

Alice Goffman (Assistant Professor of Sociology at University of Wisconsin; PhD, Princeton University, 2010)

Mark Makela/Getty Images News/Getty Images

Maintaining a certain level of objectivity and distance from the individuals one is researching can prove challenging, especially when one is immersed in their daily lives for an extended period of time. Ethical dilemmas can arise when researchers empathize too much with the people being studied. Alice Goffman found herself facing just such a dilemma when conducting fieldwork on how young black men and their families negotiate the criminal justice system in one Philadelphia neighborhood she calls 6th Street. Most of these men were on parole or probation or had outstanding warrants. They spent much of their time trying to avoid the police and incarceration. Law enforcement does not make this easy for them. Goffman observed the police harassing these men in a variety of ways, from stopping and frisking them on the streets to searching their homes, often without probable cause. The courts offer little recourse. Missed court dates and failure to pay court fees make it difficult for these men—and by extension their families and friends—to avoid the legal system.

During the six years that Goffman was in the field, she developed close relationships with two men in particular, Mike and Chuck. For a time, she even became their roommate. While establishing strong connections is important to build trust and gain access to research sites and subjects, Goffman found herself spending more time—and feeling more comfortable—with her friends on 6th Street than she did at the university at which she was studying. She also found herself engaging in legally questionable activities. One night she spent "on the run" with Chuck and his brother Reggie, hiding with them in a neighbor's house from the police. After Chuck was shot and killed, Goffman drove Mike around to try to find Chuck's killer. During one of these drives, Goffman waited in the car when Mike, who was carrying a loaded gun, got out and followed a man who he thought shot Chuck. Luckily, Mike determined that this was the wrong man and returned to the car. If Mike had shot and killed this man, Goffman could have been an accomplice in a conspiracy to commit murder. *On the Run* reveals that the decision of when to observe and when to participate is complicated both ethically and legally when conducting ethnographic research.

Supplementary Resources

- Goffman discusses her research findings from *On the Run* in her TED Talk, "How We're Priming Some Kids for College—and Others for Prison" (www.ted.com/talks/alice_goffman_college_or_prison_two_destinies_one_blatant_injustice?language=en).
- Criticisms about the reliability of Goffman's ethnographic methodology are examined in an article by Gideon Lewis-Kraus (2016), "The Trials of Alice Goffman" (www.nytimes.com/2016/01/17/magazine/the-trials-of-alice-goffman.html?_r=0).

The best-known example of sociological research involving deception and intrusion into people's lives is Laud Humphreys's (1970) study of the homosexual activities of men in public restrooms ("tearooms"). Humphreys (1930–1988) acted as a lookout outside tearooms and signaled men engaged in anonymous acts of fellatio when members of the public or the police were approaching. He interviewed some of the men with full disclosure. However, he also noted the license plate numbers of some of those he observed and tracked down their addresses. Humphreys appeared at their homes a year or so later, in disguise, to interview them under false pretenses. In this way he uncovered one of the most important findings of his study: More than half the men were married, with wives and families. They were active in the tearoom trade not because they were homosexual but because sexual relations in their marriages were problematic.

Laud Humphreys put forth that homosexual acts do not define homosexual identity. His work helped launch queer theory and increased sociological interest in the difference between public and private selves.

Humphreys deceived these men by not telling them from the outset that he was doing research on them and, with those he interviewed under false pretenses, by not revealing the true nature of the research. His research had at least the potential of revealing something that most of the participants wanted to conceal. He later admitted that if he had the chance to do the research over again, he would tell the participants about his true role and goal. But the research itself is not without merit. It helped distinguish between homosexual acts and homosexual identity. Also, homosexuals had very difficult lives in the early 1970s. Nearly half of Humphreys's participants were covertly bisexual or homosexual and faced numerous difficulties, if not danger, if they came out. Thus, there were very strong reasons for them to keep their homosexual activity hidden. Many of these men also experienced considerable stress in trying to live as married men while simultaneously engaging in impersonal homosexual activity with strangers. Humphreys's research, while ethically flawed and harmful to the unwitting participants, did have some benefit: It provided much-needed insight into the social construction of sexuality and the difficulties involved in understanding how people develop their sexual selves.

INFORMED CONSENT AND INSTITUTIONAL REVIEW BOARDS

Various ethical codes have been devised to protect people from overzealous or malicious researchers. The Hippocratic Oath taken by medical doctors offers helpful guidelines for dealing with human participants. The Nuremberg Code was developed in 1947 to protect biomedical research subjects after the Nazi experiments on concentration camp inmates were revealed (see Table 3.1). Codes like these were later broadened to a concern for all research involving human participants. Such ethical codes have helped protect research participants, but it is important to realize that they are only codes of conduct and not enforceable laws or regulations.

Following revelations of the Tuskegee experiments, the U.S. Congress passed the 1974 National Research Act, requiring ethical oversight for research funded by the federal government. Since then, the U.S. Department of Health and Human Services has required that all research in the United States receiving federal funding be approved by an institutional review board (IRB; Cameron 2015; Corwin and Tierney 2007). (In the United Kingdom and Australia, research ethics committees, or RECs, serve a similar purpose.) IRBs are designed to deal with the issue of deception in social research and the harm that social research can do to participants. Universities have their own IRBs, and board committee members are typically faculty members from a wide variety of disciplines, along with members of the community. IRBs generally protect three broad ethical principles:

TABLE 3.1 • The Nuremberg Code

	DIRECTIVES FOR HUMAN EXPERIMENTATION
1	The voluntary consent of the human subject is absolutely essential.
2	The experiment should be such as to yield fruitful results for the good of society.
3	The experiment should be so designed and based on the results of animal experimentation and a knowledge of the natural history of the disease.
4	The experiment should be so conducted as to avoid all unnecessary physical and mental suffering and injury.
5	No experiment should be conducted where there is an a priori reason to believe that death or disabling injury will occur.
6	The degree of risk to be taken should never exceed that determined by the humanitarian importance of the problem to be solved by the experiment.
7	Proper preparations should be made and adequate facilities provided to protect the experimental subject against even remote possibilities of injury, disability, or death.
8	The experiment should be conducted only by scientifically qualified persons.
9	During the course of the experiment, the human subject should be at liberty to bring the experiment to an end.
10	During the course of the experiment, the scientist in charge must be prepared to terminate the experiment at any stage, if he has probable cause to believe, in the exercise of the good faith, superior skill, and careful judgment required of him, that a continuation of the experiment is likely to result in injury, disability, or death to the experimental subject.

SOURCE: U.S. Department of Health.

- *Respect for persons.* Participants—especially those with diminished capacities, such as physical or mental disabilities—are to be treated with dignity and respect.

- *Beneficence.* As little harm as possible is to be done to participants, and every effort is to be made to be of benefit to them. However, there are exceptions where the benefits of the research are overwhelming and the harm to be done is unavoidable.

- *Justice.* Research should operate on the principle of justice, so that burdens and rewards are distributed in an equitable manner.

Of particular importance is that most IRBs require evidence of written **informed consent** of those being studied. Typically, researchers present a statement for participants to sign that ensures informed consent. It includes such details as

- What the study entails and why it is being conducted

- How and why research participants have been recruited to participate

- What participation involves

- The risks and benefits associated with participation

- The degree to which participants' privacy and confidentiality will be protected

- How the study safeguards vulnerable populations (such as children, prisoners, and the impaired)

- Whom the participants can contact at the university if they have further questions

Participants have a right not only to be aware that they are being studied but also to know about the potential harms and benefits they might experience in the course of the research. Research that does not include obtaining such consent or, more important, that poses dangers to participants is likely to be turned down by the IRB unless it is justified by extraordinary reasons.

ASK YOURSELF

What other facts, if any, do you think should be part of an informed consent document? Have you ever participated in an experiment as a subject? If so, were you told everything you wanted to know before you agreed to participate?

In addition to the statement for participants, researchers submit to the IRB a research protocol that provides an overview of the way in which the research will be conducted.

For example, if the research is interview based, the protocol might specify that the interviewer will first provide the participant with an introduction to the research and a review of the participant's role in the research, show him or her the informed consent form that will be signed by participants, and provide a basic script of the questions that will be asked during the interview. The IRB committee then reviews these materials and decides whether the proposed research plan should be approved, modified, or disapproved.

OBJECTIVITY, OR "VALUE-FREE" SOCIOLOGY

Another issue relating to sociological research is whether or not researchers are, or can be, objective. That is, do they allow personal preferences and judgments to bias their research? Many argue that value-laden research jeopardizes the entire field of sociology. The publication of such research—and public revelations about researcher biases—erodes and could destroy the credibility of the field as a whole. In the history of sociology, this discussion is traceable, once again, to the work of Max Weber (Black 2013). Taken to its extreme, *value-free sociology* means preventing all personal values from affecting any phase of the research process. However, this is not what Weber intended in his work on values, and it is instructive to take a brief look at what he actually meant.

Weber was most concerned with the need for teachers, especially professors, to be value-free in their lectures. This issue arose in Weber's day in Germany at least in part because of the growing number of Marxist-oriented teachers. Many of them wished to use the classroom to express Marxist ideology and to raise the consciousness of students about the evils of capitalism. They may even have wanted to foment revolution against the capitalist system. Weber was opposed to Marxism, but he was also more generally opposed to using the classroom to express any values. He took this position because he felt that young students were neither mature nor sophisticated enough to see through such arguments. He believed that they were also likely to be too intimidated by the position of their professors, especially in the authoritarian Germany of his day, to be able to evaluate their ideas critically. The idea of, and the need for, value-free teaching seems clear and uncontestable. However, we must realize that all professors, like all other human beings, have values. Therefore, the best we can hope for is for them to strive to be as objective as possible in the classroom.

Weber did *not* take the same position with reference to research. In fact, he saw at least two roles for values in social research. The first is in the selection of a question to be researched. In that case, it is perfectly appropriate for researchers to be guided by their personal values, or the values that predominate in the society of the day. The second is in the analysis of the results of a research study. In that analysis, sociologists can, and should, use personal and social values to help them make sense of their findings. These values are an aid in interpretation and understanding. However, they are not to be used purposely to distort the findings or mislead the reader of a report on the study.

In Weber's opinion, the only place in research to be value-free is in the collection of research data. This is a rather unexceptional argument, meaning that researchers should do everything they can to prevent bias in the data collection process. Few, if any, scientists would accept the opposing position that it is perfectly acceptable to engage in such distortions. Such a position would undermine all research and the scientific status and aspirations of sociology.

Some sociologists, especially feminist and critical scholars (Reid 2004), question whether even this limited attempt to conduct value-free research is possible. In a famous essay, Alvin Gouldner (1962) argued that value-free sociology is a myth. Even when researchers strive to be completely objective, they carry with them their own experiences, assumptions about the world, and personal biases that inevitably shape the ways in which they approach their research and collect their data. The fact that women and people of color were largely overlooked by social researchers until relatively recently is an example of how an unquestioned assumption—the belief that the experiences of men and women or of people of color and whites are all the same—can be problematic. For this reason, many scholars (such as Bourdieu 1992) argue that researchers should be extremely reflective and explicit about their own social positions and how those might influence the research process.

In contemporary terms, what Weber argued for was an attitude of objectivity during the research process. But there is another kind of objectivity, *procedural objectivity*, which entails reporting the research in such a way that any reader will understand how the research was conducted. Researchers should report as many details as possible to allow for outside assessment of the research. Among other things, details about sampling, the questions asked in interviews or on questionnaires, the statistical procedures employed, and known limitations of the research should be made available in research reports. Other researchers can then, if they choose, repeat (or replicate) the study to see if they get the same results. The ability to replicate research is a hallmark of any science.

CHECKPOINT 3.5: ISSUES IN SOCIAL RESEARCH

RESEARCH ISSUE	DEFINITION
Reliability	The degree to which a given question or measure produces the same results each time
Validity	The degree to which questions get accurate responses
Ethics	Standards by which we judge right and wrong

SUMMARY

Sociologists apply the scientific method. First, the sociologist finds a question that needs to be answered and then reviews the literature to see what has already been found. Next, the sociologist develops a hypothesis, chooses a research method, and collects data that can confirm, or fail to confirm, the hypothesis. Finally, the researcher analyzes the data in relation to the initial hypothesis. Sociology is a multiple-paradigm science, which means that no one model unifies all sociologists.

Sociologists use different research methods, depending on the research questions they are studying. Quantitative research yields data in the form of numbers, usually derived from surveys and experiments. Qualitative research is conducted in natural settings and yields descriptive information. Observation consists of systematically watching, listening to, and recording what takes place in a natural social setting over some period of time. Researchers may choose to participate and play a role in what they are observing or engage in nonparticipant observation. Ethnographic research is more likely to be based on participant observation over an extended length of time. In interviews, respondents are asked a series of questions, usually on a face-to-face basis. Survey research collects data through interviews and questionnaires. Experimentation manipulates one or more independent variables to examine their effect on one or more dependent variables.

Sociologists also often engage in secondary data analysis, in which they reanalyze data collected by others. Secondary data may consist of statistical information, historical documents and analyses, or the content of cultural artifacts and messages.

Reliability is the degree to which a given measure produces the same results time after time, and validity is the degree to which a measure is accurate. Past problems with questionable research ethics have led to the development of institutional review boards (IRBs). A key requirement is that researchers obtain informed consent from participants by explaining the purpose of the study and any sensitive or dangerous aspects of the research.

It is difficult to avoid bias altogether. However, clear and objective descriptions of research procedures will enable other researchers to evaluate and perhaps replicate those procedures.

KEY TERMS

content analysis, 73
convenience samples, 68
dependent variable, 69
descriptive statistics, 61
descriptive survey, 67
empiricism, 56
ethics, 74
ethnography, 63
experiment, 69
explanatory survey, 68

field experiments, 69
global ethnography, 64
historical-comparative
   research, 71
ideal type, 71
independent variable, 69
inferential statistics, 61
informed consent, 80
interviews, 65
laboratory experiments, 69

natural experiments, 69
netnography, 64
nonparticipant
   observation, 63
observation, 62
paradigm, 58
participant observation, 62
qualitative research, 61
quantitative research, 61
questionnaires, 67

random sample, 68
reliability, 74
sample, 68
scientific method, 56
secondary data
   analysis, 70
statistics, 61
stratified sample, 68
survey research, 67
validity, 74

REVIEW QUESTIONS

1. What steps do researchers take when applying the scientific method? How would you apply the scientific method to get answers to a question you have about the social world?

2. What does it mean to say that sociology is a multiple-paradigm science? What are the benefits and disadvantages of a multiple-paradigm science?

3. What are the differences between participant and nonparticipant observational methods? How do sociologists ensure that their observations are systematic using both approaches?

4. What is the key value of conducting ethnographic research? How would a global ethnography help you make sense of your own place in the world?

5. Researchers use interviews to gather data by asking individuals a series of questions. How do researchers choose between prestructured and unstructured interviews? What are the advantages and disadvantages of each type of interview?

6. Why do sociologists who conduct surveys rely on samples? What techniques do researchers use to avoid biases in their samples?

7. A researcher uses the World Values Survey to examine the relationship between people's religious beliefs and their level of happiness. In this study, what is the independent variable, and what is the dependent variable? What reliability and validity issues could arise in conducting this survey across countries?

8. Some experiments allow researchers to take advantage of a naturally occurring event to study its effect on one or more dependent variables. Can you think of any recent events that might have been conducive to natural experiments? What would be the dependent variable or variables in your example?

9. What are some of the ethical concerns raised by sociological research? Use specific examples from research discussed in this chapter to describe these ethical concerns. How do IRBs help keep research ethical?

10. What role do values play in the research process? According to Weber, when is objectivity most important?

PRACTICE AND APPLY WHAT YOU'VE LEARNED

► **edge.sagepub.com/ritzerintro4e**

CHECK YOUR COMPREHENSION ON THE STUDY SITE WITH:

- **Diagnostic pre-tests** to identify opportunities for improvement.

- **Personalized study plans** with focused recommendations to address specific knowledge gaps and additional learning needs.

- **Post-tests** to check your progress and ensure mastery of key learning objectives.

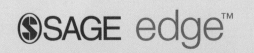

4

CULTURE

A Reflection of U.S. Culture

A jazz musician, Miles Davis, gave new life to the term *cool* in his 1957 album *Birth of the Cool*. Being cool—calm and steady as cool water—remains part of American culture, though that culture has many other characteristics. One influential cultural force today is HBO's *Girls* and its decidedly "uncool," even geeky, characters, especially its 30ish star, executive producer, writer, and director, Lena Dunham.

Girls and Lena Dunham have become cultural phenomena by portraying, and helping define, the culture of urban millennials (those born between the early 1980s and the early 2000s). The show, which is somewhat autobiographical (like Dunham's book, *Not That Kind of Girl*), deals fearlessly with a wide range of topics, particularly the many varieties of human relationships, including between female friends and the sexual politics of male-female and homosexual and lesbian relationships. The characters are young, flawed, unstable, vulnerable, self-involved, somewhat immature people whose relationships are fraught with difficulties. Their jobs and careers, such as they are, exist mainly at the bottom of the occupational hierarchy and are, if anything, more problematic than are their social relationships.

Dunham's character, Hannah, is a paradigm of a millennial woman. A writer, she is a narcissistic, striving careerist who fails more often than not. She is irrepressible but anxious, self-loathing, often depressed, frequently badly treated by friends and lovers, and in need of drugs—prescription and nonprescription—and therapy. She hates her overweight body and alternates between dieting and binge eating. When not clothed in some bizarre, unflattering outfit, she often unselfconsciously displays her nude, decidedly un-model-like body. Sex for Hannah often seems unsatisfying, and many of the problems that she and her friends have appear to stem from the fact that they are women. *Girls* seems to get at the essence of millennial culture, at least for women, in the early twenty-first century.

LEARNING OBJECTIVES

4.1 Define culture.

4.2 Identify the basic elements of culture.

4.3 Discuss cultural differences.

4.4 Explain characteristics of global culture.

4.5 Outline the characteristics of consumer culture.

edge.sagepub.com/ritzerintro4e

- Take the chapter quiz
- Review key terms with eFlashcards
- Explore multimedia links and SAGE readings

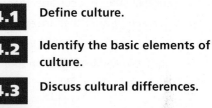

SAGE edge™

Millennials and their culture are not difficult to spot within the United States. Around the world, however, the culture of the millennial generation may take on many other forms or be nonexistent. But globalization and Americanization have spread U.S. millennial culture around a significant portion of the world.

Because you were likely born in the 1990s or 2000s, you are considered part of the millennial generation. However, you also belong to many different cultures and subcultures. For example, you are likely to be engaged to some degree or another in consumer and digital culture, as well as the culture of college life. You are continually learning the dimensions and the rules of these and other cultures. Much of that learning happens almost effortlessly, as you live your daily life. But cultures that are new to you, such as university culture, or that are evolving rapidly, such as digital culture, are likely to require much, and continuing, effort, alertness, and flexibility on your part for you to learn how to behave in them. ●

A DEFINITION OF CULTURE

Culture encompasses the ideas, values, practices, and material objects that allow a group of people, even an entire society, to carry out their collective lives in relative order and harmony. There are innumerable ideas, values, practices, and material objects associated with most cultures. As a result, no one individual can possibly know them all or what they all mean. But people must know at least the most basic and important elements of their culture. Knowledge of a shared culture leads people to behave in similar ways and to adopt a similar way of looking at the world. However, it is important to remember that there are differences within, as well as between, cultures. This point was reflected in the early 2015 murderous attacks in Paris by Islamic radicals on such cultural symbols as a French humor magazine and a kosher supermarket. There are profound differences in France today among French, Muslim, and Jewish cultures.

Closer to home, consider the cultures of the Bloods and the Crips, two street gangs with origins in Los Angeles in the early 1970s but now existing nationwide (Covey 2015; Deutsch 2014). Members of the two gangs distinguish themselves from each other in a variety of ways, but most notably by their defining colors—red for Bloods and blue for Crips. These colors and other symbols are very meaningful to gang members, helping them mark territories, easily identify friends and foes, and signify their values. The symbols—and their meanings—have been created by the group itself and passed down from one gang member to another. Symbols like these may also be passed along from a gang in one locale to those situated elsewhere. Some Mexican American gangs—for example, La Gran Raza and La Gran Familia—have adopted ideas and objects, as well as names, such as La Eme and Nuestra Familia, from predecessors in Mexico or gangs formed in U.S. prisons.

In contrast, for those who are not members of the group, an idea, a value, a practice, or an object may have little meaning, may mean something completely different, or may even have no meaning at all. For example, to members of the general public, a spray-painted gang tag may just be a scribble defacing neighborhood property. A person wearing a red shirt is simply wearing a red shirt.

The existence of a culture and common knowledge of it are so important that newcomers to any group, especially children, are taught its basic elements early. They then expand on that knowledge as they mature and become more integral members of the group.

At the same time, culture is constantly being affected by changes both internal and external to the group. Among the *internal changes* are the average age of the population within that group. Depending on whether the average age increases or decreases, a culture will need to reflect the needs and interests of either younger or older people. For example, in the United States and other aging societies, television programs and the advertisements associated with them are more oriented to older people than is the case in societies with increasing numbers of younger people (Carter and Vega 2011). A good example of this is the great popularity, especially among older viewers, of CBS's *NCIS*. On the other hand, television certainly cannot and does not ignore its younger audience. The great popularity and cultural influence of Fox's *Empire* is indicative of that.

Similarly, cultures need to adapt to other changes, such as a group's gender composition. For example, today there are more female gang members in general, and this is also true of the membership of the Bloods and the Crips (Goldman, Giles, and Hogg 2014). As a result of this shift, a gang's culture needs to change to deal with things such as the tasks to be allotted to female members (e.g., carrying concealed weapons) and, more specifically, to those who are pregnant or have young children.

Technological innovations are among the *external changes* likely to alter a group's culture significantly. For example, with the growth of smartphone use, texting has become wildly popular as a communication method (including among street gang members), and cell phone

There are few rules on what should and should not be discussed on a cell phone in places where others, especially strangers, are close enough to overhear what is being said.

conversations have become proportionally less common. Thus, not only newcomers to the group but also those who have participated for years must constantly learn new aspects of culture (e.g., gang members using prepaid "burner" cell phones that are difficult or impossible to trace) and perhaps unlearn others (using traditional cell phones) that are no longer considered desirable.

The increasing ubiquity of the smartphone has created a whole new set of realities for which clear and firm cultural rules are not yet in place. There are few rules about texting, and those few that do exist are notoriously difficult to monitor and police, especially in settings such as classrooms (Pettijohn et al. 2015). In addition, long, loud, and frequent phone conversations are not a problem in the privacy of one's home, but they may be a problem in public areas where there is an expectation of quietude, such as at a nice restaurant. I found out for myself how rude a cell phone conversation may be perceived to be, and the consequences of such a perception, on a train trip between New York and Washington, D.C. Amtrak now has "quiet cars" for those who do not want to be plagued by the cell phone conversations of strangers. I found myself in one of those cars, but I didn't know the rules of phone behavior in such a car. Soon after the trip began, my wife called, and we began a conversation. Almost immediately, a man sitting a few rows in front of me jumped up and glared at me angrily, while another passenger gently tugged on my sleeve and pointed to the "quiet car" sign. I now understood its meaning and said good-bye to my wife. This illustrates the power of

culture and also how we learn about new cultural elements and developments, sometimes the hard way. I no longer need to be reminded of the rules of, and what is expected of me in, a quiet car—and in most other social settings.

While I was gently sanctioned for violating the culture of the quiet car, such sanctions can sometimes be much more extreme. Violence is not the norm, but it is not unheard of, as in the case of Curtis Reeves, who shot and killed a man in a movie theater for texting (his babysitter) during the previews (the movie hadn't even started; Buie 2014).

A more formal set of rules regarding talking and texting on cell phones is being developed to control these activities on the part of drivers. It has become apparent—both from insurance company statistics and from experimental research—that using a handheld cell phone while driving increases the risk of accidents (Horrey and Wickens 2006). In 2015, more than a quarter of automobile crashes in the United States involved the use of cell phones while driving (Smith 2015). A very active media campaign has developed—and has been promoted by Oprah Winfrey, among others—to discourage people from using handheld cell phones while driving. As shown in Figure 4.1, many states have enacted laws against the practice, and some safety advocates are pressing for a similar federal law. If both campaigns succeed, using a handheld cell phone while driving will no longer be culturally acceptable and will in fact become illegal across the nation.

Although we generally accept and learn the various components of culture, sometimes we refuse to comply with, or even accept, them. For example, many continue to talk and text on cell phones while driving even though they know it is illegal and the larger culture and legal system are increasingly characterized by negative views on such behaviors. To take a different example, premarital and extramarital sexual relationships continue to be disapproved of by traditional American culture, but many people have come to reject these ideas and to engage increasingly in these behaviors (on premarital sex, see Elias, Fullerton, and Simpson 2015). Indeed, it could be argued that both these forms of sexual behavior have come to be widely tolerated; premarital sex in particular has become an accepted part of the culture.

FIGURE 4.1 • Cell Phone Use and Texting-While-Driving Laws, 2016

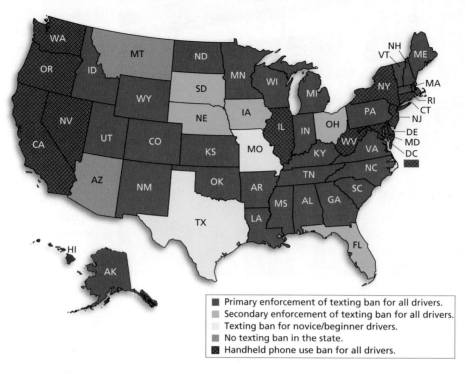

- ■ Primary enforcement of texting ban for all drivers.
- ■ Secondary enforcement of texting ban for all drivers.
- ☐ Texting ban for novice/beginner drivers.
- ■ No texting ban in the state.
- ▨ Handheld phone use ban for all drivers.

NOTE: Under "secondary" laws, an officer must have some other reason to stop a vehicle before citing the driver for using a cell phone. Laws without this restriction are called "primary." Many states that have passed handheld phone bans and texting bans provide for various exemptions for emergencies, law enforcement personnel, emergency medical technicians, firefighters, state DOT employees, and so on.

SOURCE: Map Showing Cellphone Use and Texting While Driving Laws in "Distracted Drivers." Copyright © National Conference of State Legislatures. Reprinted with Permission.

CHECKPOINT 4.1: EXAMPLES OF TYPES OF CHANGES THAT AFFECT CULTURAL GROUPS

INTERNAL	EXTERNAL
Demographics of group members, such as age and gender composition	Technology, such as smartphones

THE BASIC ELEMENTS OF CULTURE

As pointed out earlier, every group and society has a culture. Culture surrounds such diverse social phenomena as athletics, cooking, funeral ceremonies, courtship, medicine, marriage, sexual restrictions and taboos, bodily adornment, calendars, dancing, games, greetings, hairstyles, personal names, religion, and myths. However, the specific content of each of these domains, and many more, varies from culture to culture. Cultures differ from one another mainly because each represents a unique mix of values, norms, objects, and language inherited from the past, derived from other groups, and created anew by each group.

VALUES

The broadest element of culture is found in **values**, the general and abstract standards defining what a group or society as a whole considers good, desirable, right, or important. Values express the ideals of society, as well as of groups of every size.

In his classic work *Democracy in America* ([1835–1840] 1969), the French scholar Alexis de Tocqueville detailed what he perceived to be America's values. Among the things Americans valued in the early nineteenth century were democracy, equality, individualism, "taste for physical comfort," spirituality, and economic prosperity. Although Tocqueville wrote about his impressions of the United States almost 200 years ago, the vast majority of Americans today would accept most, if not all, of the values he described (Crothers 2010).

Indeed, Americans find these values so natural that they expect them to be accepted in other cultures around the world. However, this expectation has had some disappointing, even disastrous, consequences for the United States. For example, when the United States undertook invasions of Iraq and Afghanistan, one of the objectives was the creation of democratic regimes in those societies. The assumption was that Iraqis and Afghanis wanted the same kind of democracy as the one that exists in the United States. But creating democracies in those countries has proven to be extremely difficult for a variety of reasons, including the fact that their cultures lack a tradition of democratic government. It is extremely difficult, if not impossible, to impose a value, such as the value of democracy, on a society where it does not already exist, or where it exists in a very different form. As I write this in mid-2017, the terrorism practiced by the Islamic State, especially in Iraq and Syria, as well as the continuing threat posed by the Taliban in Afghanistan (Packer 2016), make it seem even less likely that those countries will become functioning democracies any time soon. Even though the Islamic State is in retreat in Iraq and Syria, its terrorism is likely to continue, and the devastating effects there will be felt long into the future.

Have you ever deliberately broken a social norm? Some of the passengers on this New York City subway are participating in an annual "No-Pants Subway Ride" event.

Researchers using data collected through the World Values Survey (WVS) have found support for the idea that democracy is a hard, if not impossible, sell in many parts of the world (Welzel and Inglehart 2009). As you may recall from Chapter 3, the WVS has gathered data from a variety of countries around the world on individual views on topics such as gender equality; tolerance for abortion, homosexuality, and divorce; desire for autonomy over authority (for example, obedience and faith); and democratic participation over security. Respondents in countries where personal freedom is not valued highly—such as Pakistan, Jordan, and Nigeria—tend to think of antidemocratic authoritarian regimes as being democratic. The data also show that citizens within these countries have little knowledge of the meaning of liberal democracy. There is little chance that American-style democracy will succeed in these countries.

Of course, there are many other reasons democracy has a difficult time succeeding in some countries. Among other things, before democracy can be established, people need to have enough to eat, to feel safe, to be able to get an education, and to trust the government. Unfortunately, many, if not all, of these needs are not being met in many parts of the world.

NORMS

Based on values, **norms** are the informal rules that guide what people do and how they live. Norms tell us what we should and should not do in a given situation (Dandaneau 2007). Many norms are informal. That is, they are not formally codified, not written down in any one place. **Laws** are norms that *have* been codified. They are written down and formally enforced through institutions such as the state. Rules prohibiting speaking and texting on handheld cell phones while driving are examples of how informal norms can come to be codified into laws.

You are expected to follow norms and obey laws, but the consequences of failing to do so are usually very different in the two cases. If you violate the law against homicide, you can expect to be arrested, incarcerated, and perhaps even executed. But if you fail to follow the norm of using utensils to eat your dinner and use your fingers instead, you can expect merely a few raised eyebrows and a "tsk tsk" or two from your dinner companions. However, reactions to violating norms are not always so gentle. For example, a gang member's violation of a norm against fleeing a fight with another gang may lead to physical violence, death, and other not-so-subtle outcomes.

Norms are reinforced through **sanctions**, which can take the form of punishments (negative sanctions) or rewards (positive sanctions). In general, when norms have been violated, punishments are used, while rewards are employed when norms have been followed. For example, dinner companions might frown when you eat with your hands and grin approvingly when you use the right utensil. Gang members would be likely to disapprove of those who flee and approve of those who stay and fight. Children who bring home report cards with lots of As and Bs may be praised, while those whose report cards are dominated by lower grades may get stern lectures from their parents. In other words, sanctions may be applied when norms are observed as well as when they are violated. Sometimes either positive or negative sanctions are enough to enforce norms. However, enforcement is generally more effective when positive and negative sanctions are used in tandem—when *both* the "carrot" (reward) and the "stick" (punishment) are applied. Most people follow norms primarily because sanctions are associated with them.

ASK YOURSELF

What norms are operating in your classroom, dorm, or apartment? What negative sanctions have you observed when these norms have been violated?

For a good example of the differences between laws and the various types of norms, consider the situations you may encounter if you travel by airplane. First, if you want to get through airport security with a minimum of hassle, you need to observe laws regarding the belongings you can carry onto the airplane and the things you must and must not say and do. There are warning signs about the laws posted in the immediate vicinity of the security checkpoint.

Norms of air travel include the following:

- Don't block the aisles when you are entering or leaving the airplane.

- Limit your carry-ons to what realistically fits through the aisle and in the compartments.

- Don't hog the armrests.

- Don't encroach on seats on either side of you.

- Don't talk to the people beside you if they are busily working on their laptops or trying to sleep.

- Don't linger in the lavatory too long—others may be waiting—and don't leave behind a total mess.

- Don't get angry at flight attendants. It's generally not their fault—whatever the problem is—and in any case they can make your life miserable for the remainder of the flight.

- If traveling with a baby, use the restroom for diaper changes—not the seat next to you.

- When it's time to deplane, wait your turn and allow people seated ahead of you to get off first.

Once on the plane, you are still subject to various laws, such as those against smoking or carrying weapons on board. In addition, you are subject to a long list of norms, although there are no signs listing or explaining them or orientation sessions devoted to them. Nevertheless, you probably know some or all of these norms, such as not intruding too much on your neighbor's space. There are more serious informal rules against things like drinking too much alcohol and wandering around the plane, disturbing other travelers. These unwritten norms, and many more, are part of the culture of airplane travel. While you and your fellow passengers know most, if not all, of them, the norms are nevertheless frequently violated. However, it is a reflection of the power of culture that you likely know when you are violating the norms as well as when others are doing so.

Not all norms are the same, are equally important, or carry with them the same penalties if they are violated. On the one hand, there are **folkways**, or relatively unimportant norms. Whether they are observed or violated, they carry with them few if any sanctions (Sumner [1906] 1940). Not intruding on the space of the passenger sitting next to you on a plane is an example of a folkway. To take another example from a different setting, many college classes have norms against texting during lectures, but those norms are frequently violated. When students' violations are detected by alert instructors, the negative sanctions, such as being asked to stop or to leave the room for the rest of class, are generally mild. In contrast, **mores** (pronounced MOR-ays) are more important norms whose violation is likely to be met with severe negative sanctions. Airplane passengers who are belligerent toward other passengers or crew members are violating mores and may be forcibly ejected from the plane. Also violating mores (as well as campus rules) are students who use their smartphones to cheat on college exams. If their actions are witnessed or discovered, they may be subjected to severe negative sanctions, such as failing a class or even being expelled from school. While a clear distinction is often made between folkways and mores, in fact they exist along a continuum; it is often hard to distinguish where folkways end and mores begin.

For a good example of the differences between laws and the various types of norms, consider the situations you may encounter at Walmart. There are laws against shoplifting, there are mores against damaging store displays, and folkways exist about lining up and waiting your turn to check out.

Sharing an armrest on a train can be a fraught experience. How do you react if someone violates what you see as an established social norm?

MATERIAL CULTURE

Values and norms exist within the realm of ideas (see the following section for a related definition and discussion of symbolic, or nonmaterial, culture). However, culture also takes material—that is, tangible—forms. **Material culture** encompasses all the artifacts, the "stuff" (Molotch 2003; Steketee and Frost 2011), in which culture is reflected or manifested (Dant 2007). A wide range of things can be included under the heading of material culture, including this book, the clothes we wear, the homes we live in, our computers and iPhones, the toys children play with, and even the weapons used by our military.

Culture shapes such objects. For instance, the value that Americans place on economic prosperity is reflected in such material objects as games like Monopoly. This game was first patented in the mid-1930s, and its icon is a well-dressed, economically successful tycoon with a monocle, named Rich Uncle Pennybags. The goal of the game is to accumulate the most property and money. There are now online versions of Monopoly, as well as countless editions of the game specially designed around various cities, sports teams, television programs, and hobbies (including a version for fashion-minded girls). There are now also nonmaterial games (such as Minecraft) and Pokémon Go that are not only enjoyed by millions of people online but are also played by thousands in quite material sports arenas for millions of dollars in very real and material prize money (Wingfield 2014b, 2014c).

Material culture also shapes the larger culture in various ways. For example, when playing Monopoly, children are learning about, helping support, and furthering a culture that values wealth and material success. To take a different example, the centuries-old American value of individual freedom and individualism has been greatly enhanced by the widespread adoption of such material objects as the automobile, the single-family home, and the smartphone. The last, for example, gives us highly individualized and mobile access to the vast world available on the phone and the internet.

Material culture exists not only in these individual objects but also in the relationships among various objects (Baudrillard [1968] 1996). For example, each brand of beer has meaning in part because of its place in the larger system of beer brands. Budweiser has its place in a system that includes lower-status, lower-priced beers (Pabst Blue Ribbon, for example) as well as much higher-status, higher-priced beers (such as some microbrews and elite beers like Chimay). Budweiser and, indeed, all beer brands derive their meaning, at least in part, from their positions within the more general system of beers.

SYMBOLIC CULTURE AND LANGUAGE

Symbolic culture includes the nonmaterial, intangible aspects of culture. In fact, we have already discussed two key forms of symbolic culture—values and norms. However, there is no clear line between material and nonmaterial culture. Most, if not all, material phenomena have symbolic aspects, and various aspects of symbolic culture are manifest in material objects. Our symbolic culture is manifest when we buy American-made rather than Japanese or Korean automobiles in a show of patriotism, purchase the latest iPhone as soon as it is released to denote our technological sophistication, or choose cloth diapers over disposables as a symbol of our commitment to "green" parenting.

One important aspect of symbolic culture is **language**, a set of meaningful symbols that enables communication. Language, especially in its written form, allows for the storage and development of culture. Cultures with largely oral traditions do manage to accumulate culture and transmit it from one generation or group to another, but written language is a far more effective way of retaining and expanding upon a culture.

Perhaps more important, language facilitates communication within a culture. Our words reflect the way in which we think about and see the world. They also shape and influence culture. Suppose a time traveler from the 1950s arrived at a modern-day supermarket to buy something to eat for breakfast. Kellogg's Frosted Flakes, with its sprinkling of sugar, was a noteworthy innovation in the 1950s. However, our time traveler would be bewildered by cereals with brand names such as Froot Loops, Fruity Pebbles, Count Chocula, Franken Berry, Lucky Charms, and so on. The exotic and varied cereals we have now would be considered a marvel by someone from the 1950s. The point, however, is that having names for many different kinds of cereals allows consumers to make much finer distinctions about breakfast and to communicate more precisely what it is they wish to eat.

The contemporary world has given us a wealth of new words. For example, in the digital era, e-mail and advertisers have given us the word *spam* for the avalanche of unwanted messages. In the world of social networking, Twitter has given us the word *hashtag* to describe a label that helps us in searching *tweets*. The term *trolls* refers to those who seek to instigate arguments on social media forums. The consumption-oriented nature of our society has also led to the creation of many new words, a large number of them brand names. For example, the now nearly extinct *iPod* was the leading portable music device for some time; it led to the development of *iTunes*. The *iPhone* is the leading *smartphone* (another new word), and it has replaced the iPod as well as led to a booming industry in *apps* (applications) of all sorts. Similarly, globalization has led to new words, including *globalization* itself, which was virtually unused prior to 1990 (Ritzer and Dean 2015). The boom in sending work to be performed in another country or countries has given us the term *outsourcing* (Ritzer and Lair 2007).

Words like these are shared by people all over the world and allow them to communicate with one another. Communication among people of different cultures is also easier if they share a mother tongue. As you can see in the simplified map of world languages in Figure 4.2, African cultures use a variety of official and national languages. People in countries where French is the official language, such as Burkina Faso and Niger, can transact their business more easily with one another than they can with nations where Arabic or Portuguese is the primary language, such as Mauritania and Cape Verde.

Communication between cultures is never as easy or as clear as is communication within a given culture. For example, the 2003 movie *Lost in Translation* deals with communication difficulties experienced by Americans in Japan. The lead, played by Bill Murray, is a famous American actor visiting Japan to do commercials. Among other things, he is unable to understand how a large number of words spoken in Japanese become, when translated for him, a very small number of English words. He suspects that the translator is purposely not telling him things. He also finds himself unable to understand what the director of the commercial wants him to do, even when the directions are translated into English.

In a world dominated by consumption, communication between cultures also takes place through the viewing of common brands. However, brand names well known in some cultures may not translate well in other cultures. As a result, brands are often renamed to better reflect the cultures in which they are being sold. The following list shows the names of some well-known brands in the United States and elsewhere and the way in which they are translated into Chinese:

Brand	Chinese Translation
Nike	Enduring and Persevering
BMW	Precious Horse
Heineken	Happiness Power
Coca-Cola	Tasty Fun
Marriott	10,000 Wealthy Elites

While such name changes are common, some Chinese brand names are simply phonetic translations of the brands' names into Chinese. For example, Cadillac is translated "Ka di la ke." Although this name means nothing to the Chinese, the fact that it is foreign gives it an aura of status and respectability. However, if Microsoft had used a phonetic Chinese translation of the name of its search engine Bing, it would have been in big trouble. In Chinese, the word *bing* translates into "disease" or "virus." To avoid being seen as disease-ridden or a carrier of a virus,

FIGURE 4.2 • Distribution of Major Languages

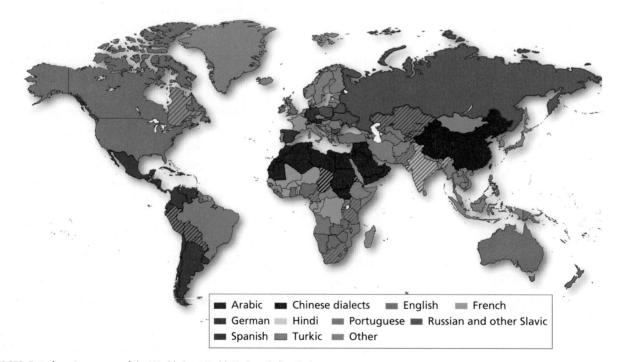

Arabic   Chinese dialects   English   French
German   Hindi   Portuguese   Russian and other Slavic
Spanish   Turkic   Other

SOURCES: Data from Languages of the World, One World, Nations Online Project.

Have you ever been in a situation, such as a trip abroad, in which understanding and communicating were difficult for you because you were unfamiliar with the language and symbols around you? How did you cope? Have you ever helped someone else who was in a similar situation? What did you do?

Microsoft changed the search engine's Chinese name to Bi ying. This has the far more appealing meaning of "responding without fail" (Wines 2011).

Even when people share a language, communication may be difficult if their backgrounds and values are too different. In the enormously popular, award-winning, and influential TV show *Breaking Bad* (2008–2013), a high school chemistry teacher, diagnosed with terminal cancer, decides to use his chemical expertise to become a crystal meth cook so that he can make money to take care of his family after his death. At least initially, he is befuddled by the norms, values, and language used in the world of illegal drug users, dealers, and killers. It's a long way from the language of high school chemistry class to that of the world of illicit drugs.

CHECKPOINT 4.2: THE BASIC ELEMENTS OF CULTURE

ELEMENT	DESCRIPTION
Values	General and abstract standards defining what a society considers good, right, or important
Norms	Informal rules that guide what people do and how they live
Material culture	Artifacts that are manifestations of culture
Symbolic culture	Nonmaterial aspects of culture

CULTURAL DIFFERENCES

As you have seen so far, we can think in terms of the culture of a society as a whole (for example, American culture), and later in this chapter we will even conceive of the possibility of a global culture. But you have also seen that there is great diversity within cultures, from gang culture to internet culture and too many other variants of culture for us to enumerate. Studying and understanding culture becomes easier, however, with the aid of a few key ideas: ideal and real culture, ideology, subculture and counterculture, culture war, and multiculturalism.

IDEAL AND REAL CULTURE

There is often a large gap, if not a chasm, between **ideal culture**, or what the norms and values of society lead us to think people should believe and do, and **real culture**, or what people actually think and do in their everyday lives. For example, as we have seen, a major American value is democracy. However, barely a majority of Americans bother to vote in presidential elections—only 60 percent of eligible voters voted in the 2016 election, about 1 percent above the figure four years earlier (United States Elections Project 2016; see Chapter 15). A far smaller percentage of those who are eligible vote in state and local elections. Worse, very few Americans are active in politics in other ways, such as canvassing on behalf of a political party or working to get people out to vote.

In another example, the cultural ideal that mothers should be completely devoted to their children (Blair-Loy 2003; Hays 1998) often comes into conflict with lived reality for many women who work outside the home and must balance their time between job and family. This contradiction is apparent in the incidence of breast-feeding, which at least for some women is once again a norm of motherhood (Avishai 2007; Stearns 2009, 2011). Breastfeeding is difficult or impossible for many mothers because it is labor- and time-intensive, and given work and all the other constraints they face in their lives, it is difficult for them to find the time and energy to do it. Despite its health benefits for baby and mother, under such circumstances breastfeeding can have adverse social and economic consequences for women. One study demonstrated that women who breastfed for more than six months suffered greater economic losses than those who did so for less time or not at all (Rippeyoug and Noonan 2012). Women who do not breastfeed, however, can feel that they have failed to live up to cultural standards of being a "good mom" (Blum 2000; Taylor, Funk, and Clark 2007).

IDEOLOGY

An *ideology* is a set of shared beliefs that explains the social world and guides people's actions. There are many ideologies in any society, and some of them become dominant. For example, in the United States, *meritocracy* is a dominant ideology involving the widely shared belief that all people have an equal chance of succeeding economically based on their hard work and skills. Many people act on the basis of that belief and, among other things, seek the education and training they think they need to succeed.

However, even with dedication and adequate education and training, not everyone succeeds. Among many other things, some people are luckier than others (Frank 2016). Even though they don't deserve it, some people succeed because of a lucky break; others who deserve to succeed

Queuing in Hong Kong and India

We are accustomed to spontaneously forming straight, orderly lines to efficiently board an airplane, order food, gain admission to an athletic event, or attend a popular concert (Fuller 2014; Helweg-Larsen and LoMonaco 2008). Queuing up is a norm within modern American society.

Standing in straight lines is less normative in other societies, however, particularly those that are less developed and less modern. For example, in India, people might begin to form a queue, but when the line grows too long, new arrivals stand next to those already in line, forming what look like new limbs on a human evergreen tree. "They hover near the line's middle, holding papers, looking lost in a practiced way, then slip in somewhere close to the front. When confronted, their refrain is predictable: 'Oh, I didn't see the line'" (Giridharadas 2010). To prevent such cutting, people (mostly men) end up standing very close to those in front of them, often close enough that they are touching.

There is a long history of queues in many other cultures, most notably British culture. However, although Hong Kong was a British colony for well over a century (as was India), queuing was not the norm at McDonald's when it opened in Hong Kong in 1975. Rather, milling crowds shouted out orders and waved money at the servers. McDonald's introduced queue monitors responsible for getting customers to form orderly lines, a practice that later became characteristic

Men in New Delhi lined up for free food, squeezing close together to prevent cutting. What happens when norms that govern this kind of group behavior break down?

of middle-class culture in general in Hong Kong. In fact, older residents often credit McDonald's with bringing the queue to Hong Kong.

More recently in India and elsewhere, the queue is being challenged by the "market mentality," as many, especially the affluent, increasingly believe that they should be able to pay to get to the front of any queue or avoid it altogether. There are lines at Hindu temples, for example, but those who can pay get in much shorter VIP lines or avoid lines entirely. Indian clubs have "rope lines" for most visitors, but purchasers of premium memberships get in faster. At the Bibbidi Bobbidi Boutique at Disneyland,

parents can pay an extra fee to have their kids get a princess or prince makeover, then skip the line in the castle area next door to meet the princess characters.

Such market-driven arrangements are more efficient for those who can afford them, but they complicate life for those who cannot, and they contribute to the creation of an increasingly stratified world.

Think About It

Do you think queuing up in an orderly fashion is a positive norm or a negative one? Why do you suppose there are no apparent social sanctions for paying extra to go to the head of the line?

don't because they are unlucky. This reflects the key fact that not all ideologies are true. For one thing, they may come from, and be true for, some groups of people (such as those in the upper classes) and not for others (those in the lower classes; Mannheim [1931] 1936). For another, they may be outright distortions used by one group to hide reality from another group (Marx [1857–1858] 1964). In this sense, it could be argued that meritocracy is an ideology created by the upper classes to hide the fact that those in the lower classes have little or no chance of succeeding. This fact is hidden from them to prevent them from becoming dissatisfied and rebellious. If the lower classes accept the ideology of meritocracy, they may be more likely to blame themselves for failing rather than the upper classes or the American economic system as a whole.

SUBCULTURES

Within any culture there are **subcultures**, or groups of people who accept much of the dominant culture but are set apart from it by one or more culturally significant characteristics. In the United States, major subcultures include the LGBTQ community (lesbian, gay, bisexual, transgender, and queer people), Hispanics, the Tea Party, Hasidic Jews, hip-hop fans, and youth. Muslims are becoming an increasingly important subculture in the United States (especially in cities such as Detroit). They already constitute a major subculture in many European countries, most notably France and Great Britain.

Subcultures arise in the realm of consumption as well. For example, "brand communities" develop around particular brand-name products (Meister 2012; Muniz and O'Guinn 2001; Stratton and Northcote 2014). Harley-Davidson motorcycle riders are one such subculture (called HOGS, for Harley Owners Group), with distinctive clothing, events, and norms. Brand communities have formed around a number of Apple products, such as the Macintosh computer (the "Mac") and the iPad. The members of these communities share a number of cultural elements, including norms. In the case of the Mac, for example, some community members positively sanction "jailbreaking," a method for hacking into Apple's software in order to get around its restrictions and limitations.

Any society includes many subcultures, such as hackers or those devoted to fishing, that develop around particular styles of life and share special vocabularies. A great deal of attention has been devoted to "deviant" subcultures (Barmaki 2016), such as those of punks, goths, and the like (Berard 2007). In Great Britain, "football hooligans," those who often engage in violence at or in regard to soccer matches, constitute a deviant subculture largely specific to that society (Ayres and Treadwell 2012; Dunning,

Murphy, and Williams 1988). However, there are also many "straight" subcultures, such as those who play online games (e.g., Pokémon-Go) or "straight" fans of clean eating (e.g., the Whole30 program [https://whole30.com] or the Paleo diet; Wood 2006).

Another example of a subculture is the world of skateboarders. The majority of skateboarders accept most of the larger society's culture, norms, values, and language, but they also differ in some ways. Many are more willing than most members of society to take physical risks, for example, by participating in the sport known as parkour, which involves using the body to overcome urban obstacles such as walls and ledges (Kidder 2012; Thorpe and Ahmad 2015). Skateboarders in general, as well as those who practice parkour, see such obstacles as enhancing the thrill of their activity.

Skateboarders also have their own vocabulary. It happens that one of my family members is a skateboarder, so I am (vaguely) familiar with these terms. However, it took me a long time to understand them. When I did, I was able to get a better sense of skateboarding and its intricacies. Of course, my understanding pales in comparison to that of those immersed in the skateboarding subculture and its distinctive language.

COUNTERCULTURES

Countercultures are groups that not only differ from the dominant culture but also adhere to norms and values that may be incompatible with those of the dominant culture (Binkley 2007; Zellner 1995). They may, in fact, consciously and overtly act in opposition to the dominant culture. The term *counterculture* was introduced by Theodore Roszak ([1968] 1995) in the late 1960s in reference to hippies, antiwar activists, and radical students.

Computer hackers are a contemporary example of a counterculture (Corbett 2014; Levy 2010). Many hackers simply seek to show their technical mastery of computers through relatively benign actions, such as writing free computer software, but a minority are devoted to subverting authority and disrupting the internet, and some are involved in stealing personal identification data ("identity theft") and money. They may write malicious code in order to interrupt or even shut down the normal operations of computers. In one famous case in 1988, Robert Tappan Morris unleashed what was thought to be the first worm that slowed down thousands of computers, making many of them unusable. Since then, many attempted and successful break-ins have threatened government and corporate computer systems (e.g., Sony in 2014); the hackers' goal has been to steal secret or personal information (e.g., gossip about movie stars in the e-mail of Sony personnel). A recent rash of break-ins into corporate computers was aimed at

Skateboarding has developed a subculture with its own norms, values, language, and environments. Do you belong to any similar subcultures?

stealing credit card numbers and account information. For example, in late 2014 the account information of 56 million Home Depot customers was compromised; information on 40 million Target accounts had been hacked the year before (Perlroth 2014). In mid-2015 hackers exposed the names of 30 million people who had accounts with Ashley Madison. This was particularly troublesome to the account holders because those who participated on the Ashley Madison website were interested in having adulterous affairs. The site's slogan was "Life is short; have an affair" (McPhate 2016). Personal accounts have also been hacked and locked until the account holders paid ransom demanded by the hackers (Simone 2015). Hacking became a huge public issue in late 2016 when the Russians were caught hacking the accounts of Hillary Clinton and her supporters during the U.S. presidential campaign. Many believe that the Russians' goal was to help Donald Trump win the election (Lipton, Sanger, and Shane 2016). This continues to be an important issue in mid-2017, and we can expect more revelations about it in the future.

In the realm of consumption, an important contemporary counterculture is formed by those who are associated with or sympathetic to the "voluntary simplicity" movement (Elgin 2010; Grigsby 2004; Zammuel, Sasson-Levy,

and Ben-Porat 2014). Sociologist Juliet Schor (1993, 1998) has critiqued the dominant American culture's emphasis on what she calls "work and spend." That is, we are willing to work long hours so that we can spend a great deal on consumption and live an ever-more elaborate lifestyle. In addition, Schor (2005) points out the ways in which our consumer culture has led to the commercialization of childhood, with advertising pervading all aspects of children's lives. As a countercultural alternative, she suggests that we both work less and spend less and instead devote ourselves to more meaningful activities. Living a simpler life means avoiding overconsumption, minimizing the work needed to pay for consumption, and doing less harm to the environment.

Globalization, especially economic globalization, has also spawned a number of very active countercultural groups. They are not necessarily antiglobalization, but they favor alternative forms of globalization (Kahn and Kellner 2007; Obara-Minnitt 2014; Pleyers 2010). In fact, many of them are part of the process of globalization. The World Social Forum (WSF) was created in 2001 following a series of antiglobalization protests, particularly one in Seattle in 1999. Its members come from all over the world. The WSF's slogan is "Another world is possible." That other world would be less capitalistic. It would also allow for more democratic decision making on matters that affect large portions of the world's population. Those who accept this kind of perspective are clearly part of a counterculture. They oppose the global spread of the dominant capitalist culture that prioritizes maximizing profits over democratic decision making.

CULTURE WARS

In the 1960s, the hippies, student radicals, and anti–Vietnam War activists vocally, visibly, and sometimes violently rejected traditional American norms and values. Among other things, they rejected unthinking patriotism and taboos against recreational drugs and sexual freedom. The term *culture war* was used to describe the social upheaval that ensued. More generally, a **culture war** is a conflict pitting a subculture or counterculture against the dominant culture (e.g., antievolutionists versus evolutionists; Silva 2014), or a conflict between dominant groups within a society. Culture wars sometimes lead to the disruption of the social, economic, and political status quo (Hunter 1992; Luker 1984).

ASK YOURSELF

Do you think a culture war between political conservatives and liberals is inevitable? Must it be ongoing? Why or why not?

In the United States today, the major culture war being fought is between those who place themselves on the conservative end of the sociopolitical spectrum and those who place themselves on the liberal end. It is largely viewed as a political battle over such things as government spending, taxes, social services, national defense, and environmental measures. Conservatives generally favor less government spending, lower taxes for the wealthy, fewer entitlements for the poor, aggressive national defense, and minimal environmental regulations. Liberals usually support higher government spending on education, health care, and services for the poor; less spending on national defense; and stricter environmental regulations. Today, this battle is epitomized by struggles between Donald Trump and his conservative allies in the Republican Party and liberal Democrats in the Congress.

There are important differences in fundamental values between these groups. Consider, for example, the long-running battle over abortion. The political battle is over legal limits to abortion and contraception. However, the underlying values have to do with varying definitions of life and attitudes toward women's role in society. Similarly, much heat is generated over "family values," with conservatives

worrying about the decline in the traditional nuclear family, the increasing prevalence of cohabitation and single parenthood, homosexual marriage, and the adoption of children by same-sex couples (Murray 2013). They place more emphasis on strict moral codes and self-discipline, whereas liberals, in contrast, place more significance on empathy, openness, and fairness (McAdams et al. 2008). Liberals tend to see the developments in the family as signs of greater acceptance of people's differences and circumstances (Gerson 2011). Within the field of sociology, in fact, there is intense debate between family scholars who argue that the family is in decline (Popenoe 1993, 2009) and those who feel that the concept of the family needs to be broadened to embrace the many ways in which people experience kin connections (Biblarz and Stacey 2010; Stacey 1998; see Chapter 12).

The conservative–liberal culture war is debated endlessly in the popular media. The media themselves tend to be increasingly divided along conservative (Fox News) and liberal (MSNBC) lines. The leading media pundits (e.g., Fox News's conservative Tucker Carlson and MSNBC's liberal Rachel Maddow) are often at war with one another.

Examples of culture wars are also to be found in the digital world. For example, open-source advocates believe that the internet, or at least large portions of it, should be protected from control by governments or corporations. They support free open-source software (e.g., Linux, Firefox, OpenOffice, GNU Image Manipulation Program) as well as free access to information. One of their models is Wikipedia, where anyone can create entries and modify them. They oppose the dominant players on the internet, including Microsoft, Google, Apple, and internet service providers. These large corporations are seen as carving up the digital world and controlling access in order to generate huge profits. There is a constant low-level conflict going on between members of these two cultures and the groups that support them. More recently, a culture war broke out between those who want to give some corporations (such as Comcast and Verizon) control over the internet and those who favor "net neutrality," in which the internet is free and open to all. The issue seemed settled when in mid-2016 a federal court ruled in favor of net neutrality, but it is far from dead. In mid-2017, the Trump administration sought to unwind some net neutrality rules. Large corporations that want to control the internet have vowed to take the issue to the Supreme Court (Kang 2016).

MULTICULTURALISM AND ASSIMILATION

A great deal of attention has been paid in recent years to another aspect of cultural diversity—**multiculturalism**, or an environment in which cultural differences are accepted and appreciated both by the state and by the majority group (Modood 2007; Pakulski 2014). The cultural groups may be based on race, ethnicity, nationality, or language. They may also be based on age and other dimensions of difference. People in the United States, for example, generally accept that young and old people have their own cultural preferences. Americans for the most part tolerate—sometimes even celebrate—the coexistence of different cultural groups within the larger culture.

When it comes to ethnicity and national origin, however, multiculturalism has not always been celebrated in this country. The dominant culture has been interested primarily in **assimilation**, or integrating the minority group into the mainstream. As a so-called nation of immigrants, the United States has always had to resolve issues of cultural diversity. Until late in the twentieth century, most immigrants to the United States were from Europe, especially Eastern and Southern Europe (see Figure 4.3). Many of these groups did assimilate to a large degree, even if their assimilation occurred over a couple of generations. Today we do not think twice about whether or not Polish Americans or Italian Americans, for instance, are "regular" Americans.

But immigrants from the next large wave, in the 1990s and 2000s, have not assimilated so well. If you refer again to Figure 4.3, you can see that the largest flow of immigrants is now from the Americas, with another large—and growing—group from Asia. These immigrants, especially those from Mexico and China, often live in largely separate enclaves and speak their native languages (see Figure 4.4 for a map depicting the percentage of the population speaking a language other than English at home). They also often retain their basic cultures, such as their tastes in food. It remains to be seen whether, and to what degree, these groups will be assimilated into mainstream culture or their culture will be accepted as a valued element of American culture.

In the past, Muslims have generally assimilated well in the United States (Freedman 2016). The future of their assimilation, however, is in doubt (Bulut 2016). This is a result of the current widespread hostility toward Muslims (especially toward radical Islamic extremists) because of their perceived association with 9/11 and terrorism in the United States and many other parts of the world. This hostility increased greatly during the 2016 presidential campaign when then-candidate Donald Trump suggested at least a temporary ban on Muslim immigration to the United States. As president, Trump has tried to implement such a ban, at least for a few primarily Islamic countries, but his efforts have thus far been stymied the courts. It remains to be seen how this will be resolved, but Muslims, as well

FIGURE 4.3 • Legal Migration to the United States by Region of Origin, 1820–2014

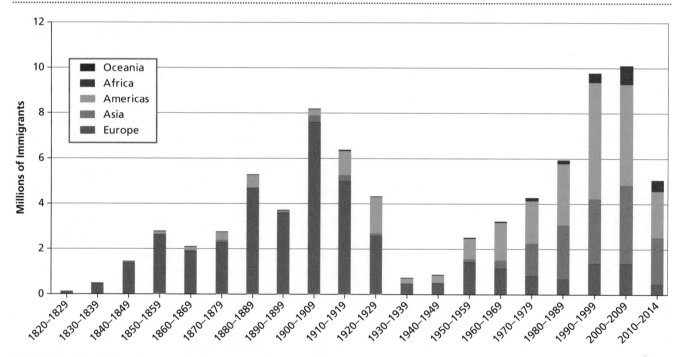

SOURCE: Data from Table 2, "Persons Obtaining Legal Permanent Resident Status by Region and Selected Country of Last Residence: Fiscal Years 1820 to 2014," Washington, Dc: U.S. Department of Homeland Security, 2014.

The Spirit Catches You and You Fall Down: A Hmong Child, Her American Doctors, and the Collision of Two Cultures (Farrar, Straus and Giroux, 2012)

Anne Fadiman (Adjunct Professor of English, Francis Writer-in-Residence at Yale University; Essayist and Reporter; BA, Harvard University, 1975)

Foua Yang weeps as she describes her daughter Lia Lee, whose 30-year struggle with epilepsy, cerebral palsy, pneumonia, and sepsis is chronicled in *The Spirit Catches You and You Fall Down.*

Ignorance and confusion about cultural differences often result in awkward social interactions that can be momentarily embarrassing. Cultural misunderstandings, however, can have life-or-death consequences. Take, for example, situations in which doctors and patients believe in different values and practice different norms. Anne Fadiman spent eight years studying encounters between immigrant Hmong parents and the American doctors who treated their epileptic daughter, Lia. Lia's condition was not diagnosed initially because she was not having seizures when she arrived at the emergency room. Further, her parents did not speak English, so they could not communicate her symptoms to the doctors on duty. After her doctors made the correct diagnosis, her condition did not improve because her parents did not dispense her medicines properly. Lia's parents did not trust Western doctors, the medicine they prescribed, or even the idea that biology was the basis of their daughter's epilepsy. They adhered to the Hmong belief that Lia's epilepsy was caused by her soul escaping her body. Her symptoms were seen as the result of a soul-stealing spirit that made Lia fall down, or have seizures. According to the Hmong, being epileptic is a sign of distinction and indicates that an individual has special powers (Fadiman 2012, 20–21). Even if Lia's parents did believe that Western medicine could help her, they could not read the instructions on giving her the right dosages. Their lack of compliance—whether intentional or accidental—resulted in Lia's being removed from their custody and placed in foster care.

Lia's parents eventually regained custody of their child by agreeing to dispense her prescriptions according to her doctor's orders. However, six months later, Lia unexpectedly suffered a massive seizure that resulted in septic shock and rendered her brain dead. The doctors removed her from life support so that her parents could take her home and presumably allow her to die there. But, to their surprise, she survived, even though her parents refused to give her more Western medicine or use a feeding tube. Using traditional Hmong rituals and medicines, Lia's mother constantly cared for her body and her soul. Though Ladiman admits that she does not know whether Lia would become a fully functioning adult, she argues that cross-cultural misunderstandings between Lia's parents and her doctors played a key role in how epilepsy affected her life (Fadiman 2012, 263). Many Hmong in the United States, like Lia's parents, want "to be left alone to be Hmong" and refuse to assimilate (2012, 183). They value self-sufficiency and believe that surgery and drawing blood from the body are taboo. When sick, they prefer to be treated by a shaman, who will come to their homes and spend hours with them (2012, 33). In contrast, American medical professionals value science and rationality. They have their patients visit them in impersonal office buildings or hospitals and often spend only a few minutes with them. Undoubtedly, the ethnocentrism expressed by both the Hmong and American doctors can be tempered with a dose of cultural relativism.

Supplementary Resources

- You can read more about Fadiman's book, including the fate of Lia and her family and how it has influenced the medical field, at www.nytimes.com/2012/09/15/us/life-went-on-around-her-redefining-care-by-bridging-a-divide.html?_r=0.

- Learn more about why cultural competency in the healthcare professions is important by watching this training video: www.youtube.com/watch?v=dNLtAj0wy6I.

FIGURE 4.4 • Percentage of U.S. Population Speaking a Language Other than English at Home, by County, 2007–2011

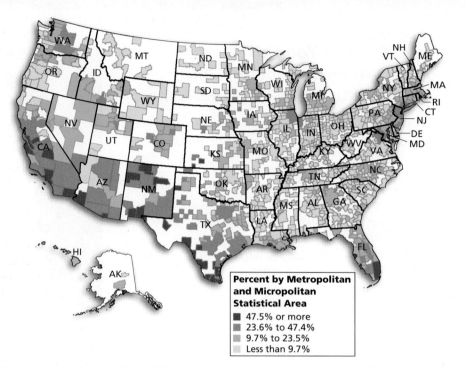

Percent by Metropolitan and Micropolitan Statistical Area

■ 47.5% or more
■ 23.6% to 47.4%
■ 9.7% to 23.5%
□ Less than 9.7%

SOURCE: Camille Ryan, "Language Use in the United States: 2011," American Community Survey Reports ACS-22, U.S. Census Bureau, August 2013, p. 12.

as members and supporters of the rights of all minority groups, have every reason to be alarmed.

Muslims who have already assimilated may face more hostility in the future, and newcomers may have a harder time assimilating. This hostility toward Muslims in the United States (and elsewhere) exists even though many of the attacks by radical Islamists have taken place in Muslim-dominated countries and Muslims have constituted a disproportionate percentage of the victims (Barnard 2016).

Multiculturalism is a relatively recent issue for many European societies, particularly the Scandinavian countries and the Netherlands. They have traditionally been almost monocultures, and even now, during a period of widespread global migration, they have a smaller proportion of foreign-born residents than the United States has. However, beginning in the 1950s, many European countries began to experience labor shortages (Fassmann and Munz 1992; Fielding 1989). Large numbers of people from poorer Southern European countries, such as Spain and Italy, migrated to Northern European countries. Later, migration flowed from less developed countries outside Europe, such as Turkestan, other largely Islamic countries, and many African countries. The fall of the Soviet Union in 1991 brought additional Eastern Europeans from places such as Albania. Many Northern European governments had intended for these immigrant workers to stay only a short time. However, the immigrants built lives for themselves,

brought their families, and chose to remain. The result is that European countries today are far more multicultural than they were several decades ago.

ASK YOURSELF

If you were born in the United States, imagine yourself as an immigrant to another country, one to which you have no cultural or genealogical ties and where you know no one. What would you do on your arrival in order to survive? Would you seek out other Americans? Why or why not? Would you try to assimilate? How?

More recent immigrants to largely Christian Europe bring with them very different cultures and very different religions (Islam, for example). They are also likely to be relatively poor. In a 2011 protest against Muslim immigration to his country, a Norwegian right-wing extremist bombed government buildings in Oslo, killing eight people. He later killed another 69 people during a shooting spree at a summer camp related to the country's ruling party. As a relatively small, monocultural country, the Netherlands has had trouble digesting its roughly 850,000 Muslim immigrants, and relations between Muslims and non-Muslims have grown increasingly polarized (Maliepaard and Alba 2016). The same is true in Belgium, which has sought to accommodate the burgeoning Muslim population by de-Christianizing its own holidays (for example, All Saints Day was renamed Autumn Holiday; Kern 2014). In spite of such efforts, concerns about the Muslim population in Belgium continue, epitomized by the coordinated attacks in Brussels in March 2016, which killed 35 people and injured hundreds of others.

Since 2014, France has experienced a number of terrorist attacks. Among them, perhaps the most infamous incident (at least so far) occurred in January 2015, when three Islamic extremists entered the Paris offices of *Charlie Hebdo,* a venerable French satirical newspaper, and shot and killed 12 people, including editors and cartoonists. In 2016, as a result of such acts of terrorism, the French authorities dismantled the Calais Jungle refugee camp, where almost 2,000 refugees—many of them Muslims—were living in makeshift shelters (McAuley 2016).

A number of the acts of terrorism in France were perpetrated against Jews. This had led to fears of increasing conflict between these two groups, as well as to a more general resurgence of anti-Semitism. In an attack related to the *Charlie Hebdo* incident, a Muslim extremist killed a policeman and later took over a kosher supermarket in Paris. In an act labeled anti-Semitic by the French president, the gunman killed four people in the market before also being killed in a police raid (Higgins and Bilefsky 2015). Southern Europeans, especially in Italy, are increasingly having difficulty in dealing with waves of immigrants from North Africa. In fact, many would-be immigrants are dying in accidents at sea before they even get to Italy as they seek to navigate the Mediterranean Sea in overcrowded and rickety boats. For years Italy and other countries sought to prevent migrants from leaving North Africa, especially the failed state of Libya. However, a 2012 ruling by the European Court of Human Rights stopped them from doing so. Now a more humane response is required, such as putting migrants, including many unaccompanied children, in holding centers until a decision can be made about what to do with them. Spain has an enclave in Morocco and has had great difficulties in dealing with mass attempts of people from all over Africa to scale the enormous fence that separates the enclave from Morocco. Their goal is to gain entrée into Spain and thereby into Europe. Despite efforts to make the fence more difficult to climb, thousands succeeded in scaling it in 2014. The resistance of Italy, Spain, and other Southern European countries to such immigration, like that in Northern Europe, is motivated in part by economics and the fear that immigrants will cost natives their jobs. However, it is also cultural in the sense that the different cultures of these immigrants are seen as a threat to Italian, Spanish, and other European cultures. In short, European countries today have more cultural diversity than ever. However, the situation is fraught with tension, conflict, and danger as people from very different cultures, religions, and languages struggle to find a way to live side by side (Caldwell 2009). Given these recent developments in Europe, the United States, and elsewhere in the world, some are declaring multiculturalism a failure. States, and especially majority groups, are growing less appreciative of, and less willing to accept, groups that represent different cultures (Gozdecka, Ercan, and Kmak 2014).

Identity Politics

While some majority groups have come to oppose multiculturalism, various minority groups have grown impatient with the dominant culture's limited view of multiculturalism and its unwillingness to accept the minority groups for who they are. Such minorities have asserted their right to retain their distinctive cultures and even their right *not* to assimilate, at least totally. These groups have engaged in **identity politics** in using their power to strengthen the position of the cultural groups with which they identify (Nicholson 2008; Wasson 2007). Identity politics has a long history; in recent decades it has included the black power, feminist, and gay pride movements in many parts of the world. The goal of such movements has been the creation of a true multicultural society, one that accepts minorities for who they are.

Identity politics has played out not only on the streets in the form of public protests and demonstrations but also in schools, especially in universities. In the latter, the central issue has been whether all students should be required to learn the "canon"—a common set of texts, sometimes referred to as the "great books"—a body of knowledge long regarded to be of central importance. For example, the works of Marx, Weber, and Durkheim are often thought to be the canonical texts in sociology. Minority cultures claim that the canon in sociology and many other fields reflects the interests and experiences of white middle- and upper-class males. They argue that alternative bodies of knowledge, such as those created by women, people of color, and the LGBTQ community, are at least as important. The result has been a proliferation of programs such as those devoted to black, Chicano, and feminist studies, where the focus is on those alternative texts and bodies of knowledge. However, such programs have been the subject of much controversy and political scrutiny. For example, Arizona's secretary of education targeted racial and ethnic studies programs in a bill passed by the state legislature in 2010, contending that these programs encourage students to think of themselves as oppressed (Lacey 2011). However, a judge ruled in 2013 that banning such programs and the courses associated with them was unconstitutional.

Cultural Relativism and Ethnocentrism

Multiculturalism and identity politics are closely related to **cultural relativism**, which is the idea that aspects of a culture such as norms and values need to be understood within the context of that culture; there are no cultural universals, or universally accepted norms and values. In this view, different cultures simply have different norms and values. There is no basis for saying that one set of norms and values is better than another (Weiler 2007). Thus, for example, those in Western countries should not judge Islamic women's use of headscarves. Conversely, those in the Islamic world should not judge Western women who bare their midriffs.

Cultural relativism runs counter to the tendency in many cultures toward **ethnocentrism**, or the belief that the norms, values, traditions, and material and symbolic aspects of one's own culture are better than those of other cultures (S. Brown 2007b; Machida 2012). The tendency toward ethnocentrism both among subcultures within the United States and in cultures throughout the world represents a huge barrier to greater cultural understanding. However, to be fair, a belief in one's own culture can be of great value to that culture. It gives the people of that culture a sense of pride and identity. Problems arise when ethnocentrism serves as a barrier to understanding other cultures, a source of conflict among cultures, or an excuse for one culture to deny rights or privileges to another.

CHECKPOINT 4.3: SOME COMPARISONS THAT DEFINE CULTURAL DIFFERENCES

COMPARE THIS CULTURAL IDEA . . .	TO THIS ONE
Ideal culture: What our norms and values lead us to think we should believe and do	**Real culture:** What we actually think and do
Subcultures: Groups that accept much of the dominant culture but are set apart by one or more significant characteristics	**Countercultures:** Groups that not only differ from the dominant culture but hold norms and values that may be incompatible with it
Multiculturalism: An environment in which cultural differences are accepted and appreciated by the majority group	**Assimilation:** The integration of a cultural minority group into the mainstream
Cultural relativism: The belief that different cultures have different norms and values, and that none are universally accepted or better than any others	**Ethnocentrism:** The belief that the norms, values, traditions, and symbols of one's own culture are better than those of other cultures

GLOBAL CULTURE

Culture is continually in the process of change, just as it is continually in the process of being transmitted from one generation to the next. Some of the ways in which today's cultures are changing are worthy of further exploration. In this section, we will focus on global culture, consumer culture, and cyberculture.

There are certainly major differences within American culture, such as those that exist among subcultures. Yet few would dispute the idea that it is possible to talk about American culture in general. However, discussing a global culture, a culture common to the world as a whole, is not as easy. Some elements of material culture, including hamburgers, sushi, cars, and communication technology, have spread widely around the world. However, the global diffusion of nonmaterial culture—values, norms, and symbolic culture—is somewhat more difficult.

THE GLOBALIZATION OF VALUES

We have already discussed how values differ, sometimes greatly, from one society to another. How, then, can we discuss global values—values that are shared throughout the world (Sekulic 2007c)? Some scholars argue that global values exist because all people share a biological structure that produces universal tendencies, including common values. Others contend that while particular values vary from country to country, the underlying structure of values is much the same across societies. However, the most persuasive argument for the existence of global values is traceable to the process of globalization. The global flow of all sorts of things—information, ideas, products, and people—produces realities in most parts of the world that are more similar than ever before in history (Lechner and Boli 2005). If these realities are increasingly similar, it seems likely that what people value will come to be increasingly similar throughout the world.

In fact, the globalization of values has been the subject of the World Values Survey, discussed previously in this chapter and in Chapter 3. One of the major findings of this research is a wide-ranging global shift from valuing economic prosperity and material success to valuing more quality-of-life issues such as lifestyle (free time to enjoy the activities and company that one prefers) and self-expression (the opportunity to express one's artistic talents). Other emerging global values are egalitarianism, especially as it relates to men and women, and liberalization of sexuality.

However, do these changes signify the emergence of truly global values? While they probably hold for the most developed societies in North America, Europe, and Asia, do they apply to most of the less developed world? Probably not! For example, there is little evidence that all societies (especially Islamic societies) are becoming more accepting of greater equality between men and women and more liberal sexual values. There are also generational differences within many societies, even those that are highly developed, with younger people being more likely to accept these quality-of-life values than the older generations (Welzel and Inglehart 2009).

In short, we can agree that globalization has brought with it greater acceptance of some values in a larger part of the world, but that is a very long way from saying that we have a global value system. For example, although many societies have welcomed greater access to information from around the world through the internet and other digital media, China has erected what has been called the "Great Firewall," seeking to restrict the ability of its people to view the entire range of internet sites and therefore the global values on view in at least some of them.

CULTURAL IMPERIALISM

Many have the strong view that what affects global culture most of all is **cultural imperialism**, or the imposition of one dominant culture on other cultures (Tomlinson 1999, 2012). Cultural imperialism tends to destroy local cultures. Let us look briefly at two examples of cultural imperialism in contemporary India:

- Saris are a key element of Indian material culture. Indian saris have traditionally been made of silk and woven by hand in a process that can take as much as two months for each sari. Elaborate designs use silk interspersed with strands of gold thread. However, India's roughly one million sari makers are now threatened by the availability of machine-made saris, especially from China (Wax 2007). A culture that emphasizes inexpensive, machine-made products is imposing itself on a realm in another culture that has emphasized local products, practices, and indigenous skilled workers. In the process, the local sari-making culture is being destroyed, and the sari itself, a distinctive Indian product, is losing its unique character.

- There is also a long tradition in India of professional letter writers, men who place themselves in prominent locations (e.g., near train stations) and offer their services writing letters for poor, illiterate migrants. Many of these letter writers are able to survive on the pittance they are paid for each letter. However, the adoption of elements of Western culture—the cell phone, texting, and so on—is rendering the professional letter writers, and the cultural traditions associated with them, obsolete.

There is certainly a great deal of cultural imperialism in the world today, much of it associated with the United States (Crothers 2010; Kuisel 1993). The process of **Americanization** includes the importation by other countries of a variety of cultural elements—products, images, technologies, practices, norms, values, and behaviors—that are closely associated with the United States. One example is the American movie industry: The popularity of American movies around the world has decimated the film industries of many countries, including Great Britain and France. (India is one exception, with its thriving Bollywood productions, including the 2009 Academy Award winner for Best Picture, *Slumdog Millionaire* [Rizvi 2012].) Another successful U.S. cultural export is Americans' taste for food, especially fast food and the way in which it is eaten (quickly, with one's hands, standing up or in the car). McDonald's is a prime example, but another of note is Starbucks (Simon 2009), which has been surprisingly successful in exporting its model of large, slowly consumed cups of coffee. In contrast, in France and Italy and other countries, the historic preference has been for tiny cups of espresso quickly consumed. There are now more than 24,000 Starbucks stores located around the world, in more than 70 countries.

Cultural imperialism certainly exists, but it would be wrong to overestimate its power. Local cultures can be quite resilient. Not all cultures suffer the fate of French movie producers and Indian sari makers and letter writers. For example:

- The powerful process of Americanization is often countered by **anti-Americanism**, which is an aversion to the United States in general, as well as to the influence of its culture abroad (Huntington 1996; O'Connor and Griffiths 2005).

- Many cultures—Chinese and Islamic cultures, for example—have long, even ancient, histories. These cultures have resisted at least some impositions from other cultures for centuries. They are likely to continue to resist changes that threaten their basic values and beliefs.

- Local cultures modify inputs and impositions from other cultures by integrating them with local realities and in the process produce cultural hybrids that combine elements of both (Nederveen Pieterse 2015). Hybridization occurs when, for instance, British people watch Asian rap performed by a South American in a London club owned by a Saudi Arabian; another example is the Dutch watching Moroccan women engage in Thai boxing. In the fast-food realm, McDonald's sells such hybrid foods as McChicken Korma Naan, which caters to those in Great Britain who have developed a taste for Indian food (including the many Indians who live there); McLaks, a grilled salmon sandwich served in Norway; and McHuevos, a hamburger with a poached egg served in Uruguay.

Thus, cultural imperialism needs to be examined in the context of the counterreactions to it, counterflows from elsewhere in the world, and the combination of global and local influences to produce unique cultural elements.

EMERGING ISSUES IN CULTURE

CONSUMER CULTURE

Recall that in Chapter 2 we discussed Thorstein Veblen's ([1899] 1994) concept of *conspicuous consumption* (Schor 2015). When this idea was introduced at the turn of the twentieth century, its focus was on the wealthy and their desire to demonstrate their wealth by flaunting mansions, yachts, designer clothes, and so on. While there is no shortage of conspicuous consumption today, it is also the case that not being so conspicuous about one's consumption and instead engaging in what we might call *inconspicuous consumption* is valued in some circles. Examples might include a well-to-do professor at an Ivy League university dressing in baggy khakis or tattered jeans, or a Hollywood star driving an economy car. Larry David, creator of *Seinfeld* and model for the character of George Costanza on the show, conspicuously drove a Prius on his HBO program *Curb Your Enthusiasm* (which aired for eight seasons between 2000 and 2011; a ninth season is slated to release in 2017). However, the Prius can be seen as representing another kind of conspicuous consumption—a conspicuous concern for the environment.

Whether it is conspicuous or inconspicuous, consumption is clearly highly valued in the United States (and elsewhere; see Nwachukwu and Dant 2014). That makes American culture a **consumer culture**, one in which the core ideas and material objects relate to consumption and in which consumption is a primary source of meaning in life (Belk 2007; Berger 2015; Sassatelli 2007; Slater 2015). In a consumer culture, meaning may be found in the goods and services that you buy, in the process of buying them (in shopping malls, cybermalls, and so on), in the social aspects of consumption (shopping with your friends or family), and even in the settings in which consumption takes place (e.g., the Venetian or some other Las Vegas hotel-casino, eBay; Ritzer, Goodman, and Wiedenhoft 2001). There are norms for the consumption process as well. For example, customers should wait patiently in the queue for the cashier, gamblers at a Las Vegas casino should not flaunt their winnings in front of other gamblers and should tip dealers, and so on.

Consumer culture is rather unique in the history of the world. In the past, culture has generally focused on some other aspect of social life, such as religion, warfare, citizenship, or work. In fact, in the not-too-distant past in the United States and other developed countries, the core ideas and material objects of culture related to work and production. People were thought to derive their greatest meaning from their work. This was true from the Industrial Revolution until approximately 1970, when observers began to realize that developed societies, especially the United States, were beginning to derive more meaning from consumption (Baudrillard [1970] 1998). Of course, work continues to be important, as do religion, warfare, and citizenship, but many people in the world now live in a culture dominated by consumption.

The roots of today's consumer culture can be traced further back in history, to when popular settings of consumption, such as large expositions, world's fairs, and department stores, began to arise (Williams [1982] 1991). France in the mid-nineteenth century was particularly important to this development as home of the trendsetting Le Bon Marché department store and several world's fairs, including the first truly international exposition. In these settings, consumption became democratized. It was no longer restricted to the aristocracy and to men. It became popular with the middle class and, as their ability to afford consumption improved, with the working class as well.

It could be said that the rise of consumer culture was linked to the rise of the modern world in the West (Campbell 1987). Today, of course, consumer culture has arguably become *the* culture of the modern West and, indeed, of modernity in general. But consumer culture has also been globalized to a great degree. It has become firmly entrenched in such non-Western places as Singapore, Hong Kong, and Dubai. Japan has been called the premier consumer culture. Even in today's China, known for its production-oriented culture, a billion-plus citizens are becoming more and more consumption oriented. Shanghai is already studded with huge modern shopping malls, and a new Disney theme park opened there in 2016.

CHILDREN IN A CONSUMER CULTURE

The most controversial aspect of consumer culture may be the involvement of children (Sparman 2015). In a consumer culture, it is important that children be socialized into, and become actively involved in, consuming (Cook 2004, 2007; Pilcher 2013). Consumption by children has not always been valued, however. In fact, there were once strong norms against it. Children were not considered to be able to make informed choices about consumption and were therefore seen as even more susceptible than adults to exploitation by advertisers and marketers.

An important change began to take place in the mid-nineteenth century with the advent of department stores. Some stores offered supervised play areas so that parents could shop more easily. A key development by the mid-twentieth century was children's sections in department stores; they were eventually subdivided into shops for babies, children, and teens. Also during this period, radio programs, movies, and TV shows were increasingly directed at children. Disney was a leader in this trend. TV shows of the 1950s, such as the Davy Crockett series (*King of the Wild Frontier*), prompted the sales of hundreds of millions of dollars' worth of simulated coonskin caps and other merchandise for children. More recently, children have come to be targeted directly by advertisers on Saturday-morning TV shows and cable channels such as Nickelodeon that specialize in children's programming.

In fact, marketing aimed at children is now pervasive. For example, the Walt Disney Company directly markets baby products, and thus the Disney brand, to new mothers in maternity wards. In schools, branded products are sold at book fairs, and corporate sponsorships adorn everything from sports stadiums to classroom supplies. Brands and logos are woven into textbook problems and examples. Market researchers observe the way in which children use and respond to products and advertising messages not just in focus groups and in the lab, but also in natural settings such as school and the home. Marketers have also discovered the importance of the "pester power" of children. This is the ability of children to nag their parents into buying things. It is effective not only for selling children's products but also for getting children to influence their parents' purchases.

Overall, children are much more immersed in consumer culture today than ever before. They learn at an early age to value it as well as the norms involved in participating in it. As adults, then, they will fit well into a culture with consumption at its core.

NONTRADITIONAL SETTINGS FOR CONSUMPTION

An interesting aspect of consumer culture is the way in which it has spread beyond the economy to other aspects of society. For example, higher education is increasingly characterized by consumer culture. Students and their parents shop around for the best colleges and the most conspicuous degrees or for the best values in a college education. College rankings, such as those published by *Kiplinger* and *U.S. News & World Report,* are a big business. For-profit colleges have become a booming industry, with enterprises such as the University of Phoenix and Kaplan University enrolling hundreds of thousands of students who pay for the opportunity to earn their degrees on a flexible schedule.

Not long ago, students were largely passive recipients of what educational systems had to offer, but now they are more active consumers of education. For example, college students shop for the best classes, or the best class times, and regularly rate their professors and choose classes on the

Some parents see buying and collecting certain toys, such as the American Girl dolls these girls are holding, as valuable activities. What cultural values are being promoted when young children are encouraged to participate actively in consumer culture?

basis of the professors' ratings. They are also much more likely to make demands for up-to-date "products" and attentive service from their professors and colleges, as they do from shopping malls and salespeople.

A key site of consumption is now the internet (Miller and Slater 2000; Zuev 2015). A good portion of the time people spend online is related to consumption, either directly (by purchasing items on sites such as Etsy or Amazon) or indirectly (by buying things on game sites such as FarmVille2 with real dollars). Among the changes wrought by the internet is a great increase in consumer-to-consumer sales on sites like eBay. In 2000, only 22 percent of Americans had used the internet to buy products online, including books, music, toys, and clothing. By 2013, that number had increased to 80 percent (Weinstein 2013). In 2014, 69 percent of American adults shopped online at least once per month (Mintel 2015). The growing importance of online consumption is reflected in the increasing amount spent each year on "Cyber Monday" (the Monday after Thanksgiving). Cyber Monday 2016 set a new record for online shopping, generating $3.45 billion in sales. In addition, in a process known as "contextual advertising," advertisements are often woven seamlessly into the content of internet sites—even into games designed for children. Beyond that, many websites carry pop-up ads for goods and services targeted to the interests of the individuals who are viewing the sites. More specifically, if you use Google to shop for shoes or Amazon for books, ads for shoes and books will pop up for days, or even months, later on many of the sites you visit.

YouTube offers several innovations in consumption, including "shopping haul" and "unboxing" videos. In shopping haul videos, consumers, often women, show viewers the results of their recent shopping trips. Haulers describe and display clothing, accessories, and cosmetics from popular chain stores (such as Superdry, Bebe, and Victoria's Secret) in malls and shopping strips around the world. Prices and bargains are mentioned frequently. Unboxing videos are a curious hybrid of unofficial marketing and product demonstration. Technology unboxers might demonstrate the features of new iPhones or computer games, while toy unboxers film children playing with various toys. Unboxers might assemble Lego kits, break open Disney *Frozen*-themed chocolate eggs, or open up McDonald's Happy Meals and then have children play with the toys.

It could be argued that people in general, and especially children and teens, are becoming more immersed in consumer culture as they become more deeply enmeshed with the internet. This is even more the case now because we increasingly carry the internet—and the ability to shop there—with us all the time on our smartphones. As a result, consumer culture has become an even more inescapable part of our daily lives. Furthermore, consumption on the internet is increasingly wedded to the material world. You can pay for parking and rental cars using smartphone apps. An iPhone app allows a driver to open the doors of her rented Zipcar with her phone and honk its horn to locate it. The Hunt is an app that brings into play a community of fashion-minded people to help us hunt down desired fashion items.

ASK YOURSELF

How much of the time that you spend online is devoted to shopping or purchasing? Try keeping a log of your internet use for a few days. Note how many times you went online and on how many of those occasions you bought something or browsed sites devoted to consumption. Are you a typical internet consumer? Why or why not?

A POSTCONSUMER CULTURE?

Technically the Great Recession lasted from late 2007 to mid-2009, but its economic effects are still being felt. In the United States, the employment situation has improved, but pay for the middle and lower classes remains stagnant (Appelbaum 2014). In some areas the housing market remains weak at least in part because of the continued existence of homes in foreclosure. The stock market has rebounded, even reached record highs, but there is great concern that its success is inconsistent with fundamental weaknesses that remain in the economy. The depth and persistence of these effects has caused observers to question many things about the economy, including the durability of consumer culture. The latter, after all, has a history of perhaps a half century, although some elements, such as the department store, go further back. The world existed for a long time without a consumer culture, or at least one as excessive as ours has become. It could do so again.

Thus, the recession has caused us to think about the possibility of a *postconsumer* culture. During the depths of the recession many consumers lost their ability and desire to consume, at least for a time. They continue to have many reasons to spend carefully ("How America Shops Now" 2014). These include unemployment and lower income, a decline in the value of retirement funds and of homes, and, most generally, a fear, almost irrespective of the individual's economic situation, that another recession is never far away. But there's more to it than lack of money: Consumers, even those who are well-off, are described as "more socially conscious and embarrassed by flashy shows of wealth"

(Bannon and Davis 2009). As a result, consumption centers throughout the world—Atlantic City, Las Vegas, Dubai, Macau—have been hurting. At least some consumption settings (especially shopping malls) have gone bankrupt or are facing bankruptcy.

Many people are also doing something that would have been unthinkable only a few years ago—saving money. The personal savings rate in the United States has changed over the past few years. In late 2007 it dipped to close to 3 percent of disposable income. At the height of the Great Recession in 2008 and 2009, it spiked to more than 8 percent. By mid-2015, even though the economy had improved considerably, the personal savings rate still exceeded 5 percent. People who are saving more of their money are obviously using less of it to consume.

These changes in the behavior of consumers and their attitudes speak to a change in the larger value system. Consuming less is a sure indication of at least a temporary decline of consumer culture. It may even be the beginning of a postconsumer culture. Among the characteristics of such a culture, beyond buying less and saving more, are sharing more things in the "sharing economy" (Belk 2014; Sundararajan 2016), renting consumer items (such as dresses on sites like Rent the Runway, www.renttherunway.com), taking pride in buying less expensive or even recycled items, buying less showy brands (a Kia rather than a BMW), dining at home more often than eating at restaurants, and showing a greater concern for the environment in terms of what we buy and, more important, do not buy. It is not clear that we are in a postconsumer culture, and if we are, it is uncertain how long it will last. However, just as we entered what is best described as a consumer culture in the last half of the twentieth century, it is at least possible that we are entering a postconsumer culture in the first half of the twenty-first century.

CULTURE JAMMING

Another chink in consumer culture has been created by organized groups actively seeking to subvert aspects of both consumer culture and the larger culture. The success of Burning Man is one indication of such subversion. Begun in 1986, this annual weeklong event in Nevada's Black Rock Desert today attracts 50,000 participants, who commit themselves during their stay to self-expression, decommodification (for example, cash transactions between participants are banned), and community building (Chen 2009; Jones 2011). This is an example of **culture jamming**, which radically transforms mass media messages, often turning them on their heads completely (Kuehn 2015; Lasn 2000). It is a form of social protest aimed at revealing underlying realities of which consumers may be unaware. The hope is that once people are made aware of these realities through culture jamming, they will change their behaviors or perhaps even band together to change those underlying realities.

The best examples of culture jamming are to be found in the magazine *Adbusters* and the media campaigns it sponsors. The magazine's main targets are in the realm of consumption, especially web and magazine advertisements and billboards. The idea is to transform a corporation's ads into anticorporate, anticonsumption advertisements (Handelman and Kozinets 2007).

The following are some additional examples of the ways in which culture jamming turns commercial messages inside out:

- "Tommy Sheep" is a spoof of a Tommy Hilfiger ad, with sheep (presumably representing the conformists who buy such clothing) pictured in front of a huge American flag.

- "Absolute on Ice," spoofing an Absolut vodka ad, depicts the foot of a corpse (presumably someone killed by excessive alcohol consumption) with a toe tag.

- "True Colors of Benetton" depicts a man wearing a Benetton shirt but with wads of money stuffed in his mouth. The ad is designed to underscore the true objective of Benetton, and of all corporations in capitalist society: money and profits.

- "Joe Chemo"—rather than Joe Camel—shows an emaciated version of the Camel character (who, of course, smokes Camel cigarettes) in a hospital bed undergoing chemotherapy, presumably for lung cancer caused by smoking.

- People for the Ethical Treatment of Animals (PETA) used the Burger King logo with the phrase "Murder King" to raise awareness of animal brutality in the beef industry.

All the above show the hidden realities (sickness, death, and other miseries) and goals (conformist consumers, obscene profits) of corporations. A broader objective is to show viewers the folly of consumer culture, which encourages the consumption of numerous harmful substances (e.g., cigarettes, alcohol) and wasteful goods and services (e.g., expensive clothing). In addition to advertisements, culture jammers create memes to spread ideas and information that challenge the status quo (Lasn 2012). For example, one meme designed by culture jammers depicts a photo of Walmart with the following words: "One of the biggest companies in the world owned by one of

"Absolut Impotence" is an example of culture jamming intended to counter the alcohol industry's influence by suggesting that alcohol will negatively impact drinkers' sex lives. Is this an effective way to change consumption?

the richest families in America . . . holds food drive for needy employees instead of paying them a living wage" (CursedByTheDiceGods 2017).

CYBERCULTURE

The internet is, as mentioned before, one site for the proliferation of consumer culture and perhaps postconsumer culture. It is also the site of an entirely new culture— **cyberculture** (F. Turner 2008). That is, the internet as a whole (as well as the individual websites that it comprises) has the characteristics of all culture, including distinctive values and norms.

Some of the distinctive values within cyberculture are openness, knowledge sharing, and access. These values have their roots in the open-source software that emerged before computing became an attractive commercial opportunity. They are also rooted in the knowledge sharing and continuous improvement that were the practice when early computer professionals survived through reciprocity (Bergquist 2003). These roots have been

maintained through the open-source movement, through actions against censorship, and through organizations such as the Free Software Foundation and the "copyleft" movement. In line with the values of a postconsumer society, these "cyber-libertarians" favor user control of information and applications and free products (Dahlberg 2010; Himanen 2001). They are in conflict with the more dominant values of profit maximization and control of the internet by large corporations. This conflict of values, a culture war by the definition offered earlier in this chapter, goes a long way toward defining the internet today.

Various norms have also come to be a part of cyberculture. Internet users are not supposed to hack into websites, create and disseminate spam, unleash destructive worms and viruses, maliciously and erroneously edit user-generated sites such as Wikipedia, and so on. Many norms relate to desirable behavior on the internet. For example, creating and editing entries on Wikipedia is supposed to be taken seriously and done to the best of one's ability. Once an entry exists, the many people who offer additions and deletions are expected to do so in a similar spirit. Those who purposely add erroneous information on Wikipedia will suffer the stern disapproval of other contributors to, and users of, the site. They may even be banned from the site by those who manage it.

There is, of course, much more to the culture of the internet. For example, in addition to a general cyberculture, there are a number of cybercultures that vary from nation to nation. But the point is that cyberculture, like all culture, is emerging and evolving as other changes take place within and around it. The biggest difference between cyberculture and other cultures is that, because the internet is so new and the changes in it are so rapid, cyberculture is far more fluid than culture is in general.

People need to be socialized in order to learn how to use the internet, and they increasingly interact online rather than on a face-to-face basis. In Chapter 5 we turn to a broad discussion of the sociological perspective on socialization and interaction.

✔ CHECKPOINT 4.5: EMERGING ISSUES IN CULTURE

TYPE OF CULTURE	EMERGING ISSUES
Consumer culture	Conspicuous consumption, marketing to children, nontraditional settings for consumption, postconsumer culture, culture jamming
Cyberculture	Openness, sharing, access

Netiquette

Social media websites are developing faster than the norms that can help guide and regulate the behavior of their users (McLaughlin and Vitak 2011:300). Online etiquette, or netiquette, tends to be implicit—there are few if any formal rules on how to use Snapchat or Instagram. Norms for these sites often emerge when users directly sanction the behavior of each other and content that they feel is inappropriate. They may flag a sexually explicit photograph or hide a person from their Facebook feed who posts too many status updates. Our understanding and practice of online norms typically reflect the habits of our close friends, whom we are more likely than acquaintances to confront with norm violations. For example, if our friends are discrete about the photos they post of us, then we will likely reproduce this norm of being considerate when we post photos that include them (McLaughlin and Vitak 2011). Reciprocity, or sharing, is one of the most important norms currently guiding online behavior. Adherence to these norms allow us to build trust and gain access to information (Palfrey and Gasser 2008, 25).

Netiquette can be complicated, considering the diversity of our online audience—what might be appropriate for our close friends to read or see might not be acceptable to our teachers or bosses. Furthermore, some sites might encourage people to behave in ways online that might not be acceptable in the real world. Snapchat can automatically delete photos, which might encourage users to post inappropriate or unflattering pictures of themselves or their friends. The legality of such practices has become an issue with teenagers when they send sexual images of themselves to each other. In some states this is considered to be the distribution of child pornography. Likewise, the anonymity of Yik Yak can prompt users to post racist or sexist comments without fear of being held accountable. These same users might never make such derogatory statements when they interact in face-to-face conversations. In addition, cyberbullying occurs on a variety of social media sites, such as Tumblr, Twitter, and Facebook, prompting some people to question whether these digital means of communication are making cruelty more normative (Boyd 2014).

Engaging the Digital World

Select one social media site and list five norms that are regulating, or you think should be used to regulate, the behavior of the site's users. Explain what you think should happen if a user violates each of these norms. Are there any behaviors that are so extreme that they should result in the user's being denied access to the site? Have you ever tried to directly sanction the behavior of someone on a social media site? If yes, what norm did this person violate, and how did he or she respond to your sanction?

SUMMARY

Culture encompasses the ideas, values, norms, practices, and objects that allow a group of people, or even an entire society, to carry out their collective lives with a minimum of friction. Values are the general, abstract standards defining what a group or society as a whole considers to be good, right, or important. Norms are the rules that guide what people do and how they live. Culture has material and symbolic elements. Material culture encompasses all the objects and technologies that are manifestations of a culture. Symbolic culture, the nonmaterial side of culture, is best represented by language.

We are surrounded by cultural differences. Subcultures include people who may accept much of the dominant culture but are set apart from it by one or more culturally significant characteristics. Countercultures are groups of people who differ in certain ways from the dominant culture and whose norms and values may be incompatible with it. Culture wars pit one subculture or counterculture against another or against the dominant culture.

Many societies tend to be ethnocentric—those living in them believe that their own culture's norms, values, and traditions are better than those of other cultures. In many cases, newcomers are expected to assimilate, or to replace elements of their own culture with elements of the dominant culture. Groups that do not want to assimilate entirely may engage in identity politics, or try to use their power to strengthen the position of the cultural groups with which they identify. A society that values multiculturalism accepts and even embraces the cultures of many different groups and encourages cultural diversity. Multicultural societies often embrace cultural relativism, or the belief that there are no cultural universals.

Some scholars argue that globalization has increasingly led to a global culture of shared norms and values. Others attribute the growing cultural similarity around the world to cultural imperialism, or the imposition of one dominant culture on other cultures. American culture in particular has been exported around the world. Bu, some countries have challenged this process of Americanization with anti-American sentiment and emphasis on their own culture.

Emerging cultural issues today include the growth and significance of consumer culture and cyberculture in our daily lives.

KEY TERMS

Americanization, 103
anti-Americanism, 103
assimilation, 98
consumer culture, 104
countercultures, 95
cultural imperialism, 103
cultural relativism, 102

culture, 86
culture jamming, 107
culture war, 97
cyberculture, 108
ethnocentrism, 102
folkways, 90
ideal culture, 93

identity politics, 101
language, 91
laws, 89
material culture, 91
mores, 90
multiculturalism, 97
norms, 89

real culture, 93
sanctions, 89
subcultures, 95
symbolic culture, 91
values, 88

REVIEW QUESTIONS

1. What do you and your peers think of the millennial culture depicted in HBO's *Girls?* Are you as "uncool" as the characters on that show? You are likely the right age to be considered a millennial, but do you feel that you are part of that culture?

2. How and why might the American value of democracy have created tensions in Iraq and Afghanistan?

3. As part of our material culture, what values do smartphones reflect? In what ways have "brand communities" or other subcultures formed around smartphones and the use of smartphones?

4. Consider the terminology that has developed around the internet. How does this language reflect changes in the world around us? In what ways does it shape the world around us?

5. Skateboarders constitute a subculture because they have certain cultural differences (in language, dress, values) that set them apart from other groups in society. What is another example of a subculture in the United States, and what elements of this culture (both material and symbolic) make it unique?

6. How does a counterculture differ from a subculture? Is it reasonable to say that computer hackers are part of

a counterculture? Can you think of other examples of countercultures?

7. What is the difference between assimilation and multiculturalism? Would you say that the United States is an assimilationist or a multiculturalist society? Would you say that multiculturalism is more a part of the ideal culture or the real culture of the United States? Why?

8. What are some of today's important culture wars? In what ways and to what degree are you engaged in them? Even if you are not active in them, how is your life affected by them?

9. What do we mean by the term *global culture?* Do you think the evolution of popular social networking sites such as Facebook and Twitter is related more to the evolution of a global culture or to Americanization? In what ways are these sites reflective of cultural hybridization?

10. To what extent are you and your friends embedded in a consumer culture? How has the development of technology (the internet, smartphones, and so forth) helped create this consumer culture?

PRACTICE AND APPLY WHAT YOU'VE LEARNED

▶ edge.sagepub.com/ritzerintro4e

CHECK YOUR COMPREHENSION ON THE STUDY SITE WITH:

- **Diagnostic pre-tests** to identify opportunities for improvement.

- **Personalized study plans** with focused recommendations to address specific knowledge gaps and additional learning needs.

- **Post-tests** to check your progress and ensure mastery of key learning objectives.

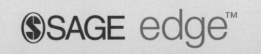

SOCIALIZATION AND INTERACTION

Socialization and Variance

Mack Beggs won his weight class in the Texas state wrestling championships in February 2017—in the girls' league. Mack is a 17-year-old transgender boy, but state rules bar him from competing in the boys' league. The rules say that boys cannot compete against girls, and that students are required to compete as the gender noted on their birth certificate. After Beggs' final competition in an undefeated season, the crowd erupted in both cheers and boos.

Beggs, who began transitioning a year and a half prior to the championship, has been taking testosterone as part of that process. Some felt that he shouldn't have been competing against girls, because the added testosterone gave him an unfair advantage. A few parents even attempted legal injunctions to prevent Beggs from competing. Ignoring the controversy, Beggs credited his success to his teammates, noting that they all worked hard together. While the public, schools, and politicians debate the fluidity of gender, transgender students like Beggs face pressure to fit in with the social expectations of their peers, their families, and the wider world—and the repercussions when they don't.

The majority of transgender students from kindergarten through twelfth grade who are out or perceived as transgender while in school experience some form of mistreatment. In 2015, 54 percent acknowledged being verbally harassed, 24 percent said they had been physically attacked, and 13 percent were sexually assaulted because they were transgender. Some (17 percent) experienced such severe treatment that they left school (James et al. 2016). Such mistreatment due to gender identity or expression is not restricted to peers and schools, but may also pervade family and work life. Transgender people have an attempted suicide rate *nine times* that of the general U.S. population.

LEARNING OBJECTIVES

5.1 Describe the development of the self.

5.2 Discuss the concept of the individual as performer.

5.3 Explain the significance of socialization in childhood and adulthood.

5.4 Describe the key aspects of interaction with others.

5.5 Identify micro-level social structures.

edge.sagepub.com/ritzerintro4e

- Take the chapter quiz
- Review key terms with eFlashcards
- Explore multimedia links and SAGE readings

$SAGE edge™

Yet despite sometimes violent disapproval from the dominant society, many transgender people continue to express their gender identity. Research suggests a biological basis for transgender identity. At the same time, behavior and experiences are as influential as biology is. You are who you are because of the people, institutions, and social structures that have surrounded you since birth (and that have been in play even before then). You have been socialized to look, think, act, and interact in ways that allow you to live harmoniously, at least most of the time, with those around you. However, at times you may come into contact with those who socialize you into ways that are at variance with the dominant culture. In extreme cases, such socialization can lead to actions such as those taken by abusers of transgender people. Discovering how socialization and social interaction shape who we are and how we act, as we will do in this chapter, is the most basic level of sociological analysis. But, in fact, sociologists are concerned with everything along the **micro-macro continuum**, which was introduced in Chapter 1. That includes the individual's mind and self, interactions among individuals, and interactions within and between groups, formally structured organizations, entire societies, and the world as a whole, as well as all the new global relationships of the "global age."

Sociology's micro-macro continuum means that rather than being clearly distinct, social phenomena tend to blend into one another, often without our noticing. For example, the interaction that takes place in a group is difficult to distinguish from the group itself. The relationships between countries are difficult to distinguish from their regional and even global connections. Everything in the social world, and on the micro-macro continuum, interpenetrates. ●

This chapter and the next will introduce you, at least briefly, to the full range of sociological concerns along the micro–macro continuum. We will start with the smallest-scale social phenomena and work our way to ever larger ones as these two chapters progress.

THE INDIVIDUAL AND THE SELF

Sociologists rarely, if ever, concern themselves with any particular individual. Rather, their concern is with individuals in general. A primary sociological question is what, if anything, distinguishes humans as individuals from other animals. Some would argue it stems from characteristics such as a larger brain or an opposable thumb. However, most sociologists believe the essential difference between humans and other animals is the distinctive interaction humans are capable of having with other humans.

An important source of this view is data about individuals who grew up in social isolation and did not experience normal human interaction during their development. For instance, we have information on cases in which children have been locked in closets or in single rooms for much or all of their childhoods (Curtiss 1977; Davis 1940, 1947). In a more recent example, five children, ages 2 through 13, were discovered by authorities in York, Pennsylvania. They had lived their entire lives with their parents in a single room in a private home without any functioning utilities; their water source was rain dripping through the roof. The children had no birth certificates and had received no formal schooling, and there was no evidence that they had ever received any medical care, including vaccinations. They suffered from physical and mental health problems and were not where they should have been in terms of educational level ("Police Discover Five Children" 2010).

Of related interest is the existence of feral, or wild, children—that is, children who have been raised by animals in the wilderness (Benzaquen 2006; Dombrowski, Gischlar, and Mrazik 2011; Friedmann and Rusou 2015; Newton 2002). Oxana Malaya is from a small village in Ukraine (Grice 2006). In 1986, after being abandoned by her parents at age three, she crawled into a hovel that housed dogs. The "Dog Girl" lived there for five years before a neighbor reported her existence. When she emerged, she could hardly speak. Like the dogs she lived with, she barked, ate with her tongue, and ran about on all fours. Years later, when she was living in a home for the mentally disabled, Oxana was found to have the mental capacity of a six-year-old. Among other things, she could not spell her name or read. She was able to communicate like other humans and talk because she had acquired some speech before she began living with dogs. She had also learned to eat with her hands and to walk upright (Lane 1975; Shattuck 1980).

Oxana has done better than other feral children have (Lane 1975; Shattuck 1980). Long after another little feral girl was discovered, efforts to socialize her had been only minimally successful. For example, she persisted in spitting and blowing her nose near and on other people (Curtiss 1977). Feral children are generally unable to talk or to show much in the way of human emotion. Oxana, in contrast, has had boyfriends, although it is doubtful she has the emotional ability to develop long-term relationships. The overall conclusion from the literature on feral children and those raised in isolation is that people do not become human, or at least fully human, unless they are able to interact with other people, especially at an early age.

The concept of feral children relates to the fundamental question of the relationship between nature and nurture. The "nature" argument is that we are born to be the kinds of human beings that we ultimately become; it is built into our "human nature" (Settle et al. 2010). The "nurture" argument is that we are human beings because of the way we are nurtured—that is, the way we are raised by other human beings, who teach us what it is to be human. Of course, both nature and nurture are important (Meloni 2014). However, the cases of feral children indicate that nurture is in many ways more important than nature in determining the human beings we become.

SYMBOLIC INTERACTION AND DEVELOPMENT OF THE SELF

As the example of feral and isolated children suggests, development as a human presupposes the existence of other humans and interaction with and among them. This brings us into the domain of symbolic interactionism, which developed many ideas of great relevance to this view of humans. In general, the interaction that takes place between parents and children is loaded with symbols and symbolic meaning.

One early symbolic interactionist, Charles Horton Cooley (1864–1929), explained how parents help children develop the ability to interact with others with his famous concept of the **looking-glass self**. This is the idea that as humans we develop a self-image that reflects how others see and respond to us. We imagine how we appear to others and how they evaluate our appearance. Based on that, we develop some sort of self-feeling, such as pride or embarrassment. Because children's earliest interactions are typically with their parents, it is that interaction that is most important in the formation of a self-image. This helps explain why feral children and others who spend their formative years in prolonged social isolation are unlikely to form a fully developed self-image: There are no others to respond to them. It is as we interact with others, especially when we are young, that we develop a sense of our selves.

The major thinker associated with symbolic interactionism (see Chapter 2) is one of Cooley's contemporaries, George Herbert Mead (186–1931). Mead ([1934] 1962) was very concerned with the micro level (the individual, the mind, the self). He prioritized the social relationship, including interaction, and the importance of symbols in social interaction. In fact, it is this prioritization of the social that distinguishes sociologists from psychologists in their studies of individuals and interaction. We will examine some of Mead's more general ideas before turning to his thinking on development, especially development of the self.

Humans and Nonhumans

Mead distinguished between humans and nonhumans. However, both are capable of making gestures (e.g., by raising a limb). By **gestures**, Mead meant the movements

George Herbert Mead's ideas strongly influenced the development of sociological theory, especially symbolic interactionism. His most famous work, *Mind, Self, and Society,* originated as lectures from his teachings at the University of Chicago.

of one individual that elicit automatic and appropriate responses from another individual.

Both animals and humans are capable of not only gestures but also *conversations of gestures,* whereby they use a series of gestures to relate to one another. Thus, the snarl of one dog may lead a second dog to snarl in return. That second snarl might lead the first dog to become physically ready to attack or be attacked. In terms of humans, Mead gave the example of a boxing match, where the cocking of one boxer's arm may cause the other boxer to raise an arm to block the anticipated blow. That raised arm might cause the first boxer to throw a different punch or even to hold back on the punch. A less aggressive example can be found in the realm of flirting (Delaney 2012; Henningsen 2004), where one person's prolonged eye contact (a subtle gesture) may cause another person to return the eye contact. The returned gaze might cause the first flirter to look away and, perhaps, quickly glance again at the other person. As in the case of animals, the gestures of boxers and those who flirt (among many others) are instantaneous and involve few, if any, conscious thought processes.

In addition to physical gestures, animals and humans are both capable of vocal gestures. The bark of a dog and the grunt of a human (boxer) are both vocal gestures. In both cases, a conversation of vocal gestures is possible, as the bark of one dog (or the grunt of a boxer) elicits the bark (or grunt) of another. However, when humans (and animals) make facial gestures (such as originating eye contact in an effort to flirt), they cannot *see* their own facial gestures. In contrast, both animals and humans can *hear* their own vocal gestures. As a result, misunderstanding is more likely when people rely on facial rather than vocal gestures. For example, men may be more likely than women to interpret making eye contact as sexual in nature.

ASK YOURSELF

In what ways do you interact with your pets in the same way you interact with humans? In what ways is the interaction different? Do you find it more satisfying to interact with people or with pets?

It is the vocal gesture that truly begins to separate humans from animals. In humans, but not other animals, the vocal gesture can affect the speaker as much and in the same way it does as the hearer. Thus, humans react to and interpret their own vocal gestures and, more important, their words. Furthermore, humans have a far greater ability to control their vocal gestures. We can stop ourselves from uttering sounds or saying various things, and we can alter what we say as we are saying it. Animals do not possess this capacity. In short, only humans are able to develop a language out of vocal gestures; animals remain restricted to isolated vocal gestures.

Many sociologists have come to reject the clear distinction between the abilities of animals and those of humans (Greenebaum and Sanders, forthcoming). For example, some sociological work has examined symbolic interaction between humans and animals (Alger and Alger 1997; Irvine 2004).

Symbolic Interaction

Of greatest importance in distinguishing humans from animals is a kind of gesture that can be made *only* by humans. Mead calls such a gesture a **significant symbol**, a gesture that arouses in the individual making it a response of the same kind as the one it is supposed to elicit from those to whom it is addressed. It is only with significant symbols, especially those that are vocal, that we can have communication in the full sense of the term. In Mead's view—although more and more research on animals tends to contradict it (Gerhardt and Huber 2002; Gillespie-Lynch et al. 2013)—ants, bees, dogs, and apes are unable to communicate by means of such symbols.

Over time, humans develop a set of vocal significant symbols, or language. According to Mead, language involves significant symbols that call out the same meaning in the person to whom an utterance is aimed as they do in the person making the utterance. The utterances have meaning to all parties involved. In a conversation of gestures, only the gestures are communicated. With language,

both the (vocal) gestures and the meanings are communicated. One of the key functions of language is that it makes the mind and mental processes possible. To Mead, thinking (and the mind; see the following section) is nothing more than internalized conversations individual humans have with themselves. Thinking involves talking to oneself. It is little different from talking to other people.

Symbols also make possible **symbolic interaction**, or interaction on the basis of significant symbols. This also allows for much more complex interaction patterns than those that occur where interaction is based only on gestures. Because people can think about and interpret significant symbols, they can interact with large numbers of people and make complex plans for future undertakings. They can interpret the symbolic meaning of what others say and do and understand, for example, that some of them are acting in accord with their own plans. Animals lack the ability to make and understand complex plans.

ASK YOURSELF

What did George Herbert Mead mean by saying that thinking is so much like talking to yourself that it is little different from talking to other people? Do you agree with him? Why or why not? Think of some examples and counterexamples.

However, since Mead's day, a great deal of research has demonstrated that many animals, especially primates, are able to think (Young and Thompson 2013). That is, they can plan and calculate, in at least a rudimentary way (Ristau 1983; Schmitt and Fischer 2009). For instance, scrub jays engage in planning behavior to store away diverse caches of food that they will not eat until the following morning (Raby et al. 2007). Meerkats, which often prey on poisonous animals, teach their young how to deal with these potentially dangerous food sources by disabling the prey they present to young meerkats (Thornton and McAuliffe 2006). Chimpanzees demonstrate deceptive behavior when it helps them access foods they like (Woodruff and Premack 1979). Most of this research suggests that while animals think, human thought is much more complex (Premack 2007).

Mind and Self

Central to Mead's ideas about the development of human beings, and the differences between humans and nonhumans, are the concepts of mind and self. As pointed out previously, the **mind** is an internal conversation using words (and also images, especially, but certainly not only, for the autistic and the deaf; Fernyhough 2014; Grandin 2000). That internal conversation arises, is related to, and is continuous with interactions, especially conversations that one has with others in the social world. Thus, the social world and its relationships and interactions precede the mind and not vice versa. This perspective stands in contrast to the conventional view that prioritizes the brain and argues that we think first and then engage in social relationships. It also differs from the view that the mind and the brain are one and the same thing. The brain is a physiological organ that exists within us, but the mind is a social phenomenon. It is part of, and would not exist without, the social world. While the brain is an intracranial phenomenon, the mind is not.

The **self** is the ability to take oneself as an object. The self develops over time. Key to the development of self is the ability to imagine being in the place of others and looking at oneself as they do. In other words, people need to take the role of others in order to get a sense of their own selves. There are two key stages in Mead's theory of how the self develops over time, the **play stage** and the **game stage**:

1. *Play stage.* Babies are not born with the ability to think of themselves as having a self. However, as they develop, children learn to take on the attitudes of specific others toward themselves. Thus, young children play at being Mommy and Daddy, adopt Mommy's and Daddy's attitudes toward the child, and evaluate themselves as do Mommy and Daddy. However, the result is a very fragmented sense of the self. It varies depending on the specific other (e.g., Mommy *or* Daddy) being taken into consideration. Young children lack a more general and organized sense of themselves.

2. *Game stage.* Children begin to develop a self in the full sense of the term when they take on the roles of a group of people simultaneously rather than the roles of discrete individuals. Each of those different roles comes to be seen as having a definite relationship to all the others. Children develop organized personalities because of their ability to take on multiple roles—indeed, the entirety of roles in a given group. The developed personality does not vary with the individual role (Mommy, Daddy) that a child happens to be taking. This development allows children to function in organized groups. Most important, it greatly affects what they will do within specific groups.

Mead offers the example of a baseball game (or what he calls "ball nine") to illustrate his point about the game stage of development. It is not enough in a baseball game for you to know what you are supposed to do in your position on the field. In order to play your position, you must know what those who play all other eight positions on the team are going to do. In other words, a player, every player, must take on the roles of all the other players. A player need not have all of those roles in mind all of the time; three or four of them will suffice on most occasions.

In Mead's game stage of the development of the self, we learn how to work with others by understanding their roles as well as our own. Do you think this learning process is ever complete?

For example, a shortstop must know that the center fielder is going to catch a particular fly ball; that he is going to be backed up by the left fielder; that because the runner on second is going to "tag up," the center fielder is going to throw the ball to third base; and that it is his job as shortstop to back up the third baseman. This ability to take on multiple roles obviously applies in a baseball game, but it applies as well in a playgroup, a work setting, and every other social setting.

In a different example, from the college classroom, students are often asked to work together on group class presentations. Each student not only will have to prepare his or her part of the project and presentation but also will need to know and coordinate with what each of the other presenters, as well as the group as a whole, will do. He or she might have to know the content of each presentation and the sequence of presentations, along with the time allotted to each. Such group work resembles that of Mead's baseball team, where all members have to be familiar with and know the roles of all the others involved to be successful as a group. This is, in essence, what children learn in the game stage, and they continue to implement and practice this ability throughout their lives.

The Generalized Other

Mead also developed the concept of the **generalized other**, or the attitude of the entire group or community. The generalized other includes the roles, prescriptions, and proscriptions that individuals use to develop their own behaviors, attitudes, and so forth. Individuals take the role of the generalized other. That is, they look at themselves and what they do from the perspective of the group or community. "What would people think if I . . ." is a question that demonstrates the role of the generalized other.

The generalized other becomes central to the development of self during the game stage. In the classroom example, the generalized other is the attitude of the group working on the collaborative project. In the family, to take still another example, it is the attitude of all family members.

In taking on the perspectives of the generalized other, children begin developing more fully rounded and complete selves. They can view and evaluate themselves from the perspective of a group or community and not merely from the viewpoints of discrete others. To have a coherent self, in the full sense of the term, as an adult one must become a member of a group or community. An adult must also be sensitive to the attitudes common to the community.

Having members who can take the role of the generalized other is also essential to the development of the group, especially in its organized activities. The group can function more effectively and efficiently because it is highly likely that individual members will understand and do what is expected of them. In turn, individuals can operate more efficiently within the group because they can better anticipate what others will do.

This discussion might lead you to think that the demands of the generalized other produce conformists. However, Mead argues that while selves within a group share some commonalities, each self is different because each has a unique biographical history and experience. Furthermore, there are many groups and communities in society and therefore many generalized others. Your generalized other in a baseball game is different from your generalized other in a classroom or in the family.

The "I" and the "Me"

Critical to understanding the difference between conformity and creative thinking and acting is Mead's distinction between two aspects, or phases, of the self—the "I" and the "me." Bear in mind that the "I" and the "me" are not things; they do not exist in a physical sense. We would not find the "I" or the "me" if we dissected the brain. Rather, the "I" and the "me" are subprocesses that are involved in the larger thinking process. An individual sometimes displays more of the "I" aspect of the self and sometimes more of the "me" aspect. In any given instance, the relative mix of "I" and "me" determines the degree to which an individual acts creatively (more "I") or more as a conformist (more "me").

The **"I"** is the immediate response of an individual to others. It is that part of the self that is unconscious, incalculable, unpredictable, and creative. Neither the person nor the members of the group know in advance what that response of the "I" is going to be. A daughter at a holiday dinner does not always know in advance what she is going to say or do, and the same is true of the other family members at the dinner table. That is what makes for frequent squabbles, if not outright battles, on such family occasions. As a result of the "I," people often surprise themselves, and certainly others, with the unexpected things they say and do.

Mead greatly values the "I" for various reasons, including the fact that it is the source of new and original responses. In addition, the "I" allows a person to realize the self fully and to develop a definite, unique personality. The "I" also gives us the capacity to have an impact on the groups and communities in which we live. Moreover, in Mead's view, some individuals, including the great figures in history, have a larger and more powerful "I." They are therefore able to have a greater impact on their groups and communities, as well as on society and even on the globe.

The **"me"** is the organized set of others' attitudes and behaviors adopted by the individual. In other words, the "me" involves the acceptance and internalization by the individual of the generalized other. While your "I" might dispose you to find inventive ways of introducing yourself to an attractive student in this class, your "me" might counter that impulse by reminding you that such socializing in the classroom is considered inappropriate by your social group (the generalized other, in this case). The "me" might lead you, then, to wait for someone to introduce you to that student or to find a way to run into that student outside of class. To Mead, the "me" involves a conscious understanding of what a person's responsibilities are to the larger group. The behaviors associated with the "me" also tend to be habitual and conventional. We all have a "me," but conformists have an overly powerful "me."

It is through the "me" that society is able to dominate the individual. In fact, Mead defines "social control" as the dominance of the "I" by the "me." Through the "me," individuals control themselves with little or no need for control by outside influences. In the "me" phase, however, individuals analyze and critique their own thoughts and actions from the point of view of the social group and what its criticisms are likely to be. Thus, in most cases, the group need not criticize individuals; they do it themselves. In other words, self-criticism is often, in reality, criticism by the larger society.

Nevertheless, people and society as a whole need both "I" and "me." For the individual, the "me" allows for a comfortable existence within various social groupings. The "I" lends some spice to what might otherwise be a boring existence. For society, the "me" provides the conformity needed for stable and orderly interaction. The "I" is the source of changes in society as it develops and adapts to the shifting environment.

The "I" and "Me" in Consumer Society

While the "me" generally provides the individual with some comfort and security, that is less the case in consumer society (Trentmann 2016). The reason is that consumer society is all about change, and as a result the "me" is constantly changing. For example, one might be expected to adopt a given fashion at one time, but soon an entirely different fashion comes to be expected. Instead of attaining stability, "consumers must never be allowed to rest" (Bauman 1999, 38). Of course, the "I" always impels the individual in unpredictable directions, such as making unusual fashion statements. However, in consumer society *both* the "I" and the "me" are at least somewhat unpredictable. This serves to make many people uneasy because they lack, at least as far as fashion is concerned, the comfort of a strong and stable "me."

While it is generally the case that consumer society is not conducive to a stable "me," the level of unpredictability is very much related to the individual's position in the stratification system. It is those in the middle class who are likely to experience the most instability. As rapidly as they change, they are led to desire many more changes than they can afford to make. This is particularly true for females because the costs of being in style, especially for clothing, are much greater for them than they are for males. The upper class is also confronted with a rapidly changing world of consumption, but those in that class can afford to change whenever it seems necessary. The lower class can afford little, with the result that those in it are unable to change what they consume to any great degree. However, the lower class experiences the uneasiness associated with not being able to keep up with changing demands of the "me."

CHECKPOINT 5.1: CONCEPTS OF THE INDIVIDUAL AND THE SELF

CONCEPT	EXPLANATION
The looking-glass self	The idea that an individual develops a self-image that reflects the way in which others respond to him or her
The mind	An internal conversation that arises from, is related to, and is continuous with social interactions
The self	The sense of oneself as an object
The generalized other	The attitude of the entire group or community that an individual internalizes
The "I"	An individual's immediate response to others
The "me"	The organized set of others' attitudes that an individual assumes

THE INDIVIDUAL AS PERFORMER

Erving Goffman (1922–1982) is another important contributor to the symbolic interactionists' understanding of the self and how it develops (Jacobsen and Kristiansen 2015). Goffman's work on the self was deeply influenced by Mead's thinking, especially the tension between the "I" and the "me." In Goffman's work, this distinction takes the form of the tension between what we want to do spontaneously and what people expect us to do (Goffman 1959).

Goffman developed the notion of **dramaturgy**, which views an individual's social life as a series of dramatic performances akin to those that take place on a theatrical stage. To Goffman, the self is not a thing possessed by the individual but the dramatic product of the interaction between people and their audiences (Manning 2007). While many performances of the self are successful, there is always the possibility that performances can be disrupted by the actions of audiences. For example, audiences can jeer at performances or even walk out on them. Goffman focuses on these possibilities and what people can do to prevent them by improving their dramatic performances or to deal with disruptions once they occur.

IMPRESSION MANAGEMENT

When people interact with others, they use a variety of techniques to control the images of themselves that they want to project during their social performances. They seek to maintain these impressions even when they encounter problems in their performances (Manning 2005). Goffman (1959) called these efforts to maintain certain images **impression management**.

For example, in your sociology class you might typically project an image of a serious, well-prepared student. Then one night you might stay up late partying and not get the required reading done before class. When the instructor asks a question in class, you might try to maintain your image by pretending to write busily in your notebook rather than raising your hand. Called on nonetheless, you struggle, in vain, to give a well-thought-out, serious answer to the question. The smiles and snickers of fellow students who know that you were out partying late the night before might well disrupt the performance you are endeavoring to put on. To deflect attention from you to them, you might suggest that they try to answer the question.

Impression management relates directly to the plots of many movies. In the world of the 2014 movie *Divergent* (see also the 2015–2017 sequels, *Insurgent*, *Allegiant*, and *Ascendant*), most people live in one of five "factions," while a few are relegated to a sixth group, "the Factionless," which exists at the bottom of the social stratification system. Assignment to a faction is based, at least in part, on a test score, but some test results are inconclusive because the test takers defy categorization; they are "divergent." To conceal their difference, which is generally considered unacceptable in their society, they engage in impression management. While all of us sometimes fail at impression management, the cost of failure to the divergents—death—is much greater than the cost to us in our social world is.

Used by permission of the Pennsylvania Gazette.

One of the most influential sociologists of the twentieth century, Erving Goffman employed qualitative methods, particularly ethnography, in much of his research. One of his main research topics was the sociology of everyday life, or the way in which people manage the impressions they make on others in face-to-face interactions.

However, in some cases—for example, Jews trying to pass as non-Jews in Nazi Germany—failure at impression management can have similarly dire consequences. While the idea of impression management is generally associated with face-to-face social interaction, it also applies to interaction on social networking sites. For instance, many people constantly change the pictures on their Facebook pages to alter the images of themselves being conveyed to others (Cunningham 2013).

ASK YOURSELF

What impression management activities do you undertake? Have they generally been successful? Do you see yourself performing more of these activities as time goes on, or fewer? Why?

FRONT AND BACK STAGE

Continuing the theatrical analogy, Goffman (1959) argued that in every performance there is a **front stage**, where the social performance tends to be idealized and designed to define the situation for those who are observing it. When you are in class, as in the previous example, you are typically performing on your front stage. Your audience is the teacher and perhaps other students. As a rule, people feel they must present an idealized sense of themselves when they are front stage (e.g., by giving that seemingly well-thought-out answer). Because this performance is idealized, things that do not fit the image must be hidden (such as the fact that you were partying the night before and are now unprepared to answer questions intelligently).

Also of concern to Goffman is the back stage. In the **back stage**, people feel free to express themselves in ways that are suppressed in the front (Cahill et al. 1985). Thus, after class you might well confess to your friends in the cafeteria that you had been partying and faked your answer to a question asked in class. If somehow your front-stage audience—the instructor, in this case—sees your back-stage performance, your ability to maintain the impression you are trying to project in the classroom, in the front stage, is likely to become difficult or impossible in the future.

The back stage plays a prominent role in our lives. For every one of our front-stage performances, there are one or more back stages where all sorts of things happen that we do not want to be seen in the front stage. For example, when summer camp is over, counselors are often "friended" by their former campers on Facebook. In order to allow the campers to stay in contact with them through Facebook, counselors might post limited, carefully edited profiles to special Facebook pages. These are, in effect, the counselors' front stages for former campers. However, the counselors might also retain back-stage versions of their Facebook profiles that the ex-campers are unable to see.

The existence of two stages, front and back, causes us all sorts of tensions and problems. We are always afraid that those in the front stage will find out about our back stage, or that elements of the back stage will intrude on the front stage.

These ideas are central to Leslie Picca and Joe Feagin's *Two-Faced Racism: Whites in the Backstage and Frontstage* (2007). The central point of this study of white college students is that what they say and do differs depending on whether they are in their front stage or their back stage. When they are in their back stage with friends and family, as well as with other whites, they often feel free to talk and act in a blatantly racist manner. Examples include telling racist jokes and mocking minority group members. However, when they are in their front stage in a public setting, especially with African Americans present, what they say and do is very different. They may act as if they are blind to a person's color or even be gratuitously polite to African Americans. Thus, while overt racism may have declined in the front stage of public settings, it persists in the back stage (Cabrera 2014; Sallaz 2010).

Alone Together: Why We Expect More from Technology and Less from Each Other

(Basic Books, 2012)

Sherry Turkle (Abby Rockefeller Mauzé Professor of the Social Studies of Science and Technology at Massachusetts Institute of Technology; PhD, Harvard University, 1976)

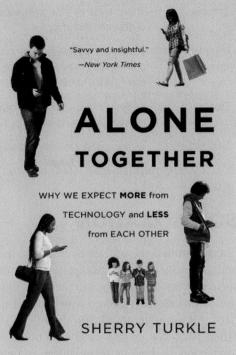

One controversial issue today is whether or not technology is contributing to a decline in meaningful social relationships. Some experts argue that technology can help us build and maintain social networks, but in *Alone Together,* Sherry Turkle offers a critical look at how different technologies are leaving us detached and afraid of face-to-face social interactions. Turkle finds that some people prefer interacting with social robots instead of real humans because they do not have to deal with unpredictable emotions that might make them feel vulnerable—robots love unconditionally, and they never die. These social robots are so technologically sophisticated that they can follow our gaze and even talk to us, making it seem like they can empathize and understand our feelings. Turkle warns that intimacy with machines is no substitute for human intimacy and that machine-human relationships cause us to reduce our expectations of other humans.

When we do engage in social interactions with other humans, many of us often do so using technology, such as smartphones or computers. These machine-mediated exchanges allow us to communicate quickly and conveniently, but not very expressively. While communicating via text, social media, and e-mail can be quite practical, it is also more impersonal and less spontaneous than face-to-face interactions are. For example, announcing a pregnancy on Facebook might be efficient, but it might also be insensitive if a person has not personally told close family members and friends first. New technologies allow us to edit and manage our impressions more than we can during face-to-face interactions, even if we cannot always verify how our messages are interpreted. Our online audience generally does not challenge our performances and most likely confirms our impressions of ourselves by "liking" what we post (if they respond at all). Social media might provide us with thousands of virtual connections; however, most of these are weak ties that require nothing consequential from us. This is why many of us feel alone at the same time that we are digitally connected.

Supplementary Resources

- Turkle explains the key themes of her book *Alone Together* in her TED Talk, "Connected, but Alone?" (www.ted.com/talks/sherry_turkle_alone_together?language=en).
- Turkle elaborates on the social implications of the digital revolution in a *Frontline* interview (www.pbs.org/wgbh/pages/frontline/digitalnation/interviews/turkle.html).

While the distinction between front and back stage is important, bear in mind that these are not "real" places, nor are they rigidly separated from one another. That is, what is the front stage at one point in time can become the back stage at another. Nevertheless, in general, people are most likely to perform in an idealized manner on their front stage when they are most concerned about making positive impressions. They are likely to perform more freely back stage, among those who are more accepting of less-than-ideal behavior and attitudes.

CHECKPOINT 5.2: CONCEPTS OF THE INDIVIDUAL AS PERFORMER

CONCEPT	EXPLANATION
Dramaturgy	The idea that an individual's social life is a series of dramatic performances
Impression management	Techniques individuals use to control the images of themselves they want to project during their social performances
Front stage	An arena where an individual defines the situation for observers
Back stage	An arena where an individual feels free to express him- or herself

SOCIALIZATION

Socialization is the process by which an individual learns and generally comes to accept the ways of a group or a society of which he or she is a part. It is during the socialization process that children develop a self as they learn the need, for example, to take on the role of the generalized other. Socialization almost always involves a process of interaction, as those with knowledge and experience teach those with a need to acquire that knowledge or to learn from others' experiences.

While socialization occurs throughout an individual's lifetime, it can generally be divided into two parts. Socialization during childhood sets the course for a lifetime and has been a central focus for researchers. However, researchers have increasingly pointed to a variety of ways in which adults continue to learn how to function within their society. Perhaps the scholar most responsible for promoting the idea of socialization across the life course was Erik Erikson (1994), who proposed eight stages of socialization, beginning at birth and ending at death, each based on what he described as a fundamental "existential question." For example, the final stage involves addressing the growing awareness of one's mortality and contemplating whether or not one's life has been meaningful and one's major goals have been achieved.

CHILDHOOD SOCIALIZATION

A central concern in the study of socialization is those who do the socializing, or the **agents of socialization** (Wunder 2007). The first and often most effective agents of socialization are the child's parents, as well as other family members and friends. These are defined as *primary agents of socialization*. In addition, broader, less personal influences, such as the educational system, the media

(Prot et al. 2015), and consumer culture, are important in socialization. These are defined as *secondary agents of socialization*. All play a part in creating an individual who can effectively operate within and shape culture. Except for education, which will be discussed in Chapter 13, we will examine each of these various agents of socialization in the following sections.

Primary Socialization and the Family

In a process known as **primary socialization**, newborns, infants, and young children acquire language, identities, cultural routines, norms, and values as they interact with parents and other family members (Laible, Thompson, and Froimson 2015; Lubbers, Jaspers, and Ultee 2009). This socialization lays the foundation for later personality development (Rohlinger 2007). Early socialization performs various functions for society, such as equipping the young to fit better into society and perpetuating the culture from one generation to the next.

In addition to a great deal of primary socialization, parents provide **anticipatory socialization**—that is, they teach children what will be expected of them in the future. Anticipatory socialization is how parents prepare children for the very important developmental changes (puberty, for example) that they will experience. Among the many other things that must be anticipated in family socialization are entrance into grade school, high school, college, the work world, and life as an independent adult. Anticipatory socialization is especially important in societies and in time periods undergoing a great deal of change. Children need to be prepared not only for changes within society but also for changes within the family and changes that will affect them more directly.

Many assumptions about primary and anticipatory socialization are changing dramatically as the nature of families and the way in which they are understood culturally undergo major transformations. The socialization process was thought to be rather straightforward when the ideal of the nuclear family, composed of a mother, a father, and two or more children all living in the same home, predominated, as it did throughout much of the twentieth century. The lesson children were required to learn, at least as far as the family was concerned, was that when they became adults, they would go on to reproduce the same kind of nuclear family as the one in which they grew up. However, assumptions about the goodness and inevitability of the nuclear family and the ease of the socialization process now seem impossible to accept (McLanahan 1999). This is the case because of increasing public awareness of the many problems associated with the nuclear family, such as divorce, abuse, and unhappiness (see Chapter 12).

Then there is the expansion of what were at one time called "alternative family forms" (e.g., single-parent households, grandparents as primary caregivers) and the

The Self in the Global Age

The self is not fixed. It changes over the course of our lives and even on a day-to-day basis, depending on the nature of the impression we want to make on others (Goffman 1959). The self also changes with large-scale transformations in the social world, and no change has been more dramatic than globalization.

Globalization brings with it the increasingly easy movement of all kinds of objects, ideas, and knowledge, as well as of people. This mobility is of great importance in itself (Urry 2007), and also because "the globalization of mobility extends into the core of the self" (Elliott and Urry 2010, 3).

On the positive side, the self can become more open and flexible as a result of all the new experiences associated with the global age. The many brief interactions that happen, for example, online or through travel can lead to a different kind of self, perhaps more oriented to the short-term and the episodic than to that which is long-term or even lifelong.

Of great concern, however, are the negative effects of globalization on the self. At the extreme, Lemert and Elliott (2006) see globalization as "toxic" for the individual, including the self.

Because people are increasingly mobile, they are likely to feel that their selves are either dispersed and adrift in various places in the world or exist even more loosely in global cyberspace. While in the past the self was increasingly likely to be shaped by close personal relationships, it is now more likely to reflect the absence of such relationships and a sense of distance, even disconnection, from others. At the minimum, this can lead to a different kind of self than what existed before the global age. At the maximum, it can lead to one that is weak because it is untethered to anything strong and long-lasting.

A more familiar pathology associated with the global age is being obsessed with digital mobile technologies. For one woman, the experience of being so deeply enmeshed in these technologies "has left the self drained and lifeless" (Elliott and Urry 2010, 41). Most people will not be affected as strongly or as adversely as this. However, globalization and its associated mobility have had a great effect on the self, and that impact is likely to grow exponentially in the future.

Is it possible to be too involved with and dependent on digital technology? What do we gain from our use of digital devices, and what do we lose?

Think About It

Is the self today shaped more by the absence of close personal friendships and a sense of distance from others than by close personal relationships? What might be some of the negative effects of this change, if it is real? How could society counteract them?

---

increasing centrality of day-care centers and their workers to the socialization process (Patterson, Farr, and Hastings 2015). The agencies doing the socializing today are much more complex and varied than they were in the era of the predominance of the nuclear family. As a result, socialization is not as straightforward as it once was thought to be. In addition, it is no longer possible to think of a seamless relationship between the agencies of socialization and the socialization process. For example, the family may be socializing its children in one way, but the day-care center may be doing it very differently.

In addition, at one time socialization was seen as one-directional, for example, from parent to child. Current thinking sees such socialization among intimates as two-directional, even multi-directional, with, for example, parents socializing children and children socializing parents, other adults, and families (Gentina and Muratore 2012). For example, children tend to be far more familiar with the latest advances in digital technology than their elders are, and they teach their parents much about both the technology itself and the digital culture. Another example is found in the large number of immigrant families in the United States and elsewhere. Children in these families are more likely than their parents to learn the language and culture of their new country (often in school). As a result, they are frequently the ones to teach, or at least try to teach, that knowledge to their parents (Mather 2009). This is **reverse socialization**, in which those who are normally being socialized are instead doing the socializing.

ASK YOURSELF

Have you experienced any instances of reverse socialization? For instance, have you taught your parents how to use their smartphones or set up Facebook pages, or has a younger relative or friend introduced you to a new smartphone app? What was this experience like?

Peers

A good deal of socialization within the schools takes place informally, through children's interaction with fellow students (see Chapter 13 for a discussion of the role of schools and teachers in the process of socialization). This is a situation where primary agents of socialization (peers) compete with secondary agents of socialization (teachers and other employees of the school system; Bukowski et al. 2015). Such informal socialization grows increasingly important as students progress through the school years, especially the high school years (Steinberg and Monahan 2007). Peers are also important sources of socialization in contexts outside of school, such as scouting groups and athletic teams of various kinds (Bennett and Fraser 2000; Fine 1987). For example, researchers have found that children involved in contact sports, such as football and wrestling, are socialized to be more physically aggressive in everyday life (Kreager 2007). Male students who participate in contact sports such as football (and their friends) are more likely to get into serious fights than are nonathletic males or males involved in noncontact sports such as baseball, basketball, and tennis.

As the child matures and spends an increasing amount of time in the company of friends, peer socialization is increasingly likely to conflict with what is being taught at home and in the schools. Peer involvement in risky and delinquent behavior exerts an influence that is often at odds with the goals set forth by parents and educators (Gardner and Steinberg 2005; Haynie 2001). In *Living the Drama: Community, Conflict, and Culture among Inner-City Boys*, David Harding (2010) examines the impact of peer relationships on teenage boys growing up in high-poverty neighborhoods with frequent gang activity. Many of the boys he interviewed were geographically limited to small pockets of their neighborhoods out of fear of crossing into rival gang areas. As a result, their peer networks drew heavily on others in their immediate social space, such as a housing project. These networks typically involved older boys and men, in their late teens and early twenties, who socialized younger boys into the ways of the neighborhood. Older peers could provide protection and status within these neighborhoods. They could also, however, provide models for behaviors such as drug dealing, drinking, and smoking marijuana. This sort of socialization can challenge messages from parents about the importance of staying in school or finding employment.

Although peer socialization is especially important in, and associated with, childhood (Perez-Felkner 2013), it continues to be important throughout the life course (Preves and Mortimer 2013). For example, peers help us learn what we are expected to do at college (Brimeyer, Miller, and Perrucci 2006), at work (Montoya 2005), in social settings (Friedkin 2001), and in civic arenas (Dey 1997), as well as how to be sports fans (Melnick and Wann 2011).

Gender

Sociologists devote a great deal of attention to gender socialization (Leaper and Farkas 2015; McHale, Crouter, and Whiteman 2003; Rohlinger 2007), or the transmission of norms and values about what boys and girls can and should do.

Even before babies are born, their parents (and many others) start to "gender" them. In the United States they do so by, for example, frequently buying blue clothing for boys and pink for girls. Parents often dress baby girls in frilly dresses and affix bows to their bald heads to signal to others that the babies are girls. These gender differences are reinforced by the toys children are often given by parents—trucks and soldiers for boys, dolls and dollhouses for girls. Boys may get toys and games organized around action, activity, and role-playing thought to be appropriate for boys. Girls may get toys and games focused on interactions, relationships, and less active play. Sociologist Emily Kane (2012) conducted in-depth interviews with more than 40 parents of preschoolers, asking about the children's toys, clothing, and socialization, among other things. She found that while parents often want to challenge gender assumptions about what constitute appropriate toys and clothing for children, they are constrained by traditionally gendered structures and social institutions. As children grow up, they learn from their parents and other significant others (as well as the generalized other) what behaviors are considered appropriate and inappropriate for their gender. They also learn the consequences, or sanctions, for deviating from these expectations. For example, parents may give a girl a great deal of sympathy when she cries, whereas they may tell a boy to "be a man" and not cry after an injury. Boys may be expected to have an interest in sports, to play roughly with each other, and to be unable to sit still. Girls, in contrast, are expected to display more "ladylike" behaviors, such as sitting quietly and sharing. Many children come to see these traditional gender expectations as "natural" expressions of being male or female. Parents trying to raise boys are more likely to socialize them into narrow gender roles. They cite biology, or "nature," as the reason for doing so. Parents also do so because they fear social sanctions if they socialize the boys differently.

The feminist movement of the 1970s challenged traditional notions about the socialization of boys and girls (Lorber 2000). Today, some parents pride themselves on their "gender-neutral"

Peers are highly influential in the socialization process, especially during adolescence and early adulthood. What role do you think fellow students play in your socialization? Which ones will most influence you?

(Auster 2016) child rearing. They socialize their children without rigid adherence to traditional binary gender roles, rejecting the ideas that boys and girls are completely different (Martin 2005). Yet many parents continue to strongly discourage boys from expressing an interest in activities that are stereotyped as "for girls" (Kane 2006). Illustrating this difference, *tomboy* can be a positive term applied to a girl who likes physical activity and plays with boys. *Sissy*, in contrast, is a derogatory term for boys who express an interest in quieter types of play or playing with girls (Thorne 1993). Traditional gender socialization remains especially strong for boys (Kane 2006). Advice about the differential socialization of boys and girls continues to dominate child-rearing and parenting books, as well as other media (Martin 2005).

Historically, traditional socialization for gender roles has been reinforced in schools, sports, and the mass media. In schools, teachers and curricula once tended to support traditional gender norms, and peer groups were likely to be segregated by gender (Thorne 1993). In sports, girls and boys were channeled into different sports; for example, girls tended to play softball, while boys played baseball (Coakley 2007). When girls did play "male" sports, their efforts were often labeled differently; for instance, girls' football competitions might be called "powderpuff" football. The passage in 1972 of Title IX of the U.S. Education Amendments, which bars discrimination on the basis of gender in educationally based sporting activities receiving federal funding, has changed such views dramatically. Since the passage of Title IX, women's athletic activities in college and even in

high school have become increasingly visible and, in some cases, more highly regarded as "real" sports. One of the best examples is women's basketball at the collegiate level. More generally, both men and women are now more likely to seek to build muscular and athletic bodies.

ASK YOURSELF

Why do you think traditional ideas about gender role socialization in childhood remain strong in U.S. culture today? Do you foresee that they will ever give way entirely to more egalitarian norms? Why or why not?

The media, especially movies, TV, and video games, have also tended to reinforce children's traditional gender role socialization. However, that, too, is changing. Television programs are increasingly featuring strong female characters (*Agent Carter, The Good Wife, Grey's Anatomy, Jane the Virgin*), and numerous shows have featured female cops and police chiefs (*Law & Order: SVU, Chicago PD, Hawaii Five-0, Rizzoli & Isles*). Other TV shows featuring strong female leads in recent years include *Scandal* (political operative), *How to Get Away with Murder* (lawyer), and *Extant* (astronaut). Female action stars (Sigourney Weaver in the *Alien* movies, Angelina Jolie in most of her films, Michelle Rodriguez in *The Fast and the Furious* series and *Avatar*) are increasingly likely to play strong and aggressive characters. Young adult novels and the movies based on them often also have strong female leading characters, such as the extremely smart

Hermione Granger in the *Harry Potter* series, Katniss Everdeen in the *Hunger Games* series, and Beatrice Prior in the *Divergent* series.

Change is less obvious in other settings. Malls tend to reinforce traditional gender roles by offering separate shops for boys and girls, and for men and women. The Disney theme parks offer highly differentiated attractions aimed at boys (Pirates of the Caribbean) and girls (It's a Small World). Modern advertisements, both in print and on television, continue to feature men and women in their "traditional" roles—men are often shown fixing things around the house or doing hard labor, while women are shown cooking, cleaning, and taking care of the kids. Most video games are targeted at boys, while girls are offered computer games focused on facial makeovers and shopping. This media emphasis on female appearance is not new. Movies, television programming, and advertisements have been widely critiqued for decades for their unrealistic portrayal of women's bodies (Bordo 1993; Cole and Daniel 2005; Milkie 1999; Neuendorf et al. 2009). Magazines such as *Rolling Stone* have featured sexualized images of men on their covers, but they still use many more such images of women. More striking is the fact that the images of women have become increasingly sexualized over time (Hatton and Trautner 2011). A study of images of girls in the magazines *Seventeen* (1971–2011) and *Girls' Life* (1994–2011) showed an increase in their sexualization over time. More specifically, there was an increase in the depictions of girls in low-cut tops and tight-fitting clothing, as well as a decrease in images of childlike girls in *Girls' Life* (Graff,

Murnen, and Krause 2013). Many of the action heroines (e.g., those in James Bond and X-Men movies) continue to embody traditional male preferences for female bodies: young, attractive, and slender. Young women comparing themselves with these versions of adult Barbie dolls become anxious about their own bodies. Media images of women may also reaffirm racial stereotypes, with young women of color often being sexualized or portrayed as poor and irresponsible (Collins 2004).

Mass Media and New Media

Until recently, much of the emphasis on the role of the mass media in socialization has been on the effects of television and the enormous number of hours per week children spend in front of their TVs (Comstock and Scharrer 2007). TV remains an important socialization agent, especially for young children. However, it is clear that as children mature, especially in the middle and upper classes, more of their socialization is taking place via the computer, smartphones, video games, and other new and emerging technologies (Rideout, Foehr, and Roberts 2010). As the range of media devices has expanded, so has the portion of time spent using them. In 2009, children and young people between the ages of 8 and 18 spent almost 11 hours per day exposed to media of various sorts, reflecting an increase of more than 3 hours from 10 years prior (Da Silva 2015). The percentage of young people who own their own media devices is high and, for the most part, increasing.

Of course, a world of wonderful information is available to children on the computer via Google and other forms of new media. However, there are also lots of worrying things online that children can easily find or stumble upon. In addition, access to computers has changed the viewing experience considerably. Watching TV programs or movies is a passive activity. Even when "adult themes" are presented, the child is an observer, not a participant. However, on computers and other new digital media, the child can play video games such as *Pokémon Go, Grand Theft Auto V,* and *Call of Duty: Infinite Warfare.* Some of these games engage children in simulations of antisocial activities, such as stealing cars and evading police

Mark Makela/Corbis via Getty Images

What do you think the impact will be of the increasing amount of time young children are spending looking at devices' screens?

chases. Clearly, the nature of the socialization implicit in such games is at odds with the lessons that parents and teachers wish to impart.

Smartphones and social networking sites play a role in socialization as well, mostly through the influence of peers. A great deal of peer socialization also takes place via sites such as Facebook, Twitter, and Snapchat (Buckingham 2008; Skoog, Sobring, and Bohlin 2015; Watkins 2009). All of this is so new, and new forms of media are emerging so rapidly, that it is hard to know exactly what role the new media will play in socialization in the future, but their role is likely to be increasingly powerful and pervasive.

Consumer Culture

Consistent with the emphasis on consumption in this book, and in the contemporary world, it is important to understand that children need to be socialized in order to consume, and especially in order to devote a significant portion of their lives to consumption (Atkinson, Nelson, and Rademacher 2015). Like many other types of socialization, much of this socialization takes place early on in the family (Meuleman and Lubbers 2016), in schools, and in peer groups. Of course, we must not ignore the role of marketing, especially to children, in how people learn to consume (Schor 2005).

However, much socialization now takes place in consumption sites themselves rather than in the family, in schools, or through advertisements. For example, preteens and teens spend a large amount of time at shopping malls, either with their families or, as they mature, on their own and in the company of peers. Although young people may be going to a movie in a mall's multiplex or just "hanging out" at the mall rather than shopping, the fact remains that those activities take place in a setting devoted to shopping and consumption (Cook 2004; Rose 2010). Children readily learn the nuts and bolts of how to consume. They also learn various norms and values of consumption, and especially to value the processes of consumption and shopping as well as the goods and services acquired through those processes. For many years, there was even a board game, *Mall Madness*, designed to socialize children, especially girls, into the realities of shopping at a mall. In the game, the "mall" has 18 different stores where players can use credit cards to shop. Children are thereby also socialized into credit card use. The object of the game is to be the first player to buy all six items on one's shopping list and return to the game's starting point. In other words, the winner in the game, and in much of consumer culture, is the best consumer.

There is also a toy line produced by Moose Toys oriented mainly to selling figurines called Shopkins to children (see www.shopkinsworld.com). More important, these products also aim at promoting unbridled consumption—"Once you shop . . . you can't stop!"—both in the present and implicitly throughout the lifespan of those who first play with the toys as children. The immediate goal is to entice children into collecting as many Shopkins and as much associated paraphernalia as possible. A broader goal is implicit in the fact that the figurines are characters associated with a wide array of items that can be purchased in stores. Among them are Kooky Cookie (a chocolate chip cookie), Polly Polish (a bottle of nail polish), and Lippy Lips (a tube of lipstick). Most broadly, the goal is to encourage a lifetime of "hyperconsumption" (Ritzer 2012a).

Online consumption and shopping sites (such as Amazon and eBay) are also socializing agents. Navigation and buying strategies are learned at digital retailers, and those have an effect on consumption in the brick-and-mortar world. For instance, many younger people who have grown up with online shopping are adept comparison shoppers. They are likely to compare products online and to search out the best possible deals before making purchases. Some storefront retailers have gone out of business as a result of online competition, further reinforcing the use of online retailers. Other storefront retailers have developed new hybrids of online and storefront retailing. They offer consumers the ability to buy online and then pick up their items at local outlets. The hope is that visits to local stores will lead consumers to make unplanned purchases. These new forms of retailing offer new ways of socializing young people into our culture of consumption.

Socialization into being a consumer also reinforces lessons about race, class, and gender (Otnes and Zayre 2012). In *Inside Toyland* (2006), Christine Williams shows that consumer choices—where to shop, what brands to buy, what products are appropriate for whom—contribute to the maintenance of social inequalities. Girls face pressure to consume beauty products that encourage them to live up to an idealized and usually unattainable level of female beauty (Wiklund et al. 2010). For example, the Barbie doll is often presented as an ideal form of the female body—a form that is physically impossible to attain in real life. Such toys socialize children not only into a consumer culture but also into one that reproduces and reinforces harmful gender expectations.

ADULT SOCIALIZATION

A great deal of adult socialization takes place in later life as people enter the work world (Ellis, Bauer, and Erdogan 2015) and become independent of their families.

Workplaces

At one time, socialization into a workplace was a fairly simple and straightforward process. Many workers were hired for jobs in large corporations (e.g., General Motors, U.S. Steel) and remained there until they reached retirement age. Especially for those who held jobs in the lower reaches of the corporate hierarchy, socialization occurred for the most part in the early stages of a career. Today, however, relatively few workers can look forward to a career in a single position within a single company. Increasing numbers of workers are changing employers, jobs, and even careers with some frequency (Bernhardt et al. 2001; Legerski 2012). Each time workers change jobs, they need **resocialization** to unlearn old behaviors, norms, and values and to learn new ones. They can no longer rely (assuming it was ever possible) on what they learned as children, in school, or in their early years on the job.

Consider the findings of one study of U.S. workers' experiences in the job market. The researchers found that the generation of workers who entered the labor market in the late 1980s were 43 percent more likely to change jobs during their lifetimes than the generation that began in the early 1960s (Bernhardt et al. 2001). In addition, the proportion of workers in their mid-thirties with less than two years' tenure on any one job increased from 35 to 45 percent. The fraction of workers who had had only one or two employers decreased from 16 to 11 percent, while the figure for those who had had seven or more employers rose from 15 to 21 percent. Clearly, workers are changing jobs more frequently and filling more different jobs over a lifetime.

Furthermore, the Great Recession caused a record number of workers to lose their jobs, and those who have been able to find new ones have needed to be resocialized into them. One study of more than 1 million people found that 16 percent reported having lost a job between 2007 and 2009. This figure is much higher than the job loss rate during the 1981–1983 economic recession, which was 13 percent (Farber 2011). Furthermore, these displaced workers were more likely to remain unemployed than were previous cohorts of displaced workers. This trend continued through 2014, although over time more workers were able to find new jobs. However, among losers of full-time jobs, those new jobs were more likely to be part-time and to be lower in pay (Farber 2015).

Total Institutions

At some point in their lives, many adults find themselves in some type of total institution (Gambino 2013; Goffman 1961a). A **total institution** is a closed, all-encompassing place of residence and work set off from the rest of society that meets all the needs of those enclosed in it.

A major example of a total institution is the prison. In 2016, 2.3 million Americans were housed in prisons and jails of various types (including, among others, military prisons and detention centers for immigrants; www.prisonpolicy.org/reports/pie2016.html; International Centre for Prison Studies 2011). On initial entry into prison, inmates undergo formal resocialization in the form of being told the rules and procedures they must follow. However, of far greater importance is the informal socialization that occurs over time through their interactions with guards and especially with other inmates (Walters 2003). In fact, other inmates often socialize relatively inexperienced criminals

In what ways are branches of the military total institutions? Why are they set up as total institutions?

Scott Olson/Getty Images

into becoming more expert criminals; prisons are often "schools for crime" (Sykes [1958] 2007; Walters 2003).

Another total institution is the military. Members generally live in military housing. They often eat together, share living quarters, and have access to all necessary services on the military base. They must follow strict rules of dress, conduct, physical appearance, and organization of their time. The image of the military as a total institution is especially clear in the films *Full Metal Jacket* (1987) and *American Sniper* (2014). For example, *Full Metal Jacket* depicts military recruits getting their heads shaved, a process that removes their control over their own appearance. They are also harassed and deindividualized by the barking orders of their infamous drill sergeant, who has complete authority over everything they do.

Other Aspects of Adult Socialization

Adult socialization and resocialization take place in many other ways and in many other settings. For example, medical schools, law schools, and graduate schools of various types socialize their students to be doctors, lawyers, nurses, and members of other professions (Becker and Geer 1958; Granfield 1992; Hafferty 2009). The students have to learn the norms that govern their appearance, conduct, and interactions with others in their professions, their patients or clients, and the public at large. Medical residents, for example, need to learn how to present their diagnoses to patients with sensitivity and confidence. They also learn to maintain and reinforce status differences between doctors and nurses.

Many consumption settings also offer formal socialization aimed mostly at adults, at least on initial visits. For a fee, the Mall of America will give newcomers an orientation tour of the mall. Las Vegas casinos helpfully offer newcomers lessons on the various forms of gambling and implicitly on how to lose their money. Cruise lines offer first-time travelers tours of their sometimes vast ships, including their onboard casinos and shops.

Like all economic depressions and recessions, the Great Recession that began in 2008 also necessitated resocialization. Many people lost their jobs and their homes. Some were reduced to entirely different existences, doubling up with family or friends or, if truly unlucky, living in their cars or on the streets. For a family to learn to live on one income instead of two requires considerable adult resocialization, and becoming unemployed and homeless obviously requires even more.

There are a number of other situations that lead to the need for adult socialization or resocialization (Brim 1968; Lutfey and Mortimer 2006; Wilson 1984):

- *Changes in societal values and norms*. Many aspects of American culture are experiencing rapid change. One

aspect, as mentioned earlier, is gender stereotypes. One study of men who set out to participate in college cheerleading squads found that their sense of masculinity adapted to the highly feminized environment (Anderson 2005).

- *Family changes*. Separation, divorce, death of a spouse, and remarriage involve particularly important transitions for the adults who are involved, not just the children. They require considerable adult resocialization into new relationships, new household organization, and new public images. One significant change in the family is the growing number of households with children where the mother is the "breadwinner." In 1960, only 11 percent of mothers were the sole source of income for their households, but in 2011, 40 percent held this role (Wang, Parker, and Taylor 2013, 1).

- *Geographic mobility*. Job change, retirement, and migration are becoming increasingly likely. People undergoing any of these transitions must be resocialized into not only new physical environments but also new subcultures.

- *Changes associated with aging*. As people age, they gradually become disengaged from work, which has implications for relationships and financial well-being. A retired person must become resocialized into this new status. People are also living much longer and therefore are likely to experience longer periods in which their health deteriorates (Kotarba 2007). According to the World Health Organization (2003), American men spend 10 percent and American women 11 percent of their lives in poor health. It may be difficult for people who see themselves as competent adults to experience the significant impact of disability on the ways in which they interact with the world.

Because we live in a global age, it is clear that adults also need to be resocialized, probably many different times as they age, into this new and ever-changing world. Some global socialization occurs on the job: As employers increasingly seek a global market and establish global outposts, employees have more opportunities to experience other cultures. Global socialization is also aided by the internet, which, of course, is itself increasingly global. Interaction with global websites, news sources, and other people throughout the world by e-mail or on social networking sites plays an important role in global socialization. We are all socialized globally to participate in consumer culture (Poff 2010), and students experience global socialization through study-abroad programs.

Digital Natives

Many of you reading this book are digital natives—members of the Millennial generation who have been socialized into a digital world since birth. Unlike the older generations of "digital settlers" and "digital immigrants," who had to go through a process of resocialization to adapt to the digital world, digital natives "learned in digital the first time around" (Palfrey and Gasser 2008, 4). Although digital natives possess the skills to use the internet and social media, that does not necessarily mean that they are cognizant of the consequences of their online behavior. Creating and managing their identities online is complicated because they must "contend with collapsed contexts and invisible audiences" (Boyd 2014, 31). For instance, teenagers in particular create their online identities for their peers, not for their teachers, parents, college admission selection committees, or future employers. But these other actors also look at their Facebook profiles and Twitter pages and often judge teenagers based on what they post, often taking the content out of its original context (Boyd 2014).

Given that versions of our online identities are so accessible and persistent, it would be wise for not just digital natives but all of us who use social media to be careful of whom we "friend" or "follow" and what we post online. But digital natives tend to be reluctant to use privacy settings because they do not want to block peers with similar interests (Boyd 2014, 32). Palfrey and Gasser (2008, 26) contend that digital natives share so much personal information online in order to establish group memberships, which they incorporate into their social identities. Online group memberships are types of reference groups that provide clues to an individual's preferences and values. While some online groups are secondary groups with weak ties, others approximate primary groups for digital natives, even if they do not involve face-to-face interaction. Although digital natives can change their online identities quickly and easily, these identities are insecure because they lack the power to control how others perceive them (Palfrey and Gasser 2008, 31).

Engaging the Digital World

One criticism directed at digital natives is that they are addicted to digital technology and social media. Instead of talking to each other before class begins, they are checking their Twitter feed on their smartphones. Some have been known to text their friends even when they are sitting in the same room. How addicted are you to digital technology and social media? Try to disengage the digital world for 24 hours—no e-mail, social media, or streaming music. Explain your experience. Did you find yourself unable to leave the digital world entirely?

CHECKPOINT 5.3: SOCIALIZATION CONCEPTS

TYPE OF SOCIALIZATION	DESCRIPTION OF PROCESS
Primary socialization	Process by which newborns, infants, and young children acquire language, identities, cultural routines, norms, and values by interacting with parents and family members
Anticipatory socialization	Process by which parents teach children what will be expected of them in the future
Resocialization	Process of unlearning old behaviors, norms, and values and learning new ones

INTERACTION

In the first part of the chapter, we focused on the socialization of individuals. However, socialization generally involves **interaction**, or social engagement involving two or more individuals who perceive, and orient their actions to, one another (vom Lehn 2007). Interaction has generally been seen as involving face-to-face relationships among people, but in the twenty-first century, interaction is increasingly mediated by smartphones and social media. Interaction is an important topic of study in itself because of its ubiquity and its influence on individuals. It is also a key building block for more macroscopic social phenomena, such as networks and groups as well as larger organizations, societies, and the global domain, which will be explored more deeply in the next chapter.

Personal interaction occurs throughout our lifetimes. Examples include interactions between parents and children, between children and their siblings, between teachers and students, between coworkers, and between medical personnel and patients. Interactions early in the life cycle, especially in the family and in schools, tend to be long-term and intense. Later in life, many interactions tend to be more fleeting (a quick hello on the street or a brief conversation at a cocktail party), although interactions with family members tend to remain intense.

Various sociological theories have been brought to bear on interaction. For example, as you learned earlier in this chapter, George Herbert Mead and later symbolic interactionists distinguished between a conversation of gestures and interaction that relies on symbols such as language. Georg Simmel believed that human interaction not only gives rise to society but also meets a basic human need to be sociable. In the following discussion, you will see references to a variety of theories that deal with interaction.

SUPERORDINATE–SUBORDINATE INTERACTIONS

Simmel saw society as being defined by interaction. Moreover, he differentiated between the forms that interaction takes and the types of people who engage in interaction. For example, one "form" of interaction is the relationship between a *superordinate* and a *subordinate* (Simmel [1908] 1971a). This type of relationship is found in many settings, for example, between teacher and student in the classroom, between judge and defendant in the courtroom, and between guard and prisoner in the jail. We tend to think of this relationship as eliminating the subordinate's independence. However, a relationship between the two cannot exist unless the subordinate has at least some freedom to be an active party to the interaction. The relationship between employee and supervisor is a good example. If the employee cannot react to the supervisor's direction, there is no interaction—only one-way communication from the supervisor to the employee. Furthermore, experimental research has demonstrated that the greater the equality in an employee–manager relationship, the greater the amount of two-way communication. In such a situation, the subordinate feels less resentment, anger, and worry when conflict arises with the manager (Johnson, Ford, and Kaufman 2000).

RECIPROCITY AND EXCHANGE

To sociologists who theorize about exchange, interaction is a rational process in which those involved seek to maximize rewards and minimize costs. Interaction is likely to persist as long as those involved find it rewarding, and it is likely to wind down or end when one or more of the parties no longer find it rewarding. An important idea in this context is the social norm of **reciprocity**, which means that those engaged in interaction expect to give and receive rewards of roughly equal value (Gouldner 1960; Mazelis 2015; Molm 2010). When one party feels that the other is no longer adhering to this norm—that is, not giving about as much as he or she is receiving—the relationship is likely to end.

Studies of exchange relationships, like much else in sociology, are now being challenged to find ways of dealing with new forms of virtual interaction: e-mail, social networking, and interaction on Skype and WhatsApp. One researcher who has explored the effects of virtual reality on interaction in the "real" world, and vice versa, concludes that "the constantly evolving avatar [or digital representation of oneself] influences the 'real' self, who now also orients toward virtual, yet all-too-real others" (Gottschalk 2010, 522). In other words, interactions in the digital realm and those in the physical realm both influence the self. Additional research questions come to mind quite readily. For example, are people compelled to cooperate to the same extent in the digital realm (such as when using e-mail communication) as they are in the material world (such as during in-person communication; Naquin, Kurtzberg, and Belkin 2008)? However, it is important to remember that the digital and material worlds are not separate from one another, but rather interpenetrate. An important issue, then, is the connection between, for example, collaborative relationships online and offline (Ritzer 2013).

"DOING" INTERACTION

Another interactionist theory of great relevance here is ethnomethodology, which focuses on people's everyday practices, especially those that involve interaction. The basic idea is that interaction is something that people actively "do," something that they accomplish on a day-to-day basis. For example, the simple act of two people walking together can be considered a form of interaction. Engaging in certain practices makes it clear that you are walking with a particular someone and not with someone else (Pantzar and Shove 2010; Ryave and Schenkein 1974). You are likely to walk close to, or perhaps lean toward, a close friend. When you find yourself walking in step with a total stranger, you probably behave differently. You might separate yourself, lean away, and say, "Excuse me," to make it clear that you are not walking with that stranger and are not engaged in interaction with her. More complex forms of interaction require much more sophisticated practices. In the process of interacting, people create durable forms of interaction, such as those that relate to gender (West and Zimmerman 1987) and the family.

Ethnomethodology also spawned **conversation analysis**, which is concerned with how people do, or accomplish, conversations (Heritage and Stivers 2012). For example, you must know and utilize certain practices in order to carry on a successful conversation: You must know when it is your turn to talk and when it is appropriate to laugh at a comment made by someone else (Jefferson 1979). Conversation analysts have taken the lead in studying conversations, and interaction more generally, in great depth. They typically record conversations using audio or video devices so that they can study them in detail. Later, they transcribe the conversations to create written records of them.

INTERACTION ORDER

While every instance of interaction may seem isolated and independent of others, each is part of what Erving Goffman (2000) called the **interaction order** (Rawls 2015). This is a social domain that is organized and orderly. The order is created informally and governed by those involved in the interaction rather than by some formal structure, such as a bureaucracy and its constraints (Fine 2012; Jacobs 2007). One example of an interaction order is a group of students who form a clique and develop their own norms to govern their interaction. In this thinking, Goffman was following Simmel's view that society is based, in a real sense, on interaction. In many ways, society is interaction.

The interaction order can be seen in many settings and contexts. One example is the 2016 shooting of police officers in Dallas by a lone sniper, which killed five officers. Before the shooting, an orderly demonstration against police brutality was taking was taking place, but the shooting destroyed this interaction order and replaced it with fear and confusion. Some sociologists have suggested that human interaction with animals is another area in which we can observe the interaction order (Jerolmack 2009, 2013). In fact, there is a relatively new sociological theory—actor-network theory—that seeks to include not only animals but also inanimate objects in the interaction order (Law and Hassard 1999).

STATUS AND ROLE

Status and role are key elements in the interaction order, as well as in the larger structures in which such interactions often exist. A **status** is a position within a social system occupied by people. Within the university, for example, key statuses are professor and student. A **role** is what is generally expected of a person who occupies a given status (Hindin 2007). Thus, a professor is expected to show up for class, to be well prepared, to teach in an engaging manner, and so on. For their part, students are also expected to attend class, to listen and sometimes to participate, to avoid texting and checking their Facebook pages during class, to complete the required assignments, and to take and pass examinations.

The concept of status can be broken down further into ascribed and achieved status. An **ascribed status** is one that is not chosen; it is beyond the individual's control.

It involves a position into which the individual is placed or to which he or she moves, regardless of what that person does or the nature of his or her capacities or accomplishments. In some cases, individuals are born into an ascribed status—for example, the status associated with race, ethnicity, social class, sex, or gender. In contrast, an **achieved status** is a position that a person acquires on the basis of accomplishment or the nature of the individual's capacities. It may be based on merit or earned, or the person may choose it—for example, by seeking out and finding someone who will be a mate for life. Spouse, parent, and career as a "successful" entrepreneur are all achieved statuses. In addition, adults can achieve improvement in their social class or socioeconomic status (children's social class is almost always ascribed).

Whether it is ascribed or achieved, a status can become a **master status**, or a position that is (or becomes) more important than any other status, both for the person in the position and for all others involved. A master status will become central to a person's identity, roles, behaviors, and interactions. Primary examples of master statuses are those associated with race, disability, gender, and even sexuality.

The social roles connected with any statuses can be congruent; that is, the expectations attached to a given status can be consistent. Student status (achieved) may have role expectations of attending class and doing homework outside of class. But roles can also come into conflict—for example, going to class and keeping up with your social life. **Role conflict** can be defined as conflicting expectations associated with a given position or multiple positions (Merton 1957; Schmidt et al. 2014). A professor who is expected to excel at both teaching and research can be seen as having role conflict. Devoting a lot of time to research can mean that a professor is ill prepared to teach her classes. Or a professor may be torn between the expectations of being a teacher (preparing for class) and those of being a parent (playing with her children). A student may need to deal with the role conflict between being a student and studying and being a friend who spends the evening helping a close acquaintance deal with a personal problem.

Much research has been done on the role conflicts experienced by workers with domestic obligations. Each role interferes with the individual's ability to satisfactorily meet the expectations associated with the other role (Moore 1995). Research has supported this idea. For example, women who work outside the home, who still tend to be responsible for the care of children and the home, experience higher levels of stress and poorer physical health than do working men (Gove and Hughes 1979; Pearlin 1989; Roehling, Hernandez Jarvis, and Swope 2005). The heavy burden of the female caretaking role inhibits women's ability to fulfill their role as caretakers of themselves.

Another role-related problem is **role overload**, in which people are confronted with more expectations than they can possibly handle (Mathews, Winkel, and Wayne 2014). Students during final exams week are often confronted with role overload in trying to satisfy the expectations of several professors and courses. One study of the American "time crunch" and mental health suggests that feeling under time pressure is likely the active ingredient in role overload, which in turn affects people's psychological well-being (Roxburgh 2004).

There is a tendency to see roles as fixed, unchanging, and constraining. However, people do have the ability to engage in **role making**. That is, they have the ability to modify their roles, at least to some degree (Turner 1978). Thus, the professor in the previous example might take her child to the office so that she can perform parent and teacher roles simultaneously. Researchers have noted that parents adopt a variety of strategies to reduce work-family conflict (Becker and Moen 1999; Bianchi and Milkie 2010). Examples of such strategies include reducing work hours, turning down promotions, and negotiating trade-offs with one's partner.

CHECKPOINT 5.4: INTERACTION CONCEPTS

CONCEPT	EXPLANATION
Interaction	Social engagement between two or more individuals
Superordinate–subordinate interaction	A relationship in which the subordinate has at least some freedom to actively participate
Reciprocity	A social norm allowing those engaged in interaction to expect to give and receive rewards of roughly equal value
Interaction order	A social domain whose order is created informally and governed by those engaged in the interaction

MICRO-LEVEL SOCIAL STRUCTURES

Through an accumulation of persistent patterns of interaction and social relationships, individuals contribute to the creation of social structures, which are enduring and regular social arrangements (Hunt 2007). Social structures include everything from the face-to-face interaction that is characteristic of the interaction order to networks, groups, organizations, societies, and the globe. This chapter focuses on micro-level social structures—interpersonal

relationships, social networks, and groups. Chapter 6 covers larger-scale social structures.

INTERPERSONAL RELATIONSHIPS

A good place to start a discussion of social structures is with another famous set of concepts created by Georg Simmel (1950) to describe the structures common to interpersonal relationships. A **dyad** is a two-person group, and a **triad** is a three-person group.

Dyads are the most basic of interpersonal relationships, but they often evolve into triads—as when a couple welcomes a new child. It would appear on the surface that the addition of one person to a dyad, creating a triad, would be of minimal importance sociologically. After all, how important can the addition of one person be? Simmel demonstrated that no further addition of members to a group, no matter how many that might be, is as important as the addition of a single person to a dyad. A good example is the dramatic change in the husband–wife relationship caused by the arrival of a first child. Another is the powerful impact of a new lover on an intimate dyadic relationship. In cases like these, social possibilities exist in the triad that do not exist in a dyad. For example, in a triad, two of the parties can form a coalition against the third: A wife and child can form a coalition against the husband. Or one member of the triad—say, the child—can take on the role of mediator or arbitrator in disputes involving the other members.

The most important point to be made about Simmel's ideas on the triad is that it is the group structure that matters, *not* the people involved in the triad or the nature of their personalities. Different people with different personalities will make one triad different from another, but it is not the nature of the people or their personalities that make the triad itself possible (Webster and Sell 2012).

SOCIAL NETWORKS

Simmel's work, especially on social forms, also informs the study of social networks (Chriss 2007; Kadushin 2012). The most basic social networks involve two or more individuals, but social networks also include groups, organizations, and societies; there can even be global social networks.

Network analysts are interested in how networks are organized and the implications of that organization for social life. They look at the nodes, or positions, occupied by individuals (and other entities) in a network, the linkages among nodes, and the importance of central nodes to other nodes in the network. Figure 5.1 shows a network with low centrality and one with high centrality. In the low-centrality network, one node appears in the center, but it is actually linked to only two other nodes. The central node in the high-centrality example is far more influential. Every other node is connected to it, and there is only one link that is independent of the central node. Those who occupy

FIGURE 5.1 • Social Network Centrality

Opposite Degrees of Network Centrality

Low Network Centrality   High Network Centrality

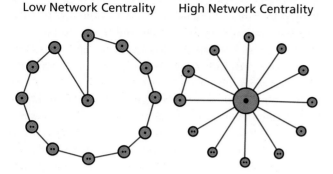

SOURCE: Social Network Centrality Is reprinted by permission of S Joshua Mendelsohn.

FIGURE 5.2 • The Strength of Weak Ties

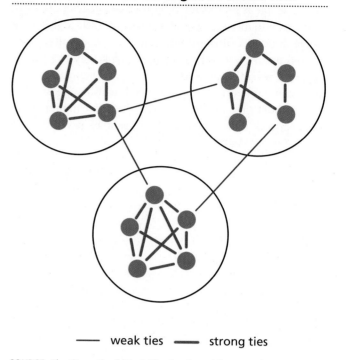

—— weak ties   —— strong ties

SOURCE: The Strength of Weak Ties is adapted from Weak Ties in Social Networks, Bokardo, a blog about interface and product design, Joshua Porter.

positions that are central in any network have access to a great many resources and therefore have a considerable ability to gain and to exercise power in a network.

A key idea in network theory is the "strength of weak ties." We are all aware of the power of strong ties between, for example, family members, or among those who belong to close-knit social groups such as gangs. However, as Mark Granovetter (1973) has demonstrated, those who have only weak ties with others (that is, they are just acquaintances) can have great power. While those with strong ties tend to remain within given groups, those with weak ties can more easily move between groups and thus provide important linkages among and between group members (see Figure 5.2). Those with weak ties are the ones who hold together disparate groups that are themselves linked internally by strong ties.

Researchers generally find that at least half of all workers in the United States have obtained their jobs through informal means, meaning referrals, rather than formal job postings (Marsden and Gorman 2001; Pfeffer and Parra 2009). It makes sense, then, to understand the strength of weak ties. If you are looking for a job, you may want to seek out the help of friends and acquaintances who have weak ties to many groups. This is because they are likely to have many diverse and potentially useful contacts with people you *and* your strong ties do not know at a number of different employers.

Those who are responsible for hiring need to keep in mind that access to network resources is largely dependent on someone's social position. Social network research has shown that socioeconomically disadvantaged individuals suffer an additional deficit in both strong and weak network ties (Bian 1997; Granovetter 1973, 1974; Lin 1999; Lin and Bian 1991; Lin, Ensel, and Vaughn 1981; Wegener 1991). Thus, they have an additional disadvantage in finding jobs. To overcome this barrier to finding talented workers, an employer may want to seek ties to networks that include the socioeconomically disadvantaged.

One point worth underscoring in any discussion of social networks is the importance of internet networks, including Facebook, Instagram, and Twitter (Gee, Jones, and Burke, forthcoming). This is another domain where weak ties can be of great importance. On Facebook, for instance, you may have hundreds, even thousands, of "friends." However, it is clear that many of these "friendships" involve weak ties—in fact, far weaker ties than analysts such as Granovetter had in mind. It is also important to note that they leave objective traces, such as e-mail messages and writings on Facebook walls. As a result, such networks are much easier to study than, for example, those that exist in face-to-face interaction, which usually leave few material traces. This is the reason the app Snapchat was developed; it forces you to arrange for traces—such as photos—to disappear within 1 to 10 seconds (Wortham 2013).

GROUPS

We have already encountered the key sociological concept of groups at several points in this chapter, especially in Simmel's ideas on the dyad and beyond. A **group** is a relatively small number of people who over time develop a patterned relationship based on interaction with one another. However, just because we see a small number of people who appear to be together—say, in a queue waiting to board a plane—that does not mean that they necessarily constitute a group. Most people in a queue are not likely to interact with one another, to have the time or inclination to develop patterned relationships with one another, or, if they do interact, to do so beyond the time it takes to board the plane and find their seats.

Types of Groups

Several key concepts in sociology relate to groups. Consider the traditional distinction between the primary group and the secondary group (Cooley 1909). **Primary groups** are those that are small, are close-knit, and have intimate face-to-face interaction. Relationships in primary groups are personal, and people identify strongly with the groups. The family is the model of a primary group, although as we will see in Chapter 12, the family is often riddled with many conflicts, and at least some members leave the family or are driven from it. Primary groups can also take unlikely forms. A 2009 study of people in New York City who tend pigeons and fly them from the rooftops documents the formation of primary group ties among members involved in this rare animal practice activity (Jerolmack 2009). Such group ties can be stronger for these individuals than can class and ethnic ties.

In contrast, **secondary groups** are generally large and impersonal; ties are relatively weak, members do not know one another very well, and members' impacts on one another are typically not very powerful. Members of a local parent–teacher association would be a good example of a secondary group.

Primary and secondary group ties can occur in the same social context. For example, the primary group for servicemen and servicewomen is usually the squad or platoon. The secondary group is typically the company, battalion, brigade, or regiment (in descending order of closeness; Siebold 2007).

Also worth mentioning are **reference groups**, or those groups that you take into consideration in evaluating yourself. Your reference group can be one to which you belong, or it can be another group to which you do not belong but nevertheless often relate (Ajrouch 2007; Merton and Kitt 1950). People often have many reference groups, and those groups can and do change over time. Knowing people's reference groups, and how they change, tells us a great deal about their behavior, attitudes, and values. We often think of reference groups in positive terms. An example would be a group of people whose success you would like to emulate. They also can be negative if they represent values or ways of life that you reject (say, neo-Nazis). The group to which one belongs is not necessarily the most powerful group in one's life.

Reference groups can be illustrated by the case of immigrants. Newly arrived immigrants are more likely to take those belonging to the immigrant culture, or even those in the country from which they came, as their reference group. In contrast, their children, second-generation immigrants, are much more likely to take as their reference group those associated with the new culture in the country to which they have immigrated (Kosic et al. 2004).

One final set of concepts that can help us understand the sociological importance of groups is the distinction between in-groups and out-groups (Sumner [1906] 1940). An **in-group** is one to which people belong and with which they identify, perhaps strongly. An **out-group** is one to which outsiders, at least from the perspective of the in-group, belong. Thus, from your perspective, the group you sit with at your regular table in the college dining hall or fast-food court would be the in-group, while other groups at other tables might be the out-groups. The differences between these groups may be insignificant (e.g., whether they get their food in the food court from McDonald's or Pizza Hut). However, they can also come to be so important ("jocks" versus "geeks") that each group not only accepts its own ways but also rejects those of the others. In extreme cases this can lead to conflict between the in-group and the out-group. Research suggests that hostility often arises when members of the in-group perceive the out-group as constituting a threat to their self-interest (Rosenstein 2008). This is particularly evident in research on immigration (Schlueter and Scheepers 2010; Schneider 2008). In that case, native-born individuals (representing the in-group) may maintain discriminatory attitudes toward a growing population of foreign-born individuals (representing the out-group). In a more specific study it was found that religious fundamentalists in Western Europe, especially Muslims, have very high levels of hostility toward out-groups (Koopmans 2015).

More prosaically, in-groups and out-groups play a prominent role in the television show *Glee* (2009–2015), which centers on a group of high school students who perform in the campus glee club (a singing group). The club includes students with a wide variety of identities. There are cheerleaders, football players, goths, nerds, and rebels. Members of the glee club consider themselves an in-group, but on their high school campus, the "glee kids" are considered the out-group, reviled by jocks and nerds alike for their focus on singing. Another example is found in the movie *Mean Girls* (2004), in which those involved in the high school's in-group are considered "fabulous but evil." Many students in the out-groups know who the "mean girls" are and at least some of the intimate details of their lives. This is because many students in the out-groups hope to become part of the in-group. Some of these aspirants are called "desperate wannabes." Members of the out-groups also model their behavior on the ways in which those in the in-group behave.

FIGURE 5.3 • Solomon Asch's Conformity Experiment Cards

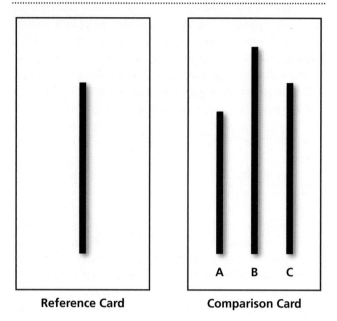

Reference Card   **Comparison Card**

SOURCE: Solomon Asch's Conformity Experiment Cards is adapted from Solomon E. Asch, Opinions and Social Pressure, *Scientific American*, 193 (1955), pp. 31–35.

Conformity to the Group

We have seen that group members generally conform to certain aspects of the group with which they prefer to identify. Some conformity is clearly necessary for a group to survive. If everyone "did his or her own thing," or went his or her own way, there would be no group. But too much conformity can have disastrous consequences. A central issue in the sociological study of groups has been the degree to which members conform to the expectations and demands of the group, despite their own misgivings. The experiments by Stanley Milgram (1974) discussed in Chapter 3 demonstrated that people tended to conform to the demands of authority figures who ordered them to administer painful shocks. Groups often develop informal authority structures that can induce the kind of conformity uncovered by Milgram. Also discussed in Chapter 3 was research by Zimbardo (1973) that showed similarly troubling tendencies toward conformity.

Another series of experiments, conducted by Solomon Asch (1952), showed that groups with no clear authority figure also promote conformity. Asch demonstrated that the power of the group is so great that it may override an individual's own judgments and perceptions (see also Kinney 2007). In one of the experiments, groups of seven to nine students were assembled. All but one

(the subject) were confederates of the researcher. All but the subject knew the details of the experiment. Only the subject believed that the experiment was investigating vision. Each group was shown two cards, one with one vertical line on it and a second with three such lines (see Figure 5.3). One of the lines on the second card was the same length as the line on the first card. The other two lines were clearly different. All the students were asked to choose the line on the comparison card that matched the single line on the reference card. As they had been instructed, each of the confederates chose, out loud, one of the wrong lines. The subjects were always positioned last in their groups. When the subjects' turns came, about a third of them conformed to their groups' erroneous choice and selected the same wrong line. They made the wrong choice, even though they apparently knew it was the wrong choice.

There is no question that some people conform to group demands at least some of the time. Conformity is especially likely when the demands come from someone in authority in the group. However, it is important to remember that about two-thirds of the choices made by subjects in the Asch conformity experiments indicated independence from the group. It is also important to note that these experiments are decades old, and many of them occurred in a period of American history more defined by conformity than the era we are in today.

This chapter has focused largely on such micro-level phenomena as individuals, interaction, and groups. In Chapter 6 we turn to the progressively more macro-level phenomena of organizations, societies, and the globe as a whole.

CHECKPOINT 5.5: TYPES OF GROUPS

TYPE	DESCRIPTION
Primary group	A small, close-knit group with intimate face-to-face interaction
Secondary group	A large and impersonal group with members who do not know each other very well
Reference group	A group you take into consideration in evaluating yourself, whether you belong to it or not
In-group	A group to which people belong and with which they identify
Out-group	A group to which outsiders—from the perspective of the in-group—belong

SUMMARY

The sociological perspective on the individual and the self focuses on the social interactions humans are capable of having with each other. Cooley's concept of the looking-glass self, the idea that humans develop self-images reflecting the way in which others respond to them, is fundamental to sociology. Symbolic interactionism posits that humans use significant symbols, such as gestures and language, to develop a sense of self. George Herbert Mead defined the self as the ability to take oneself as an object. Once individuals are able to internalize the perspective of a group or community, they come to possess a sense of the generalized other. According to Mead the self is composed of two parts, the "I" that is impulsive and the "me" that is conformist.

Erving Goffman believed that in every interaction, or performance, individuals attempt to manage projections of themselves. On a front stage, they operate in an idealized manner, but on a back stage, they can more freely express themselves.

Socialization is the process through which a person learns and generally comes to accept the ways of a group or of a society as a whole. Primary socialization begins with newborns and infants and continues over the course of their childhood during anticipatory socialization. Socialization does not end with childhood—adults continue to be socialized throughout their lives. Our families, peers, workplaces, and the media are important agents of socialization.

Socialization involves interaction, or social engagement between two or more individuals. Some interaction involves reciprocity, or the expectation that those involved in it will give and receive equally, while other interactions transpire between those with power and their subordinates. Interaction is deeply involved in people's statuses and their related roles.

Patterns of interaction and social relationships that occur regularly and persist over time become social structures. A group is one type of social structure that develops when individuals interact over time and develop a patterned relationship. A small, close-knit group with intimate face-to-face interactions is a primary group. A secondary groups is larger and more impersonal; its members do not know each other very well.

KEY TERMS

achieved status, 132

agents of socialization, 122

anticipatory socialization, 122

ascribed status, 132

back stage, 120

conversation analysis, 131

dramaturgy, 119

dyad, 133

front stage, 120

game stage, 117

generalized other, 117

gestures, 115

group, 134

"I", 118

impression management, 119

in-group, 135

interaction, 130

interaction order, 132

looking-glass self, 115

master status, 132

"me", 118

micro–macro continuum, 114

mind, 116

out-group, 135

play stage, 117

primary groups, 135

primary socialization, 122

reciprocity, 131

reference groups, 135

resocialization, 128

reverse socialization, 124

role, 132

role conflict, 132

role making, 133

role overload, 133

secondary groups, 135

self, 117

significant symbol, 116

socialization, 122

status, 132

symbolic interaction, 116

total institution, 128

triad, 133

REVIEW QUESTIONS

1. How can we use the literature on feral children to explain the importance of interaction to human development? In what ways does this relate to the "nature versus nurture" debate?

2. According to Mead, what distinguishes humans from non-humans?

3. How does the socialization process help individuals develop their sense of self? Why are games so important to the socialization process?

4. What is the difference between the "I" and the "me"? Why do people and society as a whole need both the "I" and the "me"?

5. According to Goffman, in what ways do we use impression management in our front-stage performances? Why would a sociologist say that racism has increasingly been relegated to the back stage? What is problematic about this development?

6. Why are families important agents of socialization? How do families from higher social classes socialize their children differently than families from lower social classes do? What effects might these differences in socialization have on children?

7. How are we socialized to be consumers? In what ways has the internet resocialized us as consumers?

8. In what ways is being a fifth grader in the United States both an ascribed and an achieved status? What does this suggest about the differences between roles attached to ascribed statuses versus those attached to achieved statuses?

9. In the realm of social networks, why are "weak ties" helpful to those who are looking for jobs? What effect has the internet had on the development of weak ties and strong ties?

10. In what ways do we use images in the mass media as reference groups? How do the mass media help to define in-groups and out-groups?

PRACTICE AND APPLY WHAT YOU'VE LEARNED

▶ edge.sagepub.com/ritzerintro4e

CHECK YOUR COMPREHENSION ON THE STUDY SITE WITH:

- **Diagnostic pre-tests** to identify opportunities for improvement.

- **Personalized study plans** with focused recommendations to address specific knowledge gaps and additional learning needs.

- **Post-tests** to check your progress and ensure mastery of key learning objectives.

ORGANIZATIONS, SOCIETIES, AND GLOBAL RELATIONSHIPS

Questioning Governmental Authority

Oliver Stone's 2016 biopic, *Snowden*, gave renewed life to the controversy surrounding U.S. Central Intelligence Agency contractor Edward Snowden and his leak of thousands of classified government documents. The clamor in the United States had become especially loud in mid-2013—and it has not died away to this day—when Snowden told the world that the U.S. government, through its National Security Agency, had been attempting to prevent terrorist acts by spying on ordinary American citizens. This was being done through the systematic accumulation of bulk data (or metadata) on routine phone calls. Public reaction was swift and divided, with some arguing that Snowden was a hero for revealing this fact and that the government had gone to unwarranted lengths in breaching its citizens' privacy. This view was upheld in mid-2015 by a federal appeals court ruling that such data collection was illegal. Others continue to argue that any and all steps that are necessary to uncover terrorist plots, including spying on American citizens, are defensible. Snowden, who made his revelations from Hong Kong, fled to Russia, where he received asylum and in 2014 a three-year residency permit. Snowden's revelations continue to have impacts. Some terrorist groups have altered the way in which they communicate because some of the documents Snowden released revealed information about U.S. surveillance techniques. The leaks also led to great changes in the way in which the government protects secret documents.

LEARNING OBJECTIVES

6.1 Describe the features of bureaucracies and informal organizations.

6.2 Discuss challenges that arise in contemporary organizations.

6.3 Contrast gemeinschaft and gesellschaft societies.

6.4 Describe global social organization and global flows.

The events surrounding Snowden's leaks reveal the relationship between us as individuals and the different organizations and institutions that frame our lives, such as our local and national governments. These organizations cannot exist, at least for very long, without willing members. When groups of individuals begin to question the authority and rationality of the bureaucracies that govern them, they may voice concern about, seek to change, or even rebel against those bureaucracies. The massive Hong Kong "umbrella" protests in late 2014 over the government's reneging on its commitments to create a more democratic society are another good example of such actions. Social order cannot be maintained if citizens refuse to adhere to society's shared laws and norms. How do governments, as institutions, react? Some believe that governments and institutions often overreact. Snowden is wanted by the U.S. government for violating the Espionage Act, and Hong Kong suppressed the umbrella protests.

We have seen how technology and globalization facilitate the global flow of information, fundamentally altering the way in which we communicate. But this nearly instantaneous dissemination of ideas has become a bonanza for everyone, including whistle-blowers, revolutionaries, rioters, potential terrorists, and even elected governments. For instance, revelations that swiftly followed Snowden's initial leak suggested that the United States had also been secretly conducting extensive monitoring of the communications of its European Union allies (including the prime minister of Germany). Some governments, such as that of the United Kingdom following a series of violent riots in London in 2011, have considered shutting down digital communication during public disturbances. Other countries, such as China, Syria, and Iran, routinely censor their citizens' use of the internet. China blocked the internal flow of information about the umbrella revolution. Such barriers to the flow of information, as well as efforts such as Snowden's to overcome them, are of profound interest to sociologists, public figures, and social activists alike. ●

Picking up where the previous chapter left off with groups, this chapter moves on to the more macroscopic levels of interest to sociologists: organizations, societies, and global relationships. These social structures are discussed here as if they were clearly distinct from one another. However, the fact is that they tend to blend together in many clear-cut ways, as well as in many other almost imperceptible ones.

The individuals, interaction, and groups of focal concern in Chapter 5 all exist within, affect, and are affected by the various macroscopic phenomena of concern here. In fact, neither microscopic nor macroscopic social phenomena make much sense without the other level. Individuals, interaction, and groups do not exist in isolation from macro-level phenomena, and organizations, societies, and global social relationships cannot exist without individuals, interaction, and groups. What is new in recent years is the emergence, largely because of the explosive growth of digital communication, of an increasingly networked social world where both micro-level and macro-level phenomena are ever more closely intertwined. And this contributes to the dramatic expansion of globalization as a process and of the growth of global relationships at every point in the continuum that runs from the most microscopic to the most macroscopic social phenomena. You are, of course, deeply implicated in all of this. In fact, if you are a young person, you are the most likely to participate in, and be affected by, these recent developments, especially those involving digitized interrelationships. For example, through our (micro-level) smartphones, we are able to access, participate in, and even influence everything from the most micro (our close friends) to the most macro (global) levels of the social world.

ORGANIZATIONS

The social world is awash in **organizations**, which are collectives purposely constructed to achieve particular ends. Examples include your college or university, which has the objective of educating you as well as your fellow students; corporations, such as Apple, Google, Amazon, and Walmart, whose objective is to earn profits; the International Monetary Fund (IMF), which seeks to stabilize currency exchanges throughout the world; and Greenpeace, which works to protect and conserve the global environment.

There is a particularly long and deep body of work in sociology that deals with organizations (Adler et al. 2016; Godwyn and Gittell 2011), much of it traceable to the thinking of Max Weber on a particular kind of organization, the bureaucracy. As you may recall, a **bureaucracy** is a highly rational organization, especially one that is very efficient. However, both Weber's own thinking and later sociological research (see the following section) make it clear that bureaucracies are *not* always so rational and are even as irrational as you undoubtedly sometimes find them to be. Nevertheless, the bureaucracy is a key element of Weber's

FIGURE 6.1 • Organization Chart for a Typical Bureaucracy

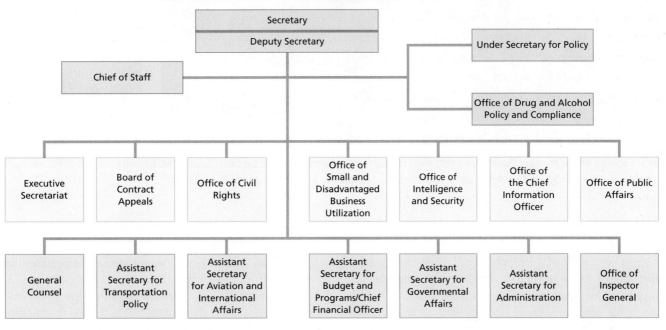

SOURCE: Organization Chart for a Typical Bureaucracy, U.S. Department of Transportation.

theory of the rationalization of the Western world. In fact, along with capitalism, the bureaucracy best exemplifies what Weber meant by rationalization. For decades, the concept of bureaucracy dominated sociological thinking about organizations, and it led to many important insights about the social world.

BUREAUCRACIES

Throughout his work, Weber created and used many "ideal types" as methodological tools with which to study the real world and conduct comparative-historical analysis (see Chapter 3). An *ideal type* greatly exaggerates the characteristics of a social phenomenon such as a bureaucracy. It is a model of how the social phenomenon is supposed to operate in some optimal sense, but rarely does. Once the model has been created, we can compare it to the characteristics of any specific example of the social phenomenon anywhere in the world. It serves to identify the ways in which the ideal type differs from the way in which the social phenomenon actually operates.

One of Weber's most famous ideal types was the bureaucracy. The ideal type of bureaucracy is primarily a methodological tool used to study real-life bureaucracies. However, it also gives us a good sense of the advantages of bureaucracies over other types of organizations. The ideal-typical bureaucracy is a model of what most large-scale organizations throughout much of the twentieth century

looked like or at least tried to resemble. Figure 6.1 is an organization chart for a typical bureaucracy. A bureaucracy has the following characteristics:

- A continuous series of offices, or positions, exist within the organization. Each office has official functions and is bound by a set of rules.

- Each office has a specified sphere of competence. Those who occupy the positions are responsible for specific tasks and have the authority to handle them. Those in other relevant offices are obligated to help with those tasks.

- The offices exist in a vertical hierarchy.

- The positions have technical requirements, and those who hold those offices must undergo the needed training.

- Those who occupy the positions do not own the things needed to do the job (computers, desks, and so on). The organization provides officeholders with what they need to get the job done.

- Those who occupy particular offices—chief executive officers, for example—cannot take the offices as their own; these remain part of the organization.

- Everything of formal importance—administrative acts, decisions, rules—is documented in writing.

Elected officials such as President Donald Trump (left) wield rational-legal authority, while King Salman of Saudi Arabia (center) has traditional authority based on his inherited position. Charismatic authority characterizes such popular leaders as Mahatma Gandhi (right).

The development of the bureaucracy is one of the defining characteristics of Western society. In Weber's view, it was a key source of the superiority of the West over other civilizations in the operation of society as a whole as well as of its major components, such as the military. Weber felt that in meeting the needs of large societies for mass administration, there is no better organizational form than, and no alternative to, the bureaucracy.

ASK YOURSELF

Have you ever been a member of a bureaucracy? How many of Weber's characteristics did it have? How well or poorly did it meet the needs of the society it was designed to serve? Why?

Authority Structures and Bureaucracy

Weber's work on bureaucracy is related to his thinking on three types of authority structures. Before getting to those types, we need two preliminary definitions. **Domination** is the probability, or likelihood, that commands will be obeyed by subordinates (Weber [1921] 1968). There are degrees of domination. Strong domination involves a high probability that commands will be obeyed; domination is weak when those probabilities are low. **Authority** is a particular type of domination: legitimate domination. The key question, then, is what makes authority legitimate as far as subordinates are concerned.

Weber differentiates among three types of authority:

- **Rational-legal authority** is domination legitimated on the basis of legally enacted rules and the right of those with authority under those rules to issue commands. For example, the president of the United States has rational-legal authority to take a variety of actions,

such as appointing federal officials, because the president is duly elected in accordance with the country's election laws. It is also legitimate for the president in the role of commander in chief to issue various commands, such as to order the use of troops in the case of an attack on the United States. However, in some cases the scope of such authority is not clearly defined. For example, throughout his tenure in office, and with increasing frequency over the years, former President Barack Obama claimed the authority to order numerous drone strikes on enemies in places such as Yemen, Afghanistan, Pakistan, Syria, and Iraq. While a number of enemy leaders were killed in those strikes, many innocent bystanders also lost their lives. The point is that President Obama believed that he had the legitimate authority to order the use of drones for such purposes. However, some would say that using drones in this way is an act of war. (President Trump is likely to be even more aggressive in exploring the limits of his authority.) As such, the drones' use should have been approved by Congress, which alone has the rational-legal authority to declare war. Similarly, but less dramatically, your professors have rational-legal authority because of the rules of the university and their positions within it. They can, for example, demand that you read this chapter, take an exam on it, and complete other course requirements.

- **Traditional authority** is based on belief in long-running traditions. For example, although the pope is elected by the college of cardinals, his authority within Catholicism is based primarily on the long traditions associated with his position. At the university, it is traditional for senior professors with many years of service, especially those who are well known on the campus or internationally, to acquire authority in their departments as well as in the university as a whole.

Gang Leader for a Day: A Rogue Sociologist Takes to the Streets (Penguin Books, 2008)

Sudhir Venkatesh (William B. Ransford Professor of Sociology at Columbia University; PhD, University of Chicago, 1997)

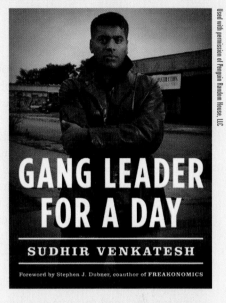

One of many provocative findings discussed in Sudhir Venkatesh's *Gang Leader for a Day* is that the organization of street gangs is similar to that of bureaucracies, such as corporations and the military. The original intent of Venkatesh's research was to study how African Americans experience urban poverty. But after Venkatesh is unexpectedly befriended by J. T., the charismatic leader of a Chicago gang, he learns that in order to carry out his study, he needs J. T.'s guidance and protection. Venkatesh discovers that J. T.'s gang, the Black Kings, controls the territory that includes one of Chicago's largest public housing projects, the Robert Taylor Homes. The absence of official authority, particularly law enforcement, and steady, full-time employment creates a vacuum of power and jobs that the Black Kings fill through its illegal drug trade. Like any other trade, the illegal drug trade requires a hierarchical organization to ensure that it operates efficiently. Careful bookkeeping and calculation are crucial to keeping a record of supply, wages, profits, and losses. Customer demand for a predictable product necessitates quality control measures. A clear division of labor and chain of command exists in the Black Kings. Numerous low-wage street dealers, or foot soldiers, sell the drugs, while only a few high-ranking officials, such as J. T., manage the trade within their respective territory. J. T. must report his affiliated gang's activities to a regional board of directors, who occupy the positions at the very top of the Black Kings hierarchy. While being the leader of a gang might appear to be a glamorous job, Venkatesh comments that J. T.'s daily routines are quite mundane, albeit with the potential risk of encountering violence from a rival gang.

Through J. T.'s friendship, Venkatesh is able to gain access to the residents of the Robert Taylor Homes, who are mostly impoverished African American women and their children. In order for the Black Kings to conduct its illegal drug trade smoothly, the gang performs certain services for these residents, such as buying school supplies for the children or cleaning up dirty hallways. J. T. even refers to himself as a philanthropist, using drug profits to help the community survive. The gang, however, holds a monopoly of power over the residents and "taxes" activities that generate any revenue, including prostitution, child care, and selling food. Money from the drug trade and these taxes fuels the informal economy coordinated by the Black Kings in the Robert Taylor Homes. It also accounts for why street gangs such as the Black Kings are prosecuted by the federal government as organized criminal enterprises under the Racketeer Influenced and Corrupt Organizations Act (RICO).

Supplementary Resources

- Venkatesh briefly describes *Gang Leader for a Day* in this video trailer: www.youtube.com/watch?v=yRq1AhFAN-4.
- Steven Levitt uses Venkatesh's research to explain the economics of gangs in his TED Talk, "The Freakonomics of Crack Dealing": www.ted.com/talks/steven_levitt_analyzes_crack_economics?language=en.
- *Dislocation* (2005) is a documentary directed by Venkatesh that portrays the demolition of the Robert Taylor Homes.

- **Charismatic authority** is based on the devotion of followers to what they define as the exceptional characteristics of a leader. Large numbers of people believed that Martin Luther King Jr. and Mahatma Gandhi had such exceptional characteristics and, as a result, became their devoted followers. A professor who is considered to be a charismatic teacher by her students is likely to attract a large number of adoring students. Such a professor is also likely to have authority over them as well as over other professors interested in learning how to improve their teaching techniques.

Each type of authority can spawn its own organizational form. However, it is rational-legal authority that is most associated with bureaucracy. In comparison to the bureaucracy, organizations based on traditional and charismatic authority are less rational. They are, for example, less efficient than is the highly efficient bureaucracy.

Rationality and Irrationality

Much sociological research on organizations in the twentieth century took Weber's highly rational model of a bureaucracy as a starting point for the study of the ways in which bureaucracies actually worked. However, much of that research found Weber's ideal-typical model to be unrealistic. For one thing, there is no single organizational model. The nature of the organization and its degree of rationality are contingent on such factors as the organization's size and the technologies that it employs (Orlikowski 2010; Pugh et al. 1968). For another, researchers found Weber's ideal-typical bureaucracy to be overly rational. This is not surprising, because for Weber ([1903–1917] 1949, 47) it was "not a *description* of reality." Weber purposely exaggerated its degree of rationality. The ideal-typical bureaucracy is a fiction designed to serve as a reference point for the study of real-world bureaucracies. However, researchers often overlooked the fact that this ideal type is a methodological tool and mistook it for an attempt to accurately describe bureaucracies. They concluded that, at best, real-world organizations exhibit a limited form of rationality, or what is called **bounded rationality** (Collet 2009; Simon [1945] 1976; Williamson 1975, 1985). That is, rationality is limited by the instabilities and conflicts that exist in most, if not all, organizations and the domains in which they operate (Scott 2014). It is also restricted by inherent limitations on humans' capacities to think and act in a rational manner. Some members of the organization are capable of acting more rationally than others are. However, none are able to operate in anything approaching the fully rational manner associated with Weber's ideal-typical organization (Cyert and March 1963).

The military is an example of an organization with bounded rationality. One source of instability in the military is the cycling of personnel in and out of it, especially in combat zones. Newcomers to the battle zone rarely know what to do. Their presence in, say, a platoon with experienced combat veterans can reduce the ability of the entire group to function. Another larger source of instability lies in the conflicts that exist between branches of the armed forces, as well as between central command and those in the field. In addition, military actions are often so complex and far-reaching that military personnel cannot fully understand them or rationally decide what actions to take. This phenomenon is sometimes referred to as the "fog of war" (Blight and Lang 2005).

A good deal of sociological research on bureaucracies has dealt with how the rational (that is, what is efficient) often becomes irrational (or inefficient). This is often referred to as the "irrationality of rationality"—the irrationality that often accompanies the seemingly rational actions associated with the bureaucracy (Ritzer, forthcoming). For example, Robert Merton ([1949] 1968) and other observers (Gupta 2012) found that instead of operating efficiently, bureaucracies introduce great inefficiency due to, among other things, "red tape." *Red tape* is a colloquial term for the rules that a bureaucracy's employees are needlessly required to follow, as well as the unnecessary online and offline questions to be answered and forms to be filled out by the clients of the bureaucracy. Bureaucracies generally demand much more information than they need, often to protect themselves from complaints, bad publicity, and lawsuits. Red tape also includes the telephone time wasted by keeping clients on hold and forcing them to make their way through a maze of prerecorded "customer service" options. In the end, clients often discover that they have been holding for the wrong office or, as is increasingly the case today, that they can resolve their problem only by visiting the organization's website.

Catch-22 is a term derived from the novel of that name by Joseph Heller (1961), which was adapted into a movie in 1970. It refers to the fact that bureaucratic rules may be written in such a way that one rule makes it impossible to do what another rule demands or requires. Heller's story takes place during World War II and focuses on a burned-out pilot who wants to be excused from flying further combat missions. One of the military's rules is that he can be excused from such missions if he has a doctor declare him crazy. However, there is another, contrary rule—Rule 22. It states that anyone rational enough to want to get out of combat cannot possibly be crazy. In other words, it is the ultimate in sanity to want to avoid life-threatening activities. If the pilot follows the first rule and does what is required to avoid flying combat missions, Catch-22 will make it impossible for him to get out of those missions.

Lawrence J. Peter and Raymond Hull (1969) intended what they called the *Peter Principle* to be a humorous characterization of a tendency in bureaucratic organizations to award promotions presumably on the basis of merit. The principle can be summarized in one sentence: "Employees tend to rise to their level of incompetence." The idea behind the principle is that if an employee does well in her position, she is rewarded by being promoted to a higher level in the organization. If she does well in that new position, she once again is offered a promotion. Promotions continue in this way until the person ends up in a position of authority and responsibility for which she does not possess the required skill set. To the extent that this possibility occurs, the result is an organization in which people in key leadership positions are not up to the task, thereby hampering the organization's ability to fulfill its mission.

Parkinson's Law was similarly conceived as a humorous attempt to point to another source of irrationality in bureaucratic organizations. It was formulated by Cyril Northcote Parkinson (1955), who worked in the British civil service and thus was intimately familiar with the ways in which large bureaucratic organizations functioned. Parkinson summarized the law when he wrote that "work expands so as to fill the time available for its completion." Thus, if a bureaucrat is assigned three reports to complete in a month, it will require a month's work to complete all three. If that same employee is assigned two reports during that time, it will take a month to complete two. And the task will still take a month even if the assignment calls for completing only one report.

Another source of irrationality is that described by Robert Merton ([1949] 1968) as the **bureaucratic personality**, someone who follows the rules of the organization to such a great extent that the organization's ability to achieve its goals is subverted. For example, an admissions clerk in a hospital emergency department might require incoming patients to fill out so many forms that they do not get needed medical care promptly. Similarly, a teacher might devote so much time and attention to discussing and enforcing classroom rules that little real learning takes place. A government bureaucrat might refuse welfare aid to a deserving person simply because a form was late or filled out incorrectly.

In these and in many other ways, the actual functioning of bureaucracies is at variance with Weber's ideal-typical characterization. However, it is important to remember that Weber was well aware of at least some of these possibilities. His ideal type was created as a methodological tool, *not* as an accurate description of reality.

Robert Merton is considered to be the founder of the sociology of science. His work, mostly in the structural-functional tradition, was influential in public policy. For instance, his research on successfully integrated communities was a key element in the U.S. Supreme Court's decision to desegregate public schools. His conceptual contributions to sociology include the bureaucratic personality, unintended consequences, and the self-fulfilling prophecy, among others.

The Informal Organization

A great deal of research in the twentieth century focused on the **informal organization**, that is, how the organization actually works as opposed to the way it is supposed to work as depicted, for example, in Weber's ideal-typical formal bureaucracy (Blau 1963). For instance, those who occupy offices lower in the bureaucratic hierarchy often have greater knowledge of and competence in specific issues than do those who rank above them. Thus, fellow employees may seek the advice of the lower-level bureaucrat rather than the one who ranks higher in the authority structure. Similarly, a recent study found that those interested in land conservation are more likely to be influenced by informal contacts outside a conservationist organization than by those in the organization

(Prell et al. 2010). The informal organization can help make up for inadequacies in the formal organization (Gulati and Puranam 2009). It might lead employees to take very useful actions that are ignored by the formal organization. For example, students constitute an informal network that offers advice about which faculty members to seek out if students are looking for undemanding courses or guaranteed high grades. Most generally, it is important *not* to examine informal and formal organizations in isolation from one another. Rather, the focus should be on the many linkages between them (McEvily, Soda and Tortoriello 2014). Informal organizations often arise to deal with problems and failures in formal organizations, and formal organizations often change in order to take account of actions in informal organizations.

Employees sometimes do things that exceed what is expected of them by the organization. However, they more often do less, perhaps far less, than they are expected to do. For example, contrary to the dictates of the formal organization, the most important things that take place in an organization may never be put down in writing. Employees may find it simply too time-consuming to fill out every form or document they are supposed to use. Instead, and contrary to the organization's rules, they may handle many tasks orally. In addition, employees handle some tasks orally so that if anything goes wrong, there is no damning evidence that could jeopardize careers and even the organization as a whole.

ASK YOURSELF

What specific bureaucracy came to mind when you read about Weber's definition of this type of organization? Is there an informal organization at work there? How is it different from the formal organization? In what ways is it more effective or less effective than the formal one is?

The problem for organizations (and individuals) is somewhat different in the digital age. Rather than too little information in writing, the danger is now that too much information is in written form, such as e-mail messages, posts on the internet, tweets, and the like. Of particular concern are posts that can exist forever and be widely and endlessly circulated. This danger was pointed out in 2010 and 2011 when WikiLeaks, a global organization, released many previously unpublished official U.S. government documents, including some relating to the war in Afghanistan. These documents revealed, among other things, secret ties between Pakistan security forces and the Taliban. The public release of this information jeopardized the lives of people in Afghanistan working undercover for the United States and disrupted already troubled Pakistan–U.S. relations. However, there are those, including those involved with WikiLeaks, who feel that secrets and secret agreements pose the greatest danger to human lives. For example, it is widely believed that Pakistan's security forces secretly helped the Taliban kill American soldiers.

Similarly, in 2016 WikiLeaks released some of the Democratic Party's e-mails. They showed that the party, which is supposed to be neutral, favored Hillary Clinton over her close rival, Bernie Sanders, for the party's nomination for the presidency in 2016. The release of the e-mails arguably contributed to Clinton's losing the election (Sanger and Perlroth 2016).

Snapchat attempts to deal with the problem of information remaining on the internet forever by automatically deleting posts and photos after a few seconds. While this seems comforting, those who receive the information and photos can save them by taking screenshots. The sender is notified about any screenshots, but there are ways for those taking them to conceal their identities. As one of the founders of Snapchat put it, "Nothing ever goes away on the internet" (Wortham 2013, A3).

While in some bureaucracies, power is meant to be dispersed throughout the offices, it often turns out that an organization becomes an **oligarchy**. That is, a small group of people at the top illegitimately obtain and exercise far more power than they are supposed to have. This can occur in any organization. Interestingly, this undemocratic process was first described by Robert Michels ([1915] 1962) in the most unlikely of organizations—labor unions and socialist parties that supposedly prized democracy. Michels called this "the iron law of oligarchy" (Martin 2015; Tolbert 2013). Those in power manipulate the organization (for example, as seen in the Democratic Party's e-mails released by WikiLeaks in 2016, by structuring elections to work to their advantage) so that the leaders and their supporters can stay in power indefinitely. At the same time, they make it difficult for others to get or to keep power. While oligarchy certainly develops in some organizations, in reality its occurrence is neither "iron" nor a law. That is, most organizations do not become oligarchical. Nevertheless, the tendency toward oligarchy is another important organizational process not anticipated by Weber's ideal-typical bureaucracy.

Weber's model also makes no provision for infighting within organizations. However, internal squabbles, and sometimes outright battles, are an everyday phenomenon within organizations. This is particularly evident in the government and other very large organizations, where one branch or office often engages in pitched turf battles with others. For example, in his book *Obama's Wars* (2010), investigative journalist Bob Woodward reveals numerous conflicts within the Obama administration over the direction of the war in Afghanistan, noting, for instance, that Vice President Joe Biden called the now-deceased Richard Holbrooke, then special representative to Afghanistan, "the most egotistical bastard I ever met" (Baker 2010, A12). In his book *Duty* (2014), published while he was U.S. secretary of defense, Robert Gates expresses his disappointment with President Obama, but he is outright contemptuous of Vice President Biden. There were also conflicts between Obama's advisers and others. For example, Afghanistan commander General David Petraeus disliked Obama adviser David Axelrod because he was "a complete spin doctor" (Baker 2010, A12). Interestingly, returning to the issue of written communications in bureaucracies, Petraeus was later disgraced, charged with a misdemeanor, and forced to resign for divulging classified information in notebooks he gave to his then-girlfriend, mentee, and biographer (Bennett 2016).

CHECKPOINT 6.1: TYPES OF ORGANIZATIONS

TYPE	DESCRIPTION
Bureaucracy	A highly rational organization characterized by efficiency
Informal organization	An organization as it really functions, as opposed to the way in which it is intended to function

CONTEMPORARY ORGANIZATIONAL REALITIES

As the social world has changed, so too has sociological thinking about many things, including organizations. New concepts are supplementing the concept of bureaucracy to enrich our understanding of these new realities. These concepts include gendered and network organizations and others that help inform our efforts to deal with organizational challenges such as sexual harassment, outsourcing of jobs, McDonaldization, and globalization.

GENDERED ORGANIZATIONS

Weber's model does not account for discrimination within organizations. In the ideal bureaucracy, any worker with the necessary training can fill any job. However, as "gendered organization" theorists, such as Joan Acker (1990, 2009), have shown, bureaucracies do not treat all workers the same (Pager, Western, and Bonikowski 2009). Jobs are often designed for an idealized worker—one who has no obligations except to the organization. Women, and sometimes men, who carry a responsibility for child rearing can have difficulty fitting this model (Williams 2001). Women may face the "competing devotions" of motherhood and work (Blair-Loy 2003; Wharton and Blair-Loy 2006). Some women who face inflexible workplaces due to gendered organizational practices and family obligations opt to become self-employed (Thébaud 2016). Organizations may also discriminate (consciously or unconsciously) in hiring and promotions, with white men (who tend to populate the higher levels of bureaucracies) being promoted over women and minorities (Alvesson and Due Billing 2009; Ortiz and Roscigno 2009). Some women in male-dominated business organizations find that they hit a "glass ceiling"—a certain level of authority in a company or organization beyond which they cannot rise (Acker 2009; Gorman and Kmec 2009; Wasserman and Frenkel 2015). This is also true in other contexts, such as medicine, as female surgeons have experienced (Zhuge et al. 2011), and higher education (Hart 2016). Women can see the top—hence the "glass"—but cannot reach it. Within other organizations, particularly

female-dominated ones, men can find themselves riding the "glass escalator" (Williams 1995). This is an invisible force that propels them past equally competent, or even more competent, women to positions of leadership and authority (Dill, Price-Glynn and Rokovski 2016; Williams, Muller, and Kilanski 2012).

In a global context, American female executives face a "double-paned" glass ceiling. There is the pane associated with the employing company in the United States, and there is a second pane women executives encounter when they seek work experience in the corporation's foreign locales. This is a growing problem, because experience overseas is increasingly a requirement for top-level management positions in multinational corporations, but corporations have typically "masculinized" these expatriate positions and thereby disadvantaged women. Among the problems experienced by women who succeed in getting these positions are sexual harassment, a lack of availability of programs (such as career counseling) routinely available to men, a lack of adequate mentoring, and male managers who are more likely to promote male rather than female expatriates. Much of the blame for this problem lies in the structure of the multinational corporations, and with the men who occupy high-level management positions within them. However, research has shown that female managers' greater passivity and lesser willingness to promote themselves for such expatriate management positions contribute to their difficulties (Insch, McIntyre, and Napier 2008).

While most of these ideas have been developed on the basis of studies of American organizations, they likely apply as well, or better, globally. For example, a recent study found that the glass ceiling exists in Durban, South Africa (Kiaye and Singh 2013). Figure 6.2 shows where women in industrialized nations have the best chance of circumventing the glass ceiling—that is, of being treated equally in the work world. New Zealand is best for working women; South Korea is the worst. The United States is in the middle of the pack.

The idea of a glass ceiling relates to vertical mobility—and its absence—for women in organizations. A related concept is the "glass cage," which deals with the horizontal segregation of women (and other minorities; Kalev 2009; Gabriel, Korczynski and Rieder 2015). The idea here is that men and women doing the same or similar jobs operate in separate and segregated parts of the organization. As in the case of the glass ceiling, women can see what is going on in other cages, but, compared with men, they find it more difficult to move between the cages. Although the cage is made of glass, the skills and abilities of women tend to be less visible, and, as a result, stereotypes about them abound. In addition, women have less communication with those outside the cage, are less likely to learn about jobs available

FIGURE 6.2 • Glass-Ceiling Index

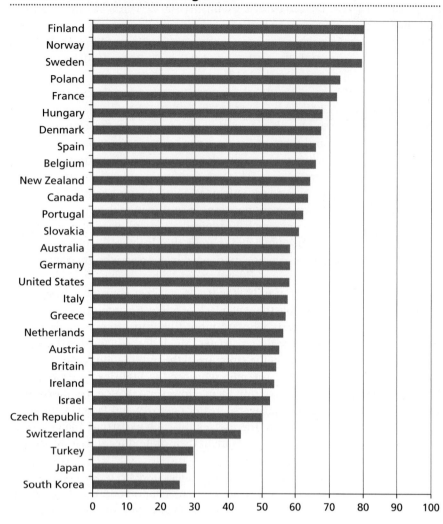

Country	Index
Finland	~83
Norway	~80
Sweden	~80
Poland	~73
France	~72
Hungary	~68
Denmark	~67
Spain	~66
Belgium	~66
New Zealand	~64
Canada	~63
Portugal	~62
Slovakia	~61
Australia	~59
Germany	~59
United States	~58
Italy	~58
Greece	~57
Netherlands	~56
Austria	~55
Britain	~54
Ireland	~53
Israel	~52
Czech Republic	~50
Switzerland	~44
Turkey	~30
Japan	~28
South Korea	~26

NOTE: 100 = best for working women.

SOURCE: © The Economist Newspaper Limited, London (March 5, 2015).

there, are not as likely to get high-profile assignments, and are less likely to get needed training. The situation confronting women would improve if there were more collaboration across the boundaries of the glass cage. Of course, the ultimate solution involves the elimination of the glass cage, as well as the glass ceiling. However, men are unlikely to want to eliminate either the glass cage or the glass ceiling because they tend to benefit from them. Many women may also accept both because they think their individual abilities will allow them to overcome those barriers.

A third interesting idea here is that of the "glass cliff" (Peterson 2016; Ryan and Haslam 2005). The glass ceiling and the glass cage represent barriers to the mobility of women within organizations. The concept of the glass cliff describes what can happen to women who experience upward mobility when the organization is going through hard times. The implication is that women who rise to high levels at such times end up in highly precarious positions.

Of course, the same would be true of men, but Ryan and Haslam found that women are more likely than men are to move into positions on boards of directors in organizations that have been performing badly. This means that they are more likely than males are to find themselves at the edge of that organizational cliff. A disproportionate number of those women (and minorities) are likely to be demoted or fall off that cliff (i.e., lose their jobs) and be replaced by males (Cook and Glass 2014). Peterson (2016) found that women in senior management positions in higher education are confronted by a similarly precarious situation. In addition, these positions grow more time-consuming, and that adversely affects their scholarly work.

OTHER PROBLEMS IN ORGANIZATIONS

Beyond the problems associated with gendered organizations, the ideal-typical bureaucracy makes no provision for an array of other problems in the organization or for problematic organizations (Friedrichs 2007). However, in the real world there is no shortage of either. The most heinous example of a problematic (to put it mildly) organization is the Nazi bureaucracy responsible for the murder of six million Jews, and others, during the Holocaust (Bauman 1989). The Islamic State, Al-Qaeda, the Mafia, and Mexican drug cartels, among many others, would also be considered by most people to be problematic organizations. In addition, many less developed countries in the world regard global organizations such as the International Monetary Fund and the World Bank as problematic because of the damaging austerity programs and other forms of "structural adjustment" they impose on recipient countries in exchange for monetary assistance and other help (Babb 2005).

Problems also occur in organizations that in themselves are not seen as problematic. For example, a scandal broke out in the National Football League (NFL) in late 2014, when the website TMZ released a video of Baltimore Ravens star running back Ray Rice knocking out his then-fiancée (and later wife) in an elevator in an Atlantic City hotel-casino earlier in the year. The NFL claimed it did not know about the incident, although it turned out that it did. When the incident became public, Rice was at first suspended for two games, but when the public furor grew, he was released by the Ravens and suspended by the NFL. The NFL could come increasingly to be seen as a problematic organization as evidence of player spousal abuse mounts, along with alarming revelations about the disastrous long-term effects of brain-related injuries incurred by players during practices and games, including dementia and suicide, stemming from concussions. The NFL seems to have learned its lesson, as is clear in the case of another scandal known as "Deflategate." Various people associated with the New England Patriots deflated footballs before the 2015 Super Bowl game (won by the Patriots) in order to give the team an advantage over the Indianapolis Colts. A quick investigation was undertaken, and as a result the Patriots were penalized in various ways: They were fined $1 million and lost two future draft picks, and superstar quarterback Tom Brady was to be suspended without pay for the first four games of the next season (Pennington 2015a). He appealed that judgment, but dropped his appeal in mid-2016, and he was suspended for the first four games of the 2016–2017 NFL season.

Sexual harassment is also a common organizational problem (Lopez, Hodson, and Roscigno 2009). **Sexual harassment** consists of unwanted sexual attention, such as sexually oriented remarks and jokes, advances, and requests that take place in the workplace or in other settings (Zippel 2007; see Chapter 11). In the United States, the federal Equal Employment Opportunity Commission (2015) was informed of 6,822 charges of sexual harassment in the workplace in 2015. However, many women (and the vast majority of victims are women) are afraid to report to management that they have been subjected to sexual harassment. Even when they are reported to management, many claims of sexual harassment never find their way into the judicial or criminal justice system.

Cases of sexual harassment also rarely get publicity, but that is changing. For example, in mid-2016 Roger Ailes, the powerful head of Fox News, was sued by a former news anchor, Gretchen Carlson, for sexual harassment (she was awarded $20 million). Other female newscasters at Fox were then emboldened to claim that they, too, had been subject to sexual harassment. In short order, Ailes was forced to resign as a result of the lawsuit and an internal investigation by Fox News of the other claims of sexual harassment by Ailes, as well as the enormous negative publicity that the case engendered (Koblin, Steel, and Rutenberg 2016). Even more strikingly, similar claims led to the firing of the star of Fox News, Bill O'Reilly, in 2017 (Leonhardt 2017).

While there is a tendency to ignore it, sexual harassment is widely practiced not only in the United States but globally, and a great many women are harmed by it. The United Nations estimates that 40 to

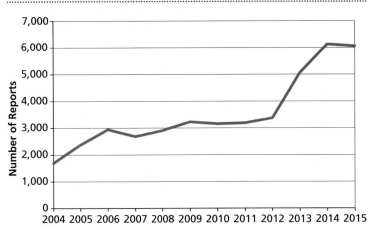

FIGURE 6.3 • Total Reports of Sexual Assault Made to the Department of Defense, 2004–2015

SOURCE: Data from U.S. Department of Defense, "Sexual Assault Prevention and Response," *Department of Defense Annual Report on Sexual Assault in the Military: Fiscal Year 2013* (Washington, DC: Author, 2014); data for 2014 onward from U.S. Department of Defense, "Appendix B: Statistics on Sexual Assault," Fiscal Year 2015 (Washington DC: Author, 2015).

50 percent of women in European Union countries experience some form of sexual harassment at work (Directorate-General for Employment, Industrial Relations and Social Affairs 1998, iii, cited in United Nations General Assembly 2006, 42; see also UN Women 2014).

To be considered illegal in the United States, sexual harassment must recur and/or be severe and result in a hostile workplace environment, or even the firing of the harassed employee. The stereotype of high-ranking men (e.g., Roger Ailes and Bill O'Reilly) demanding sexual favors from subordinates (usually women) is generally accurate, although both men and women can perpetrate and be subject to all forms of sexual harassment. About 17 percent of 2015 charges reported to the Equal Opportunity Employment Commission were filed by men (U.S. Equal Employment Opportunity Commission 2015).

In the U.S. armed forces, however, sexual harassment does seem to follow the stereotypical pattern of males harassing females. There have been many allegations of sexual harassment (and sexual assault) of female service members, and criticism of the armed services for failing to react adequately has been mounting (Schemo 2003; Shear 2013; Verkaik 2006). The U.S. Department of Defense reported that cases of sexual assault in the military increased almost 50 percent between fiscal year 2012 and fiscal year 2013 and continue to grow (see Figure 6.3). Military men and those at higher ranks perceived fewer barriers to reporting such assaults compared to military women and those at lower ranks (U.S. Equal Employment Opportunity Commission 2015).

One of the largest organizations in the world, the Catholic Church, has had to address a global organizational culture that enabled priests and other church officials to perpetuate a system of sexual assaults and abuses against children. This culture has been a huge problem not only because of the behavior of the priests and its impact on children, but also because church officials have not done nearly enough to dismiss those responsible and make it more difficult for such assaults to occur in the future (Doyle 2003; Spröber et al. 2014). This problem and the difficulties involved in uncovering it, let alone dealing with it, constitute the central theme of *Spotlight,* the 2016 Academy Award winner for best motion picture.

Disasters (and other unplanned outcomes) are deeply problematic for organizations. Such events often occur as the result of rational organizational processes (Vaughan 1996). For example, in the 1980s, the National Aeronautics and Space Administration (NASA) operated on the basis of what it considered to be a highly reliable and rational plan. As a result, it focused on, among many other things, a variety of quantifiable factors to keep the space shuttle *Challenger* on schedule for its launch. In doing so, the agency cut a number of corners and engaged in various economies. These actions made sense from the perspective of NASA as a rationalized organization. However, they contributed to the disaster on January 28, 1986, in which *Challenger's* fuel tank broke apart, causing the in-flight destruction of the shuttle and the deaths of seven crew members.

CONTEMPORARY CHANGES IN ORGANIZATIONS

In the last several decades, bureaucratic organizations have undergone a number of important changes that do not fit well with Weber's view of organizations. Indeed, the very notion, if not reality, of a bureaucracy in Weber's terms is not only changing rapidly, but in some cases disappearing completely. For one thing, contrary to Weber's thinking on the likelihood of the growth and spread of bureaucracy in organizations, many of the largest organizations, especially industrial organizations and labor unions, have been forced to downsize and, in the process, reduce the size of their bureaucracies dramatically (Cooper, Pandey, and Campbell 2012). The idea that "bigger is better" is no longer the rule in most organizations. Instead of constantly adding new functions, and more employees, organizations are now likely to focus on their "core competencies." For example, the Ford Motor Company is focusing on manufacturing automobiles and not, as it once did, on making (among many other things) the steel for the frames and the rubber for the tires. Ford also sold off the Volvo and Jaguar lines to focus on the Ford brand. In essence, organizations have come to concentrate on being "lean and mean" (Harrison 1994). They have also sought to streamline their systems of production—to develop lean methods of production using more high-tech systems and fewer employees (Janoski 2015). Many newer organizations, such as Facebook and even Google, have learned crucial lessons from the problems experienced by organizational giants such as Ford. They are smaller and far less hierarchical; they are increasingly flat structures with the characteristics of social networks discussed in Chapter 5. They seek to avoid ever losing their focus or becoming too large and diverse. As a result, it is unlikely that they will ever need to downsize or simplify to the degree that Ford has in order to accomplish these goals.

To adapt to a rapidly changing environment, contemporary organizations have also been forced to become more flexible and more agile than the ideal-typical bureaucracy suggests. For example, it appears that Ford has become flexible enough to compete with rising automobile manufacturers such as Hyundai. When today's organizations lack such flexibility, there is a strong likelihood that they will decline or disappear. For instance, the video store chain Blockbuster, which went bankrupt in 2010 and closed its last store in late 2013, failed to adapt to competition from Netflix and, at least initially, its movies by mail. More important, it failed to anticipate the streaming of movies to one's television or computer (and now to both smart TVs and regular TVs connected through devices such as Roku). Customers were no longer willing to travel to a video store when they could stream movies from the comfort of their homes via a cable provider such as Comcast or online from Netflix, Hulu, or Amazon.

The social networking site MySpace is also a victim of failing to adapt to new consumer demands. In 2006, MySpace was the most popular website in the United States, but it lost its popularity to Facebook because it maintained the anonymity of its users instead of allowing them to use their real identities. By 2015, only 50 million individuals visited MySpace per month, compared to 1.44 billion on Facebook (Schenker 2015).

Yet another important organizational development is the increasing trend toward **outsourcing**, or the transfer of activities once performed by one organization to another organization in exchange for money (Furneaux 2013; Ritzer and Lair 2007). Since the early 2000s, outsourcing has increased dramatically. For example, in 1989, U.S. companies spent between $9 billion and $12 billion per year to outsource information technology (IT) jobs (Krass 1990; Lacity and Hirschheim 1993), "from medical transcription to nanotechnology research" (Davis-Blake and Broschak 2009, 322). By 2008, that number had reached $55 billion, and it was expected to grow between 15 and 20 percent per year over the succeeding five years (Oshri, Kotlarsky, and Willcocks 2009). Companies have become more likely to outsource functions such as those handled traditionally by human resource departments (Korkki 2012). Hospitals outsource the operation of their emergency rooms to businesses that employ people—including physicians—devoted to such work. Hospitals are also increasingly likely to outsource such activities as cleaning and food preparation to outside contractors. This can adversely affect the functioning of hospitals and the well-being of patients. Most important, the decline in cleanliness can lead to an increase in hospital-based infections (Zuberi 2013). Local, state, and federal governments also outsource work to other organizations, especially private businesses. An example that received a lot of negative publicity after the Iraq war was the U.S. government's outsourcing of many military and paramilitary activities in Iraq to a company known as Blackwater. When the news media raised alarms over the company's involvement in unwarranted killings and use of unnecessary force, the company changed its name to Xe Services.

Another recent trend in organizations not anticipated by Weber's ideal-typical bureaucracy is that of turning over to clients some of the work formerly performed by officeholders. For example, we are increasingly filling out census forms on our own, thereby doing work that used to be done by census takers. We are scanning checks into our cell phones instead of handing them to tellers, reviewing restaurants and movies online rather than reading reviews by professional critics, and talking about our experiences with products or brands on social networking sites instead of passively accepting advertising messages from producers. More and more, we are scanning our own groceries; the first self-checkout machine was installed in the United States in 1992, and by 2014 it was estimated that 430,000 such machines were in operation across the country. In taking on these tasks, clients and consumers are turned into producers, at least for a time. In other words, consumers have been transformed into *prosumers*, combining the acts of consumption and production (Ritzer, Dean, and Jurgenson 2012; see Chapter 15). This is yet another wide-ranging and pervasive change that is dramatically transforming the nature of organizations and organizational life. The most recent changes are even eliminating the work performed by customers and clients and turning it over to "smart machines" (Ritzer 2015). For example, instead of requiring a person to unload a shopping cart and scan each product at checkout, a smart machine can now scan the products in the cart as the customer leaves the store and charge the total bill to the customer's credit card.

GLOBALIZATION AND ORGANIZATIONS

Most organizations of any significant size have become increasingly global. They are affected by numerous global

One form of offshore outsourcing that has become familiar to many U.S. consumers is customer service and product support provided by Indian call centers. Why are some employees in such centers encouraged to assume American identities?

realities and changes and in many cases have become global forces and players themselves. The global reach of McDonald's is well known. It has more than 36,000 restaurants in 119 countries throughout the world. However, in the fast-food industry, Yum! Brands (corporate parent of Pizza Hut, KFC, and others) is in slightly more countries—140—and has over 7,000 more restaurants than McDonald's. Walmart is another American global powerhouse, with more than 11,000 stores in 27 countries. Other organizations with a presence in the United States have their roots elsewhere in the world. Examples include IKEA, based in Sweden, with 328 stores in 28 countries; H&M, an apparel retailer from Sweden; T-Mobile, a telecommunications company originating in Germany; HSBC, a financial services provider from Hong Kong and Shanghai; and Zara International, a fashion retailer, whose home base is in Spain (Ritzer, forthcoming).

Spanning much of the globe is a challenge to any organization and forces it to adapt to global realities in innumerable ways. Ford Motor Company, for example, recognized some years ago that producing a different model car for every country or global region was very inefficient, so it focused on the manufacture and sale of a global car, the Ford Focus.

Globalization has also accelerated the transfer of work to organizations in other countries, known as **offshore outsourcing**. See Table 6.1 for a list of the world's top 20 outsourcing destinations. The top 8 destination cities are all in India and the Philippines, where a large proportion of the population is fluent in English. This is important because the United States is the world leader in offshore outsourcing. Offshore outsourcing takes many forms, but the one we are most familiar with is the outsourcing of call center work. A call center is a centralized office that handles a large volume of telephone calls from people asking an organization for information and help. At first, many U.S. organizations outsourced such work to call centers in the United States. More recently, much of that work has been outsourced offshore because it can be done outside the United States much less expensively.

India is a particularly attractive location for the outsourcing of call center work once performed in the United States (Aneesh 2012). The pay of call center workers is much lower in India than it is in the United States, and many Indians speak excellent English. In fact, many call center workers outside the United States are expected to "pose as Americans" as part of their employment. In a strategy referred to as "national identity management," they adopt, among other things, American names and hometowns (Poster 2007). For Indian women, working at call centers can provide financial autonomy. Yet the number of women working in these jobs—particularly during the night shift—has raised cultural anxieties about changing gender norms within India (Patel 2010). For example, there is worry that because unmarried women who work at call centers will be more able to support themselves financially, they will be less beholden to family demands.

In India, it is unusual for women to work at night rather than be at home. Indian call center companies go to great lengths to calm the fears of the employees and their families about this and other aspects of their work life. For example: "Separate wings require individual key card access and security guards are posted to each floor, 24 hours a day. . . . Shuttles run from 7 a.m. to 7 p.m. from the building to the nearest metro station. Private taxis, on contract with the company, are available for anyone working 8 p.m. to 6 a.m., and if there are female passengers, a security guard accompanies them" (Swanson 2012). Some call centers even have "family days" with tours of the workplace, dinner, and entertainment. Said one human resources officer, "Some of these things were just to make parents and families feel comfortable with where their daughter or son goes all day" (Swanson 2012).

In recent years, the Philippines has caught up with and passed India as the dominant locale for call center work stemming from the United States (Bajaj 2011). There were almost 700,000 Filipino call center workers in 2011, about 1 percent of the labor force (Whaley 2012), and that number was expected to almost double within a few years. That is roughly double the number of such workers in India. Filipino call center workers earn comparatively high salaries and generally are happy with the work. They also get additional perks, such as free meals and, as in India, shuttle service. The main reason U.S. companies have switched

TABLE 6.1 • Top 20 Outsourcing Destinations, 2016

RANK	COUNTRY	CITY
1	India	Bangalore
2	Philippines	Manila
3	India	Mumbai
4	India	Delhi
5	India	Chennai
6	India	Hyderabad
7	Philippines	Cebu City
8	India	Pune
9	Poland	Kraków
10	Ireland	Dublin
11	Costa Rica	San José
12	China	Shanghai
13	China	Beijing
14	Czech Republic	Prague
15	China	Dalian
16	Sri Lanka	Colombo
17	Malaysia	Kuala Lumpur
18	Vietnam	Ho Chi Minh City
19	Vietnam	Hanoi
20	South Africa	Johannesburg

SOURCE: Data from "Tholons 2016 Top 100 Outsourcing Destinations," Tholons, January 29, 2016.

from India to the Philippines as the main locale for their call centers is that the residents of the Philippines, a former American territory, are very familiar with American culture. Their American English is not as accented as the British English spoken by most Indians. Filipinos are likely to watch American TV shows, follow American sports teams, and eat hamburgers. American companies are making this choice even though Filipino workers are slightly more expensive ($300 per month per worker) than are Indian workers ($250 per month per worker). Regardless, both Filipino and Indian call center workers earn far less than the roughly $1,700 per month earned by American call center workers.

Recently, there has been a backlash against offshore outsourcing. This has occurred in a number of European countries, but it has been especially strong in the United States. During the 2016 presidential campaign, Donald Trump railed against the fact that offshore outsourcing had caused the loss of companies and the jobs they had provided. In addition, there was already a movement for *backsourcing,* or bringing businesses and jobs back into the countries that were not long ago eager to outsource them (Gylling et al. 2015). However, given the erosion and destruction of plant and equipment in those countries and the seeming paucity of workers willing to take low-wage, low-skill jobs, it remains to be seen how much backsourcing will actually occur in Europe and the United States.

McDonaldization and Bureaucratic Organizations

During the early twenty-first century, the fast-food restaurant can be seen as the best example of the ongoing process of rationalization first described by Weber (Ritzer, forthcoming). While the fast-food restaurant is a relatively new and important organizational development, it is continuous with the bureaucracy and its basic principles: efficiency, predictability, calculability, control, and the seemingly inevitable irrationalities of rationality. What, then, distinguishes McDonaldized fast-food restaurants from bureaucracies?

Many fast-food restaurants, as well as a variety of other businesses, are franchised (Dicke 1992; Grace and Palmer 2015). In a franchise system, a large business (such as McDonald's) sells various rights to franchisees, who control small, legally independent firms. The franchisees invest their own money, and much of the risk of failure falls on them rather than the big business that grants the franchise. In return for their investment, franchisees obtain the right to use, among many other things, the company name, its logo (e.g., the "Golden Arches"), its distinctive products, and its ways of operating. While each franchise is independent, it "must conform to detailed standards of operation designed and enforced by the parent company" (Dicke 1992, 2–3). Thus, a franchise system combines a small business with a large bureaucratic system in which it exists and functions. Most important, the franchise must operate on the basis of the same rational principles that characterize the large bureaucratic organization.

McDonaldization is therefore applicable to both large organizations and relatively small organizations, most of which are independent operations, not franchises. The principles of bureaucracy have tended to be applied to state governments and giant corporations such as Ford and Walmart. Such bureaucracies still exist, although in many cases they are much smaller than they once were. The principles of McDonaldization can be applied not only to large corporations such as Starbucks but also to small independent restaurants and all sorts of other small enterprises. In short, the model of the McDonaldized fast-food restaurant has much wider applicability than the bureaucratic model does. There are far more small enterprises throughout the United States and the world than there are state governments and large corporations.

McDonaldization is applicable to both consumption-oriented organizations and production-oriented organizations. The bureaucratic model is most applicable, outside of government, to large production-oriented corporations. However, the United States has moved away from a society dominated by work and production to one dominated by consumption. As a result, the large corporation involved in goods production has declined in importance, at least in the United States and other developed countries. In its place we have seen the rise of similarly large corporations, such as Subway, Walmart, and IKEA, devoted to consumption. While the corporate structures of these organizations remain highly bureaucratized, their real hearts lie in the numerous smaller outlets that constitute the sources of income and profit for the organizations. Thus, of greatest importance now is the McDonaldization of those outlets, not the bureaucratization of the larger organizations in which they exist.

ASK YOURSELF

Why do you think being customer-friendly is more important to McDonaldized systems than to traditional bureaucracies? What is the goal of this user-friendliness, and why aren't bureaucracies more user-friendly?

The key point is that bureaucratization involves a kind of rationality that is highly centralized and largely invisible to those who consume the goods and services produced by these organizations. Few people have much person-to-person contact with the U.S. Internal Revenue Service (IRS) or with the bureaucracy that runs Honda. However, McDonaldization is both very local and highly visible to those who consume in settings such as fast-food restaurants. People have a lot of direct, person-to-person contact with those who work in McDonaldized settings. This means, among other things, that the fast-food restaurant—and, indeed, almost all McDonaldized systems in the realm of consumption—need to be much more "customer-friendly" than does the traditional bureaucracy. Counter people are trained to smile and wish you a "nice day" (Leidner 1993). At Walmart there is even an employee—the greeter—whose sole task is to be warm and friendly to customers when they enter the store. Then there are those "smiley faces" that customers see throughout the store. Similarly, Mac computers maintain their physical presence through aesthetically pleasing Apple stores, which include "genius bars" staffed by friendly and knowledgeable workers who can answer questions in person and fix your laptop. In contrast, the IRS has no full-time greeters or smiley faces. In fact, it is very difficult even to speak with an IRS agent on the phone.

Despite the spread of McDonaldization, some are speculating that it, like bureaucratization, has passed its peak. The online auction site eBay is considered by some to be a new model of organizational development in the contemporary world (Ahuvia and Izberk-Bilgin 2011). Unlike McDonaldization, the basic dimensions of eBayization include variety, unpredictability, and limited control. Millions of products are available on eBay compared to only the few dozen offered at McDonalds. The predictable products of McDonald's are quite unlike the highly unpredictable products on eBay. Whereas eBay sellers interact directly with buyers of their products with little involvement from the eBay organization, McDonaldized systems exercise more widespread control. McDonald's may be fast, but eBay is vast. However, it is possible to argue that eBay is a highly McDonaldized company. For example, it takes a highly rationalized company and system to offer millions of products for sale.

NETWORK ORGANIZATIONS

The bureaucracy and the fast-food restaurant both continue to be important in the early twenty-first century. However, organizations continue to change and evolve. Further, entirely new organizational forms are coming into existence. One such new form is the network organization. As discussed in more detail below, the **network organization** is defined by its networks, especially those based on and linked together by information (Blaschke, Schoeneborn, and Seidl 2012). The network organization came about in the wake of the revolution in informational technology in the United States in the 1970s. Developments included the penetration of television deep into American life and the introduction of home computers, personal data assistants (PDAs), and the internet (Allan 2007; Van Dijk 2012). The network model is also inextricably entwined with globalization. Most of the important functions and processes in the information age are increasingly dominated by these networks, and many of them are global in scope. This revolution led, in turn, to a fundamental restructuring of the global capitalist system beginning in the 1980s. For example, multinational corporations grew in importance, in part because of great improvements in the ability to communicate globally. Those corporations that were narrowly nation based experienced serious declines or were themselves transformed into multinationals.

Characteristics of the Network Organization

This new organizational form has several notable characteristics. Of greatest importance is the idea that an organization is composed of several **networks**, or "interconnected nodes" (see the discussion of social networks

in Chapter 5). A network organization has the following characteristics:

- *Horizontal structure.* In contrast to the vertical and hierarchical structures that characterize classic bureaucracies, network organizations are flatter, meaning that there are fewer positions between the top of the organization and the bottom.

- *Fuzzy boundaries.* Network organizations are *not* seen as distinct entities with clear and definite boundaries, as would be the case with a bureaucracy. Rather, organizations intertwine with one another in many ways. Most obviously, they form strategic alliances with other organizations that have similar or complementary goals.

- *Dispersed decision making.* Many of the differences between network organizations and bureaucracies stem from a number of highly successful Japanese innovations. One such innovation is more collective decision making, or the involvement of many more people in the organization in the decision-making process.

- *Flexible production.* Manufacturing organizations with a network model have moved away from mass production and toward more flexible production methods, such as variable and limited production runs.

An organization with these characteristics is, in comparison with a bureaucracy, more open, more capable of expansion, more dynamic, and better able to innovate without disrupting the system.

In the global information economy, at least in developed nations, the nature of work is being transformed. Workers, including manufacturing employees, are dealing more with information and less with material processes (Caprile and Serrano Pascual 2011). This has reduced the total number of employees needed, even as output increases. In addition, the network organization allows for new kinds of work arrangements, because information can flow anywhere, especially anywhere there is a computer or a smartphone. Thus, for example, more people can work from the comfort of their homes, in transit on airplanes, and in hotels anyplace in the world (Alexander, Ettema, and Dijst 2010; Kaufman-Scarbrough 2006). This change is reflected in the 2009 movie *Up in the Air,* which depicts corporations' efforts to move away from firing people in person and toward doing it via computer videoconferencing. In a more personal example, I have teletaught some of my graduate-level courses at the University of Maryland from my winter home in Florida.

Informationalism

The processing of knowledge, or what Manuel Castells (b. 1942; 1996, 1997, 1998; Subramanian and Katz 2011;

Williams 2012) famously calls **informationalism**, is a key feature of the network organization. Forces of production and consumption, such as factories and shopping malls, are linked through knowledge and information. Thus, for example, the stocking of shelves at Walmart is done nearly automatically. Computerized technology at the local Walmart tracks stock on hand and transmits the information to centralized warehouses. As the stock is being depleted, new shipments are sent out automatically, so that the shelves at the local Walmart will remain well stocked.

Informationalism has five basic characteristics:

- Technologies act on information, such as the depletion of stock at Walmart.

- These technologies have a pervasive effect, as information transmitted to personal computers, tablets, and smartphones increasingly becomes a part of all human activity.

- All organizations, and other systems, using information technologies are defined by a "networking logic" that allows them to affect a wide variety of processes and organizations to which they are linked. For example, Walmart has linkages to its many suppliers throughout the world.

- The new technologies are highly flexible, allowing them to adapt and change constantly.

- The specific technologies associated with information are already merging into a highly integrated system that cuts across many different organizations and areas of the world. Thus, for example, the internet, e-mail, and text messaging link innumerable global organizations.

As a result of informationalism, a new, increasingly profitable global information economy has emerged. The productivity of firms and nations depends on their ability to generate, process, and apply knowledge-based information efficiently. Global communication systems allow those involved in this economy to operate as a unit on a worldwide scale. While it is a global system, there are regional

Manuel Castells is well known for his research in communication and the information society, including the ways in which information is increasingly becoming a part of all human activity and how the processing of knowledge has allowed for the emergence of an increasingly profitable global information economy. He is also known for his studies of social movements.

differences, even among those areas—North America, the European Union, the Asia-Pacific region—that are at the heart of the new global economy (Abdul 2015). Other regions, such as sub-Saharan Africa, are largely excluded, as are pockets of deprivation in the developed world, including inner cities in the United States.

The network organization, as well as the informationalism that defines it, is the latest organizational form to draw sociologists' attention, but it will certainly not be the last. New organizational forms are likely to emerge as society and the world continue to change.

CHECKPOINT 6.2: TYPES OF CONTEMPORARY ORGANIZATIONS

TYPE	DESCRIPTION
Gendered organization	An organization in which gender plays a large role in determining a person's position and career progression
Network organization	An organization defined by networks based on and linked by information

SOCIETIES

Sociologists have traditionally defined *society* as a complex pattern of social relationships that is bounded in space and persists over time (Ray 2007). This definition has two key characteristics: First, it is very abstract; second, this abstractness allows it to encompass the gamut of social relationships. Thus, in these terms, a triad (a three-person group) and any larger group would be a kind of society, as would the United States and other countries, as well as global organizations such as the United Nations and the International Monetary Fund.

There is a long tradition in sociology of thinking about and studying such highly diverse societal forms. A classic analysis of this type was created by Ferdinand Toennies ([1887] 1957), who differentiated between two broad types of societies—*gemeinschaft* and *gesellschaft*. He labeled traditional societies **gemeinschaft societies** and defined them as being characterized by face-to-face relations. Toennies considered families, rural villages, and small towns to be gemeinschaft societies. Such societies tend to be quite small because they are based on intimate interaction. Relationships between people are valued for their intrinsic qualities, such as familiarity and closeness, and not, or at least not merely, for their utility. Gemeinschaft societies continue to exist in many parts of the world, including the United States.

More modern societies are **gesellschaft societies**, characterized by impersonal, distant, and limited social relationships. In such societies, people tend to enter relationships for what they can gain from them rather than for their intrinsic qualities. That is, relationships are often a means to an end. Gesellschaft societies can be small in scale, and social groups and communities can have the characteristics of a gesellschaft society, such as impersonality. For instance, employees within an office may work together for 40 hours or more per week but interact with one another only in a highly businesslike way. Furthermore, after they go home to their "real lives" and intimate relationships, they are likely to interact rarely, if ever, with coworkers outside the workplace. However, gesellschaft societies are much more likely to be large-scale societies, or to exist within them.

Of course, gemeinschaft and gesellschaft are ideal types. In the real world, including today's world, aspects of both exist in all societies. The abstract and broad-ranging definition of society mentioned previously encompasses both gemeinschaft and gesellschaft societies, and everything in between. Furthermore, both concepts can be applied to every social relationship, from the smallest group, such as a dyad or triad, to the largest society, such as China.

Although the earlier general definition of society has its utility, *society* can be more narrowly and specifically—and usefully—defined as a relatively large population that lives in a given territory, has a social structure, and shares a culture. The United States, China, and Spain would be societies in this macro-level sense of the term; a triad or group or organization would not be a society. This definition also fits the thrust of this chapter, which ends with a discussion of the most macroscopic level of social organization: the global society.

ASK YOURSELF

Keeping in mind that gesellschaft and gemeinschaft societies are idealized abstractions of reality and that real societies can have characteristics of both, make a list of all the groups and communities to which you belong and decide which are more gesellschaft and which are more gemeinschaft. Why have you included each group or community in one category or the other? In which groups or communities do you prefer to spend time, and why?

One of the best-known theories of society in this sense was created by leading structural-functionalist Talcott Parsons. In fact, Parsons wrote a book entitled *Societies* (1966). As a structural-functionalist, Parsons had a very positive view of macro-level societies. He was concerned with the major structures of societies, including the economy, the political system, systems responsible for transmitting culture and its norms and values (e.g., schools), and the legal system, which is responsible for the integration of society. Clearly, these are key components of society in the macro sense of the term.

Sociologists who study societies often ask big questions about them and their changing nature. One of the most notable recent efforts to think about the issues facing society as a whole is the work of German sociologist Ulrich Beck (Anaïs and Hier 2012). Until recently, it was the norm to think of society as being dominated by industry. In "industrial society," the key issue was wealth and how to distribute it more evenly. This problem continues to concern many sociologists (see Chapter 8). However, Beck ([1986] 1992) argues that we have moved from an industrial society to a **risk society**, where the central issue is risk, and especially how to prevent, minimize, and channel it. In addition, while in an industrial society a central concern is equality, in a risk society the focus shifts to how to remain safe in the face of increasing risk. Most important, there is a big difference between the two types of societies in the ways in which solidarity is achieved. In an industrial society, solidarity is achieved by people joining together for the positive goal of creating a more equal society. In a risk society, solidarity is achieved through the largely negative and defensive goal of being spared from danger. The implication is that risk society is weaker, more individualized, and less laudable than industrial society and its humanitarian goal of increased equality.

What accounts for the emergence of risk society? The key is that the risks are far greater in scope today than ever before, and no society is safe from them; risks are increasingly global. Many societies produce various risks (e.g., climate change, the danger from nuclear plants and weapons, the global economic meltdown of 2007 that began in the United States, the Ebola epidemic that exploded in West Africa in 2014), which threaten not only those societies themselves but others as well. Furthermore, even when risk is exported, consciously or unconsciously, to other societies, it tends to boomerang back on the society that is the source of the risk. For example, terrorism is a risk to the United States and other societies. The United States has sought to cope with terrorism by combatting it outside its own borders (e.g., in Afghanistan and more recently in North Africa). However, those efforts have provoked attacks on the United States and its interests elsewhere in the world.

Globalization is the major reason why there are far greater risks to society than ever before. Risks in one society easily flow to many other societies. For example, because of relatively easy and inexpensive air travel, a flu outbreak in one society can quickly engulf many other societies. Thus, modern risks are not easily restricted to one locale or society. A nuclear accident, such as the one that occurred at Chernobyl in Ukraine (then part of the Soviet Union) in 1986, can release radiation that affects surrounding societies and ultimately much of the world (see Figure 6.4). Modern risks are also not limited by time. The Chernobyl accident led to genetic defects in Ukrainians and those living in neighboring societies for decades afterward.

Globalization has led some sociologists to call into question the equation of society and the nation-state, arguing that in the contemporary world it is necessary to think about a global society. Debates about the possibility of global citizenship are one example of how the idea of globalization is reshaping how we think about the boundaries of what we call society (Kivisto and Faist 2007, 138–140). Other sociologists have suggested that globalization requires a perspective on society that sees it as more fluid and unstable than would be implied by the work of earlier sociologists. Thus, Zygmunt Bauman contends that we live in "liquid times," where structures and institutions no longer "keep their shape for long" (2007, 1). John Urry (2000) has gone further and written about a sociology that goes beyond a focus on societies. He argues that because of all sorts of increased mobilities, we live in a post-society era. People, objects, and information, among many other things, move too often and too quickly to be encapsulated in societies or, perhaps, anything else. Urry's work has led to a burgeoning field of mobilities study in sociology (Sheller 2014) and to a new journal entitled *Applied Mobilities* (Sheller and Urry 2016).

It is clear from the preceding discussion that sociologists who still analyze societies do not stop at their borders but also examine various mobilities within, among, and between societies. As a result, the focus of such scholarship in recent years has shifted beyond societies

FIGURE 6.4 • Radiation from Chernobyl

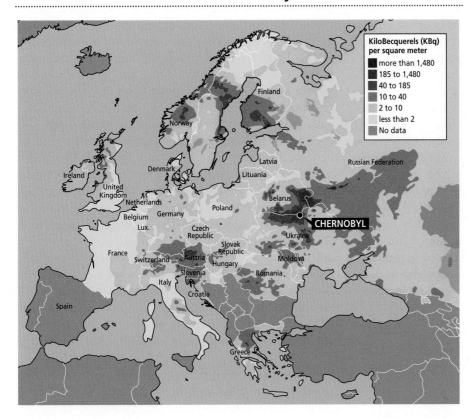

SOURCES: UNEP/GRID-Arendal, European Environment Agency; AMAP Assessment Report: Arctic Pollution Issues, Arctic Monitoring and Assessment Programme (AMAP), 1998, Oslo; European Monitoring and Evaluation Programme (MEP); Co-operative programme for monitoring and evaluation of the long-range transmission of air pollutants in Europe, 1999. Adapted from Le Monde Diplomatique, July 2000.

and even their interrelationships to the even more macroscopic global level and the mobilities (e.g., migration) that serve to define it.

GLOBAL RELATIONSHIPS

Most sociological work on the global level operates with a different set of concepts from those discussed throughout this chapter. All of these concepts are consistent with the macroscopic sense of society:

- A **nation** is a large group of people linked through common descent, culture, language, or territory. Nations can exist in contiguous geographic areas, regardless of country borders. For example, the Kurds have often been in the news as they have battled the Islamic State in a struggle to survive. As of mid-2017, they have been publicly enlisted and armed by the United States in the fight against ISIS. They live in Kurdistan, a region that overlaps Iraq, Iran, Syria, and Turkey. Nations can also be spread throughout much of the world, such as the Roma people (so-called Gypsies), who live throughout Europe and increasingly in the United States.

- A **state** is a political organizational structure with relatively autonomous officeholders (for example, in the United States, the president functions largely independent of Congress and the Supreme Court) that makes its own rules and receives its resources largely from taxes. The U.S. government would be an example of a state.

- A **nation-state** is an entity that encompasses both the populations that define themselves as a nation and the organizational structure of the state. Israel is a nation-state, because it has a state government and

encompasses a nation of Jews (although there are large numbers of Muslims in Israel and its occupied territories as well).

Of greater importance in the global age is the idea that these entities, especially the nation-state, are losing influence because of globalization and broad global processes, including mobilities and flows of all types.

CONTROLLING GLOBAL FLOWS AND MOBILITIES

The nation-state is under siege largely because it has lost or is losing control (assuming it ever had it) over a number of global flows and mobilities (Cerny 2007; Ritzer and Dean 2015). In many ways, the global flow that most threatens the nation-state is informationalism. E-mail, posts on Facebook, tweets, and WhatsApp messages, to take a few examples, flow around the world readily and quickly. There is little or nothing the nation-state can do to stop or limit those flows, although China, among others, keeps trying (see Figure 6.5 for a depiction of the levels of internet freedom in countries around the world). The Chinese government has erected the "Great Firewall of China," a virtual surveillance system that censors what its citizens can access on the internet, including a block on Google and on web sources that promote free speech and other Western, democratic values (Denyer 2016). There are many economic, financial, and technological flows around the world that involve information of various kinds. Global information flows have the potential to subvert the authority of nation-states because they cover a much larger geographic area than the nation-state. This is especially true of information that would cast a negative light on the nation-state. One example would be the distribution of information throughout China about the great inequality that exists there and China's human rights abuses.

A more specific example of the decreasing ability of nation-states to isolate themselves from global processes is the economic crisis that began in the United States in late 2007 and cascaded rapidly around the world. For example, dramatic drops in the U.S. stock market (see the movies *Margin Call* [2011] and *The Big Short* [2015] for fictionalized treatments of the origins of that economic crisis) were followed by declines in many other stock markets in the world. Similarly, bank failures in the United States were quickly followed by even more ruinous bank failures in other countries, most notably Iceland and Ireland. This series of events illustrates the importance and power of global flows and demonstrates the inability of the nation-state to do much, if anything, to limit its impact within its borders on its economy and the lives of its citizens. "In a global financial system, national borders are porous" (Landler 2008, C1). Global economic flows move more quickly than ever, if not instantaneously, and are so fluid

FIGURE 6.5 • Freedom on the Internet, 2016

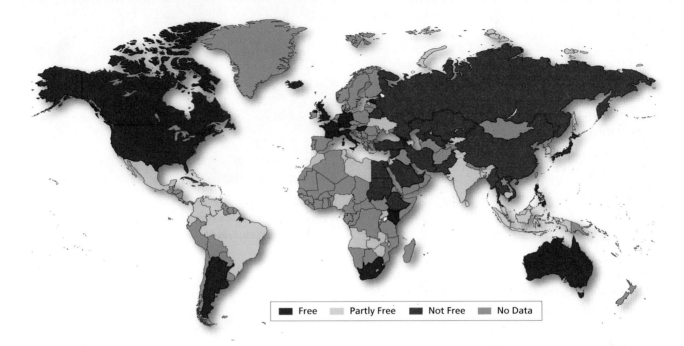

Free   Partly Free   Not Free   No Data

SOURCE: Reprinted with permission from Freedom House.

that they are difficult if not impossible to stop with the barriers available to nation-states.

The Islamic State (IS) organization has been very adept at using many types of media in a recruitment effort that reaches many parts of the world. Its communications are designed to transcend national boundaries in order to attract new supporters, who, the group hopes, will help force the creation of a new nation-state, a caliphate. Among other things, IS has released videos of threatened and actual beheadings, has been active on social media (including Twitter), and has made imitations of popular video games (such as *Call of Duty*) and movies (such as *Natural Born Killers* and *Saw*). Countries in which IS has been successful in finding recruits, such as France, England, and even the United States, would dearly love to stop its call to arms, but that is literally impossible given the nature of modern technology.

Information and economic flows are just two of the many global flows that nation-states cannot control. Among the others are flows of undocumented immigrants, new social movements, expertise in various domains, terrorists, criminals, drugs, money (including laundered money and other financial instruments), and human trafficking. Then there are global problems such as Zika virus, HIV/AIDS, H1N1 flu, tuberculosis, and the effects of climate change that flow around the world readily and cannot be handled very well by a nation-state operating on its own.

A great deal of evidence today indicates that the nation-state has become increasingly porous, but the fact is that no

nation-state has ever been able to exercise complete control over its borders (Bauman 1992). For example, people's ability to travel from one European country to another was largely unimpeded until the World War I era, when passports were introduced on a large scale for the first time. It is not the porosity of the nation-state that is new, but rather the dramatic increase in the global flows that are able to take advantage of that porosity.

Thus, the largest unit of analysis in sociology has now become the globe, and especially the global flows that best define globalization today. The concept of globalization appears throughout this book in an informal sense, but it is now time for a formal definition of *globalization:* "a transplanetary *process* or set of *processes* involving increasing *liquidity* and the growing multidirectional *flows* of people, objects, places, and information as well as the *structures* they encounter and create that are *barriers* to, or *expedite,* those flows" (Ritzer and Dean 2015, 2 [emphasis in original]; see also Chapter 17). Clearly, this is a view that goes beyond the nation-state and sees it as enmeshed in and subordinated to a global set of flows, mobilities, and structures.

OTHER GLOBAL FLOWS

Globalization is increasingly characterized by great flows of not just information, ideas, and images but also objects and people. For example, food now flows more quickly and to more people around the world (Inglis 2016). Examples of foods sold in locales far from their sources include fresh fruit from Chile (Goldfrank 2005), fresh sushi from Japan, and live lobsters from Maine. Looking at a very different kind of flow, migration within countries and from one country to another has become more common as well.

In addition, other kinds of physical objects are becoming increasingly liquid and thus able to flow more easily. Not long ago, we might have been amazed by our ability to order a book from Amazon and receive it via an express package delivery system in as little as a day. That method, however, now seems sluggish compared with the speed of downloading that book in seconds on a wireless device, such as Amazon's Kindle or Apple's iPad. That level of liquidity and flow is a major aspect of, as well as a major contributor to, globalization.

Spaces of Flows

Even places can be said to be flowing around the world. For example, immigrants often re-create in their new locales the places from which they came. The Hmong immigrants to Merced, California, described by Anne Fadiman in *The Spirit Catches You and You Fall Down* (2012), brought traditional family and societal practices with them, including rituals for healing, celebration, and many aspects of shared family life. Other examples include Indian and Pakistani enclaves in London. A different kind of example is the global spread of chains of nearly identical fast-food restaurants. Furthermore, places such as airports and shopping malls are increasingly defined not by their physical settings but by the flow of people and objects (food, airplanes) through them. You go to the airport not for the physical setting but to travel from one place to another. You similarly go to the mall not so much to visit the stores but to see and be seen and to experience the events and amenities within the mall.

Manuel Castells (1996) has made an important distinction regarding the flow of places. He argues that over time we have experienced a change from "spaces of places" to "spaces of flows" (Sassatelli 2010). **Spaces of places** are settings that have well-defined borders and can limit flows of all kinds and even stop them, at least for a time, from crossing those borders completely. Spaces of places are likely to have some solidity and to be long-lasting; people are likely to identify with them strongly. A walled city of the Middle Ages would be such a place. Today's old city of Jerusalem is a space of places, made up of separate Jewish, Muslim, Armenian, and Christian quarters. Traditional ethnic enclaves, such as Muslim communities in Europe or Indian pueblos in the United States, also have many of the characteristics of spaces of places.

Today, in contrast, we are witnessing the emergence of an increasing number of **spaces of flows**, which are settings that are unlikely to have clear and defensible borders. What happens within them is likely to be quite fluid and more

These traditionally dressed Hmong girls are celebrating their New Year not in their native region of Southeast Asia but in Merced, California. What global flows have contributed to the movement of people and cultures around the world?

temporary than the processes in spaces of places. People are less likely to identify strongly with the fleeting flows. An airport is an excellent example of a space of flows and indeed is a telling example of spaces in the global age. The Tom Hanks movie *The Terminal* (2004) further illustrates the nature of an airport. Hanks's character is forced to remain in an airport for months because he lacks the papers necessary to enter the United States. The discomforts associated with the fact that he is unable to move, that for him the airport has become a space of place, only serve to make it still clearer that an airport is fundamentally a space of flows. Drive-through windows at fast-food restaurants are another good example of spaces of flows; virtually all there is to these spaces are the flows. Yet another good example is the shopping mall. The movie *Paul Blart: Mall Cop* (2009; as well as *Paul Blart: Mall Cop 2,* 2015) demonstrates the fluid and temporary nature of relationships in the mall. Because of this, no one in the mall takes things very seriously, including the work of the mall cop.

ASK YOURSELF

Do you agree with Manuel Castells that we are in a transition from spaces of places to spaces of flows? Or do you believe that spaces of places still exist, such as in gated communities and exclusive resorts, and that spaces of flows have always been with us, such as in medieval fairs and marketplaces? Justify your answer.

Landscapes

Although global flows and globalization contribute to some degree of homogenization of the social experience around the world, they also contribute to greater global cultural diversity and heterogeneity. A very important contribution to thinking on the latter aspects of global flows is Arjun Appadurai's (b. 1949; 1996) work on what he calls **landscapes**—*scapes* for short. These are fluid, irregular, and variable global flows that produce different results throughout the world. As we will see below, these scapes can involve the flow of many different things, including people and ideas. At the heart of Appadurai's thinking are five types of landscapes that operate independent of one another to some degree, and may even conflict with one another:

- **Ethnoscapes** allow the movement, or fantasies about movement, of various individuals and groups, such as tourists and refugees. The ethnoscape of undocumented immigrants is of particular concern these days. They are often poor people who have in the main been forced to move because of poverty and poor job prospects in their home countries. They have also moved because of the belief, sometimes the fantasy, that economic conditions will be better for them elsewhere in the world, especially in the more developed countries of the United States and Western Europe.

- **Technoscapes** include mechanical technologies such as the containerized ships now used to transport freight, informational technologies such as the internet, and the materials (e.g., refrigerators and e-mail) that move so quickly and freely throughout the world via those technologies.

- **Financescapes** use various financial instruments to allow huge sums of money and other items of economic value (e.g., stocks, bonds, and precious metals, especially gold) to move through nations and around the world at great speed, almost instantaneously. The great global economic meltdown that began in late 2007 demonstrated quite clearly the importance and the power of financescapes in the contemporary world.

- **Mediascapes** include both the electronic capability to produce and transmit information around the world and the images of the world that these media create and disseminate. Those who write blogs and download photos (e.g., on Tumblr) and videos (e.g., on YouTube), global filmmakers and film distributors, global TV networks (e.g., CNN and Al Jazeera), and even old-fashioned newspapers and magazines create a variety of mediascapes.

- **Ideoscapes**, like mediascapes, include images, although they are largely restricted to political images

in line with the ideologies of nation-states. Also included here are images and counterideologies produced by social movements oriented toward supplanting those in power or at least gaining a portion of that power. Thus, for example, the United States has one ideoscape that disseminates negative images and information about the Islamic State (IS); in turn, IS has an ideoscape that responds with similarly negative images and information about the United States. News conferences by the U.S. president attacking IS's terrorism are met with videotapes of IS leaders critiquing American imperialism. Ideoscapes may be disseminated through mediascapes and technoscapes (for example, through the use of containerized shipping to send propaganda-laden books around the world).

Further increasing the global heterogeneity that results from the interaction of these landscapes is the fact that the impact of one can be at variance, or even in conflict, with another. In addition, these landscapes are interpreted differently by people and groups in different parts of the world. Interpretations depend on both the cultures in which people exist and the people's own subjective perspectives on the scapes. Powerful forces create at least some of these scapes. Nonetheless, those who merely live in them or pass through them have the power not only to redefine them in idiosyncratic ways but also ultimately to subvert them in many different ways. For example, those on a guided tour designed to show a given locale in a positive light can break off from the tour and see and hear things that lead to a very different impression of the locale. When the tourists return home, they can portray that locale in a way that contradicts the image presented by the tour creators and guides.

GLOBAL BARRIERS

The globe and the flows that increasingly pervade it are of central concern to sociology. However, there is another aspect of globalization that is of growing concern to sociology—the various global barriers to these flows. The world is made up of not just a series of flows but also structures such as trade agreements, regulatory agencies, borders, customs barriers, and standards (Inda and Rosaldo 2008). Any thoroughgoing account of globalization needs to look at the ways in which structures alter and even block flows as well as how they produce and enhance flows. In other words, there is interplay between flows and structures, especially between flows and the structures that are created in attempts to inhibit or stop them (Shamir 2005).

As mentioned previously, the most important and most obvious barriers to global flows are those constructed by nation-states. There are borders, gates, guards, passport controls, customs agents, health inspectors, trade regulations, and so on in most countries in the world. Although

Digital Currency

One relatively recent addition to the global financescape is Bitcoin, a digital currency, which is popularly referred to as "digital gold." It is a universal currency that can be used in all countries, so a Bitcoin user does not need to exchange it for local currencies when he or she crosses national borders (Popper 2015). Bitcoin was created in 2008; since then, more than 41 million Bitcoin accounts have been opened around the world. Unlike national currencies that are created by central banks and controlled by national governments, Bitcoin is decentralized and overseen by volunteers, who authenticate encrypted electronic signatures on transactions (Kharif 2014; Popper 2015). Bitcoins can be accrued through extensive data mining or purchased on Bitcoin currency exchanges. These online exchanges require consumers to open an account and create a digital wallet. They can then transfer money into the digital wallet, buy and sell bitcoins, and purchase products and services from individuals and companies that accept bitcoins. Bitcoin ATMs allow users to deposit cash into their digital wallets at physical locations in their communities (Ember 2014). Concern exists, however, over the actual value of a bitcoin and whether or not this digital currency will crash eventually.

Libertarians and anarchists were early supporters of Bitcoin because of its decentralized organizational structure and the lack of government regulations for its use (Kharif 2014). Because of the digital nature of bitcoins, they are easy to transfer and difficult to trace, especially their sources and destinations,

Bitcoin ATMs, like this one, allow users to exchange their currency for the digital money.

which remain anonymous. Thus, they are favored by those involved in criminal activities, as well as by those active in the dark web, where cyberpunks challenge the dominance of large global financial institutions (Popper 2015). Criminals appreciate the anonymity of bitcoins because they can use them to buy and sell illegal goods and services on websites such as the Silk Road. The utility of bitcoins for criminals was manifest most dramatically (so far) in a May 2017 global cyberattack (Reuters 2017). Those whose computers were attacked by this "ransomware" were instructed to pay a minimum of $300 in bitcoins, or else they would lose at least some of their computerized data.

While still tainted by its association with criminality, Bitcoin has begun to move into the mainstream. Parents are using the digital currency to pay babysitters or distribute allowances to their children (Kharif 2014). It is a quick and convenient way to electronically transfer money to a friend in another country without having to wait for a bank to open or a personal check to clear. Many mass retailers and big box stores, such as CVS and Home Depot, now accept bitcoins.

Engaging the Digital World

You can find the Bitcoin ATM nearest to you at http://coinatmradar.com, and you can learn where you can use Bitcoin at www.coindesk.com/information/what-can-you-buy-with-bitcoins or https://coinmap.org.

Where would you be most likely to use Bitcoin, and what would you purchase with it? Why? How do you think using PayPal is similar to or different from using Bitcoin?

Cricket in India

The sport of cricket has attracted attention from those interested in globalization in general and sports in particular (Appadurai 1996; Kaufman and Patterson 2005). Cricket was brought to India by the British colonialists. India played its first professional match against the British in 1932 ("Story of Cricket" 2004), giving many Indians a sense of nationhood 15 years before independence from Great Britain in 1947.

Arjun Appadurai argues that over the years, cricket has become decolonized and indigenized in India, to the point that it is "no longer English-mediated" (1996, 104). Imperial England needed to create cricket teams in its colonies that the English could play against and presumably defeat easily. However, the Indians transformed cricket and made it their own.

Of particular importance in this transformation was the role played by the media and language. Mass Indian publications—books, magazines, and pamphlets—liberated cricket from its "Englishness" and dealt with cricket matches in native terms. That is, they "vernacularized" it. The game came to be played widely in the streets, on playgrounds, and in villages. Indians also read about their favorite teams and stars and heard about them on the radio and saw them on TV. This served to make cricket an important part of the fantasy lives of many Indians. Top Indian cricket players are among the highest-paid celebrities in one of the world's fastest-growing economies.

The traditional British game of cricket has been changed by global flows. For example, India and Pakistan have appropriated and transformed the game. Will this kind of change create more global barriers between nations or help eliminate them?

In India, and elsewhere in former English colonies, cricket has become a much more aggressive game, less "sportsmanlike" and, perhaps most important, much more spectacular. Appadurai asserts that cricket "now belongs to a different . . . world" (1996, 107). It has become an "instrument for mobilizing national sentiment in the service of transnational spectacles" (1996, 109). Thus, to take one example, matches between rivals India and Pakistan resemble a war. When the two countries faced off in the semifinals of the 2011 Cricket World Cup, the game held India's (and undoubtedly Pakistan's) attention, with many Indians skipping work to watch (Betegeri 2011). In such matches,

"England . . . is no longer part of the equation" (Appadurai 1996, 109).

While there is much merit in Appadurai's analysis, today's distinctive form of Indian cricket emerged from the interaction between the game brought by the British and that produced by Indians. In today's world, many cultural forms yield such combinations and unique outcomes.

Think About It

Do you think it was inevitable that the version of cricket now popular in India would become so different from the sport brought by the British? Why or why not? What cultural purpose did the transformation of cricket in India serve for the new Indian nation?

undocumented immigrants, contraband goods, and digitized messages do get through those barriers, some other phenomena that nation-states deem counter to their national interests are successfully blocked or impeded. For example, in 2016 the U.S. government prevented Philips from selling the majority stake of its lighting business, Lumileds, to Asian buyers for "security reasons" (Sterling 2016). Congress also cited America's national security as a reason why the federal government should block the acquisition of the Chicago Stock Exchange by a Chinese company (Rogin 2016). Some have noted that as nations focus more on nationalism and militarism, their openness to international trade and other formalized flows across borders decreases (Acemoglu and Yared 2010). This was nowhere clearer than in

Donald Trump's 2016 campaign for the presidency. He adopted nationalistic and militaristic positions in order to argue for greater barriers to international trade, a ban on Muslim immigrants, and the mass deportation of 11 million undocumented immigrants, to say nothing of the idea of building of a wall between the United States and Mexico (even though immigration from Mexico has slowed to a crawl). As president, Trump has been forced to modulate some of these actions and to postpone others, but his basic position does not seem to have changed.

Are Global Barriers Effective?

However, many of the barriers created by nation-states are not effective. For instance, it is highly doubtful that the very expensive fence (to say nothing of Donald Trump's proposed wall) that has already been constructed between Mexico and the United States, combined with the use of cameras, lights, satellites, and drones, will be able to curtail the flow of undocumented immigrants into the United States. It has become more difficult, costly, and dangerous to enter the country illegally, but the fence has not stopped such entry. Moreover, the fence has had the unintended consequence of making it harder for Mexican nationals who are already in the United States illegally to move back to Mexico. The fence between Spain's African enclave—Melilla—and Morocco has not stopped some migrants, who have scaled it to gain entry to Spain and thereby to the EU (Associated Press 2014). Similarly, it is not clear whether the wall between Israel and the West Bank (or the more recently erected wall between Israel and Egypt) will stop the flow of terrorists into Israel the next time hostilities in the Middle East flare up. On the positive side, the wall is not stopping Palestinians and Israelis from communicating person to person via digital media. While there is no wall around the Gaza Strip, there is a closely watched and guarded wire fence. Nevertheless, beginning in 2014, and continuing to this day (Hadid and Waheidi 2016), the Israelis have found that Hamas fighters have dug numerous tunnels that they have used to commit terrorist acts in Israel.

In the European Union, until recently, barriers to movement between member countries had been greatly reduced, if not eliminated. In creating a structure that allows people (including, unfortunately, terrorists) and products (including, regrettably, illicit drugs and weapons) to move much more freely and quickly, the EU attempted to make Europe much more a space of flows than a space of places. However, that has changed recently, as a reaction against what were perceived to be the excesses of such openness (swarms of refugees—a few of whom turned out to be terrorists—swamping a country) gained force. For example, a number of EU countries (e.g. Hungary, Bulgaria, Slovenia) began building fences in an effort to keep out refugees (Lyman 2015a, 2015b). In mid-2016, Great Britain voted to leave the EU, in large part because of the influx of immigrants (Taub 2016). It will take several years for Great Britain's exit ("Brexit") from the EU to be finalized. When this does happen, it is presumed that one of the first things that Great Britain will do will be to create greater barriers (in terms of both number and size) to the entrance of immigrants into the country.

Globalization involves a dialectic of flows and barriers to those flows. While the barriers seem to be in ascent at the moment, it is likely that the flows will continue and find ways of breaching the new barriers.

Organizational Barriers

There are many different kinds of organizations that, though they may expedite flows for some, create all sorts of barriers for others. One example is found in the two-tier system of passport control at international airports, where citizens usually pass through quickly and easily, while foreigners wait in long lines. Another example is the protectionist tariff systems (Reuveny and Thompson 2001) that nation-states create in order to help their own farms send agricultural products (such as wheat) and to help their own manufacturers send goods (such as automobiles) across the borders of other nation-states while inhibiting the inflow of goods from their foreign competition. In January 2017, President Trump canceled the then-pending trade accord in Asia—the Trans-Pacific Partnership (TPP), involving the United States and 11 nations on the Pacific Rim. He believed that the elimination of tariffs among the countries involved (i.e., the creation of a free-trade zone) would adversely affect American companies. It would, in his view, lead to the further loss of American jobs as industries and jobs moved to low-wage countries involved in the TPP (Granville 2016).

Multinational corporations usually use market competition rather than trade policies to achieve global success. Toyota, for instance, is devoted to optimizing the flow of its automobiles to all possible markets throughout the world. It also seeks to compete with and outperform other multinational corporations in the automobile business. If it is successful, the flow of automobiles from competing corporations is greatly reduced, further advantaging Toyota.

Labor unions are also organizations devoted to promoting the flow of some things while working against the flow of others (Bronfenbrenner 2007). Unions often oppose, for example, the flow of undocumented immigrants because immigrants are likely to work for lower pay and fewer benefits (e.g., health insurance) than are indigenous, unionized workers. Similarly, labor unions oppose the flow of goods produced in nonunion shops, in other countries as well as their own. They do so because the success of nonunion shops puts downward pressure on wages and benefits. This adversely affects unionized shops and, in turn, hurts the union and its members. On the other hand, many employers are willing to hire undocumented immigrant labor despite laws against their doing so. Because these laborers lack documentation, they are easy to exploit. Employers can threaten to deport them if they demand higher wages and better working conditions or threaten to organize. Unions also tend to opposed free trade agreements such as the TPP and the North American Free Trade Agreement (NAFTA) because of the belief that jobs are lost to countries with lower wages (Kaufman 2016). Unions have a complex and complicated relationship with global flows and barriers.

ASK YOURSELF

What kinds of global flows does your college or university allow or promote? What kinds of global flows does it impede, and how?

More Open Organizations?

Organizations of many types that seek to control global flows are facing increasing competition from organizations that are becoming more fluid and open. The best-known computer operating systems are produced by Microsoft (Vista and Windows 10). They cost a great deal and are closed. Only those who work for the company can, at least legally, work on and modify them. In contrast, IBM, a traditional closed organization, has embraced Linux, a free computer operating system that welcomes changes contributed by anyone in the world with the needed skills to do so. IBM has also opened up more and more of its own operations to outside inputs. Another example is Apple, which has traditionally kept its Macintosh operating system closed but is now allowing outsiders to produce applications for its iPhone and iPad. Many other manufacturers of smartphones have followed suit. The free online encyclopedia Wikipedia and wikis more generally encourage virtually anyone, anywhere in the world, to contribute. In contrast, traditional and very costly dictionaries such as *Merriam-Webster's Collegiate Dictionary* and reference works such as *Encyclopedia Britannica* and *The Blackwell*

Encyclopedia of Sociology (Ritzer 2007a) are closed to contributions from anyone other than selected and invited experts.

Even with the new open systems, structural realities help some and hinder others. For example, to contribute to Linux or Wikipedia, one must have a computer, computer expertise, and access—preferably high-speed access—to the internet. Clearly, those without economic advantages—people in the lower classes in developed countries and people who live in the less developed countries of the Global South—are on the other side of the "digital divide" and do not have access to the tools required for making such contributions. As a result, they are unable to contribute to, or to gain from, open systems to the same degree that those in more privileged positions can. The fact that women are less likely than men to contribute to Wikipedia suggests that there are additional social factors to be considered here as well (Cohen 2011). Indeed, it is argued that women experience—and need to break through—a glass ceiling (see the previous discussion in this chapter) in order to contribute to Wikipedia (Jemielniak 2016). This further suggests that women in the Global South are doubly disadvantaged when it comes to access to these open systems—and much else.

Thus, despite the new openness, most organizations and systems remain closed to various flows. These barriers usually benefit some (elites, males) and disadvantage others (the poor, females).

CHECKPOINT 6.4: TYPES OF GLOBAL FLOWS

FLOW	DESCRIPTION
Spaces of places	Settings with well-defined borders that can limit flows of all kinds, such as walled cities
Spaces of flows	Fluid spaces where many kinds of flows are encouraged, such as airports and shopping malls
Landscapes	Fluid, irregular, and variable global flows that produce different results throughout the world

SUMMARY

Much sociological work on organizations is based on Max Weber's model of bureaucracy. However, one criticism of this model is that bureaucracies are not as highly rational as Weber believed them to be. The informal organization refers to how organizations actually work as opposed to how they are intended to function. While bureaucratic power is supposed to be evenly dispersed, this is not always the case. For example, an oligarchy might develop if a small group of people at the top of an organization

illegitimately obtain and exercise more power than they should.

Contemporary organizations face several challenges. Women often encounter a glass ceiling as a result of gender discrimination, which prevents them from achieving vertical mobility. They also might suffer from sexual harassment. Workers have to contend with outsourcing when corporations transfer their jobs to other countries. A new type of organization, the network organization, is emerging that is based on information and is more open and flexible than class bureaucracies are.

Two ideal-typical societies exist—gemeinschaft and gesellschaft societies. Gemeinschaft societies are characterized by face-to-face relationships, while gesellschaft societies are more impersonal and distant. Today, most of us in the Global North live in a risk society, where we are focused on trying to stay safe, as opposed to an industrial society, where individuals are more concerned about wealth distribution.

A key structure in global analysis is the nation-state, which is composed of a population that defines itself as a nation and the organization structure of a state. The nation-state as a form of social organization is under siege because of global flows over which it has little control. Consequently, sociologists are coming to focus more attention on global relationships and global flows. Manuel Castells, for instance, argues that globalization has brought a change from spaces of places to spaces of flows. Arjun Appadurai focuses on five different types of global landscapes. Some barriers to global flows include nation-states and labor unions.

KEY TERMS

authority, 144
bounded rationality, 146
bureaucracy, 142
bureaucratic
  personality, 147
charismatic authority, 145
domination, 144
ethnoscapes, 163
financescapes, 163

gemeinschaft societies, 158
gesellschaft societies, 158
ideoscapes, 163
informal organization, 147
informationalism, 157
landscapes, 163
mediascapes, 163
nation, 156
nation-state, 160

network organization, 156
networks, 156
offshore outsourcing, 153
oligarchy, 148
organizations, 142
outsourcing, 152
rational-legal
  authority, 144

risk society, 158
sexual harassment, 151
spaces of flows, 162
spaces of places, 162
state, 160
technoscapes, 163
traditional authority, 144

REVIEW QUESTIONS

1. What are the characteristics of the ideal-typical bureaucracy? What are some of the ways in which the ideal-typical bureaucracy is unrealistic?

2. It is often the case that those who occupy offices lower in the bureaucratic hierarchy have greater knowledge and competence than those who rank above them. What does this suggest about the ideal-typical bureaucracy? Can you think of examples from your own experiences where this has been the case?

3. According to Weber, what are the three types of legitimate authority? How is rational-legal authority related to Weber's concept of bureaucracy?

4. Over the last several decades, what changes have bureaucratic organizations undergone? How are these changes reflective of increasing globalization?

5. What is informationalism, and how has it affected the global economy? How is the emergence of informationalism related to the development of new communication technologies, such as the internet, social networking sites, and smartphones?

6. How has the process of globalization threatened the nation-state? What sorts of barriers have nation-states developed to limit global flows? What sorts of flows have nation-states been unable to limit?

7. In what ways has globalization created a shift from spaces of places to spaces of flows? What have been the benefits and disadvantages of this shift?

8. Discuss each of Appadurai's landscapes, with special focus on the disjunctures among and between them (including examples). What are the implications of these disjunctures for the process of globalization?

9. How are network organizations different from classic bureaucracies? What are the main characteristics of networks?

10. How are open-source technologies reflective of a more fluid and open world? What structural barriers have transnational corporations created to limit these open-source technologies? What do you think is going to be the direction of the future? Why?

PRACTICE AND APPLY WHAT YOU'VE LEARNED

▶ edge.sagepub.com/ritzerintro4e

CHECK YOUR COMPREHENSION ON THE STUDY SITE WITH:

- **Diagnostic pre-tests** to identify opportunities for improvement.

- **Personalized study plans** with focused recommendations to address specific knowledge gaps and additional learning needs.

- **Post-tests** to check your progress and ensure mastery of key learning objectives.

⑤SAGE edge™

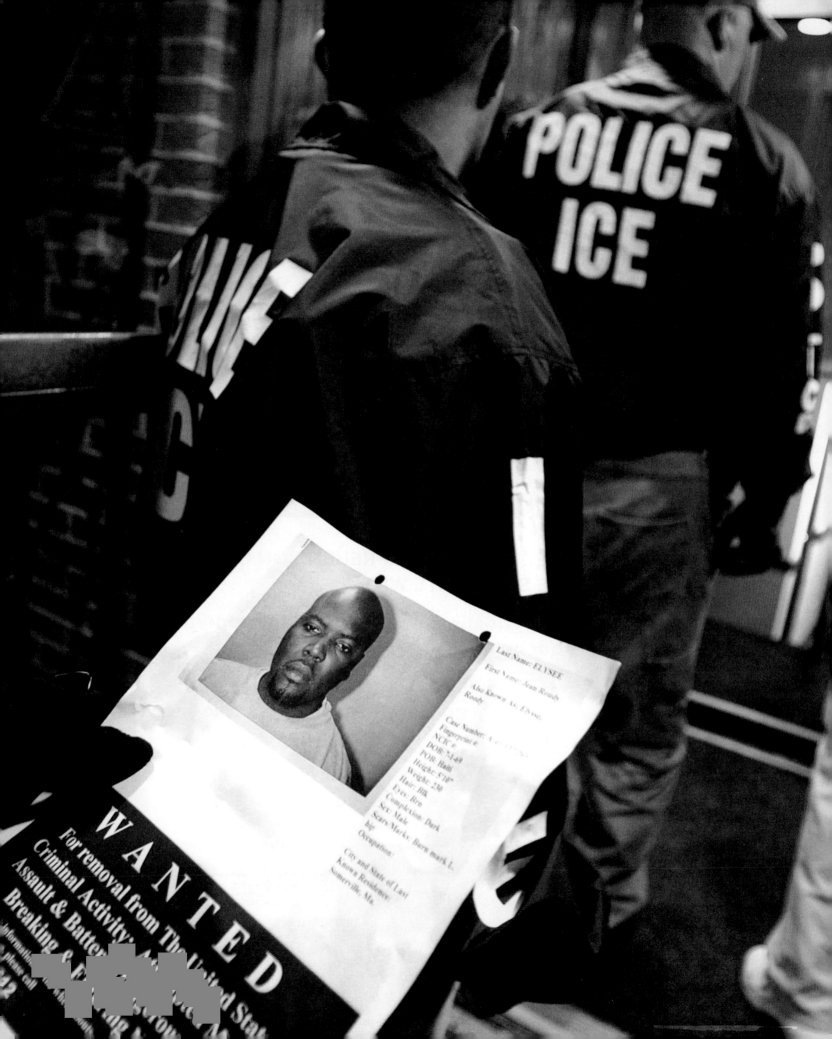

DEVIANCE AND CRIME

Norms, Labels, and Judgment

When he was running for president, Donald Trump labeled immigrants entering the United States from and through Mexico as criminals. He said, "They're bringing drugs. They're bringing crime. They're rapists" (Mandell 2016). As a result, he announced the need to build a wall between Mexico and the United States. Such views and plans contributed much to the support for Trump's campaign and to his eventual victory in the presidential election, even though rival Hillary Clinton received a majority of the popular vote.

In the early days of Trump's administration in 2017, he initiated steps to implement his plan to keep immigrants, especially those who are undocumented, from entering the United States from Mexico. However, as of mid-2017, no progress had been made on the wall, due to widespread opposition to it, as well as to scandals that had rocked the Trump administration. Even Trump's contention that Mexico would ultimately pay for the wall no longer seemed likely. (Needless to say, Mexico did not agree with Trump's position. Taking to Twitter, former Mexican president Vicente Fox responded repeatedly to Trump, stating, "Mexico has spoken; we will never ever pay for the #F******Wall" [Fox 2017].)

Do the data actually demonstrate the need for a wall and such an enormous expenditure? Are immigrants more likely to commit serious crimes? No. Rather, the data show that immigrants are *less* likely to commit the kinds of crimes that cause them to end up in prison (Ewing, Martinez, and Rumbaut 2015). More specifically, census data from 1980 to 2010 show that for men between 18 and 49 years of age, immigrants were only somewhere between one-fifth to one-half as likely to be in prison as those born in the United States. In addition, among those incarcerated in federal and state prisons, a smaller percentage of them are noncitizens than are represented in the population as a whole. Further, while undocumented immigrants had crime

LEARNING OBJECTIVES

 7.1 Define deviance.

 7.2 Describe explanatory and constructionist approaches to theorizing about deviance.

7.3 Discuss the criminal justice system and different types of crimes.

7.4 Summarize the relationship between globalization and crime.

rates higher than those of immigrants who had entered the United States legally, even they had lower crimes rates than did U.S. citizens (Perez-Pena 2017). In fact, communities with large numbers of immigrants are safer than most other communities (Sampson 2008).

This demonstrates a key point in the sociology of crime: Criminalization is not always based on the facts, and it does not occur of its own accord. Some interest group—or an authority figure, in the case of the proposed wall on the U.S.-Mexico border—must seek to have a type of action or a group of people criminalized. This is a political decision, and it is linked to the desire on the part of one powerful group—or its leader—to exert social control over another group. ●

This chapter deals with two closely related social phenomena: deviance and crime (Atkinson 2014; Downes, Rock, and McLaughlin 2016; Forsyth and Copes 2014; Goode and Thio 2007). Most forms of deviance—for example, having full-face tattoos—are not crimes. However, all crimes—theft, murder, rape—are forms of deviance. To become a crime, a form of deviance must be negatively sanctioned by the legal system, a process known as **criminalization** (Hillyard 2007; Jenness 2004; Muniz 2014).

DEVIANCE

What exactly is deviance, and where is the line between deviance and nondeviance? Without giving it much thought, many people would likely express the absolutist view that certain things are deviant in all places, for all groups, and at all times (Little 2007). However, from a sociological perspective, no act, belief, or human characteristic is inherently deviant (Perrin 2007). Thus, even genocide, while morally reprehensible and indefensible, has not been defined as deviance in some societies and at certain points in time (such as in Nazi Germany). Therefore, to the sociologist, deviance is socially defined. **Deviance** is any action, belief, or human characteristic that is considered to be a violation of group norms by a large number of members of a society or a social group and for which the violator is likely to be censured or punished (Ben-Yehuda 2012; Goode 2007a).

If a powerful interest group wants to have a form of behavior defined as deviant, it is likely to be so defined. At the same time, powerful interest groups are likely to use their power to resist the efforts of others to define the powerful group's behaviors as deviant (McCaghy et al. 2016). For example, in the wake of the collapse of the home mortgage market in 2008 (the effects of which are still being felt in Las Vegas and elsewhere in the United States [Healy 2016]), bankers fought, largely successfully, against being seen as deviant and even as criminal for their fraudulent predatory loan policies (Braithwaite 2010). However, borrowers who lied about their financial situation were less successful in avoiding being seen as deviant, and they suffered far greater negative consequences (Nguyen and Pontell 2011). They were likely to lose their homes, often their jobs, and sometimes even their health. Those interest groups that have social, political, legal, and/or financial power have a great deal of influence over whom is (or is not) defined as deviant and who suffers the negative consequences of such a definition.

SHIFTING DEFINITIONS OF DEVIANCE

In addition to being influenced by power relationships, what is thought to be deviant varies from one time period to another, from one geographic location to another, and from one group to another. For example, being tattooed used to be seen as a stigmatizing form of deviance, but for many it now seems normal, or at least far less stigmatized (Dombrink and Hillyard 2007; Larsen, Patterson, and Markham 2014). Until a couple of decades ago, most people in the United States would have considered tattoos and body modification more generally, including body piercing (Koch et al. 2010) and "flesh hook pulling" (Horton 2013), to be "discredited bodily states." A tattoo was seen as deviant in and of itself, or it was assumed to signify membership in some deviant (or countercultural) group, such as a biker gang. Today, a much greater proportion of Americans consider tattoos normal, and, indeed, about 45 million Americans have tattoos themselves. In the public realm, we accept the sight of athletes—especially professional basketball players—covered with tattoos. Once associated with the working class and men in the military, tattoos have become much more common today throughout society, including among college students. Once restricted largely to men, tattoos are more and more popular today with women as well. Some women, such as Kat Von D, have also gained fame as tattoo artists, a historically male-dominated occupation that has become so accepted that many in it aspire to be, or consider themselves to be, professionals. And tattoo parlors, once limited to the marginal areas of town, are now found on Main Street, as well as in the local shopping mall, perhaps next to the maternity shop or the toy store. Tattoos have become just another product of our consumer society (Patterson and Schroeder 2010; Trebay 2008).

As another example of the movement from deviance to normality, consider U.S. attitudes toward premarital sex (Regnerus and Uecker 2011). Just a few decades ago, a leading textbook on the subject of deviance devoted a chapter to "premarital sex" (Bell 1971). Today, premarital sex is so common and widely accepted (or at least tolerated) that it is considered normal in most groups (Wellings et al. 2009). In fact, it is now often the case that *not* having premarital sex, or being a "late bloomer" sexually, can be stigmatizing (Gesselamn, Webster, and Garcia 2016).

"Hooking up"—engaging in "something sexual" outside of committed romantic relationships—is common among teens and twentysomethings today, but it was considered deviant behavior by earlier generations (Bogle 2008; Lewis et al. 2012; Manning, Giordano, and Longmore 2006; Reay 2014; Wade 2017). Much the same can be said about cohabitation before marriage (see Chapter 12): It once was defined as "living in sin," but today the pendulum has swung entirely in the other direction, to the point where many people might consider couples who do *not* live together before marriage to be deviant. In other words, cohabitation has become normative, and for some it occurs instead of, or at least before, marriage (Kuo and Raley 2016; Popenoe 2009; Sassler and Miller 2011). Homosexuality is another form of sexual behavior that has changed in the public's perception; many no longer consider it a form of deviance (see Chapter 11). Its normalization is reflected in a host of social changes, such as the inclusion of same-sex partners in family benefits offered by employers, the repeal of the military's "don't ask, don't tell" policy, the 2011 reversal of the federal government's position on the Defense of Marriage Act (Savage and Stolberg 2011), and the 2015 U.S. Supreme Court decision legalizing same-sex marriage (see Figure 7.1 for a look at changing attitudes of U.S. adults toward same-sex marriage). Popular actors such as Ian McKellen (Gandalf in the *Lord of the Rings* movies) and Neil Patrick Harris (TV's *How I Met Your Mother* and the movie *Gone Girl*), musicians such as Adam Lambert and Lance Bass, and professional athletes such as Jason Collins (basketball), Michael Sam (football), and Billy Jean King and Martina Navratilova (tennis) have publicly identified themselves as gay and are (or were) able to maintain successful careers. Gay and lesbian characters have also featured prominently on television shows such as *Modern Family, Orange Is the New Black,* and *Pretty Little Liars.*

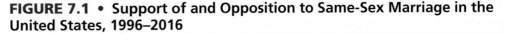

FIGURE 7.1 • Support of and Opposition to Same-Sex Marriage in the United States, 1996–2016

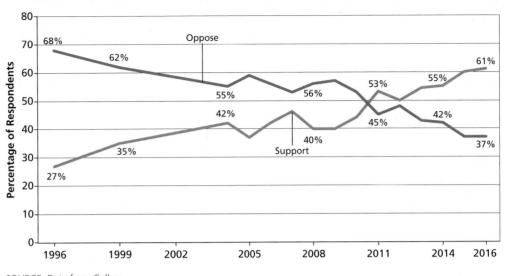

SOURCE: Data from Gallup.

Of course, some members of American society cringe at the idea that homosexuality, premarital sex, and cohabitation before marriage are becoming normative. Religious fundamentalists, for example, may believe in an absolute moral standard according to which these behaviors are deviant, no matter how many other people consider them to be normal. Fundamentalists believe that only married heterosexuals should live together and have sexual intercourse with one another (Hendershott 2002; Powell et al. 2010).

There are great differences from one geographic area to another in the ways in which some behaviors are defined. At one time, smoking cigarettes was an accepted, even admired, form of behavior in the United States. For example, the characters in the TV show *Mad Men,* which dealt with the advertising industry in New York City about a half-century ago, were often seen pleasurably smoking and drinking heavily in their offices. Now, of course, smoking is widely considered deviant by many groups in the United States. However, it is certainly not viewed as deviant in most parts of Europe, and it is considered quite normal in China (Kohrmann 2008), which consumes more tobacco than any other country in the world. In 2012, there were about 281 million smokers in China; more than half of all Chinese men were smokers (Qin 2014). While there is evidence of recent decline in smoking among Chinese men (Luo and Yu 2015), smoking still is considered normal in China.

Smoking marijuana in public is another behavior defined differently according to geographic location. It is considered deviant by most groups in the United States, but in the Netherlands, marijuana smoking, while technically illegal, is quite normal. As the "Globalization" box on page 176 indicates, however, some changes are taking place in the Dutch attitude toward marijuana.

Even groups within a given society often differ on what is and is not considered deviant. For example, the residents of a typical retirement community would likely consider marijuana smoking deviant (although that is likely to depend on whether they lived in a state where marijuana sale and use was legal, especially for medical purposes). In contrast, students on many college campuses might see it as normal. To take another example, in the top-rated high schools in the United States, students who score high on intelligence tests are considered quite normal, but in typical or underperforming public high schools, such students might be considered, and consider themselves to be, deviant (Margolin 1994).

While there are great differences in what is considered to be deviant, it is important to remember that deviance has existed for all groups, in all parts of the world, and in all times. Virtually all groups define themselves by specifying the limits of acceptable behavior for their members. Such limits, and their violation, help a group sharpen its norms and values. Without limits and at least occasional violations, norms and values might become increasingly unclear and grow weaker over time.

ASK YOURSELF

Can you think of other behaviors that were once considered deviant and are now accepted or even normative? What brought about the change in their status? Can you identify any behaviors that were once normative and are now considered deviant, such as using your cell phone while driving or failing to clean up after your dog?

GLOBAL FLOWS AND DEVIANCE

Deviance can be seen as a global flow. Obviously, like many others, people who are defined as being deviant can move around the world quickly and easily. In addition, definitions of deviance flow even more easily from society to society. For example, through its "war on drugs," the United States has made a strong effort to have the use of certain drugs defined as a form of deviance throughout the world and to make drug use illegal wherever possible. While there have been successes, many societies and cultures have resisted this effort and persist in viewing at least some drug use as normal. For example, use of the stimulant drug khat is normal in Yemen. The flip side of that phenomenon is that alcohol use, which is thought to be quite normal in the United States, is considered deviant in Yemen.

Global trends toward normalizing what was defined at one time and in some places as deviant are even clearer and more pronounced. This is particularly the case with changes in the acceptability of various forms of sexuality.

Ever greater portions of the world are accepting premarital sex, cohabitation before marriage, and, to a lesser degree, homosexuality. According to the International Lesbian, Gay, Bisexual, Trans and Intersex Association (ILGA), as of May 2014, "deviant" sexuality was protected by anti-discrimination laws in 76 countries, and same-sex unions were recognized in 47 countries (see Figure 7.2). However, the barriers to normalizing such forms of sexual behavior remain in place and are quite powerful in large parts of the world. As Figure 7.2 indicates, deviant sexual behavior is punishable by imprisonment in 78 countries and by death in 6. Such punishments are especially common in Islamic societies, which tend to be more absolutist on matters relating to sexual deviance and where deeply held religious beliefs serve as a barrier to normalization. In spite of the barriers, these behaviors exist, often covertly, in these societies and may well be expanding in the wake of increasing global acceptance.

DEVIANCE AND CONSUMPTION

The most obvious relationship between deviance and consumption is the use of goods and services that are illegal or considered deviant. This form of consumption often involves committing deviant, or illegal, acts in order to be able to afford to consume. For example, many people addicted to drugs are forced into committing criminal acts such as prostitution, shoplifting, mugging, and breaking and entering in order to pay for the high cost of their illegal drugs.

Poverty drives some to commit illegal and/or deviant acts so that they can afford to consume what is necessary for survival (Edin and Lein 1997; Livermore et al. 2011). There are many reasons for engaging in prostitution, including the need to pay for illegal drugs, a history of abuse and rape, and being forced to do so through human trafficking or other coercion, as well as simply a last-ditch effort to survive (Kennedy et al. 2007; Weitzer 2009). However, many women—and men—engage in prostitution to earn the money they need to afford to consume various conventional goods and services.

A striking example of the relationship between deviance and consumption is found in the "mall girls" of Warsaw, Poland, the subject of a 2010 documentary film of the same name. These teenage girls (15 years of age or younger) are so drawn to the malls and the goods and services offered there that they are willing to engage in sex in these settings (in the restrooms or outside in the parking lot), not for cash but for the goods and services themselves. Thus, they exchange sex for pricey sushi dinners in the mall, Chanel scarves, "designer jeans, Nokia cell phones, even a pair of socks," especially those with brand names and expensive designer labels (Bilefsky 2010, A8). Because no money is exchanged, the girls do not see themselves as prostitutes.

FIGURE 7.2 • Lesbian and Gay Rights around the World, 2016

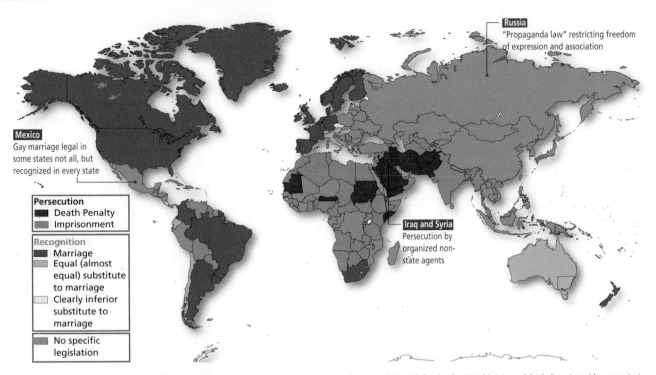

Russia
"Propaganda law" restricting freedom of expression and association

Mexico
Gay marriage legal in some states not all, but recognized in every state

Persecution
- Death Penalty
- Imprisonment

Recognition
- Marriage
- Equal (almost equal) substitute to marriage
- Clearly inferior substitute to marriage
- No specific legislation

Iraq and Syria
Persecution by organized non-state agents

SOURCE: International Lesbian, Gay, Bisexual, Trans and Intersex Association, "Lesbian And Gay Rights in the World," June 2016. Reprinted by permission of the International Lesbian, Gay, Bisexual, Trans and Intersex Association.

They call their clients "boyfriends," "benefactors," or "sponsors." Some observers have linked this phenomenon to a postcommunist decline in values and the declining power of the Catholic Church in Poland. The maker of the documentary film has argued that "the shopping mall has become the new cathedral in Poland" (Bilefsky 2010, A8).

Defining Deviant Consumption

As with all sorts of deviance, definitions of what constitutes deviant consumer behavior are frequently in dispute. For instance, deviant consumers often do not see a relationship between deviance and their consumption patterns. Most of those in the United States who use the services of prostitutes or smoke marijuana may well see such consumption as justifiable and therefore not as a form of deviance. Their actions are partly due to the fact that the laws prohibiting consumption of the services of prostitutes and the use of marijuana are rarely enforced. "Johns" and "Janes" are rarely arrested, and if they are, they ordinarily get only a legal slap on the wrist. Purchasing and smoking marijuana in states where these actions continue to be illegal are treated in a similar fashion, at least for those who are white and middle-class.

However, those who consume the "wrong" drugs are more likely to be considered deviant than are those who consume the "right" drugs. Thus, people who consume alcohol, even if they consume it excessively, are far less likely to be considered deviant than people who use marijuana. And the purchase and use of "harder drugs," such as crack cocaine and heroin, are dealt with more harshly (especially by the law) than is the purchase of marijuana where it continues to be illegal (Chriqui et al. 2002, ix; Jackson-Jacobs 2005, 835). This is the case largely because the use of hard drugs is associated with people in weaker and more vulnerable positions. Similarly, there are extensive differences along racial and ethnic lines in arrests for drug offenses (Mitchell and Caudy 2015; Ousey and Lee 2008). For example, the greatest disparity in arrest rates between blacks and whites is seen in cases involving drugs. Between 2001 and 2010, blacks were four times more likely than whites to be arrested for possession of marijuana ("Racial Disparity" 2013). More generally, blacks are more than three times more likely than whites to be arrested for any drug offense (see Figure 7.3).

"Dangerous Consumers"

In the era before the Great Recession, deviants in the realm of consumption were often considered to be the individuals who did not consume enough. They have been called "dangerous consumers" (Bauman 1997; Ritzer 2001). They included the unemployed, the poor (Hamilton Project 2013), "dropouts," those who voluntarily sought to simplify their lives, and those who saved rather than spent their

Rethinking the Dutch Approach to Marijuana Use

The Netherlands has long been the model of an open and tolerant society. It was the first nation in the world to allow same-sex marriage and euthanasia. It is also one of the most secular nations in the world. However, recent changes related to globalization seem to be threatening at least some of this openness. The threats can be seen in many areas of Dutch life, especially in the growing hostility toward mass immigration (Lechner 2008). Globalization is also threatening one of the things the Netherlands is most famous for: its openness to drug use in general, and especially to the sale and use of marijuana and hashish. Although marijuana use is technically illegal in the Netherlands, smoking marijuana in public is not unusual, and there are "coffee shops" throughout the country where marijuana is sold openly. Many cafés have marquees, resembling those in fast-food restaurants, that offer customers choices among many varieties of the drug; "Amnesia," "Big Bud," and "Gold Palm" are just a few examples.

Tourists have been drawn to these shops for decades. In recent years, however, Dutch citizens have begun to see "drug tourism" (Uriely and Belhassen 2005) as a social problem. This is especially the case in border cities like Maastricht, which lie just a few miles from Germany, France, or Belgium. Selling marijuana is illegal in these neighboring countries, but the European Union's open borders have made it easy for people to drive to the Netherlands to get marijuana. As a result, Maastricht and other Dutch border cities are plagued with traffic jams, noise, and, more important, crime. The large numbers of visitors in search of marijuana have attracted criminals who want to sell them other, harder drugs, which are definitely illegal. What is worse, these criminals have been involved in shootouts and killings. The Dutch have been shocked by this development because they have long seen their openness to marijuana as a way of keeping their young people safer, not endangering them in new and unforeseen ways.

As a result, the Dutch passed a law, which took effect on January 1, 2013, prohibiting the sale of marijuana to nonresidents. However, the mayor of Amsterdam announced that the 220 shops selling marijuana in that city would remain open. He feared that the closure of the shops would lead to a massive increase in the illegal sale of the drug across the city (Jolly 2012). In fact, illegal sales of marijuana have increased in Maastricht, which enforces a ban on sales of the drug to foreigners in its coffee shops (Amsterdam has no such ban; Corder 2014). The nationwide ban on marijuana is in effect in the Netherlands, but local officials have been given the power to override it.

Lee Snider/Corbis Documentary/Getty Images

Many "coffee shops" in Amsterdam, including this one, allow the purchase of marijuana, even though it is technically illegal. How does the Dutch attitude toward marijuana compare to the American attitude? Will current changes in marijuana laws lead to such coffee shops in the United States?

Think About It

Would you say, based on their laws and their behaviors, that the Dutch see marijuana use as normative or as deviant? Do you think they are likely to be successful in their attempts to manage marijuana use within their borders? Why or why not?

money. Their insufficient consumption posed a threat to the success of consumer society and to an economy that had come to depend on high levels of consumption. Similarly, those who did not go into debt to the credit card companies and to banks for car and home loans were also considered to be dangers to the economy. This was the case even though lesser consumption may be better for the long-term sustainability of humanity, the environment, and even the economy.

ASK YOURSELF

Do you think those who voluntarily reduce their consumption, especially of nonrenewable energy and disposable goods that contribute to the wasteful use of finite resources, should be considered deviant? Might some forms of deviance actually be admirable? Under what circumstances?

Recent changes in the economy demonstrate, once again, the relative nature of deviance. After the onset of the Great Recession, those who came to be defined as deviant or dangerous were those who consumed too much and who went too deeply into debt. For example, those who bought homes even though there was no way they could afford the mortgage payments, at least after an initial period of uncommonly low interest rates and monthly payments, came to be seen as deviants. They had jeopardized not only their own way of life but also the economy as a whole. Now that we live in an era from which we have (largely) recovered from the Great Recession, not consuming enough is once again considered to be deviant, at least to some degree and by some people.

Similarly, while savings had been considered deviant during boom times, as the Great Recession ebbed, the view emerged that it was preferable—normal—to save. As a result, the savings rate in the United States rose dramatically, at least in the short run (see Chapters 4 and 12). Those who saved money came to be seen as normal, and those who went into debt, especially too deeply, were now viewed as the deviants. In 2009, 76 percent of Americans polled by the Pew Research Center indicated that they had "changed their savings or investments, delayed or canceled buying a new home or adjusted their retirement plans," in many cases because of worries that their economic situations might worsen. As late as 2014 a *Consumer Reports* survey of just over 1,000 U.S. adults found that consumers continued to feel scarred by the Great Recession ("How America Shops Now" 2014). While they were consuming again, they were doing so very cautiously. Even

in late 2016, a large number of Americans indicated that they were still not confident in the economy.

CHECKPOINT 7.1: DEFINING DEVIANCE

TYPE OF BEHAVIOR	DESCRIPTION OR EXAMPLES
Deviance	Any action, belief, or human characteristic that members of a society or social group consider to be a violation of group norms and for which the violator is likely to be censured or punished
Behaviors no longer considered deviant	Tattoos, premarital sex, homosexual behaviors
Behaviors no longer considered acceptable by many	Smoking (in the United States)

THEORIES OF DEVIANCE

Deviance is a very good topic to study if you want to better understand the utility of, and contrasts between, the main types of sociological theories—structural/functional, conflict/critical, and inter/actionist. But before we get to these theories, it is important to make a key distinction between explanatory and constructionist theories of deviance:

- **Explanatory theories** seek to explain why deviance does or does not occur (Goode 2007b; Meier 2015). These theories are also thought of as being scientific, or "positivistic," because they view deviant behavior as objectively real, and they suggest that these forms of real behavior can be studied empirically. Explanatory theories assume that deviant behavior is determined by a wide variety of factors, such as the biological makeup of the person labeled as deviant and the structure of the larger society. For example, the structure of the social class system ensures that large numbers of people will live in poverty, at the bottom of the hierarchy, and that some of them will commit acts defined as deviant and criminal in order to survive (Meier 2007a, 2007b). Some of the earliest theories of deviance were explanatory in nature. The Italian physician Cesare Lombroso (1835–1909),

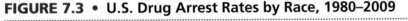

FIGURE 7.3 • **U.S. Drug Arrest Rates by Race, 1980–2009**

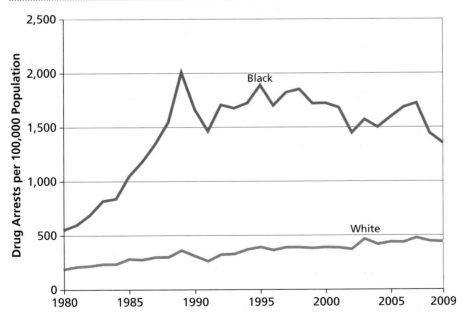

SOURCE: Data from Decades of Disparity: Drug Arrests and Race in the United States, March 2009, Human Rights Watch.

for example, focused initially on the role of biological factors—primitive, "apelike" characteristics—in people who committed deviant acts, especially criminal acts such as theft, rape, and murder. Lombroso's biological approach was discredited, but recently some sociologists have returned to this question of biological roots of deviance. One team of researchers has shown that juvenile delinquency could be explained, in part, by genetic characteristics, but that the social environment could reduce or moderate the effects of genetics (Guo, Roettger, and Cai 2008; Li, Liu, and Guo 2015). In other words, genetics is not decisive but rather interacts with the social environment. This has been made clear in a recent book by a prominent neuroscientist and professor who discovered that he himself had some of the genetic characteristics—but none of the behaviors—of a psychopath (Fallon 2013).

- **Constructionist theories** are concerned with achieving a greater understanding of the process by which people define and classify some behaviors as normal and others as deviant. In other words, these theories focus on how people construct deviance (Henry 2007). Whereas explanatory theories focus mainly on people labeled as deviant and what they do or embody (being poor, apelike, prone to juvenile delinquency), constructionist theories concentrate on those who are in power and the actions they take to create and define deviance in the first place. This means that research and theorizing are directed at those who create and enforce the moral order and their definitions of deviance instead of at those who commit so-called deviant acts. Rather than seeing deviance as "real," this perspective sees it as a social construction. For example, the Boy Scouts of America constructed transgender boys and homosexual boys and adult leaders as deviant by banning them from becoming members of its organization for more than a century. It ended its ban on gay youths in 2013 and on gay adult leaders in 2015. In early 2017 the organization permitted transgender boys to join, too (Chokshi 2017). The inclusion of these previously excluded groups demonstrates that definitions of deviance can change over time through the actions of influential organizations. By accepting gay and transgender males, the Boy Scouts of America is signaling that these people are now "normal" instead of "deviant." Of the three types of theories to be discussed below, the structural/functional and conflict/critical theories fall into the explanatory category, while the inter/actionist theories fit within the constructionist approach. However, whatever their theoretical approach, many sociologists use elements of both explanatory and constructionist approaches.

STRUCTURAL/FUNCTIONAL THEORIES

A good place to start is with the thinking of Émile Durkheim, one of the classical sociological theorists and creator of what later came to be known as structural-functionalism. While Durkheim focused on crime, it is possible to extend his thinking to deviance more generally. His basic argument was that because deviance and crime have existed in all societies at all times (and in that sense are "normal"), they must have positive functions for the larger society and its structures. In other words, deviance would not have existed in the past and continue to exist were it not for the fact that it was and is functional; deviance served and continues to serve various purposes.

The most important function of deviance in Durkheim's view is that it allows societies, or groups, to define and clarify their collective beliefs—their norms and values. Were it not for deviance, norms and values would not come into existence. More important, the norms and values that limit or prohibit deviance would grow weak without the need to be exercised on a regular basis in response to deviant acts. The public as a whole, officials, and even potential deviants would grow progressively less aware of, and less sensitive to, the existence of these prohibitions. Thus, in a sense, society needs deviance. If periodic violations of standards of conduct did not occur, those standards would become less clear to all concerned, less strongly held, and less powerful (Dentler and Erikson 1959; Jensen 1988).

ASK YOURSELF

Do you agree with Durkheim that deviance is, in a sense, normal and therefore functional? To support this argument, can you think of an example of a deviant act or behavior that has helped society define its standards of conduct?

Strain

A more contemporary structural-functional approach to deviance is known as **strain theory**. According to strain theory, there is a discrepancy between the larger structure and culture of society, especially regarding what is valued, and the structural means available to achieve what is valued. Strain exists when the culture values something—say, material success—but the structure of society is such that not everyone can achieve or realize that value in a socially acceptable way. Strain theory exemplifies a structural-functional approach in two major ways. First, it is concerned with structures, especially those structures, such as the educational system, that provide the institutionalized means to achieve cultural goals. Second, it deals with structural relationships between those goals and institutionalized means (e.g., between success and hard work).

The most obvious and important example in the United States, and in many other developed societies throughout the world, is the strain produced by the fact that although a high value is placed on material success, the structure of society does not give everyone an equal chance of attaining that success. Thus, contrary to the ideal of equal opportunity and a "level playing field," in reality most poor people in the United States have little or no chance of gaining the experience, training, education, and stable career that are the prerequisites of economic success. Nevertheless, they are still likely to value economic success, and to at least some find alternative ways of achieving it (Bourgeois 2003; Duneier 1999).

For example, in poor and minority areas in the United States, especially in the big cities, dealing drugs can be a means of making money—for some, big money. Many young men are willing to risk jail terms and even their lives selling drugs because they believe it offers them an attainable route to economic success (Dunlap et al. 2010; Levitt and Venkatesh 2000). Sociologist Sudhir Venkatesh (b. 1966; 2002) studied the Robert Taylor Homes housing project in Chicago. He spent a great deal of time talking to and observing J. T., a man who was able to make quite a lot of money by being a gang leader and drug dealer. J. T. was not uneducated and was a person of considerable ability. However, he had concluded that he was more likely to achieve material success through deviant, gang-related activities than he would by finishing college and pursuing a more acceptable and conventional career. Even within this deviant career, however, there was a hierarchical structure of opportunity and pay. While J. T. made a great deal of money, the dealers who worked under him barely made the equivalent of minimum wage. This wage gap explains "why drug dealers still live with their mothers" (Levitt and Dubner 2005).

Adaptations to Strain

The most important version of strain theory was developed in the mid-1900s by one of the leading structural-functionalists, Robert K. Merton. The issue at the heart of Merton's theory is the way in which people relate to the institutionalized means (e.g., getting a college degree and working hard) needed to achieve such cultural goals as economic success. Of greatest interest in this context is the strain placed on some people by the relationship between means and ends. Merton identified five possible relationships between means and ends and associated them with five types of adaptation:

- **Conformists** are people who accept both cultural goals, such as making lots of money, and the traditional means of achieving those goals, including hard work. Conformists are the only ones among Merton's types who would not be considered deviant.

- **Innovators** accept the same cultural goals the conformists do, but they reject the conventional means of achieving them. Innovators are deviants in that they choose nonconventional routes to success. Joaquín Guzmán, aka El Chapo, is a Mexican drug lord who rose swiftly through the ranks to achieve his financial success. By the 2010s, Guzmán had achieved a Robin Hood–like status among some for his provision of much-needed services in Mexico's Sinaloa mountains, but his illegal methods of operation saw him extradited from Mexico to the United States in early 2017. Other innovators choose legal routes to success. An example is Michael Phelps, the most decorated athlete in Olympic history, with 28 medals—23 of them gold. Phelps made his career as a record-breaking swimmer who persevered through setbacks with intense training and focus.

- **Ritualists** realize that they will not be able to achieve cultural goals, but they nonetheless continue to engage in the conventional behavior associated with such success. Thus, a low-level employee might continue to work diligently even after realizing that such work is not going to lead to much economic success. Merton saw such diligent work with no realizable goal as a form of deviance.

- **Retreatists** reject both cultural goals and the traditional routes to their attainment. Retreatists have completely given up on attaining success within the system. One example is the Brown family documented on the Discovery Channel's reality show *Alaskan Bush People*. This family has lived off the grid for more than 20 years in the Alaskan bush. They hunt, fish, and build their own homes on a remote island. They barter when needed, such as exchanging fish for dental work.

- **Rebels** are like retreatists in that they reject both traditional means and goals. However, they substitute nontraditional goals and means to achieving those goals. In a sense, that makes them doubly deviant. Revolutionaries such as Ernesto "Che" Guevara can be seen as fitting into the rebel category. Guevara rejected success as it was defined in Cuba during the 1950s. Instead, he chose to assist Fidel Castro in his effort to overthrow the country's dictatorial system. Furthermore, he chose unconventional means—guerrilla warfare waged from the mountains of Cuba and, eventually, Bolivia—to attain his goals.

Adaptations of means to ends exemplify a structural-functionalist approach, because some of the adaptations are highly functional. Conformity certainly has positive consequences in the sense that it allows the social system to continue to exist without disturbance. Innovation is functional because society needs innovations in order to adapt to new external realities. No society can survive without innovation. Even rebellion can be seen as functional because there are times when society needs more than gradual innovation—it needs to change radically.

Structural-functionalism is concerned not only with functions but also with dysfunctions. For example, ritualists and retreatists can be seen as largely dysfunctional for society, or at least as having more dysfunctions than functions. The unchanging behavior of ritualists contributes little or nothing to the requirements of an ever-changing society, and retreatists contribute even less because they are uninvolved in, and have withdrawn from, the larger society.

More Recent Developments in Strain Theory

While Merton focused on several specific strains often related to economic matters, Robert Agnew (1992; Patchin and Hinduja 2011) has sought to develop a theory that focuses more generally on what happens to those who experience strain. Among other things, he argues, they are likely to feel frustrated and angry about the strain. Those feelings predispose them to committing more deviant and even criminal acts. Whereas Merton focused on the strain associated with the failure to achieve positively valued goals, such as economic success, Agnew adds two other types of strain. One results from the loss of something—an example is the unwanted termination of a romantic relationship. The second type comes from experiencing an adverse situation, such as being mistreated by the police (Santoro and Broidy 2014). While many people suffer such strains, only those who feel angry or frustrated about them are likely to engage in deviant acts. For example, those who are mistreated by the police, especially black men, may be more likely to engage in rioting, such as what took place in Ferguson, Missouri, in 2014 in the wake of the police shooting of a young black man. Rioting also occurred in Baltimore, Maryland, in 2015 after a young black man died from injuries suffered while riding in a police van. Such acts are often aimed at doing something about the source of the strain. The most deviant reaction to strain in this context is the murder of police officers, especially the systematic murder of several officers in both Dallas, Texas, and Baton Rouge, Louisiana, in 2016.

Another important contribution to strain theory is Stephen Messner and Richard Rosenfeld's (1997) more macroscopic approach to strain (Ziyanak and Williams 2014). While Agnew focuses more on individual feelings and what people seek to do about the source of their strain, Messner and Rosenfeld are concerned, as are structural-functional theories in general, with the relationship among large-scale structures. On one side are cultural and social structural pressures to succeed, especially economically. On the other are social institutions such as the family, the political system, and religion, which are supposed to reduce these pressures. However, if the latter institutions are weak, or if they exert weak controls over the sources of pressure to succeed, people are more likely to engage in deviant behavior to enhance their chances of success, especially economically. To put it simply, poor people are more likely to engage in deviance or crime if there is no social institution powerful enough to reduce the pressure to commit such acts.

Social Control

Travis Hirschi's (1969) **social control theory** is also included under the heading of structural/functional theories. Hirschi's theory focuses on the reasons why people do *not* commit deviant acts. In brief, people are less likely to commit deviant acts if they have a variety of social bonds. Conversely, they are more likely to commit such acts if those bonds are weak. While Hirschi's theory has wide application to deviance in general, he was most interested in young people and juvenile delinquency.

Social control involves the structures of society and the people who formally act on behalf of those structures. In a sense, Hirschi sees those structures and the people who work on their behalf as functional for society. People who are involved in those structures and are responsive to those who act on their behalf are more likely to be conformists and less likely to become deviants. However, those who are more likely to become deviants are not deeply involved in those structures and not responsive to their demands or to people who act on their behalf. In terms of the latter situation, Hirschi contends, "If a person does not care about the wishes and expectations of other people . . . then he is to that extent not bound by the norms. He is free to deviate" (1969, 18). One structure of great importance to Hirschi is the school. If a young person is not involved in school and with teachers, he or she is likely to be more inclined toward deviant behavior. More informal factors are also important. For example, those who do not have close personal relationships, or who are not involved in extracurricular activities such as sports, are also more inclined toward deviance. The lack of a job and involvement in the work world has similar effects. Without such attachments and involvements, young people are less likely to accept conventional goals or internalize the norms of society. Lacking attachments to family and conventional norms and goals, there is little to prevent a person from becoming a deviant, a juvenile delinquent, or even a career criminal. The lack of other vested interests, such as owning a house, is also likely to contribute to deviant behavior. People in such a situation have little or nothing to lose in violating norms and laws.

In later work, Hirschi (2004, 545) describes these circumstances as "inhibitors," or "factors that one takes into account in deciding whether to commit a criminal act." If young people lack such inhibitors as ties to schools and teachers, they are more likely to become juvenile delinquents (Intravia, Jones, and Piquero 2012).

This view is consistent with structural-functionalism in that it focuses on larger structures (school, work, and the housing market), those who exist in those structures and act on behalf of them (teachers, supervisors), and the positions that people do or do not hold in those structures. Involvement in these structures is likely to inhibit non-conformist behavior, while a lack of such involvement makes such behavior more likely.

While acknowledging the importance of structures and those who act formally on their behalf, Sampson and Laub (1993, 2005) have expanded on Hirschi's control theory, which tends to focus more on the formal aspects of social control. Sampson and Laub deal with both the formal and informal aspects of control. In terms of informal control, they are most interested in the interpersonal bonds that serve to control what people do and prevent them from engaging in deviance and crime. Furthermore, while Hirschi focuses on young people and delinquency, Sampson and Laub deal with the relationship between control and deviance over the full course of people's lives. Informal social control in the family, in schools, and among peers is crucial to determining whether or not young people engage in deviant behavior. A lack of such control is a key cause of juvenile delinquency. However, informal social control also plays an important role in adulthood, influencing whether or not adults engage in deviant and criminal behavior. For adults, the most important informal social controls are those that relate to the family and work. Adults with strong interpersonal ties in those contexts are less likely to engage in criminal behavior.

Interestingly, according to Sampson and Laub's research, whether or not an adult engaged in delinquent behavior as a youth does not affect the likelihood of adult criminal behavior. For both those who have and those who have not been delinquents, the key to adult behavior is the existence and nature of later informal interpersonal relationships. While what happens to children is important, social ties in adolescence and adulthood also affect later criminal behavior. That is, irrespective of childhood involvement in delinquency, informal interpersonal bonds can serve to make it more *or* less likely that adolescents and adults will commit crimes. Those who lack nurturing, supportive, and controlling relationships in adulthood and throughout the life course are more likely to be persistent offenders. Those who are involved in such relationships

How does social control serve to prevent or discourage deviant behavior, such as shoplifting?

later in life are less likely to be criminals. In other words, being a delinquent does not necessarily mean that one will be a criminal in later life. That depends, among other things, on the nature of interpersonal ties and social controls at various stages throughout the life course. In sum, informal social control is negatively associated with crime throughout the life course.

Broken Windows

A very different aspect of control as it relates to deviance and especially crime is found in the highly controversial "broken windows" theory (Harcourt and Ludwig 2006; Wilson and Kelling 1982). The theory acknowledges that people worry about criminals who have the potential to mug or rob them. However, it is also the case that in public places, especially in large cities, people tend to be disturbed by a variety of less dangerous forms of urban disorder. They perceive this disorder as stemming from a variety of types of people encountered far more frequently than criminals interested in doing them harm. These types include panhandlers, loiterers, prostitutes, those who are mentally disturbed, public drunks and drug addicts, and noisy teenagers. The perception is that these types of people are permitted to behave in a disorderly manner because no one, including the authorities, cares enough about the neighborhood to stop them. The same point holds in regard to buildings that are covered with graffiti and have many broken windows, as well as other signs of neighborhood deterioration, such as abandoned and vandalized automobiles. Furthermore, untended broken windows and vandalized cars tend to invite more of each, leading to an increasingly disorderly neighborhood. Neighborhoods that lack the informal controls needed

FIGURE 7.4 • New York City Violent Crime Rate, 1985–2015

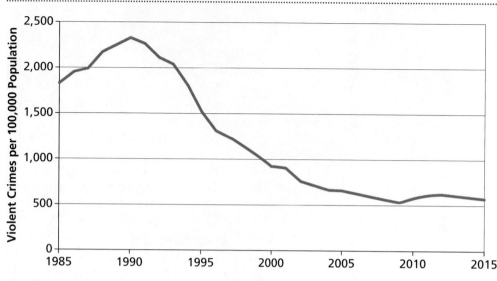

SOURCE: Federal Bureau of Investigation, Uniform Crime Reporting.

have contributed to the decline is "hot-spot policing." Because crime seems to recur in a small number of locales, the police have tended to concentrate their attention on these "hot spots." However, in addition to the contributions of such newer approaches, it is also the case that at least some of the decline may be traceable to the presence of fewer broken windows, reductions in graffiti, and the arrests of more people for minor violations.

to prevent these developments and to maintain order are those that may allow criminal elements to gain a foothold and to thrive. In other words, crime is likely to flourish in disorderly neighborhoods. The clear answer, then, is to make neighborhoods more orderly. To do so, greater control needs to be exercised, both informally by residents and more formally by the police. The formal control by the police is needed to supplement informal control by residents. This control is designed to deal early with such things as rowdy behavior, broken windows, and abandoned automobiles so that they do not proliferate and create an environment in which more widespread criminal behavior can take root.

However, there are a variety of fears associated with the broken windows approach. For one thing, there is the concern that it gives the police wide discretion to deal with people, even to arrest them, although they have done no actual harm. The other is that such police behavior will lead to discrimination against minorities. For example, in New York City in 2014, a black man who had been engaged in the minor crime of selling illegal cigarettes died after an arresting police officer placed him in a chokehold (Goldstein and Schweber 2014). This event is one of the factors that have led some to reconsider the broken windows approach (Bellafante 2015). Nevertheless, the broken windows theory has enjoyed great popularity in recent years, with New York City crediting its success in reducing crime at least in part to the application of this theory (Zimring 2011). In fact, violent crime there dropped by about 74 percent between the early 1990s and 2015 (see Figure 7.4). Astoundingly, this occurred when, for at least part of that period, the prison population was declining (Tierney 2013). Of course, many other factors have been associated with this decline in crime, such as an older population less likely to commit crimes and the moderation of the crack cocaine epidemic that caused so many crimes. One recently popular approach that may also

Self-Control

The preceding discussion has focused on the external control exerted over those who might deviate, but there is another approach that is concerned with the role of self-control in deviance and crime (Gottfredson and Hirschi 1990). The central point of this approach is that those with low self-control are more likely to engage in deviant and criminal acts. Family upbringing is a key factor in the development of enough self-control to resist committing such acts. High levels of self-control are likely to develop when parents monitor their children, supervise them, and recognize and deal with their antisocial behavior. Parental failure in these and other areas is likely to lead to low self-control. A tendency to have low self-control is likely to persist throughout a person's life. Those with low self-control are unable to resist various temptations. They are also unlikely to be able to foresee the negative consequences of acting on those temptations. Of course, such actions depend on the existence of opportunities to do so. A child might be tempted by a brand-new BMW, but he is unlikely to steal it if he does not know how to drive.

Overall, it is likely that whether or not people engage in deviant and criminal behavior is best explained by a combination of formal and informal external controls, in interaction with self-control.

ASK YOURSELF

Is it likely that disordered neighborhoods are really more crime-ridden than others? Why or why not? Given your answer, do you think that making neighborhoods more orderly and better controlled serves to reduce crime? If not, what might be more effective?

CONFLICT/CRITICAL THEORIES

Proponents of structural/functional theories trace the source of deviance to the larger structures of society and the strains they produce or the fact that they do not exercise adequate social control. Conflict/critical theorists, especially conflict theorists, are also interested in those structures and their effects on people, but they adopt a different orientation toward them. A major focus is the inequality that exists in those structures and the impact that it has on individuals. In conflict theorists' view, inequality causes at least some of the less powerful individuals in society to engage in deviant—and criminal—acts because they have few, if any, other ways of succeeding in society (Goode 2007b). In this way, they are similar to the innovators in Merton's taxonomy of adaptations to strain. Conversely, those in power in executive or managerial positions in organizations are more likely to commit crimes, especially corporate or white-collar crimes (Simpson 2002; Simpson 2013; Simpson and Weisburd 2009). This the case because the nature of their high-level positions in various social structures (business, government) makes it not only possible but also relatively easy for them to do so. Their positions also allow them to better conceal their crimes. White-collar criminals are more likely to use deception in committing their crimes and bribery in order to conceal them; their crimes are more likely to be clandestine and to remain hidden (Van Slyke, Benson, and Cullen 2016, ix). While collar crimes are also less likely to require, and to involve, the use of physical force. For all of these reasons, and others, such crimes are difficult to uncover. Further, conflict theorists argue, those in power in society create the laws and rules that define certain things as deviant, or illegal, while others are defined as normal. They do so in a self-serving way that advantages them and disadvantages those who lack power in society.

The conflict view of deviance has been extended to many other acts on the basis of racial, sexual, gender, age-related, and other social inequalities (Collins 1975). For example, questionable acts committed by racial minorities are more likely to be labeled as deviance or crime than are the same acts committed by majority group members. Before the repeal of state antisodomy laws by the Supreme Court in 2003, police in some states could arrest homosexuals for having sex with one another in the privacy of their own homes. Heterosexuals engaging in sodomy—that is, having oral or anal sex—in their own homes would almost never be arrested for such acts, but technically these acts were illegal in some locales. Some geographic areas have curfews for teenagers, meaning that a teenager who is out after a certain time can be labeled as deviant. In contrast, curfews for adults are almost unheard of, except during emergencies, such as in the aftermath of natural disasters. Again, this list can be extended greatly, but the point is that conflict theorists tend to see those who rank low in the system of social stratification, on any dimension, as more likely to be labeled as deviant.

Deviance and the Poor

Conflict theories can be applied to social inequalities throughout the ages. For instance, they form the basis of research by William Chambliss (1964) on vagrancy laws in medieval England. These laws came into existence as feudalism was falling apart; the first vagrancy law was enacted in England after the Black Death, around 1348. In the feudal system, serfs were forced to provide labor for landowners, but with the end of feudalism, and therefore of serfdom, a new source of labor was needed. Not coincidentally, the former serfs now lacked permanent homes and sources of income and wandered about the countryside. Those in power saw them as a likely group to provide the needed labor at little cost, so they created vagrancy laws. Under these laws, it was illegal for those without work or a home to loiter in public places, and some of the itinerants were arrested. As a result, many people who otherwise might not have worked for the landowners were forced to do so in order to avoid arrest and imprisonment.

Contemporary conflict theorists, heavily influenced by Marxian theory, have come to see deviance as something created by the capitalist economic system. Today's definitions of deviance serve the interests of the capitalists, especially by further enriching them. Conversely, they adversely affect the proletariat, especially the poor, who grow even poorer. This view is well summed up by Jeffrey Reiman and Paul Leighton in *The Rich Get Richer and the Poor Get Prison* (2012). As the title of this book implies, the best examples of this process lie in the realm of crime rather than that of deviance, although to be seen as a crime, an act must first be defined as deviant. For example, as we saw previously, at the close of the Middle Ages, it was in the interest of elite members of society to define vagrancy as deviance and as a crime. Such a definition seems fair and evenhanded, until we realize that elite members of society are rarely, if ever, going to be without work and a home. They are therefore unlikely to be defined as vagrants. It is only the poor who are going to find themselves in that situation, with the result that they are just about the only ones who are going to be affected by the laws against vagrancy. As the great novelist Anatole France ([1894] 2011) once commented sarcastically, "The law, in all its majestic equality, forbids the rich as well as the poor to sleep under bridges on rainy nights, to beg on the streets, and to steal bread."

Conflict theorists do not argue that have-nots never commit crimes or deviant acts. Rather, they argue that it is because of the laws (e.g., those against sleeping under bridges) created by societal elites that the actions of the have-nots are singled out for notice and for sanctions. Furthermore, the costs to society of elite deviance are much higher than the costs associated with crime and deviance among society's have-nots. Compare, for example, the approximately $65 billion the disgraced and now imprisoned Bernie Madoff cost his clients by engaging in illegal activities to the few dollars a con artist or a mugger wrests from his victims.

Deviance and the Elite

Great efforts are made to legitimate elite crimes and acts of elite deviance (Simon 2012) and, failing that, to pay little or no attention to them. Those who rank high in such hierarchies as business, government, and the military have a much greater ability to commit deviant acts (such as sexually harassing subordinates), to have these acts be seen as legitimate, and to get away with them.

Once powerful and widely revered, Penn State assistant football coach Jerry Sandusky was sentenced to at least 30 years in prison for his part in a scandal involving the sexual abuse of children. Conflict theorists believe that wrongdoing by elites rarely comes to light or is punished.

However, as is clear in the imprisonment of people like Bernie Madoff, there are limits to the ability of elites to get away with deviant and criminal behavior. There are times when the acts are so extreme that they can no longer be hidden. They come to light and become great public issues. Once this happens, even the most elite members of society have a difficult time escaping negative judgment and perhaps even punishment and imprisonment.

In fact, there is a long list of scandals involving elite public figures of various types who have been found to have committed deviant acts. In the main, their acts were so extreme, or the revelations about them became so public, that they could not be ignored. However, what has often caused difficulties for those involved has been their awkward efforts to lie about, or cover up, their offenses once they first became public. In many cases, especially in this era of the internet, evidence is uncovered or witnesses come forward that make it clear that the public figure has been deceiving the public and the authorities. The following are a few notable examples in the U.S. context (there are innumerable others everywhere in the world):

- In perhaps the most famous example of all, President Richard Nixon resigned in 1974 as he faced imminent impeachment for his role in the infamous Watergate break-in and for his efforts to conceal his and his associates' roles in it from the public.

- Gracious-living guru and media magnate Martha Stewart served five months in jail in 2004 and 2005 for lying about a 2001 stock sale. Stewart sold off her ImClone stock just before its price plunged, suggesting she might have benefited from insider trading.

- In 2011, Congressman Anthony Weiner was forced to resign from Congress when it was revealed that he had tweeted sexually suggestive photographs of himself to a young woman; in 2013, he was forced withdraw from the mayoralty race in New York City because of similar texting, and his sexting appears to continue to this day.

- In 2015, New England Patriots football star Aaron Hernandez was convicted of first-degree murder. He was serving a life sentence in prison without the possibility of parole when he took his own life in April 2017, after being acquitted of murder charges in a second case. Shortly thereafter, a Massachusetts judge vacated Hernandez's murder conviction, although the local district attorney planned to appeal the ruling.

The view of conflict theorists is that, as lengthy as this list of elite deviants and criminals might be, it is merely the tip of the iceberg. Because elites have a wide variety of means at their disposal to conceal their actions, many, many more of their acts of deviance and criminality escape detection and punishment. Such acts by elites can persist for years, decades, or even a lifetime.

INTER/ACTIONIST THEORIES

The third major type of theory employed in this book, inter/actionism, can also be used to analyze deviance (Rubington and Weinberg 2016). For example, to the rational choice theorist, a person chooses deviance because it is a rational means to some desired goal. Gang members join gangs because of the camaraderie and perceived protection offered by the gang (Melde, Taylor, and Esbensen 2009), as well as for access to a world in which the member can obtain money and achieve recognition and high status (Bell 2009; Decker and Curry 2000). Ethnomethodologists are concerned with the ways in which people "do" deviance—that is, the everyday behaviors in which they engage that produce deviance. People need to adopt methods of speech and forms of behavior that make their deviance invisible to most others. In a classic ethnomethodological study, Harold Garfinkel (1967) described the painstaking steps taken by Agnes, a transgender woman, to "pass" as a woman. She not only changed her manner of dress, posture, and demeanor but also underwent bodily changes. However, there are times when those who are deviant want to talk and act in ways that make it clear that they are deviant. For example, gang members may use certain phrases, dress in certain ways, and display certain tattoos to make their allegiance clear to other members of the same gang—and to members of opposing gangs (see Chapter 5). However, when they interact with the public or the police, gang members may speak and dress in ways that conceal, or at least attempt to hide, their membership in the gang.

ASK YOURSELF

Has engaging in any form of deviance ever seemed rational to you, in the sense that inter/actionist theories use the term? If so, was the deviance visible or invisible to others? Did it help you (or would it have helped you) achieve a goal?

Labeling

Symbolic interactionism is of great utility in analyzing and furthering our understanding of deviance. One variety of symbolic interactionism—labeling theory—is particularly useful in thinking about deviance. From that perspective, at least two things are needed for deviance to occur:

- A **symbol**, or in this case a "label." In the realm of deviance, a number of labels are particularly powerful negative symbols: *alcoholic, drug addict, pedophile, adulterer,* and so on. The golfer Tiger Woods is a good example of the power of labels. He had become a well-known public symbol, even a brand. His name conjured up images of not only a great golfer but someone who was "squeaky-clean" as well. In 2009, he was involved in a car crash that led to revelations that he had cheated on his wife with multiple women. The labels *adulterer* and

sex addict were linked with his name, and his reputation and public image were badly tarnished. Even though the accusations had nothing to do with golf, several of his corporate sponsors dropped him because they no longer wanted to be associated with a person who was labeled so negatively. They feared that his spoiled reputation would extend to them and adversely affect their businesses and profits. After a slump, Woods regained at least some of his former greatness as a golfer from 2011 to 2013. He also has regained at least some of his reputation. This was helped by, and reflected in, the fact that President Barack Obama played golf with him in 2013. Back surgeries in 2014 and 2015 set him back again, and by 2016 he was no longer ranked among the 500 leading golfers in the world. Negative labels continue to haunt him, and may do so for the rest of his life.

- Interaction between the person or group doing the labeling (the labeler) and the person or group to whom the label is applied (the labelee). During this interaction, one or more of these labels is applied to the deviant; a deviant is someone who others say is a deviant. Deviance is a matter of social definition. Those who do the defining—the labeling—are known as **social control agents**. Some of these agents (police, psychiatrists) are performing official functions, but far more often it is friends or family who label others as, for example, drunks or womanizers. When public figures are labeled as deviant, the media and their representatives are often the ones who do the labeling.

From the perspective of **labeling theory**, a deviant is someone to whom a deviant label has been successfully applied (Becker 1963; Goode 2014; Restivo and Lanier 2015). This stands in contrast to the view of the public and many sociologists, who focus on what an individual does in order to be labeled a deviant. Also of interest in labeling theory is the way in which the person labeled as deviant is affected by the label (Dotter and Roebuck 1988; Gove 1980; Walsh 1990). The person can accept the label to varying degrees or make efforts to resist, reject, or shed the label. People also vary greatly in how they react to, and feel about, being labeled as deviant. For example, some might be mortified by being labeled sex addicts, but others might take pride in it.

Labeling theory is also concerned about the actions and reactions of social control agents, as well as about their interactions with those being labeled (Pontell 2007). From the labeling perspective, "deviance is not a consequence of the act the person commits, but rather a consequence of the [creation and] application by others of rules and sanctions to an 'offender'" (Becker 1963, 9). A focus on social control agents, rather than deviants, leads to the view that deviant labels are not necessarily applied uniformly. Some people and some forms of behavior are more likely than others to be labeled as deviant. Thus, murderers and the act of murder are almost uniformly labeled as deviant (and criminal). However, in many other cases, the process is more selective and less clear-cut: "Some men who drink too much are called alcoholics and others are not; some men who act oddly are committed to hospitals and others are not; some men who have no visible means of support are hauled into court and others are not" (Erikson 1964, 11–12). Overall, people are more likely to be socially defined as deviant when they are poor, work in low-status occupations, or are in similarly devalued circumstances (Goffman 1959). A person in a more advantageous social situation often escapes being defined or labeled as deviant, despite manifesting the same forms of behavior. Similarly, the poor are more likely to be labeled as criminals for their acts of deviance, while that is not the case for those in the middle and upper classes. For example, almost none of the leaders of financial institutions implicated as playing a large role in causing the Great Recession (such as Jamie Dimon of JPMorgan Chase) were ever convicted of being, or even thought of as, criminals, even though their investment houses have been fined billions of dollars by the government (Brinded 2014).

Primary and Secondary Deviance

An important distinction that flows from labeling theory is that between primary and secondary deviance:

- **Primary deviance** consists of early, random acts of deviance, such as an occasional bout of drinking to excess or an isolated act considered strange or out of the ordinary. Virtually all of us commit such acts; we all have engaged in various forms of primary deviance (Lemert [1951] 2012; Wallerstein and Wyle 1947). Isolated acts of primary deviance rarely, if ever, lead to the successful application of a deviant label. Primary deviance consists of acts and behavior, not identities or labels.

- Of far greater interest to labeling theorists is **secondary deviance**, or deviant acts that persist, become more common, and eventually cause people to organize their lives and personal identities around their deviant status (Liberman, Kirk, and Kim 2014). Secondary deviance usually occurs after an individual has been stigmatized and judged for deviant behavior and possibly labeled as deviant. In response, the individual begins to see and define him- or herself as deviant. Thus, if a person moves from occasionally having short-term sexual encounters with strangers to being obsessed with such encounters and seeking them out whenever and wherever possible, that person may be labeled a sex addict. It is possible, as in the case of Hank Moody (the lead character on the Showtime comedy *Californication*), and perhaps Tiger Woods, that the label of sex addict will become more important than all other definitions of the self. When that happens, sex addiction becomes a

form of secondary deviance. In one recent study, body modifications such as tattoos and body piercings were shown to be acts of primary deviance that were related to forms of secondary deviance such as drug abuse and juvenile delinquency (Dukes and Stein 2011).

While labeling theory tends to focus on others labeling an individual as deviant, it is possible, or even likely, that individuals will label themselves in this way (Thoits 1985, 2011), that they will do so before anyone else does (Norris 2011), and that they will act in accordance with their self-imposed label (Lorber 1967). This is consistent with the view of the leading symbolic interactionist, George Herbert Mead, who saw the mind as an internal conversation with oneself. Such an internalized conversation may certainly lead to labeling oneself as deviant.

Key Ideas in the Labeling Process

Social control is the process by which a group or society enforces conformity to its demands and expectations. One way in which this is accomplished is through the creation and application of rules and labels. This leads to the distinction between rule creators and rule enforcers. **Rule creators** are usually elite members of society who devise its rules, norms, and laws (Ryan 1994). Without rule creators and their rules, there would be no deviance. Rule creators are usually (but not always) distinct from **rule enforcers**, who threaten to or actually do sanction the rule violators (Bryant and Higgins 2010). Another important idea here is that of **moral entrepreneurs**, or those individuals or groups of individuals who come to define an act as a moral outrage and who lead a campaign to have it defined as deviant and to have it made illegal and therefore subject to legal enforcement (Becker 1963; Lauderdale 2007; Nordgren 2013). Drugs provide a good example, especially globally, because moral entrepreneurs (particularly those located in the United States) have taken it upon themselves to have drugs themselves defined as illegal and their use labeled as deviant. They have done so, even though the use of many of these drugs (such as marijuana) is common and accepted not only in many societies throughout the world but also among a large portion of the American population. One famous example of a moral entrepreneur is U.S. senator Joe McCarthy, who in the 1950s created a public fervor over the existence of communists in the government and elsewhere (such as Hollywood). As a result, many people were labeled communists (often falsely) and therefore came to be seen in a negative light, perhaps for the rest of their lives.

Moral Panics

Moral entrepreneurs can stir up such a fuss that they can cause a **moral panic**, or a widespread and disproportionate

Moral panics—such as the witch-hunting crazes of Renaissance Europe—rely in part on the use of labels to identify perceived threats. What might help prevent the development of a moral panic?

reaction to the form of deviance in question (Goode and Ben-Yehuda 1994, 2009; Hier 2011; Krinsky 2013). It could be argued that today we are witnessing, in Europe and to a lesser degree in the United States, concern about Muslim immigrants that is quickly becoming a moral panic (Morgan and Poynting 2012). This moral panic is related, at least in part, to the increasing threat of terrorism posed by radical Islamic groups, especially the Islamic State and al-Qaeda (among many examples from around the world are the early 2015 murder by Islamist extremists of 12 people at the Paris satirical newspaper *Charlie Hebdo* and 4 people at a Jewish supermarket; the killing of 49 people at a nightclub in Orlando, Florida, in June 2016, as well as an attack on Ataturk Airport in Turkey in the same month that killed 45 people; and the killing of 84 people at a Bastille Day celebration in Nice, France, in July 2016). In spite of these gruesome and highly publicized attacks, it is important to remember that very few Muslims are Islamist extremists, let alone terrorists.

A good historical example of a moral panic is the witch craze that occurred in Europe between the fourteenth and sixteenth centuries (Ben-Yehuda 1980, 1985). The idea of witches had existed before this time, but it was seen as a more complex phenomenon involving both bad and good witches. In any case, no assumption had been made about a conspiracy between women and Satan to corrupt the world. However, in this era, Dominican friars took the lead in defining witchcraft as such a conspiracy and as a crime subject to corporal punishment, in this case, burning at the stake. The friars were the moral entrepreneurs in this example. They played a key role in generating a moral panic that came to involve large numbers of people. That panic, in turn, led to the painful deaths of hundreds of thousands of people, mostly women.

Moral panics are, by definition, exaggerated. Thus, the threats posed by witches in the fifteenth century, communists in the 1950s, and immigrants and even terrorists today have been made out by many, especially moral entrepreneurs, to be greater than they really are. One of the ways to do this is to create a "folk devil" who stands for what is feared. In the case of communism, it was Joseph Stalin or Mao Zedong; more recently, terrorism made Osama bin Laden a folk devil.

Stigmas

Erving Goffman's *Stigma* (1963) is a very important contribution of symbolic interactionism to our understanding of deviance. A **stigma** is a person's characteristic that others find, define, and often label as unusual, unpleasant, or deviant. Goffman begins his book with analyses of physically stigmatized individuals, such as those missing a nose. He then introduces a wide array of other stigmas, such as being on welfare. In the end, readers come to the realization that they have been reading not only about people who are unlike them, with major physical deformities, but also about themselves: "The most fortunate of normals is likely to have his half-hidden failing, and for every little failing there is a social occasion when it will loom large, creating a shameful gap" (Goffman 1963, 127). Goffman's idea of stigma has attracted many scholars and has been applied to many forms of deviance, such as prostitution (Scambler and Paoli 2008; Wong, Holroyd, and Bingham 2011), mental illness (Payton and Thoits 2011), Asperger's syndrome (Hill and Liamputtong 2011), and tattooing (Dickson et al. 2014).

There are two types of stigmatized individuals. The individual with a **discredited stigma** "assumes his differentness is known about already or is evident on the spot." In contrast, those with a **discreditable stigma** assume that their stigma "is neither known about by those present nor immediately perceivable about them" (Goffman 1963, 4). An example of a discredited stigma might be the bodily symptoms of having advanced AIDS, having a lost limb, or being a member of a minority group viewed negatively by others, while discreditable stigmas include having done poorly in school or having a prison record. As is to be expected with a symbolic interactionist perspective, of great importance is the symbolic nature of the stigma and the individual's interaction with others, especially those thought to be normal. Because the physical nature of a discreditable stigma is not visible to others, neither are the stigma's symbolic qualities. Nevertheless, the people with such a stigma want to make sure it remains secret and thus try to conceal the stigmatizing information during most interactions. However, in the case of a discredited stigma (such as being morbidly obese), those with the stigma must deal with the tension associated with interacting with people who view them negatively because of the stigma.

The idea of discreditable stigmas has wide applicability to the contemporary world. For example, the court records of juvenile offenders are often hidden from the public or expunged to avoid stigmatizing otherwise promising young people for a lifetime. People with mental illnesses or substance abuse problems often go to great lengths to hide the real reasons for unscheduled absences from work. Parents of children with mental disabilities, especially those with mild impairments, "mainstream" their children in standard classrooms, in part so that the children's disabilities will be more likely to be discreditable than discredited. The theme of hiding stigmatizing conditions is common in popular entertainment as well: In the movie *Philadelphia* (1993), actor Tom Hanks plays a high-powered lawyer in a prestigious law firm who is diagnosed with HIV during the early years of the epidemic. As the disease progresses, he tries but ultimately fails to conceal the signs, such as skin blemishes associated with Kaposi's sarcoma. When it becomes clear to the leaders of his firm that he has AIDS, he is fired.

This movie realistically portrays the painful, destructive effects of revealing a discredited stigma.

Positive Deviance

Deviance is usually defined in negative terms. In fact, the discussion to this point of the chapter has focused on negative examples of deviance. However, there is increasing attention in sociology, and other fields, to positive forms of deviance (Heckart and Heckart 2015). **Positive deviance** can be defined as actions that violate norms but are defined by society as having beneficial effects on it. Unlike most deviance, positive deviance is usually seen as socially acceptable. Among the broad types of positive deviance are altruistic acts (such as jumping in front of a moving car to save a child crossing the road), heroic acts performed by charismatic individuals (such as the long fasts of people like Gandhi aimed at bringing attention to important social issues; see Chapter 6 for a definition of charismatic authority), innovative acts (such as Steve Jobs's iconic contributions to Apple, including the Mac computer and the iPhone), and acts by "supra-conformists" that exceed basic normative expectations and demands (such as being a "gifted student" or getting straight As in college). At the most extreme are the positive deviants who are most likely to bring about needed dramatic changes in society. While positive deviance usually has positive outcomes, there can be negative consequences of positive deviance. For example, that leap in front of an oncoming car could cost both the do-gooder and the endangered child their lives; the pursuit of straight As could lead to cheating on exams or little actual education as students learn to game the exam system; and the effort to win sports championships can lead, as has often been demonstrated, to cheating (e.g., the many individual doping cases in amateur and professional sports, most notably Lance Armstrong in bicycle racing and, more generally, the 2016 revelations that Russian athletic success, especially in the Olympics, was fueled by a state-run doping system).

CHECKPOINT 7.2: COMPARING THEORIES OF DEVIANCE

EXPLANATORY THEORIES	CONSTRUCTIONIST THEORIES
Explanatory theories attempt to explain why deviance does or does not occur.	Constructionist theories seek a greater understanding of the process by which people define and classify some behaviors as normal and others as deviant.
Structural/functional theories: strain, social control, broken windows, self-control	Inter/actionist theories: labeling
Conflict/critical theories: inequality	

CRIME

While there are many ways to define it, **crime** is simply a violation of the criminal law (Whitehead 2007). As pointed out previously, it is the fact that the law is violated that differentiates crime from other forms of deviance. **Criminology** is the field devoted to the study of crime (S. Brown 2007a; Maguire, Morgan, and Reiner 2012; Rosenfield 2011; Siegel 2014). Many, but certainly not all, criminologists are sociologists. While many criminologists are now found in university departments and schools devoted to the study of criminology, a large number work in sociology departments. There is a sociology of crime, but the field also includes those from many other disciplines, such as psychologists, economists, biologists, and anthropologists, as well as officials who once worked in the criminal justice system. In fact, the field today has become increasingly multidisciplinary, even interdisciplinary (Wellford 2012).

While there is growing interdisciplinarity in the study of crime, sociology plays an important role in it. Clearly, a variety of sociological factors (including social class and race; Chilton and Triplett 2007a, 2007b) are involved in who commits crimes and which crimes they commit. The same sociological factors are involved in who gets caught, prosecuted, and incarcerated, as well as how much of their sentences they actually serve. And such factors are involved in what happens to people after they serve their sentences and whether or not they are likely to end up back in prison.

The "father of criminology" is Cesare Lombroso, who published *The Criminal Man* in 1876 (McShane and Williams 2007). The title of the book reflects the fact that the focus of early criminologists was on criminals and their innate physical or psychological characteristics. Criminals were seen as being defective in various ways, and the goal was to study the defects and those who had them scientifically in order to deter crime. While the major causes were considered to lie within the individual, they were seen as being beyond the individual's control. In fact, Lombroso's main focus was on the "born criminal." Hence, early criminologists adopted the view that such people needed the external control of the criminal justice system. Lombroso was also prone to gross and indefensible generalizations, such as the claim that Gypsies "murder in cold blood in order to rob, and were formerly suspected of cannibalism. The women are very clever at stealing" (cited in Williams and McShane 2007, 2663).

In more recent years, criminology has shifted away from its focus on criminals and their defects and toward a concern with the social context of criminal actions and the effects of those actions on the larger society. A key figure in bringing a sociological perspective to criminology was Edwin Sutherland (1883–1950). Sutherland studied a variety of issues in criminology, such as white-collar crime, the death penalty, and prisons, but his greatest influence was his textbook *Criminology* (1924). The book went through 10 editions and was used by students for nearly 70 years. Sutherland was a symbolic interactionist. This perspective helped shift the focus in criminology from the criminal and his or her misdeeds to society, especially the societal reaction to those actions, including the labels placed on criminals.

Sutherland's most important contribution to the sociology of crime is **differential association** theory. The main point of the theory is that people are *not* born criminals; they learn criminal behavior. Therefore, whom a person associates with is crucial. One's family and friends—the primary group—are important sources of attitudes toward crime, knowledge about how to commit crimes, and rationalizations that help one live with being a criminal. Today, we would need to add the fact that criminal behavior can also be learned through television, songs, and especially the internet (e.g., the impact of the internet on the Islamic State's ability to recruit terrorists). Many criticisms were leveled at differential association theory; even Sutherland later came to criticize it on various grounds. For example, it did not explain why some people became criminals, while others exposed to the same situations did not. One of Sutherland's own criticisms was the fact that the theory did not give enough attention to the role of opportunity in committing crimes.

ASK YOURSELF

Can you think of any reasons some people become criminals, while others exposed to the same situations do not? Consider the theories of deviance discussed previously as you prepare your answer.

While the previous discussion focuses on the causes of crime, especially those that are sociological in nature, criminology has long had a second focus on the criminal justice system (Siegel and Worrall 2014; Wellford 2012). This interest is traceable to another early Italian scholar, Cesare Beccaria (1738–1794; McShane and Williams 2007). Beccaria was a lawyer by training and received a doctorate in law. He is best known for his book *On Crimes and Punishments* ([1764] 1986), and its concern with such issues as the origins of law and the criminal justice system. His work led to an interest not only in this system as a whole but also in whether its major components—law enforcement, courts, and corrections (Culver 2007)—are fair, effective, and just. In terms of the latter, much work has been done on the (un)fairness, especially as far as race is concerned, of arrest decisions by the police, the length of sentences, and the likelihood of receiving the death penalty.

FIGURE 7.5 • Prison Population around the World, 2015

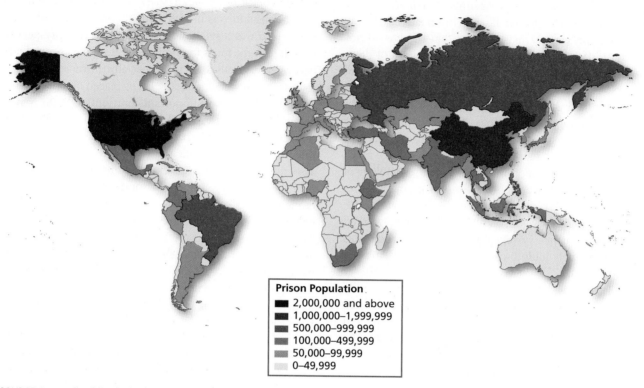

Prison Population
- 2,000,000 and above
- 1,000,000–1,999,999
- 500,000–999,999
- 100,000–499,999
- 50,000–99,999
- 0–49,999

SOURCE: International Centre for Prison Studies.

THE CRIMINAL JUSTICE SYSTEM

The criminal justice system in the United States consists of various loosely connected government agencies and the individuals who work in those agencies. It is involved in the apprehension, prosecution, and punishment of those who violate the law. It also seeks to prevent such violations before they occur. Finally, the criminal justice system has much more general responsibilities, such as ensuring public safety and maintaining social order (Culver 2007, 851). The major components of the criminal justice system are law enforcement, the courts, and the correctional system.

As a general rule, the criminal justice system is not supposed to operate on an automatic basis. That is, the individuals who work in the system are expected to use their professional judgment in their decisions. As a result, police officers do not give tickets to all speeders, prosecutors do not bring all cases to court, and judges do not give the same sentence to all who violate the laws against possession of marijuana. Such discretion at all levels is needed to allow the system to operate in a reasonably efficient fashion. For example, if all people convicted of a minor crime like marijuana possession were sentenced to long jail or prison terms, the jails and prisons would be even more overcrowded than they are now. (By the way, the distinction between jails and prisons is that the former are locally controlled, whereas the latter are controlled by the states or the federal government.)

Even though there is much discretion in the American criminal justice system, an enormous number of people are being held in the jail and prison system. In 2014, 2,217,947 adults were incarcerated in U.S. jails and federal and state prisons. The United States has the highest rate of incarceration (about 0.7 percent of the adult population) in the world. It has approximately 568,140 more prisoners than China and almost 1.6 million more than Russia (see Figure 7.5 for the prison population around the world). Although the United States has only 4.4 percent of the world's population, it has about 25 percent of the world's prisoners (Cullen, Jonson, and Nagin 2011). This is a very costly system to operate (Bratton 2011). It is estimated that in 2013, local, state, and federal governments spent about $71 billion on corrections, much of it on incarceration (Schmidt, Warner, and Gupta 2010). Further complicating matters is the fact that the economic problems facing the United States in general, and state and local jurisdictions in particular, mean that fewer prisons and jails are being built, while an increasing number of Americans are being sentenced to them. The growing number of prisoners creates other problems, including overcrowding of the prisons as well as increased violence among prisoners. Given the huge numbers involved, prisons have become little more than warehouses for prisoners. The ability of prisons to rehabilitate inmates has declined, and the focus on punishment has strengthened (Phelps 2011).

The millions of people in prisons, and the billions of dollars spent on them, became hot public issues in 2016. One of the concerns was mandatory minimum sentences for nonviolent offenders (Williams 2016), which have helped lead to a sharp increase in the number of nonviolent offenders (often involved in drugs) in prison. Many of those offenders—roughly 160,000—are serving life sentences. This is more than four times the number of those serving such sentences in 1984. Obviously, putting people in prison for life is very costly. In any case, such sentences are highly questionable as punishment for minor, drug-related crimes.

Much of this recent increase in the prison population is traceable to the 1994 Clinton crime bill (Yassky 2016). That law was passed at a time when crimes rates and public concern about crime were increasing dramatically. The heart of the law was a provision to add many more police officers throughout the United States and to have many of them operate by the old-fashioned policy of "walking the beat." This helped lead to a halving of the violent crime rate. However, it came at two great costs: One was the development of "mass incarceration." The second was the inappropriate and unconstitutional "stop-and-frisk" practice of officers on the beat, which especially affected young black and Latino men. At least some of these men have ended up in prison, causing the prison population to swell. In addition, the anger produced by the stop-and-frisk policy, as well as by police abuse associated with it (including what many regard as the unnecessary deaths of many black men and women), played a major role in the emergence of the Black Lives Matter movement in 2013. Many of the police officers involved in the injury or death of black suspects were either not prosecuted or not convicted. However, as mentioned earlier in this chapter, there has also been a simultaneous increase in the death of police officers, with targeted killings of officers occurring in 2016, although these killings are not on par with the death toll in the black community.

Beyond the more than 2 million people in prisons and jails in 2014, more than 4.7 million people were under the control of the criminal justice system because they were either on parole (856,900) or on probation (3,864,100; Kaeble, Maruschak, and Bonczar 2015). **Parole** is the supervised early release of a prisoner for such efforts as good behavior while in prison. Parole officers work with those on parole to help them adjust to life outside prison and to be sure that they are not violating the conditions of their release. If they do violate those conditions, they can have their parole revoked, and they can be sent back to prison. Those who are convicted of less serious crimes may

be placed on **probation**, whereby they are released into the community with supervision. They are also released under certain conditions, such as that they must be enrolled in and complete a substance abuse program. If the offender does not adhere to these conditions, is arrested, or is convicted, probation can be revoked. In that case, a new, more restrictive probation can be imposed, or the offender can be sent to prison (Culver 2007). Both parole and probation require the participation of bureaucracies, and especially the parole and probation officers who are employed by them. These systems, like the prison and jail system, are very costly.

It might be argued that the enormous cost of prisons—as well as the parole and probation systems—would be justifiable if incarceration taught people that "crime does not pay." In other words, a case might be made for mass imprisonment if it rehabilitated prisoners so that they were less likely to commit crimes after they were released. But does a prison term serve as deterrence to the commission of crimes after an inmate is released from prison? It is obvious that prisoners are deterred from further crime while imprisoned, although some seem to be able to engage in crimes while in prison. After a prisoner is released, those involved in the criminal justice system are interested in the issue of **specific deterrence**, or whether the experience of punishment in general, and incarceration in particular, makes it less likely that the ex-prisoner will commit crimes in the future. In other words, the issue is whether an individual will be "scared straight" by punishment, especially incarceration (Apel and Nagin 2011).

Most research in the field has shown that prisons do a poor job of rehabilitating prisoners, and as a result they do not reduce **recidivism**, or the repetition of a criminal act by one who has been convicted of a prior offense (Smith 2007). Those who serve time in prison learn new and better criminal techniques during their incarceration. In other words, prisons have a "criminogenic" effect, leading to more rather than less crime (Cullen et al. 2011). Nonetheless, no expert would argue for the elimination of punishments, including imprisonment, for most crimes. However, there is a need for more focused forms of specific deterrence (Braga and Weisburd 2012). Furthermore, important individual and situational differences can have impacts on the effectiveness of such deterrence. What is needed is a focus on what forms of specific deterrence will be effective on what types of criminals and under what circumstances (Piquero et al. 2011).

General deterrence deals with the population as a whole and whether individuals will be less likely to commit crimes because of fear that they might be punished or imprisoned for their actions (Apel and Nagin 2011). Although it is not clear how many people do not commit crimes because of fear of punishment, it is clear that such fear constitutes some level of deterrence to some who might otherwise become criminals.

The ultimate example of both forms of deterrence is capital punishment, or the death penalty (Hood and Hoyle 2015; Paternoster, Brame, and Bacon 2007). Someone who is executed clearly cannot commit another crime. However, there is evidence that even the threat of capital punishment is not a strong general deterrent to crime (Cohen-Cole et al. 2009).

Although a number of countries have abolished the death penalty, the United States is one of a handful that continue to employ it. Figure 7.6 shows the legality of the death penalty across U.S. states, as well as data on the number of people on death row per state and the number executed since 1976. The four leading countries in the world, in terms of the number of people executed, are China, Iran, Pakistan, and Saudi Arabia. These are countries that the United States would not like to be associated with, especially on this issue. The United States ranks fifth, with 28 executions in 2015 (Death Penalty Information Center

2016). This is far fewer than the 200 or so who were executed in each of two consecutive years in the 1930s. There have been nearly 1,437 executions in the United States since 1976. Overall, there have been more than 15,269 known executions in the United States (Paternoster 2007). There has also been a trend toward more "humane" execution (if such a thing is possible). Prior to 1930, most executions were done by hanging. Many of these were mishandled, resulting in those who were condemned gradually choking to death. From 1930 to 1967, the majority of executions in the United States were by electrocution. This did not seem to be much of an improvement, as the initial electrical charge, at least in some cases, did not cause death or even unconsciousness and in some cases caused the condemned to catch fire. Beginning in 1977, there was a movement toward the use of lethal injections, and about 88 percent of executions are now performed in that way. However, a number of recent botched executions by injection have caused long and painful deaths.

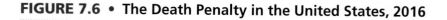

FIGURE 7.6 • The Death Penalty in the United States, 2016

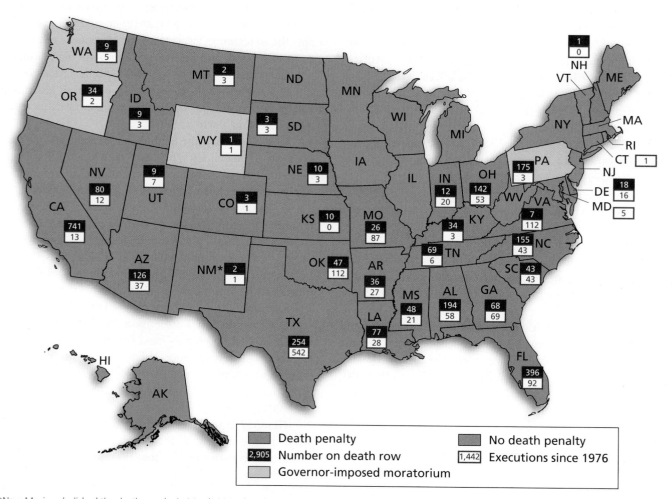

*New Mexico abolished the death penalty in March 2009, but the law was not made retroactive, so two remain on death row.

SOURCE: Based on data from Death Penalty Information Center, http://www.deathpenaltyinfo.org.

The New Jim Crow: Mass Incarceration in the Age of Colorblindness (The New Press, 2012)

Michelle Alexander (Associate Professor of Law at Ohio State University; JD, Stanford University, 1992)

African-American inmates at the Pitchess Detention Center in Castaic, California speak to clergy and community activists. According to Alexander's research, up to 75% of young, black men will be incarcerated in their lifetime in some communities.

Rates of incarceration have been increasing more quickly in the United States than in any other nation. In the 1980s, the federal government initiated the war on drugs, which imposed mandatory prison time for minor, nonviolent drug offenses. Drug users became criminals and subject to punishment in prisons instead of treatment in rehabilitation facilities. Today more than 2 million people are in U.S. prisons, serving time related to drug convictions. From Michelle Alexander's perspective, the most distressing aspect of mass incarceration is the high percentage of racial and ethnic minorities who are imprisoned. Poor, young black men are significantly overrepresented in U.S. prisons. In some poor communities, up to 75 percent of young black men will be incarcerated at some point in their lives. As Alexander details, this is not because they use or sell drugs more often than others do, but because of racial discrimination in the criminal justice system. Law enforcement possesses enormous discretion in regard to search-and-seizure practices and ultimately in terms of who is arrested. In the past, police officers routinely stopped and frisked individuals without probable cause and searched vehicles during traffic violations. Overwhelmingly, they stopped, searched, and arrested young black men more than anyone else (Alexander 2012, 6–7, 61).

Alexander argues that mass incarceration has become the new Jim Crow—a legal form of racial discrimination that aims to socially control and exclude black men from mainstream society. Social control and exclusion do not stop with the end of a prison sentence. Former prisoners are stigmatized—labeled as criminals even after they have served their sentences. Felons on parole and probation are legally barred from voting in most states. They experience difficulty finding employment because the law requires them to disclose that they have a felony conviction on job applications. They can be denied food stamps and other public benefits. Similar to the racial segregation created by the old Jim Crow laws of the early to mid-twentieth century, mass incarceration is creating an underclass that is legally prevented from achieving upward social mobility. But unlike the overt racism of the past Jim Crow era, Alexander asserts that the new Jim Crow is being practiced in a so-called colorblind society that fails to recognize the institutional racism prevalent in the criminal justice system. Even the civil rights movement, which was fundamental in dismantling the old Jim Crow laws, neglected the impact of mass incarceration in black communities; however, the popular reception of Alexander's book may be starting to change this.

Supplementary Resources

- You can watch Bill Moyer interview Alexander about how difficult it is for those who have been incarcerated to achieve the American dream at https://www.youtube.com/watch?v=om2hx6Xm2JE.
- Read about the popular reaction to *The New Jim Crow* in *The New York Times* at http://www.nytimes.com/2012/03/07/books/michelle-alexanders-new-jim-crow-raises-drug-law-debates.html?_r=0.

The application of capital punishment continues to be highly controversial. In fact, many death sentences are accompanied by active campaigns against them and vigils protesting executions both before and as they occur. There are many who feel that it is morally wrong for the government to kill anyone. Others are opposed to the death penalty because it is likely that at least some wrongly convicted people are killed in the process (Aronson and Cole 2009). Finally, there is strong evidence of bias, especially racial bias, in capital punishment. Many studies have shown that

FIGURE 7.7 • Reported Violent Crime in the United States, 1994–2015

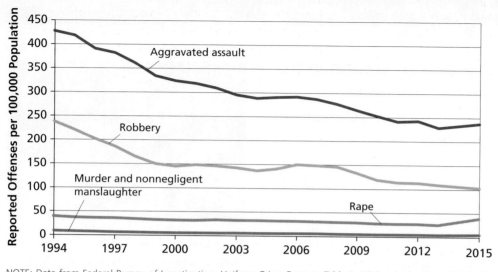

NOTE: Data from Federal Bureau of Investigation, Uniform Crime Reports, Table 1: "Crime in the United States by Volume and Rate per 100,000 Inhabitants, 1994–2013," 2013.

FIGURE 7.8 • Reported Property Crime in the United States, 1994–2015

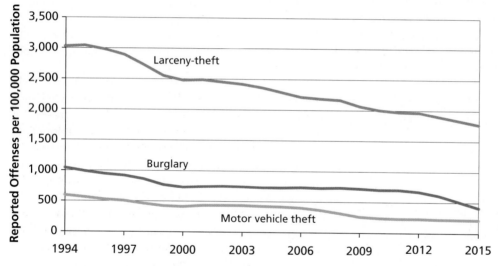

SOURCE: Crime in the United States, 2013. U.S. Department of Justice, Federal Bureau of Investigation.

tracked by the FBI are murder and nonnegligent manslaughter, forcible rape, robbery, and aggravated assault. Figure 7.7 shows the reported violent crime rates in the United States for 1994 through 2015. In recent years, although they do not appear in the UCR, increasing attention has been paid in the United States and elsewhere to violent crimes related to terrorism, as well as globally to war crimes (Gartner 2007). **Property crimes** do not involve injury or force, but rather are offenses that involve gaining or destroying property. While there are others (such as shoplifting and forgery), the major property crimes are burglary, larceny-theft, and motor vehicle theft. About three-fourths of all U.S. crime is property crime (Copes and Null 2007). Figure 7.8 shows the property crime rates in the United States for 1994 through 2015. Another important way of categorizing crimes is by separating **felonies**, or more serious crimes punishable by a year or more in prison, from **misdemeanors**, or minor offenses punishable by imprisonment of less than a year.

blacks, and nonwhites more generally, who are convicted of killing whites are more likely to get the death penalty than are whites who kill other whites (Lee, Paternoster, and Rowan 2016; Paternoster 2007).

TYPES OF CRIMES

Data on crime across the United States are found in the Federal Bureau of Investigation's Uniform Crime Reports (UCR), which include data on crimes reported to police departments and police arrest statistics. Two broad types of crime are reported. **Violent crime** includes the threat of injury or the threat or actual use of force. The violent crimes

- **White-collar crimes** are those committed "by a person of responsibility and high social status in the course of his occupation" (Geis 2007b, 850; Simpson 2013).

- **Corporate crime** involves legal organizations that violate the law. It includes such illegal acts as antitrust violations, stock market violations (e.g., insider trading), and false advertisements (Geis 2007a).

- **Organized crime** can involve various types of organizations, but it is most often associated with syndicated organized crime, especially the Mafia, which uses violence or the threat of violence and the corruption of public officials to profit from illegal activities (Griffin 2007). Other examples of criminal organizations are Mexican drug cartels, the Russian Mafia, and the Islamic State.

- **Political crimes** can be either offenses against the state to affect its policies, such as the assassination of one of its officials, especially its leader (as in the assassination of John F. Kennedy), or offenses by the state, either domestically (e.g., spying on citizens) or internationally (e.g., state-sponsored terrorism, bribery of a foreign official; Tunnell 2007).

- **Hate crimes** are those that stem, in whole or in part, from the fact that those who are being victimized are in various ways different from the perpetrators. These differences include race, religion, sexual orientation, gender, national origin, and disability status. Victims are held in contempt by the perpetrators (Levin 2007).

- **Cybercrime** targets computers (for instance, by hacking; Hill and Marion 2016). Cybercriminals use computers to commit traditional crimes, such as stealing from a bank account or theft of a credit card number. They also use computers to transmit illegal information and images to carry out such activities as insider trading, identity theft, child pornography, plans for terrorist acts, and "cyberterrorism," with some experts even worrying about the possibility of a "cyber Pearl Harbor" (Nunn 2007; Perlroth 2015).

- **Consumer crimes**, or crimes related to consumption, include shoplifting and the use of stolen credit cards or credit card numbers.

ASK YOURSELF

Why are all crimes not considered equally serious? White-collar crime, for instance, can have far-reaching effects and untold numbers of victims. Consider the definitions of crime in your answer.

Although all the offenses described previously are classified as crimes, they are not all considered equally abhorrent. In line with the idea that deviance is defined by elites, so are crimes and criminal punishments. Thus, white-collar and corporate crimes are often downplayed, while the crimes usually associated with those in the lower social classes—for example, violent crimes, especially felonies, and property crimes—receive a great deal of attention from the police, the media, and the public.

Nonetheless, violent crime is a major issue in the United States, especially murder committed with widely available and readily obtainable guns. In 2014, 8,124 Americans were killed by guns—27 per day (Quealy and Sanger-Katz 2016). That amounts to about 31 homicides per million people. In comparison, about 2 out of every million people are shot to death in Germany, the Netherlands, and Austria; in Poland and England, the number who die from gunshots is 1 per million; and in Japan, the rate of gun deaths is 1 in 10 million (about the chances of an American being killed by lightning).

CHECKPOINT 7.3: SOCIOLOGISTS' CONCEPTS OF CRIME

CONCEPT	DESCRIPTION
Crime	A violation of the criminal law
Differential association theory	A theory arguing that people learn criminal behavior from those with whom they associate
Specific deterrence	The reduced likelihood of committing future crimes because of experiencing punishment
General deterrence	The reduced likelihood that the population as a whole will commit crime, for fear of punishment

GLOBALIZATION AND CRIME

The amount of global, or cross-border, crime has increased with globalization (Aas 2013; Andreas and Nadelmann 2006; Shelley, Picarelli, and Corpora 2011; also see the journal *Global Crime*). Globalization makes cross-border crime increasingly possible and more likely. International crime has existed for centuries in such forms as piracy on the oceans and the African slave trade. However, today there seems to be far more of it. This may be due to the fact that, because of the increase in global criminal flows, much more public and government attention is devoted to these crimes. Fortunately, action against crime flows almost as easily as do the crimes themselves.

The growth in global crime is largely traceable to increasing concern about illicit drug use in the United States in the late 1960s and early 1970s, as well as Western Europe's interest in terrorism during roughly the same period. Drugs and terrorism now top the list of concerns about the "global illicit economy" (Andreas 2015), but others include "clandestine trade in sophisticated weaponry and technology, endangered species, pornographic materials, counterfeit products, guns, ivory, toxic waste, money, people [i.e., trafficking in human beings; Farr 2005; Weitzer 2015], stolen property, and art and antiquities" (Andreas and Nadelmann 2006, 5). All of these involve flows of all sorts—drugs, money, human victims (for example, prostitutes or, more recently, terrorists and those fleeing war

Digital Piracy

Music and video piracy is undoubtedly the most widespread form of criminal activity on the internet. Many of us listen to songs or watch movies online without thinking about whether or not they have been uploaded illegally. But if these songs and movies are being shared and accessed without the permission of the individuals who created them, we are violating copyright laws. Music, movies, photographs, books, and other forms of creative expressions and innovations are considered the intellectual property of their creators, who have "exclusive ownership and rights to use, produce, and distribute" their work (Piquero 2010, 89). Every time we engage in music and video piracy, we are stealing someone's intellectual property and failing to financially compensate that person for his or her work. According to research in the Recording Industry Association of America's 2015 digital music report, 52 percent of respondents from 13 countries agreed that downloading and streaming copyrighted material without permission constituted theft, and 53 percent wanted licensed content to appear before pirated content on internet search engines (Recording Industry Association of America 2015).

Although individuals who engage in digital piracy are certainly at fault for violating copyright laws, web companies are also to blame. The 1998 Digital Millennium Copyright Act requires that web companies remove URLs that contain pirated content; however, instead of making these companies monitor possible cases of digital piracy, the Act expects the creators of the original

Fredrik Neij, co-founder of The Pirate Bay, a site that allows users to share entertainment content and software, was convicted of enabling copyright infringement. He and the other founders were ordered to pay fines and sentenced to a year in prison. Do you think this was a fair outcome?

work to do so. Creators who find illegal content then have to make a request that the companies remove it. Given how fast and easy it is to upload illegal content, this is a time-consuming and burdensome chore to place on individual creators (Taplin 2016). Google, the web company with the most removal requests, received more than 20 million requests per week in 2016 (Molla and Ovide 2016). The good news is that web traffic on torrent websites that actively facilitate digital piracy appears to be decreasing. BitTorrent, a site where users can swap and watch pirated movies, saw its web traffic decrease from 13 percent of all web traffic in 2011 to only 4 percent in 2015. At the same time YouTube, which is owned by Google,

experienced an increase in total web traffic from 10 percent in 2011 to 17 percent in 2015 (Molla and Ovide 2016). This is a worrisome trend, considering the "rampant piracy" on YouTube (Taplin 2016).

Engaging the Digital World

Do you believe that sharing music or video files online is deviant? Should it be criminalized? Who benefits, and who is harmed? What type of punishments should be established to prevent digital piracy, and who should enforce them? Conduct an online search of your favorite movie or song. How many URLs do you find? How many do you suspect link you to pirated material? What clues do these links contain that make you think they are pirated?

or oppression and trying to gain illegal entry into Europe (Glenny 2015). They also include various illegal content that flows through the internet (e.g., child pornography, laundered funds, computer viruses, calls to commit terroristic acts).

These illegal flows have been aided by the decline of the nation-state and its increasing inability to reduce or halt such flows. Furthermore, global criminal cartels have come into existence to expedite illegal flows and to increase the profits that can be derived from them. In his book *McMafia* (2008), Misha Glenny attributes much of the cartels' success to increasingly sophisticated organizational methods (including economies of scale, global partnerships, and the opening of new markets) copied from leading legitimate businesses such as McDonald's. New technologies have also been employed to make at least some criminal flows more successful. For example, one cartel used a primitive submarine to transport drugs. The internet has made a number of illegal flows (e.g., child pornography and internet scams) much easier and is largely impervious to efforts at control by individual nation-states.

Criminalization of Global Activities

As pointed out earlier, crime (and deviance) is always a matter of social definition or social construction. So, although the power of nation-states has generally declined in the global age, it continues to matter greatly as far as what come to be *defined* as global forms of deviance and crime. In the era of globalization, the nation-states of Western Europe and the United States have played the central role in criminalizing certain activities. It is *their* sense of morality and *their* norms of behavior that have come to be the rule in much of the world (Andreas and Nadelmann 2006). The global criminalization of drug use is a good case in point.

However, while there have been a number of efforts to define drug use as deviant and illegal, they have not always been successful. The global drug trade has in fact expanded in spite of great efforts by the United States and other nation-states to at least reduce it.

Much of the publicity about drugs and the ways in which they are implicated in globalization involves cocaine and heroin. Great attention is devoted to, for example, the growing of poppies in Afghanistan and drug production in Guatemala, and the ways in which drugs from those areas and many others make their way around the world. A more recent global drug is methamphetamine (meth), made easily and cheaply in home-based "cooking facilities" from pseudoephedrine, the main ingredient in a number of cough, cold, and allergy medications. The AMC television show *Breaking Bad* dealt with the cooking of meth by a former high school chemistry teacher in New Mexico and meth's often violent relationship to the drug trade in nearby Mexico. Once largely an American phenomenon, the production

and use of methamphetamine is beginning to expand globally. For example, it is the drug of choice in Indonesia (Reuters 2016b), and there was fear as long as a decade ago that it would spread throughout the European Union and to many other parts of the world as well (Kulish 2007).

Several aspects of cross-border crime, especially as it relates to drugs, help account for why global as well as national efforts to counter this type of crime have been largely unsuccessful. First, those who commit the crimes do not require a great many resources to do so. Second, they do not need very much expertise to commit the crimes. Third, such crimes are easy to conceal. Fourth, in many cases the crimes are not apt to be reported to the police or other authorities. Finally, the crimes are those for which great consumer demand exists and for which there are no readily available alternative products (e.g., drugs) or activities (e.g., prostitution; Andreas and Nadelmann 2006).

However, it would be wrong to judge global efforts to control drugs and other illegal substances and activities as complete failures. The fact is that while drugs continue to flow readily throughout the world for the reasons suggested previously, the United States has had considerable success in internationalizing its views, laws, procedures, and efforts at enforcement. As mentioned earlier, powerful societies are often able to get weaker societies to adopt their ways of doing things. Foreign governments have

- Altered their laws and methods of law enforcement to more closely match U.S. laws on drugs

- Acceded to demands by the United States to sign law enforcement treaties

- Adopted American investigative techniques

- Created specialized drug enforcement agencies

- Stationed law enforcement representatives in other countries

- Enacted various laws on conspiracy, asset forfeiture, and money laundering related to drugs

- Provided greater assistance to the United States and changed their laws on financial secrecy

In other words, we have seen an Americanization of law enforcement throughout much of the world. However, a wide variety of failures, most notably in the so-called "war on drugs," in both the United States and globally, has led to more questioning of many of these changes in law enforcement (*New York Times* 2016b).

Global Crime Control

The growth in global crime has been met, of course, with the expansion of international policing and of the role of the police in international relations (Andreas and Nadelmann 2006; Bowling and Sheptycki 2012). In addition to its role regarding drug trafficking, the United States has taken the lead in countering other forms of global crime and in influencing other nations to work against those types of crime. In the early twentieth century, the focus was on "white slavery" (prostitution); during the Cold War, it was the control of weapons and advanced technology; and in the mid-1980s, the focus shifted to the regulation of securities markets, especially insider trading. Following the onset of the Great Recession, the focus shifted again to abuses in the global financial system as well as illegal economic activities. These include the existence of secret bank accounts in other countries, especially Switzerland, as well as the creation of shell companies in, among other places, Panama. (Shell companies have few assets and exist mainly to evade taxes.) An international scandal arose in 2016 when the leak of more than 11.5 million documents from a Panamanian law firm revealed its involvement in the creation of shell companies, as well as the names of many of them (Semple 2016).

Since 9/11, there has been a dramatic erosion of distinctions in the world of criminal justice in an effort to forestall further terrorist attacks and to catch or kill people defined as terrorists. For example, the distinction between law enforcement and intelligence operations has eroded as law enforcement authorities seek to gain intelligence on potential terrorists. The distinction between law enforcement and security has also eroded. The USA PATRIOT (Uniting and Strengthening America by Providing Appropriate Tools Required to Intercept and Obstruct Terrorism) Act, signed into law on October 26, 2001, has played a key role in this erosion by, for example, extending the concern of law enforcement agencies to domestic terrorism. In addition, surveillance of the border between the United States and Mexico, as well as in immigrant communities in the United States, has increased. In the process, many immigrants have been defined as criminals, apprehended, and then returned to Mexico. It is important to note that far less attention is devoted to surveillance on the much longer border with Canada, and those who do cross that border illegally are much less likely to be defined, or apprehended, as criminals.

As we have seen (see Chapter 1), some European countries have recently instituted a similar toughening of border controls and surveillance. However, within the European Union, border law enforcement has become more homogeneous as criminal justice norms and procedures have become more similar and law enforcement contacts and exchanges of information among member states have become more regular. Of great importance has been the formation of Europol, the EU's law enforcement agency, which enables better and increased communication and cooperation among national police agencies.

While these efforts have improved global crime control, they have a variety of downsides. For one thing, democracy and civil rights may be threatened by these efforts. Crime control efforts are not always as transparent as they should be, and the officials involved often need to be more accountable. For another, tougher border and immigration controls have led to more daring and dangerous efforts to cross borders, leading to more deaths in the process. Those who have been denied entry often suffer in poorly constructed and overcrowded border camps. In addition, the global antidrug campaign has generated high levels of crime, violence, corruption, disease, and so on. Efforts by the United States to deal with trafficking in women and children have focused more on criminalizing that traffic than on protecting the human rights of the women and children being trafficked. Finally, the attention and money devoted to international crime and its control have tended to distract attention, and to take money away, from efforts to deal with a wide range of fundamental issues within nation-states, including the welfare of large portions of society.

Public efforts to control global crime have been far from totally successful. For example, in 2014, 43 Mexican college students were murdered by a drug gang. The murders were committed at the behest of the mayor of Iguala, who was later arrested, as were some members of the gang (Archibold 2015). Between 2007 and 2011, approximately 40,000 people were killed in the wars between drug gangs, and the wars continue to ravage Mexico (although, as noted previously, to a declining degree), and they have spread across the border into the United States. The police in Mexico have failed to halt the carnage, and even the use of the Mexican military has not met with much success. The news media, often intimidated by the gangs, have often failed to provide needed and accurate information about criminal activities.

Many Mexican citizens have given up hope of help from the state and the media. They have begun to try to help themselves, most notably through crowdsourcing information via social media such as Twitter and Facebook (Sullivan 2010). For example, social media have been used to warn of shootouts involving drug gangs and of roadblocks set up by the drug cartels. In one case, 35 bodies were dumped on a Veracruz highway at rush hour in late 2011. Before police and the mainstream media arrived on the scene, Twitter was alive with messages such as "Avoid Plaza Las Americas" and "There are gunmen . . . they're not soldiers or marines; their faces are masked" (Cave 2011, 5). In this case, unfortunately, the Mexican drug gangs struck back. Two mangled bodies were found hanging from a bridge in a city bordering the United States next to a sign that read, "This will happen to all the internet snitches" (Cave 2011, 5). However, while the drug lords have been successful in intimidating centralized media, police, and the military, it may be more difficult to control the decentralized masses who are anonymously crowdsourcing information about drug-related violence.

While social media have been used elsewhere in the world (e.g., Tunisia, Egypt, Ukraine) to help bring about social revolution, in Mexico they have been employed to help people deal with crime. They provide people with not only needed information but also a sense of social support, as well as offer a bit of certainty in a highly uncertain world.

SUMMARY

Deviance is any action, belief, or human characteristic that violates the norms of a group or society. Deviance changes over time—certain actions that were considered norm violations in the past, like cohabitation, are not anymore. Norm violations are an important way in which groups and societies define acceptable behavior and form cohesion.

Explanatory and constructionist theories are two different ways to understand deviance. Explanatory theories attempt to explain why deviance does or does not occur. Constructionist theories are more concerned with the process of how some behaviors are defined and classified as deviant. Structural/functional theories are explanatory. Strain theory, for example, posits that deviance is caused by a discrepancy between the larger structure and culture of society. Social control theory suggests that deviance is a result of weak social bonds, while broken windows theory suggests that deviance is a result of social disorder. Conflict/critical theories are also explanatory and focus on how the elite are less likely to be defined as deviant than

are the poor. Inter/actionist theories are constructionist, highlighting how social control agents label certain behaviors as deviant. Individuals that are stigmatized by social control agents organize their lives and identities around their deviant status. Not all deviant actions are necessarily harmful or even objectionable. Positive deviance can have beneficial effects on society and is socially acceptable.

Crime is a form of deviance that violates criminal law. The major components of the criminal justice system are law enforcement, the courts, and the correctional system. There are a number of different types of crime, but the broadest distinction is between violent crimes that involve the threat or use of force and property crimes that involve gaining or destroying property. Globalization has been associated with increases in cross-border crime, particularly the international drug trade. Illegal flows are aided by nation-states' declining ability to halt them. International policing has expanded to contend with the growth in global crime.

KEY TERMS

conformists, 179
constructionist
  theories, 178
consumer crime, 195
corporate crime, 194
crime, 189
criminalization, 172
criminology, 189
cybercrime, 195

deviance, 172
differential
  association, 189
discreditable stigma, 188
discredited stigma, 188
explanatory
  theories, 177
felonies, 194
general deterrence, 191

hate crimes, 195
innovators, 179
labeling theory, 185
misdemeanors, 194
moral entrepreneurs, 186
moral panic, 186
organized crime, 194
parole, 191
political crimes, 195

positive deviance, 188
primary deviance, 186
probation, 191
property crimes, 194
rebels, 179
recidivism, 191
retreatists, 179
ritualists, 179
rule creators, 186

rule enforcers, 186

secondary deviance, 186

social control, 186

social control agents, 185

social control
    theory, 180

specific deterrence, 191

stigma, 187

strain theory, 178

symbol, 185

violent crime, 194

white-collar crime, 194

REVIEW QUESTIONS ··

1. What do sociologists mean when they say that deviance is socially defined? Given a sociological approach, in what ways is tattooing deviant, and in what ways is it not?

2. How can we understand deviance as a global flow? How do countries differ in terms of their interpretations of what is deviant? In an increasingly globalized world, what are the consequences of these differing interpretations?

3. How does consuming the "wrong" products and services make someone a deviant? What does this suggest about the relationships between power and deviance?

4. Adolescents value a certain level of independence from their parents, often wanting more control over their own lives. They want to be able to do what they want to do without needing permission from their parents. Apply Merton's strain theory to an understanding of how adolescents might behave, given this desire for more independence.

5. Why do those who rank high in such hierarchies as business, government, and the military have a much greater ability to commit deviant acts, to have those acts seen as legitimate, and to get away with them? What does this suggest about the "fairness" of deviance?

6. What are the differences between a discredited stigma and a discreditable stigma? What is an example of each?

7. How is crime different from deviance? Why do some forms of deviance become criminalized, whereas others do not?

8. How do you explain the fact that the United States has so many people in prison? Why is the U.S. incarceration rate the highest in the world?

9. Is the death penalty useful as a form of general deterrence? Are you in favor of the death penalty? If so, for what crimes?

10. What sorts of barriers have countries attempted to implement to limit the global flow of drugs? Why have these been relatively unsuccessful?

PRACTICE AND APPLY WHAT YOU'VE LEARNED

▶ edge.sagepub.com/ritzerintro4e

CHECK YOUR COMPREHENSION ON THE STUDY SITE WITH:

- **Diagnostic pre-tests** to identify opportunities for improvement.

- **Personalized study plans** with focused recommendations to address specific knowledge gaps and additional learning needs.

- **Post-tests** to check your progress and ensure mastery of key learning objectives.

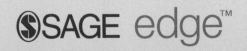

SOCIAL STRATIFICATION IN THE UNITED STATES

Student "Haves" and "Have-Nots" in Higher Education

The world of higher education is stratified in various ways. For example, a status hierarchy is formed by graduates of high-ranking Ivy League universities, mid-level state universities, and lower-level community colleges. Whatever the level of the higher education system from which you graduate, another aspect of stratification, and one that undoubtedly interests and may even trouble you, is the high cost of your education. Cost is not much of a problem for the very wealthy or those brilliant (or athletically gifted) enough to earn full scholarships. However, for most students, it is a major issue, and for many (and likely their parents), it can be a hardship if not an overwhelming barrier to attending and ultimately graduating from college. The ability to afford a college degree is closely related to social class position.

Students from the middle and lower classes deal with the cost of education in various ways, such as by holding part-time jobs, attending lower-cost state and especially community colleges, and taking out loans, either on their own or through their parents. Whatever route they take, they are disadvantaged in comparison to those who have no problem affording whatever college they wish to attend.

Student loans represent an especially big problem for many students. Private loans are likely to have variable interest rates and offer little protection in case of default. This stands in contrast to federal student loans, which have fixed rates and many protections, including against default. Total student loans in the United States amount to more than $1.36 trillion, a fourfold increase between 2000 and 2016. Many students leave college owing $35,000 or more, and they are then likely to find themselves unemployed or with low-paying jobs. As a result, many are unable to make the payments due on their loans, and they may remain saddled with college debt for a large part of their lives, perhaps even into old age.

LEARNING OBJECTIVES

8.1 Describe the three dimensions of social stratification.

8.2 Identify factors contributing to economic inequality.

8.3 Identify different types of social mobility.

8.4 Discuss theories of social stratification.

8.5 Explain the relationship between consumption and social stratification.

edge.sagepub.com/ritzerintro4e

- Take the chapter quiz
- Review key terms with eFlashcards
- Explore multimedia links and SAGE readings

$SAGE edge™

Of great and particular concern is debt incurred by students who attend for-profit colleges such as the University of Phoenix, as well those institutions that don't even deserve to be thought of as colleges (or universities), such as the scandalous Trump "University," where students lost tens of thousands of dollars (Carey 2016). Such colleges are most likely to be attended by those who are underprepared for higher education, are economically disadvantaged, and rank low in the stratification system. These students may receive a poor education, have a lower-than-average graduation rate, and incur higher-than-average student debt, even if, as is often the case, they do not complete their degrees. For-profit colleges enroll only 11 percent of all college students in the United States, but they account for almost 35 percent of student defaults on loans (Douglas-Gabriel 2016; Shen 2016). Further complicating matters for such students is the fact that they are preyed upon by debt-relief companies that charge high fees and/or often do not deliver on their promises to cut or eliminate the debt. These students' debt is high both because they have fewer economic resources with which to avoid or repay the debt and because for-profit colleges are often more expensive than other colleges are.

The educational experience is just another example of the highly stratified character of many areas of U.S. society in which the poor pay more—and get far less. ●

We often hear that American society, as well as the world as a whole (see Chapter 9), is unfair. This is generally taken to mean that a relatively small number of people have way too much, while most of the rest of us have far too little. In the United States, this unfairness is made abundantly clear when we see news reports about the excesses of the super-rich, such as multimillion-dollar bonuses, private jets, and mansions, or condos in New York or London worth tens or hundreds of millions of dollars. At the other extreme, the gap is just as clear when we encounter homeless people begging on street corners and at turn lanes on heavily traveled roads.

What is it that some people have, or are thought to have, and others lack? The most obvious answer is money and what money buys. However, **social stratification** involves hierarchical differences not only in economic positions but also in other important areas, such as status, or social honor, and power. Social stratification has a profound effect on how monetary and nonmonetary resources are distributed in American society and around the globe (global stratification is discussed in more detail in Chapter 9).

DIMENSIONS OF SOCIAL STRATIFICATION

Any sociological discussion of stratification draws on an important set of dimensions derived from the work of the great German social theorist Max Weber ([1921] 1968; Bendix and Lipset 1966). These three dimensions are social class, status, and power.

SOCIAL CLASS

One's economic position in the stratification system, especially one's occupation, defines one's **social class**. A person's social class position strongly determines and reflects his or her income and wealth. Those who rank close to one another in wealth and income can be said to be members of the same social class. For example, multibillionaire entrepreneurs such as Bill Gates and Warren Buffett belong to one social class; the janitor in your university building and the mechanic who fixes your car at the corner gas station belong to another. Terms often used to describe a person's social class are *upper class* (for example, large-scale entrepreneurs and many large investors, especially in hedge funds), *middle class* (nurses, teachers, veterinarians, air traffic controllers, travel agents, and firefighters), *working class* (manual, clerical, and full-time service workers in industries such as fast food), and *lower class* (part-time service and other workers and the unemployed). Figure 8.1 illustrates the relationships among occupation, income, and social class in the United States (Gilbert 2015). Its teardrop shape represents the percentage of Americans in each class; there are substantially more people in the working and lower classes than there are in the upper class. As we will soon see, the United States is even more stratified than Figure 8.1 suggests.

As discussed in Chapter 2, Karl Marx had a conception of social class that was different from Weber's. To Marx, social class was defined by ownership of the *means of production,* or the resources necessary for production to take place, such as factories, machines, tools, and raw materials. Those who owned the means of production were the *capitalists,* and they stood at the pinnacle of the stratification system. Members of the *proletariat* lacked the means of production. Therefore, they had to sell their labor time to the capitalists in order to work and be productive. This created a hierarchal stratification system, with the capitalists on top and the proletariat standing far lower in the hierarchy. This constituted a class system in the sense that the capitalists kept the vast majority of profits for themselves, had higher incomes, and accumulated great wealth. In contrast, the capitalists barely paid the proletariat enough to survive. Thus, the proletariat found it impossible to accumulate wealth.

While Marx's conception of social class is still useful, changes in the economic system have made it less relevant today. For example, it is now much harder to argue

FIGURE 8.1 • Social Classes, Occupations, and Incomes in the United States

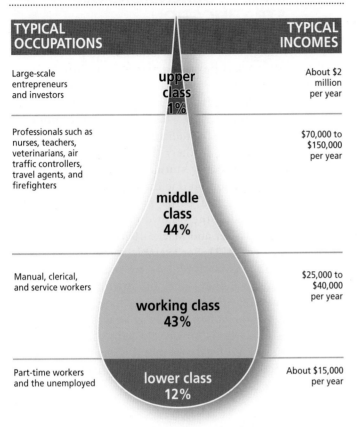

TYPICAL OCCUPATIONS		TYPICAL INCOMES
Large-scale entrepreneurs and investors	**upper class 1%**	About $2 million per year
Professionals such as nurses, teachers, veterinarians, air traffic controllers, travel agents, and firefighters	**middle class 44%**	$70,000 to $150,000 per year
Manual, clerical, and service workers	**working class 43%**	$25,000 to $40,000 per year
Part-time workers and the unemployed	**lower class 12%**	About $15,000 per year

SOURCE: Adapted from Gilbert, D. L. (2015). *The American class structure in an age of growing inequality.* Thousand Oaks, CA: SAGE.

that capitalists are defined by, and gain their position in the stratification system from, their ownership of the means of production. Such capitalists (like Facebook founder Mark Zuckerberg) have come to be replaced at the center of the economic system by corporations (like Zuckerberg's Facebook). The stocks and bonds of these corporations are owned by thousands, hundreds of thousands, or even millions of shareholders and bondholders. However, the people who stand at the pinnacle of the stratification system (like Zuckerberg) today own a disproportionate number of these stocks and bonds, and many have become fabulously wealthy, with a net worth of billions of dollars (Zuckerberg's was in excess of $50 billion in early 2017). They do not own the means of production, such as factories, at least not directly. They may also hold executive positions at or near the top of the corporations, but, again, those positions alone do not give those who hold them ownership of the means of production.

Today, members of the proletariat still occupy lower-level positions in these corporations; they still must sell their labor time for access to the means of production, and they continue to be relatively poorly paid. However, they may

be minor stockholders in these corporations through, for example, 401(k) or profit-sharing retirement plans. Still, there is a vast economic difference between those who occupy high-level positions in corporations and/or own large blocks of stocks and those at the bottom who own few (if any) shares. Bill Gates (of the Microsoft Corporation) was the richest person in the United States as of mid-2017, a position he has held for twenty-three straight years (Dolan and Kroll 2014; www.forbes.com/forbes-400). Compare his net worth, estimated at $81 billion, to the near-total absence of wealth among the lower-level, often temporary, Microsoft employees. (This disparity will be addressed further later in this chapter, in the discussion of the growing income and wealth gaps in the United States.)

STATUS

The second dimension of the stratification system, *status*, relates to the prestige attached to a person's positions within society. The existence and importance of this dimension demonstrate the fact that factors other than those associated with money are considered valuable in society. For example, in a 2015 Harris Poll of 2,223 U.S. adults, the well-paid doctor was ranked the most prestigious, followed by the less well-paid scientist, and in third place the comparatively modestly paid firefighter. However, the often exorbitantly paid and rewarded corporate executive was not even in the top 10 occupations in terms of prestige (Harris Interactive 2016).

POWER

A third dimension of social stratification is **power**, or the ability to get others to do what you want them to do, even if it is against their will. Those who have a great deal of power rank high in the stratification system, while those with little or no power are arrayed at or near the bottom. This is clearest in the case of politics, where, for example, the president of the United States ranks very high in power, while millions of ordinary voters have comparatively little political power. Still lower on the political power scale are disenfranchised citizens, such as convicted felons, and noncitizens, including undocumented immigrants.

Power, of course, is not restricted to the political system but also exists in many other institutions. Thus, top officials in large corporations have greater power than do workers, religious leaders have more power than do parishioners, and those who head households are more powerful than are their spouses or children (Collins 1975).

Greater income is generally associated with more power, but there are exceptions to this rule. In the late 2000s, an increasing number of media stories focused on the phenomenon of "breadwinner wives" and "breadwinner moms," or those wives and moms who are the sole or primary providers of

FIGURE 8.2 • Percentage of Married Women Who Earn More than Their Husbands, 1960–2011

% based on married couples with children under age 18

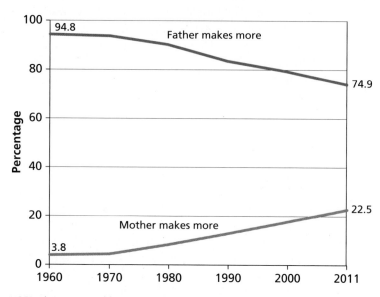

NOTE: The category of father and mother having the same income not shown.

SOURCE: Who Makes More in the Family? 1060–2011, from p. 12 in *Breadwinner Moms,* May 29, 2013. Reprinted by permission of Pew Research Center, Washington, DC. Data from Wendy Wang, Kim Parker, and Paul Taylor, "Breadwinner Moms," Pew Research Center, Pew Social and Demographic Trends, May 29, 2013.

income for their families. Only 11 percent of households with children under 18 had breadwinner moms in 1960, but that had risen to 40 percent in 2011 (Wang, Parker, and Taylor 2013). Then there are "alpha wives and moms"—women who earn more than their husbands (Chae 2015; Mundy 2012; Roberts 2010). As shown in Figure 8.2, only 3.8 percent of wives in 1960 had income greater than that of their husbands, but by 2011, 22.5 percent of married women were alpha wives.

In spite of their greater income, breadwinner wives and moms may not have greater power in the marital relationship, and in many cases, they are compelled to be content with sharing power with their husbands (Cherlin 2010). In fact, many high-earning women have great difficulty even finding mates, and they face disapproval for breaking gender norms. Expectations regarding gender, and other types of minority status, can clearly complicate power relations.

ASK YOURSELF

Is your position in the social stratification system characterized by inconsistency? That is, do you rank higher on one dimension of stratification than on the others? Are the positions of other people you know well inconsistent in the same way?

CONSISTENCY/INCONSISTENCY ACROSS DIMENSIONS OF STRATIFICATION

Some people rank similarly across all three dimensions of social stratification. For example, a midlevel supervisor within a U.S. corporation is likely to earn a middle-class income, to enjoy middling prestige, and to have some power. This is known as **status consistency**, or *crystallization status* (Lenski 1954). However, it is likely that many people will be characterized by **status inconsistency**. That is, their position on one dimension of stratification will be different, perhaps very different, from their positions on the other dimensions of stratification (Stryker and Macke 1978; Wang, Elder, and Spence 2012). For example, famous movie stars, musicians, and athletes are likely to earn huge sums of money—they are high in social class—but they are not likely to have much power. While they often acquire great wealth, celebrities (such as Chris Brown and Bill Cosby) with well-publicized legal and moral issues (such as drug addiction and sexual harassment) are likely to have little status.

CHECKPOINT 8.1: THE DIMENSIONS OF SOCIAL STRATIFICATION

DIMENSION	DESCRIPTION
Social class	A person's economic position, reflecting and determined by income and wealth
Status	The prestige attached to a person's position within society
Power	The ability to get others to do what you want them to, even if against their will

ECONOMIC INEQUALITY

A major concern in the sociological study of stratification is **inequality**, a condition whereby some positions in society yield a great deal of money, status, and power, while others yield little, if any, of these. While other bases of stratification exist, the system of stratification in the United States, and in much of the contemporary world (see Chapter 9), is based largely on money. Money is not inherently valuable and desirable—it has these characteristics only when it is so defined in a money economy, such as in the United States, as well as in much of the rest of the world today (Simmel [1907] 1978). In such an economy, the occupational structure is characterized by a payment system in which those in higher-level positions, and those who perform well in these positions, are rewarded with larger paychecks. The use of money as a reward makes money seem valuable to people. They come to desire it for itself as well as for what it will buy.

We continue to use, although to a decreasing extent, bills printed on paper-fabric blends and metal coins, but they are being rapidly replaced by the use of digital, or electronic, payments and currency. Online money transfers such as PayPal are already well established. Apple Pay allows for money transfers using mobile devices. Much attention is now devoted to a revolutionary, open-source currency, Bitcoin, which exists only electronically and does not require the involvement of banks or other institutions. Many believe that it represents the future of e-money.

Other kinds of economies existed before the development of the money economy and continue to exist, at least to some degree, in some areas, such as northern Ecuador (Ferraro 2011; Hirth and Pillsbury 2013). One is the barter economy, in which people exchange goods with one another without money mediating the exchanges. In such economies, there is little or no need for money. There are ways of recognizing people's relative contributions other than through the size of their bankrolls. It is worth noting that even within advanced money economies, we find a great deal of barter. Thus, it is not unusual for people to exchange services, or to do services in exchange for products. This is often done, illegally, to avoid the taxes that would likely need to be paid if money did change hands. Of course, there are also transactions—such as illegal drug transactions and payment for under-the-table labor—where money changes hands without any records that might attract the attention of the Internal Revenue Service.

French social theorist Jean Baudrillard ([1976] 1993), among many others, criticized the money economy and the economic exchange that lies at its base. Baudrillard (1929–2007) argued instead for an economy and a society characterized by symbolic exchange. In **symbolic exchange**, people swap all sorts of things, but, most important, the process of exchange is valued in itself and for the human relationships involved. It is *not* valued because of the economic gains—the money—that may be derived from it. A greater contribution to the group's well-being may be rewarded with higher ranking in the group rather than with more money. In such a system, you might acquire a high-level position by helping others more than they help you and by gaining recognition for your helpfulness.

Still, while other bases are possible, money remains at the root of the American stratification system. Money can take the form of income or wealth. **Income** is the amount of money a person earns from a job, a business, or returns

Jean Baudrillard's idea of "symbolic exchange" laid the basis for thinking about an alternative to the system of stratification in capitalist society. This and other ideas of Baudrillard's, as well as his published works, earned him noted recognition and made him one of the most famous social theorists of the twentieth century.

on various types of assets (e.g., rents on real estate) and investments (e.g., dividends on stocks and bonds). Income is generally measured year by year. For example, you might have an income of $25,000 per year. **Wealth**, on the other hand, is the total amount of a person's financial assets and other properties less the total of various kinds of debts, or liabilities. Assets include, among others, savings, investments, homes, and automobiles, while debts include home mortgages, student loans, car loans, and amounts owed to credit card companies. If all your assets total $100,000 but you owe $25,000, your wealth (or net worth) amounts to $75,000.

Wealth can be inherited from others, so that a person can be very wealthy yet have a modest income. Many elderly widows and widowers find themselves in this position. Conversely, people can earn substantial incomes and not be very wealthy because, for example, they squander their money on expensive vacations or hobbies, or on alcohol or drugs.

INCOME INEQUALITY

Sociologists (and economists) are interested in inequality in status and power, but they tend to be most concerned about economic inequality. In many parts of the world, incomes became more equitable from the late 1920s until the 1970s. However, since the 1970s, there has been a substantial increase in income inequality in many countries, with a few individuals earning a great deal more and many earning little, if any, more. Even in the United States, which we historically and erroneously (Massey 2008) regard as an egalitarian society, income inequality has been rising since the 1970s and now rivals levels that existed in the late 1920s (DeSilver 2013). That was at the peak of the boom years of the Roaring Twenties and just before the bursting of the economic bubble that heralded the beginning of the Great Depression. In 1928, the top 1 percent of families, the main beneficiaries of the economic boom of the 1920s, received almost 24 percent of all pretax income, while the bottom 90 percent of families earned only about 51 percent of that income. The Depression and World War II altered the economic landscape and led to greater equality. By 1944, the top 1 percent was receiving *only* about 11 percent of income, while the bottom 90 percent was earning more than 67 percent of that income. However, the situation began to change again in the 1970s, and by 2015, the top 1 percent of American families earned nearly 17 percent of all income, up from 10.03 percent in 1960 (see Figure 8.3)—this was almost as much (in percentage terms) as in 1928. At the same time, the share of the bottom 90 percent was below 50 percent, even less than in 1928.

Income inequality today is even greater if we focus not on the top 1 percent but on the elite of the elite, the top 0.1 percent of households. In 2012, the average annual household income for the top 0.1 percent was a whopping $6,373,782. By comparison, the top 1 percent had to make do with an income of *only* $1,264,065. How about the bottom 90 percent? Their average household income was $30,997. In other terms, the top 0.1 percent earned 206 times as much as the bottom 90 percent, while the top 1 percent made 41 times the income of those at the bottom. This gap, too, has worsened over time. In 1980, the multiples were 47 and 14; in 1990 they were 87 and

21 (Lowrey 2014). Thus, it's a great time to be rich, but it is an even better time to be uber-rich.

However, there is even further stratification within the ranks of the very rich. Those in the top one-hundredth of 1 percent—the billionaires and those with hundreds of millions of dollars—are in an economic world of their own compared to *mere* millionaires (Frank 2014). As a result, while demand for less expensive light private jets has been declining, demand for the most desirable and expensive jet—Gulfstream's G650, which costs $65 million—has been increasing. Similarly, sales of megayachts (longer than 300 feet) are booming (one 330-footer sold for $250 million), while demand for smaller yachts is declining, along with price. Plans are afoot to build even bigger yachts, perhaps rivaling the 590-foot yacht now owned by the president of the United Arab Emirates.

Enterprises of all sorts are now catering in new and ever-more elaborate ways to the super-rich (Schwartz 2016b). There are now, for example, ships-within-cruise-ships for the elite. They are separate areas that are largely inaccessible and invisible to other people on the cruise. They can offer a concierge, 24-hour butler service, as well as a private pool, sun deck, and restaurant. A "Royal Suite" on Royal Caribbean's *Anthem* costs $30,000 for a seven-day cruise, compared to $4,000 for a run-of-the-mill stateroom elsewhere on the ship. The super-rich in the "royal" area of the cruise ship never need to mingle with the merely rich, let alone the middle class on the rest of the ship. We are increasingly living in an era where the elites are segmented from the rest of the population and treated to a lifestyle that most people can only fantasize about. This segmentation, however, might not make everyone happy. As one corporate advisor put it, "If I'm in the back of the plane, I want to hiss at the people in first class. . . . If I'm up front, I cringe as people walk by" (Schwartz 2016b, 22).

FIGURE 8.3 • Income Share of the Top 1 Percent of Families in the United States, 1950–2015

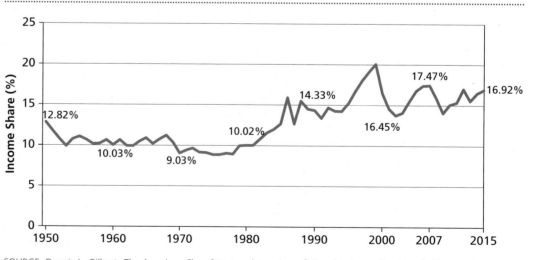

SOURCE: Dennis L. Gilbert, *The American Class Structure in an Age of Growing Inequality*, 9th ed. (Thousand Oaks, CA: SAGE, 2015); personal communication with Dennis L. Gilbert.

FIGURE 8.4 • Most and Least Stratified States in Average Income, 2013

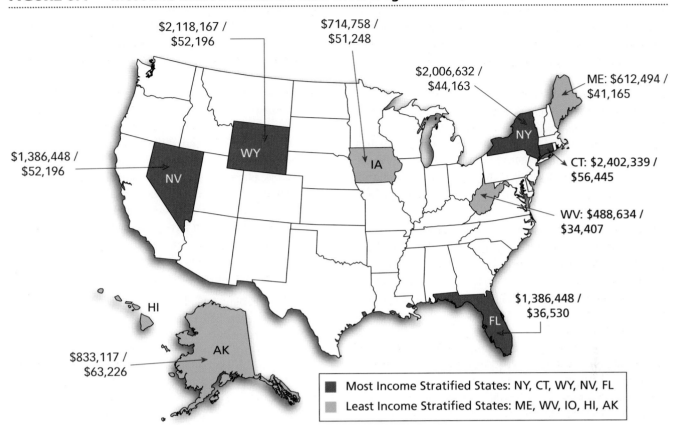

$2,118,167 / $52,196

$714,758 / $51,248

$2,006,632 / $44,163

ME: $612,494 / $41,165

$1,386,448 / $52,196

CT: $2,402,339 / $56,445

WV: $488,634 / $34,407

$1,386,448 / $36,530

$833,117 / $63,226

■ Most Income Stratified States: NY, CT, WY, NV, FL
■ Least Income Stratified States: ME, WV, IO, HI, AK

SOURCE: Estelle Sommellier, Mark Price and Ellis Wazater, 2016. *Income Inequality in the U.S. by State, Metropolitan Area and County.* Washington D.C.: Economic Policy Institute, 2016: pp. 8–9; www.epi.org/files/pdf/107100.pdf.

While income inequality is a national (and, even more, an international) problem, it is greater in some parts of the United States than in others. As one might expect, New York and California have the greatest income inequality, but inequality exists throughout the United States as well (Sommellier, Price, and Wazater 2016). Between 2009 and 2013, the top 1 percent captured *all* of the gains in income in fifteen states; in another nine states, they captured half to nearly all of those gains. For the United States as a whole, the top 1 percent captured 85 percent of income growth in that period. In 2013, the top 1 percent of families earned 25.3 times as much as did the bottom 99 percent. To be in the top 1 percent, a family would need a yearly income of almost $390,000, and that number is much higher in more affluent areas. For example, in Connecticut, a family would need to earn nearly $660,000 a year to be in the top 1 percent; in the Bridgeport-Stamford-Norwalk area of Connecticut, a yearly income of $1 million would be needed to make the cut.

It is important to note that this concentration of wealth represents a sharp reversal of historic trends. Between 1928 and 1979, the top 1 percent's share of income *dropped* in every state but Alaska. See Figure 8.4 for the most and least stratified states when looking at average income.

Several broad reasons have been put forth to explain recent increases in income inequality:

- *Deindustrialization.* The decline of U.S. industry, as well as of industry in other developed countries, has led to the loss of many higher-paying industrial jobs (Bluestone and Harrison 1984; Kollmeyer and Pichler 2013). Many who achieved middle-class status and relatively high incomes through such jobs have been reduced to lower-paying service jobs in, for example, the fast-food and tourism industries, or have become unemployed. The latter have found themselves without income, and in many cases out of the work force completely.

- *Decline of labor unions.* Deindustrialization is also related to the decline in the power of labor unions, which had helped many industrial workers obtain higher pay and generous benefits. Many nonindustrial workers also joined and benefited from unions, but most of those unions have declined as well.

- *Technological advances.* The highest-paying new jobs in recent years have been created in high-tech, high-skill areas, such as information technology (IT). Many Americans have not received the training necessary to shift from industrial to high-tech work. In fact, there is an insufficient supply of people adequately trained to handle such highly skilled work. As a result, income inequality due to technological advances may be a short-term problem that will be rectified as more people are trained for such jobs. However, many people, including former industrial workers, likely lack the education needed to acquire the skills necessary for success in tech jobs. They may also be too tied down by other obligations at this point in their lives to move to new job locations. And they may be too "tainted" by their long-term unemployment to even be considered for the new jobs. Furthermore, there may not be nearly enough of these high-tech jobs to make up for the lost industrial jobs.

- *Political climate.* A variety of political decisions help explain the increase in income inequality (Levy 1999; Sacchi and Salotti 2014). There is, for example, political opposition in the United States (mainly from Republicans and their wealthy supporters and backers) to raising the federal minimum wage, currently $7.25 per hour, or to raising it very much (Ritzer 2015b). This is the case even though various polls indicate that a significant majority of Americans favor an increase in the minimum wage (see, for example, Drake 2014). In his 2013 inaugural address, Barack Obama pushed for an increase in the federal minimum wage to $9.00 per hour, but the proposal did not succeed; in fact, as of mid-2017, the minimum wage was still $7.25 per hour in most states (see Figure 8.5 for a look at minimum wages by state). In real dollars, the minimum wage has actually declined in recent years. Those who hold minimum-wage jobs have lost ground to those in higher-paying occupations. As a result of the low minimum wage, an increasing number of people, especially men, are choosing not to work. The percentage of men 25 to 54 years of age who are not working (16 percent) has tripled since the late 1960s (Appelbaum 2014).

- *Increasing power of those at the top.* Those at the pinnacle of many hierarchies, such as business (Lowrey 2014), finance, politics, sports, entertainment, and the professions (physicians and lawyers), have used their power to grab more income and many other goodies as well. This is a symptom of what has been called a *winner-take-all* society (Frank and Cook 1995, 2013). In such a Darwinian economy, the rich use their advantages to succeed wildly, and the

poor, with few (if any) advantages, grow increasingly worse off (Frank 2011).

A series of more recent and narrower changes have also contributed to the huge and growing income gap:

- Tax cuts made in the early years of President George W. Bush's administration (2001–2009) favored the rich and disadvantaged most others; the Congressional Budget Office contended that federal taxes were doing less to equalize income in 2007 than they had in 1979. That is, taxes had grown less progressive. Most of the Bush-era tax cuts remain in place, and tax cuts for the rich have meant that the tax system continues to foster income inequality. In fact, as we saw previously, income inequality has grown dramatically. President Trump has discussed tax cuts that would greatly favor the rich and create even more inequality.

- Federal benefits are doing little to address inequality, and may even be exacerbating it. For example, Social Security payments go to the increasing number of older Americans, irrespective of their income and their economic status. Like clockwork, older wealthy Americans get their Social Security payments every month. Further, wealthy Americans tend to live longer than do poorer citizens, meaning that they get more from Social Security than do those who need it the most (Irwin 2016). However, the relationship between federal benefits and

FIGURE 8.5 • Minimum Wage Rates in the United States, 2017

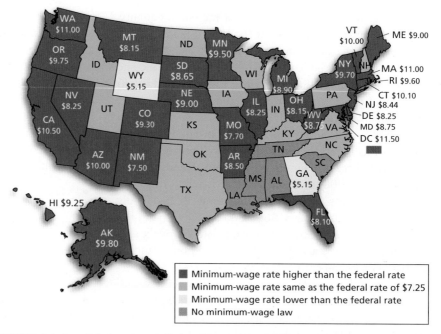

SOURCE: Data from U.S. Department of Labor, Wage and Hour Division, "Minimum Wage Laws in the States," January 2017.

ASK YOURSELF

Which of the proposed reasons for the steady increase in income inequality do you think has had the greatest impact on people you know? What about in society at large? Why?

inequality changed somewhat with the implementation of the Affordable Care Act of 2014, which added millions of people to the ranks of those with health insurance. This did more to address inequality than any federal program had since the 1960s. However, in the early days of his administration, President Trump began the process of dismantling the structures created by the Affordable Care Act. This could mean more inequality in the coming years. Tax policies have shifted to favor income derived from wealth (see the following discussion), especially long-term capital gains. Such gains involve income derived from investments in capital such as real estate, stocks, and bonds that are held for more than one year. Although the capital-gains tax increased slightly in recent years, at the maximum, long-term capital gains are still taxed at only slightly more than half the top rate for ordinary income. Those with the highest incomes pay 20 percent on capital gains, while the top tax rate on ordinary income is 33 percent to 40 percent. This is a huge advantage for the after-tax income of mainly the rich, although farmers have also benefited to some degree. The super-rich, who own a disproportionate share of the capital, reap the vast majority of the benefits of the low capital-gains tax.

WEALTH INEQUALITY

As unfair as income inequality may seem, the greatest disparities in society—the largest differences between the haves and the have-nots—are found in the enormous differences in wealth (that is, economic assets) in society. Wealth inequality tends to be much greater than income inequality. The two are linked, however, because wealth tends to produce various sources of income, such as dividends and interest. Those with significant amounts of income from such sources are far more likely to rank toward the top of the stratification system in terms of income than are those who rely mainly on wages and salaries. Thus, wealth itself is important, as is the seemingly endless stream of income that wealth tends to produce.

Like income inequality, wealth inequality has tended to increase in recent years in the United States and other Western countries (Mishel and Bivens 2011; Wilterdink 2007),

and the U.S. tax system is of *decreasing* utility in reducing that inequality (Looney and Moore 2016). More than 80 percent of the wealth gain in the United States between 1983 and 2009 went to the wealthiest 5 percent of the population. Over the last three decades, the wealth of the top 0.1 percent of households has increased from 7 to 22 percent of the total. In contrast, the poorest 60 percent of the population saw a 7.5 percent *decline* in wealth. Their wealth has eroded because of such factors as the decline of many housing values and stagnant wages (Saez and Zucman 2014), as well as the large number of people who have given up and left the labor force, thus earning no income and acquiring no wealth (Appelbaum 2014).

As with income inequality, the super-rich (the top 0.01 percent in terms of wealth) are growing dramatically better off in terms of wealth (see Figure 8.6). The share of the wealth for the top 0.01 percent grew from about 3 percent in 1960 to about 11 percent in 2012.

As we saw previously in the case of cruise ships, those with great wealth live lifestyles beyond the wildest dreams of those who live on the lowest rungs of the economic ladder. Wealth brings with it a wide range of advantages:

- It can be invested to generate income and ultimately even greater wealth.

- It can be used to purchase material comforts of all sorts: mega-homes, vacation retreats, luxury cars, and custom-tailored clothes, as well as the services of housekeepers, gardeners, mechanics, personal trainers, and so forth.

- It can afford a high level of financial security, allowing the wealthy, if they wish, to retire at an early age with the means to live well for the rest of their lives.

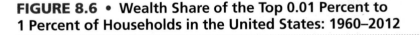

FIGURE 8.6 • Wealth Share of the Top 0.01 Percent to 1 Percent of Households in the United States: 1960–2012

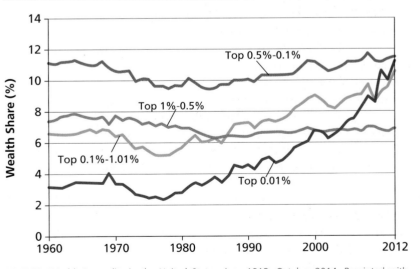

SOURCE: Wealth Inequality in the United States since 1913. October 2014. Reprinted with permission from Emmanuel Saez (UC Berkeley) and Gabriel Zucman (LSE).

- It purchases far more freedom and autonomy than less wealthy individuals can acquire. An example would be the freedom to leave unsatisfactory employment—or not to work at all—without worrying about how the bills will be paid.

- It allows the wealthy to get the benefit of the doubt from the criminal justice system. In the unlikely event that they are even arrested and charged with crimes, the wealthy can hire expensive lawyers who are likely to be able to fashion favorable outcomes for them. And white-collar criminals of any class tend to be only lightly sanctioned (drawing probation instead of parole for embezzlement and fraud, for example).

- Most wealth can be passed on to offspring, even generations away, guaranteeing that they will live a similarly privileged lifestyle.

Wealth and the growing disparities in wealth received enormous academic and media attention with the publication of economist Thomas Piketty's *Capital in the Twenty-First Century* (2014; see also Antonio 2014). Piketty sees wealth as being of greater importance than income. Rather than relying on pay or a salary (even though it might be high) for their labor, those with wealth rely much more on the income their wealth produces, such as earned interest, rental from properties, dividends on stocks and bonds, and royalties. Overall returns from such sources have historically outstripped increases in salaries and pay. With growth in pay projected to remain slow in the years to come, those who live off the income from their wealth will further outstrip those who live off their wages and salaries.

Those with wealth also stack the deck in their favor by, for example, influencing the government to pass laws that favor wealth enhancement (such as a lower tax rate on capital gains from the sale of stocks than on income). Furthermore, wealth can be passed from generation to generation through inheritance, meaning that the advantages of the wealthy grow exponentially over time. The top 10 percent in the United States already own 75 percent of the nation's wealth, and that fraction is likely to grow, while the bottom 50 percent own only 2 percent of the wealth, and that is unlikely to increase. The only hope, as far as Piketty (2014) is concerned, is a significant and progressive tax on global wealth (it must be a global tax, because wealth itself is so mobile globally), with the wealthy paying a significantly higher rate. That is the only way to halt the growing gap between the wealthy and the rest of society. However, the barriers to instituting a global tax on wealth are almost insurmountable. The wealthy and their political supporters will oppose it with the extensive resources at their disposal. Furthermore, it is difficult to imagine the many diverse societies across the globe agreeing to such a transformation.

Status, Power, and Wealth

Perhaps of greatest importance is the fact that wealth not only accords a high-level position on one dimension of stratification, social class, but it is also an important factor in gaining similar positions on the other dimensions of stratification, status and power. Those who have great wealth tend to rank high in social class because class is, to a considerable degree, defined economically and wealth is a key indicator of it. Those with great wealth are also generally able to buy or to otherwise acquire whatever gives them high status and great power. There are exceptions, however, to the link between great wealth and high social class. An example is those who retain a high social ranking even though they have lost much or most of their wealth over time. Another exception is the *nouveau riche* (some might consider Donald Trump to be in this category), whose extravagant and inelegant tastes and behaviors may lead others in the upper class to refuse to accept them as members of their class. However, in general, those with great wealth *are* members of the upper class.

In terms of status, the wealthy can afford an increased level and better quality of education. They can, for example, send their children to very expensive and exclusive prep schools and Ivy League universities. In some elite universities, being a "legacy" applicant—the son or daughter of an elite who attended the same school—can increase the chances of gaining admission, perhaps by as much as 45 percent (Mandery 2014). The practice of favoring legacy applicants is sometimes called "affirmative action for the rich" (Kahlenberg 2010). At Princeton, in 2009, for example, 41.7 percent of legacy applicants were admitted, compared with 9.2 percent of nonlegacies. The wealthy can also purchase more of the trappings of high culture, such as season tickets to the opera or multimillion-dollar paintings by famous artists. The wealthy can also achieve recognition as philanthropists by, for example, attending $1,000-per-ticket charity balls or even donating the money needed to build a new wing of a hospital.

Power over employees is a fact of life for wealthy individuals who own businesses or run other organizations. Their needs for financial, household, and personal services give the wealthy another source of power. They have the ability to direct the activities of many charities and civic groups. And if that weren't enough, the wealthy can buy more power by bribing political officials or making generous campaign contributions to favored politicians. Such contributions often give donors great behind-the-scenes power. In some cases, the wealthy choose to use their money to run for public office themselves; if successful, their families may come to occupy positions that give them great power. These families can even become political dynasties, with two or more generations attaining high political office. Joseph P. Kennedy used the large sums of money he earned during the Great Depression to become a powerful political figure. His money and his political influence helped get his sons elected to office:

Stratification in the New Sharing Economy

In the sharing economy, instead of buying or renting in the usual ways, we share goods and services—at low cost or free of charge—with others (Gansky 2010; Stein 2015). Instead of renting a hotel room, we can get a room in a private home, or even an entire home, through the online site Airbnb. Instead of hailing a taxi, we can use Uber's smartphone app and get a prepaid ride in a private automobile. Instead of waiting for a table at a "hot" restaurant, we can hire someone online to do so through TaskRabbit.

The sharing economy is clearly the wave of the future. But while some sharing is free of profit making and the exchange of money (Atsushi 2014), big businesses have become deeply engaged, and the sharing economy is growing highly stratified.

At the top are the founders, executives, and financiers of the most successful companies. Uber is now valued at about $68 billion (Austin, Canipe, and Slobin 2015), and its founders are likely to be millionaires or even billionaires. But for most of the drivers, the job is part-time and the pay low. Drivers use their own cars, pay their own expenses, and lack benefits and job security. As a result, they are likely to land in or near the lower class. Worse, their success is costing traditional taxi drivers their jobs. Uber cars now outnumber yellow taxis in New York City by more than three to one (Hu 2017; Pramuk 2015).

Airbnb, valued at about $25 billion, has created a similar stratification system, with founders and executives on top and many who list their apartments and homes nearer the bottom. However,

Russell Hart/Alamy Stock Photo

Smartphone apps, such as those of Uber and Airbnb, create a divide between those who control the sharing economy and those who work in it. Is such increased stratification inevitable?

few of those participants are actually individuals sharing space with others. While New York City is attempting to crack down on this, commercial operators there supply more than one-third of Airbnb rental units and earn more than one-third of the profits; 6 percent of the hosts earned 37 percent of the revenue, and one had 272 units, earning revenue of $6.8 million. Some critics argue that, at least in this case, "the very term 'sharing economy' is ridiculous" (Austin, Canipe, and Slboin 2015; Streitfeld 2014, A1).

Belk (2014) argues that in all these cases and many others, sharing is being transformed into "pseudo-sharing" by, among others, profit-making organizations that have found this to be a way

to grow rich. As Ritzer (2017) puts it, there is "woefully little sharing" in the sharing economy. The sharing economy is creating a new stratification system, or at least new positions in the current system. Many people will be at or near the bottom.

Engaging the Digital World
Do you think that the stratification taking place in the sharing economy is inevitable? Why or why not? Should consumers avoid participating in this economy, even if the services offered are desirable and affordable? Why or why not? If you participate in the sharing economy, explain what types of services you use (or provide) most often and what the alternatives would be to each of them.

John F. Kennedy as president, Ted Kennedy as U.S. senator, and Bobby Kennedy as U.S. senator before he was assassinated while running for the presidency. Prescott Bush made his money on Wall Street and became a U.S. senator. His son, George H. W. Bush, became president of the United States, as did his grandson, George W. Bush. Another grandson, Jeb Bush, former governor of Florida, was a (failed) candidate for the Republican nomination for president in 2016.

The lifestyles that large amounts of money can buy are a source of interest and fascination for many people. In the 1980s, Robin Leach hosted a popular TV show called *Lifestyles of the Rich and Famous*. The show took viewers behind the scenes to explore the mansions of the elite. On a modern version of this show, MTV's *Cribs*, celebrity musicians and athletes show off their homes, pools, cars, and other trappings of wealth. Reality TV shows, such as Bravo's *Real Housewives* series and E!'s *Keeping Up with the Kardashians* and *Rich Kids of Beverly Hills,* feature the daily lives of an elite group of the extremely wealthy. These shows highlight the gap between the wealthy and everyone else. For example, many of the real-life elites do not know how to do things that seem commonplace to most of us, including pumping their own gasoline and waiting in line at the Department of Motor Vehicles for a driver's license. The prevalence of such entertainment suggests a deep curiosity about how people with a great deal of status, money, and/or power live.

The Perpetuation of Wealth

One of the great advantages of the wealthy is their ability to maintain their social class across generations. Their ability to keep their wealth, if not expand it, often allows the members of the upper class to pass their wealth, and the upper-class position that goes with it, to their children. Financial mechanisms (for example, generation-skipping trusts) have been devised that allow the wealthy to pass on their wealth not only to the next generation but also to many generations to come. Thus, wealth tends to be self-perpetuating over the long term.

The wealthy are able to perpetuate their wealth in large part because they have been able to use their money and influence to resist taxation systems designed to redistribute at least some of the wealth in society. For example, the wealthy have fought long and hard against the estate tax, which places a high tax on assets worth more than a certain amount that are left behind when an individual dies. Many of the wealthy prefer to refer to the estate tax in more negative terms, as a "death tax."

The year 2010 was fascinating from this point of view because the estate tax law was allowed to expire, the result being that *no* estate taxes were paid by the estates of millionaires and billionaires who died that year. One particular beneficiary was the family of George Steinbrenner, then owner of the New York Yankees, who died that year with an estate estimated to be worth slightly over $1 billion. Even more extreme was the case of the much less well-known Dan Duncan, whose estate was estimated at about $9 billion. The Steinbrenner and Duncan families saved hundreds of millions, perhaps billions, of dollars in taxes because these billionaires happened to die in 2010.

The estate tax was renewed in 2011. In 2015, the estate tax exemption was set at a generous $5.43 million per person, rather than the $3.5 million exemption in force in 2009. In other words, a single person pays *no estate tax* on the first $5.43 million of his or her estate (the exemption is $10.86 million for a married couple). Beyond 2015, the exemption was set to increase in line with the rate of inflation. Thus, for 2016, the exemption increased only modestly, to $5.45 million per person. Only a few Americans have anything approaching an estate of that magnitude, with the result that proposals to reduce or eliminate the estate tax are of little or no relevance to them. Reducing or eliminating that tax will serve only to make the rich even richer.

Like having a great deal of wealth, having little wealth tends to be self-perpetuating. Those who have little or no personal wealth can be fairly sure that their children, and generations beyond them, will also lack wealth. Of course, there have been, and will be, many exceptions to this pattern, but in the main there is great consistency from generation to generation. This contradicts the Horatio Alger myth (Alger was a late nineteenth-century author of cheap, but very popular, rags-to-riches novels), which tells us that anyone can get ahead, or rise in the stratification system, through hard work and effort. This myth is functional in that many people believe in it and continue to strive to get ahead (and some even succeed), often in the face of overwhelming barriers and odds. But it is also dysfunctional in that it tends to put all the burdens of achieving success on the shoulders of individuals. The vast majority of people are likely to fail and to blame themselves, rather than the unfairness of the highly stratified system, for their failures.

Recent research has shown that people throughout the stratification system greatly overestimate the amount of upward mobility in U.S. society, although such overestimation is greater among those who rank lower in that system (Kraus, Davidai, and Nussbaum 2015). Overestimation of upward mobility by those at the top of the stratification system serves to legitimate their position because it makes it seem that positions at the top are open to a great many people. More important, and consistent with the Horatio Alger myth, overestimation of upward mobility offers those at or near the bottom of the stratification system the hope that they will be able to ascend to higher positions in that system.

THE DECLINE OF THE AMERICAN MIDDLE CLASS

Much has been written in recent years about the decline, or the hollowing out, of the American middle class (Frank 2013). While there is no clear economic dividing line that separates the middle class from the upper and lower classes,

How are poverty and social class related? Is poverty inevitable in a stratified society?

we can say that to be considered part of the middle class, a family of four must have earnings (adjusted for inflation) between $35,000 and $100,000 per year (Searcey and Gebeloff 2015). The proportion of the U.S. population in the middle class *declined* from 53 percent in 1967 to 50 percent in 2015 (Parlapiano, Gebeloff, and Carter 2015). Some of those in the middle class have been able to rise into the upper class, which grew from 7 percent to 21 percent of the U.S. population between 1967 and 2015. However, many have dropped into the lower class (which, nonetheless, dropped from 40 percent to 29 percent of the population in that period).

The major reason for the decline of the middle class is the decline of middle-income jobs, such as better-paid, often unionized, positions in manufacturing, usually owing to technological change. In other cases, those jobs have been lost to successful companies elsewhere in the world. Some displaced workers have been able to get better-paying jobs and thereby move up the stratification hierarchy. However, many more have had to take lower-paying service jobs, such as in the fast-food industry. They have likely dropped into the lower class, as have those who have been unable to find jobs or have been unwilling to accept poorly paid work. Said one man who was once a highly paid electrician but has now been out of work for four years: "I'd work for them [Chick-fil-A], but they're only

willing to pay $10 an hour. . . . I'm 49 with two kids—$10 just isn't going to cut it" (Appelbaum 2014, A1). While many middle-class people are counted among the unemployed, others—like this electrician—are not, because they are not looking for work. They have given up hope of finding the kind of work they want, or any kind of work at all.

Another major factor in the decline of the middle class is wage stagnation in the kinds of jobs that members of this class are likely to continue to hold (Greenhouse 2015; Wisman 2013). They may still have the same jobs they had a decade or two ago, but the wages associated with them have tended to increase little, and actually have been more likely to decline in real terms over that time. As a result, they are worse off because they are trying to pay for various goods and services whose prices have risen, sometimes dramatically, over time, but with wages that have not kept pace with those price rises. As a result, many may still be considered part of the middle class, but they may not feel that way because their expenses have risen faster than their income—they may no longer be able to afford the things usually associated with a middle-class lifestyle.

The Great Recession badly hurt the middle class. For example, many lost their homes because they could no longer afford their mortgage payments. Government efforts in the wake of the recession (such as bailing out banks and investment companies) greatly aided the upper class, but they did little or nothing for the middle class (the government bailed out few homeowners in danger of losing their homes; Hacker and Pierson 2010).

The decline of the middle class is of great concern, especially to those who are no longer in it, or who can no longer aspire to be part of it. From a large-scale perspective, this decline creates a stratification system that splits into the upper and lower classes, with an increasingly massive hole in the middle. This leads to growing inequality and to increasingly less hope for those in the lower classes of finding middle-income positions that will allow them to rise in the stratification system.

POVERTY

While some in the middle class have become poor and dropped into the lower class, poverty is obviously a problem mainly for the much more numerous and often long-term members of that class. Poverty and the many problems associated with it are of great concern both to sociologists and to society as a whole (Desmond 2016; Edin and Schaefer 2015; Iceland 2007, 2013). The poor are likely to be underemployed or unemployed, or to have given up hope of finding a job and to be out of the workforce completely (see Chapter 15). Those who are seeking a full-time job and are able to find only a part-time job, at, for example, McDonald's or Walmart, are unlikely to have enough income to live on and must often rely on others or welfare payments of various kinds.

Poverty is troubling for many reasons, the most important of which is its negative effect on the lives of the poor themselves. The lack of a job, or having one that does not offer a living wage, is likely to be associated with many troubling conditions. Those suffering from poverty are likely to suffer from food insecurity—that is, to have difficulty getting enough to eat. They are also likely to be in poor physical and mental health and, as a result, to have a lower life expectancy. In fact, the poor are falling increasingly behind the rich as the gap between the rich and poor in terms of lifespan has widened dramatically over the years. For men born in 1920, those in the top 10 percent of earners could expect to live six more years than those in the bottom 10 percent of earners. For men born in 1950, the gap had more than doubled to 14 years. For women over the same time period, the gap had grown from 4.7 years to 13 years (Tavernise 2016). Major causes of these growing disparities in lifespan are significant class differences in smoking, obesity, and involvement in the prescription drug epidemic, especially among poor whites.

Beyond its effects on the poor themselves, poverty hurts the economy in various ways. The economy is less likely to benefit from the contributions of those who are only in the workforce part time or, worse, out of it completely. The vibrancy of the economy is reduced because poverty adversely affects the ability to work of at least some of those who do have a job. For example, they may be less productive or lose more work time due to illness. Further, the level of consumption in society as a whole is reduced because of the inability of the poor to consume very much. Crime, social disorder, and revolution are more likely where poverty is widespread.

ASK YOURSELF

Do you believe that the poor are victims? If so, of whom? Or do you believe that the poor have chosen not to raise themselves from poverty? If so, what sociological factors would explain this choice?

The great disparity between the rich and the poor is considered by many to be a moral problem, if not a moral crisis, for society as a whole. The poor are often seen as not doing what they should, or could, to raise themselves out of poverty. They are seen as disreputable, which makes them objects of moral censure by those who have succeeded in society (Damer 1974; Matza 1966; Shildrick and MacDonald 2013). They may be blamed for the degradation of society and may even blame themselves for that degradation as well as for their own poverty. However, some see poverty as an entirely different kind of moral problem. They argue that the poor should be seen as the "victims" of a system that impoverishes them (Ryan 1976). The existence of large numbers of poor people in otherwise affluent societies is a "moral stain" on those societies (Harvey 2007). Something must be amiss in the economic and political systems in societies that perpetuate so much poverty. Not only are the poor blamed for poverty; they must also suffer most of the burdens associated with it. However, poverty adversely affects all of us and society as a whole in various ways (Rank 2014). We pay a steep economic and social price for poverty. We would all benefit from less poverty, and even more from the elimination of poverty completely.

ANALYZING POVERTY

It may be tempting to blame the poor for the existence of poverty, but a sociological perspective notes the larger social forces that create and perpetuate poverty. To the sociologist, poverty persists for three basic reasons:

- Poverty is built into the capitalist system, and virtually all societies today—even China—have capitalist economies. Capitalist businesses seek to maximize profits. They do so by keeping wages as low as possible and by hiring as few workers as possible. When business slows, they are likely to lay off people, thrusting most of them into poverty. It is in the interest of the capitalist system to have a large number of unemployed, and therefore poor, people. This population serves as what

Marx called the "reserve army of the unemployed." This is a readily available pool of people who can be drawn quickly into the labor force when business booms and more workers are needed. The presence of this reserve army also keeps existing workers in line and reluctant to demand much, if anything, from management.

- Competition among social classes encourages some elite groups of people to seek to enhance their economic position by limiting the ability of other groups to maintain even their lower economic positions. The elites do so by restricting the poor's access to opportunities and resources such as those afforded by various welfare systems.

- Government actions to reduce poverty, or to ameliorate its negative effects on people and society, are generally limited by groups of people who believe that the poor should make it on their own and not be afforded the aid of the government. They also believe that government aid reduces people's incentive to do what they need to do on their own to rise above the poverty line. These beliefs are fairly common among political conservatives.

There are two broad types of poverty:

- **Absolute poverty** is a measure of what people need in order to survive. No matter the standard for measuring poverty, absolute poverty remains constant over time, although its level is revised to take inflation into consideration. The United States, for instance, uses the poverty line (see the following section), based on income level, as the measure of absolute poverty. By contrast, the level of consumption is used to determine poverty in the developing world, where income can be essentially nothing. Thus, absolute poverty might be defined in a developing nation as the consumption of goods valued at less than $2 per day. While the poor in the United States may be impoverished according to some absolute standard and in some absolute sense, they are often much better off than the poor in most other places in the world. However, as recent research has discovered, there is a surprising number of American families suffering from "extreme poverty" and living on as little as $2 per day (Edin and Schaefer 2015). The researchers estimate that 1.5 million households, including 3 million children, are in that category. They might survive, for example, from income obtained through donating their blood plasma.

- **Relative poverty** is defined not by some objective standard but rather by the fact that some people, irrespective of income, are, or consider themselves to be, poor, relative to others to whom they relate. Townsend offers such a relative view when he argues that poverty occurs when "resources fall seriously short of the resources commanded by the average individual or family in the community in which they live" (2010, 99). Thus, even middle-class people (especially those who have experienced wage stagnation or have lost their jobs) and some upper-class people can see themselves as poor in comparison with those around them who have greater incomes and more of the trappings that go with such incomes (such as bigger homes and more luxurious cars). While relative poverty is a reality, it is harder to feel much sympathy for the relatively poor when they are compared with those in absolute, let alone extreme, poverty.

Poverty in the United States

While many sociologists adopt a more relativistic view of poverty, governments, including the U.S. government, tend to use absolute measures. A **poverty line**, or threshold, in terms of income is set, and then the income of a household is compared with it. A household whose income falls below the threshold is considered poor. Poverty lines vary from country to country. In the United States, the Social Security Administration sets the poverty line. The formula involves multiplying the cost of what is deemed to be a nutritionally adequate food plan by three. This is because a family is assumed to spend a third of its budget on food. It is worth noting that many people criticize this calculation for not considering other necessary expenses, such as child care, housing, and transportation. The poverty line in 2017 for a family of four was a pretax income of $24,600, and $12,060 for a single adult (U.S. Department of Health and Human Services 2017). In 2014, 15 percent of the U.S. population, or 46.7 million people, lived below the poverty line and were therefore officially categorized as poor (DeNavas-Walt and Proctor 2015).

Of course, millions who exist at or slightly above that line would also be considered poor by many people in society. In the wake of the Great Recession's lingering effects, there have been calls for a stronger focus on the "near poor" (DeParle, Gebeloff, and Tavernise 2011; Hokayem and Heggeness 2014). Those who have income that is less than 25 percent above the poverty line would be included in this category. Using this measure, it has been estimated that in 2014, almost 15 million people in the United States were considered near poor. If we combine that number with the number of the poor, we see that almost 60 million Americans are poor or very close to it. There is no question that poverty is a huge problem in the United States, but it is almost certainly far greater than most of us imagine.

Looking at the longer-term trends shown in Figure 8.7, we can see that there has been considerable variation in the numbers of people living in poverty from year to year since 1959. What is striking, however, is the sharp increase in poverty that coincided with the beginning of the Great Recession; 6 million more households were below the poverty line in 2015 as compared with 2009.

FIGURE 8.7 • Poverty in the United States, 1959–2015

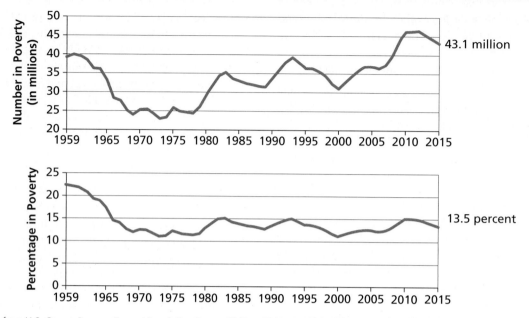

SOURCES: Data from U.S. Census Bureau, Current Population Survey, 1960 to 2015 Annual Social and Economic Supplements; Bernadette D. Proctor, Jessica L. Semega, and Melissa A. Kollar, Figure 4: "Number in Poverty and Poverty Rate: 1959 to 2015," in *Income and Poverty in the United States: 2015,* Current Population Reports P60–256(RV), U.S. Census Bureau, September 2016.

One indicator of the level of poverty in the United States is the number of people receiving aid from the Supplemental Nutrition Assistance Program (SNAP), or what were called food stamps before 2008 (Bartfeld et al. 2016). At the beginning of 2010, 44.1 million people received SNAP; by October 2016, 43.2 million were receiving such aid (https:// www.fns.usda.gov/sites/default/files/pd/34SNAPmonthly .pdf). This is a modest decline, but the fact remains that well over 40 million Americans are on SNAP, and the program cost the U.S. government $74 billion in 2015.

As you might expect, given their disadvantages in income and wealth, minorities suffer disproportionately from poverty. The poverty rate in 2014 for non-Hispanic whites was 10 percent. The 12 percent poverty rate for Asians was down significantly from 16 percent in the mid-1980s, but still higher than the rate for non-Hispanic whites. Even more telling, the poverty rate was over 20 percent for both blacks (26 percent) and Hispanics (24 percent; DeNavas-Walt and Proctor 2015; U.S. Census Bureau 2014b).

Figure 8.8 looks at poverty by family type. Three types of families are covered here: those headed by a married couple, those with a male householder and no wife present, and those with a female householder and no husband present. Families headed by women with no husband present have long had dramatically higher poverty rates than have the other family types. For example, in 2014 the poverty rate for families headed by women was almost double that of families headed by men. Meanwhile, poverty rates are much lower for married-couple families than for single-parent households, although rates for married-couple families increased slightly in 2014 from the year before.

One indication of poverty and its effect on the family is the increase in the number of families experiencing "doubling up" (Bitler and Hoynes 2015). Doubled-up families are those that include at least one additional adult who is 18 years old or older and not in school, the householder, and the spouse (or one cohabiting with the householder). Between 2007 and 2011, there was an 11 percent increase in

FIGURE 8.8 • Poverty Rates by Family Type in the United States, 1973–2014

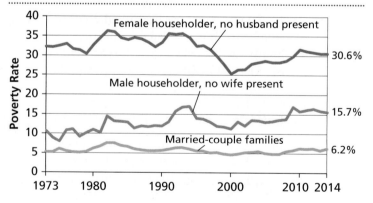

SOURCES: Data from U.S. Census Bureau, Current Population Survey, 1960 to 2014 Annual Social and Economic Supplements; Carmen DeNavas-Walt and Bernadette D. Proctor, *Income and Poverty in the United States, 2014,* Current Population Reports P60–252, U.S. Census Bureau, September 2015.

the number of doubled-up households. Further, there was a 26 percent increase during that period in the number of 25- to 34-year-olds living with their parents (Johnson 2011). The latter trend should be especially worrisome to many readers of this book.

The Feminization of Poverty

A central issue in the study of poverty is the degree to which women and children are overrepresented among the poor (Abercrombie and Hastings 2016; Hinze and Aliberti 2007). In 2014, 15 percent of U.S. women were below the poverty line, whereas only 12 percent of men lived in poverty (U.S. Census Bureau 2015). Poverty levels vary by age: Women between the ages of 45 and 64 are less likely to be poor than are those 18 and below and 65 and above. Female poverty levels also vary based on race and ethnicity: Both black and Latino women are more than twice as likely to be poor as are white women. Also, as noted previously, female-headed households with no husband present have far higher rates of poverty than do families headed by married couples.

The **feminization of poverty**, first framed as a concept in 1978, means that those living in poverty are more likely to be women than men (Goldberg 2010; Pearce 1978). Although in recent years the improved position of women in the work world, as well as increases in women's earnings, would seem to indicate that the poverty gap is narrowing,

the gender gap persists (McLanahan and Kelly 1999). One of the reasons for that persistence is the fact that the trend toward gender wage equalization has been more than offset by the increasing tendency for a greater proportion of men to raise their earnings through "overwork"—that is, by working more than 50 hours per week (Cha and Weeden 2014).

A variety of demographic factors and changes help explain the feminization of poverty:

- Women are more likely than men to live alone (because, for example, single women marry later, and divorced women are less likely to remarry than are divorced men).

- Women have lower average earnings than men do. This is the case even when they do the same work.

- More children are being born to unmarried women, who tend to earn less than married women and who are more likely to be fully responsible for their dependents.

- Women have longer life spans than men do, increasing the likelihood that older women will be living on their own.

Economically, women suffer from a variety of disadvantages. Historically, males were considered to be the main breadwinners, and women, if they worked, were thought of as secondary earners. Women today exist in a sex-segregated labor force in which the best and highest-paying positions

FIGURE 8.9 • **Female-to-Male Earnings Ratio and Median Earnings of Full-Time Workers in the United States by Gender, 1960–2014**

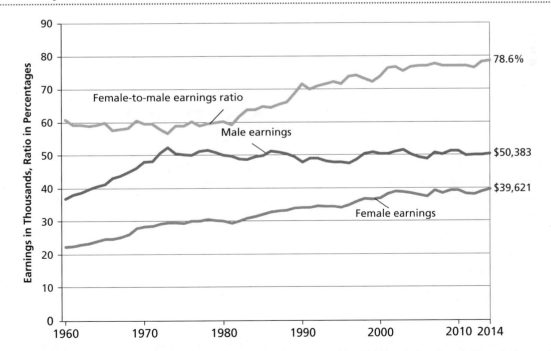

SOURCES: Data from U.S. Census Bureau, Current Population Survey, 1961 to 2014 Annual Social Economic Supplement, Figure 2; Carmen Denavas-Walt and Bernadette D. Proctor, Table A-4: "Number and Real Median Earnings of Total Workers and Full-Time, Year-Round Workers by Sex and Female-to-Male Earnings Ratio: 1960 to 2014," In *Income and Poverty in the United States, 2015,* Current Population Reports P60–252, U.S. Census Bureau, September 2015.

go largely to men. The subordinate economic position of women is reinforced by the systematic wage discrimination practiced against them. They are routinely paid less than men, even for the same work. In regard to income, women are also adversely affected by the fact that they are more likely than men to work part-time, to hold temporary jobs, or to work at home (Presser 2005). Female workers have gained some ground in recent years: They earned about 61 percent of male earnings in 1960 but 79 percent in 2014 (DeNavas-Walt and Proctor 2015), in part because of stagnation in male earnings. In spite of the improvement, the gender gap in earnings persists to this day (see Figure 8.9).

CHECKPOINT 8.2: FACTORS IN ECONOMIC INEQUALITY

FACTOR	DESCRIPTION
Income inequality	This is substantially higher since the 1970s, due to deindustrialization, technological advances, and political choices.
Wealth inequality	This is much greater than income inequality, because it can be passed on to the next generation.
Decline of the middle class	Because of job loss and wage stagnation that have struck the middle class most severely, society is increasingly dividing into the upper and lower classes.
Poverty	This can be absolute or relative, and tends to affect women and children disproportionately.

SOCIAL MOBILITY

Those who live in poverty are understandably eager to improve their lot. However, virtually everyone in a stratified system is concerned about **social mobility** (Hout 2015: van Leeuwen and Maas 2010), or the ability or inability to change one's position in the hierarchy. *Upward mobility,* the ability to move higher (Kupfer 2012; Miles, Savage, and Bühlmann 2011), is obviously of great personal concern to many Americans. In addition, the possibility of such mobility for most is what lends legitimacy to the U.S. stratification system, indeed the entire U.S. economic system (Leventoglu 2014). This is especially the case for those who are poor. Upward mobility is the route out of poverty. However, as a major recent study in Baltimore demonstrated, upward mobility for most poor people is more myth than reality. The poor tend to end up in about the same place in the stratification system as where they started; they have little upward mobility (Alexander, Entwisle, and Olson 2014). This is undoubtedly what causes many of the poor to question the legitimacy of our economic system.

Those in the middle class are more likely to be upwardly mobile and may have an even greater desire to be mobile—and to continue to be mobile—than the poor do. The reason is that they are likely to have experienced at least some of the improved possibilities associated with upward mobility. They have some class, status, and power, but they tend to want more. They often want to move into the upper class. Even those in the upper class are interested in and concerned about upward mobility. They often want to move to higher-level positions than those occupied by their rivals within the upper class. They are also interested in keeping tabs on those below them who may be moving up the ladder. Those who are on the move up the stratification system threaten to supplant them, and perhaps even reach positions higher than their own.

People in all social classes are also concerned about *downward mobility* (Wilson, Roscigno, and Huffman 2013). That is, people worry about descending to lower levels within their social class or to lower classes (for example, dropping from the upper to the middle or even lower class). Downward mobility causes people real hardships, and even its mere possibility is a great cause of concern. Immigrants and refugees who move to a new country almost always experience serious difficulties, such as language differences (Guo 2013), and as a result they are likely to experience downward mobility during the first generation in their new locale. This is especially true of those who held high-level occupations in their countries of origin (Gans 2009). More generally, it is likely that, given the current economic problems in the United States and Europe, many people will experience downward mobility relative to their parents' status. As one newspaper columnist put it, "Young people today are staring at a future in which they will be less well off than their elders, a reversal of fortune that should send a shudder through everyone" (Herbert 2011).

ASK YOURSELF

Why should the public "shudder" at the prospect that young people today will be less well off in the future than their elders? What negative effects could this future reality have on social institutions, such as schools, workplaces, and industries like banking and real estate? Would it be likely to have any positive effects, perhaps on consumerism or the natural environment? How might it affect the world standing of the United States as a society? Explain your answers.

TYPES OF SOCIAL MOBILITY

To this point, we have discussed upward and downward mobility, but there are a number of other types of social mobility as well. Upward and downward mobility are the key components of the general process of **vertical mobility**. Also of interest is **horizontal mobility**, or movement within one's social class. For example, the chief executive officer (CEO) of a given corporation may experience horizontal mobility by becoming the CEO of a different corporation. At the other end of the spectrum, the taxi driver who becomes a driver for Uber also exhibits horizontal mobility (Ultee 2007a).

Sociologists are also concerned about two other types of mobility. One is **intergenerational mobility**, or the difference between parents' position in the stratification system and the positions achieved by their children (Corak 2013; Park and Myers 2010). Children who rise higher in the stratification system than their parents have experienced upward intergenerational mobility. Those who descend to a lower position on the ladder have experienced downward intergenerational mobility. Chetty et al. (2014) found that children born today have about the same chance of upward mobility as did children born in 1970.

Intragenerational mobility involves movement up or down the stratification system in one's lifetime. It is possible for some to start their adult lives in the lower class and to move up over the years to a higher social class. However, it is also possible to start out in the upper class and slide down the stratification ladder to a lower class in the course of one's lifetime (Corak, Lindquist, and Mazumder 2014; Ultee 2007b).

Much of the concern about mobility relates to the work that people do or the occupations they hold. **Occupational mobility** involves changes in people's work, either across or within generations (Blau and Duncan 1967; Treiman 2007). Research on occupational mobility has generally focused on men, even though such mobility obviously also applies to women (Mandel 2012). For example, in the case of intergenerational mobility, the focus has been on the difference between a man's occupation and that of his father.

All the previously discussed types of mobility are concerned with individual mobility. **Structural mobility** describes the effects of changes in the larger society on the positions of individuals in the stratification system, especially the occupational structure (Gilbert and Kahl 1993; Miller 2001). For example, China under communism offered people little mobility of any type. Now that China has a booming capitalist economy, the country has experienced a vast increase in structural mobility, because many more higher-level positions (especially occupations) are now available (Lui 2014; Vogel 2011). Millions have moved out of the peasantry and into an expanding hierarchy of nonagricultural occupations and thus higher social positions.

STRUCTURAL MOBILITY IN THE UNITED STATES

There have been many changes in the occupational structure of the United States over the last century. These changes have profoundly affected occupational mobility and, ultimately, all the other types of mobility. For example, in 1900, the largest single occupational category was farming. A male born in 1900 was likely to have a father who was a farmer. However, over time, farm work became a smaller part of the economy, and there were few opportunities for a son in farming. He might end up in a wide range of occupations, but wherever he ended up, he was likely to experience occupational mobility. He was also likely to experience upward intergenerational mobility, because his occupation was apt to be of higher status and offer higher pay than his father's did. Even if the son had started in farming, he was unlikely to end up in farming. Thus, he would experience upward intragenerational mobility as well.

If we fast-forward to 1930, we find that the largest occupational category was no longer farming but manual, or blue-collar, work. Fathers, and perhaps their sons, were likely to do manual work in factories. However, since that time, manufacturing work has also declined dramatically in the United States. The production of textiles, steel, automobiles, and other manufactured goods has largely shifted to other parts of the world, especially Asia. An American worker today is much more likely to be in a white-collar occupation (professional, managerial, clerical, service, or sales) than in a manual occupation. In other words, she is likely to have experienced intergenerational mobility. Some contemporary workers who started out as factory workers and then moved into some sort of white-collar work have also experienced intragenerational mobility.

Great inter- and intragenerational upward mobility were characteristic of the United States throughout the twentieth century. This was due to the fact that the country prospered and the number of high-level occupational positions expanded greatly. There were certainly people in the twentieth century who experienced downward mobility, but they were far outnumbered by those who experienced upward mobility. However, with the American economy in decline in the early part of the twenty-first century and other global economies rising dramatically (especially India and China), it is likely that we will see a rise in downward mobility and a decline in upward mobility in the United States (Levy 1987; Room 2011; Strobel 1993). Downward occupational mobility in the United States increased from 19 percent to 27 percent among males between the 1970s and 2000 (Gilbert 2011). As described previously, young people today are going to have a hard time maintaining the positions in the stratification system held by their parents. It is also possible that because of change in the occupational structure in the rest of the twenty-first century, many people, especially the young, will experience downward intragenerational mobility as more high-status, high-paying jobs are lost.

American women's mobility has been somewhat different from men's in recent years. It may well continue to be different in the decades to come. While women's intergenerational mobility is similar to that of men, their intragenerational mobility is much greater as a result of the changing structure of the labor force (Park and Myers 2010). Women have many more opportunities today to attain high-status occupations, such as professional and managerial positions, than they did in the past. Upward intragenerational mobility has thus grown more likely for women in recent years. They, too, will be affected by the declining fortunes of the American economy in the twenty-first century, but the effect will be muted because changes in the labor force will continue to operate to their advantage—at least relative to the fortunes of men.

The good news for U.S. workers is that intragenerational mobility can be affected by access to human capital resources. For example, a college education is very helpful for obtaining initial employment. Also very helpful is education pursued throughout a career. Ongoing education can be a resource for maintaining employment, and it is likely to increase the chances of upward mobility (Carnevale, Rose, and Cheah 2009). Figure 8.10 shows that more education pays off economically for both males and females. With each increase in educational level, there is a significant increase in earnings. However, males earn more than females at *all* educational levels. Male advantage remains even though females are getting more than their share of college degrees. This reflects the continuing sexism and institutional discrimination in the work world.

ACHIEVEMENT AND ASCRIPTION

Thus far, we have been describing a system of social stratification defined by status, power, and class—especially economic class. This, however, is but one type of stratification system. A chief characteristic of this system is the idea that social positions are based on **achievement**, or the accomplishments—the merit—of the individual. For example, a person becomes a physician, and thereby attains a high-level position in the stratification system, only after many years of education, hard work, and practical experience. Conversely, some people believe that a person at or near the bottom of the stratification system is there because he or she lacks the accomplishments necessary to achieve a higher level. These people might suggest that a homeless person is homeless because that individual has not worked hard enough to earn a living wage. The idea that achievement determines social class is accurate to some extent, but the fact is that where a person ends up in the stratification system may have little or nothing to do with achievement. Instead, it can be explained by external factors over which the individual has little control.

A person's status usually has a great deal to do with **ascription**, or being born with, or inheriting, certain characteristics, such as race, gender, wealth, and high status (or, conversely, poverty and low status; Bond 2012). Thus, a person's position in the social hierarchy may be due to nothing more than the accident of being born a man or a woman,

FIGURE 8.10 • Educational Attainment and Earnings in the United States by Gender, 2012

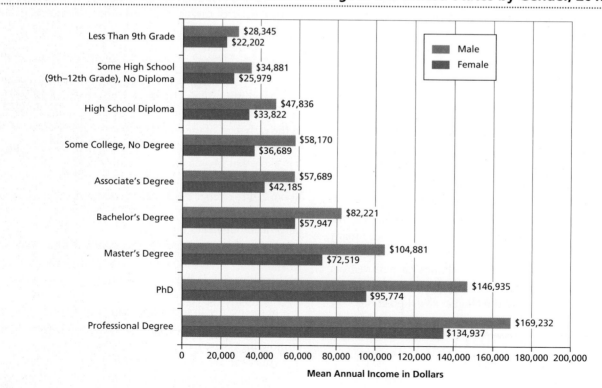

SOURCE: U.S. Bureau of the Census, 2013.

or black or white. At the extremes, ascribed status has little or nothing to do with a person's accomplishments, skills, or abilities. Further, once in a given position in the stratification system, a person is likely to remain in that position throughout his or her lifetime.

CHECKPOINT 8.3: TYPES OF SOCIAL MOBILITY

TYPE	DESCRIPTION
Vertical	Upward or downward movement through the social hierarchy
Horizontal	Movement within the same social class
Intergenerational	Movement by children to a different social class than their parents'
Intragenerational	Upward or downward movement over the course of one person's lifetime
Occupational	Changes in people's work across or within generations
Structural	Changes in the larger society that affect the positions of individuals in the stratification system

THEORIES OF SOCIAL STRATIFICATION

Within the sociology of social stratification, the dominant theoretical approaches are structural/functional theory and conflict/critical theory. These approaches are also involved in the major theoretical controversies within this area of sociological study (de Graaf 2007). Also to be discussed here are inter/actionist theories of stratification.

As in all areas of the social world, different theories focus on different aspects of social stratification. Instead of choosing one theory over another, it may make more sense to use all of them. Structural/functional and conflict/critical theories tell us much about the macro structures of stratification, while inter/actionist theories offer great detail about what goes on within those structures at the micro levels.

STRUCTURAL/FUNCTIONAL THEORIES

Within structural/functional theory, it is structural-functionalism that offers the most important—and controversial—theory of stratification. It argues that all societies are, and have been, stratified. Further, the theory contends that societies need a system of stratification in order to exist and to function properly (Davis and Moore 1945). Stratification is needed, first, to ensure that people are motivated to occupy the less pleasant, more difficult, and more important positions in society. Second, stratification is needed to ensure that people with the right abilities and talents find their way into the appropriate positions. In other words, society needs a good fit between people and the requirements of the positions they occupy.

The structural-functional theory of stratification assumes that higher-level occupations, such as physician and lawyer, are more important to society than are lower-level occupations, such as laborer and janitor. The higher-level positions are also seen as being harder to fill because of the difficulties and unpleasantness associated with them. For example, both physicians and lawyers require many years of rigorous and expensive education. Physicians are required to deal with blood, human organs, and death; lawyers have to defend those who have committed heinous crimes. It is argued that in order to motivate enough people to occupy such positions, greater rewards, such as prestige, sufficient leisure, and especially large amounts of money, need to be associated with them. The implication is that without these high rewards, high-level positions would remain understaffed or unfilled. As a result, structural-functionalists see the stratification system as functional for the larger society. In this case, it provides the physicians and lawyers needed by society.

CONFLICT/CRITICAL THEORIES

Conflict/critical theories tend to take a jaundiced view of stratified social structures because they involve and promote inequality. These theories are especially critical of the structural-functional perspective and its view that stratification is functional for society. Conflict/critical theories take a hard look at who benefits from the existing stratification system and how those benefits are perpetuated.

Critical theorists focus on the control that those in the upper levels of the stratification system exercise over culture (Kellner and Lewis 2007; Lash and Lury 2007). In contrast to Marx's emphasis on the economy, they see culture as of utmost importance in the contemporary world. Elites are seen as controlling such important aspects of culture as television and movies, and as seeking to exert increasing control over the internet and such major social networking sites as Facebook and Twitter. Elites use the media to send the kinds of messages that further their control. Furthermore, the amount of time that people lower in the stratification system are led to devote to TV, video games, movies, and the internet is so great that they have little time to mobilize and oppose, let alone overthrow, those in power.

ASK YOURSELF

Do you agree with the structural-functional perspective that stratification provides an important function for society? Or do you believe, as conflict/critical theorists do, that stratification exists to perpetuate benefits for the elite and expand their control? Justify your choice.

Social Rewards and Status

While critical theorists focus more on culture, conflict theorists are mainly concerned about social structure (Huaco 1966; Tumin 1953). Conflict theorists ridicule the idea that higher-level positions in the social structure would go unfilled were it not for the greater rewards they offer. They ask, for example, whether higher-level positions in the stratification system are less pleasant than those at the lower end of the continuum. Is being a surgeon really less pleasant than being a garbage collector? The argument being made by structural-functionalists seems preposterous to conflict theorists and to many others.

Conflict theorists accept the idea that higher-level positions, such as being a lawyer, may be more difficult than lower-level positions, such as being a garbage collector. However, they wonder whether higher-level positions are always more important. Is a lawyer who engages in shady deals or who defends environmental polluters more important than a garbage collector? In fact, the garbage collector is of great importance to society. Without garbage collectors, diseases that could seriously threaten society would develop and spread.

Conflict theorists also criticize the idea that those at the upper levels of the stratification system require the large rewards offered to them. Many people would be motivated to occupy such positions as CEO of a multinational corporation or hedge fund manager without such extraordinary rewards. Fewer economic rewards for those at the top, and more for those at the bottom, would reduce the economic gap and make for a more equal society. Conflict theorists also argue that providing huge sums of money is not the only way to motivate people to pursue an advanced education or whatever else is necessary to occupy high-ranking positions. For example, the status or prestige associated with those positions would be a strong motivator, as would the power that comes with them. It may even be that economic rewards motivate the wrong people to occupy these positions. That is, perhaps those who are motivated to become surgeons are more interested in maximizing their income than in doing right by their patients. Focusing on the nonmonetary rewards associated with making positive contributions to society would likely improve the way in which medicine, law, business, finance, and other high-status occupations function.

Gender, Race, and Class

Operating from another variant of conflict/critical theory, feminist theorists tend to focus on the issue of stratification in the work world. Because men owned the means of production in the development of capitalism, they gained positions of great power and prestige that yielded major economic rewards (Hartmann 1979). Women, by contrast, were

Despite some notable exceptions, such as Indra Nooyi, CEO of PepsiCo, women are still vastly underrepresented in the executive suite. How does feminist theory explain this imbalance?

relegated to subordinate positions. Over the years, women's position in the U.S. stratification system has improved with the entrance of more women into the workforce and greater legal protections against workplace gender discrimination. There are now many more women in such high-ranking positions as executive, physician, and lawyer. Yet, compared with men overall, women still occupy a subordinate position in the stratification system. They can also find it harder to rise very high in that system.

Feminist theorists have dealt with this issue under the heading of *occupational gender segregation,* or the unequal allocation of occupations to men and women (Reskin 1993). Women have been disadvantaged by occupational gender segregation in various ways. They have tended to get inferior occupational training and therefore to be hired at lower-level, lower-paying positions than men. Women have also tended to be hired, and to remain, in female-dominated occupations. These factors have led women into careers in which they do not rise as high in the employing organization and are not paid as much as men. Women are also likely to confront more problems in the day-to-day operations and procedures of their employing organizations. For example, organizational policies on day care are far more likely to have adverse effects on female employees than on male employees. Further, while males have been advantaged by their ability to engage in overwork and earn extra income (see the previous discussion), females, especially in male-dominated occupations, are likely to be disadvantaged, and even forced to leave the labor force entirely, because of excessive work-related demands (Cha 2013). Such factors are far more likely to impede women's career progress.

While the occupational situation for women has improved in recent years, the occupational world remains segregated on the basis of gender (Gauchat, Kelly, and

Wallace 2012). For example, women face a "motherhood penalty" (Budig, Misra, and Boeckman 2012, 2016; Correll, Benard, and Paik 2007) in the workplace that limits upward mobility among women with children. Mothers seeking jobs are less likely to be hired, are offered lower salaries, and are seen by others as less committed to the workplace. Illustrating how pervasive this penalty is, the wage gap between women without children and mothers is greater than the wage gap between men and women (Boushey 2008; Hausmann, Ganguli, and Viarengo 2009). Even women at the highest levels of the corporate world continue to face barriers unique to their gender. Recent research finds that women tend to boast less about their accomplishments and to give themselves lower self-ratings than do men. This internalized modesty about work performance contributes to lower upward mobility over and above external factors such as the glass ceiling (Hutson 2010; Smith and Huntoon 2014).

INTER/ACTIONIST THEORIES

From an inter/actionist theory perspective, social stratification is not a function of macro-level structures but of micro-level, individual actions and interactions. While both structural/functional and conflict/critical theorists see stratification as a hierarchical structure, inter/actionists see it as much more of a process or a set of processes. As a process, stratification involves interactions among people in different positions. Those who occupy higher-level positions may try to exert power in their interactions with those below them, but the latter can, and usually do, contest such exertions of power.

To the symbolic interactionist, inequality ultimately depends on face-to-face interaction. It is what happens in face-to-face interaction that leads to inequality. One symbolic interactionist approach identifies four processes that produce and reproduce inequality (Schwalbe et al. 2000). First, the dominant group defines the subordinate group into existence. Second, once in existence, the subordinate group finds ways of adapting to its situation. Third, efforts are made to maintain the boundaries between the two groups. Finally, both groups must manage the emotions associated with their positions in the stratification system. For example, those at the top must not show too much sympathy for those below them, and those at the bottom must not display too much anger toward those above them.

Symbolic interactionists see social stratification as much more fluid than do structural/functional and conflict/critical theorists. While the theories discussed previously focus mainly on economic factors, symbolic interactionists are more concerned about the struggle over things that are symbolically important to those at various positions in the stratification system. Those in higher-level positions define what they have as of great importance. Those below them may accept that definition and work to gain those symbols. However, the latter can also reject that definition and find or create other symbols that are of importance to theirs and that serve to elevate them and their positions. For example, those in lower-level positions may reject the long hours and high stress associated with higher-level positions. Instead, they may place a higher value on positions that involve less responsibility and offer more reasonable hours, and therefore more time to enjoy leisure activities.

Ethnomethodologists note that people may exist within a stratified structure, but what really matters is what they *do* within such a structure. As in other aspects of the social world, people use commonsense procedures to operate and make their way in such structures. These procedures are used by elites and the downtrodden alike to "do" their positions in the system. For example, elite members of society are likely to carry themselves with authority and self-importance. In contrast, those at the bottom rungs of the stratification system are more likely to appear overburdened and to slouch throughout the day. In other words, one of the ways in which people do stratification is in their body language.

People can and do use the system of stratification to accomplish their goals. On the one hand, elites may get others to do their bidding merely by acting in ways they think elite members of society should, along with sporting the trappings of their position, such as driving a luxury car. On the other hand, those at the bottom may use their position to extract handouts at street corners or from charitable agencies. Alternatively, they may use their position to obtain loans or scholarships that allow them to move up the stratification system.

Clearly, sociological theory regarding stratification entails a vibrant, ongoing discussion offering a variety of insights and perspectives.

CHECKPOINT 8.4: THEORIES OF SOCIAL TRENDING: STRATIFICATION

TYPE OF THEORY	MAIN HYPOTHESIS
Structural/functional theories	All societies need stratification to exist and to function properly.
Conflict/critical theories	Stratified social structures promote inequality and control by those in higher-level positions.
Inter/actionist theories	Social stratification is a function of micro-level individual actions and interactions among people in different positions.

TRENDING

Evicted: Poverty and Profit in the American City (Crown Publishers, 2016)

Matthew Desmond (John L. Loeb Associate Professor of the Social Sciences at Harvard University; PhD, University of Wisconsin–Madison, 2010)

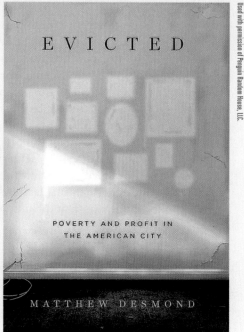

Used with permission of Penguin Random House, LLC.

....

Lack of access to safe and affordable housing is a serious problem in the United States, especially for poor families who are forced into the private rental market. Though many of us might assume that these families live in public or government-subsidized housing, most (67 percent) receive no federal assistance (Desmond 2016, 303). Matthew Desmond lived in a trailer park on the south side of Milwaukee and a rooming house on the north side of the city to better understand the relationship between renters who live at or below the poverty line and their landlords. He discovered that landlords can make a substantial profit from impoverished renters. Landlords hold considerable power over their poor tenants, charging them high rents for properties that have broken toilets or are infested with cockroaches. Tenants are reluctant to complain, because they fear that if they do, they will then be evicted. Even if they do not complain, millions of families across the country are evicted every year because they do not have enough income to make their rent payments on time.

Once a person is evicted, it can be difficult to find a new place to live; many landlords refuse to rent to someone with an eviction record, deeming it too risky.

The feminization of poverty is evident in Desmond's study: Women of color and their children are most likely to be evicted. But they are not alone. Whites, the elderly, widowers, people with physical and mental disabilities, and those addicted to opioids join their ranks. Many of these poor renters spend up to 70 or 80 percent of their income on housing, so they have little left for food, clothing, or utilities. The few personal possessions they do own are often lost when they are evicted—unless they can afford to put them in storage until they find new housing. In terms of stratified consumption, Desmond describes how landlords judge their tenants in terms of their personal possessions. If a tenant who is behind on her rent buys herself a new pair of shoes, the landlord might feel slighted and demand that the rent be paid immediately or threaten eviction. Tenants, however, also judge their landlords this way. A landlord who drives around in an expensive truck or wears what they consider to be too much jewelry might be viewed as greedy and not in need of rent payments. Yet landlords can also be generous, purchasing groceries for their tenants or letting them miss rent payments for a few months. This generosity, however, is mitigated by tenants enduring substandard housing, living in dangerous neighborhoods, and, most important, eventually paying their late rent. In sum, impoverished renters suffer from a variety of injustices because of a lack of affordable, quality housing in the United States.

Supplementary Resources

- You can watch Desmond discuss *Evicted* on C-SPAN BookTV at https://www .c-span.org/video/?405981-1/ evicted.

- Sociologist Barbara Ehrenreich explains the social significance of *Evicted* in her book review that appeared in *The New York Times:* http://www.nytimes .com/2016/02/28/books/review/ matthew-desmonds-evicted -poverty-and-profit-in-the -american-city.html?_r=0.

CONSUMPTION AND SOCIAL STRATIFICATION

Much of this chapter relates to issues of production and work, but social stratification is also related to consumption in various ways. For one thing, different positions in the stratification system involve differences in consumption. Most obviously, those in the upper classes are able to afford to consume products (such as yachts, Maserati automobiles, and Dom Pérignon champagne) and services (such as those provided by maids, chefs, and chauffeurs) that those in the middle and especially the lower classes cannot even contemplate. For another, the nature of consumption itself forms a stratification system. The consumption of certain sorts of things accords a higher position than does consumption of other kinds of things.

STRATIFIED CONSUMPTION

In addition to the class differences on cruise ships discussed previously, fashion is a good example of a stratified form of consumption. Georg Simmel ([1904] 1971) argued that those in higher levels of the stratification system continually seek to distinguish their consumption from that of those below them. This is evident in the realm of fashion, where the elites adopt new fashions, thereby displaying that they can afford the latest styles. However, elites soon find that those below

Kim Kardashian West epitomized the concept of conspicuous consumption when she carried a Hermès bag worth $120,000 to a casual lunch.

them have copied their fashions with cheaper, if not cheap, imitations. Thus, fashion, as well as other choices by elites, has a tendency to "trickle down" the social stratification ladder to the middle and eventually the lower classes. To distinguish themselves from the masses, elites must continually move on to new and different fashions. This phenomenon most obviously applies to fashions in clothing, but there are fashions in many other things as well, such as cars, homes, vacations, and even ideas (Lipovetsky [1987] 2002, 2005).

ASK YOURSELF

Do you think Simmel's concept of trickle-down fashion or Veblen's notion of conspicuous consumption is a more accurate description of the relationship between consumption and social stratification? Why? Can you provide examples to support your answer?

Simmel's contemporary Thorstein Veblen ([1899] 1994) also theorized about stratification and consumption. In Veblen's view, the elite members of society want to be "conspicuous." In the past, they had been conspicuous about their accomplishments in the work world, but over time, these feats became less and less visible as they came to be concealed by the walls of factories and office buildings. As a result, elites shifted more toward *conspicuous consumption,* wanting others to see what they were able to consume, especially those things that served to differentiate them from those in lower social classes (see Chapter 2). Thus, their money came to be invested in mansions, fancy furnishings, fine riding horses, expensive automobiles, designer dresses, and exquisite jewelry, because such things can easily be seen and admired by others.

This is a key difference between Simmel's and Veblen's theories. Simmel's concept of trickle-down fashion assumes that the middle and lower classes will, in a sense, copy the consumption patterns of the elite. In contrast, Veblen believed that because the things that the elite consume are very expensive, their consumption patterns cannot be copied so easily by those who rank lower in the stratification system. Therefore, elite status is expressed and solidified through conspicuous consumption. What appears to involve unnecessary expense has a payoff in supporting and enhancing the status of elites. In fact, in Veblen's view, the factor that distinguishes elites from others is their ability to engage in wasteful consumption.

SOCIAL CLASS AND TASTE

A person's taste in consumption also helps indicate the social class to which that person belongs. For example, if you read the *New York Times* (whether online or in hard copy), you are likely to be classified as being in the middle or upper class.

However, if you read *USA Today* or don't follow the news at all, you would be classified by most as standing lower in the stratification system. While taste can be demonstrated in the purchase and display of expensive consumer goods, it also can be shown much more subtly in the way in which one talks, the kind of music one listens to, and the books one reads. Good taste in these and other areas demonstrates and enhances the position of elite members of society. It supposedly shows that they have good breeding, come from a good family, and have a good education, and especially that they value things according to their merit and not simply because of how much they cost. Those without such taste, who have a taste for the necessary rather than the good taste of elites (Holt 2007)—in music, for example (Prior 2011)—are likely to be relegated to the lower reaches of the stratification system.

Taste must be considered not only in terms of how others classify you but also in terms of how you classify yourself through your demonstration of taste, lack of taste, or, more extremely, tastelessness. For example, at a formal business luncheon, wearing a conservative suit would show good taste, while wearing either a tuxedo or a sports jacket would show a lack of taste; being either over- or underdressed demonstrates a lack of taste regarding appropriate attire. A T-shirt and jeans would be considered completely tasteless for such an occasion and might result in your losing a business opportunity. Demonstrations of taste or tastelessness are not simply indications of individuality but also indications of linkages to the larger social world, especially the social class system.

The Quest for Distinction

Both Simmel and Veblen focus on the economic aspects of consumption, but a more contemporary sociologist, Pierre Bourdieu (1930–2002; 1984; Bennett et al. 2009), adds a cultural dimension to the analysis of consumption and stratification. What animates Bourdieu's work is the idea of **distinction**, the need to distinguish oneself from others. Both Simmel and Veblen address the desire of elites to distinguish their superior economic position through the wasteful things it enables them to buy. An example would be, as discussed previously, paying $30,000 per week for a suite on cruise ship that offers perfectly nice cabins for $4,000 and that takes everyone to the same ports of call. Although Bourdieu, too, recognizes the economic factors involved, Bourdieu adds the more cultural dimension of taste to the analysis of consumption and stratification (Gronow 2007; Marsh 2012). That is, elites seek to distinguish themselves from others by their good taste. With members of the lower classes constantly imitating the tastes of the upper classes, the latter are continually forced to find new ways to achieve distinction. In other words, in Bourdieu's view, in order to achieve distinction, elites are forced to become ever more refined, sophisticated, and exclusive in their tastes.

Perhaps the most important aspect of this work on distinction and taste is that it is closely related to struggles for

Pierre Bourdieu was a major intellectual figure of the twentieth century. His research in part focused on people's practices and developing theory related to those practices, which reflected some Marxist ideas that Bourdieu rejected early in his career but continued to express in his work. For instance, among his contributions is the idea that society's elites define high and low culture because they have won a power struggle with the masses.

power and position within the stratification system. On the one hand, elites use culture to obtain and maintain their position. They might do this by focusing on high culture, such as opera or art (see Chapter 4). Such taste helps elites gain high-level positions in the stratification system and make those below them accept their lesser positions in that system. The focus of elites on high culture serves to exclude the lower classes from higher-level positions in the stratification system by discouraging them from even thinking of trying to move into those positions. Even those from the lower classes who manage to acquire considerable wealth are often not likely to have or to develop the level of cultural sophistication needed to appreciate something like ballet. Like Marxian theorists, Bourdieu and his followers see the stratification system as an arena of ongoing struggle. However, while Marxists tend to see this as largely an economic struggle, Bourdieu sees it as a cultural struggle, although he certainly recognizes its economic aspects.

Elites as Cultural Omnivores

The idea of *cultural omnivores* (Katz-Gerro and Jaeger 2013; Peterson and Kern 1996) offers a very different view of the relationship among social class, consumption, and taste. From this perspective, elites are not seen as refined and exclusive in their tastes; they are not viewed as "snobs." Rather, they are seen as having very diverse tastes, ranging from those that are highly refined to those that are unrefined, even coarse. Their tastes are not exclusive but rather wide-ranging and inclusive. In other words, elites are omnivores who appreciate all sorts of things. Thus, elites might attend both the opera and kickboxing matches, might download highbrow books on their Kindles as well as pornography on their hard drives, and might buy both opera arias and country and western music from iTunes. In contrast, those in lower classes have been seen as having more limited tastes, which might be more oriented toward kickboxing, pornography, and country and western music; in other words, those in the lower classes are less likely to be omnivores. However, this is likely changing dramatically, as the lower classes, and non-elites more generally, are gaining access to much more highbrow (as well as lowbrow) culture on the internet. Similarly, elites have greater access to lowbrow (and highbrow) culture online than ever before.

Another example of the amalgamation of high and low culture is found in "fast fashion," a retailing strategy led by such Europe-based firms as H&M and Zara. Although they have become global firms, these brands are rooted in Europe because the fashion capitals of the world, the centers of expensive haute couture (high fashion), are there—in particular, Paris and Milan (Lipovetsky [1987] 2002). This is important because the styles of fast-fashion firms are heavily influenced by the creations of the world's great fashion houses. As soon as these creations are shown, they are quickly copied (Steele 2011), produced (Menkes 2008), and shipped rapidly around the world by the fast-fashion firms (Joy et al. 2012). The copies created by the fast-fashion companies are helping erode the difference between stratified tastes.

As we have seen, there are several contrasting views on the social stratification of consumption—on why people at various levels of society consume what they do. The overriding point, however, is that many people in the world, especially in the United States, are enmeshed in consumer culture. Whether we buy tickets to the ballet or a kickboxing match, we are participating in a highly stratified consumer culture.

CHECKPOINT 8.5: STRATIFIED CONSUMPTION

FORM OF STRATIFIED CONSUMPTION	DESCRIPTION
Trickle-down theory	Elites adopt a fashion that is copied by the classes below them, prompting elites to adopt a new fashion so that they can differentiate themselves.
Conspicuous consumption	Elites display their wealth and class position through consumer goods.
Distinction	Elites distinguish themselves from others by their cultural tastes.
Cultural omnivores	Elites possess a wide variety of tastes, not just refined ones.

SUMMARY

Social stratification results in hierarchical differences and inequalities. Three important dimensions of stratification are social class, status, and power. In the money-based stratification system in the United States, wealth and income are the main determinants of social class. Since the 1970s, the United States has experienced increasing income inequality. However, the greatest economic differences in U.S. society are due to differences in wealth. People with great wealth often have high class, status, and power and can usually pass most of these advantages to future generations. Those who have little have a difficult time amassing their own wealth. The middle class in the United States has declined in recent decades, leaving a large hole in the stratification system between the lower and the upper classes. In the United States, the measure of absolute poverty is the poverty line, the level of income that people are thought to need in order to survive in our society. Members of minority groups, women, and children are overrepresented among the poor.

While individuals in the United States have generally experienced intergenerational upward mobility, it seems likely that young people in the twenty-first century will experience more downward mobility. Sociologists are also concerned about structural mobility, or changes in the occupational structure.

Structural-functional theories of stratification argue that societies need a system of stratification in order to function properly. Conflict theorists challenge this assumption, particularly the idea that positions at the higher end of the stratification system are always more important. Finally, symbolic interactionists view stratification as a process or set of interactions among people in different positions.

Social stratification is related to consumption in a number of ways. Those in the higher classes can afford expensive items that those in the lower classes cannot. Elites use their patterns of consumption to distinguish themselves, sometimes conspicuously, from those beneath them.

KEY TERMS

absolute poverty, 217
achievement, 222
ascription, 222
distinction, 228
feminization of
   poverty, 219

horizontal mobility, 221
income, 207
inequality, 206
intergenerational
   mobility, 221
occupational mobility, 221

poverty line, 217
power, 205
relative poverty, 217
social class, 204
social mobility, 220
social stratification, 204

status consistency, 206
status inconsistency, 206
structural mobility, 221
symbolic exchange, 207
vertical mobility, 221
wealth, 207

REVIEW QUESTIONS

1. According to Max Weber, what are the various dimensions of social stratification? What are some examples of people who rank high on each of these dimensions? Other than the examples discussed in the chapter, can you identify individuals who are status-inconsistent?

2. How does the system of social stratification in the United States differ from the symbolic exchange system of stratification discussed by Jean Baudrillard? How are the two systems of social stratification related to values in society?

3. What is the difference between income and wealth? Which is more important to explaining the differences between the haves and the have-nots? Why?

4. How has inequality in the United States changed since the 1970s? In what ways are the explanations for these trends related to globalization?

5. What has happened to the U.S. middle class in recent decades? What accounts for the change?

6. What are the differences between absolute and relative poverty? How can we use inter/actionist theories to understand relative poverty?

7. What do we mean when we refer to the feminization of poverty? What factors help explain the position of women in the system of social stratification?

8. How has the nature of individual social mobility in the United States changed since the 1900s, and in what ways are these changes related to structural mobility?

9. According to structural-functional theories, how is inequality beneficial to society? How can the income and wealth of celebrities and sports stars be used as a criticism of this model?

10. How does access to the internet and new technologies relate to the system of stratification? How can the internet be used to alter the system of stratification?

PRACTICE AND APPLY WHAT YOU'VE LEARNED

▶ **edge.sagepub.com/ritzerintro4e**

CHECK YOUR COMPREHENSION ON THE STUDY SITE WITH:

- **Diagnostic pre-tests** to identify opportunities for improvement.

- **Personalized study plans** with focused recommendations to address specific knowledge gaps and additional learning needs.

- **Post-tests** to check your progress and ensure mastery of key learning objectives.

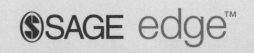

CHEESEBURGER

10 KR

CRISPY CHICKEN

20 KR

GLOBAL STRATIFICATION

Something Is Right in Denmark

Hampus Elofsson has a low-skill service job at a Burger King in Copenhagen. At the end of his workweek, he makes sure his bills are paid, enjoys a night out with friends, and even sets aside some money for savings. He can afford to do this because he earns $20 per hour, the base salary for a fast-food worker in Denmark. As Elofsson notes, "You can make a decent living here working in fast food. You don't have to struggle to get by."

The benefits for fast-food workers in Denmark do not end there. They also enjoy five weeks of paid vacation each year, full health insurance (Denmark has universal health care), paid maternity and paternity leave, a pension plan, and overtime pay for working after 6:00 p.m. and on Sundays. These benefits contrast sharply with the wages and benefits of fast-food workers in the United States, who earn an average of $8.90 per hour. For example, Anthony Moore is a shift manager at a Burger King near Tampa, Florida, where he earns $9.00 per hour. He works 35 hours per week, and his weekly take-home pay is about $300. While his daughters, ages two and five, qualify for Medicaid, he has no health insurance. He says he sometimes asks him-self, "Do I buy food or do I buy them clothes?" His earnings are often not enough to pay his electricity and water bills. Moore's situation is illustrative of other workers' experiences in low-wage work in the United States, where workers do not earn enough money to meet basic living expenses, let alone to set aside any savings. One in five U.S. households with a family member working in fast food lives below the poverty line. Wages in the fast-food industry in the United States are so low that more than half of the industry's workers rely on some sort of public assistance.

Note: Paul Dean coauthored this chapter; his help is much appreciated.

LEARNING OBJECTIVES

9.1 Identify positions in global stratification.

9.2 Describe forms of global equality.

9.3 Discuss the changing positions in global stratification.

9.4 Summarize theories of global stratification.

9.5 Explain how consumption is connected to global stratification.

edge.sagepub.com/ritzerintro4e

- Take the chapter quiz
- Review key terms with eFlashcards
- Explore multimedia links and SAGE readings

$SAGE edge™

The reasons for such vast differences across countries are complex. One of the most important factors is that in contrast with workers in the United States, all fast-food workers in Denmark are represented by a union that bargains for their wages and benefits. The union agrees not to participate in strikes, demonstrations, and boycotts in exchange for higher wages and benefits. Companies like Burger King, McDonald's, and other fast-food chains still earn a profit in Denmark, but their profits are not as high as they are in the United States. Other laws and regulations in Denmark, such as universal health care, further help workers. ●

Immanuel Wallerstein's world-systems theory focuses on the world as the unit of analysis, rather than discrete nations.

The inequality in the global fast-food industry described in the vignette pales in comparison to the broader levels of global inequalities. This chapter examines many of these inequalities, including how they originated and how they are changing. Building on Chapter 8, which focused on social stratification in the United States, we shift here to the global level to understand how wealth, income, status, and power are distributed unevenly throughout the world. As is clear in the theories of Immanuel Wallerstein (b. 1930; 1974), nations of the world form a stratified system. At the top are those that tend to be better off economically, to wield great power in many parts of the world, and to be looked up to around the globe. Conversely, the nations at the bottom of the global stratification system are likely to be very poor, to have little power outside (and perhaps even inside) their borders, and to be looked down upon by many throughout the world. Global stratification is a macro-level phenomenon that has profound effects at the micro level of individuals and their relationships and opportunities. As you read this chapter, you should consider how you fit into this global stratification structure. How have the circumstances of your birth, not only within your own country but also within the world, shaped your life chances?

POSITIONS IN GLOBAL STRATIFICATION

THE GLOBAL NORTH AND SOUTH

Stratification on the global level is often seen as a divide between those nation-states located in the Northern Hemisphere (more specifically, the north temperate climate zone), or the Global North, and those located in the tropics and Southern Hemisphere, or the Global South (Williams, Meth, and Willis 2014). For centuries, the North has dominated, controlled, exploited, and oppressed the South. Today the North encompasses the nations that are the wealthiest

and most powerful, and have the highest status in the world, such as the United States, China, Germany, France, Great Britain, and Japan. The South, on the other hand, has a disproportionate number of nations that rank at or near the bottom in terms of global wealth, power, and prestige. Most of the nations of Africa and South America would be included here, as well as others, especially in Asia, such as Yemen.

A society's position in the global stratification system greatly affects the stratification within that society. A nation that stands at or near the top of the global stratification system, such as the United States, has a large proportion of middle- and upper-class positions. In contrast, a low-ranking nation, like Somalia, is dominated by lower-class positions and the poverty associated with them. The problems associated with this stratification system have been recognized by institutions such as the International Monetary Fund, which distributes funds from countries in the Global North to those in the Global South.

While the terms *Global North* and *Global South* are widely used to describe positions within the global hierarchy, they do not always clearly relate to positions on the world map. For example, Australia is in the Southern Hemisphere, but is clearly part of the Global North economically. Similarly, there are several very poor countries (e.g., Afghanistan) in the Northern Hemisphere that are economically part of the Global South. This is one of several reasons why some analysts prefer to differentiate countries in terms of average income per person.

HIGH-, MIDDLE-, AND LOW-INCOME COUNTRIES

The wide variation among and between countries is hidden when they are simply categorized as part of either the Global North or the Global South. For example, countries in the same category may have more or less inequality. The United States and France are generally placed in the same category (Global

North, high income), but the United States has a greater percentage of people at the bottom of the stratification system living in poverty than France does. Similarly, Vietnam and Nigeria are in the same category (Global South, middle income), but Nigeria has a larger number of wealthy elites than does Vietnam. In other words, the level of income inequality within Nigeria is far greater than that in Vietnam. Argentina has a high standard of living compared with the immense poverty found in many African countries, such as Sudan. However, both countries are considered to be part of the Global South. The Global North–South dichotomy ignores many of the important economic (and political) differences between nations within each category, Global North or Global South. Furthermore, whatever a country's category may be, immense economic inequalities exist between strata within the country, making daily life very different for the inhabitants at different levels.

A slightly more nuanced category system focuses on low-income, middle-income, and high-income economies (and their countries; see Figure 9.1; Ferrarini and Nelson 2016). As a general rule, low-income countries are concentrated in the Global South, while high-income countries are found in the Global North. Middle-income countries exist in both parts of the world, but a disproportionate number of them are in the Global South.

High-income economies exist in countries with the highest incomes in the world. Countries with gross national income (GNI) per capita of $12,476 are in this category (World Bank 2015a). Currently, 79 countries have GNI that high or higher. As a result, they occupy lofty positions in the global hierarchy. They include countries long considered part of the Global North (e.g., the United States, Canada, Japan, and those in Western Europe). However, they also include countries that are traditionally thought of as part of the Global South, including Chile and Uruguay (South America), Equatorial Guinea (Central Africa), and Oman (Middle East). Some of these countries have been considered to have high-income economies since the Industrial Revolution, while others (e.g., Japan) have industrialized—and grown wealthy—more recently. Still other high-income countries are not yet highly industrialized but derive their income from natural resources, such as oil (e.g., Equatorial Guinea and Oman). The levels of wealth in the latter countries offer a standard of living unimagined in many other parts of the world.

Middle-income economies are found in countries that have average levels of income on a global level. Countries are placed in this category if they have a GNI per capita between $1,026 and $12,475. This encompasses a significant range that begins at or near the bottom of per capita income, with the Kyrgyz Republic in central Asia (average GNI of $1,200 per capita), and includes Cabo (Cape) Verde and Sudan (Africa), Nicaragua (Central America), and Vietnam (Asia). Toward the top of this range are upper-middle-income countries including Argentina and Brazil (South America), Cuba (Central America), South Africa, and Thailand (Asia). The World Bank considers 108 countries to be in the

FIGURE 9.1 • High-Income, Middle-Income, and Low-Income Economies

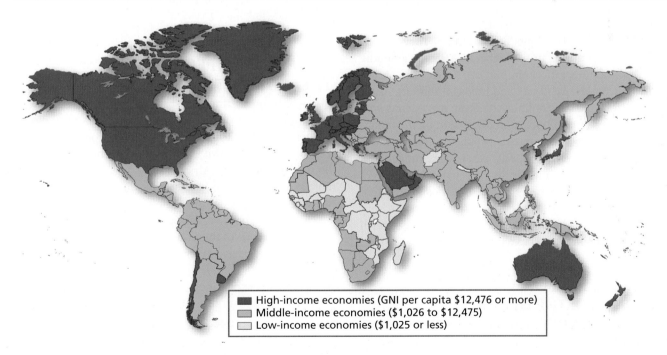

High-income economies (GNI per capita $12,476 or more)
Middle-income economies ($1,026 to $12,475)
Low-income economies ($1,025 or less)

SOURCE: Data from World Bank.

STEPHANE DE SAKUTIN/AFP/Getty Images

While social stratification involves the relative positions of people within a society, global stratification demonstrates that widespread poverty and lack of opportunity can leave an entire nation near the bottom of the global pecking order. This boy is on his way to collect water in an encampment in Madagascar.

a focus on such relationships tends to obscure the full extent of global inequality. A recent report by the global charity Oxfam offers a stunning picture of the concentration of wealth in the world (Hardoon 2015): As of 2015, the richest 1 percent of people in world owned 50 percent of the wealth. That left only exactly half—50 percent—for the other 99 percent of the world's population. Furthermore, Oxfam has projected that the top 1 percent may soon have *more wealth* than everyone else in the world combined. Even more extreme, the 62 richest people in the world (among the top are four U.S. men, Bill Gates, Warren Buffett, Jeff Bezos, and Mark Zuckerburg) are worth $1.76 trillion, about the same as the poorest 3.6 billion people in the world combined.

The situation is growing ever more unequal. Since 2010, the wealth of the world's wealthiest 62 people has risen by 44 percent ($542 billion), while the wealth of the bottom 50 percent declined by 41 percent in that same time. In 2014, all of those in the lowest 10 percent of the world's population are in debt. Further, no individual in the lowest 50 percent has more than $3,650 in assets (Wolfers 2015). Said Oxfam's executive director: "Do we really want to live in a world where 1 percent own more than the rest of us combined? . . . The scale of global inequality is quite simply staggering" (P. Cohen 2015).

middle-income category. Many countries in this range, such as China (and most of Asia), began industrializing relatively recently (the 1970s or later). Other middle-income countries were formerly communist countries. They were highly, albeit primitively, industrialized, but they declined industrially and economically after the collapse of the Soviet Union in the late 1980s.

Low-income economies are in countries that are home to many of the world's poorest people, have very little of the world's wealth, and are largely agrarian societies with low levels of industry. The World Bank counts 31 low-income countries with GNI per capita below $1,025. They include many of the countries in sub-Saharan Africa, Cambodia and North (Democratic Republic of) Korea (East Asia), Afghanistan and Nepal (Asia), and Haiti (Caribbean). As we will see later, scholars continue to debate the reasons why these countries remain poor. Compared with their counterparts in higher-income countries, people in these countries are much more likely to experience disease, hunger, and malnutrition and have a lower life expectancy. Increasingly, they are moving into densely populated cities in search of economic opportunities, only to find themselves in very crowded and unsafe living conditions. They constitute much of the "bottom billion," to be examined further below.

THE RICHEST PEOPLE IN THE WORLD: THE GLOBAL CONCENTRATION OF WEALTH

There is certainly great inequality between the North and the South, or between high-income and low-income countries, but

THE POOREST PEOPLE IN THE WORLD: THE BOTTOM BILLION

Also worth considering is the broader category that includes the world's poorest people—the "bottom billion" of global residents (Collier 2007, forthcoming; Murphy and Walsh 2014). The vast majority (70 percent) of the people in the bottom billion are in Africa, but countries such as Haiti, Bolivia, and Laos also have significant numbers of people who are part of the bottom billion.

Wherever they live, the bottom billion have incomes of only about a fifth of those in other countries in the Global South. They also have many other serious problems, such as

- A low life expectancy of about 50 years (the average is 67 in other nations in the Global South)

- A high infant mortality rate (14 percent of the bottom billion die before their fifth birthday, versus 4 percent in other countries in the Global South)

- A higher likelihood of malnourishment (36 percent of the bottom billion show symptoms of malnutrition, as opposed to 20 percent in other countries in the Global South; Collier 2007)

The nations in which most of the bottom billion live rank at or near the bottom of the global stratification system. These countries are extremely poor (with low incomes), exert little or no power on the global stage, and have little prestige. Furthermore, their situations worsened in recent years as a result of the global recession (Alexander 2010). In addition, many of their best-trained and most productive people are migrating to high-income countries in the Global North (Collier 2013). However, these nations still aspire to move up the global ladder.

Some of the bottom billion who live in middle-income countries, such as India and especially China, have had great success in recent decades in improving their positions in the global stratification system. By developing economically, some people within India and China have moved out of the bottom billion, although the pace of such upward movement has slowed in India. However, most nations at the bottom face huge, if not insurmountable, barriers to improving their positions, including frequent conflicts with neighbors, civil wars, and revolutions (Collier 2007). They are also likely to have experienced one bad government after another. Some, like Somalia, Yemen, and Libya, are "failed states" that have virtually no national government and, as a result, have lost control of much, or even all, of their own countries. Perhaps of greatest importance is the fact that the situation in such countries has grown worse in recent years, and there could now be far more than 1 billion people experiencing desperate poverty (Murphy and Walsh 2014). Many have fallen further behind not only the Global North but the others in the Global South as well.

CHECKPOINT 9.1: POSITIONS IN GLOBAL STRATIFICATION

LEVELS OF GLOBAL STRATIFICATION	DESCRIPTION
Global North and South	The Global North encompasses the wealthiest and most powerful nations. They dominate the South, which has little or no power.
High-, middle-, and low-income economies	High-income economies have a GNI per capita of $12,746 or more, middle-income economies have a GNI per capita between $1,046 and $12,745, and low-income economies have a GNI per capita below $1,046.
The richest people in the world	The richest 1 percent own 48 percent of the world's wealth.
The bottom billion	The bottom billion have incomes one-fifth of those in the Global South.

GLOBAL ECONOMIC INEQUALITIES

THE GLOBAL DIGITAL DIVIDE

According to the most recent statistics, there were about 3.5 billion internet users worldwide at the end of 2016, and that number will certainly continue to grow (www.statista.com/statistics/273018/number-of-internet-users-worldwide/). At least theoretically, the internet allows for participation by anyone, anywhere in the global, digital economy. However, in reality there is a daunting and persistent global digital divide (Drori 2006, 2012; Pick and Sarkar 2015). The International Telecommunications Union found that the percentages of individuals using the internet in 2016 remained very low in many low-income countries in the Global South, such as Ethiopia (4.2 percent), Tanzania (5.3 percent), Cambodia (11.1 percent), Iraq (13 percent), Haiti (12.1 percent), and Nicaragua (19.4 percent). Compare these figures with the Global North, the world's most developed countries, where internet usage is usually above 80 percent, including in the United States (88.5 percent), Australia (85.1 percent), Germany (88 percent), Finland (92.5 percent), Denmark (96.3 percent), and Sweden (93.1 percent). Figure 9.2 shows the difference in internet access between households in the developed world (Global North) and those in the developing world (Global South).

The main barrier to global equality in access to, and use of, the internet, and information and communications technology (ICT) more generally, is the lack of infrastructure within the less developed countries of the Global South. Also important are the low incomes in those areas that make complex digital technologies, and therefore access to the internet, prohibitively expensive (Wakefield 2013). Language represents another source of inequality on the internet. Most websites are in English, and increasingly in Chinese, as well as eight other languages (see Figure 9.3); comparatively few sites are in the world's other languages (Bowen 2001; EnglishEnglish.com, n.d.). Clearly, those who do not speak any of these 10 languages—the overwhelming majority of whom live in the Global South—are at a huge disadvantage on the internet. They may even find the internet completely inaccessible because of the language barrier. Those who are illiterate are even worse off in a world increasingly dominated by the internet.

However, there are signs that the digital divide is being reduced. This was clear, for example, in the wide-scale use of social media in the 2010–2011 Arab Spring revolutions in Tunisia, Libya, and especially Egypt (see Chapters 1 and 18). More recently, the narrowing of the digital divide has been evidenced by the adept use of the internet by the terrorist organization calling itself the Islamic State of Iraq and

FIGURE 9.2 • Percentage of Households with Internet Access by Level of Development, 2002–2016

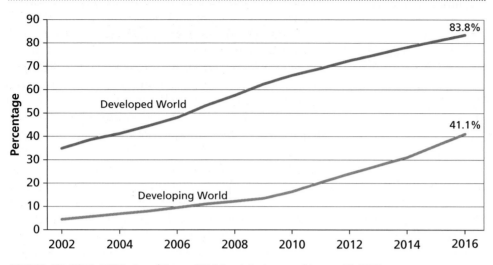

SOURCE: ITU. 2016. "ICT Facts and Figures 2016," p. 4. Last accessed January 30, 2017.

Syria (ISIS) to, for example, disseminate video of people being beheaded and, in 2015, being burned alive in cages. ISIS is also adept at using social media to recruit supporters throughout the world (Shane and Hubbard 2014). The United States has struck back by using (of course) social media to lure people away from ISIS: "These new efforts include using Facebook videos, Instagram ads and other social media that have been designed to convince young men and women that joining the militants' fight means breaking their mothers' hearts, tearing apart their families and leaving their loved ones to lives of emptiness" (Cooper 2016).

The digital divide is beginning to be bridged by the rising accessibility of relatively simple and inexpensive smartphones, laptops, and tablets that are essentially minicomputers. Industry analysts indicate that mobile internet access is ramping up significantly faster than desktop internet access ever did.

An important reason for the rapid expansion of mobile access is that mobile devices are not only relatively inexpensive; they also do not require the expensive, hardwired infrastructure needed by traditional computers and computer systems. Cellular signals provide internet access at increasingly high speeds. Some nations have avoided having to build fixed phone line systems by moving straight to mobile phone technology. Figure 9.4 shows the growth of mobile-broadband subscriptions based on level of development worldwide. More leapfrogging of the use of computers and traditional computer systems and the further adoption of smartphones instead promises to greatly reduce the global digital divide in a relatively short period. In the future, much of the Global South will also be able to leapfrog stages of other kinds of technological development that were required in the Global North. For example, some countries in the Global South (South Africa, Ghana, Kenya) have leapt straight to solar power rather than erecting huge power plants run by coal, oil, or nuclear energy (Amankwah-Amoah 2015, 16). By adopting solar energy, these countries avoid the enormous infrastructure investments needed for diesel generators, transmission lines, distribution networks, and transformers. They are able to provide solar energy at a fraction of the cost of the energy produced by diesel generators.

FIGURE 9.3 • Most Frequently Used Languages for Internet Sites, 2016

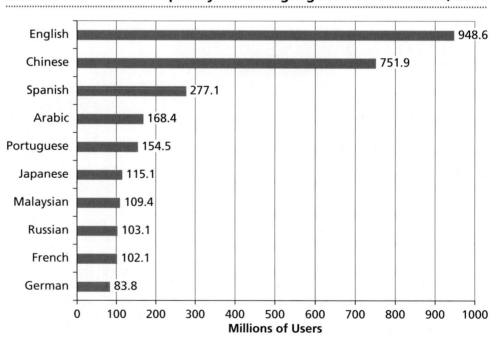

SOURCE: Data from Internet World Stats. 2016.

FIGURE 9.4 • Mobile Broadband
Subscriptions, 2016

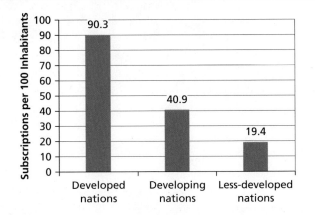

SOURCE: ICT Facts and Figures. The World in 2016. ITU World Telecommunication/ICT Indicators database. Reprinted with permission.

GLOBAL HEALTH INEQUALITY

While globalization has been associated with increased aggregate life expectancy throughout the world, it also has tended to widen global disparities in lifespan and in health (Hashemian and Yach 2007; Vogli et al. 2014; Winchester et al. 2016; see also Chapter 16). For example, Johns, Cowling, and Gakidou (2013) found that the widening gap between the world's rich and poor is continuing to increase differences in life expectancy. According to the World Health Organization (2016), the average life expectancy of newborns in high-income countries is at least eighty years. In contrast, newborns in sub-Saharan African counties will live less than sixty years on average. Economic inequality drives many of these health disparities.

Those in poor nations tend to have poorer health as a result of limited access to health services, education, sanitation, adequate nutrition, and housing. In turn, the poor health of residents tends to limit economic growth in those nations, mainly by adversely affecting productivity. The Global South has a disproportionate share of mortality and morbidity, much of which could be prevented inexpensively and treated effectively if the money were available to do so. Of the total burden of disease in the world, 90 percent is concentrated in low- and middle-income countries, which account for only 10 percent of health care expenditures. Similarly, only 10 percent of research money in the United States is devoted to the health problems that account for 90 percent of the global disease burden (Al-Tuwaijri et al. 2003). Furthermore, the Global South has lower levels of education, which lessens the likelihood of residents' knowing about preventive strategies and obtaining knowledge about how to control their own health (Rinaldo and Ferraro 2012). The improvements that have been seen in the Global South tend to be in those countries (e.g., Brazil, Egypt,

Malaysia) that are more deeply integrated in the global economy and have become, or are becoming, middle-income countries. However, for most of the rest, especially the low-income countries, globalization has brought with it a decline in economic growth, an increase in poverty, and, as a result, a decline in health.

Countries in the Global South also suffer disproportionately from hunger and malnutrition (Serra-Majem and Ngo 2012). Roughly 850 million people there are affected by these problems, and "19 countries suffer from levels of hunger that are either 'alarming' or 'extremely alarming'" (von Grebmer et al. 2013, 3). Recent political catastrophes have led to hunger crises in 2016 in Syria, the Ukraine, Chad, Mali, the Central African Republic, and South Sudan, among others. Environmental crises, such as droughts and hurricanes, are other major causes of people going hungry. Hunger involves inadequate or almost totally unavailable food supplies and a lack of assured and continual access to food, as well as poor and unbalanced diets. These problems are especially important for children, who are likely to die young from malnutrition. Poor nutrition causes nearly half of all child deaths in the world (Reuters 2016a). Furthermore, those children who survive even though their growth is stunted because of a lack of food are likely to be less physically and intellectually productive when they become adults, and to suffer more chronic illnesses and disabilities. This pattern carries on intergenerationally, as the ability of such adults to provide adequate nutrition for their children is compromised.

To complicate matters, there is a dramatic increase in obesity among other segments of the poor in the Global South (Global Nutrition Report 2016; McNeil Jr. 2016). It is estimated that there are 41 million overweight children under five years of age in the world today, an increase of 10 million from 1990 (Reuters 2016a). Those in the Global South are therefore now increasingly likely to suffer from a "double nutritional burden"—that is, some do not have enough to eat, and others eat too much, especially of the wrong kinds of foods (e.g., foods that are high in fat and cholesterol).

Finally, poor countries are less likely to provide extensive health care for their populations. Low-income countries tend to have fewer hospitals, less capacity for research on health and disease, and fewer people covered by medical insurance programs. These problems can be addressed through economic growth when national governments prioritize spending on health care. For example, the World Health Organization reported that in just four years, China added 172 million previously uninsured people to its health coverage programs. Coverage in rural areas, where poverty is especially high, increased from 10 percent to 97 percent. From 2009 to 2013, the Chinese government built 2,400 county-level hospitals and more than 40,000 grassroots medical facilities, dramatically expanding health coverage. This can be contrasted with India, which, despite its significant economic growth, has done little to extend health coverage to its poor.

Differences between countries in health care were especially apparent during the outbreak of Ebola from 2013 to 2015. Ebola hemorrhagic fever is a deadly viral disease, killing between 50 percent and 90 percent of those who contract it. It is not spread by casual contact, but rather through direct contact with the blood, body fluids, and tissues of those infected with the disease. It can also occur through the handling of chimpanzees with the disease or those that have died from it. The most recent outbreak of Ebola, and the largest in history, began in several West African countries (mostly in Guinea, Liberia, and Sierra Leone) in 2014. In the end, 28,600 people were infected by the Ebola

The extent of inequality in access to health care around the world was made starkly apparent by the 2015 outbreak of the deadly and highly contagious Ebola virus in Africa. While stricken medical workers evacuated to the West were likely to survive, inadequate diagnostic and treatment facilities and even lack of information and transportation were blamed for the thousands of deaths that occurred in Africa before the epidemic subsided. Here a health worker sprays a dying man with disinfectant on a Liberian road while a crowd looks on.

virus and 11,300 died from it (Benko 2016). The figures on Ebola cases and deaths included many medical workers treating Ebola patients, among them more than 300 medical workers who died in West Africa (Fink 2014). One man, who contracted the disease and traveled from Liberia to Dallas, Texas, before he was diagnosed, died from Ebola in the United States. Two medical workers who contracted the disease in the United States recovered. People who contracted the disease in West Africa were also successfully treated in Germany, Norway, France, Italy, Switzerland, and the United Kingdom ("Ebola" 2014). Some who contracted the disease in Africa died in spite of being transferred to U.S. and European hospitals for treatment, but others recovered.

As was the case in the past, it is likely that outbreaks of Ebola will occur again in the future. In fact, isolated cases continued to be reported in 2016. There are ongoing efforts to find a vaccine (Gladstone 2016a). However, practicing basic hygiene—such as routine hand washing and avoiding contact with blood and bodily fluids—holds out the best hope of dealing with the spread of the disease, at least in the short run.

Much in the news in 2016 was the mosquito-borne Zika outbreak in South America. The disease causes babies still in the womb to suffer from microcephaly and to be born with abnormally small heads. Microcephaly will cause these children many mental problems (retardation, brain damage) and a variety of other health problems as they mature. Many of them will die prematurely. After

outbreaks in Africa as recently as 2015, Zika arrived in Puerto Rico and southern Florida in the middle of 2016 (Belluck 2016). The ability of the United States to afford large-scale public awareness campaigns about the dangers posed to pregnant women, as well as vigorous efforts at mosquito control, are likely to limit its effects there.

The differences across countries in the experiences of people infected with Zika and Ebola reveal how global stratification shapes health inequalities. Guinea, Liberia, and Sierra Leone are all low-income countries with weak health care systems. Compared with high-income countries, they have fewer trained doctors (many doctors who are sufficiently trained are enticed to work in high-income countries, where they can earn higher salaries), fewer resources to expend on fighting an outbreak, and far fewer people covered by health care systems. As such, these countries are more prone to outbreaks, and individuals in them are more likely to die when outbreaks occur. To make matters worse for these members of the "bottom billion," these types of outbreaks involve a self-perpetuating cycle. Margaret Chan, director-general of the World Health Organization, warned that the Ebola virus could deliver a "potentially catastrophic blow" to the economies of the countries involved (Gettleman 2014; O'Grady 2014). While it was predicted that all affected countries would be devastated by the Ebola outbreak, it negatively affected three African countries (Guinea, Liberia, and Sierra Leone). Initial evidence was that the economies of these countries were, in fact, badly hurt (Nossiter 2014). During such outbreaks, the economies of poor countries are adversely affected because money that could be used elsewhere (such as on new industries) is instead spent fighting the disease. In addition, the labor force is negatively affected by deaths, illness, and fear of contracting the disease. Borders are sealed, often unnecessarily, hurting cross-border commerce. In the case of Zika, South American nations such as Brazil struggled with preventive measures and treatment for those affected, while the government of the wealthier United States had the luxury of arguing over how to respond.

It is worth noting that a society's wealth does not always correspond to health coverage or better health outcomes. For example, the United States spends the most in the world on health care, but it ranks significantly lower than other high-income countries on a number of public health indicators. Compared with their counterparts in other high-income countries, Americans tend to live shorter lives, are more likely to experience violent deaths, are more likely to be obese, and have higher rates of many diseases. Unlike the residents of all other countries in the Global North, many Americans (particularly those with low incomes) do not have health coverage.

Twenty million more Americans gained health care coverage with the implementation of the Affordable Care Act (widely known as Obamacare), and the number of uninsured Americans decreased dramatically (Pear 2016). Nevertheless, just over 10 percent of Americans (28.5 million) still lacked health insurance in 2015. Although the Trump administration promises to replace the plan with something new (and "better"), that number could rise if the administration succeeds in its promise to rescind the Affordable Care Act.

The United States is also one of the most economically unequal among high-income countries. Research shows that the greater the economic inequality in a country, the lower the health of its overall population (Pickett and Wilkinson 2011). With a highly inefficient private health insurance system, Americans pay more money for lower-quality health care.

GLOBAL WASTE AND THE CHUREQUEROS

The flows and uses of waste, or garbage, are also indicative of global stratification. For example, all parts of the world produce garbage that is dangerous, at least potentially. Examples of concern here include electronic waste, or e-waste, such as discarded television sets, computers, printers, and cell phones. However, it is the highly developed countries of the Global North, with their higher rates of consumption, that produce a disproportionate amount of such waste. Once products have outlived their usefulness (or even long before that) and are disposed of as waste, those in high-income countries want no more to do with them. They seek to send much of this waste to low-income

countries, which, for their part, are anxious to receive the garbage because it can be transformed into work, jobs, and profits. Very often the waste that is unloaded on these countries includes valuable components and elements (gold, silver, copper) that are difficult and time-consuming to extract. From the perspective of global corporations and governments, the poorly paid workers of low-income countries are ideal for this unskilled work. Few in high-income countries want to do this work, especially for the pay that those in low-income countries receive.

Some individuals and families in the Global South exist in situations so dire that they actually *live and work* in garbage dumps. In Managua, the capital of Nicaragua, there is one official garbage dump that receives 1,200 tons of garbage daily (another 300 tons of garbage each day end up in drainage ditches and in hundreds of illegal garbage dumps around the city; Hartmann 2013). The official dump is not filled with garbage from wealthier countries; rather, it is a municipal dump, fueled by urbanization and the spread of "global throwaway culture." Known as La Chureca, the dump covers 116 acres and is home to more than 250 families, who live near or literally on top of the garbage. Another 1,500 men, women, and children come to La Chureca daily to pick through its garbage. The *churequeros* (trash pickers) look through the garbage in search of recyclables that they can sell, as well as discarded food, clothing, and other goods for their personal consumption (for a chilling video of working conditions in La Chureca, see https://www.youtube.com/watch?v=ebSWvKO2TIs). This form of extreme poverty obviously exposes the *churequeros* to a variety of health risks. To make matters worse, the dump was not subject to any regulations for approximately four decades. As a result, it has contaminated the air, water, and soil, leading to a variety of health problems for others throughout Managua. To put all this in context: Managua's *churequeros* are part of an estimated 64 million people in the Global South who make their livings by picking through solid waste (Medina 2007).

GENDER STRATIFICATION

Inequality in Employment, Occupations, and Wealth

While men's labor force participation rates worldwide have decreased slightly over the last several decades, a notable increase has occurred in women's labor force participation, particularly in the Americas and Western Europe. There are significant variations within and across regions, but women's labor force participation has also risen substantially in sub-Saharan Africa, North Africa, Eastern Europe, Southeast Asia, and East Asia over this period (Cagatay and Ozler 1995; Elborgh-Woytek et al. 2016; Heintz 2006; Kivisto and Faist 2010; Moghadam 1999). While the progress in women's employment status is linked at least in part to

E-waste

Many people who use smartphones, tablets, and computers are unaware of the toxic heavy metals that these electronic devices contain, such as mercury, lead, and cadmium. Most are also ignorant of what happens to their electronic devices when they upgrade to new models and discard old ones. Electronic waste, or e-waste, is a growing problem in the digital age that is global in nature and has long-term environmental consequences. The Basel Convention prohibits affluent, developed countries from exporting their hazardous waste, including e-waste, to poorer, developing ones for disposal. However, it does not prevent the exportation of hazardous waste for the purposes of recycling or repair, which is how most e-waste eventually ends up in developing countries, particularly in China (Pickren 2015). The town of Guiyu, China, has become an e-waste haven. Many of its residents are involved with recycling e-waste that is hazardous to their health and to the environment. Burning circuit boards creates air pollution that affects workers' lungs and eyes, as does the mercury that is released into the atmosphere when flat screen televisions are disassembled. Lead and cadmium pollute Guiyu's soil and water, which in turn contaminate local water sources and food supplies (Watson 2013). As the Global South leapfrogs into the digital age, it has to deal with not only hazardous e-waste imported from the Global North, but also the e-waste of its own residents.

Workers in Guiyu unload e-waste, including discarded keyboards and telephones. The devices are broken down to recover small quantities of valuable raw materials, but toxic byproducts have polluted the environment and sickened workers, as well the larger population.

There are many ways in which we can try to solve the problem of e-waste. Manufacturers can use fewer or no toxic chemicals in the electronic devices they produce. In addition, they can participate in extended producer responsibility programs that require them to properly dispose of or recycle all electronic goods that they produce. Consumers can use their electronic devices longer instead of upgrading to new models so frequently. Governments in developed countries can do a better job of tracking and monitoring e-waste, so that it does not end up creating more e-waste havens in poorer countries. The United States in particular needs to better regulate e-waste. Not only has the United States failed to ratify the Basel Convention; it has no federal laws on recycling e-waste.

Engaging the Digital World

Find out what happens to the e-waste generated at your university or college. If your school has an e-waste program, with whom does it have a contract to collect its e-waste? Where does this e-waste go once it leaves your campus? Is there a designated place where you can drop off your used laptop, tablet, or smartphone to be collected? If there is one, have you used it, or will you use it? Why or why not?

gender equality movements, the key factor in this change is the better integration of an increasing number of areas into the world economy through trade and production. Nevertheless, in no part of the world are women as involved as men are in the labor force (see Figure 9.5). In some areas—South Asia, the Middle East, and North Africa—women's labor force participation is markedly lower than that of men.

In much of the Global North, educated middle-class women have made inroads into professional (law, banking, accounting, computing, and architecture) and managerial employment. In the global paid labor market, women predominate as service and clerical workers and in elementary occupations, such as agriculture and manufacturing (United Nations Department of Economic and Social Affairs 2015a). They are likely to work as teachers and university professors, as nurses and doctors in public hospitals, and as workers and administrators in government offices (Moghadam 1999). Women have also made inroads in professional services.

However, according to the World Bank, women earn less and participate in the labor force less than men do. Globally, Gallup polling finds that men are twice as likely as women to have full-time jobs. The wage gap found in the United States is also a global phenomenon, and the gap is especially large in the Middle East and in North Africa. Mothers' wages are lower than fathers' in many countries (Misra and Strader 2013). The historical belief persists that fathers are supporting entire families (and thus need a higher wage), while mothers are not. Despite the gains made by women, high-pay and high-status occupations continue to be dominated by men in both the Global North and the Global South. Even in countries like the United States and those in Western Europe, men still have easier access to, and therefore hold a much larger percentage of, professional and managerial jobs.

Women and Informal Employment

At the same time that some women are finding success in the paid labor force, others are being limited by the nature of their arrangements with employers. Women are more likely than men to have informal jobs (Limoncelli, forthcoming). Informal employment, which has increased in many countries, includes temporary work without fixed employers, paid employment from home, domestic work for households (de Regt 2009), and industrial work for subcontractors. Informal sectors are characterized by low pay and a lack of secure contracts, worker benefits, and social protections. Workers in the informal economy do not have wage agreements, employment contracts, regular working hours, or health insurance or unemployment benefits (Kabeer, Sudarshan, and Milward 2013). They often earn below the legal minimum wage and may not be paid on time. Many formal jobs have been replaced by informal ones as lower labor and production costs have increasingly become the major organizing factor in global production.

While greater informal employment characterizes the entire labor force globally, women and men are concentrated in different types of informal work (Vanek et al. 2014). Men are concentrated mainly in informal wage-based jobs and agricultural employment, while women are typically concentrated in nonagricultural employment, domestic work, and unpaid work in family enterprises. Compared with men's informal employment, women's employment is much more likely to have lower hourly wages and less stability. To reduce labor costs, most multinational corporations establish subcontracting networks with local manufacturers employing low-paid workers, mostly women, who can be laid off quickly and easily. In these production networks, women are more likely to work in small workshops or from home. Many women accept

FIGURE 9.5 • Men's and Women's Labor Force Participation Rates by World Region, 2014

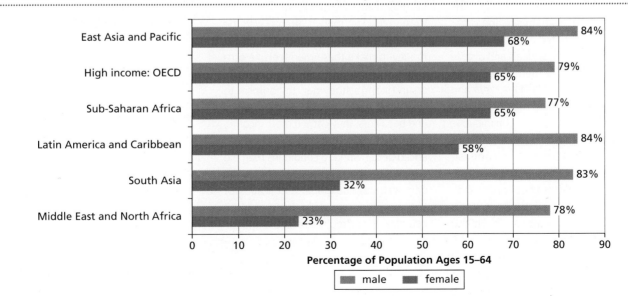

SOURCE: Data from The World Bank, "World DataBank: Gender Statistics.

Dealing in Desire: Asian Ascendancy, Western Decline, and the Hidden Currencies of Global Sex Work (University of California Press, 2015)

Kimberly Kay Hoang (Assistant Professor of Sociology at the University of Chicago; PhD, University of California–Berkeley, 2011)

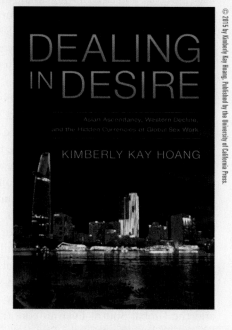

Though not often recognized, the labor of female sex workers is a critical segment of the global economy. Kimberly Hoang spent five years working in different types of hostess bars in Ho Chi Minh City. Her goal was to better understand the relationships between female sex workers, their male clients, and global capital. She situated her study in the context of the economic rise of Asia and the subsequent economic decline of Western countries after the 2008 recession, which created a new global hierarchy of men. The wealth, status, and power of men from the Global North began to decrease during this time, but increased for Asian men. While most of the women in Hoang's study were from poor rural or urban families, the men occupied different class and status positions that helped determine what type of hostess bars they patronized and their relationships with sex workers. She found that local Vietnamese and other Asian men frequented exclusive hostess bars to broker business deals and display their power to other men. Vietnamese men who lived abroad (*Viet Kieu*) and visited their homeland may have used hostess bars to engage in conspicuous consumption and differentiate themselves from Western men. In contrast, Western expatriate businessmen patronized establishments that catered to their insecurities due to their decline in status relative to Asian businessmen. Hoang

found that Western budget tourists were most likely to visit hostess bars to purchase sex directly, affirming the power and masculinity abroad that they had lost at home.

Sex workers in the all the different types of hostess bars performed a variety of duties for their clients. Paid sex was not a job requirement for any of them. Most women earned money from tips that they received for pouring drinks, playing drinking games, singing karaoke, dancing, or just talking with their clients. Some hostesses, especially those who catered to Western expatriate clients, tried to develop long-term relationships with their clients as a way of securing a steady source of income. This was often accomplished by making a man believe that a particular hostess was his exclusive "girlfriend" whom he had "won" in a competition with other men, confirming his masculinity. Hostesses who targeted Western budget tourists often played the role of a "third-world" victim who needed money to make these men feel like economic providers. Though the sex workers in Hoang's study had to conform to sexualized stereotypes about their bodies and behaviors, they earned more income, possessed more autonomy, and experienced better working conditions than did their counterparts in factories. As Hoang demonstrates, the global stratification of the contemporary sex industry is quite complex, with "multiple niche markets"

that "cater to global and local men . . . for business and leisure" (2015, 39).

Supplementary Resources

- You can watch Hoang participate on a panel about sex workers at a conference entitled "From Prosecution to Empowerment: Fighting Trafficking and Promoting the Rights of Migrants." She discusses her book 21 minutes into this video clip: https://www.youtube.com/watch?v=TEBAg4bS0ZY.
- Toni Mac, a sex worker and activist, discusses different legal models being used to legislate sex work around the world in her TED Talk, "The Laws That Sex Workers Really Want": https://www.ted.com/talks/toni_mac_the_laws_that_sex_workers_really_want?language=en.

the lower wages and less formal working arrangements of home-based work in order to be able to continue to carry out household responsibilities.

The differences in wealth between men and women are much more extreme than the differences in labor force participation, occupations, or incomes. According to the United Nations Development Programme (2014), men own 99 percent of the world's wealth, while women hold only 1 percent. This provides men with a huge advantage in economic power. Because women own comparatively little property and other wealth, and because they are much more likely than men to be employed in irregular jobs, they also have a more difficult time obtaining loans. Nearly 75 percent of women in the world cannot get a bank loan.

Women in Global Care Chains

Another form of global gender inequality occurs within families through caregiving work. As men and women from low-income countries migrate to find better-paying jobs, women especially find employment in domestic work. Arlie Hochschild (b. 1940; 2000) argues that the migration of domestic workers creates **global care chains** that involve a series of personal relationships between people across the globe based on the paid or unpaid work of caring (Yeates 2012). Care includes social, health, and sexual care services, and usually involves menial tasks such as cooking, cleaning, and ironing. In global care chains, women supply their own care labor to their employers while consuming other women's care labor, both paid and unpaid. Thus, instead of care chains, it might be better to think of this as "care circulation" (Lutz and Palenga-Mollenbeck 2016). Migrant domestic workers often rely on female relatives, neighbors, and daughters as well as paid domestic workers for the care of their children back in their home countries. For instance, while a mother works as a nanny in a high-income country, her young children may be cared for by an older daughter or by a nanny who migrated from a middle- or low-income country. On one end of the chain is a woman in the North pursuing professional employment and finding herself unable to fulfill her duties within the family. On the other end is a domestic worker's oldest daughter taking over her mother's familial duties. With the increasing use of the internet, mothers (aka "Skype mothers") can play a more active role in their families back home, but such a form of motherhood obviously has great limitations.

Referred to also as the *international transfer of caretaking,* the *global nanny chain,* and the *racial division of reproductive labor,* the transfer of reproductive labor (which may include gestational surrogacy, or the use of surrogate mothers) from women in high-income countries to those in low-income countries points to a paradoxical situation in women's empowerment through participation in the labor force. While women in the North are able to undertake careers, they tend to pass their household duties and reproductive labor on to low-wage immigrant workers. Rather than pushing for a redistribution of household responsibilities among family members, women as employers maintain the gender division of labor by transferring the most devalued work to disadvantaged women. As a result, the worth of reproductive labor (and of women) declines even further (Parreñas 2001). In this sense, women's labor force participation does not necessarily result in a change in traditional gender roles, but rather in the greater exploitation of immigrant women by middle- and upper-class women.

The provision of reproductive labor by migrant domestic workers is not new. It has been obtained by class-privileged women for centuries. However, the flow of reproductive labor has increased due to globalization and the growth of the global economy. There is a substantial and increasing demand for migrant domestic workers in the North, and the bulk of the supply comes from the South.

CHECKPOINT 9.2: GLOBAL ECONOMIC INEQUALITIES

TERM	DEFINITION
Global digital divide	Inequality resulting from the comparative lack of access to the internet in the Global South
Global health inequalities	Inequalities in life expectancy, disease, nutrition, and health care between the Global North and South
Global gender stratification	The systematic advantages in wealth, occupations, employment, and income conferred on men around the world, relative to women
Global care chains	Personal relationships between people across the globe based on the paid or unpaid work of caring

CHANGING POSITIONS IN GLOBAL STRATIFICATION

Despite the several forms of global inequality discussed previously, it is possible for countries to develop economically and change their positions within the global stratification system. This section examines the risky strategy of a race to the bottom in offering cheap labor, the importance of industrial upgrading, and the controversial use of foreign aid as a means of development.

RACE TO THE BOTTOM

Those countries that rank low in the global stratification system often have to engage in a so-called economic race to the bottom in order to have a chance of eventually moving

Domestic Workers in Kuwait

Because oil usually commands a high price on the global market, Kuwait, a small Persian Gulf nation-state with vast oil reserves, is exceptionally wealthy. Kuwait's wealth conveys many advantages to its citizens, who enjoy state-funded education, health care, and retirement income, as well as virtually guaranteed employment, usually in the oil industry or investment banking. Wealth allows Kuwaitis to hire domestic workers, mostly women, from many relatively poor countries, including the Philippines, Sri Lanka, Nepal, and Indonesia (Fahim 2010). Attracted to Kuwait by higher wages than they could earn elsewhere, these workers can send large sums home, but power relationships between them and their employers are starkly unequal (Fernandez 2010).

While some workers are treated well, a large number have complained of sexual and/or physical abuse, unpaid wages, and withholding of their passports. One maid said she was allowed to sleep only two hours per night and finally left when asked to wash windows at 3:00 a.m. A Sri Lankan maid escaped what she claimed had been 13 years of imprisonment, without pay, by her Kuwaiti employer. A Filipina maid was reported to have been tortured and killed by her employers, who tried to make her death appear to be an accident. When one Filipina domestic worker sought help because she was being abused by the family she worked for, her employers threw her out a third-floor window, breaking her back. Many domestic workers have fled to their home countries' embassies for protection, sleeping there on their luggage or on the floor in crowded rooms.

Globalization is drawing large numbers of poor people far from home in the hope of finding work; some are trafficked illegally. In many places, including the United States, such immigrants have few, if any, rights and are subject to a wide range of abuses. Existing at the bottom of often very highly stratified societies without rights, representation, or resources, they are often powerless.

Think About It

What accounts for the huge disparity in power between wealthy employers and the immigrants who work as their household help? Why do agencies that try to help these employees tend to focus on individual cases and not on the wider problem of power inequality? Would addressing power issues be more effective in the long run? Why or why not?

Despite efforts by organizations like the Human Rights Watch, sponsor of the event seen here, laws to protect domestic workers from exploitation in Kuwait have been slow in coming. Why?

---

up the global hierarchy. The basic method is to offer lower prices than the competition does—usually other low-ranking countries. Such nations may lower prices by reducing costs, which they do by offering their citizens lower wages, poorer working conditions, longer hours, ever-escalating pressure and demands, and so on. Figure 9.6 shows wage disparities among countries; pay special attention to the disparities between the Global North and South. An especially desperate nation will go further than the others to reduce wages and worsen working conditions in order to lower costs and attract the interest and investments of multinational corporations. However, the "winning" low-income nation remains a favorite of the multinationals only until it is undercut by another low-ranking country eager for jobs. In other words, the countries that get the work are those that "win" the race to the bottom. These, of course, are almost always questionable victories, because the work is poorly paid and subjects workers to horrid circumstances.

FIGURE 9.6 • Minimum Wage Rates for Selected Countries, 2013

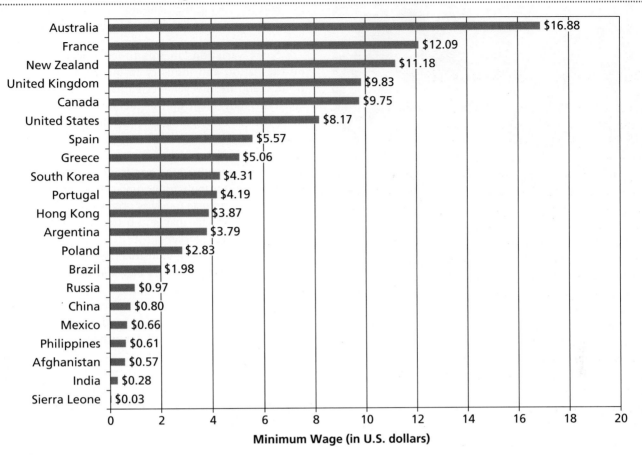

SOURCE: Data from the Matthew Boesler, "Here's How America's Minimum Wage Stacks Up against Countries Like India, Russia, Greece, and France," Business Insider, August 19, 2013.

A similar point is made by Pietra Rivoli (2015) in her study of the global market for T-shirts. If one takes the long historical view, the nations that won the race to the bottom centuries ago are now among the most successful economies in the world. In textiles, the race to the bottom was won first by England, then the United States, then Japan, then Hong Kong. The most recent winner of this race was China, which now is moving up industrially and economically. If anything, the race to the bottom has sped up in recent years as a result of such changes as the rise of the rapid turnover in fashion, or "fast fashion," as found in global chains such as Zara and H&M (Rivoli 2015, 272–275).

ASK YOURSELF

What could the Global North do to reduce other countries' need to engage in the race to the bottom? Why have such efforts so far been few and generally ineffective? How would slowing or even ending the race to the bottom affect the trend toward consumerism in the countries of the Global North?

Rivoli generalizes examples from the global textile industry to argue that nations must win the race to the bottom in order ultimately to succeed. Victory in this race is, in her view, the "ignition switch" that turns the economy on and gets it rolling. Thus, she concludes, those who criticize globalization are misguided in their efforts to end this race.

Rivoli's view seems to endorse the race to the bottom for all countries interested in development. However, we must take note of the fact that the race initially leads them deeper into poverty, at least for a time. It also greatly advantages the wealthy North, which is guaranteed a continuing source of low-priced goods and services as one country replaces another at the bottom. Winning the race to the bottom is no guarantee of moving up the global stratification system, but it is a guarantee of low wages and poverty in developing countries in the South *and* of cheap goods for the middle and upper classes in the North.

In actuality, winning the race to the bottom might mean that a country remains at or near the bottom. For example, some countries compete in the world economy by focusing on agricultural exports and employing cheap, local labor to plant and harvest crops. As countries battle with

Maquiladoras, global manufacturing operations housed in Mexico, have been transformed from labor-intensive providers of finished products, like the Samsung plant in Tijuana shown here, to highly automated suppliers of cars and appliances. They are increasingly relying on smaller numbers of highly skilled technical and engineering professionals for research and development. Given this transformation, why are *maquiladora* workers' wages still so low?

one another by paying workers less money, they make their agricultural goods cheaper on the global market. But if these export sectors do not eventually transition to other types of goods and services, with higher wages, the countries might never lift themselves off the bottom.

INDUSTRIAL UPGRADING

In focusing on the losers in the race to the bottom, we must not ignore evidence of improvement in middle-income countries and their industries (Bair and Gereffi 2013; Gereffi 2012). At least some of the countries that enter the global economic market at or near the bottom begin to move up over time by becoming more competitive economically. *Industrial upgrading* generally takes place as nations, firms, and even workers take on progressively more complex and higher-value production activities (Gereffi 2005, 171). Industrial upgrading often occurs in four stages:

1. Assembly: for example, incorporating electronic components from high-income countries into a smartphone in a process that has been designed by the client and will be sold elsewhere under the client's brand name

2. Original equipment manufacturing: for example, designing and producing televisions to the client's specifications and under the client's brand for distribution by the client

3. Original brand-name manufacturing: for example, designing and selling automobiles under one's own brand name

4. Original design manufacturing: for example, designing and producing high-end audio equipment, which is simply purchased and resold by the client

Some variations in this process occur, depending on the nation and industry in question; apparel, electronics, and fresh vegetables all have different processes. However, movement up this hierarchy tends to occur in those nations undergoing industrial upgrading. For example, the early success of industry in China was based on the country's victory in the race to the bottom, but the Chinese are now moving away from low-end production (such as T-shirt manufacturing) and toward the production of higher-value products (such as original brand-name automobiles) with higher pay and better working conditions for many Chinese workers.

Another example of industrial upgrading is to be found in Mexico, especially in its *maquiladora* manufacturing operations (Bair and Gereffi 2013; Gereffi 2005). The first-generation *maquiladoras* were labor-intensive, employed limited technologies, and assembled finished products for export—apparel, for example—using components imported from the United States. Second-generation *maquiladoras* became more oriented toward manufacturing processes, using automated and semiautomated machines and robots rather than human labor. They were more likely than their predecessors to be centered in the automobile, television, and electrical appliance industries. Third-generation *maquiladoras,* now supplanting second-generation operations, do more research, design, and development and are more dependent on highly skilled labor, such as engineers and technicians. *Maquiladoras* have gone from relying on inexpensive labor to being competitive on the basis of their productivity and high quality, although the wages of *maquiladora* workers are still far below those of U.S. workers.

While the *maquiladoras* may have advanced, a lot of workers have not kept pace with this development. Many of the *maquiladoras* employ women, who are seen as more docile and agile than men are. Such factory work has provided women with new economic opportunities, but it has also opened them up to new possibilities of exploitation and violence. In the 1990s and 2000s, researchers and journalists began to draw attention to the "*maquiladora* murders" (Arriola 2006–2007; Pantaleo 2010) in Ciudad Juárez, a Mexican city directly across the border from El Paso, Texas. While the numbers are debated, conservative estimates are that 300 to 400 women working in *maquiladoras* disappeared, with many of their bodies turning up in the desert (Arriola 2006–2007). The conditions within the *maquiladoras* themselves also present health hazards. Filmmakers Vicky Funari and Sergio de la Torre highlight these conditions in their documentary film *Maquilapolis* (2005). The film follows a group of women who work in a *maquiladora* in Tijuana, Mexico, who organize to protest unsafe working conditions, such as exposure to toxic chemicals and the practice of toxic dumping in their poor neighborhoods. As they push for change in their lives, the globalization of labor begins moving production away from Mexico. In the end, the workers are unsure whether they will still have jobs or the *maquiladoras* will cross the seas to China in search of cheaper labor. The process of industrial upgrading within a nation is always threatened to some extent by the race to the bottom, but if industry can skillfully move up the hierarchy to more complex and highly valued forms of manufacturing, it can reduce the sting.

FOREIGN AID AND DEVELOPMENT[1]

Another way in which global economic inequality can be addressed is through the use of foreign aid to improve a poor country's position within the world economy. **Foreign aid** is defined as economic assistance given by countries or global institutions to a foreign country in order to promote its development and social welfare. In the form that we now know it, foreign aid began following the economic devastation of World War II with the United States' Marshall Plan to help struggling European economies. Foreign aid has continued to expand since that time, totaling $131.6 billion in 2015, according to the Organisation for Economic Co-operation and Development (OECD; 2016).

The OECD, which sets standards for official development assistance (ODA), states that aid may take the form of grants or subsidized loans and must promote development and welfare. This can include funding or other resources for education, health, debt relief, social or economic infrastructure, humanitarian assistance, or other development projects. To qualify as "aid," loans must be given with interest rates at least 25 percent below market rates. Most aid is bilateral, or given directly from one country to another. Aid can also be multilateral, where resources of many donors are pooled through a third party like the World Bank, which then distributes the aid. This ideally cuts bureaucratic costs and reduces political motivations for giving. The 34 members of the OECD, which include the United States, Western European countries, Canada, Japan, Australia, South Korea, and New Zealand, provide the majority of foreign aid. Other providers of significant aid are Brazil, China, India, Kuwait, Qatar, Saudi Arabia, Taiwan, Turkey, and the United Arab Emirates (Williams 2014). The United States is by far the largest donor in terms of dollars, giving more than $31 billion in foreign aid in 2015 alone. However, when measured as a percentage of gross national income, the United States gives only 0.17 percent, which is considerably short of the target of 0.7 percent set by the United Nations (see Figure 9.7). The countries that typically give the most in foreign aid as a percentage of GNI include several Nordic countries (Norway, Denmark, Finland, and Sweden), Luxembourg, the United Kingdom, and the Netherlands. They tend to meet or surpass the 0.7 percent target. However, in 2015, the United Arab Emirates gave 1.09 percent of GNI as foreign aid (not shown in Figure 9.7), the highest percentage of any country besides Sweden, which gave 1.40 percent. The average percentage of GNI donated is about 0.3 percent (OECD 2016).

The aim of all this aid is to generate economic growth and domestic savings in recipient countries, but efforts have achieved varying levels of success. Some of the top receivers of aid (in terms of both raw dollars and percentage of GNI), such as Afghanistan, continue to experience significant economic and political turmoil despite long histories of receiving aid.

An examination of studies on who receives aid and how much they receive reveals several important trends. Disproportionate amounts of aid go to countries with smaller populations when analyzed on a per capita basis, primarily because smaller countries show more noticeable changes as a result of aid than do extremely populous countries like China and India. Additionally, countries that have colonial histories and that align themselves politically with major donor countries receive more aid than countries that do not. These characteristics are much better indicators of how much aid a country will receive than are levels of poverty or democratization or economic openness (Alesina and Dollar 2000).

There are many criticisms of foreign aid, focusing on issues such as its questionable effectiveness, the political agendas of donors and recipients, and the adverse effects it can have on the countries seeking assistance. Donors often seek to promote the economic growth of nations to enhance their own economic interests, preserve access to natural resources, and benefit their political positions. One example of this is the correlation between countries serving as members of the United Nations Security Council and those receiving increased IMF funding (Dreher, Sturm, and Vreeland 2009). Foreign aid is also frequently tied to very specific stipulations about how countries may spend it. Donor countries often provide aid for specific purposes, some of the most common of which are education, transportation and communications infrastructure, and the development of government and civil society institutions. Issues can arise concerning such stipulations when the intentions of the donor country are not in line with those of the receiving country. Causes of this can be

---

[1]Miranda Ames made significant contributions to this section.

FIGURE 9.7 • **Aid Outflows in Billions of Dollars and as a Percentage of Gross National Income, 2015**

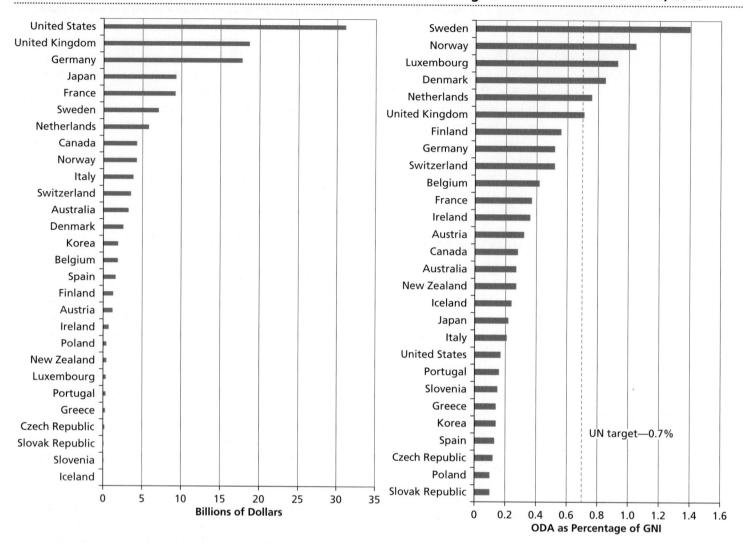

SOURCE: Data from Organisation for Economic Co-operation and Development, "Development Aid Rises Again in 2015, Spending on Refugees Doubles," April 13, 2016.

anything from miscommunication to blatant corruption, and the end result can be the misuse or misdirection of billions of dollars. While the purposes stipulated by donor countries may seem beneficial, these requirements add levels of bureaucracy, time, and other additional costs to aid-funded development projects (Easterly and Pfutze 2008). Finally, any military or military logistical assistance provided to foreign nations cannot be counted toward ODA, but this does not preclude countries that receive foreign aid from using the aid to free up and redirect their own funds toward the military. In short, it can be argued that while foreign funds are being used for development purposes, there is still the potential for military budgets to increase as an indirect result, thereby fueling further conflicts.

While foreign aid has the potential to address dramatic global inequality, it has long been and will likely continue to be a contentious issue. First, the ability of some countries to give foreign aid clearly reflects existing forms of inequality.

Second, the aid can reinforce existing inequalities as well as global power structures.

CHECKPOINT 9.3: CHANGING POSITIONS IN THE GLOBAL ECONOMY

CONCEPT	EXPLANATION
Race to the bottom	Poor nations compete to decrease wages and working conditions in order to reduce costs and attract multinational corporations.
Industrial upgrading	Nations, firms, and workers take on progressively more complex and higher-value production activities.
Foreign aid and development	A country or global institution gives economic assistance to a foreign country to promote development and social welfare.

THEORIES OF GLOBAL STRATIFICATION

As noted in Chapter 8, the dominant theoretical approaches to social stratification are structural/functional theory and conflict/critical theory. Not only are these the most common theoretical approaches; they are also hotly debated among scholars and practitioners.

STRUCTURAL/FUNCTIONAL THEORIES

A dominant structural/functional theory of global stratification is **modernization theory**, which explains unequal economic distributions based on the structural (especially technological) and cultural differences between countries. It is the focus on structure and culture that makes it clear that modernization theory is a variant of structural/functional theory. According to this theory, the development of certain structures (especially technologies) and cultural realities (values, norms) is essential for societies to modernize (Jacobsen 2015).

One of the thinkers best known for articulating and promoting modernization theory is Walt Rostow (1960, 1978), an economic theorist who served as an adviser to President John F. Kennedy. In his theory of modernization, which had a major influence on U.S. foreign policy during the Cold War, Rostow argued that low-income countries must abandon their traditional values and ways of life in order to improve their economic standards of living. He saw countries as progressing through four stages in a very linear path on their way to economic development:

1. Traditional stage. People in traditional societies have lived their lives in the same way for many generations and know only the lives of their ancestors. Such societies are characterized by hardship and a lack of material comfort, conditions that they accept as inherent and inevitable features of life. With traditional values, people are encouraged to follow the paths of others in their families and communities. This acceptance of one's position in life, along with a cultural focus on family and community, does not give people the incentive to work harder, save money, and acquire more material goods. Before the industrial era, this stage characterized much of the world; it can still be found today in the poorest countries and in regions within middle-income countries (e.g., China and India). From the perspective of modernization theorists, the poverty of these areas is a result of the cultural flaws of the people themselves.

2. Takeoff stage. When people in poor countries begin to abandon their traditional values, they think more ambitiously about the future. They start to save and invest, trading with others to acquire profit, and new markets are developed for these exchanges. This stage is marked by greater individualism and a growing desire for material goods, with less emphasis placed on family and community. This kind of economic growth occurred in Great Britain by the end of the 1700s, quickly followed by the United States around 1820. Some countries currently in the takeoff stage might include Malaysia, Peru, and Belize. Advocates of this approach would encourage further modernization in these countries by approving foreign aid to develop infrastructure, promoting advanced technology to develop new industries, and recommending communications systems that would help stimulate consumer culture.

3. Drive to technological maturity. A country in this stage continues to experience economic growth with the development of more advanced industries, high levels of investment, increasing urbanization, and higher standards of living. Institutions and societal values become more oriented toward production and consumption, with individualism trumping traditional values and norms. As people demand more material comforts and gain more education, they continue to promote economic advancement. The United States reached technological maturity around the mid-1800s, and countries such as Mexico, Brazil, and the Czech Republic are currently reaching this stage.

4. High mass consumption. For Rostow, a country is fully modernized when large numbers of its people are able to enjoy the high standard of living associated with mass consumption and brought about by economic growth. In the mass consumption stage, people come to expect the everyday conveniences, and even luxuries, of consumer society. Absolute poverty falls significantly as people have more material comforts. However, societal values largely move away from family and community. Much of Western Europe, Great Britain, and the United States achieved this stage by 1900.

Among the critics of modernization theory are those associated with dependency theory (a variant of conflict-critical theory, discussed in the following section). They see modernization as having a negative economic effect on less developed countries, making them, among many other things, more dependent on developed countries. However, some have argued that modernization theory (and dependency theory) focuses too narrowly on economic production. Edward Tiryakian contends, "It seems patent that 'modernization' in the world today means more than upgrading the conditions of economic production, although it means that also. It also means upgrading the conditions of the life space of individuals and collectivities which have been circumscribed by political arrangements of the state that are viewed as illegitimate" (1991, 172).

Putting forth a theory of **neomodernization**, Tiryakian argues that technological and cultural differences between countries are important for explaining both economic and social development. He notes that economic modernization can come at a high cost to forms of political and social life. A thriving civic culture, in which people can meaningfully participate in political processes, is also important for a country to be considered modern. The emphasis on cultural values is, therefore, extended beyond ideas such as individualism and competition to include democratization. Corruption and clientelism (where, for example, politicians pay for votes), which can minimize trust in government functioning and democratic participation, are inconsistent with views of modernization—even if they are coupled with the drive toward mass consumption.

It is possible to think about China today through the lens of neomodernization. As noted previously, China has varying levels of economic modernization, ranging from traditional values maintained in many villages to increasing levels of technological advancement and consumption in its urban centers, but on the whole, it is clearly on a path toward economic modernization. However, the political arrangements that have brought about this modernizing process have relied on the silencing of political dissent, close monitoring of the internet, and the systematic denial of human rights. A narrow focus on economic modernization ignores such dramatic social and political costs.

CONFLICT/CRITICAL THEORIES

At the global level, several conflict/critical theories have implications for the study of stratification. These theories tend to focus on a relationship of dependency (see the previous discussion) between wealthy countries and their transnational corporations that exploit poor countries.

Colonialism, Imperialism, and Postcolonialism

Theories of colonialism deal with the various methods employed by one country to gain control, sometimes through territorial conquest, of another country or geographic area. **Colonialism** generally involves settlers as well as formal mechanisms of control over a country's colonies (Williams and Chrisman 1994). The colonial power often creates an administrative apparatus to run a colony's internal affairs. Once the stronger country is in power, it then seeks to exercise political, economic, cultural, and territorial control over that area. Of course, the main point is to exploit the weaker area for the stronger country's benefit. In some cases—most famously in the case of the British Empire—many areas of the world have been colonized by one country (see Figure 9.8).

Imperialism involves control *without* the creation of colonies, the associated settlers, or the formal methods of

FIGURE 9.8 • Developing Countries by Primary Western Colonizer

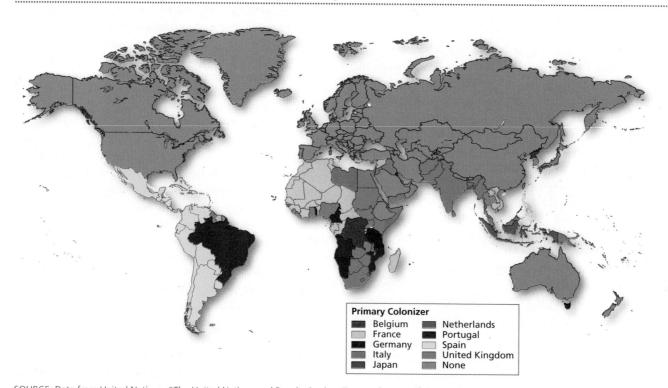

Primary Colonizer
- Belgium
- France
- Germany
- Italy
- Japan
- Netherlands
- Portugal
- Spain
- United Kingdom
- None

SOURCE: Data from United Nations, "The United Nations and Decolonization: Trust and Non-Self-Governing Territories (1945–1999)."

control. Imperialism is defined more by economic control and exploitation, while colonialism is more about political control. Of course, the two are often combined. The British were both imperialists *and* colonialists.

Today few, if any, colonies remain, the result being that we can now think in terms of **postcolonialism** (Bhambra 2007; G. Steinmetz 2014). Clearly, the term implies the era in a once-colonized area *after* the colonizing power has departed. However, postcolonial thinking and work are often already well underway before the colonizing power departs. The most notable work on postcolonialism is Edward Said's *Orientalism* ([1979] 1994), which deals with this problem in the context of negative stereotypes developed in the West about those who live in the East, including both Asia and the Middle East. The issue raised is the difficulty experienced by "Orientals" in developing a positive identity in light of all the negativity about them in the West, which dominated the East in various ways, including through imperialism and colonialism, until very recently. The problem from the point of view of social stratification is that while "Orientals," and "natives" more generally, acquire high-level positions when the colonial powers leave, they may lack the positive sense of self needed to handle these positions adequately. Thus, colonialists and imperialists may continue to exercise economic and political control behind the scenes: While they may no longer actually occupy high-level positions in the stratification system, they may be able to control the locals who do hold these positions.

World-Systems Theory

World-systems theory focuses on the current stratification system by viewing the world as a single economic entity (Wallerstein 1974). It envisions a world divided mainly between the *core* and the *periphery*. The core includes the wealthiest industrialized countries, such as Western European countries, the United States, Australia, and Japan. The nation-states associated with the periphery are dependent on, and exploited by, the core nation-states. The periphery includes most of Africa and parts of Asia (Indonesia, Vietnam, Afghanistan), the Middle East (Iran, Syria), and South America (Peru, Bolivia). There are also a number of states in the middle, the *semiperiphery*, including much of Eastern Europe, Thailand, India, China, South Africa, Brazil, and Argentina.

The current world system has its roots in the early process of colonization. Wealthy European countries searched the globe for natural resources and slave labor. They set up colonies throughout Africa, Southeast Asia, South America, and other places in order to keep resources and labor flowing back to the wealthy core countries. For example, as a British colony, India sent much of its natural resources and foods to England. When droughts hit India in the late

1800s, millions of Indians died because the majority of the food produced in India was being redirected from its own people to Britain as the colonizing power (Davis 2002). In other colonized countries around the world, gold, timber, and other natural resources were extracted from colonized countries (i.e., the periphery) for the benefit of the colonizers (i.e., the core).

More recently, the core has been able to benefit from the periphery in other ways. Core nation-states have helped keep the countries of the periphery focused on narrow export-oriented economies rather than on developing their industrial capacity. The "race to the bottom" discussed previously benefits the core by providing the periphery's cheap labor and helps keep profits flowing back to the core. The core can also make loans to peripheral countries, but because of the power imbalance, the core is able to dictate the terms of the loans. Currently, poor countries owe the United States and other core countries more than $4 trillion in debt, leaving them in a weak economic position relative to the core.

World-systems theory argues that because of this relationship between the core and periphery, we cannot understand an individual nation's wealth today by simply understanding how much wealth or what level of income the country might have. Instead, we can understand a nation's position in the world system only by examining its current relationship to other countries. Of course, countries in the core, periphery, and semiperiphery can shift positions over time. At one time, Great Britain was the dominant core nation-state in the world, but by the time of World War II, it had been replaced by the United States. Today, the United States is slipping, and China, at one time a peripheral country, shows every sign of moving to the core.

ASK YOURSELF

In the context of world-systems theory, could a time come when the United States is in the semiperiphery or even the periphery? What do you think would make this result more likely? What could perhaps prevent it?

World-systems theory is a conflict/critical theory, strongly influenced by Marxian ideas, that offers a very different view of social stratification than is typical in most Marxist approaches. As you will recall, Marxists generally focus on stratification within societies, especially between the capitalists at the top of the stratification system and the proletariat at or near the bottom. World-systems theorists focus not on a particular country but on the world as a whole. Instead of being concerned about the capitalists exploiting the proletariat, world-systems theory focuses on the exploitation of the periphery by the core.

TYPE OF THEORY	MAIN HYPOTHESIS
Structural/functional theories	Technological and cultural factors explain countries' varying levels of economic and social development.
Conflict theories	Wealthy countries and transnational corporations exploit poor countries and make poor countries dependent on them.

CONSUMPTION AND GLOBAL STRATIFICATION

Consumption is especially interesting from the perspective of global stratification. As discussed below, consumption can simultaneously reflect, reinforce, and be used to address global stratification.

GLOBAL CONSUMER CULTURE AND INEQUALITY

This chapter has highlighted the inequalities in wealth, occupations, and income that permit varying levels of consumption. One way to think about these different levels of consumption is to consider how they enable different standards of living. For example, proponents of modernization theory argue that a society is fully modernized when its people can enjoy the fruits of their labor by enjoying mass consumption. In other words, having a large, spacious house, air-conditioning, a car for every family member, a smartphone and tablet, a large-screen TV, and other consumer items can make life more comfortable and enjoyable. To the degree that there are global inequalities in consumption, there are inequalities in the levels of comfort in people's lives. But there is another way to think about how mass consumption relates to inequality.

In Chapter 4, we discussed the rise of consumer culture, in which core ideas and material objects relate to consumption and consumption is a primary source of meaning in life. We noted there that consumer culture is becoming increasingly globalized, with previous production-oriented cultures (e.g., China) focusing more and more on consumption. Some conflict/critical theorists argue that this rise of mass consumerism, and consumer culture itself, helps reinforce existing inequalities.

As usual, McDonald's, as well as the fast-food industry in general, offers wonderful examples of the globalization of consumer culture. McDonald's offers types of food in many parts of the world that, while highly McDonaldized (see Chapter 1), are adapted to local tastes, as the examples in Table 9.1 illustrate.

Horkheimer and Adorno ([1944] 1997) argued that all people, and especially those experiencing poor economic conditions, are seduced into passivity through consumption. As a result of corporate branding and advertising, people are seduced into wanting all sorts of consumer items. For example, through the marketing efforts of Apple (the most profitable brand in the world), we have come to interpret iPhones, Mac computers, iPads, and Apple's other lines of consumer electronics, such as Apple Watches, as hip, cool, and unique. People intensely desire these consumer items for themselves and come to feel that they cannot be cool or happy without them. When a new iPhone is released, consumers wait in long lines just to be among the first to get one. Or, to quote Tyler Durden (played by Brad Pitt) in the popular film *Fight Club*, "The things you own end up owning you."

This phenomenon relates to global stratification through the spread of consumer culture. Leslie Sklair's theory of globalization focuses on the "culture-ideology of consumerism," the goal of which is to "persuade people to consume not simply to satisfy their biological and other modest needs but in response to artificially created desires in order to perpetuate the accumulation of capital for private profit" (2002, 62). This consumer culture promotes consumption as a value and constructs both the desire for it and the means to achieve it. As a result of globalization, people around the world have had this particular type of culture imposed on them. It is facilitated by information and communication technologies, which have proliferated through the spread of the internet, computers, and smartphones. Beginning at very

TABLE 9.1 • McDonald's Cuisine in Select Countries

COUNTRY	MENU ITEM
Japan	Black Burger (so named because the buns are dyed with squid ink)
Korea	Shrimp Burger
Canada	Poutine (french fries with brown gravy and cheese curds)
Mexico	McMollettes (English muffins with refried beans, salsa, and cheese)
India	McAloo Tikki Burger (a bun with a pea-and-potato patty)
New Zealand	Georgie Pie (one version includes Steak Mince 'N' Cheese)
Philippines	Chicken (fried leg) McDo with Rice
Italy	Pizzarotto (dough filled with cheese and marinara sauce)
France	Le M Burger (burger served on a ciabatta roll baked in a stone oven)

SOURCE: Caitlin Morton, "McDonald's Abroad: 25 Fast Food Items You Can't Get in the U.S.," Condé Nast Traveler, November 14, 2014.

early ages, people are bombarded with images and other messages that create new wants and encourage the pursuit of such wants.

This emphasis on consumption draws people's attention away from the dramatic inequalities documented in this chapter, such as in wealth, income, and health. Rather than becoming dismayed at the injustice of such inequalities, people are seduced into focusing on the types of consumer products on which these systems rely. Instead of acting to change the economic system, they buy into it by consuming more and more goods. However, each consumer item provides satisfaction for only a short period of time. The need to keep up constantly with the most recent iPhone or other consumer gadget keeps people working harder and harder to consume more and more. From this perspective, this continuous desire helps corporations and their wealthy home countries by maintaining steady flows of profits, but it does not actually make people any happier, and it does not address the inequalities in the system of stratification itself. Low-income countries that become more oriented toward consumer culture are likely to dig themselves further into debt and grow ever more reliant on large corporations and wealthy countries for steady streams of money and consumer goods.

The fair trade system aims to help coffee farmers like this one earn a decent price for their crop and insulate them from price fluctuations while also aiding their communities.

ASK YOURSELF

How can consumption reinforce global stratification? When a country's economy is developing, do you think mass consumption should be the ultimate goal? Why or why not?

FAIR TRADE

The concept of fair trade offers a different way of approaching consumption and global stratification (Brown 2013; Moberg 2015; Raynolds and Bennett 2015). **Fair trade** is an alternative way of organizing highly unequal global trade, with the aim of mitigating global inequalities. The fair trade system links consumers in the Global North to producers in the Global South, so that consumers know where their products come from and under what conditions they were produced. Fair trade producers are given better prices for their products, with the goal of addressing the income and power imbalance between producer and consumer countries. Fair trade is meant to reduce global economic inequalities by helping empower workers and alleviate poverty in the Global South.

One of the most common products in the fair trade system is coffee, and it offers a good example of how the system works. Coffee is one of the world's most important primary products. Much of the world's coffee is produced by small-scale farmers in the Global South. Producing coffee is very labor-intensive, and it offers low financial return. In the global market, conventional (i.e., non–fair trade) coffee is subject to fluctuations in pricing on the global market. Prices can drop as low as $0.43 per pound (in 2015, farmers were paid an average of $1.11 per pound). When prices fluctuate so unpredictably and can drop so low, many farmers cannot earn enough money from their coffee to sustain themselves. In other words, farmers' costs of production can exceed the price that they are paid for their coffee. In these instances, farmers are likely to experience extreme poverty, hunger, and malnutrition; they may not be able to send their children to school and can lose their farms and livelihood, increasing local unemployment.

The fair trade system seeks to address these hardships in several ways. First, it guarantees farmers a minimum price for their coffee, rather than allowing the price to be subject to the whims of the global market. In 2016, farmers in the fair trade system were paid a minimum of $1.40 per pound for coffee (or $1.70 per pound if it was also certified organic). Unlike coffee growers in conventional markets, fair trade farmers are also given advance payments for their coffee—they do not have to wait for payment until an entire crop is harvested. This helps farmers by giving them a steady stream of income to feed their families and cover other basic personal and business expenses. Fair trade coffee farmers are also required to be part of a cooperative, and wholesale buyers of fair trade coffee make additional payments of $0.20 to 0.30 per pound to the cooperative for use in the community. This premium is often used to build schools, to establish community health centers, and to improve farming techniques.

To participate in the fair trade system, farmers must meet a set of conditions regarding their production practices that are meant to empower workers and improve environmental sustainability. Participants must be small-scale farmers who own their own farms and are organized into self-governing cooperatives with democratic decision-making procedures. They must meet certain working conditions and cannot employ child labor. They are required to follow protocols regarding the use of fertilizers, pesticides, and other farming practices to promote environmental sustainability. In addition to needing to meet quality standards, farmers who sell fair trade coffee are regularly monitored to ensure that they meet these social and environmental standards.

When consumers in the Global North (e.g., the United States, Canada, England, or Australia) buy fair trade coffee, they tend to pay a little more than they would for other coffee, for moral or ethical reasons (Brown 2013). Given their position within the global stratification structure, Global North consumers use their higher incomes to pay a fair price and to address at least some of the economic injustices inherent in the global system. In the case of coffee, these premiums go back to the 30 countries where fair trade coffee is produced, with the majority of fair trade coffee coming from Colombia, Brazil, Peru, Nicaragua, and Costa Rica.

The first fair trade product (coffee) appeared on the market in 1988. While coffee remains the most important fair trade commodity (accounting for 25 percent of all retail sales), fair trade has expanded tremendously. Other food products include bananas, cocoa, dried fruit, fresh fruit and vegetables, honey, juices, nuts, oil, quinoa, rice, spices, sugar, tea, and wine. There are also non-food fair trade

products, such as beauty products, cotton, cut flowers, ornamental plants, sports balls, gold, platinum, and silver. In the United States, public awareness of fair trade grew from 12 percent in 2004 to 34 percent by 2011 and 59 percent by 2016 (Fairtrade USA 2016). In countries where fair trade is most common (e.g., the United Kingdom, Germany), 90 percent of consumers recognize fair trade logos. Worldwide it is estimated that 5.9 billion euros (nearly $7.3 billion) were spent on certified fair trade products in 2014 (Fair Trade International 2015). A few markets are now coming to be dominated by fair trade goods. For example, in Switzerland, 55 percent of all bananas sold are certified fair trade, and in the United Kingdom 42 percent of all bagged sugar meets fair trade standards.

Of course, conflict/critical theorists like Horkheimer and Adorno would be critical of fair trade for its focus on the use of consumption to address global inequalities. They might argue that using consumption to make change helps perpetuate consumer culture and consumerism. Only consumers who have higher incomes can afford this type of "ethical consumerism." It reinforces the inequalities inherent within capitalism by creating a new market segment that corporations can exploit for profit. Instead, critics might suggest, emphasis should be placed on the need to pay people a living wage and the development of new economic systems that end worker exploitation and are not based on consumption, especially mass consumption.

CHECKPOINT 9.5: CONSUMPTION AND GLOBAL STRATIFICATION

CONCEPT	DESCRIPTION
Global consumer culture	The idea that consumption is the primary source of meaning in life, which helps strengthen the power of capitalist corporations and reinforces inequality
Fair trade	An alternative way of organizing global trade that gives producers better prices for their products

SUMMARY

Global stratification refers to the hierarchical differences and inequalities among countries and individuals across the world. This stratification is evident in the oppression of the Global South by the Global North, the differences among high-, middle-, and low-income countries, and the differences between the richest and poorest people in the world.

Global economic inequalities take many forms. For example, there is a large and persistent global digital divide that limits the ability of some people in less developed countries from accessing and using the internet. Differences in wealth also lead to global health inequalities, including

vastly different life expectancies, levels of nutrition, and disease rates. Though gender stratification exists throughout the world, it is more pronounced in some countries. Typically, men have greater access to high-pay and high-status occupations and wealth, while women are more likely to be found in low-skill jobs that offer less pay and status.

While global inequalities are highly persistent, it is possible for countries to develop economically and to change their positions within the global stratification system. Some scholars argue that poor countries can compete to offer the lowest wages possible in order to attract further development or focus on industrial upgrading. Foreign aid may also be offered to countries to encourage development and to improve social welfare, although such aid is at least at times in the self-interest of the giving nation.

The dominant structural/functional theory of global stratification is modernization theory, which argues that technological and cultural factors explain countries' varying levels of economic and social development.

In contrast, conflict theorists argue that rich countries oppress and exploit poor countries, thus keeping them poor. Consumption is related to global stratification in several ways. For example, different levels of economic wealth enable different levels of consumption and standards of living. The increasing global desire for consumer goods helps reinforce existing power structures. Fair trade is one way in which people can engage in ethical consumerism to address global power imbalances.

KEY TERMS

colonialism, 252
fair trade, 255
foreign aid, 249
global care chain, 245

high-income
    economies, 235
imperialism, 252
low-income
    economies, 236

middle-income
    economies, 235
modernization theory, 251
neomodernization, 251

postcolonialism, 253
theories of
    colonialism, 252
world-systems theory, 253

REVIEW QUESTIONS

1. Compare and contrast the different ways of classifying countries in the global stratification system. What does each classification emphasize?

2. How does access to the internet and new technologies relate to the global system of stratification? How can the internet be used to alter this system?

3. How much health inequality exists in the world? Using the recent Ebola outbreak as an example, explain how differences in wealth affect health outcomes.

4. How are men and women affected differently by the global economy? Do you expect these differences to change significantly in the future? Why or why not?

5. How are families affected by global stratification?

6. Does a race to the bottom provide opportunities for economic development? How would world-systems theory explain the race to the bottom?

7. Which method of economic development would best help countries move up in the global stratification structure? Explain.

8. According to structural/functional theories, how is culture related to global stratification?

9. Is foreign aid an effective way of addressing global poverty? How might conflict theories explain the role of foreign aid in global stratification?

10. What are the benefits and limitations of promoting consumption, even through fair trade, to address global stratification? What are the effects of global consumer culture on inequality?

RACE AND ETHNICITY

Minorities Acquire Political Power

In 2005, Evo Morales, a widely popular union leader and political activist, was elected president of Bolivia on the basis of an unorthodox leadership style and a reformist agenda. He was reelected in a landslide in 2009, and he won a third term, once again by a wide margin, in 2014. However, in 2016, a referendum thwarted his effort to run for a fourth term. A pioneer in many respects, Morales not only brought the democratic republic of Bolivia a new socialist mandate and a reformed constitution, but as an Aymara, he also became the developing nation's first indigenous president.

The Aymara are a racially and ethnically distinct people who have lived in central South America for more than 2,000 years. Conquered first by the Incas and then by Spanish colonists, they lived as an indentured minority group until Bolivia won its independence in 1825. Despite achieving legal freedom, however, the Aymara continued to be stereotyped, discriminated against, and marginalized by the country's Spanish-descended majority.

After nearly two centuries of marginalization, the Aymara rose via a number of social movements to achieve social equality and political power for Bolivia's indigenous populations. Organizations such as the militant Tupac Katari Guerrilla Army and Evo Morales's own Movimiento al Socialismo (MAS) challenged racist norms and championed sweeping reform. Running on a string of successful MAS actions (including the ousting of the previous president) and a populist platform of farmers' rights and antimilitarism, Morales transcended old stereotypes and expectations, rising to his country's highest office.

Like Nelson Mandela before him in South Africa and Barack Obama, his U.S. contemporary, Evo Morales is a living symbol of a particular culture's ongoing struggle with prejudice, racism, and institutional discrimination. His presidency marks an important step in Bolivia's social evolution, but it by no means signifies that the Aymara have

LEARNING OBJECTIVES

10.1 Contrast historical and recent views of racial categories and ethnic identities in the United States.

10.2 Describe majority–minority relations.

10.3 Discuss the foundations of racism.

10.4 Explain race and ethnicity in a global context.

edge.sagepub.com/ritzerintro4e

- Take the chapter quiz
- Review key terms with eFlashcards
- Explore multimedia links and SAGE readings

$SAGE edge™

achieved social equality. Racism and ethnic discrimination have permeated Bolivia for hundreds—if not thousands—of years. During that time, the country's dominant groups have accumulated wealth, power, and prestige—assets they have been reluctant to share.

It took roughly eight generations for Bolivia to elect its first indigenous president and slightly longer for the United States to elect its first biracial one. These accomplishments have led some to suggest that we have achieved a postracial, or "color-blind," world. Racism, xenophobia, ethnic conflict, and ethnocentrism are sensitive topics for most people. However, denying that these difficult problems persist will only perpetuate them. ●

A discussion of race and ethnicity flows naturally from a discussion of social stratification. Racial and ethnic differences per se are not a problem. Problems arise when these differences are defined in such a way that people are ranked at or near the bottom of the stratification system *because* of their race or ethnicity. In addition, those in these groups confront prejudicial, often racist, attitudes and discriminatory conduct. **Racism** consists of defining a minority group as a race, attributing negative characteristics to that group, and then creating the circumstances that keep that group at a disadvantage relative to the majority (Law 2012b).

While many scholars and citizens have come to believe that racism is on the wane and that the chances for racial integration and a postracial society have improved (Alba 2009; Khanna and Harris 2015; Wise 2010), others contend that racism not only continues to exist but also remains highly virulent (Bonilla-Silva 2015; Feagin 2012; Jung, Vargas, and Bonilla-Silva 2011). To understand the conflicting claims, we need to put the issue of race into a broader context and define concepts basic to a sociological understanding of race, ethnicity, and majority–minority relations.

THE CONCEPTS OF RACE AND ETHNICITY

Globally, many groups of people have been singled out for differential treatment on the basis of "race." They include people whose complexions or skin colors are different—white, black, brown, red, and yellow—as well as those who share a lineage, such as Roma, Jewish, Arab, Navajo, Tibetan, Finnish, and Serbian. You may notice a difference between these two sets of groups. The reason is that **race** is a *socially constructed* definition based on some real or presumed physical, biological characteristic, such as skin color or hair texture, as well as on a shared lineage (Law 2012a; Omi and Winant 1994). However, races are usually defined according to social and historical ideas about what has been deemed biologically important. While race is often based on real or presumed bodily characteristics, it is more about what people define it to be than about any meaningful physical differences. **Ethnicity** is also socially defined, but on the basis of some real or presumed cultural characteristic, such as language, religion, traditions, or cultural practices. Ethnic groups may define themselves on the basis of their ethnicity, or they may be so defined by others. **Ethnic groups** have a sense of shared origins and relatively clear boundaries, and they tend to endure over time. These boundaries may be recognized by both insiders and outsiders (Carter and Fenton 2010).

While races and ethnic groups have been defined separately, the line between race and ethnicity is not always clear (Kivisto and Croll 2012, 8–13). Races are often considered ethnic groups, and ethnic groups are often considered races. For instance, *white* is a racial category that is frequently subordinated to ethnic categories such as Italian American or White Russian. Similarly, *black* has become "ethnicized." For example, Davis (1991) argues that blacks in the United States are now a self-conscious social group with an "ethnic identity." The creation of Kwanzaa, soul food, and the development of hip-hop all speak to the significance of *African American* as a cultural identity—not just a racial one. On the other hand, Jews, most notoriously in Nazi Germany during the Holocaust, have frequently been thought of not simply as an ethnic group but, as mentioned previously, also as a race. However, Jews do not all come from the same genetic stock; some have Semitic features, and others have European features. They do tend to have some ethnic characteristics in common, most notably a religion and a shared cultural history. Thus, as you read this chapter, which at times discusses race and ethnic groups separately, bear in mind the strong overlap between race and ethnicity.

HISTORICAL THINKING ABOUT RACE

The concept of race has an ancient history. It has taken many different forms over the centuries, but it always serves as a way of differentiating among groups of people and creating hierarchies that empower some and disempower, or disadvantage, others (Song 2007). Race has also played a key role in most imperial conquests, often with whites imposing their will on, and then exploiting, other races. During the

What is race, and what is ethnicity? This Ethiopian boy, newly arrived in Israel, is a member of an ancient Jewish community.

peak of the British Empire, for example, the British controlled India, the West Indies, and West Africa, all of whose dark-skinned populations were subordinated to the British. The rationalizations for this pattern of dominance included both "scientific" and cultural explanations.

"Scientific" Explanations

Following the Enlightenment, and especially in the nineteenth and early twentieth centuries, folk ideas about race were supplemented with "rational" (which today are seen as pseudoscientific) justifications for treating people of other races differently (Blatt 2007). While Enlightenment thinkers believed in the unity of humankind, they also believed in classifying people along a continuum from primitive to modern. One result was classification schemes based on race. These schemes ranged from those identifying as few as four races, such as Carolus Linnaeus's 1740 distinction among American, European, Asiatic, and African races, to schemes identifying as many as 30 or more races (Arthur and Lemonik 2007a).

A more ominous result was the use of allegedly fixed biological characteristics not simply to differentiate among groups of people but also to "scientifically" justify the unequal distribution of wealth, power, prestige, access to resources, and life chances to subordinate racial groups. In 1795, a German naturalist invented the idea of the Caucasian race as the first and most perfect race. In 1800, a French scientist argued that race was involved in social hierarchies and that whites stood on top of those hierarchies.

Evolutionary thinking spurred interest in racial categories. The idea of social Darwinism, associated with sociologist Herbert Spencer, was taken to mean that racial differences were the result of evolutionary differences among the races. One race was better off, and another was worse off, because of evolution. Further, society was not to

try to tamper with, reduce, or eliminate these differences; it was not to interfere with a natural process. Spencer defined this in terms of the "survival of the fittest" (1851, 151).

Also during the nineteenth century, Gregor Mendel's work on genetics and heredity led to the idea that the races could be distinguished from one another on the basis of their genetic makeup. This idea played a role in the development of the eugenics movement, which notoriously argued that the human population could be improved genetically through scientific manipulation. Especially in the first half of the twentieth century and during the Nazi era, eugenicists defended racial segregation, opposed interracial marriage, and sought the restriction of immigration and the compulsory sterilization of those considered "unfit."

ASK YOURSELF
Do you think the ideas behind the eugenics movement would be widely accepted by many people today? Why or why not?

Others criticized these extreme ideas while still arguing the existence of genetically based racial differences in behavior. With the creation of the IQ test in the early 1900s, IQ was used not only to differentiate among races but also to demonstrate racial superiority and inferiority. Later scholars argued that it is possible to make predictions based on race about intelligence (Herrnstein and Murray 1994), the likelihood of inheriting certain diseases (Hatch 2009), and the propensity to engage in criminal activities (Duster 2003). In 2007, Nobel laureate James Watson (co-discoverer of the structure of DNA) controversially contended that races with darker skin have a stronger sex drive than do those with lighter skin. He also stated that he was "gloomy about the prospect of Africa" because blacks scored lower on intelligence tests than whites. Watson later recanted, saying that he did not believe that Africans were "genetically inferior" (Law 2012a).

The pseudoscientific focus on race as the source of significant social differences has gotten a recent boost because of the growing interest in genetics and the success of the international Human Genome Project, which seeks to create a map of human biological differences (Hauskeller, Sturdy, and Tutton 2013). However, the goal of this project is simply "to understand the genetic factors in human disease, paving the way for new strategies for their diagnosis, treatment and prevention" and to "accelerate the pace of medical discovery around the globe" (U.S. Department of Health and Human Services 2011). Relative intelligence, personality types, and behaviors are not a focus of study.

Threats to the Roma

The Roma, often called Gypsies, have long been discriminated against for their dark skin, mysterious origins, and Romani language; their distinctive dress; and their itinerant lifestyle, along with their refusal to integrate into any society in which they find themselves. They tend to form tight-knit groups, marry within the Gypsy community, and form strong family ties (see the 2016 documentary *The People Uncounted: The Untold Story of the Roma*).

A group of Roma may appear one day on the outskirts of a community and live there until they are eventually asked to leave. When they do, they may not go very far and may well return again in the future. Thus, they are an excellent example of what Georg Simmel ([1908] 1971b) called the "stranger." They are never too close to or too far from the mainstream community.

The Roma live in many parts of the world today, including the United States and Brazil, but their population has long been concentrated in Europe (Vlase and Voicu 2014). In 2011, it was estimated that between 7 million and 8 million Roma were living in Europe (Lydaki 2012). Figure 10.1 indicates where in Europe they are concentrated.

During World War II, between 200,000 and 600,000 Roma died in Nazi concentration camps (Lydaki 2012). Recently, hostility against them has again increased throughout Europe, and while they tend to live in nomad camps under tight police controls and close surveillance, the Roma survive and continue to reinforce their distinct cultural identity.

Given the European Union's open borders, many more Roma than before have traveled from Eastern Europe to wealthy Western European countries,

FIGURE 10.1 • Roma Population in Eastern Europe

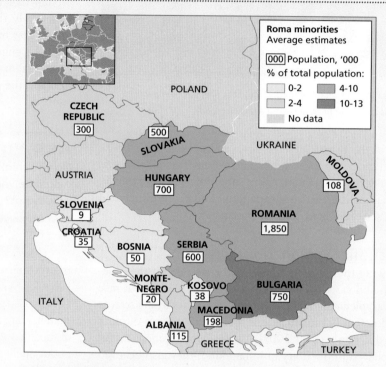

Roma populations
Selected western European countries

	Roma population in thousands	Percentage of total population
Spain	725	1.57
France	400	0.62
Britain	265	0.43
Italy	145	0.24
Germany	105	0.13

SOURCE: Council of Europe–Table of the estimated numbers of Roma in 2012. http://www.coe.int/en/web/portal/roma

seeking relief from poverty and limited prospects. However, many European countries have violated the human rights guaranteed to the Roma by a 2009 European treaty (Phillips, Connolly, and Davies 2010). Some have expelled the Roma, seeing them as a threat to national identity (Bancroft 2005). In 2010, the then-president of France, Nicolas Sarkozy, ordered recently arrived

Roma ousted from the country and had their camps dismantled (Saltmarsh 2010).

Sarkozy had offered the Roma several hundred dollars each to return to Romania or Bulgaria (Simons 2010a, 2010b), leading to a storm of protest over efforts to bribe a minority into leaving France (Erlanger 2010a, 2010b). Human rights groups threatened France with legal action for failing to protect the rights of the Roma, who are, after all, EU citizens (Castle 2010). Some critics said that the Roma would take the money, leave, and then return, having received from France the equivalent of a paid vacation. In late 2014, the mayor of a town in France refused to provide burial space for a Roma child, although the furor that ensued eventually led to the child's being buried in early 2015 (Breeden 2015). Later that year, about 300 Roma were forcibly evicted from a "shantytown" in the outskirts of Paris (*New York Times* Editorial Board 2015).

Ironically, Roma culture today is threatened by the Roma's own activities. Many are settling in cities, posing a threat to their itinerant way of life. Their traditional jobs (such as peddling) are undermined by social and technological change. A high rate of illiteracy persists among the Roma, and children in the camps rarely attend school. Their lack of education will almost undoubtedly lock them into a marginal position in society for the foreseeable future, ensuring that relationships between the Roma and the dominant society remain problematic.

Think About It

Why have the Roma not assimilated into the majority culture in any areas in which they live? Do you think they are unlikely to do so in the future, despite the changes occurring in their way of life? Why or why not?

Contemporary sociologists typically reject single-minded "scientific" explanations of race (Hughey and Byrd 2015; Hatch 2016), including the view that genetic differences are responsible for socially significant differences among racial groups. Rather, most see the historical, structural, institutional, and oppressive contexts of race as explanations for observable differences among racial groups. Sociological research focusing on genetics tends to take the stance that genes matter, but so does environment (Guo, Roettger, and Cai 2008). Conceptualizations by sociologists of race (and ethnicity) acknowledge that socially constructed racial categories overlap with some biological/genetic differences among racial groups. However, biological/genetic differences within racial groups are often as important as those between such groups.

Cultural Explanations

Even though "scientific" explanations of race continue to exist, explanations based on social and cultural factors such as religion, language, and national origin are more prevalent today. In the second half of the twentieth century, ideas of cultural superiority and inferiority increasingly replaced those associated with biological superiority and inferiority. For example, African Americans have been described as having a "culture of poverty," which suggests that they have a sense of learned helplessness and powerlessness (Cohen 2010). While this argument has been used against poor people more generally, it has often been racialized to explain the disproportionately high rates of black poverty (according to the U.S. Census Bureau, in 2015 about 24 percent of African Americans were poor, while about 14 percent of all people living in the United States were impoverished; Proctor, Semega, and Kollar 2016). As is the case with "scientific" explanations, there are often problems with cultural explanations. For instance, the concept of the culture of poverty has been used to legitimate racial

differences in class position rather than to explain these differences in terms of the structural lack of economic opportunity that African Americans have faced throughout their history. Very recently, there has been a revival of interest in serious cultural explanations that avoid the excesses of the culture of poverty argument yet deal critically with aspects of black culture (e.g., the tendency to devalue traditional coparenting). However, such cultural explanations must not ignore the structural problems facing the black community (Patterson and Fosse 2015; Sanneh 2015). Racial differences, like poverty, are complicated and multivariate in cause, effect, and scope. Needless to say, biological, cultural, and structural explanations should not be used, on their own or collectively, to legitimate racial (or ethnic) differences in positions in the system of social stratification.

THE FLUIDITY OF RACIAL CATEGORIES

Sociologists point to the fact that racial categories are often blurred and subject to change; race is a dynamic and fluid social concept. There are many examples of the fluidity and variability of the race concept in the United States. For example, former president Barack Obama is the offspring of a white mother and a black African father. However, he is referred to as black or African American, not "half black" or "half African American." This is a legacy of the **hypodescent rule**, also known as the "one drop" rule or the "one Black ancestor rule" (Davis 1991). In Virginia, people with as little as one-sixteenth African ancestry were considered by law to be black; in Florida it was one-eighth, and in Louisiana it was one-thirty-second. In the early twentieth century, several states, including Tennessee and Alabama, adopted the rule that a person with the slightest trace of African ancestry was considered to be black. While its effect is muted today, the one-drop rule continues to affect how at least some black Americans think of themselves (Guo et al. 2014).

TABLE 10.1 • Race in the U.S. Census, 1790–Present

RACIAL CATEGORY	YEAR(S) USED IN CENSUS	DESCRIPTION
White or black	1790–1850	Only *white* and *black* categories were used (*mulatto* was also used if not "fully" black); *black* was divided into "free" and "slave"
Mulatto	1850–1870, 1890, 1910, 1920	Mixed race, one mixed-race parent and one white parent
Quadroon	1890	Mixed race, one-quarter African ancestry
Octoroon	1890	Mixed race, one-eighth African ancestry
Hindu	1910–1940	South Asian Indian
Mexican	1930	Parent or individual was Mexican-born; this was the first and only time this was listed as a race
Hispanic	1980–present	Anyone of Spanish-speaking descent, regardless of race or physical appearance
More than one	2000–present	First time in U.S. history when a person could identify with more than one specific racial category

SOURCE: Race in the U.S. Census, 1790–Present is Reprinted by Permission of Lisa Speicher Muñoz.

The amount of African blood borne by a person was considered to be so important to society that at various times several variations were encoded into U.S. laws (see Table 10.1): A *quadroon* (one-fourth black) was classified as black, despite the fact that three of four grandparents were white. *Octoroons* (one-eighth black) were defined as black, even though seven of eight immediate ancestors were white and they generally had few, if any, of the physical traits associated with people generally recognized as "black." *Mulatto* originally referred to a child with one "all-white" parent and one "all-black" parent, but it was later changed to mean the child of one mixed-race parent and one white parent (Davis 1991).

Often, individuals who were not white under a hypodescent rule but had light skin and hair and Caucasoid features tried to "pass" for white in order to reap the benefits of being in the privileged group. For example, Homer Plessy was an "octoroon" who was able to pass as "white." When it was discovered that he was "colored," Plessy was forced to leave a "whites only" train car. Plessy fought this in court, and his case eventually led to the "separate but equal" doctrine in the 1896 Supreme Court decision *Plessy v. Ferguson*. This decision legitimated segregation until the Court overturned the ruling in *Brown v. Board of Education of Topeka* in 1954.

The fluidity and variability of the race concept are even clearer when we adopt a global perspective. In South Africa during apartheid (1948–1994), there were three racial categories: white, black, and colored. Whites were descended from Europeans and blacks from Africans. The colored category was more complex, including both those with mixed racial backgrounds (who might also have been labeled black) and those descended from Asians. In many Caribbean and Latin American countries, especially Brazil, race is a matter of gradations between black and white, with indigenous descent and social status factored in as well. In this case, it is especially clear that the color of an individual's skin does not determine whether that person is "black" or "white." It is also true that someone defined as black in the United States might be considered white in, say, Peru. Clearly, racial categories embrace far too much variation to claim a scientific basis. As pointed out previously, variation within racial categories is often as great as, or greater than, variation between racial categories.

Race data have been collected by the United States since its first census in 1790. However, the categories have changed across time, reflecting the social, economic, and political climate of the era. It wasn't until 1970 that individuals were allowed to choose their own race in responding to census questionnaires. Prior to that time, census takers had filled in the race category, based at times on asking the individuals and at other times on their own assumptions (Passel 2010). Although many people have identified as "mixed race" for generations, it wasn't until the 2000 census that such individuals were allowed to identify officially with two or more races.

Table 10.2 shows the racial composition of the U.S. population based on data from the 2000 and 2010 censuses. Of great interest in this table is the strong increase between 2000 and 2010 in the Hispanic or Latino and Asian populations and the slow growth of the Black or African American population.

RACIAL AND ETHNIC IDENTITIES

Because oppression and subordination are often based on race and ethnicity, many individuals from racial and ethnic minorities go to some lengths to identify with the dominant group. They might adopt the cultural values and practices of the dominant culture. For instance, linguistic

TABLE 10.2 • Racial Composition of the U.S. Population, 2000 and 2010

	2000		2010		CHANGE, 2000 TO 2010	
	NUMBER	PERCENTAGE OF TOTAL POPULATION	NUMBER	PERCENTAGE OF TOTAL POPULATION	NUMBER	PERCENTAGE
Hispanic or Latino	35,305,818	12.5	50,477,594	16.3	15,171,776	43.0
Not Hispanic or Latino	246,116,088	87.5	258,267,944	83.7	12,151,856	4.9
White alone	194,552,774	69.1	196,817,552	63.7	2,264,778	1.2
One race	274,595,678	97.6	299,736,465	97.1	25,140,787	9.2
White	211,460,626	75.1	223,553,265	72.4	12,092,639	5.7
Black or African American	34,658,190	12.3	38,929,319	12.6	4,271,129	12.3
American Indian and Alaska Native	2,475,956	0.9	2,932,248	0.9	456,292	18.4
Asian	10,242,998	3.6	14,674,252	4.8	4,431,254	43.3
Native Hawaiian and Other Pacific Islander	398,835	0.1	540,013	0.2	141,178	35.4
Some Other Race	15,359,073	5.5	19,107,368	6.2	3,748,295	24.4
Two or More Races	6,826,228	2.4	9,009,073	2.9	2,182,845	32.0

SOURCE: Racial Composition of the U.S. Population 2000 & 2010 from "Overview of Race and Hispanic Origin: 2010," Table 1, p. 4. *Census Briefs*, March 2011. United States Census Bureau, U.S. Department of Commerce.

assimilation—adopting English, perhaps leaving the old language behind—has almost been inevitable among nearly all ethnic minority groups in the United States. In the past it was common for individuals to change their names to have a more "Anglo" sound; some changed their names when they immigrated to the United States (Cannato 2009). Some individuals defined as part of a minority racial or ethnic group may physically resemble the dominant race or ethnic group, and they may go so far as to straighten, curl, or color their hair or lighten their skin to increase that resemblance (Campbell 2010). They might even undergo cosmetic surgery (Luo 2013).

At the same time, many members of minority groups have strong and positive attachments to their racial or ethnic identities. They make this evident in various ways, including by supporting racial or ethnic organizations, participating in group-specific celebrations, taking pride in the achievements of highly successful members of their groups, and resisting dominant cultural expectations, such as those regarding beauty (Lloréns 2013).

CHECKPOINT 10.1: EXPLAINING RACE AND ETHNICITY

SCIENTIFIC EXPLANATIONS	CULTURAL EXPLANATIONS
Race and ethnicity are biologically determined and fixed.	Race and ethnicity are based on social and cultural factors and fluid.

MAJORITY–MINORITY RELATIONS

Race and ethnicity can be understood in the context of a wide range of relationships that can be subsumed under the heading of *majority–minority relations* (Farley 2011; Yetman 1991). The focus in work on such relations is often on the difficulties experienced by minority groups, especially racial and ethnic minorities. Many of these problems are traceable to majority group prejudice and discrimination (Jackson 2007). Those in a dominant group are prone to exploiting and marginalizing members of subordinate groups.

However, the distinction between *majority* and *minority* raises a number of questions. How can the white race, to take one example, be considered a majority group when it is outnumbered by a wide margin in the world by those in other races? Whites are still numerically dominant in the United States, but the U.S. Census Bureau has projected that by 2044 the non-Hispanic white population in the country will be in the minority when compared with the combined nonwhite population groups, although whites will still outnumber any single racial/ethnic group (Colby and Ortman 2015). The 2010 census terms this demographic situation a **majority-minority population**, defined as a case "where more than 50 percent of the population is part of a minority group" (U.S. Census Bureau 2011;

FIGURE 10.2 • Majority-Minority Counties in the United States, 2012

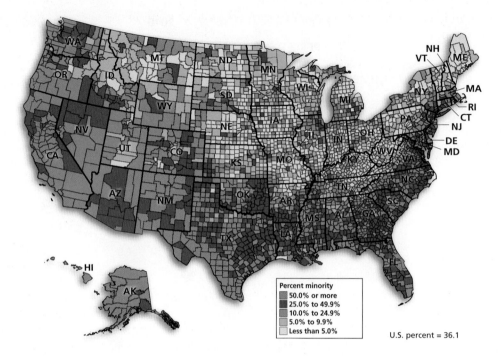

Percent minority
- 50.0% or more
- 25.0% to 49.9%
- 10.0% to 24.9%
- 5.0% to 9.9%
- Less than 5.0%

U.S. percent = 36.1

SOURCE: U.S. Census Bureau, Population Division, Vintage 2012 Population Estimates.

see also Lichter 2013). Majority-minority populations already exist in California, Texas, Hawaii, New Mexico, and the District of Columbia. Figure 10.2 shows the percentage of minorities residing in each county in the United States in 2012.

Similarly, the Kaiser Family Foundation (2015a) reports that there are 157 million women (51 percent) and 151.8 million men (49 percent) in the U.S. population. How can women be a minority when they outnumber men? The answer to this question lies in the sociological definitions of *majority* and *minority,* which do not rely on the numerical size of groups. Rather, these definitions are concerned with differences in levels of money, prestige, and power possessed by groups. As the classic social theorist Max Weber defined the terms, a **minority group** is in a subordinate position in terms of wealth, power, and prestige (status), while a **majority group** is in a dominant position on those dimensions. While these three factors often vary together, a higher ranking in only one or two can be enough to accord a group majority status and, by implication, define another as a minority group. Women are a minority group because although they are in the numerical majority, as a group they have less wealth, power, and prestige than do men.

The same principles apply at other times and in other places. The British colonialists in India were a distinct numerical minority. In fact, this was true of British (and other) colonials virtually anywhere they went. It is something of a marvel that the British were able to control the vast land area of India and its huge population with a comparative handful of soldiers and administrators. The British were the dominant group—with great wealth, power, and prestige in pre-independence India. In spite of their huge numbers, India's natives were the minority group.

THE SOCIAL CONSTRUCTION OF DIFFERENCE

Earlier in human history, quite incredibly, white people discussed whether black persons had souls and whether they were more beast than human. Their descriptions said less about the observable characteristics of black people than about their own need to construct a clear boundary between black people and themselves (Wimmer 2013). Today the white majority no longer denies that blacks and other racial and ethnic minorities are fully human. But the insistence on significant differences between the majority and minorities persists.

We tend to think of majority and minority statuses as being objective in the sense that they are based on such externally observable characteristics as skin color, sex, and age. However, the fact is that all majority and minority statuses are products of social definitions, including social definitions of seemingly objective traits. Because they involve social definitions, majority and minority statuses also differ—those definitions vary over time and from one locale to another. The emphasis on social definitions is based on one of the classic arguments in sociology: "If men define situations as real, they are real in their consequences" (Thomas and Thomas 1928, 572).

ASK YOURSELF

What does it mean to say that if we define a situation as real, it is real in its consequences? How does this sociological argument apply to majority and minority statuses? How might it also apply to social constructions that you have studied in other chapters?

STEREOTYPES, PREJUDICE, AND DISCRIMINATION

A **stereotype** is a generalization about an entire category of people that is thought to apply to everyone in that category. Stereotypes are frequently manifested in daily social interaction. For example, people might assume that a clean-cut, young, white student-athlete at the elite Stanford University would be highly trustworthy. However, just such a man (and there are a number of others like him), Brock Turner, was convicted in 2016 of felony sexual assault on an intoxicated, unconscious female student. In contrast, stereotypes about racial and ethnic minorities tend to work against them. In department stores, security guards may follow black customers without apparent cause, salespeople may view black shoppers with suspicion, cashiers may avoid physical contact with black customers when giving change, and white customers may exhibit nervousness when joined by a black man in an elevator (Staples 1986). This all occurs because of a stereotype relating black people with criminal behavior. In restaurants, servers operate with a stereotype that black diners are "rude" or "demanding." Sociologists Zachary Brewster and Sarah Rusche (2012) studied 200 mostly white servers in 18 restaurants in North Carolina and found that because of that stereotype, 38.5 percent of their subjects admitted to giving black people poorer service. Nearly 53 percent reported seeing other servers treat black customers poorly.

Stereotypes are the basis for prejudice and discrimination. **Prejudice** consists of preconceived negative attitudes, beliefs, and feelings toward minorities, typically derived from unfounded opinions or stereotypes. **Discrimination** is the unfavorable, unjust treatment of minorities arising from the negative stereotypes associated with prejudice (Law 2007). Racial discrimination is unequal treatment based on race (Pager and Shepherd 2008). Discrimination occurs both formally (e.g., on the job) and informally (e.g., in interpersonal situations). It can occur in any social realm, including in schools, workplaces, healthcare institutions, housing, and the criminal justice system. Members of the majority group unfairly deny minority group members access to opportunities and rewards that are available to the majority. In the United States today, much overt discrimination has been outlawed.

Discrimination and prejudice do not necessarily occur in concert with one another. People can be prejudiced without discriminating; they need not act on their prejudices. However, stereotypes, prejudice, and discrimination often interact with one another. For example, black women often face stereotypes that identify them as overly sexual and financially irresponsible (Collins 2004; Rosenthal and Lobel 2016). These stereotypes can have negative real-life consequences. Black women who receive welfare aid have been compelled to undergo compulsory sterilization at some points in U.S. history. In fact, children as young as 12 were coerced to undergo sterilization procedures in some states up until the 1970s (Flavin 2008). The assumption in these cases is that black women will have too many children and be unable to support them financially.

The stereotype of black men as dangerous criminals (Bolton and Feagin 2004; Dow 2016; Ferguson 2001) has persisted from the end of slavery to the present and has created grave difficulties for black citizens. Recent examples of those difficulties are evident in the 2012 acquittal of a Florida man accused of murdering a black man, Trayvon Martin, whom the defendant claimed was a suspicious person. Then there was the killing in late 2014 of an unarmed young black man, Michael Brown, in Ferguson, Missouri, by a white police officer who had assumed that the young man was dangerous. In 2016, police officers in Chicago shot and killed an unarmed black teen fleeing on foot from officers; he had allegedly stolen a car. Numerous other examples exist.

Those killings and resulting demonstrations led to and fueled the development of a powerful new social movement called "Black Lives Matter." It focuses on dealing with the prejudice and discrimination facing black people throughout the United States and other parts of the world. More specifically and extremely, it is concerned with the phenomenon of black lives that are "systematically and intentionally targeted for demise." More positively, it involves an "affirmation of Black folks' contributions to this society, our humanity, and our resilience in the face of deadly oppression" (blacklivesmatter.com). While concerned about violence and many other aspects of black lives in America and internationally, Black Lives Matter is primarily concerned with "state violence," especially extrajudicial violence waged by police officers. Black Lives Matter became more visible in 2014 after helping mount protests over the deaths of several black men at the hands of the police, including Michael Brown in Ferguson, Eric Garner in New York City in 2014, and Freddie Gray in Baltimore, Maryland, in 2015. The killings and protests continued in 2016, most notably involving the murder, also by police officers, of Alton Sterling in Baton Rouge, Louisiana, and Philando Castile in St. Anthony, Minnesota. While expressing concern for this issue, 2016 Democratic presidential candidate Hillary Clinton argued that "all lives matter," while others have argued that "white lives matter" as much, or more than, black lives.

Beyond all this, there are those who feel that this focus on police victims, while legitimate, fails to represent the point of view of the police and the dangers and risks they face on a daily basis. That perspective was underscored by the murders of three police officers in Baton Rouge, Louisiana, and five more in Dallas, Texas, in July 2016. The black perpetrator in Dallas was intent on killing white people, especially white police officers. Although he had no direct ties to the Black Lives Matter movement, he was influenced by it, and angry about recent police shootings and by the prejudice and discrimination practiced by white people in general (Fernandez, Perez-Pena, and Bromwich 2016).

Blacks and other racial minorities are legally entitled to receive fair treatment from the police, as well as in jobs, housing, and education. While they may get fairer treatment in at least some of these areas than they used to, prejudice has been harder to root out. Many minorities still face negative stereotypes. They are constantly reminded that their social group has been defined as "different" from the majority group. George Yancy has described lingering prejudice as being reinforced on a daily basis through "the white imaginary," a "perspective that carries the weight of white racist history and everyday encounters of spoken and unspoken anti-Black racism" (2008, 5). This white imaginary, or racist social construction of "difference," has a cumulative effect that can alienate, disempower, and psychologically oppress blacks (Trepagnier 2010).

Members of the majority group do not experience discrimination or prejudice on a regular and ongoing basis and thus may have trouble empathizing with members of minority groups (Croll 2013). Members of the majority do not have to consider repeatedly whether their daily experiences reflect or do not reflect discrimination and prejudice. Peggy McIntosh (2010) sees this freedom from daily consideration of such issues as "white privilege," which she defines as obliviousness to the sorts of challenges that minorities experience on a regular basis.

INTERSECTIONALITY

Many groups may be described as minority groups. Individuals may belong to more than one such group—for instance, gay Filipinos or Native Americans with disabilities. People's experiences as one type of minority may overlap and intersect with other experiences common to another type of minority. **Intersectionality** is the idea that

Patricia Hill Collins is noted for her research on how members of minority groups are affected by the intersection of a number of minority statuses. Her book *Black Feminist Thought* has received multiple awards.

members of any given minority group are affected by the nature of their position in other systems or other forms of social inequality (P. Collins 1990, 2012; Collins and Bilge 2016; Collins and Chepp 2013). This concept was developed initially to analyze the situation confronting women of color, who face discrimination along both gender and racial lines. It has subsequently been expanded to include other variables, such as age, disability, and sexual orientation.

Minority group members are seen as being enmeshed in a "matrix of oppression" that involves not only race but also gender, ethnic group, sexual orientation, age, social class, religion, ability status, and the part of the globe, North or South, in which they live. The problems associated with being a member of multiple oppressed minority groups are not simply additive; rather, the disadvantages multiply, as do their effects (Kivisto and Croll 2012, 66).

The converse is also true. That is, a person who holds a number of statuses that are highly valued by society is likely to be extremely advantaged. One of the most esteemed groups consists of people who are male, white, Anglo-Saxon, upper-class, heterosexual, and adult. This could be seen as a "matrix of power and advantage."

A dramatic example of how gender and race intersect is provided by black transgender men—individuals who were categorized as "female" at birth but who physically

Race in Cyberspace

Although whites, blacks, and Hispanics use social media at similar rates, recent findings from a Pew Research study indicate that whites and minorities tend to prefer different platforms. Facebook is the most popular social media site for all races, with about 70 percent of all people using the platform. Twitter users are roughly equally distributed, with 25 percent of Hispanics, 27 percent of blacks, and 21 percent of whites using this social media site. But people of color use Instagram more frequently than do whites, and whites are most likely to use Pinterest (Krogstad 2015a). Another Pew study found that the viewing of race-related content on social media platforms was significantly different, depending on a person's race. Twenty-four percent of blacks reported that most of the content they viewed on social media was about race or race relations, compared to only 6 percent of whites (Anderson and Hitlin 2016). While social media has been lauded as having the potential to transcend racial differences (Kang 2000), research has found that racial segregation offline is often replicated online (Boyd 2014). For example, Boyd discovered that teenagers were more likely to be friends both online and offline with other teens of the same race—though the teens themselves understood their behavior through a lens of personal preference rather than racism (2014, 168).

One of the most significant instances of race on social media is the Black Lives Matter movement, which began as a hashtag on Twitter in 2013. #BlackLivesMatter centers on exposing injustices experienced by African Americans, including police brutality, incarceration, and poverty. Pew Research

The #BlackLivesMatter (or #BLM) hashtag spread quickly on Twitter, calling attention to the injustices faced by African Americans and prompting in-person protests. When did you first hear the phrase "Black Lives Matter"?

has found that social media platforms, especially Twitter and tweets associated with #Ferguson and #BlackLivesMatter, have brought greater awareness to racial inequality in the United States. While most of the tweets associated with #BlackLivesMatter have been supportive, following the July 2016 shooting of police officers in Dallas, there was a significant increase in comments that were critical of the movement and a rise of tweets from followers of #AllLivesMatter and #BlueLivesMatter (Anderson and Hitlin 2016). Some scholars argue that #BlackLivesMatter needs to be more inclusive in regard to gender and sexuality, calling for a greater presence of digital intersectionality (Tynes, Schuschke,

and Noble 2016). *Digital intersectionality* refers to the connections between myriad social categories, such as race, ethnicity, gender, sexual orientation, socioeconomic class, and religious affiliation, that an individual or group may identify with online.

Engaging the Digital World

How racially diverse are your online social networks? Do they mimic your offline social networks? If yes, in what ways? How often does content related to race and racial inequality appear on the social media platforms that you frequently use? Do you think this influences your limits on, or expands your understanding of, race in the United States?

transition, with the aid of hormones and surgeries, to become men. They find that their lives as black men are radically different from their previous lives as black women. They come to realize that many white women are afraid of them when they pass on the street, an experience they did not face as black women. As men, they face the experience of being pulled over by police for "driving while black." Whereas white transgender men find that they gain some social privileges as white men that they did not enjoy as white women, black transgender men can experience greater social constraints and discrimination (Schilt 2010).

The allocation of Social Security benefits to the elderly yields another good illustration of the concept of intersectionality. Women over the age of 65 rely on Social Security benefits to a greater extent than do men in their age group, and racial minorities rely on such benefits more than do whites (Angel, Montez, and Angel 2010; Calasanti and Slevin 2001). In the calculation of Social Security and pensions, however, work and income history matters. People who earn more and work more during their lifetimes receive higher Social Security payments in retirement. Because women and minorities face labor force discrimination and thus lower lifetime wages, their retirement income is lower. Black women are particularly vulnerable, as they face both gender and racial discrimination (Calasanti and Slevin 2001). Because black women are less likely than white women to be married, they also gain less from spousal benefits. Whites, especially men whose work lives are not interrupted for childbearing, are more likely than blacks and Hispanics to receive pensions from employers. The disadvantages of being female and a member of a racial minority thus accumulate over time.

Workplace experiences also reflect the concept of intersectionality. Women who work in male-dominated jobs—occupations ranging from high-level professional jobs, such as finance, to blue-collar jobs, such as construction—often face discrimination and limits to advancement. Men who work in female-dominated jobs, such as nursing and elementary school teaching, can find themselves, in contrast, quickly successful and promoted to positions of influence and authority. Christine Williams (1995) has labeled this the "glass escalator" effect. One recent study of the great success of gay men in the fashion design industry offers yet another example of the existence and operation of the glass escalator in a traditionally female-dominated occupation (Stokes 2015). But not all men have access to this glass escalator. Rather, men who are racial minorities can find themselves facing both gender- and race-based discrimination in traditionally female professions (Harvey 2009). In other words, they do not benefit in the same way as white men do because of the ways in which racialized stereotypes interact with gender expectations. Williams (2013) acknowledges that because "class inequalities" have "exploded," her work needs to be updated to reflect new intersectional occupational realities. Workers at the bottom of pay scales confront intersections of class, race, and gender.

PATTERNS OF INTERACTION

When members of majority and minority groups interact, the outcomes tend to follow one of four patterns: pluralism, assimilation, segregation, or genocide.

Pluralism exists in societies where many groups are able to coexist without any of them losing their individual qualities. For example, in pluralistic societies, there may be multiple races, ethnic groups, and religions and many languages spoken.

Assimilation occurs when a minority group takes on the characteristics of the dominant group and leaves its old ways behind. In the United States, assimilation has occurred when immigrant groups have chosen to give up their native languages for English or when they have adopted mainstream American cultural values and customs. Sometimes, however, assimilation has been forced on certain groups. During the late nineteenth and early twentieth centuries, many Native American children were forced into boarding schools where they were given new names, forced to speak English (and punished for speaking their native languages), and taught Christianity.

The United States has leaned more at times toward pluralism and at other times toward assimilation. Even when minorities feel that their differences are respected, all majority–minority relations are fraught with at least the potential for conflict. Members of the majority group act to maintain or enhance their positions, and minority group members struggle to improve theirs, or at least strive to prevent theirs from declining any further. These conflicts, potential or real, are generally resolved in favor of the majority group because it has far greater resources (money, power) than does the minority group.

ASK YOURSELF

If your parents or grandparents came to the United States from another country, did they arrive during a period when pluralism or assimilation was the norm? How did this prevailing norm affect their experience as immigrants? Do you think it has had an effect on your life, or on the life of your family?

This issue was in the news during the 2016 presidential campaign, when then Republican candidate Donald Trump suggested that Muslim communities within the United States (representing about 3.3 million people; roughly 1 percent of the population) constituted a potential source of danger to the country. He also attacked American pluralism

While segregation still exists informally in the United States, especially in schools, it is no longer supported by the law, as it was when this photo was taken in the American South.

and urged at least a temporary "total and complete shutdown of Muslims entering the United States." He proposed that customs agents ask travelers to the United States if they were Muslim; if they said yes, the agents were to turn them away (Rappeport and Haberman 2016).

In the early days of Trump's presidency in 2017, he followed through on these proposals by prohibiting, at least initially for 90 days, entry into the United States of those coming from Syria, Iran, Iraq, Somalia, Sudan, Libya, and Yemen. Christians were to get priority when—and if—refugees from those countries would be permitted to enter beyond that deadline (Walsh 2017). Within hours of the announcement of this new policy, people from those countries began to be refused to be allowed to board planes bound for the United States.

Trump's views and initial actions as president were so outrageous that they led to an outcry from not only Muslims but also many in the majority group in the United States, as well as many people throughout the world.

Segregation is the physical and social separation of majority and minority groups. Historically, segregation was mandated by law in the United States (and elsewhere). As a result, whites and minorities were not able to attend the same schools, live in the same neighborhoods, or share the same public facilities (such as restrooms, theater seating areas, swimming pools, or courtrooms). *Brown v. Board of Education* (1954) is seen as the beginning of the end of legally mandated segregation in the United States. While levels of segregation have declined, such history set into motion practices that continue to segregate majority and minority groups. For example, schools are generally still segregated, a reflection of the persistence of residential

segregation (Logan, Minca, and Adar 2012). Further, residential segregation is key to majority–minority, especially racial, stratification (Massey 2016).

Genocide—an active, systematic attempt at eliminating an entire group of people—is a fourth outcome of majority–minority group relations. A genocidal campaign was conducted against Native Americans from the early days of European settlement in the United States through the 1800s. This was committed even though an official governmental policy of extermination did not exist. In this regard, the tragedy of the Native Americans is not the same as the genocide experienced by Jews, the Roma, and homosexuals during the Nazi reign of terror known as the Holocaust (Berger 2012) or the Tutsi ethnic group during the genocide in Rwanda. In those cases, genocide *was* official government policy.

Given the conceptual background presented previously, we turn now to a discussion of two (among many) areas in which race and ethnicity are important—education and the economy (specifically, consumption).

RACE, ETHNICITY, AND EDUCATION

Economic success is in large part predicted by educational opportunity and achievement. As you can see in Figure 10.3, which shows the relationship between race/ethnicity and educational attainment, Hispanics are the group least likely to complete high school. This is in line with their higher-than-average rate of poverty. Hispanics and blacks are the least likely to get a college degree or beyond. The groups that are more likely to complete a bachelor's

FIGURE 10.3 • Educational Attainment by Race and Ethnicity in the United States, 2015

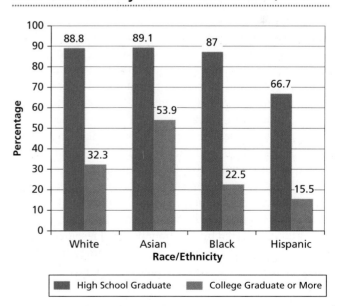

NOTE: Data are for those ages 25 and older.

SOURCE: Data from U.S. Census Bureau, "Statistical Abstract Of The United States: 2012," U.S. Census Bureau.

degree or higher, Asians and whites, are also the two groups with the lowest percentage of members living below the poverty line.

Racial and ethnic disparities in learning outcomes are a critical dimension of inequality. Black and Hispanic students have lower levels of educational attainment. The most obvious explanation for these differences is that black and Hispanic students are significantly more likely than white students to come from poor families. Black and Hispanic families have lower levels of education than whites, and black children are especially likely to grow up in single-parent families. Family background is the strongest predictor of how well a student does in school. Thus, the black–white gap in achievement is considerable in the prekindergarten years (Aud and Hannes 2011). However, among elementary school students with similar family backgrounds, black and white students have similar levels of academic achievement (Yeung and Pfeiffer 2009).

Things change as students enter high school. Many black adolescents disengage in school because they are exposed to an "oppositional" peer culture. Black students often equate doing well in school with "acting white." Consequently, to fit in with their peers and to affirm their racial identity, black students tend to exert less effort in their schoolwork and thus attain lower grades.

Black students are much more likely than white students to attend segregated schools: 74 percent of black students attend schools that are 50 percent or more minority, almost 40 percent attend schools that are 90 percent or more minority, and 16 percent attend schools that are virtually all minority (Aud and Hannes 2011; see Figure 10.4). Much of this is due to residential segregation in the United States: Black families live in predominantly black neighborhoods, and students are typically assigned to schools based on where their families live. School segregation contributes to the black–white gap in learning, because data show that students learn less as the percentage minority in a school increases (Hanushek and Rivkin 2006). Black students are also strongly affected by variation in school resources. Both teacher quality and class size are more important predictors of learning for black students than they are for white students. Thus, school-based reforms, such as better teachers and smaller class sizes, can potentially play an important role in reducing or erasing the black–white gap in learning.

The black–white achievement gap is an important reason why black students are less likely than white students

FIGURE 10.4 • Three Measures of School Segregation for Black Students, 1968–2010

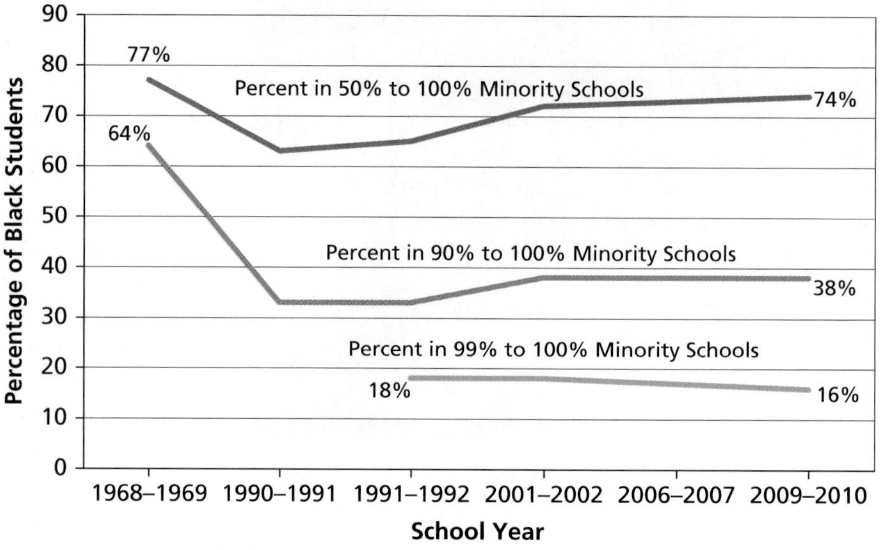

NOTE: 2010 is the most recent date for which data is available.

SOURCE: *E Pluribus . . . Separation: Deepening Double Segregation for More Students,* by Gary Orfield, John Kucsera & Genevieve Siegel-Hawley. September 2012. The Civil Rights Project.

to attend, and to graduate from, a four-year college (Perna 2006). Black students who attend more racially diverse schools are more likely to pursue a college degree and more likely to graduate.

Hispanic students share numerous disadvantages with black students, including having fewer family resources than white students do and attending segregated schools. However, they also face some unique challenges. First, many Hispanic students are recent immigrants to the United States. Interestingly, more-recent Hispanic immigrants to the United States typically do better than those who have been here longer. Much of this "immigrant paradox" is explained by students' orientation toward school and their experience in the broader culture (Suárez-Orozco, Rhodes, and Milburn 2009). New immigrant families typically value hard work and see it as the key to success. In contrast, immigrants who have resided in the United States for a longer time are more aware of the structural barriers to success and do not fully believe that hard work pays off (Portes and Zhou 1993).

Second, Hispanic students have more diverse ethnic backgrounds than do black students. For example, Mexican students typically have the lowest achievement among Hispanic students, while Cuban students rank highest in achievement (Reardon and Gallindo 2008). As Portes and Zhou (1993) note, Cuban students are especially advantaged (compared to other Hispanics) because Cuban immigrants have organized small, tightly knit enclaves that provide resources and support for their children. The same appears to be true for Chinese and Japanese immigrant children (Tsuda 2014; Zhou 2014).

Finally, some Hispanic students may struggle in school if English is their second language. Many schools provide special bilingual programs that help students learn the curriculum in their native language until they are proficient enough in English to enter English-instruction classes. Yet these programs may only further inequalities by limiting access to other kinds of courses and enhancing negative labeling by other students and by teachers (Stromquist 2012). The Hispanic–white gap in learning decreases dramatically from kindergarten through fifth grade, partly reflecting increased facility with English.

RACE, ETHNICITY, AND CONSUMPTION

In the United States and many other countries, people of all races and ethnicities are active in the economy, specifically in consumer culture. However, there are huge differences in the nature of their involvement. Elite members of the white majority in the United States have their pick of the best and most expensive goods and services in the world. Others in the white majority also do well in consumer culture.

Some of those in racial and ethnic minorities are also actively involved in, and well served by, consumer culture. However, minorities face some particular limits and opportunities in their consumption patterns. They also consume goods and services within their own frames of reference (Chin 2007). For example, both black and white American children may own traditional Barbie dolls, but these toys have different meaning for a black child in inner-city Detroit than they do for a white child in an upscale suburb of New York City. In order to address this issue, in early 2016, Mattel, the manufacturer of Barbie, announced that dolls with a variety of skin color tones would be introduced (Abrams 2016).

The history of each race has an important influence on minority consumption. Black slaves themselves were a product for consumption. Only a little more than a half-century ago, blacks and other ethnic and racial minorities were unable to participate in various whites-only consumption settings. One of the most important acts of nonviolent protest during the civil rights movement of the 1950s and 1960s was that of blacks taking seats as paying customers at previously all-white lunch counters. By the late twentieth and early twenty-first century, black and Latino Americans had become an important market segment for consumer culture, largely because of the significant increase in middle-class members of these groups and their growing wealth (Landry 1988; Landry and Marsh 2011).

Still, many other minority group members scrape along at the bottom of the American consumption system, and some—including the chronically unemployed and homeless—are excluded almost completely. Living in a consumer culture is doubly hard for those who cannot participate, or whose participation is limited due to lack of income.

Many minority group members must learn to do without many things, even as they are literally surrounded by the trappings of consumer culture that they cannot afford.

Marketing to Minorities

Clearly, businesses will market to the black and Latino (and many other minority) communities as long as they believe that there is money to be made from them (Jamal, Penaloza, and LaRouche 2015). Such marketing efforts lead to higher levels of consumption of various goods and services within these groups and to deeper involvement of blacks and Latinos in consumer culture.

Corporations interested in maximizing profits and the consumption of their goods and services often use race and ethnicity to sell to minority group members. Certain foods, clothing styles, haircare products and cosmetics, financial services, and so on are sold exclusively, or nearly so, to particular racial or ethnic groups. In addition, advertising and marketing campaigns for goods and services sold to the general public may also target particular racial or ethnic groups.

ASK YOURSELF

Should companies be allowed to create marketing campaigns specifically targeting racial and ethnic minorities? Why or why not? Could preventing such marketing actually be a form of discrimination against minorities? Explain your answer.

One example of this kind of racialized marketing is found in menthol cigarettes. Black smokers are four times as likely as white smokers to choose menthol cigarettes over unflavored cigarettes. This preference for menthol cigarettes has been relentlessly reinforced by advertising campaigns, creating what one research scientist has called "the African Americanization of menthol cigarette use" (McNichol 2011). As early as the 1950s, makers of Kool menthol cigarettes used black sports celebrities and musicians as spokespersons. In the 1980s and 1990s, Kool sponsored jazz and hip-hop festivals—two forms of music typically consumed by blacks. In the late 2000s, the federal government considered banning menthol cigarettes. To mobilize the black community against such a ban, the makers of Newport cigarettes, another popular menthol brand, ran ads featuring black men and women that framed such a ban as an assault on civil rights (McNichol 2011). Some leaders in the black community also fought the ban, saying that it unfairly targeted one particular racial group. The U.S. Food and Drug Administration chose not to ban menthols, although it admitted that, according to some research evidence, menthols may be more addictive than unflavored cigarettes (McNichol 2011). Unfortunately, then, the continued marketing of menthols could widen racialized health disparities.

The Cosmopolitan Canopy: Race and Civility in Everyday Life (W. W. Norton & Company, 2011)

Elijah Anderson (William K. Lanman, Jr., Professor of Sociology at Yale University; PhD, Northwestern University, 1976)

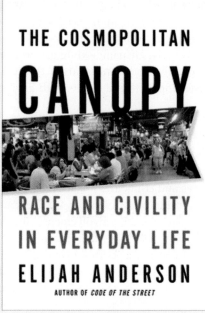

W.W. Norton. Used with permission.

Elijah Anderson explores public spaces in the city of Philadelphia in order to observe the everyday interactions between individuals from different racial and ethnic backgrounds. He finds that most urban residents act with civility and coexist peacefully in what he calls "cosmopolitan canopies," or "settings that offer respite from the lingering tensions of urban life and an opportunity for diverse peoples to come together" (2011, xiv). Cosmopolitan canopies are relaxed environments that encourage "people watching" without fear of offending strangers, because "ethnocentric feelings" are kept in check (2001, xvii). Two places in particular exemplify cosmopolitan canopies: Philadelphia's Reading Terminal Market and Rittenhouse Square. Reading Terminal Market is a crowded public space with a variety of shops, kiosks, and restaurants, where interracial interactions and cross-cultural exchanges are common and do not engender anxiety or conflict. Rittenhouse Square is an historic public park where a diverse population gathers to observe others and be observed without feeling self-conscious. Though Anderson discovers that interracial eye contact, or "eye work," can be complicated here, most "people watching" across color lines and other social categories, such as gender and sexuality,

is understood as a form of entertainment and as harmless fun.

Outside of cosmopolitan canopies, racial and ethnic differences are more likely to be emphasized and can result in discomfort and tension. In these spaces, individuals often form racially homogenous "clumps" and avoid interracial interactions (Anderson 2011, 226). For example, many whites will not sit by young black males on public transportation because they look "ghetto" and are perceived as possibly dangerous (2011, 217). The black middle class often experiences uncomfortable encounters outside of cosmopolitan canopies because the dominant white society views them as lower class. This is one reason why, Anderson argues, they conspicuously display their wealth by wearing expensive clothes or driving luxury cars. Anderson finds that middle-class blacks feel the color line acutely in upscale restaurants, where they clearly confront racial prejudice and discrimination. They are stereotyped as "difficult, demanding customers, who don't tip" and are often seated at the worst tables (2011, 235–236). Many prefer to patronize chain restaurants, where they feel they receive better service—if they choose to eat out at all. Anderson argues that we need to extend the civility and openness of

cosmopolitan canopies to not just racially segregated public spaces but also our neighborhoods and workplaces in order for all of us to become more comfortable with diversity.

Supplementary Resources

- Listen to a free podcast of Anderson delivering a talk on his book *The Cosmopolitan Canopy* at https://libwww.freelibrary .org/podcast/episode/650.

- You can read an article by Anderson based on his popular ethnographic study *Code of the Street* in *The Atlantic* at http://www.theatlantic.com/ magazine/archive/1994/05/the -code-of-the-streets/306601.

White Consumption of Black Culture

Many whites are interested in consuming products associated with ethnic minorities. Consider the popularity of sushi restaurants and salsa as a condiment, among many other things. Whites have a strong, longstanding interest in consuming aspects of black culture (P. Collins 2009). There is, for example, a lengthy history of white interest in jazz, much of which comes from the black community. More recently, various aspects of black music (e.g., rap), and black culture more generally (e.g., ways of dressing, talking, and walking), have been of great interest to whites, especially youths.

However, white consumption of black culture has been highly selective. For example, white teenagers often want to be "black" on Saturday night in terms of things like the clothes they wear and their music preferences. However, their desire for blackness is likely limited to clothes, music, and the like, whereas the rest of the time they, and indeed whites in general, avoid and even criticize black culture.

White consumption of black culture is selective in another, more important, sense. It could be argued that whites are interested in consuming "everything but the burden" associated with black culture (cited in P. Collins 2009, 141). White entrepreneurs tend to select out of black culture only what they think is desirable, especially what they think is marketable and from which they can earn a profit. Interestingly, whites, especially youth, seem to prefer to consume aspects of black lower-class culture. More

damagingly, whites often glorify the negative aspects of black culture.

White interest in consuming "everything but the burden" could also be taken to mean that whites are unwilling to accept their responsibility for the problems that exist in the black community and that can be traced to white racism. Acceptance and consumption of a few aspects of black culture can be seen as helping assuage white responsibility, at least collectively, for the difficulties that exist within the black community.

ASK YOURSELF

Do you think the "consumption of everything but the burden" hypothesis is correct? Why or why not? Give examples to support your answer.

Commercialization of Ethnicity

Minority groups sometimes seek to commercialize themselves—to sell themselves and their unusual or unique offerings to a larger public. For example, many tourists visiting Hawaii are attracted to luaus, which are marketed as a unique indigenous custom. Similarly, tourists in the southwestern United States may time their travels to coincide with Native American powwows. Locales like the Hollywood Forever cemetery in California draw thousands of tourists annually for the one-day "Day of the Dead" (*Dia de los Muertos*) event unique to Mexican cultural traditions. At such events, members of the ethnic group sell arts, memorabilia, and other cultural products to the "consumers" of the experience. In this way, they can be said to be commercializing themselves.

There is an international market for cultural and ethnic products, which people in some parts of the world seek to exploit. Some ethnic groups in southern Africa have become like business corporations in their attempts to capitalize on what they have to offer to the global market (Comaroff and Comaroff 2009). Some ethnic and racial minorities go so far as to seek exclusive rights to their cultures through legal means (Kasten 2004). If they control their "brand," they can sell parts of it themselves (e.g., by sole rights to its distinctive products), or they can sell the rights to aspects of that culture to third parties (e.g., majority-group tour operators taking tourists on "Zulu tours" to Africa).

These participants in a Day of the Dead celebration at the Hollywood Forever Cemetery wear costumes and pose before an altar honoring the family's dead. During this annual event, art, memorabilia, and other tourist-oriented products are sold. Are cultural minorities adversely affected by the commercialization of their culture?

CONCEPT	DESCRIPTION
Prejudice	Negative attitudes, beliefs, and feelings toward minorities
Discrimination	Unfavorable treatment of minorities based on negative stereotypes or prejudice
Intersectionality	Belonging to more than one type of minority group
Pluralism	The coexistence of many groups that retain their individual qualities
Assimilation	A process in which a minority group takes on the characteristics of the dominant group, leaving its old ways behind
Segregation	The physical and social separation of majority and minority groups

RACISM

As noted at the beginning of this chapter, racism involves defining a group as a race and attributing negative characteristics to that group (Elias and Feagin 2016). It also involves creating the circumstances that keep that group at a disadvantage relative to the majority. Racism can be seen as a subtype of xenophobia, or "fear of strangers." **Xenophobia** involves the beliefs, attitudes, and prejudices that reject, exclude, and vilify groups who are not part of the dominant social group.

Note that the definition of racism used here allows us to discuss negative attitudes and treatment based on either race or ethnicity. Cultural characteristics that are different

FIGURE 10.5 • How Much Discrimination Is There against African Americans?

% saying ...

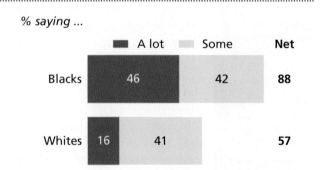

NOTE: Blacks and whites include only those who are not Hispanic.

SOURCE: For African Americans, discrimination is not dead, by Carroll Doherty. June 28, 2013. Reprinted by permission of Pew Research Center, Washington, DC.

from the mainstream, the hallmark of ethnic identity, are almost always associated with racial groups, so cultural discrimination is central to racial discrimination. In short, racism is based on ethnocentrism, or the belief that the norms, values, and customs of one's own group are superior to those of other groups (S. Brown 2007b; Sumner [1906] 1940).

If you were to ask any American on the street whether he or she is racist, you would be almost certain to be told that the person is not prejudiced and considers people of all races and ethnicities to be equal. Yet racist attitudes and behaviors persist. Minority members are likely to have experienced, or to know someone in their group who has experienced, discrimination at the hands of a white person or within the structure of an organization or society as a whole. A Pew Research Center poll of U.S. adults found that blacks are far more likely than whites to say there is "a lot of discrimination" against blacks (Doherty 2013): 46 percent of black respondents agreed with this statement, while only 16 percent of whites agreed (see Figure 10.5).

Erving Goffman's ideas on dramaturgy can be used to analyze this disparity (Slatton and Feagin 2012). Whites often quite unconsciously conceal or play down their racism in their *front stage*. However, when they are *back stage* with those they are confident hold similar views, they are quite comfortable making overtly racist comments or telling racist jokes (see Chapter 5 for a discussion of the concepts of front and back stage). If they happen to be in a place where outsiders, especially minority group members, might intrude, they may use code words or symbols instead of overt racial slurs.

FOUNDATIONS OF RACISM

Social Structure and Racism

In the United States, whites disproportionately occupy higher-level positions, and blacks are more likely to be near or at the bottom of the racial hierarchy. However, this is an overly simplistic picture of U.S. racial stratification (Song 2007). There are blacks (and other minorities) scattered throughout every level in that hierarchy, even in its highest reaches, as exemplified, most notably, by the recent presidency of Barack Obama (2009–2017). Undocumented immigrants to the United States are predominantly Latino, and they are much more likely than blacks to exist at the lowest rungs in the racial hierarchy. About 21 percent of Hispanics in the United States are poor, ranging from 42 percent in Kentucky to 15 percent in Virginia and the state of Washington and 12 percent in Washington, DC. Large numbers of whites also exist at or near the bottom rungs in that hierarchy: About 13 percent of whites in the United States are poor (Kaiser Family Foundation 2015b).

As is clear in the preceding discussion, one of the main indicators of racial stratification is the extent to which poverty is linked to race. Figure 10.6 shows the relationship between race/ethnicity and poverty between 1959 and 2015. The fact that 24.1 percent of blacks and 21.4 percent of Hispanics were below the poverty line in 2015—compared with 11.6 percent of whites and 11.4 percent of Asians—is a strong indicator of economic disadvantage for the first two groups. Also worth noting is the strong increase in poverty among blacks and Hispanics beginning in 2008, right after the onset of the Great Recession. The historical influences of segregation and legal discrimination in generations past, coupled with the economic benefits of white privilege, help link economic disadvantage and racism.

Culture and Racism

Some sociologists argue that a part of the larger culture of the United States involves a "white racial frame" through which whites, and to some degree blacks, view race (Feagin 2010, 2013; Slatton and Feagin 2012). The **white racial frame** includes an array of racist ideas, racial stereotypes, racialized stories and tales, racist images, powerful racial emotions, and various inclinations that discriminate against blacks (as well as other minorities, including Latinos [Feagin and Cobas 2014]). To a certain extent, blacks themselves have adopted elements of this frame. This is exemplified in "gangsta" style being identified as part of black culture. It is also found in measures of success—such as graduating from college, gaining a professional job, or living in the suburbs—that are seen by black culture as selling out, or "acting white." This white racial frame is largely responsible for perpetuating racial stereotypes, as is seen throughout movies, music videos, and television shows.

This set of ideas is pervasive throughout American culture and is found in and affects many, if not all, of its structures and institutions. These ideas come to "operate as a taken-for-granted, almost unconscious common sense" (Winant 2001, 293) in the minds of the individuals who accept them. Thus, for example, we have the widely held belief that the Puritan work ethic underlies educational and occupational success, ignoring the role played by external social factors. Americans firmly believe, often despite evidence to the contrary, that "equal opportunity" and individual habits, like "hard work," are all a person needs to succeed (DiTomaso 2013).

Racism has often been, and can still be, a matter of physical domination of minorities by, for example, the state. However, racism is now more a matter of **hegemony**. That is, one race now subordinates another more on the basis of dominant ideas, especially about cultural differences, than through force.

Throughout this discussion, whiteness as a racial category has either been ignored or, especially in the case of the white racial frame, dealt with negatively as the source of prejudice and discrimination against blacks and other minorities. However, white is a "racial category," and whites can be considered a "racial group" (Hartigan 2014; Smangs 2016). Whiteness can be, and for some people is, a positive source of identity. It can also be seen as a source for good, not only for whites but also for minorities. Many whites are antiracist, and large numbers of them embrace other races. In any case, as we saw earlier in this chapter, in not too many decades,

FIGURE 10.6 • Poverty Rates in the United States by Race and Ethnicity, 1959–2015

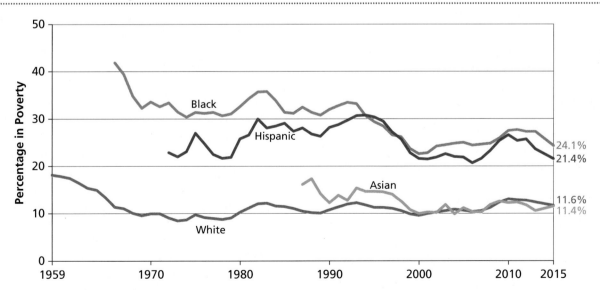

SOURCE: Data from Bernadette D. Proctor, Jessica L. Semega, and Melissa A. Koller. 2016. "Income and Poverty in the United States: 2015." Current Population Reports, P60–256(RV). September. Last accessed January 26, 2017.

A woman who opened a temporary mosque in Temecula, California, offers a flower in response to protesters near the site of a planned Islamic center. How have increased global flows of people affected your community?

whites will be a numerical minority in the majority-minority United States. As a group, whites will then need to be dealt with in very different ways in any discussion of race in the United States, more in line with the approach taken concerning minorities in this chapter. Nevertheless, the relationship of whites to minorities and the role of whiteness in prejudice and discrimination need to remain the focus of attention in work on majority–minority relations, as well as in efforts to create a more equitable society.

Racist Motives

One reason racism is so difficult to eradicate is that it serves a number of functions for individuals. Law (2010, 2012b) identifies the following motives for racism expressed toward black Americans—all of which can apply to any form of racial or ethnic animosity:

- *Ideological motive.* Simply stated, racism fits with some people's fundamental beliefs about the world. For example, they may view whites as a "superior" race and therefore come to the conclusion that all other races are "inferior" to whites.

- *Bigotry motive.* Racism may stem from a stereotype-based hatred or fear. Journalism scholars such as Austin Scott have remarked on the role of the press in reinforcing bigotry and "white fright." A 1981 *Los Angeles Times* article headlined "Marauders from the Inner-City Prey on L.A.'s Suburbs" described "a 'growing wave' of Black and Latino youth leaving their neighborhoods, 'staging grounds for robbers and burglars and thieves' and riding the freeways 'like magic carpets' to the suburbs where they would 'wreak senseless havoc' on white residents" (Scott 1982, 3).

- *Emotional motive.* People may engage in racist acts because of anger or fear, but also because they enjoy it or because engaging in those acts makes them feel better. This is sometimes seen among those who are insecure or otherwise have low social status and who act to boost their self-esteem or improve their relative social status by demeaning others.

- *Criminal-materialist motive.* Majority group members who are engaged in criminal activities may express race hatred toward minorities involved in similar activities

REUTERS/Mike Blake

that threaten their livelihood. More generally, those engaged in quite legal activities may feel that their economic well-being is threatened and express similar hatred toward those they see as threats. For example, whites may feel that they have not gotten jobs, or lost jobs, because of **affirmative action**, which aims to increase diversity and equal opportunity by taking race and other minority group factors into consideration when it comes to decisions about hiring, among other things (Kennedy 2013).

- *Political-territorial motive.* Majority group members may feel that a given area—ranging anywhere from a single street or even a building to an entire country—belongs to them and thus that minority group members are not welcome there. For example, racism might be involved in a struggle between a white gang and a black gang over control of a street corner, a neighborhood, or a high-rise building in a housing project.

- *Group norm motive.* Racism may stem from group norms that define racism as acceptable, even desirable. The way in which anti-Islamic bigotry seemed commonplace immediately following 9/11, and to some degree remains so to this day, is an example of the group norm motive.

- *Structural motive.* Racism may be traced to larger structures (bureaucratic, military, and so on) where it is either demanded or at least implicitly expected. While this is now illegal, it continues to exist in subtle and informal ways. For example, majority group members who occupy lower levels in a hierarchy may sense that their superiors expect them to behave in a racist manner. Thus, they may discriminate on the basis of race, even though no one has explicitly ordered or instructed them to do so.

INSTITUTIONAL RACISM

While there is a general tendency to emphasize individual prejudice and discrimination in discussing racism, from a sociological perspective, it is institutional discrimination—more specifically, institutional racism (Bonilla-Silva 2009; Carmichael and Hamilton 1967; Ward and Rivera 2014)—that is the far bigger problem. **Institutional racism** is race-based discrimination that results from the day-to-day operation of social institutions and social structures and their rules, policies, and practices (Arthur and Lemonik 2007b). In other words, racism is more than attitudes (prejudice) or behavior (discrimination); it is "systemic" within society, especially American society, and within its most important and powerful social structures (Feagin 2006, 2010, 2013).

Institutional discrimination is found in many settings:

- *Educational systems.* Schools in which the student body is disproportionately black or Latino are often underfunded (Lee 2012).

ASK YOURSELF

Do employment policies that favor seniority work against the goals of affirmative action? If so, how? What type of workplace layoff policy might be less racially and ethnically discriminatory than "last hired, first fired," given that minorities lack seniority as a whole? Do you think the setting of such policies should be up to employers or mandated by law? Why?

- *Labor markets.* Equally qualified black candidates are less likely than their white counterparts to obtain interviews and jobs. Bertrand and Mullainathan (2004) sent out 5,000 résumés in response to real job ads. The only significant difference in the résumés was whether a name sounded very white (Emily or Greg) or very black (Lakisha or Jamal). The authors found that people with white-sounding names received 50 percent more callbacks than did people with black-sounding names. Labor market discrimination (indeed, all forms of discrimination) affects others as well. A study of Muslim women who applied for jobs while wearing headscarves (*hijab*) revealed the effects of more formal discrimination (on the likelihood of callbacks) and more interpersonal discrimination (on the negativity felt from interviewers; Ghumman and Ryan 2013).

- *The courts and prison system.* Drug laws and enforcement heavily penalize the selling and possession of the kinds of drugs, especially narcotics, that young black and Latino men are more likely to use or sell. In contrast, laws against use of the drugs of preference among affluent whites—especially cocaine—are less likely to be enforced by the system (Alexander 2012).

- *The healthcare system.* Blacks and Latinos are likely to receive no treatment at all or are more likely to receive poorer-quality treatment in, for example, emergency rooms, rather than in the offices of physicians in private practice (Lara-Millán 2014).

- Most social institutions and structures in the United States are not overtly designed to discriminate on the basis of race. Many policies and practices are designed to be fair. Nevertheless, they may have an unintended discriminatory effect. Take, for example, the employment policy that favors seniority in decisions regarding which employees are laid off during economic downturns. This is not an unreasonable idea, but minority members are overrepresented among less senior personnel due to historically limited opportunities. Thus, such "last hired, first fired" policies unintentionally result in the disproportionate firing of blacks and Latinos.

The Role of Individuals in Institutional Racism

Often, individual racism is rooted in, and supported by, racism in institutional structures. Thus, while much research indicates that prejudice and racism at the individual level are declining (Alba 2009), the larger structures in which those attitudes and behaviors are embedded continue to operate to the detriment of blacks and other racial minorities (Bonilla-Silva 1997; Slatton and Feagin 2012). A good example is to be found in the idea of "dog-whistle" politics (Lopez 2015). A dog whistle is one that only dogs, not humans, are able to hear. While on the surface contemporary politics is less overtly racist than it has been in the past, a variety of coded statements are aimed at, and interpreted by, the targeted audience as being just that. It is dog-whistle politics because the words and phrases are likely to sound racially motivated only to the audience at which they are aimed. For example, Ronald Reagan never mentioned race when using phrases like "welfare queens" driving Cadillacs. However, the racially tinged message was quite clear to a receptive white audience. That audience heard the dog whistle loud and clear. Donald Trump was often accused of engaging in such politics during the 2016 presidential campaign. Trump's belated and reluctant repudiation of the former Louisiana imperial wizard of the Ku Klux Klan (KKK)—"I repudiate, *okay?*"— was a dog whistle to racists (Hochschild 2016, 226). In fact, he had used such dog whistles much earlier when, for example, in 2013 he made a comment that could be interpreted as a dog whistle for anti-Semites: "I'm much smarter than Jonathan Leibowitz—I mean, Jon Stewart" (Weisman 2016). Individuals such as Ronald Reagan and Donald Trump, as well as their millions of followers, may not necessarily be racists, but they are embedded in, and strongly influenced by, structures characterized by institutional racism.

Similarly, discriminatory policies may be carried out by people who are not racists and do not actually believe in those policies. For example, in 1935, the Federal Home Loan Bank Board asked the Home Owners' Loan Corporation (also a federal agency) to map the relative security of property investments by neighborhood. The evaluation of "risk" included the racial composition of the neighborhood, and this resulted in minority-dominated neighborhoods being judged ineligible ("redlined") for property investment. After World War II, the government poured a significant amount of money into home loan programs for veterans through the Federal Housing Administration. However, redlined neighborhoods were not eligible, despite many minority residents' individual creditworthiness. Thus, individual lenders who may have been sympathetic and wished to approve loans for minority veterans could not do so if the veterans were trying to purchase homes in redlined neighborhoods. While perhaps not as intentional or overt, the practice of racial discrimination in housing continue to this day (Massey 2015; Turner et al. 2013). Blacks and Latinos are more likely than whites to be turned down for mortgage loans and more likely to be given less desirable mortgages when they are approved (Bocian, Li, and Ernst 2010). Racial discrimination has been embedded in the structure of mortgage lending in the United States, and individual lenders have often conformed to its structural demands (Massey et al. 2016).

At a more microscopic level, organizations can be characterized by institutional discrimination as well. For example, an employee may be expected to discriminate against minorities to please her superiors and to succeed on the job. Before laws against such practices were instituted, many real estate agents would not sell to black clients because they were afraid of alienating their white clients and thereby losing the income derived from selling homes to them. Selling to black clients would also anger white bosses, who might fire agents who sold homes to blacks and thereby jeopardized future sales to whites.

The "Invisibility" of Institutional Racism

Individual acts based on racism are often out in the open and easier for all to see than institutional racism can be. However, institutional discrimination is far subtler—often even invisible. Individual acts that are reflective of prejudice (shouting a racial epithet) or discrimination (a taxi driver refusing to pick up a black passenger) are easy to discern. However, the mundane operations of a large organization are often difficult to see.

In addition, large numbers of whites benefit from the racism of larger structures by being awarded higher-paying jobs, better working conditions, and power over others, including over blacks and other minorities. These beneficiaries have a deep, if perhaps unacknowledged, interest in seeing institutions continue to operate to their benefit but to the detriment of blacks and other racial minorities.

Because their day-to-day operations are largely invisible, institutions that operate in a racist manner are much less likely to be seen as a problem than are individual acts of prejudice or discrimination. This is the case in spite of the fact that institutional racism and discrimination represent a far greater problem for blacks and other minorities than do individual discrimination and prejudice. In addition, the comparative invisibility of institutional racism makes it far more difficult to find ways of combating it.

SOCIAL MOVEMENTS AND RACE

Hate Groups

Most hate groups in the United States are white supremacist movements, with the Ku Klux Klan (KKK) being an archetype. It is best known for its antiblack positions and activities, but the KKK originated as a nativist, anti-Catholic, and anti-Semitic group. KKK activity began at a time of high European immigration from places like Ireland, Italy, and other non-WASP (white Anglo-Saxon Protestant) nations. These new arrivals were seen as a threat to national identity.

Other well-known racist hate groups include the neo-Nazis and skinheads. In 2016, the Southern Poverty Law Center (SPLC) identified 892 active hate groups in the United States (www.splcenter.org/hate-map). The SPLC has cited a rise in ethnic-based hate crimes following 9/11. It reports that an increasing number of hate crimes are directed toward immigrant populations, thus reflecting continued xenophobia in American society. Activities of hate groups include rallies, speeches, marches, leafleting, publishing, the maintenance of websites, and criminal activities including vandalism, arson, sexual assaults against immigrant women, and other violence. Figure 10.7 reports the breakdown of hate crimes in 2014 and shows that almost half of them were motivated by race.

Participation in racial hate groups was long considered to be the domain of white men. When white women participated in such movements, they were assumed to have been brought into the movement through husbands and boyfriends. However, sociologist Kathleen Blee (2002), one of the first researchers to study gender in racist hate movements, found that these women have a variety of reasons for joining that do not include the influence of men. She conducted in-depth interviews with 34 women

FIGURE 10.7 • Breakdown of the 5,462 Single-Bias Hate Crime Incidents Reported in 2014

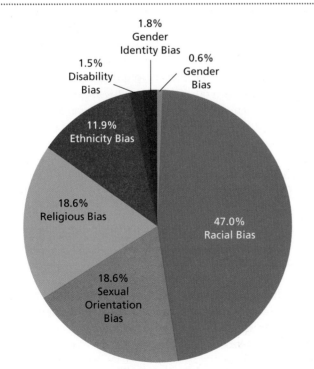

1.8% Gender Identity Bias

0.6% Gender Bias

1.5% Disability Bias

11.9% Ethnicity Bias

18.6% Religious Bias

47.0% Racial Bias

18.6% Sexual Orientation Bias

SOURCE: Data from Federal Bureau of Investigation, Uniform Crime Reports, 2015. "Latest Hate Crime Statistics Available," November 16.

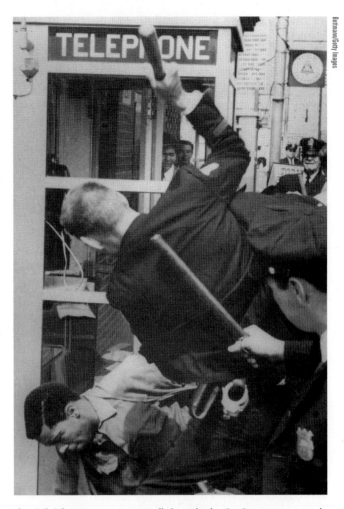

The civil rights movement eventually brought the Jim Crow era to an end, but racism and discrimination are still with us. Why?

involved in several groups. Some women had joined after experiencing life tragedies that they, rightly or wrongly, blamed on another racial group. Others had moved into social circles that supported and propagated racist views, often attributing a variety of social ills to blacks, Hispanics, and Jews. Blee showed that white women are not just auxiliary members but rather are integrated into positions of power within many of these organizations.

The Civil Rights Movement

While we have focused here on various forms of oppression of blacks and other minority groups, there also has been, and continues to be, resistance to this oppression by blacks and others. One major example is, of course, the modern civil rights movement, which arose in the mid-1950s and 1960s, largely in the South, to deal with black oppression maintained by the Jim Crow system (Morris 1984, 2007). Under Jim Crow laws, which were instituted after the Civil War and Reconstruction, blacks were denied political and social rights and were exploited economically. (See the Trending box in Chapter 7, page 193.)

Blacks and progressive allies had long opposed and fought against this system. However, it was the civil rights movement that brought Jim Crow to an end. It did so by honing a variety of techniques, such as "boycotts, mass marches, mass arrests, sit-ins, freedom rides, attempts to register at all-white schools, lawsuits, and other unruly tactics" (Morris 2007, 510). For their part, racist whites and their representatives often responded with "bombings, billy clubs, high-pressure water hoses, and attack dogs" (Morris 2007, 510). These responses often took place in front of TV news cameras, and the national coverage served to put pressure on the federal government and white public opinion to reform the system.

As a result, between 1955 and 1965, Jim Crow was dismantled. The civil rights movement of that era led to the passage of the Civil Rights Act of 1964 and the Voting Rights Act of 1965, formally striking down legal discrimination in various aspects of public life. While blacks today tend to suffer from many of the same problems as they did before the civil rights movement, the problems are now caused more by institutional racism than by the law or racial hatred of individuals.

Collective Identity and "Power" Movements

After the successes of the civil rights movement in the mid-1960s, several social movements arose in the late 1960s and early 1970s that sought to energize racial minorities. Winning legal rights was one thing, but many individuals continued to feel belittled and oppressed. The Black Power movement was the best-known attempt to raise a racial minority out of its sense of inferiority. Its slogan was "black is beautiful."

The visibility of the Black Power movement contributed to racialization among Hispanics. The Brown Berets saw themselves as analogous to the Black Panthers. The Brown Berets adopted the slogan "brown power" (and later "*Viva la raza*," or "Long live the race"). The 1968 East L.A. Chicano Student Walkout was an important historic event. More than 2,700 students walked out of schools to protest institutional racism that included prohibitions against speaking Spanish in class and guidance counseling that pushed Latino students to consider menial labor instead of college. Police beat and arrested some students and arrested some of the teachers who helped students mobilize (Global Nonviolent Action Database 2011). More recent politicized racial identities among American Latinos include the *indigena* movement, which elevates South American Indian ancestry to a matter of pride.

RACE AND ETHNICITY IN A GLOBAL CONTEXT

Historically, ethnic identities have been closely tied to nation-states. For instance, until the modern era, the population of Ireland embraced almost exclusively the Gaelic language and Irish culture. However, nation-based ethnic identity has declined over time. One major factor in this decline is **diaspora**, or the dispersal, typically involuntary, of a racial or ethnic population from its traditional homeland and over a wide geographic area. In recent years, mass migration in an age of globalization has had a powerful impact on ethnic identities and has reduced their association with given nation-states.

Such population movement has led to the existence of multiple identities on the global stage. This, in turn, has increased the possibility of people having hybrid ethnic identities. That is, an increasing number of people identify not only with, say, the ethnic group into which they were born, but also with other ethnic groups in geographic areas to which they may have migrated. Thus, migrants from India to China may see themselves as both Indian and Chinese.

ETHNIC IDENTITY AND GLOBALIZATION

Some see globalization as a threat to ethnic identity; they see globalization as leading toward a world of homogeneous identities. However, others disagree, citing the following reasons:

- Ethnic identities are not nearly as fragile as is often believed. Ethnicity is inculcated from birth, within the family, and then often in school and by the surrounding culture. Thus, it usually becomes part of a person's core identity.

- Globalization can be a force, maybe the most significant force, in the creation and proliferation of ethnic

CHECKPOINT 10.3: RACISM

CONCEPT	DESCRIPTION
Racism	The process of defining a minority group as a race, attributing negative characteristics to it, and keeping it at a disadvantage relative to the majority
Xenophobia	The presence of beliefs, attitudes, and prejudices that reject, exclude, and vilify groups outside the dominant social group
Ethnocentrism	The belief that the norms, values, and customs of one's own group are superior to those of other groups
White racial frame	An array of racist ideas that discriminate against blacks
Hegemony	A situation in which one race subordinates another, more on the basis of dominant ideas and cultural differences than through force
Institutional racism	Race-based discrimination that results from the day-to-day operation of social institutions and structures

identity (Tomlinson 2000). Ethnic groups and many aspects of their culture flow around the globe, creating new pockets of ethnic identity and reinforcing that identity in particular locales. Global pressures toward a homogenized identity may also stiffen a person's resolve to maintain ties to an ethnic culture.

- Ethnic identity and globalization are part of the same modern process. For example, through the development of advanced forms of communication, globalization allows ethnic group members to stay in touch with one another for the express purpose of maintaining familiar traditions. This more powerful sense of ethnic identity can be exported back to the home country through the same global media. This is part of the broader process of transnationalism (Faist, Fauser, and Reisenauer 2013).

ASK YOURSELF

Do you believe that globalization threatens ethnic identity by making the world more homogeneous through information and cultural flows? Or do you feel that ethnicity is a strong enough identity factor to survive globalization, and that global communication flows can help preserve ethnic identities by keeping emigrants in touch with their home countries? Explain your answer.

FIGURE 10.8 • Chinese Ethnolinguistic Groups

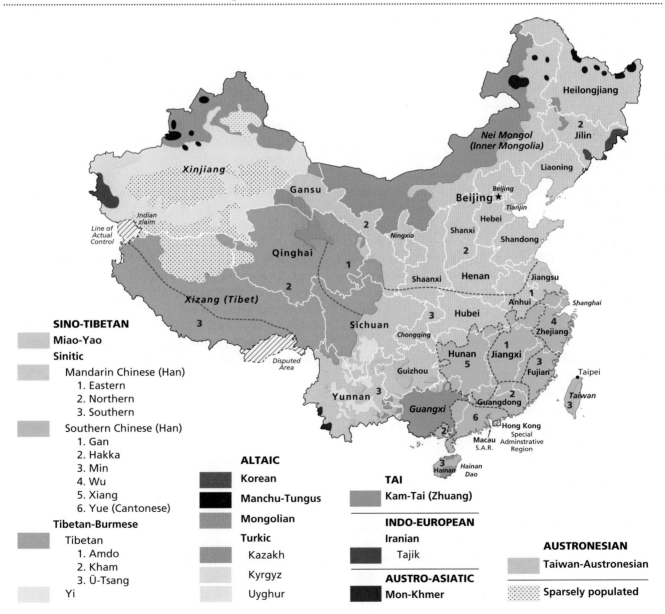

SOURCE: Courtesy of the University of Texas Libraries, The University of Texas at Austin.

GLOBAL PREJUDICE AND DISCRIMINATION

To this point, we have focused on majority–minority relations within specific nation-states, especially the United States. But we can also examine majority–minority relations in a global context. The North–South distinction is a key factor. Most of the "bottom billion," or the poorest billion people in the world (Collier 2007, 2012), are minority group members in the Global South. Few from the bottom billion are in the North. In fact, the richest billion people in the world are largely in the Global North and are mainly members of the majority groups.

It has long been the case that the Global North and its majority groups have dominated, controlled, exploited, and oppressed the Global South and its minority groups. Historically, imperialism, colonialism, economic development, Westernization, and Americanization have worked in large part to Northerners' advantage and to the disadvantage of Southerners. The system that dominates globalization today—neoliberal economics—helps those in the advantaged categories in the Global North and hurts, often badly, those in the disadvantaged categories in the Global South (Harvey 2005).

Majority groups from the Global North have often "invented" minority groups in the Global South. One example is the creation of "Indians" as an oppressed minority group after the British colonized India. Until that point, Indian society had had its own highly developed system of majority and minority castes. Another example derives from **Orientalism**, a set of ideas and texts produced by the Global North that served as the basis of systems designed to dominate, control, and exploit the Orient (the East) and its many minority groups (Said [1979] 1994).

Racism is not exclusive to the West in general, or to the United States in particular, but exists in many societies throughout the world. For example, in Japan, differences in skin color, hair, and even body odor have been used to distinguish among races such as the Ainu and Buraku. Japanese citizens whose ancestry is partly Caucasian or African are also subject to prejudice within their own country. China has 56 officially recognized ethnic groups, totaling about 105 million people; nearly 92 percent (1.2 billion) of all Chinese are in the Han ethnic group. Figure 10.8 shows the geographic distribution of ethnolinguistic groups in China; note the concentration of Han in the heavily populated coastal areas. Uyghurs, a Muslim, Turkic-speaking minority in northwestern China, are discriminated against—job listings specify that applicants must be ethnic Han or be Mandarin Chinese speakers (A. Jacobs 2013). Uyghurs have consequently held many protests against the Chinese government (Holdstock 2014).

GLOBAL FLOWS BASED ON RACE AND ETHNICITY

One way to think about globalized majority–minority relations is in terms of global flows. Both race and ethnicity can be said to flow around the world. One manifestation is the migration of people of various races and ethnic groups, who move around the world today with greater ease and rapidity than ever before. People from the North are more likely to be tourists or retirees who visit or take up residence in the nations of the South because of the good weather and low cost of living (Croucher 2009). In contrast, residents of the South typically migrate to wealthy nations in the North in search of employment, be it in low-skilled or high-skilled positions (Kivisto and Faist 2010, 49–54).

Another form of global flow involves the social and cultural aspects of race and ethnicity. As we have seen, neither race nor ethnicity is defined by objective characteristics such as "blood," genes, or skin color. Rather, both are defined socially and culturally. As social constructions—as ideas—race and ethnicity flow across borders and around the world effortlessly. A good example is the global spread of anti-Muslim prejudice today. Globalized mass communication helps spread these ideas, but they are also carried by people who are taking advantage of inexpensive means of travel, especially by air.

Paul Gilroy's *The Black Atlantic: Modernity and Double Consciousness* (1993) is an important work on majority–minority relations that stresses global flows. As the title makes clear, Gilroy is particularly interested in the flows that relate to blacks in the Atlantic region (Figure 10.9 shows those flows, as well as another flow of slaves from Africa to Asia): "I have settled on an image of ships across the spaces between Europe, America, Africa and the Caribbean as a central organizing symbol. . . . The image of a ship . . . in motion" (Gilroy 1993, 4). This image encompasses the flow of slaves from Africa to the eastern coast of the Americas and the later return of some blacks to Africa. It also encompasses the circulation of activists, ideas, books, works of art, and the like that relate to blacks and race relations. All are seen as involved in "displacements, migrations, and journeys" (Gilroy 1993, 111). Gilroy argues that in trying to understand global flows based on race, we should focus not on national boundaries but rather on the "Black Atlantic," which he portrays as a transnational space.

Positive and Negative Flows

Those in the Global North are able to create structures that greatly enhance positive or protective flows. For example, in the United States, the 911 phone system quickly summons help, and medical alert systems are available that allow elderly people and others who may not be able to get to a telephone to call for aid by pressing a button. Setting up the complex networks to handle these emergencies is

FIGURE 10.9 • Slave Trade Routes, 1518–1850

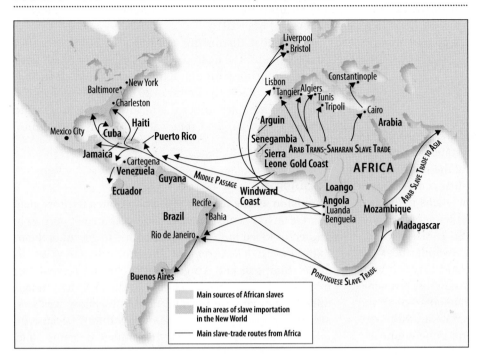

SOURCE: LatinAmericanStudies.org

they are far better able to insulate and protect themselves from them. Furthermore, those in majority groups often initiate negative flows (armaments, global warming) that have profoundly negative effects on minority groups.

Racism itself can be seen as having wide-ranging negative consequences for minority group members as the ideas and practices associated with it flow around the world (Goldberg 2009). This flow of racism around the world has been referred to as the "racialization of the globe" (Dikötter 2008; Treitler 2016). Nevertheless, racist ideas and practices are certainly not the same throughout the world, but rather are adapted and modified in each locale. They are affected by local ideas as well as by local economic, political, and military realities. As a result, racism as it involves blacks is not the same in Great Britain as it is in Ghana or the United States. Racism also changes over time, as reflected today in the flow of anti-Islamic racism through many parts of the world, especially the United States and much of Europe.

Racial and Ethnic Barriers

In all aspects of globalization, there are not only flows of various kinds but also barriers to flows. Thus, members of racial and ethnic minorities may be locked into particular racial or ethnic identities, or they may be physically unable to move from particular areas (such as ghettos) that define them in a certain way. They are also likely to reside in countries in the South from which it may difficult to move (because of poverty, for example).

Just as majority groups have the advantage when it comes to positive flows, they are better able than minority groups to create barriers between themselves and negative flows. These barriers can include border controls in the nation-states dominated by advantaged groups; local actions, such as creating gated communities patrolled by guards; and even individual actions, such as having alarm systems installed in their homes. Minorities can afford few, if any, of these kinds of protective barriers.

Minority group statuses are likely, in and of themselves, to serve as "subtle" barriers that impede many positive flows. People in those categories are not likely to participate, or at least participate equally, in such positive flows. For example, there are no physical barriers—no

expensive. In the Global South, minorities have little or no access to such networks and therefore to the positive flows expedited by them. Those in minority categories are far less likely to participate in the globe's positive flows of money, commodities, food, health care, technologies, and the like. Conversely, those in the majority categories are likely to be in the thick of these positive flows, both as creators and as beneficiaries.

On the other hand, the structures that expedite negative flows are more likely to dump into, and to be found in, areas dominated by minority groups. For example, illegal structures allow the relatively free flow of weapons into and through many poor areas of the world. Much stronger structures are in place to prevent their flow into the wealthier regions of the globe. Another example is the tendency for people in the Global South to live in close proximity to disease vectors, such as malaria-bearing mosquitoes and chickens carrying avian flu. The result is that they are at greater risk of contracting vector-borne diseases. In contrast, majority group members in the Global North are far more likely to live at some distance from, or to be heavily protected from, disease-carrying mosquitoes or live chickens, to say nothing of the vectors for many other diseases.

Those in minority groups throughout the world are more likely to be on the receiving end of such negative flows as borderless diseases, crime, corruption, war, and most environmental problems. Those in the majority groups certainly cannot completely avoid these negative flows, but walls—between Hispanics and Anglos in the United States, but the mere fact of being Hispanic, or being perceived as such, serves as a barrier to all sorts of positive flows (e.g., jobs, useful information) for members of this minority group.

ETHNIC CONFLICT WITHIN NATION-STATES

Greater ethnic diversity has increased the possibility of ethnic conflict within many nation-states. Of course, such ethnic conflict is not new. Among the most notable examples in the twentieth and twenty-first centuries have been conflicts between Turks and Armenians in Turkey; between Germans, especially Nazis, and Jews in Germany; between Tamils and the Sinhalese in Sri Lanka; between the Tutsi and Hutu in Burundi and Rwanda; between Arabs and ethnic Africans in Darfur; and between various ethnic groups—Slovenes, Croatians, Serbs, Bosnians, Montenegrins, Macedonians, and Albanians—after the breakup of Yugoslavia in 1991. However, today, with more members of ethnic groups in more and more countries, there is the potential for a great increase in the number, if not the intensity, of ethnic conflicts.

One example occurred in Paris in 2008. The 19th Arrondissement on the edge of Paris is very large, poor, and ethnically and racially diverse and has high crime rates. The area is divided into three enclaves, dominated, respectively, by Arabs largely from North Africa, blacks mainly from Mali and Congo, and Jews. Youth gangs in each area are major factors in ongoing conflict among the groups. The youths not only live in separate enclaves; they also go to separate schools. According to the deputy mayor in charge of youth affairs, this creates a situation in which "the kids don't know each other and that creates a logic of rivalry" (Erlanger 2008, A11). The conflict reached a peak in 2008 when a 17-year-old Jewish youth was beaten into a coma by a group of young blacks and Arabs because he was wearing a skullcap.

This episode is consistent with hate crime patterns in the United States, where whites are least likely to be victimized and where, when minority group members are aggressors, they tend to victimize members of other minority groups (Bodinger-deUriarte 1992, 24).

Of course, the possibility of ethnic conflict within nation-states has reached a whole new level in recent years with the vast migration of various peoples from the Middle East and North Africa to Europe. The sheer number of migrants has challenged many countries and locales. Beyond that, the migrants bring with them cultures, religions, and practices that are greatly at variance from those that exist in their destinations. These migrants compete with local populations for jobs, creating further tension. As a result, there has been a tendency to ghettoize these migrants, thereby increasing polarization between groups and creating greater alienation among both migrants and nationals (Fisher 2016).

The most disturbing examples of ethnic conflict tend to involve the majority group's efforts to "deal" with ethnic minorities through expulsion, ethnic cleansing, or genocide. Recently, Ferrara (2015) has combined the latter two examples under the heading of "demographic surgery"—the surgical removal of one or more ethnic minorities.

Expulsion

Expulsion, or the removal of a group from a territory, may seem relatively benign because minorities are not purposely injured or killed in the majority's efforts to get rid of them. Expulsion can take two forms: direct or voluntary (Costalli 2016; Simpson and Yinger 1985). In *direct expulsion*, minority ethnic groups are ejected by the majority through military or other government action. In *voluntary expulsion*, a minority group leaves "of its own volition" because its members are being harassed, discriminated against, and persecuted. Of course, in the real world, these two forms of expulsion occur in concert with one another. And although physical harm may be relatively light, social and economic harm can be considerable. The people who are forced to leave typically lose much of their property, and their social networks are often irretrievably broken.

The state of California engaged in both forms of expulsion against Chinese immigrants in the 1800s. The 1879 California Constitution delegated "all necessary power to the incorporated cities and towns of this State for the removal of Chinese" to outside the city limits, which constituted direct expulsion. The constitution also encouraged voluntary expulsion by making it illegal for corporations in California to "employ directly or indirectly, in any capacity, any Chinese or Mongolian" and further established that "no Chinese shall be employed on any State, county, municipal, or other public work, except in punishment for crime."

Two U.S. Supreme Court decisions also supported expulsion. Discriminatory curfews for Japanese Americans were upheld in the 1943 case of *Hirabayashi v. United States,* and the direct expulsion of Japanese Americans from their homes was upheld in a 1944 case, *Korematsu v. United States* (Gressman 2005).

Many of the racial and ethnic groups involved in diasporas have experienced both forms of expulsion. This has been particularly true for Jews and the Roma, who have often been forcibly ejected (e.g., Jews were ejected from Jerusalem by the Romans in the second century and from Spain and Portugal in the fifteenth century) or moved voluntarily (e.g., some Jews left the Stalinist Soviet Union because of harassment).

Ethnic Cleansing

Ethnic cleansing is the establishment by the dominant group of policies that allow or require the forcible removal, abuse, and even murder of people of another ethnic group (Oberschall 2012; Sekulic 2007a, 2016). Of course, Nazi actions against Jews and Roma fit the definition of ethnic cleansing.

Ethnic cleansing achieved more recent notoriety during the wars associated with the dissolution of Yugoslavia in 1991. The ethnic groups that dominated various regions sought to create areas that were ethnically homogeneous, and they did this by expelling and even killing members of other ethnic groups. For example, Croatians were expelled from parts of Croatia inhabited by Serbs. Bosnia, which declared independence in 1992, was composed of three major ethnic groups—Slavic Muslims (the largest single group), Serbs, and Croats. Serbian armed forces created ethnically homogeneous enclaves by forcibly removing and murdering members of the other ethnic groups, especially Muslims.

In situations of ethnic cleansing, women and girls often have been targeted for physical violence and murder, as well as sexual violence in many cases. In Bosnia in the 1990s, Serbian men systematically raped an estimated 50,000 Muslim and Croatian women as part of their campaign of terror. Because the Serbian police were in positions of power, it was difficult, if not impossible, for the women who were victims of rape to get help or to prosecute their attackers. As of 2010, only 12 of as many as 50,000 cases had been prosecuted (Cerkez 2010).

Mass rape as a weapon of war has also occurred in the region of Darfur within Sudan, with the government-supported Janjaweed militiamen raping Darfuri women and girls held in refugee camps. In 2008, Sudan's president, Omar Hassan Ahmed Bashir, was accused (and later indicted) by the prosecutor of the International Criminal Court (ICC) of The Hague of not only mass genocide but also propagating rape as a weapon of war and terror (Scheffer 2008). Bashir has yet to be tried by the ICC, but the accusations and the indictment did not prevent him from being reelected president of Sudan in 2015, with 94 percent of the vote (Kushkush 2015). Sudanese armed forces have continued to carry out mass rapes (and killings) in Darfur to this day (Gladstone 2015).

U.S. citizens of Japanese descent were forced into internment camps during World War II in actions that were upheld by the Supreme Court but are now seen as discriminatory. Contrast these camps with steps the government is taking today to try to ensure national security.

Genocide

The most extreme cases of ethnic conflict involve an active, systematic attempt at eliminating an entire group of people, or genocide. *Genocide* was defined in 1948 by the United Nations Convention on the Prevention and Punishment of the Crime of Genocide as "acts committed with the intent to destroy, in whole or in part, a national, ethnic, racial, or religious group" (cited in Karstedt 2007, 1909–1910). It is seen as the crime of the twentieth century, and it shows every sign of continuing to define the twenty-first century.

Figure 10.10 shows select genocides of the twentieth and twenty-first centuries. The earliest genocide depicted here dates back to 1914, but there were many other instances of genocide long before that.

The 1948 UN convention on genocide was prompted by the Nazi Holocaust (Karstedt 2007). At first, the Holocaust occurred within the confines of Germany, but it later spread to the European countries allied with, or conquered by, Germany. It was in that sense transnational, and it would have undoubtedly become far more of a global phenomenon had the Nazis achieved their goal of world conquest. For example, had the Nazis succeeded in conquering the United States, we would undoubtedly have seen the genocide of American Jews.

A parallel example of large-scale genocide is the mass killings that took place during the rule of Joseph Stalin throughout the then-vast Soviet empire. In the main,

FIGURE 10.10 • Select Genocides around the World, 1914–Present

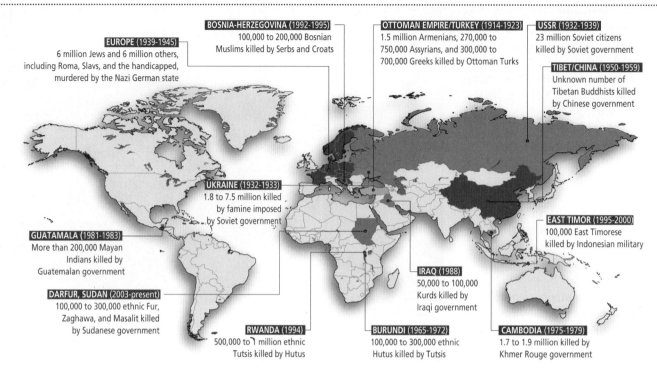

BOSNIA-HERZEGOVINA (1992-1995)
100,000 to 200,000 Bosnian
Muslims killed by Serbs and Croats

EUROPE (1939-1945)
6 million Jews and 6 million others,
including Roma, Slavs, and the handicapped,
murdered by the Nazi German state

OTTOMAN EMPIRE/TURKEY (1914-1923)
1.5 million Armenians, 270,000 to
750,000 Assyrians, and 300,000 to
700,000 Greeks killed by Ottoman Turks

USSR (1932-1939)
23 million Soviet citizens
killed by Soviet government

TIBET/CHINA (1950-1959)
Unknown number of
Tibetan Buddhists killed
by Chinese government

UKRAINE (1932-1933)
1.8 to 7.5 million killed
by famine imposed
by Soviet government

GUATAMALA (1981-1983)
More than 200,000 Mayan
Indians killed by
Guatemalan government

EAST TIMOR (1995-2000)
100,000 East Timorese
killed by Indonesian military

DARFUR, SUDAN (2003-present)
100,000 to 300,000 ethnic Fur,
Zaghawa, and Masalit killed
by Sudanese government

IRAQ (1988)
50,000 to 100,000
Kurds killed by
Iraqi government

RWANDA (1994)
500,000 to 1 million ethnic
Tutsis killed by Hutus

BURUNDI (1965-1972)
100,000 to 300,000 ethnic
Hutus killed by Tutsis

CAMBODIA (1975-1979)
1.7 to 1.9 million killed by
Khmer Rouge government

SOURCE: Adapted from Online Resources from The Choices Program, Brown University.

however, genocide continues to be practiced within nation-states. Examples include the murder of nearly 2 million people by the Khmer Rouge in Cambodia in the mid- to late 1970s, the killing in 1974 of as many as 1 million people (mostly minority Tutsis) by the majority Hutus in Rwanda, the murder of tens of thousands of Bosnians and Croats in the 1990s by Bosnian Serbs, and the killing of hundreds of thousands of ethnic Africans in Sudan since 2003 by ethnic Arabs.

The global age has brought with it the globalization of genocide, as instances of it have flowed around the world (Karstedt 2012, 2016). That is, genocide has become another negative flow making its way from one part of the world to another. Genocide may become more likely in the future because of proliferating and accelerating global flows of ideas, agitators, and arms. Added to this is the increased inability of nation-states to block many of these flows.

CHECKPOINT 10.4: RACE AND ETHNICITY IN THE GLOBAL CONTEXT

CONCEPT	DESCRIPTION
Diaspora	Dispersal, often involuntary, of a racial or population group from its homeland
Orientalism	Ideas and texts produced by the Global North that served as the basis of systems designed to dominate and exploit the East
Expulsion	The removal of a group from a territory
Ethnic cleansing	Policies established by the dominant group to allow or require the forced removal, abuse, or murder of another ethnic group
Genocide	Active and systemic efforts to eliminate an entire group of people

SUMMARY

Race has historically been defined on the basis of a shared lineage and some real or presumed biological characteristic. In the second half of the twentieth century, race began to be defined more as a cultural phenomenon, making it a more fluid than fixed type of identity. Ethnic groups are typically defined on the basis of some real or presumed cultural characteristic such as language, religion, traditions, or cultural practices.

Race and ethnicity have always served as a way of stratifying individuals into groups with more or less power. The majority group, even if it has fewer members, has the power to act on it prejudices and discriminate against members of minority groups. Intersectionality, or belonging to more than one type of minority (for example, being black and female), often compounds disparities. Majority–minority relations devolve into racism when the majority defines a group as a race and attributes negative characteristics to that group. It is the combination of xenophobia and ethnocentrism that makes racism so powerful. Current racism is also a matter of hegemony, or the majority group foisting its culture on minority groups and the persistence of institutional racism.

Putting majority–minority relations in a global context, the North has more majority group members and dominates and oppresses those in the South. Majority groups are better positioned than minority groups to create structures that enhance positive or protective global flows. Greater ethnic diversity within nation-states has opened up more possibilities for internal ethnic conflicts. At the extreme, ethnic conflict leads to expulsion, ethnic cleansing, and genocide of minorities by the majority within a territory.

KEY TERMS

affirmative action, 279
diaspora, 282
discrimination, 267
ethnic cleansing, 287
ethnic groups, 260
ethnicity, 260
expulsion, 286

genocide, 271
hegemony, 277
hypodescent rule, 263
institutional racism, 279
intersectionality, 268
majority group, 266

majority-minority
  population, 265
minority group, 266
Orientalism, 284
pluralism, 270
prejudice, 267
race, 260

racism, 260
segregation, 271
stereotype, 267
white racial frame, 277
xenophobia, 276

REVIEW QUESTIONS

1. What is the difference between race and ethnicity? What are the similarities? How have biological and cultural explanations helped create racial and ethnic differences?

2. Barack Obama is the child of a white mother and a black African father, but more often than not he is referred to as black. What does this suggest about the nature of race in the United States? What are the consequences of this perception?

3. What criteria do sociologists use to define a majority group? How do majority groups maintain their positions of privilege?

4. Considering some of the examples provided in this chapter, do your consumption patterns reflect your racial and ethnic identity?

5. Do you think it is a good idea for ethnic groups to commercialize ethnicity? What do they stand to gain? What do they stand to lose in the process? Are the gains worth the costs?

6. What are the different motivations for racism? What are some mechanisms that minorities have used to resist racism?

7. What is institutional racism, and what are some examples of institutional racism? In what ways is institutional racism more problematic than individual racism is?

8. How would you characterize majority–minority relations on a global level? What sorts of advantages do majority groups have on the global level?

9. How is globalization changing the nature of ethnicity on a global scale? In what ways have ethnic groups been able to use advances in communication and media to retain their ethnic identity?

10. Do you agree that globalization is creating a universal culture? Why or why not?

GENDER AND SEXUALITY

Challenging Gender Stereotypes

In a *favela* (slum) in Rio de Janeiro, Brazil, a thoughtful, handsome man named Marcio talks about his life. "My dream was to be a father," he says, standing with his son and wife. Sending a kite into the gray sky, he continues, "For some people, maybe it's a career, for others, maybe to travel somewhere, but my dream was always to be a father. And to give my son something I never had." Marcio explains that his childhood was marked by constant violence; his father beat his mother, and the community stood by and accepted it. "He had to show he was a man," he says of his father. Marcio learned from his father that manhood meant having many women, drinking, partying, and staying out all night.

As he cries at the memory of his father's absence and lack of attention, Marcio explains how he managed to avoid becoming like his father by finding a group of men who had had similar experiences. As they met, talked, and cried together, Marcio saw how traditional cultural gender stereotypes of masculinity and femininity had been harmful. He came to be willing to challenge his culture's sex and gender norms in order to create a better life for himself, his wife, and his son. With the help of a global organization called Promundo, he now works with other men to support their efforts to challenge traditional gender expectations. As Marcio puts it, "The rain doesn't come all at once; it comes a drop at a time. And then it becomes a strong river." Change in the lives of a few can lead to change in the lives of many and, indeed, even in an entire nation or culture.

Beliefs and attitudes about gender and sexuality differ across countries as well as over time. Globalization, technological advancements in communication, and growing awareness of the consequences of gender inequalities are among the factors changing what we think about gender and sexuality. As the founders of Promundo listened to

---

Note: The author thanks Rebecca Plante for her help in revising this chapter.

LEARNING OBJECTIVES

11.1 Identify the cultural influences on gender and discuss gendered inequalities.

11.2 Describe how social forces constrain sexuality.

11.3 Explain the effects of globalization on gender and sexualities.

11.4 Examine global flows related to gender.

edge.sagepub.com/ritzerintro4e

- Take the chapter quiz
- Review key terms with eFlashcards
- Explore multimedia links and SAGE readings

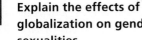

accounts of men committing violence against women and children around the world, they saw an opportunity and a need for reform. Promundo now works with local community stakeholders and agencies such as the World Health Organization in 22 countries, helping men and boys change themselves and their communities. For the people involved in Brazil—and elsewhere—the ongoing struggle between tradition and freedom is exhilarating and terrifying, joyful and heart-wrenching. For sociologists, it's a testament to the intricate beauty of a living, breathing culture that is always changing. ●

Sex and gender are terms that are often used interchangeably and confused with one another. However, it is important that they be distinguished clearly. Sex is principally a biological term, usually expressed as *female* or *male*. Sex is typically reflected in a person's chromosomes, gonads, genitalia, and hormones. Gender is a cultural term, connected to societal definitions of expected behaviors, attitudes, and personalities, and is usually reflected in terms like *woman* or *man*, or *girl* or *boy*. Gender consists of the physical, behavioral, and personality characteristics that are defined as appropriate for one's sex. The key difference is that sex is based mainly on biology, whereas gender is based on social distinctions (Ryan 2007). Western conceptualizations of gender assume that there are strong, clear gender differences based on sex. Westerners often assume that genitalia are "not only the primary marker of gender identity, but indeed, the underlying *cause* of that identity" (Helliwell 2000, 797; emphasis added). But bodies and biology are socially constructed as the basis for gender. "Gender builds on biological sex, but it exaggerates biological difference, and it carries biological difference into domains in which it is completely irrelevant" (Eckert and McConnell-Ginet 2013, 2). There is nothing in human biology to explain why, for example, we think that only women should wear high heels, or that men should not paint their nails.

Sex and gender are typically assigned at birth, although we often begin gendering babies in utero, when ultrasounds give some idea of a fetus's sex. Expectant parents might tell family and friends that they are "having a boy" or "having a girl." People throw "gender reveal parties," complete with ultrasound images baked into cakes or boxes of pink or blue balloons waiting to be opened in front of friends and family (for other party ideas, see, for example, www.pinterest.com/babycenter/gender-reveal-ideas). Parents choose gendered names for their unborn children and often begin shopping for "gender-appropriate" infant clothing and toys.

GENDER AND SEX

Gender and sex are examples—another is race—of a master status, or a position that is more important than any others, both for the person in the position and for all others involved. Master statuses dominate all other statuses, including achieved (such as education) and ascribed (such as age) statuses, and are therefore of great consequence (see Chapter 5).

Biological sex has long been linked with gender as a social construct, but the two are not as neatly entwined as we have been taught. Furthermore, sex and gender, especially gender, are not simply natural, biological processes. They are both—again, especially gender—strongly affected by social and cultural forces.

ASK YOURSELF

Why is gender so important in many cultures? Do you think we could make gender less important in the United States? Should we make gender less important? What would need to happen in order to minimize the importance of gender in our interactions with others?

Although we tend to think in terms of only two biological sexes, in fact there is a continuum of sex (Fausto-Sterling 1999). **Intersex** is a "general term used for a variety of [medical] conditions in which a person is born with a reproductive or sexual anatomy that doesn't seem to fit the typical definitions of female or male" (Intersex Society of North America 2008). Only a few intersex conditions represent "true medical emergencies," in that the genitalia are a sign of an underlying metabolic medical issue needing immediate treatment. The majority of intersex conditions do not require hasty or immediate medical interventions. Until quite recently, intersexed people were stigmatized with the label *hermaphrodite,* and doctors often surgically altered infants' and children's genitalia to attempt to match more typical male or female anatomy (Coventry 2006). Thanks to intersex advocacy and increased awareness among medical personnel, today intersexed people who may have been subject to surgery in the past have much more choice about whether, and how, to proceed (Zeiler and Wickstrom 2009).

Most aspects of maleness and femaleness are on a continuum as well. For example, both males and females have the hormones estrogen and testosterone. However, the amounts vary greatly from individual to individual within and between sexes, as well as over time (Liaw and Janssen 2014). Both sexes also have breasts, so although breast cancer is largely a female disease, some males develop it. Facial hair is usually thought of as a male characteristic, but some females grow enough facial hair to need to shave regularly. Biologically, the differences between males and females are few, but much of

These Lebanese men walked a mile in women's shoes during a 2015 event calling for an end to violence against women. Men have routinely worn high-heeled shoes in the past—for instance, during the time of King Louis XIV of France (1638–1715). Why don't they do so now?

U.S. culture is based on assumptions about sex (and gender) differences. Unfortunately, we rarely encounter "separate but equal" social structures based on notions of such differences. Instead, beliefs about difference are often translated into constructions of superiority and inferiority.

FEMININITIES AND MASCULINITIES

The terms *femininities* and *masculinities* refer to the cultural definitions of the traits associated with being a "woman" or a "man" acquired during the socialization process (Laurie et al. 1999; Lind 2007). They are plural because there are many forms of both, connected to other characteristics such as race, ethnicity, age, nationality, and social class (see Chapter 10 for a discussion of intersectionality). Cultural interpretations of femininities and masculinities are subject to change, depending on place and historical era. There is a tendency to develop stereotypes about what it means to be a woman and to be feminine (motherly, nurturant, emotional) and to be a man and masculine (fatherly, tough, unemotional). However, in reality, these stereotypes are not natural or biological; rather, they are socially constructed. As Simone de Beauvoir famously put it, "One is not born, but rather becomes, a woman" ([1952] 1973, 301). The same is true, of course, for a man. Yet the distinction between masculine and feminine persists. Sociologist Raewynn (née Robert W.) Connell (1944–, 1987, 1997, 2009; Gough, forthcoming) coined the terms *hegemonic masculinity* and *emphasized femininity* and analyzed the roles that these ideas have played in global gender inequalities. *Hegemonic* means dominant. Therefore, **hegemonic masculinity** refers to the dominant form or most idealized vision of masculinity. We take this form for granted as "natural." It is linked to patriarchy, a form of society that is dominated by men and focused on men and hegemonic masculinity (Johnson 2005). Hegemonic masculinity is the vision of masculinity that underlies patriarchal systems. **Emphasized femininity** is a set of socially constructed ideas about "model womanhood." These ideas are organized around accommodating the interests of men and the patriarchy. Emphasized femininity focuses on social ability (rather than intellect), ego stroking, and acceptance of the roles of mother and wife (Spade and Valentine 2011). It represents a subordinate heterosexual femininity. Specific manifestations of femininity and masculinity are measured against these dominant forms.

Hegemonic masculinity and emphasized femininity adversely affect both men and women. Men who do not live up to the stereotype of hegemonic masculinity, including gay and working-class men, as well as men of color, are negatively affected. Generally, the rigid expectations of hegemonic masculinity mean that many men, even heterosexual, white, middle-class men, will be viewed, and will view themselves, as falling short of the ideal. Many women are adversely affected because they do not and cannot live

Raewynn (née Robert William) Connell has made important contributions to the study of social stratification and the study of gender, including the idea that gender is a large-scale social structure, not just a matter of personal identity. She frequently uses biographical interviewing in her research and was one of the first people to study the social construction of masculinity.

up to the ideals associated with emphasized femininity (Butler 1990).

While some men benefit greatly from hegemonic masculinity, their advantages have, at least until recently, been largely invisible to them. Not having to think about masculinity, or what it means to "be a man," has been one of the dividends (or privileges) of gender inequality. In contrast, women often think a great deal about the disadvantages of masculinity and gender stereotypes, because they are oppressed by the system of gender inequalities in many different ways.

Masculinities and femininities can be detached from biological sex, the body, and gender. Men can act in socially defined "feminine" ways by nurturing others, and women can behave in a socially defined "masculine" manner by competing aggressively. As is true of the continuum of male and female sexes, we should not think in simple either/or terms about gender. There is a continuum of masculinities *and* femininities, resulting in part from the variety of socialization patterns that we experience over the life course. People adapt throughout their lives, emphasizing different aspects of gender and interpreting the gender role expectations constructed by society. We merge gendered expectations with those of other intersectional statuses, including race, class, and sexual orientation. Moreover, individuals can be high in both masculinity and femininity, or low in both. Gender performance is fluid, not static, and allows room for individuals to make some choices about how to perform gender within socially defined roles (Fields, Copp, and Kleinman 2007; Goldschmied and Kowalczyk 2016).

ASK YOURSELF

What did Simone de Beauvoir mean by saying, "One is not born, but rather becomes, a woman"? Do you agree with her view? Why or why not? Do you think she would say the same thing today?

TRANSGENDER AND NONBINARY GENDERS

As is the case with sex, we often think of gender in binary terms. We think of a *gender binary* involving only two genders, man and woman. But just as sex, most notably in the case of the intersexed, is not a simple binary, gender has multiple aspects, forms, and expressions; it is not a simple, neat binary. It is socially constructed and variable across cultures, times, and places. Individuals who might identify themselves as one of the two dominant genders—namely, as a man or a woman—enact a wide range of gender portrayals, roles, and identities, including being transgender.

Most basically, **transgender** is an umbrella term for people whose gender identity and/or gender presentation

LGBTQ advocate Laverne Cox, a star of the Netflix series *Orange Is the New Black,* is the first openly transgender actor to be nominated for a Primetime Emmy Award. She has been named one of *People* magazine's most beautiful women of the year and one of *Time*'s 100 most influential people.

differs from the gender assigned to them at birth or in infancy. **Gender identity** is a person's internal sense of gender (Bornstein 1994; Wood and Eagly 2015). Trans individuals may have **gender roles**—the social presentation of gender, which includes clothing, hairstyle, and attitudinal and behavioral traits—that differ from or correspond with their gender identities.

Trans individuals do not follow a single path. They may or may not locate themselves somewhere in the broad matrix of gender. They may or may not identify with either of the two culturally dominant genders. They may or may not wish to use hormones or obtain surgeries to change aspects of their physical sex. Trans individuals may choose identities and/or create self-applied labels—such as *genderqueer, agender,* or *gender fluid*—that do not fit neatly within the gender binary. People who are *agender* may not identify with any gender, while those who are *gender fluid* may feel that their identities change depending on the context. *Genderqueer* is a broad umbrella term that encompasses a range of gendered identities, feelings, and self-determined labels.

The official number of Americans who identify as transgender is 1.4 million, which is double previous estimates based on a smaller federal database (Hoffman 2016). Although only about 8 percent of U.S. adults say they personally know someone who is trans (Pew Research Center 2013), general awareness of trans people has increased in recent years. Not long ago, *Time* magazine ran a cover story, "The Transgender Tipping Point," featuring actor Laverne Cox, a "proud African American transgender woman" (K. Steinmetz 2014). Kye Allums is a "queer fluid trans artist and athlete" who played Division I college basketball and was the first NCAA player to come out as trans (see http://time.com/3537849/meet-the-first-openly-transgender-ncaa-athlete). Cox and Allums do advocacy work and education

Gender-Swapping in Online Games

Virtual reality allows individuals a variety of opportunities to experiment with their identities, including their gender. **Gender-swapping**, or gender-switching, occurs when an individual represents himself or herself online as a gender that is different from his or her offline gender. Gender-swapping is particularly evident in massive multiplayer online role-playing games, such as World of Warcraft and Second Life, which require players to create avatars to play the games (Hussain and Griffiths 2008; Martey et al. 2014). An avatar "marks" a player's identity and offers a "visual representation of the player" (Song and Jung 2015, 435). Players are free to construct their visual representations by selecting skin, hair, and eye color, hairstyle, body type, clothing, and accessories, such as glasses, for their avatars. While some players choose to create avatars that closely mimic their offline appearances, others opt to create fantasy avatars—for fun and aesthetic or strategic purposes. For example, some male players create female avatars because "they prefer the esthetic of watching the female avatar form," particularly from behind, which is where most role-playing games visually position the gaze of their players (Martey et al. 2014, 289). Other male players explain that they create female avatars because other players treat them better and more readily give them gifts or hints that they need to advance to subsequent game levels (Hussain and Griffiths 2008; Song and Jung 2015). Thus, gender-swapping may be less an expression of one's identity than a "rational choice based

Participants in online gaming may choose an avatar that bears no physical resemblance to their actual appearance or even one of the opposite gender.

on practical benefits" (Song and Jung 2015, 435).

Even if gender-swapping is not necessarily an extension of an individual's offline identity, studies have found that players who engage in this practice find themselves adopting the gendered behaviors of their avatars during online play. Song and Jung (2015, 444) discovered that gender-swapping males acted more feminine and displayed "socially amiable behaviors" when playing as female avatars. Martey et al (2014, 295) found that they adopted female linguistic behaviors, such as using more emotional phrases, than men who did not gender-swap. Other research has revealed that the avatars of females who gender-swap tend to display more aggressive, achievement-oriented behaviors (Song and Jung 2015, 238). Interestingly, gender-swapping appears to be reinforcing heteronormativity and traditional gender stereotypes instead of encouraging gender diversity.

Engaging the Digital World
Create a virtual avatar "superhero" that is different from your offline gender at http://marvel.com/games/play/31/create_your_own_superhero. Describe the appearance of this avatar (eyes, hair, body type, accessories) and how it conforms (or not) to traditional gender stereotypes. Explain how the options available to you on this website constrained or enabled you to adhere to or deviate from traditional gender stereotypes.

across the United States; Cox has appeared in many venues, working tirelessly on behalf of trans people, especially trans youth. In 2011, *Dancing with the Stars* featured Chaz Bono, a trans man whose parents are entertainers Sonny and Cher, and in 2015, Olympic gold medalist Bruce Jenner—now Caitlyn Jenner—came out as transgender.

ASK YOURSELF

What might explain hate-based violence against trans people? Do you think there is a connection between this violence and the recent increase in the visibility of trans people? Why or why not?

Trans history and context runs deeper than is suggested by a few years of increased public visibility. Sylvia Rivera (1951–2002), a "drag queen [and] bisexual transgender activist," was a "loud and persistent voice for the rights of people of color and low-income queers and trans people" (Sylvia Rivera Law Project 2015). She was among those who clashed with police in the 1969 New York Stonewall bar riot, in which gay, queer, and trans people resisted police harassment. That riot is often seen as the start of the modern U.S. lesbian, gay, bisexual, and trans rights movement (see Chapter 18). The Transgender Day of Remembrance (TDOR) began in 1999, when trans woman of color Rita Hester was the victim of a hate murder. Between January 2008 and December 2015, 2,016 trans people were murdered around the world; most of these crimes occurred in Central and South America (Trans Murder Monitoring Project 2016). Life is particularly hellish for trans individuals who find themselves in prison, where rape is an ever-present danger (Sontag 2015). Trans women of color in the United States—and elsewhere—are disproportionately targeted and beaten, abused, or murdered (National Coalition of Anti-Violence Programs 2014). The TDOR is now the culmination of an annual November Transgender Awareness Week. Violence is only one of many issues that trans people face in a society that remains largely inflexible about gender diversities. However, one exception to this is the official policy of the U.S. military, which was changed in mid-2016 to allow transgender Americans to serve openly. In addition, transgender people in the military no longer could be discharged simply because they were transgender (Rosenberg 2016).

GENDER DIVERSITY

Globally, there are many cultures with various nonbinary genders. Some North American Native and First Nations tribes include roles for *two-spirit* individuals. They are socially defined as truly distinct, neither man nor woman, nor a combination of the two, and are respected in their tribes (Roscoe 1998). Another kind of gender diversity can be found in some mountain villages in Afghanistan (Nordberg 2014), where a rigidly constructed culture dictates that sons are necessary for families hoping for prestige (Arbabzadah 2011). In order to gain such prestige, some families without male children present young girls as boys (called *bacha posh*), with the clothing, haircuts, and behavioral shifts common to boys. At puberty, they are "changed" into girls. In some rural areas of Albania, some women became men, adopting men's dress, habits, privileges, and responsibilities (Bilefsky 2008). They swore off marriage, sex, and children and were accepted by men and respected as if they were men.

Evidence of fluid definitions of gender and sex may also be found in the Dayak farming community of the Gerai, in Indonesian Borneo. Christine Helliwell (2000) discovered that the Gerai do not use genitalia to determine a person's gender. Instead, they link gender to tasks and accomplishments, such as learning to choose rice seeds according to growing conditions. For the Gerai to concede that Helliwell might be a woman, she had to begin learning what Gerai women did and then become competent at those tasks.

In southern Oaxaca State in Mexico, there is a group of people—*muxes*—who do not identify as male or female, although they were born with male bodies. There is a long tradition of a mixed-gender way of life in Mexico. *Muxes* have been widely accepted, and their "embroidery, hairstyling, handicrafts, and cooking" are greatly admired (Burnett 2016, A4). Nevertheless, in recent years protests have arisen about *muxes'* use of women's restrooms.

GENDERED INEQUALITIES

As a master status and a primary basis for the persistence of structural, institutional inequalities, gender is a key variable in understanding life chances in the United States. Gender is structured into all our social institutions or systems—education, families, the economy, the law, and so on. Social institutions are powerful established sociocultural pathways that exist to meet our collective needs (Acker 1992). In the United States, we socialize people into the binary gender system through our social institutions and then channel them into differently valued activities, attributes, and pursuits. In this chapter, we will explore several aspects of institutional and cultural inequality in the United States. The way in which we gender individuals and social institutions has real consequences for almost everyone.

Gender inequality is not just a problem in the United States; it is also a global problem (see Chapter 9 on global stratification). The World Economic Forum (2016) measures gender inequality in terms of gender gaps in health care, education, economy, and politics. Statistics on men's and women's salaries, participation in paid labor, access to education, representation in political bodies, and life expectancy contribute to the score. No country in the world has a score of one; no country has full equality between men and women. Scores closer to one indicate that a country has a relatively narrow gap between men and women—that women are doing nearly as well as men. As you can see in Figure 11.1, Iceland is the most equal country in the world in terms of gender, with a score of 0.881, while Yemen is the least equal, with a score of 0.484. The United States, with a score of 0.74, ranks 28th.

There are global differences in the ways in which societies deal with gender differences and inequalities. Change.org petitioners in the United Kingdom and Ireland have sought to send a message to toy retailers: Stop labeling some toys for boys (construction sets, cars, and the like) and others for girls (princess outfits, play kitchens, etc.). In London, the Selfridges department store has recently eliminated clothing departments segregated by sex or gender. Management argued that individuals should be able to shop without the constraints of marketers' decisions about which clothes should be in "men's" and "women's" departments. Some Swedes strongly support the idea that traditional gender norms enhance inequalities. They argue for gender-neutral pronouns as a way of promoting equality. Swedish preschools and elementary schools have begun to use the gender-neutral pronoun *hen* (Braw 2014).

GENDER AND EDUCATION

Educational systems constitute an important site and source of gender inequality throughout American society and across the globe. Historically, families invested relatively little in the education of girls because they were expected to grow up to stay at home as wives and mothers. Thus, there has long been a gender gap in education in many countries, including the United States.

Clearly the formal educational system, especially at the primary and secondary levels, has been a major cause of that gap, and it continues to pose some persistent problems for women. One aspect of that system, and a root cause of the gender gap in education, is often the **hidden curriculum**, or a school's unofficial norms, routines, and structures that transmit dominant cultural norms and values (De Lissovoy and García 2013; Giroux and Purpel 1983). Schools reproduce unquestioned social norms, such as obedience to authority, hard work, and the value of hierarchy. Most schools foster competitiveness, a push for achievement, and an understanding of the social hierarchy within the school (Scott and Schwartz 2008). Because boys are socialized from infancy to enact these preferred values, they are likely to get more attention in class from teachers, to be asked more questions, to get more constructive criticism, and, at least in the early years of school, to monopolize class discussions (Sadker and Sadker 1994; Sharp 2012).

FIGURE 11.1 • Global Gender Gap Index, 2015

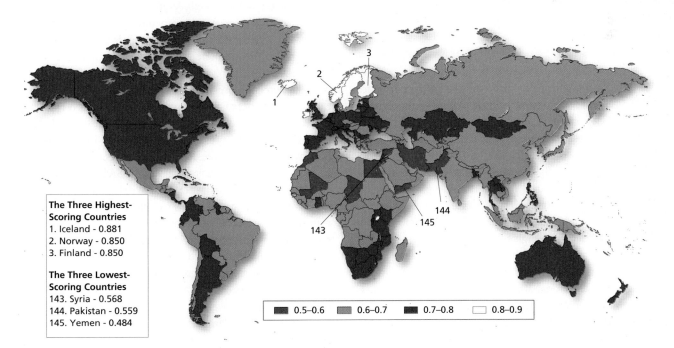

The Three Highest-Scoring Countries
1. Iceland - 0.881
2. Norway - 0.850
3. Finland - 0.850

The Three Lowest-Scoring Countries
143. Syria - 0.568
144. Pakistan - 0.559
145. Yemen - 0.484

0.5–0.6   0.6–0.7   0.7–0.8   0.8–0.9

SOURCE: Data from World Economic Forum, *The Global Gender Gap Report 2015* (Geneva: World Economic Forum, 2016).

There is a deeply hidden curriculum regarding gender conformity and norms (Surtees 2008). Analyses of elementary teacher training materials and in-depth studies of elementary school classrooms suggest that most teachers are not well trained to deal with gender (or sexuality) issues at school. A small, exploratory study found that elementary school teachers were afraid of the prospect of having a transgender student (Payne and Smith 2014). Lack of formal training, education, and institutional support, combined with individual-level discomfort, creates this fear. Institutional policies against discussing sexuality, as well as the mistaken perception that gender identity is linked to sexuality, hampered teachers' ability to deal with transgender students (Payne and Smith 2014; Surtees 2008).

Increasing awareness of the gender gap in education has led to significant efforts to overcome it and subsequently to great educational gains for women (Dorius and Firebaugh 2010). Nevertheless, a gender gap in education persists. In spite of this continuing gender gap, some girls, especially those who are white, experience success in primary and secondary schooling due, in part, to gendered socialization. They are more engaged in school and more likely to comply with school rules, such as doing homework and responding to teacher requests (Buchmann and DiPrete 2006). Such "noncognitive" skills are strong predictors of academic success. They partly explain why girls outperform boys on most academic indicators.

ASK YOURSELF

Think back to your elementary and high school years. Did the schools you attended have a hidden curriculum? You may have been unaware of it at the time, but can you now identify any specific examples of the way in which it manifested itself?

Another explanation for girls' success in primary and secondary school is structural, related to long-term job success. Many occupations continue to be segregated by sex. The most consistently male-segregated occupations (e.g., truck driver, auto mechanic, firefighter) do not require postsecondary schooling, whereas several of the most consistently female-segregated occupations (e.g., preschool teacher, registered nurse, dental hygienist) do require schooling beyond high school. Young women therefore must maintain some success in high school in order to get into the college programs needed for future job training. This occupational segregation is increasingly responsible for women's advantages in educational attainment (Jacobs 1996).

Changing societal attitudes about gender roles and declining sexism have had dramatic effects on women's educational attainment as they advance through the educational system. Women are significantly more likely than men to

FIGURE 11.2 • Gender Differences in Undergraduate Enrollment in the United States, 1970–2025 (projected)

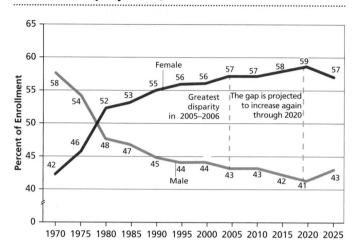

SOURCE: "The Condition of Education 2016." U.S. Department of Education, National Center for Education Statistics. Washington, DC: U.S. Government Printing Office.

graduate from high school and to attend either a two- or four-year college (Carbonaro and Covay 2010). In 1960, women represented less than 40 percent of college undergraduates in the United States; today, roughly 56 percent of students at both two- and four-year colleges are women (Goldin, Katz, and Kuziemko 2006). Women are more likely than men to receive bachelor's or master's degrees (Alon and Gelbgiser 2011; Bauman and Ryan 2015; Buchmann and DiPrete 2006). Figure 11.2 depicts the dramatic gap between men and women enrolled as undergraduates in the United States, which is expected to remain large. By 2025, women are projected to make up almost 57 percent of undergraduates, while men will make up 43 percent. This constitutes an almost complete reversal of the situation in 1970, when almost 58 percent of undergraduates were men and only 42 percent were women. We can also see this trend in the dramatic increases in law and medical degrees earned by women. However, men continue to be more likely to be trained in the most prestigious colleges and universities and to obtain doctoral degrees. In part this is because elite institutions highly value (perhaps overvalue?) SAT scores, and men continue to perform better on the SAT (Bielby et al. 2014).

Even with women's gains in higher education, a significant pay gap exists between men and women once they leave school and begin their careers (Charles and Bradley 2009; Jacobs 1996). While in college, women are more likely to major in sex/gender-segregated academic fields, such as education, English, and psychology, which tend to lead to jobs that do not pay as well as jobs dominated by men. While there are differences among the fields, women continue to be less likely to major in science, technology, engineering, and math (STEM fields) in college. Majoring in these fields tends

FIGURE 11.3 • Bachelor's Degrees Awarded to Women in Select STEM Majors in Postsecondary Institutions in the United States, 1949–2014

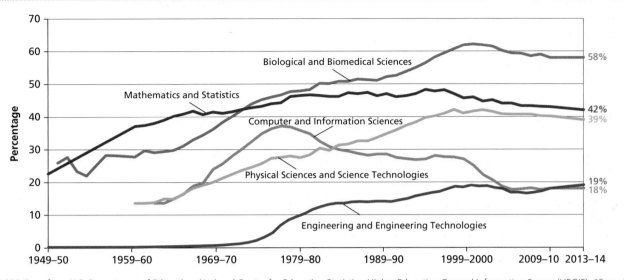

SOURCES: Data from U.S. Department of Education, National Center for Education Statistics, Higher Education General Information Survey (HEGIS), "Snapshot Report—Degree Attainment," January 26, 2015; and "Degrees and Other Formal Awards Conferred" surveys, 1970–71 through 1985–86; Integrated Postsecondary Education Data System (IPEDS), "Completions Survey" (IPEDS-C:87–99); and IPEDS fall 2000 through fall 2012, completions component.

to lead to higher-paying jobs. Figure 11.3 shows that women now earn a majority of degrees in biology, and they have shown strong gains in the physical sciences and mathematics/statistics. However, they continue to be less likely than men to earn degrees in STEM fields. Worse, women lag far behind men in bachelor's degrees in computer science and information science, as well as in engineering. Part of the reason for this underrepresentation is the fact that women continue to be likely to be stereotyped as being less capable scientifically and technically. Larry Summers, a noted economist and former president of Harvard University, once said that genetic differences explain why boys outperform girls in science and math. Female chemistry professor Donna Nelson responded, "I have heard men make comments like this my entire life, and quite honestly, if I had listened to them, I would never have done anything" (Goldenberg 2005). This kind of sex and gender stereotyping in education is frequent and continues to be not only an American problem but also a global one.

GENDER, FAMILY, AND WORK

The relationship between gender and work is one of the most studied issues in the field of gender (Thorn 2007). A primary concern has been documenting the intersections of gender, work, and family. As you can see in Figure 11.4, heterosexual families with men and women in the paid labor force earn more than all other family types. Even when their wives are not in the paid labor force, married men earn more than unmarried men (Ahituv and Lerman 2007; Ashwin and Isupova 2014). However, unmarried women's household income is far below that of all men and of married women.

Many of these inequities are based on historical, traditional gender roles in families.

Separate Spheres

Prior to the Industrial Revolution, women and men together occupied both the private sphere (domestic life in and around the home) and the public sphere (the job sector and public life). That is, women and men shared the breadwinner and domestic roles. Industrialization brought about the separation of the public and private spheres. Men tended to become the breadwinners, venturing forth into the public world of work; women were less likely to work outside the home and were apt to be relegated to the private sphere (Kerber 1988). The "cult of domesticity" that arose around the private sphere argued that women should display

- Submissiveness to their husbands and other male authorities

- Piety as moral exemplars within the home

- Purity in being virgins at marriage and strictly monogamous thereafter

- Domesticity, having been well trained in the domestic arts and caretaking (Connellan, forthcoming; Welter 1966)

The public–private division applied almost entirely to white families in the United States. Men of color were not allowed to become breadwinners; women of color were not permitted to keep house in a private sphere (Glenn 2002). African American and single women were often in the

FIGURE 11.4 • Median Income of Families in the United States, by Family Type, 1950–2015

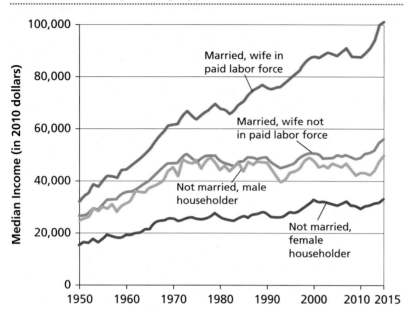

SOURCE: U.S. Census Bureau, Current Population Surveys, Selected Characteristics of Families by Total Money Income.

industrialized labor force, enabling white middle- and upper-class women to be involved in the cult of domesticity.

The once clear-cut, gender-based differentiation between the public and private spheres in the United States has been breaking down since the mid-twentieth century. Now women are more likely not only to be in the work world (England 2010) but also, increasingly, to be the principal—or even the only—wage earner in the family. The family characterized by a division between male/ breadwinner and female/home-maker has increasingly given way to more blended roles, and even to role reversals, especially in dual-earner families (McClelland, Mok, and Pierce 2014). Figure 11.5 shows the steadily increasing percentage of mothers who earn most of the family income (breadwinners), along with those who are co-breadwinners.

Dual-Earner Households and the Stalled Revolution

A key issue in the study of gender, work, and family is the difference between heterosexual

men and women in the ways they use their time in the era of dual-earner families. Arlie Hochschild (1989, 2012) argues that in U.S. dual-earner families with children, wives who work outside the home tend to be saddled with additional labor—the traditionally gendered tasks of childcare and housework—when they get home from their paid work. Such women can be said to be working a "second shift." Figure 11.6 presents 2015 data on gender differences in performing three household tasks: cleaning the house, preparing and cleaning up after meals, and caring for and helping children. On an average day, 70 percent of women did meal preparation or cleanup, while only 43 percent of men performed these tasks. More extremely, 50 percent of women cleaned the house on an average day, while only 22 percent of men did such work. In terms of caring for and helping household children, 26 percent of women perform these tasks, compared to only 16 percent of men.

However, other recent research indicates that the differences between heterosexual women and men in performing household tasks may be narrowing (Bianchi, Robinson, and Milkie 2006). While the second shift continues to exist for women, they are now spending more time at work and less at home. Thus, they have less time for, and are less involved in, the second shift. Between 1965 and 2015, the amount of time American women spent per week on housework decreased, on

FIGURE 11.5 • Share of Mothers Who Are Breadwinners or Co-breadwinners in the United States, 1967–2012

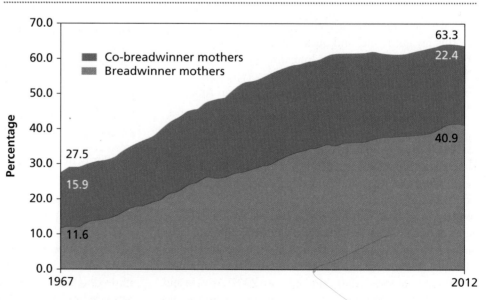

SOURCE: Sarah Jane Glynn, "Breadwinning Mothers, Then and Now," Center for American Progress, June 2014: Figure 1, page 6. This material was published by the Center for American Progress, www.americanprogress.org.

FIGURE 11.6 • Division of Household Labor in the United States, by Gender, 2015

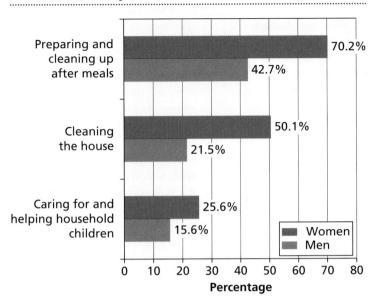

SOURCE: Data from U.S. Department of Labor, Bureau of Labor Statistics, "Daily Household Labor in the United States by Gender," in *American Time Use Survey Summary*, June 18, 2014; 2015 data from "American Time Use Survey—2015 Results," June 24, 2016: 9.

average, from 32 to 16 hours (Liss 2014). Men are spending less time at work and more time at home, participating more in the tasks associated with the second shift. Between 1965 and 2015, their average weekly time devoted to housework increased from 4 to 10 hours. However, according to the United Nations, women worldwide continue to shoulder vastly more household responsibilities than do men.

Men's tendency to do less domestic work than women (Lachance-Grzela and Bouchard 2010; Miller and Sassler 2010) has been attributed to a "stalled [gender equality] revolution," especially in the United States (Coontz 2013; England 2010). Explanations for the stalled revolution are complex and extend beyond the bounds of individual families (Thebaud and Pedulla 2016). Both men and women in the white-collar paid labor force in the United States are expected to work comparatively more hours than those in similar jobs in many other developed countries. The U.S. model of a two-week vacation each year also lags behind other developed countries, where four to eight weeks are standard. As a rule, the United States is not friendly to parents, whether heterosexual dual earners or single parents, or those creating other family forms. The gender equality revolution has stalled, at least in part, because work-life policies lag behind domestic realities. For example, the United States has no federal maternity leave policies. The Family and Medical Leave Act grants 12 weeks of unpaid maternity leave, but only for full-time employees who have worked 1,250 hours in the year preceding the leave and who work in companies with 50 or more

employees. Thus, part-time employees and full-timers in workplaces that employ fewer than 50 people are not covered. Even full-timers may not be able to afford time off without pay for the responsibilities associated with childbirth and beyond. Papua New Guinea and the United States are the only countries that do not have federally supported paid time off for mothers. There is a similar situation with paternity and home care leave. Unlike Sweden (which offers a total paid leave of 60 weeks), Germany (58 weeks), and Canada (52 weeks), the United States offers zero paid leave days. In fact, the United States ranks at the bottom globally in government-supported time off for new parents (see Figure 11.7).

ASK YOURSELF

Did your mother or grandmother work a "second shift"? How many women do you know who are doing so now? Do you know any men who could be said to be working a "second shift" to the same degree as women?

In the past half-century or so, there has certainly been a revolution in the United States (and elsewhere), with women participating in the paid labor force at much higher rates. Feminism and other movements for greater equality are having a wider effect on society as a whole, on men and women in the labor force, and on the family. However, it would be premature to argue that the revolution is now complete or that there is true equality in men's and women's work, either in the home or in the labor force.

Gender Inequality at Work

In nearly every kind of job and work setting, gender inequalities persist and begin to intersect with racial inequalities. Perhaps the most widely cited inequality is the wage gap, the difference between men's earnings and women's earnings, usually expressed as a percentage of men's earnings. In the United States in 2016, the wage gap was 80 percent. According to the U.S. Bureau of Labor Statistics, overall, women earn (on average) 80 cents for every dollar earned by white men. As is evident in Figure 11.8, a wage gap exists at all levels of the occupational ladder. Women in entry-level jobs or positions (for example, cashiers and food preparers) earn much less ($407) per week than do similarly employed young men ($471). The gap between well-educated men in white-collar jobs and similarly situated women is large. For example, female financial managers earn $1,130 per week, while male financial managers earn $1,732.

When women begin moving into occupations (such as working in parks or being ticket agents) in large numbers,

FIGURE 11.7 • Government-Supported Paid Leave for New Parents in Select Countries

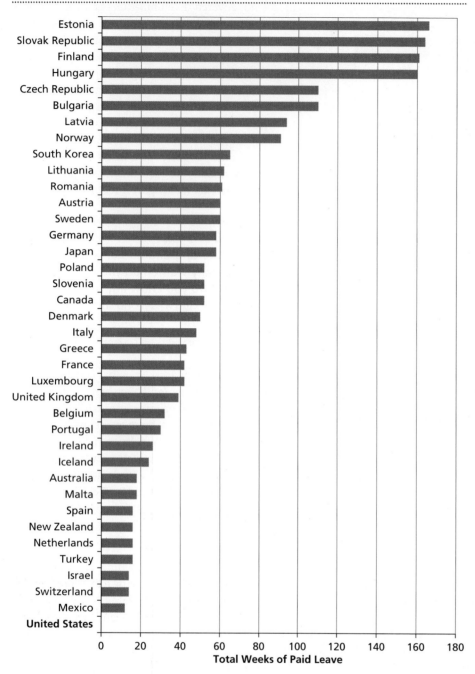

Total Weeks of Paid Leave

NOTE: Total paid leave represents maternity, parental, and home care leave available to mothers. The data do not address paid leave or other accommodations that individual employers make available to employees or guarantees provided by a few individual states.

SOURCE: Data on paid leave from Organisation for Economic Co-operation and Development, "PF2.1: Key Characteristics of Parental Leave Systems," OECD Family Database, Table PF2.1.A, p.3, February 28, 2016; Data on protected leave from OECD via Gretchen Livingston, "Among 38 Nations, U.S. Is the Outlier When It Comes to Paid Parental Leave," Pew Research Center, Fact Tank, December 12, 2013.

the pay tends to go down. Conversely, when males move into occupations such as computer programming, pay tends to rise. Of the 30 best-paying jobs, 26 are dominated by males. On the other hand, 23 of the 30 lowest-paying jobs are dominated by females (Miller 2016).

Some explanations for the wage gap are structural and institutional. Women remain strongly clustered in some relatively low-paid occupations (for example, nursing and elementary school teaching), although they have made inroads into historically male-dominated fields, such as law, medicine, and business (Blau, Brummund, and Liu 2012). Occupations and specialties within certain occupations that are male-dominated tend to have higher salaries than occupations and specialties that are, or have been, female-dominated. The higher the percentage of women in an occupation, the lower the average wages. Another explanation is more personal or family based. Historical gender roles and stereotyping, particularly in the middle class, have led to the expectation that women who have children will take time off from their paid employment to care for them. Such career disruptions certainly contribute to the wage gap. Women who take time away from the paid labor force lose ground in terms of salaries and rate of advancement into higher-paying positions.

Many different consequences stem from the inequality of workplaces and work structures. Pudrovska and Karraker (2014) discovered that women with authority on the job—the ability to hire, fire, and influence—had more diminished mental health than did women without job authority and men *with* authority. They argue that women in authority deal with a host of negative interpersonal stressors, stereotyping, and resistance from both subordinates and superiors. Mental health may be most adversely affected by contradictory social, gendered expectations (Cook and Glass 2014). On the one hand, women in leadership positions may be viewed as not assertive or confident enough. On the other hand, when they do display these characteristics, they are judged negatively for not being

FIGURE 11.8 • Median Weekly Earnings of Full-Time Wage and Salary Workers by Occupation in the United States, 2015

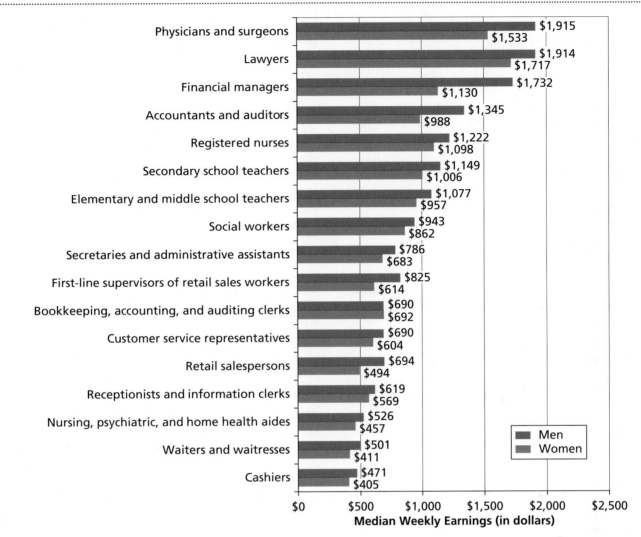

SOURCE: Data from U.S. Department of Labor, Bureau of Labor Statistics, Table 39: "Household Data: Annual Averages," 2015.

feminine enough. Snyder (2014) studied 248 performance reviews of 180 people (105 men and 75 women) from 28 companies. She found that "words like *bossy, abrasive, strident,* and *aggressive* are used to describe women's behaviors when they lead; words like *emotional* and *irrational* describe their behaviors when they object. . . . *Abrasive* alone is used 17 times to describe 13 different women." The only word on this list that shows up in men's reviews is *aggressive.* Snyder saw it three times, but on two of those occasions, the reviewer was encouraging the male employee to be *more* aggressive.

GENDER AND CONSUMER CULTURE

In consumption, as in many other aspects of the social world, gender matters (Casey 2015). Since the Industrial Revolution, production has been centered outside the household and has primarily been the function of white men. White middle- and upper-class women, largely

relegated to the home, were assigned the role of consumers (Williams and Sauceda 2007). This is both different and unequal, because historically production has been far more highly valued than consumption.

Consumption, Work, and Family

Women were not just defined as the prime consumers—their consumer practices were also closely tied to their domestic practices and their roles in the home. Women consumed goods and services to care for, and on behalf of, their families (De Laat and Baumann 2016; DeVault 1991). Much of women's shopping was related to love, especially their love of family members (Miller 1998); it was an instrumental way of showing caring and love. In one way or another, women generally made purchases for their families and to fulfill their responsibilities in the home and to those who lived there. Women are still thought to constitute a "multiple market"—they purchase things for significant others, family members, and friends. As marketing expert Bridget Brennan observes: "If somebody, somewhere needs a gift, chances are there's a woman thinking about it; tracking it down; wrapping it; making sure it's accompanied by a personal message and then arriving to the person on the appointed day. I sometimes think entire industries would collapse overnight if women stopped being so thoughtful. Consider the impact to the greeting card industry alone" (2013).

As women have entered the paid work world in increasing numbers, their consumption patterns have changed. They are now more likely to consume an array of subcontracted services, such as cleaning and childcare. Much of this work is done by other women—women are subcontracting work to other women (Bowman and Cole 2009). In addition, they are increasingly more likely to consume for themselves than for others. For example, greater involvement in the work world requires the use of a wider variety of clothing: business casual, conservative office work wear, and uniforms, to name a few. This certainly contributes to the amount that U.S. women spend on clothing—$116 billion in 2013 (Madhok 2014).

Women and Girls as Consumers

As one sociologist put it, "For a large number of girls in modern America, participating in the consumer realm is the defining feature of life as a girl" (Best 2007, 724). Several historical events mark the development of greater interest in girls, and children more generally, as consumers (Cook 2007). One was the emergence of the department store in the middle and late 1800s, along with the celebration of Christmas, and its associated gifts, by department stores such as Macy's. Children's consumer culture gained further impetus when department stores began to have separate departments for toys and, more important, separate departments for boys' and girls' clothing. In the early 1900s, department stores everywhere from Paris (Galeries Lafayette) to London (Selfridges) to New York (Macy's) encouraged women of means to approach shopping as leisure and entertainment (van Eeden 2006). Stores like these were seen as safe extensions of the domestic private sphere, keeping upper- and middle-class women safe while allowing them to be in public, unaccompanied by male protectors. The idea of recreational shopping, or "shopping for fun," seems to have originated at this time. Consumption is a marker of status for young women, as it is for adults.

As girls gain some freedom from gendered expectations and spend more of their own money, they are being courted more aggressively by advertisers and marketers (Deutsch and Theodorou 2010; Verde Group 2007). Now, of course, all children, including girls, are being targeted on their computers, their smartphones, and myriad other new and yet-to-be-created technologies that have a ready audience among teenagers and younger children (Kahlenberg and Hein 2010; Sheldon 2004). Some teen women court others in the form of shopping "haul" videos, "the YouTube equivalent of calling a best friend and gushing about a recent shopping spree" (Khrais 2013). More than 1 million such videos have been posted online, with shoppers often partnering with clothing and cosmetic companies. Haul videos help drive young women's consumption—about 4 in 10 buy a product after seeing it discussed in a haul video (Parker 2012).

This focus on consumption is particularly clear in the efforts made by the cosmetics and clothing industries to sell to young women by advertising in magazines aimed at this age group (*Seventeen, Teen Vogue*) and through pop-up advertisements on the internet. "Women/girls . . . are expected to consume their way into attractiveness" (Deutsch and Theodorou 2010, 234). One of the unfortunate consequences of this for young girls is increased rates of eating disorders and body dysmorphia—an obsession with perceived flaws in one's body—as well as the hypersexualization of their lives (Hesse-Biber 1996; Kimmel 2012). Hypersexualization has become such a concern globally that the Norwegian minister of family affairs urged chain stores to remove sexualizing clothing (for example, string bikini underwear; Rysst 2008).

Men and Boys as Consumers

Men and boys are different from women and girls in the ways in which they consume and are targeted by marketers. Consumer analysts now spend a lot of time exploring distinctions between and among men and women, developing typologies, patterns, and thus strategies for selling (Mortimer 2013). This wasn't always the case. For a long time, market researchers assumed without question that the most important consumers to study were women (Peñaloza 2000). When they did study men, they believed that men were not interested in shopping or viewed it as something to do only for a purpose or specific goal, such as purchasing sports gear. Shopping as leisure was thought to be something only women did (Otnes and McGrath 2001). Men's consumption habits differ by generation. For example, compared to older men, younger men are much more comfortable shopping online (Brosdahl and Carpenter 2012). Retailers and advertisers are now increasingly recognizing that there is a growing subset of men who see that clothing is "an outward sign of self-image and a symbol of success" (Parker, Simmers, and Schaefer 2014). Upper-middle-class and upper-class men are spending more money shopping online via smartphones, patronizing Amazon, and buying luxury brands like Rolex and Louis Vuitton, according to the digital marketing experts at iProspect (www.iprospect.com). Men's (and women's) shopping habits certainly vary globally. For example, one study reports that Indian men spend more ($17.3 billion to $15.5 billion) on clothing than do Indian women (Madhok 2014).

What has inhibited the recognition that men are important consumers is, quite simply, gendered stereotyping. Heterosexual men are thought to be wary of paying too much attention to their looks and appearance (Brosdahl and Carpenter 2012). Thus, we develop other labels for them—hipster, lumbersexual (Compton and Bridges 2014)—and define their consumption habits accordingly. Currently, one of the most stereotyped narratives about men's consumption is that of the "man cave," which the *Urban Dictionary* (www .urbandictionary.com) defines as a room or space reserved for a man to engage in his hobbies. "This area is usually decorated by the male" who uses it, without "female influence." There are stores designed specifically to cater to men who want to shop for their man caves. Mantiques and More, in Corpus Christi, Texas, is designed as a store for men, because "an antique store can be seen as anything but cool, hip, and manly" (Salinas 2014). Men involved in this market talk about wanting spaces that are clearly masculine (Moisio and Beruchashvili 2014). Further, man caves represent a form of productive consumption that enables men to combine leisure with work, like building shelves for the man cave.

Advertising and Gender

Much of advertising and marketing is targeted to only women or men. For example, in the first half of the twentieth century, advertising targeted at middle-class women focused on household products that helped with their home and family responsibilities. The media also influenced mothers to focus on maintaining domestic happiness (Douglas and Michaels 2006). As more middle-class women entered the labor force, at least some advertising came to focus on the needs of working women (e.g., labor-saving devices in the home). Feminist critiques of advertising, beginning in the 1970s, attacked advertisements' emphasis on slimness and beauty. Feminists argued that the ads set up ideals that few women could approximate, adversely affecting their self-esteem (Bordo 1993). In line with general trends in society, advertising has recently begun to focus more on encouraging women to purchase what they need to be unique individuals (Zukin 2004). Of course, there is a huge contradiction in offering generally available, brand-name products as a way of achieving uniqueness (Maguire and Stanway 2008).

ASK YOURSELF

Think back to Chapter 2, about sociological theory. How might sociological theorists explain the link between gender and social inequalities? How can theory help you see why gender and inequalities persist in most of the world?

Interrelated aspects of consumer culture, and the social world more generally, come together to define women's and men's consumption behavior. For example, gender ideals in advertising are reinforced by the spatial segregation of women's and men's television networks (E! mainly for women, ESPN mainly for men), television shows (*The Bachelor/Bachelorette* versus *Monday Night Football*), movies ("chick flicks" versus action movies), lifestyle magazines (*Vogue* and *O, the Oprah Magazine* versus *GQ* and *Esquire*), and departments in department stores and shops in malls. However, as with consumption in general, adult women and men are not simply passive in the face of these pressures. They are able to resist, or even actively reconstruct, the messages being communicated to them (Fransen et al. 2015).

CHECKPOINT 11.1: GENDER CONCEPTS

CONCEPT	DESCRIPTION
Sex	Principally a biological term and typically reflected in a person's chromosomes, gonads, genitalia, and hormones
Gender	A cultural term, connected to societal definitions of expected behaviors, attitudes, and personalities
Intersex	A term to describe a person who is born with reproductive or sexual anatomy that does not conform to typical definitions of biological sex
Transgender	A term for people whose gender identity differs from the gender assigned to them at birth or in infancy

THE SOCIOLOGY OF SEXUALITY

Sexuality is the ways in which people think about, and behave toward, themselves and others as sexual beings (Kimmel 2014; Plummer 1975). Sexuality is, of course, related to both sex and gender, and includes sexual attitudes, behaviors, sensuality, values, anatomy, biochemistry, identities, and orientations. It is of central interest to sociologists, perhaps because of its complicated and seemingly opposed elements. Sexuality is both individual and personal *and* collective and public; it is biological and biochemical as well as cultural, social, and historical. There is variation in degrees of sexuality among individuals and across cultures and time periods.

There is now a large and growing body of literature on the sociology of sexuality (Plummer 2012). While bodies and biology are involved, the bulk of this work deals with the social, social psychological, and cultural aspects of sexuality. Sociologists have become increasingly interested in sexuality for a number of reasons:

- The growing number of sexually linked social problems, including sexual violence, HIV/AIDS, and the recent discovery that Zika can be transmitted sexually (Davidson et al. 2016)

- Social changes in attitudes and behaviors, including the increase in "hooking up" (see the discussion later in this section) and casual sexual relationships

- The greater visibility of sexuality-related social movements, especially those associated with gays, lesbians, bisexuals, and transgender people

- Technological changes, such as the arrival and exploding popularity of erectile dysfunction (ED) drugs like Viagra and Cialis

- The media's presentation of sex in its many forms

- The globalization of sexuality, for example, through sex tourism (both male and female) and human/sex trafficking (Frank 2012; Lerum and Brents 2016)

- The increase in overt expressions of sexuality in consumer culture—not only widespread commerce in sexual activity but also the use of sex to sell virtually everything

- The increasing popularity of the internet, especially its ever more vibrant commercial sex culture (Waskul 2015)

Sexuality is rarely simply a matter of sexual release or so-called reproductive imperatives. It is complex, contradictory, and often confusing (Plante 2015). For example, we are told that "having sex"—meaning, usually, engaging in heterosexual activities (Seidman 2003)—is "natural" and that reproduction is the key goal of these activities. Similarly, we are told that people "naturally" have hormones, sexual urges, and needs that must be fulfilled. However, we are also told that people should control themselves for religious, social, or cultural reasons (Plante 2014). Culture gives us patterns, rules, and codes to manage our sexualities and sexual identities. Laws and formal sanctions, along with informal sanctions, are intended to regulate cultural and individual sexualities. Contemporary and historical gender roles and power dynamics affect our sexualities, as do race and class (Scott and Schwartz 2008). Culture provides the big picture for our sexualities by communicating our shared attitudes, values, goals, and practices. Language and socialization convey these aspects of culture. However, the existence of a wide variety of subcultures means that there is great diversity in our sexualities.

SEXUAL SELVES

We often ask people to explain the development of their sexualities. Those who are labeled as "deviant" are especially expected to spell out "how they got that way." Normally, heterosexuals are not expected to explain their sexualities. We tend to assume that what we have labeled as normal does not need explanation. But who has the power to define what gets called deviance? Without a society or culture to act as judges, sexualities are not "deviant." They can come to be defined that way only through cultural consensus. If enough people, and especially those with power, agree that something should be called "deviant," societal expectations will change to reflect this consensus.

The stories that people tell and do not tell about their sexualities are of great significance and symbolic importance. They tell us a lot about not only the storytellers and their listeners but also the societies in which we live. In the United States, for example, we have "virginity loss stories" that follow a scripted path (Carpenter 2011). We tell such a story with particular details, including the where, when, how, who, and why, and we use patterned concepts, such as virginity as *something to lose,* or virginity as *a gift to give* (Carpenter 2005). We have "coming out" stories, in which gay, lesbian, bisexual, asexual, and queer people detail the origins of their sexual orientations (Plummer 1995). Unfortunately, these kinds of stories can include the mistaken idea that coming out is a clear, staged process (Klein et al. 2015).

Sexual Identities and Orientations

In the United States, we believe in the concept of **sexual identity**, an internal sense of one's sexual self (Manning 2015). The idea that people have sexual orientations and identities is fairly new in human history. Until as recently as 1923, one could still find *heterosexual* defined in the dictionary as a *medical* term (it was not an *identity* term) meaning "morbid sexual passion for one of the opposite sex" (Katz 2004, 44). In the past 125 years or so, we have begun to classify and label people according to culturally powerful decisions about what is "normal." One element of sexual identity is **sexual orientation**, which identifies whom you desire (fantasies), with whom you want to have sexual relations (behavior), and with whom you have a sense of connectedness (feelings; Scott and Schwartz 2008). Sexual orientation is actually quite complicated. We have tended to oversimplify it by assuming that there are only a few orientations—gay or lesbian, bisexual, and heterosexual.

Although there are cultural, social, and historical contexts for our sexualities, sexual expression varies among individuals. For example, someone may define herself as bisexual, and may be sexual with men and women, but may prefer romantic relationships with women. Another person may define himself as an asexual heteroromantic, someone with no sexual attractions but who is interested in a romantic relationship with a woman (DeLuzio Chasin 2011). Like sex and gender, sexualities and identities are also on continua. In fact, it may be most accurate to conceive of these aspects of ourselves as a matrix. And our interests, fantasies, tastes, and desires may change quite a bit through the life course (DeLamater 2012).

Our attitudes about sexual identities reflect changes in the larger society. Recently the changes have been profound, as have their effects. The best-known example today is the increasing openness many people feel about identifying as gay, lesbian, bisexual, or transgender. In many settings, it is no longer necessary to hide those identities. It is increasingly possible to be very public, and to feel very good, about having such an identity (Plummer 2007a). The Pew Research Center (2013) conducted a nationally representative survey of 1,197 lesbian, gay, bisexual, and transgender adults, and found that 92 percent of respondents said that compared to 10 years ago, U.S. society is now more accepting of LGBTQ people. But the increasing multiplicity of sexualities and sexual communities makes conflicts over the boundaries of sexualities increasingly likely (Köllen 2013). Thus, while LGBTQ people are more accepted, it is also the case that more hate crimes are now aimed at them than at African Americans, Jews, and Muslims (Park and Mykhyalyshyn 2016).

Some of the conflicts *seem* individual and interpersonal, as you can see in Figure 11.9. For example, nearly 40 percent of the Pew survey respondents reported that they had been rejected by a close family member or friend, 30 percent had been physically threatened or attacked, and almost 60 percent had been verbally attacked. These statistics have social and historical roots in homophobia and heterosexism. **Homophobia** is defined as "the fear of being, appearing, or seeming gay; fear of anyone or 'anything' gay. . . . At its most virulent, homophobia inspires hate crimes, murders, assaults (sexual, physical, and emotional), rapes, batteries, and other forms of violence" (Plante 2015, 212). **Heterosexism** is the belief that heterosexuality is superior to other sexual orientations, along with individual and institutional discrimination against those with other orientations. Heterosexism and homophobia combine to drive some of the alienation and aggression experienced by lesbian, gay, bisexual, and trans people.

FIGURE 11.9 • Discrimination against LGBTQ People in the United States

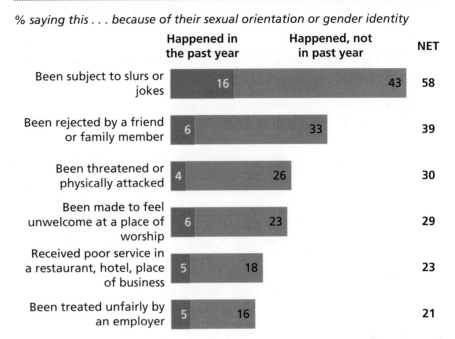

% saying this . . . because of their sexual orientation or gender identity

	Happened in the past year	Happened, not in past year	NET
Been subject to slurs or jokes	16	43	58
Been rejected by a friend or family member	6	33	39
Been threatened or physically attacked	4	26	30
Been made to feel unwelcome at a place of worship	6	23	29
Received poor service in a restaurant, hotel, place of business	5	18	23
Been treated unfairly by an employer	5	16	21

SOURCE: A Survey of LGBT Americans, June 13, 2013. Reprinted by permission of Pew Research Center, Washington, DC.

Gendered Sexual Scripts

Gendered differences between men and women appear to be greater in sexuality than in any other aspect of our intimate lives (Naples and Gurr 2012). Although biology of course plays some role, the sociological view is that social and cultural factors are of far greater importance. Socialization plays a key role, as we learn sexual and gendered scripts by observing and learning from others. We are taught by socialization agents—parents, peers, mass media, teachers, and so on. Particularly important are gender-appropriate **sexual scripts**, the culturally produced, shared, and reinforced social norms that serve as blueprints, or maps, to guide sexual and gender behavior (Gagnon and Simon 1973; Wiederman 2015). Scripts include the *who, what, where, when, how, and why* of socially constructed sexualities. Gagnon and Simon (1973) argued that there are three broad levels of scripting—cultural, interpersonal, and intrapsychic (i.e., mental, in our minds)—and Rebecca Plante (2015) has added the concept of subcultural scripting.

ASK YOURSELF

Where and how do we learn sexual scripts? Do you think we can unlearn them, or learn new ones? Why or why not? How?

Dude, You're a Fag: Masculinity and Sexuality in High School (University of California Press, 2012)

C. J. Pascoe (Associate Professor of Sociology at University of Oregon; PhD, University of California–Berkeley, 2006)

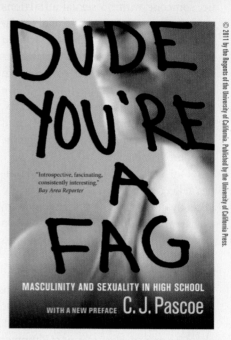

A common assumption is that the word "fag" is a derogatory term for the sexuality of homosexual boys and men. However, after spending 18 months observing and interviewing teenage boys at a high school in California, C. J. Pascoe found that there was more to fag discourse than simply denoting sexuality. It was directed not just at homosexual males, but also at heterosexual males. Many of the heterosexual teenage boys in her study called other heterosexual teenage boys "fags" if their behaviors were viewed as feminine and weak. Thus, calling someone a "fag," whether or not he is homosexual, reaffirms hegemonic masculinity. Another way in which the heterosexual boys in her study asserted their masculinity was through sexualizing teenage girls and women. The boys were expected by their peers to brag about their sexual exploits with females—or at the very least publicly express their heterosexual desires. These practices served to protect them from being called fags and thereby having their masculinity questioned (2012, 85–87). When Pascoe experienced being objectified sexually as a desirable female during her study, she attempted to adopt a "least-gendered identity" by wearing baggy pants, smiling less, and talking about her athletic interests, including weight-lifting (2012, 181).

Heterosexual normativity, or the assumption that heterosexuality is the norm, is reinforced at the institutional level by schools through curriculum, pedagogy, informal teacher-student interactions, and rituals. For instance, Pascoe witnessed a classroom discussion about state laws and marriage that ignored same-sex marriage. She also heard homophobic jokes between teachers and students in stereotypically male spaces (e.g., the weight room and auto shop class). She observed only one teacher reprimanding students for voicing homophobic slurs (2012, 35, 38). School rituals, including dances, assemblies, and football games, that Pascoe attended were rife with what she calls compulsive heterosexuality. Most of these rituals "naturalized heterosexual pairings" and gave boys the opportunity to publicly perform their masculinity by watching, "getting," and touching girls (2012, 41). These rituals also provided the occasion for boys who had been labeled "fags" to renounce this identity by being seen kissing or touching a girl. Interestingly, when these boys engaged in one-on-one, private interactions, they were less likely to objectify girls sexually or to feel compelled to prove their masculinity (2012, 107).

Supplementary Resources

- Pascoe discusses bullying, masculinity, and the "spectre of the fag" in this microLECTURE: https://www.youtube.com/watch?v=5Ha2kSDJ9dY.
- This article from the *New York Times* Opinion Pages situates Pascoe's findings in the context of sexual identity and adolescent socialization: http://opinionator.blogs.nytimes.com/2009/04/16/who-are-you-calling-gay/?_r=0.

Spotlight on "Hooking Up"

What exactly is hooking up? It is *not* a clearly socially defined relationship such as dating, seeing someone, having a boyfriend or girlfriend, or being engaged to be married. It *can be* somewhat committed or somewhat casual, emotionally and physically intense or not, sporadic or fairly regular, sober or intoxicated; it can involve friends or strangers (Plante 2014). Hooking up involves the occurrence of some sort of sexual event—very broadly defined—usually between only two people, and sometimes including alcohol or other drugs. It may include only kissing and making out, or it may involve a range of behaviors from touching to oral sex, penile–vaginal sex, and/or anal sex. Hooking up is intended to be an ambiguous concept. Some of our most unquestioned cultural scripts argue that sex "should be" spontaneous, mysterious, even magical (Kleinplatz 1992). The ambiguity, spontaneity, and apparent lack of rules or expectations for hookups fit these expectations well.

Researchers have observed that hooking up maintains the heterosexual gendered double standard (Hamilton and Armstrong 2009). The **heterosexual double standard** describes a cultural belief system in which men are expected to desire and seek sex from whomever, whenever, while women are expected to be sexual only within committed, romantic relationships. Those who hold this double standard may also believe that women's sexual behavior is different from men's and should be judged differently (Allison and Risman 2013; Reid, Elliott, and Webber 2011). For instance, they may judge women negatively for seeking sex and pleasure outside relationships, while they judge men less harshly, if at all, for the same behavior (Armstrong, England, and Fogarty 2012).

Although there is some evidence that belief in the double standard is weakening, we still see it in heterosexual hooking up. For instance, it may lead to what Hamilton and Armstrong (2009, 594) call "sexual dilemmas," in which young women in particular find that social rules and expectations for gender and social class contradict each other. Heterosexual women are told they should be sexual only in romantic, committed relationships, but also that they should avoid the baggage (and feelings) of committed relationships in favor of self-development and the achievement of academic and career goals. Researchers have explored the sexual dilemmas of hooking up by examining the ways in which heterosexual young women are expected to look and act appropriately sexy—the "just right," or Goldilocks, amount (Plante 2015)—while also "distanc[ing] themselves from the troubling figure of the 'drunken slut'" (Griffin et al. 2012, 187).

SOCIAL CONSTRAINTS ON SEXUALITY

There is a growing sense, not without reason, that sexuality has become increasingly free of social constraints. This seems especially true in the way in which the media treat sexuality. The last 15 years have seen an abundance of increasingly relaxed, open-minded portrayals of sexual experiences and attitudes. TV series, from *The Good Wife* to *Orange Is the New Black* to *Unbreakable Kimmy Schmidt*, are obvious examples. Historical dramas depict lusty sex from the past, and fantasy dramas such as *Game of Thrones* and *The Outlander* feature frequent sexual content. The popularity of *Fifty Shades of Grey* and its sequels, in both book and movie form, depicting bondage and sexual domination, suggests that we have become more open about sexuality. (The movie sequel *Fifty Shades Darker* was released in early 2017.)

Examples of changing consensus about sexualities and social constraint are abundant in modern culture. In 1969, only 21 percent of Americans said that sex between unmarried men and women was morally acceptable (Pennington 2003). By 1973, 43 percent were saying that it was acceptable morally. A majority of Americans (68 percent) now say that sex between unmarried men and women is morally acceptable (Riffkin 2014). The rapid shift in perceptions of the morality of premarital heterosexual sex is an excellent example of changing consensus. Surprisingly, perhaps, American attitudes about heterosexual marital monogamy remain stable. For decades, Gallup has found that 93 percent of Americans believe that "married men and women having an affair" is "morally unacceptable" (Riffkin 2014). Curiously, Americans' attitudes about polygamy have shifted comparatively little: 5 percent viewed it as "morally acceptable" in 2006, but this was before television shows such as *Sister Wives* and reality shows featured the practice. Now, 16 percent of Americans say that polygamy is morally acceptable.

While there is much to support the idea of increasing sexual freedom, human sexuality is never totally free from social and cultural constraints and regulatory attempts. For example, a public school in Mississippi canceled its senior prom because a lesbian student wanted to bring her girlfriend as a date (Joyner 2010). The school was afraid of the message it would send if it allowed a same-sex couple to attend. Society's social institutions, such as schools, families, the law, the police, and formal religions, along with cultural customs and mores, constrain our sexualities. But generally speaking, culturally oppressed minorities' relationships and sexualities are more likely to be constrained than those of the hegemonic, or dominant, group. Sodomy laws, which loosely defined acts of sodomy as "crimes against nature" or "unnatural copulations," were intended to punish sexual activities and romantic relationships between homosexual men. People of color have also been subject to numerous dehumanizing laws, customs, and discourses that constrain their sexualities (Garcia 2012; Rousseau 2011).

CULTURE AND CONSENT

Important to a discussion of social constraints on sexuality are the concepts of consensual sexual activities, sexual assault, and rape. All involve issues of the relative power of the individuals involved, along with complicated sociocultural histories and contexts regarding gender and sexualities. **Consensual sexual activities** are those agreed upon by the participants, any of whom have the right to decide to stop at any point and for any reason. **Informed (or "effective") sexual consent** has been in the news recently, as hundreds of college campuses have been investigated for poor enforcement of rape and sexual assault laws. Informed, effective consent can be defined as follows:

- Informed: Both parties demonstrate a clear and mutual understanding of exactly what they are consenting to.

- Freely and actively given: There is no coercion, force, threats, intimidation, or pressuring.

- Mutually understandable: Consent is expressed in words or actions that indicate a clear willingness to do the same thing, at the same time, in the same way, with each other. Silence does not equal consent.

- Consent is not indefinite; furthermore, consent may be withdrawn at any time, and at that time all sexual activity must cease unless and until additional effective consent is given (Reed College 2015).

These Penn State students and supporters are protesting a campus fraternity's depiction on Facebook of sleeping or unconscious women in the nude. Why are women victimized in this way more often than men are?

Under such informed consent, consenting to one behavior does not obligate an individual or imply consent to any other behaviors. Consenting to a person or an act on one occasion also does not obligate an individual or imply consent on any other occasion.

Sexual assault encompasses sexual acts of domination, usually enacted by men against women, other men, and children. Such assaults can occur between strangers, but they usually occur between acquaintances or intimates. **Rape**, also a form of domination, is defined as "penetration, no matter how slight, of the vagina or anus with any body part or object, or oral penetration by a sex organ of another person, without the consent of the victim" (Federal Bureau of Investigation 2014).

Communities vary in the probability of sexual violence and the effectiveness of legal, social, and moral constraints on the kinds of behaviors that often lead to such violence. In many religious communities, strong expectations for modesty and for expressing sexuality only within marriage keep sexual violence to a minimum. In contrast, the nature of residential colleges' sexual climates can promote a "rape culture" (Boswell and Spade 1996; Plante and Smiler 2014), an environment conducive to sexual assaults and rape. Rape cultures tend to be prevalent in and around college campuses because of several factors, including gender imbalances (more women than men enrolled), the routine presence of alcohol and other drugs at social events and parties, the age of the population, and the relatively unsupervised nature of life "at college." Structural aspects of college campuses that can reproduce gender imbalances include party systems controlled by fraternities and social life environments that actively or passively promote settings combining alcohol

use with assumptions about sexuality (Corprew and Mitchell 2014; Flack et al. 2007).

Sexual assaults and rapes have, to put it mildly, very serious consequences. According to the Rape, Abuse, and Incest National Network (RAINN), the largest anti–sexual violence network in the United States, survivors are more likely to suffer from depression and posttraumatic stress disorder, contemplate and attempt suicide, and use illicit drugs than the general public. Sexual violence is endemic in the United States, where it has been estimated that 17.7 million women have been victims of completed or attempted rapes, along with 2.78 million men. Most sexual assault victims (54 percent) are under the age of 30. Men and women of color are disproportionately likely to be victimized, particularly Native Americans (RAINN, n.d.). The mental and physical consequences of assaults combined with systematic racism are profound (McGuffey 2008).

SEX AND CONSUMPTION

Regardless of constraints on sexuality, everyday life has been sexualized to a large degree—the world has been "made sexy" (Rutherford 2007). In our consumer society, sex is used to encourage consumption of all sorts of things that are not inherently sexual. Advertisements use sexualized images to promote innumerable products, from cars to toothpaste and from clothing to soft drinks. The implication in many of these ads is that use of the products leads to sexual relationships. The well-known media adage that "sex sells" shows no signs of going out of fashion, and it is certainly applied to sexual products, such as Viagra. However, researchers have found that women usually have a strong negative reaction to explicit sexual content in advertising and are less likely to buy merchandise promoted with these types of ads, unless the sexual content is promoting an expensive item (Vohs, Sengupta, and Dahl 2014). In comparison, men tend to feel positively about such ads.

More blatant than the use of sexual images to sell products and services is the way in which human sexualities have been increasingly turned into commodities and marketed (Sanders 2013; Y. Taylor 2007). Of course, the consumption of sex is nothing new—after all, prostitution is often referred to as the "oldest profession" (Bazelon 2016). What is new since the mid-twentieth century is the rise of a huge sex industry, one whose reach and influence spans the globe. This sexual marketplace may be described as being composed of five interlocking markets (Plummer 2007b):

- *Bodies and sexual acts.* This market includes sex work, such as transactional sexual acts, as well as stripping and table and lap dancing. "Real sex" involving "real bodies" is available for purchase by those who choose to pay.

- *Pornography and erotica.* Sexual images and text are not generally thought to involve "real sexuality" or "real bodies." However, pornography and erotica can be associated with, or lead to, real sexual acts and relations, including masturbation and sexual intercourse. The production, distribution, sale, and consumption of pornography are taking place largely on the internet. There is, in fact, no clear line between "real sexuality" and sexuality on the internet.

- *Sexualized objects.* Sexualized objects include sex toys (e.g., inflated blow-up dolls), drugs that are thought to enhance sexual sensations ("poppers," or nitrate inhalers), costumes for sadomasochistic sex, dildos, vibrators, and lingerie (Comella 2013).

- *Sexualized technologies.* People around the world increasingly consume contraceptives, as well as drugs like Viagra and Cialis (Katsulis 2010). The latter are supposed to be used to treat erectile dysfunction (ED), although men without ED use these drugs to enhance the sexual experience by sustaining erections for hours. Other sexualized technologies include surgeries for making oneself more sexually attractive (breast enhancement surgery, rehymenization, vaginal rejuvenation, penile enlargement, genital reconstructive surgery) to building vaginas, vulvas, and phalluses as part of gender transitions. Digital technologies, such as smartphones and the internet, have been similarly sexualized.

- *Sexualized relationships.* One example of a sexualized relationship is the mail-order bride. In addition, bars and other consumption sites are often locales for beginning sexualized relationships. Help for improving a sexualized relationship can be purchased from highly paid sex therapists, from self-help books of all sorts, and now increasingly from a number of internet websites.

CHECKPOINT 11.2: SEXUALITY CONCEPTS

CONCEPT	DESCRIPTION
Sexuality	The ways in which people think about and behave toward themselves and others as sexual beings
Sexual identity	An internal sense of one's sexual self
Sexual orientation	Identification of those whom you desire, with whom you want to have sexual relations, and with whom you have a sense of connectedness
Homophobia	The fear of being, appearing, or seeming gay; also, the fear of anyone or anything gay
Heterosexism	The belief that heterosexuality is superior to other sexual orientations; also, individual or institutional discrimination against those with other orientations
Heterosexual double standard	A cultural belief system in which men are expected to desire and seek sex from whomever, whenever, while women are expected to be sexual only within committed, romantic relationships

SEXUALITY, GENDER, AND GLOBALIZATION

SOCIAL CHANGE AND THE GLOBALIZATION OF SEXUALITY

Globalization is one of a number of forces that are affecting and interacting with sexuality in the twenty-first century (Plummer 2012). The globalization of sexuality is linked to a variety of social changes that are altering not only sexuality but also much of what transpires in the social world:

- *The globalization of media and technologies.* Sexuality is a growing presence in the global media. The internet—and the social networks it has engendered—is most important. However, photos, movies, music, advertising, and television have also gone global. These media have been sexualized; they can even be said to have undergone a process of "pornographication" (McNair 2002; Ogas and Gaddam 2012; Tyler and Quek 2016).

- *Increasing urbanization.* Urbanization is a key trend across the globe, and it has contributed both to increased freedom of sexual expression and to the globalization of sexuality (Bell 2007; Hubbard, Gormley-Murray, and Nash 2015). Cities are at the center of freedoms of all sorts (Simmel [1903] 1971), including sexual freedoms. Residents of global cities learn a great deal about what is possible and what is "cutting-edge" from one another, including the latest developments in sexuality. Further, sex trafficking and sex tourism take place primarily in the world's cities. The world's major cities, including London, Hong Kong, and Shanghai, are the nodes in global "sex-scapes" (Kong 2010; Maginn and Steinmetz 2015).

- *Globalized social movements and social change.* A wide range of sexualities-related social movements have arisen, facilitated by the spread of technologies such as Twitter and Instagram. Women's and gay, lesbian, bisexual, and trans movements (see Chapter 18), as well as more specific social change efforts focused on repressive sex laws, are global. Activists, change agents, and ideas flow, spread, and adapt to their specific contexts (Parker, Garcia, and Buffington 2014).

- *Increased mobility.* It is relatively easy now for people to travel to locales far from home. Thus, travel for sex itself is a global and commercial phenomenon, in the form of sex tourism and sex holidays (Altman 2001; Frank 2012).

GLOBAL FLOWS RELATED TO SEX AND SEXUALITY

Sexuality "flows" around the world in many other ways, such as through sex trafficking, sex work, gay global parties, and the sexual diaspora, as members of various sexual subcultures move around the world and from one society to another. In addition, all sorts of sexual goods and services are shipped and sold globally, especially via the internet. Globalization has had a real effect on sexual interactions, identities, and relationships (Wieringa and Sívori 2013). Altman (2001) has argued that sexualities and globalization are integrally linked. Sex, like nearly every other aspect of

social life, is influenced by cultural, political, and economic factors. Thus, there are now a number of globally applied sexuality laws, such as those attempting to outlaw the sexual exploitation of children. Organizations like UNICEF monitor these laws and seek to protect the vulnerable from sexual abuse and violence. Laws dealing with sexual crimes, such as rape, have grown increasingly similar (DiMaggio and Powell 1983). At the cultural level, norms and values about sex have been changing, and those changes have tended to flow around the world.

As a result, some norms and values have grown increasingly similar in many parts of the world. For example, there has been a general movement away from trying to control sexuality and procreation while attempting to maintain the collective order. At the same time, there has been a movement toward viewing sexuality as a series of acts that are mainly about pleasure and self-expression. Premarital (or nonmarital) sex has also become increasingly normative in many (but certainly not all) parts of the world.

Another example of global cultural change involves the global diffusion of such sexual identities as straight, gay, and bisexual. The terms *gay, lesbian,* and *transsexual,* as well as the idea that they refer to identities, are exports from the Global North. Almost anywhere you go in the world, you may be able to find similar identities, norms, and values relating to sexuality.

Lesbian, Gay, Bisexual, Transgender, and Queer Sexualities in a Global Context

A key issue for lesbian, gay, bisexual, transgender, and queer (LGBTQ) people is the barriers that inhibit their movement around the world or encourage their movement from one place to another (Altman 2001; Carrillo and Fontdevila 2014; Lewis 2014). Such barriers may be erected within the home country as well as between countries. Barriers at home that might *push* LGBTQ people to migrate include legal

Homosexuality remains a highly controversial subject in Uganda, spurring protests on both sides of the issue. Some opponents of gay rights view homosexuality as an unwelcome import from the United States.

prohibitions of consensual sex acts and relationships with same-sex partners, lack of equal opportunity in the workplace, and bans on same-sex marriages. State-sanctioned physical assaults and even murders of LGBTQ people can force them to seek better lives elsewhere in the world. They can also be *pulled* elsewhere in the world by better conditions, such as more opportunities to work, marry, and live more freely with less fear. Urban environments are attractive, because large and visible groups of other LGBTQ people often create communities and neighborhoods in cities around the globe (Nash and Gorman-Murray 2014).

Other aspects of globalization, such as inexpensive air travel, the internet, and sex tourism, have made it easier for LGBTQ people to communicate and be together anywhere in the world. Globalization has also contributed to the rise of gay and lesbian global social movements and to the increasing acceptance of same-sex sexual relationships in large parts of the world (Stone and Weinberg 2015).

Yet while globalization has aided sexual minorities, it has also facilitated the spread of homophobia and other forms of prejudice and discrimination (Binnie 2004; Kaoma 2014). A recent film about the twin global forces of U.S. conservatism and homophobia, *Call Me Kuchu,* shows the effects of fear of homosexuality and misunderstandings about it (Wright and Zouhali-Worrall 2012). In the film, the editor of the Ugandan edition of the U.S. music and culture magazine *Rolling Stone* laughs on camera, seemingly oblivious to his role in inciting violence against gays and lesbians. His magazine published a list of Ugandans accused of being gay, along with their photographs and the charge to "hang them!" Globalization clearly has not been an unmitigated good as far as LGBTQ people are concerned.

The Global Sex Industry

Industries based on sex have become increasingly important to global capitalism. Bars, dance clubs, massage parlors, pornography, sex work establishments, international hotel chains, airline companies, and the tourist industry create, and help meet, the demand for sexual labor around the globe. It is almost impossible to get accurate numbers on those involved in the global sex industry, and at least some of the data are likely fabricated (Steinfatt 2011). Although sexual labor has a very long history, its current explicitly global quality is a more recent phenomenon.

Sex trafficking, a commercial sex act that includes force, fraud, or coercion and transporting and obtaining a person for sex acts, is truly a global issue. It is one sector of human trafficking, which the U.S. State Department calls "modern slavery" or forced labor, and includes child soldiers, debt bondage, and domestic servitude. The International Labour Organization (2017) estimates that 21 million people are victims of human trafficking around the world; 4.5 million of these victims are involved in forced sexual labor,

which generates $99 billion in revenue annually. According to the U.S. State Department's annual *Trafficking in Persons Report* (2016), in 2015, there were 18,920 prosecutions for human trafficking, but only 6,609 convictions. The flow of people in the global sex industry moves not only from the South to the North but also in the other direction. Over the past 30 years, the global sex tourism industry has grown to be a multibillion-dollar enterprise (Weitzer 2012; Wortmann 2007). **Sex tourism** occurs when individuals travel to other countries specifically for the purpose of buying sex from men, women, and sometimes children; sex is the primary or sole purpose of these trips. These encounters can be complicated by the fact that locals and tourists usually do not have the same levels of economic privilege. For one thing, tourists have the disposable income to take such trips (Dewey 2015). While some sex tourism involves people traveling to the developed countries of the North (e.g., to Amsterdam in the Netherlands), most of it involves customers traveling from the North to the less developed countries of the South (Katsulis 2010). For example, Thailand receives millions of sex tourists every year from the United States, Western Europe, Australia, and Japan, bringing in billions of dollars (Hepburn and Simon 2013).

Several factors have contributed to the rise of sex tourism. The internet expedites it, as information about destinations is readily available through websites, chat rooms, e-diaries, blogs, promotional videos, and guidebooks (Wortmann 2007). Websites offer advice on the best tourist sites to visit, the best sex workers at those sites, how to arrange visits, and even how to negotiate with sex workers to get the lowest prices (Katsulis 2010). It is even possible to buy a customized package tour of the best locations in the world for sex tourism, joining other sex tourists from the Global North. Low-cost travel has permitted more sex tourists to circle the globe in search of sexual relations (Brennan 2004).

What else might explain sex tourism? Many popular locales have histories of having been dominated by colonial empires (Dewey 2015). Tourists may see such destinations through a "conquering" lens. Social norms are seen as suspended on sex tourism trips, and participants may perceive host countries to be welcoming of such tourism (Padilla 2007). North American and Western European tourists may stereotype Global Southerners as hypersexualized, exotic, and exceptionally interested in sex with them (Kempadoo 1996–1997). Some gay male sex tourists argue that their presence improves the gay climate in the locales to which they travel and "liberates" the local men (Mitchell 2011). Many sex tourists—men and women—believe that their money, attention, and transactions are welcome to the local men, women, and children. That may be so, as poverty leads large numbers of people in sex tourism destinations to participate in the industry.

CHECKPOINT 11.3: SEXUALITY-RELATED ASPECTS OF GLOBALIZATION

ASPECT	DESCRIPTION
Sex trafficking	Transporting and obtaining a person for sex acts through force, fraud, or coercion
Sex tourism	Traveling to other countries for the purpose of buying sex from men, women, and sometimes children

GLOBAL FLOWS RELATED TO GENDER

THE FEMINIZATION OF MIGRATION

The global economy has contributed to an unprecedented increase in women's migration: "Women are on the move as never before in history" (Ehrenreich and Hochschild 2002, 2). Some have referred to this trend as the "feminization of migration" (Gabaccia, forthcoming). Much of this flow involves women from the Global South moving, legally and illegally, to the Global North to handle work that was historically performed by Northern women (Runyon 2012). Large numbers of women are emigrating from China, India, Indonesia, Myanmar, Pakistan, the Philippines, Sri Lanka, Thailand, and Bangladesh. The migrants often become nannies (Eckenwiler 2014), maids (Ehrenreich 2002; Gündüz 2013), or sex workers (Brennan 2002). Most immigrant women are in service occupations (33 percent) and business/managerial positions (33 percent; see Figure 11.10).

This migrant labor enriches the Global North and enhances its already elevated lifestyle. Domestic work is now considered the largest labor market for women worldwide. Many female labor immigrants clean the homes and care for the children of affluent families while trying to send money (remittances) to their own families in their home countries (Faist, Fauser, and Reisenauer 2013; Hondagneu-Sotelo 2000). They believe that this work will bring with it better pay and improved working conditions, increasing the immigrants' quality of life and that of their families.

Undocumented and informal migration, which is common for women migrating to the North for domestic work, exposes women to the worst forms of discrimination, exploitation, and abuse (Adams and Campbell 2012; Jones 2008; United Nations 2006). They can be held as debt

FIGURE 11.10 • Occupational Fields of Female Immigrants in the United States, 2015

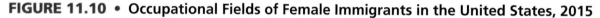

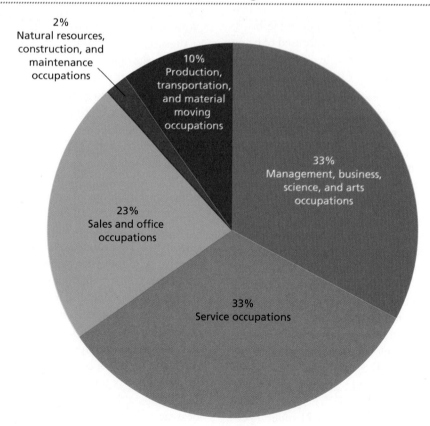

NOTE: Data total more than 100 due to rounding.

SOURCES: Ariel G. Ruiz, Jie Zong, and Jeanne Batalova, "Immigrant Women in the United States," Figure 7, Migration Policy Institute, March 20, 2017.

hostages by recruitment agencies until their transportation and placement fees are paid, imprisoned in the houses of their employers, treated inhumanely, and sometimes murdered. Increasing numbers of migrant women are victims of sexual abuse (including rape), sex trafficking, and prostitution, as discussed previously.

THE FEMINIZATION OF LABOR

There has been a notable increase in women's labor force participation rates worldwide, particularly in the Americas and Western Europe. In the United States, 57 percent of women 16 years and older were employed in 2015, compared to 69 percent of men (see Figure 11.11). In 1948, only 31 percent of women were employed, in comparison to 84 percent of men. Even though there are significant variations within and across regions, women's labor force participation has also risen substantially in sub-Saharan Africa, North Africa, Eastern Europe, Southeast Asia, and East Asia over this period (Cagatay and Ozler 1995; Heintz 2006; Kivisto and Faist 2010; Moghadam 1999). As noted in Chapter 9, while the progress in women's employment status is linked at least in part to gender equality movements, the key factor in this change has been the better integration of an increasing number of areas into the world economy through trade and production.

The increasing participation of women in the labor force has been termed the **feminization of labor** (Standing 1989). This refers to the rise of female labor participation in all sectors and the movement of women into jobs traditionally held by men. This global trend has occurred in both developing and developed countries (Hawkesworth 2006).

The Feminization of Poverty and Female Proletarianization

The feminization of labor, especially in developing economies, is often accompanied by **female proletarianization** as an increasing number of women are channeled into low-status, poorly paid manual work. Female proletarianization is closely related to the feminization of poverty (see Chapter 8; Brady and Kall 2008). Globally, more women are being drawn into labor-intensive and low-paying industries, such as textiles, apparel, leather products, food processing, and electronics (Chen et al. 2013; Villareal and Yu 2007). Jobs in these industries are characterized by the flexible use of labor, high turnover rates, part-time and temporary employment, and a lack of security and benefits. Female employees are preferred in these industries because of the persistence of a number of stereotypes that often have little basis in reality. Such stereotypes include the idea that women will typically work for lower wages and that they are easier for male employers and managers to supervise (English 2013). They are considered not only to be more docile but also to have greater patience and more dexterity than men in performing standardized and repetitive work. Female employment is also characterized by poorer and more dangerous working conditions and more compulsory overtime with no extra pay.

FIGURE 11.11 • Employment in the United States, by Gender, 1948–2015

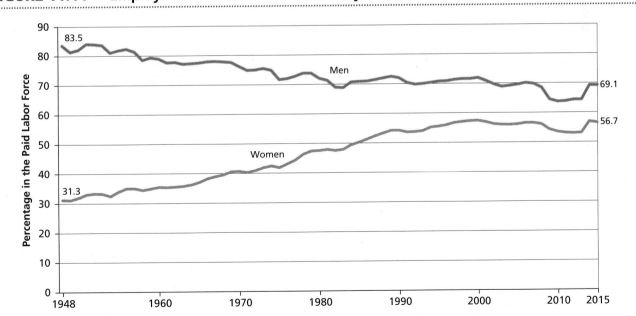

SOURCE: Data from U.S. Department of Labor, Bureau of Labor Statistics, "Women in the Labor Force: A Databook," *BLS Reports*, December 2014; data for 2014 from Bureau of Labor Statistics, "Civilian Labor Force Participation Rate by Age, Gender, Race, and Ethnicity," December 2015; data from 2015 from the Department of Labor, "Latest Annual Data: Labor Force Participation Rates," retrieved February 2, 2017.

Women in the Global South, such as these workers in China, are much more likely than their counterparts in the more industrial Global North to be employed in assembly line work or other low-wage labor. Why does this situation persist?

A great deal of attention has been focused on the place of women in what has been called the "global assembly line" (Collins 2003). While high-status research and management positions are likely to be found in the North, assembly line work is relegated to the less developed nations of the South (Ward 1990). Women are much more likely to be employed in the latter than in higher-level positions in developed countries.

ASK YOURSELF

What is the relationship between the feminization of labor and the feminization of poverty? Is this relationship inevitable? What social, structural, and gender-related factors might account for it?

In corporate economic centers, especially global cities, large amounts of low-wage labor are required, and, again, women often fill the bill. They help maintain the offices and lifestyles of entrepreneurs, managers, and professionals through clerical, cleaning, and repair work and labor for companies, providing software, copying paper, office furniture, and even toilet paper (Sassen 2004). Furthermore, the vast majority of child tending and caring for the elderly and for homes is done by immigrants, primarily women (Acker 2004).

Women in Export Processing Zones

Export processing zones (EPZs) are special industrial areas, often in developing countries, designed to draw foreign companies and capital investment. EPZs offer multinational companies incentives, including exemption from labor and environmental regulations, taxes, tariffs, and quotas. A wide range of products are produced in EPZs, especially textiles, clothing, and electronics for the mass market. EPZs are characteristically unstable, as companies are continually setting up new ones where labor is cheaper and regulators are more compliant.

It is often suggested that EPZs reduce poverty and unemployment and, as a result, facilitate the economic development of the host countries. Even if these outcomes do occur, they do not occur without serious costs (Attanapola 2006). Working conditions are brutal in most EPZs, where violence and abuse are daily routines. A workday may consist of impossibly long shifts with unpaid overtime, nonpayment for workers on sick leave, insufficient

GL🌐BALIZATION

Rape as a Weapon of War

Rape as a weapon of war is an ancient practice, but we don't need to go back very far in history to find examples of its use. As the Soviet army marched through Germany in 1945 at the close of World War II, Russian soldiers were ordered to take revenge against German civilians, including by raping German women. American troops also engaged in this practice when they raped Vietnamese women in the 1960s. In a civil war that ran from 1960 to 1996, Guatemalan soldiers engaged in the systematic rape of indigenous Mayan women. Today, fighters from the radical group the Islamic State rape ethnic Yazidi women and force them into sexual slavery (Wood and Cohen 2015). In Nigeria, the extremist group Boko Haram kidnaps and rapes women and children (Searcey 2016), and South Sudanese forces use mass rape against women and girls in the conflict there (Cumming-Bruce 2016).

While these examples illustrate that rape as a weapon of war is not uncommon, there are instances in which the atrocity has been taken to an even more extreme level. For instance, during the war in Bosnia (1992–1995), Bosnian Muslim women were systematically raped by Serbian soldiers and officers. The Serbs set up camps to hold the women, with the goal of impregnating them (Salzman 2000). This is a technique of ethnic cleansing (see Chapter 10). The children born to Bosnian women as a consequence of rape would not have "pure" Bosnian blood; they would have some Serbian "blood." Ultimately, the numbers of the invader's descendants in the invaded country would rise.

Rape as a tool of war is also used to traumatize its victims and humiliate the enemy by "taking" their women. As is true of rape in general (Kellezi and Reicher 2014; Rudrappa 2012), rape in

A sign in the Democratic Republic of Congo (SEXUAL VIOLENCE? NO!) is part of a campaign to change perceptions about the acceptability of rape and sexual assault against women. How else might nations try to stem the use of rape as a weapon of war, a problem that has been particularly widespread in the Congo?

warfare is not a sexual act, but rather an act of power (Brownmiller 1975). Beyond immediate rape and sexual assault in times of warfare, women may also be forced into prostitution or slavery, as Korean women experienced from the mid-1930s to mid-1940s, when Japan forced Korean "comfort women" to serve Japanese soldiers.

However, rape seems to have reached new heights since the late twentieth century in the African nation of the Democratic Republic of Congo. The Congo has been characterized by more or less constant warfare and ongoing rebellions since 1996. A number of African nations and a couple of dozen armed groups have been involved there in a shifting pattern of violence and exploitation (Hochschild 2011). Rape has been so commonplace and virulent in the Congo that the UN special representative on sexual violence in

conflict called it the "rape capital" of the world (Mawathe 2010). In 2011, it was estimated that about 2 million women in the Congo had been raped; women were being raped at a rate of one per minute (Gettleman 2011). And the warfare and the rape continue to this day.

Women can suffer severe consequences from their experiences. Because of social and culture mores, many are rejected by their husbands and families, who call them "dirty" and cast them out (Mawathe 2010). Other survivors are severely injured, both physically and emotionally. The psychological trauma leaves some women emotionless and paralyzed. Rape survivors may find expert medical care and the support of other survivors at specially established medical centers, if such centers are available, but their despair is likely to persist for years, if not for a lifetime. In addition, the trauma of their rapes may also affect any resultant children, who, like their mothers, may be cast out of society. The Women Under Siege project is helping raise awareness of how sexual violence is used as a tool of war and aims to prevent mass sexual assaults in future conflicts (http://www.womenundersiegeproject .org/blog/entry/what-are-the-solutions -to-wartime-rape).

Think About It
Why does rape as a tool of war persist? Is it an act of sex, or one of power and violence? Can its incidence be reduced? If so, how?

health and safety measures, monitored access to bathrooms, sexual harassment, physical abuse, and in some cases forced consumption of amphetamines to ensure efficiency. These working conditions are particularly hard on women, especially those who are pregnant or have infants. In most EPZs, mandatory pregnancy testing is a condition for employment and for maintaining a job. In some cases, gender bias intersects with age discrimination: EPZs tend to hire mostly young and single women; women over 25 years of age are usually not hired, because they are seen as more likely to bear children (Pun 1995). Because of the harsh working conditions and low pay, female (and male) workers often burn out; the turnover rate in EPZs is very high (Sivalingam 1994).

GENDER, WAR, AND VIOLENCE

Men are certainly more likely than women to be killed or wounded in warfare. However, a 2015 Human Rights Watch report describes the ways in which women bear the brunt of war, violence, and failed peace efforts. More specifically, women are more likely to be the noncombatant victims of wars and other forms of organized collective violence, including being raped (see the Globalization box in this chapter) and killed (Gerami and Lehnerer 2007; Human Rights Watch 2015; Liebling-Kalifani et al. 2013). Women are also likely to suffer as a result of local and global terrorism and political violence (Gentry and Sjoberg 2015).

Several changes have made it more likely that women will be the victims of international violence. One is the change in the nature of warfare. For example, "asymmetric warfare," or warfare involving forces of unequal capabilities, often takes the form of shootouts in the streets. Obviously, civilians—women, children, and the elderly—are more likely to be victims in such cases than they are when conventional ground battles take place. This is evident, for example, in the brutal civil wars that continue to engulf Syria, Iraq, Libya, and Yemen as of this writing. Generally, the line between combatants and civilians has blurred, with the result that more civilians, including women, have become the victims of warfare. Finally, more women are in the armed forces and in terrorist groups (e.g., the Islamic State, Boko Haram) in various countries, and this greatly increases their chances of being the victims of violence. In some cases, terrorist groups use women to carry concealed explosives and to detonate them in or near targets, killing themselves and those in the vicinity (Gentry and Sjoberg 2015).

Women who are fortunate enough not to experience such horrors as being raped or murdered may still find their lives, as well as the locales in which they live, badly disrupted by international violence. Women are likely to be impoverished by such violence, and their homes and livelihoods may be destroyed. Shortages of all sorts during times of war are likely to affect those at home, especially women. One organization estimates that women make up 70 percent of those internally displaced by conflicts (International Organization for Migration 2005).

Women may be called on to care for the wounded, and they may be injured not only physically but psychologically. The larger community in which they live may also be disrupted, because, for example, the women may no longer be able to devote much attention to their normal duties and responsibilities as mothers.

One unintended consequence of war is that women can sometimes benefit from warfare and its disruption of business as usual. Among other things, they can gain greater economic independence, more freedom to act, and greater mobility. With the norms and values of society disrupted, women can do things they could not do before: acquire a more public role in the community and society, gain greater responsibility for decision making, and generally acquire more power. Such was the case during World War II, when labor shortages caused by the mobilization of men for military service resulted in work opportunities for women. The iconic image of Rosie the Riveter working in a factory reflected this new reality, as women entered the blue-collar workforce that had been dominated by males.

THE GLOBAL WOMEN'S MOVEMENT

As you have seen, globalization and the rise of a global economy have created or exacerbated a variety of inequalities faced by women. One response has been expansion of the international women's movement (see Chapter 18). It has grown dramatically in recent years because of problems created for women by globalization. It has also expanded because of the increased ability of those working on behalf of the movement to travel globally and to communicate with one another. The international women's movement has a long history, traceable to the late 1800s (Rupp 1997). It has focused on issues such as sexual violence, reproductive rights, labor issues, and sexual harassment. Its greatest triumphs have related to women's right to vote in countries around the world (Ramirez, Soysal, and Shanahan 1997).

The larger global movement is concerned with a variety of issues: human rights (Yuval-Davis 2006), economic concerns, the environment, health care, and violence against women. The movement has also come to focus on the adverse effects of global capitalism (e.g., increased global trafficking in women), the lack of women's voices in global civil society, the growth of antifeminist fundamentalist movements (the Taliban, IS, Boko Haram), and the HIV/AIDS epidemic. More generally, the international women's movement has focused attention on issues of global justice for women and other minorities. Feminist activism around the world takes many forms. It has had a strong impact on the United Nations and has helped create strong linkages among the United Nations, national governments, and nongovernmental organizations (George 2007).

Women throughout the world not only have been active in the global women's movement but also have responded at local and regional levels to common problems caused by globalization. They also localize global political activities undertaken by the international women's movement and global human rights groups. In addition, they organize against global activities such as militarism and conflict and use global organizations (such as the United Nations and international nongovernmental organizations) to help in local and regional activities (Naples and Desai 2002). However, even the activities that have been primarily or exclusively local in nature have had profound effects globally. Even with all the local variations, feminism can be seen as "a truly global phenomenon" (Ferree and Tripp 2006, viii).

CHECKPOINT 11.4: EFFECTS OF GLOBAL FLOWS RELATED TO GENDER

WHAT IS FEMINIZED	RELATED GLOBAL FLOW
Migration	Women travel from the South to the North in search of work.
Labor	Women workers are concentrated in labor-intensive, low-wage jobs.

SUMMARY

Sex is principally a biological concept, while gender is a cultural term connected to societal definitions of expected behaviors, attitudes, and personalities. Femininities and masculinities are socially constructed and subject to change and variation. Transgender and intersexed individuals confront the difficulties of living in a society that is still based on binary understandings of gender and sex. Gendered inequalities persist in numerous domains, including in education, at home and in families, and at work.

Sexuality is related to both sex and gender and is experienced both individually and collectively. A person's sexual orientation is an important aspect of one's sexual identity. Sexual orientation is more complicated than the few categories we typically use to express it, such as heterosexual, gay, or lesbian. Heterosexism refers to the belief that heterosexuality is superior to other types of sexual orientation. Social constraints exist that shape what types of sexual expressions and activities are appropriate (or not). Consensual sexual activities are those agreed on by the participants, in contrast to those that are not, such as sexual harassment and rape.

Globalization reinforces but also destabilizes preexisting gender structures on a global scale. The greater flow of people creates more opportunity for traffickers to transport women and children for sexual exploitation and for people to travel for sex tourism. Globalization is linked to the increasing number of women working in the Global South, although many are drawn into low-status, poorly paid, and sometimes dangerous manual work. Women are often victims of international violence, including being subjected to rape as a weapon of war.

KEY TERMS

consensual sexual
   activities, 309
emphasized
   femininity, 293
female
   proletarianization, 315
feminization of labor, 315
gender, 292

gender identity, 294
gender role, 294
gender-swapping, 295
hegemonic
   masculinity, 293
heterosexism, 307
heterosexual double
   standard, 309

hidden curriculum, 297
homophobia, 307
informed (effective)
   sexual consent, 309
intersex, 292
rape, 310
sex, 292
sex tourism, 313

sex trafficking, 313
sexual assault, 310
sexual identity, 306
sexuality, 305
sexual
   orientation, 306
sexual scripts, 307
transgender, 294

REVIEW QUESTIONS

1. What is the difference between sex and gender? How does sex affect gender? How does gender affect sexuality?
2. What do sociologists mean when they say that there are no clear-cut biological differences between men and women?
3. What are the differences in the ways in which men and women experience hegemonic masculinity and emphasized femininity? How do these constructs help create and reinforce gender stratification?
4. How do men and women differ in terms of their educational experiences? In what ways does the hidden curriculum of educational systems reinforce gender stratification?
5. Why are women and men treated differently as consumers? What events in recent decades have changed the way in which women are thought of as consumers?
6. What are the differences in the ways in which men and women approach sexuality? How are the differences

related to the socialization process? Do you think increasing equality between men and women will affect sexualities?
7. In what ways has the sex industry become increasingly important to global capitalism? How is this sex industry reflective of gender stratification? How is it reflective of inequalities between the Global North and South?
8. In what positive and negative ways have lesbians, gays, bisexuals, and trans people been affected by globalization?
9. What do sociologists mean by the "feminization of poverty"? By "female proletarianization"? How are these concepts related to one another and to the more general process of the feminization of labor?
10. What types of violence are women most likely to experience when they live in places experiencing war and other types of armed conflict?

$SAGE edge™ **Want a better grade?**

Get the tools you need to sharpen your study skills. Access practice quizzes, eFlashcards, video and multimedia at **http://edge.sagepub.com/ritzerintro4e**.

PRACTICE AND APPLY WHAT YOU'VE LEARNED

▶ **edge.sagepub.com/ritzerintro4e**

CHECK YOUR COMPREHENSION ON THE STUDY SITE WITH:

- **Diagnostic pre-tests** to identify opportunities for improvement.

- **Personalized study plans** with focused recommendations to address specific knowledge gaps and additional learning needs.

- **Post-tests** to check your progress and ensure mastery of key learning objectives.

$SAGE edge™

12

FAMILIES

Fictional Families Get Real

The family has been a staple on television since the medium's early years. Fictional, very traditional families were a staple, perhaps most notably on the long-running and top-rated shows *I Love Lucy* (1951-1957) and *The Adventures of Ozzie and Harriet* (1952-1966). Interestingly, while these shows were fictional, the actors playing husband and wife in both cases were married in real life. The best-known early series to deal with a real family in a nonfictional way, and TV's first reality show, was the groundbreaking *An American Family,* which aired on public television in the 1970s. It was intended simply to chronicle the happy, mundane lives of a husband and wife and their five children, but over the course of the series, cracks in the family's calm and stable facade became apparent, exposing events never before seen on U.S. television. The public witnessed the husband and wife's real-life separation and subsequent divorce, for example, and the eldest son's coming out as television's first openly gay person.

Since then, family-based television shows, both fictional and nonfictional, have flourished and become increasingly "real," going far beyond the kinds of problems depicted in *An American Family*. The fictional *Transparent* (2014-) portrays a family with an array of difficulties, most notably drug addiction and challenges traceable to the discovery that the father is transgender and frequently appears in public wearing dresses. The reality show *Keeping Up with the Kardashians* (2007-) depicts the family and a number of relatives who deal with divorce, have numerous affairs, perform in a sex tape, are arrested for drunk driving, and so on. The popular sitcom *Modern Family* (2009-) features several different types of families, including a heterosexual couple with three children, a same-sex white couple with an adopted Asian daughter, and a heterosexual couple that consists of an older male married to a much younger woman from Colombia, her son from a previous relationship, and their own son. Compared to early TV shows about the family, those on the air today not only are more honest (in

LEARNING OBJECTIVES

12.1 Explain basic sociological concepts of the family, marriage, and intimate relationships.

12.2 Describe current trends that are changing marriage and the family.

12.3 Apply structural/functional, conflict/critical, and inter/actionist theories to the family.

12.4 Describe current problems associated with the family.

12.5 Identify the effects of globalization on the family.

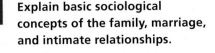

edge.sagepub.com/ritzerintro4e

- Take the chapter quiz
- Review key terms with eFlashcards
- Explore multimedia links and SAGE readings

$SAGE edge™

reality, the stars of *I Love Lucy* had a troubled marriage, leading to divorce) but also reflect the dramatically changing nature of the family.

It should come as no surprise that family-based TV shows are enormously popular. Family, after all, is a universal social institution. It constitutes a person's first group and primary socializer, and, for many, a lifelong source of companionship and security. Because the institution of family is such a central part of life, it is natural that we are fascinated by—and even feel connected to—the intimate relationships, conflicts, and problems experienced by families.

As television shows indicate, the structure of a family can take a great number of forms. Extended and nuclear families have proven popular over the last 100 years, but recent social changes have opened a wide variety of other options. Some couples involve a man and woman, but homosexual and lesbian marriages are increasingly common (and legal). Some couples, whatever their gender, marry for love, others do so for purely economic reasons, and an increasing number choose not to marry at all. Some have children in the double digits, while others have one or none. Some maintain exclusive partnerships until death, others divorce and sometimes remarry, and still others incorporate new members into existing relationships.

Family-based TV shows paint a picture of domestic dynamics and realities that is captivating and intriguing but by no means complete. They largely sidestep issues critical to sociology, such as poverty, gender inequality, and the prevalence of domestic abuse. Also, unlike sociology, most shows in the United States have not adopted a global perspective, choosing instead to focus on American families. That leaves us with much to learn and study. ●

FAMILY, MARRIAGE, AND INTIMATE RELATIONSHIPS

What is family? Who is in your family? Does it include only people related to you by blood? Are there people who are no longer in your family? The U.S. Census Bureau defines the **family** as "a group of two people or more (one of whom is the householder) related by birth, marriage, or adoption and residing together." Families are especially important in socializing children so that they are able to fit into the larger society. Although families often fail in this role and many other things, sociologists continue to view the family as a universal social institution that is central to social

life (Powell and Branden 2007). Sociologists are interested in such issues as the relationship between family and marriage, the different forms taken by families, and how families are formed and maintained, expand and contract, and even dissolve (Cohen 2014; Farrell, VandeVusse, and Ocobock 2012).

SOME BASIC CONCEPTS

In this section, we will define such basic concepts and ideas as marriage, intimate relationships, and love and explore their roles in the family.

Marriage

Marriage is the socially acknowledged and approved and often legal union of two people, allowing them to live together and to have children by birth or adoption. Families govern various issues that relate to marriage, such as the "meanings of marriage" as well as "the number of marriage partners" (Shaw and Lee 2009, 378). **Monogamy** has traditionally been defined as marriage between one wife and one husband. However, given changing laws related to gay marriage, monogamy today might involve two wives or two husbands. There are also many other forms of marriage, such as **polygamy**, which allows multiple spouses. **Polygyny**, in which a single husband has multiple wives, is a more common form of polygamy than **polyandry**, in which a single wife has multiple husbands. **Cenogamy** is group marriage.

Historically and around the world, rules, customs, and laws have been created to define and control marriage. Key to understanding marriage (and thus most families) is the concept of **endogamy**, or marriage to someone with similar characteristics in terms of race, ethnicity, religion, education level, social class, and so on (Penn, forthcoming). In contrast, **exogamy** involves marriage to someone with characteristics that are dissimilar in these dimensions. Throughout history, families have been defined much more by endogamy than by exogamy. In recent years, though, endogamy has declined in importance, and there is more exogamy. For example, there has been an increasing tendency of Americans to marry persons of other races (Qian and Lichter 2011). However, as a general rule, families continue to be characterized more by endogamy than by exogamy.

In the last several decades, the nature of family and marriage has undergone a series of rapid and dizzying changes. It is less and less clear exactly what constitutes marriage or a family. One thing is clear, however: The close linkage between marriage and the family has been greatly weakened, if not broken. Nevertheless, most people in the United States end up being married one or more times during their lifetimes. And those who marry often create families, although they may not stay together as long as families did in the past. Being married and in a family does not mean that the marriage or the family will remain the same for decades, or

Endogamy, or marriage to a partner who is culturally, socially, and racially similar, is still much more common in the United States than exogamy, or marriage to someone who is different in these dimensions. Do you think this situation will change in the future?

even years. Nevertheless, while marriage and the family will remain important intimate relationships, they will not be the only, or even the dominant, forms of intimacy in the future.

Intimate Relationships

The word *intimacy* is often associated with sexual relationships, in which people are "intimate" with one another. More generally, however, **intimacy** can be defined as a close and personal relationship that is built over time (Jamieson 2011). Thus, an **intimate relationship** occurs between partners who have a close, personal, *and* domestic relationship with one another. This intimate relationship is a byproduct of courtship rituals in which two people are attracted to each other, develop intimacy, enjoy each other's company, and identify as a couple after a period of dating.

The nature of intimacy is not static, but changes over time. Fifty or one hundred years ago, couples could be intimate without necessarily sharing very much about themselves with each other, especially their most private thoughts. However, in Western culture today, intimacy increasingly involves disclosing much, if not everything, about oneself to one's partner (Jamieson 2007). Levels of disclosure tend to be gendered (Kimmel 2012). Women tend to function as emotional caretakers within heterosexual relationships. They do so because they are generally socialized to engage in communication in which they express their emotions, whereas men are socialized to suppress their emotions and communicate little about them. In other words, women tend to be the ones to share first and to help males share by drawing out their emotions. The assumption made by most women is that such self-disclosure will strengthen a relationship because there are no secrets and therefore there will be no surprises, or at least there will be fewer of them, as the relationship develops.

Love

Intimacy in domestic relationships is, of course, often associated with love (Frieze 2007). **Passionate love** has a sudden onset, inspires strong sexual feelings, and tends to include idealization of the one who is loved (Hatfield, Bensman, and Rapson 2012). Passionate love brings with it great intimacy, but it is an intimacy very likely to be short-lived. In contrast, **companionate love** develops more gradually, is not necessarily tied to sexual passion, and is based on more rational assessments of the one who is loved. Companionate love is more likely than passionate love to lead to long-lasting intimate relationships. However, these two types of love are not clearly distinguished from one another. This is clearest in the fact that long-term intimate relationships often start out with passionate love, but in those that succeed over time, it tends to be combined with, or even supplanted by, companionate love.

Passionate love, also known as romantic love, has a long and interesting history. For example, some of our more recent senses of love are traceable to 1950s consumer culture (Shaw and Lee 2009). It was then that love became closely associated with consumption and travel. The movie, automobile, fashion, and makeup industries capitalized on, and disseminated ideas about, romantic love. Each of these industries, in its own way, glamorized romance and conveyed the message that romance was associated with commodities that were available for a price.

ASK YOURSELF

What do you think of Bauman's concept of "liquid love"? Do you agree that love is fleeting, and that this impermanence is a reflection of a society in which nothing lasts? Why or why not? Would you find the experience of liquid love troubling, or liberating? Why?

Zygmunt Bauman has sought to get at the essence of love in the contemporary world in his book *Liquid Love* (2003). On the cover of the book is a heart drawn in the sand. However, the sea is nearby, and the implication is that love will soon be washed away by the waves. To Bauman, love, like everything else in today's liquid society, is fleeting. This clearly applies to passionate love, but to Bauman, even companionate love is constantly at risk of erosion and disappearance. This represents a major challenge to all intimate relationships, especially marriage, and to all those involved in them. However, liquid love can also be seen as offering people freedom from lifelong loveless relationships. It also offers the possibility of innumerable experiences with love and the possibility of many different relationships built on love.

It can be argued that our main concerns in this chapter—family and marriage—are also increasingly liquid.

Because they are now so liquid, the borders of marriage and the family are increasingly difficult to define. More important, many traditional forms of marriage and the family are confronting the possibility of being washed away. As a result, many sociologists have moved away from a focus on the family and marriage and prefer to discuss vaguer phenomena such as "relationships" and "personal life." Nevertheless, most people, including most sociologists, continue to think in terms of marriage and the family (Powell et al. 2010). We will do the same in this chapter, but with an understanding that both are changing dramatically and refer to phenomena that are far more liquid than they were in the past.

CHECKPOINT 12.1: TYPES OF MARRIAGE

TYPE OF MARRIAGE	DESCRIPTION
Marriage	The socially acknowledged and approved and often legal union of two people, allowing them to live together and to have children by birth or adoption
Monogamy	Marriage between one wife and one husband (or two wives or two husbands)
Polygamy	Marriage to multiple wives (polygyny) or multiple husbands (polyandry)
Cenogamy	Group marriage
Endogamy	Marriage to someone of a similar race, ethnicity, religion, education level, social class, and so on
Exogamy	Marriage to someone of a dissimilar race, ethnicity, religion, education level, social class, or other such characteristic

BROAD CHANGES IN MARRIAGE AND THE FAMILY

We will discuss two major changes in this section: the decline of marriage and changes in the family household.

DECLINE IN MARRIAGE

In 1970, married couples constituted 71 percent of all U.S. households (see Figure 12.1); by 2012, only 49 percent of all households were married couples. Similarly, the traditional **nuclear family** consisting of two adults and one or more children dropped from 40 percent of all households in 1970 to not quite 20 percent of all households in 2012.

Another way to get a sense of the dramatic change in marriage and the family is to look at the percentage of those who have never been married, which has changed significantly in the past few decades. Figure 12.2 shows that in 2016, 28 percent of men and 24 percent of women in the United States ages 25 and older had never been married, compared to 10 percent of men and 8 percent of women in 1960.

However, it remains the case that as people age, they are more likely to marry. Figure 12.3 shows that in 2016, 43 percent of men and 33 percent of women had never been married by age 35. But by age 45, 17 percent of men and 12 percent of women had never married. In comparison, in 1960, only 7 percent of men and 6 percent of women had never married by the age of 45.

PERSPECTIVES ON THE DECLINE IN MARRIAGE

The decline in marriage (and the family) has led to some fascinating new perspectives on the status of marriage today.

The Deinstitutionalization of Marriage

Andrew Cherlin (2004; Brown, Manning and Payne 2015a; Treas, Lui, and Gubernskaya 2014) focuses on the "deinstitutionalization of American marriage." By **deinstitutionalization**, he means that the social norms relating to marriage have weakened. As a result, people increasingly question their actions, or those of others, as they relate to marriage. While Cherlin focuses on this deinstitutionalization in the United States, he recognizes that a similar process is occurring in much of Europe as well as in Canada (and elsewhere, including in Asia; see Davis and Friedman 2014). In the mid-twentieth century, especially in the United States, few questioned marriage and the creation of a nuclear family. As a result, most plunged into both, sometimes successfully, but more often with dubious or even disastrous results. Now, with marriage and perhaps the nuclear family and the family household deinstitutionalized, it is much easier for people *not* to rush into such arrangements. They are freer to experiment with many other arrangements.

Five factors have been influential in the deinstitutionalization of marriage:

- First, as more women entered the labor force, the clear division of labor in the family between homemaker and breadwinner began to break down. The once clear norms about what men and women were to do in a marital relationship were eroding. This contributed to a more general lack of clarity about marriage as well as the family.

- Second, the norms about having children within the context of marriage and the family were also eroding. This was demonstrated in the dramatic increase in the rate of childbirth outside of marriage, which increased

FIGURE 12.1 • U.S. Households by Type, 1970 to 2012

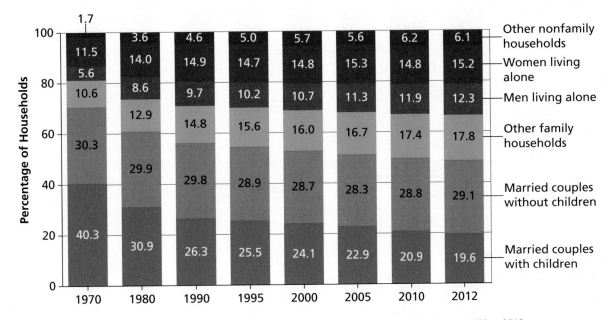

SOURCE: U.S. Census Bureau, Current Population Survey, Annual Social and Economic Supplement, selected years, 1970 to 2012.

from one in six in the late 1970s to one in three in the early twenty-first century.

- Third, the high and increasing divorce rate between 1960 and 1980 contributed to the deinstitutionalization of marriage. Although the divorce rate has declined in recent decades, the high rate between 1960 and the late 1970s and early 1980s had a seemingly irreversible impact on attitudes toward marriage.

- Fourth has been the growth in cohabitation, which began in the 1970s and accelerated as the twentieth century ended.

- Finally, same-sex marriage began to increase in the 1990s and has grown even more prevalent in the twenty-first century.

These factors in deinstitutionalization are embedded in a long-term model of change. In the early twentieth century, **institutional marriage** was the predominant form. The focus in such a marriage was on the maintenance of the institution of marriage itself. There was less concern that those involved would love or be good companions to one another. Today, many see the time of institutional marriage as past; others,

however, see it as alive and well and as having a future (Lauer and Yodanis 2010).

By the middle of the twentieth century, a model of **companionate marriage** (see the previous discussion of companionate love) had become predominant (Amato et al. 2007; Burgess and Locke 1945). Companionate marriage

FIGURE 12.2 • Share of Never-Married Adults in the United States, by Gender, 1960–2016

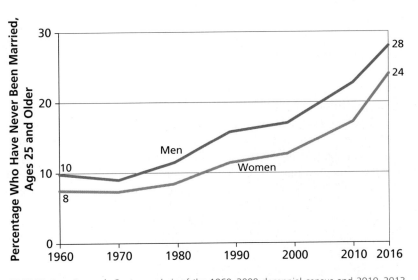

SOURCE: Pew Research Center analysis of the 1960–2000 decennial census and 2010–2012 American Community Survey, Integrated Public Use Microdata Series (IPUMS), September 24, 2014. Data for 2016 from U.S. Census Bureau, "America's Families and Living Arrangements: 2016: Adults," Table A1.

FIGURE 12.3 • Share of Never-Married Adults in the United States, by Age, 2016

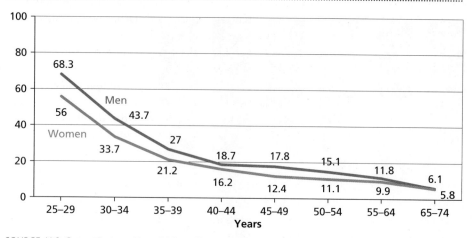

SOURCE: U.S. Census Bureau, "America's Families and Living Arrangements: 2016: Adults," Table A1.

meshed well with the nuclear family. It involved a clear division of labor between the single-earner breadwinner—almost always the male—and the female homemaker. In spite, or perhaps because, of the strict division of labor, husbands and wives were held together by bonds of sentiment, friendship, and sexuality. They were supposed to be each other's companions, which included being each other's friends, confidants, and lovers. Romantic love was an essential component of companionate marriage.

In the 1960s, a dramatic shift began to take place in the direction of **individualized marriage** (Lauer and Yodanis 2011). The goal of companionate marriage was the satisfaction of the couple, the family as a whole, and the roles the couple played in the family. However, that focus began to shift increasingly in the direction of the satisfaction of each individual, as well as toward individuals' ability to develop and express themselves. In addition, instead of being as rigid as companionate marriage, individualized marriage became increasingly open and flexible. Furthermore, couples were becoming more open with each other in communicating about and dealing with problems. Many couples, as well as many observers, applauded the greater freedoms and sensitivities associated with individualized marriage, although the changes may not be as clear-cut as was first believed (Yodanis and Lauer 2014).

A major factor in the rise of individualized marriage was the changing place in society of women, especially middle-class women. For example, as more women went to work, they were no longer restricted to the homemaker role and reliance on the male breadwinner. As more women obtained higher education, their occupational prospects were enhanced. This put them in a context where ideas associated with companionate marriage were increasingly open to question. Greater access to contraception and to abortion enabled

more women to plan their reproductive lives, releasing them from some of the constraints of companionate marriage as they related to producing and socializing children.

As a result of all these changes, people today feel freer to never marry, to marry later, to end unhappy marriages, and especially to engage in many other types of intimate relationships. Yet, in spite of these changes, the vast majority of people—as many as 90 percent or more—will eventually marry, although many of their marriages will end long before they reach the "till death do us part" stage. Thus, marriage has not been deinstitutionalized to the degree anticipated by Cherlin, and it is likely to survive, although it will not be nearly as important as it once was (Lauer and Yodanis 2010).

Marriage as a Carousel

In *The Marriage-Go-Round* (2009), Cherlin adopts a somewhat different perspective involving a "carousel of intimate partners." Some of those intimate partners are to be found in marriages, but those marriages are more likely to end; people are likely to remarry, perhaps more than once. Rounds of separation and divorce add to the merry-go-round and its increasingly dizzying speed. Then there may be a series of cohabitations into and out of which people move. Thus, many people have not given up on the idea and even the practice of marriage, but they exist side by side with the often conflicting notion of individualism. People want to be legally defined as couples and as families, but they also want to be free of constraints and to act as they wish as individuals. Current sociological research underscores this paradox. On the one hand, researchers are told that most people, including young adults, want an "exclusive, lifelong intimate partnership, most commonly a marriage" (Hull, Meier, and Ortyl 2010, 37). Hoffnung and Williams (2013) surveyed about 200 female college seniors in 1993. A follow-up of those women in 2009 found, unsurprisingly, that 91 percent of them had married, nearly 75 percent were mothers, and 57 percent were combining motherhood and full-time work outside the home. The women contended that the most satisfying thing they had ever done was mothering. On the other hand, people often indicate by their behavior that they want to be free of such bonds. Americans remain committed to the ideal of marriage, but in reality they spend fewer of their adult years married than previous generations did.

Self-Disclosing Intimacy and Pure Relationships

British sociologist Anthony Giddens (1992) offers an ambivalent view on the new individualized forms of marriage and of relationships more generally. The key to this new form of relationship is what Giddens calls "self-disclosing intimacy" (Duncan 2014; Funk and Kobayashi 2016). Couples are disclosing much more to each other. As a result, much more intimate relationships are likely to develop. This is contrasted with companionate marriages, which were more likely to be based on secrets and half-truths. Thus, companionate marriages in the past, and even the many that continue today, may survive for decades or a lifetime even though they may be based on deceptions that leave one or both partners in the dark. The partners often remain in such marriages for reasons other than their openness and honesty. They may stay together because of social norms against divorce or "for the sake of the children."

Giddens recognizes the advantages of self-disclosing intimacy, but he also argues that intimate relationships based on full disclosure are made much more fragile by such disclosures, especially as the disclosures continue and proliferate over time. The more weaknesses someone reveals to a partner, the more likely that partner is to become disappointed with the relationship. Despite this, Giddens, as well as many others today, seems to prefer relationships based on mutual disclosure because he believes they are likely to be more mutually satisfying, equal, and democratic. Further, he contends that almost anything is preferable to being locked into the kind of dishonest and unsatisfying relationship often associated with companionate marriage.

Because marriage of any kind can be confining and limiting, Giddens (1992) has coined the term *pure relationships* to describe a new reality. A **pure relationship** is one that is entered into for its own sake, or for what each partner can get from it, and those in it remain only as long as each derives enough satisfaction from it. While pure relationships can exist within marriage, they are more likely to exist outside such legal relationships. As a result of the increasing predominance of this idea, at least among young people, a relationship is likely to be ended when the couple no longer find it satisfying. It is also likely that another, different pure relationship (or several) will be formed in relatively short order, or perhaps even simultaneously with the existing one. This fits with the increasing individualization of contemporary society as well as the closely related phenomenon of individuals wanting more choices and greater freedom of choice. It represents an even greater degree of individualization than that found in individualized marriage. Less constrained by marriage, or more likely not to be married at all, couples are free to individualize their lives to a much greater degree. Marriage is seen as just one of a wide range of lifestyle choices open to couples. In whatever type of intimate relationship people find themselves today, the possibility that it will dissolve is never very far from their consciousness. This may be one of the reasons why young adults are putting off developing intimate relationships. They are more likely to consider an intimate, committed relationship as the last stage of adult development, unlike in the 1950s, when such relationships were more likely to develop in early adulthood (Rauer et al. 2013).

The idea of the pure relationship has its origins in Western society, but, like many such ideas in the global age, it has flowed readily around the world to many locales.

Questioning the New Ideas on Marriage and Relationships

Some observers have questioned the range of new ideas about intimate relationships, like those discussed previously. For example, Lynn Jamieson (1998, 2012) has questioned the importance of self-disclosing intimacy. There are many forms of intimacy other than those based on self-disclosure, and good relationships are based on more than such disclosures. For example, negotiating an equitable division of labor in the home may do more for increasing intimacy than a wide range of self-disclosures.

Interestingly, a major critique of these new ideas on marriage and the family is implicit in the work of one of sociology's classic social theorists, Georg Simmel (see Chapters 1, 2, and 5). In his famous essay on secrecy, Simmel ([1906] 1950; Coll 2012) argues that while there is always a temptation to reveal all to a partner in an intimate relationship, especially marriage, making such revelations is a big mistake. In his view, all relationships require a certain proportion of both openness and secrecy, and marriage is no exception. Even if it were possible to disclose everything about one's self, and it almost certainly isn't, this would only serve to make marriage boring and matter-of-fact, because all possibility of the unexpected would be eliminated. Finally, most of us have limited internal resources, and every revelation reduces the (secret) treasures that we have to offer our mates. Only those few with great storehouses of personal assets and accomplishments can afford numerous revelations to a marriage partner. All others are left denuded—and perhaps less interesting—by excessive self-revelation. The contrast is striking between Simmel's ideas, written more than a century ago, and the current thinking of many who emphasize the importance of revealing all to intimate partners.

THE RESILIENCE OF MARRIAGE

In spite of all the changes discussed previously, there are those who remain committed to the traditional notion of marriage. "Marriage naturalists" view "marriage as the *natural* expected outcome of a relationship that has endured for a period of time" (Kefalas et al. 2011, 847). In contrast, "marriage planners" need to deal with a number of practical realities before they can consider marriage. These include finding a well-paying job and being able to create and support a separate household. Marriage naturalists "see marriage as being a prerequisite to being an adult," and marriage planners "want to establish themselves as adults *before* they wed" (Kefalas et al. 2011, 870). In either case, however, the goal is to marry.

While they are going about creating those realities, both marriage planners and marriage naturalists may have premarital sexual/romantic relationships, cohabit, and bear children outside of marriage. All these phenomena have been found by sociological researchers to have risen in recent years. Kefalas and colleagues (2011) found that marriage naturalists are more likely to be rural, while marriage planners have to arrange their intimate lives around the realities of urban life. In addition, the views of marriage naturalists are closer to the realities of marriage in the mid-twentieth-century United States, while those of marriage planners better fit the realities of postindustrial America and the wait-and-see attitude more characteristic of the early twenty-first century.

Only about one fifth of the young adults studied by Kefalas and colleagues (2011) were marriage naturalists; the rest were marriage planners. However, the marriage planners, even those who regarded marriage as only a distant possibility, still desired to marry eventually. More striking is the fact that there was little discussion among these young adults of passion or love.

ASK YOURSELF

Among the married couples you know, how many were marriage naturalists and how many were marriage planners? Have you observed other approaches to marriage among those who are committed to the institution? If so, what are they?

Today there is a debate between those who see marriage as in decline and those who emphasize its resilience (Amato 2004). Those who see marriage in decline focus on such variables as the rising divorce rate and the increase in the number of children born outside legal marriages. These events are seen as social problems in themselves and as indicators of larger problems, such as excessive focus on the individual and inadequate concern for the collective. Those who focus on the resilience of marriage argue that, for example, divorce allows people to escape from marriages that they ought to escape, especially marriages that are dysfunctional in various ways, such as abusive marriages. Having children outside legal marriage may have the positive effect that fewer children will be locked into families in which they are socialized poorly or even abused physically and psychologically. However, observers such as Amato and his colleagues (2007) acknowledge that neither perspective—marriage in decline or resilient—is complex enough to fully explain marital and familial change.

FIGURE 12.4 • Percentage of U.S. Households with One Person, 1960–2016

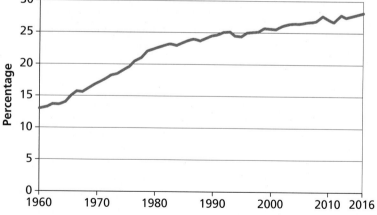

SOURCE: U.S. Census Bureau, Current Population Survey, 1960 to 2011. Annual Social and Economic Supplements; data for 2016 from U.S. Census Bureau, "America's Families and Living Arrangements: 2016: Households," Table H1.

NONFAMILY HOUSEHOLDS

A **nonfamily household** is one in which a person lives either alone or with nonrelatives. Of greatest interest is the growth of one-person households, or people living alone. As is clear in Figure 12.4, the United States has witnessed an increase in such households, from 13 percent in 1960 to more than 28 percent of all households in 2016.

One-person households, or "singletons," are the subject of Eric Klinenberg's *Going Solo: The Extraordinary Rise and Surprising Appeal of Living Alone* (2012). (See Trending box on p. 331.) Detailed in this work is the long-term increase in the number of people living alone. Overall, 31 million Americans now live alone. The fastest-growing segment of the population going solo is young adults between ages 18 and 34. In 1950, only a half million of those in this age group lived

TRENDING

Going Solo: The Extraordinary Rise and Surprising Appeal of Living Alone (Penguin Books, 2012)

Eric Klinenberg (Professor of Sociology and Director of the Institute for Public Knowledge at New York University; PhD, University of California–Berkeley, 2000)

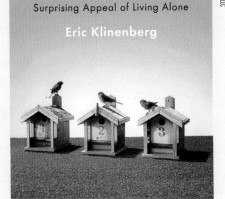

An interesting trend—the rise of singletons, or individuals who live alone—is changing the dynamics of family, marriage, and intimate relationships around the world. Today, 27 percent of all U.S. households contain only one occupant. Sweden has the largest percentage in the world (47 percent) of households with only one occupant. In contrast, India has one of the smallest percentages of people living alone, at 3 percent. Klinenberg explains that relatively affluent people in the global North are choosing to live alone because they have the economic wealth and social security to do so. There are several reasons for the increase in singletons. First, increasing economic affluence has made it possible for more people to afford the greater costs associated with living alone. Second, living alone is consistent with the growth of individualism in the United States and much of the developed world. Third, the rising status of women and their higher levels of education and higher-paying jobs enable more of them to live alone (although their wages continue to be lower than men's and they are more likely than men to be poor). With greater independence, they are more likely to marry later, separate, or divorce. Fourth, the communications revolution has allowed people to communicate with other people, and to be entertained, while they are home alone. Fifth, mass urbanization has made the active social life of the city available to more people. Finally, the population is aging, and as people live longer, they are more likely to find themselves alone.

Klinenberg and his research assistants spent seven years conducting in-depth interviews with more than three hundred singletons, finding some demographic differences in why and how individuals live alone. Younger singletons prefer to live alone because it provides them with the opportunity to be independent and to focus on self-discovery. Most have strong social networks that they can rely on if they feel lonely or need support. Older, widowed singletons prefer to live alone rather than remarry or move in with family members; however, they face social isolation if they do not develop robust social networks. In general, women are stigmatized more than men for being single and must more often defend their singleton status. Even though women are achieving higher status in society, their femininity may be questioned if they choose to remain single and not have children. For those who do not have good financial resources, being single can be extremely difficult due to the lack of affordable housing. The infirm elderly who need to live alone in nursing homes or assisted living facilities also suffer from a lack of quality care and services. To address these social changes and challenges, Klinenberg suggests that we need to redesign our cities and suburbs to better integrate all singletons into society, such as building more apartments instead of houses for nuclear families (2012, 207).

Supplementary Resources

- You can read an interview with Klinenberg that appeared in the *New York Times* at http://www.nytimes.com/2012/02/12/fashion/America-Single-and-Loving-It.html.
- You can watch Klinenberg discuss his book at a presentation he gave for Talks at Google: https://www.youtube.com/watch?v=C8E8usVe7-s.

alone, while today the total of 5 million is 10 times the number in the mid-twentieth century. Among those who are middle-aged (35 to 64), 15 million live alone, while 10 million of the elderly are singletons. More women (17 million) than men (14 million) live alone. Going solo is mainly an urban phenomenon; more than half of dwellings in Manhattan are one-person residences. (See Trending box in this chapter, p. 331.)

THE FAMILY HOUSEHOLD

A **family household** consists of two or more people who occupy a given domicile and are related by blood, marriage, or adoption. It is distinguished by the fact that those involved are related but not necessarily married, and by their occupation of a specific domicile. One member of the family household—the *householder*—owns or rents the property as well as maintains it.

As a form of an intimate relationship, the family household, like the family itself, has been declining in the United States and in the Global North more generally. For example, in 1940, 90 percent of households were family households, but that declined to 81 percent in 1970 and to 66.4 percent in 2010. This means, of course, a corresponding increase in nonfamily households over this period of time (Casper 2007; Jacobsen, Mather, and Dupuis 2012).

One countertrend worth noting is the increase in millennials—18- to 34-year-olds—who are returning home and are more likely to live with a parent than with a romantic partner (Lewin 2016). In other words, they are returning to the family household. A turning point came in 2014, when 32.1 percent of millennials lived with a parent, while slightly fewer—31.6 percent—lived with a partner or spouse.

In this sense, the United States is growing more like Italy, where even more young adults live with their parents. Young American men are more likely to live with their parents, but the number of young women living this way is also growing. While minority group members are more likely to live with a parent, the number of white young adults living with a parent has increased substantially.

A variety of other changes in the family household are worth mentioning:

- People are living longer. More are able to maintain their households and family structure for many more years than they were in the past.

- Women outlive men. This means that late in life, many women live alone in nonfamily households (34 percent of women 65 years of age and older lived alone in 1970, but by 2015 that number had grown to 36 percent).

- Families have been growing smaller. For example, between 1970 and 2016, there was a decrease in households including five or more people, from 21 percent to 10 percent of all households, while households with only one person increased from 17 percent to 28 percent (see Figure 12.5). Overall, the number of people per household declined in that timespan from 3.1 to 2.6.

- Declines in the family household are related to declines in births to married women in two-parent families, increases in births to unmarried women (leading to more one-parent families), and increases in the proportion of divorced people (from 2 percent to 9.2 percent among men and 3 percent to 9.7 percent among women between 1970 and 2009; Casper 2007).

FIGURE 12.5 • Households by Size in the United States, 1970–2016

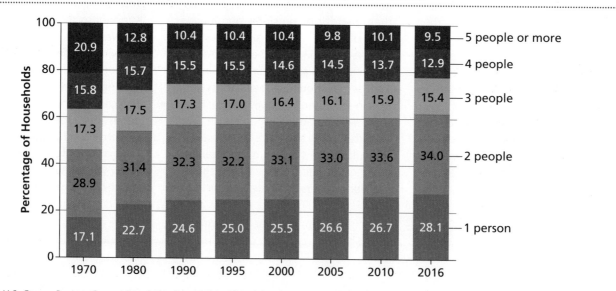

SOURCE: U.S. Census Bureau, Current Population Survey, Annual Social and Economic Supplement, selected years, 1970 to 2012; data for 2016 from U.S. Census Bureau, "America's Families and Living Arrangements: 2016: Households," Table H1.

Online Dating

In the past, a person was likely to be introduced to a potential partner by family members or friends or to meet him or her at school, work, or church. Today, one can use an additional intermediary: online dating websites and mobile apps. Match.com claims that one in five relationships begin on online dating sites. eHarmony commercials boast that matches made on its website have resulted in more marriages than other online dating services. Unlike traditional intermediaries, online dating sites require us to actively participate in finding and selecting our own partners (Shepherd 2016, 29). eHarmony users, for example, have to complete the site's 29 Dimensions of Compatibility questionnaire, which asks them to provide information about such topics as their family background, personality traits, communication skills, and appearance (Shepherd 2016, 44–46). After these data have been collected and analyzed via a set of algorithms, compatible users are "matched" to each other. Match.com operates in a similar manner, although

it also allows users to state their preferences about their ideal partners (Shepherd 2016, 57). Perhaps the most important difference between eHarmony and Match.com is that eHarmony does not permit its users to browse the profiles of all of its members—only profiles that the service has officially "matched" together (Shepherd 2016, 49). Both, however, charge members for their services.

While eHarmony and Match.com cater to heterosexuals interested in eventually getting married, mobile apps connect people more interested in a quick hookup or in a gay or bisexual relationship. Tinder users can swipe right on their smart phones to find a willing partner for a quick sexual encounter. Grindr, which has 2 million daily users, connects gay and bisexual men looking for a partner. Though Tinder and Grindr are free of charge, paid subscriptions for premium services on Tinder are available. Paying for dating assistance has been a subject of debate, with critics arguing that it commodifies love. Others wonder

whether meeting someone online is as authentic as unexpectedly finding love through a chance encounter in real life. Being "matched" with a potential partner through an online dating service might take the romance out of getting to know someone over time, because you can read a profile to discover a person's hobbies or favorite color (Rosewarne 2016). Many Americans are not troubled by these concerns. The use of online dating sites and mobile apps has increased, from 10 percent in 2013 to 27 percent in 2015 for young adults (18–24 years old), and from 6 percent in 2013 to 12 percent in 2015 for middle-aged adults (55–64 years old; Smith 2016).

Engaging the Digital World
Have you ever used online dating sites or mobile apps? If so, state which ones, describe how they work, and describe your experience, including whether you eventually went on a real date with a person to whom you were "matched." If not, would you consider using one? Why or why not?

Elliott, Young, and Dye examined the impact of the Great Recession on a specific form of family household, the complex family household, involving the presence of "an individual in a household who according to the household roster is related to the householder, but is not a member of the householder's immediate nuclear family" (2011, 8). There was a slight increase in such households, reflecting, perhaps, the hard economic times and higher unemployment (for a contrasting view, see Schaller 2013). There might well be cost savings for all concerned by bringing in more extended family members during hard economic times. Cost savings is also a major motivator for millennials returning to the family household.

ALTERNATIVE FORMS OF FAMILIES

Recent social changes have made it possible for people to choose nontraditional family structures for themselves, such

as cohabitation, single-parent families, families with nonresident parents, stepfamilies or blended families, or lesbian or gay families (Few-Demo and Demo 2016).

Cohabitation

Cohabitation is defined as an arrangement in which a couple shares a home and a bed without being legally married (Kroeger and Smock 2014; Manning and Cohen 2012; Sassler 2010; Thornton, Axinn, and Xie 2007). There are clearly more cohabiting couples today than there were previously, although they still compose only a small proportion (about 5.5 percent) of all U.S. households. The United States ranks low among developed countries in terms of cohabitation. For example, cohabitation is much more common in France, Estonia, Denmark, and the United Kingdom (see Figure 12.6).

FIGURE 12.6 • Percentage of Cohabiting Households in Selected Countries, Couples Ages 20 Years and Older

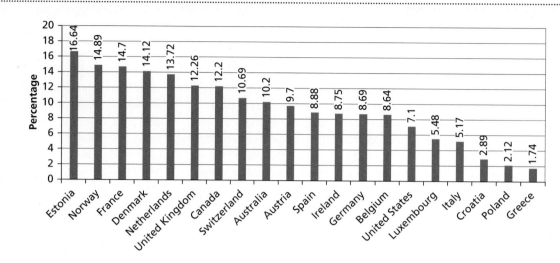

SOURCE: Data from Organisation for Economic Co-operation and Development 2011.

It is unclear exactly how many people are living in such relationships, because cohabitation is not a formally constituted relationship and it leaves no legal records. Furthermore, it is not clear how many nights, weeks, months, or years a couple must be together to be categorized as cohabiting. It is clear, however, that more young men and women (especially those between the ages of 25 and 35) are living together outside marriage, even if they are not considered, or do not consider themselves, to be cohabiting couples (Manning and Cohen 2015). Living together in this way has come to be considered a common tryout for, and pathway to, marriage, although few people actually plan to marry when they begin cohabiting. Then again, marriage may never occur or even be discussed, and cohabiting couples may break up and move on to other relationships. A declining number of cohabiting couples—less than 40 percent—end up getting married.

At one time, cohabitation was associated with being poor, less educated, or in the lower classes; it was seen as the "poor man's marriage." More recently, cohabitation has become increasingly common among those with advanced education, even college degrees. In the past, black women were more likely to cohabit than were white women, but in recent years the cohabitation rates for white women have increased dramatically, and they are now more likely to cohabit than are black women (Manning 2013). There are differences between these groups in the function of cohabitation. For instance, for blacks, cohabitation is more likely to be an alternative to marriage; for whites, it is more likely a prelude to marriage (England and Edin 2009; Smock and Manning 2004). Whatever the differences, most of those who cohabit have a variety of reasons for making the decision to live together: support, friendship and companionship, as well as love and commitment.

Huang and colleagues (2011) sought to better understand why young adults have cohabited or would cohabit. They found that the percentages of women who had ever cohabited ranged from 40 percent (Latinas) to 54 percent (both white and black women), consistent with previous studies of this phenomenon. The major findings of the study relate to people's rationales for cohabiting, as well as to gender differences in those rationales.

The first rationale was simply a desire to spend more time with one's partner. This was seen as a way of enhancing the relationship and desirable because it solved a variety of logistical problems, for example, by eliminating lengthy trips to see one's partner. The second rationale was the belief that the partners would save money cohabiting because they were sharing expenses rather than paying for everything on their own. Third, cohabitation was seen as a kind of "test drive" of the relationship to assess the partners' compatibility.

Perhaps the most interesting results of the study related to gender difference in terms of the ways in which cohabiting enhanced the relationship: Women focused on love, while men focused on sex. As one man put it, "Most girls want to have the connection with the guy and know it's a relationship. 'Cause women, their number one thing in life is to have good relationships with people. . . . Guys, the thing they strive for is sex, so it's kind of a tradeoff" (Huang et al. 2011, 887).

The biggest gender differences revolved around cohabitation's disadvantages. Women saw it as less legitimate and as entailing less commitment than marriage. Men were most concerned about the decline in freedom compared with being single. In terms of the latter, men focused on their loss of personal autonomy with regard to space, social activities, choice of friends, and sexual freedom. Overall, however, for both men and women, the benefits of cohabitation outweighed the disadvantages.

Rates of cohabitation vary greatly around the globe. Sweden has a long history of cohabitation, and the process is well institutionalized there. In excess of 90 percent of first partnerships are cohabitations, and more than 40 percent of all first births are to cohabiting couples (Perelli-Harris and Gassen 2012). The legal status, or the rights and privileges, of those who cohabit is virtually the same as that of married couples in terms of such things as social security and taxes (Wilk, Bernhardt, and Noack 2010). The high rate of cohabitation has led to a decline in the importance of marriage and of the customs, rituals, and ceremonies associated with it. Couples who cohabit and then marry might well give the date they met as their anniversary. Instead of making a decisive break, young people are likely to drift away from their families of orientation, perhaps in stages, and then settle down and cohabit with someone else (Popenoe 1987). However, since 1998 there has been evidence of a change in this pattern, as more Swedes are marrying. This reverses a long-term decline in marriage in Sweden between the 1960s and the 1990s (Ohlsson-Wijk 2011). Other, mainly Catholic, European countries—Italy and Spain—have much lower rates of cohabitation. There is evidence of the spread of cohabitation throughout much of Europe, including Eastern Europe, and elsewhere.

Single-Parent Families

Among the developed countries, the United States has the highest rate of single-parent families (29.5 percent of all households with children), while Japan has the lowest (10.2 percent). In Europe, the northern countries—for example, the United Kingdom (25 percent), Ireland (22.6 percent), and Denmark and Germany (both 21.7 percent)—have the highest rates of single-parent families. It is mainly the southern European countries—Greece and Spain (5 percent), Portugal (6 percent), and Italy (7 percent)—that have the lowest rates of such families.

One of the reasons that the United States has the highest rate of single-parent families is that several minorities are disproportionately likely to have such families. More than half of black children live with a single parent, while almost a third of Hispanic children exist in such a family. However, not all minorities have a high rate of single-parent families; the rate of such families is only 13 percent among Asian children. That is even lower than the 21 percent of non-Hispanic white children in single-parent families (Vespa, Lewis, and Kreider 2013).

Nonresident Parents

Nonresident parents are fathers and mothers who live apart from their children (Smyth 2007). Most nonresident parents are fathers, although the number of mothers in this category is increasing. Historically, there have been many reasons for fathers to be absent from their families, including work, war, and incarceration. Today, although those reasons continue to exist, the major reasons are nonmarital childbearing with the parents never having lived together, the breakdown of cohabiting relationships, and marital dissolution.

In the popular media, nonresident parents have been viewed negatively, often being labeled "deadbeat dads" or "bad moms." In the case of absent fathers, the term *masculinization of irresponsibility* has been used to describe "the refusal of fathers to provide economically for their children" (Kimmel 2012, 173). However, recent evidence tends to indicate that such labels are unfair. Many nonresident parents want to be active in their children's lives, but they face major problems in their efforts to play such a role. There are various emotional issues involved, such as the heartache associated with brief and intermittent visits with children. The major difficulties are practical in nature, including a lack of adequate time to handle parental responsibilities. This has given rise to terms like *Disneyland dads* (although there are *Disneyland moms* as well), because such fathers have time only for brief visits or recreational trips

Some nonresident parents are in the armed forces. This Air Force servicewoman marches with her son during a Memorial Day parade in Indiana. How are the stresses on military families different from those faced by others with nonresident parents?

(Stewart 1999). When nonresident fathers are able to spend time with their children, however, research shows that the children have higher academic achievement (Kimmel 2012). Other difficulties confronting nonresident parents include a lack of financial resources due to the demands of child support, lack of adequate space in the new home for children, difficulty in maintaining sufficient contact with children, additional responsibilities associated with a new home and perhaps a new family, and the difficulty of meeting the children's needs as far as things like extracurricular activities are concerned. Many nonresident parents—somewhere between 20 percent and 50 percent—cannot deal with some or all of these difficulties, with the result that they have little, or even no, interaction with their children. This, in turn, can cause many problems for the children involved, including poor performance in school.

Women typically have greater problems as nonresident parents than do men. They generally have fewer financial resources, and this makes it more difficult for them to perform the role of parent. They are therefore less likely than men to pay child support. Women may also believe that from a financial perspective, fathers are in a better position to raise the children involved. Or, in the case of transnational mothers (Dominguez and Lubitow 2008; Hondagneu-Sotelo and Avila 2005), providing financial resources for their children may be the only way they can engage with their children while also tending to and nurturing the children of others. Gender roles, such as being nurturing and being caretakers of children, also put more pressure on women to be highly active as nonresident parents. Gender roles may also lead women to be labeled negatively for living apart from their children. In spite of these difficulties, nonresident mothers are more likely than nonresident fathers to see their children, to see them more frequently, to have richer and more open encounters with them, and to maintain contact with them through telephone calls, e-mail, or text messaging.

The issue of nonresident parents is highly related to globalization and to the tendency for at least one parent to migrate in search of work. The physical distance created by work migration makes it difficult to perform adequately the role of mother or father, although that is ameliorated by the internet and interaction through e-mail, Skype, Facebook, and text messaging through services such as WhatsApp. Such services have helped create new "cyberparents." While much of the focus has been on the negative effects of globalization on both nonresident parents *and* their children, it is possible that we are seeing a restructuring of global parenting—and the creation of a new category of transnational parent—with a number of benefits, especially for the children. For example, parents who emigrate for work may end up being better off economically. This is especially true for mothers who may be empowered and better able to take on the "breadwinner" role. They are likely to be better able to send remittances and "care packages" back to their families

(R. Cohen 2015). Such parents, especially mothers, become more of providers for their children and are less able to play a nurturing role. At the minimum, they are performing a different nurturing role. Clearly, the success of transnational parenting is closely related to the economic situation of the parents. Poor parents who emigrate for economic reasons are in a far different position than are well-paid, high-level executives who are transferred to a different location but for some reason are not able to take their families with them (for example, the family is already well-adjusted in its current location).

Stepfamilies and Blended Families

A **stepfamily** consists of two adults who are married or cohabiting, at least one of whom has a child or children from a previous marriage or cohabitation living with him or her (Coleman, Ganong, and Russell 2013; Ganong and Coleman 2017). A **blended family** includes some combination of children from the partners' previous marriages or relationships, along with one or more children of the currently married or cohabiting couple (Martin-Uzzi and Duval-Tsioles 2013). Stepfamilies and blended families have become very common in the United States, because about half of all marriages include a partner who was previously married. According to a 2011 Pew Research Center survey, 42 percent of all U.S. adults have at least one step-relative. The U.S. Census Bureau estimates that 50 percent of children under the age of 13 live with one biological parent and that parent's partner (Stepfamily Foundation, n.d.). Although the differences are not great, stepchildren tend to do less well in school and have more behavior problems than do children who grow up living with their original pair of parents. One explanation is that stepfamilies are "incomplete institutions" (Cherlin 1978). That is, in dealing with problems, stepfamilies do not have the institutionalized guidelines, resources, and support that exist for first-marriage families.

There are a variety of differences between stepfamilies and first-marriage families. First, stepfamilies are more complex, because the children are likely to spend time with a stepparent as well as with the mother or father from their first-marriage family. Second, stepfamilies often have insufficient time to develop the family routines and rituals that are likely to have existed in first families. Children may well have difficulty adapting to these new, nonroutinized ways of living. Third, the bonds between first-marriage parents and children are better established and closer, at least at first, than are the new spousal bonds in stepfamilies. This can make circumstances difficult for the stepparent, at least early in the relationship, although the situation improves over time as the stepparent finds roles to play in the new family. Fourth, the lack of a legal relationship between stepparents and their stepchildren can cause a variety of problems, such as lack of any rights in regard to stepchildren after a divorce.

Family relationships can be difficult for both stepfathers (Edwards and Hadfield 2007) and stepmothers (Coleman and Ganong 2007a, 2007b; Coleman, Ganong, and Chapman, forthcoming). Stepfathers are far more common than stepmothers because mothers are far more likely than fathers to get custody of their children after divorce. For stepfathers, the relationship with stepchildren can be difficult because it is mediated by a third party, the mother and perhaps a nonresident father (Edwards, forthcoming). Stepfathers might, for example, resent all the time the mothers are spending with the children. If stepfathers have their own biological children, this can create conflicts over loyalties and the allocation of scarce money and time. Stepfathers might also have difficulties serving as father figures within stepfamilies. However, stepmothers might well have greater difficulties than stepfathers because they feel the expectations of them are ambiguous. For example, it may be unclear how they should act toward their stepchildren or whether they are impinging on the role of the biological mother. Stepmothers may also be frustrated by a lack of support from their partners. Having children with stepfathers can create problems, as stepmothers are likely to feel closer to those children than they are to their stepchildren.

The U.S. Supreme Court issued a historic decision in the summer of 2015 ruling that the Constitution allows gay and lesbian couples to marry.

Lesbian and Gay Families

It is very difficult to get accurate numbers on the gay and lesbian population as a whole, let alone on gays and lesbians involved in long-term relationships, including those in which children are present. Gays and lesbians were largely invisible a half-century ago due to cultural and legal biases and sanctions against them. That began to change in the era of sexual liberation of the 1960s and 1970s. A major factor in the gay and lesbian community in general, and in gay and lesbian family formation in particular, has been the HIV/AIDS epidemic that emerged in the 1980s (Heaphy 2007a). The gay and lesbian community reacted by building institutions to better deal not only with HIV/AIDS but with many other concerns as well. One of the institutions that was buttressed in this period was the gay and lesbian family. Previously, gay and lesbian couples had often come together because of the need for support and comfort in the face of a hostile environment. Today, such linkages have become more affirmative in nature, especially as the larger society has become more accepting of homosexuality and of gay and lesbian families as an institution. Lesbian and gay politics have devoted more attention to these individuals' right to marry, adopt children, and be parents.

Gay and lesbian couples have various similarities to, as well as differences from, straight families. One important difference is that gay and lesbian couples tend to be more reflexive and democratic in their family decisions and practices than straight couples. This is particularly the case concerning housework and other domestic duties, contentious issues for heterosexual couples who both work outside the home. Gay and lesbian couples are less constrained by social and institutional gender roles, with the result that they are freer in their negotiations over relational and family practices. Scripts for sexual relationships are less institutionalized among gay and lesbian couples as well, leading to some creative adaptations. Although monogamy is often assumed (but often violated) by straight couples, same-sex male couples are not as wedded to the idea or practice of sexual exclusivity. They negotiate over this issue and develop clear ground rules for nonmonogamous sexual relationships (Adam 2006; Barrett and Pollack 2011). Gay male relationships tend to be more fragile, while lesbian relationships tend to be far more stable. Some of the reasons for these gender differences are related to gender socialization patterns and sexual scripts (see Chapter 11; Kimmel 2012).

Studies of children of same-sex couples have tended to indicate that growing up in these families does not have adverse effects on children, such as psychological or developmental problems, or at least any more or different adverse effects than those experienced growing up in straight families. While there is no evidence of adverse effects on the children of same-sex couples, that does not mean that there are no differences between them and children of opposite-sex parents. For example, there is some evidence that same-sex parents are less worried about gender nonconformity among their children, spend more time with their children pursuing common interests, and are less likely to use corporal punishment on them (Moore and Stambolis-Ruhstorfer 2013).

ASK YOURSELF

Why do you think it took the Supreme Court as long as it did to declare same-sex marriage constitutional? What factors finally changed the Court's position?

However, most of this research has focused on children who were brought into same-sex families but were conceived, and spent at least some time, in previous heterosexual families. Now, however, same-sex couples are more likely to become parents themselves in various ways, such as through artificial insemination (Mamo 2007), adoption, becoming foster parents, or becoming surrogate parents. While we do not yet know much about the children in such families, there is no reason to assume that they are adversely affected by these methods of achieving same-sex parenthood. In fact, there is every reason to believe that they do at least as well as children raised in traditional heterosexual families.

The polar views on same-sex marriage are, on the one hand, that it is an expression of greater tolerance in the population as a whole and, on the other hand, that it is yet another threat to religion, morality, and heterosexual marriage. Whatever the perceived dangers, same-sex marriage has become increasingly common in the United States and in many other countries (Biblarz and Stacey 2010; Heaphy 2007b). As recently as the 1990s, there was no legal recognition of such marriages *anywhere in the world,* and the prospect of such marriages faced considerable hostility and intolerance. A key event occurred in September 2000, when the Netherlands extended the right to marry to same-sex couples. In the ensuing decade, a number of other countries throughout the world (Argentina, Canada, Belgium, Norway, Portugal, Sweden, Spain, South Africa, and Uruguay, as well as Mexico City) came to permit same-sex marriages.

After same-sex marriage had been legalized in a number of U.S. states, the U.S. Supreme Court finally declared same-sex marriage constitutional in mid-2015, making it legal in all 50 states.

There is considerable ambivalence in the gay and lesbian community toward legal same-sex marriage. Some welcome the validation it offers. They also appreciate gaining the same legal rights and benefits enjoyed by straight married couples in terms of child support, medical decision making, and inheritance. Many gays and lesbians also welcome legal marriage because of the challenge it poses to the dominance of heterosexual norms and values. Others see marriage as surrender to *heteronormativity,* or the view that heterosexuality is the normal sexual orientation, and as a threat to the distinctive character of gay and lesbian culture

and ways of life. From this perspective, same-sex marriage represents submitting to outmoded notions of commitment and to rules that can stifle the uniqueness and creativity of the gay and lesbian community, especially in regard to relationships. As a result of this ambivalence (Reczek 2016), while many gays and lesbians feel that they ought to have the right to marry, far from all would actually choose to marry if they had the opportunity (Considine 2012). They are likely to see their current relationships as offering greater possibilities for freedom, creativity, and equality than what would be offered in marital relationships.

CHECKPOINT 12.2: CHANGES IN MARRIAGE AND THE FAMILY

RELATIONSHIP	DESCRIPTION
Nuclear family	A family consisting of two married adults and one or more children
Companionate marriage	A marriage emphasizing a clear division of labor between a breadwinner and a homemaker and held together by sentiment, friendship, and sexuality
Individualized marriage	A marriage characterized by greater freedom for the partners to develop and express themselves
Nonfamily household	A household consisting of a person who lives alone or with nonrelatives
Family household	A household comprising two or more people who are related by blood, marriage, or adoption
Cohabitation	A couple sharing a home and a bed without being legally married
Nonresident parents	Fathers and mothers who live apart from their children
Blended family	A family that combines children from the partners' previous marriages or relationships with the children of their current marriage or relationship

THEORIZING THE FAMILY

Whatever the family form, the main types of theories outlined in Chapter 2 and used throughout this book—structural/functional, conflict/critical, and inter/actionist theories—can be used to think about and shed light on the family (Cheal 2007; White 2013).

STRUCTURAL/FUNCTIONAL THEORIES

Writing in the mid-twentieth century, in the heyday of marriage, the nuclear family, and the family household, Talcott Parsons, the preeminent structural-functionalist, saw the family as a structure with very important functions for society as a whole. The nuclear family was especially important in the America of Parsons's day. Its structure freed family members from the obligations of an **extended family**—two or more generations of a family living in the same household or in close proximity to one another—and allowed them the mobility needed in the industrial society of the time. Parsons also argued that the family system of the day functioned efficiently and effectively because of the clear distinction between "expressive (female) and instrumental (male)" roles (Kimmel 2012, 147).

Of greatest concern to Parsons, and to structural-functionalism, was the need for order in society. A very important source of that order is the socialization of children into how they are supposed to act, as well as the process by which they learn the norms, values, and morality of society. What is communicated during childhood socialization tends to be internalized by children and becomes part of what is generally called their "conscience" (Parsons 1951). The personality in general, and the conscience in particular, is shaped during childhood socialization and remains relatively stable throughout the life course. The family, especially in the heyday of the nuclear family, played a crucial role in socialization. Furthermore, such a family was more likely than any other family form to communicate a coherent sense of society's culture and morality. Parsons certainly did not see the family as devoid of problems or the process of socialization as seamless, but he did not emphasize the problems associated with either. Rather, he saw the family and socialization as functional for society.

This kind of thinking has been picked up by those sociologists who emphasize the functions of the family:

- First, society must at least replace those who die. This is accomplished through childbearing, which traditionally has been preferred to occur within the family.

- Second, the family fulfills the need to provide physical and emotional care to children.

- Third, the family fulfills the socialization function discussed previously.

- Fourth, the family shares resources to meet its economic needs.

- Fifth, the family provides intergenerational support as parents continue to support their adult children economically, emotionally, and in many other ways.

Was structural/functional theory more relevant to nuclear families of the 1950s than it is to today's socially diverse families?

- Sixth, the family has traditionally served to control sexual behavior. That control varies greatly from one society to another; in American society, whatever control the family previously had over sexuality is in decline.

- Finally, the family is a mechanism for helping children find a place in society, especially in its stratification system.

There are many criticisms of the structural-functional theory of marriage and the family, not the least of which is that it applied best to the realities of the 1950s and is increasingly out of touch with today's realities. It simply "doesn't take into account the diversity of family structures and roles found in American marriages and families" (Scott and Schwartz 2008, 349). Moreover, structural-functional theory has a conservative bias that "tends to promote and rationalize the status quo," including that of marriage and the nuclear family. Furthermore, it tends to "understate disharmony and conflict" and, more generally, the array of family-related problems that will be discussed in the following section (Scott and Schwartz 2008, 349).

CONFLICT/CRITICAL THEORIES

Unlike structural-functionalists, conflict theorists have never seen the family as a coherent unit or as contributing in an unambiguously positive way to the larger society. For one thing—as pointed out previously and as we will discuss later in this chapter—the family itself is riddled with stresses, strains, and conflicts that lead to all sorts of problems for the family, its members, and society as a whole (Noller and

Karantzas 2012). The family is an especially rich arena for conflicts based on gender and age (e.g., sibling rivalries, children versus parents). Such conflicts are closely related to the issue of power within the family—who has the most power, how it is used (and abused), and so forth. Above all, conflict can arise when one or more family members seek to wrest power from those who possess it.

ASK YOURSELF

If you have siblings, have you ever thought of any conflicts you may have had with them (or with your parents) as power struggles? If you didn't think so at the time, can you see them as power struggles now, in light of conflict theory? Does this view help you understand such disagreements better? Why or why not?

In contrast to Talcott Parsons's harmonious view of the family, Randall Collins (1975) looks at conflict within the broader system of social stratification, as well as within formal organizations and the family. Collins sees the family as an arena of gender conflict in which males have historically been the winners, leaving female family members in an inferior position. Similarly, when it comes to age-based conflict within the family, parents are generally victorious and children relatively powerless.

A key issue in looking at inequality and conflict within the family is found in the resources possessed by the various parties involved. In terms of the conflict between adults and children, parents have a variety of resources, including greater size, strength, experience, and ability to satisfy the needs of the young, and as a result, the young are likely to be dominated by the adults. Among the few resources possessed by the young are their physical attractiveness and physical prowess. As a result, "girls are taught to capitalize on good looks, cuteness, and coyness [and] boys discover that athletic ability and performance are what count for males" (Kimmel 2012, 157). However, as children mature, they acquire other resources and are better able to resist adults. The result is more conflict between the generations as children mature.

Feminist Theory

Feminist theory tends to be critical of the dominant family model—male-dominated, white, middle-class, heterosexual, with dependent children. What distinguishes feminist theory from conflict theory in general is the adoption of a conflict view of the relationship between genders and, more specifically, as that relationship exists within the family (Allen and Jaramillo-Sierra 2015). Feminist theorists see the family as being internally stratified on the basis of

gender: Men and women possess different economic and social positions and interests, and they struggle over those differences. Males have been able to create and to impose a gendered division of labor within the family that benefits men and adversely affects women. The family is seen as a patriarchal structure in which males exercise power and oppress women. Male control is enhanced by an ideological mechanism whereby traditional family norms are upheld. For example, girls tend to learn to accept the idea that they should put family responsibilities ahead of everything else, including their personal development and satisfaction. This tends to engender and support masculine power and privilege. Some consequences of masculine privilege and power include men's "expecting or taking for granted personal and sexual services, making and/or vetoing important family decisions, controlling money and expenditures, and so forth" (Shaw and Lee 2009, 387). According to the staunch feminist Emma Goldman, "the institution of marriage makes a parasite of woman, an absolute dependent" (cited in Shaw and Lee 2009, 298). By buying into the ideology of masculine power and privilege, women are, in effect, supporting and enabling their own oppression. This ideology is seen as a major impediment to the liberation of women in the family and elsewhere in society. Overall, it could be argued that from a feminist perspective, the family is a concept and a structure created and disseminated by males in order to serve their own interests and not those of females. Yet it is important to note that "the balance of power in marriage (or any domestic partnership) depends in part on how couples negotiate paid labor and family work in their relationships" (Shaw and Lee 2009, 388).

INTER/ACTIONIST THEORIES

The inter/actionist theories discussed in this section, symbolic interaction and exchange theory, look at the family from a more microscopic perspective than structural/functional or conflict/critical theories do.

Symbolic Interactionism

Symbolic interactionism focuses on the meanings attached to identities, roles, and social relationships, treating meaning as socially constructed. This approach has long been used in family research (Stryker 1959). For example, men may attach different levels of significance to the role of father, and marital partners may redefine their relationship over time. Examples of research carried out from a symbolic interactionism perspective include Derek Ball and Peter Kivisto's (2006) study of couples considering divorce in marriage counseling settings and David Aveline's (2006) study of the reframing of identities that occurs when parents learn that a child is gay.

Exchange Theory

Exchange theorists look at the family from the perspective of choices made on the basis of rewards and costs. People enter marital relationships because they think the rewards associated with marriage will outweigh the costs. They also tend to think marriage will be more rewarding than the alternatives to it: remaining single or becoming involved in other kinds of intimate relationships. Heterosexual marriage benefits men and women; however, men generally benefit the most. "All psychological measures of indices of happiness and depression suggest that married men are much happier than unmarried men. . . . Husbands report being more satisfied than wives with their marriages; husbands live longer and enjoy better health benefits than unmarried men" (Kimmel 2012, 153). However, both married men and married women live longer, have fewer health problems, have more sex, save more money, and have fewer psychological problems, such as depression, than do unmarried men and women.

A marriage is likely to break down when the reward–cost calculation leads the partners involved to see the marriage as no longer profitable or to realize that other alternatives are more profitable. From this perspective, a marriage is likely to break down for two reasons. First, it will collapse if the individuals involved come to the conclusion that their marriage is not as profitable to one or both partners as other marriages with which they are familiar. In other words, they come to feel deprived relative to these other married couples. Second, it is likely to break down if they come to believe that greater rewards or lower costs are to be found in alternatives, such as becoming single again, marrying someone else, or becoming involved in some other type of intimate relationship, such as cohabitation. In the last case, the rewards of a different partner might be offset by the costs, such as the effect such a change will have on any children involved.

CHECKPOINT 12.3: SOCIOLOGICAL THEORIES ABOUT THE FAMILY

THEORY	MAIN HYPOTHESIS
Structural/ functional theory	The family is a structure that functions efficiently because the "expressive" (female) and "instrumental" (male) roles are clearly defined.
Conflict/ critical theory	The family is a rich arena for conflicts based on gender and age and the use and abuse of power.
Inter/ actionist theory	The family is a meaningful relationship people enter into because they think the rewards will outweigh the costs.

PROBLEMS IN THE FAMILY

There are a wide variety of family troubles, but we will focus on a few of the major ones in this section.

FAMILY CONFLICT

Conflict is endemic to family life, with numerous flash points between husband, wife, and children in a traditional nuclear family, and innumerable other possibilities for conflict in the wide array of other forms of intimate relationships. While divorce is usually seen as the major result of family conflict, conflict often exists long before a divorce, and it may not even lead to divorce. Much conflict simmers below the surface in many families, surfacing only now and then. Family conflicts may arise over such issues as the family's objectives, resources, and the need to protect the interests of various family members.

The five basic models of family conflict (Kellerhals 2007; Kellerhals and Widmer, forthcoming) are the deficit model, the overload model, the cultural tensions model, the conflict-of-interest model, and the anomie model.

The Deficit Model

The deficit model contends that deficits in the socialization of family members contribute to family conflicts. Poor socialization can be attributed to parents getting married at too young an age and therefore not having progressed through enough of the socialization process themselves to do a good job of socializing their children. Other deficits in socialization that contribute to family conflict include growing up in an unstable, conflict-laden, poverty-stricken, or economically insecure family where opportunities for proper socialization and learning how to relate to others are limited. Inadequate education can adversely affect parents' ability to socialize children, as well as to communicate and negotiate within the family structure. Another deficit is a lack of ties with kin or the larger social structure. Such linkages can help prevent conflict within the family.

The Overload Model

The overload model is traceable to the work of Phillipe Aries (1978), who argued that because the public sphere has declined, the private sphere, including the family, has had to take up the slack, thereby overloading it with responsibilities. With the state and other aspects of the public sphere doing less, the family has had to compensate by meeting more and more of the needs of family members, such as providing money to aged, retired family members. An overburdened family is likely to be subject to much more conflict, stemming from having so many expectations as well as being unable to satisfy many of them.

The Cultural Tensions Model

The cultural tensions model focuses on strains traceable to the existence of family commitments and responsibilities on the one hand and the increasing emphasis in society on the self and individualization on the other hand (Beck and Beck-Gernsheim 2002). Individuals are seen as torn between these two phenomena, and the inability to address both can lead to conflict in the family. This is especially the case when family members focus too much on themselves and downplay or ignore family responsibilities.

The Conflict-of-Interest Model

The conflict-of-interest model involves the tension between the increasing equality in the family and the structural inequalities that exist in society as a whole, especially in employment. Thus, while many now believe that there should be equality within the family, structural realities mean that women who work are likely, as we have seen, to continue to handle an inordinate amount of responsibility at home as well. The injustice felt by many can lead to heightened conflict in the family.

The Anomie Model

According to the anomie model, conflict stems from the fact that contemporary families are left to their own devices in negotiating and organizing their relationship (see Chapter 2). This stands in contrast to what occurred in the past, where extended families and larger social groups, as well as broader norms and values, were of much more help in organizing family relationships. Among the difficult things that need to be worked out within the family are the definition of priorities, the division of work and labor both inside and outside the family, how economic and material resources should be shared, how much contact there will be outside the family and how intensive that contact will be, and what is private and what is not. All of these issues can, and often do, become areas over which family members conflict.

ABUSE AND VIOLENCE WITHIN THE FAMILY

Heightened conflict within the family can lead to abuse and violence. This can take various forms, but the most common are parental abuse of children and violence by husbands against their wives (who are considered "battered women"; Dunn 2005; LaViollete and Barnett 2014). Far less common is women abusing and behaving in a violent manner toward their children and even their husbands. Violence within the family can take emotional or psychological forms (Ellin 2016). It can also involve physical and sexual abuse (Carmody 2007; Pennington 2015b). Although norms that relate to the acceptability of such behavior have changed in recent years, such abuse and violence are still common and accepted in some groups and parts of the world. In such cases, parents feel justified in abusing children, and husbands think it is acceptable to batter their wives. While there are exceptions, we should remember that the vast majority of those who engage in such behavior are not considered to be criminals (Straus 1980).

Child Abuse

Hundreds of millions of children throughout the world are abused, maltreated, and exploited (Bell 2011; Whittier 2016). According to the World Health Organization, "child abuse or maltreatment constitutes all forms of physical and/or emotional ill-treatment, sexual abuse, neglect, or negligent treatment or commercial or other exploitation, resulting in actual or potential harm to the child's health, survival, development, or dignity in the context of a relationship of responsibility, trust, or power" (cited in Polonko 2007, 448). In the United States alone, reports indicate that several million children (15 percent) are severely maltreated, but this number reflects only official reports—the actual number is much higher. Furthermore, the official number includes only those who have been the victims of severe abuse and who clearly have been injured. The most common forms of child abuse are parents hitting their child with an object (20 percent), kicking or biting their child or hitting their child with their fists (10 percent), or physically beating up their child (5 percent; Kimmel 2012). Fathers and father surrogates are most likely to commit these offenses.

The impact of child abuse is great, especially for the children involved, but also for the parents (or other adults) and the larger society. Physical and emotional abuse and violence experienced in childhood can lead to an increased likelihood of cognitive impairment (lower IQ and levels of educational attainment), impaired ability to reason morally (a weakly developed conscience), and a greater likelihood of engaging in violence and crime. Children who have been abused are themselves more likely to be violent toward other children, including siblings, and later in life to abuse their own children, their spouses, and even elderly parents.

There is often a cycle of violence and abuse toward children that stretches across several generations (Steinmetz 1987). Many of the parents who mistreat and abuse their children were themselves victims as children and, as a result, may have developed mental and substance abuse problems that can increase their own likelihood of mistreating others.

There is also a cost to society. The Centers for Disease Control and Prevention (2012) has estimated that in the United States alone, the lifetime economic cost associated with one year's worth of child abuse (for the population as a whole) is more than $124 billion. This cost is traceable to such things as social services provided to families, the lesser contributions of victims to society, and related criminal justice and healthcare activities. While there are things

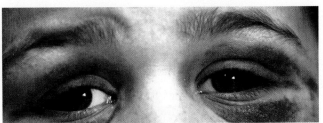

Conflicts in some families can turn violent. This boy's father was arrested for beating and torturing his wife and children.

that can be done to deal with the adults involved in terms of intervention and prevention, the structure of society as a whole needs to be addressed in various ways to reduce this problem. Of greatest importance is the need to change a culture in which children are viewed as property that parents and other adults can treat, and abuse, in any way they want. Children also need to be seen as having human rights. In addition, children need to be better protected, helped, and treated by the various agencies involved. More generally, society and the government need to believe in and support a wide range of policies that are of benefit to children, such as more and better child care.

Domestic Violence

Domestic violence entails the exertion of power over a partner in an intimate relationship through behavior that is intimidating, threatening, harassing, or harmful (Carmody 2007). The partner can be harmed physically and/or sexually, emotionally, and psychologically; the violence can occur multiple times (Goodlin and Dunn 2011). A debate in this area is whether the concept of domestic violence should be restricted to physical violence, or whether abuse in all of these areas qualifies as domestic violence.

A great deal of research has been done on domestic violence, and several general conclusions can be drawn from this work:

- Women are about five times more likely than men to be victims.

- Women are about six times more likely to be assaulted by those they are intimate with (partners or former partners) than by strangers.

- One of the leading causes of injury to women is domestic violence.

- Among minority groups, blacks have the highest rate of such violence.

- Most likely to be victims are poor females between 16 and 24 years of age.

- It is difficult to leave a violent relationship, and the risk of serious, even fatal, injury is greatest when one does try to leave such a relationship.

- Domestic violence is a major cause of homelessness.

- About one third of all female homicide victims are killed by those who are intimates.

Figure 12.7 shows that from 1994 to 2011, intimate partner violence dropped by more than 60 percent for both males and females. From 1994 to 2011, such violence was down 49 percent for females and 46 percent for males. From 2000 to 2005, the rate of intimate partner violence against females dropped an additional 31 percent, while male victimization rates remained nearly steady. The rate of intimate partner violence against females remained almost stable from 2005 to 2011, while males experienced a decline from 1.7 to 1.5 victimizations per 1,000 males age 12 or older.

Because gender socialization often leads men to see violence as an appropriate means of communication, it follows that most abusers tend to be male. Heterosexual men and gay men can suffer intimate partner violence, however, as can lesbian, bisexual, and queer people (Dutton and White 2013; Messinger 2014). Men who experience such violence are often discouraged from reporting the crime or

FIGURE 12.7 • Intimate Partner Violence, by Sex, 1994–2011

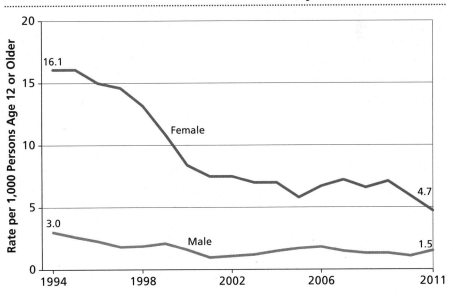

NOTE: Estimates based on two-year rolling averages beginning in 1994. Includes rape or sexual assault, robbery, aggravated assault, and simple assault committed by current or former spouses, boyfriends, or girlfriends.

SOURCE: Bureau of Justice Statistics, National Crime Victimization Survey, 1993–2011, Appendix Table 1.

seeking social support. Societal assumptions that domestic violence cannot be perpetrated against men, combined with masculine socialization, can make male victims reluctant to report it.

In addition to being very costly to victims and their families, domestic violence is costly to society. Those abused are not likely to be able to function as well in the larger society as those who are not victimized. For example, the abused have higher levels of absenteeism from work. Furthermore, society often needs to pay the costs associated with medical treatment, police involvement, court expenses, and shelters for those who have been victimized.

Elder Abuse

The elderly do not escape abuse merely because of their advanced age. This is certainly an ancient problem, although it has come to wide-scale public attention only in the last half-century. In a large national study, about 10 percent of elderly respondents reported some type of abuse (Acierno et al. 2010). The elderly are abused in various ways, including physically, psychologically, financially, sexually, and through neglect. Among other things, we know that elderly women are more likely to be abused than men, the very elderly (over 80 years of age) are most likely to be victims, and adult children and spouses are most likely to perpetrate the abuse. Beyond the elder abuse committed by family members, such abuse also takes place in residential care facilities for the elderly (Burns, Hyde, and Killett 2013).

ASK YOURSELF

Do you believe that any of the five models of family conflict can help explain why elder abuse is most often committed by members of the victim's family? Which model or models can explain this phenomenon, and how?

POVERTY AND THE FAMILY

There is a close relationship between family structure and poverty (Lichter 2007). For example, the poverty rate in 2015 in the United States for married-couple families was 54 percent, but for female-headed families it was 28 percent—almost five times as much. The likelihood of poverty for female-headed families is much less in many other developed countries, largely because of more generous social welfare programs. The concentration of poverty among female-headed households tends largely to reflect the consequences of gender inequality.

The big debate here is not over the facts, but over whether the family structure causes poverty or poverty causes problems within the family. On the one hand, the argument is made that a weak family structure—one, for example, where women are left alone to raise children—causes poverty. Such women are apt to be poor because they are unlikely to be able to work, and the children are poor because they are not adequately supported by these women or their absent fathers. On the other hand, it is contended that poverty causes families to crumble. Women are left alone to raise children as the men leave because they cannot support them or because the mothers are more likely to qualify for welfare if the father is absent. The emotional and economic stresses associated with being poor are likely to put intolerable strains on the family.

Being unmarried is likely to be associated with poverty for women with children. Divorce is also likely to drive women, especially those who are already in a marginal economic situation, into poverty. More generally, divorce is likely to affect almost all women adversely. The only debate in this area concerns how badly women are affected and how much they are hurt economically, as well as in other ways.

GENDER INEQUALITIES

Intimate relationships, especially marriages, are unequal as far as the men and women involved are concerned. Marriages can be so different from the points of view of men and women that they seem like completely different systems. These inequalities take several forms (Shehan and Cody 2007).

The first is inequality in the amount of time devoted to household and childcare tasks (Patton and Choi 2014). Figure 12.8 shows the average number of hours per week mothers and fathers spent on paid work, housework, and child care in 1965 and 2011. In 2011, mothers on average spent almost twice as much time (18 hours per week) on housework as did fathers (10 hours). Mothers also spent 7 hours more per week on child care than did fathers. Although the gap has been shrinking since 1965, gender inequalities are still clearly prevalent in the home, even as women's hours of paid work have increased dramatically. We know that the intersection of race and class can affect the likelihood of men's greater participation in housework. In addition, men spend more time on tasks that are discretionary, at least to some degree, while women are more likely to perform regular, repetitive labor. Mothers are more likely to maintain the children, while fathers are more likely to engage in recreational activities with the children. The disparity is even greater when it comes to the care of the ill and the elderly; this is almost always the near-total responsibility of females.

Then there are various gender inequalities in power and decision making. As in sociology in general, *power* here is defined as the ability to impose one's will on others despite their opposition. This can involve forcing a spouse to do something or to define a situation in a particular way. In heterosexual marriages, men are favored in terms of power within the marital relationship because of their greater size and strength. They are likely to earn more money, and they

FIGURE 12.8 • Hours per Week Mothers and Fathers Spend on Paid Work, Housework, and Child Care, 1965 and 2011

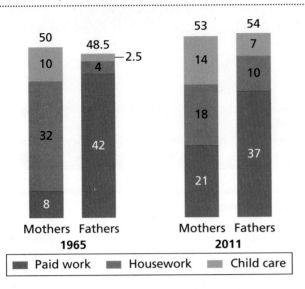

NOTE: Based on adults ages 18–64 with own child(ren) under age 18 living in the household. Total figures (at the top of each) may not add to component parts due to rounding.

SOURCE: Modern Parenthood Roles of Moms and Dads Converge as They Balance Work and Family, March 14, 2013. Reprinted by permission of Pew Research Center, Washington, DC.

are likely to dominate conversations, thereby swinging decisions their way. In addition, male power tends to be institutionalized and supported by religious groups and their customs (especially by Evangelical Christians, Hasidic Jews, Muslims, the Amish, and Mormons) as well as by governments and their policies. The latter often assume that husbands are the household heads and are responsible for the support of wives and children, and that wives are supposed to take care of the household and the children.

As we saw previously, women are more likely than men to be the victims of intimate partner violence, even though men are more likely to be victimized by violence in general. In 1993, the United Nations adopted the Declaration on the Elimination of Violence against Women. Within the United Nations, UN Women (previously UNIFEM) is particularly concerned with the violence perpetrated globally against women and girls, especially in the family (see www.unwomen.org/en/about-us). There is a strong preference for male children throughout much of the world, with the result that female embryos are more likely to be aborted, female infants are more likely to be the victims of infanticide, and female children are more likely to be the victims of violence.

Globally, wife beating is the most common form of family violence. In some parts of the world, this is taken to extreme lengths, with wives beaten to death. Brides may be burned to death because of (supposed) infidelity, because the bride's family was unable to pay the dowry in full to the husband, or even because a pregnant 14-year-old bride refused to work in the fields, in one specific case (Mashal 2016). In some parts of the world, women are stoned to death for such offenses. The movie *The Stoning of Soraya M.* (2008), based on a 1994 novel of the same name, tells the true story of an Iranian woman who was stoned to death by members of the community, including her father and sons, on the basis of a false accusation by her husband—who wanted another woman—that she had been unfaithful to him. Some cultures support so-called honor killings, or killings of females because they have engaged in such "dishonorable" behaviors as infidelity, same-sex sexual relations, wanting out of arranged marriages, seeking marriage on their own, or even refusing to adhere to the dress code. There has been a good deal of publicity about, and public uproar over, honor killings in places such as Pakistan, Egypt, Turkey, and Iran.

DIVORCE

Rates of divorce increased in Western nations during the twentieth century. The United States has one of the highest divorce rates in the world (Amato and James 2010). However, the often-repeated "statistic" that half of all U.S. marriages end in divorce is inaccurate.

In 2014, the divorce rate per thousand in the United States was 3.2 (www.cdc.gov/nchs/fastats/marriage-divorce.htm). The once dramatic differences in divorce rates between the United States and Europe have declined, mostly because of increases in divorce across Europe; Europe has become more like the United States in terms of divorce. For example, "between 1971 and 2007, the crude divorce rate increased from 0.73 to 2.8 [per thousand] in Belgium, from 0.88 to 2.0 in the Netherlands, from 1.2 to 2.4 in the United Kingdom, from 0.42 to 1.2 in Greece, and from 0.32 to 0.80 in Italy" (Amato and James 2010, 3).

Factors in Divorce

Regardless of how prevalent or rare it is, divorce is the best-known way of leaving a marriage. Divorce is a formal and legal mechanism that relates to legal marriages. Many marriages end with separations that become permanent without divorce. Other intimate relationships, even those that last a long time, do not require divorce; they end as informally as they began.

Divorce is often the result of a litany of family problems—for example, violence and abuse—that may have occurred over a long period of time before a divorce was ever contemplated, let alone takes place. Divorce itself can be seen as a problem, as well as one that creates many other problems, but it also can be seen as a solution to many problems. Divorce allows a spouse to get out of a bad, even disastrous, relationship. In fact, to some, it is the relationship, especially a "bad" marriage, that is the problem and not the divorce. Thus, we should not simply assume—as many do—that divorce is in itself a problem.

An important factor in divorce today in the United States, and in the Global North in general, is the increasing emphasis on the self and individualism. This is also linked to the idea of the pure relationship discussed previously. As we have seen, in such a relationship, including a marital relationship, the partners do not necessarily feel that they are locked into it for a lifetime, or even an extended period of time. Rather, they feel that they are in a relationship as long as it continues to work for *them*. Once individuals come to the conclusion that the relationship is no longer working for them, they are free to leave. Indeed, some take the view that they have an obligation to themselves to leave because they should not jeopardize their own need to have a satisfying life.

In the past, there was a tendency to value positively all marriages that remained intact—that did not end in divorce or in other ways. In many ways, a bad marriage can be a far greater problem than one that ends in divorce. For example, children in unhappily married families tend to feel highly neglected and humiliated (Kimmel 2012, 179). As acceptance of divorce has spread, the negative attitudes and social sanctions aimed at those who divorce have declined. Thus, remarried adults are more accepting of divorce and more likely to take steps toward it when experiencing marital distress than are those in first marriages. This indicates a weaker commitment to marriage among those married more than once (Whitton et al. 2013).

ASK YOURSELF

What are some of the reasons why divorce has become more socially acceptable? What specific norms and values about individuals, families, and the institution of marriage have changed to make this acceptance possible? Do you think the increase in the number of divorces has had an impact on society at large? If so, what sort of impact?

Not only have negative attitudes, norms, and values as they relate to divorce declined, but the material circumstances and barriers surrounding divorce have declined as well. Of prime importance is the fact that women today are likely to be better equipped materially to handle divorce than were women in the past. Among other things, they are better educated and more likely to be in the labor force. Thus, they may be more willing to seek divorce because they can better afford to be on their own. Furthermore, dissatisfied husbands are more likely to leave their marriages when they know that their wives can not only survive economically without them but will be financially independent after divorce. Changes in the law are another important material factor that has followed from changes in the norms and values that relate to divorce. One important example is no-fault divorce (i.e., where there is no need to show that either party has been guilty of wrongdoing), which not only has made it

As negative attitudes toward divorce have declined, many of the barriers to divorce have eased.

easier for people to divorce but also seems to be associated with an increase in the divorce rate. No-fault divorce laws have also acted on the larger culture, helping it become even more accepting of divorce.

A long list of risk factors has been associated with the likelihood of divorce, including having relatively little education; marrying as a teenager, whether or not the couple cohabited before marriage; poverty; having divorced parents; infidelity; alcohol or drug abuse; mismanaged finances; and domestic violence. The reasons for divorce in Europe are very similar to those found in the United States. In terms of the nature of the relationship, marriages are more likely to be stable, and less likely to end in divorce, when couples handle their disagreements and anger well, such as by having a sense of humor about disagreements. Conversely, divorce is more likely when couples are contemptuous of or belligerent toward each other or react defensively to disagreements (Gottman et al. 1998; Hetherington 2003). In one recent study, the two most common reasons for divorce were found to be "growing apart" and "not able to talk to one another" (Hawkins, Willoughby, and Doherty 2012).

✓ CHECKPOINT 12.4: **FACTORS IN DIVORCE**

FACTOR	DESCRIPTION
Deinstitutionalization of marriage	The social norms associated with marriage have weakened.
Domestic violence	The exertion of power over a partner in an intimate relationship.
Pure relationship	Emphasis on individual satisfaction within a relationship makes long-term commitments more flexible.
Increasing status of women	Educational attainment and labor market participation by women provides financial security independent of a spouse.

GLOBAL FAMILIES

Just as the nation-state is eroding in the face of globalization, it could be argued that the traditional family, deeply embedded in a national context, is also declining. It is no longer necessary for family members, especially those who are relatively well off, to live in the same country, have the same passport, be of the same ethnicity, or share a household in a given locale. Characteristics that used to separate people and made creating global families difficult or impossible are less important in the global age. National hostilities, religious differences, and even great geographic distances matter less to family formation today than they did in the past (Beck and Beck-Gernsheim 2012).

On the one hand, this clearly makes possible, and even highly likely, a wide range of new family types and configurations. For example, it is increasingly possible for family members, even spouses, to live in different countries, even on different continents, and to function quite well as a family (Nobles 2011). Of course, this again is true for those with the means to afford such a family life—means that are well beyond the capacities of most people in the world.

On the other hand, these new realities also create many new possibilities for conflict within the family. That is, family members are now bringing to the family new and far broader stresses and strains of various types; clashes of different languages, cultures, religions, and races create new points of potential conflict and hostility. However, these differences are also likely to enrich the family, as well as the larger society, in various significant ways. As globalization increases, new hybrid forms of the family will be created, resulting in innovative and interesting differences within and between families. New combinations of, and interactions between, hybrid cultures will result in unforeseen sociological developments, such as wholly new customs and traditions. Another way of putting this is to say that global families are increasingly liquid (Bauman 2000). That is, they no longer—if they ever did—form solid and immutable structures that are impervious to outside, especially global, influences. Families are subject to global flows of all types, and they and their members are increasingly part of those global flows.

While there are great variations in family forms throughout the world, there are also great commonalities. Thus, many of the general ideas discussed throughout this chapter apply globally. It is well beyond the scope of this section to describe similarities and differences in the family throughout the world. There are sociologists who spend their entire careers doing just that—engaging in the comparative analysis of families in various societies (Goode 1963; Ingoldsby and Smith 2006; Yeh et al. 2013). Globalization on the whole is more about global flows and how these flows relate to the family than it is about comparing families across the world (Ritzer and Dean 2015). In this section, then, we will examine at least some of the global flows that involve or affect the family. It is clear that many families are actively engaged in global flows of one kind or another, and that no family is totally unaffected by those global flows (Karraker 2013; Trask 2010).

GLOBAL FLOWS THAT INVOLVE THE FAMILY

Global flows that involve the family take four major forms. First, entire families, even extended families, can move from one part of the globe to another with relative ease (assuming they have the resources to do so). They can do so on vacation, in relationship to temporary job changes, or permanently.

Second, individual family members can move to a different part of the world and then bring the rest of the family along later. It is ordinarily the case that males are those doing the initial moving. Once they are secure enough economically in their new locations, they are then able to bring over the rest of their family members. Of course, it sometimes happens that males make new lives for themselves in the new locales and leave their families behind in their countries of origin. With increasing economic independence, women are now moving first more often, and then bringing the remainder of their families over (or not). However, many women move globally into low-paying, low-status jobs—for example, as care workers—or are moved, by force, into the global sex trade. Such women are unlikely to be in a strong enough economic position to enable other family members to join them.

Third, individuals can immigrate to create new families. For example, there are many marriage bureaus in developed countries that are in the business of bringing together men from those countries with women who are usually from less developed countries. Various differences between such men and women often create enormous problems for their relationships, however. For one, there is great economic disparity between the spouses. For another, the women often come from societies that are unstable politically and economically, and this makes it difficult for them to adapt to a more stable environment. Finally, marriage bureaus often portray the women as fitting traditional gender expectations, but when they arrive, it may turn out that they do not really measure up to those expectations. Overall, these differences put females in a weak position vis-à-vis males, and they are therefore more vulnerable to abuse of various kinds.

Fourth, transnational adoptions generally involve the flow of children from less to more developed countries (Briggs 2012; Marre and Briggs 2009; Seligmann 2013). The United States is the world leader in the adoption of children from other countries, while very few American children are adopted elsewhere. Adopting a child from another part of the world transforms the family in many ways. There are

Chris and Cori Schmaus of South Dakota have adopted three children from Africa. Couples in the United States lead the world in adopting children from abroad. What do such children gain from the adoption process? What do they lose?

also various problems associated with such adoptions, such as the health risks associated with being born in, and having spent at least some time in, less developed countries. There are also stresses involved in the differences between the culture from which the children came and the culture of the country to which they are sent. This is especially a problem if the adopted children are not infants.

GLOBAL FLOWS THAT AFFECT THE FAMILY

As a liquid phenomenon in a liquid world, the global family is affected by, and affects, all the other liquid phenomena that make up the global world. We will examine just a few of them in this section.

Global Economic Flows

Families are likely to be affected in various ways by global shifts in the economy. For example, a weak economy at home and a boom in another part of the world can lead or even force family members to seek work in the locale that is booming. They are likely to be compelled to leave the rest of the family behind, at least temporarily. This movement of workers can take many forms, such as low-wage male construction workers moving from India or Bangladesh for work in Dubai, female care workers in the Philippines being drawn to Singapore to care for young children, or mostly male workers from between 75 and 90 countries who are drawn to the many low-status, often seasonal jobs available

in the American cruise line industry (Oyogoa 2016). In such cases, families can be broken up for long periods at a time, and the stress of those periods can have permanent negative effects on the marriage, as well as on the children. This has been reduced somewhat in the contemporary world of cell phones, the internet, and social networking, which help maintain family relationships or at least reduce the possibility of them fraying or breaking.

Global Migration

The global family is affected by population flows of various kinds. Of utmost importance is the high rate of global migration (Castles 2013), both legal and illegal (see Chapter 17). Among other things, this means that very different people from very different parts of the world are coming together in greater numbers than ever before. Some will settle and marry in diasporic communities composed of people like them; many others will not. Those who do not are likely to create families with mates who are very different from themselves in terms of place of origin, race, ethnicity, religion, and the like (Qian and Lichter 2011). As you recently learned, those entering hybrid families are likely to encounter various difficulties and hostilities. Such problems are likely to be greatest for undocumented immigrants, whose family problems are compounded by the fact that they are in the country illegally. This became a major issue during the 2016 U.S. presidential campaign, when then Republican candidate Donald Trump threatened, if elected, to deport the approximately 11 million undocumented immigrants in the United States and their children, many of whom were born in the country and are therefore U.S. citizens. It remains to be seen whether—and, if he does, in what ways—President Trump will implement this campaign promise.

Global Trafficking

Human trafficking involves selling and buying humans as products. It is likely to affect the family in many ways (Jakobi 2012). Children are sometimes trafficked for the purpose of illegal adoption. As with legal adoption, the children generally flow from poor, weak countries to those that are rich and powerful. Recall from Chapter 11 that women are trafficked for purposes of prostitution and forced marriage, both of which have the potential to disrupt family life. Then there is the illegal global traffic in human organs. People in developed countries who need organ transplants but cannot

The Role of Cuban Families in Improving U.S.–Cuban Relations

In mid-2015, the United States and Cuba restored diplomatic relations between the two countries. This restoration of ties marked another step on a long political road greatly influenced by the Cuban families who sought refuge in the United States after upheaval in their home country.

A communist regime headed by Fidel Castro took power in Cuba in 1959; the United States subsequently placed an embargo on Cuba in 1962, and by 1963 all travel between the two countries was banned. A number of Cubans fled to the United States before the travel embargo; others left later, many illegally on rickety boats that cost many people their lives. Most settled in south Florida, especially in the Miami area (which has a "Little Havana" neighborhood). More than 1 million Cuban Americans live there today and represent a potent economic and political force. Many, especially the early immigrants, were middle-class and opposed to communism and the Castro regime, which seized their property and sought to redistribute their wealth more equitably among Cubans. For decades, these immigrants resisted U.S. efforts to improve relations with Cuba, but that began to change in the run-up to the 2015 agreement.

Many who fled Cuba left family members behind, and for decades it was difficult or impossible for them to visit. However, visits to Cuba by children and other family members gradually increased over the years. It was these family-based relationships rather than the hostility between the governments that, over time, proved to be the stronger force and helped lead to the formal rapprochement between Cuba and the United States. While older generations of Cubans remain hostile to the Cuban government, those who arrived after

the mid-1990s are more open to it and, more important, have an extensive web of family and friends in the country. They want to see them and stay in touch with them. It is family, not politics or ideology, that is their major motivator. One expert on Cuba argued that well before the restoration of relations, Cuban Americans were "normalizing relations one by one" (Alvarez 2011, A3).

Restrictions on shipping and travel between the two countries were loosened in 2009 under President Obama, and since then there have been no restrictions on flights by Cuban Americans to visit family members in Cuba. For its part, Cuba began allowing its citizens to own cell phones and computers, easing their ability to contact family members in the United States. Cuba also made it easier for Cubans to buy homes and businesses. As a result, Cuban Americans began sending all sorts of products to their families in Cuba, enabling them to open an array of small businesses. Furthermore, increasing amounts of money began flowing to Cuba from Cuban Americans seeking to help family members buy (and sell) property. All these changes accelerated in light of the 2015 agreement. For example, regular cruises to Cuba from Miami began in Spring 2016. Six airlines were also approved to fly between the United States and Cuba, and commercial flights began in late 2016, though by mid-2017 some of these flights had been scaled back because of a lack of demand on the part of American travelers.

These developments have not been viewed positively by all Americans, however; some in the United States (and in Cuba) would still like to limit relations between the two countries. Some Americans, especially Cuban Americans in Congress, fear that the Cuban regime, which still regards itself as communist,

Joe Raedle/Getty Images News/Getty Images

Because of the restoration of diplomatic relations between the United States and Cuba, families like this one have been reunited after many years. Such scenes may soon be repeated as relations between Cuba and the United States continue to normalize. What challenges will reunited families face? Will they be the same as or different from those that confronted the family in this photo?

will be strengthened by improved relations. As a result, the embargo on trade with Cuba remains in place. It is likely that most Cuban families in both the United States and Cuba will oppose such limitations and push for even more open relations ("Return Visit to Communist Cuba" 2015). Nevertheless, as of this writing, in mid-2017, the openness to improved relations with Cuba was being questioned by President Trump. He may push to close at least some of the openings to Cuba initiated by President Obama.

Think About It

What flows between the United States and Cuba could change as a result of the restoration of diplomatic relations between the two countries in 2015? Can the desire for family reunification overcome efforts by hard-liners in the United States and Cuba to maintain the separation between the two countries?

obtain the organs locally are better able to survive because of this traffic. Poor people in less developed countries sell organs not critical to their lives, which are then transported to developed countries and implanted into well-to-do recipients (Negri 2016; Scheper-Hughes 2001). Although the poor in less developed countries do receive some money for their organs, this is but another form of exploitation of the global poor by the global rich. It is a particularly heinous form of exploitation, because the poor must sacrifice one or more of the things that make them human in order to survive.

Global Conflict

Global conflict can affect the family in a number of ways. For one thing, family members, if not entire families, can be forced to flee, sometimes to neighboring countries or even to other parts of the world. For example, after the Vietnam War, more than 2 million people fled Indochina. Many families did not survive intact; in fact, almost 60,000 of the survivors were unaccompanied children. They often were not only traumatized, but also suffered from neglect and abuse in the camps in which they found themselves.

Another impact is the fact that it is young combatants who are the most likely to die in war. This can create a "marriage squeeze," leaving women without a sufficient number of suitable males from which to choose partners (Akers 1967; Bethmann and Kvasnicka 2013). Such a squeeze occurred in Vietnam in the 1970s and 1980s. Another has occurred in Lebanon, which has been afflicted with armed conflict for decades (Karraker 2013). Although it is not necessarily true for all wars, it has been discovered that those who served in World War II have had higher divorce rates (Pavalko and Elder 1990). Deployment of American troops in more recent wars in Iraq and Afghanistan has also been associated with higher divorce rates (Negrusa and Negrusa

2014; Negrusa, Negrusa, and Hosek 2014). It is also likely that civilians in countries that have experienced armed conflict will have higher rates of divorce.

Then there is the reality of life for military families, especially those associated with the U.S. military. Many can become "military nomads," moving from bases throughout the world over the course of their military careers (Ender 2002). While the U.S. military has put a lot of supports in place, such perpetual movement can wreak havoc on families, especially in times of deployment during warfare.

The main point is that the family today is an integral part of globalization, which it is both affecting and being affected by. There is no such thing as a typical global family; at best, there are many global families. More to the point, the people involved in today's families are part, and at the intersection, of innumerable global flows and as a result are enmeshed in constantly changing intimate relationships of all sorts. This may be as good a definition of the family as any in the global age.

✓ CHECKPOINT 12.5: THE EFFECTS OF GLOBALIZATION ON THE FAMILY

GLOBALIZATION FACTOR	DESCRIPTION
Global migration	Global moves, such as for vacation, a job change, the adoption of a child, or migration
Human trafficking	The buying and selling of humans, or human body parts, as products
Global conflict	A cause of "marriage squeeze"; leaves women with too few suitable males from which to choose partners

---

SUMMARY

The family is a crucial social institution that is central to social life. Marriage is a legal union of two people. It can involve monogamy, polygamy, or cenogamy. In an intimate relationship, partners have a close, personal, and domestic relationship with one another. Some relationships are characterized by passionate love with short-lived intimacy, while others involve long-term companionate love based on rational assessment.

Marriage has declined over the years, and so has the traditional nuclear family, which now accounts for only about

one fifth of all households. The social norms associated with marriage have weakened, resulting in a loss of institutional and companionate marriages and the growth of individualized marriages. Many households today are nonfamily households, with a single person who lives alone, or are cohabiting households, comprised of couples who are not legally married. Other contemporary households include single-parent families, blended families, and lesbian and gay families. Structural/functional theorists posit that the family is important to society because of its ability to control adult behavior and socialize children.

Conflict/critical theorists see the family primarily as a relationship involving inequality and conflict, particularly between those of different ages and genders. Inter/actionists focus on the meanings and identities associated with the family.

Five basic models of family conflict are the deficit, overload, cultural tensions, conflict-of-interest, and anomie models. Abuse and domestic violence severely affect many families, as does poverty. Gender inequality in marriages is visible in partners' decision making and power distribution, and in the different amounts of time they devote to household tasks. Some people find their lives enhanced by divorce, whereas others who divorce experience negative effects. For example, divorce tends to have an adverse economic effect on women.

Global flows that affect the family take four major forms: Entire families can move from one part of the globe to another; individual family members can move to a different part of the world and bring the rest of the family later; individuals can immigrate to create new families; and transnational adoptions can bring children from less developed to more developed countries. Global migration, trafficking, economics, and conflict all affect the global family.

KEY TERMS

blended family, 336
cenogamy, 324
cohabitation, 333
companionate love, 325
companionate marriage, 327
deinstitutionalization, 326
domestic violence, 343

endogamy, 324
exogamy, 324
extended family, 339
family, 324
family household, 333
individualized marriage, 328
institutional marriage, 327

intimacy, 325
intimate relationship, 325
marriage, 324
monogamy, 324
nonfamily household, 330
nonresident parents, 335
nuclear family, 326
passionate love, 325

polyandry, 324
polygamy, 324
polygyny, 324
pure relationship, 329
stepfamily, 336

REVIEW QUESTIONS

1. What is marriage? What are the different types of marriage?
2. What factors account for the deinstitutionalization of marriage over the past few decades?
3. What are the five basic models of family conflict? Give an example of such conflict, then apply each of the five models in turn. Which rings most true for you? Is it possible that each model applies to family conflict?
4. According to structural/functional theorists, why are families so important to society? What criticisms do conflict/critical theorists have of structural/functional theories?
5. What forms can intimate relationships take? Do you think that some forms of relationships in the United States are valued more highly than others? Do you think these values will change in the future? Why or why not?

6. Explain the growth of nonfamily and cohabiting households. Do you find either of these household arrangements more desirable than a family household? Why or why not?
7. What are the causes and consequences of divorce? What are the benefits and disadvantages of divorce?
8. What are some general conclusions sociologists have made about domestic violence? Where is there still debate concerning such violence? What are some other common problems that arise within families?
9. Many sociologists see a close relationship between family structure and poverty. What is this relationship? What role does gender play? What are some contrasting viewpoints?
10. In what ways has globalization affected the family?

EDUCATION

13

Going to the "Right" Parties on Campus

Remember your freshman year? Maybe you lived on campus, in a dorm that seemed exactly the same as every other freshman dorm. You moved in, set up your room, started getting to know your roommate, and began wondering how you would spend your evenings. Now, imagine one Friday evening early in the year, as you wandered around campus looking for a party. Pretty innocent, right? Wrong! There is a "party pathway" at colleges and universities (Armstrong and Hamilton 2013). (This chapter's Trending box on page 375 explores this further.) The path you choose—or, rather, are allowed onto—and how far you progress on it are of great importance to you and your future.

If you come from a family with money, you are likely to be invited to, and choose, the "right" path and its associated parties (at high-status fraternities). There, you are likely to make friends with others from well-to-do families and network with them in school. They are likely to become an even more important occupational network in later life. As a result, your chances of finding a good job and having a bright career are greatly enhanced. You might even meet the "right" person at such a party, who later becomes your spouse. He or she is likely to come from a family that offers access to elite career networks, as well as being the kind of spouse who is very helpful in furthering your career.

However, the situation is likely to be very different if you come from a nonprivileged family. You might not be able to enter a party pathway at all (because you need a part-time job that doesn't give you time to party), or, if you are, you are not likely to be invited to the parties at high-status fraternities, for example. The events you do attend are far less likely to bring you into contact with the right friends or the right future spouses. As a result, your party pathway is not likely to be as helpful to you in later life; it might even hinder you.

LEARNING OBJECTIVES

13.1 Apply structural/functional, conflict/critical, and inter/actionist approaches to the social institution of education.

13.2 Discuss the relationships between education and consumption.

13.3 Describe inequality in education, its sources, and its effects.

13.4 Compare the educational system in the United States to the system in other countries around the world.

edge.sagepub.com/ritzerintro4e

- Take the chapter quiz
- Review key terms with eFlashcards
- Explore multimedia links and SAGE readings

$SAGE edge™

But can't partying, especially too much partying, be a problem for all students? If you are a student from a privileged family, with the help of your parents' advice and financial support, you are likely to overcome problems that may occur as a result of your partying. On the other hand, if you come from a less well-to-do family, you are less likely to be able to overcome such problems because of your parents' comparative lack of resources.

In the end, those who are well-to-do are well served by the party system at colleges or universities, while those who are less privileged are not. Thus, the party system serves to reinforce the existing system of social stratification. Because universities, even state universities, support the party system and the fraternities and sororities that undergird it, they serve to reinforce, if not worsen, the stratification system. ●

Education is closely related to the process of socialization discussed in Chapter 5. In fact, there is no clear line between the two, because both involve the learning process. As a general rule, socialization tends to be a more informal process, while education takes place more formally in schools of various types (Zerelli 2007). Much socialization—for example, learning not to eat with one's hands—takes place largely within families in children's early years. Children also usually learn to talk and in many cases to read before they begin formal schooling. By the time most U.S. children are five years old, the focus has shifted from the highly informal process of socialization in the family to the more formal educational process in schools. Formal educational settings, such as preschools, elementary, middle, and high schools, and colleges and universities, build on and expand the base of knowledge acquired through the early socialization process. In addition, classroom rules teach children about order, respect for authority, and the benefits of conformity. In adulthood, much new learning takes place during socialization processes, such as when starting a new job, but adults also increasingly participate in adult education programs. Overall, some education takes place during socialization processes, and socialization (e.g., orientation when beginning college) occurs in educational settings.

While five years of age is the norm for starting school in the United States and other developed countries, much younger children are increasingly entering preschools. Infants as young as a few months old are being placed in daycare centers. While all schools shift the processes of socialization and education from parents to others, a number of social and educational issues arise when many two- to three-year-olds, and especially two- to three-month-olds, are turned over to schools for large portions of the day.

Of course, preschool is only the beginning of the educational process. In the United States, as in all other advanced industrial countries, education continues for many years, through grade school, middle school, high school, college, graduate school, and professional school, and even beyond in formal adult socialization programs (Kotarba 2007). Most people do not progress through all these stages, though the stage at which someone's formal education ends has profound implications for that person's future.

Clearly, educational attainment is closely related to employment and earnings. Figure 13.1 shows the correlation between educational attainment and employment and income in 2015. Individuals ages 25 and over with less than a high school diploma were almost three times more likely to be unemployed than were those with a bachelor's degree; they were almost five times more likely to be unemployed than were those with a doctorate. A person's likelihood of being unemployed decreases as he or she ascends the educational ladder.

Higher levels of education serve as a protection against unemployment, especially in hard economic times. During the Great Recession that began in late 2007, the hardest-hit segment of the population was people with less than a high school diploma. The recession's smallest negative effect was on those with doctoral and advanced professional degrees. According to the U.S. Department of Labor's Bureau of Labor Statistics (see Figure 13.1), the unemployment rate in 2015 for individuals with doctoral degrees and advanced professional degrees was nearly 2 percent. At the same time, the rate for individuals with less than a high school diploma was 8 percent, whereas it was 5 percent for people with no more than a high school diploma.

Individuals' median weekly earnings increase significantly with level of education, although there is a slight decrease for those with a doctoral degree compared to those who hold a professional degree. Those with a professional degree have the highest median weekly earnings, at $1,730, nearly four times the earnings of those without a high school degree, and almost three times the earnings of individuals with a high school degree. While there are many other measures of success in life, levels of education and earnings are obviously of great importance (Blau and Duncan 1967). Other individual benefits of having more education (Brennan, Durazzi, and Séné 2013) include being less likely to commit a crime and being better off in terms of overall health (Smith et al. 2015); those with more education are also more open politically (Bills 2007; Buchmann and Hannum 2001).

Education makes a huge difference not only at the individual level but also at the level of the nation-state. Thus, if we compare nation-states on a global basis, nations with strong educational systems and high levels of education tend to be more economically prosperous.

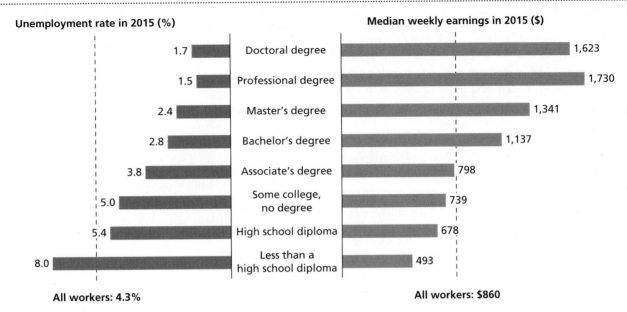

Unemployment rate in 2015 (%)		Median weekly earnings in 2015 ($)
1.7	Doctoral degree	1,623
1.5	Professional degree	1,730
2.4	Master's degree	1,341
2.8	Bachelor's degree	1,137
3.8	Associate's degree	798
5.0	Some college, no degree	739
5.4	High school diploma	678
8.0	Less than a high school diploma	493
All workers: 4.3%		**All workers: $860**

NOTE: Data are for persons age 25 and over. Earnings are for full-time wage and salary workers.
SOURCE: U.S. Department of Labor, Bureau of Labor Statistics, Employment Projections.

THINKING ABOUT EDUCATION

As is true of examinations of other institutional spheres of society, analyses of education lend themselves nicely to the broad theories that inform this book. The following sections discuss education in terms of the structural/functional, conflict/critical, and inter/actionist approaches.

STRUCTURAL/FUNCTIONAL THEORIES

The structural-functional orientation to education is traceable to one of the founders of sociology, Émile Durkheim. Durkheim was a professor of the science of education and sociology at the famous French university the Sorbonne. He felt that the task of sociology was to provide needed theory and empirical research, while the educational arena was a crucial area to which that theory and research were to be applied. Durkheim saw education as a structure concerned with the process by which an individual acquires the physical, intellectual, and moral tools needed to function in society. Thus, to Durkheim, and to later structural-functionalists, education is a structure that is functional for both individuals and society.

Durkheim on Education

Durkheim ([1925] 1973) believed that the educational system should provide individuals with two types of training.

First, schools should provide them with training for life in the broader society (Prus 2011). Each society is unique, with its own needs, and has a culture with its own moral codes, values, and norms. Durkheim hoped that schools would provide those guidelines as well as the social "glue" that would help a highly differentiated society remain normatively coherent and, in so doing, keep the levels of anomie (see Chapter 2) to a minimum.

Second, Durkheim believed that individuals need specialized training for the specific "milieus" they will occupy in life. In referring to "milieu," Durkheim was especially concerned about the many diverse occupations that were arising in modern societies. He contended that there is greater occupational specialization in highly differentiated and complex modern societies than there is in traditional societies. Durkheim believed that schools should not provide every member of society with the same type of education. Individuals need to learn the technical skills required to do their jobs well, and the complex division of labor means that a person's education should be aligned with his or her future occupational aspirations. Schools should help all workers acquire the skills they need to increase economic productivity in their occupational contexts. Durkheim also believed that schools need to socialize workers for social life within occupations so that they can more easily interact with people at work.

Durkheim argued that educational systems should differ depending on a society's particular circumstances and needs. Thus, we should expect school systems to vary by time and place. For example, Roman society sought to make all students "men of action, devoted to military glory, and indifferent to letters and the arts" (Durkheim [1922] 1956, 64). In contrast, modern society values individualism and personal autonomy, and the educational system in a modern capitalist society should teach those values to the younger generations. Durkheim noted that such an education would have harmed Roman society and failed to allow it to maintain itself.

A Later Structural-Functional Approach

Robert Dreeben (1968) provided a later structural-functional account of the role of educational institutions in socializing the young into industrial societies. Schools teach students four main values that are critically important for success in such societies. First, schools encourage independence. Children must learn that adults in the broader society are less available to them than their parents are. They must learn to function on their own. Second, schools teach children to value achievement. While families tend to accept and value each child unconditionally, a teacher's acceptance of a student often depends on successful performance in the classroom. Third, while families are particularistic and treat each child as a unique person, schools are universalistic, treating children as members of general social categories, such as "third graders," "special needs," "gifted," and "honor students." Finally, schools teach the norm of "specificity." While families think of the "whole child," schools are interested only in specific aspects of a given student. Math teachers judge students on their math skills and are uninterested in students' performance in other subjects, let alone their behavior outside the classroom. Together, the daily practices and underlying structure of schooling socialize students for life in the broader society by ensuring that they possess the values considered necessary for society to function properly.

ASK YOURSELF

Was your educational experience in elementary and high school (or the equivalent) characterized by a focus on the four values identified by Robert Dreeben? Were any of these values enforced more strongly than the others? If so, which one(s), and why? If other values were taught besides these four, what were they, and how well do they reflect the values of your community?

In sum, Durkheim and later structural-functionalists believe that school systems are at worst benign institutions and at best highly positive systems necessary to the successful functioning of society and to individual success. As we will see, conflict/critical theorists question this assumption and suggest that the educational system serves the interests of some social groups much better than others.

CONFLICT/CRITICAL THEORIES

There are two main approaches under the conflict/critical heading that have proposed very different views of the role played by education in society. However, the overarching view of both perspectives is that education serves to reproduce social inequalities and reinforces the system of social stratification. In other words, as this chapter's opening vignette shows, the education system tends to help those at or near the top and to adversely affect those at or close to the bottom of the stratification system.

Capitalist Systems and Education

The first conflict/critical perspective on education is largely inspired by Karl Marx's critique of capitalism (Anyon 2011). Marx believed that a capitalist society's dominant social institutions, including its schools, support and reproduce the capitalist system.

Working within this perspective, Bowles and Gintis (1976) argued that in order to maximize profits, capitalists must find ways to motivate their workers to work hard, even though they earn a disproportionately small share of the profits. Schools address this problem by training students to be submissive, docile, punctual, and hardworking—all of the traits that make for "good" workers in the capitalist system. As in the factory and the office, students in schools are required to show up regularly and follow a schedule; follow the orders of authority figures, such as teachers; do boring work that has little meaning; and pursue external rewards, or grades, rather than the intrinsic meaning in their work, or learning. Bowles and Gintis labeled this the "hidden curriculum" of schools. Students who display the traits of punctuality, dependability, perseverance, and consistency receive the highest grades in school.

Bowles and Gintis (1976) also recognized that some workers, such as managers, professionals, and other highly skilled workers, need different skill sets to perform their roles well in the capitalist order. It could be argued that curricular tracking arose in schools in order to deal with this problem (Cara, Cortina, and Eccles 2014). Students who were likely to attain jobs that required creativity, independence, and problem-solving skills were placed in advanced classes with an enriched curriculum that instilled these values. Oakes (2005) studied the curricular content and experiences of students in high- and low-track classes. She found support for Bowles and Gintis's theory: High-track students were exposed to a more sophisticated curriculum and were encouraged to be independent problem solvers, while low-track students were rewarded for rote learning, conformity, and docility.

Willis (1977; McGrew 2011) offered a different interpretation of how the capitalist system reproduces the economic order. He studied working-class students—"lads"—in Great Britain. He found that they did not passively submit to the normative climate of schools. Rather, they actively resisted attempts to make them docile and subservient to authority. The lads formed an "oppositional culture," and they openly mocked teachers and students who bought into the schooling system. Ultimately, however, by rejecting school, the lads embraced working-class culture and ended up reproducing the capitalist order by becoming factory workers like their parents. Willis highlighted the role of students as *active agents* in the process of social reproduction.

Overall, conflict/critical theorists inspired by Marx conclude that the educational system is a system of **social reproduction**, in which class relations and the capitalist order are systematically reproduced with each new generation of students.

Were you aware of the "hidden curriculum" when you were in grade school? As you think back, can you see signs of its existence in your elementary school experiences?

Industrialized Society and Education

A second conflict/critical perspective on education is largely inspired by the writings of Max Weber. Weber recognized that modern societies were becoming increasingly dependent on the rise of rationalized bureaucracies. While governmental bureaucracies had long existed, large bureaucratic organizations associated with industry were something new in Weber's day—the late 1800s and early 1900s. Formal, bureaucratized education and specialized certifications came into being largely to serve the needs of governmental and industrial bureaucracies. This was because careers in bureaucracies were not obtained, as they had been in the past, through inheritance from father to child, but rather on the basis of merit, including educational attainment.

However, Weber did not believe that the main purpose of schooling is to enhance the skills of workers in bureaucratic systems. Rather, schooling helps certain social groups exclude outsiders from entering their trades or professions, and thereby monopolize and control access to these economic positions. Schooling could become the basis for new forms of inequality. Weber referred to this process of exclusion as "closure" (Klein 2016). In short, Weber saw education as central to a status competition among groups within society. Thus, while the ideal of merit suggests the possibility of everyone having an equal chance to achieve success in the bureaucratic order, there is a darker side to merit.

Randall Collins (1979) extended this idea by focusing on the educational credentials, such as college degrees of all sorts, needed to succeed in society (Brown et al. 2014).

He examined the expansion of educational institutions in the United States from the late 1800s through the 1930s. Collins found that functionalist accounts of increased skill demands at work did not explain the growth in secondary and postsecondary schooling during that period. The growth in credentials expanded much faster than the number of jobs requiring complex skills did. According to Collins, educational expansion was due to **credentialism**—the linkage between educational degrees and high-status positions (Tholen, forthcoming). As low- and high-status groups both pursued upward mobility, Collins argued, high-status groups maintained their social position by acquiring more education and more educational credentials. Low-status groups found it more difficult to attain the same credentials as high-status groups, and therefore found it difficult to improve their social position by obtaining the higher-status and higher-paying occupations that increasingly required such credentials.

ASK YOURSELF

Do you agree that credentialism serves to solidify social statuses and justify the existence of educational systems? Why or why not?

It is important to recognize that Collins argued that there is often little substance to these "inflated" credentials. Additional schooling does not really make workers more productive. Rather, it mainly serves as a social signal to employers that an applicant is the "right" kind of person for the job. Thus, Collins believed that educational expansion driven by status competition is inherently wasteful and inefficient for society.

The master of business administration (MBA) degree is often criticized as such a "hollow" credential, and such criticism increased after the onset of the Great Recession. After all, it was people with MBAs who occupied many high-level financial and corporate positions. They had played a key role in plunging the American, and the global, economy into a deep recession. The norms and values taught in MBA programs—the emphasis on maximizing the profits of one's employer and the shareholders as well as one's own income, irrespective of costs—were key factors in overheating the economy and in the emergence of the recession. In fact, in light of the recession, many graduate schools of business began rethinking their MBA programs in order to make them less hollow—and thus to better equip MBAs to avoid producing the next catastrophic recession. Thus, considerable attention was given to expanding courses related to business ethics (Datar, Garvin, and Cullen 2010). However, in line with the view of critical theorists, it became clear within only a few years that there is powerful resistance to the expansion of ethics courses in business schools (Floyd et al. 2013). This resistance exists despite continuing evidence of the need for such courses. Students who enter business schools are often focused on materialism, power, and winning above all else. Furthermore, they are dubious about business ethics and the need to lead ethical lives (Giacalone and Promislo 2013).

The master of fine arts in creative writing (MFA-CW) has recently been described as a "useless" credential (Childress and Gerber 2015). For one thing, critics contend that students in such programs generally do not learn—that

is, they cannot be taught—to be better writers. For another, the programs do not help in the development of a professional writing career. In the terms used previously, such programs also do not help in creating "closure." That is, completing such a program does not prevent those without such degrees from becoming professional writers. Indeed, the vast majority of such writers do *not* have such advanced degrees. While it may have other functions (for example, as a symbolic resource of professional identity for those with the degree), an MFA-CW can be seen as another advanced degree that is wasteful and inefficient.

Critical theorists see education as part of the larger culture. In capitalism, that culture is seen as producing a mass culture that is administered and inauthentic (Jay 1973). The ideas associated with that culture are designed to repress, pacify, and stupefy students. In this view, education is designed to keep people in their place and not to teach them the sorts of things that might lead them to think creatively, let alone to resist or rebel (McGrew 2011).

Educational systems are also part of what critical theorists call the "knowledge industry" (Schroyer 1970). The use of the term *industry* here is meant to suggest that education is not that much different from traditional industries, such as the automobile and computer industries. This means, for example, that educational systems such as universities and research institutes have sought to extend their cultural influence throughout society and well beyond their original educational mandate. In recent years, the American educational system has become increasingly industrial, in the sense that more and more of it is characterized, and affected, by profit-making organizations (Giroux 2012). This became a scandal in 2016 when Donald Trump's candidacy for the presidency led to many revelations about his for-profit "university." Among other things, costs to already economically vulnerable students could run into the tens of thousands of dollars, the university relied on high-pressure tactics to extract that money, its instructors had few if any qualifications, and Trump himself played little or no active role in the school (Barbaro and Eder 2016). After Trump was elected, and in spite of numerous assertions over the years that he never settles lawsuits, he ended the controversy surrounding the scandal by paying the claimants $25 million in late 2016 (Eder 2016).

We will discuss several of more of these profit-making educational organizations later in this chapter, in the section on education and consumption. In addition, education,

Why have educational credentials multiplied so much faster than the jobs that require them? What does this imbalance mean for young graduates and their future careers?

like much else, has become increasingly digital, and critical theory is now being extended to that realm (see the "Digital Living" box in this chapter on massive open online courses, or MOOCs; Berry 2014).

INTER/ACTIONIST THEORIES

Symbolic interactionism tends to focus more microscopically on the school, the class, the physical setting, the interaction between teachers and students and among students, and so on (Barker, Quennerstedt, and Annerstedt 2015). One concern is how the system of patterned advantages and disadvantages discussed previously is reinforced in the classroom. This sometimes becomes an application of labeling theory (discussed in Chapter 7). In the classroom, students acquire a variety of labels, such as *good* or *bad*, or *smart* or *slow*. Such labels tend to reinforce the students' own previous experiences as well as teachers' experiences with them or what they've heard about the students. Such reinforcement serves to reproduce both positive (*good, smart*) and negative (*bad, slow*) behavior in the classroom. Students are very much aware of the labels being applied to them. They come under enormous pressure from themselves and others to live up to the expectations associated with those labels.

The classroom, especially in primary and high schools, is an "interaction order" (see Chapter 5), and the teacher has a great responsibility to maintain order in it (Way 2007). However, this involves a delicate balance—too much control can stifle the educational process, and too little can lead to chaos and little or no possibility of any meaningful learning. Student behavior can be unruly and aggressive, but it often takes much more mundane forms (such as dressing provocatively) that, nonetheless, can disrupt the class (Stebbins 1977, 45–46). This kind of seemingly trivial, everyday classroom behavior is an important issue for symbolic interactionists, as is what, if anything, teachers and peers do about it. Of course, there are far more serious discipline problems in the classroom. Examples include delinquency and gang activity, which are of great public concern, and these issues interest symbolic interactionists as well. Symbolic interactionists have also examined communication channels between school administrators and both teachers and students. They see such communication as an ongoing process of appearing transparent while actually shifting back and forth between concealing and disclosing information (Gawley 2008).

Ethnomethodologists are interested in the everyday methods that students and teachers employ to accomplish such tasks as taking exams or having discussions about current events (Baker 1997; Maynard and Marlaire 1992), or, more specifically, in putting a lived physical education curriculum into practice (Figueiredo et al. 2016). These are the kinds of things that are taken for granted by most people, including most sociologists. Much of the work of ethnomethodologists who focus on education involves detailed analysis of conversations in the classroom. The key point here is that ethnomethodologists refuse to treat students as **cultural dopes**, that is, as being controlled unthinkingly by a variety of external forces, such as school rules or teacher demands. Rather, these researchers view students—and teachers—as being actively and thoughtfully involved in accomplishing discussions of, for example, current events. The ethnomethodologist must attend to what the students say and do in the classroom. In fact, in a real sense, what students and teachers say and do in the classroom *is* the class. For ethnomethodologists, this is the topic of study, whereas structural/functionalists and conflict/critical theorists tend to see what transpires in the classroom as being determined largely by such structural forces as the structure of the classroom, the school, and the educational system as a whole.

CHECKPOINT 13.1: APPLYING SOCIOLOGICAL THEORIES TO EDUCATION

THEORY	MAJOR HYPOTHESIS ABOUT EDUCATION
Structural/ functional theory	Education should provide individuals with training for life in the broader society and specialized training for the specific occupation each person will occupy.
Conflict/ critical theory	Schools support and reproduce the capitalist system by training students to be submissive and hardworking.
Inter/actionist theory	Schools confer labels that reinforce and reproduce students' earlier behavior.

EDUCATION AND CONSUMPTION

In the broadest sense, students have always been consumers of education. What is different today is the emergence of an all-encompassing consumer society, as well as the increasing commercialization of education (T. Norris 2011a). Although students have always consumed education, they have not always done so in ways that yield profits to commercial enterprises.

Education takes place in various societies where consumption is pervasive. American society is the prime example. Consumption is not restricted to obvious places like the shopping mall, the supermarket, and the fast-food restaurant, but is manifest throughout society. Students are deeply immersed in that society and can't help but bring its ethos into the educational setting. At the college level, education, or at least the degree, is increasingly seen by students as a product to be purchased and consumed. As with most consumption, the emphasis is on evaluating educational alternatives to find the one that promises the greatest return for the least amount of money. Parents who are likely to foot the bill for most college expenses are especially oriented toward looking at college education from a cost-benefit perspective.

For their part, colleges and universities increasingly look and function like commercial establishments (Singer 2011). This is clearest in the football and basketball stadia at major universities, which resemble the ones in which professional teams play. They are also often named after big businesses, which not only pay for the "naming rights" but also foot the bill for part of the costs associated with the facilities. Then there is corporate sponsorship of college—and even large high school—athletic teams (by, for example, Nike and Under Armour) as well as of major tournaments, such as the NCAA basketball tournament (Eder 2014). Dorms increasingly look like hotels. And student unions are hard to differentiate from shopping malls, especially the food courts, which offer the same array of fast food purveyors to be found in the malls themselves (Ritzer 2010b, 126). There are also credit cards associated with given colleges and universities, and some schools award exclusive licenses to corporations such as Visa and MasterCard. Similar licenses are awarded to soft-drink companies such as Coke and Pepsi, and in some cases the only soft drinks available on campus are those of the company awarded the license. While a more traditional view of the university continues to coexist with this commercial view, the trend is strongly in the commercial direction (Kleinman and Osley-Thomas 2016).

Beyond the commercial pressures in traditional, nonprofit colleges and universities, there has been, at least until recently, an increase in explicitly for-profit colleges, such as the already mentioned Trump University, as well as much more broadly by corporate-run colleges such as the University of Phoenix, the largest for-profit university in the United States. However, the number of University of Phoenix students has dropped precipitously, from a high of about 600,000 in 2010 to about 155,000 today.

The University of Phoenix was purchased by the Apollo Group—a group of investors and a private equity firm—for $1.1 billion in early 2016. The sale to Apollo Group was a kind of "fire sale" because of the university's enormous drop in students. This drop and the low sale price were, in turn, the result of the many allegations of corruption against the University of Phoenix, as well as other for-profit colleges. Such allegations included lying about job placement rates, "shady recruiting, deceptive advertising . . . questionable financial aid practices," and a propensity to prey "upon veterans and low-income students, saddling them with outsize student loan debt and subpar instruction" (Cohen and Bray 2016). Students at for-profit colleges often end up deeply in debt, and their degrees, while much more expensive than those from community colleges, tend to lead to lower-paying jobs and greater unemployment. Thus, after a meteoric rise (the number of bachelor's degrees from such schools septupled between 1990 and 2010), for-profit colleges have experienced a similarly dramatic fall. In fact, in May 2015, the second largest for-profit—Corinthian Colleges—went bankrupt (Surowiecki 2015).

These institutions have relied on the easy availability of federally subsidized student loans and generally operate with open admissions policies. Critics complain that many of the students brought into these institutions are not adequately prepared for higher education. This fact is borne out by the high attrition rate and, linked to it, the high rate of default on student loans. As shown in Figure 13.2, the student loan default rate for private for-profit colleges was 15 percent in 2013, compared with 11 percent for public institutions and only 7 percent for private nonprofits. Part of the reason for this is that students emerge from for-profit colleges with poor career prospects and almost twice as much debt as do those who attend private colleges (Mettler 2014).

FIGURE 13.2 • Student Loan Default Rates at Postsecondary Institutions, 2013

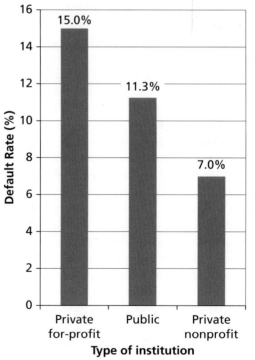

NOTE: Default occurs when a borrower fails to make a payment for 270 days.

SOURCE: Data from Office of Federal Student Aid, Comparison of FY 2013 Official National Cohort Default Rates to Prior Two Official Cohort Default Rates.

For-profit colleges were dealt a serious blow with the Obama administration's 2016 "gainful employment" regulations. The federal government wanted to reduce its involvement in educational programs that did not lead to good jobs. This was a result of the conclusion that billions of government money was being spent on education, especially at for-profit colleges, with little payoff for the students in terms of their ability to graduate, leave school with manageable levels of debt, and find decent-paying jobs. It remains to be seen how these regulative changes will play out in the years to come, but it seems clear that unless for-profit colleges are dramatically restructured, they face a problematic future. However, if there is money to be earned, businesses are likely to find a way to resuscitate for-profit colleges.

Problematic, if not fake, for-profit colleges are not easy to control, especially those that exist online and are headquartered outside of the United States (see the "Digital Living" box on the digital revolution in education on page 362). A scandal arose in mid-2015 when it was revealed that a Pakistan-based company—Axact—was selling fake degrees from elegant-sounding but nonexistent universities (Walsh 2015). Its videos featured professors boasting that they were part of a highly renowned faculty, but the "professors" were actually paid actors. The day after the sham was reported, Pakistani officials raided the offices of Axact and shut down the company's offices (Imtiaz and Walsh 2015). This doesn't help those who paid large sums of money for useless phony degrees, and it is likely that other companies will take Axact's place in the global market for online education and educational credentials.

Then there are corporations such as Kaplan and Sylvan that run for-profit learning centers. They perform a variety of educational functions, such as tutoring children with problems in school. However, their big moneymakers are the courses that prepare students for such national tests as the SAT.

Perhaps of greater importance is the increasing intrusion of profit-making corporations into traditional public grade and high schools. This accelerated after the Great Recession as a funding crisis hit schools and they grew desperate for funds. Corporations were willing to fill the economic void, at least in part, as long as they could use the opportunity to advertise their products in the schools. For example, one local retailer of high-tech products donated computers to some schools in the Toronto school system. In return, the retailer required the schools to repaint classrooms in the colors and patterns of its logo. In addition, the only schools that received computers were those within shopping distance of one of the retailer's stores (T. Norris 2011b).

The best-known example of the intrusion of commercialization into education is Channel One News, a corporation that donates video and other communications equipment to public middle and high schools, a reach of about 5 million students, in return for the right to broadcast programming in the schools. The programming consists of news stories interspersed with commercials, and students are often unable to differentiate between the two. Furthermore, because the commercials are being shown in a school setting, they are seen as more credible than when they are viewed outside the school setting (T. Norris 2011a, 2011b). In many ways, schools are becoming just another setting dominated by the media and infused with consumer culture.

CHECKPOINT 13.2: EDUCATION AND CONSUMPTION

SOCIAL ISSUES IN EDUCATION TODAY

Education today is seen as a product to be purchased and consumed.

Like any other product, education is being evaluated based on what provides the greatest return for the lowest cost.

Digital education offers customized and mobile learning in settings other than schools, but can also result in widening of the digital divide.

INEQUALITY IN EDUCATION

A **meritocracy** is a system based on a dominant ideology involving the widely shared belief that all people have an equal chance of succeeding economically based on their hard work and skills (see Chapter 4). A meritocratic social system also requires that people's social origins, such as class background, and ascribed characteristics, such as race and gender, be unrelated to their opportunities to move up in the social system. Education is a centrally important institution in a meritocracy, because it has the potential to level the playing field and provide equal opportunities for students to learn, work hard, and compete to move up in the social hierarchy.

Structural/functionalists see meritocracy as a positive development because society benefits from having the most important positions filled by the most hardworking, skilled, and capable individuals. Conflict/critical theorists argue that within a meritocracy, advantaged groups are able to secure better opportunities for their children and thereby reproduce their social and economic status across generations (Au 2013).

WHO SUCCEEDS IN SCHOOL?

In a meritocratic society, we would expect to find that social origin and ascribed status (see Chapter 5) have little effect on how much students learn and how far they go in school.

Massive Open Online Courses (MOOCs)

In recent years, many came to believe that the future of college education in the United States and the world lay in the expansion of online education, especially massive open online courses, or MOOCs (Heller 2013). MOOCs

- Are designed to enroll *massive* numbers of students
- Are *open* to anyone
- Are offered only *online*
- Are *courses* designed to educate

In 2011, three Stanford University MOOCs each enrolled more than 100,000 students, from nearly every country in the world. By 2012, a corporation named Coursera had enrolled more than 2 million students in its MOOCs. Corporations such as Udacity and edX joined the trend, and a number of universities explored this new educational frontier as well.

A driving force in the MOOC craze was the fact that many traditional college classes were overcrowded, too large to be taught well, or closed to many students who needed to take them. Even more important was the increasing cost of traditional higher education; MOOCs

are able to reach far more students at a much lower cost (a single instructor can teach 100,000 students or more).

One MOOC begun in 2012 was an Introduction to Sociology course taught by Professor Mitch Duneier at Princeton University and offered to approximately 40,000 students worldwide on Coursera (Lewin 2012). However, like many others, Duneier has become disillusioned with MOOCs; he has ceased teaching his course, at least for the time being. He expressed concern about taking students away from economically hard-pressed state colleges, contributing to reduced funding for these colleges, and costing their teachers their jobs. He also commented on the questionable pedagogical quality of MOOCs (Parry 2013).

Disillusionment with MOOCs is also based on the low completion rates of those who enroll (Lewin 2014). Further, MOOCs have not served to democratize education. The vast majority of students enrolled in MOOCs in two universities in the United States, as well as in universities in several other countries, were *not* those who lacked access to higher education, but rather those who already had college degrees (Selingo 2014).

Finally, while MOOCs are currently free, this is not a sustainable business model. How to collect fees and what to charge remain unanswered questions (Lewin 2013). A survey of more than 2,800 academic leaders asking whether MOOCs represent a sustainable way to offer courses revealed that in 2012, 28 percent of respondents believed that MOOCs were sustainable, while 26 percent thought they were not. Two years later, only 16 percent believed that MOOCs were sustainable, while the proportion who thought they were not had nearly doubled, to 51 percent (Babson Survey Research Group 2015).

It is not time to write an obituary for MOOCs, but they certainly need to be rethought. Given the huge and growing importance of the internet, it is difficult to believe that education, including higher education, will not be a significant part of the online world.

Engaging the Digital World

Do you think that MOOCs have a future in higher education? Would you ever enroll in one? What do you think would be the strengths and weaknesses of a MOOC compared to a traditional college course?

However, there is a clear pattern of inequality in the United States that suggests that our educational system is not meritocratic. Students with the highest reading and math scores at the end of high school are those whose parents have the most education. The same pattern is evident if we look at family income and parental occupational status. In terms of race/ethnicity, we see in Figure 13.3 that Asian and white students, both male and female, are more likely than black or Hispanic students to complete high school and attain either a bachelor's or master's degree, or higher. Looking at sex differences in the figure, we see that females generally have better high school completion rates than their male

counterparts and are more likely to obtain a bachelor's or master's degree (or higher).

Clearly, social origins and ascribed characteristics (race, gender) are strongly related to educational outcomes. To many observers, this suggests that American society is decidedly unmeritocratic.

THE COLEMAN REPORT: HOW MUCH DO SCHOOLS MATTER?

The first large-scale study of American schools was conducted in the 1960s by James Coleman. Coleman's study

The Globalization of Education

Education has long seen global exchanges, often in the form of a semester of study abroad or school-organized cultural trips overseas, but over the last several decades, education has become increasingly globalized. First, American college students are increasingly spending part of their undergraduate years overseas. This goes well beyond the traditional junior year abroad. The most extreme version of this is offered by Minerva Schools at Keck Graduate Institute, where students can spend as much as three-quarters of their college years overseas (Miller 2015).

Second, many foreign students have long come to the United States to study, and some U.S. colleges are now going to great lengths to recruit them. One is Houston Community College (HCC), which has more foreign students than any other community college in the United States. Among its 56,000 students, HCC has more than 5,200 international students from more than 200 countries, including about 900 students from Vietnam, 500 from Mexico, and 200 each from Angola, Nigeria, and Kazakhstan (Fernandez 2015). This large international population is the result of an aggressive effort by community colleges to recruit students from overseas (as well as to send their own students to faraway places). The goal is to prepare students for "a global life of unpredictable velocity and volatility." Aggressive recruiting of students from overseas is fraught with problems. In some cases, the students who are actively recruited in places like India do not meet the U.S. university system's standards. Universities are increasingly seeking paying foreign students because of cuts in state funding. In the case of Western Kentucky University, it used a private recruiting company, Global Tree Overseas Consultants, and paid them

Yale University and the National University of Singapore opened an independent liberal arts college in Singapore in 2012. The small first graduating class included students from more than 25 countries.

a commission of roughly $2,000 per student. Some of these students are subjected to high-pressure sales tactics, such as online postings that say such things as "hurry up," "spot admissions," and "letter in one day" (Saul 2016).

Third, U.S. universities have long been active overseas, but many now have constructed branch campuses in other countries (Clotfelter 2010; Lewin 2008a, 2008b, 2008c; Sutton 2014), including China, India, Singapore, and especially the nations of the Persian Gulf area. Why the Persian Gulf? Nations in that region are awash in oil revenues and can afford to host such educational centers and to pay for many students to attend them. For example, the president of New York University was led to create a branch campus in Abu Dhabi by a $50 million gift from that country's government. Education City has developed in Doha, Qatar. Local students there are able to study at branch campuses of leading institutions, such as Weill Medical College of

Cornell University, Georgetown, Carnegie Mellon, Virginia Commonwealth, and Texas A&M. U.S. universities are becoming *global universities*, with faculty and students traveling to their various branches around the globe.

An obvious question is to what degree these international campuses will reflect U.S. culture or the cultures of the host nations. Yale University has created a joint venture, Yale–National University of Singapore College (Yale–NUS College), with the National University of Singapore. It began accepting students in 2012. Critics, including some Yale faculty, have questioned the institution's commitment to freedom and equality, because this alliance was established in a city-state known for its excessive control over people and institutions. Like all students in Singapore, students at Yale–NUS are prohibited from engaging in any kind of protest movement (Gooch 2012). NYU's Abu Dhabi campus created a controversy when reports revealed that the immigrant laborers who built it were treated cruelly, underpaid, and forced into substandard housing (Kaminer and O'Driscoll 2014).

Then there is the issue of whether campuses like these are really exposing students to other cultures. The campuses are relatively self-contained and tend to reflect the hyperefficient, hyperrationalized culture of the United States in general, and of U.S. education in particular, rather than local culture. To the degree that students are exposed to the local culture, it is likely to be a simulated version (see Chapter 2; Daley 2011).

A variety of other issues have been raised as well. Is it in the United States'

interest to export its educational systems? Some believe that training people in other nations will adversely affect the ability of the United States to compete globally. Will these transplanted universities attract hostility as simply a new version of U.S. imperialism? Finally, what will happen to these campuses if, for example, Abu Dhabi falls to a radical Islamic regime hostile to the United States and the Global North in general?

Think About It

What benefits might you, as a local student, gain from foreign students

attending your university? Do you think education abroad is a desirable college experience? Why or why not? Do you think the extension of U.S. universities abroad is overall a positive or a negative development for the societies in which they are opening? Why? Is the cultural and informational flow that these campus branches represent good or bad for the United States? Why? Would you welcome the arrival of an extension of, say, Oxford or Cambridge University or the Sorbonne in your state? What about Cairo University, or Qatar University? Why or why not?

---

was commissioned by the U.S. Congress, and everyone anticipated that the findings would support the conventional wisdom of the time: Differences in student learning reflect inequalities in school quality. Coleman's findings, published in what has become known as the Coleman Report, were a surprise, and they changed the way that sociologists understand educational inequality. They led to a rethinking of the assumption that

educational institutions can create equal opportunities that will overcome existing class and racial inequalities in the larger society.

First, Coleman (1966) estimated how much schools differ in "quality." He collected data on teachers' salaries, teacher quality, the number of books in the library, the age of school buildings, the curriculum, and numerous other features of schools. On average, schools were much more similar in these respects than was commonly believed. Subsequent research has supported this finding, and reforms in the past half-century have made schools even more similar than they were when Coleman conducted his study.

Second, Coleman found few school characteristics that were related to student learning. School resources, such as per-pupil spending, the books in a library, and so on, did not predict student achievement. In terms of achievement, Coleman found that the most important school characteristics were teacher quality and the family background and racial composition of the students attending the school. Students learned more in schools with better

FIGURE 13.3 • Educational Attainment of Persons 25 to 29 Years Old, by Race/Ethnicity and Sex, 2016

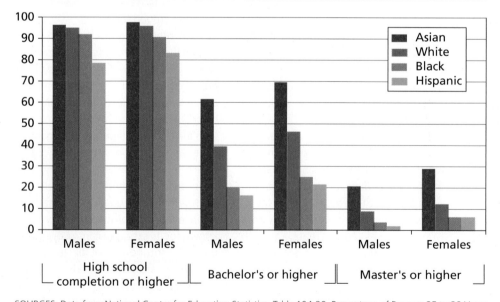

SOURCES: Data from National Center for Education Statistics, Table 104.20, Percentage of Persons 25 to 29 Years Old with Selected Levels of Educational Attainment, by Race/Ethnicity and Sex: Selected Years, 1920 through 2016.

teachers and white, middle-class peers. Finally, Coleman found that the most important predictor of student learning was a student's family background.

ASK YOURSELF

What resources—social, material, and other—does the institution of the family provide to account for Coleman's finding that family background is the most important predictor of student learning? Does it surprise you to learn that schools are very similar in terms of their physical and material features? Why or why not?

Recent research on "school effects" has generally been supportive of Coleman's conclusion that school differences in resources contribute less to educational inequality than has often been assumed. The key point is that schools play a role secondary to that of the different levels of cultural capital students bring to the classroom due to their socioeconomic backgrounds. There have been many studies of the importance of school funding for student learning, and generally the results have been mixed. Numerous studies of public–private differences in student learning have indicated at best only a small advantage in learning for Catholic high school students (Elder and Jepsen 2014), mostly due to more rigorous coursework (see Bryk, Lee, and Holland 1993; Carbonaro and Covay 2010). In elementary and middle school, public school students actually outperform private school students in math, and they do equally well in reading (Lubienski 2006).

Finally, recent large-scale surveys indicate that socioeconomic and racial and ethnic differences in student ability are sizable when children *begin* kindergarten. Furthermore, these differences can be detected when children are as young as two years of age (Aud and Hannes 2011). Clearly, schools cannot be blamed for producing educational inequalities if the inequalities are present *before students even enter school.* In short, Coleman's study and subsequent research undermine the simplistic explanation that educational inequality merely reflects unequal opportunities available to students while they are in school.

This is not to argue, as some have, that family backgrounds are determinative and schools are irrelevant. They are not. Indeed, they play a significant role. Coleman conducted his study during the height of the civil rights movement, and one of his concerns was the impact

of segregated schools. Using standardized test results, he observed that blacks did not do as well as whites did. However, he found that black students did best when they were in integrated schools rather than in predominantly black ones. Integration, in other words, was a resource just like teacher quality was. Unfortunately, efforts aimed at school integration led to massive "white flight." The integration of public schools peaked in the 1980s, and since then the nation has witnessed the resegregation of schools (Orfield 2001). For example, in 2012, African Americans and Latina/o students were in schools that were almost as segregated as they were before the seminal Supreme Court case *Brown v. Board of Education* in 1954 (Decuir-Gunby and Taliaferro 2013). Figure 13.4 shows that in Boston during the 2014–2015 school year, 77 percent of the public school student population was black and Hispanic, and only 13 percent was white. In Washington, D.C., public school enrollment was 84 percent black and Hispanic, and in Atlanta, the figure was 82 percent. In Los Angeles, where 74 percent of public school students were Hispanic, only 10 percent were white. The educational achievement gap between blacks and whites (Condron et al. 2013) narrowed between the 1960s and 1990s, but since that time it has remained basically unchanged (Camera 2016; Gamoran and Long 2006).

While it is certainly not the last word on the debate over the Coleman Report, Downey and Condron (2016) have recently made the case for a more nuanced and balanced position on the relationship between inequality and schools. That is, some inequalities might be reproduced or

FIGURE 13.4 • Racial Composition of U.S. Public Schools in Selected Cities, 2014–2015

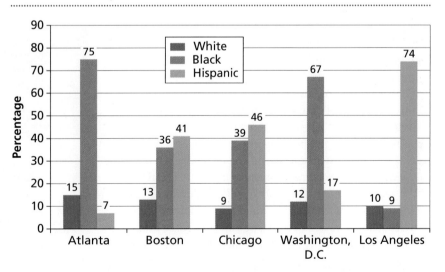

SOURCE: Data from Georgia Department of Education, Atlanta Public Schools (761), Enrollment by Ethnicity/Race, Gender and Grade Level (PK-12)—Fiscal Year 2015–3 Data Report; Boston Public Schools, Boston Public Schools at a Glance 2014–2015; Chicago Public Schools, School Data: Demographics (2015–2016 school year); District of Columbia Public Schools, DCPS at a Glance: Enrollment; Education Data Partnership, Los Angeles Unified: Demographics.

even increased by schools, but others (disparities in cognitive skill) may be reduced.

INTELLIGENCE AND SCHOOL SUCCESS

One possible explanation for Coleman's findings, and those of others, focuses on what are hypothesized as innate differences in intelligence. Richard Herrnstein and Charles Murray offered the most detailed and widely cited argument in support of this thesis in their controversial book *The Bell Curve* (1994). They argued that educational inequalities are due mostly to "natural" differences in intelligence in human populations rather than systematic differences in educational opportunities.

Herrnstein and Murray claimed that differences in learning and schooling are largely determined by differences in intelligence. In addition, they argued that differences in intelligence are largely inherited (up to 80 percent) and fixed. These two claims will be evaluated here because they are the most relevant to our discussion of meritocracy and schooling. If intelligence determines how much students learn and intelligence is largely inherited and fixed, efforts to equalize opportunities in schools are futile, and nothing much can be done to eliminate differences in student learning.

Herrnstein and Murray's claim that learning and school success are determined by intelligence is consistent with the finding that students who learn more in school have higher IQs. However, intelligence is by no means the only, or even the most important, predictor of learning. Angela Duckworth and Martin Seligman (2005; see also Duckworth and Carlson 2013) conducted a study in which students' "self-discipline," such as their work habits and perseverance, was measured and correlated with their grades at the end of the year. The researchers found that a student's self-discipline had a substantially greater impact than intelligence on that student's grades at the end of the year. These findings are consistent with both structural/functional and conflict/critical theories, which suggest that students who master the school's "hidden curriculum"—by, for example, developing the best work habits—are the most likely to be rewarded in school.

Herrnstein and Murray's claim that intelligence is largely inherited and fixed has been vigorously challenged by many researchers. Herrnstein and Murray relied on data on identical twins raised in separate families to derive their estimates of the high "heritability" of IQ. The IQs of identical twins raised in different families are almost as similar as the IQs of those who are raised in the same families. These findings suggest that intelligence is affected more strongly by a person's genes than by the family in which the person is raised.

However, several studies have raised doubts about this conclusion. First, a high percentage of adoptive families are upper-middle-class; almost none are lower-class (Stoolmiller 1999). In addition, adoptive family environments are much more similar than those of nonadoptive families. Thus, twins reared apart by different adoptive families are likely raised in very similar family environments. This makes it unsurprising that they have similar IQs. Second, a French study examining IQs among children adopted into upper- and lower-class families found that being born to upper-class parents boosted a child's IQ by about 12 points (Capron and Duyme 1989). However, being adopted by and raised in an upper-class family also raised a child's IQ by 12 points. Finally, scores on intelligence tests have increased dramatically in many nations in the past 50 years (J. Flynn 2007; Lynn 2013). Such dramatic increases in intelligence across generations in so short a time are inconsistent with the claim that intelligence is largely genetically determined and fixed. Most recently, Conley and Dominique (2016) have concluded that while genetics can predict educational attainment, there is little evidence to support the view that our population is becoming increasingly genetically stratified.

Especially troubling were Herrnstein and Murray's conclusions about racial differences, and it was precisely these findings that made *The Bell Curve* so controversial. Herrnstein and Murray claimed that whites had discernibly higher intelligence levels than blacks and Latinos (interestingly, Asians had the highest ranking). Their research has been subjected to rigorous analyses by numerous social scientists, who have found that Herrnstein and Murray's conclusions were based on a number of methodological and interpretive errors. The consensus of the social scientific community, including Conley and Dominique (2016), is that there are no grounds for contending that there are innate intelligence differences along racial lines (Fischer et al. 1996).

Students who learn more may have higher IQs, but even more important to their academic success are their solid work habits, self-discipline, and perseverance, as well as mastery of the "hidden curriculum." How do these conclusions reflect the propositions of structural/functional and conflict/critical theories?

CLASS DIFFERENCES IN EARLY CHILDHOOD

If both school-based and "natural" explanations of educational inequality fail, what remains? Many social scientists have turned their attention to inequalities in children's earliest experiences—the home environment. Betty Hart and Todd Risley (1995) did a fascinating in-depth study of 42 families with children. Each child studied was seven to nine months old when the study began. The researchers visited each family once every month until the children were three years old. For each hour-long visit, Hart and Risley recorded every spoken word and took notes on what happened. They found that the three types of families in their study—professional, working-class, and welfare—differed markedly in how they spoke to and interacted with the children. By the time the children were three years of age, there were massive differences in the numbers of words that had been addressed to them among these different families: 35 million words in professional families, 20 million in working-class families, and fewer than 10 million in welfare families. Hart and Risley also found that children in professional families experienced the most encouragement and fewest discouragements by their parents, as well as the greatest diversity in language. In terms of interaction styles, parents in professional families tended to use questions rather than commands to direct children's behavior. They were also more responsive to their children's requests.

Did these differences in home environments matter for early learning outcomes? By age three, children's exposure to differences in parenting practices and styles is highly correlated with vocabulary growth, vocabulary use, and intelligence. These effects persist when intelligence is measured at ages nine and ten. In addition, class differences in early cognitive outcomes are explained almost entirely by differences in parenting. Hart and Risley's classic study provides compelling evidence that children enter formal schooling with large differences in ability because they are exposed to very different home environments from an early age.

While the Hart and Risley study emphasized the role of the social class of the family—professional, working-class, or welfare—in learning, a recent analysis emphasized not social class but the quality and nature of parents' educational behavior (Rindermann and Baumeister 2015). However, social class remains important, and the quality of education provided by parents is certainly related to social class.

PRESCHOOL

Can we change children's educational outcomes by changing the cognitive culture that they experience when they are very young? Several intensive preschool programs have shown impressive results. From 1962 to 1967, 123 black children whose families were living in poverty in Ypsilanti, Michigan, participated in a fascinating policy experiment (Heckman et al. 2010; Schweinhart, Barnett, and Belfield 2005). Half of the children were assigned to an enriched preschool program (High/Scope Perry Preschool), while the other half—the control group—received no preschooling (Stoolmiller 1999). By the time the program ended, children who had attended the Perry Preschool program for two years were experiencing larger gains in intelligence than the control group. However, this IQ advantage faded only a few years after the program ended. The Perry students performed better in school because they were more motivated to learn. Researchers followed these two groups of students well into adulthood (age 40) and found that the Perry students did substantially better as adults than did members of the control group. The Perry students were more likely to finish high school and college and to hold steady jobs, and they had higher earnings than the control group. Those in the control group were more likely to be arrested, to use public assistance, and to have out-of-wedlock children.

James Heckman (2006) has estimated that in the long run, every dollar spent on the Perry Preschool program saved $7 in tax revenue. Because the differences in cognitive ability between the two groups were negligible, he attributed the success enjoyed by Perry students as adults to the better social skills they learned in preschool.

ASK YOURSELF

How strong do you think the connection is between social skills learned in preschool and adult success? Why? What advice would you give educational policy makers based on your conclusions?

SEASONAL LEARNING AND CLASS DIFFERENCES IN ACHIEVEMENT

Differences in early childhood experiences explain why socioeconomic and racial and ethnic differences are present when children enter school. However, achievement gaps grow larger as children progress through school. This pattern suggests that unequal learning opportunities in school are important factors driving educational inequality. One method of examining the role of schools in producing educational inequality is to measure learning gains during the school year and then compare them with learning gains during the summer, when students are not in school.

Entwisle, Alexander, and Olson (1998) studied children in the Baltimore school system. They tested the children at the beginning and end of each school year in grades K through 5. Students clearly learned at a faster rate during the school year than they did during the summer. Students who were high or low in socioeconomic status (SES) learned at roughly *the same* rate during the school year. In contrast, during the summer, high-SES students kept learning, while low-SES students did not. When Entwisle and colleagues compared school-year and summer gains from kindergarten through fifth grade, they found that virtually all of the growth in the SES gap in learning occurred during the summer. Downey, von Hippel, and Broh (2004) found that the SES gap grows three times faster during the summer than it does during the school year. Alexander, Entwisle, and Olson (2007) found that summer learning has a variety of long-term effects, such as whether or not students are placed in college preparatory tracks, complete high school, or attend four-year colleges.

Why do high-SES students learn more during the summer than low-SES students do? To explain this pattern, Alexander and colleagues (2007) offer the metaphor of schooling as a faucet. When school is in session, the faucet is open for both high- and low-SES students, and differences in family backgrounds matter little for student learning. However, during the summer, the school spigot is turned off, and inequalities in family resources become much more important for student learning. High-SES students attend summer camp, visit the library, take educational summer vacations, and have many more educational resources in the home. Low-SES families provide far fewer resources for their children during the summer. Consequently, they have fewer opportunities to reinforce or expand upon learning gains from the school year.

Research on seasonal learning affirms the power of schooling to compensate for differences in family backgrounds and to act as an "equalizer" that actually reduces educational inequality (Downey et al. 2004). Coleman was correct in concluding that differences among schools, or "school effects," play a small role in generating educational inequality. However, that conclusion does not mean that schools are unimportant for student outcomes. Indeed, schools reduce inequality in student outcomes because school environments are much more similar than family environments.

INEQUALITY WITHIN SCHOOLS: TRACKING AND STUDENT OUTCOMES

Many studies have examined whether students who attend the same school receive similar learning opportunities. It is common at all levels of schooling in the United States to group students by ability, which is typically measured by standardized test scores and/or grades. This is commonly known as *tracking*. Barr and Dreeben (1983) examined first-grade reading groups in which students were grouped by their reading abilities at the beginning of the year. Students in higher-ability groups learned more new words and improved their reading skills more rapidly than did students in low-ability groups. Better readers were placed in high-ability groups at the beginning of the year. They received

more instructional time, were exposed to more new words, and experienced a faster pace of instruction than students placed in low-ability groups. In short, higher-performing students received more learning opportunities than did lower-performing students. Consequently, the gap between high- and low-achieving students grew larger during the year. This process is known as **cumulative advantage**—the most advantaged individuals are awarded the best opportunities, and this increases inequality over time (DiPrete et al. 2006).

ASK YOURSELF

Does the practice of educational tracking tend to support the conflict/critical view of education as a system of social reproduction? Why or why not?

As students progress through middle and secondary school, curricular differentiation takes the form of different classes with different content. Traditionally, these curricular tracks are aligned with students' future ambitions: The "high" track entails coursework that prepares students for four-year colleges and professional careers, and the "low" track focuses on basic and/or vocational skills for semi-skilled occupations that do not require a college degree. Research consistently finds that high-track classes offer better learning opportunities to students because they are taught by more experienced, higher-quality teachers who have higher expectations of their students (Kelly 2004). Higher-track classes cover more material, and students receive higher-quality instruction (Gamoran et al. 1995). Students in high-track classes are more engaged and exert greater effort in school (Carbonaro 2005), which also helps them learn at a faster rate. Research consistently shows that otherwise similar students learn more when placed in a higher-track class because of higher expectations (Karlson 2015), greater effort, and better learning opportunities. Ultimately, high-track students are more likely to attend college than are low-track students.

What determines how students are assigned to different ability groups, tracks, and classes? In a meritocracy, achieved characteristics—hard work and prior academic success—should determine which students have access to high-track classes. Most studies show that prior achievement and grades are indeed the most important predictors of track placement. Because students from high-SES families are more likely to be high achievers, they are much more likely than low-SES students to take high-track classes. However, when students with the same test scores and grades are compared, students from higher-SES families are still more likely than their low-SES counterparts to be enrolled in high-track classes (Gamoran and Mare 1989). Thus, high-SES students are doubly advantaged in the track placement process.

What accounts for the SES advantage in track placement? Useem (1992) studied how families affect students' placement in middle school math classes. She found that college-educated parents had several key advantages in the placement process that ensured that their children would end up in the high-level classes. First, college-educated parents were much more knowledgeable about which classes were the most demanding and which were linked to high-level classes in high school. Indeed, some less educated parents seemed unaware that math classes were tracked. College-educated parents also better understood how the placement process worked, and they knew how to intervene successfully on their children's behalf. Second, college-educated parents were much more integrated into social networks in the school—through parent–teacher associations and volunteering, for example. They used these connections to gain information about classes and teachers in the school. Finally, college-educated parents influenced their children in selecting classes by encouraging them to challenge themselves and think about the long-term consequences of their choices.

Is religious education as relevant in the United States today as it was in the past?

ALTERNATIVES TO TRADITIONAL PUBLIC SCHOOL

Not everyone attends public schools. For one thing, elite families often send their children to private boarding schools, where they can interact with members of their own upper-class stratum and remain apart from members of other classes (Khan 2011). For another, members of some religious groups opt to send their children to parochial schools to reinforce particular worldviews. Catholics have created an extensive system of parochial schools with teaching staff made up primarily of nuns and other members of religious orders. Many immigrant Catholics prefer to send their children to parochial schools because they think this will protect the children from the undue influence of Protestantism reflected in the dominant culture and its institutions, including public schools. In both cases, families pay to send their children to these alternative institutions. In addition, after the Supreme Court's 1954 ruling in *Brown v. Board of Education,* which stated that segregation in public schools violates the U.S. Constitution, many white families either fled cities for suburbs to avoid sending their children to integrated schools or sent their children to alternative "Christian academies." All three of these alternatives continue to exist, although funding difficulties have led to the closing of many parochial schools. However, many parents are unable, or hesitant, to send their children to such alternatives because of the high costs involved.

In this general context, three other alternatives to public school have emerged in the past few decades: vouchers, unschooling and homeschooling, and charter schools. Proponents of the various alternatives have much in common with one another. First, they are highly critical of existing public schools, either for what they claim are shortcomings in educational achievement or for promoting values at odds with their particular beliefs. Regarding the latter, their stances may include opposition to the teaching of evolution, sex education, and what is seen as endorsement of gays and lesbians. Second, they view education as a commodity that customers purchase. They believe that a market must include alternative products from which savvy consumers can choose. Indeed, a hallmark of this way of thinking hinges on the concept of choice, which often takes on an ideological quality.

Vouchers

School **vouchers** are government-issued certificates that allow students to use public tax dollars to pay tuition at private schools. Parents seeking to remove their children from underperforming public schools find vouchers an attractive alternative. As of 2013, 17 U.S. states offered 33 programs relying on vouchers (Santos and Rich 2013).

Many voucher schools are religious schools. This raises constitutional issues about the separation of church and state and using public money to support religious schools. Moreover, whereas public schools are required by law to accept all students, this does not apply to private schools.

Thus, private schools are not required by law to provide special education services if they would have to make major adjustments to do so.

Proponents of school vouchers argue that voucher programs provide parents—particularly poor parents—with options (such as to avoid inadequate public schools) for their children's education that they otherwise would not have. (Betsy DeVos, confirmed as secretary of education in early 2017 under the Trump administration, is a major advocate of these vouchers [Stewart 2016].) In addition, voucher proponents' contend that under these programs, the increased competition the local public schools face from private schools stimulates them to enact changes to improve their educational programs (Figlio and Hart 2014). Opponents counter that vouchers encourage the creaming off of the best students from public schools. They question the constitutionality of voucher programs on the basis of the First Amendment (Harris, Herrington, and Albee 2007). They also express a concern that vouchers will reduce funding levels for already underfunded public schools.

There has been limited research on whether students in voucher schools do better than their counterparts remaining in public schools. In a study in Florida, a state that has been very active in promoting vouchers, Rudolfo Abella (2006) found that over a two-year period, voucher students did about as well as students remaining in public schools (the exception was math, in which they performed more poorly). This is a surprising finding, because parents are presumably using vouchers to send their children to better schools. Researchers do not have a ready reason for this disparity. One possible explanation is that because most private and parochial schools pay their teachers less than public schools do, they attract less capable teachers, especially in areas such as math and science, where demand for teachers is highest.

Unschooling and Homeschooling

The Unschool of New Haven opened its doors to high school–age students in 1971, in a rented church basement near Yale University. With start-up funding and tuition based on ability to pay, it was the brainchild of Peter Lallos, a teacher whose counterculture views led him to seek an alternate vision of education. Unschoolers believe that the educational institutions in which most of us spend many years are seriously flawed.

The Unschool's students were overwhelmingly white and middle-class. Self-styled rebels, they hated regimentation and resented the power of teachers to make all decisions about learning. At the Unschool, every student and teacher had an equal voice in which classes would be taught, by whom, and for how long. Conventional courses about contemporary U.S. literature complemented courses in yoga and alternative medicine, as well as once-only courses taught by community volunteers. Students

decided what was important to them at the moment. One who hitchhiked to a Tennessee commune and spent several months there requested course credit when he returned. As was the practice, the entire student body voted on the request, which was approved. Colleges open to alternative education programs expressed a willingness to admit Unschool graduates.

The Unschool experiment proved short-lived, ending in 1975. Unschooling was influenced by John Holt (1923–1985), who spent his early career seeking to reform the public school system. Later Holt abandoned these efforts and became a key proponent of homeschooling. The idea of unschooling remains in, among other places, the homeschooling movement, which focuses on educating children at home rather than in schools. Holt's book *Teach Your Own* (with Pat Farenga, 2003) is often called the "bible" of homeschooling. Holt warned parents not to simply take over the role of teachers, but instead to appreciate that children do not need to be coerced to learn. Contending that children are naturally inquisitive, he urged parents to let their children decide what they need to learn and when. Moreover, he argued, children know *how* to learn. One homeschooling parent who embraces this perspective has written in her blog: "We decided that Cassidy would determine what, when, where, how much and with whom he would learn. We never used school books or taught lessons. We answered his questions when he asked and helped him to gain access to the real world when he wanted it. We called it unschooling" (Shosie 2011).

The popularity of homeschooling has grown over the years (Rich 2015). About 3 percent of the U.S. school-age population was homeschooled in 2011–2012. The vast majority of these approximately 2 million children were white (68 percent). Among the minority children being homeschooled, 15 percent were Hispanic, 8 percent were black, and 4 percent were Asian or Pacific Islander (U.S. Department of Education, National Center for Education Statistics 2014). Homeschooling is also growing in many other countries (Lois 2013; Stevens 2001, 2007), but the United States has the largest percentage of school-age children currently being taught at home (Kunzman and Gaither 2013).

As shown in Table 13.1, many parents of children who are homeschooled (74 percent) are dissatisfied with the quality of the instruction offered in the public schools and believe that their children are not adequately challenged in those schools. Even more parents (91 percent) express concern about environmental factors in schools, such as safety, drugs, and negative peer pressure. However, a large number of parents homeschool their children to ensure that they receive religious (64 percent) and moral (77 percent) instruction that the parents do not think can be found outside the home and in traditional schools. Many parents (44 percent) desire a nontraditional approach to their child's

TABLE 13.1 • School-Age Children Who Were Homeschooled, Ranked by Reasons Parents Gave as Important and Most Important for Homeschooling, 2011–2012

REASON	IMPORTANT[a]		MOST IMPORTANT	
	NUMBER	PERCENTAGE	NUMBER	PERCENTAGE
A desire to provide religious instruction	692,299	64	176,338	16
A desire to provide moral instruction	831,842	77	51,210	5
A concern about the environment of other schools[b]	986,643	91	268,628	25
A dissatisfaction with academic instruction at other schools	799,336	74	204,312	19
A desire to provide a nontraditional approach to child's education	474,545	44	56,045	5
Child has a physical or mental health problem	166,878	15	50,652	5
Other reasons[c]	404,313	37	226,423	21

NOTE: Homeschooled students are school-age children (ages 5–17) in a grade equivalent to at least kindergarten and not higher than grade 12. Excludes students who were enrolled in public or private school more than 25 hours per week and students who were homeschooled only because of temporary illness.

a. Respondents could choose more than one reason.

b. Based on the response to the question, "Are you concerned about the school environment, such as safety, drugs, or negative peer pressure?"

c. Parents homeschool their children for many reasons that are often unique to their family situation. "Other reasons" parents gave for homeschooling included family time, finances, travel, and distance.

SOURCE: U.S. Department of Education, National Center for Education Statistics, Parent and Family Involvement in Education Survey of the National Household Education Surveys Program (NHES), 2012.

education. A smaller number (15 percent) opt for homeschooling because their child has a physical or mental health problem.

To avoid isolation and offer their children options that one family alone cannot offer, many families that homeschool have formed organizations. These groups arrange field trips and participate in various activities such as theater and sports. In addition, curricula and textbooks have been created specifically to meet the needs of homeschoolers. A more difficult challenge arises when parents who are homeschooling lack effective teaching skills or expertise in certain topics, such as advanced math and physics.

As the numbers of homeschooled students have risen, universities have begun to address the need to assess such students as they apply for admission. Based on standardized tests, homeschooled children may on average perform slightly better than their public school counterparts, but this is not the case in all regions of the country. Critics point to limitations in much of the research in this area, but, more important, they identify two topics that standardized tests do not address. The first has to do with whether homeschooled students have the social skills to function in a diverse society. The second raises concerns about the critical abilities of homeschooled students and whether they look at the world unreflectively, embracing their parents' worldviews.

ASK YOURSELF

Why might homeschooled children be at risk of lacking the social skills and worldviews necessary to succeed in a diverse society? Is it important for homeschooling parents to address this risk? Does your answer to this question agree with your thoughts about the connection between social skills learned in preschool and adult success (see above)? Why or why not?

Charter Schools

Charter schools entered the educational arena in 1992, but they have grown dramatically in recent years. In the 15 years between 1999 and 2014, they almost quadrupled in the United States, to well over 6,000 such schools, with about 2.5 million children (Berends 2015). Charter schools are a hybrid: They are intended to be alternatives to traditional public schools, but nevertheless they remain part of the public school system. They receive funding from public tax dollars, although they can also receive private funding. However, they are not run by the government (although they are accountable to it); they have a separate governance structure that can include parents, teachers, and community and private groups. Charter schools were intended to be schools of choice,

Andrea Forte conducts the day's math lesson with her children as part of their homeschooling. Should homeschooling be more heavily regulated by the government, or less?

alternatives for parents dissatisfied with the local public schools and interested in sending their children to schools over which they had greater control. Unlike private or parochial schools, charter schools do not charge tuition. In other words, they are publicly funded but privately operated. Unlike homeschools, charter schools employ teachers. However, one of the things that distinguishes them from mainstream public schools is that their teachers are not members of teachers' unions. The idea behind charter schools was that they would be more responsive to the concerns of parents and more accountable in terms of ensuring solid student outcomes.

Given the fact that public schools have not managed to provide students in poor communities with the education necessary to become upwardly mobile, a great deal of the interest in charter schools has revolved around assisting the poor—in particular, racial minorities living in neighborhoods characterized by concentrated poverty. These schools are granted greater autonomy than are traditional public schools. They define their own missions and establish criteria for determining whether or not they achieve their objectives. Charter schools have sponsors, and they are accountable to those sponsors and to the states in which they are located. One of the chief objectives of early proponents of charter schools was to reduce racial segregation in schools by bringing together people who shared a vision of what they wanted for their children's education. At the same time, because the traditional public schools would end up competing with charter schools, proponents argued that the traditional schools would be forced to improve in order to remain viable.

The results from a quarter-century of experience with charter schools are mixed at best (Berends 2015). For one thing, the schools have experienced managerial problems. Somewhere between 10 percent and 15 percent of charter schools have failed and closed. This has led some to propose larger-scale administrative organizations that would overcome some of the shortcomings of existing local charter management (Farrell, Wohlstetter, and Smith 2012). Second,

the evidence does not support the idea that racial segregation is being reduced by charter schools. On the contrary, it appears that the self-selection process built into the idea of choice actually increases levels of racial segregation (Garcia 2008; Roda and Wells 2013). Even in a city like Washington, D.C., where charter schools might be expected to address the problems of racial, economic, and linguistic segregation, the role of choice has resulted in the establishment of segregated schools (N. Jacobs 2013). Third, there is no clear evidence supporting the idea that charter school competition results in improved performance of traditional public schools (Silvernail and Johnson 2014; Zimmer and Buddin 2009).

But do charter schools perform better than their traditional public school alternatives do? That, after all, was the reason that they were established in the first place. Here the evidence is not particularly encouraging. A 2013 study conducted by the Center for Research on Education Outcomes at Stanford University found that charter schools are improving. But the findings reveal wide differences across states. While in some states, charter schools achieve better results than their traditional counterparts do, in other states, their results are significantly worse. Table 13.2 shows the performance of charter schools relative to that of the traditional public schools in their markets. Students in 25 percent of charter schools demonstrated significantly stronger academic growth than did their public school counterparts in reading, 56 percent were not significantly different, and 19 percent had significantly worse growth than did students in public schools. In math, 29 percent of students in charter schools had stronger academic growth than their public school counterparts, 40 percent had growth that was not significantly different, and 31 percent had growth that was significantly worse. Overall, this is a decidedly mixed picture and does not represent a clear case for or against charter schools. Berends (2015) offers a slightly more positive position. In his view, while the evidence is mixed on student achievement in charter schools, charter school students seem to do better in terms of graduating from high school and attending college.

An ethnographic study of three charter schools in California—one serving a predominantly white suburb, another a working-class Latino community, and the third an inner-city African American neighborhood—showed that they offered very different experiences. Charter schools in the wealthier community were far more capable of achieving their educational goals than were those in the two poorer neighborhoods. The charter schools in the African American community fared worst (Bancroft 2009).

THE POLITICS OF PUBLIC EDUCATION

Part of the playbook of contemporary American political campaigns calls for candidates, particularly presidential candidates, to focus on education. Calls for educational reform have been part of such campaigns for more than a

TABLE 13.2 • Academic Performance of Charter Schools Compared to Local Noncharter Schools

	READING (PERCENT)	MATH (PERCENT)
Significantly better	25	29
No significant difference	56	40
Significantly worse	19	31

SOURCE: Center for Research on Education Outcomes, Stanford University, "National Charter School Study 2013." © 2013 CREDO.

quarter of a century. As the public sector has been attacked with the mantra that government is the problem and not the solution, conservative critics have proposed various private-sector, market-based alternatives, including the three discussed previously. Although the Trump administration and Betsy DeVos are likely to ramp up these efforts, the evidence to date suggests that these alternatives have not delivered on their initial promises (Fabricant and Fine 2012).

This is not to say that choice does not benefit those who have the capital—financial, social, and cultural—to make it work to their advantage. But the goal of public education for all was that this particular institution might play a major role in leveling the playing field for all citizens. Public education was intended to serve everyone equally, and support for it was based on the idea that as citizens we are concerned not only about our own private interests (including the well-being of our own children) but also about the interests of our fellow citizens. This was the ideal of public education advanced by such influential educational philosophers as John Dewey.

Focusing solely on the private interests of individuals as consumers and taking out of the equation the role of individuals as citizens has undermined the American system of public education, creating a situation that can contribute to greater levels of inequality (Orfield and Frankenberg 2013). Diane Ravitch (2011), an astute observer of educational policies who once embraced many of these reform efforts, has concluded that the market models that shape them are mistaken. She has rejected privatization, charter schools, vouchers, the inappropriate and punitive use of standardized testing, and similar elements of the "reform" movement of recent decades. Instead, she calls for a return to the ideal advanced in earlier generations by thinkers such as Dewey.

WHO GOES TO COLLEGE?

Student learning is an important outcome of schooling, but successfully obtaining educational credentials is critically important for numerous life outcomes, such as income, occupational status, health, and well-being. Figure 13.5

FIGURE 13.5 • College Enrollment in the United States, by Income Level, 1975–2014

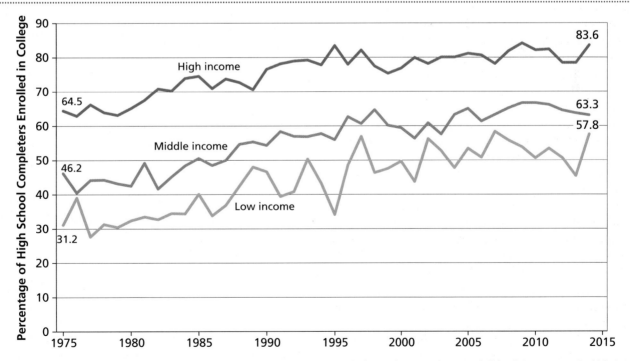

NOTE: *Low income* refers to the bottom 20 percent of all family incomes, *high income* refers to the top 20 percent of all family incomes, and *middle income* refers to the 60 percent in between.

SOURCE: Data from National Center for Education Statistics, Percentage of Recent High School Completers Enrolled in 2-Year and 4-Year Colleges, by Income Level: 1975 through 2014.

shows that students with more advantaged family backgrounds are more likely to graduate from high school and to enroll in college. Although college enrollment for students from low-income households rose from 31.2 percent in 1975 to nearly 58 percent in 2014, these students still lagged far behind middle-income students. In 2014, middle-income students were 16 percent more likely than low-income students to enroll in college, and high-income students were 26 percent more likely to enroll in college.

Family background is important not only in regard to college enrollment but also in regard to graduation from college. Studies from the 1950s through the 1980s found that students from high-income families had a greater likelihood of receiving a college degree. More recent studies, however, suggest that virtually all students—regardless of family background—want and expect to complete a college degree (Schneider and Stevenson 1999). This trend reflects a "college for all" mentality on the part of policy makers, school counselors, and the general public (Rosenbaum 2001, 2011). This is not only true in the United States; it is a global trend (Marginson 2016).

However, students from high-income families are more likely to attend and to graduate from college because they encounter a "college-going habitus" at home and in school; they learn and internalize the "rules of the game," in terms of getting into the right colleges and how to succeed in them (Lareau 2015). A **habitus** is an internalized set of preferences and dispositions that are learned through experience and social interactions in specific social contexts (Bourdieu and Passeron 1977). For example, children raised in families with highly educated parents may constantly be exposed to justifications of the importance of education in adult life. They may also hear dismissive and derogatory comments that devalue people with less education. It may become clear that education is a critical part of being accepted as a member of the group. Ultimately, children in this situation may not see the pursuit of a college degree as a "choice"; rather, they may see it as an obligation. As students experience different social contexts that correspond with their family backgrounds, they form different ideas about the importance of college and the role it plays in their lives.

CHECKPOINT 13.3: INEQUALITY IN EDUCATION

STRATIFICATION AND EDUCATION IN THE UNITED STATES

High-achieving U.S. students are those whose parents have the most education.

Black students are much less likely than white students to finish high school or graduate from college.

Hispanic students are the most disadvantaged in terms of attainment.

Women are much more likely than men to finish both high school and college.

GLOBALIZATION AND EDUCATION

We have spent much time discussing educational inequality in learning outcomes in the United States. Is the American system typical? How do other school systems around the world differ, and with what consequences?

PISA Rankings

The Program for International Student Assessment, or PISA, is a worldwide study of student educational performance (Meyer and Benavot 2013). The Organisation for Economic Co-operation and Development (OECD) created the program in 1997. Since 2000, it has measured the proficiency of 15-year-olds in reading, math, and science every three years. Critics have pointed to shortcomings in the assessment, but it remains the best comparative portrait we have today. Figure 13.6 shows the top-performing nations in 2015, when the most recent test was carried out. Students in Asian countries consistently garnered the highest scores in math, reading, and science. Especially worrisome for the United States is the fact that American students ranked toward the bottom of the list of countries—37th in math, 24th in reading, and 25th in science (for more details, see Weisenthal 2013).

Educational experts have been especially fascinated by Finland's consistently high rankings over the years and have pondered whether it may be possible to translate the lessons of the Finnish case to other countries. What does the Finnish educational system look like? First, teachers are well trained. Gaining acceptance into teacher-training programs in universities is competitive. Teachers are not extravagantly paid, but they are paid well, and the teaching profession remains highly respected. Teachers are unionized, a fact that undercuts the argument of conservatives in the United States and elsewhere that teachers' unions have been detrimental to the delivery of quality education. Indeed, there is evidence that teachers in Finland exhibit a high level of accountability, not because of imposed standards but because of their commitment to their profession.

Second, Finland has not embraced any of the policies pursued in recent decades in the United States, including charter schools, vouchers, merit pay for teachers, and evaluation of teachers and schools in terms of how well they perform on standardized tests (Ravitch 2012, 19).

Third, Finnish schools perform at remarkably similar levels. In other words, there is less variation in achievement across the educational system than there is in other countries (Sahlberg 2011). This has led educational reformer Diane Ravitch to conclude that Finland comes "closest to achieving equality of educational opportunity" (2012, 19). This commitment to equal opportunity means, among other things, that school funding is uniform and equitable. The school system reflects the larger national culture, which has been shaped for many decades by a social democratic commitment to equality and to a welfare system that promotes it.

TRENDING

Paying for the Party: How College Maintains Inequality (Harvard University Press, 2013)

Elizabeth Armstrong (Associate Professor of Sociology and Organizational Studies at the University of Michigan; PhD, University of California–Berkeley, 1998) and **Laura Hamilton** (Associate Professor of Sociology at the University of California–Merced; PhD, University of Indiana, 2010)

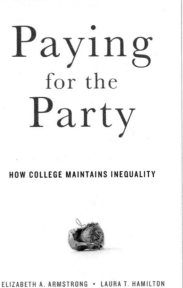

Historically, the purpose of four-year public universities was to help disadvantaged in-state students achieve social mobility by providing affordable, quality education. This purpose has been compromised over the past few decades as these schools have suffered from a drop in federal and state funding at the same time that their budgets have increased. In order to cover their costs, public universities not only have raised tuition, but have started to enroll more affluent out-of-state students. These students are from families that have the financial resources to pay full tuition rates—and they are "primed to party." Such students may often be less interested in education than in the social activities that these schools offer, especially Greek life.

Elizabeth Armstrong and Laura Hamilton (2013) argue that catering to these privileged students has shifted the purpose of public universities away from the social mobility of disadvantaged groups and toward providing pathways for the elite to party. Unfortunately, less affluent students suffer when these schools prioritize the "partying" of their elite students rather than paying for quality educational programs, advising assistance, and investments in teaching.

Armstrong and Hamilton spent five years studying 53 women at a large

public university in the Midwest, which we will refer to as MU. During the first year of their study, they lived in a residence hall with the students, observing their initial reactions to university life as freshmen. Armstrong and Hamilton quickly learned how the socioeconomic positions of these students shaped their motives for attending MU and their expectations for what they would achieve after they graduated.

Affluent students, many from out-of-state, attended MU to party and socialize; many majored in easy subjects and assumed that they would marry a successful man to support them. A few affluent students chose MU for academic reasons. They pursued the "professional pathway" in higher education and envisioned themselves as independent career women after they graduated.

Women from lower-income backgrounds were motivated to attend MU to achieve social mobility and escape their hometowns. Unlike their affluent peers, the lower-income women had to depend on student loans and part-time work instead of their families to fund their educations. Most felt isolated at MU and transferred to smaller, regional campuses near their hometowns. Few achieved secure upward mobility—some ended up working minimum-wage jobs

that did not require a college degree. Armstrong and Hamilton argue that unless public universities eliminate the party pathway, such as by abolishing the Greek system, then they are culpable for reproducing class inequality.

Supplementary Resources

- You can read an interview with Hamilton that appeared in the *New York Times* at http://www.nytimes.com/2013/08/04/education/edlife/elizabeth-a-armstrong-on-her-book-paying-for-the-party.html.
- You can learn more about the cost of higher education and the student loan crisis, and also watch a clip of the documentary *Ivory Tower* (2014), at http://www.takepart.com/ivorytower.

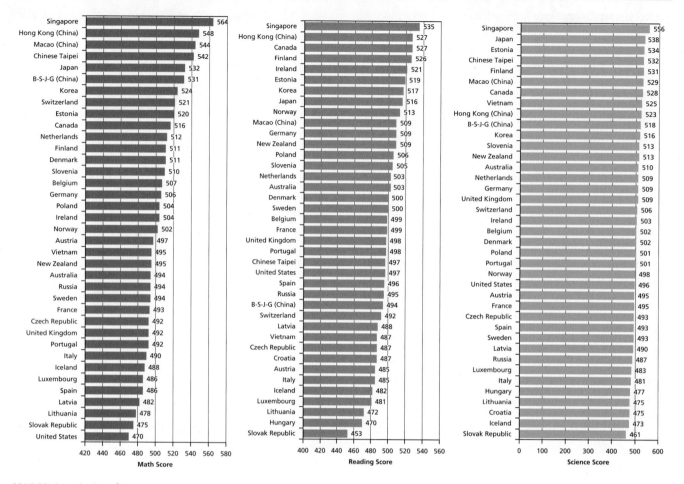

SOURCE: Organisation of Economic Co-operation and Development (OECD), PISA Results in Focus: 2015.

Finland is a small country of slightly more than 5.5 million people, and the population is quite homogeneous. Moreover, it is one of the most equal societies among the world's advanced industrial nations. For these reasons, detractors have contended that it cannot serve as a model for large and heterogeneous societies such as the United States. Pasi Sahlberg (2011), one proponent of the Finnish system, counters this claim by pointing out that the varied reforms that have been initiated in many countries share in common a belief in market principles as applied to education, and he concludes that the results have been less than impressive.

To appreciate the fact that different societies have tackled educating future generations differently, we turn to an examination of the education systems in three large industrial societies: the United States, Germany, and Japan.

U.S., German, and Japanese Education Systems

As we have seen, the U.S. schooling system does not create inequality in student learning outcomes. Sometimes it compensates for other inequalities, sometimes it reinforces these inequalities, and sometimes it increases educational inequality. Other nations have structured their educational systems differently. These institutional differences have important implications for inequalities in learning among students.

Three schooling systems—those in Germany, Japan, and the United States—are compared below to illustrate how different nations allocate learning resources to students who will occupy different positions in the social hierarchy.

In Germany, all elementary school students attend *Grundschule,* which does not practice ability grouping; all children are exposed to the same curriculum. At the end of fourth grade, teachers make a recommendation to each child's family regarding the type of secondary school the child should attend, based on his or her test scores and the teachers' subjective assessments of the student's ability. There are three types of schools that represent academic and vocational tracks: lower-level *Gymnasium* (the college track), *Realschule* (the middle track), and *Hauptschule* (the lowest track). Each of these has its own curriculum, which is designed to correspond with the future occupational trajectories of its students. Only 30 percent of students are placed in the *Gymnasium* level. Transferring to a different track is possible, but it is difficult and rare. Between-school tracking continues at the next level of schooling, and only students who attend upper-level *Gymnasium* can proceed to the university system and attain the equivalent of a baccalaureate degree.

Japan has a very different system of educational stratification. From school entry through ninth grade, there is little or no ability grouping among students, either between or within schools. For the first nine years of school, Japanese students are exposed to a remarkably uniform curriculum. At the end of ninth grade, Japanese students take a high-stakes test that determines which type of high school they will attend. About 75 percent of students attend *futsuuka,* which has a college preparatory curriculum. The remaining 25 percent of students attend a variety of technical and vocational schools. Family background still plays an important role in educational success for Japanese students because of a "shadow education" system, in which informal schooling opportunities outside school give more advantaged students better preparation for both high school and college entrance exams.

The German and Japanese systems highlight key features of the U.S. public schooling system. Education in the United States has always been organized around the "common school" ideal: All American students, regardless of their class origins and their future aspirations, attend the same types of schools. In the United States, tracking occurs within schools, not between schools. The United States also has more variability in school quality by geographic region. The German and Japanese systems are much more centralized than the U.S. system is. The United States has 50 different educational systems (one run by each state) with different levels of funding and varying curricula. In the United States, more so than in Japan and Germany, the quality and character of a student's education is likely to be affected by where the student's family lives.

These differences have implications for achievement outcomes in each nation (Montt 2011). Germany has the highest levels of achievement inequality because of its highly stratified system. Japan has higher average achievement than Germany but much less inequality in outcomes because it does not practice curricular differentiation until very late. The United States actually has the lowest average achievement and the least variability of these three nations.

Two features of educational systems are significant for student outcomes. First, nations with highly differentiated school systems—with between-school tracking—have more unequal learning outcomes for students, and family background tends to matter more for student outcomes (Van de Werfhorst and Mij 2010). Second, standardization—the degree to which the curriculum and examinations are the same across schools—produces less inequality in student outcomes and a weaker correlation between family background and achievement. Thus, institutions do matter greatly, and the choices that nations make have important consequences for how learning is distributed within society.

CHECKPOINT 13.4: GLOBALIZATION AND EDUCATION

COUNTRY	EDUCATIONAL IDEOLOGY
United States	Meritocracy, equal chances of succeeding based on hard work
Finland	Equality of educational opportunities with less variation in achievement
Germany	Secondary school tracking based on academic and vocational aptitudes
Japan	Uniform curriculum and no ability grouping until the end of ninth grade

SUMMARY

Education is closely related to the process of socialization, although it most often takes place more formally in schools. Structural/functionalists view education as a social structure functional for both individuals and society. Conflict/critical theorists believe that education serves to reproduce social inequalities and reinforce social stratification. Symbolic interactionists focus on the micro aspects of education and often analyze how social inequality is reinforced at this level.

The educational system in the United States is becoming increasingly commercialized. Education is now seen as a product to be purchased and consumed and is evaluated based on the greatest return for the lowest cost. The cost of higher education has soared in recent years, forcing many students to take out student loans. Some of these indebted students, especially those who attend postsecondary for-profit institutions, have difficulty paying back these loans because their degrees do not guarantee them high-paying jobs.

Though structural/functionalists insist that education provides equal opportunities for all students to learn and achieve social mobility, research has found that inequalities exist in the educational system that prevent many from succeeding. Coleman found that teacher quality, family background, and racial composition of the student body were the most important factors affecting student achievement. In addition, the use of tracking in schools often leads to a cumulative advantage for students placed in higher tracks. Other researchers have discovered that differences in the home environments of very young children also explain differences in educational ability and attainment. Family background also helps determine who is most likely to pursue postsecondary education. Students with more advantaged family backgrounds are more likely to graduate from high school and to enroll in and graduate from college.

Educational inequality also exists around the world. Countries vary greatly in their ability to educate students and educate them well. The Program for International Student Assessment (PISA) measures the proficiency of 15-year-olds in reading, math, and science every three years. Students in the United States fall near the bottom, while students in Singapore rank at the top.

KEY TERMS

credentialism, 357

cultural dopes, 359

cumulative advantage, 368

habitus, 374

meritocracy, 361

social reproduction, 357

vouchers, 369

REVIEW QUESTIONS

1. How do structural/functional explanations of education differ from conflict/critical approaches? Which theoretical perspective is best suited to explain current changes in education?

2. What is a meritocracy, and why is the educational system an important component of a meritocratic society? In what ways is the U.S. education system meritocratic, and in what ways is it not meritocratic?

3. According to the Coleman Report, how important is the quality of schools to student achievement? What other factors affect student achievement? What factors have not been found to affect student achievement to any great extent?

4. Describe overall trends in student achievement by race and ethnicity and by gender. In what ways are these changes reflective of larger societal changes? Do you think that new technologies can be used to close achievement gaps across groups? Why or why not?

5. Homeschooling has grown in popularity in recent years. What are the main reasons why parents opt to educate their children at home rather than sending them to either public or private schools? What are some of the drawbacks to homeschooling?

6. Charter schools operate within the public educational system but are designed to be alternatives to traditional public schools. They have proven to be very controversial. Identify the pros and cons of charter schools, and provide an overview of the evidence to date about how well charter schools do.

7. What is the relationship between income of parents and the ability of their children to enroll in and graduate from college?

8. Several Asian countries are at or near the top in the PISA rankings. What aspects of Asian culture might account for these high scores? Can you explain the comparatively low U.S. scores? What are the implications of those scores for the future of the United States?

9. Compare and contrast the U.S., German, and Japanese educational systems. How do these systems' differences affect achievement outcomes in these countries? How do their attitudes toward grouping reflect the countries' respective cultural norms and values?

10. What are MOOCs? What are the pros and cons of using MOOCs in higher education? Will we see more or fewer of them in the future? Why?

PRACTICE AND APPLY WHAT YOU'VE LEARNED

▶ **edge.sagepub.com/ritzerintro4e**

CHECK YOUR COMPREHENSION ON THE STUDY SITE WITH:

- **Diagnostic pre-tests** to identify opportunities for improvement.

- **Personalized study plans** with focused recommendations to address specific knowledge gaps and additional learning needs.

- **Post-tests** to check your progress and ensure mastery of key learning objectives.

14

RELIGION

Commercialism Encroaches on a Holy City

Mecca, a city in Saudi Arabia, is the holiest city in Islam. At its center is the Sacred Mosque, with its black cubed structure—the Kaaba—the most sacred site in the Islamic world. The Sacred Mosque and the Kaaba are major destinations for the annual pilgrimage—or *hajj*—which in 2016 attracted nearly 2 million Muslims from all over the world. In addition, 5 million more people come throughout the year for the minor pilgrimage known as *umrah*, and millions of Saudi citizens also visit as tourists.

In recent years, more than 98 percent of Saudi Arabia's historic sites—some dating back to Muhammad in the sixth and seventh centuries CE—have been destroyed to make way for development. Some changes have been made to better accommodate all the pilgrims, but others, including in the immediate surroundings of Mecca's holy center, have been made for commercial reasons, with little regard for history or religion. A Hilton hotel was built on the site of the house of the first caliph of Islam, and other hotels have followed nearby. Rooms with a view of Kaaba can cost up to $2,700 per night during the hajj. Expensive high-rise apartment buildings surround the holy center of the city. The closer the buildings are to the central mosque, the more costly the apartments are. This is especially true of apartments with a view of the mosque. The people who occupy them are able watch from on high the milling masses during the hajj.

Most striking is the Disneyesque Mecca Royal Clock Tower, built by the Saudi Bin Laden Group, a management conglomerate with links to Osama bin Laden and his family; the tower is modeled after—and five times bigger than—Big Ben in London. It is one of the tallest buildings in the world and towers over the city center, with 48 searchlights on top that make it especially visible at night. The tower includes an 800-room hotel (where a suite can cost $10,000 per night) and a five-story shopping mall; shopping halts during calls to prayer. As a

LEARNING OBJECTIVES

14.1 Explain how Marx, Weber, and Durkheim viewed the role of religion in society.

14.2 Define religion.

14.3 Identify the major components of religion.

14.4 Describe the types of religious organizations.

14.5 Apply structural/functional and conflict/critical theories to religion.

14.6 Describe the relationship between globalization and the world's major religions.

Orhan Akkanat/Anadolu Agency/Getty Images

result of all of these changes, the hajj itself has been transformed for many from a trek that traditionally has involved great effort and hardship to a journey including shopping at high-end stores, stays at luxury hotels, and packaged tours in which pilgrims are transported in groups from hotel to hotel and religious site to religious site.

These changes are part of a wider range of transformations affecting religion throughout the world. One of the most important is secularization, or the declining significance of religion. In the case of Mecca, religion seems to be increasingly taking a backseat to commercial and economic interests. The comfort of the consumers of the hajj, as well as the profits to be earned from them, seem to be gaining priority over the religious experience. ●

Religion is of great importance to billions of people throughout the world. As a result, the early giants in the field of sociology were all in one way or another affected by, interested in, and sometimes critical of religion.

EARLY SOCIOLOGISTS AND RELIGION

According to Karl Marx, religion brings pleasure or consolation to believers who think they are incapable of changing their distressing social conditions. It is a response to the alienation people experience in the social world. However, in Marx's view, religion is not capable of changing the conditions, especially in capitalism, that cause that distress.

Max Weber wanted to better understand the ways in which world religions helped create different kinds of societies and different personality types within those societies. From a critical perspective, his research convinced him that various trends originating within Western Europe were serving to erode the power of religious conviction. In his view, religion was being increasingly compartmentalized and separated from other spheres of social life and from secular institutions. He foresaw the emergence of new religions and efforts to revitalize traditional religions as likely responses to the challenges to religious belief.

Émile Durkheim believed that despite massive social changes "there is something eternal in religion which is destined to survive" ([1912] 1972, 243). He analyzed less developed societies in order to discover and better understand those eternal factors. He was also interested in how they had contributed to the development of religious beliefs, practices, and institutions. He wanted to describe

and understand everything from the simplest to the most complex forms of religion. In doing so, he thought he could understand what seemed to make religion functional for people in every historical period.

Of particular importance to Durkheim's understanding of religious phenomena was the role of social interaction in producing feelings about a powerful force that not only comes to stand beyond the ordinary world but also influences it in various ways. He described this force as the *sacred* and distinguished it from the *profane* that characterized daily life. Hand in hand with the emergence of a belief in the sacred was the development of rituals, or regularly repeated, prescribed, and traditional behaviors that serve to symbolize some value or belief (Kurtz 2016). Rituals in early human societies were directed toward totems, or animals and plants that served as symbolic representations of the sacred.

Durkheim contended that religion is the basis of the *collective conscience* (see Chapter 2). He believed this was the source of the fundamental categories of thought that provide people with a stable and coherent worldview. Their worldview includes the way people think about space, time, causality, categorization, and related issues (Durkheim and Mauss [1903] 1963). The collective conscience was also the main way in which early societies created solidarity and social integration. In these early societies characterized by *mechanical solidarity* (see Chapter 2), a strong system of shared beliefs was the glue that held the social order together. These shared beliefs included moral values that proscribed certain kinds of conduct and defined societal expectations and individual obligations.

In modern societies characterized by *organic solidarity* (see Chapter 2), consensus on beliefs and values is no longer possible or essential. Value pluralism—or differences

In a ritual commemorating the anniversary of the Emancipation Proclamation, which freed slaves during the Civil War, members of the African Methodist Episcopal Church in Charleston, South Carolina, and many other black congregations gather to pray on New Year's Eve, as free blacks and abolitionists did on the same day in 1862.

Is religion a source of pleasure and consolation to most people in the world? Or is it more a source of conflict and pain?

in values—does not necessarily threaten modern society. Nevertheless, Durkheim believed that religion would remain important as a source of meaning and social support in the modern world.

Given this history of theorizing about the great significance of religion to society, it is not surprising that religion became—and still is—a central concern within sociology (Davie 2013).

CHECKPOINT 14.1: EARLY SOCIOLOGISTS AND RELIGION

SOCIOLOGIST	ROLE OF RELIGION
Karl Marx	Religion can console believers, but cannot change social conditions.
Max Weber	Religion can be the basis for social conduct and can help create new societies.
Émile Durkheim	Religion is the basis of collective conscience or social solidarity.

WHAT IS RELIGION?

The worship service at the Holiness Church of God in Jesus' Name in eastern Tennessee, located in the heart of Appalachia, preserves a unique regional tradition that can be traced to the early twentieth century. In an austere church building, without stained glass windows or a steeple, the worshipers gather to participate in an emotionally charged service. The presence of electric guitars and drums does not make this church different from many other Pentecostal and Holiness churches in the area. Nor do the personal testimonies about being lost to sin and then found make this church particularly distinctive. Not even the fact that as the service proceeds some present begin to speak in tongues (known as *glossolalia*) makes this church unique.

What does make the service different from that of other churches in the area can be found in the crude wooden boxes at the foot of the pulpit, which bear inscriptions such as "Lord Jesus" and "Mark 16:18." It can also be found in the contents of the mason jars sitting on the pulpit. The gathering, which will last for hours, comes to an emotional peak when the boxes are opened and their contents—poisonous snakes—are distributed to the assembled throughout the room. People hold the snakes above their heads, wrap them around their necks like scarves, and in other ways "take up serpents." Some of the faithful also lift the mason jars to their lips and drink the strychnine contents. The congregants undertake these dangerous activities with the full knowledge that others before them have died while engaging in the same practices. They also know that they are violating state law (Burton 1993).

So why do they do it? Like others who claim to be Christian fundamentalists, these serpent-handling believers argue for a literal interpretation of the Bible. What distinguishes them from other literalists is the particular importance they attach to a passage in the book of Mark in which Jesus appears after the Resurrection to proclaim: "All these signs will accompany those who believe: in my name they will cast out demons; they will speak in new tongues; they will pick up serpents; and if they drink any deadly thing, it will not hurt them."

Why do the thousand or so people who handle serpents and drink poison do so, while the overwhelming majority of people affiliated with Christian congregations do not? Why do the former believe that a literal interpretation of scripture is required? Why is this particular scriptural passage given such importance? What sociological or psychological variables are involved in inclining an individual to join a snake-handling church?

These are the kinds of questions that sociologists of religion seek to address. But they are not only, or even mainly, interested in marginalized religious groups, such as the one in this example; they are also interested in the beliefs and practices of more conventional, mainstream religions. Sociologists are also interested in religious institutions and in the ways that they contribute to shaping a society's cultural values.

We have come this far in the chapter without actually defining religion. Religion is difficult to define because it is so complex and perceived so differently by different societies, and even by individuals within any given society (James [1902] 1960; Weber [1920] 1963). Nevertheless, we need a definition to shape our discussion and analysis of the sociology of religion (Hargrove 1989).

The definition of religion employed here is largely derived from Émile Durkheim's ([1912] 1965) classic statement: **Religion** is a social phenomenon that consists of beliefs about the sacred; the experiences, practices, and rituals that reinforce those beliefs; and the communities that share similar beliefs and practices (Kurtz 2016). Before proceeding to examine the components of religion identified in this definition, it is important to note that *sociologists of religion do not judge the truth claims of differing religious systems*. Instead, they put these claims aside and address the effects of such beliefs on believers and the consequences for the larger society. Because sociologists rely solely on data from the everyday world (the profane realm), they have no access to the sacred and thus are not in a position to say one way or the other whether religious beliefs are "true." Instead, sociologists begin with the assumption that if people believe something is real, whether or not it is the case, the consequences of their beliefs are real. And this is what they can and do study.

CHECKPOINT 14.2: WHY SOCIOLOGISTS STUDY RELIGION

PURPOSE OF STUDY

To understand the belief and practices of marginalized religious groups

To understand how religious institutions shape cultural values

To understand the societal consequences of religious beliefs

COMPONENTS OF RELIGION

Three of the major components of religion are beliefs, rituals, and experiences. The fourth, community, will be discussed in a later section. Beliefs and rituals have grown out of and influenced each other for millennia. They have persisted but also changed as believers of various religious traditions have diffused globally and interacted with other religions in the lands they have passed through and in which they have settled. Moreover, neither belief nor ritual is created in isolation; rather, both are created as responses to people's experiences and particular times in particular places. Beliefs and rituals, in turn, shape these experiences.

BELIEF

Every religion has a set of interrelated **beliefs**, or ideas that explain the world and identify what should be sacred or held in awe—that is, the religion's ultimate concerns. Religious beliefs have been shaped over thousands of years; they are embedded in religious traditions and also serve as the "raw material" for new religions.

Durkheim wrote that religion deals with "things which surpass the limits of our knowledge" ([1912] 1965, 14). This view was echoed by Rudolph Otto (1923), who referred to

this domain as the realm of the holy. Others have used such words as *supernatural, supramundane,* and *sacred* to describe this realm. Durkheim, as noted previously, preferred the last of these terms, as he argued that all human experience could be divided into two categories. The **sacred** is what is extraordinary, set aside, and of ultimate concern and leads to awe and reverence. The **profane**, in contrast, *is* the ordinary and mundane. People can come to *believe* that virtually anything is sacred—a deity, a place (Jerusalem, Mecca), a particular time or season (Ramadan, Diwali), an idea (freedom), or even a thing (an animal, a mountain, a tree, a canyon, a flag, or a rock). The sacred is treated with respect, and one's relation to it is often defined in rituals: You might genuflect when passing in front of an altar or take off your shoes when entering a temple. People believe that anything that is not considered sacred is profane.

Each religious tradition weaves together a fabric of many different and interdependent beliefs. These include beliefs about creation and suffering, as well as ethical standards for judging proper behavior. For example, when Muslims declare in their daily prayers that they believe God is the most merciful and the most compassionate, it means that their behavior must reflect God's mercy: "The imperative to be merciful—to bring benefit to the world and avert harm—must underlie a Muslim's understanding of reality and attitude toward society" (Abd-Allah 2005, 6).

Beliefs are often presented in sacred stories and scriptures. They address questions about the origin and meaning of life, theories about why the world was created, and explanations of suffering and death. They first express a *worldview,* that is, a culture's most comprehensive image of the ways in which life—nature, self, and society—is ordered (Geertz 1973). That worldview, in turn, shapes an *ethos,* which "expresses a culture's and a people's basic attitude about themselves and the world in general" (Geertz 1973, 173).

These beliefs are at the same time both models of and models for reality. They provide believers with information and a framework for interpreting the world around them. As models *for* reality, however, beliefs show how the world should be versus how it really is, often prompting the believer to act. Mahatma Gandhi believed that the world was ultimately grounded in truth and nonviolence, and that a just god ruled the world. His noncooperation with the British Empire on behalf of the struggle for Indian independence was not only political resistance but also an act of faith. He saw no reason to be fearful of unjust political powers that were simply under the illusion that they were in control of the world. Hindu and Buddhist theories of *ahimsa,* nonharmfulness or nonviolence, not only explained the real power behind the universe for Gandhi but also gave him a guide for how to act.

Most religious belief systems include a *cosmogony,* a story about how and why the world was created, which usually links the believers to the act of creation.

The waters of the Ganges are considered sacred to the pilgrims who bathe there. What do you consider sacred?

Finally, every religious tradition provides an explanation for the presence of evil, suffering, and death. Most explanations of this type identify the source of evil in the world. How a religion recommends confronting evil may affect everything from individual beliefs and decisions to a nation's foreign policy. We can find a wide range of explanations in the world's religions for the existence of suffering: It may be seen as punishment for sinful behavior, the result of a battle between evil and good, or just part of the natural cycles of life and death.

One of the most difficult dilemmas for any religion is to explain why good people suffer and bad people sometimes flourish. While the suffering of the righteous is problematic, most religious explanations suggest that ethical behavior will eventually be rewarded. Most mainstream religions suggest that suffering is just part of the way the universe functions, so everyone is subject to it at one time or another. It is how you deal with suffering that is most important.

RITUAL

In most religious traditions, simply believing is never enough; one also has to act. The belief systems of religious traditions are loaded with rituals that reinforce those beliefs, serve as reminders, and help believers enact their beliefs in the world. As defined earlier, **rituals** consist of regularly repeated, prescribed, and traditional behaviors symbolizing a value or belief. Rituals are enacted during ceremonies and festivals, such as funerals, weddings, and baptisms. Rituals are a central part of the **rites of passage** that accompany major transitions in life, such as birth, puberty, marriage, economic crises (O'Loughlin 2016), and death (van Gennep 1961). Also included under the heading of rituals are ongoing spiritual practices, such as personal prayer and attending worship services of faith communities, as well as elements of everyday language that serve as religious reminders for many people.

Rituals come in many forms. Some, such as prayer, chanting, singing, and dancing, help people communicate with or show devotion to the gods. Some, such as mantras and meditations, help believers organize their personal and

social lives. Some frame daily life, such ass those relating to diet, hygiene, and sexual practices, while others celebrate cycles of nature and build community, such as holidays, seasonal festivals, and processionals.

Rituals solve problems of personal and collective life by providing time-tested actions, words, and sentiments for every occasion. When addressing a serious problem, such as death, violence, natural disaster, or social crisis, people often use rituals to

1. Identify the source of the problem

2. Characterize it as evil

3. Mark boundaries between "us" and "them"

4. Arrive at some means of working toward a solution, or at least the satisfaction that they are doing something about the problem

In times of crisis, rituals can help people deal with tragedy and offer an opportunity to strengthen social bonds. Consider the ways in which people create and repeatedly visit memorials at the sites of tragedies. Recent examples include memorials at the site of the 2015 attack on the Bataclan concert venue in Paris, France, and the 2016 shooting at the Pulse nightclub in Orlando, Florida. These memorials often involve prayer candles and services with clergy, similar to what one would find in a house of worship. Such rituals build a sense of solidarity that provides support for the suffering and reinforces the authority of the social order and the institutions that sponsor the rituals, especially when they are being threatened. Rituals can also provide a theory of evil and focus participants' attention on some abstract issue, a personified devil or mythical figure, or a human enemy who needs to be denounced or attacked.

Makeshift memorials, like this one at the site of a shooting at an elementary school in Connecticut, are a form of ritual that can provide comfort after a tragedy. Do you participate in any religious rituals?

Which religious rituals have you been involved in or witnessed in your life? Consider those of your own religion, if any, and those of other religions to which you have been exposed through friends or relatives. What was the stated purpose of these rituals? Were there other reasons for these rituals that were less obvious? If so, what were they?

Participants usually believe that their rituals are effective and remember the stories from their culture or religion that remind them of the rituals' efficacy. Although partly a rational process, rituals as symbols also evoke sentiments and emotions that go beyond rationality. When a traditional ritual is used to solve personal or social troubles, it gains new authority and helps sustain old habits and preserves the society and its institutions.

Religious rituals are also crucial for social change and cultural innovation, especially when traditional rituals can be transformed for revolutionary purposes. One example is Mahatma Gandhi's use of religious processions, prayers, and scripture readings to mobilize his fellow Indians, as brothers and sisters of the same god, to demand their freedom from the British Empire. In another example, in 1989, the Christian rituals of Eastern Europe provided spaces for nonviolent political resistance against communist regimes. And in Egypt in 2011, the Muslim Friday prayers became occasions for large gatherings that moved from prayer to protest and to regime change.

Moreover, religious rituals often mark a **liminal period**, or a special time set apart from ordinary reality (Turner 1967). The sacred time during a religious ceremony may involve an inversion of apparent reality, giving hope for the oppressed that they will be liberated, for the sad that they will be comforted, and for the last that they shall be first. In the traditional Catholic Carnival ritual preceding Lent (a period of penitence), Old Man Winter is dethroned by the young Princess Spring. The norms of appropriate behavior appear to be suspended as the celebrants sing, dance, and drink to excess. This helps encourage the revelers to overthrow masculine authority. In the liminal period, where stodgy patriarchy is defeated by youthful feminine energy, the cycles of nature replace winter with spring, resurrecting hope in the hearts of the celebrants.

EXPERIENCE

The combination of beliefs, rituals, and other practices forms the variety of religious experiences for believers, regardless of which tradition they celebrate. Much of the human community views the world through a religious lens and constructs an identity around religious affiliation and experiences, such as prayer or attendance at religious services. In a survey of 40 countries, large numbers of people, especially in sub-Saharan Africa, the Middle East, and parts of Asia, reported that religion is very important in their lives (see Figure 14.1). Interestingly, a negative relationship exists between wealth and religiosity, with people living in poorer nations being

FIGURE 14.1 • The Importance of Religion Worldwide

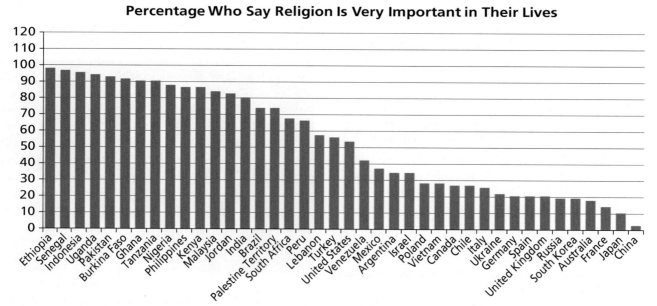

SOURCE: Angelina E. Theodorou, "Americans Are in the Middle of the Pack Globally When It Comes to Importance of Religion," Pew Research Center, Washington, DC, December 23, 2015.

FIGURE 14.2 • Religious Affiliation by Age Group, 2011

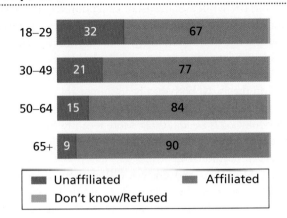

Age	Unaffiliated	Affiliated
18–29	32	67
30–49	21	77
50–64	15	84
65+	9	90

■ Unaffiliated   ■ Affiliated
■ Don't know/Refused

SOURCE: ""Nones" on the Rise" Pew Research Center, Washington, DC (October, 2012) http://www.pewforum.org/2012/10/09/nones-on-the-rise/.

more religious than those in wealthy countries. The major exception is the United States, where 53 percent of respondents report that religion is very important to them. Religion is much more important to Americans than it is to people living in other wealthy nations, such as Germany and Britain (21 percent), Japan (11 percent), and France (14 percent). In many sub-Saharan countries, no fewer than eight in ten people report religion as very important. Nine in ten of those in the predominantly Muslim countries (such as Indonesia and Pakistan) view religion as very important.

While religion remains important to most Americans, young people do not necessarily accept this view. They—and many others—are increasingly religiously unaffiliated. Almost one third of those between 18 and 29 years of age are unaffiliated (see Figure 14.2). However, this does not mean that religion is completely unimportant to them; more than two thirds say they believe in God. In comparison, only 9 percent of those over age 65 report being unaffiliated.

CIVIL RELIGION

The experiences discussed to this point in this section relate to organized religion. However, many religious experiences occur outside of, and side by side with, those that occur in the context of those religions. One set of such experiences has been very important to Americans in particular—**civil religion**, or the beliefs, practices, and symbols that a nation holds sacred (Turner 2014; Yamane 2007). This idea has a long history in philosophy and sociology, including the work of Jean-Jacques Rousseau, Alexis de Tocqueville, and Émile Durkheim. However, it was a 1967 essay by Robert Bellah (1927–2013) titled "Civil Religion in America" that gave this idea broad visibility in the sociological study of religion. Bellah argued that civil religion has existed in U.S. society since the nation's founding. It exists, among other places, in presidential addresses, from those of George Washington to those of Donald Trump (Gorski 2011); in

texts, such as the Constitution; at revered geographic locations, such as the battlefield at Gettysburg and Arlington National Cemetery; and in community rituals, such as parades and fireworks on the Fourth of July. Civil religion becomes especially prominent and important in difficult times, such as after 9/11. In the immediate aftermath of this tragedy, many Americans sought to express their shared national identity by flying the U.S. flag. This was a powerful moment during which people felt a deep bond with their fellow Americans. With the passage of time, the site of the main attack on the World Trade Center has become a sacred geographic area. The 10-year anniversary of the attack witnessed a communal ritual on the site, as well as one involving a large portion of the American population via the mass media. Large numbers of people make pilgrimages to the site where the World Trade Center once stood.

What is the function of civil religion? As the examples of communal rituals at and pilgrimages to the World Trade Center illustrate, it provides a sense of a collective national identity. It does so by promoting and reaffirming shared ideas and ideals. Civil religion reinforces a sense of solidarity, defining who the "we" is in "we the people." Many Americans experience civil religion by reading the sacred texts, visiting key places in the nation's history, and participating in rituals such as those associated with the Fourth of July. By actively participating in this distinctive American religion, Americans serve to legitimate the state (Bloom 1992). While many Americans continue to believe in the country's civil religion, others contend that it is less important today than it was when Bellah first developed the concept. Divisions within American society, especially between liberals (as reflected in the policy proposals of failed 2016 Democratic candidate Bernie Sanders) and conservatives (expressed most extremely in the 2016 presidential campaign and spurred on by the election of Donald Trump and his extremely conservative policies and cabinet selections), suggest that there may no longer be a consensus on the major components of America's civil religion. While the divide across political views makes consensus difficult, Bellah was well aware of this possibility. The nation was also very divided during the era of the civil rights movement and the Vietnam War—in fact, it was likely more divided than it is today. Bellah (1975) wrote about this era as one of a "broken covenant," but he thought that it could be fixed. Of course, another crisis such as the one associated with 9/11 would, at least for a time, serve to reduce today's differences and lead to a reaffirmation of America's civil religion. But even beyond moments of national crisis, as long as nations continue to exist, citizens of those nations need to share certain values and beliefs, which are the glue that holds the country together.

ASK YOURSELF

Do you think civil religion is more important to American society now than it was when, say, you were a child? Why or why not? Give examples to support your answer.

SECULARIZATION

Secularization is defined as the declining significance of religion (Bruce 2013; Calhoun, Juergensmeyer, and VanAntwerpen 2011; Dobbelaere 2007; Perez-Agote 2014; C. Taylor 2007). It occurs at both the societal and individual levels. At the societal level, it can involve the declining power of organized religion as well as the transfer of functions such as education from religion to the state. At the individual level, secularization means that individual experiences with religion are less intense and less important than are other kinds of experiences.

Secularization includes historical developments in the modern world that undermine the authority of religion. Among the mechanisms that are seen as contributing to it are the following:

1. The rise of scientific thinking as an alternative way of interpreting the world (the scientific perspective encourages skepticism and doubt, thereby challenging the certainty of religious belief)

2. The development of industrial society, particularly when it results in relative affluence and thus encourages materialism and downplays otherworldly concerns

3. The rise of governments that do not mandate or promote an established religion

4. The encouragement of religious tolerance, which leads to a "watering down" of religion in general and religious differences in particular

5. The existence of competing secular moral ideologies, such as humanism (Smelser 1994, 305–306)

Given the combined impact of these developments, by the 1960s, proponents of secularization theory (such as Berger 1969; Wilson 1966) assumed that religion would continue to decline. It was thought that people would be less likely to believe in God, attend religious services, join religious institutions, or embrace religious beliefs. This was already happening in the wealthy industrial nations of Western Europe, the first to become "modern," and it was believed that it would inevitably happen elsewhere, too, at some point in the future. The churches in Europe were largely empty, and religious convictions were waning. But even as these views about secularization were being articulated, there was awareness that they were problematic. For one thing, religion continued—and continues—to be vibrant in most of the world. For another, the United States remains a religious nation. In the 1980s, sociologist and priest Andrew Greeley (1989) found that more than 90 percent of Americans said they believed in God (and 40 percent reported that they attended religious services every week). While the belief in

God has declined in United States since the 1980s, the fact that 79 percent of Americans still believe in God makes it clear that the United States is an exception to the secularization thesis (see Figure 14.3). In fact, given this reality, as well as the rise of Islam in much of the world, it is the more secularized Europe that increasingly looks like the exception.

There are still some proponents of the original secularization thesis. Nobody has been more explicit about this than Scottish sociologist Steve Bruce in his provocatively titled book *God Is Dead* (2002). More recently, Bruce (2013) has admitted that such views, and more generally secularization, are "unfashionable."

Recently, Voas and Chaves (2016) have, like Bruce, embraced the idea of secularization, arguing that, in fact, the United States is *not* the exception to the secularization rule. First, they argue and present evidence that religiosity (religious commitment) in the United States has been slowly declining for decades. This is the case even though Americans remain remarkably religious, especially in comparison to others in the West. Second, as in Europe, this is because each successive generation is less religious than the previous one.

However, many sociologists today have been attracted to the idea of a "postsecular" society. While there is a lot of debate about what that term actually means, the growing view is that two contradictory trends can be observed: on the one hand, increasing religiosity, and on the other, an entrenched and expanding secularization (Goldstein 2009; Gorski et al. 2012; Nynäs, Lassander, and Utriainen 2012; O'Brien and Noy 2015).

FIGURE 14.3 • Percentage in the United States Who Believe in God, 2016

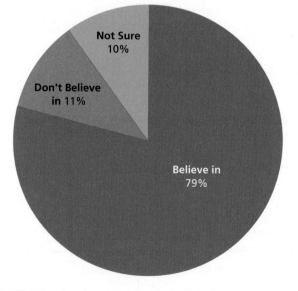

SOURCE: "Most Americans Still Believe in God," Gallup, June 29, 2016.

Practicing Virtual Faith

Instead of being threatened by new technologies like the internet, many religious institutions are finding that their success, even their continued existence, is dependent on these technologies. Virtual religious services help recruit and sustain members, especially the infirm, those without access to transportation, or students or military personnel who temporarily move away. Catholics can attend a virtual mass officiated by Pope Francis, Buddhists can follow the blog of a Tibetan monk, and Muslims can listen to an imam's prayer service on YouTube. Some churches rely on virtual tithing via PayPal and credit cards for financial support. Facebook pages and internet chat rooms can be a source of spiritual sustenance and a means of building virtual religious communities. One recent study found that evangelical Christians use religious internet chat rooms to expand their sexual knowledge and improve their nonvirtual sex lives within the confines of heterosexual marriage (Burke 2016).

To generate revenue and sustain followers, many religious institutions use the internet to sell traditional religious objects, such as rosaries, yarmulkas (skullcaps), and prayer beads. In addition, they even sell more commercial items, such as religiously themed T-shirts and bumper stickers. The selling of actual

Many religious institutions have increasingly accepted technology, including social networks. Pope Francis joined Instagram in 2016 and tweets regularly. Do you ever use the internet in the practice of religion?

religious rituals also occurs and may become more common as religious diasporas, such as the Hindu one, grow. For instance, the religious market in India is a multibillion-dollar industry that profits from the sale of online pujas, or religious ceremonies, to Hindus who live in India and abroad. Companies like Shubhpuja .com hire Hindu priests to perform virtual pujas, which customers purchase to pray for a variety of things, like getting a promotion at work, celebrating a wedding, or healing from an illness. Prices for a puja range from $10 to $500 and are typically conducted via Skype (Bengali 2016).

Engaging the Digital World

Learn more about a religion of your choice by visiting the following website: www.bbc.co.uk/religion/religions.

Write a brief report that describes what you have learned about the history, beliefs, rituals, and practices of the religion you have selected.

RELIGION AS A FORM OF CONSUMPTION

An extensive religious, or spiritual, marketplace (Roof 2001) exists in societies that have a great deal of religious diversity and in which people are free to choose their religion. Roger Finke and Rodney Stark (2005) have built on this idea by describing religious institutions in terms of a "religious economy" that operates like commercial economies do. In this context, religious institutions are like business firms seeking to serve a market, and in so doing, they enter into competitive relationships with other "firms" in order to maintain or expand market share and attract more "consumers" (believers). Not only do religions market themselves; consumers "shop" for religion much as they shop for most other things (Gonzalez 2010; Warner 1993). It is in this context that religions must compete against each other and for consumers of religion in much the same way that manufacturers and shopping malls compete for customers.

Many churches, especially large megachurches, are increasingly oriented toward making themselves consumer-friendly (Sanders 2014). The Hartford Institute for Religion Research defines **megachurches** as churches having at least 2,000 people in attendance at worship services each week. Among the more well-known megachurches are Willow Creek Community Church, led by the Reverend Bill Hybels in suburban Chicago, Rick Warren's Saddleback Church in Southern California, and Joel Osteen's Lakewood Church in Houston. In these churches and others like them, the founders "have created sanctuaries that can only be intended to be entertainment spaces, complete with stages, lighting, and even theater-style seats" (Drane 2012, 105). The fanciest megachurches may have Christian rock music (Bowler and Reagan 2014), aerobics classes, food courts, and bowling alleys, as well as multimedia Bible classes presented in ways that resemble MTV videos (Niebuhr 1995). At crusades, and in some cases in churches themselves (such as Canterbury Cathedral in England), people exit through bookstores/gift shops that sell all sorts of religious and nonreligious items. On Sunday morning, big screens project scripture verses and lyrics to pop-style religious songs so that everyone in the congregation can see and follow along (Niebuhr 1995). The pastor of one Baptist church who sought to make services more "fun" urged his staff to study the techniques used by Disney World

AP Photo/Houston Chronicle, Eric Kayne

How do megachurches like this one exemplify the features of McDonaldization—efficiency, predictability, calculability, and control? What are the advantages for the church? For its congregation? Are there any disadvantages?

(Barron 1995). Once a distinctly American phenomenon, megachurches can now be found elsewhere in the world, including Singapore (Yip and Ainsworth 2014).

Consumers of religion have different tastes, which can be influenced by class, race, gender, educational attainment, age, region, and similar factors. When consumers "purchase" religious institutions, they do so for different reasons. Some might seek a family-friendly place with quality child care on the premises, some might emphasize worship that is very traditional, others may value contemporary worship formats, and still others might place a premium on the religious leaders' stances on various social and moral issues.

One measure of the degree to which the leaders of religious organizations have become conscious of the need to market their "product" can be seen in the increasing stress placed on treating potential members as customers engaged in a particular form of consumption. Religion thus can be seen as an arena in which to market religious experiences (Drane 2008). Like all other aspects of consumer culture, religions need to respond to the demands of those who consume them and advertise what they have to offer (Roof 2001). Among the more obvious examples, which are certainly not new phenomena, are efforts to sell all sorts of goods and services linked to religion (Moore 1997). All major holidays are associated with one form of consumption or another, but this is most clearly true of Christmas (Belk 1987, 2013). Christmas, and its associated forms of consumption, has become increasingly globalized. For example, it is even celebrated in tropical locales that have no Christmas tradition (Prideaux and Glover 2014).

There are even religious theme parks devoted to the consumption of religious shows, rides, attractions and souvenirs (O'Guinn and Belk 1989; Paine 2016). For example, in Williamstown, Kentucky, the theme park Ark Encounter offers a "life-size" re-creation of Noah's Ark, featuring a variety of religious exhibits and activities. In Pigeon Forge, Tennessee, the Biblical Times Theater offers dinner theater performances of biblical stories not far from Dolly Parton's Dollywood. In Orlando, Florida, near Disney World, the Trinity Broadcasting Network runs the Holy Land Experience. At this theme park, customers can visit such places as the Garden of Eden, Bethlehem, and the Garden of Gethsemane. Then there is the Creation Museum, founded in Petersburg, Kentucky, in 1992. To date, it has had 1.6 million visitors, and there are plans to build a $100 million theme park around it (Watkins 2014).

Visiting religious theme parks is only one aspect of the relationship between religion and a broader form of consumption-tourism (Stausberg 2011). Much more common is pilgrimage tourism involving visits to landmark religious sites, such as the old city of Jerusalem, Mecca (see the chapter introduction), and the Vatican, where opportunities to spend money on hotels, admissions, and religious souvenirs abound. The religiously oriented tourist also may attend an array of religious events (dances, festivals, even variety shows) that are likely not only to charge admission but also to offer yet another opportunity to purchase souvenirs.

While religion has become increasingly like much more secular forms of consumption, it can be argued that consumption has become our new religion. As a result, shopping malls and fast-food restaurants, among many other settings, have become places where people go to practice their consumer religion. For example, at the opening of a McDonald's in Moscow, a worker spoke of it "as if it were the Cathedral at Chartres . . . a place to experience 'celestial joy'" (Keller 1990). A trip to Disney World has been described as the "middle class hajj, the compulsory visit to the sunbaked city" (Garfield 1991).

Shopping malls have much in common with traditional religious centers (Zepp 1997). In line with religious centers, shopping malls fulfill various human needs, such as connecting with other people; gaining a sense of community as well as receiving community services; being in the presence of nature in the form of water, trees, plants, and flowers found in the atria; and participating in the nonstop festivals that are, and that take place in, shopping malls. Malls also provide the centeredness usually associated with temples. They are characterized by a similar balance, order, and symmetry. Play is generally an integral part of religious practice, and malls are certainly a place to play. Similarly, malls offer places where people can partake of ceremonial meals. In these and other ways, the shopping mall has religious qualities and therefore can truly be considered a "cathedral of consumption" (Ritzer 2010a). It is in such cathedrals, and in the process of consumption, that many people have what can be described only as religious experiences. That being said, malls are now in decline, due, in part, to the difficulty they have in competing with online malls such as Amazon.com. They will need to reinvent themselves if they are to survive, let alone continue to provide religious experiences (Merrick 2014).

CHECKPOINT 14.3: CONCEPTS THAT HELP DEFINE RELIGION

CONCEPT	DESCRIPTION
Beliefs	Ideas that explain the world and identify what should be sacred—that is, the religion's ultimate concerns
Rituals	A set of regularly repeated, prescribed, and traditional behaviors that serve to symbolize some value or belief
Civil religion	The beliefs, practices, and symbols that a nation holds sacred
Secularization	The declining significance of religion

TYPES OF RELIGIOUS INSTITUTIONS

In modern societies, defined as secular or postsecular, we often think of religion as a private matter. However, it is the faith communities that sustain and nurture religious experience in individuals. Religious traditions that persist become institutionalized. In the twenty-first century, reflecting the societies in which they exist, many have become bureaucratized.

Like all other aspects of religion, religious institutions are highly diverse, both between and within religious traditions. On the one hand, these institutions tend to reflect the organizational forms prominent in any specific society. On the other, there is always tension between the large established, formalized institutions and newer or less formal religious groups that either come and go or end up becoming tomorrow's establishment. Moreover, religious institutions with pluralistic religious worldviews and diverse populations tend to be decentralized institutionally, whereas those with more homogeneous populations and belief systems may tend to be more centralized. Hinduism and Buddhism tend to be less centralized and hierarchical, whereas Christianity has become more formalized, in part as a response to the universalism of its membership.

Sociologists have worked with various typologies to describe the most common religious institutions. Much of this work begins by distinguishing between two basic kinds of religious organizations, the *sect* and the *church*. These concepts were first developed by German theologian and church historian Ernst Troeltsch, who borrowed from and expanded on Weber's work on the sociology of religion (Swatos 2007, n.d.; Troeltsch 1932). These two terms are appropriately conceptualized as poles on a continuum, from the sect at one end to the church on the other (Ren 2007).

SECTS

A **sect** is a small group of people who have joined the group consciously and voluntarily to have a personal religious experience. They see themselves as the "true believers" who have privileged access to religious truths, which makes them critical of other religious institutions. The members' religious experiences and general behavior tend to be spontaneous and unregimented. A sect's leadership is usually composed of laypersons rather than those with specialized training. As such, the organizational structure is nonbureaucratic and nonhierarchical. Leaders often arise because they are seen as possessing charisma and thus should be obeyed without question. Sects tend to be antiestablishment, and the members often feel alienated from, and as a result are prone to reject, society and the status quo. In fact, sects can be seen as breakaway, dissident groups that leave established religious institutions. They do so because they think such institutions have compromised too much with "the world" and therefore have polluted the religion's teachings.

Sects frequently draw their membership from the lower classes, who are more interested either in changing society or in remaining apart from it than in maintaining the status quo. Sects tend to set themselves apart from the larger society and admit only those who rigorously conform to the group's norms. There is a demand for high levels of commitment on the part of members. Likewise, doctrinal purity is emphasized, and a diversity of opinions within the group about such matters is not permitted. Sect members frequently set themselves apart from society in terms of such things as how they dress and what they eat. In addition, they might even segregate themselves physically and live in areas that are largely isolated from the rest of the community. Sect members may not be in a position to effectively challenge religious competition, but they do not believe in tolerating other religious organizations.

The Puritans in the seventeenth century are a good example of a sect. Forced to leave England because of their religious convictions, they created a closed community in New England. They considered themselves to be God's chosen people who had what they described as an "errand in the wilderness." They did not tolerate dissenters. Many who ran afoul of the Puritan leadership in Massachusetts were forced to flee. One particularly famous example is Roger Williams, who ended up helping establish Rhode Island as a place that promoted religious tolerance (a statue of Williams can be found on top of the state capitol building's dome).

Numerous sects within the Christian tradition have long histories in the United States, including the Amish, Hutterites, Seventh-Day Adventists, and Jehovah's Witnesses. Sects with twentieth-century origins include the Soldiers of the Cross and the snake-handling groups described earlier in this chapter. Sunni and Shia are the major sects in Islam. Within Judaism, Hasidic Jews are an example of a sect.

The Puritans were a sect that had enormous influence in the American colonies and in the development of the United States. What other sects are you familiar with? Have you been actively involved in any of them?

CHURCHES

In contrast, a **church** is a large group of religiously oriented people into which members are usually born (instead of joining consciously and voluntarily). The church's leadership is composed of professionals who have highly specialized training. The church as a whole tends to have a highly bureaucratic structure and a complex division of labor (Diotallevi 2007). Churches tend to draw members from throughout society and across all social classes. While a sect tends to restrict membership to true believers, a church seeks to include as many people as possible. Churches often actively seek out new members, sometimes by employing missionaries. A church's belief systems tend to be highly codified, and rituals are often elaborate and performed in a highly prescribed manner. In comparison with members of sects, church members tend to have a lower level of commitment, and much less is expected of them. While sects tend to reject the status quo, churches accept it.

Using the term *church* strictly as laid out by Troeltsch, there are no churches in the United States. This is because, according to his definition, the church is closely connected to the state. It seeks a religious monopoly, attempting to eliminate, marginalize, or co-opt the religious competition. Thus, it seeks to be the all-embracing religious affiliation of all or at least the vast majority of the nation's population. Churches function to legitimate the existing society, culture, and political system. This function was evident during the 2013 funeral of Margaret Thatcher, the long-serving and extremely divisive conservative former prime minister of her nation. The flip side of this relationship is that the state ensures that the church has a privileged position.

The Roman Catholic Church during the Middle Ages is perhaps the best illustration of the strict meaning of *church,* existing in relatively pure form. It still has the status of church in some Western European nations. In the Nordic countries, the Lutheran Church is an official state church (although this is changing at present in some of them). As the example of Thatcher's funeral suggests, the Church of England (or Anglican Church) is another example.

While *sect* and *church* are presented here as if they are totally distinct, in reality there is no clear dividing line between them. They are discussed previously as "ideal types" (see Chapter 3) so that they can be clearly distinguished. In fact, over time there is a tendency for a sect to become transformed into something that takes on the organizational features of a church. As sects become larger, they need, among other things, ever-larger bureaucratic structures with less charismatic leadership and more leadership based on expertise. The behavior of sect members becomes less spontaneous and more formal. The key point is that when we use these terms, they are static. In other words, they capture an organization at a particular moment in time.

DENOMINATIONS

The church–sect distinction does not fully and accurately reflect the realities of mainstream religion in the United States. H. Richard Niebuhr (1929) long ago noted that although many religious institutions in the country look in some respects like churches, in other ways they are different. He referred to the latter institutions as denominations. Like a church, a **denomination** is an organized form of religious expression that is usually supportive of the social order and of other religious forms. Because the United States has no established religion, all religious institutions must survive in the religious marketplace. Denominations do this in a general spirit of tolerance and acceptance of other religious bodies. In this regard, they are quite different from sects.

Like a church, a denomination has a positive view of the larger society. It supports the culture and nonreligious institutions such as public schools. Unlike a sect, a conversion experience—such as being born again—is not required. Religious services of denominations, like those of churches, are formal and reserved, with an emphasis on teaching rather than on an emotional religious experience.

Denominations are hierarchical and bureaucratic. Local organizations are not independent but part of larger regional or national institutional structures. They rely on specialized, professionally trained, full-time clergy. The clergy are generally trained in seminaries run by the denominations to ensure conformity to doctrines.

FIGURE 14.4 • Protestant Christian Groups with the Largest Number of Adherents, by County

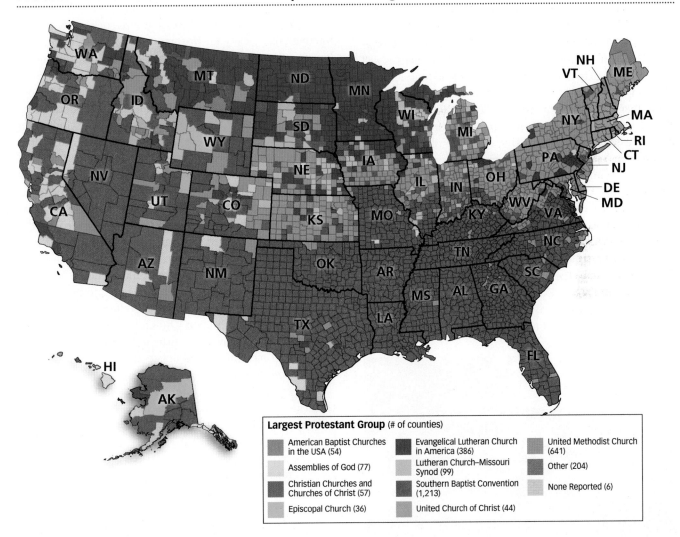

Largest Protestant Group (# of counties)

- American Baptist Churches in the USA (54)
- Assemblies of God (77)
- Christian Churches and Churches of Christ (57)
- Episcopal Church (36)
- Evangelical Lutheran Church in America (386)
- Lutheran Church–Missouri Synod (99)
- Southern Baptist Convention (1,213)
- United Church of Christ (44)
- United Methodist Church (641)
- Other (204)
- None Reported (6)

*The "Other" category includes 37 groups with less than 20 counties each. Six of these had at least 10 counties where each was the largest group: Lutheran Congregations in Mission for Christ (16 counties), Wisconsin Evangelical Lutheran Synod (16), Church of the Nazarene (15), Amish Groups, undifferentiated (13), National Baptist Convention, USA, Inc. (12), and African Methodist Episcopal Church (10).

SOURCE: Clifford Grammich, Kirk Hadaway, Richard Houseal, Dale E. Jones, Alexei Krindatch, Richie Stanley, and Richard H. Taylor. 2010 U.S. Religion Census: Religious Congregations & Membership Study. Nazarene Publishing House, Kansas City, Missouri. 2012. © Association of Statisticians of American Religious Bodies (ASARB).

Among major Christian denominations today are a long list of Protestant groups, including American Baptist, Assemblies of God, Church of Christ, Episcopal, Evangelical Lutheran, Lutheran, Presbyterian, Southern Baptist, United Church of Christ, and United Methodist (Figure 14.4 shows the largest Protestant Christian groups at the county level). But this list would also include Roman Catholics and the Eastern Orthodox Church. Denominationalism accepts a pluralistic view of religion and is in line with political pluralism (see Chapter 10).

CULTS AND NEW RELIGIOUS MOVEMENTS

A cult resembles a sect in many ways, but it is important to distinguish between the two (Stark and Bainbridge 1979). While a sect is a religious group that breaks off from a more established religion as a result of a schism in order to revive itself and rediscover the original beliefs and practices of that organization, a **cult** is a new, innovative, small, voluntary, and exclusive religious tradition that was never associated with any religious organization. A cult is often at odds with established religions as well as the larger society. Those who found cults tend to be religious radicals who want to go back to religion's origins, to import ideas from other religions, or to create totally new ideas. Like sects, cults demand high levels of commitment and involvement on the part of members. Because they are new, cults, even more than sects, tend to be led by charismatic figures.

The term *cult* has fallen out of favor in sociology because it is has come to be associated in the popular mind and press with such destructive groups as Charles Manson and his "family," who murdered a number of people, including actress Sharon Tate, in 1969. The Manson cult was not actually a religious organization, but a number of religiously based cults have proved to be very destructive. These include Jim Jones's People's Temple, David Koresh's Branch Davidians, and Heaven's Gate. All of these groups ended in tragedy. In the case of the People's Temple, the end involved the 1979 mass suicide and murder of 918 of

More than 900 people died as part of Jim Jones's People's Temple, including Jones himself, when he ordered his followers to drink cyanide-laced grape Flavor Aid.

Jones's followers in their jungle compound in Guyana. In the case of the Branch Davidians, the leader and members died in a controversial confrontation in Waco, Texas, with federal officials from the Bureau of Alcohol, Tobacco, and Firearms. And in the case of Heaven's Gate, a charismatic leader convinced his followers that Comet Hale-Bopp was hiding a mother ship that would take them to a better world. The result was that 39 members committed suicide. Other cults have directed violence outward. In Japan, the Aum Shinrikyo cult was involved in the release of sarin gas in the Tokyo subway system, killing 12 people and injuring thousands of others (Juergensmeyer 2003; Reader 2013). There are a variety of other violent groups, ranging from Christian militias associated with the Aryan Nations and other extremist groups (Simi 2013) to al-Qaeda, the Islamic State, and Boko Haram (Gulmohamad 2014; Juergensmeyer 2009).

However, none of these are true cults in the sense of the definition offered previously. Among those that better fit the definition are more benign groups such as Baha'i; the International Society for Krishna Consciousness, commonly known as Hare Krishnas; the Transcendental Meditation movement; Rastafarians; the Peace Mission of Father Divine; Silva Mind Control; Rosicrucianism; and the Divine Light Mission. The most widely studied cult is that founded in South Korea by the Reverend Sun Myung Moon, known as the Unification Church. It began recruitment efforts in the United States in the 1950s, billing itself as a religion that fuses the core teachings of all the major world religions. It defines itself as a world-transforming movement that seeks to restore all of humanity to a positive relationship with God. To accomplish its goal, it has aggressively sought new recruits. This activity, along with the practice of mass arranged marriages, has led to much criticism, and members of the organization have often been belittled as "Moonies." Nevertheless, the Unification Church has substantial financial resources, which it has used to promote the view that the group is acceptable. This effort to promote the legitimacy of the Unification Church includes its ownership of one of the two daily newspapers in Washington, D.C., the *Washington Times*. Moon died in late 2012, at which time his wife and sons took control of the Unification Church.

Given the negative connotations associated with the term *cult,* many sociologists today have discontinued using it. However, others continue to view *cult* as a useful sociological concept (Shepard 2007).

The term *new religious movements* has gained broad acceptance in the sociology of religion. It encompasses sects, cults, and a wide array of other nontraditional, often innovative, religious groups (Lewis and Tollefson 2016). The concept was created because of a dissatisfaction with existing ideas and concepts as they relate to religious groups and their organization (Bromley 2016). Furthermore, it became clear that a much broader conceptual umbrella was needed to encompass the increasingly large number of very diverse religious organizations. Use of the term *new religious movement* is also intended to eliminate or reduce the negative connotations associated with cults, as well as other nontraditional religious organizations. It also emphasizes the idea that each unconventional religious organization should be examined objectively based on its own characteristics.

New religious movements tend to be typified by their zealous religious converts, their charismatic leaders, their appeal to an atypical portion of the population, their tendency to differentiate between "us" and "them," a distrust of others, and a proneness to rapid fundamental changes (Barker 2007). One example is the New Age movement, characterized by a belief in the coming of a global renewal in the "age of Aquarius" as well as an individually oriented, loving spirituality (Introvigne 2007).

The substitution of the idea of a new religious movement for religion does not solve the problem of what to make of Scientology. Some in the United States accept Scientology as a legitimate religion. It actively recruits new members, making use of substantial resources provided by high-profile celebrity members such as Tom Cruise and John Travolta. At the same time, it has provoked considerable controversy in this country (and elsewhere; Wright 2013). It is highly debatable whether Scientology can be considered a religion, but it certainly can be seen as a movement with *some* characteristics of a religion. However, other characteristics such as its business orientation and its scientific pretensions make it more of a hybrid form. Many feel that scientology wraps itself in a cloak of religiosity in order to enhance its ability to make money, reduce taxes, and keep government interference to a minimum. The HBO documentary based on Wright's book, *Going Clear: Scientology and the Prison of Belief,* details some of the abuses associated with Scientology, including its aggressive pursuit of power and profit, as well as the disillusionment of some past believers. Actress and producer Leah Remini, a former adherent, has

overseen the documentary *Scientology and the Aftermath,* which offers stories from former church members and their families. (The church itself claims that these stories are false.)

THEORIZING RELIGION

Because religion is such an important sociological subject, it should come as no surprise that sociologists have examined it from the perspectives of the major sociological theories. The following sections address religion through the lenses of structural/functional and conflict/critical theories. While the former purports that religion fulfills important social functions—and perhaps simultaneously causes a panoply of dysfunctions—the latter argues that religion serves merely as a distraction from economic and social inequalities.

STRUCTURAL/FUNCTIONAL THEORIES

Early sociologists such as Auguste Comte and Émile Durkheim believed that religion fulfills important social functions. The structural-functionalist perspective that emerged from their work focuses not only on the functions, or social purposes, served by religion but also on its dysfunctions.

Functions of Religion

In *The Elementary Forms of the Religious Life,* Durkheim emphasizes the solidarity produced by religion: "It is by uttering the same cry, pronouncing the same word, or performing the same gesture in regard to some object, that they become and feel themselves to be in unison" ([1912] 1965, 230). In addition to solidarity, religion provides a number of other functions for individuals and societies.

First, as Peter Berger (1969) suggests, religious and cultural traditions become a "sacred canopy" that covers a people, provides a sense of security, and answers questions about *meaning,* or the purpose of life. A religion's answers to these questions include an overall vision of the universe, a worldview, and perceptions of how best to organize life, individually and collectively.

Second, Durkheim ([1912] 1965) observes that religion provides explanations for puzzling aspects of life. Of particular importance are *theodicies,* theories that help us better understand and deal with suffering and death.

A third and vital function of religion for any society and its individuals is to provide a set of ethical guidelines (or ethics). These guidelines identify taboo lines marking what is unacceptable, or immoral, behavior. Ethical guidelines also promote positive action, such as sharing and caring for others. Each religious tradition also has a theory about what happens when people violate the norms, the most important of which are codified in a society's laws.

A fourth function of religion is to provide guidelines for a better style of life. While the evidence is mixed, research has shown that some Americans who are actively religious are more likely to have better physical and mental health (Ellison

ORGANIZATION	DEFINITION
Sect	A small group of people who see themselves as true believers and who voluntarily join a group, usually broken off from a more established religion, in order to have a personal religious experience
Church	A large group of religiously oriented people into which members are usually born (instead of joining consciously)
Denomination	A religious group that exhibits a general spirit of tolerance and acceptance of other religious bodies
Cult or new religious movement	A small, new, and exclusive group whose religious tradition has never been associated with any established religious organization and is often at odds with the rest of the religious community

1999; Ferraro and Kim 2014; Weber and Pargament 2014). One way religion may accomplish this is by helping people develop social support networks and ways of coping with various types of stress.

ASK YOURSELF

Do you think it is possible to develop community, ethics, social change, and compassion for all without religion? Why or why not?

Fifth, religious systems can provide individuals and groups with hope for the future, including what happens after death, giving believers a sense of self-confidence. If you believe that the universe is friendly, or at least that you are on the right side of larger forces or that they are protecting you, it is easier to have a sense that the future will turn out well, even if the present seems dark.

Finally, religion plays a crucial role in the process of social change. Although religious institutions are often intertwined with ruling elites, they also provide the foundation for major changes in a society. Examples include the Reverend Dr. Martin Luther King Jr.'s condemnation of racism in the United States, the antiapartheid movement's challenge to the South African government, and the uprisings in Eastern Europe in 1989 and the Arab world in 2011.

Dysfunctions of Religion

Although religion can facilitate the creation of community, it also might lead to ethnocentrism involving intolerance, conflict, and sometimes violence between religious groups. This is the "paradox of community": The same things that draw us together tear us apart (Ekland-Olson 2012). Although being a Hindu in South Asia may give one a sense of belonging to a significant community, for some it is at the expense of bonds with Muslims. In forging their identities in terms of negative comparisons, these communities tend to cultivate disrespect for each other. This mutual disrespect sometimes becomes violent.

Moreover, the very functions of religions may be dysfunctional. Further, what is functional from one point of view is dysfunctional from another. Religion may promote solidarity and order, but to the detriment of oppressed minority groups or those exploited by the system by helping keep injustice in place. It may provide explanations for suffering and evil that single out some groups as responsible for a society's problems. It therefore provides a rationale for the subordination of those groups or for hostility against them.

ASK YOURSELF

Can you think of any other social institutions besides religion that present a paradox of community? If so, what are they and how do they serve this double function?

A Palestinian man and an Israeli policeman face off in the Old City of Jerusalem. How does the solidarity of a religious group encourage a sense of the "otherness" of outsiders? Is this result inevitable?

The flip side of social solidarity is antipathy toward the other, which is a hallmark of religious history in many times and places. Exclusivist, "chosenness" theologies that promote the status of one group or society at the expense of another can be functional not only for a given community or society but also for regional and international relations. Those traditions that accentuate differences between "us" and "them," and imbue those differences and "our" perceived superior status with sacred endorsement, are almost inevitably going to engage in conflict with others. Religious communities with an ethnocentric view of the world and a belief that they are chosen by God—that only people who follow their beliefs and rituals are God's elect—are more vulnerable to rhetoric of exclusion and the condemnation of outsiders. In the midst of communal conflicts, each community may see the other as the focus of evil in the world and the source of all its problems. Religious justifications for these social divisions—such as the scapegoating of Jews in Nazi Germany—intensify emotions and sometimes give the conflicts themselves a sacred meaning (Kurtz 2005). In short, escalating communal conflict can lead to violence and even war. This is clear today in, among many other places, the Middle East (and increasingly elsewhere), where there is a state of perpetual war between Jews and at least some Muslims. A similar situation exists within Islam in the conflict between Shiites and Sunnis in much of the Middle East and parts of Asia, especially in recent years in Syria and Iraq.

The final and perhaps most dangerous dysfunction of religion, therefore, is the fact that it sometimes promotes violence and even evil behavior. A major reason for this is that religion provides a rationale for the use of violence against others. Most individuals who are going to harm others have to use what are called "mechanisms of moral disengagement" to avoid having guilty feelings for carrying out such behavior (Bandura et al. 1996). Among the most effective of those mechanisms, often facilitated by religious beliefs, are the practices of dehumanization, blaming the victim, and advantageous comparison. That is, if others are evil and condemned by God, they are more easily dehumanized and rationalized as unworthy of respect or dignity.

CONFLICT/CRITICAL THEORIES

A discussion of the dysfunctions of religion leads nicely into the conflict/critical approach to religion. Much of this approach continues to be informed by Karl Marx's original thinking in general, especially on the base and superstructure of capitalist society. To Marx ([1859] 1970), the *base* of capitalist society is the economy, while everything else—ideas, the state, and religion—is part of the *superstructure*. The things that are part of the superstructure in capitalist society are erected on an economic base. Thus, the nature of ideas, the state, and religion is ultimately traceable to that base. As a result, it is the capitalist economy that controls religion—as well as the state and ideas—and religion serves to enhance and protect the economic base.

According to Marx, religion performs this function by serving as an ideology that, like all ideologies, distorts and hides the underlying realities of capitalist society. Religious ideologies also serve to distract people and to obscure those economic and social realities. They are like drugs that put people into a daze so that they cannot see the social world accurately. It is this view that leads Marx ([1843] 1970) to his famous idea that religion is the "opium of the people." People who are drugged by religion are not only unable to have an accurate view of social problems; they are also unable to act on those problems, let alone overthrow the capitalist social structure that is the source of those problems.

Religion can be seen as what critical theorist Jürgen Habermas (1975) calls **legitimations**, or systems of ideas generated by the social system to support its own existence. Thus, the ideas associated with religion legitimate not only it but also the social, economic, and political systems in which it exists. To critical theorists, legitimations serve to "mystify" all of these systems, making it unclear exactly what is happening, especially the negative effects these systems are having on large numbers of people.

Another way of thinking of religion is that its distortions and illusions lead people into *false consciousness* (see Chapter 2). That is, because of religion and many other social forces, large numbers of people do not have a clear and correct sense of their true interests. For example, members of the working class do not realize that they are being exploited in a capitalist system. To critical theorists, false consciousness, including that induced by religion, prevents people from acquiring *class consciousness,* or a true sense of their interests. Without religion, people would be better able to see that their interests would be furthered by the overthrow of the capitalist system as well as the religious system that supports it (Lukacs [1922] 1968).

CHECKPOINT 14.5: THEORIES ABOUT RELIGION

THEORY	MAIN HYPOTHESIS
Structural/ functional theory	Religion fulfills social functions, such as producing solidarity; explains life's puzzling aspects, such as suffering and death; and provides a set of ethical guidelines.
Conflict/ critical theory	Religion is a system of ideas generated by the social system to support its own existence.

RELIGION AND GLOBALIZATION

Every major religious tradition was originally a local, even tribal, expression of faith that grew out of a specific environment and then diffused across certain regions and eventually the globe. All the global religions originated in Asia: The Eastern religions, including Hinduism, Buddhism, Confucianism, and Taoism, originated in South Asia and then spread east into China and East and South Asia. The Western religions, including Judaism, Christianity, and Islam, came from West Asia, or the Middle East.

Today, as Figure 14.5 shows, Christians make up 33 percent of the world's population (Britannica 2012; Kurtz 2012, 46). About 22 percent are Muslims, 14 percent are Hindus, and smaller proportions are followers of Buddhism (7 percent), Sikhism (0.36 percent), Judaism (0.21 percent), and the Baha'i faith (0.11 percent). Atheists (those without any religious belief) account for 2 percent of the world population.

The study of the relationship between religion and globalization is relatively recent, but it is clear that religion globalized before anything else. In fact, by this accounting, globalization is at least 2,000 years old (Beyer 2006). Although religion, like globalization, is a highly contested concept, we can focus on institutional religion and, under that heading, on two aspects of its relationship to globalization.

First, there is the issue of the importance of religion in transnational migration, in the bringing of institutional religion to new locales. Migrants transplant religions into new places, making those places more multireligious. This is evident in the movement of large numbers of Muslims into Europe, especially in the highly contentious influx that has occurred in recent years. Migrants also generate in those locales new and different versions of the local religions, even as the migrants' versions are influenced and altered by local religions. This, in turn, can alter religion in the migrants' homeland. Thus, transnational migration globalizes religion spatially and contributes to the further pluralization of religion around the world. Migrants play a variety of other roles in globalization. They help unify various parts of the world by, for example, making

FIGURE 14.5 • The World's Dominant Religions, by Percentage of Believers

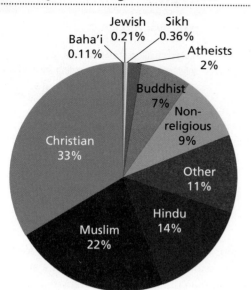

SOURCE: CIA World Factbook. (2013). *World.*

pilgrimages to religious sites like Mecca and the Wailing Wall, posting prayers in cyberspace, and sending money to religious centers in their homelands.

Second is the spread of religious organizations and movements through independent missions. Here the Christian Church, especially the Roman Catholic Church, has played a central role through its missionaries. In fact, Christianity became the first worldwide religion. Messengers for Islam created the most global system prior to the modern era (see the discussion of Islam below). Many other religions have expanded globally, but special note must be made of Islam and Buddhism and their renewed expansion and utilization of new possibilities and technologies, especially those associated with the internet.

It is also important to keep in mind that the spread of institutionalized religion was not unrelated to other institutions and other aspects of globalization. For example, the spread of Christianity from the sixteenth century through the eighteenth century was closely related to the spread of European political power and influence.

ASK YOURSELF

Have any other social institutions spread as widely as religion has? What do you think accounts for religion's staying power in the places to which it has been transported? Why are religions still expanding globally today?

THE MOST SIGNIFICANT GLOBAL RELIGIONS

In this section we will deal with several globally important religions—Judaism, Buddhism, Hinduism, Islam, and

Christianity. Although Mormonism is not a large global religion, and debate continues about whether it should be defined as a Christian denomination or a new religion, we will also examine it here because of its very contemporary efforts to become a global religion. However, as is clear in Figure 14.6, many of the world's dominant religions, despite their spread, are still to a large extent concentrated in particular parts of the world.

Judaism

Founded more than 3,000 years ago, Judaism is today one of the smallest of the world's religions, with roughly 14.3 million people in the world defining themselves as Jews (Goldberg 2007; Goldscheider 2012). However, for a variety of reasons, Judaism's importance both historically and contemporarily has been far greater than one would think by simply looking at the numbers involved. By the late nineteenth century, there were 12 million Jews in the world, many of whom had migrated from the Middle East and were spread in mostly small enclaves across many countries. There was and continues to be a large concentration of Jews in Europe, but migrations to North America, as well as to Palestine (then under Ottoman control), began during this period. By the onset of World War II, the number of Jews in the world had grown to 16.6 million, but the atrocities of the Nazis led to a reduction in the population to about 10 million. The founding of Israel in 1948 marked an important turning point for Jews, and that nation's population is now more than 6 million people. Another large concentration of Jews—approximately 6 million—is found in North America, mostly in the United States. The vast majority of the more than 14 million Jews alive today live in either North America or Israel, with fewer than 2 million living elsewhere, mostly in Europe. Just a few of the factors that give Judaism great global significance are the spread of Jews throughout the world, Zionism (which helped lead to the founding of Israel), the Holocaust, anti-Semitism, and the conflict between Israel and its Arab neighbors over Palestine.

Hinduism

Although no precise starting date can be determined, Hinduism began sometime between 800 and 200 BCE (Abrutyn 2012). While it has ancient origins, Hinduism became firmly established in India as the country opposed foreign occupation by Muslims (999–1757) and later the British (1757–1947). Today, the vast majority of Hindus (about 966 million) live in India. Hinduism is strongly defined by the *Vedas,* which are both historical documents and enumerations of incantations needed for successful rituals. Hinduism is also closely associated with India's caste system.

While it continues to be heavily concentrated in India, Hinduism is a global religion spanning six continents. It has been spread by both migrants and itinerant religious teachers (Madan 2007). Although it is heavily concentrated geographically, Hinduism has been important as part of the "Easternization of the West" (Campbell 2007) in, for

FIGURE 14.6 • The World's Dominant Religions

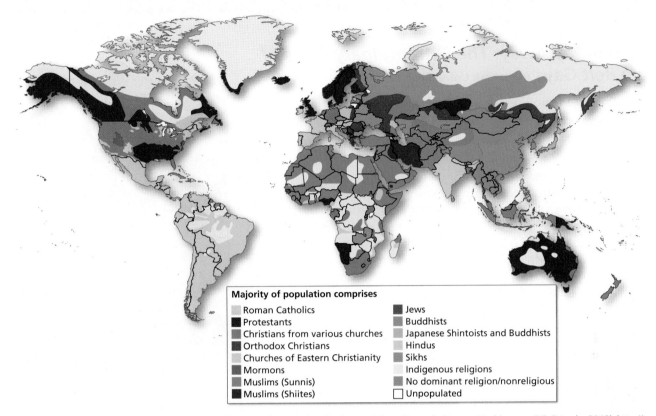

Majority of population comprises

- Roman Catholics
- Protestants
- Christians from various churches
- Orthodox Christians
- Churches of Eastern Christianity
- Mormons
- Muslims (Sunnis)
- Muslims (Shiites)
- Jews
- Buddhists
- Japanese Shintoists and Buddhists
- Hindus
- Sikhs
- Indigenous religions
- No dominant religion/nonreligious
- Unpopulated

SOURCE: "Faith on the Move - The Religious Affiliation of International Migrants" Pew Research Center, Washington, DC (March, 2012) http://www .pewforum.org/2012/03/08/religious-migration-exec/.

example, the spread of yoga (including now "he-man" yoga; Bluestein 2014), Transcendental Meditation, and so on. (And, of course, there has been a parallel, but much stronger, Westernization of the East [Sander and Cavallin 2015]). However, Hinduism has not been nearly as expansionistic as Christianity, Islam, or even Buddhism.

Buddhism

Buddhism arose in the Indus Ganges basin in about the sixth century BCE and began to have a transnational influence about three centuries later (Nichols 2012; J. L. Taylor 2007). Today there are somewhere around 488 million Buddhists across the globe, although the vast majority are in Asia. China has the largest number of Buddhists, followed by Japan. Other Asian countries with majority Buddhist populations include Thailand, Cambodia, Myanmar, Bhutan, Sri Lanka, Laos, and Vietnam. Thus, while Buddhism moved out from its origins in India, it has remained primarily concentrated on the Asian continent. The *Journal of Global Buddhism* is devoted to the study of the globalization of Buddhism (www.globalbuddhism.org).

Islam

Islam was founded by the Prophet Muhammad, who was born on the Arabian Peninsula and lived between 570 and 632 CE. The lands encompassed by Islam were seen as the center of the world, with all else subordinate to it. Important to Islam's spread (see Figure 14.6) was its universalistic worldview; Muslims did not view themselves as a chosen people but believed that they and all of humanity had a common destiny. Islam's universalistic ideas (God-given standards that lead everyone to search for goodness) had to be diffused throughout the world. Such beliefs led to a global mission to rid the world of competing idea systems, such as idolatry and superstition. On the other hand, Islam saw itself as building on, but going beyond, Judaism and Christianity. Thus, "Islam was the first of the world's great religious civilizations to understand itself as one religion among others" (Keane 2003, 42).

Believers in Islam, as well as their armies, spread westward into Spain and France and eastward into Byzantium, Persia, and eventually India and China. They traveled with the belief that they were the messengers and that everyone was eagerly awaiting, if not being actively denied, their message. Thus, the belief emerged that "Islam would prevail among the world's peoples, either by willing acceptance, or by spiritual fervour, or (in the face of violent resistances) by conquest" (Keane 2003, 42). Because there was only one God and therefore only one law according to Islam, such a view—and mission—meant that followers of Islam took no notice of nation-states and their borders.

In the end, of course, the efforts of Islam's early missionaries were thwarted. One factor in this failure was the

Pray the Gay Away: The Extraordinary Lives of Bible Belt Gays (New York University Press, 2012)

Bernadette Barton (Professor of Sociology and Women's Studies at Morehead State University; PhD, University of Kentucky, 2000)

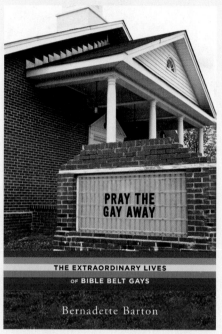

New York University Press. Used with permission.

In *Pray the Gay Away*, Bernadette Barton describes how homophobic attitudes of fundamentalist Christians are entrenched not just in religious institutions, but in families, workplaces, schools, politics, and social networks in the Bible Belt. Evangelical fundamentalists consider the Bible to be a source of authority and practice "witnessing," or spreading the word of Christ at every opportunity they can find, such as while standing in line at a grocery store or by placing religious flyers on a neighbor's doormat (2012, 2, 10). Bible Belt Christians often begin a conversation with what might seem like a relatively benign question: "What church do you belong to?" But Barton discovers that the answer to this question reinforces a form of "compulsory Christianity" that positions a person's Christian identity at the center of daily social interactions (2012, 4). Political and cultural ideologies are conveyed through identifying as a Bible Belt Christian, especially when it comes to sexual orientation. Regardless of denomination, Bible Belt Christians believe that homosexuality is sinful and contrary to the teachings of Jesus.

As a lesbian living (but not raised) in the Bible Belt of eastern Kentucky, Barton's encounters with Bible Belt Christians made her curious about the experiences of gay men and lesbians who grew up there. Using a variety of qualitative methodological techniques, including participant observations and interviews with 59 gay men and lesbians in Kentucky and Texas, Barton learned that most were forced to live in a "toxic closet" and hide their homosexuality or "risk rejection and ostracism" from their families and friends (2012, 5). Because they were taught that same-sex attraction is a sin, many literally tried to pray their gay away at their churches. The shame that many feel living in their toxic closets is amplified by having to confront compulsory Christianity on a daily basis. Barton likens this to living in a prison where gay men and lesbians are forced to monitor their daily lives for signs of Christian identity, such as a person wearing a fish belt buckle or a scripture printed on a store receipt. Such objects signify their social exclusion and alert them as to whether they should disclose their sexual identity (2012, 23).

Supplementary Resources

- You can watch a short clip of Bernadette Barton describing her book *Pray the Gay Away* at www.youtube.com/watch?v=sb4D62KQKoI.
- Learn more about the controversy surrounding praying away homosexuality in this episode of Dr. Drew's show that aired on HLN: www.youtube.com/watch?v=ESSOnnB5KCk.

efforts of alternative religions, especially Christianity and its various militaristic campaigns against Islam. Another was that the principle of *jihad,* or the duty to struggle on behalf of God against those who doubt him or are his enemies, was rarely pursued unconditionally. Thus, Islam was willing to compromise with its opponents (although that now seems to be changing, at least among some fundamentalists), and this proved fatal to its ambitions. Furthermore, because ultimate victory was ensured, Muslims believed that contact, trade, and traffic with nonbelievers was acceptable, even encouraged. These efforts ultimately had only limited success because of the Crusades as well as military defeats that forced Muslims out of Italy, Spain, and Portugal. However, the history of such efforts remains strong among many devotees of Islam and helps inform the contemporary thinking of jihadists and Islamic fundamentalists (Sayyid 2012).

Christianity

Christianity and Islam are the two fastest-growing religions in the world today (Garrett 2007; Thomas 2012). Christianity spread in the Middle East following the death of Jesus of Nazareth. By 1000 CE, a schism had developed between Roman Catholicism in the West and Orthodoxy in the East, with more Christians living in the East than in the West. A major series of events in the history of globalization was the Crusades, which began in 1095 CE and lasted for centuries. The Crusades were designed to liberate the Holy Land from Muslims and others who had gained control of Jerusalem in 638 CE. This is still a sensitive issue for Muslims, as reflected in protests that erupted when President George W. Bush used the word *crusade* in a speech shortly after the 9/11 terrorist attacks.

Christianity today is declining in Europe, but that is more than compensated for by strong growth in the Global South, including parts of Asia, Africa, and Latin America. Growth is so strong in the Global South that it is predicted that by 2050, 80 percent of the world's Christians will be Hispanic. Furthermore, Christianity is different in the Global South— "more . . . morally conservative, and evangelical" (Garrett 2007, 143). However, it is important to remember that there were not just outflows from Europe, but also reverse flows and cross-flows, producing original variants of Christianity.

Pentecostalism (see the Globalization box in this chapter), a charismatic movement, offers another example of the spread of Christianity around the globe (Anderson 2013). This religion had its origins in revivals attended by poor blacks and whites in Los Angeles in 1906. It is now the second-largest and fastest-growing form of Christianity, with about 280 million adherents, and has come to exceed in size all forms of Christianity except Catholicism. Its growth has been especially great in Asia, Africa, and Latin America (Lechner and Boli 2005). In fact, today only 69 percent of adults in Latin America say they are Catholic, compared to 90 percent throughout much of the twentieth century. The growth of Pentecostalism is a major factor in this decline (Paulson 2014). Pentecostal missionaries from Asia, Africa, and Latin America now often travel to the United States and Europe in search of converts. Many variations and localized forms of Pentecostalism are linked through publications, conferences, electronic media, and travel.

Mormonism

Mormonism, or the Church of Jesus Christ of Latter-Day Saints, has shown substantial growth in the last 60 years. Founded in the United States in the nineteenth century, Mormonism had fewer than 2 million members in 1960, but today the number has risen to approximately 15 million (McCombs 2013).

The Church of Jesus Christ of Latter-Day Saints is centrally controlled from its headquarters in Salt Lake City, Utah. The organization exercises considerable oversight over its churches in the United States and around the world from these headquarters. It also transmits much content, such as conferences and leadership training, via satellite throughout the world. And, of course, it maintains websites for the use of its global members.

Once almost exclusively an American religion, today Mormonism has more members outside the United States and thousands of churches and meetinghouses in most of the world's countries and territories. Eighty thousand missionaries spread Mormonism across the globe. Although the church banned blacks from becoming priests until 1978, today it is growing rapidly in Africa and has about half a million members there (Jordan 2007).

The global expansion of Mormonism is not only an example of globalization but also the result of a variety of global processes. First, as noted previously, the church has made extensive use of the internet, especially its well-known website (www.mormon.org). Second, it broadcasts, via satellite, church services, conferences, and leadership training conducted at the church's headquarters to 6,000 Mormon churches around the world. Third, it continues to follow the traditional path of global and globalizing religions by sending tens of thousands of missionaries around the world. The global acceptance and expansion of Mormonism is especially notable because of the church's sect-like character and practices. For example, the church has a history of polygamy and the marriage of preteen girls to older men—practices that some fundamentalist branches of Mormonism continue to this day. Such traditions are not easily accepted in many cultures and parts of the world. Other unusual practices include having a family "sealed" so that it can stay together after death and *tithing*, whereby one-tenth of a member's income is given to the church.

In contrast to other globally successful religions, Mormonism has not significantly adapted to local customs and realities. For example, unlike the far more rapidly expanding Pentecostalism, Mormonism has *not* incorporated a variety of indigenous customs (such as drumming and dancing) into its African Sunday services. Said one member who had moved to Nigeria and married a Nigerian: "No matter where you go in the world, the service is the same . . . the buildings, baptismal fonts, services and hymns in Lagos were nearly identical to those back home in the United States" (Jordan 2007, A13). Through watching Salt Lake City services via satellite, worshippers elsewhere in the world can easily see that the services and the teachings are the same—or at least very similar.

FUNDAMENTALISM

Religious **fundamentalism** is a strongly held belief in the fundamental or foundational precepts of any religion (Stolow 2004). It is also characterized by a rejection of the modern secular world (Kivisto 2012a). Fundamentalists see the world in stark terms (Koopmans 2015), dividing it into true believers (the in-group), who are saved, and the rest of the world's population (the out-groups), who are damned. There is often hostility between the in-group and out-groups. Fundamentalists seek to replace doubt and ambiguity with

Tongues of Fire

Pentecostalism is the fastest-growing Christian religious movement in the world, with dramatic increases in membership in Africa, Asia, Eastern Europe, and especially Latin America, despite the movement's modest origins (Miller, Sargeant, and Foley 2013). At the beginning of the twentieth century, a charismatic itinerant preacher named William J. Seymour set up operations in a decrepit former church in Los Angeles's black ghetto. Here he managed to attract large and enthusiastic interracial audiences to what came to be called the Azusa Street Revival (Robeck Jr. 2013).

The term *Pentecostal* derives from the New Testament account of the Holy Spirit coming to Jesus's followers after his resurrection, an event called Pentecost, during which tongues of fire appeared on their heads and they spoke in tongues. Central to this narrative is the occurrence of an emotionally intense religious experience expressed with exuberance.

So it was with the revival meetings Seymour conducted at Azusa Street beginning in 1906. They often took all night, with people caught up in the emotional intensity of the moment, falling to the ground and writhing about, possessed by the spirit so that they, too, spoke in tongues. The movement attracted both sympathizers and critics. Enthusiasm persisted for about a decade, after which attendance dropped off.

But by that time Pentecostals had begun to send missionaries around the world to spread their belief system, which emphasizes speaking in tongues, faith healing, and prophesying. Nowhere has the growth of Pentecostalism been more

Snake handling is a religious ritual in a small number of Pentecostal churches in the United States. Pastor Mack Wolford of the Jolo (West Virginia) Church of the Lord Jesus died after refusing medical treatment for a rattlesnake bite he suffered during a sermon. What might sociologists try to learn about the role of a snake-handling church in the lives of its members?

evident than in Latin America, almost entirely Roman Catholic until recently (Chesnut 2015). Guatemalans have been particularly inclined to convert, especially after intense missionary efforts following a 1976 earthquake. A brutal civil war then sent many Guatemalan Pentecostals to the United States, where they established churches with connections to those left behind. Pentecostalism thus came full circle: U.S. missionaries working in Guatemala succeeded in converting many people who later migrated to the United States.

Many Pentecostal congregations preach the "health and wealth gospel." Unlike the view of the Pentecostals on Azusa Street, which held that the

sufferings of this world will be rewarded in heaven, the message of these churches is that we can get ahead through individual initiative, and that aspiring to be economically successful is serving the will of God. At the same time, these groups continue to enact their religion in ways William Seymour would have understood (Liana 2007; Miller and Yamamori 2007).

Think About It

What accounts for the recent surge in the Pentecostal population? Do you think a focus on earthly success, such as the "health and wealth gospel," is compatible with the spiritual role religion plays in many people's lives? Why or why not?

---

crystal-clear certainty. All of the major world religions have fundamentalist elements, as do many smaller religions.

One example of fundamentalism is strict adherence to *sharia*, or traditional Islamic law. This includes mod-

est dress for women, abstention from alcohol, and public prayers. Sharia law has been seen as the basis of a governmentally enforced legal structure among Islamic fundamentalists, most notably the Taliban in Afghanistan and more recently the terrorist organization the Islamic State (IS) in Iraq and Syria. Moreover, it has been used to justify such inhumane practices as cutting off the hands of thieves, the stoning to death of people convicted of committing adultery, and the mass murder—most visibly and alarmingly by public beheading—of infidels, especially those who refuse to convert.

Fundamentalism has increased in importance in light of such developments as the growth of the Christian right in the United States; the Iranian Revolution of 1979, when Islamic fundamentalists led by Ayatollah Khomeini overthrew the pro-Western government of the shah; and, more recently, terrorist attacks by Islamic fundamentalists in various places in the world. The internet has become increasingly important to fundamentalist groups in getting out their messages, as well as in the efforts of groups such as the Islamic State to recruit supporters and fighters from throughout the world, including the United States (see the "Digital Living" box earlier in the chapter for more on how religious groups use technology).

Fundamentalism can be seen as being involved in globalization in at least two major senses (Brouwer, Gifford, and Rose 2013; Lechner 1993). First, it is often expansionistic, seeking to extend its reach into more and more areas of the world and to extend its power in those areas. Second, it is profoundly affected by various globalizations. For example, the globalization of one fundamentalist religion, such as that of Islamic militants, is likely to lead to a counterreaction by another, such as that of Hasidic Jews. Another important reaction involves movements against various forces seen as emanating from the modern world, including secularism, popular culture, rationalization, and the United States and the West in general. Much of the momentum for the recent rise of fundamentalism can be seen as traceable to a reaction against such forces. For example, IS is reacting against artificial borders in the Middle East drawn and imposed by the West largely after World War I, as well as the West's military involvement and cultural imperialism in that region. In a subtler sense, it has become a global expectation that people will develop a communal identity through involvement in fundamentalism.

FAITH ON THE MOVE

The globalization of religion—and the growing diversity of religions around the globe—is also the result of the movement of people. While the number has probably grown, the United Nations estimates that in 2010, there were 214 million immigrants globally. This figure represents just over 3 percent of the total population of the world. Recently, an attempt was made to determine what that movement of people meant in terms of the movement of religions across international borders. The Pew-Templeton Global Religious Futures Project provided a broad overview of the movement of major world religions in a study led by Phillip Connor (2012). Figure 14.7 summarizes the findings. It is perhaps not surprising that the world's two largest religions—Christianity and Islam—contribute the largest numbers of immigrants. Christians account for 2.3 billion adherents worldwide, and nearly half of all immigrants. Islam has 1.6 million adherents, and Muslim immigrants amount to 27 percent of all immigrants. Hinduism is the third-largest religion, but only 5 percent of Hindus are migrants. Jews, though the smallest of the world's religious groups, constitute 2 percent of all immigrants. Buddhists constitute 3 percent of all migrants, even though their religion has many more members than does Judaism. This indicates that just as Jews have historically been a diasporic people (that is, a people scattered around the world), they remain so today. Further, because of the rise of anti-Semitism, especially in Europe, we are likely to see an increase in Jewish immigration, especially to Israel and the United States. In fact, in light of the *Charlie Hebdo* massacre in 2015 (and similar and even more recent events elsewhere in France, Great Britain, and Europe more generally), the prime minister of Israel encouraged the mass immigration of Jews from Europe (Kershner 2015).

In terms of country of origin, more Christian immigrants are from Mexico than from any other nation. For Muslims, the largest point of origin is the Palestinian Territories. Most Palestinians are not recent migrants, but

FIGURE 14.7 • Religious Composition of International Migrants

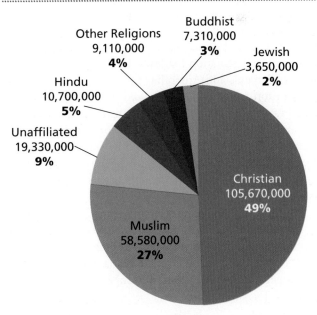

SOURCE: "Faith on the Move—The Religious Affiliation of International Migrants" Pew Research Center, Washington, DC (March, 2012) http://www.pewforum.org/2012/03/08/religious-migration-exec/.

The growing Muslim population in Europe has sparked controversy, including over the modest attire of some Muslim women. Some cities have even attempted to ban the "burkini" swimsuit.

rather became refugees after the establishment of Israel in 1948. For Jews, the largest point of origin is Russia; for Hindus, it is India; and for Buddhists, it is Vietnam. China, a major country of emigration, is the top country for both "other religions" and the unaffiliated.

Turning to destination countries, the United States is the number one country for Christians, followed by Russia, Germany, Spain, and Canada. The United States is also the number one country for Buddhists, followed by India, Australia, and Canada. Furthermore, the United States is the primary destination for the unaffiliated, followed by Russia, Germany, and Canada. Israel is the main destination for Jews, followed by the United States, Canada, and Australia. Saudi Arabia is the main destination for Muslims, followed by Russia, Germany, and France. India is a rather curious case, for it is both the number one country of origin for Hindus and the number one destination, followed by the United States, Bangladesh, and Nepal. Finally, those in the "other" category end up in the United States, Ivory Coast, Japan, and the United Kingdom.

In this detailed listing, two things are clear. First, some countries are especially important destinations. These include three countries with long histories of immigration: the United States, Australia, and Canada. They also include the larger countries of Western Europe: France, Germany, and the United Kingdom. In these countries, worship centers for new immigrant groups have been created, sometimes amid controversy. Thus, in various locales, efforts to "purpose-build" mosques (with minarets and other distinctive features) have been resisted by residents hostile to a growing Muslim presence in their communities. This has been a far bigger issue in Europe than in the United States, reflecting the fact that Europe has a much larger Muslim population. Thus, voters in Switzerland voted to prohibit the construction of any more minarets on mosques, even though there are only four in the entire country. Similarly, the wearing of veils by Islamic women has become a highly charged political issue in several European countries (Mirza 2013), particularly France (Joppke 2009). A more recent controversy involves the wearing of full-body Burkini swimsuits by Islamic women in the West (Rubin 2016). The United States has not been immune to such resistance and controversy. For example, efforts were made in Murfreesboro, Tennessee, to prevent a mosque from opening, even though an Islamic worship community had lived in the area for two decades.

CHECKPOINT 14.6: MOST POPULAR LOCATIONS OF THE WORLD'S DOMINANT RELIGIONS

RELIGION	DOMINANT GEOGRAPHIC LOCATION
Judaism	Israel, North America
Hinduism	India
Buddhism	China, Japan
Islam	North Africa, the Middle East
Christianity	Europe, North and South America

SUMMARY

Marx argued that religion is a response to the alienation people feel in the real world and therefore cannot be the basis for social change. Weber argued that religion helped create different types of societies, but that over time all societies became less religious and more rational. Religion played a central role in Durkheim's work. He believed that religion was the basis of collective conscience and that societies create rituals that serve to symbolize important beliefs and values.

Religion is a social phenomenon that consists of shared beliefs, rituals, and experiences. Sociologists study religion not to judge the truth claims of different religions, but to understand the social consequences of different beliefs. Beliefs are ideas that explain the world and identify what should be sacred (or extraordinary) and profane (or mundane). Rituals are repeated behaviors that symbolize beliefs and are often a central part of weddings and other rites of passage. Civil religion consists of the beliefs, rituals, and symbols that a nation holds sacred. Secularization refers to the declining importance of religion.

Sociologists have identified different types of religious institutions. These include sects, churches, cults, and new religious movements. A sect is a small group of "true believers" who voluntary join together to have a personal religious experience. A member of a church is typically born into a specific religion instead of voluntarily choosing it. In contrast to a sect, a church is hierarchically organized, with professional leaders. Similar to sects, cults are small, voluntary groups that are not associated with any religious organization; however, cults are newer and more innovative than sects. Both sects and cults are part of the new religious movements that are characterized by zealot converts, charismatic leaders, and proneness to rapid fundamental change.

Structural/functionalists focus on the social purposes of religion, such as providing a sense of security, belonging, and hope for people in addition to ethical guidelines. Religion may also be dysfunctional for a society if it affords solidarity and order for one group at the expense of another. Conflict/critical theorists view religion as an ideology that distorts and hides the causes of inequality in a capitalist society. Religion not only serves to distract people from engaging in social change, but also acts to legitimize the status quo.

The spread of religion is not new, but it has accelerated with increased globalization. The most significant global religions are Christianity, Islam, Hinduism, Buddhism, and Judaism. Christianity and Islam are the two largest religions in the world and are growing, while Judaism is the smallest global religion. One factor contributing to growing global religious diversity is global migration.

KEY TERMS

beliefs, 384
church, 392
civil
   religion, 387
cult, 394

denomination, 393
fundamentalism, 401
legitimations, 397
liminal
   period, 386

megachurches, 390
new religious
   movements, 395
profane, 384
religion, 383

rites of passage, 385
rituals, 385
sacred, 384
sect, 391
secularization, 388

REVIEW QUESTIONS

1. Religion is one of sociology's longest-running concerns. Based on your reading of this chapter, in what ways has sociology helped you have a better understanding of religion?

2. How do we define religion? What are the basic elements and components of religious institutions? In what ways have religions changed over time?

3. What are the major religions of the world? How are people distributed among the major religions of the world? In what ways are religions global?

4. What is the difference between a sect and a church? Provide one example of a sect and one of a church. Why has the term *cult* fallen out of favor with sociologists of religion?

5. What is ritual? Why is it an important component of religion? Offer examples of ritual practice from one of the major global religions discussed in the chapter. Provide another example, this time from a new religious movement.

6. Provide a definition of civil religion and discuss its function. The text describes several examples of civil religion. Offer additional examples.

7. What is secularization? Five factors are cited that sociologists think have contributed to secularization. Which ones do you think are most important, and why?

8. What does it mean to speak of a religious or spiritual marketplace? Provide examples that illustrate how religion is marketed to consumers.

9. Nondenominational megachurches have become very common today. What is their appeal to religious consumers, and what might turn some people off about them?

10. Most Christians, including those who claim to read the Bible literally, do not handle poisonous snakes during religious services. Offer a sociological explanation for how those thousand or so who do are different from the vast majority of Christians. Why are they willing to engage in such a dangerous practice?

PRACTICE AND APPLY WHAT YOU'VE LEARNED

▶ edge.sagepub.com/ritzerintro4e

CHECK YOUR COMPREHENSION ON THE STUDY SITE WITH:

- **Diagnostic pre-tests** to identify opportunities for improvement.

- **Personalized study plans** with focused recommendations to address specific knowledge gaps and additional learning needs.

- **Post-tests** to check your progress and ensure mastery of key learning objectives.

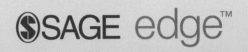

BREXI
HT RACIS
THE. SCAPEGOATING
mmigrants
END FREEDOM
OVEMENT
FOR JUSTICE By Any Means Necessary

POLITICS AND THE ECONOMY

The Interrelationship of Government and the Economy

"It's the economy, stupid" is a phrase attributed to Democratic political consultant James Carville and offered as advice in 1992 to successful presidential candidate Bill Clinton. The phrase was specific to the campaign against sitting Republican president George H. W. Bush, who was saddled with an economic recession. It was designed to remind Clinton to address the economy whenever he could, because that was what was most on peoples' minds and was likely to attract the most votes. However, it is a phrase—and a reality—that has lived on and continues to be applicable to most, if not all, political campaigns. Except in the rare case of an economic boom, it is almost always the economy that is key as far as politics is concerned, and, conversely, economies are always deeply political.

We were reminded of that once again in 2016 as the political landscape in several countries was drastically altered by a series of dramatic developments. The most extreme example was Brexit, or the British exit from the European Union (EU). The EU is a political organization that, at least in part, grew out of the European Economic Community (EEC), or "Common Market," which was created in 1957. As the name suggests, the EEC was created to bring about economic integration among member nations. It was absorbed into the political European Union (EU) in 1993.

Many Europeans, however, grew dissatisfied with the centralized political control exerted by the EU, which mandated open borders between EU-member countries, among other things. That contributed to massive flows of immigrants from poorer countries, threatening those with well-paying jobs in the richer countries of the EU. Other economic problems included the inability of poorer countries in the EU to devalue their currencies because they were all using the euro. Historically, poorer countries have been able to compete

LEARNING OBJECTIVES

 15.1 Contrast democracy and dictatorship.

 15.2 Outline who rules the United States using the perspectives of structural/functional and conflict/critical theories.

15.3 Explain how global politics affect war and terrorism, geopolitics, and the nation-state.

 15.4 Describe the U.S. economy's transition from industrialization to deindustrialization.

 15.5 Discuss how work, consumption, and leisure shape our understanding of the economy.

 15.6 Describe the effects of globalization on the world economy.

edge.sagepub.com/ritzerintro4e

- Take the chapter quiz
- Review key terms with eFlashcards
- Explore multimedia links and SAGE readings

$SAGE edge™

Rex Features via AP Images

economically in times of recession by devaluing their currencies, thereby making their products cheaper and therefore more competitive.

In the context of this dissatisfaction with the EU, Britain engaged in what was considered to be a *pro forma* vote on whether or not it should remain in the EU. To the surprise of many, however, the British public voted against remaining in the EU, and unless something dramatic happens, Britain will leave the organization in a few years. Brexit could have dire economic consequences for Great Britain (and much of Europe), but it had great, immediate political consequences for British Prime Minister David Cameron, who had opposed Brexit and felt compelled to resign as a result of the vote.

Surprisingly, the decision by the British reverberated in the United States, especially among a large number of lower- and middle-class people who were suffering economically. They had never really recovered from the Great Recession and had few prospects of ever recovering fully. Republican presidential candidate Donald Trump appealed to that population, its economic frustrations, and its fear of the Other, especially in the form of undocumented immigrants from Mexico, including the fact that they would work for less than American workers. This led, among other things, to Trump's famous call to build a great wall between the United States and Mexico . . . and to make Mexico pay for it.

Politics is economics . . . economics is politics. Sociology looks at how people make political and economic choices and how societies deal with the personal, national, and global consequences of those choices. ●

POLITICS: DEMOCRACY OR DICTATORSHIP

Society can be seen as a collection of groups that compete to determine whose members get what, as well as when and how they get it (Lasswell 2012). When groups operate through established governmental channels to do so, this competition is referred to as **politics**. The state is the political body organized for government and civil rule. By putting pressure on the state, a group can advance a given position or promote policies that benefit its members. Therefore, politics is one way of exercising power in society.

DEMOCRACY: CITIZENSHIP AS A RADICAL IDEA

Democracies are political systems in which people within a given state vote to choose their leaders and in some cases vote on legislation as well. In modern democracies, people vote to choose their legislators rather than actually managing their own political affairs and directly making decisions about the things that affect their lives. Nevertheless, contemporary theorists of democracy often suggest that the power to rule in democracies comes from the *consent* of the people.

Sometimes these systems are called **representative democracies**. The people, as a whole body, do not actually rule themselves but rather have some say in who will best represent them in the state. In **direct democracies**, by contrast, the people have a say in decisions that directly affect them.

Democratic states are organized into bureaucracies (see Chapter 6), with clear hierarchies as well as established and written codes, laws, and rules. The authority that legislators have under democracies is based on legal codes that confer this authority on them. Democracies tend to extend rights to **citizens**, the people represented by the state and most often born within its territories. **Citizenship** means that the people of a given state can vote for their representatives and that they have rights and responsibilities as citizens (Soysal 2012; Turner 2011). It should be noted, however, that citizenship has not always been universal. In the past, it was often conferred only on men or property owners. Under *universal citizenship*, the rights of citizenship are generally conferred on most people residing in a given state's territory. At times, however, citizenship is still denied to groups of immigrants residing within that territory. In the United States, citizens have certain rights and can vote on who will be president and on who will represent them in Congress.

Most democratic states guarantee citizens the right to freely express dissent, the right to due process and equality before the law, the rights of freedom of speech and of the press, and the right to privacy. These rights and others are sometimes extended to noncitizens. Even in modern liberal democracies, these "rights" are highly contextual. Consider, for example, how the right to dissent was treated in the United States during the Red Scare of the late 1940s and early 1950s, when the state, led by Senator Joseph McCarthy, saw to it that dissidents were ostracized and harassed (see Chapters 7 and 18). At his first press conference after being elected president, Donald Trump threatened, not for the first time, the freedom of the press. He repeatedly refused to answer a question from a CNN reporter because, he claimed, the news network was a purveyor of "fake news." Freedom House, an organization committed to monitoring

FIGURE 15.1 • Freedom in the World, 2015

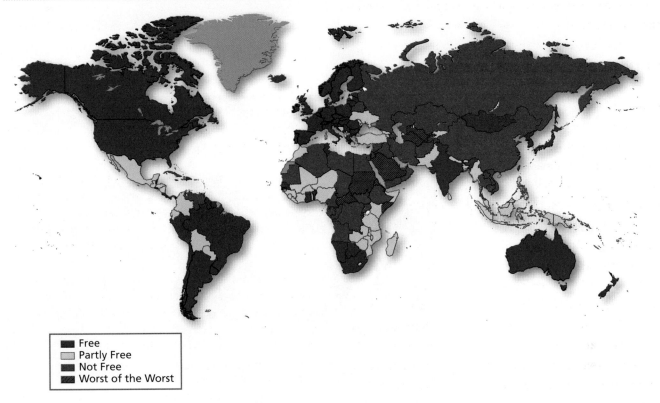

Free
Partly Free
Not Free
Worst of the Worst

SOURCE: Data from Freedom House, "Freedom in the World," 2016.

democratic trends and human rights around the world, publishes an annual survey on 195 countries rating political rights and civil liberties (see Figure 15.1). In 2016, of the 195 countries assessed, 86 (44 percent) were rated "free," 59 (30 percent) were rated "partly free," and 50 (26 percent) were rated "not free." Ratings for the Middle East and North Africa were the worst in the world, followed by Eurasia. Syria, a dictatorship mired in civil war, ethnic division, and uncontrolled terrorism, received the lowest score of any country in more than a decade. The other "worst of the worst" countries are the Central African Republic, Equatorial Guinea, Eritrea, North Korea, Saudi Arabia, Somalia, Sudan, Turkmenistan, and Uzbekistan.

Democracies are not without their critics, even from within. Some have argued that voters are typically uninformed about many political issues. For example, many of those in Great Britain who voted for Brexit were not fully aware of its implications for them. Many working-class voters in the United States did not anticipate that Donald Trump would appoint billionaires and millionaires to his cabinet who would likely be unresponsive to their needs and interests (Duhigg 2017). Other critics argue that liberal democracies extend *too many* rights and tend to allow too much diversity of thought and interest, making them unstable.

DICTATORSHIP: THE SEIZURE OF POWER

Dictatorships are states that are usually totalitarian and ruled either by a single individual or by a small group of people. Dictatorships are governments *without* the consent of the people being governed. In the modern period, dictatorships are often formed in formerly democratic states that have been seized by small groups of political fanatics.

In the years just before and during World War II, the world saw an alliance of dictatorships based on fascist principles. These dictatorships shared some very basic institutional arrangements and principles. They

- Were totalitarian in that they attempted to control every facet of social life

- Had a "cult of masculinity" that organized political life and the public sphere around men and punished perceived deficiencies in masculinity, such as homosexuality

- Saw conflict and war as natural states and methods for human betterment

- Were viciously opposed to liberalism, anarchism, and any form of socialism or communism

Hacktivism and State Interference

Digital technologies have enabled hackers to access private computer servers and leak or sell personal information, such as Social Security numbers, credit card accounts, and e-mails. Hackers target not only individuals, but also governments, corporations, universities, and internet search engines, such as Yahoo and Google. While some hackers engage in such behavior to prove that they have the technical skills to do so, others profit from selling information they obtain to the highest bidder. Some so-called hacktivists view themselves as digital activists who can change the world with the information that they hack and target powerful individuals and organizations. The website WikiLeaks permits hackers to post leaked information, which it archives for the public to access.

Recently, U.S. political figures and organizations have been targeted by hackers, which has had a profound effect on the political process. For example, in the summer of 2016, more than 30,000 e-mails from Hillary Clinton's private server when she served as secretary of state were leaked and posted on WikiLeaks. Thousands of leaked e-mails from the Democratic National Committee were also posted on WikiLeaks that summer, leading to the resignation of its chair, Debbie Wasserman Schultz. According to American intelligence

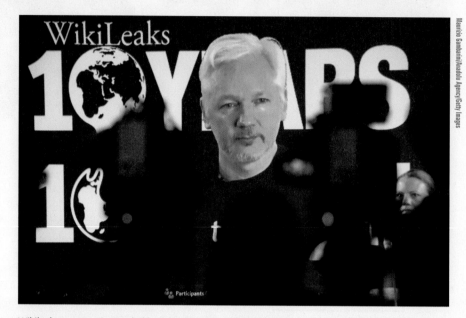

Wikileaks, an organization led by Julian Assange, has posted thousands of hacked documents, including personal e-mails of politicians and campaign workers.

agencies, Russian hackers interfered in the 2016 U.S. presidential election and leaked documents from Democratic Party organizations to WikiLeaks, in the process possibly influencing the election in favor of Donald Trump (Sanger and Shane 2016). Russian hackers also targeted Democratic House candidates in the election, leaking documents from the Democratic Congressional Campaign Committee to journalists in Florida (Lipton and Shane 2016).

Engaging the Digital World

How concerned are you about hackers accessing and leaking your personal information? What do you think the U.S. government's response should be to international hackers leaking e-mails and documents of politicians and government agencies to WikiLeaks? Is using our "cyberarsenal" against the Russian government an appropriate action? Why or why not?

Dictatorships did not end with the defeat of the fascist powers in World War II. Indeed, in the postwar era, the Soviet Union and its satellites in the Eastern Bloc were often organized as dictatorships, with small groups of Communist Party officials controlling society. Latin America has had a number of dictatorships since World War II. Among dictatorships elsewhere in the world today, North Korea is arguably the most dangerous, given its fraught relationship with

South Korea and its frequent testing of nuclear weapons. The United States has often sponsored dictatorships and fought against democracy. This has occurred particularly where democratically elected leaders might turn toward political orientations (such as socialism or, as in Turkey today, Islamism) that would make their governments problematic for American political and business interests (Chomsky 1985).

FORM OF GOVERNMENT	DESCRIPTION
Democracy	A political system in which people in a given state vote to choose their leaders
Dictatorship	A political system that is usually totalitarian and ruled without the consent of the governed

WHO RULES THE UNITED STATES?

Even though the United States is a democracy, the issue of who rules the nation is a source of continuing debate among sociologists (and political scientists).

THE STRUCTURAL/FUNCTIONAL PERSPECTIVE: PLURALISM

Within structural-functionalism, the typical position put forward regarding who rules America is pluralism (see Chapter 10). This is the view that the United States is characterized by a number of powerful competing interest groups, and no one of them is in control all of the time. In other words, there is a kind of balance of power among these interest groups. In addition, there is a **separation of powers** in the government. That is, the three major branches of government—legislative, executive, and judicial—are separate and counterbalance one another so that there is little danger that any one branch of government can wield too much power.

Among pluralists, there are two major strands of thought. **Group pluralism** focuses on society's many different interest groups and organizations and how they compete for access to political power to attempt to further their interests (Drache 2008; Fung 2004). For group pluralists, this jockeying for power by various organizations provides stability for society. They see a *balance of group power,* where no one group retains power indefinitely and any group can always be challenged by another group. Further, there are *crosscutting group memberships,* with group members belonging to a variety of organizations that see to their needs and interests. This allows people to be political actors in a variety of collective processes. Group pluralists also believe that there tends to be a general *consensus of values* in society. As a result, the state is expected and pressured to legislate according to the common good and according to the cultural values largely held in common by members of society.

Group pluralists not only focus on existing organizations and groups that act for their political interests in society but also see *potential groups* as a source of stability. Accordingly, if, for example, the state expects that particular legislation might mobilize people in opposition to it, that threat might hold political actors back from taking action. There might not yet be an oppositional interest group, but the expectation of *mobilization of latent interests* can serve to pressure politicians to legislate for the common good. To group pluralists, then, organizations do not have to exist to help create societal stability. The mere *possibility* of future organizations can have the same effect.

Elite pluralism focuses specifically on how political elites form similar interest groups and organizations that vie for power (Higley and Burton 2006; Lipset 1981; Rose 1967). While voters may decide which elites represent them, the ultimate decision-making power rests in the hands of those elites. Similar to group pluralists, elite pluralists look at political elites as a diverse social body that organizes into groups to compete with one another for votes. This competition for votes ensures that no one group retains political power indefinitely. Stability is achieved in the system because these political elites must forge agreements with one another in order to pass legislation. This allows for a diversity of interests to be satisfied through those agreements, which tend to represent the common values of the larger society.

George Bush Presidential Library and Museum.

In his college days, George H. W. Bush (standing nearest the clock, on the left) belonged to the elite and secret Yale University society called Skull and Bones. How does membership in such groups confer advantage on members later in life?

THE CONFLICT/CRITICAL PERSPECTIVE: THE POWER ELITE

Pluralism is often juxtaposed to a theory produced by conflict/critical theorists: C. Wright Mills's (1956; Maclean, Harvey, and Chia 2010) **power elite theory**. This theory holds that power is not dispersed throughout a stable society—either among citizen groups or among elite groups. Rather, power is concentrated among a small number of people who control the major institutions of the state, the corporate economy, and the military. The powerful people who make up these institutions may have minor disagreements about policy, but for the most part they are unified in their interests and in the business of owning and operating much of American society.

These elites develop a common worldview. First, they undergo a process of *co-optation*, whereby they are taught the common ideology of the elite. Further, they forge a shared ideology through their common *class identity*. That is, members of the power elite tend to come from wealthy families, go to similar schools, and belong to similar clubs. These clubs count as their members many of the most powerful people in the world, including corporate leaders, politicians, and top military brass. The clubs provide private spaces where friendships and common policies are forged (Clogher 1981; Domhoff 1974, 2013).

The power elite within the military, the state, and the corporate world are also often *interchangeable*. That is, the people who hold leadership positions within these three major institutions play a sort of institutional "musical chairs," switching from one powerful institution to another.

In sum, to power elite theorists, the state is not some neutral institution existing in a stable society where everyone (or every group) has an equal chance of having their interests met. Rather, the state is an institution controlled by the elites.

WHICH PERSPECTIVE IS CORRECT?

We can see strengths and weaknesses in both pluralism and power elite theory. The pluralist idea that latent interests influence politicians cannot be verified empirically. The assumption that society is stable is also problematic. It avoids issues such as for whom society might be stable and in which contexts. Finally, pluralism assumes that the state is a neutral institution, rather than an institution with its own interests, and one that tends to be controlled by wealthy elites.

Power elite theory also has various problems. For example, it assumes that elites share a common worldview and common interests to an extent that may not match reality. Indeed, can we assume that the power elite is monolithic and has little diversity of thought? Further, is the power elite untouchable by the masses of people? Does it control society to the extent that power elite theorists would have us believe, or are there avenues for changing society from below that those theorists are ignoring? And if the members of the power elite all but control our society, how is it that legislation that benefits some sections of society at their expense is passed? How did we end up with minimum-wage laws, social welfare, Medicaid, the Affordable Care Act ("Obamacare"), and so on?

CHECKPOINT 15.2: THEORIES ABOUT WHO RULES THE UNITED STATES

THEORY	MAIN HYPOTHESIS
Structural/ functional theory	The United States has many powerful and competing interest groups, but pluralism ensures that no one of these is in control all the time.
Conflict/ critical theory	Power elite theory suggests that power is concentrated among a few who control the major institutions of the state, the corporate economy, and the military.

GLOBAL POLITICS

Politics has long been global (Heywood 2014; Kaarbo and Ray 2010), but it is convenient to trace modern political globalization to the end of World War I in 1918. After the war, efforts at peace led to the creation of the League of Nations in 1920. While this organization was weak, in part because the United States never joined, it created an important forum for global political dialogue and relationships. Of course, peace failed, leading to the start of World War II in 1939. Many of the world's nations became immersed in global warfare. The war had disastrous consequences for much of the world, but it did lead to the formation of the United Nations in 1945. While far from an unmitigated success, the UN persists to this day as an important site and source of political globalization. Many other global political organizations have been formed within the United Nations (e.g., the UN Educational, Scientific, and Cultural Organization, known as UNESCO) or alongside it (e.g., the now troubled European Union).

These organizations have helped bring about greater dialogue among the world's nations, and in the last six decades, we have not witnessed anything like the carnage of World Wars I and II (Pinker 2011). However, such organizations have not led to world peace. Since the formation of the UN, there have been several major interstate wars— conflicts fought between different countries—including the Korean War, the war in Vietnam, the various wars involving

FIGURE 15.2 • Civil Wars and Interstate Armed Conflicts, 1946–2012

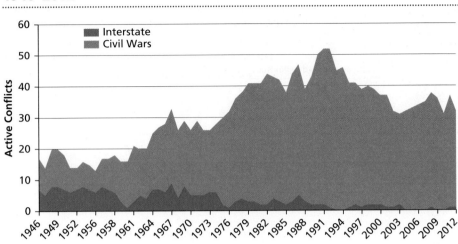

SOURCE: Trends in Armed Conflict, 1946–2014, PRIO Conflict Trends, 01, 2016, Figure 1, p. 2.

that the state sees this use as legitimate. These firms operate both domestically, as in security details for private corporations, and abroad. The state also determines when private citizens have the right to use violence. If someone uses violence against another and it is deemed self-defense by the courts, that violence is seen as legitimate. The state creates and maintains the regulations and rules that one must abide by to commit an act of violence. At times, this is in defense of oneself, but in some cases it is in defense of one's property. There are also legal codes dealing with when people can use violence in defense of someone else or of their property.

Israel and its Arab neighbors, and the conflicts in Iraq, Afghanistan, and Syria. The number of interstate wars has decreased significantly since the UN's founding, but internal conflicts such as civil wars continue to endure, as shown in Figure 15.2. In addition to continued internal conflict, the world has been plagued by a number of terrorist (and antiterrorist) incidents, especially since September 11, 2001. While many of the nations of the world communicate with one another in various global forums, they still manage to engage in conflict and to slaughter each other's citizens. Further enhancing the likelihood of conflict is the existence of terrorist groups such as the so-called Islamic State, which are not interested in dialogue and do not participate in such forums. There was, however, a more hopeful development in late 2016 when Colombia reached an agreement with the rebel group FARC (Revolutionary Armed Forces of Colombia) ending fifty years of warfare (Casey 2016).

IMPLEMENTING POLITICAL OBJECTIVES: LEGITIMATE VIOLENCE, WAR, AND TERRORISM

When authority rests in its hands, the state maintains order through its claim to the legitimate use of violence in a given territory. Thus, through the police force and the military, the state is able to use legitimate violence to enforce order. Much of the power of the state rests in this monopoly on legitimate violence.

The state also legitimates the forms of violence that might be used by people not directly acting as its agents. Private security firms can legitimately use violence, provided

War

War occurs when a nation uses its military in an attempt to impose its will on others outside the nation (Malesevic 2010). It also occurs when a nation uses its military to impose its political will within its borders—the case of civil war. War is one method of "doing politics," or dealing with political disagreements.

Why does war occur? First, there needs to be a cultural tradition of war. Second, a situation must exist in which two political actors have objectives that are incompatible. Finally, a "fuel" must bring the situation from thinking about war to actually *making war* (Timasheff 1965).

In the United States, the cultural tradition of war is all around us. We are often taught in our history classes about U.S. involvement in foreign wars, in which we are depicted as saviors, the bringers of democracy, and so on. In our own history, we can see antagonistic situations that brought us into military conflict with other nations or peoples. Acts of aggression, such as the Japanese attack on Pearl Harbor and the September 11 terrorist attacks, have served as the fuels that ignited war.

Terrorism

Terrorism typically involves nongovernmental actors engaging in acts of violence targeting noncombatants, property, or even military personnel in order to influence politics (Vertigans 2011). The term *terrorism* is often controversial, because it is usually the powerful who define who is and who is not a terrorist. Consider, for example, that if property

FIGURE 15.3 • Deaths from Terrorism Worldwide, 2000–2015

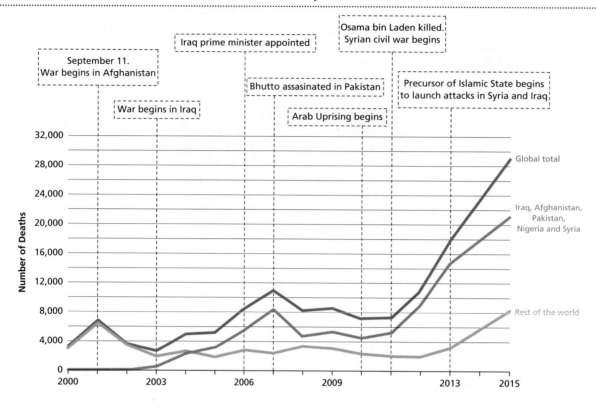

SOURCE: Based on data from Global Terrorism Database, as reprinted in *Global Terrorism Index, 2016: Measuring and Understanding the Impact of Terrorism*, The Institute for Economics and Peace.

destruction as a way to express political grievances constitutes terrorism, the people who were part of the Boston Tea Party fit the description. And where is the line between terrorists and revolutionaries fighting against invading or occupying armies? Who gets to draw that line and why? Can states be terrorists?

Nevertheless, all over the world, people refer to acts such as suicide bombings and the targeting of civilians of enemy nations or groups as examples of terrorism. More specifically, in the West today, a group is likely to be labeled terrorist if it has a history of engaging in violence against the citizens of a government (Beck and Minor 2013). Terrorist attacks are quite common in the early twenty-first century and do not seem to be on the decline. While terrorism is particularly likely when one nation occupies another and attempts to police its population, many acts of contemporary terrorism, especially those committed by the Islamic State, are far more wide-ranging and not limited by national borders. Figure 15.3 shows that the number of people who have died from terrorist activity each year has increased fivefold since 2000. In 2015, approximately 29,000 deaths resulted from terrorist attacks. The vast majority of these incidents (72 percent) occurred in Iraq, Afghanistan, Pakistan, Nigeria, and Syria.

These countries experienced 21,150 fatalities. Excluding these five countries in 2015, the rest of the world lost 8,226 lives due to terrorism. From 2000 to 2015, more than 169,000 people around the world died from terrorist incidents. Not included in these numbers are acts lacking a political, economic, religious, or social goal; thus, they may exclude domestic, or home-grown, terrorism, such as school shootings (Kellner 2008).

ASK YOURSELF

It is often pointed out that those revered in U.S. history as the instigators of the American Revolution could be characterized as terrorists in another light. Do you agree with this characterization? What is the difference between a terrorist and a revolutionary hero?

GEOPOLITICS

As the previous section indicates, geopolitics continues to define global political relationships (Black 2016; Steinmetz 2012). **Geopolitics** entails political relationships that involve broad geographic areas, including the globe as a whole. On the one hand, geopolitics is concerned with how politics affect geography. One example is the ways in which national borders are redrawn after the end of a war. On the other hand, geopolitics is concerned with the ways in which geography affects politics. One example is the (usually) constant low-level warfare between Israel and its neighbors. This conflict occurs, at least to some degree, because Israel is a tiny nation surrounded by much larger hostile nations. After World War II, much of geopolitics focused on the relationship between the United States and the Soviet Union and their allies. There was great concern over the global expansion of communism. The United States and the Soviet Union clashed, usually indirectly, over their political influence in Germany, Korea, Cuba, Vietnam, and so on. While the Soviet Union sought to expand geopolitically, the United States followed a policy of containment of Soviet efforts to expand communism. For decades, the United States acted based on what was known as the *domino theory*: If one nation was allowed to fall to communism, many neighboring nations would also fall. For example, the United States feared that if Vietnam fell to the communists, neighboring countries like Laos and Cambodia would be next. The United States and its relationships with Russia, China, and the Islamic world are at the center of geopolitics today.

THE NATION AND THE NATION-STATE

As discussed in Chapter 6, geopolitics relates to core concerns in the global age: the future of the nation and the nation-state. A *nation* is a group of people who share, often over a long period of time, similar cultural, religious, ethnic, and linguistic characteristics (Chernilo 2012). Jews are a nation by this definition, and, ironically, so are their frequent geopolitical enemies, the Palestinians. While many Jews and Palestinians live in the Middle East, many others, especially Jews, are spread throughout the world. They are scattered or dispersed; as described in Chapter 10, they exist in a *diaspora* (Fiddian-Qasmiyeh 2012). The ongoing war in Syria (and Iraq) has forced millions to flee creating a new diaspora.

All diasporas share certain characteristics. First, they involve people who have been dispersed from their homelands. Second, the people in the diaspora retain a collective and idealized memory of the homeland that they transmit to their offspring as well as to other members of the diaspora. Third, as a result of this idealization, they are often alienated from their host countries; the realities of the host country cannot measure up to the idealizations associated with the homeland. Fourth, those in the diaspora often take as a political goal the idea and the objective of returning to the homeland (Cohen 1997). Many of those involved

in a nation, especially those in the diaspora, may have no direct contact with the homeland or with those who live there. Their linkages to them may be largely or purely imaginary. In other words, they exist in what Benedict Anderson (1991; Roudometof 2012) calls **imagined communities**, or communities that are socially constructed by those who see themselves as part of them. Thus, Jews who have never been to Israel, or who may never even want to visit there, may still be part of an imagined community rooted in Israel. The same is true of the relationship between Palestine and many Palestinians scattered throughout the world, and this fate likely awaits many Syrians and Iraqis who have recently fled their countries.

The *nation-state* combines the nation with a geographic and political structure. In other words, in addition to encompassing people with a shared identity and culture, a nation-state exists in a bounded physical location and encompasses a government to administer the locale. In these terms, Syria remains a nation-state, even though it has lost control over much of its territory.

Nation-states exist within a global context, but they are affected, even threatened, by globalization in various ways (Hershkovitz 2012). First, global flows of various kinds—undocumented immigrants, drugs, terrorists, and so on—easily pierce the borders of nation-states and serve to erode their national sovereignties. Second, even if it does not threaten national sovereignty, globalization serves to alter the nation-state's structure and functions. For example, corporations have become increasingly important on the global stage and have come to operate more autonomously from states. Third, the government itself has to change to adjust to global changes. For example, the United States created the Department of Homeland Security in 2002 to deal with, among other things, the global threat of terrorism. Fourth, there is the possibility that global flows can strengthen the nation-state. For example, external threats can lead citizens to put their differences aside, at least for the time being, and rally around the government and the nation-state more broadly. There are many serious internal divisions in Israel, but external threats often lead Israelis to put those differences aside and present a united front.

In spite of changes such as those described previously, we continue to think of nation-states as being all-powerful. However, not only have states experienced the kinds of problems described here; a number of them have failed, or are on the verge of failing, to fulfill the "basic conditions and responsibilities" of sovereign states (Boas 2012, 633). Among the characteristics of a failed state are a "lack of control over own territory, widespread corruption and criminality, huge economic recession and/or hyperinflation, failure to provide basic services, and large flows of refugees and internally displaced persons" (Boas 2012, 633). In addition, states that

FIGURE 15.4 • Fragile States Index, 2016

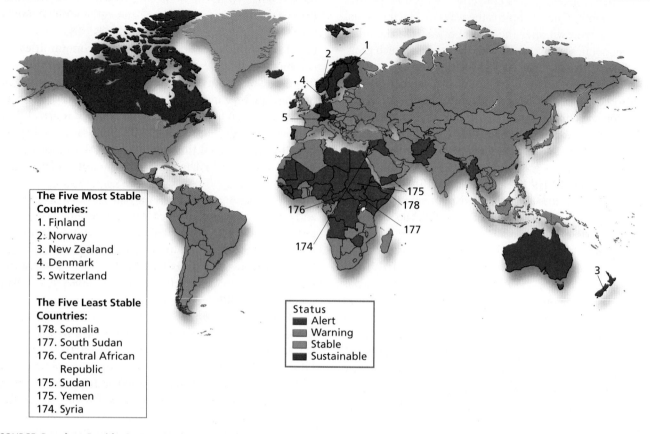

The Five Most Stable Countries:
1. Finland
2. Norway
3. New Zealand
4. Denmark
5. Switzerland

The Five Least Stable Countries:
178. Somalia
177. South Sudan
176. Central African Republic
175. Sudan
175. Yemen
174. Syria

Status
- Alert
- Warning
- Stable
- Sustainable

SOURCE: Data from Fund for Peace, "Fragile States Index 2016."

do not have economic and political institutions that include broad segments of society are more likely to fail. Failed states also tend to exploit one segment of society (the middle and lower classes, for example) for the benefit of another subset, especially the rich (Acemoglu and Robinson 2012). The Fragile States Index, an annual ranking of 178 nations, highlights weak and failing states around the world based on their levels of stability (see Figure 15.4). In 2016, the countries that received the worst scores were South Sudan, Somalia, Central African Republic, Congo, Sudan, Yemen, Syria, and Chad.

Failed states cause many problems for themselves and their residents, but from a global perspective, it is the problems they cause for others that are the main concern. Pirates based in Somalia roamed the high seas for years and succeeded in a number of acts of high-stakes piracy, such as holding huge oil tankers for millions of dollars in ransom. The Somalian government, to the extent that it exists, was unable to control the pirates or their activities. This piracy, however, has been has been greatly reduced in recent years by the formation of a combined task force to patrol the seas around Somalia (Gladstone 2014).

CHECKPOINT 15.3: GLOBAL POLITICS

FACTOR	DESCRIPTION
War	Occurs when a nation uses its military to impose its will on others outside the nation
Terrorism	Occurs when nongovernmental actors engage in violence against noncombatants, property, or military personnel to influence politics
Geopolitics	Political relationships that affect broad geographic areas, even the entire globe
Nation	A group of people who share cultural, religious, ethnic, and linguistic characteristics over a long period of time
Imagined community	A community socially constructed by those who see themselves as part of it
Nation-state	A political entity that combines the nation with a geographic and political structure

THE U.S. ECONOMY: FROM INDUSTRIALIZATION TO DEINDUSTRIALIZATION

The **economy** is the social system involved in the production, consumption, and distribution of goods and services. The devastating effects of the Great Recession reminded us, if we ever really need a reminder, that the economy is of overwhelming importance to everyone (Orr 2012; Smith et al. 2011). For those who had forgotten, or who might have grown complacent about the economy because of the economic boom throughout most of the first decade of the twenty-first century, the recession and its devastating effects were a rude awakening. While the economy in the United States and elsewhere has strengthened significantly since the recession ended, and stock markets have boomed, there is always the danger of another recession or even a Depression like the one that began in 1929.

SOCIOLOGY OF THE ECONOMY

The economy is, of course, the focal topic in the discipline of economics. What distinguishes the sociological approach to the economy from that of economics? Economists focus on the rational economic behavior of individuals and take such behavior as the basis for more general analyses of, and arguments about, the economy. Sociologists are also concerned about individual economic behavior, but they do not necessarily assume that people act rationally. In addition, sociologists focus more on national economies as a whole, as well as on global economic systems. In addition, they focus on the large-scale components of those systems, such as labor unions, corporations, occupations, and financial institutions, as well as on the ways in which these interrelate. More important, sociologists devote greater attention to the linkage between the economy and noneconomic macro phenomena such as politics, the family, and culture (Fourcade-Gourinchas 2007). Sociologists are also often more concerned about the micro–macro link as it relates to the economy, such as how the global recession affects individuals who lose their jobs as a result of the economic downturn. For example, Matthew Desmond (2010, 2016) has shown how evictions during the recession disproportionately affected black women.

The economy is the first and longest-running concern of sociology (Ramella 2007). All of the major figures in early sociology had a focal interest in the economy: Marx, of course, was interested in capitalism, Weber in the rationalization of the economy, Durkheim in the economic division of labor, Simmel in money, and Veblen in consumption (see Chapter 2). Today, the subfield of economic sociology continues to be quite vibrant (Aspers and Dodd 2015; Granovetter and Swedberg 2011; Swedberg 2007).

Over the last 200 years, the U.S. economy has moved from reliance on industrial employment and mass production to the decline of manufacturing and a corresponding increase in the service and information sectors.

THE INDUSTRIAL REVOLUTION

The key development in the emergence of the modern economy was the nineteenth-century Industrial Revolution (see Figure 15.5), which introduced the factory system of production (Hobsbawm and Wrigley 1999). Instead of making products alone at home or in small groups in workshops, large numbers of workers were brought together in factories. Eventually, manual factory work with hand tools gave way to work in conjunction with machines. In addition, human and animal power were replaced by power supplied by steam and other energy sources. While there were skilled workers in these early factories, they tended over time to be replaced, because skills were increasingly likely to be built into the machinery. This meant that less skilled or even unskilled workers, less well-trained and lower-paid workers, and even children could be—and were—hired to do the work. They tended to work increasingly long hours in harsh working conditions and at ever lower pay. Another defining characteristic of this factory system was an elaborate division of labor by which a single product was produced by a number of workers, each performing a small step in the overall process.

The factories of the early Industrial Revolution were quite primitive, but over time they grew much larger, more efficient, more technologically advanced, and more oriented toward the mass production of a wide variety of goods. **Mass production** has a number of defining characteristics, including large numbers of standardized products, highly specialized workers, interchangeable machine parts, precision tools, a high-volume mechanized production process, and the synchronization of the flow of materials used in production, with the entire process made as continuous as possible. The logical outcome of this was the assembly line, which came to fruition in the early twentieth century in the mass production of Ford automobiles. By the mid-twentieth century, these systems had reached their fullest application in the United States and had spread to many other parts of the world. After World War II, the Japanese—and later manufacturers in other nations, such as Korea—adopted these American innovations and came to outstrip the United States in many industries, most notably the production of electronics and automobiles. Today, it is China that leads the world in many forms of mass production.

FROM FORDISM TO POST-FORDISM

Fordism consists of the ideas, principles, and systems created by Henry Ford and his associates at the beginning of

FIGURE 15.5 • Timeline of the Industrial Revolution, 1712–1903

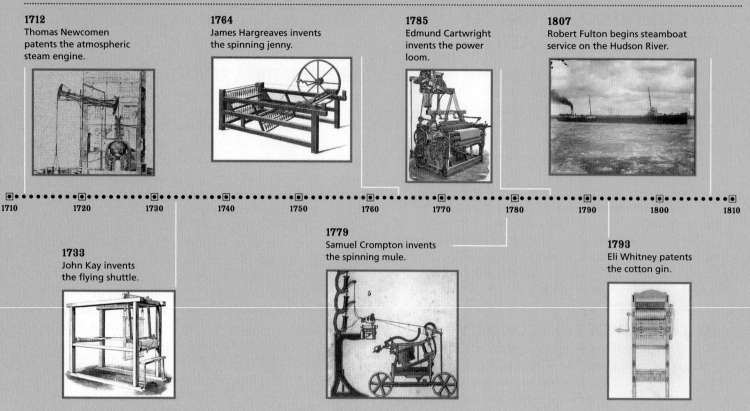

1712
Thomas Newcomen patents the atmospheric steam engine.

1764
James Hargreaves invents the spinning jenny.

1785
Edmund Cartwright invents the power loom.

1807
Robert Fulton begins steamboat service on the Hudson River.

1710 1720 1730 1740 1750 1760 1770 1780 1790 1800 1810

1733
John Kay invents the flying shuttle.

1779
Samuel Crompton invents the spinning mule.

1793
Eli Whitney patents the cotton gin.

SOURCE: Adapted from Industrial Revolution: Timeline, Facts, and Resources, Research by B. Sobey, TheFreeResource.com.

the twentieth century. Ford is generally credited with the development of the modern mass production system, primarily through the creation of the automobile assembly line. Among the characteristics associated with Fordism are the mass production of homogeneous products, reliance on inflexible technologies such as the assembly line, the use of standardized work routines, economies of scale, and the creation of a mass market for products, like automobiles, that flow from the assembly line (Beynon and Nichol 2006; Bonanno 2012).

Fordism dominated much of the twentieth-century American automobile industry and many others. It coincided with, and played a major role in, the "golden age of capitalism" (Vidal 2016). It declined in the 1970s, especially with the 1973 oil crisis and the rise of the Japanese automobile industry. It was also done in by the fact that consumers were no longer content with homogeneous products. They demanded greater choice in their automobiles and their components. **Post-Fordism** is associated with smaller production runs of more specialized products, especially those high in style and quality; more flexible machinery, made possible by advances in technology largely traceable to the computer; more skilled workers with greater flexibility and autonomy; less reliance on economies of scale; and more differentiated markets for those more specialized products (Amin 1994; Beynon 2016; Janoski and Lepadatu 2013; Prechel 2007).

CAPITALISM, SOCIALISM, AND COMMUNISM

From its inception, the Industrial Revolution was capitalist in nature. The United States is beginning to lose its grip on the position of being the preeminent capitalist society in the world. This is especially the case in heavy industries such as automobile manufacturing. China is already outstripping U.S. industry in many areas, and some observers project that China will replace the United States as the dominant force in global capitalism in a few years (Tabassum and Ahmed 2014), or at least by the middle of the twenty-first century (Jacques 2009). This is ironic because of China's recent history as a communist power and the fact that it continues to think of and describe itself, at least politically, as a communist nation.

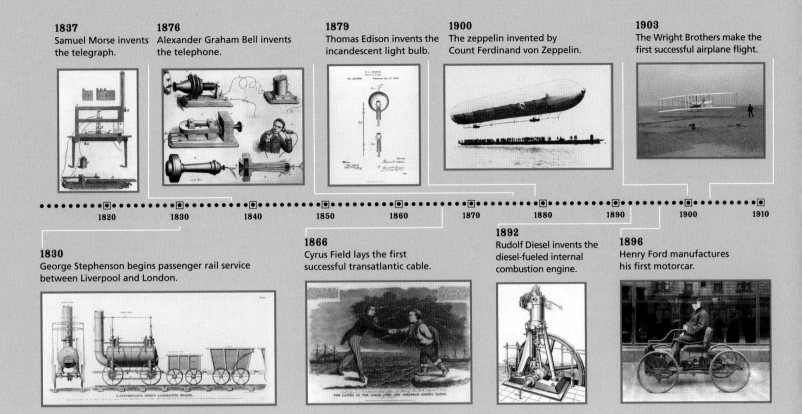

1837
Samuel Morse invents the telegraph.

1876
Alexander Graham Bell invents the telephone.

1879
Thomas Edison invents the incandescent light bulb.

1900
The zeppelin invented by Count Ferdinand von Zeppelin.

1903
The Wright Brothers make the first successful airplane flight.

1820 1830 1840 1850 1860 1870 1880 1890 1900 1910

1830
George Stephenson begins passenger rail service between Liverpool and London.

1866
Cyrus Field lays the first successful transatlantic cable.

1892
Rudolf Diesel invents the diesel-fueled internal combustion engine.

1896
Henry Ford manufactures his first motorcar.

Socialism and Communism

The terms *socialism* and *communism* are often used more or less interchangeably. However, it is important to differentiate between them.

In Chapter 2, you learned that communism is a social system associated with Karl Marx. **Socialism** is an economic system oriented to the collective, rather than the private, ownership of the means of production. The means of production are the tools, machines, and factories that in capitalism are owned by the capitalists and are needed by the workers—the proletariat in Marx's terms—in order to produce. Marx hoped that the exploitation of the proletariat would lead them to revolt against the capitalist system. That, in turn, would lead to collective rather than private ownership of the means of production, resulting in a communist economy. Control of the economic base would lead to control of everything else of importance, including the political system.

From a Marxian perspective, **communism** can be seen as a historical stage following socialism. It involves the effort by society to plan and organize production consciously and rationally so that all members of society benefit from it (Cox 2007; Shevchenko 2012). The collective control of the means of production in communism is a first step, but in itself it is not enough to run a society. Once in control of the means of production, the collectivity must set about the task of creating a rational centralized economy (and society) that operates for the good of all and creates social and economic equality.

The ideas associated with communism and socialism are less important today than they were only a few decades ago, before the fall of the Soviet empire in late 1991. There is little that passes for communism in the world today, except in North Korea ("North Korea Country Profile" 2015) and possibly Cuba. China continues to see itself as a communist society, even though it is, as we have seen, on the cusp of becoming the most powerful capitalist country in the world. In China, a political commitment to communism coexists uncomfortably with a highly capitalistic economic system.

Welfare States

In the contemporary world, socialism is more vibrant than communism. However, even Israel, not long ago a strongly socialist economy, has moved decidedly in the direction

This Russian poster of 1920 depicts Soviet leader Vladimir Lenin sweeping the exploiting classes off the Earth. Would a social change as radical as that depicted in the cartoon ever be likely?

Тов. Ленин ОЧИЩАЕТ землю от нечисти.

of capitalism (Ram 2007; Zilberfarb 2005). Although there are no fully socialist societies in the world today, many societies have socialistic elements. Many Western European countries have become **welfare states** (Cousins 2005). They have powerful social welfare programs that are socialistic in nature, in that they are run consciously and rationally by centralized authorities. Welfare states seek both to operate their economic markets efficiently, as capitalism does, and to do so equitably, which capitalism does *not* do (Esping-Anderson 1990; Gangl 2007; Lessenich forthcoming). Their goal is to provide for the welfare—the well-being—of their citizens (Peoples 2012). There are many examples of social welfare programs, including national health plans, old-age plans, childcare and parental leave systems, and social safety nets of various kinds (e.g., unemployment insurance).

Even the United States has social welfare programs, such as unemployment insurance, Social Security, and Medicare. However, the United States lags far behind leaders in Western Europe (and Canada) in these kinds of programs. And there are powerful forces in the United States aligned with capitalism that strongly resist efforts to expand social welfare programs. For example, President Barack Obama was criticized for being a socialist because of his efforts to reform the U.S. healthcare system (through the Affordable Care Act, which came into effect on January 1, 2014, and which faced frenzied efforts to change it in 2017, led by the newly elected President Trump and his conservative supporters). Still, for all the criticism in the United States, socialism remains alive and well in many parts of the world today. In the United States, Bernie Sanders, an avowed socialist (although he played that down during the 2016 campaign), garnered enormous support in his failed effort to defeat Hillary Clinton for the Democratic nomination for president. However, the defeat of Sanders and Clinton and the victory of Donald Trump does not auger well for the future, at least in short run, of socialistic programs in the United States.

While the United States struggles to implement more social welfare programs, the most developed social welfare states in Europe are experiencing something of a crisis and finding it difficult to maintain existing programs (Kangas 2007). In fact, some, especially Great Britain, are retrenching in various ways, such as offering less generous benefits and programs, making it more difficult for people to qualify for them, and making people take greater responsibility for providing for their own welfare. Threats to, and declines in, social welfare programs have spread throughout Europe as a result of both the Great Recession and the euro crisis (see below) that threatened the European economies. Those countries worst hit by the latter—Greece and Spain—had to cut back dramatically on these programs. Programs are in danger even in countries such as Sweden, which has long been at the forefront in social welfare programs.

Welfare states have been threatened before. However, they are being threatened much more today than ever before by the realities of the global economy. With today's markets for virtually everything becoming increasingly global and highly competitive, the lion's share of global business is very likely to go to the countries, and the industries in them, where costs are lowest (see Chapter 9). This advantages countries like China, India, and Vietnam, where social welfare costs are minimal or nonexistent. By contrast, the costs of production in Western European countries are far higher, in part because of the extraordinary social welfare expenses that must be factored into the cost structure. This has made Western Europe, and the United States to a lesser degree, less competitive or even uncompetitive in various global markets. Many observers see this situation as a profound threat to these economies and societies. Some argue that these countries must reduce social welfare expenditures to compete in the global marketplace. Others contend that the more generous welfare states lower costs of business in

Fordlandia in Brazil

Beginning in the late 1920s, Henry Ford decided that he needed greater control over the supply of rubber required for the tires of the cars he was manufacturing. The best and closest source of rubber was a remote jungle area near the Amazon River in Brazil. This was a wild and untamed area inhabited by people unaccustomed to the modern, standardized, and rationalized world that Ford had played such a huge role in creating.

Ford sought to apply to his Brazilian rubber plantations the principles and methods that had made him successful in the production of automobiles. However, the wilds of the Amazon were far from the urban realities of Detroit, and they proved far more resistant to Ford's methods of operation.

Ford created a town—Fordlandia—as the hub of his rubber operations in Brazil (Grandin 2010). This was a version of small-town America with suburban-type houses built in perfect rows along neatly laid-out streets. It was out of place in the jungles of Brazil. For example, the houses that already existed there

had thatched roofs. They functioned reasonably well in the extremely hot and humid climate because they allowed hot air to escape easily. Ford had his new houses built with modern metal roofs lined with asbestos. They retained much more heat than did those with thatched roofs and were thus transformed into ovens.

In the wild, rubber trees tend to grow in a haphazard manner and at some distance from one another. This makes obtaining the rubber very time-consuming. However, it is also more difficult for diseases and insects to attack trees that are widely dispersed throughout the jungle. The Ford people had their rubber trees planted close to one another in neat rows. This made it much easier for the trees to contract disease and to be assaulted by insects. Many of them died, and Ford's rubber plantation eventually failed.

Ford management also decided that it would be more efficient for Fordlandia employees to be fed cafeteria style. However, the native workers were unfamiliar with this modern mode

of food service. A resulting riot by the workers destroyed much of Fordlandia, although it was later rebuilt.

Fordlandia represented the battle to apply modern techniques to a wilderness and to a people who operated on the basis of their own very different principles. In the short run, the wilderness and the natives and their ways won out. However, in more recent years, Brazil has become one of the world's rising economic powerhouses, a good portion of the Amazon basin has undergone deforestation, and major metropolises have burst forth out of the forest. It may be that Henry Ford was just way ahead of his time.

Think About It

Could Ford's management have prevented any of the problems that arose in Fordlandia? If so, how? Why did plans for the settlement fail to take account of the area's biological, environmental, and cultural realities? If they had done so, would the result have been different? Why or why not?

---

some sectors and help make the workforce more productive (Hall and Soskice 2001). They assert that greater spending on social welfare programs can contribute to a more educated, healthier, and more flexible workforce.

Capitalism

Karl Marx lived during the era of **competitive capitalism**, characterized by a large number of relatively small firms. No single firm or small subset of firms could completely dominate and control a given area of the economy. The capitalism of Marx's day was highly competitive.

However, in the late nineteenth century and into much of the twentieth century, this situation changed. Huge corporations emerged and, alone or in combination with a few other similarly sized corporations, came to dominate, or

monopolize, certain markets. This was **monopoly capitalism** (Baran and Sweezy 1966). Perhaps the best example is the American automobile industry, which for much of the twentieth century was dominated by three huge corporations—General Motors, Ford, and Chrysler.

Of course, capitalism has changed once again, and a number of foreign companies (Toyota, Honda, Nissan, Hyundai, BMW, Mercedes) now compete successfully with the U.S. firms. We may have seen the end of monopoly capitalism in the United States, but it is likely that we will see the emergence of a global system of monopoly capitalism in which a small number of corporations come to dominate a global, not just a national, market.

Whether or not capitalism once again becomes monopolistic, in recent years it has certainly become increasingly global. This can be seen as **transnational capitalism**, where it is no longer national but transnational economic practices that predominate (Kauppinen 2013; Sklair 2002). Thus, the global flow of automobiles and even money has become far more important than their existence and movement within national boundaries.

It could also be argued that the center of capitalism no longer lies in production, but rather in consumption. That is, the focus is on inducing large numbers of people throughout the world to consume at high levels. While the capitalism of Marx's day was described as producer capitalism, we now live more in an era of consumer capitalism. Within the realm of consumption, some of the leading transnational corporations are Walmart, IKEA, H&M, and McDonald's.

I have recently argued that we are living in yet a later stage of capitalism—"prosumer capitalism" (Ritzer 2015b). While the producer produces and the consumer consumes, the **prosumer** is *both* producer and consumer, often at the same time. Producer and consumer capitalism will continue to exist, but they will gradually be subsumed and supplanted by prosumer capitalism. Prosumption is occurring increasingly in all of the businesses mentioned at the end of the last paragraph (e.g., the consumer putting together—"producing"—a bookshelf purchased—"consumed"—at IKEA), but it is most notable on the internet, where there is virtually no distinction between producer and consumer. For example, one must produce the order for what one wants to consume on Amazon.com or eBay. With the increasing ubiquity of 3-D printers, prosumers will be able to produce at home more and more of the things they are now interested in consuming.

While all of this seems to give the prosumer more power—and it does—the fact remains that this is a form of capitalism. Why are capitalists attracted to a system that gives people more power when it has historically been oriented toward exerting as much control as possible over them? The simple answer is that such a system means much lower costs to them—little or no need to pay employees or to pay the costs associated with offices or factories in which they work. Prosumers generally work at home (or in their own cars, if they drive for Uber), purchase all their own equipment, and pay all of the costs (e.g., electricity) associated with what they are doing. And lower costs—or, better yet, in some cases, no costs at all—mean more profits. Some of the most powerful companies today, and those that will dominate even more in the future, such as Amazon and eBay, rely mainly on prosumers and will employ fewer and fewer workers. An even better example is Facebook, which will become increasingly profitable on the basis of accumulating—in the form of "Big Data"—all the information provided to them by prosumers free of charge on those Facebook pages, likes, and so forth (Lazer, forthcoming). They will sell, and already are selling, that information in

IKEA exemplifies the idea of prosumer capitalism. Customers are not only consumers, but producers, assembling the furniture themselves—often with great difficulty!

anonymous batches of Big Data to corporations, which can then use that information to target just the right consumers for their goods and services. If Ford is a model of producer capitalism, and McDonald's is a paradigm of consumer capitalism, then Facebook is likely the model of the coming predominance of prosumer capitalism.

DEINDUSTRIALIZATION IN THE UNITED STATES

Industry and industrial employment were clearly crucial to economic development in the United States and other developed nations. However, a number of developed nations, especially the United States, have been undergoing a process of deindustrialization (Porter 2016b). **Deindustrialization** involves the decline of manufacturing as well as a corresponding increase in various types of services (Bluestone and Harrison 1984; Dandaneau 2012; N. Flynn 2007; Koistinen 2013; Wren 2013).

We tend to think of deindustrialization in the United States as a process that has been going on for decades, is now far advanced, and may even be near completion. The focus tends to be on the Rust Belt in middle America and the demise, beginning in the 1960s, of such steel cities as Pittsburgh, Youngstown, and Bethlehem, Pennsylvania, as well as Akron, Ohio, the heart of the rubber industry (see Figure 15.6). These industries are all but gone, and these cities have suffered greatly, although in a few cases, such as Pittsburgh, they have been able to reinvent themselves. The decline of the auto industry began a bit later, but it, too, has clearly undergone massive deindustrialization. This is reflected in the decline of many American cities, but in no city is it more evident than in Detroit, Michigan (Silver 2015). In early 2013, conditions had gotten so bad in Detroit that the state of Michigan appointed an emergency manager to take control of the city's finances (Vlasic 2013). The city filed for bankruptcy in mid-2013, but a plan to eliminate billions of dollars of debt allowed it to begin exiting bankruptcy in late 2014. However, while Detroit is now slowly revitalizing, it is highly unlikely that its economic woes are over. Deindustrialization in the United States has not yet run its course, and other industries, such as the glass industry, are now experiencing this process as well (Uchitelle 2010).

Factors in Deindustrialization

Several factors were (are) responsible for deindustrialization in the United States. First was the aging technology in many American industries. This made them vulnerable to foreign competitors, which were often building new, state-of-the-art factories. Another technological factor was the rise of automation, which greatly reduced the need for many blue-collar workers (Noble 2011) and, more recently, robotization, which eliminated the need for many other types of workers (Ford 2015). Furthermore, the increased efficiency of automated technologies made it possible for corporations to close unnecessary factories, thus cutting many more jobs.

Second was globalization, which brought with it industrial competition from low-wage workers in less developed countries. This was especially true in the early years of the emergence of China as an industrial power. Now, of course, China is developing rapidly, but its low wages and seemingly endless stream of workers will make it nearly impossible for American industries to compete with Chinese industries. For example, most of the work that goes into manufacturing Apple's iPhone is done in China at Longhua Science and Technology Park (Duhigg and Bradsher 2012). At least 230,000, and maybe many more, people work there, often six days per week and for as many as 12 hours per day. Workers sleep in onsite

FIGURE 15.6 • The U.S. Rust Belt

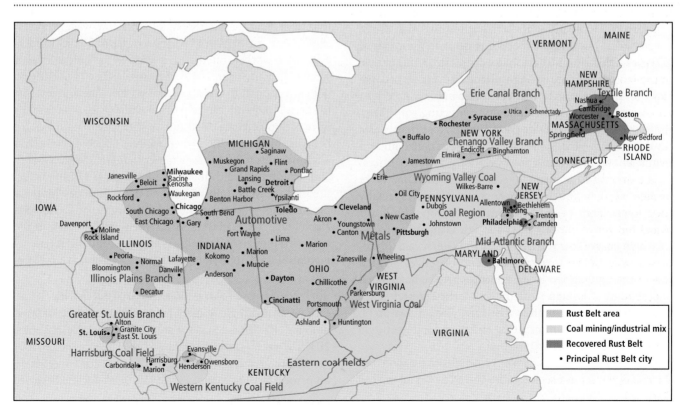

barracks provided by the company, and only a few years ago many earned less than $17 per day. How many American workers would be willing to work in such enormous factories, work such long hours, and live in company barracks, all for $17 per day? However, there is a glimmer of hope that as the wages—and living standards—of Chinese workers rise, we may also see an increase in the price of Chinese goods (Schuman 2016). It will take quite some time for Chinese wages—and prices—to rise to a level that approximates those in the United States, but the trend is in that direction, especially as wages for American workers have risen little in recent years.

Another aspect of globalization as it relates to deindustrialization is the closing of American factories and, in some cases, their movement, or at least the relocation of their jobs, elsewhere in the world, especially to Mexico. For example, great controversy arose in 2016 when Carrier announced it was closing its Midwestern plant that made furnaces and heating equipment and shifting many of its 1,400 jobs to Carrier plants in Mexico. While devastating in the United States, the move made economic sense for the company. Permanent workers in the Carrier plant in Mexico earn about $19 *per day,* while comparable workers in the United States earn between $15 and $26 *per hour* (Schwartz 2016a). However, under pressure from Donald Trump, in late 2016 Carrier announced that it would *not* close its Midwestern plant and that it would keep the majority of the 1,400 jobs there. Other companies, such as Ford Motor Company, took similar steps to placate Trump. It remains to be seen whether in the long run politics will continue to "trump" economics.

A third factor in deindustrialization was the rise of consumer society and the increasing demand for goods of all types. This should have helped American industries, but it led many more foreign manufacturers to become eager to sell products to that consumer market. American industries have had great difficulty competing with them. In terms of the demand for goods, there arose, partly as a result of the low prices offered by foreign manufacturers, a mania among American consumers for ever lower prices. This worked to the advantage of foreign manufacturers because of their much lower cost structures, especially their lower labor costs. Consumer obsession with lower prices for things like fast food and fast fashion has led to the "high cost of low price" (Spotts and Greenwald 2005), or the unfortunate unanticipated consequences of such low prices. Among those consequences are the heightened exploitation of foreign workers, an increasing preference for goods produced by low-cost foreign manufacturers, and a decline in the number of American manufacturers and the jobs they offer.

A fourth factor responsible for deindustrialization was the rise of the service sector in the United States (as well as

in other developed countries; Wren 2013). In the last half of the twentieth century, an increasingly affluent U.S. population demanded not only more and cheaper goods but also a dramatic increase in services of all types (Kollmeyer 2009). Increasingly wealthy Americans seemed to prefer spending their newfound money on services rather than on industrial products. Among other things, this led to the expansion of service industries, such as the health, education, and personal and social services industries. More recently, other service industries have increasingly come to the fore, such as the financial, real estate, tourism, and hospitality (hotels, cruise ships) industries.

Service jobs proliferated, and some proved to be not so desirable. Millions of such jobs have been created for U.S. workers of all age groups, even seniors, in the retail sector, most notably at Walmart and Target. Women are disproportionally represented in these service occupations. The best example of less-than-desirable jobs is provided by the fast-food industry (Leidner 1993; Ritzer 2015a). Fast-food workers generally earn the minimum wage, although there is now a growing movement in the United States to raise that wage (and the hourly pay of other low-wage workers) significantly, perhaps to $15 per hour (Barro 2015). In addition, these workers often are not allowed to work a 40-hour week (Allegretto et al. 2013). As a result, they frequently do not earn enough to rise above the poverty line and are able to survive only with the help of government assistance in the form of Supplemental Nutrition Assistance Program (SNAP) benefits, Medicaid, the earned income tax credit (which is a refundable credit on taxes rather than an additional tax), and Children's Health Insurance Program (CHIP) benefits. It costs taxpayers almost $7 billion per year to pay for these programs for workers in the fast-food industry. McDonald's alone costs U.S. taxpayers $1.2 billion annually. This is the case even though McDonald's is hugely profitable; it had net income of $5.47 billion in 2012 (Sauter, Frohlich, and Hess 2013).

The Decline of American Labor Unions

Closely related to deindustrialization is the decline of labor unions in the United States (Fantasia and Voss 2007; Timms 2012; Western and Rosenfeld 2012). The American labor movement grew from 3 percent of the labor force in 1900 to 23 percent by the close of World War II. A decline began in

FIGURE 15.7 • U.S. Union Membership among All Wage and Salary Workers, 1973–2015

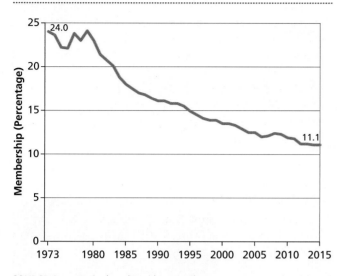

SOURCE: Barry T. Hirsch and David A. Macpherson, "Union Membership and Coverage Database from the Current Population Survey: Note," Industrial and Labor Relations Review, Vol. 56, No. 2, January 2003, pp. 349–54; Hirsch and Macpherson (Current Population Survey); U.S. Historical Tables: Union Membership, Coverage, Density and Employment, 1973–2015. © 2002, 2015 by Barry T. Hirsch and David A. Macpherson.

the 1960s, at about the same time as the onset of deindustrialization and the rise of the service sector. As of 2015, only 11.1 percent of the U.S. labor force belonged to labor unions (see Figure 15.7).

There are a number of reasons for this decline in unionization, although deindustrialization, the decline of manufacturing, and the loss of blue-collar jobs rank at the top of the list. Many of those jobs either left the United States or were automated out of existence (and many more will disappear in the coming years). Prosumers are now doing work for nothing (serving themselves at fast-food restaurants or doing the work of bank tellers at ATMs), or for comparatively little pay (as Uber drivers, or as part of the growing "gig economy" for part-time jobs)—work that many people were paid pretty well to do not too long ago. The great increase in service and white-collar work involved a population that, in the main, had been hostile to unionization.

For their part, unions were very slow to adopt the new methods needed to appeal to and organize these workers. In many cases, they never did adapt fully to them and their needs and interests. For example, among these new workers were large numbers of young people, especially in service jobs like those in the fast-food industry. However, unions had grown rigid and could not find effective ways to attract and organize these young, part-time workers (Freeman and Medoff 1984). Then there is the fact that many jobs that

existed in the northeastern and midwestern United States had flowed to the South, where unions had always been much weaker (Roscigno and Kimble 1995).

Finally, beginning in the 1970s, there was a strong movement toward aggressive antiunion activism by both government and industry (Fantasia 1992; Goldfield 1987). There had always been a powerful current of anti-unionism in the United States, and it was emboldened by an increasingly conservative mood among the American public and the decline of the union movement's traditional industrial power base. Laws were put into effect to expedite the decline of unions. Companies hired management consultants to find ways to avoid unions and employed lawyers highly skilled in "union busting."

Today, the union movement is dramatically smaller, but its membership seems, at least for now, to have stabilized, buttressed by some successes, especially in the public realm. In fact, in 2009, for the first time, a majority of union members were employed by the government (Greenhouse 2011). One area of success has been teachers and their unions, especially the nearly 3-million-member National Education Association (NEA) and the 1.6-million-member American Federation of Teachers (AFT). However, even that outcome has been threatened by movements in some states (Ohio, Wisconsin, and Illinois) to eliminate collective bargaining by teachers, as well as by public-sector employees more generally (Goldfield and Bromsen 2013). One of the most effective efforts took place in Wisconsin, where Governor Scott Walker set out to limit teachers' unions by, among other things, stripping them of the right to bargain collectively (Samuels 2015). In the end, in being successful doing so, he may have crippled them. Teacher membership in both the AFT and NEA dropped precipitously. Walker also may have created a model for other states interested in limiting or eliminating not only teachers' unions, but those representing other public service workers. If Donald Trump's new secretary of education, Betsy DeVos, has her way, public schools will begin to give way to private initiatives such as charter schools where there is unlikely to be much, if any, of a role for teachers' unions.

THE POSTINDUSTRIAL SOCIETY

Clearly, deindustrialization, the decline in industrial jobs and industrial unions, set the stage for the emergence of postindustrialism in the United States and in the developed world in general. An increasing emphasis on consumption and the dramatic growth in service jobs, many of which exist to serve a consumer-oriented society, pushed the United States even further from industrialization and toward a truly postindustrial society (Bell 1973; Hage and Powers 1992; Smart 2011; Vogt 2016).

TRENDING

The Tumbleweed Society: Working and Caring in an Age of Insecurity (Oxford University Press, 2015)

Allison Pugh (Associate Professor of Sociology at the University of Virginia; PhD, University of California–Berkeley, 2006)

By permission of Oxford University Press, USA

THE
TUMBLEWEED
SOCIETY

*Working and Caring
in an Age of Insecurity*

ALLISON J. PUGH

Deindustrialization has helped create a culture of insecurity—a "tumbleweed society"—that affects not just the economy and our jobs, but also our personal relationships and our self-identity. Allison Pugh discovered through her interviews with eighty mothers and fathers that this culture of insecurity profoundly shapes their expectations of commitment, loyalty, and obligation. Flexibility in the workplace has weakened employer commitment, but not the work ethic of the labor force. Some workers value flexibility because it gives them more freedom and mobility. This is especially true for well-educated professionals, who are better positioned financially to relocate for a new job. Women in general have also gained more independence in the labor force as a result of deindustrialization. But others, particularly unskilled males, feel angry that their hard work does not guarantee stable employment. Interestingly, this anger is directed not against their bosses, but at themselves for being too dependent on their jobs. Pugh describes this as a "one-way honor system" that holds individual workers responsible for their job successes and failures, not employers.

Job insecurity transcends the workplace, influencing what kinds of expectations we have about commitment in our personal relationships. More affluent workers and their spouses try to protect their homes from the unpredictability of the economy and commit to stable, long-term relationships with each other. Less affluent workers more often take a stance of either independence or duty in their commitment to others. Low commitment expectations in the labor force parallel low commitment expectations in intimate relationships for those who pursue independence. Though extremely loyal to their children, these individuals, particularly women, do not expect their intimate relationships to endure. In contrast, those who feel angry about job insecurity, especially men, possess a strong of sense of duty in maintaining constancy in their personal lives to compensate for the instability that they experience in the labor force. These individuals desire enduring relationships with their significant others, and feel betrayed and abandoned when this does not occur. Pugh argues that we need to move beyond the tumbleweed society and establish a coral society based on "radical pluralism" that supports stable employment, committed personal relationships, and diverse types of families.

Supplementary Resources

- You can listen to Pugh discuss *The Tumbleweed Society* in a podcast posted on the Society Pages: https://thesocietypages .org/officehours/2015/09/01/ allison-pugh-on-the -tumbleweed-society.
- Read an interview with Pugh that appeared in *The Atlantic* at www.theatlantic.com/business/ archive/2015/05/work-is-about -more-than-money/392342.

A **postindustrial society** is one that was at one time industrial, but the focus on the manufacture of goods has been replaced by an increase in service work. The latter is work in which people provide services for one another rather than producing goods. It encompasses a wide range of service-oriented occupations, including lawyer, physician, teacher, financial adviser, and computer geek, as well as salesperson, clerk, and counter person at a fast-food restaurant. Employment in such occupations has increased dramatically in the United States in the last century, while there has been a similarly dramatic decline in work relating to goods production. Agricultural work declined earlier and even more steeply.

CONCEPT	DESCRIPTION
Industrial Revolution	The era that introduced the factory system of production, leading to the assembly line and mechanized mass production
Fordism	The modern mass production system promoted by Henry Ford, relying on machines, routines, economies of scale, and inflexible technologies
Post-Fordism	A production system for more specialized products in differentiated markets, relying on smaller production runs, more flexible machinery, and skilled workers
Deindustrialization	The decline of manufacturing and a corresponding increase in the provision of services
Postindustrial society	A onetime industrial society in which the focus on manufacturing has been replaced by an increase in service work

WORK, CONSUMPTION, AND LEISURE

Much of the preceding discussion has dealt with the economy in terms of general trends and developments. However, most people connect to the economy either through their work or through the process of consumption, to be discussed below. The relationship between people and their work is undergoing rapid change.

EMPLOYMENT, UNEMPLOYMENT, AND UNDEREMPLOYMENT

Not long ago, we tended to think of people as taking jobs, perhaps in large and stable organizations, and embarking on lifelong careers. Those careers entailed at least some upward mobility, sufficient earnings for workers and their families to live on, and retirement with ample pensions—perhaps in sunny Florida or Arizona—when workers reached their early 60s.

However, there are several problems with this romantic scenario. First, even in its heyday from about 1950 to 1990, it applied to only a very small proportion of the population. Employment has ebbed and flowed over time. It has always been the case that a number of people have been unable to get any jobs at all. In the United States, **unemployment** is defined as being economically active

and in the labor force (e.g., not retired), able and willing to work, and seeking employment but unable to find a job (Nordenmark 2007). The unemployment rate in the United States has generally run at about 5 percent of the labor force. However, in the midst of the recession in 2009, it reached 10 percent, although by December 2016 it had dropped to 4.7 percent (see Figure 15.8). Many observers believe that is an underestimate, because many people have given up searching for work and are therefore not included in the unemployment statistics (see the discussion of discouraged workers below).

William Julius Wilson (1935–; 1997) focuses on long-term unemployment and the problems it creates for black Americans. Many observers have traced these difficulties (e.g., children without involved fathers, drug abuse) to social structural problems (e.g., institutional racism) that are difficult, if not impossible, to solve. However, Wilson links them directly to unemployment and thus sees them as solvable through a number of reforms, including the creation of more work for all black Americans. At the moment, black Americans experience not only greater unemployment but also a long list of additional difficulties associated with being unemployed, not the least of which is a higher incidence of poverty. In 2015, the unemployment rate for black Americans was double the rate for whites and Asians and three percentage points higher than that for Hispanics (see Figure 15.9).

The statistics on unemployment understate the problem of lack of work because they deal only with those who are in the labor force and who are actively seeking work. Another large group of people who are marginally attached to the workforce includes **discouraged workers** (Heslin, Bell, and Fletcher 2012). To be categorized as such, people must have sought work within the last year or since their last job ended, if that was less than a year previous, and must have not sought work in the last four weeks. Other reasons to be considered marginally attached to the labor force include being prevented from working because of family responsibilities or because of a lack of transportation.

ASK YOURSELF

The government's reported rate of unemployment includes those who are actively seeking employment. Why do you suppose it does *not* include those who have given up looking for work, or who have settled for less employment than they need or would like, such as part-time instead of full-time work? What would happen to the unemployment picture if the reported unemployment rate did include these people, and how might that difference affect economic policy making about labor?

FIGURE 15.8 • U.S. Unemployment Rate, 2005–2016

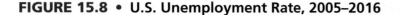

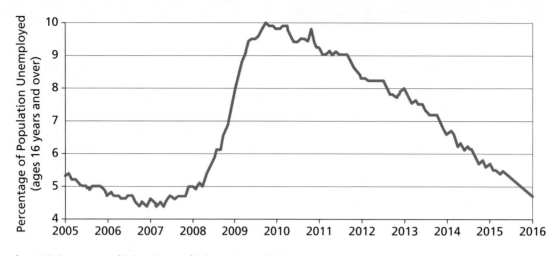

SOURCE: Data from U.S. Department of Labor, Bureau of Labor Statistics, 2016.

The number of marginally employed, and especially discouraged, workers is, like unemployment, a chronic problem. Even worse, both marginal employment and unemployment increase in recessionary times. In early 2009, the number of marginally attached workers had risen by 35 percent over the preceding year to 2.1 million people; of that total, a little more than 700,000—an increase of 70 percent in the same period—were in the discouraged category. Young people and blacks are overrepresented among discouraged workers. Discouragement can stem from either real or imagined problems in finding work, including believing that no work is available, being unable to find work, lacking needed training or education, being perceived by employers as either too young or too old, and thinking one is—or actually being—discriminated against on various bases. The number of marginally employed workers pales in comparison with the number of unemployed, which rose by 5.5 percent between late 2008 and late 2009 and involved 13.5 million people (U.S. Department of Labor, Bureau of Labor Statistics 2009). While distressing, this number should be seen in the context of the fact that the number of employed Americans exceeded 140 million in early 2009. Another 79 million were not in the labor force because they were too young, too old, and so on.

A large number of Americans must also cope with the problem of **underemployment** (Dooley and Prause 2009). This involves (a) being in jobs that are not up to one's training and ability, such as a college professor driving a taxi at night; (b) being an involuntary part-time worker, that is, working part-time because one cannot find full-time work; or (c) working in jobs that are not fully occupying, such as in a seasonal industry like agriculture, where work slows down dramatically or disappears in the off-season.

The U.S. government has an alternative measure of what it calls "labor underutilization." Among the underutilized are the unemployed and those marginally attached to the labor force (including discouraged workers and those employed part-time for economic reasons [i.e., they would like to work full-time, but have had to settle for part-time work]). Under this restrictive definition (for example, it doesn't include those in jobs that are not fully occupying), it estimated the underutilization in mid-2016 to be more than 10 percent of the civilian labor force, more than double the unemployment

FIGURE 15.9 • U.S. Unemployment Rate by Race/Ethnicity, 2015

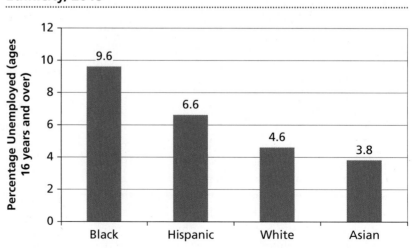

SOURCE: Data from U.S. Department of Labor, Bureau of Labor Statistics, Labor Force Statistics from the Current Population Survey.

William Julius Wilson has published research on race, social class, and the city and is particularly known for his contributions regarding the reasons for the persistence of poverty and inequality for African Americans. He has received many awards and holds forty-four honorary degrees.

rate at that time (4.9 percent). However it is defined and measured—marginally employed, discouraged, or underutilized—it is clear that the problem of lack of work is far greater than is revealed by the simple unemployment rate.

The welfare states of Europe have done better than the United States in dealing with these problems, but even there, these problems and others are on the rise. In part, this is because of the large influx of immigrants, many of them undocumented, who are much more likely to have difficulty finding work. Employment difficulties in Europe are also related to the continent-wide economic crisis and the myriad problems experienced with the euro—but more on that later.

Being without a job is a major problem. However, as pointed out previously, most Americans who want jobs have them, although they might not always have the jobs that they want. An even bigger problem is that many jobs (especially service jobs) do not pay a *living wage,* an income that is high enough to meet the most basic family expenses. This has led, among other things, to a call for a national minimum wage of $15 per hour, a call that is unlikely to be met any time soon, although it has been promised in several locations in the United States, such as New York and California, where it will be phased in by 2023.

CONSUMPTION AND THE POSTMODERN SOCIETY

Recall from Chapter 1 that consumption is the process by which people obtain and utilize goods and services (Cook and Ryan 2015; Sassatelli 2007; Wiedenhoft Murphy 2017b). More specifically, it is a process involving the interrelationship among consumer objects and services, consumers, the consumption process, and consumption sites (Ritzer, Goodman, and Wiedenhoft 2001). First, consumption involves what is to be consumed, largely consumer objects (clothes, cars, electronic gear) and services (help from computer experts, medical services). Second, consumption requires consumers, or people who do the consuming. Third, there must be a process of consumption. Fourth, this process often takes place at consumption sites, such as farmers markets, shopping malls, theme parks, cruise ships, and, increasingly, Amazon.com and other online sites.

Many of these sites can be seen as **cathedrals of consumption** (Ritzer 2010a; see also Ostergaard, Fitchett, and Jantzen 2013). These are the large, sometimes lavish, consumption sites created mostly in the United States in the last half of the twentieth century and into the early twenty-first century. The use of the term *cathedrals* is meant to indicate the fact that consumption has in many ways become today's religion. We go to the cathedrals of consumption to practice that religion. Thus, for example, many middle-class children make a pilgrimage to Disney World at least once in their lives.

Outdoor strip malls are traceable to the 1920s, and the first indoor malls were built in the 1950s, but it is the megamall, which arrived in the 1980s and 1990s (e.g., the Mall of America in Minneapolis in 1992), that is the crucial innovation here. What defines the megamall is the combination under one roof of a number of cathedrals of consumption, especially a shopping mall and a theme park. The theme park itself is a second cathedral of consumption—the first landmark development for theme parks was the opening of Disneyland in Southern California in 1955. Third is the modern cruise ship, the first of which set sail in 1966 (Clancy 2012). The final major cathedral of consumption is the hotel-casino, most notably of the type that defines Las Vegas. The first of these—the Flamingo—was built in 1946. It was the idea of the mobster Bugsy Siegel.

Of course, there are many other important cathedrals of consumption—superstores such as Bed Bath & Beyond and Best Buy, huge discounters such as Walmart and Costco, and online retailers and malls such as Amazon.com and eBay. These cathedrals, along with other consumption sites, especially chain stores such as McDonald's and Starbucks, have come to define not only the sites themselves but also much of consumption as a whole.

In the past we had to travel, sometimes long distances, to cathedrals of consumption such as department stores (Howard 2015), but now many of them are available via the internet on our home computers or on the smartphones in our pockets or bags. As a result, brick-and-mortar cathedrals of consumption, such as department stores, shopping malls, and casinos, are in decline. Nevertheless, consumption continues to grow, even though much of it has shifted from offline to online cathedrals.

Consumption is generally considered to be the hallmark of postmodern society. That is, while modernity is defined by production and work, postmodernity is defined by consumption. This change is best seen in the United States, which moved from being the preeminent industrial society in the world in the mid-twentieth century to being the world's most important consumer society in the late twentieth and early twenty-first centuries. This is reflected in, for example, the fact that consumption accounts for approximately 70 percent of the U.S. economy today.

ASK YOURSELF

Why is a farmers market not a cathedral of consumption? What other places in which you can engage in consumption are not cathedrals of consumption? Are internet sites such as Amazon.com cathedrals of consumption? Why or why not? If not, could they ever become cathedrals of consumption?

Consumption is central to the idea of a postmodern society precisely because it represents a shift from the focus on production in modern society. However, in another sense, there is such a thing as postmodern consumption that is different from, and stands in contrast to, modern consumption (Hamouda and Gharbi 2013; Venkatesh 2007, 2015). In modernity, consumption is seen as a secondary activity, as well as something to be avoided as much as possible so that people can focus on the far more important activities of production and work. This, of course, is the view associated with Max Weber's ([1904–1905] 1958) famous conception of the Protestant ethic. According to this ethic, people are to concentrate on work because it is there (especially in terms of being successful in one's work) that the signs of religious salvation can be found. People are expected to consume minimally, to be frugal, to save their money, and to reinvest what they earn from productive activities.

Postmodern consumption is best thought of as **consumerism**, an obsession with consumption (Barber 2007). We have become consumed by consumption. This

Is it possible not to consume in a society that values consumption so much that it offers innumerable shopping malls, theme parks, and hotel-casinos? What would happen to the economy if large numbers of people consciously limited their consumption?

reflects the view, outlined in Chapter 2, that postmodern theory can be seen as a new kind of critical theory. For example, Baudrillard ([1970] 1998) argues against the conventional view that consumption is about the satisfaction of needs. He contends that if that were the case, consumption would cease when one's needs are satisfied. However, in contemporary consumerism, as soon as one need is satisfied, a new and different need comes to the fore, requiring additional consumption. Baudrillard further argues that what consumption is really about is difference. That is, it is through consumption that people seek to demonstrate that they are different from others in, for example, their taste in clothes or in cars. In the postmodern world, where an endless and ever-expanding set of differences is created, consumption becomes a never-ending process of demonstrating those differences.

Postmodernists are very prone to appending the prefix *hyper-* to many things (Lipovetsky 2005). Appending *hyper-* to any modern characteristic tends to turn it into something associated with, and critical of, the postmodern world. For example, the postmodern world is associated with hyperconsumption, or buying more than you want, need, and can afford (Ritzer 2001). Related to the idea of hyperconsumption, especially consuming more than you can afford, is the idea of **hyperdebt**, or borrowing more than you should, thereby owing more than you will be able to repay (Ritzer 2012a).

However, some postmodernists have a more complex view of consumption, whereby a more positive perspective coexists with this critical orientation (Venkatesh 2007, 2015). For example, they tend to see consumption as an aesthetic undertaking, or as a form of art. Consumers are seen as artists in, say, buying and putting together, in highly creative ways, the various elements of different outfits. This is particularly related to the postmodern idea of *pastiche* (see Chapter 2), or the mixing together of various elements, especially those that most would not see as fitting together. While a modern consumer might purchase an outfit composed of matching elements (e.g., skirt and top) predesigned and preselected by the manufacturer, the postmodern consumer is seen as creatively and artistically putting together components from a wide range of manufacturers and styles. Furthermore, new and used clothing, or clothing from different time periods, is combined in unique ways to create outfits that can be seen as works of art.

LEISURE

One of the dominant trends of our time is that more and more of our leisure time is devoted to consumption. For example, in golf, consumption includes acquisition of the equipment and proper clothing, payment of greens fees, and perhaps even the purchase of membership in a country club. Leisure time also takes place in settings that are entirely devoted to consumption, such as cruise ships or online casinos. Furthermore, for many people, consumption *is* leisure. Going to the shopping mall, on- and offline, and making a variety of purchases can be very relaxing for some.

Leisure is defined as a means of escape from the obligations associated with work and family. It involves social activities that are not coerced. They are relaxing, perhaps informative, and set apart in time and often in space (Dumazadier 1967; Parker 1971; Rojek 2005, 2007b; Scraton 2007; Stebbins 2007). People engaging in leisure are not just free from their usual obligations; they are also free to think differently and to do different things. It is presumed that when people are at leisure, they have much more freedom of choice than they have at work or at home.

However, much leisure activity takes place in settings that are designed to control and to limit the thoughts and actions of those at leisure. The best example is Disney World, where all sorts of conveyances are provided to lead people to move around the park and its attractions quickly, efficiently, and in given directions. Even during the times when visitors seem to be wandering around the park on their own, subtle kinds of controls are being exercised over them. Examples include preset paths, directional arrows, and signs. Most interesting from this perspective is what Walt Disney called "weenies," or highly visible attractions—mountains, castles, and the like—to which virtually all visitors will be drawn. Thus, they move in the direction of the weenies, the way that Disney management wants them to move. They do so without anyone telling them where they should go and how they should get there. This allows for the efficient movement of large numbers of visitors. On the way, they are led past many kiosks, shops, restaurants, and the like, where they can spend even more money.

This controlled and limited image of leisure seems at variance with the increasing diversity of experiences available to those at leisure. There is a world of global choices now open to people who can afford the high costs involved. For example, a cruise ship is a vast world unto itself, where tourists have a wide array of options open to them from early morning until late at night. While this greater choice exists, it is also the case that the managers of such settings have not given up on their efforts to control those at leisure. Rather, the controls have become more varied and sophisticated. Thus, on a cruise ship, a variety of preprogrammed tourist trips are arranged for each stop along the way, and numerous TV cameras monitor virtually everything that passengers do.

Ultimately, the success of a cruise ship, and of any other setting in which leisure takes place, depends on how much people can be induced to spend on consumption. Cruise ships are very expensive to build and operate. Whether or not a cruise is economically successful depends on how much people lose in the casino, spend on alcohol, and buy in the shops in the onboard mall, and on how many costly side trips they take during the voyage.

Leisure time is strongly affected by social class. Many leisure activities (cruises, golf, etc.) are very expensive. Those in the lower rungs of the stratification system in the Global North, and most of those in the Global South, are largely excluded from them. Of course, there are many inexpensive and even

A mah jong game takes place in a home in Kunming, China. What is it that makes leisure time desirable? What makes it possible?

free forms of leisure available to virtually everyone, but these are not generally deemed the most desirable forms in today's world. Furthermore, the demands of work, and even of survival, make it difficult for the have-nots of the world to have much time for, or to get great enjoyment from, leisure-time activities.

Women's leisure, in comparison with men's, has also tended to be more constrained by economic factors (Holland 2013). That is changing somewhat, as women in the middle classes are increasingly likely to have substantial incomes associated with occupations of their own (see Chapter 11). These occupations also tend to give them more demarcated time for leisure (e.g., vacation time), something that historically has been the province of men. Yet, because women still spend more hours per week on child care and household maintenance than men do (see Chapter 11), a gendered leisure divide remains.

CHECKPOINT 15.5: EMPLOYMENT, CONSUMPTION, AND LEISURE

CONCEPT	DESCRIPTION
Unemployment	The state of those in the labor force who are able and willing to work and are seeking employment but are unable to find jobs
Discouraged workers	People who have sought work within the last year but not within the last four weeks
Underemployment	The state of workers who are involuntarily working only part-time or working beneath their training and ability
Consumerism	An obsession with consumption
Leisure	A means of escape from the obligations of work and family

GLOBALIZATION AND THE ECONOMY

Globalization is associated with many changes in the economy. One of the most remarkable changes has been in **macrofinance**, or globalization as it relates to money and finance. Not long ago, money and finance were closely tied to the nation-state that issued the money and to the financial transactions that took place therein. Moving money and financial instruments—for example, stocks and bonds, as well as new instruments such as derivatives—from one part of the world to another was difficult and cumbersome. Travelers needed to change their own country's currency into the currency of the country to which they were traveling. And if they were going to many different countries, they needed to repeat this transaction for each one. Now, however, all a traveler needs is a debit card, which can be used in most nations in the world to rapidly and efficiently pay for goods and services with the currency of each of the nations visited. As Dodd (2012, 1446) puts it, "We are witnessing the end of money's geography."

As a result, money is increasingly liquid, and it flows around the world quite readily. This is clearly true for tourists and businesspeople, but it is true in other ways as well: Substantial flows of money are associated with the informal economy, criminal networks, the international drug trade, and money laundering. For example, a 2016 scandal involved Panamanian law firm Mosseck Fonseca, which, among other things, was involved in the proliferation of shell companies and tax havens for the very rich that allowed them to evade taxation in their home country (Semple, Ahmed, and Lipton 2016). This became a global scandal that even resulted in the resignation of Iceland's prime minister.

To take another, more mundane example of the fluidity of money globally, much money flows in the form of remittances, largely from migrants in the Global North to family and friends back home in the Global South. In fact, in 2015, recorded remittances totaled $432 billion—though much more probably went unreported (www.worldbank .org; Ratha and Mohapatra 2012). While this sounds like a great deal of money, it pales in comparison with other types of global financial transactions. For example, in only one aspect of the global financial market, the market for the world's currencies, about $5 trillion changes hands *every day* (Knorr Cetina 2012; getafirstlife.com/forex-trading).

The largest amounts of money by far flow easily and quickly through electronic transmissions associated with global financial markets (Knorr Cetina 2012). People and businesses are increasingly dependent on electronic transfers for the credit they need, or think they need, in today's world. Individuals usually need credit to purchase such things as homes and automobiles. Credit is also central to the growth and investments of corporations and governments.

Even more important is global trade in a series of obscure financial instruments. Questionable banking practices and speculative financial instruments tied to the U.S. housing market set off a global chain reaction in 2007–2008 that devastated international economic flows and triggered a global recession. Central to these problems was the fact that financial markets in both the United States and much of the rest of the world were deregulated to a great degree. Without governmental oversight, many of these markets were allowed to run wild. For example, rampant speculation in exotic financial instruments produced an economic bubble that burst violently, causing the recession to develop and gather momentum.

The bursting of the bubble created a global liquidity crisis because nations and their banks were reluctant to lend to one another. They were afraid the economic crisis would render other nations and banks unable to repay their loans. Without these loans, many nations were plunged into deep recessions. This was especially true in the European countries that constitute the *eurozone,* the 19 of 27 European nations that use the euro as a common currency.

Over the years, this led to the *euro crisis,* which grew particularly intense in late 2011 and early 2012 (Riera-Crichton 2012). The wealthier European societies, especially Germany, were able to deal with the recession well. Other countries, especially Greece, Portugal, Ireland, Spain, and later Italy and Cyprus, were not (Stewart 2013). They suffered huge economic problems, such as the collapse of their housing markets and high unemployment. Several of these countries had their credit ratings diminished. In such a situation, the typical course of action for a country is to devalue its currency, thereby reducing its costs. This makes its products cheaper and more competitive in the global economy, allowing its economy to begin to grow again. However, because those troubled countries were part of the eurozone, they were unable to devalue their currency. The troubled European economies were left without the traditional method of dealing with recessions and depression.

Further worsening the situation for these countries was the fact that it became more difficult for them to borrow money to keep their economies functioning. Lenders increasingly believed that the troubled nations might not be able to repay those loans. The result was that the troubled eurozone countries had to pay ever-higher interest rates to get loans.

Countries like Ireland, Cyprus, and Greece had to get bailouts (and Greece continues to need bailouts) from European sources. In exchange for those bailouts, they had to agree to practice greater austerity. For example, they fired government employees and cut back welfare programs. Paradoxically, this austerity further weakened their economies, at least in the short run, because many people had less money to spend. As of this writing, in mid-2017, Greece continues to suffer badly from the economic crisis and from the austerity it promised to practice in order to get needed bailouts.

There were many catastrophic fears associated with the euro crisis. While the worst of them did not occur (e.g., abandonment of the euro, the economic collapse of some European countries), the underlying problems remain. For example, the huge economic differences between prosperous northern European countries like Germany and comparatively impoverished southern countries like Greece—and to a lesser extent Spain and Italy—remain a reality. In the event of another economic crisis, it seems less likely—if not unlikely—that the northern European countries will bail out those in the south. Furthermore, southern European countries remain locked into the shared euro currency. That means that those countries will not be able to help themselves in times of economic crisis by devaluing their national currencies in order to make their goods and services more competitive.

There will be another economic crisis—such crises recur with some regularity—and some of the catastrophic fears associated with the last euro crisis may come to pass in the next one. If they do, the economic calamity may well not be limited to Europe—it may well become a global economic calamity.

CHECKPOINT 15.6: GLOBALIZATION AND THE WORLD ECONOMY

FINANCIAL CONCEPT	DESCRIPTION
Macrofinance	A globalization process that relates to money and finance
Deregulation	The lifting of government oversight of banking practices, which allowed wild speculation and economic bubbles that worsened the U.S. and larger global recession
Eurozone	The 19 European nations that use the euro as their currency
Euro crisis	An economic crisis in the eurozone caused by the inability of countries to adjust their currencies to changing economic realities

SUMMARY

Politics is one way to advance a given position or policy through the use of, or by putting pressure on, the state. Democracy is a political system in which people within a given state vote to choose their leaders and, in some cases, to approve legislation. This is in contrast to dictatorships, which are usually totalitarian governments operating without the consent of the governed.

The question of who rules the United States is a source of continuing debate. In analyzing politics, structural-functionalists emphasize pluralism, while conflict theorists focus on power elite theory. One way of dealing with political disagreements is through war. Terrorism involves nongovernmental actors engaging in violence targeting noncombatants, property, or military personnel.

Sociologists define the economy as the social system that ensures the production and distribution of goods and services. In the last 200 years, the capitalist U.S. economy has transitioned from industrialization to deindustrialization. There have been dramatic changes in the nation's labor force as a result of this transition. The number of unemployed, discouraged, and underemployed workers rose during the recent recession. Deindustrialization and the decline of labor unions, as well as the growth of service jobs and an increasing focus on consumption, set the stage for a postindustrial society, in which the focus on the manufacture of goods has been replaced by an increase in service work. One of the dominant trends of the last several decades is the increasing amount of leisure time devoted to consumption.

Capitalism has become increasingly global in that transnational, not national, economic practices predominate. The eurozone has faced, and may again confront, a euro crisis that threatens to destabilize Europe and possibly the world.

KEY TERMS

cathedrals of consumption, 432
citizens, 410
citizenship, 410
communism, 421
competitive capitalism, 423
consumerism, 432
deindustrialization, 424
democracies, 410
dictatorships, 411

direct democracies, 410
discouraged workers, 429
economy, 419
elite pluralism, 413
Fordism, 419
geopolitics, 416
group pluralism, 413
hyperdebt, 433
imagined communities, 417
leisure, 433

macrofinance, 434
mass production, 419
monopoly capitalism, 423
politics, 410
post-Fordism, 420
postindustrial society, 428
power elite theory, 414
prosumer, 424
representative
  democracies, 410

separation of powers, 413
socialism, 421
terrorism, 415
transnational
  capitalism, 424
underemployment, 430
unemployment, 429
war, 415
welfare states, 422

REVIEW QUESTIONS

1. What factors help explain the emergence of democratic political systems? How is democracy related to bureaucracy and rational-legal concepts that you learned about in previous chapters?

2. In what ways is citizenship an important component of a democratic political system? Do you think low voter turnout in the United States is due to a failure of the nation's citizens? Or do nonvoters in the United States express their political interests in other ways? In what ways could new technologies facilitate political involvement?

3. The question of who rules the United States is still being debated. In what ways does a pluralist understanding of power and politics in the United States differ from the power elite perspective? Do you think globalization has an effect on who rules the United States? Why or why not?

4. How are socialism and communism alternatives to capitalism? What elements of welfare states are socialistic, and what forces in the United States are resistant to social welfare programs?

5. What factors help explain deindustrialization in the United States, and how does deindustrialization relate to the decline of labor unions? What effects has deindustrialization had on other countries?

6. In what ways has the internet changed the nature of work? What are some examples of the ways you use the internet as a producer and/or consumer?

7. How is our society characterized by rampant and insatiable consumerism? How do we use consumption to satisfy our needs in the world today? Do you agree that we tend to consume beyond our needs?

8. In what ways might consumption today be described as the new religion?

9. How do leisure activities create distinctions between groups of people? In what ways are these distinctions reflective of the system of social stratification?

10. What was the euro crisis? In what ways was it an economic crisis? In what ways did it show the linkage between the economy and government? Were the great fears associated with the crisis well founded?

THE BODY, MEDICINE, HEALTH, AND HEALTH CARE

The Debate Over Medical Marijuana

As of early 2017, 28 states and the District of Columbia had legalized marijuana for medical use. That means that as of this writing, 22 states continue to ban the drug. In addition, eight states and the District of Columbia have legalized pot for recreational use. Nevertheless, the federal government continues to define marijuana as a dangerous Schedule I drug (along with heroin and LSD), making it illegal nationally. We are in the odd situation where marijuana is legal in more U.S. states than not while still being considered illegal at the federal level.

Many fear that federal legalization allowing unlimited medical use of the drug would lead to the legalization of recreational marijuana use throughout the United States. Their opposition is motivated by a fear that the use of marijuana can be harmful, especially addictive, and that it is a portal to the use of other illegal and more dangerous drugs. This concern is amplified by worry that we have insufficient knowledge of marijuana's effects. Research on pot's effects has been greatly limited because of the federal government's definition of it as an illegal substance.

These limitations have prevented research scientists from ascertaining whether marijuana is a useful medical treatment for a long list of diseases and medical problems, including cancer, HIV/AIDS, hepatitis C, multiple sclerosis, seizures, severe nausea, glaucoma, and chronic pain. Yet there is consensus among the medical community that the drug *is* beneficial for such medical problems. About a million people in the United States now use medical marijuana. However, even in states where such use is legal, patients fear, at least theoretically, prosecution by the U.S. government for violating federal narcotics law.

LEARNING OBJECTIVES

 16.1 Discuss sociological concepts that relate to the body.

 16.2 Outline the issues studied in medical sociology.

16.3 Describe the influence of globalization on health and health care.

edge.sagepub.com/ritzerintro4e

• Take the chapter quiz
• Review key terms with eFlashcards
• Explore multimedia links and SAGE readings

§SAGE edge™

In addition, in the states where marijuana use is legal, there is wide variation in the diseases that qualify for treatment with the drug. The quality and potency of marijuana also goes largely unregulated by those states.

Some who smoke marijuana for medical reasons are concerned about the fact that doing so exposes them to carcinogens. Others are disturbed by the psychoactive effect—the high—that is the great attraction for most other users. Said one ophthalmologist, "None of my 60-year-old patients are interested in being stoned to treat their glaucoma." However, the cause of the high—tetrahydrocannabinol (THC)—can be removed, especially when the drug is given in pill form, which also removes various contaminants.

Because of the great demand for marijuana and its apparent utility in the treatment of many medical problems, there have been strong efforts to ease federal prohibitions on its medical use. In early 2015, a bill was introduced in Congress to remove it from the most dangerous drugs category and make it a Schedule II drug. This change would have acknowledged that marijuana is medically useful but with high potential for abuse. However, in late 2016 the Drug Enforcement Agency (DEA) decided not to change marijuana's categorization. ●

The central concerns of this chapter—the body, medicine, health (including mental health), and health care—are at the top of the social, as well as almost everyone's personal, agenda. Globally, there is much concern about epidemics such as AIDS, malaria, the flu, Ebola, and Zika, as well as the great inequalities in health and health care that exist throughout the world. At the societal level, the United States has been—and may well continue to be—wracked by an acrimonious debate over reforming health care. Among other things, reformers have sought to address flagrant inequalities and increasing costs in health care. Some changes in health care (to be discussed later in this chapter) have been instituted, although they have been far less significant than many had hoped. Millions of Americans still do not have health care, even though governmentally mandated reforms took effect in 2014. These global and societal issues affect the health and health care of individuals. Among those most concerned about such issues are those who are, or will be, patients—that is, virtually everyone—as well as the large and growing number of people who work in health care.

Ultimately, much of the interest in health comes down to a growing focus on, and concern about, the state of our bodies. However, interest in the body manifests itself in different ways for various social groups. If you are young, your main concerns, and those of your friends, are likely to be how to remain good-looking, healthy, and fit through diet, exercise, and perhaps even a nip or a tuck here or there. These are likely to be lifelong concerns. However, as you age, your focus will shift to the increasing likelihood that you may develop various diseases—breast cancer for women and prostate cancer for men, as well as heart disease for both men and women. You will also become increasingly concerned about how to avoid those diseases, if possible. If you are diagnosed with one, your focus will be on how to deal with it—*if* it can be dealt with. Gender affects the types of health-protective behaviors that you employ. Women tend to be more active participants in their health maintenance than men. Health-protective behaviors include screenings, self-examinations, and regular checkups.

Some of you will fall ill, be hospitalized, and perhaps die in middle age (or even earlier). However, most of you will face health-related issues with increasing frequency and intensity as you move into old age. New health-related concerns will then emerge, such as the possibility of developing Alzheimer's disease. As shown in Figure 16.1, it is estimated that the number of people age 65 and older with Alzheimer's disease will almost triple between 2010 and 2050. The number of people 85 years of age and over with the disease—and there will be many more in that age group in the coming years—will quadruple. As you age, you may wonder whether you are going to have the funds, or the insurance, needed to pay the often astronomical health care costs associated with the inevitable illnesses of your last years, and you may worry about how you will die and whether you will be able to do so with dignity.

For these reasons as well as others, the body has emerged in recent years as a major concern in sociology (Adelman and Ruggi 2015; Garlick 2014; B. Turner 2008). However, before we turn to a discussion of the body, it is important to remember that the mind and mental processes have long been of concern and of interest to many sociologists. (For example, see the discussion of Mead's work on these topics in Chapter 5.) Furthermore, while the introduction to this chapter has focused on physical illnesses, mental illnesses such as depression, schizophrenia, and attention-deficit/hyperactivity disorder (ADHD) are also major concerns at the global, national, and individual levels (Clark 2014; Koivusalo and Ollila 2014). There is no clear line between the mind and the body. The brain, which houses the mind, is, after all, a body part. Mental processes affect the body (such as through psychosomatic illnesses), and the body affects the mind. One example of the latter is

FIGURE 16.1 • Number of People Age 65 and Over in the U.S. Population with Alzheimer's Disease, 2010–2050 (projected)

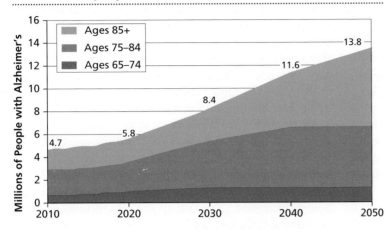

SOURCE: Figure 4, Projected Numbers of People Age 65 and Over in the U.S. Population with Alzheimer's Disease, 2000–2050, p. 23 from *2016 Alzheimer's Disease Facts and Figures*. Reprinted with permission from the Alzheimer's Association.

postpartum depression, which is caused, at least in part, by hormonal imbalances (Mollard 2014). Another is depression that develops following a diagnosis of breast or prostate cancer, or heart disease (Love, Thompson, and Knapp 2014). However, it is important to remember that mental processes can also have positive effects on the body and its well-being. A strong sense of self-efficacy can be helpful to an individual who is trying to quit smoking or lose weight, or who is recovering from a heart attack, among other things.

THE BODY

While sociology has always had some interest in the body, the recent explosion of such interest is largely traceable to the work of French social theorist Michel Foucault (1926–1984).

THE THINKING OF MICHEL FOUCAULT

The body is a central issue in several of Foucault's most important works. In *Discipline and Punish: The Birth of the Prison*, Foucault ([1975] 1979) is concerned, at least initially, with the punishment of the criminal's body. The book opens with a description of the punishment inflicted on a condemned murderer in 1757:

[His flesh was] torn from his breasts, arms, thighs and calves with red-hot pincers, his right hand . . . burnt with sulphur, and, on those places where the flesh will be torn away, poured molten lead, boiling oil, burning resin, wax and sulphur melted together and then his body drawn and quartered by four horses. . . . When that did not suffice, they were forced to cut off the wretch's thighs, to sever the sinews and hack at the joints. (Foucault [1975] 1979, 3)

Clearly, at this point in the history of punishment, the focus was on the body.

Between 1757 and the 1830s, the abysmal treatment of criminals and their bodies gave way to the rise of what seemed to be more humane treatment in prison. There, prisoners' bodies were contained and controlled rather than tortured. However, Foucault argues that in some ways, the prison system was far *less* humane than the earlier systems of physical torture. Imprisonment, as well as the continual surveillance associated with it, involved constant mental torture of what Foucault called the "soul" of the prisoner. Today, it can be argued that the souls of prisoners and nonprisoners alike are being tortured to an increasing degree because surveillance is so much more pervasive (Bauman and Lyon 2012; Smith 2015). We are being watched by omnipresent video cameras, through scanners at airports, and on the computer, where Google and others keep tabs on the websites we visit (Andrejevic 2009). Most of us are not aware of much of this surveillance. Even when we are, we may not mind it, and we may even enjoy doing the things that allow us to be watched, such as writing on Facebook walls. However, all this surveillance, especially when taken together, has the potential to be used in ways we might not want, including gathering the information needed to exert great control over us.

Frenchman Michel Foucault is perhaps best known for his research on disciplinary power and governmentalities, particularly the idea of the panopticon, an all-seeing surveillance tower whose existence tends to control behavior. Much of Foucault's work focused on the relationship between power and knowledge—how knowledge leads to power and how those in power are better able to gain knowledge. He also studied the body and its relationship to society and culture.

In *The Birth of the Clinic* (1975), Foucault begins with an analysis of medicine prior to the nineteenth century. At this time, in order to diagnose a disease, doctors focused on lists of diseases and their associated symptoms. However, in the nineteenth century, the gaze of doctors shifted from such lists to human beings, especially their bodies and the diseases that afflicted them. Of great importance was the ability to see and touch diseased or dead bodies. In terms of the latter, the focus shifted to performing autopsies—cutting into bodies and body parts—to learn about diseases, their courses, and their effects on bodies and their organs. The medical gaze often depersonalizes patients by viewing them as objects. Instead of treating the whole patient, the gaze reduces a person to localized pains or diseases that affect specific parts of the body. The medical gaze ignores not only personal problems, but also social issues that may contribute to a patient's suffering (Holmes 2013, 115).

In *The History of Sexuality,* Foucault (1978) emphasizes the importance of sexuality and the role of the body in obtaining sexual pleasure. He asserts that society uses sexuality, and restrictions on it, to gain access to the body in order to control, discipline, and govern it. He suggests that people reject such constraints on the body as well as constricted forms of sexuality. Instead, Foucault argues, people should focus on sexuality that is about "bodies and pleasures" (1978, 157). One way to do that, Foucault writes, is to push one's body to the limit in sexual experiences—to make sexuality a limit experience. While most people do not come close to what Foucault means by "limit experiences," today there is much more openness and freedom as far as sexuality is concerned. Experiences often include, for example, oral and anal sex, as well as sex with multiple partners. Although these behaviors were certainly practiced in the past, most people would have blushed, or at least pretended to be shocked, if they were discussed publicly.

With the work of Foucault and many others as a base, the study of the body has become increasingly important. It is defined by a general focus on the relationships among the body, society, and culture (Turner 2007a, 2007b; 2012). It also includes a wide range of more specific concerns, including the gendered body, sexuality, body modifications such as tattooing, bodily pain, and abominations of the body (such as stigmas; see Chapter 7). Of course, the issue of the body is also central to the main focus of this chapter, the sociology of health and medicine.

THE HEALTHY BODY: LIFESTYLE, BEAUTY, AND FITNESS

We live in an increasingly reflexive society. In the context of health, **reflexivity** creates a heightened awareness of the body and of ourselves more generally. Nevertheless, many of us engage in risky behaviors (for example, basking for hours in the summer sun; having unprotected sex with an acquaintance) that endanger our health as well as the way we look and our physical fitness. However, reflexivity can lead us to be more likely to avoid risky situations, protect ourselves when we are in those situations (for example, by using sunblock or condoms), and seek out more beneficial ones. More generally, many of us focus on creating lifestyles that we hope will make us fit, attractive, and healthy. We may feel a responsibility to take care of ourselves, and especially to do everything possible to avoid becoming sick and dying. Our bodies, and our health, have become "projects" to be worked on continually. In spite of this, there is no shortage of times—that trip to the fast-food restaurant, one too many beers on Saturday night, "hooking up" with a stranger—during which health and the body take a backseat. We are likely to mold, and perhaps even alter, our bodies throughout the course of our lives (Brumberg 1998; Strandbu and Kvalem 2014).

ASK YOURSELF

Do you view your body and health as "projects" you work on? Do you know others who do? What beliefs and activities can you identify that characterize this outlook on the body and health?

Reflexivity often leads to dissatisfaction with the body, especially as a result of the influence of peers and the media. We live in what might be called an "appearance culture," that is, one in which appearance is of central importance to peers and in the media. That culture includes ideas about what makes an appearance "attractive," and such ideas can negatively affect people's feelings about their own appearance. This is particularly true for adolescents, especially young women. Derogatory comments about their bodies and appearance-related teasing, among other influences, can have profoundly damaging effects on young people (Webb, Zimmer-Gembeck, and Donovan 2014). This is also true of derogatory comments about images of body parts (breasts, penises) derived from sexting and circulated to others (Ringrose and Harvey 2015).

More generally, both boys and girls have concerns about their bodies, although the nature of those concerns is often different. For example, little boys tend to want strong bodies in order to engage in sports, while little girls are apt to want bodies that "look good" (Tatangelo and Ricciardelli 2013). Boys who do not have strong bodies and girls who do not look good are likely to feel dissatisfied with their bodies. However, beliefs about the body are socially contextualized and socially constructed, and they vary by, among other things, race. For example, Latina college students report more dissatisfaction with specific areas and features of their bodies than do their white and black counterparts (Warren 2014).

Blood Sugar: Racial Pharmacology and Food Justice in Black America

(University of Minnesota Press, 2016)

Anthony Ryan Hatch (Assistant Professor of Science in Society at Wesleyan University; PhD, University of Maryland–College Park, 2009)

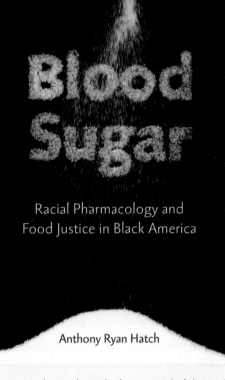

Anthony Ryan Hatch became a subject of "the political forces that aim to manipulate, control, and profit from the metabolic processes within [his] body" (2016, ix) after he was diagnosed with type 1 diabetes as a teenager. He likens his regime of monitoring his blood sugar several times per day to the self-surveillance of prisoners who learn to discipline themselves because they internalize the gaze of authority figures. In Hatch's case, he internalized the scientific discourse on metabolism constructed by biomedical researchers, pharmaceutical corporations, and the government. Diabetes is one biomarker of metabolic syndrome, which refers to a combination of high blood sugar, high blood pressure, high cholesterol, and high body mass index. According to Hatch, metabolic syndrome is a measurement or a "statistical construct" of how likely an individual is to develop one of the biomarkers that could lead to a metabolic disease. Over the past 30 years, not only has biomedical research on metabolic syndrome increased in the United States, so has the number of individuals diagnosed with it and the amount of money spent on pharmaceutical drugs to prevent and treat it.

Hatch describes metabolic syndrome as an endemic problem instead of an epidemic one because it is a discriminating and long-term phenomenon (2016, 7).

In contrast, epidemic problems are more widespread and occur at specific times, like the seasonal flu. Focusing on the discriminating aspect of metabolic syndrome, Hatch uses genealogy as a methodology to uncover the racial inequalities associated with how it is constructed and regulated. African Americans and other racial minorities, for example, have higher death rates and complications from metabolic diseases like diabetes than do whites (2016, 10). Genetics and racial food preferences for sugar are often blamed for these higher death rates and complications, instead of structural factors, such as access to access to health care, health insurance, and prescription drug coverage. Biological explanations for the cause of diseases, such as genetics, fail to take into account social and environmental factors. Those who argue that a person's lifestyle can cause certain diseases assume that individuals are voluntarily choosing to become sick and therefore can easily make different choices and prevent their own suffering. Blaming individuals for metabolic syndrome allows powerful actors, such as the corporate food industry that produces unhealthy food, to remain unsullied in spite of their role in the syndrome. It also encourages an individualistic approach to treating metabolic syndrome through pharmaceuticals instead of changes in society as a whole.

Supplementary Resources

- You can watch Hatch discuss the findings from his book *Blood Sugar* in an interview on *Rising Up with Sonali* at https://vimeo.com/167320079.

- Learn more about the role of food deserts and public health and explore the Food Access Research Atlas at this website maintained by the United States Department of Agriculture: www.ers.usda.gov/data-products/food-access-research-atlas/about-the-atlas.

Even desired skin tone and complexion have cultural and social determinants. In one study, adult British whites were found to want darker skin tones, while British South Asians and British African people from the Caribbean wanted lighter skin tones (Swami et al. 2013).

Reflexivity is manifested in many other ways in the contemporary world. However, here we are concerned with the fact that individuals are increasingly likely to reflect on the way they live their lives and how that affects their appearance and physical fitness.

This Gucci ad was banned in Britain by the Advertising Standards Authority because of the model's "unhealthily thin" appearance. In what ways does this billboard reveal the influence of the "appearance culture"?

Beauty: Cultural Contexts

The social construction of beauty made it onto more people's radar after the publication of Naomi Wolf's book *The Beauty Myth* ([1991] 2002). Wolf argues that the media present the vast majority of people with an unattainable standard of beauty. The "objectifying gaze," rooted in patriarchal and Eurocentric ideals of beauty and attractiveness and expressed through media, includes a narrow standard for beauty and desirability (Gervais, Holland, and Dodd 2013). Heterosexual men and women report feeling more positive toward women who meet that standard—for example, women who have a typical hourglass shape (small waist, curvy chest and hips).

Some argue that the elevation of the importance of beauty has its roots in evolution (Singh and Singh 2011). That is, beauty may be an indicator of health and fertility. As a result, beautiful heterosexual women are more likely to be selected for mating. They are also more likely to have children who are beautiful and who have a greater chance of survival and success. Regardless of the potential biological roots of beauty, we use beauty as a means of determining who is attractive and as a way to distribute socially valuable resources. Economist Daniel Hamermesh (2011) has studied the economic effects of beauty, finding that those deemed beautiful earn more and are more successful at work. It even matters in choices made among candidates for the House of Representatives. Those who are less informed politically are more likely to choose candidates who are physically attractive (Stockemer and Praino 2015). We often are not even consciously aware of the ways in which stereotypical beauty matters in the decisions we—and others—make (Kwan and Trautner 2011).

Race, ethnicity, and class are implicated in stereotypical conceptualizations of beauty. One study compared satisfaction with body shape and skin tone, finding that biracial women were most satisfied with their skin tone, while Afro-Caribbean and African women were more satisfied with their body shapes compared to African American women (Mucherah and Frazier 2013).

Efforts to attain a high standard of stereotypical beauty may include excessive dieting, bingeing, and purging. Women are particularly susceptible to these actions. However, such actions often lead to failure, negative self-image, and low self-esteem (Daniels 2009; Rosenberg 1979). Some gay men feel compelled to diet excessively in order to fit the "twink" body type, a very slender physique deemed particularly attractive by some within the gay male community (Jones 2015; Kimmel 2012). Similarly, increased media attention to men's bodies leads to a preoccupation with ideas about the ideal male form. Internalization of ideals about the superiority of muscular bodies influences some men's drive to develop muscular physiques (Pritchard and Cramblitt 2014). However, male desire for a muscular body is not universal. For example, comparative research reveals that college-age men in Hong Kong have less positive attitudes about muscularity than do American college-age men (Jung, Forbes, and Chan 2010).

The Quest for the Ideal, the Consumption of Beauty, and the Fit Body

The rewards for being beautiful are so great for women (and for men, for being muscular) that many try to at least approximate the mythic ideal. In consumer culture, beauty has become a commodity that can be bought (or at least we think it can) through great effort, often pain, and almost always expenditures of large sums of money. This is clear, for example, in the hundreds of billions of dollars (Hamermesh 2011) spent in the United States on cosmetics, fitness, and clothing. The global beauty product industry is, of course, much larger. Most of the American and global consumers of beauty products are women.

The most extreme efforts to become beautiful involve cosmetic surgeries of all sorts (Gimlin 2007). Beauty is deemed so important in Brazil that cosmetic surgeries are offered to all who can pay for the anesthesia. Poor and rich Brazilians alike can thus buy procedures to create the culturally ideal physique. For women, that physique features small breasts, a small waist with a large derriere, and a slim nose and lips (Edmonds 2010).

About 90 percent of cosmetic surgical procedures in the United States (and the United Kingdom) are undergone by women (Tranter and Hanson 2015). As Table 16.1 shows, the most popular modifications are breast augmentation, nose reshaping, eyelid surgery, liposuction, and facelift. Far less common are procedures that illustrate just how many aspects of the human body can be changed: rib removals that produce smaller waists, pinky toe removals to enable preferred shoes to fit better, and, for some fantasy fiction fans, transformation of the ears from a rounded to a pointed "elfin" shape. Some people have genital cosmetic surgeries intended to enhance sexual response (clitoral hood reduction, vaginal tightening) or to improve genital aesthetics (vulvaplasty; Braun 2010). These procedures are not to be confused with surgeries linked to gender or sex assignment, which some transgender people may elect to have (for example, mastectomy or vaginal construction).

TABLE 16.1 • The Five Most Popular Cosmetic Procedures in the United States, 2015

PROCEDURE	NUMBER
Breast augmentation	279,000
Nose reshaping	222,000
Eyelid surgery	218,000
Liposuction	204,000
Facelift	128,000

SOURCE: American Society of Plastic Surgeons, "2015 Top Five Cosmetic Surgical Procedures" is reprinted with permission.

Looks-related stress affects both men and women, although young women are particularly susceptible. The greater likelihood of such stress among young women can be found in many places around the world; looks-related depression and low self-esteem have been found among young women in Sweden, South Korea, and New Zealand (Jose, Kramar, and Hou 2014; Landstedt and Gådin 2012; Julie Lee 2012).

Naomi Johnson (2010) found that consumption related to beauty and appearance pervades teen romance novels, which link a young woman's romantic and sexual desirability to her use of brand-name products and types of body modification. Like many movies, the books engage in product placement to earn money and sell advertisers' products. Products mentioned in such books include clothing (Valentino tank tops), negligées (La Perla), shoes (Jimmy Choo high heels), cosmetics (Chanel Vamp lip gloss), and body modifications (Brazilian body waxes).

Interest in the way we look, while not new, has grown dramatically in the current era of increasing reflexivity. We are more aware of how we (and others) look. We are more conscious not only of the steps we can take to improve our appearance but also of the many means available to us for doing so. The increase in pure relationships (see Chapter 12) may add greater importance to this focus on appearance, because others are more likely to leave relationships with us if they are dissatisfied with the way we look (and vice versa). Our good looks are seen as a resource, or a form of capital, that is socially constructed (Hakim 2011).

Fitness and the Healthy Body

Closely related to the emphasis on beauty is the focus among both females and males on physical activity, physical fitness, sports, and bodybuilding (Klein 1993; Scott 2011). All these are seen, at least in part, as ways of obtaining a body that is not only more beautiful but also healthier (Waddington 2007)—or at least one that appears that way.

Hutson (2016) recently discussed the results of such efforts under the heading of "bodily capital." That is, the work involved in becoming fitter, more muscular, healthier, and more beautiful can all be seen as efforts to accrue more bodily capital. People invest much time, energy, and money in order to acquire—and to retain—bodily capital. More bodily capital can, in turn, be used to increase people's status and enable them to be on a more equal footing with those who have more of other kinds of cultural capital. Thus, for example, female trainers in fitness centers can use their fitness to develop higher status than (and power over) their male clients (who might otherwise have more power and occupy a higher-status position because they are males), occupy higher-status positions, or both. Female trainers are able to use their fitness to alter the usual interactional power dynamics and to gain a measure of control over an interaction that otherwise might be controlled by male clients.

We must distinguish among the array of methods employed to acquire bodily capital. Walking, cycling, jogging, and at-home workouts typically do not include competition and are clearly good for most people. Through those activities, people can hone their bodies and in the process acquire bodily capital. However, the increasingly competitive nature of many sports may actually have adverse effects on health and appearance. Such sports require great exertion and are often violent. They can be damaging, even dangerous, to the body and reduce, or even eliminate, bodily capital. Consider the increasing alarm over the effect of concussions and other brain traumas on those involved in various sports, especially professional football. See, for example, the extensive coverage of this topic by the *New York Times* in recent years (e.g., Belson 2014; "Head Injuries in Football" 2010), as well

as in the 2015 movie *Concussion* based on those media revelations. Attention is now also being focused on youth football, with a lawsuit being filed in late 2016 against Pop Warner leagues for ignoring the risk of head traumas to children involved in the league (Belson 2016).

Some contact sports, such as wrestling and boxing, require competitors to qualify for, and remain in, very restrictive weight classes. This requirement can lead participants to engage in bouts of starvation and dehydration in order to "make the weight." Such practices, in turn, can evolve into "manorexia," a male analogue of the mainly female disorder of anorexia, by which women strive to attain slimmer bodies (Kershaw 2008). There is also a phenomenon known as "bigorexia," or the Adonis complex (Kimmel 2012; Mosley 2009), which may affect men who have grown up with G.I. Joe action figures or photos of bodybuilders and who aspire to have similar physiques. Such men are likely to feel that their biceps, to take one example, are inadequate in comparison to those of such idealized models. They might be led to lift weights obsessively and to consume mainly, or only, proteins. Such practices are especially rampant among competitive bodybuilders. In addition, bodybuilders might binge on sugars on the day of a competition to make their veins more prominent. Such veins are considered a sign of fitness, even beauty, in these competitions. All these examples illustrate the fact that some sports, taken to extremes, can have a variety of deleterious effects on the body in both the short and the long term and thereby reduce bodily capital.

Exercise, sports, and physical activity often take as their goal the improvement of the body and of health more generally. They are increasingly oriented toward outcomes, such as losing weight and strengthening muscles. In other words, the focus is on acquiring bodily capital. However, such a focus means that people often

Fitness is possible at any age, indoors or out, alone or in groups. Does your fitness routine improve or adversely affect your body?

overlook the enjoyment associated with exercise and, more generally, the process involved in acquiring such capital (Wellard 2012). As a result, people do not explore the full potential of various kinds of physical activities.

ASK YOURSELF

Consider any sports you have played in your life so far. What was your goal? Were you forced to play during gym or fitness class, or did you play for fun, or to earn a college scholarship? What effect did your motives have on your level of engagement and the outcomes for your health? Do you still play?

BODY MODIFICATIONS

Practices of body modification have been nearly universal across societies and throughout history (Ferreira 2014; Pitts 2003). However, in recent years, there has been something of a boom in such practices in the United States and elsewhere. There are several major forms of body modification, including tattooing (Atkinson 2003; Dukes and Stein 2011), scarification (scarring or cutting of the skin; see Dargent 2014), piercing (Vail 2007; Wessel and Kasten 2014), and even intentional self-injury (Adler and Adler 2011). At one time, body modification was associated with deviants of various types (see Chapter 7), including gang members, prisoners, and prostitutes. It was also associated with certain conventional groups, such as those in the military, particularly the navy.

Today, some body modifications, especially tattoos, have become so widespread and common that they are now mainstream (Adams 2009). For example, tattooing occurs these days in tattoo parlors found in shopping malls. The media are full of images of movie stars and especially star athletes adorned, if not covered, with tattoos. Consider, for example, former soccer player David Beckham, football player Chris Johnson, and basketball players Kevin Durant, LeBron James, and J. R. Smith. Historically associated with men, body modifications now seem to be much more common among women (Botz-Bornstein 2013; Thompson 2015;), including star professional basketball player Brittney Griner and actress Ruby Rose. Parents seem less likely to reject the idea of tattoos on their children. They may even have tattoos themselves, though perhaps concealed most of the time by clothing. They are likely more concerned about whether their tattoos, or those of their children, are concealable or aesthetically pleasing. In many ways, body modification is now in fashion and is itself a fashion statement. Figure 16.2 shows the percentages of U.S. adults with one or more tattoos, grouped by age and sex. In 2015, more than one in five adults had at least one tattoo (29 percent), an increase of 13 percentage points from 2003. Adults ages 30–39 are most likely to have a tattoo (55 percent), compared to those both younger (42 percent of those 25–29 and 35 percent of those 18–24) and older (33 percent of those 40–49, 13 percent of those 50–64, and 11 percent of those 65 and older). Women are now more likely than men to have a tattoo (31 percent versus 27 percent).

Body modification reflects the increase in reflexivity. Ever-greater reflexivity is required with each succeeding decision about which new form or style of body modification to have. Among the issues to be decided are whether the modification—say, a new tattoo—should be visible, where it should be placed, and how traditional or creative and unique it should be. Furthermore, a variety of different tastes in tattooing have emerged, many of which are gendered (Anastasia 2010; Atkinson 2003), raced, and classed (Santos 2009).

A study of tattooed Mexican American women in Los Angeles revealed that some preferred symbolically feminine images, such as flowers, for their tattoos, while others preferred images that reflected their

FIGURE 16.2 • Percentage of the U.S. Population with One or More Tattoos, by Age and Sex, 2015

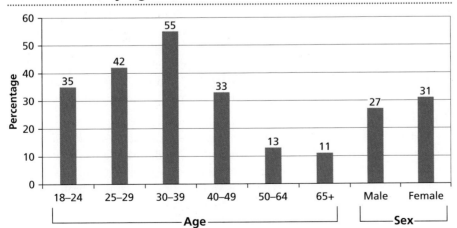

SOURCE: Larry Shannon-Missal, "Tattoo Takeover: Three in Ten Americans Have Tattoos, and Most Don't Stop at Just One." *The Harris Poll,* February 10, 2016. Harris Interactive.

heritage, such as the Mexican flag (Santos 2009). Men tend to get tattoos that reinforce conventional ideas of masculinity, while women favor symbols that challenge or reinforce conventional ideas of femininity (Kang and Jones 2007). Gang members tend to prefer tattoos that identify them as such and that have autobiographical elements. Bikers often want tattoos that not only distinguish them from the general population but also tend to intimidate or frighten people. Collectors of tattoos are likely to prefer personalized and highly distinctive designs (Vail 1999). Various groups also gain status for different types of tattoos. For example, a full-back tattoo, a "back piece," is highly valued in artistic circles.

As tattoos have grown more mainstream and even common among some groups, the people originally drawn to them have sought other ways of distinguishing their bodies from those of others. Many have been drawn to piercings of various types (Schorzman et al. 2007). Most popular are tongue and eyebrow piercings. However, as those, too, have become more common, more people are piercing other parts of the body, even the genitals (Thomas, Crosby, and Milford 2015), and are getting more body piercings in general.

ASK YOURSELF

Thinking back on the definition of deviance, can you identify body modifications that you think are deviant, if any? What about modifications that others might see as deviant that are normal to you? What makes the difference between these two categories?

Dukes and Stein (2011) studied preferences for tattoos and piercings among ninth- to twelfth-grade students. Slightly more boys than girls reported having tattoos, but a much higher percentage of girls (42 percent) than boys (16 percent) had piercings (other than pierced earlobes). Tattoos were less prevalent than piercings, perhaps because they are more or less permanent. The scars left by piercings are likely to heal and are less likely than tattoos to be obtrusive. Overall, girls reported fewer deviant behaviors than boys. However, girls with piercings reported more deviant behavior than girls who were not pierced. Those with piercings were also less school oriented than were girls with tattoos. The older the students became, the more likely they were to have body modifications. Body modification has been linked to a variety of risky behaviors (King and Vidourek 2013), such as self-cutting, drinking, and drug use.

RISKY BEHAVIOR

The German sociologist Ulrich Beck ([1986] 1992) argues that we live in a "risk society." The idea of risk has become a central concern in many areas of sociology, and one of those is the way in which it relates to the body and to health. Interestingly, this meshes well with Foucault's ideas on limit experiences, because it is in such experiences that risks are greatest. Indeed, it is the risks that draw at least some people to these experiences. Few go to the extremes suggested by Foucault, but many people take risks that endanger their health, their bodies, and their lives. That is, they take actions that adversely affect all of these things (Lupton 2007).

People take a wide range of risks that have the potential to jeopardize their health. On the one hand, there are the things people do *not* do, such as see their physicians, have regular medical checkups, and take prescribed medicines. Another example is the failure, or refusal, to be vaccinated against various diseases. This was made clear in the outbreak of measles in the United States caused, at least in part, by the refusal of some parents to have their children vaccinated. The outbreak was traced to visits to Disneyland in late 2014, and by early 2015 it had spread to a number of states and had infected more than 100 children (Grady 2015).

On the other hand, people engage in many behaviors that they know pose health risks:

- *Cigarette smoking, which is at, or near, the top of the list.* Smoking itself can be considered a disease, but it is also a major risk factor in a number of diseases, including lung cancer as well as many other cancers, chronic obstructive pulmonary disease (COPD), stroke, high blood pressure, and heart disease (Brody 2016).

- *Taking illegal drugs of various sorts, especially those that are addictive.* This is clearly very risky, as are the illegal activities often required to support a drug habit.

- *Drinking alcohol to excess or driving (or boating) under the influence of alcohol.* Especially dangerous is the combination of alcohol and caffeine (Goodnough 2010). Cocktails combining alcohol and caffeine are popular. The natural inclination with alcohol consumption is to grow sleepy and stop drinking, but this effect is counteracted when caffeine is added to the mix. The result is that some people go on drinking well beyond normal inebriation and, as a result, end up in hospital emergency rooms.

- *Consuming energy drinks such as Red Bull and 5-Hour Energy.* There has been a dramatic growth in visits to emergency rooms associated with these drinks. Among the symptoms are anxiety, irregular heartbeat, and even heart attacks (Meier 2013).

- *Having unprotected sex.* This is highly risky, especially with multiple partners, and having such sex has been linked to other risky behaviors, such as drug and alcohol abuse.

- *Overeating, allowing oneself to become obese, and staying that way.* The overwhelming evidence linking obesity to various illnesses makes it clear that this a risky behavior.

- *Talking on cell phones and texting while driving.* People engage in these behaviors even though they are illegal in many states and the increased risk of having an accident associated with them has received a great deal of publicity (see, e.g., Caird et al. 2014).

In some cases, the nature of work is risky. One example is the exposure to radiation risked by nuclear weapons workers, which can make them ill and perhaps kill them (Cable, Shriver, and Mix 2008). Of course, there are many occupations, such as coal mining (Chen and Zorigt 2013), that carry with them a variety of health risks. Figure 16.3 shows the total number of fatal work injuries and the fatal work injury rate by industry.

In 2015, construction workers accounted for the most fatalities (937), with transportation and warehousing second, with 765 fatalities. The agriculture, forestry, fishing, and hunting industries had the highest injury rate, at 22.8 fatalities per 100,000 full-time workers. Mining, quarrying, and oil and gas extraction also had a high fatal work injury rate, with 11.4 deaths per 100,000.

There is, however, another side to engaging in risky behavior. It may well be that taking some risks makes some people happier and mentally, and perhaps even physically, healthier. This connection may help account for the growing interest in extreme sports, such as surfing and snowboarding. Of course, these positive outcomes do not negate the fact that participants in such sports are exposed to extraordinary physical and health risks, as borne out by the death of snowmobiler Caleb Moore after he attempted a backflip during the 2013 Winter X Games (Branch 2013).

FIGURE 16.3 • Number and Rate of Fatal Occupational Injuries, by Industry Sector, 2015

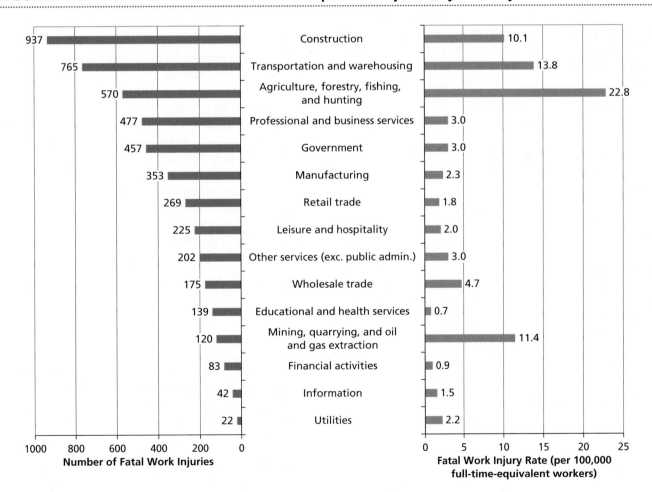

NOTE: Fatal injury rates exclude workers under the age of 16 years, volunteers, and resident military.

SOURCE: Data from U.S. Department of Labor, Bureau of Labor Statistics, "National Census of Fatal Occupational Injuries in 2015," December 16, 2016.

CHECKPOINT 16.1: SOCIOLOGICAL CONCEPTS OF THE BODY

CONCEPT	DESCRIPTION
Health and beauty	In an increasingly reflexive society, the body and its health have become "projects" that are continually worked on.
Body modifications	Tattooing and piercing have become mainstream, another manifestation of reflexivity.
Risky behaviors	Reflecting Foucault's notion of "limit experiences," many today take actions that endanger their health and their bodies.

THE SOCIOLOGY OF HEALTH AND MEDICINE

Medical sociology is the largest specialty area within sociology (Cockerham 2016). It is concerned with the "social causes and consequences of health and illness" (Cockerham 2007, 2932). Social factors are also deeply involved in the delivery of health care. This has become an increasingly important issue in the United States and much of the rest of the world. Medical sociology addresses a wide variety of specific issues, including the following (Hankin and Wright 2010):

- Racial/ethnic differences in health care

- The basic causes of health inequalities in terms of social class, gender, and race/ethnicity

- The linkage between stress and health

- The relationships between patients and health care providers

- The increasing use of advanced medical technology

- The astronomical and spiraling cost of medical care

- The changing nature of the medical profession

Among the changes taking place in the medical profession are its declining status, the trials and tribulations of obtaining reimbursement from insurance companies and government agencies for medical services rendered, the more active role of patients as prosumers of their own health care, the more complicated relationships between patients and health care providers, and the fact that those relationships are likely to last longer because people are living longer and suffering from more chronic ailments.

THE MEDICAL PROFESSION

In the mid-twentieth century, a great deal of power was accorded to the health care system and especially to the medical profession, the key player in that system. Physicians exercised significant power over virtually everyone else involved in the health care system—nurses, hospital administrators, and so on (Hafferty and Castellani 2011). They also gained and retained great power over birth and death. This was an era in which the professions of medicine, law, and other fields not only exercised great power but also acquired great autonomy. In fact, a **profession** is distinguished from other occupations mainly by its high level of power and considerable autonomy. Other characteristics often associated with the professions are advanced education, mastery of knowledge and skills, the need to be licensed, and high prestige (Young and Muller 2014).

Historically, physicians in the United States have been disproportionately male (and white). However, that profile has changed dramatically, at least in some ways, in the last half-century. For example, women earned only 6.9 percent of medical degrees in 1966, but by 2016 they earned 46 percent of those degrees (down slightly from 2014; see Figure 16.4; Williams, Pecenco, and Blair-Loy 2013). However, white male physicians' historical power continues to be evident in their starting salaries, which are consistently higher than those of their female counterparts. In fact, a salary gap exists even for physicians who teach at medical schools. On average, with the exception of radiology, female academic physicians at medical schools earn 80 percent ($206,600) of the earnings of their male counterparts ($258,000). Women earn less than men in every medical specialty, including those they dominate, such as pediatrics, where they earn only 66 percent of what male pediatricians earn.

The professions generally, and the medical profession in particular, continue to enjoy considerable power, autonomy, and high status. However, there has been a marked decline in all of those dimensions in the last half-century. In fact, in the last several decades, the professions have been characterized by a process of **deprofessionalization**. That is, their power and autonomy, as well as their high status and associated wealth, have declined, at least relative to the exalted position they once held (R. Brooks 2011; Epstein 2014). A variety of factors are involved in the declining power of the medical profession, including the increasing power of patients, especially their ability to use the internet to inform themselves about their medical problems and options; third-party payers, such as the government through Medicare and Medicaid; and the pharmaceutical industry. However, while the medical profession is weaker than it once was, it remains a powerful force in the practice of medicine and in the larger society. In other words, the medical profession has proven itself to be quite resilient (Timmermans and Oh 2010).

FIGURE 16.4 • Percentage of Women among Medical Student Graduates in the United States, 1966–2016

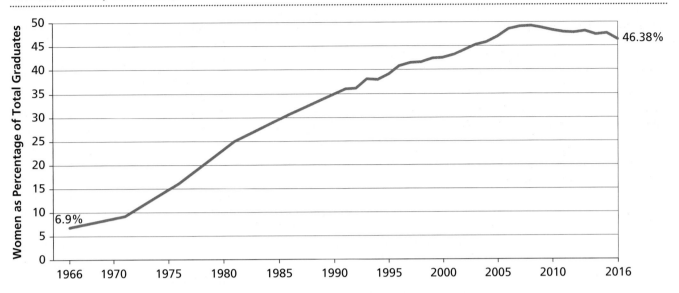

SOURCE: Data from the Association of American Medical Colleges; Associate of American Medical Colleges, Table B-2.2 Total Graduates by U.S. Medical School and Sex, 2011–2012 through 2015–2016.

How do we account for the deprofessionalization of physicians? First, they simply had acquired too much power a half-century ago to be able to sustain it at that level for very long. Second, the public, which had granted (or at least ceded to) the medical profession that power and autonomy, came to question the medical profession. One basis of this increasing doubt was a growing awareness of the extraordinary wealth and power acquired by many physicians. Another was the revelation of medical malpractice, which demonstrated that physicians did not always adhere to their own code of ethics (Ocloo 2010). The growth in malpractice suits was aided, if not instigated, by the other major profession, law, which reaped great economic rewards from medical malpractice lawsuits. Third, the government came to exert more power over the medical profession through, for example, Medicare and Medicaid. Fourth, as discussed in the coming pages, patients became much more active and aggressive consumers of physician services as well as of other aspects of the medical system. Fifth, and perhaps most important, private health insurance companies like United Healthcare became the most powerful players in the medical care system. Among other things, the insurance companies (along with Medicare and Medicaid) squeezed physicians' income by reimbursing them for office visits and medical services at much lower rates than the amounts billed.

Because of these changes, many young people have elected not to pursue careers in medicine. Older physicians are retiring early. Others are leaving traditional private practice for what are called "concierge" or "boutique" practices.

In 2012 about 4,400 of the 600,000 practicing physicians in the United States were in concierge practices (O'Brien 2013). Physicians who move into boutique concierge practices generally charge each patient a retainer of between $1,500 and $25,000 per year, although the average is about $1,800. For that fee, the patient gets easy-to-obtain, often same-day, doctor visits; more leisurely appointments; perhaps house calls; and an annual physical. However, the patient must also pay for each visit to the doctor, although the fee may be reimbursed by the patient's insurance after he or she has filed the correct forms. The patient must also pay for, or have insurance to cover, medical procedures, medications, specialist visits, and hospitalizations (Sack 2009).

Concierge practice is obviously a form of medicine that only the well-to-do can afford. More important, it serves to widen the gap in health care between the wealthy and the poor. Many of the poor still lack insurance and may be relegated to using hospital emergency rooms for everyday medical concerns, or may receive no medical care at all. The well-to-do, who use concierge services or other elite medical practices without concern for whether they are covered by insurance, have high-quality physicians and other medical services at their disposal at virtually all times.

Of course, there are many other kinds of workers in the health care system—physicians assistants (PAs) are increasingly ubiquitous (Cockerham and Hinote 2015), but most notable and important are nurses (Riska 2007). Historically, nurses were unable to achieve full professional status. Nursing was often thought of as a semiprofession (Etzioni 1969).

It lacked anything approaching the power, status, income, and autonomy of the medical profession. Much of this failure had to do with the enormous power wielded by physicians and their desire to keep occupations that had the potential to compete with theirs in a subordinate position (Ocloo 2010). However, a more important factor was the fact that nursing is an occupation that was—and still is—dominated by females (Apesoa-Varano 2007, 250–253). Males in powerful positions, not only as physicians but also as high-level executives such as hospital administrators, were generally opposed to according professional status to occupations dominated by women. (Schoolteachers and social workers suffered much the same fate as nurses.)

As a result, team-based, collaborative care involving both physicians and nurses has been adopted only to a limited degree (Bell, Michalec, and Arenson 2014). A major factor in this relative failure is the continuation of gender discrimination in medicine and the fact that physicians are predominantly men and nurses continue to be overwhelmingly women. Nevertheless, doctors, adhering to traditional definitions of the roles of women and nurses, have come to rely heavily on nurses because they engage in, among many other things, "emotion work," or the emotional maintenance of patients (Lorber and Moore 2002; Rees 2013). This reliance on nurses is reinforced by the fact that, historically, "most people believed that caring came naturally to women, and this belief continues to be widely held to this day" (Weitz 2013, 363). The result has been that while physicians have almost all of the formal power and do not deal with nurses as co-equals, nurses often have a great deal of informal power over the day-to-day decisions and operation of hospitals and doctors' offices.

Of course, patients and the health care professions and occupations are only a small part of the American health care system. That system also includes, among many other elements, medical schools; public, private, and government-run hospitals; medical insurance companies; health maintenance organizations (HMOs); pharmaceutical companies; and state and federal government programs such as Medicaid and Medicare.

WEAKNESSES IN THE U.S. HEALTH CARE SYSTEM

There has been a broad consensus that the U.S. system of health care is badly flawed, although many aspects of it improved substantially as a result of the changes associated with the Affordable Care Act (ACA; Galston, Kull, and Ramsay 2009). One major problem that actually worsened was the high cost of medical care. In 2015, health care spending in the United States reached $3.2 trillion, almost $9,990 per person (Centers for Medicare and Medicaid Services 2015). The Trump administration and the Republican-dominated Congress are, as of mid-2017, working on major changes in the ACA. Many fear that this will, in various ways, make health care worse,

especially for the millions who are likely to lose their coverage in order to reduce costs associated with the program.

The United States spent almost 17 percent of its gross domestic product (GDP) on health care in 2015—the highest percentage among OECD (Organisation for Economic Co-operation and Development) countries by a considerable margin (see Figure 16.5). In fact, the United States spends a higher percentage of its GDP on health care than any other country in the world (World Bank 2016).

Costs of health insurance are rising rapidly. Many Americans are forced into bankruptcy because of their inability to pay their medical bills (Sanger-Katz 2016). Among the reasons for the high cost of American medicine are

- The American love affair with expensive advanced medical technologies, such as magnetic resonance imaging (MRI)

- The profit motive at the base of decisions by health insurance companies, for-profit hospitals, large medical equipment and pharmaceutical manufacturers, and physicians in private practice

- These entities' use of lobbyists in Washington to resist efforts to cut costs and reduce profits

- The cultural notion that Americans have a right to the best health care possible

- An aging population that spends more proportionately on health care than other age groups

- The large numbers of well-off Americans who drive up costs for all because they are willing to spend almost anything to remain healthy or recover from illness

In spite of spending more than almost any other country absolutely and per capita, the U.S. health care system

Hero Images Inc./Alamy Stock Photo

While many men have entered the nursing profession in recent years, nursing is still seen as a female occupation. Why?

DIGITAL LIVING

Telemedicine

Americans spend 2.4 billion hours visiting their doctors every year (Frakt 2016). Most of this time is not actually spent with doctors, but on travel and in waiting rooms. A patient who has to take time off from work for a medical appointment can lose wages. As a student, your grade in a course might drop if you have to miss class to visit a doctor. **Telemedicine**, that is, using technology to consult with doctors rather than going to their office, has the potential to save us time and make health care more convenient, especially for people who live in rural areas. E-mails and video chats are popular ways to communicate with health care providers without having to leave the comfort of our homes, workplaces, or schools. Some workplaces and schools have installed telemedicine kiosks for their employees and students. One recent review of telemedicine research found no health care outcome differences between video conferencing and face-to-face delivery

for patients experiencing mental health issues, substance abuse problems, and dermatological conditions (Flodgren et al. 2015). This same review also found that telemedicine helped diabetics control their blood sugar levels better than did traditional doctor visits.

Telemedicine is not without obstacles. While video chatting with our therapist when we are experiencing anxiety or e-mailing our dermatologist a photo of a bug bite that looks infected might seem like reasonable issues to manage with telemedicine, not all health care problems can be handled by distance health care delivery. Telemedicine may prove more beneficial in helping us manage chronic health conditions than in diagnosing initial symptoms. Also, the digital divide prevents those without internet access from taking advantage of telemedicine, and not all insurers cover e-visits. In addition, telemedicine requires our active participation. We are required

to inspect, monitor, and care for our bodies more closely than required for face-to-face medical visits. This increases our own responsibility over the state of our health—and perhaps self-blame if we fail to monitor it adequately.

Engaging the Digital World

Imagine that you have the following sets of health symptoms:

1. Fever, sore throat, and a runny nose
2. Irregular heartbeat, shortness of breath, and a headache
3. Profuse sweating, dizziness, and anxiety

If given the choice between telemedicine and a face-to-face doctor's visit, which one would you prefer for each set of symptoms? Why? What do you think are the future promises and limits of telemedicine?

---

fares poorly in comparison to the health care systems in other countries. Life expectancy in the United States is among the lowest of the high-income nations in the world (Woolf and Aron 2013). More broadly, the United States ranks 43rd in the world in terms of life expectancy (Central Intelligence Agency 2015). Infant mortality is higher in the United States than in most other industrialized countries, and, startlingly, it is worse than that of many less developed (e.g., Mexico, Bangladesh, Ethiopia), and even war-torn (e.g. Iraq, Syria, Libya), nations (Central Intelligence Agency 2015). Although there is hope that the situation will improve in the future, more than 25,000 Americans still die each year because of a lack of medical care (Wilper et al. 2009).

Inequalities in U.S. Health Care

There are great inequalities in the American health care system. The well-off in the United States can afford any medical care they wish (including that offered by concierge medical

ASK YOURSELF

Why does the U.S. health care system achieve such comparatively low-quality outcomes, considering the huge financial costs it imposes on U.S. society? Why do Americans accept such poor-quality health care? What might be standing in the way of Americans' receiving the level of care experienced by citizens of other industrialized societies? What can be done to remedy this situation?

practices). They are also able to purchase "Cadillac" health insurance policies that pay a large proportion of medical costs (a plan to tax such plans was delayed by Congress until 2020). In contrast, even with the ACA, millions of Americans have no health insurance, and many others are underinsured.

The inequalities in health and health care that exist in the United States—and everywhere else in the social

FIGURE 16.5 • Total Expenditures on Health as a Percentage of Gross Domestic Product, OECD Countries, 2015

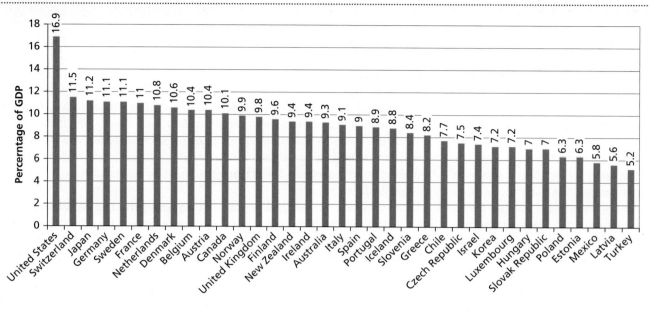

SOURCE: Data from OECD Health Statistics 2016, Health Expenditure and Financing.

world—are unjust, artificial, undesirable, and likely avoidable (Lahelma 2007, forthcoming). Among the major inequalities are those based on social class, race, and gender.

Social Class and Health. There is a largely constant relationship—the "health inequalities invariance"—between social class and health. That is, the lower one's social class, the poorer one's health is likely to be (Elo 2009; Warren and Hernandez 2007). This relationship holds across countries (although there are variations from country to country) and over time (Pascoe et al. 2016). In fact, inequalities based on social class have generally increased over the years.

There are a number of causes of social class differences in health (Lahelma 2007). First, the conditions in which children live matter a great deal, because early differences may have long-lasting health consequences. Thus, living in poverty or in a broken home can contribute to ill health in childhood and therefore later in life (Duncan, Ziol-Guest, and Kalil 2010). Second, conditions in the adult years also affect health. Contributors to poor physical and mental health among adults include poor living conditions, especially those associated with living in unhealthy urban neighborhoods (Cockerham 2012); working lives that are unrewarding economically and psychologically; and high levels of stress. Third, a variety of health-related behaviors contribute to inequalities in health. These include the greater likelihood that those in the lower classes will use illegal drugs, smoke, drink to excess, and be obese as a result

of poor eating habits and a lack of sufficient exercise. Finally, the presence or absence of health care in general, and high-quality health care in particular, can play a huge role in health inequalities. Those who see physicians in high-priced concierge practices are likely to have better health than those who get no health care or get it sporadically from hospital emergency rooms (Gawande 2011).

A good example of the relationship between social class and health is the adverse health consequences associated with smoking (Marmor 2005). In the 1950s, those in the upper social classes were more likely than those in the lower classes to be smokers. This difference was due, in part, to the influence of the movies, which glamorized smoking, associating it with travel and romance (Kimmel 2012). However, by the 1960s, those in the lower social classes were more likely to smoke. It was during this period that medical knowledge about the adverse health effects of smoking became better known and publicized. While that knowledge was disseminated quickly in the upper classes, it had a much harder time working its way to and through the lower classes (Phelan et al. 2004, 269; Phelan, Link, and Tehranifar 2010). A key factor here was the lower educational level among members of the lower classes, who thus had less ability to access and understand the research and data available on the negative effects of smoking (Layte and Whelan 2009). In any case, to this day, the lower classes suffer much more from the ill effects of smoking than do the upper classes.

Another example of the relationship between health and social class involves the likelihood of participating in clinical trials for new surgical procedures, disease screenings, or drug therapies. The fact is that the vast majority of people who participate in such trials are people from the middle and upper classes. It is they who are most likely to benefit from medical advances at early stages in their development and to disseminate knowledge about them, most often to others in their social classes (Braveman et al. 2005; Clougherty, Souza, and Cullen 2010).

Race and Health. The relationship between race and health is closely related to that between social class and health. In the United States, for example, whites are more likely to be in the middle and upper classes, while blacks and Hispanics are disproportionately in the lower classes. Overall, whites tend to have better health than blacks (and Hispanics). As a result, blacks in 2014 had a life expectancy 3.6 years *shorter* than that of whites (Centers for Disease Control and Prevention 2016a). Why do blacks have poorer health than whites? Racism, both today and as a legacy of the past, plays a major role. Given the history of experiments on black women's bodies during slavery, as well as notoriously unethical clinical trials such as the Tuskegee experiments (see Chapter 3), many black women and men have great distrust of the American medical system because of what they see as its practice of medical racism (Westergaard et al. 2014). Blacks continue to have great difficulty getting the education they need to gain higher-status occupations and the higher incomes associated with them. Even with such education, they may still be unable to obtain those jobs. As a result, they remain in the working class and are less likely to have the best health insurance, or they may have none at all. They are also less likely to have the money to visit health care professionals, at least on a regular basis. The health care they do get from hospital emergency rooms, public hospitals, or more marginal physicians is likely to be inferior. Even if they can afford better care, offices and centers that offer such health care may be far from their homes, in forbidding white middle- and upper-class neighborhoods.

Blacks are also more likely to be poorly treated, or even mistreated, by the health care system (Perloff et al. 2006; Quach et al. 2012; Wasserman, Flannery, and Clair 2007), even if they are suffering from life-threatening diseases such as cancer (Merluzzi et al. 2014). As a result, they are likely to underutilize that system, to not utilize it at all, or to use alternative medicines (such as folk and faith healers). They are also likely to be put off by the underrepresentation of blacks in high-status health care positions and occupations—only about 5 percent of physicians are black (Tweedy 2015).

Working-class and lower-middle-class blacks are more likely to be relegated to neighborhoods and conditions that adversely affect their health. Examples include living near waste dumps where the land, air, and water are contaminated and in apartments or houses with lead-based paint that poses a health risk, especially to young children (Crowder and Downey 2010). And stress associated with racism throughout the life course increases the mortality rates of black adults and infants (David and Collins 2014; Nuru-Jeter et al. 2009).

It is possible, even likely, that health conditions began to improve for blacks and other racial minorities in 2014, when the ACA went into effect—a topic that will be discussed in more detail later in the chapter. More specifically, as a result of the ACA, the U.S. Department of Health and Human Services (2014) put a plan in place to reduce racial and ethnic health disparities. Also pointing in the direction of such improvement is the fact that unless researchers receive a special dispensation, research funded by the National Institutes of Health must now include proportionate numbers of racial minorities. In part, this is a result of outcries from sociologists, minority activists, and others (Epstein 2009). Knowing more about the health problems of blacks should lead to improved prevention and treatment.

ASK YOURSELF

What could social institutions such as schools, employers, the insurance industry, the medical profession, and local governments do to reduce the racial disparities in health that we observe in the United States? What costs would such efforts incur, and who is likely to bear them? Does anyone benefit from these health disparities? If so, who, and how?

Gender and Health. On the surface, inequality in health does not appear to be a problem that afflicts females, because their life expectancy throughout the Western world exceeds that of males by a significant margin. However, as we saw in Chapter 11, while women live longer, there is a widespread, although not fully accepted, view that they have poorer health than men during their lifetimes (Shinberg 2007).

A good example of an area in which women *are* disadvantaged in comparison to men is coronary heart disease. Men are more likely to have this disease than women, but the gap is narrowing, partly as a result of the fact that more women are smoking. Heart disease is the leading killer of *both* men and women. Medical care helps in the prevention and treatment of coronary heart disease, but it has reduced the disease more for men than for women. Doctors are less likely to give women with coronary symptoms close attention and the needed diagnostic tests (Adams et al. 2008; Ayanian and Epstein 1991). Women are more likely not to get treatment until the disease is well advanced. They are also more likely

Medical Tourism

Medical tourism has increased dramatically in recent years, and it is estimated that it has now become a $100 billion industry (Fetscherin and Stephano 2016). Rapidly growing numbers of people, especially from the United States and other developed counties, are engaging in medical tourism. That is, they travel to other, usually less developed, countries for medical care, often nonemergency surgery. The main reason is that such care can be had at a fraction of the cost of similar care in more developed countries. In addition, the quality of that care is deemed by many to be as good as or better than the quality obtainable at home (L. Turner 2007). Medical tourism is also attractive because such trips can be combined with vacations, which are easily paid for with the savings associated with overseas medical care. Thailand, to take one example, is now a major tourist destination both because of its affordable, high-quality health care and because of its weather and sites of interest. For similar reasons, Mexico is another favorite destination for medical tourism (Medina 2012).

Medical tourism is a good illustration of both globalization and the increasing degree to which medical treatment is seen as a form of consumption. From a global perspective, people increasingly flow around the world in search of medical treatment. In addition, medical knowledge, associated advanced technologies, and medical professionals flow around the world and are therefore available in an increasing number of locales. From the point of view of consumption, medical treatment is increasingly seen as a service to be consumed as cheaply (assuming it remains at a high quality) and in as pleasant a locale as possible. It is not unusual for less developed countries and the medical facilities associated with them to market themselves as destinations for medical tourists. For example, Argentina promotes itself as a destination for cosmetic surgery (Viladrich and Baron-Faust 2014).

It is primarily the well-to-do from developed countries who are able to avail themselves of these medical services and the associated vacation opportunities. And only the wealthy from less developed countries can afford to travel to developed countries for medical care and pay the high costs associated with it. Medical tourism also underscores the stratification in the destination countries in that the quality of care, the technologies used, and the state-of-the-art facilities are likely to be out of reach of most of those native to those countries (Buzinde and Yarnal 2012).

However, medical tourism has its risks. In an effort to recover from a stroke, Jim Gass spent $300,000 for stem cell therapy in Mexico, China, and Argentina (Kolata 2016). While the treatments had some initial success, Mr. Gass eventually developed an unusual tumor that has resisted treatment. While "stem cell tourism" is clearly risky, it might well be that people should think twice before spending large sums of money to have other kinds of treatments in less developed countries.

Think About It

If being treated for a serious medical problem in the United States would leave you with debt that would take years to repay, would you consider leaving the country for treatment? Would you go to another country for treatment if you simply wanted to save some money?

---

to have emergency surgery for it. Less is known about heart disease in women because in the past epidemiological studies and clinical trials tended not to include female subjects. Even though the disease is somewhat different in women and men, the medical profession has simply treated women based on the findings from research on men.

Coronary heart disease is related to stress, and women appear to experience more stress than men (Wiegner 2015). This is largely because they are less likely than men to be in control of the settings in which they find themselves. At work, they are more likely to be in lower-status jobs that give them less control over what they do as well as offer less security and fewer financial rewards. Many women who work outside the home have the additional stress of having to continue to handle household responsibilities, including child rearing (see Chapter 11).

Women have experienced the medicalization of aspects of their lives that are specific to them. **Medicalization** is the process of labeling and defining aspects of life as medical problems that were not previously so labeled and defined (McHugh and Chrisler 2015). It also involves a tendency to exaggerate the ability of medicine to deal with certain phenomena or syndromes (Conrad 1986; Conrad, Mackie, and Mehrota 2010; Conrad and Schneider 1980). Medicalization

What are some of the arguments for and against the Affordable Care Act? Which arguments are most persuasive for you? If the ACA is repealed, what—if anything—should replace it?

is particularly clear in the case of childbirth, a natural process now defined as a medical problem that can be dealt with only by physicians in hospital settings. Perhaps the most infamous example of an aspect of life that was once medicalized is the female orgasm. This was long seen not as a natural aspect of female sexuality but rather as an element of "hysterical" disease that required medical attention (Maines 2001). Many other aspects of women's health have been medicalized in recent years, including premenstrual syndrome (PMS), which has been renamed premenstrual dysphoric disorder (PMDD) and is argued to affect potentially as many as 85 million menstruating women. Part of the medicalization of PMDD has included renaming the antidepressant Prozac as Sarafem and marketing it as treatment for PMDD symptoms (Gehlert et al. 2009). Infertility and menopause have also been medicalized. Overall, it could be argued that women receive too little medical attention in some crucial areas (such as coronary care) and too much medical attention in others (such as reproductive health).

Health Care Reform in the United States

In the wake of the kinds of problems discussed previously, especially those that relate to social class differences, the Patient Protection and Affordable Care Act of 2010 (ACA, or "Obamacare") was enacted into law. The law came fully into effect in 2014. Initially, it was expected that the law would extend health insurance coverage to an additional 32 million people. However, by late 2016, only about 20 million people had enrolled in it. Nevertheless, one of the desired goals was achieved as the have-nots—especially immigrants and minorities—experienced the sharpest rise in health care coverage under the law (Tavernise and Gabeloff 2016), as did those with preexisting conditions who could not previously receive coverage. Nevertheless, by late 2016, 24 million Americans still lacked health care coverage.

Key aspects of the Affordable Care Act include the following:

- Providing health care to millions of Americans

- Expanding Medicaid coverage for the poor, allowing them an income of up to 133 percent of the federal poverty line (as noted in Chapter 8, the poverty line in 2017 was $12,060 for an individual and $24,600 for a family of four; U.S. Department of Health and Human Services, Assistant Secretary for Planning and Evaluation 2017)

- Requiring Americans to have health insurance—if they do not, they must pay a tax penalty of up to 2.5 percent of their income

- Requiring employers with more than 50 employees to provide health insurance for the employees or be fined

- Forbidding health insurance companies from rejecting applicants because they have preexisting conditions, charging excessive rates, or canceling policies after policyholders become sick (Cockerham 2012)

Although the health care reform law has many laudable characteristics, it did not create the public option desired by many. That would have provided affordable, low-cost public insurance for those who could not afford private insurance. The public option would have helped lower the cost of private health insurance by forcing private insurers to offer rates that were competitive with the public option.

By 2016, an array of problems with the ACA had become clear. Premiums were rising, making insurance less affordable for many who needed it. Major health insurance companies (e.g., Aetna, UnitedHealthcare) were exiting—or threatening to exit—the program in some states because their outlays there were higher than expected. This was due, in part, to the fact that to many of the "wrong" kind of people (the elderly and those among the poor who were more likely to become sick and therefore were most costly to the system) were signing up. Conversely, not enough younger, healthier, and therefore less costly people were enrolling.

After Donald Trump was elected president, it was expected that there would be a strong and immediate effort to repeal the ACA. There was much early talk of "repeal and replace," but no replacement plan was ready in the early days of the Trump administration. At least some elements of the ACA are likely to be with us for some time to come. It now seems likely that it will be impossible to scuttle it completely. In any case, health care reform, and how to pay for it, will remain an enduring issue.

CONSUMERISM AND HEALTH CARE

Historically, thinking about health care involved a tendency to focus on the "producers" of health care, especially physicians, nurses, other health care workers, hospitals, and government agencies. Also included here are the insurance companies, Medicare, and Medicaid. While much attention continues to be paid to all of those producers of health care, the focus began to shift several decades ago in the direction of the consumers of that care. Larger numbers of patients began to realize that they did not simply have to accept what was offered to them by physicians, hospitals, and others. They came to the recognition that they were consumers of those services in much the same way they were consumers of many other services (and goods).

This was due, in part, to the deprofessionalization of physicians. As physicians came to be seen as less powerful professionals, it was increasingly easy for patients to question them. At the same time, the increasing questioning furthered physicians' decline in status and power. The entry of consumerism into medicine meant that more patients began to shop around for physicians and to question doctors' diagnoses and treatment recommendations.

The best example of increasing consumerism in contemporary medicine is associated with pharmaceutical companies' decision to improve sales of prescription drugs through direct appeals to consumers, using catchy advertisements in newspapers and magazines, online, and on television. The avalanche started in 1997 when the U.S. Food and Drug Administration began to relax restrictions on direct-to-consumer prescription drug advertisements. Since that time, the pharmaceutical companies have increasingly used direct-to-consumer advertising to supplement their marketing to physicians through advertisements in medical journals, salespeople, and free samples. Direct marketing targets the ultimate consumer of pharmaceuticals—the patient (Morgan 2007). The irony is that, in general, patients cannot go out and obtain the advertised drugs on their own; they need prescriptions from their physicians. Thus, the idea is to motivate patients to ask their doctors for, and in some cases demand, the desired prescriptions. The evidence is that this works, and as a result the pharmaceutical companies have become increasingly ubiquitous presences in the media (e.g., Singer 2009). We are all now familiar with endless advertisements for the leading and most profitable prescription drugs, such as Lipitor (to treat high cholesterol), Plavix (a blood thinner), Nexium (for heartburn), and Advair (an asthma inhaler), and especially the seemingly ubiquitous advertisements for drugs that treat erectile dysfunction, especially Viagra and Cialis. All of these ads suggest, either directly or indirectly, that viewers ask their physicians to prescribe these medications for them.

ASK YOURSELF

Overall, do you think the shift to consumerism is a positive or a negative development for patients? Why? What about for the medical profession? Why? Would a structural-functionalist see medical consumerism as functional for society? Why or why not?

THE INTERNET AND THE CONSUMPTION OF HEALTH CARE

The internet has become implicated in the consumption of health care (e-health) in various ways. The first and most obvious way is by allowing people to find health care providers of all sorts more easily. The internet is a vast resource for finding providers by specialty, and on the local, national, and even global levels.

Not only is it possible to find the names and addresses of providers on the internet; in addition, and more important, lots of information about them is available there. For example, one can get rankings of health care providers as well as information from previous patients about their experiences and recommendations. There is also a wealth of information and evaluation available on pharmaceuticals, medical technologies, and alternative treatments.

The increasing amount of health care–related data of all sorts on the internet allows people to become much more knowledgeable consumers of health care services and products. At the moment, most of the information is scattered, widely and unsystematically, across the internet. Another problem is that it is not linked to individuals, their diseases, and their specific needs. Increasingly, however, consumer-patients can comparison shop for medical care on the internet in much the same way that they shop for automobiles, TVs, hotels, and airfares (Konrad 2009). For example, there are sites such as Health in Reach (www.healthinreach.com) and Healthcare Bluebook (www.healthcarebluebook.com) where people can compare prices on everything from flu vaccines and annual physicals to mastectomies and bowel surgeries. One patient ultimately paid $300 for an MRI, for which her local hospital had quoted her a price of $2,500. Health insurance companies are also increasingly providing information online about benefits, stating, for example, what they pay out for office visits and various medical procedures. However, it is often difficult for consumer-patients to compare medical procedures because there are no standard terminological codes, available information is highly jargonistic, and the same procedure may have a dozen different prices at the same hospital because of separate negotiations with different health insurers.

The internet has become a global source of medical information. One specific example is the Clearinghouse on Male Circumcision for HIV Prevention (www.malecircumcision.org), a website devoted to providing information about, and debunking the myths related to, circumcision and HIV/AIDS (McNeil 2009). Access to such information is especially important in Africa, where HIV/AIDS is rampant (as we will discuss later). The website notes that studies based in Africa have shown that circumcision reduces the risk of sexually transmitted HIV/AIDS by as much as 60 percent. Also addressed are myths such as the erroneous belief that after circumcision men no longer need to use condoms to prevent HIV/AIDS. Of course, the existence of the digital divide (see Chapter 9) and the lack of access to computers and the internet make it particularly difficult for such information to make its way to the people in Africa—and elsewhere—who are most in need of it.

The internet also opens a global range of views, possibilities, and alternatives to the consumers of medical goods and services. Consumers are better able to make themselves aware of alternatives available elsewhere in the world, obtain information and advice about them, and find ways of obtaining them. On the positive side, this gives medical consumers better access to most goods and services and many more choices and options. The internet allows people to explore a wide range of alternative medical goods and services, some of which could prove to be useful, even lifesaving. Consumers can also search for and compare prescription drug prices, which vary widely, in local pharmacies (for example, at www.rxpricequotes.com). On the negative side, this is all relatively new and unregulated global territory, and consumers need to be aware of the danger that they may obtain fraudulent medical products and services.

The net result of the above is that a patient who uses online resources can become a much more sophisticated, knowledgeable, and independent consumer of medical services and products. For example, consumers can obtain many products and services legally or illegally—and often more inexpensively—through the internet without going through intermediaries associated with the health care system (Krauss 2004; Napoli 1999). Also available online are a variety of tests that can be done at home, such as a DNA test that can be had for $99 at two different websites: 23andMe (www.23andme.com) and AncestryDNA (http://dna.ancestry.com). Individuals and couples can use such tests to discover on their own whether they are carriers of life-threatening diseases, such as cystic fibrosis, that could show up in their children. However, there are concerns that these tests may not be reliable, that they may give test takers a false sense of assurance, that the costs are too high, that the privacy of the test results may not be ensured, and that those who rely on these tests will not get the expert advice of trained medical professionals (Brody 2009).

Other problems associated with using the internet for health-related consumption include the possibility of getting counterfeit, and perhaps ineffective, medications, as well as bogus services and information of various types (Lavorgna 2015). At the height of the global scare over a 2009 H1N1 flu pandemic (another lesser outbreak occurred in 2014), the internet was rife with false claims about healing gels and "ionic silver" sprays, as well as ads for fake Tamiflu, an antiviral medication (Wayne 2009). While consumers may become more sophisticated by exploring medical information on the internet, they are usually not trained in medicine and therefore are likely unable to fully understand the advantages and disadvantages of what is available. As a result, they are more likely to be duped in various ways.

The internet is also an increasingly important resource for health care providers, who can use it to access information on new research, pharmaceuticals, and technologies. A variety of computer programs and apps are available for medical professionals to use to improve patient care. For example, in cases where patients have been exposed to the AIDS virus, a screening process has been developed that allows physicians to ask the right questions and get needed information quickly. It is important to know when exposure to the virus took place and to start treatment quickly (Rabin 2009). Another example involves online registries for various diseases (e.g., cystic fibrosis), which can be important sources of information on the effectiveness of medications and physical therapy (Freudenheim 2009).

✓ CHECKPOINT 16.2: DEVELOPMENTS IN MEDICAL SOCIOLOGY

FACTOR	DESCRIPTION
Deprofessionalization	Recent years have seen a decline in the power and autonomy of the medical profession.
Medicalization	Labeling aspects of life as medical problems that were not previously so labeled.

GLOBALIZATION AND HEALTH

A nearly endless array of issues could be discussed under the heading of globalization and health (Linn and Wilson 2012). We can do little more than touch on a few of them in this section.

GROWING GLOBAL INEQUALITY

While globalization has been associated with increased aggregate life expectancy, it also has tended to widen global disparities in health (Hashemian and Yach 2007; McMichael 2013). Women and children tend to be the most vulnerable populations globally, due to such things as economic inequality (Goli, Doshi, and Perianayagam 2013) and poor access to health care (Fillipi et al. 2006). As noted in Chapter 9, people in poor nations tend to have poorer health as a result of limited access to health care services, poor education, inadequate sanitation, and inadequate nutrition and housing. In turn, poor health tends to limit economic growth in those nations, mainly by adversely affecting productivity. Developing countries have a disproportionate share of mortality and morbidity, much of which could be prevented inexpensively and treated effectively if the money were available to do so.

For the reasons mentioned previously, and others, there is a significant gap in life expectancy between developed and less developed, or high- and low-income, countries. Figure 16.6 shows life expectancy at birth for select countries around the world. Note the 35-year age difference in life expectancy between highly developed Japan at the top of the list and the far less developed Chad at the bottom. The greatest increases in life expectancy have occurred in developing countries such as Brazil, Egypt, and Malaysia, which have tended to be increasingly and successfully involved in economic globalization. However, for most of the rest, especially the least developed, low-income countries in the Global South (such as Chad, the Central African Republic, and Afghanistan), globalization has been accompanied by a decline in economic growth, an increase in poverty, and, as a result, a decline in health.

Disease

The vast majority of not only acute but also chronic diseases occur at younger ages and in low- and middle-income countries. The rising cost of dealing with chronic diseases in developing countries will adversely affect the countries' ability to deal with acute infectious diseases. Of special importance from the point of view of globalization is the increasing global marketing of tobacco, alcohol, sugar, and fat—the latter two especially aimed at children—and the consequent global spread of the diseases (lung cancer, cirrhosis of the liver, diabetes, heart disease) associated with these products.

Although most observers have noted an increase over time in health disparities between the developed and the less developed countries, Firebaugh and Goesling (2007) found a decline in recent years in between-nation inequality in health. However, they recognize that the continuation of that decline is threatened by the HIV/AIDS epidemic and, more recently, the Ebola outbreak in Africa. Even if we accept the argument about a decline, great disparities remain between and within nations in terms of health.

FIGURE 16.6 • Life Expectancy at Birth among Select Countries, 2016

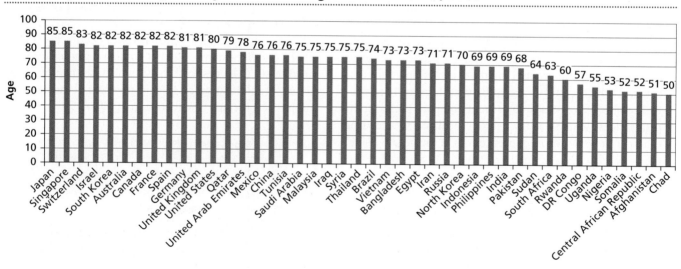

SOURCE: Data from Central Intelligence Agency, *World Factbook*.

Malnutrition

As discussed in Chapter 9, countries in the Global South suffer disproportionately from hunger and malnutrition (Van de Poel et al. 2008). Roughly 795 million people there are affected by these problems, which are the result of inadequate, or totally unavailable, food supplies and poor and unbalanced diets (www.wfp.org/hunger/stats). Dealing with hunger and malnutrition is especially important for children, because those who are underweight are, as adults, likely to be less physically and intellectually productive and to experience more chronic illnesses and disabilities. This carries on across generations as the ability of such adults to provide adequate nutrition for their children is compromised.

Undernutrition is a form of malnutrition involving an inadequate intake of nutrients, including calories, vitamins, and minerals. The other form of malnutrition involves obesity, which is caused by an excessive intake of nutrients, especially calories. Developing countries now increasingly suffer from a "double nutritional burden," with some people not having enough to eat and others eating too much, especially the wrong kinds of food (e.g., food that is high in fat and cholesterol; Vogli et al. 2014). Although obesity is increasing in the less developed world, undernutrition remains the greatest problem there, particularly for mothers and children. Undernutrition creates difficulties that continue throughout the life cycle and is responsible for stunted growth, lower levels of schooling, lower productivity, and chronic diseases; undernourished women also give birth to low-birthweight infants. Undernutrition has also been linked to rapid weight gain and obesity among formerly underweight children (Serra-Majem and Ngo 2012).

Undernutrition is related to problems not only for individuals but also for societies as a whole. It leads to underdevelopment and tends to perpetuate poverty. Without adequate nutrition, the human capital needed for economic development cannot develop.

Food insecurity is a major cause of undernutrition in less developed countries, and it is even an important issue in developed countries like the United States and the United Kingdom (Purdam, Garratt, and Esmail 2015). Such insecurity exists when people do not have sufficient access to safe and nutritious food—a condition necessary for leading a healthy and productive life. There are many causes of food insecurity. Poverty is a centrally important cause everywhere, but an especially important cause in less developed countries is the lack of adequate agricultural development. A number of global programs have been undertaken to help deal with this problem through the creation of agricultural diversification programs, community gardens, farmers' markets, and the like.

SMOKING

Smoking is an important cause of health problems around the world. In spite of those health problems, however, a highly profitable tobacco industry continues to be central to the global economy (Fulbrook 2007). According to a World Health Organization (2017) estimate, about 6 million people die each year from tobacco use, and unless there are dramatic changes, that number will rise to 8 million by 2030. It is also projected that 1 billion people will die in the twenty-first century from smoking-related diseases.

With the Western market for cigarettes shrinking because of growing awareness of the risks associated with smoking, the tobacco corporations have shifted their focus to Africa and Asia. India accounts for almost one third of the world's tobacco-related deaths. China is now the world's biggest market for cigarettes (Gu et al. 2009), with 2.5 trillion cigarettes smoked every year. The Chinese consume about 30 percent of the world's cigarettes, although China has about 20 percent of the world's population. There are about 300 million Chinese smokers. Many appear to have little knowledge of the health hazards associated with smoking (World Health Organization 2010a). As a result, the deaths of about 1 million Chinese are traceable to smoking cigarettes. By 2030 the number of smoking-related deaths in China could increase to 3 million people (*New York Times* Editorial Board 2014). For their part, the Western powers are the major exporters of cigarettes to the rest of the world. The United States is the single largest exporter of cigarettes as well as of globally recognized cigarette advertisements and brands.

While China has become the world's biggest market for cigarettes, only one in five people there are aware of smoking's dangers. What would it take for this situation to change? Who would benefit, and who would be harmed?

The hazards of smoking are well known in the United States. Should it be legal for tobacco companies to export their products to markets where such information is not widely known or is disregarded? Why or why not? What would a conflict/critical theorist say is happening here?

BORDERLESS DISEASES

Another negative aspect of globalization as far as health is concerned is the flow of borderless diseases (Ali 2012). While borderless diseases have become much more common in recent years, they are not a new phenomenon. Tuberculosis (TB) was known in ancient times. Today the World Health Organization (WHO) estimates that more than one third of the world's population is infected with the cause of the disease—the TB bacillus (Linn and Wilson 2012). Almost 10 million people in the world have the disease and a little over 1 million of them are expected to die from it (World Health Organization 2015a). Sexually transmitted infections (STIs) of various types have long diffused globally. A specific example is syphilis, which has spread globally and continues to circulate, especially throughout a number of less developed countries. However, the roots of the disease were probably in Europe, and it was originally spread by European colonialism and military exploits. In fact, for many in the less developed world, the disease was closely associated with French soldiers, and it came to be known in some parts of the world as the "French disease."

Then there is the increasing prevalence of other borderless diseases, many of them relatively new. Examples include severe acute respiratory syndrome (SARS); bovine spongiform encephalopathy (BSE, or "mad cow disease"), which is often found in cattle and can cause a brain disease in humans (Ong 2007); avian flu; Ebola; Zika; and HIV/AIDS. The nature of these diseases and their spread—either in fact (HIV/AIDS, Ebola) or merely, at least so far, as a frightening possibility (avian flu)—tells us a great deal about the nature and reality of globalization in the twenty-first century. The pathogens that cause these diseases flow, or have the potential to flow, readily throughout the globe.

Several factors help explain the great and increasing global mobility of borderless diseases (Zhou and Coleman 2016). First, there is the increase in global travel and the increasing rapidity of that travel (Rosenthal 2007). Tourists both carry borderless diseases and can be infected by them in tourist destinations throughout the world (Baker 2015). Second, there is growing human migration and an increasing ease with which people can cross borders. As a result, people often bring with them diseases that are not detected at national borders. Third, the expansion of massive urban areas, such as Lagos, Nigeria, has created vast mixing bowls where large numbers of people in close and frequent proximity can easily infect one another. Until 2014, outbreaks of Ebola were limited to relatively small African villages, but the explosion of cases in late 2014 was traceable to the fact that the virus had found its way into more densely populated areas. Figure 16.7 shows the African nations affected by Ebola. While the spread of the disease abated in early 2015, as of January 14, 2016, there had been 28,637 cases and 11,315 deaths worldwide, the vast majority of them in Liberia, Sierra Leone, and Guinea. Yet this disaster pales in comparison to what might have happened if the disease had spread to, and grown out of control in, a huge city like Lagos. A fourth factor in the global flow of disease is increasing human presence in previously untouched natural habitats. There, people can have contact with pathogens for which they have no immunity and that can spread rapidly throughout the world (Ali 2012). It is believed that humans initially caught Ebola (and other diseases) from wild animals.

The flow of efforts to deal with these diseases must be equally global. That is, there is a need for global responses to the increasing likelihood of the spread of various diseases. However, some nations have proven unable or unwilling to respond to this global need. For example, China and Vietnam were unwilling to provide the WHO with samples of the avian flu that had become a serious problem in those countries. Such samples were needed to study the spread of the disease and the ways in which the flu was evolving. This information could have been useful in heading off the further spread of the disease and might have sped up the development of a vaccine to prevent it. More recently, there have been many criticisms of the slowness of the global response to Ebola and the relatively small amounts of money committed to fight the disease.

Could medical practitioners or governments have anticipated the possibility that germs and viruses might begin to flow more easily around the world, along with people, goods, and information? Communicable diseases have always existed, so why is their ability to travel globally of such concern? Does the Global North bear any particular responsibility for dealing with potential outbreaks? Why or why not?

HIV/AIDS

HIV/AIDS was first recognized in the United States in 1981 and has since been acknowledged as a scourge throughout not only the United States but also much of the world

FIGURE 16.7 • Ebola Outbreaks in Africa as of January 2016

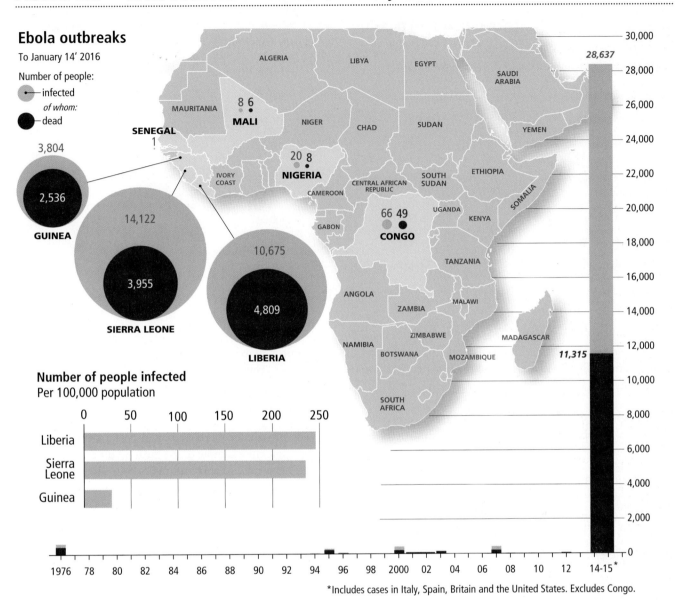

Ebola outbreaks

To January 14' 2016

Number of people:
— infected
of whom:
— dead

3,804
2,536
GUINEA

14,122
3,955
SIERRA LEONE

10,675
4,809
LIBERIA

8 6
MALI

SENEGAL
1

20 8
NIGERIA

66 49
CONGO

28,637

11,315

30,000
28,000
26,000
24,000
22,000
20,000
18,000
16,000
14,000
12,000
10,000
8,000
6,000
4,000
2,000
0

Number of people infected
Per 100,000 population

0   50   100   150   200   250

Liberia
Sierra Leone
Guinea

1976 78 80 82 84 86 88 90 92 94 96 98 2000 02 04 06 08 10 12 14-15*

*Includes cases in Italy, Spain, Britain and the United States. Excludes Congo.

SOURCE: © *The Economist* Newspaper Limited, London.

(Whiteside 2008, 2012). In 2015, it was estimated that 35 million people worldwide had died from AIDS since the first diagnosis. Nearly 37 million, many of whom would die from the disease, were living with AIDS in 2015. The numbers of people infected with HIV and living with AIDS vary widely around the globe. Table 16.2 shows that Africa has been hit hardest, with nearly 70 percent (24.7 million) of the world's HIV population living on this continent. Of the 2.1 million people newly infected in 2015 around the world, 960,000 million live in Eastern and Southern Africa. About 2 million people live with HIV in Latin America and the Caribbean combined, including 100,000 newly infected in 2015. Eastern Europe and Central Asia, with

an adult HIV prevalence rate of 0.9 percent, is the third-hardest-hit region in the world, after Eastern and Southern and Western and Central Africa. An estimated 5.1 million people are living with HIV in Asia and the Pacific. The huge population of this region means that even relatively low prevalence rates translate into large numbers of people infected with HIV. In contrast, people in the Middle East have the lowest rate of HIV, at 0.1 percent, or less than 230,000 HIV-infected persons.

HIV/AIDS cannot be contracted through casual contact with people who have the disease. The disease spreads only through intimate human contact with body fluids, especially through unprotected sex and intravenous drug use. Thus, in

TABLE 16.2 • HIV Prevalence and Incidence by Region, 2015

REGION	TOTAL NUMBER (PERCENT) LIVING WITH HIV	NEWLY INFECTED	ADULT PREVALENCE (PERCENT)
Global total	36.7 million (100%)	2.1 million	0.8
Eastern and Southern Africa	19.0 million (52%)	960,000	7.1
Western and Central Africa	6.5 million (18%)	410,000	2.2
Asia and the Pacific	5.1 million (14%)	300,000	0.2
Western and Central Europe and North America	2.4 million (7%)	91,000	0.3
Latin America and the Caribbean	2.0 million (5%)	100,000	0.5
Eastern Europe and Central Asia	1.5 million (4%)	190,000	0.9
Middle East and North Africa	230,000 (<1%)	21,000	0.1

SOURCE: The Global HIV/AIDS Epidemic January 19, 2017; Kaiser Family Foundation.

spite of the large numbers of people with AIDS, it is *not* an easy disease to contract. For instance, fellow passengers on an international flight will not contract AIDS simply because they sit next to, or talk with, a fellow passenger with the disease.

The spread of AIDS is linked to globalization, especially the increased global mobility associated with tourism (notably, sex tourism), the greater migration rates of workers, increased legal and illegal immigration, much higher rates of commercial and business travel, the movement (sometimes on a mass basis) of refugees, military interventions and the movement of military personnel, and so on.

People who have the disease can travel great distances over a period of years without knowing they have been infected. They therefore have the ability to transmit the disease unknowingly to many others in widely scattered locales. When people with HIV/AIDS travel to other countries and have sexual contact with people there, they are likely to transmit the disease to at least some of them. Similarly, those without the disease can travel to nations where HIV/AIDS is prevalent, contract it, and then bring it back to their home country. In either case, the disease moves from region to region, country to country, and ultimately globally, carried by human vectors.

One well-known way in which HIV/AIDS has spread across the African continent is through truck drivers working their way from country to country. If they have the disease, they may infect those who live in areas that were previously free of the disease.

The disease, as well as the many burdens associated with it, is having an adverse effect on all aspects of social and economic life throughout Africa. Some observers

predicted the failure of African states and the complete economic collapse of some as a result of the spread of the disease. The economies of many African nations have already contracted as average life expectancy has declined and it has become harder to find healthy adults to perform basic tasks.

The prevalence of HIV/AIDS in Eastern and Southern Africa is just one example of the greater vulnerability of the world's have-nots to this and many other borderless diseases. This is a question not just of economic marginality but also of social and political marginality. Compounding the problem is the fact that it is precisely this *most* vulnerable population that is *least* likely to have access to the high-quality health care and the very expensive drugs that can slow the disease for years, or even decades. However, there is now hope that the worst of the AIDS epidemic is over, and some are predicting that it will end by 2030. Part of this hope is traceable to the increasing availability of highly active antiretroviral treatments (HAARTs), which were first discovered in the mid-1990s. In addition, a number of improved prevention and coping strategies have been developed to deal with the disease (Simooya 2016)

New Forms of Flu

In 2009 and 2010, the world witnessed an avian flu pandemic (H1N1), but it proved to be a relatively mild form of the disease. Prior to that, there had been fear of a pandemic of a potentially far more deadly strain of avian flu. Because we live in a global age, the spread of the flu would be faster and more extensive than that of earlier pandemics. However, it is also the case, as will be discussed in a moment, that the ability to deal with such a pandemic is enhanced as a result of globalization. For example, global monitoring has increased, and there is greater ability to get health workers and pharmaceuticals rapidly to the site of an outbreak.

Some flu subtypes can spread through casual human contact with an infected animal, but there is little evidence of human-to-human spread of the avian flu virus. The relatively small number of humans in the world who have gotten the disease, including the even smaller number who have died from it, contracted it through direct contact with infected birds. Those in less developed nations are more likely to have direct contact with birds—some literally live with their birds. This is usually because birds and their eggs are central to their food supply or because birds and their eggs are an important business for them. In contrast, in the developed world, relatively few people have direct contact with birds, so contracting bird flu in this way is highly unlikely.

There is some fear, however, that the virus that causes bird flu might eventually transform itself into a strain that can be spread by casual human-to-human contact. This fear stems from the fact that viruses have taken this route before and caused global human pandemics, such as the infamous "Spanish flu" of 1918–1920, which killed half a million people in the United States and tens of millions worldwide (Kolata 1999). Were this virus transformation to occur, the increased global mobility of people would lead to rapid spread of the disease. While there would be efforts to quarantine those who clearly have the flu, some asymptomatic individuals would inevitably slip through and bring the disease with them to many areas throughout the world.

Superbugs

There is growing concern in the United States and globally about superbugs, which are bacteria that are resistant to all known drugs. These are garden-variety germs rather than the more exotic ones like Ebola already discussed. Superbugs are often picked up during hospitalizations and have been cured easily in the past with antibiotics. Bacteria that are resistant to certain drugs can pass that resistance on to other germs that may already be resistant to other drugs. Over the years, bacteria—for example, the one associated with TB—have grown resistant to an increased number of overused drugs (e.g., penicillin). For example, in the United States, we are down to the last drug, Colistin, that can treat carbapenem-resistant-bacteria (CRE). When bacteria become resistant to that drug, CRE bacteria will be unstoppable. According to the director of the Centers for Disease Control and Prevention, this is one of many indicators that we are entering a "post-antibiotic world" (cited in Tavernise and Grady 2016). Just as diseases of

all sorts can move readily around the world, so, too, can bacteria, and their associated diseases, that are resistant to all known drugs.

THE IMPACT OF WAR ON HEALTH

War and the preparations for it have a profound effect on the health and well-being of people, again, especially in developing countries. For example, in the developing world, four times as much is spent on the military as is spent on health and education. Of the casualties in war, 90 percent are civilians, many of whom are severely wounded and need significant amounts of long-term health care. Warfare also affects the nutrition of all people, as agricultural lands and crops are overrun and the ability of the economy as a whole to function is adversely affected. People, in the form of the human capital they have to offer to the economic system, are diminished. The result is a decline in the quantity and quality of the labor force.

Warfare also has a measurable impact on mental health. For example, child soldiers in Africa are more likely to exhibit antisocial behavior, depression, and paranoia as a result of participation in battle (Honwana 2007). Children who do not fight in battle but live near war zones are more likely not only to be wounded but also to feel that they have less control over their surroundings. This can lead to greater feelings of insecurity and depression and to an increased inability to make meaningful connections with others (Sagi-Schwartz 2008). Children as well as many others who experience being in battle or being close to it can suffer from posttraumatic stress disorder (PTSD). For example, among American soldiers who returned from Afghanistan, PTSD was associated with such problems as alcohol and drug abuse, depression, violence toward others, and thoughts of suicide (www.va.gov).

GLOBALIZATION AND IMPROVEMENTS IN HEALTH AND HEALTH CARE

We have focused in the last few sections on the negative effects of globalization on health. It is clear, however, that globalization has also brought with it an array of developments that have improved, or at least should improve, the quality of health throughout the world. One example is the growth of global health-related organizations, such as the World Health Organization (WHO), the Red Cross, and Médecins sans Frontières (Doctors without Borders; Inoue and Drori 2006). Of course, as with much else about globalization, the effects have been uneven and affected by a variety of local circumstances.

Increasing interpersonal relations among and between various regions throughout the world means that positive developments in one part of the world are likely to find their way to most other parts of the world, and quite rapidly. In addition, there is a ready flow of new ideas associated with health and health care. In the era of the internet and online journals—in this case, medical journals—information about new medical developments flashes around the world virtually instantaneously. Of course, how those ideas are received and whether, and how quickly, they can be implemented vary enormously. There is great variability around the world in the number of professionals able to comprehend and utilize such information. Thus, surgeons in the developed world might be able to implement a new surgical technique almost immediately, but those in less developed countries would find it harder to learn about and utilize such a technique. Furthermore, the institutions in which such ideas can be implemented vary greatly. Thus, hospitals in developed countries would be able to implement changes to reduce the risks of hospital-based infections, but those in less developed countries would find such changes difficult or impossible because of the costs involved.

New medical products clearly flow around the world much more slowly than new ideas, but because of global improvements in transport, they are much more mobile than ever before. Included under this heading would be pharmaceuticals of all types. Clearly, the superstars of the pharmaceutical industry are global phenomena. In fact, while North America (primarily the United States) accounted for about 48 percent of the over $1 trillion in pharmaceutical sales worldwide in 2014, sales in emerging markets outside the United States are growing more rapidly than U.S. sales (Alazraki 2010; Herper and Kang 2006; Statista 2015). As new drugs (especially oncologics to treat cancer) are approved and come to be seen as effective, they are likely to flow around the world, especially to developed countries and to the elites in less developed countries.

Of course, the drugs that are most likely to be produced and distributed globally are those that are considered likely to be most profitable. Those are the drugs that address the health problems of the wealthier members of global society, such as hypertension, high cholesterol, arthritis, mental health problems, impotence, and hair loss. The well-to-do are most able to afford the diets that lead to high cholesterol, acid reflux, and heartburn, and they are therefore the likely consumers of Lipitor, Zocor, Nexium, and Prevacid. Because they produce the greatest earnings for pharmaceutical companies, these drugs are most likely to achieve global distribution.

Conversely, drugs that might save many lives are not apt to be produced (Moran et al. 2009). Few, if any, of the pharmaceutical companies surveyed in the United States, Europe, and Japan devote research and development money to creating drugs that would help those in less developed countries who suffer from diseases such as sleeping sickness and malaria. Such drugs are unlikely to yield great profits because those who need them are mainly the poor in less developed countries. If the drugs are produced, their flow to those parts of the globe is likely to be minimal. Thus, as we have seen, Africa is a hotbed of many diseases, such as malaria, some of which kill millions of people each year. However, these are largely poor people in impoverished countries, and the major drug companies based primarily in the West and wealthy developed countries are little interested in doing the research and paying the start-up and production costs necessary to produce drugs that are not likely to be profitable and may even lose money. To be fair, we are beginning to see a glimmer of hope for drugs to treat sleeping sickness and malaria (P. Kennedy 2013; Willyard 2014), but they are a long way from mass production and distribution. In the meantime, millions continue to die from these diseases.

There has been no vaccine for Ebola largely because, prior to 2014, there had been too few cases *and* because those infected were poor people from impoverished African countries. Now that we have seen tens of thousands of cases, and thousands have died, great progress seems to be taking place in the development of an Ebola vaccine. A cynic would also say that now that the developed countries have themselves had to deal with a few cases and have recognized at least the potential for some threat of an Ebola epidemic there, the drug companies have suddenly discovered the ability to test and create an Ebola vaccine at warp speed.

Similar points can be made about the flow of advanced medical technologies, including MRIs and CAT scans, throughout the world. These are extraordinarily expensive technologies found largely in the wealthy developed countries of the Global North. The machines are not only more likely to exist in these developed countries but also more likely to be used extensively there because patients, either on

A worker for Doctors without Borders helps children in South Sudan, where the World Health Organization hopes to carry out a massive vaccination campaign against cholera. What challenges does this effort face, given that unrest in that country has displaced almost 1 million people?

their own or because of health insurance, are able to afford the very expensive scans and tests associated with them. Also concentrated in developed countries are the highly trained personnel needed to administer and interpret the results of, say, an MRI. In contrast, relatively few of these technologies flow to less developed countries in the Global South; they are used there less extensively, and there are relatively few trained people there capable of conducting the tests and interpreting the results (Debas 2010; World Health Organization 2010b).

In terms of networks of people, much the same picture emerges. Medical and health-related personnel in the Global North are tightly linked through an array of professional networks. As a result, personnel can move about within those networks. More important, the latest findings and developments in health and medicine are rapidly disseminated through those networks. The problem in the Global South is not only that fewer professionals are involved in these networks but also that the flow of new information to them is more limited (Godlee et al. 2004; Horton 2000). More important, even if they are able to get the information, they generally lack the resources and infrastructure to use it, or to use it adequately.

At a more general level, we can say that the health and medical institutions in the Global North are highly interconnected, while those in the Global South are only weakly interconnected with those in the Global North as well as with one another (Buss and Ferreira 2010). This is another, more general reason that important new developments in health and medicine do not flow rapidly to the Global South.

CHECKPOINT 16.3: GLOBAL HEALTH CONCERNS

HEALTH FACTOR	DEFINITION
Undernutrition	A form of malnutrition caused by the inadequate intake of calories, vitamins, and minerals.
Food insecurity	Lack of access to safe and nutritious food.
Borderless diseases	The increasing global mobility of diseases like SARS, HIV/AIDS, and Ebola, as a result of migration, tourism, and urbanization, as well as the spread of antibiotic resistant superbugs.

SUMMARY

The growth of sociological interest in the body can be traced to Michel Foucault, whose work focused on the relationship between the body and society and culture. The field encompasses a wide range of concerns, such as sexuality, bodily pain, and body modifications.

The medical profession has gone through a process of deprofessionalization, characterized by a decline in power and autonomy as well as in status and wealth among members. Challenges to the authority of physicians include the threat of medical malpractice, the creation of government medical programs and policies, and the rise of private health insurance programs. Patients have become more active prosumers in the health care system,

too, using the internet to shop for the lowest prices for medical procedures and reading fellow patients' reviews.

Disparities in health and health care have often been tied to globalization. Individuals in the Global South suffer disproportionately from hunger, forms of malnutrition, and food insecurity. The spread of diseases such as HIV/AIDS and Ebola is linked to increased global mobility and urbanization in the Global South. The ability to implement new medical technologies and afford new treatments varies by region, with the Global South lagging far behind the Global North, but the rise of antibiotic-resistant superbugs poses a danger to the treatment of some diseases in all parts of the world.

KEY TERMS

deprofessionalization, 450
food insecurity, 461

medicalization, 456
medical sociology, 450

profession, 450
reflexivity, 442

telemedicine, 453
undernutrition, 461

1. We live in an increasingly reflexive society with a heightened awareness of our bodies. According to Naomi Wolf, how does the beauty myth perpetuate such reflexivity?

2. How is risk-taking behavior related to Michel Foucault's idea of limit experiences? What satisfaction do people get from risk-taking behavior?

3. What are the pros and cons of our obsession with our appearance and the fitness of our bodies?

4. What are the characteristics of a profession? What factors can help explain why physicians have become increasingly deprofessionalized?

5. What are the weaknesses of the health care system in the United States? How are these weaknesses related to systems of stratification?

6. Explain the increasing medicalization of society. How has it affected women in particular?

7. How have the internet and new social media technologies affected the consumption of health care? What are some of the disadvantages of having access to more information about health care?

8. In what ways are patients increasingly prosumers of health care? How has this change affected the power of physicians?

9. How has globalization tended to widen global disparities in health care? What kinds of health problems are you most likely to find in the Global South? What could be done to avoid some of these problems?

10. What are the major borderless diseases? In what ways are they made worse by globalization? Can globalization also play a role in curing them, or at least in reducing their prevalence?

$SAGE edge™ **Want a better grade?**

Get the tools you need to sharpen your study skills. Access practice quizzes, eFlashcards, video and multimedia at **http://edge.sagepub.com/ritzerintro4e**.

PRACTICE AND APPLY WHAT YOU'VE LEARNED

▶ **edge.sagepub.com/ritzerintro4e**

CHECK YOUR COMPREHENSION ON THE STUDY SITE WITH:

- **Diagnostic pre-tests** to identify opportunities for improvement.

- **Personalized study plans** with focused recommendations to address specific knowledge gaps and additional learning needs.

- **Post-tests** to check your progress and ensure mastery of key learning objectives.

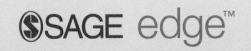

17

POPULATION, URBANIZATION, AND THE ENVIRONMENT

Reaching a New Global Milestone

At two minutes to midnight on October 30, 2011, the world's population reached 7 billion; by early 2017, the number was approaching 7.5 billion. While it would have been impossible to identify the actual 7-billionth human born among the several hundred who came into the world at that moment in 2011, Danica May Camacho, born in Manila, Philippines, was the first of several babies chosen by the United Nations to represent this major milestone. A series of media events and press conferences were held throughout the following "Day of 7 Billion" to draw attention to the challenges posed by an ever-growing population.

For media outlets around the world, reaching the 7 billion mark proved a fascinating but passing diversion. Some reports were celebratory, others contemplative, but most were over once the next big news story broke. For sociologists, demographers, ecologists, and other scientists, however, the growing global population is a major and ongoing social phenomenon that has had—and will continue to have—enormous consequences for where and how we live. Along with environmentalists, these scientists have voiced serious concerns about what continued population growth means for the planet's finite and fragile resources.

Population growth and other demographic changes over the last 150 years, such as shifts in the proportions of young and old in many countries and the increasing concentration of people in urban environments, have helped give rise to new patterns of living. Urbanization,

LEARNING OBJECTIVES

17.1 Explain the causes and effects of population growth and decline.

17.2 Describe the growing urbanization of the world's population.

17.3 Summarize the development of global cities.

17.4 Discuss major environmental problems and responses to solve them.

edge.sagepub.com/ritzerintro4e

- Take the chapter quiz
- Review key terms with eFlashcards
- Explore multimedia links and SAGE readings

for instance, has brought with it the emergence of megacities, edge cities, and megalopolises. The rising global consumption that accompanies population growth has contributed to serious environmental problems on a worldwide scale, such as climate change, unchecked pollution, the rapid accumulation of human and manufactured waste, and a new scarcity of potable water. These effects will further challenge the way we perceive and interact with our environments, both natural and social.

While Danica May Camacho's birth had no direct effect on urbanization trends or the environment, the rapid growth of the global population that her arrival represented certainly has. As long as new births outpace deaths and the population climbs, Earth's cities and its environment will be challenged, and we will need to adapt. Bear in mind that the challenges will only increase as the global population continues to grow in the coming years. ●

This chapter covers three broad topics—population, urbanization, and the environment. While each is important in its own right, they are covered together here because of the many ways in which they interrelate. For example, population growth leads to more densely populated cities, and an increased population is likely to wreak ever more havoc on the environment.

POPULATION

Demography is the scientific study of population (Bianchi and Wight 2012; Weeks 2011; Wight 2007), especially its growth and decline, as well as the movement of people. Those who study these population dynamics are **demographers**. Demography is both a distinct field of study and a subfield within sociology.

POPULATION GROWTH

A great deal of attention has been devoted to population growth and the idea of a population explosion, or the "population bomb" (Ehrlich 1968). Some of that fear has dissipated in recent years. This has happened, at least in part, because of the ability of the world's most populous country, China, to slow its population growth through, among other things, its one-child policy. Although that policy was discontinued at the beginning of 2016, China's population is already huge and will continue to grow, although it will soon be surpassed by India's in size. Population increases are important and of

interest not only in themselves but also because of the need for greater resources to support a growing population. Also of concern is the strain such increases place on national and city services, as well as on the environment.

While overall fertility rates are dropping globally, the world's population continues to increase, although at a declining rate. It was not until the early 1800s that the global population exceeded 1 billion people; it reached 2 billion in just one century (by 1930), then 3 billion in 30 more years (by 1960). In the next 14 years, it reached 4 billion (1974); 13 years later, and it was 5 billion (1987); and in another 12 years, it reached 6 billion (1999; Roberts 2009). As pointed out in the introduction to this chapter, in 12 more years the world's population exceeded 7 billion people—37 percent of them in China and India alone (Population Reference Bureau 2010). It will likely take only another decade—to the spring of 2026—to achieve the next milestone of 8 billion people (Worldometers 2015). This recent slowdown in population growth is in stark contrast to the rapid growth after World War II. It was the latter that led to dire predictions about the future of population growth. However, it is now estimated that *only* about 9.4 billion people will be in the world by 2050 (see Figure 17.1; Bianchi and Wight 2012). While this is a dramatic reduction in future estimates, it still represents a major increase in the world's population (an additional 2 billion more people in the next three-plus decades). This growth is occurring, and will continue to occur, in spite of high death rates in many parts of the world due to high infant mortality, war, starvation, disease, and natural disasters. The death rate may increase dramatically in the twenty-first century if, as many expect, the disastrous effects of climate change accelerate, although that increase is unlikely to have much of an impact on overall population projections. Nevertheless, although there is less talk these days about a population explosion, there is little doubt that the world's population is increasing, perhaps at an unsustainable rate.

Taking a longer time perspective, it is estimated that by 2100 there will be as many as 12.3 billion people in the world (Gerland et al. 2014). The reason for the significant increase is largely that in many countries (such as Ethiopia and Niger), population growth continues to be very rapid. In fact, in spite of the ravages of warfare and of diseases such as malaria, AIDS, and Ebola, the population of Africa as a whole is expected to double by 2050 (United Nations Department of Economic and Social Affairs 2015b).

POPULATION DECLINE

Historically, population decline has not been considered as important as growth, but it has recently come to the fore in various parts of the world, especially in a number of European countries (Italy, Germany, Russia) and Japan (Coleman and Rowthorn 2011). By 2050, the population of

FIGURE 17.1 • World Population, 1950–2050 (Projected)

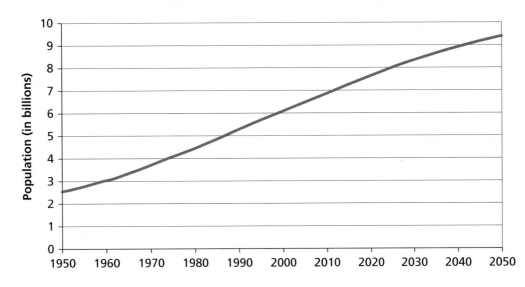

SOURCE: Data from U.S. Census Bureau, World Population 1950–2050.

Germany is projected to *drop* from 82.4 million to 81 million, while Japan's population is projected to decline from 127.7 million to 100.6 million (Coleman and Rowthorn 2011, 220; U.S. Census Bureau 2012). Also of concern is the decline expected to occur in Russia, from 142.8 million to 136.4 million in 2050. A variety of problems, such as high alcoholism rates and greatly unequal development across the country, have led to predictions of the "depopulation" of Russia. Similar declines, and problems, are expected in a number of former Soviet Bloc countries, such as Ukraine, Bulgaria, and Latvia. Population decline can be caused by a low **birthrate**, the number of childbirths per 1,000 people per year. It can also be caused by a high death rate, more emigration than immigration, or some combination of the three. In countries with aging populations, birthrates are often below the level needed to maintain the population.

Of interest here are not only the various causes of such declines but also their impact on society as a whole. For one thing, population decline can weaken nations in various ways, including militarily (Yoshihara and Sylva 2011). This is because the power of nations is often associated with having large populations; a smaller population generally translates into a smaller military (Israel is an exception). For another, population decline can weaken a nation's economy because the total number of productive workers declines. Third, the fact that population decline is generally accompanied by an aging population brings with it various problems, including a "financial time bomb." This is because of the high costs associated with caring for the elderly—especially government pensions and health-related expenses. A parallel decline in the number of younger people in the labor force means that there are fewer people who are able to help pay those costs through taxes (Singer 2010). Among other

things, this financial time bomb will bring with it a great increase in national debt. This, of course, is already a concern in many countries. However, there are actions that can be taken to mitigate this problem, such as raising the retirement age so that older people can support themselves longer. Another possibility, although it is difficult politically, is for nations to reduce pensions and medical coverage, especially for the elderly.

ASK YOURSELF

What are some of the problems nations would face in reducing expensive government benefits in attempts to defuse the "financial time bomb" of an aging population? Who would benefit from such reductions? Who would be harmed, and how could governments protect them?

It would be wrong to conclude that population decline brings with it only a series of problems. Among the gains would be a reduction of the ecological problems caused by a growing population. For example, a smaller population would produce fewer automobile emissions and create less pollution. In addition, the pressure on the world's diminishing supplies of oil and water would be reduced.

While some nations will be hurt by an aging population, others, especially developing countries, will get a "demographic dividend" (Desai 2010; Lee 2007) because they have a favorable ratio between those who are able to work and those who are dependents, such as the aged and children. The dividend results, in part, from the presence of a large younger population able to work and earn money. At the same time, there are relatively few in need of their support. A significant part of the dividend is traceable to education and the greater productivity associated with a better-educated younger generation (Cuaresma, Lutz, and Sanderson 2014).

THE PROCESSES OF POPULATION CHANGE

Beyond some of the specific issues outlined previously, three basic processes are of concern to demographers. The first is **fertility**, or people's reproductive behavior, especially the number of births. Key to understanding fertility is the birthrate. Second is **mortality**, or deaths and death rates within a population. Finally, there is **migration**, or the movements of people, or *migrants,* and the impact of these movements on both the sending and the receiving locales (Bianchi and Wight 2012; Faist, Fauser, and Reisenauer 2013). While these are dynamic processes, demographers are also concerned about more structural issues such as population composition, especially the age and sex characteristics of a population.

Fertility

Theoretically, women could average as many as 16 births throughout their reproductive years. In reality, women rarely reach that number. In 2014, the global fertility rate was 2.45 births per woman. However, fertility levels vary widely around the globe. In 2014, they ranged from 1.2 birth per woman in Macao and the Republic of Korea to 6 or more per woman in several African countries; Somalia was the highest, at 6.5 births per woman (World Bank, n.d.). In this section, we deal with the economic and social factors affecting fertility, regional differences in fertility, and fertility trends in the United States.

Economic Factors. Fertility is affected by a variety of economic factors. For example, we know that record low points in population growth were associated with the Great Depression. Low points were also recorded in the 1970s, when an oil crisis led to a dramatic jump in oil prices and rampant inflation.

Social Factors. Fertility is also affected by a variety of social factors. For instance, there is the obvious impact of age on fertility. Most childbearing involves women between the ages of 15 and 45. Especially important in the context of age is the fertility and childbearing of adolescents (less than 20 years old). Globally, adolescents give birth to an estimated 16 million babies per year: The rate is as high as 200 per 1,000 births in some African countries, 24 per 1,000 in most developed countries, and only 7 or fewer per 1,000 in China, Japan, and Korea (Cooksey 2007). The United States has the highest rate of births to teenage mothers of all industrial nations; it is more than four times the rate of many

FIGURE 17.2 • Teenage Birthrate in the United States, 1940–2015

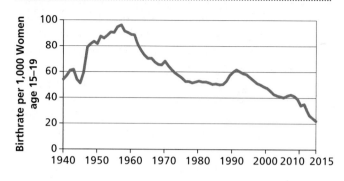

SOURCE: Data from CDC/NCHS, Division of Vital Statistics

Western European countries (World Health Organization 2014). However, the teenage birthrate in the United States has been declining dramatically in recent years. The peak year was 1957, with a birthrate of 96.3 per 1,000 teenage women ages 15–19. By 2015, the birthrate for such women had reached a record low of 22.3 (see Figure 17.2). Even if it has become less of a problem in the United States, a high birthrate among adolescents remains a problem in many parts of the less-developed world. Among the concerns are that these young mothers, as well as their children, experience more birth-related health complications and that they may not be ready to care for their children. This lack of readiness is largely tied to inadequate education, especially sex education, as well as adolescent mothers' subordinate gender roles (Weiss and Lonnquist 2009). As a result, adolescent mothers generally lack the knowledge and power they need to make informed decisions on childbearing and child rearing.

A second, and related, issue involves the broader category of nonmarital fertility; not all of such fertility is accounted for by adolescents (Musick 2007). Nonmarital fertility has increased dramatically in the United States, rising from only 5 percent of all births in 1960 to one-third in 2000; it now accounts for almost 44 percent of all births (Bianchi and Wright 2012; Centers for Disease Control and Prevention 2016b). The United States is not unique among Western industrialized countries in this: Its rate of nonmarital fertility is higher than some, such as Germany's and Ireland's; on a par with others, such as Austria, Spain, and Finland; and lower than others, such as Mexico and Iceland, where almost two-thirds of children are born outside marriage (Haub 2013).

Regional Factors. While countries in many less developed areas of the world still worry about high birthrates, officials in many developed countries have grown increasingly concerned about *low* birthrates. A birthrate of 2.1 is needed to replace an existing population. However, in the early twenty-first century, the average fertility in developed countries was 1.6 children for each woman; in some of those countries, it approached the "lowest low fertility" of fewer than 1.3 children. In other words, the birthrates in these countries are inadequate to replace the current population. This is a particular concern throughout Western Europe and has led to worry over the issues discussed previously in terms of an aging population. Another concern is the future of the historical cultures of various European countries where the birthrates of immigrants (especially Muslims) far exceed those of "natives" (Caldwell 2009). This fact has contributed to increasing animosity between natives and immigrants and the growing conflict between them. In fact, nativist movements have grown in much of Europe (and even in the United States), fueled by the growth in immigrants, especially Muslims, and increasingly frequent terrorist attacks, especially in France and Great Britain.

U.S. Fertility Trends. When the United States was founded, the average birthrate was slightly less than 8 per woman; that rate declined throughout the nineteenth century and throughout most of the first half of the twentieth century. Then World War II led to an increase in the birthrate, and it remained high throughout the 1950s. In fact, the rise in the birthrate between 1946 and 1960 is referred to as the *baby boom*. The peak in fertility in the United States was reached in 1957, after which the birthrate declined for almost two decades, reaching a low of 1.7 in 1976. Today the birthrate is 1.84 (see Figure 17.3; Centers for Disease Control and Prevention 2017). In other words, fertility in the United States is just below "replacement level"—the number needed to replace the population.

Mortality

As an indicator of change, a population's mortality—or death rate—is certainly as important to demographers as its birthrate. A population's death rate is measured as the number of deaths per 1,000 people. Life expectancy is the number of years an individual can be expected to live.

Life Expectancy. In prehistoric times, life expectancy in the world ranged between 20 and 30 years; by 1900, that number had increased slightly, and today it has reached an average of 69 years. Nearly half of the decline in mortality in developed countries took place in the twentieth century. Life expectancy is now 77 years in the more developed countries, 67 years in less developed countries, and 56 years in the least developed countries (Bianchi and Wight 2012). Life expectancy in Africa is only 60 years (World Health Organization 2015b). As we saw in Chapter 16, the highest life expectancy is found in Japan, where women live an average of 88.5 years and men are apt to live 81.7 years. Life expectancy for women in the United States is about 82.1 years;

FIGURE 17.3 • Number of Children per Woman in the United States, 1911–2015

SOURCE: Data from CDC/NCHS, National Vital Statistics System.

for men it is 77.5 years (Central Intelligence Agency 2016). By 2050, U.S. women can expect to live between 90 to 95 years, while men can expect to live between 80 and 85 years.

Macro-social Factors. Although death is, of course, a biological inevitability, increased life expectancy and lower death rates in a population can be affected by a variety of macro-social factors. Major factors in the decline in mortality (with a few examples) include the following (Elo 2007):

- A general improvement in standards of living (better housing quality, improved nutrition)

- Better public health (improved sanitation, cleaner drinking water)

- Cultural and behavioral factors (stronger norms regarding healthy lifestyles)

- Advances in medicine and medical technologies, which not only led to an aging population but also reduced infant mortality rates (antibiotics and newer drugs, immunizations, improved surgical techniques)

- Government actions (control of diseases such as malaria)

Of course, important factors that keep death rates high continue to exist (including infectious diseases such as malaria, Ebola, and AIDS), and other factors that could increase the death rate, including global flu epidemics, loom on the horizon.

Mortality is greatly affected by one's position in the system of social stratification (see Chapters 8 and 9). In the United States, those in the lower classes are likely to have shorter life spans than those who rank higher in the stratification system. As for race, blacks have a lower life expectancy than whites, but black males are more disadvantaged in comparison to white males than black females are compared to white females. Lower life expectancies among black men are the result of the fact that they are more likely to live in rural areas, where life expectancy in general is lower, are less likely to seek health care, are at higher risk of death by homicide, and are more likely to engage in substance abuse (Sabo 1998; Singh and Siahpush 2014).

In terms of gender, women have a longer life expectancy than men in spite of the various disadvantages they confront that stem from the system of gender stratification (see Chapter 11). This difference is due, in part, to the fact that women engage in more health-protective behaviors than men, such as visiting physicians more often. Gender roles also tend to protect women from fatal disease and injury (Rieker and Bird 2000). For example, women are less likely than men to engage in potentially disabling or deadly activities, such as using illegal drugs, driving dangerously, and engaging in violent behavior. Higher death rates for male fetuses, as well as for male infants in the first four months of life, suggest that females may be more viable organisms than males. However, in general, "women now live longer than men not because their biology has changed, but because their social position and access to resources have changed" (Weitz 2010, 52). Nevertheless, in some parts of the world, such as Swaziland and Botswana, females have a lower life expectancy than males. This is traceable, at least in part, to the fact that females in some regions are more likely to die in infancy, perhaps because of parental neglect or female infanticide, or when giving birth to their own children.

Micro-social Factors. Mortality is also affected by a number of micro-social factors, especially those associated with poor lifestyle choices, including smoking, failing to exercise, overeating, and eating unhealthy foods. Obesity has long been related to higher death rates from heart disease and stroke. A more recent discovery is the linkage between obesity and death from various forms of cancer, including breast and endometrial cancer. More than 100,000 new cases of cancer per year in the United States can be traced to obesity. Conversely, healthy lifestyle choices can lead to longer lives. For example, religious groups that restrict the use of tobacco products, alcohol, coffee, and addictive drugs, such as the Mormons, tend to have longer life expectancies. Globally, the lifestyle of the Japanese, which includes eating more fish and less red meat, is closely related to their greater longevity.

In this context, special mention must be made of the increasing role of drug abuse (and addiction)—especially of heroin and prescription opioids (Kolodny et al. 2015)—in mortality. Heroin and opioids are similar molecularly. Almost half of opioid deaths come from the over-prescription of drugs such as oxycodone and methadone. Opioids killed more than 28,000 Americans in 2014 (in a high-profile example, music superstar Prince died from abuse of the drug

fentanyl in 2016). That is quadruple the number of such deaths in 1999, and it represents a 14 percent increase from the year before. While adverse publicity has finally led to a decline in opioid prescriptions, the amount of the drug prescribed is still high by historical standards (*New York Times* Editorial Board 2016a). More than 8,000 people per year die from heroin overdoses; fatal overdoses tripled between 2012 and 2014 (Quinones 2015). Heroin use and abuse, once largely a low-income, minority, inner-city problem, occurs increasingly throughout society. Many recent users are middle-class whites who live outside major cities. At least some of these people started on opioids prescribed by their physicians, but eventually graduated to the more accessible and less expensive heroin. The following statement by one drug abuser sums up the opioid-heroin situation well: "All of my friends use heroin and I know multiple people who will sell it to me or help me find someone who has it. Also if I have money I wanna spend it on something I know will get me high. If I buy pills I might not have enough money to make sure I get high" (Cicero et al. 2014).

The Demographic Transition

The issues of fertility and mortality are central to a major theory of population: demographic transition theory. According to this theory, population changes are related to the shift from an agricultural society to a more industrialized and urbanized society (Davis 1945; Weeks 2007). Four stages are associated with the *demographic transition* (see Figure 17.4).

In the first, or preindustrial, stage, there is a rough balance between high death rates (mortality) and high birthrates (fertility). As a result, the population growth rate, while high, is fairly stable.

FIGURE 17.4 • The Demographic Transition Model

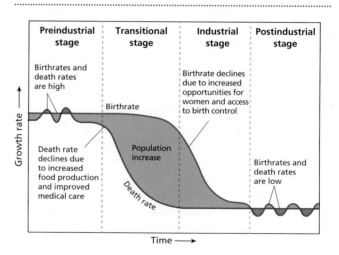

SOURCE: Adapted from *A Dictionary of Geography,* 2nd edition by Susan Mayhew (1997). Figure 20, p. 122. By permission of Oxford University Press.

In the second, or transitional, stage, the death rate declines dramatically while the birthrate remains high (although it begins to decline slowly toward the end of this stage). The total population grows rapidly under these circumstances. In this stage, death rates decline first in developed countries for various reasons, including improvement in food production, a higher standard of living, a better-informed population, improved hygiene, and better health care. This was the situation in most of the developed countries of Europe beginning in the eighteenth century.

In the industrial stage, the death rate drops more slowly over time, to its lowest level. The deep decline in the death rate leads to more children in the family and the community. As a result, people begin thinking about limiting the number of children. Women begin to have greater access to, and are more likely to use, birth control. In addition, fewer children are required because not as many workers are needed on the family farms. Many family members move into the cities and take jobs in industries and other organizations. Thus, another main cause of the decline of the birthrate in the industrial age is the fact that women have increased work-related opportunities. For these and other reasons, it is to the family's advantage to limit family size. Eventually, the birthrate drops to a level roughly equal to the low level of the death rate.

In the postindustrial stage, while there is some variation over time, birthrates and death rates remain low. As a result, in the postindustrial stage, as in the latter part of the industrial stage, population growth remains slow or stabilizes.

As a general rule, birthrates drop more slowly than death rates largely because it is difficult to overcome the positive value individuals and cultures place on children and on life more generally. In contrast, reducing the death rate is relatively easy, at least when the means to do so exist, because postponing death *is* consistent with valuing life. This contradicts the myth that a population grows because of a rise in the birthrate. Rather, such growth is better attributed to a decline in death rates with birthrates remaining largely unchanged.

In Western Europe, the entire demographic transition took about 200 years, from the mid-1800s until the mid-twentieth century. The process continues today in much of the rest of the world. However, in recent years, in less developed countries, the process has taken significantly less time. This is traceable to the much more rapid decline in the death rate because of the importation of advanced, especially medical, technologies from developed countries. Because birthrates have remained high while death rates have declined, population growth in less developed countries has been extraordinarily high.

Given this recent rapid population growth in less developed countries, the issue has become what can be done about it, especially in the areas of the world where fertility remains high. In other words, how can the birthrate be reduced in those areas?

Reducing Fertility. Adopting the view that development is the best contraceptive, one approach to reducing fertility is to stress economic development. This follows from what has been learned from the demographic transition in Europe and the United States, where economic development did lead to lower fertility. A second approach is voluntary family planning. This includes providing people with information about reproductive physiology and the use of contraceptive techniques, actually providing such things as birth control pills and condoms, and developing societal or local informational programs to support the use of contraception and the ideal of small(er) families. A third approach involves a change in the society as a whole, especially where large numbers of children have been considered both advantageous and desirable. In many societies, children are still needed to work to help the family survive and to provide for the parents in their old age. Changes such as compulsory childhood education and child labor laws can counter the fact that these realities lead families to have large numbers of children. They serve to make children less valuable economically because they cannot work when they are in school and they are kept out of the labor force for years by child labor laws. As a result, at least some parents have fewer children. Another important step is to be sure that women acquire public roles beyond the family realm. When women have greater educational and occupational opportunities, their fertility declines, and families have fewer children (Fillipi et al. 2006; Hwang and Lee 2014). However, solutions that require changing cultural ideas about women and reproduction can be difficult and slow to achieve.

ASK YOURSELF

What happens to families that depend on children's earnings for survival when those children are required to attend school instead of working? Should society help address the loss of income to such families, and, if so, how? Should companies that hired child workers in the past be responsible for these families' survival? Why or why not?

The practice of infanticide is an unfortunate reality in some parts of the world, and the selection of females for infanticide is especially problematic for various reasons, including its impact on fertility. The selective killing of female fetuses ("female infanticide") subsequently affects fertility because males end up outnumbering females in a population and there are fewer potential mothers (Bhatnagar, Dube, and Dube 2006). Infanticide is most common in South and East Asia, although it is also found in other areas of the world, including North Africa and the Middle East (United Nations 2006).

A Second Demographic Transition. In the 1980s, some scholars began thinking in terms of a second demographic transition to describe the general decline in the fertility rate and of population growth, especially in developed countries (Lesthaeghe 2010, 2014; Lesthaeghe and van de Kaa 1986; Ochiai 2014). This decline is linked to parents coming to focus more on the quality of life of one child, or a few children, as well as on the quality of their own lives. Better occupational prospects, and therefore a more affluent lifestyle, have come to be associated with having fewer children.

The second demographic transition is seen as involving three stages. The first stage, between 1955 and 1970, is of greatest importance. The key factor during this period was the end of the baby boom, aided by the revolution in contraception that made it less likely that people would have unwanted children. Also beginning at this time was the gender revolution, which meant, among other things, that women began to marry later and to divorce more. They also entered the work world in greater numbers. This tended to reduce the birthrate, as did the fact that there were fewer women at home to care for children. These and other factors can be said to be associated with a second demographic transition involving subreplacement fertility, lower birthrates, and a declining rate of population growth (Lesthaeghe 2007). This transition has also been accompanied by the proliferation of a variety of living arrangements other than marriage and an increasing disconnect between marriage and procreation (Klinenberg 2012).

Migration

Although migration certainly takes place within national borders (Crowder and Hall 2007), our primary concern here is cross-border, international (Kritz 2007), or global migration—with migration as a central aspect of globalization (Faist 2012; Scherschel 2007). In the United States, migration drew a great deal of media and political attention in 2014 for various reasons, not least of which was the massive influx of unaccompanied minors from Central America through the border with Mexico. This led to questions about what to do with the children once they were in the country and how to pay for any solutions (Chishti, Hipsman, and Bui 2014).

Since then, the focus has shifted to the more general issue of illegal migration through and from Mexico. This is the case largely because of the 2016 presidential campaign in the United States. Donald Trump made the centerpiece of his campaign stopping illegal migration by, among other things, building a much larger and stronger wall between Mexico and the United States (and forcing Mexico to pay for it). He made this suggestion in spite of the fact that the flow of illegal immigration through Mexico and to the United States has slowed dramatically, largely because of improved economic conditions in Mexico (Porter 2016a). Trump continued to contend that the wall would be built in the early days of his presidency, but it would be likely to cost much more than he estimated and take much longer to complete.

Globally, concern about migration reached a crescendo in 2015 and 2016 as massive numbers of people fled their home countries because of warfare, failed states, and hostility to minority groups. Syria, Iraq, Libya, and Yemen were sites of catastrophic warfare and can be considered failed, or at least failing, states. Minority groups such as the Yazidi in Syria and Iraq fled as a result of persecution and even genocide at the hands of the Islamic State (Cumming-Bruce 2015). In Myanmar (and Bangladesh), many Rohingya, a Muslim minority, fled to escape violence perpetrated by the Hindu majority in that country (Fuller and Cochran 2015). Ironically, many Rohingya who fled Myanmar found their way in late 2016 and early 2017 to, of all places, Bangladesh (Barry 2017). For its part, in early 2017 Bangladesh announced plans to relocate its Rohingya refugees, many in camps close to the country's major resort, to a remote island that floods for much of the year (Sattar 2017). In the seas around Europe and Southeast Asia, many rickety boats (some of which sank) carried people to what they thought would be safe havens in other countries. However, at least some countries did not welcome these people or even rejected them—fearing, among other things, the cost of maintaining them until they could be integrated into those countries.

Controlling Migration. Prior to the beginning of the fifteenth century, people moved across borders rather freely, although they were greatly hampered by limitations in transportation. However, with the rise of the nation-state in the fifteenth century, much more notice was taken of such movement, and many more barriers were erected to limit and control it (Hollifield and Jacobson 2012). Nevertheless, as late as the end of the nineteenth century, there was still much freedom of movement, most notably in the great Atlantic migration to the United States from Europe. It is estimated that about 50 million people left Europe for the United States between 1820 and the end of the nineteenth century (Moses 2006). Prior to 1880, entry into the United States was largely unregulated—virtually anyone who wanted to could get in. In 1889, the International Emigration Conference declared: "We affirm the right of the individual to the fundamental liberty accorded to him by every civilized nation to come and go and dispose of his person and his destinies as he pleases" (cited in Moses 2006, 47). It was World War I that changed attitudes and the situation dramatically; nation-states began to impose drastic restrictions on the global movement of people. Today, while there is variation among nation-states, "there is not a single state that allows free access to all immigrants" (Moses 2006, 54). With legal migration restricted in various ways and border controls more stringent, one unintended consequence (Massey and Pren 2012) has been an increase in illegal immigration (Hadjicostandi 2007), often involving human smugglers (Martinez and Slack 2013; Shane and Gordon 2008).

A great deal of population movement is associated with globalization (Kritz 2008; Kritz, Lim, and Zlotnik 1992). In the early twenty-first century, about 3.2 percent of the global population lived outside their countries of origin (United Nations Population Fund 2015). To some observers, this represents a large and growing number, and, in fact, it constitutes a substantial increase of 36 percent since 1990 (although the rate of increase has declined dramatically in recent years). However, to other observers, the sense that we live in a global era of unprecedented international migration is exaggerated because the actual rate was higher in the late nineteenth and early twentieth centuries (Guhathakurta, Jacobson, and DelSordi 2007).

While it is true that the rate is lower than it was a century ago, migrants do make up significant proportions of the populations of many countries (Kivisto and Faist 2010). For example, in 2013, migrants accounted for about 12 percent of the population in Germany, France, and the United Kingdom, and more than 14 percent of the U.S. population (United Nations Department of Economic and Social Affairs 2015a). In the case of the United States, the proportion of migrants in the total population will reach 15 percent between 2020 and 2025, and it will rise to 19 percent by 2050, but only if the migratory wave persists. This will exceed the previous high of nearly 15 percent achieved in the late nineteenth century (Roberts 2008).

Several interesting and important changes have affected the nature of today's international migrants. For one thing, the proportion of such migrants from the developed world has actually declined. For another, there has been a large increase in the number of migrants from the developing world, and a very significant proportion of them (70 to 90 percent) are moving to North America.

Unlike much else in the modern world (trade, finance, investment), legal restrictions on the migration of people, especially labor migration, have *not* been liberalized (Tan 2007). The major exception has been within the European Union, and only for the citizens of member nations. In what would have been another exception, in late 2014 President Obama issued a controversial executive order that served to protect about 4 million undocumented immigrants from deportation and to allow them to work in the United States legally (Shear 2014). However, in mid-2016 the Supreme Court blocked President Obama's order. In 2017, President Trump began his tenure by seeking to impose new and severe restrictions on Mexico and several predominantly Muslim countries. In mid-February he announced measures to enforce existing immigration laws, regardless of past presidents' leniency. All unauthorized immigrants, criminal or not, may now be subject to deportation.

Elsewhere in the world, restrictions on migration remain in place, as they do in the EU for non-EU citizens. In some places, and for some less welcome migrants, restrictions have not only been increased but in some cases also militarized (Schuster 2012b). In some locales, European borders have been sealed (e.g., between Hungary and Croatia [Lyman 2015b]; between Greece and Macedonia; around the entrance in France to the Chunnel). There is also talk of walls being constructed in other places throughout Europe to stem, if not totally block, the flow of unwanted migrants. Beyond the physical barriers, the president of the European Council issued a stark warning to illegal migrants: "Do not come to Europe" (Kanter and Chan 2016).

ASK YOURSELF

What social function do restrictions on immigration serve? What would a conflict theorist say about the privatization of immigration controls?

However, there are daunting problems involved in attempting to control global human migration. For one thing, the sheer numbers of such people make control extremely difficult. According to one estimate, "tens of millions of people cross borders on a daily basis" (Hollifield and Jacobson 2012, 1390). The greatest pressure is on the United States and Europe, which are the most desirable destinations for migrants, both legal and illegal. For another thing, controls are very costly, and few nations can afford to engage in much more than token efforts. Untold billions of dollars would be needed to implement Trump's plan to build a huge 2,000-mile wall across the border between the United States and Mexico. In addition, there's the far greater economic (and the greater social) cost of another aspect of Trump's campaign plan—to deport as many as 11 million people. While his initial efforts as president have been more limited and met with legal roadblocks, there is no doubt that he will seek to deport many people, especially those he has characterized as "bad hombres."

Then there is the fact that attempts to control migration inevitably lead to heightened and more sophisticated efforts to evade those controls. A lucrative market opens up for those, such as smugglers, who are in the business of transporting people across borders illegally (Alderman 2016). Finally, the increased efforts at control lead to increasingly desperate efforts to evade them. This, in turn, leads to more deaths and injuries. For example, between January and September 2014, there were 230 known deaths of people who sought to cross the U.S.–Mexican border illegally. This pales in comparison to the many thousands who died seeking to reach Europe, especially those who sought to cross the Mediterranean in leaky boats and rafts from places like Turkey and North Africa. While many have died, others have been saved in harrowing rescues from death by drowning (Associated Press 2016). Deaths and rescues involving those fleeing by boat from Turkey declined markedly in mid-2016. This was the result of a deal struck between Turkey and the EU that, among other things, involved $6.6 billion in aid to Turkey to help pay for migrants who remained there (Chan 2016).

To prosper economically, a nation-state must try to retain its own labor force, comprising highly paid skilled workers and professionals of various types as well as masses of low-paid semiskilled and unskilled workers. If a nation-state (e.g. Syria, Libya) routinely loses large numbers of either of these types of workers, but especially the former, its ability to compete in the global marketplace suffers. However, nation-states also need both skilled and less skilled workers from other locales, and it is in their interest to allow these workers entry, either legally or illegally. Yet too many such immigrants can be threatening to the societies that they seek to enter. For example, even a wealthy country like Germany is struggling to absorb the roughly 1 million migrants it has admitted in recent years. The backlash against migration threatened the position of Prime Minister Angela Merkel, who engineered the migrants' admission.

Explaining Migration. More generally, migration is influenced by a combination of push and pull factors. Among the *push* factors are the desire of migrants for better or safer lives; problems in the home country, such as unemployment and low pay, making it difficult or impossible for migrants to achieve their goals; and major disruptions, such as war, famine, political and religious persecution, and economic depression. *Pull* factors include features of the host country, such as its being a liberal nation at peace and having a favorable immigration policy, a prosperous economy, higher pay and lower unemployment, a strong social welfare program, available food, a good educational system, formal and informal networks that cater to immigrants, labor shortages, and language and culture similar to those of the home country.

In addition to these traditional factors are factors specific to the global age. There is, for example, the global diffusion of information, which makes it easier for migrants to find out about, and become comfortable in, a host country. Then there is the interaction of global–local networks, either through formal networks mediated by modern technologies, such as mobile phones and the internet (especially e-mail and Skype), or through more informal family and social networks that might well employ the same technologies. All of this makes it much easier for migrants to relocate and to be more comfortable in new settings, while it is simultaneously becoming easier for them to send money (remittances) to family and friends back home.

Types of Migrants. **Refugees** are migrants who are forced to leave their homeland, or who leave involuntarily because they fear for their safety (Haddad 2003; Kivisto 2012b; Loyal 2007). The Office of the United Nations High Commissioner for Refugees is charged with determining whether migrants will be defined as refugees.

Asylum seekers are people who flee their home country, usually in an effort to escape political oppression or religious persecution. They seek to remain in the country to which they flee. They are in a state of limbo until a decision is made on their request for asylum (Schuster 2012a). If and when that claim is accepted, the asylum seeker is considered a refugee. If the claim is rejected, it is likely that the asylum seeker will be returned to the home country.

Labor migrants are those who move from their home country to another country because they are driven by push and pull factors (Kritz 2008; Schwartzman 2013). Examples of labor migrants are the Mexican and South American women who immigrate to the United States to find employment as domestic workers. Among the push factors for such women are "tenuous and scarce job opportunities," civil wars, and economic crises in their home countries (Hondagneu-Sotelo and Avila 2005, 308). The major pull factor is the existence of jobs paying higher wages than those back home.

Undocumented immigrants are those residing in a receiving country without valid authorization (Torpey 2012; Yamamoto 2012). This category overlaps with some of the previously discussed types of migrants; both asylum seekers and labor migrants may be undocumented immigrants. There are three broad types of undocumented immigrants. The first are those who manage to

Thousands of migrants have died attempting to reach Europe, including this child and the 33 others whose boat sank on the voyage from Turkey to Greece. What impact does increased control on migration have?

gain entry without passing through a checkpoint or without undergoing the required inspection. The second type comprises those who gain entry legally but then stay beyond the period of time permitted by their visas. Third are those who immigrate on the basis of false documents. As shown in Figure 17.5, the number of undocumented immigrants to the United States increased from about 3.5 million in 1990 to a high of 12.2 million in 2007, before declining to about 11.1 million in 2014. Immigrants from Mexico account for the majority of undocumented immigrants. Of the 11.1 million undocumented immigrants in 2014, just under 6 million were of Mexican descent (Krogstad, Passel, and Cohn 2016).

It is estimated that more than 9 percent of Mexico's total population lives in the United States. As of 2014, the majority of Mexican immigrants were in the United States illegally (Hoefer, Rytina, and Baker 2010). They migrate because, although they may be paid poverty wages by U.S. standards, that may be more than they could earn in Mexico. Many undocumented Mexican immigrants work on U.S. farms picking fruits and vegetables and suffer from working long hours and living in substandard housing (Holmes 2013).

Another reason many immigrants enter the United States is for educational opportunities that are not available in their home countries. Many become undocumented students. Harmon and colleagues estimate that

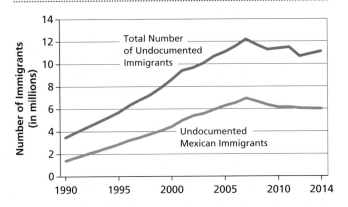

FIGURE 17.5 • Undocumented Immigration to the United States: Total Number versus Mexican Immigrants, 1990–2014

SOURCE: Population Decline of Unauthorized Immigrants Stalls, May Have Reversed, Passel, Cohn, and Gonzalez-Barrera. September 23, 2013; Jens Manual Krogstad, Jeffrey S. Passel, D'Vera Cohn. 2016. "5 Facts about Illegal Immigration in the U.S." Pew Research Center, November 3.

"approximately 1.1 million undocumented immigrants are under 18 years of age with an estimated 65,000 students graduating from public high schools annually" (2010, 69). Furthermore, because the U.S. Supreme Court holds that states cannot deny undocumented students access to pri-

People fleeing violence, like these members of the minority Yazidi sect walking toward the Syrian border, are usually considered refugees rather than simply migrants. War and fighting in the Middle East and Africa have forced millions of people from their homelands in the last few years. What obligation toward them do the rest of the world's people have?

mary and secondary education, "education plays a central role in social mobility" for these students (Harmon et al. 2010, 75).

The Case for Limited or No Migration Restrictions.

Public opinion is divided over immigration policies in general and dealing with the undocumented in particular. While those (like Donald Trump) who argue for the need to restrict migration get a lot of media attention, there are powerful arguments on the side of those who favor limited or no restrictions on migration (Moses 2006).

Economically, immigration has had positive—*not* negative—effects on the economies of the United States and other developed nations. Contrary to what many believe, it is not clear that immigrants compete with natives for jobs. It is also not clear that immigrants have less skill than natives. While the wages of native, less skilled workers may be negatively affected, wages overall are not affected by the presence of immigrants in the workforce. Immigrants are not a drain on public finances and may even pay more in taxes and into Social Security than they cost in services. A very strong economic argument in support of more open immigration in developed countries is the fact that because these countries are dominated by aging workforces (Germany is one example), they need an influx of young, vibrant, and "hungry" workers. Yet another economic argument relates to the high cost of border controls to restrict immigration. If border controls were eased, this money could be put to other uses.

Politically, freer immigration can contribute in various ways to greater democratization and less authoritarianism. In terms of sending countries, the fact that people, especially the most highly educated and skilled, can and do leave because of a lack of democracy puts pressure on their political systems to reform themselves. More generally, such migration strengthens the ability of individuals to influence political regimes and to push them in the direction of increased democratization. In a world of freer movement, nation-states also compete with one another to be better able both to keep their best people and to attract those from elsewhere. This could make nation-states the world over more democratic and enhance international exchanges.

There are two basic moral arguments in support of freer migration. First, as an end in itself, free mobility is "a universal and basic human right" (Moses 2006, 58). Second, instrumentally, free migration is a means of achieving greater economic and political justice. In terms of the latter, greater freedom of movement would lead to a reduction in global economic inequality and would mitigate global tyranny.

CHECKPOINT 17.1: POPULATION CHANGE

POPULATION FACTOR	DESCRIPTION
Fertility	Births and birth rates
Mortality	Deaths and death rates
Demographic transition	The decline in mortality and fertility rates when an agricultural society becomes industrialized. In the postindustrial stage, population growth slows and becomes stabilized.
Cross-border migration	The movement of people across national borders

URBANIZATION

We turn now to a discussion of urban areas, the traditional destinations for many migrants and the locales most affected by population changes of various types.

The world has, until very recently, been predominantly rural; even in 1800, there were only a handful of large urban areas in the world. As late as 1850, only about 2 percent of the world's population lived in cities of more than 100,000 residents. Urban areas have, of course, grown rapidly since then. In the first decade of the present century, a "watershed in human history" occurred as for "the first time the urban population of the Earth" outnumbered the rural population (Davis 2007, 1). However, there are great differences among the nations of the world in terms of their degrees of urban development: In the United Kingdom, 83 percent of the population is urban, and in the United States, 82 percent is, while only 29 percent of Rwanda's population is urban (World Bank 2015b). It is projected that by 2050, 66 percent of the world's population will live in urban areas (54 percent do today; United Nations 2014). In the more developed areas of the world, 86 percent of the population will live in cities. The greatest growth will be in developing areas, where 67 percent of the population will be urban dwellers.

The importance of **cities**, or large, permanent, and spatially concentrated human settlements, has progressively increased. Even when there were not very many of them, cities were at the heart of many societies. Max Weber ([1921] 1968) accorded great importance to the rise of the city in the West in the Middle Ages. The Western (Occidental) city had a number of distinctive characteristics, including being surrounded by walls, having political autonomy, and having a distinct urban economy (Le Gales 2007). The city became increasingly central, and it has become much more important in the context of today's "global" and "world" cities (discussed later in this chapter).

The term *urban* generally refers to city dwelling (Coward 2012), but it also has a more specific and technical meaning, although what is considered urban varies from society to society (Parrillo 2007). To be considered urban in the United States, an area must have more than 50,000 inhabitants. In comparison, to be classified as urban in Iceland, an area need have only 200 residents. The U.S. government labels a city of 50,000 residents or greater an "urbanized area," or a "metropolitan statistical area" (Farley 2007; United Nations 2016). **Urbanization** is the process by which an increasing percentage of a society's population comes to be located in relatively densely populated urban areas (Orum 2007). It is clear that urbanization occurred even in ancient times when large numbers of people moved to Rome, Cairo, and Peking; however, it has accelerated greatly in the modern era. **Urbanism** is the way of life that emerges in, and is closely associated with, urban areas. That way of life includes distinctive lifestyles, attitudes, and social relationships. In terms of the last, one example would be the greater likelihood of relating to strangers (Elliott 2012).

Skyscrapers distinguish New York City's financial district in lower Manhattan. New York is one of the world's largest megacities.

EVER-LARGER URBAN AREAS

Cities have grown considerably larger in recent decades. (We will discuss the world's largest cities—megacities—below when we turn to the issue of globalization.) However, cities have become part of even larger spatial forms. After 1920 in the United States (and later elsewhere), there emerged a new urban form—the **metropolis**—a large, powerful, and culturally influential urban area that contains a central city and its surrounding communities, known as **suburbs**, which are economically and socially linked to the center but located outside the city's political boundaries (Friedman 2007; Lacy 2016). Suburbs often create band-like structures around cities. While suburbs in the United States have tended, at least until recently, to be populated by the middle class, suburbs in other societies, such as France and South America, are more likely to be dominated by the lower class, including many recent immigrants. As we will see, suburbs in the United States are coming to resemble those other suburbs to an increasing degree.

A **megalopolis** is a cluster of highly populated cities that can stretch over great distances (Gotham 2007; Gottman 1961).

There are currently 11 megalopolises in the United States, with "BosWash," the area between Boston and Washington, D.C. (including northern Virginia), being the classic example. Another now stretches from San Diego to San Francisco and ultimately may extend as far as Seattle and even Vancouver. The cities that surround the Great Lakes constitute another megalopolis.

SUBURBANIZATION

The process of **suburbanization** has traditionally occurred, at least in the United States, when large numbers of people move out of the city and into nearby, less densely populated environs. They are often impelled by urban problems such as crime, pollution, poverty, homelessness, and poor schools. The "American dream" of the last half of the twentieth century of an affordable one-family home was more likely to be found in the suburbs than in the city.

Various criticisms have been directed at suburbanization. One is that it led to the creation of vast areas characterized by a seemingly endless sprawl of tract houses and the businesses created to serve them (Duany, Plater-Zyberk, and Speck 2010). More recently, many others have noted the problem of suburban sprawl promoting high levels of traffic congestion and environmental degradation.

In the past few decades, suburban development has seen the emergence of **gated communities**. While usually associated with the United States, gated communities have developed globally in many places, including Hungary (Kovacs and Hegedus 2014) and China (Wu, Wei, and Wang 2014). In gated communities, gates, surveillance cameras, and guards provide residents with a feeling of security from the dangers they think, sometimes wrongly, they have left behind in the city (Atkinson and Blandy 2005; Blakely and Snyder 1997). For example, there are fewer burglaries in such communities (Addington and Rennison 2015), although some gated communities offer better protection than others (Breetzke, Landman, and Cohn 2014). Nevertheless, as Setha Low notes in *Behind the Gates: Life, Security, and the Pursuit of Happiness in Fortress America* (2003), no matter the reality, such communities tend to produce a heightened sense of fear and insecurity among residents.

Recently, a variety of new developments have affected suburbanization in the United States (Lacy 2016). First, we are witnessing the suburbanization of poverty; the number of the poor in the suburbs has increased more rapidly than in urban areas. Second, increasing numbers of immigrants have made their way into the suburbs and are making these areas their home. Third, more blacks, especially those in the middle class, are living in the suburbs.

While suburbanization was first associated with the United States, it long ago became a global phenomenon. However, there is considerable variation around the world in this process and the nature of suburbs. It would be a mistake to assume that the American model fits suburbs elsewhere in the world (Clapson and Hutchison 2010; Herzog 2015).

A Postsuburban Era?

Suburbanization peaked in the United States in the late twentieth century. Today, there is much talk about the decline of American suburbs. Instead, some argue that we live in a postsuburban era (Phelps and Wu 2011). This is related to the growing realization that a way of life that includes large, energy-devouring private homes and vast thirsty lawns is ecologically unsustainable. High gasoline prices and home heating and air-conditioning costs further help make the cost of a suburban home prohibitive for many. Renting an apartment in or close to the city is back in vogue. This trend toward a post-suburban era is also occurring in other parts of the world, but it takes different forms because, in part, the suburbs themselves are different throughout the world. While post-suburbanization is not a well-defined era, and it is taking different forms, it is clear that many of the old boundaries—between cities and suburbs, and between suburbs and the forms to be discussed next, exurbia and edge cities—are eroding.

Exurbia. Cities and suburbs continue to push outward, to where land and housing costs are lower. These outlying areas, at the "crabgrass frontier," are called **exurbia** (Crump 2007). While suburbs are usually seen as the dominant development outside of cities, Taylor and Hurley (2016) argue that the major development is now in exurbia, which involves the push beyond suburbs into rural areas. The houses there are

less expensive, as is the land on which they are built. Those houses exist on larger, low-density tracts of land, often in scenic areas. The people who live in these areas are seeking a more rural lifestyle, but still require most, if not all, of the modern conveniences. They are seeking a closeness to nature that they believe has been lost in both the cities and suburbs.

Edge Cities. Associated with the rise of exurbia is the emergence of what have come to be called edge cities (Garreau 1991; Phelps and Wood 2011). As the name suggests, **edge cities** are developments at the outermost rings surrounding large cities that in many ways function more like cities than suburbs. As part of exurbia, edge cities become indistinguishable from the hinterlands, giving rise to the idea of the "edgeless city." Like suburbs and exurbs, edge cities originated in the United States, but such cities are becoming increasingly global (Bontje and Burdack 2005). They are now found, among other places, in Canada, as well as in China.

The New Urbanism. While exurbia and edge cities represent movement further away from cities and even suburbs, new urban and suburban forms continue to emerge. One is the shopping mall designed to look and function like a small town. Combined in one setting might be a few streets with shops, an indoor mall, and apartments and condominiums. These settings are supposed to look and feel more like towns than shopping malls and to overcome the separation between living and shopping that exists in most of suburbia.

These developments are part of a movement known as "new urbanism," where the goal is the creation of a simulation (a fake copy) of a traditional American small town with neighborhoods, "walkability," and various facilities within close proximity for residents (Duany and Plater-Zyberk 1990). The most famous new urban development is the Disney-created community of Celebration, which began functioning in 1994. More recent is "landscape urbanism," which focuses on the design of the landscape rather than the buildings in the landscape. Among other things, this adds a greater sense of ecological sustainability to new urbanism (Duany and Talen 2013).

THE CHANGING NATURE OF MAJOR U.S. CITIES

While there has been much talk about the decline of major American cities, and much of that decline continues, it is also the case that at least some American cities (e.g., New York,

Chicago, San Francisco, Los Angeles, San Diego, and Seattle) have been booming in recent years (Kimmelman 2016).

Nevertheless, many major American cities (e.g. Detroit, Michigan; Akron, Ohio) that developed with the industrialization of the nation underwent substantial deterioration as a result of deindustrialization, or the decline in the manufacturing sector (see Chapter 15). This decline was accompanied by *white flight*—the exodus of whites from cities—which led not only to highly segregated urban areas but also to areas that had declining tax bases and deteriorating infrastructure (roads, water and sewage systems, public transportation, especially the subway systems in the northeastern cities of New York, Boston, and Washington, D.C. [Fitzsimmons 2016]) and thus declining ability to provide basic services for residents (Williams 1999).

In some cities, the water supply is compromised in various ways. One notable example is the contamination of the water in Flint, Michigan. This is a city whose population is predominantly black, and many residents are poor. The contamination occurred in early 2014 when, in a cost-saving measure, the city switched from a satisfactorily treated water supply drawn from Lake Huron to water it was supposed to treat itself from the Flint River. The city's treatment was inadequate (due mainly to lead leaching from ancient pipes), and the water was eventually deemed undrinkable, even dangerous to the health of those who drank it. As of early 2017, the city's water is still undrinkable and remains a health hazard. The contamination of Flint's water can be seen as an example of *environmental racism,* or the "disproportionate exposure of blacks to polluted air, water and soil" (Eligon 2016, A1).

While all this has had a negative impact on those who remained in the cities, especially less well-off blacks, it has had some positive effects. For example, the lower-priced homes left empty by the flight of white households allowed more blacks to afford home ownership (Boustan and Margo 2013).

In some cases, cities have rebuilt at least some of their infrastructure in a process of urban renewal (Crowley 2007). A related process is **gentrification,** in which real estate capital is reinvested in blighted inner-city areas to refurbish housing for the upwardly mobile middle class (Lees, Slater, and Wyly 2010; Patch and Brenner 2007). A recent instance is the change that has taken place in the working-class Mission District in San Francisco (Pogash 2015). Another prominent example is the borough of Brooklyn, New York, which in the 1940s and 1950s was largely shunned by New Yorkers because of its industrial-era slums. Today, much of Brooklyn, with its famous brownstones, has been transformed into a model postindustrial landscape. Town houses and condominiums have been renovated, and many are ultraexpensive. Brooklyn has become the least affordable home ownership market in the United States (Gopal 2014).

Restaurants, bars, and other businesses catering to the new residents have sprung up all over the borough (Osman 2011). Pioneers in the process of gentrification are often young professionals, hipsters, younger gay men, and artists (Zukin 1982). Gentrification allows the wealthier residents (the "gentry") who grew up in the suburbs to return to the city. The expectation is that they will rebuild its depressed areas not only physically but also economically, socially, and culturally. In the process, working-class and poor residents are often forced out.

Beyond gentrification, the ultra-rich have been increasingly drawn to major American cities. As a result, there has been a boom in expensive high rises in the downtown areas of cities like New York, where apartments can cost $100 million or more. A similar trend is seen in global and world cities (see the Globalization box on p. 489) such as London and Singapore (Brass 2015).

ASK YOURSELF

Does gentrification serve a social purpose? If so, what is it? Does conflict theory apply to the fate of the working class and the poor in this process? If so, how?

Our old notions of the city need to change in light of the decline of many cities (in spite of gentrification and the boom in housing for the super-rich) and the development of suburbs, megalopolises, exurbs, edge cities, new urbanism, and so on. We used to think of a city as having a nucleus around which all other areas revolved. Now, it is best to think of a city—Houston, Texas, for example—as having a number of different nuclei that sprawl over a vast geographic area. The central city, the central business district, is no longer a magnet for many people. Instead, many separate and

Detroit's return to prosperity may be a long and slow process. Vacant homes like this one have become a common sight after years of declining tax revenues and population flight. What are some possible effects of blight on those who remain behind?

specialized centers are found across a wide area, and different types of people are drawn to different areas (Gotham 2012).

Toward a More Regional Perspective

This new, more expansive way of conceptualizing urban areas may not go far enough as new, looser regional formations emerge (and will continue to emerge) in the United States (and elsewhere) that are not as tied to cities or even to states or countries (Khanna 2016). As is clear in Figure 17.6, Khanna divides the United States into seven mega- or super-regions that have common economic and demographic characteristics. They are also held together by "existing lines of infrastructure, supply chains and telecommunications." The seven mega-regions are the Great Northeast, the Southeast Manufacturing Belt, the Great Lakes, the Gulf Coast, the Great Plains, the Inland West, and the Pacific Coast. Within these mega-regions, Khanna includes not only the main metropolitan hubs in the United States (e.g. Boston–New York, Washington D.C.),

but some newly emerging ones, such as Phoenix to Tucson (Arizona's Sun Corridor) and Atlanta to Charlotte, North Carolina (the Piedmont Atlantic cluster). This new conceptualization encompasses the major cities, metropolises, and megalopolises—and acknowledges their continuing importance—but it redraws the map and reorients us to broader, less city-centric ways of thinking. Just as these regions are not limited by state borders, national borders are also not a barrier. There is for example, Detroit–Windsor (Ontario), the largest U.S.–Canada cross-border area. The key issue is connectivity, not territory.

Similar areas of connectivity that are not limited by traditional notions of geography are to be found throughout the world. Examples include areas around Beijing and Shanghai in China and Rome and Turin in Italy. Those cities have, in fact—and in some cases, legally—merged into the surrounding areas. While such regional thinking makes increasing sense going forward, we continue to be in the thrall of cities and many changes associated with them.

FIGURE 17.6 • U.S. Mega Regions

SOURCE: Parah Khanna, "A New Map for America," *The New York Times*, April 15, 2016.

LOCATION	CHARACTERISTICS
City	A large, permanent, spatially concentrated human settlement
Suburbia	Communities that surround cities
Exurbia	Developments located between the suburbs and rural areas
Edge cities	Cities on or near major highways, with corporate offices that offer employment to many, as well as important commercial and consumption centers

CITIES AND GLOBALIZATION

From the beginning, cities have been central to both scholarly and popular work on globalization (Sassen 2012; Timberlake and Ma 2007). Cities are seen as being **cosmopolitan**, or open to a variety of external and global influences (Beck 2007). In contrast, small towns and rural areas are more likely to be viewed as **local**, or inward rather than outward looking. Cities therefore came to be seen as inherently global, and they grew more so as they came to encompass a range of populations, cultures, ethnicities, languages, and consumer products from around the world. Cities also exerted a powerful influence over surrounding areas.

Cities today are part of global flows of people, products, information, and more. This has been described as "mobile urbanism" (McCann and Ward 2011). Urban policies and ideas on how to improve the city flow easily throughout the world's urban areas. The many city-based organizations are linked through elaborate networks to organizations in other cities throughout the home country and the world. Furthermore, the people in those cities are themselves involved in a wide range of global networks and are linked to people throughout the world.

GLOBAL AND WORLD CITIES

At the top of the world's hierarchy of cities are the global cities. New York City, London, and Tokyo are generally included in this elite category. Saskia Sassen (1991) embeds her notion of global cities in the process of economic (capitalistic) globalization. In this context, she accords priority to the three cities mentioned previously on the basis of their place in the world economy. Specifically, they are **global cities** because they are

- The key locations for leading industries and market-places and the high-level management and specialized services they require

- The centers of the production and creation of innovative, cutting-edge financial services

- The homes of new financial, legal, and accountancy products

- The settings from which businesses and organizations exercise global command and control

Much of what global cities achieve is made possible by a wide range of new electronic technologies. In light of the history of the Great Recession, we also know that these cities, with their great financial centers, are likely to be at the epicenter of monumental collapses in the global economy and, presumably, of economic renaissances.

To Sassen and others, global cities are central nodes in a new international division of labor. Of great importance are the linkages among and between these global cities and the flows, both positive and negative, among and between them. In many ways, the global cities have more in common with one another than with the smaller cities and the hinterlands within their own countries. They are also more integrated into the global economy than those hinterlands. The direct linkages between global cities point to the fact that nation-states are less important in the global age than they were previously. They are unable to control the flows between global cities. As Sassen puts it, the global city "engages the global directly, often bypassing the national" (2012, 189). In addition, the nation-state is unable to stem such global flows as undocumented immigrants and illegal drugs.

A similar, but somewhat more expansive, concept is **world cities**, a much larger group of cities that perform most of the same functions as global cities (Friedmann 1986; Lin 2012; Ma and Timberlake 2013). World cities are important, but perhaps not yet as important as global cities. Friedmann (1986) includes a total of 30 cities under the heading of world cities. Tokyo, New York, and London are included in his list, but so are Paris, Los Angeles, and Chicago. Excluded, however, are now-booming Chinese cities, including Shanghai and Beijing. Any contemporary listing of world cities would likely include them, as well as perhaps other currently exploding Chinese cities (Timberlake et al. 2014). Also of increasing note are Indian cities, such as Mumbai, and Brazil's Rio de Janeiro.

Like global cities, world cities are centers of communities of immigrants who interact with family and friends in their homelands as well as in many other parts of the world. For example, studies of Dominican immigrants in Boston and Mexicans in New York City have shown such linkages with people back home as the sending of remittances, participation in cross-national political lobbying, and involvement in binational religious groups (Levitt 2001; Smith 2006). Another study of Chinese immigrants to the United States showed that they regularly fly to China and back. In addition, they are flexible citizens who are involved in politics in both countries (Zhou 2009).

MEGACITIES (AND BEYOND)

Megacities are defined as cities with populations greater than 10 million. Of course, the global cities discussed previously meet that criterion, but what is striking is the large and growing number of cities in the less developed world that can be defined as megacities (Krass 2012). In 2016, there were 31 urban areas qualifying as megacities (up from 10 in 1990), led by Tokyo, with almost 38.1 million people (see Figure 17.7). China alone has six megacities, and both it and India will likely have seven by 2030 (United Nations 2016). Extant cities are expected to grow dramatically in the coming years.

Such population concentrations bring with them enormous problems associated with the large numbers of very poor people living in these cities, especially those in less developed countries. More generally, Mike Davis envisions a planet of urban slums that are a far cry from what early urban visionaries had in mind:

> The cities of the future, rather than being made out of glass and steel as envisioned by earlier generations of urbanists, are instead largely constructed out of crude brick, straw, recycled plastic, cement blocks, and scrap wood. Instead of cities of light soaring toward heaven, much of the twenty-first-century urban world squats in squalor, surrounded by pollution, excrement, and decay. (2007, 19)

These megacities, even the most blighted of them, have wealthy residents as well. Thus, they are sites of some of the most profound inequalities in the world. A stunning example of this inequality is found in Mumbai, where Mukesh Ambani, the richest person in India, built a 27-story, single-family home that may be valued at as much as $1 billion. Among other things, it has nine elevators, a six-level garage, helipads, "airborne swimming pools," a spa, hanging gardens, a 50-person theater, and a grand ballroom. To function, the structure requires hundreds of servants and staff. All this is found in a city noted for its poverty, where about 60 percent of the population lives in slums (Yardley 2010).

FIGURE 17.7 • The World's Megacities, 2014

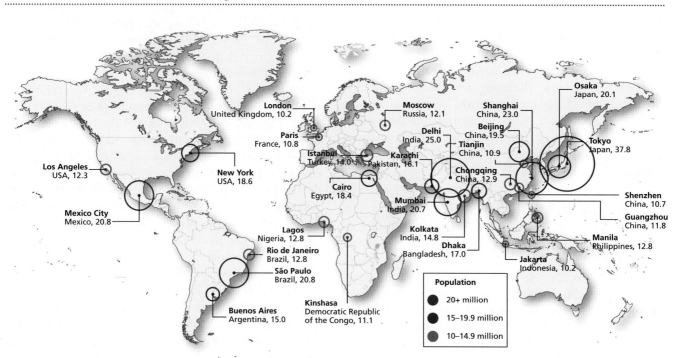

SOURCE: United Nations, Department of Economic and Social Affairs, Population Division (2014). *World Urbanization Prospects: The 2014 Revision, Highlights (ST/ESA/SER.A/352).*

GL🌐BALIZATION

The Flow of the Super-Rich to the World's Great Cities

The world has become increasingly stratified, with the super-rich ever more able to afford things that 99 percent of the world would find unimaginable. Among these things are homes in the world's great cities, especially New York and London. The wealthy from various countries (Russia, for example) are paying astounding prices for these residences. The resulting flow of global money is driving up other housing prices in those cities, making it increasingly difficult for ordinary people to live in them. For instance, a residence in the Belgravia area of London can cost between $7.5 million and $75 million. A Ukrainian recently paid $204 million for two penthouse condominiums at One Hyde Park and then spent another $90 million for renovations (Lyall 2013). In New York City, $8 billion is spent each year on residences that cost more than $5 million each; in 2015, one New York condo sold for more than $100 million (Story and Saul 2015).

Even more striking is that many who buy such ultraexpensive residences live in them for only a few days per year (say, the Christmas holidays), or not at all if they are buying them as long-term investments or rental properties. They move between several extremely costly residences throughout the world, spending very little time in any one of them. This means that the prime areas of the world's great cities are largely devoid of people for much of the year.

Investigative reporting in New York City uncovered the fact that many of the actual purchasers of elite real estate—such as the owners of the condos at the Time Warner Center, which houses at least 17 billionaires—are not only rarely (if ever) seen but also difficult to identify (Story and Saul 2015). The reason is that the purchases are often made in the name of shell companies, trusts, or limited liability companies in order

to conceal the identities of the actual owners, who want to keep a low profile. However, some buyers have also been found to have been arrested or fined for engaging in corrupt practices in their home countries. They might not be accepted by the condominium associations were their true identities known, although associations anxious to sell properties at greatly inflated prices might prefer *not* to know. Owners of condos and officials of the global cities in which they exist are often eager to have the super-rich as residents, no matter who they are and even if only for a few days per year.

Think About It

Is there anything that the world's great cities can or should do about the influx of the global super-rich and the fact that the resulting increases in real estate prices are driving out the middle class, to say nothing of the poor?

THE MAIN SITE OF GLOBAL PROBLEMS

Global and world cities are home to the rich and powerful, the main beneficiaries of globalization. However, it is also the case that cities, including the global and world cities, are especially hard-hit by a wide range of global problems. Among other things, some of the world's great cities—New York, London, Madrid, and especially Paris—have been the targets of major terrorist attacks; they are the destinations for large numbers of immigrants, many of them undocumented; they are the settings where large numbers of those affected by global health problems are likely to end up and in need of medical help; and so on. This has led Zygmunt Bauman to contend that "cities have become dumping grounds for globally begotten problems" (2003, 101).

In spite of these problems' global nature and source, dealing with them becomes a local political problem, and city officials often lack the economic resources needed to address the issues. For example, the mayor of London is limited in what he can do to deal with the forces that lead many to migrate to his city—the roots of Islamic State–inspired

terrorism, the global HIV/AIDS epidemic, and climate change (see the discussion later in the chapter) generated elsewhere. To take a very recent example, Zika arrived in Miami from South America in late 2016, but in the long run, the city may be unable to afford the costs of dealing with the mosquitos that carry the disease and those, especially babies, who are victimized by it. To quote Bauman again: "Local politics—and particularly urban politics—has become hopelessly overloaded" (2003: 102)

THE CENTER OF CULTURE AND CONSUMPTION

Much of this discussion of the city has tended to emphasize its problems, or dark side. However, it is also the case that cities have played a highly positive role in the development of societies throughout the world. Compared with rural areas, cities tend to have better-educated residents, promote more tolerance, are more likely to generate new ideas, have the best hospitals, offer more jobs, and so on. Much of what we think of as culture, especially "high culture," has its origins, and has become centered, in the city. Thus, a large number of the world's great universities, museums, symphony orchestras, opera companies, theaters, and restaurants are found in the world's great cities. It is also the case that much of pop culture—such as hip-hop and rap—emanates from the city.

The city is also the source of many developments in the world of consumption. For example, shopping arcades (Benjamin 1999), world's fairs, and department stores had their origins in nineteenth-century Paris and other European cities (Williams [1982] 1991). In the twentieth century, U.S. cities became the world leaders in such consumption sites, most notably New York City, with its world-famous department stores (Macy's and Gimbels) as well as the 1939 and 1964 World's Fairs. When those who lived outside the city could afford to travel and wanted to consume, they often made regular treks to the city to shop, go to the theater, and so on. Cities like Paris and New York also played other key roles in consumption, such as being national and global centers of fashion (Lipovetsky [1987] 2002; Simmel [1904] 1971). Furthermore, cities, especially New York and its famed Madison Avenue, became centers for the advertising industry, which functions to drive consumption (Schudson 1987). A number of cities have become more specialized centers of consumption, the most notable examples being gambling centers such as Las Vegas and Macau. Dubai has undergone a massive building boom in an effort to become the commercial and consumption center for a good part of the world, stretching from Cairo to Tokyo.

Fantasy City. A **fantasy city** is one in which great emphasis is placed on creating a spectacle, especially in the areas of consumption, leisure, tourism, and real estate, dominated by impressive buildings and other developments. Hannigan (1998, 2007) sees only two cities as full-scale fantasy cities: Las Vegas, Nevada, and Orlando, Florida (home of Disney World and many other tourist attractions). However, many others, especially Dubai, have moved in that direction.

Fantasy cities are characterized by infrastructure dominated by such "cathedrals of consumption" (Ritzer 2010a) as "themed restaurants, nightclubs, shopping malls, multiplex cinemas, virtual reality arcades, casino-hotels . . . sports stadiums and arenas, and other urban entertainment centers" (Hannigan 2007, 1641). The whole idea is to draw people, especially tourists, to fantasy cities, and once they are there to lure them into the various cathedrals of consumption, where they will spend large sums of money. Like many developments in the realm of consumption, the fantasy city was largely a U.S. creation, but it has now become increasingly global, and it is possible to identify fantasy cities in Australia, Singapore, Malaysia, and China, as well as the United Arab Emirates.

Although people are drawn to fantasy cities to consume, what they find especially attractive is the spectacle of the city. For example, many American cities have built huge and spectacular sports arenas and concert halls (the $1 billion–plus

Yankee Stadium in New York and the $130 million Walt Disney Concert Hall in Los Angeles are prime examples) as places in which to spend large sums of money (Hoffman, Fainstein, and Judd 2003). In Las Vegas, the spectacle is the famous Strip, Las Vegas Boulevard, with its themed hotel-casinos, such as Paris Las Vegas (with its replicas of both the Eiffel Tower and the Arc de Triomphe), the Venetian (with its canals and gondolas), the Bellagio (including its famous fountains), and Treasure Island (with its regular outdoor sea battles). In Orlando, the spectacle is Disney World and its many parks and attractions, as well as other theme parks (Universal Studios, Busch Gardens, SeaWorld). Other cities have sought to draw tourists and consumers in similar ways.

Decline. In recent years, the central role of cities, especially in consumption, has been reduced. First, suburban shopping malls supplanted urban shopping centers and department stores as the prime destination for many shoppers. More recently, the shopping malls themselves have been being supplanted by online shopping (e.g., Amazon.com, eBay). Globally, such major players in the world of consumption as IKEA (from Sweden, with Dutch ownership) and Carrefour (French) are most likely to be located outside cities. Entertainment giant Disney has placed its theme parks outside some of the world's great cities—Los Angeles, Orlando, Paris, Tokyo, Hong Kong, and Shanghai (which launched most recently, in 2016).

In many ways, roles have been reversed, and instead of cities being the source of innovations in consumption, external developments are increasingly finding their way into the cities. They are making the distinctions among cities, suburbs, edge cities, and other geographic areas less clear and meaningful. For example, fast-food restaurants (especially McDonald's) were originally suburban and small-town phenomena, but they have increasingly become urban phenomena as well. In the process, they have tended to displace distinctive urban cafés and restaurants, driving many of these establishments out of business and into oblivion. Similarly, discount retail chains (e.g., Target and Kohl's) have increasingly made their way into American cities. Even New York City, long known for its highly distinctive consumption sites, has come to look more and more like the rest of the United States (and much of the world) with its large numbers of McDonald's and KFC restaurants, and now even Kohl's stores.

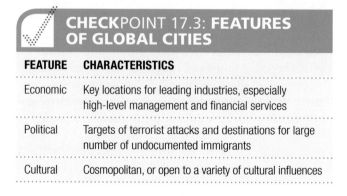

CHECKPOINT 17.3: FEATURES OF GLOBAL CITIES

FEATURE	CHARACTERISTICS
Economic	Key locations for leading industries, especially high-level management and financial services
Political	Targets of terrorist attacks and destinations for large number of undocumented immigrants
Cultural	Cosmopolitan, or open to a variety of cultural influences

Children of Katrina (University of Texas Press, 2015)

Alice Fothergill (Associate Professor of Sociology at the University of Vermont; PhD, University of Colorado–Boulder, 2001) and **Lori Peek** (Associate Professor of Sociology and Co-director of the Center for Disaster and Risk Analysis at Colorado State University; PhD, University of Colorado–Boulder, 2005)

Children of Katrina

ALICE FOTHERGILL AND LORI PEEK

In August 2005, Hurricane Katrina made landfall in the United States, causing storm damage that devastated areas in the Gulf Coast, especially the city of New Orleans. Eighteen hundred people died as a direct result of the disaster, and more than 1 million became environmental refugees, dislocated from their homes, families, and friends—some temporarily, others permanently. Children's lives were particularly disrupted when their homes, schools, and churches were destroyed. Alice Fothergill and Lori Peek spent 7 years studying 650 children and youth who were between the ages of 3 and 18 at the time Katrina hit. They used multiple methods to study these children, including observations, focus groups, and interviews. They discovered that creative techniques, like drawing and molding playdough, encouraged the children to talk about their experiences. Because many of the children and their families were forced to leave their homes in New Orleans and relocate, Fothergill and Peek traveled to other cities in Louisiana, Dallas, Texas, and Denver, Colorado, to conduct their research. Their observational sites included disaster relief centers, FEMA trailers, playgrounds, and restaurants. To develop trust with the children and their families, Fothergill and Peek offered to take them out for lunch or dinner, sent gifts, and took the effort to maintain longstanding contact by phone, e-mail, or even letters.

Fothergill and Peek were interested in learning about the long-term effects of a disaster like Katrina for children. They selected seven children to investigate in depth because these children represented three distinctive post-disaster trajectories: declining, finding equilibrium, and fluctuating. The lives of children experiencing a declining post-disaster trajectory were worse after Katrina, while the lives of children on the equilibrium trajectory remained the same. Some children fluctuated between the stability of equilibrium and the disruption of decline. These trajectories were influenced by several key spheres in each child's life, including family, housing, peers, physical and mental health, and extracurricular activities. Children with limited financial and social resources before Katrina encountered the most difficulties and were most likely to face continuous disruptions in the key spheres of their lives on the declining post-disaster trajectory. But even children who had these types of resources pre-Katrina could end up on the declining trajectory, because of multiple displacements that isolated them from their friends and social networks back home. Katrina caused an initial disruption for some children, but those whose families had financial and social resources regained equilibrium and stability in their lives. Children in families that had extended social networks outside of New Orleans, for example, could stay in homes with family members or friends instead of temporary shelters. Other children in Fothergill and Peek's study were located on the fluctuating trajectory, suffering disruptions in some but not all key spheres.

Fothergill and Peek warn that we should not assume that all children are resilient and "bounce back" after disasters; many have continuing needs years after the initial response period. Equally important, they stress that we should not view children as passive victims, but as active agents who are capable of preparing a parent or sibling for an imminent disaster and helping others during the response and recovery process.

Supplementary Resources

- Read more about the children of Katrina in this article from *The Atlantic:* www.theatlantic.com/education/archive/2015/04/the-lost-children-of-katrina/389345.
- This short clip from the *CBS Evening News* portrays children affected by Katrina 10 years after the disaster: https://www.youtube.com/watch?v=RqCP0-zl1fg

THE ENVIRONMENT

In recent years, there has been an explosive growth of a wide range of environmental problems (e.g., flooding, increasingly powerful storms). This has led to greatly increasing attention to them. Because of concern over, and even fear of, those problems, many sociologists have been drawn to, and even led, the study of the environment, especially of environmental problems (Dunlap and Jorgenson 2012; Hannigan 2014; Pellow and Brehm 2013). There is now even a journal entitled *Environmental Sociology*, which had its inaugural issue in 2015. The field was inspired, as was public interest as a whole, by such highly influential books as Rachel Carson's *Silent Spring* (1962), which focused on poisons such as insecticides and weed killers and the threats they posed to the food supply. This interest has expanded exponentially, and for some it has grown to alarm, as the public has been exposed to, and made aware of, the threats posed by environmental problems.

Some environmental sociologists have been very concerned with how various environmental matters come to be defined as problems. However, there has been a dramatic shift in the direction of conceiving of these problems as "real" (not just in people's minds as social definitions), as in need of serious empirical study, and in many cases as needing action now or in the near future. Environmental problems, as well as sociological attention to them, are likely to increase dramatically in the coming years, especially as those problems become increasingly global in scope (Lidskog, Mol, and Oosterveeer 2015).

THEORIES OF THE ENVIRONMENT AND ITS PROBLEMS

Sociological approaches to the environment differ depending on the theoretical perspective employed (Preisendorfer and Diekmann 2007). Structural/functional theories tend to focus on large-scale structures and systems and their impact on environmental problems, as well as on the ability to deal with them. For example, one line of thinking is that because large-scale structures are differentiated functionally (politically, economically, legally), they have difficulty coming together to deal with environmental problems. The conflict/critical perspective focuses on free-market capitalism and the need for corporations to grow and to show ever-increasing profits (Klein 2014). In other words, capitalism creates a treadmill of production whereby everyone in the system depends on continuous productive growth (Gould, Pellow, and Schnaiberg 2008). Such capitalistic needs lead to the exploitation of nonrenewable natural resources and other negative effects on the environment. For example, one recent study showed that tourism, driven by capitalism's treadmill of production, has an adverse effect on the environment in the Caribbean (Griffin, Pavela, and Arroyo

This energy plant in Cattenom, France, is nuclear powered. Sociologists study the way we define and grapple with the environmental consequences of our actions.

2015). Among the inter/actionists, symbolic interactionists focus on the ways in which we come to define various environmental issues as problems. We also define ourselves in relationship to environmental issues. This can include our views of ourselves if we engage in sustainable ("green") consumption, as well as how others view such consumption (Noppers et al. 2014). Rational choice theorists focus on the fact that there have been great rewards, such as high profits and pay, for those who adversely affect the environment. Conversely, there have been weak, or nonexistent, rewards and even high costs (lower profits, lower wages, higher prices for environmentally friendly products) for those who are interested in being more environmentally responsible by, for example, consuming less. Clearly, from this perspective, the reward and cost structures need to be changed if we hope to induce people to change their behavior and to take actions that help, rather than hurt, the environment. We need to see, for example, that we can live better by consuming less and, at the same time, have the rewards associated with being more responsible as far as the environment is concerned (Jackson 2014).

URBAN AREAS AND THE ENVIRONMENT

The relationship between the city and the environment is a link to the preceding section and is also an issue of great importance in itself (Berrone, Enric Ricart Costa, and Duch T-Figueras 2016; York and Rosa 2007).

Environmental problems can lead to urbanization. The extraordinary demands placed on the rural environment by large urban populations can lead to a decline in the ability of rural areas to support those who live there. For example, the need for more natural resources in the city can lead to the depletion of those resources in rural areas. An insatiable need for timber for building purposes can lead to deforestation and the elimination of jobs in the rural lumber industry.

Similarly, overuse and abuse of farmland can lead to declining productivity and less farm-related work in rural areas. As a result, many rural residents are forced to move to the city in search of work, thereby increasing urbanization. There are also many ways in which cities, which account for only 2 percent of the Earth's surface, contribute disproportionately to environmental degradation (Berrone et al. 2016; Seto, Güneralp, and Hutyra 2012). Environmental problems associated with cities include the following:

- Cities account for 60 to 80 percent of the Earth's energy consumption.

- Cities account for about 70 percent of pollution from carbon dioxide, or greenhouse gases, through emissions from the large numbers of motor vehicles and centralized power plants that characterize modern cities. (However, suburban and rural areas may actually have larger carbon footprints than cities because, for example, city residents have shorter commuting distances and may even forgo driving cars altogether. The latter trend is likely to increase with the expansion in cities of car services such as Lyft and Uber.)

- Green spaces and natural habitats are destroyed to make way for cities, contributing to the loss of biodiversity associated with increasing urbanization.

- Heat retention in the "treeless concrete jungles of cities" can greatly worsen the negative health effects of heat waves (York and Rosa 2007, 1423).

- Cities create byproducts in the form of organic matter rich in nutrients, which can be used as fertilizer to benefit the environment in rural areas but becomes waste requiring disposal in urban settings (via sewage treatment plants, which use a lot of energy).

In addition, environmental toxins spread within cities, and the presence of environmental pollutants has led to rising rates of health problems, such as respiratory illnesses (asthma) among children and adults, especially for the urban poor.

Although cities have been the cause of these and many other environmental problems, this linkage is not inevitable. New forms of urban development could be less ecologically destructive. Majora Carter, founder of the Majora Carter Group (MCG), has noted that "it was a pollution-based economy that brought us to the environmental breaking point we face today." She advises that we "restructure that system so that a new green economy will benefit us in many more ways than simply raising our GDP (gross domestic product)" (Majora Carter Group 2009). Carter's consulting group works to create simple green projects that not only physically improve urban neighborhoods but also foster local community economies, provide "green" and sustainable jobs, and reduce health and social problems (www.majoracartergroup.com). And, by creating green spaces, community residents develop a stronger sense of their ability to accomplish important tasks.

GLOBALIZATION AND THE ENVIRONMENT

The environment performs three general functions for humans and other species (Dunlap and Catton 2002; Dunlap and Jorgenson 2012). First, the environment is a kind of "supply depot" that provides us with the natural resources needed for life to exist. Among the renewable and nonrenewable resources provided are air, water, food, shelter, and the materials needed for industries to operate. However, overuse of such renewable resources as water and such nonrenewable resources as fossil fuels can deplete, if not empty, the supply depot.

Second, in consuming those resources, humans produce wastes of various kinds. The environment serves as a "sink" to absorb or dispose of the waste. However, it is possible to produce so much waste that the environment cannot absorb it all. For example, too much sewage can lead to water pollution. There are ongoing efforts to find various uses for the waste we produce. For example, human excrement is being converted into fuel for everything from buses to rockets (Buck 2014; Sullivan 2014).

Third, the environment provides us with living space, or a "habitat—where we live, work, play, and travel" (Dunlap and Jorgenson 2012, 530). However, having too many people in a living space creates numerous problems associated with overcrowding and overpopulation.

In terms of all three functions, it could be argued that humans are beginning to exceed the "carrying capacity" of Earth.

There is great global inequality in these three functions. Basically, the developed nations adversely affect the ability of the less developed nations to perform these functions. For example, they use less developed nations as supply depots for natural resources for which they have historically underpaid. In the process, they often adversely affect the ability of the less developed nations to continue to produce these resources. Developed nations also often ship e-waste—that is, discarded electronic equipment—to developing countries, polluting them and their people with the minerals and chemicals in this dangerous debris. This, in turn, despoils the living spaces and the ecosystems of those developing countries.

While environmental problems can and do affect specific countries, the vast majority of these problems are global in nature and scope. As a result, one of the most enduring and important issues in the study of the environment involves its relationship to globalization (Newell and Roberts 2017; Stevis 2005). The environment is inherently global. That is, we all share the atmosphere, are warmed by the sun, and are connected by the oceans (Yearley 2007). Further, much that relates to the environment has an impact on and flows around the world, or at least large portions of it (such as through weather patterns).

In spite of this, the earliest work on globalization tended to ignore the natural environment, or at least to underplay its significance (Munton and Wilkening 2007). In the 1980s and 1990s, however, the environmental movement made great progress (Rootes 1999): A number of notable problems, especially the depletion of the ozone layer (Liftin 2007), global climate change, and the rise in sea levels, among others, brought the environment to the fore as a global issue.

Although many environmental problems *are* global issues, this view has been challenged in various ways:

- Not everyone or every part of the world is equally to blame for the most pressing global environmental problems. Those from the most developed countries are disproportionately responsible for them, but those in developing countries also play a major role (Olivier, Janssens-Maenhout, and Peters 2012).

- Such problems do not, and will not, affect everyone and all areas of the world in the same way. For example, the rise of the level of the seas as a result of climate change will mostly affect those who live in coastal areas or on islands. Such areas will also be most affected by the expected increase in the number and severity of hurricanes. Tornadoes are also expected to increase, although they are likely to affect some geographic areas, such as the American Midwest, more than others. In addition, because of their greater wealth, those in the Global North will be better able than those in the Global South to find ways of avoiding or dealing with all but the most catastrophic of the problems caused by climate change.

- There are global differences in the importance accorded to, and the dangers associated with, these problems. For example, many in the developed North are highly concerned about climate change, while many in the Global South feel that they are faced with more pressing problems, such as health problems related to disease and malnutrition as well as the decline of available drinking water.

- The main sources of environmental problems change. For example, the center of manufacturing, with its associated pollutants, has been moving from the United States to China.

ASK YOURSELF

Do you think environmental problems are local, global, or both? Why? Do you think it matters who is responsible for creating them, if we are to solve them? Why or why not?

While these views have credence, they should not distract us from the global implications of, and threats posed by, a wide range of environmental problems.

THE LEADING ENVIRONMENTAL PROBLEMS

There are many important environmental problems, and we have touched on several in the preceding sections. In this section, we will deal with a few in more depth: the destruction of natural habitats, adverse effects of human activity on marine life, the decline in freshwater, and global warming.

Destruction of Natural Habitats

Natural habitats such as "forests, wetlands, coral reefs, and the ocean bottom" are being destroyed across the globe, often as the result of population growth and the conversion of some of those natural habitats into human habitats (Diamond 2006, 487; Mackay 2014). The forests that have not yet been destroyed are being divided into smaller and more isolated, less self-sufficient fragments surrounded by human environments. Both their smaller size and their human surroundings threaten their continued existence (Haddad et al. 2015). The most notable deforestation in the world has been taking place in the Amazon rain forest

PATRICK HERTZOG/AFP/Getty Images

Brazil's rain forest continues to be depleted. However, the country's minister for the environment reports that this depletion, a process that threatens untold numbers of plant and animal species, has begun to slow down. How can sociologists contribute to the protection and preservation of Earth's natural habitats?

(mostly in Brazil), where more than half of the tree species are under threat (St. Fleur 2015; "Welcome to Our Shrinking Jungle" 2008), but other parts of the world are also destroying or losing their forests. In fact, more deforestation may now be occurring in Indonesia than in the Amazon basin (Margono et al. 2014). The Amazon forest is being decimated to allow the area to be "developed"— to create farms and areas for livestock to graze—and for the creation of more human settlements. Brazil's forests are so huge, and they play such a large role in the global ecology, that their destruction will have negative effects on the world as a whole. For example, the burning of all those felled trees releases huge amounts of carbon dioxide, which drifts into the atmosphere and flows around the globe, contributing to climate change The loss of the forest leads to other problems for humans, including a diminished supply of timber and other raw materials. This is of great concern also because, especially in the areas undergoing deforestation, forests protect against soil erosion, are essential to the water cycle and prevention of drought, and they provide habitats for many plants and animals. The loss of other natural habitats, such as wetlands, coral reefs, and the ocean bottom, will also have a variety of negative consequences for life on Earth. For example, the decline of coral reefs due to runoff from agriculture adversely affects the sea life that exists in and around these reefs.

Adverse Effects on Marine Life

A large portion of the protein consumed by humans comes from fish. Aquaculture, which involves growing seafood under controlled conditions such as fish farms, is not an adequate replacement for the loss of natural fishing areas, because it causes a whole series of ecological and other problems (de Kerckhove, Minns, and Chu 2015; Goldburg 2008).

Marine life in the world's oceans has been greatly diminished by overfishing. According to the United Nations Food and Agricultural Organization, 69 percent of the world's most important fisheries can be considered either "fully exploited" or "overexploited." An early twenty-first-century study concluded that industrial fishing had led to a 90 percent decline in "big fish" such as swordfish, tuna, and marlin populations (Khatchadourian 2007).

A major culprit in the decimation of marine life is industrial fishing. As the amount of sea life declines, the fishing industry compensates by using much more industrialized and intensive techniques. Among these industrial techniques is the use of huge nets that catch large numbers of fish, including many that are not wanted and are discarded. Modern industrial fishing is also characterized by the use of factory ships that process the fish on board rather than waiting until the ships return to port. These technologies contribute to overfishing and in the process destroy complex ecosystems.

The Decline in Freshwater

Water is becoming an increasingly critical global issue (Conca 2006; Hoekstra 2012). Many observers have expressed concern about the "water crisis" in some parts of the world, including California and Nevada in the United States (Nagourney 2015; Subramaniam, Whitlock, and Williford 2012). However, it is the less developed countries in the world that are most likely to be negatively affected by a water crisis as water-dependent manufacturing industries locate themselves within their borders. In addition, they are the least likely to have environmental regulations to prevent problems or to be able to do very much about problems once they begin. Among the concerns about water are the following:

ASK YOURSELF

What can individuals do to help alleviate potential problems in the world's freshwater supply? Is it realistic to think that individuals can make a difference in this environmental challenge? Why or why not?

- *Water inequality.* The United States has a water footprint double that of the world average and four times that of China. While many in the world have little access to water, many Americans "water their gardens, fill their swimming pools, and . . . consume considerably more meat than the world average, which significantly enlarges their water footprint" (Hoekstra 2012, 2207).

- *Water pollution.* Humans contribute to the pollution of water through manufacturing processes, mining, agriculture, and inadequate treatment and management of waste (especially fecal matter). One result of this pollution is an increase in waterborne diseases, especially those that affect children (Jorgenson and Givens 2012).

- *Marine pollution.* This involves "a disruption to the natural ecology of water systems, particularly oceans, as a direct or indirect result of human activity" (Burns 2012, 1324). Among the most important causes of marine pollution is the dumping into the oceans of the herbicides, pesticides, and fertilizers used in modern industrial agriculture.

- *Flooding.* Experts contend that because warmer air holds more moisture, heavy precipitation is expected to increase in some regions as a result of climate change.

- *Increasing scarcity of water.* There is a possibility that the flow of water could slow or stop completely, at least in some locales (Veldkamp et al. 2014). Some nations are forced to choose between essential uses of water, such as drinking and irrigating crops (Martin 2008). There are tensions within nations and between nations—and even the possibility of war—over increasingly scarce water supplies (Dunn 2013).

Desertification is the decline in the water supply as a result of the degradation and deterioration of soil and vegetation (Glantz 1977; Reed and Stringer 2016). Water, once considered a public good, is increasingly becoming a valuable and privatized commodity as many places run low on drinkable water. Another preventable decline in water supply is caused by the wasting of those supplies; for example, nearly two-thirds of all water used for irrigation, in addition to as much as half of city water supplies, is wasted due to leaky pipes.

Although we usually think of water as abundant and readily accessible, the fact is that more than 1 billion people do not have reliable sources of safe drinking water, and more than 2.5 billion do not have adequate sanitation systems (Conca 2007; World Health Organization 2015c). The poorest areas of the globe and the poorest people within those areas experience a disproportionate share of water-related problems. The situation is apt to grow worse in coming years; it is possible that half the world's population will be faced with water-related problems by the 2030s.

A less visible water problem involves international trade, especially in agricultural and industrial products. For example, when Japan buys crops (which are water-intensive to produce) from the United States, pressure is put on American water supplies. People throughout the world are using water from elsewhere on the globe. This is called "virtual water" because almost all the water has been used in production of some commodity (Vos and Hinojosa 2016). If people do not realize that they are using or abusing water, how can they do anything about it?

Global Warming

Global warming is a concept often used interchangeably with climate change, but here we will treat it as the most significant aspect of climate change. The year 2016 was the hottest on record globally, and it was the third consecutive year of record-breaking heat (Patel 2017). All ten of the hottest days since 1880 have occurred since 1998 (Gillis 2015). As the planet heats up even more, some parts of the world will become wetter, but other parts will grow drier. As a general rule, already wet areas will grow wetter and already dry areas drier; both floods and droughts will intensify. It is in the latter that we are likely to see increasingly desperate and expensive efforts to find water by, for example, drilling ever deeper for underground water supplies (Struck 2007). Among the areas likely to grow drier are Southern Europe, the Middle East, South Australia, Patagonia, and the southwestern United States. In May 2008, Barcelona became the first major city in the world to begin importing large amounts of water by ship to help deal with a long-term drought and a precipitous drop in water resources. There are predictions of Dust Bowl–like conditions in the American Southwest and the resulting possibility of mass migrations.

FIGURE 17.8 • Global Temperature and Carbon Dioxide Concentration, 1880–2012

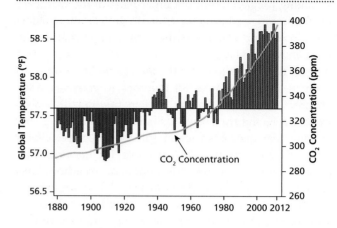

SOURCE: Global Climate Change Indicators, National Oceanic and Atmospheric Administration.

In Mexico, similar conditions may lead to mass migrations to Mexican cities and to the United States. Such increases threaten to create even greater problems and animosities than those that already exist in the United States as a result of both legal and, especially, undocumented immigration from Mexico. In more general terms, we are increasingly likely to see the emergence of an entirely new group of people in the world—climate refugees (Gray and Mueller 2012). The United States is planning to resettle its first climate refugees from a waterlogged area, Isle de Jean Charles, in Louisiana; they won't be the last. Estimates are that worldwide between 50 and 200 million people will be displaced by rising water (Davenport and Robertson 2016).

Another problem traceable to global warming is the melting of mountaintop glaciers that are important sources of drinking water for many people in the world (Filkins 2016). As those glaciers melt and fail to re-form fully, they will produce less and less water for those who need the water to survive. The affected populations, too, are likely to become climate refugees, and they are apt to come into conflict with residents of the still water-rich areas to which they are likely to move.

Humans have produced greenhouse gases that have damaged the atmosphere and, in the view of most experts, are leading to a dramatic rise in the temperature of Earth. During the twentieth century, Earth's temperature rose by about 0.74 degrees centigrade; projections for the twenty-first century are for a rise of between 2 and 8 degrees centigrade. Because of the accumulation of greenhouse gases, heat generated by the sun that would ordinarily be reflected back into the atmosphere is trapped and "radiated back to the Earth at a greater rate than before" (Beer 2012). Great concern these days is focused on the burning of fossil fuels (coal, gas, oil), the resulting emission of carbon dioxide, and the role that this plays in the accumulation of greenhouse gases and global warming. Rates of carbon dioxide emissions, mainly from industrialized countries, increased by 80 percent between 1970 and 2004 and have grown by 3 percent per year since 2000. Figure 17.8 shows the relationship between global temperature and carbon dioxide concentration.

There is little or no doubt, at least among scientists, that global warming and more generally climate change are real phenomena with human-made causes (Cook et al. 2013). Furthermore, the predominant view is that global warming is already well advanced and is progressing rapidly. Many scientists have further added that some negative effects of global warming, such as the thawing of *permafrost*, soil that has been at or below the freezing point of water for more than two years, will be irreversible once they start. Global warming is expected to affect humans adversely in a number of different ways (D. Brown 2007). It will bring with it more, and more intense, heat waves, and excessive heat can be deadly. A heat wave in Europe in 2003, the worst in almost 500 years, caused about 30,000 deaths from heat-related illnesses. A recent study concludes that heat waves such as the one in 2003 will be "commonplace" in Europe by 2040 (Jolly 2014). The aging of the population throughout much of the developed world makes more people vulnerable to being made ill and dying due to excessive heat. Urbanization also increases the likelihood of death, because cities can become heat islands. Other factors that make death from excessive heat more likely are being very young, ill, or poor, or lacking the ability to move away from superheated areas. There are things that can be done to mitigate the dangers of heat stress, such as greater use of air-conditioning, but many people in the world have no access to air-conditioning or cannot afford it. Further, the use of air-conditioning causes other problems, such as a huge demand on energy resources.

Sea levels are projected to rise dramatically, especially as the glaciers melt. A conservative estimate is that sea levels will rise about 1 meter during the twenty-first century. Approximately 100 million people in the world, mostly in Asia and in island nations, live within a meter of sea level, and their homes would be washed away by such a rise. However, this estimate does not take into account the melting of the Greenland and West Antarctic ice sheets, which could add 10 or more meters to the rising seas. In such a case, much larger areas of both the less developed and developed worlds would be inundated.

Global warming and climate change more generally will lead to a wide range of problems, some of which are already upon us:

- A 2008 typhoon caused the death of almost 140,000 people in Myanmar.

- In the United States, the residents of coastal areas (e.g. the east coast of Florida, the Gulf Coast, southern Louisiana) are in particular danger due to storm surges. In fact, storm-related flooding has already occurred in recent years all along the East Coast in, for example, Norfolk, Virginia; Tybee Island, Georgia; and Fort Lauderdale, Florida, especially in 2016 (Gillis 2016).

- Carlisle, a small city in northwest England, was hit by a crippling flood in 2005. Flooding of that magnitude was supposed to happen every 200 years, but the city has since been flooded, in 2009, and then again in 2015 (Schlossberg 2016).

- The Pacific islands and coral atolls of the nation of Kiribati are in the process of being swamped (Ives 2016).

- Coral reefs around the world are being threatened by mass bleaching caused by heat stress (Innis 2016).

- Lake Poopo, the second largest lake in Bolivia, went dry in December 2015, killing all its fish. This destroyed the way of life of those who lived around lake. It also created a group of climate refugees (Haner 2016).

Extreme variations in weather may also lead to more droughts and shortages of water. Food production may not increase as rapidly as expected, with the result that the number of the world's hungry will increase. Figure 17.9 shows all the natural catastrophes around the world in 2015, including extreme weather events.

Rising temperatures will speed up chemical reactions and worsen pollution from ozone and soot. Deaths from ozone pollution (mostly among those with lung or heart problems) could increase by 5 percent by 2050. Pollen production could increase, adversely affecting those with allergies, asthma, and other respiratory conditions.

In addition, waterborne diseases (e.g., cholera) will increase with higher temperatures and more torrential rains. Food-borne infections (e.g., salmonella) will also increase with hotter weather.

The incidence of diseases caused by animals and insects may increase. For example, it is expected that diseases such as malaria, dengue, and Zika will become more widespread. Exposure to malaria is expected to increase by 25 percent in Africa by 2100. However, actions can be taken to mitigate the spread of the disease, such as controlling the mosquito population with pesticides, greater use of bed nets (especially by pregnant women and children), and better medical care. Other diseases of this type that are likely to become more prevalent are yellow fever, also carried by mosquitoes, and Lyme disease, carried by ticks (D. Brown 2007). Ebola is now well established in the human populations in West Africa and will be difficult, if not impossible, to eradicate completely. In any case, increasing numbers of people will come into contact with the wild animals that carry the disease.

FIGURE 17.9 • Natural Catastrophes Worldwide, 2015

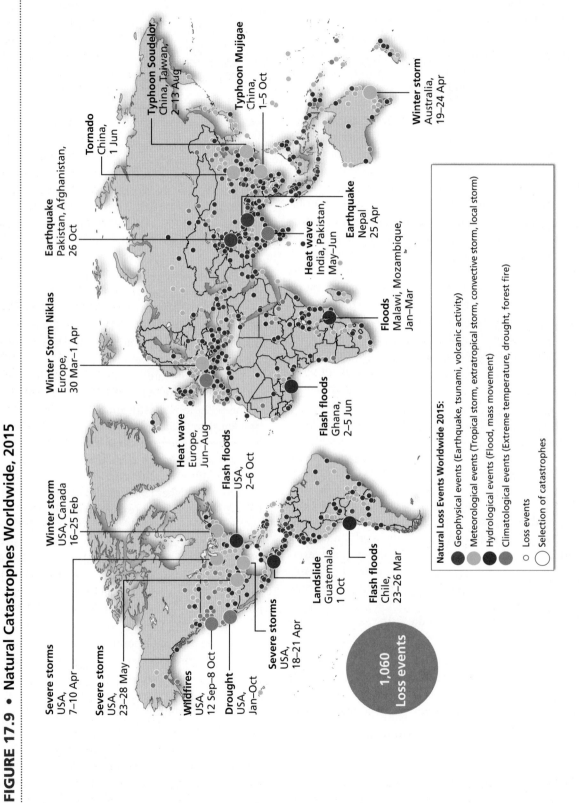

Severe storms
USA,
7–10 Apr

Severe storms
USA,
23–28 May

Wildfires
USA,
12 Sep–8 Oct

Drought
USA,
Jan–Oct

Severe storms
USA,
18–21 Apr

Landslide
Guatemala,
1 Oct

Flash floods
Chile,
23–26 Mar

Winter storm
USA, Canada
16–25 Feb

Flash floods
USA,
2–6 Oct

Heat wave
Europe,
Jun–Aug

Winter Storm Niklas
Europe,
30 Mar–1 Apr

Tornado
China,
1 Jun

Earthquake
Pakistan, Afghanistan,
26 Oct

Typhoon Soudelor,
China, Taiwan,
2–13 Aug

Typhoon Mujigae
China,
1–5 Oct

Winter storm
Australia,
19–24 Apr

Earthquake
Nepal
25 Apr

Heat wave
India, Pakistan,
May–Jun

Floods
Malawi, Mozambique,
Jan–Mar

Flash floods
Ghana,
2–5 Jun

**1,060
Loss events**

Natural Loss Events Worldwide 2015:

● Geophysical events (Earthquake, tsunami, volcanic activity)
● Meteorological events (Tropical storm, extratropical storm, convective storm, local storm)
● Hydrological events (Flood, mass movement)
● Climatological events (Extreme temperature, drought, forest fire)

○ Loss events
○ Selection of catastrophes

SOURCE: Natural Catastrophes, 2015 World Map. © 2016 Münchener Rückversicherungs-Gesellschaft, Geo Risks Research, NatCatSERVICE.

Wind turbines like these in Honduras hold the promise of supplying cleaner and more affordable energy, but this technology is not without problems. What intergenerational concerns arise in the process of attempting to reduce human reliance on fossil fuels?

GLOBAL RESPONSES

Many global environmental problems, including climate change, are traceable to capitalist economic development (Antonio and Brulle 2012). That is, as economies grow and generate greater wealth, they are likely to do increasing damage to the environment. As concerned as nation-states are becoming about damage to the environment, they are not about to either give up the fruits of economic development or cease seeking to become more developed.

As a result, a variety of efforts have arisen to at least reduce the magnitude of environmental problems. We have seen the emergence of a number of environmental movements and organizations, such as Greenpeace, oriented toward this goal (Caniglia 2012). In addition to these movements and organizations, but more general in nature, is an increase in environmental activism (Fisher 2012). Environmental activists are generally interested either in protecting some aspect of the environment, such as a coral reef or a virgin forest, or in protesting environmental hazards, such as toxic waste or the use of a particular site as a garbage dump. In terms of globalization, activists might oppose the global exportation of environmental problems or support international efforts and treaties to mitigate these problems. While some environmental movements and activists may want to slow or stop economic development, many favor sustainable development.

Sustainable Development

Sustainable development involves economic and environmental changes that meet the needs of the present, especially of the world's poor, without jeopardizing the ability to meet the needs of the future (Blewitt 2014). While the focus of sustainable development is primarily physical sustainability, it is also concerned with promoting equity within the current generation and for future generations.

Globalization can be seen as either a threat or a boon to sustainability. Globalization can threaten sustainable development by reducing the regulatory capacities of governments over environmental threats. On the other hand, globalization can aid sustainable development through the spread of modern, less environmentally destructive technologies and the creation of standards for more efficient resource utilization. Globalization can also lead to a greater demand for cleaner environments.

There are a number of dimensions to the relationship between globalization and sustainability. First, there is the *economic* dimension and the issue of whether economic development irretrievably destroys the environment or whether it gives countries the desire and the ability to better control factors that are adversely affecting the environment. Second, *technology* can be seen as both producing environmental degradation and creating the possibility of limiting the damage. Third, there is the dimension of *awareness*—whether the global media create greater awareness of environmental problems and their causes or whether consumerism, also pushed by the global media, increases people's blindness to these issues. Finally, there is the *politics* of environmentalism, with some global organizations, such as the World Trade Organization (WTO), pushing for more economic growth, while many others, such as Greenpeace, are seeking to reduce it or to limit its negative impact on the environment. Overall, many aspects of globalization adversely affect efforts at sustainable development.

Technological Fixes

There is growing interest in finding technological fixes for at least some global environmental problems, especially those related to climate change There is a longstanding attraction to finding technological solutions to all social problems. To many, creating new technologies seems far easier and less painful than the much harder task of getting large numbers of people to change their behavior. That is, people tend to be reluctant to change their consumption patterns and thus prefer the hope of technological fixes for any resultant ecological

Smart Cities

Smart cities use digital technology in their attempts to achieve environmental sustainability, quality public services, and an efficient infrastructure for their residents. In addition to bridging the digital divide and ensuring that everyone has access to digital data through wireless networks and web-enabled devices, smart cities are focusing on three key sectors to help residents improve their quality of life: energy, transportation, and security. For example, a smart city might use high-tech sensors to measure how full waste containers are, to gauge how many seats are available on the next bus or subway, or to turn streetlights on and off (Etezadazdeh 2016, 37, 43). Daily air pollution reports and one-time emergency alerts can be delivered to residents via smartphones. Police and fire departments in smart cities can use digital networks and real-time information to help them respond to emergencies faster. Interactive digital kiosks in these cities can help tourists reserve a table at a popular restaurant or buy a dress at a local shop that can be delivered to their hotel room.

Given that more than 60 percent of the world's population will be living in cities by 2050 and that cities currently consume 75 percent of the world's energy, the growth of smart cities is imperative (MIT Technology Review Custom 2016; United Nations Human Settlements Programme 2016). Digital technologies can help meet future population demands for energy and transportation in an environmentally sustainable and efficient manner. For example, Kansas City, Missouri, has developed smart streetlights that reduce energy consumption. Adelaide, Australia, is using an environment-monitoring system to collect and share data on carbon dioxide, air quality, and temperature (MIT Technology Review Custom 2016). The top five smart cities in the world are Barcelona (Spain), New York City, London (England), Nice (France), and Singapore (High 2015). In order to increase the number of smart cities around the world, partnerships between private technology firms and municipal governments need to be encouraged.

Engaging the Digital World

How "smart" is your college campus? What do you think could be done to make it smarter? Do you see any downsides to living in a smart community? If yes, what are they?

---

problems. Furthermore, many industries have a vested interest in the continuation of high levels of consumption. Thus, even though the burning of fossil fuels is a major cause of global warming, innumerable industries and people are wedded to it. Automobile culture, which exists in both the developed and developing worlds, is one consequential example.

Enter "geoengineering" and a series of relatively new and controversial proposals for dealing with global ecological problems, especially global warming, while leaving untouched and unaddressed the underlying and growing causes of climate change (Asayama 2015). Among the ideas that have been discussed are cooling the Earth's poles by injecting chemicals into the upper atmosphere and putting mirrors in space (Dean 2007). More recently, the focus has been on capturing and storing harmful carbon dioxide emissions, which would permit the Earth's atmosphere to retain less heat, or on reflecting sunlight and its heat away from the Earth (Fountain 2015). Scientific support for these and other, sometimes outlandish, possibilities has generally been muted for several reasons:

- There is concern that talk of such solutions may encourage people to continue, if not increase, their use of fossil fuels.

- There is great fear that even if some of the proposals might work, they could have a series of unanticipated consequences that would create problems as great as or greater than those they are designed to help solve.

- These innovations in geoengineering are untried, incredibly difficult to implement, and likely to be extraordinarily expensive.

- Many other climate-related problems, such as the increasing acidity of the oceans, would be unaffected by any global climate changes produced by such technologies.

Undertaking such projects would require truly global efforts and a massively funded global governance structure. The hope is that already functioning global governance, such as that which organizes air traffic control, will be a model for what is needed to deal with global climate problems (Dean 2007). However, it seems unlikely that geoengineering, or any other technological fix, will solve a set of problems that are at their base caused by human actions (Huesemann and Huesemann 2011). While technology can help, the only real solution lies in dramatically changing those behaviors.

The Paris Agreement

Efforts to deal with climate change climaxed, at least for the time being, with the Paris Agreement of the United Nations Climate Change Conference. Negotiated at the end of 2015, the agreement was signed by 174 countries on Earth Day, April 22, 2016. Most notably, the countries involved agreed to limit carbon emissions—largely from the burning of fossil fuels and forest destruction—as soon as possible. Each country will need to set a target to reduce or limit its emissions, but the "nationally determined contribution" will be voluntary. There are no enforcement mechanisms or penalties for failure to meet the targets. Each country also agreed to do its best to keep the temperature increase globally to well below 2 degrees Centigrade (3.6 degrees Fahrenheit). Virtually all countries involved realized that these steps were not sufficient, or strong enough, to slow down, let alone stop, the increase in ecological problems. As a result, they set up a system to regularly monitor and review the global ecological situation. As Gillis (2015) put it, even with this agreement, the "great ice sheets remain imperiled, the oceans are still rising, people are dying by tens of thousands in heat waves and floods, and the agriculture system that feeds seven billion human beings is still at risk." Even though it is a weak agreement, in mid-2017, President Trump announced that the United States would withdraw from it. Although this decision has the potential to further weaken the agreement, or even undermine it completely, it remains to be seen what effect it will actually have, especially in light of strong outcries from the American public and other world leaders about the importance of continuing to uphold the agreement's principles.

✓ CHECKPOINT 17.4: RESPONSES TO ENVIRONMENTAL PROBLEMS

RESPONSE	DESCRIPTION
Sustainable development	A model of economic development that minimizes environmental destruction
Geoengineering	Using new technologies to minimize environmental destruction

SUMMARY

While overall fertility rates are dropping globally, the world's population continues to increase, although at a declining rate. Demographers focus on three main processes of population change: fertility, or people's reproductive behavior; mortality, or death and death rates; and migration, the movements of people. Demographic transition theory posits that over time both fertility and mortality rates will decrease, resulting in stabilizing population growth.

Urbanization is the process by which an increasing percentage of a society's population comes to be located in relatively densely populated urban areas. Suburbs are communities adjacent to but outside the political boundaries of central cities. Looking for cheaper land and housing, people have pushed even farther out into areas between the suburbs and rural areas, known as exurbia.

Global cities are the most important of the world's cities and are key locations for leading industries in innovation and financial services. Some global cities are megacities that have populations of greater than 10 million. Global cities are cosmopolitan in regard to cultural influences and often attract large numbers of immigrants. Their world appeal and large populations make them potential targets of terrorist attacks and global health problems.

Increasing environmental problems have led sociologists to examine the environment more closely. Most environmental problems are global in nature and scope. The relationship between globalization and sustainability has a number of dimensions, including economic, technological, and political, as well as media awareness. Cooperation between nations is crucial for achieving sustainability, particularly in terms of reducing carbon emissions from burning fossil fuels.

KEY TERMS

asylum seekers, 480
birthrate, 473
cities, 482
cosmopolitan, 487
demographers, 472

demography, 472
desertification, 496
edge cities, 484
exurbia, 484
fantasy city, 490

fertility, 474
gated communities, 483
gentrification, 485
global cities, 487
labor migrants, 480

local, 487
megacities, 488
megalopolis, 483
metropolis, 483
migration, 474

REVIEW QUESTIONS

1. How does the "demographic dividend" differ from the "financial time bomb"? Overall, is the United States in a period of a demographic dividend or a financial time bomb? Why?

2. According to demographic transition theory, what role do technological advances play in changing demographics? Why is "development the best contraceptive"?

3. How does the nature of today's migrants differ from the nature of migrants in the past? In contrast, how are the barriers to migration consistent with those of the past? How have the "push" and "pull" factors associated with migration changed in the global age?

4. Distinguish among refugees, asylum seekers, labor migrants, and undocumented immigrants.

5. What are the arguments in favor of international migration? How do these fit into today's popular and political dialogue regarding immigration in the United States?

6. Discuss the contradiction between the two roles played by the world's cities—as the sites of some of the world's worst problems and as the sites of some of its greatest achievements.

7. What makes cities cultural and consumption centers? How is a "fantasy city" different from a traditional urban area? In what ways are fantasy cities related to processes of Americanization?

8. This chapter cites environmental problems arising in cities, yet points to the possibility of new forms of urban development that could be less ecologically destructive. How can sustainable development create a more ecologically friendly city? How would this development differ from that of the last 200 years?

9. What are the world's major environmental problems? Are there technological fixes that can deal with our environmental problems? If so, what are they?

10. Do you think that globalization is ultimately a threat or a boon to sustainability? What current evidence would you cite to support your position?

$SAGE edge™ Want a better grade?

Get the tools you need to sharpen your study skills. Access practice quizzes, eFlashcards, video and multimedia at **http://edge.sagepub.com/ritzerintro4e**.

PRACTICE AND APPLY WHAT YOU'VE LEARNED

▶ edge.sagepub.com/ritzerintro4e

CHECK YOUR COMPREHENSION ON THE STUDY SITE WITH:

- **Diagnostic pre-tests** to identify opportunities for improvement.

- **Personalized study plans** with focused recommendations to address specific knowledge gaps and additional learning needs.

- **Post-tests** to check your progress and ensure mastery of key learning objectives.

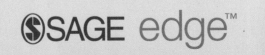

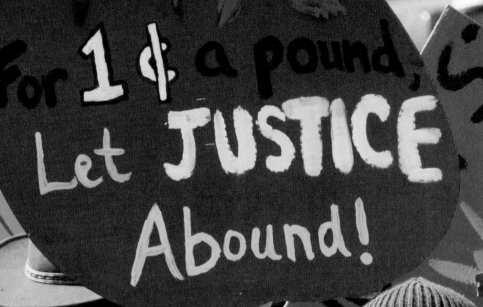

SOCIAL CHANGE, SOCIAL MOVEMENTS, AND COLLECTIVE ACTION

Workers' Rights, Consumer Activism, and Social Change

The fruits and vegetables you purchase in the grocery store were most likely harvested by undocumented workers from Mexico or Central America. These workers pay smugglers thousands of dollars to help them cross the border illegally into the United States. The lucky ones find work on farms for meager pay and substandard working conditions. Hundreds die each year from dehydration, heat stroke, or direct violence as they attempt to cross the border; others are caught by Border Patrol agents and deported (Holmes 2013). Some become trapped in a debt bondage system referred to as modern slavery; they are forced to work off the payment of their border crossing to farm camp operators. Typically, these undocumented farmworkers are not paid in wages, but by the weight of the produce they harvest. Being paid by weight compels many of them to work 10 hours or more per day with few breaks. Those in debt bondage rarely earn enough to pay off their debt and remained enslaved (Tammelleo and Lombardi 2014, 105). This was the scenario for undocumented workers who picked tomatoes in Immokalee, Florida, until the Coalition of Immokalee Workers (CIW) launched a boycott against Taco Bell in 2001.

CIW issued three demands to Taco Bell: (1) that it establish a program to stop human rights violations in its supply chain; (2) that it pay 1 penny more per pound of tomatoes, which would go to the workers; and (3) that it encourage other major retailers to follow its lead

LEARNING OBJECTIVES

18.1 Discuss the significance of social movements in the United States.

18.2 Explain how social movements emerge.

18.3 Identify different types of collective action.

18.4 Describe contemporary examples of global social change.

(Tammelleo and Lombardi 2014, 105). With pressure from consumer activists, particularly college students and members of religious organizations, Taco Bell agreed to these demands in 2005. More recently, McDonald's, Burger King, Trader Joe's, and Whole Foods have also agreed to these demands. Currently, CIW is boycotting Wendy's and Publix, two large purchasers of tomatoes who refuse to consent to its demands. In March 2017, CIW coordinated the Return to Human Rights Tour in Columbus, Ohio, near Wendy's headquarters, to exert more public pressure on this fast-food chain to treat its workers better.

CIW boycotts could not succeed without consumers using their purchasing power as a tactic to persuade corporations to change their unjust business practices. Boycotts, or the threat of withholding consumer spending from unethical companies, have a long history in the United States. In the nineteenth century, abolitionists refused to purchase sugar and other commodities that were produced with slave labor. In the early twentieth century, the National Consumers' League organized consumer boycotts of various products in order to force corporations to improve working conditions for women and to eliminate child labor. During the same time, the American Federation of Labor issued boycotts against businesses that refused to sell union-made products and companies that would not hire union workers (Forno 2013; Glickman 2009; Wiedenhoft Murphy 2017a). In 2017, a national "Day Without Immigrants" encouraged immigrant workers to stay home from their jobs to highlight their significant contributions to the U.S. economy. Consumer activism can also take the form of buycotts—that is, using purchasing power to support ethical business practices. For example, the Fair Trade movement encourages consumers to buy products that have been produced by workers who receive living wages (see Chapter 9). As corporations come to hold increasing amounts of wealth and power around the world and social media allows for widespread and rapid communication and organization, consumer activism can be a critical and effective way to hold corporations accountable for their actions. ●

S ocial change involves variations over time in every aspect of the social world, ranging from changes affecting individuals to transformations having global impacts (G. Massey 2016; Sekulic 2007b; Sztompka 1993; Weinstein 2010). Sociologists are concerned with social change itself, as well as with the ways in which social changes affect the self-concepts of individuals, the structures of society, global economic and political systems (McMichael 2011), and much more.

The issue of social change has been at the heart of sociology since its inception. This interest continues to this day, and it will be at least as strong, if not stronger, in the future. Sociology emerged during periods of great social upheaval in Europe in the nineteenth century. Early research was shaped by the aftermath of great political and social revolutions in France and the United States and by the major economic transformation wrought by the Industrial Revolution and the rise of capitalism. For example, Alexis de Tocqueville focused on the nature of democracy brought about by revolution in America (see Chapter 4), while Karl Marx sought to understand the economic upheavals associated with capitalism (see Chapter 2). The changing nature of the political system and the economy—specifically regarding democracy and capitalism—will, among other changes, continue to be of prime interest to sociologists.

The social movements in Arab countries that began in late 2010 dramatically changed much of the Arab world (Worth 2016). These movements, referred to collectively as the Arab Spring, have been discussed several times throughout this text. However, the label "Arab Spring" no longer seems appropriate, considering that many of the changes wrought by these movements were not successful—"springtime" does not seem to have arrived in many of the countries involved. Among other things, we have seen a return to authoritarianism in Egypt, anarchy in Libya, continuing civil war in Syria and Iraq, and the possibility that Syria will be permanently dismembered. This has led Roger Cohen (2016), and others, to describe the Arab Spring as an "epic failure."

The most important change wrought, at least initially, by the Arab Spring was the 2011 overthrow of longtime Egyptian dictator Hosni Mubarak and the coming to power of a former leader of the Islamic Brotherhood, Mohamed Morsi. However, Morsi's rule was uneasy and marked by much protest and disorder. In fact, Morsi was overthrown in a military coup in July 2013, and the general—Abdel Fattah el-Sisi—who led the coup became the new Egyptian president, with dictatorial powers. The dictator of Tunisia, Zine El Abidine Ben Ali, was also overthrown in 2011, but his successor was forced from office in early 2013 as a result of a continuing conflict between Islamists and secularists. An election in December 2014 resulted in the first freely elected president in that country's history. In Libya, another dictator, Muammar Qaddafi, was killed in 2011. Libya now has a weak and highly unstable political system with local tribes, militias, and warlords battling for control of parts of the country. President Ali Abdullah Saleh of Yemen was badly injured in a bomb attack and was forced out of office in late 2011. The government of Yemen disintegrated, and the country is now being ravaged by Houthi rebels. As of this writing, in mid-2017, an extremely bloody rebellion in Syria has been ongoing for more than six years, with President

Protestors rally to support Turkey's president, Recep Tayyip Erdoğan, after a failed attempt to overthrow him. What happens to a society when a revolution fails?

Bashar al-Assad clinging to control over an ever-smaller part of the country (Lynch, Freelon, and Aday 2014; Ma'oz 2014). The rest of Syria is in disarray, with various groups, especially the Sunni-based terrorist organization the Islamic State, vying for control. Syria abuts Israel, which could be drawn into the conflict in various ways, especially if Islamic State fighters draw close to its borders and engage in direct conflict with the Israeli military. That could lead Arabs in Gaza and Israel's Occupied Territories to grow more restive. The social movements associated with, and set in motion by, the Arab Spring continue to reverberate throughout the world, especially the Middle East (Lynch 2013; Moss 2013).

What is most important for our purposes is that even though it now seems misnamed, the Arab Spring is an excellent illustration of the major sociological ideas to be discussed in this chapter. It brought about *social change,* and it exemplifies both *collective action* and *social movements.* We begin this discussion with the latter idea.

SOCIAL MOVEMENTS

A **social movement** is a sustained and intentional collective effort, usually operating outside established institutional channels, either to bring about or to retard social change (Cross and Snow 2012; Della Porta and Diani 2015; Snow 2013b; Snow et al. 2013). The social movements associated with Arab Spring sought to bring about social change, while the Tea Party (Skocpol and Williamson 2016; see also the following discussion) seeks to retard, or even reverse, changes in the United States associated with liberalism, such as President Obama's Patient Protection and Affordable Care Act (ACA). Having already touched on the Arab Spring movements, we discuss other examples of social movements later in this chapter. Beyond the Tea Party, the chapter addresses the feminist movement, the gay and lesbian movement, and the civil rights movement. Following brief overviews of those movements, various sociological concepts and ideas that help us better understand these social movements will be discussed.

THE TEA PARTY

The Tea Party (www.teaparty.org) is a national movement named for the Boston Tea Party of 1773. In the contemporary context, the word *tea* in the name serves as an acronym for "taxed enough already." The Tea Party is *not* a political party, but it wields great power over and within the Republican Party.

Strangers in Their Own Land: Anger and Mourning on the American Right

(The New Press, 2016)

Arlie Russell Hochschild (Professor of Sociology at the University of California–Berkeley; PhD, University of California–Berkeley, 1969)

A sign placed by St. Amant, Louisiana resident Doug Ford welcomes Republican Presidential candidate Donald Trump, who toured flood-ravaged Louisiana on the campaign trail.

The election of Donald Trump to the presidency in 2016 caught many liberals by surprise. They questioned why so many poor and working-class Americans would vote for a Republican who vowed to dismantle government programs such as the Affordable Care Act, which were enacted to help them. Arlie Russell Hochschild spent five years in Louisiana, a strongly conservative "red" state, to learn about what she calls the Great Paradox: People who need federal assistance the most are turning away from it and toward marketplace solutions to their economic problems (2016, 9). Hochschild found that one of the main reasons for this is the emotion that shapes opinions and actions relating to such matters. Political feelings are dividing Americans, many of whom retreat into segregated "emotionally toned enclaves" and surround themselves with like-minded friends and acquaintances (2016, 6). Examples of emotionally toned enclaves may be found on social media, where friends and followers are likely to share similar beliefs. Most troublesome is the fact that invisible "empathy walls" are being constructed that "can make us feel indifferent or even hostile to those who hold different beliefs" (2016, 5). These empathy walls are particularly pronounced in the case of controversial issues, such as immigration and same-sex marriage. Hochschild explains that conservatives believe that liberals are trying to force them to feel "happy for the gay newlywed, [and] sad at the plight of the Syrian refugee," while liberals reduce conservatives' lack of requisite feelings in such cases to prejudice or ignorance (2016, 15).

In order to better understand the empathy walls dividing liberals and conservatives, Hochschild interviewed a core group of 40 highly conservative Tea Party advocates. From this group, she selected six people to profile. She engaged in participant observations of their lives, including attending political rallies, community meetings, and church services with them. Hochschild focused her research on one specific example of the Great Paradox: resistance to government regulation of environmental hazards caused by private companies. Louisiana is a state that suffers from some of the worst environmental hazards, such as air and water pollution, created by petrochemical corporations, but has some of the most lenient environmental regulations. Hochschild finds that conservatives want a clean environment, but many do not believe that government regulation is the best way to achieve it. Some of them view environmental risk as natural or inevitable, while others think it is a gamble one has to take in order to increase job opportunities. Even people in her study who were forced to relocate because their homes had been swallowed by an enormous sinkhole caused by a drilling company refused to turn to the government for help. Some even blamed government agencies for their lack of oversight instead of the negligent practices of the company. While it is easy to blame the victims of the Great Paradox for contributing to—if not

creating—their own hardships, Hochschild warns that this reasoning is too simplistic and reinforces empathy walls. It dismisses structural and cultural reasons why some individuals might oppose "big government" and support companies that promise them jobs. Climbing empathy walls by deliberating interacting with individuals who espouse different beliefs from our own is admittedly difficult at a time when political polarization is high. However, it might help us acknowledge the intense emotions supporting these walls and encourage those on both sides to be more inclusive and trusting.

Supplementary Resources

- Watch Hochschild discuss her book *Strangers in Their Own Land* on *Democracy Now!* at www.democracynow .org/2016/9/28/what_drives_ trump_supporters_sociologist_ arlie.

- Learn more about Hochschild's findings and the individuals she interviewed in this article that appeared in the *New Yorker*: www.newyorker.com/news/ benjamin-wallace-wells/arlie -russell-hochschilds-view -of-small-town-decay-and -support-for-trump.

It emerged in the United States in 2009 as a protest against high taxes and other government actions (Pullum 2013; van Dyke and Meyer 2014). It especially targeted the Obama administration's efforts to address the Great Recession and the associated housing crisis, as well as efforts to stimulate the economy through the American Recovery and Reinvestment Act of 2009. The Tea Party also opposed passage of the Affordable Care Act (ACA), or "Obamacare" (Barstow 2010), which was signed into law in 2010 and implemented to a large degree in 2014 (see Chapter 16). Similarly, the movement was later enraged by President Obama's 2014 executive order—blocked by the Supreme Court in 2016—shielding as many as 5 million undocumented immigrants from deportation (Peters 2014). Since the 2016 election, the Tea Party has been in an even stronger position to see its agenda enacted, now that sympathetic conservative Republicans control two branches of the federal government. In fact, it could be argued that Republicans actually control all three branches, now that President Trump's nominee for the Supreme Court, Neil Gorsuch, has been approved by the Senate and installed on the bench.

The initial impetus for the Tea Party movement was a February 19, 2009, on-air rant by commentator Rick Santelli on the conservative and pro-business cable TV network CNBC. Among other things, Santelli said, "The government is promoting bad behavior. . . . How many of you people want to pay your neighbor's mortgage, that has an extra bathroom, and can't pay their bills? Raise their hand! . . . We're thinking of having a Chicago Tea Party in July. . . . I'm going to start organizing" (quoted in Williamson, Skocpol, and Coggin 2011, 37). Sarah Palin, the 2008 Republican vice presidential candidate, became the most visible public figure associated with the Tea Party, although she was later supplanted by the failed 2012 Republican vice presidential candidate, Congressman Paul Ryan. Senators Rand Paul (Kentucky), Ted Cruz (Texas), and Marco Rubio (Florida) and Governor Scott Walker of Wisconsin are other Tea Party favorites who have also been failed Republican presidential candidates.

Interest in the Tea Party boomed in 2009 and beyond. However, it remains a loosely organized group of local and national conservative organizations. According to one estimate, there are only a few hundred active Tea Party groups in the United States, and only a fraction of them have more than 500 members (Williamson et al. 2011). The organization's impact has been greatly magnified by the media, especially the "advocacy journalism" of cable television news networks. Of greatest importance have been the conservative and pro–Tea Party Fox News and the liberal and anti–Tea Party MSNBC (Boykoff and Laschever 2011). Thus, for example, in a highly positive portrayal of the Tea Party on Fox News, Sean Hannity stated, "I've been to some Tea Party rallies . . . they are some of the best people. They are patriotic people. They believe in America'" (Boykoff and Laschever 2011, 351). In contrast, in an equally negative portrayal on MSNBC, Keith Olbermann said, "If racism is not the whole of the Tea Party, it is in its

Is the Tea Party a social movement, a political party in the making, or a flash in the pan?

heart, along with blind hatred, a total disinterest in the welfare of others . . . or the narrowness of their minds" (Boykoff and Laschever 2011, 350). Whatever else such overheated media coverage managed to accomplish, it brought a degree of attention and influence to the Tea Party far out of proportion to the number of active participants in the movement.

The Tea Party is unlikely to become a new political party, in part because the United States has long been dominated by a two-party system. However, if the Tea Party were to become a full-fledged political party and become institutionalized, it would no longer be a social movement. It would also no longer be a social movement if it were to peter out and die. It is possible that the Tea Party will remain what it is, a social movement, for some time to come.

Like the other examples to be discussed later, the Tea Party has *the basic characteristics of a social movement:*

- It is a *collective effort* because it includes *a significant number of people* from throughout the United States.

- It has been *sustained* for a number of years.

- It was certainly brought into being *intentionally.*

- It has been *outside established institutional channels,* because it was not, and still is not, formally affiliated with either major political party.

- It has been an *effort to retard some political changes,* such as President Obama's tax increases and health care reform act.

- It has been an *attempt to bring about substantial political change* in the Republican Party and the government as a whole. The Tea Party sought to change the Republican Party by moving it further to the right and to change the American government by forcing it to reduce taxes, better control government spending and debt, and shrink its size and power. With the election of Donald Trump, many of those goals are likely to be achieved.

Since the election of Donald Trump, the Democratic Party has started to copy some of the tactics of the Tea Party by mobilizing activists at the grassroots level. Democratic activists are attending the hometown meetings of their Republican representatives, making phone calls, and sending them e-mails to protest their support of Donald Trump. They are also organizing marches and rallies across the country to express their discontent with Trump's policies and misogynist remarks (Martin 2017; Nguyen 2017). Almost half a million people attended the Women's March in Washington in January 2017 to demonstrate their outrage with the Trump administration, with millions more attending sister marches across the country (the total number of marchers across the United States was estimated to be between 3 and 5 million) and even in cities around the world.

FEMINIST MOVEMENTS

The movements of concern here are based on **feminism**, or the belief that women are equal to men, especially socially, politically, and economically (see Chapter 11). These movements have all the characteristics of a social movement outlined previously (Crossley and Hurwitz 2013). The people involved certainly have intended to bring the movements into being and to maintain them. Feminist movements—often called women's movements—have, at least until recently, had to work outside established institutional channels. Historically, women were likely to be denied access to these channels by the men in control of the institutions. For example, U.S. women did not gain the right to vote until 1920. The movements have certainly demonstrated durability, as you will soon learn, both in the United States and around the world (Basu 2010). And they are oriented toward dramatically improving the position of women throughout the world.

The Women's Movement in the United States

The women's movement can be traced back to England and Mary Wollstonecraft's 1792 book *A Vindication of the Rights of Women,* which made the case for women's equality (Reid 2014; Tetrault 2014). The first wave of the women's movement in the United States is traditionally traced to the 1840s (Reger 2007). It was focused largely on the issue of suffrage, or gaining the right to vote for women. It had its roots in the early involvement of women in the anti-alcohol (temperance) movement and especially the antislavery movement. However, women were largely subordinated and ignored in these movements. Anger about such treatment led to the 1848 Seneca Falls Convention, which focused on such issues as restrictions on women's roles within the family, women's rights in terms of education and property, and, especially, women's suffrage (Wellman 2004). Decades of meetings, protests, marches, and social activism followed, including

the arrest of prominent suffrage leaders (for attempting to vote). Several national organizations were formed to push forward women's right to vote. The movement included battles between black and white women, with prominent white suffragist Susan B. Anthony saying, "I will cut off this right arm of mine before I will ever work or demand the ballot for the Negro and not the [white] woman" (quoted in Wilson and Russell 1996, 30). Black suffragists, including Ida B. Wells and Anna Julia Cooper, were routinely excluded from the white women's marches and protests. Although the Nineteenth Amendment gave women voting rights as early as 1848, it did not become law until August 26, 1920. (Figure 18.1 shows when women won the right to vote in select countries in the twentieth century.) By the 1930s, black women's voting rights had become severely circumscribed; their political disenfranchisement lasted until the civil rights movement of the 1960s.

The second wave of the women's movement began in the 1960s. It drew from the first wave but went beyond it in various ways. Several key books, including Simone de Beauvoir's *The Second Sex* ([1952] 1973) and Betty Friedan's *The Feminine Mystique* (1963), had a strong effect on the movement and articulated a number of its key ideas. More practically, the second wave, like the first, grew out of the dissatisfaction of activists with their involvement in other social movements, especially the New Left and civil rights movements (Houck and Dixon 2011), and their failure to deal with gender issues. Activists were also angered by the fact that these movements themselves were patriarchal. An important event in the midst of the second wave was the founding of the National Organization for Women (NOW) on October 29, 1966. The founders were women in government dissatisfied with the government's failure to deal with sex discrimination against women in the workplace. NOW eventually came to focus on a much wider range of issues, such as discrimination against women in education, the rights of women within the family, and the problems of poor women.

The second wave reached its peak between 1972 and 1982. A number of developments occurred during this period, including the founding of *Ms.* magazine; the appearance of women's studies programs on college campuses; the passage of Title IX of the U.S. Education Amendments, ending discrimination on the basis of sex in publicly funded education; and the 1973 Supreme Court decision in the case of *Roe v. Wade,* legalizing abortion. However, the second wave was soon wracked by internal conflicts. Some women—women of color, lesbians, working-class women—protested that their interests were not being adequately reflected in or addressed by the more publicly visible women's movement (Boris 2012; Roth 2004). These internal conflicts resulted in a polarization of feminism. More conservative feminists, the reformists, were primarily concerned about gender equality in the workplace (hooks 2000). Revolutionary feminists criticized the limited

FIGURE 18.1 • When Women Won the Right to Vote in Selected Countries, Twentieth Century

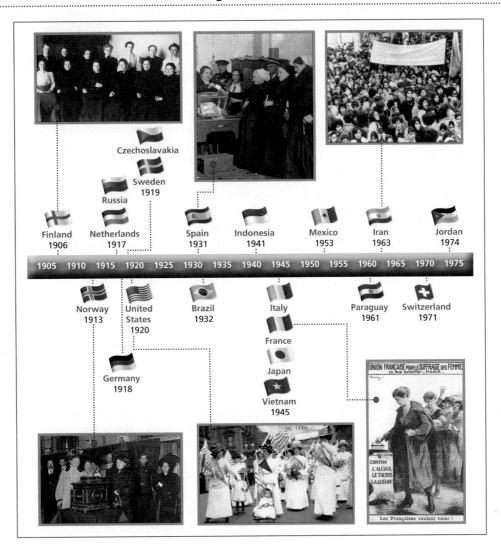

SOURCE: Data from "Women's Suffrage: When Did Women Vote?" Interactive Map. Scholastic.com.

goals of the reformists, who focused primarily on the concerns of white middle-class women. They also emphasized the ways in which conservative feminists often acted in a patriarchal and sexist manner toward other women.

In addition, feminism lost its edge because of a decline among women engaging in feminist dialogue in "consciousness-raising" groups (hooks 2000). College campuses had served as one of the few arenas in which feminist politics were discussed. Consequently, feminist politics grew stunted, and some dissatisfied radical feminists left the movement. The rise of opposition groups and the emergence of a powerful conservative movement in the United States in the 1980s contributed to the development of a sense, at least among some observers and participants, that the country had entered a postfeminist era (Hall and Rodriguez 2003).

By the early 1990s, it was clear that feminism was once again alive and well as a third wave of the women's movement emerged. This wave, which is ongoing, has been marked by a reaction against the problems confronted by the movement in the 1980s. The defining characteristics of the third wave are greater racial and ethnic inclusivity and more focus on problems such as racism, classism, transphobia, and homophobia. The movement also addresses the place of women in the larger culture and a variety of specific issues, such as the wage gap between men and women, sexual harassment, violence against women, and sexual assault and rape.

Cyberfeminism and activism on the internet can be seen as part of the third wave (Carty 2013; Haraway 1991; Wajcman 2010), although there are those who see these developments as marking the dawning of a fourth wave (Baumgardner 2011; Munro 2013). Feminists discuss, debate, and mobilize on a variety of websites, including the Crunk Feminist Collective (www.crunk feministcollective.com), The F-Word (www.thefword.org .uk), and Feministing (http://feministing.com). They use social media and write blogs to raise awareness about the right to bodily autonomy and share knitting patterns for pink pussyhats. The emerging fourth wave of feminism is centered on the idea that gender and sexuality are fluid and aims to "queer" the binary bias of these identities (Sollee 2015). Reproductive justice is also a key issue in fourth-wave feminism, as is the struggle for women to achieve full human rights. These rights include not just gender equality in social institutions, like the workplace and school, but also the physical and emotional well-being of women and girls. Among the very contemporary issues being faced by the women's movement is the fact that many online video games (such as *Grand Theft Auto V*), among many other aspects of contemporary society, are sexist and misogynistic, to say nothing of being racist and classist (Fox and Tang 2014). Men who play these games are more likely than those who do not to develop sexist attitudes (Stermer and Burkley 2015). Given the internet's booming importance, online abuses and other negative effects of internet use take on special importance for many interest groups, including the women's movement. "Gamergate" is a label for the problems posed by the internet, particularly concerning video games, for women (in particular those who have the audacity to criticize the sexism of the video game industry; Wingfield 2014a). Because sexism remains a problem on the internet—and in many other contexts—new and future developments will continue to reflect negative feelings toward women and become new targets for a continuingly evolving women's movement.

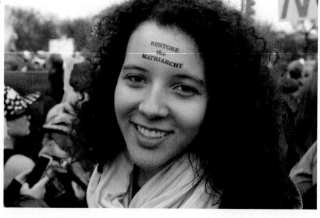

The Women's March in January 2017, held in cities around the world, drew an estimated 5 million participants in total. What is the role for a women's movement today, and what should be its goals?

The Global Women's Movement

Organizing women on a transnational basis began between the 1830s and the 1860s (Berkovitch 1999, 2012). At first, this was highly informal, but formal organizations did emerge, such as the World Women's Christian Temperance Union (WWCTU), founded in 1874. While the WWCTU focused on the problem of alcohol, it was concerned about other issues as well, such as political equality for women. By the time of its first international convention in 1891, the WWCTU had branches in 26 countries. Members adopted the view that "universal sisterhood" existed and that women throughout the world experienced a common fate. Suffrage became an increasingly important issue globally, and that led to the founding of the International Woman Suffrage Alliance (IWSA) in 1904 (Rupp and Taylor 1999).

One of the most striking events in the early twentieth century was the gathering of more than a thousand women in the Netherlands in 1915 at the International Congress of Women. This meeting took place in spite of the fact that World War I raged around the attendees, which made it very difficult to pass through national borders. The main goal of the meeting was to find ways to resolve conflicts and prevent future wars. After World War I, the founding of the League of Nations and the International Labour Organization (ILO) created new opportunities for global action by women (and others). However, women's activities in and through these organizations achieved few tangible results, in part because leaders within the organizations tended to be "elite, White, Christian women from Northern and Western Europe" (Freedman 2009, 48). Many women within these groups supported colonialism despite the presence of fellow members who suffered under colonial rule. Moreover, the reproduction of colonial relationships within the movement was yet another facet of the contentious beginnings of an international women's movement. In reaction to this, black women from Africa and the United States formed the International Council of Women of the Darker Races in 1920. They called for support in their struggle not only for personal independence but also national independence from colonial domination (Alexander and Mohanty 2013; Freedman 2009).

Much greater strides were made as a result of the founding of the United Nations after World War II. Instrumental in this progress was the UN Commission on the Status of Women. Its initiative led to a world conference on women in 1975 and to the declaration of that year as the UN International Women's Year. Yet men dominated the speeches and leadership positions at the 1975 conference; they tended to represent the interests of their respective governments rather than those of women's organizations. Women continued to press for equality, however, and were eventually granted more leadership roles to foster discussions about the gaps between male and female opportunities. This was followed by the UN Decade for Women (1976–1985), conferences during that decade, and follow-up conferences held in 1995 (30,000 people attended the UN Fourth World Conference on Women in Beijing) and 2005. Because of such meetings, women from all over the world were able to interact on a face-to-face basis and to develop various transnational interpersonal ties (Davis [1991] 1999). As a result of these associations, many local and transnational women's organizations emerged (Fernandes 2013).

In addition to these formal organizations, many transnational feminist networks have developed in recent years (Ferree and Tripp 2006). These are more fluid organizational forms, lacking formal membership and bureaucratic structures. They have been aided in their formation and interaction by new communication technologies, especially the internet. However, rather than these developments leading to a single global sisterhood, fractures and divisions have grown stronger in the global women's movement. For example, women of the Global South often resist initiatives supported by women of the Global North. This resistance is due in part to Southern women's need to prevent the imposition of Northern notions of superiority and to recognize that injustice and emancipation can take various forms (Freedman 2009). In spite of these divisions, the women's movement today is far more global than ever. It is not only having an impact on the position of women throughout the world but also shaping, and being shaped by, globalization (Basu 2010; Crossley and Hurwitz 2013). This can be seen, for example, in the millions of women around the world who participated in the Women's March on January 21, 2017.

ASK YOURSELF

Does it surprise you to learn that the women's movement and its global arm are characterized by fractures? What might heal these divisions? Do men need to play a role in women's movements? Why or why not?

LGBTQ MOVEMENTS[1]

The origins of the U.S.-based lesbian, gay, bisexual, transgender, and queer (LGBTQ) movement can be traced back to the 1890s (Shroedel and Fiber 2000). There were earlier LGBTQ movements in other places, such as Germany (Newton 2009), and there are, of course, LGBTQ movements throughout the world today (Tremblay, Paternotte, and Johnson 2013). These movements still have much work to do. For example, same-sex acts remain illegal in at least 72 countries (Carroll 2016; Hildebrandt 2014).

The focus here is mainly on LGBTQ movements in the United States (Ghaziani, Taylor, and Stone 2016; Valocchi

[1]This section is printed with the permission of Tracy Royce and Danielle Antoinette Hidalgo.

2013). The LGBTQ movement will be discussed as the successor to such previous movements as gay liberation, lesbian feminism, and queer activism. It encompasses those earlier movements, but goes beyond them to "embrace bisexuality and transgender issues" (Ghaziani, Taylor, and Stone 2016, 171).

World War II and the Lavender Scare

Some problems for gays and lesbians (such as mobilization against them in the military) developed during the World War II era (Bérubé 2010). However, in general, that period was something of a golden age for gays and lesbians in the United States. Men and women engaged in new experiences as they left home, settled in new living situations, and found themselves in same-sex milieus in the military or in civilian workplaces. This period has been described as "somewhat of a nationwide coming out experience" (Allan Bérubé, quoted in Johnson 2004, 51). The war years allowed for increased possibilities and opportunities for sexual encounters, as well as an "anything goes" mentality. However, beginning in 1948, the United States entered a period of mounting public criticism of the "moral decay" of homosexuality, as well as of communism.

What came to be known as the "Lavender Scare" signaled a turning point for the history of gay and lesbian movements in the United States. Starting in 1950, the Lavender Scare was a government-sponsored attack on sexual minorities—those who engaged in, or were suspected of, same-sex sexual behaviors (Johnson 2004). As in the better-known Red Scare (a response to fears of communism), government agents attempted to ferret out employees who were considered security risks. In this case, those suspected of engaging in "sexual perversions" or homosexuality were vulnerable because it was feared they might reveal government secrets to foreign agents under pressure to prevent their sexual activities from being made public. Thousands were discharged from the government; some committed suicide. This institutionalized attack on homosexuality also sparked political organization among gays and lesbians. The Mattachine Society (see further discussion in the next section), founded by a government worker, marked the start of 25 years of efforts to dismantle federal job discrimination laws. In 1975, it became illegal to discriminate against gays and lesbian in hiring and firing decisions. Thus, the "crackdown" on homosexuals, "perverts," and those engaged in "immoral" sexual relations fostered a long-lasting collective movement to fight for the rights of gays and lesbians.

The U.S.-Based Homophile Movement

Early efforts to organize "homophile" (i.e., gay rights) movements crystallized in 1950–1951 in the formation of the Mattachine Society, originally based in Los Angeles. Other cities started chapters, and by 1966 there were 15 gay and lesbian rights organizations in the United States; by 1969 there were 50 (D'Emilio 1983; Hay 2012). The Daughters of Bilitis (DOB), an offshoot of the Mattachine Society focusing on the rights of gay women, was founded in 1955 (Rutledge 1992; Valocchi 2007). These organizations emphasized education and largely embraced assimilationist strategies in order to gain mainstream acceptance. Although gay and lesbian activists worked alongside each other, gender privilege (particularly male) remained and was a source of dissatisfaction for lesbians active in the homophile movement. As one lesbian activist stated, "There wasn't a Women's Movement yet. . . . We knew our place—we were always the coffee makers. . . . There was a clear set of chores for women" (Shroedel and Fiber 2000, 99).

Stonewall

The 1969 uprisings at Greenwich Village's Mafia-owned gay bar the Stonewall Inn are regarded by many as pivotal in the twentieth-century struggle for gay rights and as denoting the beginning of the modern gay rights movement (Armstrong and Crage 2006, 2013; Duberman 1994). On June 27, 1969, the patrons of the Stonewall

Inn—"Puerto Rican drag queens, lesbians, effeminate men, and young street people" (Nardi, Sanders, and Marmor 1994, 14)—reacted violently to a police raid. Law enforcement officials and members of the gay community alike credited this event with inspiring gays and lesbians to more aggressively demand equality and freedom from abuse. Within a few years, there were more than 800 gay and lesbian groups all over the United States. Today, gay pride days and marches continue to commemorate the assertion of collective queer identity and entitlement to rights that emerged as a result of Stonewall. However, some question LBGTQ history's emphasis on the Stonewall uprisings. They remind us that new forms of the gay and lesbian movement owe much to the foundational work of homophile groups, as well as to twentieth-century civil rights, antiwar, and feminist organizations (Jay 1999).

Lesbian Herstory

Given the underlying male privilege that was embodied in groups such as the Mattachine Society, many lesbians were dissatisfied with their organizing experiences alongside gay men. And although lesbians found a respite from sexism in the mainstream second-wave women's movement, the heterosexism and sometimes overt hostility encountered by lesbians in feminist groups made these organizing spaces less than hospitable. Consequently, many lesbians split off from the mainstream gay and feminist movements. Numerous lesbian separatist groups emerged, such as the Furies, who framed lesbianism as a political choice in opposition to male supremacy.

Patrons of the Stonewall Inn in Greenwich Village fought back when police raided the gay enclave in 1969, in what proved to be a watershed moment. Do you agree with those who feel the civil rights, antiwar, and feminist movements had an impact on the struggle for gay rights? If so, what was that impact?

Not all lesbians politicized their sexual identities in this way. For women who desired other women in butch/femme (traditionally male/traditionally female) space, a masculine–feminine relationship continued. But lesbian separatists argued that in order to truly be feminists, women had to remove themselves completely from the male sphere. In practice, this resulted in the formation of women-only communities or "womyn's lands" and lesbian-driven, woman-centered activism. These women "wanted to create entirely new institutions and to shape a women's culture that would embody all of the best values that were not male" (Faderman 1991, 216).

ASK YOURSELF

Why do all gays and lesbians not have the same goals or try to achieve equality by the same means? Do their philosophical and practical divisions help or hinder their efforts? Why?

Homosexuality in the *DSM*

One of the early post-Stonewall political victories of the gay and lesbian movement was the removal of homosexuality as a category of mental illness from the American Psychiatric Association's (APA's) *Diagnostic and Statistical Manual of Mental Disorders* (*DSM*). Since the latter half of the twentieth century, the *DSM* has served as the definitive differential diagnostic guide for psychiatrists, psychologists, and other mental health professionals. It has therefore been influential in medicalizing and pathologizing behaviors and identities. The *DSM*'s inclusion of homosexuality as a mental illness framed same-sex behavior and desire not only as a disease, but as one that is treatable.

The efforts of both social scientists and gay and lesbian activists fostered the removal of homosexuality from the 1973 edition of the *DSM*. Radical and moderate activist groups employed a variety of strategies to express their opposition to the APA's pathologizing of homosexuality.

However, homosexuality was replaced with "ego-dystonic homosexuality" in the 1980 revision of the *DSM*, known as the *DSM-III*. This new diagnosis could be applied to those who claimed to feel distress as a result of their unwanted homosexuality. However, opposition to this diagnosis led to its later removal from the next revised edition, the *DSM-III-R*. The APA has since adopted numerous formal policies in support of the dignity of gay men and lesbians and in opposition to their stigmatization. However, both individual clinicians and organizations such as the National Association for Research and Therapy of Homosexuality (NARTH) continue to advocate clinicians' "right" to provide "psychological care" for those with "unwanted homosexual attraction."

Harvey Milk

Although several openly lesbian political candidates were elected to office prior to Harvey Milk's 1977 election to the city of San Francisco's board of supervisors, Milk was the first openly gay candidate to be elected to major political office in the state of California. His political career was tragically cut short by his assassination in late 1978, but he continues to be lauded by many as a martyr, a hero, and a visionary.

Milk was elected to public office after three unsuccessful attempts. Although he held office for less than a year, he accomplished much during his abbreviated term.

For example, he sponsored a sweeping civil rights bill that protected gays from discrimination. He advocated that gays and lesbians demolish prejudice by increasing their visibility and by "coming out" to the people in their personal and professional lives. He also devoted considerable time and effort to campaigning to defeat California's Proposition 6, the Briggs Initiative, which if passed would have required public schools to fire gay teachers and their supporters.

Milk's life and career have been memorialized in director Rob Epstein's 1984 documentary *The Times of Harvey Milk* as well as in Gus Van Sant's award-winning movie biopic *Milk* (2008).

HIV/AIDS, ACT UP, and Queer Nation

The recognition of HIV/AIDS in 1981 by the Centers for Disease Control and Prevention had a tremendous impact on gay and lesbian politics and communities. The activism that emerged from this period was embodied in the early efforts of the AIDS Coalition to Unleash Power (ACT UP; Stockdill 2013). In 1989, ACT UP pressured pharmaceutical company Burroughs Wellcome to make its new antiretroviral drug, AZT, more affordable for HIV-positive patients. ACT UP embodied a new kind of activism that included civil disobedience, activist art, and other forms of creative activities and representations. ACT UP chapters opened throughout the nation. In 1990, some ACT UP activists formed a new group, Queer Nation, which, although short-lived, served as the beginning of a public and direct representation of LGBTQ issues. Out of HIV/AIDS activism and via the efforts of Queer Nation, the gay and lesbian movement shifted into a politics of queer spaces and identities.

LGBTQ Comes of Age

All of the above can be seen as predecessors to, or early examples of, the LGBTQ movement. If we need to identify the beginnings of that broader movement, they are both the Stonewall uprisings (discussed previously; Prince 2004) and, a year later (on June 28, 1970), the first of what has become the annual "Pride Day" parades in New York City. There was also a week-long series of events around Pride Day. This has since expanded into a "Pride Month," with month-long parades and celebrations around the world.

At first, there was a tendency by the gay movement to not be accepting of bisexual and transgender people. However, by the late 1980s, that position began to change. That change is reflected in the beginning of the wide-scale use of the term LGBTQ to encompass, and reflect the mutual acceptance of, gay, lesbian, bisexual, and transgender people, as well as others outside of the mainstream (those who identify more as "queer").

The Ongoing Fight for Marriage Equality

Almost from the inception of the LGBTQ movement, marriage equality was a part of its national agenda. That effort really took off when the movement legally challenged the 1996 Defense of Marriage Act (Ghaziani, Taylor, and Stone 2016). That act restricted marriage to "one man and one woman" and barred federal recognition of same-sex marriages. The efforts of the LGBTQ movement—and others—met with considerable success, and in 2011 President Obama determined that the act was unconstitutional and directed the Justice Department to stop defending the law in court. In 2013, the U.S. Supreme Court struck down the section of the act that defined marriage as involving one man and one woman. It also declared unconstitutional the barring of federal recognition of same-sex marriages. As a result of the 2013 Supreme Court decision, gays and lesbians gained many federal and state benefits that were formerly denied to them and that are automatically conferred on heterosexual couples. By mid-2015, the Supreme Court legalized same-sex marriage for the nation as a whole. Globally, same-sex couples also enjoy the legal right to marry in a number of other countries—Argentina, Belgium, Brazil, Canada, Colombia, Denmark, Finland, France, Iceland, Ireland, Luxembourg, the Netherlands, New Zealand, Norway, Portugal, Spain, South Africa, Sweden, the United Kingdom, Uruguay, and some jurisdictions in Mexico. Gays and lesbians continue to fight for other benefits that are still denied to them.

In spite of these successes, resistance to gay marriage continues to come from both outside and within the gay rights movement. Religious conservatives oppose same-sex marriage, arguing that it threatens the sanctity of marriage and the traditional family. But queer-identified groups have also offered criticisms of gay marriage. For example, an emphasis on the central importance of securing legal marriage is criticized for failing to address the inequalities inherent in the institution of marriage itself (BeyondMarriage.org 2006). The rights associated with marriage do not benefit everyone equally. Nor do they compensate fully for unjust deficiencies in contemporary public policy. To challenge the institution of marriage and to address the needs of varied family forms across the LGBTQ community, a number of alternatives to the mainstream LGBTQ movement's focus on marriage are suggested:

- Legal recognition of a diverse range of relationships and family forms

- Basic resources, such as health care and housing for all persons, regardless of their marital or citizenship status

- Separation of church and state in all matters

- Freedom from state regulation of sexual lives and gender choices

FIGURE 18.2 • Views on Same-Sex Marriage in the United States among LGBTQ Adults by Race/Ethnicity, Age, and Political Affiliation, 2014

% saying they . . . allowing gays and lesbians to marry legally

	Oppose (Net)	Strongly favor	Favor
ALL U.S.	41	24	25
ALL LGBTQ	7	74	18
Among LGBTQ adults . . .			
Lesbians	2	85	12
Gay men	4	80	17
Bisexuals	8	69	22
White	6	78	15
Hispanic	7	67	26
Black	12	58	28
Ages 18–29	3	82	13
Ages 30 and older	8	71	20
Democrat/Lean Dem	4	81	15
Republican/Lean Rep	19	15	33

NOTE: "Strongly oppose" and "oppose" responses not shown separately. Those who did not answer are not shown. LGBTQ adults who identify as transgender are included in the LGBTQ total, but the sample size is too small to analyze separately. Whites and blacks include only non-Hispanics. Hispanics are of any race.

SOURCE: Jens Manuel Krogstad, "What LGBT Americans Think of Same-Sex Marriage," Pew Research Center, Fact Tank, January 27, 2015.

Figure 18.2 shows levels of support for and opposition to same-sex marriage among LGBTQ adults by race/ethnicity, age, and political affiliation. Although a substantial share of LGBTQ adults in all demographic categories either favor or strongly favor same-sex marriage, there are some who continue to have reservations about it. For example, blacks are considerably less supportive of same-sex marriage than whites. Support for same-sex marriage is much weaker among those who identify with the Republican Party than it is among those oriented to the Democratic Party. Support is also somewhat weaker among LGBTQ adults age 30 and older, in comparison to those in the 18–29 age group.

The gay marriage debate and activist efforts relating to it continue to be fraught with tension both within and beyond the LGBTQ community. While the LGBTQ movements discussed in this section are global in scope, the movements have had mixed success globally. For example, while at least some forms of homosexuality are legal in some parts of the world, in a much larger part of the world, homosexuality is illegal or same-sex couples are not recognized. There are even parts of the world, mostly Islamic, where homosexuality is subject to large penalties, life in prison, or even death.

THE CIVIL RIGHTS MOVEMENT

Arguably, the most notable social movement in the United States was, and may still be, the civil rights movement (Andrews 2013; Morris 1984, 2007; Fleming and Morris 2015; Santoro 2015). (Some would contend that the anticolonial [Schock 2013] and labor movements [Fantasia, Voss, and Eidlin 2013], among others, were of greater importance, especially globally.) Perhaps the key event in the history of the civil rights movement was the successful 1955 boycott of segregated city buses in Montgomery, Alabama. At the time, blacks had to ride in the back of public buses. While the movement was organized locally, it was led by the Reverend Martin Luther King Jr. ([1958] 2010). His success there cata-

Perhaps no one symbolizes the civil rights movement so well as Martin Luther King Jr. Here King waves to supporters from the steps of the Lincoln Memorial during the 1963 March on Washington.

pulted him into the position of leader of the national civil rights movement. The Montgomery boycott served as a model for future civil rights action and all other subsequent social movements. It emphasized nonviolent action, made it clear that the black community could overcome internal divisions to become an effective force for change, showed the central role that the black church could play in such a social movement, and demonstrated that the black community was able to finance these actions with little or no outside help.

The success of the Montgomery bus boycott led black organizations to become more involved in civil rights activities. These included the National Association for the Advancement of Colored People (NAACP), formed in 1910, and the Congress of Racial Equality (CORE), organized in 1942. It also led to the formation of new organizations, especially the Southern Christian Leadership Conference (SCLC), and to the creation and active involvement of innumerable local groups. The actions spurred on by these groups and organizations encountered significant opposition from whites, sometimes leading to violence. A key development in 1960 was the large-scale involvement of black college students in sit-ins at segregated lunch counters throughout the South. These students were crucial to the formation of another new organization, the Student Nonviolent Coordinating Committee (SNCC), in 1960. The SNCC, in turn, drew many white students into the movement.

In the 1960s, the civil rights movement became a significant force through boycotts, sit-ins, freedom rides, mass marches, and mass arrests. Both blacks and their white allies participated. In some cases, media coverage of vicious attacks against black activists gave the movement great visibility and elicited much sympathy from those not initially inclined to support it.

Many of the "invisible leaders" of the civil rights movement were black women, such as Fannie Lou Hamer, Septima Poinsette Clark, and Ella Baker. Their invisibility in leadership positions was an unfortunate byproduct of the gender hierarchy as it existed in the 1950s. When women spearheaded successful civil rights campaigns, more "visible" men in the movement took the credit and usurped women's leadership positions (Olson 2002). The many women who participated in the movement served as volunteers, and their numbers far surpassed those of their male counterparts.

ASK YOURSELF

Why are the black women who served as "invisible leaders" of the civil rights movement not more widely known today? Do you think women who are fighting racism today, whatever their color, are sufficiently recognized by the public? Why or why not?

The movement had great success, manifest especially in the Civil Rights Act of 1964, which banned discrimination on the basis not only of race but also of sex, religion, and national identity. Of course, the larger goal of eliminating racism in America eluded the civil rights movement and continues to elude it to this day (Pager, Western, and Bonikowski 2009).

The global nature of the civil rights movement is especially clear in the antiapartheid movement led by Nelson Mandela in South Africa (Van Kessel 2013). Apartheid was a system of racial separation that had been made legal in 1948. Soon thereafter a social movement against it emerged, led by the African National Congress. It garnered great international support and succeeded in achieving its goals in less than half a century (Waldmeir [1997] 2001). By 1994, both apartheid and white hegemony in South Africa had ended.

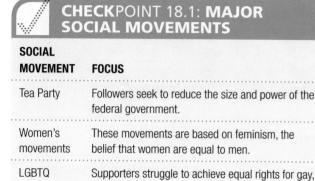

CHECKPOINT 18.1: MAJOR SOCIAL MOVEMENTS

SOCIAL MOVEMENT	FOCUS
Tea Party	Followers seek to reduce the size and power of the federal government.
Women's movements	These movements are based on feminism, the belief that women are equal to men.
LGBTQ movement	Supporters struggle to achieve equal rights for gay, lesbian, bisexual, transgender, and queer people.
Civil rights movement	Nonviolent action is aimed at eliminating racism and other forms of discrimination.

EMERGENCE, MOBILIZATION, AND IMPACT OF SOCIAL MOVEMENTS

A variety of conditions determine whether or not a social movement will emerge. To start with, there must be grievances, or matters that large numbers of people find troublesome (Snow 2013a). In the case of the Tea Party, for example, grievances included those against high taxes, the economic stimulus, and health care reform. Grievances about the unfair treatment of women, gays and lesbians, and blacks animated the other social movements discussed previously. However, grievances alone are not sufficient for a social movement to arise. Individuals and organizations must be mobilized in order to do something about them. All of the movements discussed previously were successful in mobilizing people to act.

FACTORS IN THE EMERGENCE OF A SOCIAL MOVEMENT

Assuming a set of grievances and efforts at mobilization, certain other conditions must exist for a social movement to emerge. First, there must be openings or opportunities within the political system. For example, a deep and stubborn recession, high unemployment rates, a massive bailout of banks and large corporations, and a dramatic escalation in the national debt provided an opening for the rise of the Tea Party (Macdonald 2010; Pace 2010). That opening was widened as these and related problems, as well as public concern about them, increased (Crutsinger 2010).

A second factor involves various spatial arrangements, such as the physical proximity of those involved. Clearly, social movements develop more easily when those who at least have the potential to become involved come into contact with one another fairly easily or on a regular basis. Another spatial factor is whether or not there are "free spaces" where those involved can meet. It is in such spaces that a movement can develop, out of the limelight and free of external surveillance and control. Women on college campuses existed in close proximity to one another, and this helped in the formation of the women's movement, while free spaces such as churches were especially important to the development of the civil rights movement.

A third factor is the availability of resources. This is the concern of **resource mobilization theory**, one of the most popular approaches to understanding social movements today (Edwards and Gillham 2013; Jenkins 1983; Walder 2009). The focus is on what groups of people need to do in order to mobilize effectively to bring about social change. This theory assumes that there is some strain within the larger society and that there are groups of people who have grievances that result from those strains. One of the most important works in this tradition is that of Jack Goldstone (1991; Rojas and Goodwin 2013) on *revolutions*. These are social movements in which the strains produced by state breakdown (e.g., failure of the government to function properly, fiscal distress) play a key role in the development of revolutionary movements. Major examples of revolutions include the French, American, and Russian Revolutions. Once a strain exists, the issue, then, is what resources are needed for these groups to become social movements, perhaps even successful social movements.

RESOURCES AND MOBILIZATION OF SOCIAL MOVEMENTS

Five types of resources have been identified as important to the mobilization of social movements. First are *material resources* such as money, property, and equipment. It is costly to mount a successful social movement, and money and other material resources are mandatory (Snow, Soule, and Cress 2005). Notable in this regard is the backing of the Tea Party by conservative billionaires. Second are *social-organizational resources,* which include infrastructure (internet access is especially important today), social networks (insiders with access to important groups and organizations), and the organizations that are formed by the social movement (e.g., Tea Party, NAACP, ACT UP; Stepan-Norris and Southworth 2007). Third are *human resources,* such as the leadership (Stevenson 2016), expertise, skills, and day-to-day labor of those in the organization (Tsutsui and Wotipka 2004). More specific resources might be dynamic public speakers (such as Martin Luther King Jr.) and spokespersons, skilled web designers, or people skilled in organizational dynamics. Fourth are *moral resources,* such as the degree to which the larger public regards the movement as legitimate. Other moral resources include a sense that there is a high level of integrity among the leaders as well as in the membership as a whole (Lowe 2002). Finally, *cultural resources* are important—such as bodies of knowledge or skills that are tacitly shared by at least some members of the movement. These might include knowledge of how to organize a protest, hold a news conference, or run a meeting. Overall, the keys to the success or failure of a social movement are the available resources and the ability to use some or all of them in order to mobilize effectively to pursue desired social change.

Another important issue is the source of such resources. One source is simply having members who are themselves able to produce the resources by, for example, raising money, developing networks, or socializing their children to become part of the movement as adults. Another is aggregating external resources, such as soliciting donations from a wide range of donors. Also of importance is the need to locate patrons who can be relied on to support the group monetarily and in many other ways (e.g., by providing staff members). Finally, a social movement can coopt the resources of other organizations. For example, social movements in the United States have often coopted the resources of churches by, for example, using their buildings, their staff, and their moral authority.

Participation

Once a social movement is under way, methods must be found to ensure member participation. First, people need to be asked to participate. For that to occur, they need to be embedded in social networks involving other movement members. Second, a variety of social psychological factors are involved. These include personally identifying with the movement and its causes, being aroused emotionally by the issues involved and becoming committed to dealing with them, and being at a point in life—retired, unemployed, in college—where one is available to participate in the movement. Third, incentives need to be offered so that the gains to members for their involvement outweigh the risks and costs. For example, for participants in the civil rights movement, the achievement of greater rights for blacks outweighed the risk of being beaten or murdered and the cost of lost time and income. While material incentives are important, of far greater importance are the social incentives associated with joining with others as part of the movement, as well as the moral incentive of being involved in something one believes in strongly (Quadagno and Rohlinger 2009).

Goals, Strategies, and Tactics

Once formed, a social movement needs to have goals, a strategy, and a variety of tactics in order to succeed. *Goals* relate to what the movement seeks to do, such as cut taxes or make society more equal. *Strategy* involves the movement's long-term plan for achieving its goals. Once a strategy is in place, tactics become important. *Tactics* are more short-term in nature. They need to be quite fluid and able to adapt quickly in light of changes taking place in the immediate or larger environment. In the case of the civil rights movement, the strategy was to create situations that brought the plight of black Americans, especially those who lived in the South, to the attention of the media, the public, and political leaders. Tactics, in this case, involved engaging in *civil disobedience,* or nonviolent public acts that are against the law and aimed at changing the law or government policies (Tescione 2013). For example, blacks attempted to order food at segregated lunch counters. The acts of civil disobedience produced

Members of an environmental organization called Robin Wood protested the use of fossil fuels from hammocks hung above railroad tracks leading to a coal-fired power plant in Germany. What other strategies and tactics relating to climate change are you aware of? Which do you think will be successful?

reactions (e.g., white protests, police action) that attracted media and public attention and eventually public outrage. Of particular importance are the actions of countermovements and government officials. For example, the civil rights movement had to adapt to the hostile actions of both white supremacists and many local government officials.

Factors in Success

A variety of factors help determine whether or not a social movement will succeed (Cross and Snow 2012; Rochon 1990). One is its sheer *size*. All social movements start small, but those that succeed are likely to have recruited large numbers of activists and supporters. Another is *novelty*, or the uniqueness of the movement and its goals. Uniqueness and size are important because they lead to a great deal of media attention, which, in turn, is likely to generate additional supporters and funds. The latter are two of the many *resources* social movements need to succeed (see the previous discussion). *Violence*, as in the case of the Stonewall riots, can be useful in achieving results. However, it also can be counterproductive by turning off potential supporters and members. Perhaps more important, it can lead to violent reactions that can end in the suppression of the movement. *Militancy* can also be double-edged, because a highly militant social movement might be able to achieve its goals quickly, but militancy, like violence, can lead to counterreactions and suppression. *Nonviolence* has been a successful method for social movements because it avoids the powerful counterreactions engendered by violent and militant social movements. The nonviolent approach is traceable largely to Mahatma Gandhi and his use of such means as noncooperation with the British-controlled government to gain Indian independence in 1947. Today, a large number of social movements, including the Tea Party and the women's and LGBTQ movements, have adopted a nonviolent approach. Globally, many organizations associated with the environmental movement, as well as those associated with the World Social Forum (see the Globalization box in this chapter) and operating in opposition to at least some aspects of globalization, rely almost exclusively on nonviolent methods. More generally, the ability of social movements to network—with individuals involved, as well as with other movements nationally and internationally—is increasingly a key to success (Castells 2015). Part of that, and important in itself, is the ability of the movement and its members to utilize social media (see below) to ramp up and maintain broad support (Molaei 2015).

Although various aspects of social movements themselves strongly affect whether or not they will be successful, many other factors are in play. Of great importance is the ability of individuals, groups, or the state (especially the police, the military, and the state more generally) to suppress a social movement (Davenport 2015; Earl 2007). Efforts at suppressing social movements can be covert, such as the FBI's wiretapping of the phones of members of dissident groups, especially suspected communist and civil rights groups, in the United States in the mid-1950s through the early 1970s. They can also be overt, a major example being the violent suppression in 1989 of antigovernment protests in Tiananmen Square by the Chinese government and the military. Another example is the violence committed by local law enforcement officers and white supremacists against civil rights activists in the United States in the 1960s. Yet another is the police raid in 1969 of the Stonewall Inn, which was frequented by LGBTQ people.

THE IMPACT OF SOCIAL MOVEMENTS

Whether or not they are successful, social movements often leave their mark, which is sometimes a quite powerful imprint. A government may be able to suppress a social movement, but it is likely that aspects of the government and the way it operates will be affected by the movement as well as by the efforts to suppress it. For example, in the 1940s and 1950s, the U.S. government was able to suppress efforts to increase the influence of communism throughout the country. However, while it was successful in those efforts, it engaged in a variety of highly questionable actions. Major examples include the activities of the House Un-American Activities Committee (HUAC) and especially those of the infamous Senator Joseph McCarthy. Recall from Chapter 7 that McCarthy conducted hearings with the ostensible goal of rooting communists out of the government and elsewhere, most notably Hollywood and the U.S. Army. McCarthy and his associates often made wild public accusations without presenting any supporting evidence. Long-lasting changes were brought about in the government as a result of the public's revulsion over the reprehensible tactics used by McCarthy and his supporters. Since that time, government actions that even hint at the kind taken during the 1940s and 1950s are labeled "McCarthyism" and, as a result, are unlikely to succeed.

Nevertheless, the government retains the ability to suppress social movements, and in many ways that ability and its extent have increased. This is a result, in part, of the fact that distinctions among activism, terrorism, and extremism are being eroded by government agencies, especially those concerned with law enforcement (Monaghan and Walby 2012). The danger here is that many activist social movements with positive goals and legal methods may end up being suppressed along with terroristic and extremist movements that pose a genuine threat to the United States.

Social movements, especially those that achieve some success, often leave strong legacies for, and have powerful impacts on, later movements. For example, the civil rights movement was an inspiration and a model for many later movements in the United States, such as the student, antiwar, environmental, gay and lesbian, and disability movements.

Social movements outside the United States—for example, South Africa's antiapartheid movement, the Solidarity movement in Poland, and the democracy movement in China—have also been strongly affected by the civil rights movement.

While social movements are oriented toward changing society, they also have strong impacts on the individuals involved, both members of the movements and those who oppose them. The greatest impact is usually on the large numbers of people who actively participate in movements (Roth 2007). Their attitudes, and perhaps the entire courses of their lives, are often altered greatly by their involvement. Much the same is true of those who take an active role in opposing social movements. Senator McCarthy, for example, was embittered by his failures and died soon after he was discredited.

THE INTERNET, GLOBALIZATION, AND SOCIAL MOVEMENTS

Two of the most important recent developments as far as social movements are concerned relate to globalization (Agrikoliansky 2013; Maiba 2005) and the internet (Carty 2013; Molaei 2015), as well as other new media technologies, such as smartphones (Castells 2015).

The internet has proven to be an important means of involving and organizing large numbers of people, perhaps millions of them, who are widely separated from one another, perhaps even in different parts of the world. In other words, people no longer need to be in close physical proximity to be involved in social movements. People can also now communicate more easily through the use of smartphones, even from the sites of events. This communication offers new possibilities for mobilizing those engaged in social movements. It is possible for participants in a movement not only to communicate verbally with others in the movement but also to snap pictures or shoot videos with their smartphones and send them instantaneously via YouTube or Facebook to large numbers of interested parties. This allows people to see for themselves what is transpiring in the social movement. As noted previously, the Islamic State (IS) has been effective in using the internet to recruit supporters, many of whom have trekked to Syria to participate in conflict there and in the region. IS has been particularly successful at using Facebook to attract female adherents from the West (Erlanger 2014). There are also now online activists (e-activists) who are creating electronic social movements (e-movements; Dolata and Schrape 2016). At least some e-movements have the possibility of becoming social movements in the nonvirtual world.

The internet and other technologies enable social movements to cover wide geographic areas and even to become global. Like much else in the world today, social movements are less constrained than ever before by national borders. It seems likely that the future will bring an increasing number of global social movements. We will discuss the internet and globalization further later in this chapter.

CHECKPOINT 18.2: RESOURCES OF SUCCESSFUL SOCIAL MOVEMENTS

RESOURCE	DESCRIPTION
Material	Money, property, and equipment
Social-organizational	Infrastructure and social networks
Human	Leadership and day-to-day labor
Moral	Legitimacy and integrity
Cultural	Knowledge and skills

COLLECTIVE ACTION

Collective action is generated, or engaged in, by a group of people to encourage or retard social change (Oliver 2013, 210). Social movements are one kind of collective action (Ayres 2014); others include crowds, riots, and disasters. Like all other forms of collective action, social movements usually occur outside established institutional channels. However, social movements are different from all other forms of collective action in at least two ways. First, most forms of collective action are short-lived compared to social movements. Thus, a crowd, for example, can come together and disperse within hours, but a social movement can be sustained for years or decades. Second, a social movement is intentional; other forms of collective action are not. For instance, a community that comes together immediately after a disaster such as an earthquake or a flood does not do so intentionally. It has been brought together and springs into action because of some unanticipated external event. After the 2011 earthquake and tsunami in northern Japan, newspapers reported that a strong sense of community emerged and helped people survive the aftermath (Fackler 2011). In 2014 through 2016, killings of black males by white police officers across the United States—in Ferguson, Missouri; Cleveland, Ohio; Staten Island, New York; Charlotte, North Carolina; and Baltimore, Maryland—brought together blacks in those communities, as well as multiracial groups throughout the country, in an effort to deal with the problem and its roots. More recently, the wildfire that destroyed many properties in Gatlinburg and Pigeon Forge, Tennessee, saw collective efforts to raise funds to help those communities recover, including a telethon organized by country music singer Dolly Parton.

While social movements have been theorized separately and somewhat differently (resource mobilization theory), the dominant approach to thinking about other forms of collective action is **emergent norm theory** (Arthur and Lemonik 2013; Turner and Killian 1987). This theory is based on the idea that new norms emerge in light of some precipitating

A rash of widely publicized violence by white police officers against black males in several states led to many instances of collective action, including this rally in Charlotte, North Carolina, to protest the deaths of Michael Brown, Eric Garner, and others. Have you ever taken part in collective action? If not, what would it take to motivate you to do so?

event. These norms guide the often nontraditional actions that characterize collective behavior. Implicit in this theory is the idea that in collective behavior, conventional norms cease to be as effective or as important, at least to some degree. Contrary to popular opinion, however, collective behavior is not irrational, random, or out of control. It is rational and guided by the new norms that develop in the situation.

This conclusion was supported in a study of a 2003 Rhode Island nightclub fire in which 100 people were killed and nearly 200 people were injured (Aguirre et al. 2011). There was little evidence of irrational panic or panic-like behavior among those seeking to escape the fire. They didn't follow their impulses and try to save their own lives without regard for the lives of others. Instead, a norm quickly emerged whereby, rather than saving themselves, people had to help one another, even though there was a dire, life-threatening emergency. This was especially true for those who had close relationships with others also caught up in the event. People put themselves in danger of injury or even death to try to help those who were important to

them. More generally, people's behavior in such situations is affected by commitments they have to one another before the incident.

CROWDS

The clearest application of emergent norm theory to collective action involves the case of a **crowd**, a temporary gathering of a relatively large number of people in a common geographic location at a given time (McPhail 2007; Snow and Owens 2013). We are all familiar with all sorts of crowds, such as those that gather at the sites of celebrations or catastrophes, but a relatively new type is the flash crowd (or flash mob). Flash crowds have become easier to generate as a result of the internet, e-mail, and social networking sites. A flash crowd might gather, for example, to engage in a pillow fight. In fact, in 2008 a kind of global pillow fight took place, involving participants in two dozen cities around the world. In recent years, largely teenage flash crowds have come together in Philadelphia; they have been disorderly, gotten into fights, and attacked bystanders, and

Crisis Mapping

The proliferation of information and communication technologies such as mobile phones, social media, and wireless internet access has provided new tools that allow individuals to participate in humanitarian action and disaster response efforts. One of the most popular forms of "digital humanitarianism" is crisis mapping. This involves collecting data from "live" events, such as a natural disaster or political uprising (Givoni 2016; Ziemke 2012). This data may consist of text messages, tweets, or photos posted on Facebook by victims in need of assistance. All of this—and much more—is mapped by volunteers around the world on platforms like MicroMappers. MicroMappers provides an app called "Clickers" that volunteers—referred to as "digital jedis"—can easily use to organize tweets and photos into designated categories, such as "population displacement" or "infrastructure damage." Other data that might be mapped to help victims and first responders include emergency locations of refugee camps and triage centers.

Crisis mapping also involves creating maps of "unmapped" areas before disasters occur. The Missing Map Project asks "remote volunteers to trace satellite imagery into OpenStreetMap," a collaborative, openly licensed map of the world. Local volunteers on the ground digitally add more detailed data to the map, such as street names. The map is used by humanitarian agencies, principally Doctors Without Borders and the American and British Red Cross (www.missingmaps.org; Givoni 2016). Crisis mapping proved a critical tool in the humanitarian efforts to aid victims of the 2010 Haiti and the 2015 Nepal earthquakes.

Crisis mapping depends not only on digital technologies, but also on the social practices of crowdsourcing and crowdlearning (Ziemke 2012, 105). In fact, crisis mappers understand the crowd to be the main actor that makes digital humanitarian possible. Crowdsourcing is the foundation of crisis mappers. Data is freely shared over the internet by a large number of volunteers as a collaborative form of social action. Thus, the crowd is free from the control of any one organization that might attempt to standardize its behavior, set an agenda on what disasters deserve the most attention, or dictate how to respond to the disaster. During a disaster, the crowd learns "from watching others" (Ziemke 2012, 105–106). One of the most significant lessons that the crowd learns is that it has the power to create maps and empower victims to coordinate response efforts at the local level through the use of social media. However, Givoni (2016, 1039) cautions that because the crowd is "open-ended," it is too "fragile" to challenge the dominance of the global humanitarian organizations that are trying to manage it.

Engaging the Digital World
Visit Google's Crisis Map of weather hazards and emergencies (www.google.org/crisismap/weather_and_events), MicroMappers (http://micromappers.wordpress.com), or the Missing Map Project (www.missingmaps.org) and write a short report on your findings. How helpful do you think the maps and information provided are to residents, first responders, and agencies trying to collect donations to help victims in a disaster? How likely would you be to volunteer your time and to provide information that could help map a crisis?

police have cracked down on them in unnecessarily aggressive ways (Massaro and Mullaney 2011).

In the modern age, virtual crowds are becoming the new norm, such as through **crowdfunding** sites (Kickstarter, GoFundMe). People come together online from all across the country, or even the world, to fight for a common cause by offering financial support. Examples of crowdfunding include efforts to fund medical bills or travel fees, to raise money that will buy land to protect the environment, or even to support an author in publishing independent stories. Through crowdfunding, people can choose to support charities, businesses, education, and other endeavors. Together, all kinds of people achieve the same goal and represent the interconnectedness of the world through the internet.

One concern in the literature on crowds is the degree to which individuals behave differently in crowds than they do in other social contexts. Emergent norm theory suggests that they do behave differently, but that is because they are conforming to a different set of norms than exist elsewhere in the social world. That is more comforting than the alternative view, which sees people in crowds as losing control of their cognitive processes, complying blindly with the suggestions of crowd leaders, copying mindlessly what is done by those around them in the crowd, and acting selfishly. A large body of research has failed to find any support for the latter view (Postmes and Spears 1998; von Sivers et al. 2014).

Social media (Facebook, Twitter, etc.) help spread the word about crowdfunding opportunities, and people can also go directly to sites like GoFundMe and Kickstarter to look for opportunities to support causes. This is the opposite of the all-too-common social media phenomenon of trolling, where people whose names and faces are hidden by the anonymity of the internet will argue, disparage, and even threaten violence against others.

ASK YOURSELF

Do you behave differently when in a crowd than you do when alone? How, and why? Have you ever participating in crowdfunding? What prompted you to do so?

RIOTS

A **riot** is temporary unruly collective action that causes damage to persons or property (Myers 2007, 2013). There have been a number of major riots in the last half-century in the United States, including race riots in the 1960s in Los Angeles, Detroit, and Washington, D.C. One notable set of race riots occurred in Los Angeles in 1992 following the acquittal of four police officers charged with the beating of motorist Rodney King. A more recent, if less violent, riot occurred after the 2014 shooting death of an unarmed black man, Michael Brown, by a white police officer in Ferguson, Missouri. Riots, of course, have happened elsewhere in the world; they are a global phenomenon. For example, significant rioting and extensive looting and arson took place in London and in other cities in England in August 2011. Five people died in the riots.

Negative Views of Riots

We are likely to have negative views of riots and rioters. However, riots may not be irrational outbursts (Waddington 2015). Rather, they may be motivated by frustrations over various kinds of abuses and the inability to do much about them under normal circumstances (Auyero and Moran 2007). It is hard to generalize about rioters, but there is little support in the research for the idea that rioters are more likely to be criminals, unemployed, or uneducated. A few things seem clear about those who participate in riots. They are more likely to be men, to be young, to have been physically close to where the riots occur, and to feel that their actions can make a difference. The literature on police involvement in riots is also ambiguous, with police being seen as having the ability both to quell riots and to incite them further with repressive actions.

It is also worth noting that the mass media can contribute to rioting through the ways in which they treat riots. For one thing, live coverage of riots can inflame them by drawing in additional participants. Live, immediate media reports on rioting are also more likely to be inaccurate and to involve inflammatory reporting. For another thing, media reports of riots can suggest that this is a form of action to be emulated at other places and times. Social media can also quickly draw large numbers of people to riot sites.

Positive Effects of Riots

Riots can have positive effects. The Los Angeles riots of 1992, known as the Rodney King riots, undoubtedly led to changes and improvements in the way the police deal with suspects and the general public, although similar incidents continue to be reported. More generally, riots have at times led to various programs designed to deal with the conditions that were seen to be at their source, such as poverty and unemployment. However, the lasting power of these changes is unclear, and, in any case, people are injured and die, and communities are ruined, in riots. In some cases, it takes decades for riot sites to recover (Cannon 1997; Schoch and Lin 2007; Spencer 2004).

DISASTERS

Disasters are often dealt with in sociology in the same context as social change and social movements. The reason is that disasters can result from social change (such as the "reign of terror" in the aftermath of the French Revolution) and social movements (such as the millions of deaths as a result of the rise of Nazism). Disasters can also cause various social changes (such as the building of earthquake-resistant buildings after a devastating earthquake) and lead to social movements (such as for democracy in Germany at the end of World War II in the wake of the disaster caused by the Nazis).

Disasters are events that suddenly, unexpectedly, and severely disrupt and harm the environment, the social structure, people, and their property (Silver 2007). They are distinguished from accidents (e.g., automobile and airplane crashes) by their far greater impact. Many U.S. disasters have resulted in billions of dollars' worth of damage, and the numbers of such huge disasters have increased in recent years (see Figure 18.3). One disaster in the news in 2010 was the earthquake in Haiti that decimated a significant portion of that Caribbean nation, which shares an island (Hispaniola) with the Dominican Republic. No one knows the exact numbers, but it is estimated that more than 200,000 people were killed and another 300,000 were injured. Innumerable poorly constructed homes, schools, and other buildings were destroyed. The government virtually ceased functioning as its offices collapsed, literally and

FIGURE 18.3 • Billion-Dollar Weather and Climate Disasters in the United States, 1980–2016

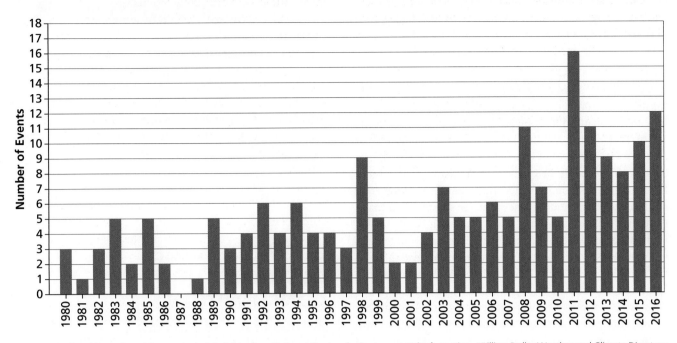

SOURCE: National Oceanic and Atmospheric Administration, National Centers for Environmental Information, "Billion-Dollar Weather and Climate Disasters: Time Series," 1980–2016.

figuratively, and many officials were killed or injured (Bhatty 2010). By as late as 2014, little progress had been made in rebuilding homes and the infrastructure in Haiti ("Haiti, Unfinished" 2014; Sontag 2012). While it is a stark example, the earthquake in Haiti represents just one of many natural disasters that have occurred in recent years. Most notable in 2015 was a devastating earthquake in Nepal that killed more than 8,000 people and destroyed much infrastructure, including many poorly constructed homes and buildings (Associated Press 2015).

Human Involvement in Disasters

Disasters such as earthquakes are natural phenomena, but humans often play a role in bringing disasters about and in exacerbating the consequences of natural disasters. People frequently build in areas—for example, on geological fault lines or on floodplains—where there should be no significant building. Furthermore, what they build is often quite flimsy and likely to be destroyed in a natural disaster. Building stronger structures can be very costly, and impoverished nations such as Haiti simply cannot afford it (Interlandi 2010).

There are, of course, disasters that are the result of human error or corruption. On April 20, 2010, a huge explosion on the BP *Deepwater Horizon* oil rig in the Gulf of Mexico killed 11 workers and left oil gushing into the gulf for three months ("Louisiana Oil Rig" 2010). During that period, 206 million U.S. gallons of oil flowed into

the water, affecting nearly 1,000 miles of coastline (Morris et al. 2013). There had been warnings for decades about the dangers associated with deep-sea drilling and oil wells. However, such drilling was pushed forward by the desire for ever-escalating profits on the part of corporations like BP and the voracious need for oil in the United States and other developed nations. Once the *Deepwater Horizon* oil gusher occurred, it became clear that no one quite knew how to go about stopping it; the well was not finally capped until July 15. The spilled oil caused great damage to the gulf's marine life, its beaches, and the businesses that depend on tourists drawn to the area.

Recall from Chapter 6 that the space shuttle *Challenger* disintegrated a little over a minute into its flight on January 28, 1986, killing all seven crew members (Altabbakh et al. 2013; Vaughan 1996). To get needed funds and to launch space shuttles in a timely manner, NASA had ignored warnings, taken risks, and tolerated mistakes and deception. While Vaughan (1996) views this disaster as a unique occurrence, Charles Perrow (1999) sees such accidents as "normal." That is, highly complex systems such as those associated with NASA and the space shuttle will inevitably have such disasters, although they happen only rarely.

Human-made disasters also can be political in nature, and they are associated with revolutions, riots, and acts of terrorism. For example, in mid-2010, the center of Bangkok, Thailand, was ravaged by riots aimed at overthrowing the government. And then, of course, there was the 9/11 disaster caused by hijackers crashing planes into the World Trade Center towers and the Pentagon, as well as the downing of one plane before it reached its target. These terrorist attacks resulted in the deaths of nearly 3,000 people.

The Effects of Disasters

Disasters have enormous negative long-term consequences for the people and areas involved. Individuals and collectivities are traumatized for long periods after disasters (Erikson 1976). People's lives are disrupted for years, if not decades, as are the social networks in which they are enmeshed. Disasters also worsen existing inequalities. For example, females in Haiti suffered disproportionately from the effects of the 2010 earthquake. Furthermore, they were less likely than males to receive humanitarian aid in the aftermath of the quake. Haitian women were more likely than their male counterparts to live in tents, which, among other things, provided them little protection and security. They were especially vulnerable to "unwanted sexual advances and assault" (Jean-Charles 2010). Negative effects on social life persisted for years. Among other things, family life was disrupted. More specifically, there was an increase in the proclivity to commit physical and sexual violence against intimate partners for a year or two beyond the quake (Weitzman and Behrman 2016).

However, some people and groups are in a better position than others to handle disasters. Disasters can also bring people and communities together in unprecedented ways to deal with the aftereffects. The heroism of many of those involved in helping after the 9/11 disaster—firefighters, police officers, and citizens—is one example of this (Fritsch 2001; Rozdeba 2011; Saxon 2003). Within Haiti, a number of aid agencies are working to continue to provide aid to women and girls, including the UN Population Fund, the World Food Programme, and World Vision. In addition, "cash for work" programs, instituted by the Haitian Ministry of Women's Affairs, helped 100,000 women displaced by the earthquake survive (Jean-Charles 2010). Moreover, in response to the increased vulnerability of women and girls, Femmes Citoyennes Haiti Solidaire, or Women Citizens Haiti United, formed an alliance of activists to continue addressing gender inequality and injustices within Haiti.

However, efforts to help sometimes cause great problems. In the case of Haiti, some of the UN peacekeepers who were brought in to help introduced cholera from Nepal. A UN-commissioned contractor dumped the contents of the peacekeepers' septic tanks, teeming with the bacteria that causes cholera, into a river. As a result, by 2016, 10,000 Haitians had died from the disease, and thousands more are being infected every month At first, the UN denied that its peacekeepers were responsible for the outbreak despite early evidence to the contrary. The UN's denial and failure to act to deal with the crisis led to many more people contracting cholera and to many more deaths from the disease (Piarroux 2016).

CHECKPOINT 18.3: COLLECTIVE ACTION

TYPE OF ACTION	DESCRIPTION
Crowd	A temporary gathering of a large number of people in the same location
Riot	A temporary unruly collective action that causes damage to persons or property
Disaster	An event that unexpectedly and severely disrupts and harms the environment, the social structure, and people

SOCIAL CHANGE: GLOBALIZATION, CONSUMPTION, AND THE INTERNET

Social change is intimately connected to the topics discussed in the first part of this chapter. Social movements, especially those that are successful, often lead to major social changes. For example, the women's, LGBTQ, and civil rights movements have all led, and continue to lead, to such social changes. Collective action is less likely to lead to social change, but there have certainly been many examples of crowd behavior, riots, and disasters that have led to change. For example, the Los Angeles race riots of 1992 and the more recent demonstrations in Ferguson, Missouri, led to changes not only in police behavior but also in efforts to deal with the underlying causes of the riots.

Although social change occurs throughout the social world, it is particularly characteristic of the three areas that are the signature concerns of this book—globalization, consumption, and the internet. Globalization is, of course, a social process of relatively recent origin; it is changing the world in which we live and is likely to lead to a variety of even more dramatic changes in the future. For example, the changing nature of the global economy, especially the shift of its center away from the United States and in the direction of China and Asia more generally, means that the job prospects of Americans are changing and apt to change even more in the future. Some economic prospects have declined, especially those that relate to the production of goods and the jobs associated with it. However, others have improved. New jobs have arisen—especially those that involve computers and the internet. Clearly, the internet is important not only in this sense but also because it is an arena in which great and extremely rapid change has taken place in recent years. It is an arena that will certainly continue to change and to affect our lives in innumerable ways. The changes discussed here—globalization, the economy, and the internet—are related to the changing nature of our other core concern—consumption. Consumption has itself become increasingly global as, for example, more of the things we buy come from outside the United States. The American economy has shifted away from one dominated by production to one dominated by consumption. It is clear that more consumption is taking place through the internet, and that trend can only accelerate in the future.

GLOBALIZATION AS THE ULTIMATE SOCIAL CHANGE

Prior to the current epoch of globalization, one of the things that characterized people, things, information, places, and much else was their greater solidity. That is, all of them tended to (figuratively) harden over time and, therefore, among other things, to remain largely in place. As a result, people did not venture very far from where they were born and raised. Their social relationships were limited to those who were nearby. Much the same could be said of most objects (tools, food), which tended to be used where they were produced. The solidity of most material manifestations of information (stone tablets, books) also made them at least somewhat difficult to move very far. Furthermore, because people didn't move very far, neither did information. Places, too, were not only quite solid and immovable but tended to be surrounded by solid barriers (mountains, oceans, walls, borders) that made it difficult for people and things to exit or to enter.

Global "Liquids"

At an increasing rate over the last few centuries, and especially in the last several decades, what once seemed so solid has tended to "melt." Instead of thinking of people, objects, information, and places as being like solid blocks of ice, we need to see them as tending to melt and as becoming increasingly liquid (Beilharz 2012). Needless to say, it is far more difficult to move blocks of ice than it is to move the water that is produced when those blocks melt. Of course, to extend the metaphor, there continue to exist blocks of ice, even glaciers, in the contemporary world that have not melted, at least not completely. Solid material realities, such as people, cargo, and newspapers, continue to exist, but because of a wide range of technological developments in transportation, communication, and the internet, they can move across the globe far more readily.

Thus, following the work of Zygmunt Bauman (1925–2017; 2000, 2003, 2005, 2006), the perspective on globalization presented here involves increasing liquidity (Lakoff 2008; Ritzer and Dean 2015). There is a constant interplay between liquidity and solidity, with increases in what is

Zygmunt Bauman first studied sociology while he served in the Polish military and went on to teach at universities in Europe and Israel. Among his notable contributions to the field are his work on the problems associated with the rationalized modern world and the increasing liquidity associated with late modernity and globalization.

liquid (e.g., terrorist attacks launched against Israel from the West Bank) leading to counterreactions and the erection of new solid forms (a fence between Israel and the West Bank). However, at the moment and for the foreseeable future, the momentum lies with increasing and proliferating global liquidity.

Global "Flows"

Closely related to the idea of liquidity, and integral to it, is another key concept in thinking about globalization, the idea of "flows" (Appadurai 1996; Inda 2012). After all, liquids flow easily, far more easily than solids. Because so much of the world has "melted," or is in the process of "melting," globalization is increasingly characterized by great flows of increasingly liquid phenomena of all types, including people, objects, information, decisions, and places. In many cases, the flows have become raging floods that are increasingly less likely to be impeded by place-based barriers of any kind, including the oceans, mountains, and especially the borders of nation-states. This was demonstrated once again in late 2008 in the spread of the American credit and financial crisis to Europe and elsewhere: "In a global financial system, national borders are porous" (Landler 2008, C1).

Looking at a very different kind of flow, as we saw in Chapter 17, many people in many parts of the world believe that they are being swamped by migrants, especially poor undocumented migrants (Moses 2006). This is especially true of concerns in the United States about migrants from Latin America and in Europe about Muslim immigrants (Ahmed 2013). Whether or not these are actually floods, they have come to be seen as such by many people, often aided by politicians and media personalities who have established their reputations by portraying migrants in that way. Places, too, can be said to be flowing around the world, as immigrants re-create the places (and cultures) from which they come in new locales (Logan, Alba, and Zhang 2002; Sarwal 2012).

Ideas, images, and information, both legal (blogs) and illegal (child pornography), flow everywhere, undoubtedly because of their immateriality. They do so through interpersonal contact and the media, especially now via the internet. Much of what would have been considered the height of global liquidity only a few years ago now seems increasingly sludgelike. This is especially the case when we focus on the impact of the computer and the internet on the global flow of all sorts of things. For example, instead of scouring an import VHS catalog and waiting weeks for an anime movie to ship from Japan, a person can simply open the Netflix app on her console and stream any number of anime movies instantly.

ASK YOURSELF

What aspects of your life can you imagine as "liquids"? Which seem like "flows"? What do you imagine these elements looked like 20 years ago, before the advent of globalization?

GLOBALIZATION AND THE INTERNET

Since its birth in the 1990s, the internet has profoundly affected almost every aspect of life, especially in the developed world. The internet has expedited the globalization of many different things and is itself a profound form and aspect of globalization (Powell 2012). The internet is global in several senses, but the most important is that while its users are not equally divided between North and South, rich and poor, and so on, they *do* exist virtually everywhere in the world (Drori 2006, 2012). It is also global in the sense that it was produced and is maintained by a number of global and transnational corporations and organizations, including multinational corporations (such as Intel), intergovernmental organizations, and international nongovernmental organizations. For instance, the World Intellectual Property Organization regulates intellectual property rights, the Internet Corporation for Assigned Names and Numbers coordinates domain names, and the UN Educational, Scientific, and Cultural Organization promotes computer and internet use in schools throughout the world.

Computer Viruses

The idea of a computer virus made its first appearance in science fiction in the late 1960s and early 1970s. More than a decade later, a graduate student wrote the first program that was able to replicate and propagate itself. His professor, seeing its similarity to a biological phenomenon, suggested that it be called a "computer virus." The first global computer virus was likely created in Pakistan in 1986. Since then, of course, many different viruses—some benign, some malicious (malware)—have been created, have circled the globe, and in some cases have caused great damage to computer systems. For example, some of these viruses (Win32/Fareit, Mariposa) "infect" personal computers and access users' information, such as credit card numbers, which the cyberthieves then use to purchase all sorts of goods and services illegally. At the same time, global organizations, including law enforcement agencies, have emerged to try to warn people about new viruses and malware—so-called *Trojans* and *worms*—and to develop countermeasures to protect against them (Chanda 2007). To the degree that they are successful, the latter are barriers to the largely free flow of computer viruses around the globe.

It is clear that no change has done more to further the process of globalization than the advent of the internet (Subramanian 2012). It occupies pride of place in many analyses of globalization. Perhaps the most famous of these is Thomas Friedman's (2005) analysis of globalization as involving a "flat world"; the major example of such a world is the internet. The internet is flat in the sense that virtually anyone, anywhere can, at least theoretically, become involved in it. However, it is important to remember that many poor and undeveloped communities still lack internet access.

Cyberactivism

For those who do have internet access, the opportunity to connect with like-minded individuals across the country and around the world has contributed to the rise of **cyberactivism**, or using social media and other internet-based communication methods to create, promote, or manage activism. Recent examples of cyberactivism include the ALS (Amyotropic Lateral Sclerosis) Ice Bucket Challenge, which raised several million dollars to increase awareness about that disease; Greenpeace's Greenwire, which digitally connects volunteers with environmental campaigns; and the Women's March on Washington, which was organized online and generated global demonstrations involving millions of women and men. While cyberactivism has taken some dramatic new directions, it came of age with the creation of the World Social Forum.

The relationship between globalization and cyberactivism has been demonstrated more recently in a wide range of forms of e-activism, including hashtag activism. The latter term is derived from the use of hashtags (#) on Twitter to

World Social Forum

The World Social Forum (WSF) was formed in 2001. It has its roots in the 1999 protests against the World Trade Organization in Seattle. A key concern of the protesters was the lack of democracy in global economic and political affairs. The WSF is, by design, not a social movement; rather, it is an arena in which like-minded people can exchange ideas on specific social movements and global issues. The very diversity of the movements and people involved in the WSF makes the development of concrete political proposals, not to mention actions, difficult. The WSF continues to struggle with this issue and its identity and role in globalization.

The WSF is a huge social network, and it is based on the "cultural logic of networking" (see Chapter 6 for a discussion of network organizations). Such networking includes the creation of horizontal ties and connections among diverse and autonomous elements, the free and open communication of information among and between those elements, decentralized coordination among the elements that involves democratic decision making, and networking that is self-directed (Juris 2005).

The internet has given the WSF in particular, and more generally those opposed to globalization (or to some specific aspect of it), a powerful series of tools with which to mount their opposition on a regional and even a global basis. Those tools include social media such as Facebook, Twitter, and You Tube, as well as the smartphones that link activists to those sites anytime and virtually anywhere. Indeed, even the now-primitive forms of those tools played an important role in the origins of the anti-globalization social movement at the World Trade Organization meetings in Seattle in 1999. It was based on cyberactivism, as were the ensuing protests in Washington, D.C., Prague, Genoa, and elsewhere in the world (Pleyers 2010). The WSF itself was made possible by such activism (Kohler 2012; Sen et al. 2004; Smith et al. 2011).

The WSF was born of the idea that protests about the evils of globalization are insufficient. That is, there is a need for more positive and concrete proposals to deal with such issues, as well as for a forum in which these proposals can be generated. The WSF's slogan has been "Another world is possible" (Teivainen 2007). That is, there must be, and there is, an alternative to the free market capitalism that has dominated the world economically and politically (Smith 2008). Although the slogan is powerful and has facilitated the coordination of large and diverse groups, the WSF has not yet produced concrete actions and policies to make "another world" a reality.

spread the word about a particular cause. Those involved are not required to take any action; they merely indicate their support by, for example, liking a tweet or retweeting something they approve of.

ASK YOURSELF

What would it take to make an alternative to free market capitalism a reality? What would such a system be like? Would it be viable for the long term? Why or why not?

WikiLeaks, Edward Snowden, and Global Surveillance. WikiLeaks is one of the most notable and controversial examples of cyberactivism. A global audience for its release of private documents has developed. The release of such documents often exposes behavior and planning hidden from the public. While WikiLeaks' home was originally in Sweden, it is now hosted by a number of servers around the world.

In 2010, WikiLeaks began releasing classified diplomatic cables between Washington and many of its consulates around the world. Later that year, documents were released—some classified as confidential or secret—relating to the Afghanistan and Iraq wars. The documents implicated numerous officials around the world in questionable, if not illegal, acts. Many lost their positions or suffered other adverse consequences as a result of the documents' release. In addition, revelations from leaked cables from the U.S. Embassy played a key role in launching the revolution in Tunisia and thereby ultimately in the wider rebellion known as the Arab Spring.

Edward Snowden is an American computer specialist and whistleblower who was employed by a contractor associated with the National Security Agency (NSA; see the 2016 movie *Snowden*). Claiming that he was disturbed by the misuse of U.S. surveillance programs, Snowden copied and eventually released through the conventional news media (e.g. *The New York Times*, *The Guardian*) classified NSA information (Greenwald 2014). Early on, he was

Graffiti outside the World Social Forum in Mumbai seems to reflect the group's stance against the lack of democracy in world economic and political decisions. Although inspired by the conviction that concrete alternatives to free market capitalism must be developed, the group has yet to offer any. What alternatives should the WSF offer?

helped by WikiLeaks personnel when he fled first to Hong Kong and then to Moscow, where he has been ever since. However, Snowden has been critical of WikiLeaks for insufficient oversight over the information it released. It did not edit and remove sensitive information, especially about the identity of people mentioned in the leaks (Chokshi 2016). As a result, Snowden chose to release further information through the more traditional news media because he felt that he could exercise greater control over what information was—and was not—released. While the initial news releases appeared in the United States, Great Britain, and Germany, the information was quickly disseminated globally.

The information released by Snowden revealed that the NSA, in cooperation with similar agencies in Australia, Canada, and the United Kingdom, had been operating a global surveillance system. Among other things, these agencies derived user data from online service providers (e.g., Google), read e-mails, tracked peoples' browsing patterns and histories as well as their social media activities, and so on. These revelations were explosive, particularly when it was revealed that the NSA was spying on leaders of allied nations, such as Germany.

From the point of view of globalization, the key points are, first, that the NSA's surveillance program involved global power alignments among secret government agencies (Lyon 2015a, 2015b). Second, the revelations about the program and its excesses were publicized globally. Finally, the implications of, and reactions to, the program were similarly global in scope. To some degree, at least, reforms also took place globally.

While some people see Snowden as a hero for revealing some of the government's dirty secrets, others see him as committing treason in revealing classified information that adversely affected what the U.S. government (and others) considered to be important surveillance operations.

Edward Snowden has been celebrated by many privacy advocates and others concerned with government overreach. Balloons like this one, attached to a replica of the Statue of Liberty in Paris, were part of an effort by Amnesty International to press President Barack Obama to pardon Snowden before leaving office. Do you believe Snowden deserves a pardon?

While the U.S. government continues to threaten to arrest Snowden if he leaves Russia, in 2016 human rights groups urged that he be pardoned by President Obama, who did not do so. Needless to say, his unlikely to be pardoned by President Trump. Nevertheless, human rights groups continue see such a pardon as important in preventing abuses of power, protecting whistleblowers, and, more generally, in maintaining a free society (Naheem 2015; Savage 2016).

CONSUMPTION AND GLOBALIZATION

There has been a tendency to associate consumption with America and, as far as the globe is concerned, with Americanization. This is largely traceable to the affluence of the United States after the close of World War II and the economic difficulties encountered by most other societies in the world during that period. Thus, the United States developed an unprecedented and unmatched consumer society for several decades after the end of the war. At the same time, it began exporting consumer society—and its various elements—to much of the rest of the world. Much of American consumer society came to be adopted elsewhere in the world. However, it was also modified in various ways, even in the immediate aftermath of World War II, in the European nations ravaged by the war and being aided through America's Marshall Plan (Kroen 2006). Stillerman (2015) argues that, in fact, the major areas for the expansion of consumer society are not in the Global North (mainly the United States and Europe), but in the less developed Global South. While much about consumption there is the same or similar, there are also distinctive patterns of consuming an array of unique products and services. Beyond its sources in the United States and the Global North, consumption has roots in many other places in the world. Consumption as a central life interest is now a truly global phenomenon; we have increasingly become "a world of consumers" (Trentmann 2016)

The latter point brings us to the issue of globalization and consumption (Brandle and Ryan 2012; Chen and Ritzer 2015). The emphasis in the global economy is on greatly increasing flows of everything related to consumption and greatly decreasing any barriers to those flows. Especially important is expediting global flows of consumer goods and services of all types and of the financial processes and instruments that facilitate those flows. Thus, for example, the relatively small number of credit (and debit) card brands with origins in the United States, especially Visa and MasterCard, are increasingly accepted and used throughout the world (Ritzer 1995). They are usable at ATMs and at checkout counters at various businesses throughout the world. Especially notable in this regard are online consumption sites, some of them global in reach, that allow people to consume many of the same products using their credit cards.

Credit cards serve to expedite not only global consumption but also the flow of global consumers, including tourists.

Local and Regional Differences

There was, and continues to be, a significant American component to the globalization of consumption. However, it is important to recognize that the heyday of the United States in this area is long past. In any case, there has always been much more to the globalization of consumption than Americanization (Brewer and Trentmann 2006). That is, local areas have certainly not always, or perhaps ever, been overwhelmed by American imports, but have integrated them into local cultural and economic realities. Furthermore, other nations and regions have been significant exporters of important aspects of consumer society, such as Mercedes-Benz and BMW automobiles from Germany. Finally, much of consumption remains largely, if not totally, local in character. One example is the growing consumption of a mild stimulant, khat, or *qat,* in Kenya, where it is defined in a highly positive way locally. In addition, there is active resistance to external definitions of it, especially the U.S. definition of khat as a dangerous drug (Anderson and Carrier 2006).

Consumption also plays itself out differently in different parts of the world. For example, both the United States and Japan can be seen as consumer societies, but Japanese consumers differ from their U.S. counterparts in many ways. The Japanese have never fully embraced the idea of a consumer society. More specifically, unlike Americans, the Japanese continue to manage to save significant amounts of money (Garon 2006).

While many consumer objects and services remain highly local (e.g., the khat mentioned previously, the services of street-based letter writers for illiterate Indians), an increasing number have been globalized. On the one hand are the global objects, such as automobiles from the United States, Germany, and Japan. On the other hand are global services, such as those offered by accounting firms like KPMG International, as well as package delivery services like DHL.

The Globalization of Consumers

Increasing numbers of people throughout the world are spending more and more time as consumers. Not long ago it was very different, as most people spent most of their time as producers, or workers. Not only do more people spend more time consuming; they are also increasingly likely to define themselves by what they consume—Bimmers, Patek Philippe watches, and so on—rather than by their jobs or the companies for which they work. Furthermore, consumers are on the move throughout the world, often as tourists. Tourism itself is a form of consumption, and much tourism is undertaken by people seeking to consume the goods and services on offer at other locales throughout the world (Gotham 2015; Weaver 2012).

Increasing numbers of people throughout the world know what is expected of them as consumers. They generally know what to do in the consumption process wherever they happen to be in the world. This includes knowing how to work their way through a tourist resort or a shopping mall, use a credit card, and make a purchase online. Others have not yet encountered, let alone learned how to handle, these processes, but many of them certainly will in the not-too-distant future. Where these processes of consumption are known, there is remarkable similarity throughout the world.

Global Brands

A **brand** is a symbol that serves to identify and differentiate one product or service from others. A brand can be contrasted with, and seeks to differentiate itself from, generic commodities such as flour and soap (Arvidsson 2012; Holt 2004; Muniz 2007; Schroeder 2015). The process of branding a product or service is undertaken because, if successful, not only is the brand distinguished from the basic commodity—also, more of it can be sold and at a higher price. We are all familiar with the most successful brands in the world (Apple, Coca-Cola, McDonald's, Walmart, Mercedes, and so on), and much consumption is oriented toward the purchase of brand-name products and services. Furthermore, even people come to be brand names (Michael Jordan, Angelina Jolie) and as such are "consumed" globally to a large degree. As brands themselves, they come to be closely associated with various brand-name products, the best-known example being the association of Michael Jordan with Nike and Hanes (Andrews and Mower 2012).

Nike is one of those brands that has made itself so important that it can be said to have created a culture, and, to some degree, we live in Nike culture (Goldman and Papson 1998; Hollister 2008). However, that culture is but a part of the larger *brand culture* in which we live. That is, brands are a key part of the larger culture: They infuse it with meaning, and contemporary society as a whole is profoundly affected by brands (Schroeder 2007).

Brands are of great importance not only within the United States and many other nations but also globally. Indeed, much money and effort is invested in creating brand names that are recognized and trusted throughout the world. Klein ([2000] 2010) details the importance of brands in the contemporary world and the degree to which they are globalized—corporate logos are virtually an international language—and have global impacts.

CHECKPOINT 18.4: GLOBAL PROCESSES AND SOCIAL CHANGE

PROCESS	DESCRIPTION
Global liquids	The ability for both nonmaterial and solid material realities to move more readily across the world
Global flows	The increasing mobility of global liquids

SUMMARY

Social change creates variations over time in every aspect of the social world. Social movements are sustained and intentional collective efforts, usually operating outside established institutional channels, either to bring about social change or to prevent it. Prominent social movements include the Tea Party, feminist movements, the LGBTQ movement, and the civil rights movement.

The emergence of a social movement requires a set of grievances, efforts at mobilization, opportunities within the political system, the proximity of people, the availability of free space to meet, and the availability of resources. Factors that affect the success of a social movement include its size and uniqueness, as well as other groups' ability to suppress the movement. When successful, a social movement can leave a lasting legacy. Unlike social movements, some collective action is short-lived and spontaneous. For example, crowds are temporary gatherings of a large number of people in a common geographic location. Riots, responses to disasters, and cyberactivism are other types of collective action that lack the organizational structure, resources, and leadership of social movements.

Globalization is arguably the most important change in human history and is characterized by great flows of liquid phenomena across the globe. The internet is both a form and an aspect of globalization and has expedited globalization. The global economy focuses on increasing the flows of everything related to consumption and reducing the barriers to these flows.

KEY TERMS

brand, 532

collective action, 521

crowd, 522

crowdfunding, 523

cyberactivism, 528

disasters, 524

emergent norm
  theory, 521

feminism, 510

resource mobilization
  theory, 518

riot, 524

social change, 506

social
  movement, 507

REVIEW QUESTIONS

1. What about the Tea Party makes it a social movement? What were the conditions that brought about the emergence of the Tea Party movement?

2. What have been the three different waves of the women's movement? How did the goals and strategies of the women's movement change during each of these three waves?

3. How have new communication technologies like the internet and social networking sites (Facebook and Twitter) aided global social movements? What types of resources move more easily because of these new technologies?

4. According to resource mobilization theory, what do groups of people need in order to mobilize effectively? How can we apply this theory to the discussion of the civil rights movement in this chapter?

5. What mechanisms do social movements use to ensure member participation? How are these mechanisms related to the LGBTQ movements discussed in this chapter?

6. What factors are used to determine whether a social movement is successful? How has the Tea Party movement been

successful to date? Has there been any resistance to the movement? What has given it renewed impetus? How might these things affect the movement's future success?

7. According to emergent norm theory, why are individuals likely to behave differently when they are in crowds? How can we explain some deviant behavior in bars (such as fighting or public displays of affection) using emergent norm theory?

8. The 2011 earthquake and tsunami in Japan and the 2015 earthquake in Nepal are examples of disasters. In what ways did humans exacerbate the consequences of these natural disasters? What sorts of negative long-term consequences can be expected from disasters like these?

9. In what ways is globalization the "ultimate social change"? How has the world become more liquid because of globalization? What role have new communication technologies played in making the world more liquid?

10. Why is branding an important process to transnational corporations? In what ways is branding reflective of the process of Americanization?

GLOSSARY

absolute poverty: An absolute measure—such as the U.S. poverty line—that makes it clear what level of income people need in order to survive.

achieved status: A position acquired by people on the basis of what they accomplish or the nature of their capacities.

achievement: The accomplishments, or the merit, of the individual.

affirmative action: A process aimed at increasing diversity and equal opportunity by taking race and other minority group factors into consideration in making various decisions, especially those related to hiring.

agency: The potential to disrupt or destroy the structures in which one finds oneself.

agents of socialization: Those who socialize others.

alienation: In a capitalist system, being unconnected to one's work, products, fellow workers, and human nature.

Americanization: The importation by other countries of products, images, technologies, practices, norms, values, and behaviors that are closely associated with the United States.

anomie: The feeling of not knowing what is expected of one in society or of being adrift in society without any clear, secure moorings.

anti-Americanism: An aversion to the United States in general, as well as to the influence of its culture abroad.

anticipatory socialization: The teaching (and learning) of what will be expected of one in the future.

ascribed status: A position in which individuals are placed, or to which they move, that has nothing to do with what they have done or their capacities or accomplishments.

ascription: Being born with or inheriting certain characteristics (wealth, high status, and so on).

assimilation: The integration of minorities into the dominant culture.

asylum seekers: People who flee their home country, usually in an effort to escape political oppression or religious persecution.

authority: A particular type of domination: legitimate domination.

back stage: The part of the social world where people feel free to express themselves in ways that are suppressed in the front stage.

beliefs: Ideas that explain the world and identify what should be sacred or held in awe—that is, a religion's ultimate concerns.

birthrate: The number of births per 1,000 people per year.

blended family: A family that includes some combination of children from the partners' previous marriages or relationships, along with one or more children of the currently married or cohabiting couple.

bounded rationality: Rationality limited by, among other things, instabilities and conflicts within most, if not all, organizations, as well as by the limited human capacity to think and act in a rational manner.

brand: A symbol that serves to identify and differentiate one product or service from others.

bureaucracy: A highly rational organization, especially one that is highly efficient.

bureaucratic personality: A type of bureaucrat who slavishly follows the rules of the organization, to such an extent that the ability to achieve organizational goals is subverted.

butterfly effect: The far-ranging or even global impact of a small change in a specific location, over both time and distance.

capitalism: In Marx's view, an economic system based on one group of people (the capitalists, or owners) owning what is needed for production and a second group (the proletariat, or workers) owning little but their capacity for work.

capitalists: Those who own what is needed for production—factories, machines, tools—in a capitalist system.

cathedrals of consumption: Large and lavish consumption sites, created mostly in the United States in the last half of the twentieth century and into the early twenty-first century.

cenogamy: Group marriage.

charismatic authority: Authority based on the devotion of the followers to what they define as the exceptional characteristics, such as heroism, of the leaders.

church: A large group of religiously oriented people into which members are usually born (instead of joining consciously and voluntarily).

cities: Large, permanent, and spatially concentrated human settlements.

citizens: The people represented by a given state, most often born within its territories.

citizenship: The idea that people of a given state can vote for their representatives within the state, but also that they have access to rights and responsibilities as citizens.

civil religion: The beliefs, practices, and symbols that a nation holds sacred.

class consciousness: According to Marx, a mental state in which the workers (proletariat) come to truly understand capitalism, their collective role in it, and their relationship to one another, as well as to the capitalists; this exists when large numbers of people have a true sense of their interests.

cohabitation: An arrangement in which a couple share a home and a bed without being legally married.

collective action: Action generated, or engaged in, by a group of people to encourage or retard social change.

collective conscience: The set of beliefs shared by people throughout society.

colonialism: A method of gaining control over another country or geographic area; generally involves settlers as well as formal mechanisms of control.

companionate love: A kind of love typified by gradual onset and not necessarily tied to sexual passion, but based on more rational assessments of the one who is loved.

companionate marriage: A marriage emphasizing a clear division of labor between a breadwinner and a homemaker and held together by sentiment, friendship, and sexuality. The predominant model of marriage in the mid-twentieth century. *See also* companionate love.

competitive capitalism: A form of capitalism where there are a large number of relatively small firms, with the result that no one or small subset of them can completely dominate and control a given area of the economy.

conflict theory: A theory that sees society as held together by coercion and focuses on its negative aspects.

conformists: People who accept both cultural goals and the traditional means of achieving those goals.

consensual sexual activities: Sexual activities agreed upon by the participants, any of whom have the right to decide to stop at any point and for any reason.

conspicuous consumption: The public demonstration of wealth through consumption.

constructionist theories: Theories of deviance that seek a greater understanding of the process by which people define and classify some behaviors as normal and others as deviant.

consumer crimes: Crimes related to consumption, including shoplifting and using stolen credit cards or credit card numbers.

consumer culture: A culture in which the core ideas and material objects relate to consumption and in which consumption is a primary source of meaning in life.

consumerism: An obsession with consumption.

consumption: The process by which people obtain and utilize goods and services.

content analysis: Systematic and objective analysis of the content of cultural artifacts in print, visual, audio, and digital media, using both qualitative and quantitative analysis.

convenience samples: Readily available groups of people who fit the criteria for participating in a research project.

conversation analysis: Analysis of how people accomplish conversations.

corporate crime: Violation of the law by legal organizations, including antitrust violations and stock market violations.

cosmopolitan: Open to a variety of external and global influences.

countercultures: Groups whose culture not only differs in certain ways from the dominant culture but also adheres to norms and values that may be incompatible with those of the dominant culture.

credentialism: The linkage between educational degrees and high-status positions.

crime: A violation of the criminal law.

criminalization: The process by which the legal system negatively sanctions some form of deviant behavior.

criminology: The study of all aspects of crime.

critical theories of race and racism: A set of ideas arguing that race continues to matter and that racism continues to exist and adversely affect blacks.

critical theory: A set of critical ideas derived from Marxian theory but focusing on culture rather than the economy.

crowd: A temporary gathering of a relatively large number of people in a common geographic location at a given time.

crowdfunding: Collective action in which people come together online from all across the country, or even the world, to financially support a common cause.

crystallization status: *See* status inconsistency.

cult: A new, innovative, small, voluntary, and exclusive religious tradition that was never associated with any religious organization.

cultural dopes: People who are controlled unthinkingly by a variety of external forces, such as school rules or teacher demands.

cultural imperialism: The imposition of one culture, more or less consciously, on other cultures.

cultural relativism: The idea that aspects of culture such as norms and values need to be understood within the context of a person's own culture and that there are no universally accepted norms and values.

culture: A collection of ideas, values, practices, and material objects that mean a great deal to a group of people, even an entire society, and that allow them to carry out their collective lives in relative order and harmony.

culture industry: The rationalized and bureaucratized structures that control modern culture.

culture jamming: The radical transformation of an intended message in popular culture, especially one associated with the mass media, to protest underlying realities of which consumers may be unaware.

culture war: A conflict that pits subcultures and countercultures against the dominant culture or that pits dominant groups within society against each other.

cumulative advantage: The process by which the most advantaged individuals are awarded the best opportunities, which increases inequality over time.

cyberactivism: Using social media and other internet-based communication methods to create, promote, or manage activism.

cybercrime: Crime that targets computers, uses computers to commit traditional crimes, or uses computers to transmit illegal information and images.

cyberculture: An emerging online culture that has the characteristics of all culture, including distinctive values and norms.

dangerous giant: An entity that has agency.

debunking: Looking beneath and beyond the surface of social structures, which are seen as facades that conceal what is truly important.

deindustrialization: The decline of manufacturing as well as a corresponding increase in various types of services.

deinstitutionalization: Weakened social norms, especially with regard to the institution of marriage.

democracies: Political systems in which people within a given state vote to choose their leaders and in some cases vote on legislation.

demographers: Those who study population dynamics.

demography: The scientific study of population, especially its growth and decline, as well as the movement of people.

denomination: A religious group not linked to the state that exhibits a general spirit of tolerance and acceptance of other religious bodies.

dependent variable: A characteristic or measurement that is the result of manipulating an independent variable.

deprofessionalization: The process whereby a profession's power and autonomy, as well as high status and great wealth, have declined, at least relative to the exalted position the profession once held.

descriptive statistics: Numerical data that allow researchers to see trends over time or compare differences between groups in order to describe some findings based on a phenomenon in the real world.

descriptive survey: A questionnaire or interview used to gather accurate information about those in a group, people in a given geographic area, or members of organizations.

desertification: A decline in the water supply as a result of the degradation and deterioration of soil and vegetation.

deviance: Any action, belief, or human characteristic that a large number of people who are members of a society or a social group consider to be a violation of group norms and for which the violator is likely to be censured or punished.

diaspora: The dispersal, typically involuntarily, of a racial or ethnic population from its traditional homeland and over a wide geographic area.

dictatorships: States that are usually totalitarian and are ruled either by a single individual or by a small group of people.

differential association: A theory that focuses on the fact that people learn criminal behavior; therefore, what is crucial is whom a person associates with.

direct democracies: Political systems in which people directly affected by a given decision have a say in that decision.

disasters: Events that suddenly, unexpectedly, and severely disrupt and harm the environment, the social structure, people, and their property.

discouraged workers: Those who have sought work within the last year or since their last job ended, if that was less than a year ago, and have not sought work in the last four weeks (and are therefore not in the labor force).

discreditable stigma: A stigma that the affected individual assumes is neither known about nor immediately perceivable.

discredited stigma: A stigma that the affected individual assumes is already known about or readily apparent.

discrimination: The unfavorable treatment of black Americans and other minorities, either formally or informally, simply because of their race or some other such characteristic.

distinction: The need to distinguish oneself from others.

domestic violence: The exertion of power over a partner in an intimate relationship through behavior that is intimidating, threatening, harassing, or harmful.

domination: The probability or likelihood that commands will be obeyed by subordinates.

double consciousness: Among black Americans, the sense of "two-ness," that is, of being both black and American.

dramaturgy: The view that social life is a series of dramatic performances, akin to those that take place in a theater and on a stage.

dyad: A two-person group.

dysfunctions: Observable consequences that negatively affect the ability of a given system to survive, adapt, or adjust.

economy: The social system involved in the production and distribution of a wide range of goods and services.

edge cities: Cities that are on or near major highways, have corporate offices that offer employment to many, and have important commercial and consumption centers, in particular shopping malls.

effective sexual consent: *See* informed (or effective) sexual consent.

elite pluralism: The formation by political elites of similar interest groups and organizations that vie for power.

emergent norm theory: A theory arguing that, in light of some precipitating event, new norms emerge that guide the often nontraditional actions that characterize collective behavior.

emphasized femininity: A set of socially constructed ideas about "model womanhood" organized around accommodating the interests of men and the patriarchy.

empiricism: The gathering of information and evidence using one's senses, especially one's eyes and ears, to experience the social world.

endogamy: Marriage to someone with similar characteristics in terms of race, ethnicity, religion, education level, social class, and so on.

ethics: A set of beliefs concerning right and wrong in the choices that people make and the ways those choices are justified.

ethnic cleansing: The establishment by the dominant group of policies that allow or require the forcible removal of people of another ethnic group.

ethnic groups: Groups typically defined on the basis of some cultural characteristic, such as language, religion, traditions, or cultural practices.

ethnicity: A sense, shared by members of a group, of belonging to and identifying with a given ethnic group.

ethnocentrism: The belief that one's own group or culture—including its norms, values, customs, and so on—is superior to, or better than, others.

ethnography: Observational (sometimes participatory) research, usually intensive and conducted over lengthy periods, that leads to an account of what people do and how they live.

ethnomethodology: An inter/actionist theory focusing on what people do rather than on what they think.

ethnoscapes: Landscapes that allow the movement, or fantasies about movement, of various individuals and groups.

exchange relationships: Stable and persistent bonds between individuals who interact, generally formed because their interactions are rewarding.

exchange theory: A set of ideas related to the rewards and costs associated with human behavior.

exogamy: Marriage to someone with characteristics that are dissimilar in terms of race, ethnicity, religion, education level, social class, and so on.

experiment: The manipulation of a characteristic under study (an independent variable) to examine its effect on another characteristic (the dependent variable).

explanatory survey: A questionnaire or interview used to uncover potential causes for some observation.

explanatory theories: Theories of deviance (or some other social phenomenon) that try to explain why it occurs.

exploitation: A feature of capitalism in which the workers (proletariat) produce virtually everything but get few rewards, while the capitalists, who do little, reap the vast majority of the rewards.

expulsion: Removal of a minority group from a territory, either by forcible ejection through military and other government action or by "voluntary" emigration due to the majority's harassment, discrimination, and persecution.

extended family: Two or more generations of a family living in the same household or in close proximity to one another.

exurbia: Outlying areas between the suburbs and rural areas.

fair trade: An alternative way of organizing global trade that gives producers better prices for their products and other benefits, with the goal of addressing the power imbalance between producer and consumer countries.

false consciousness: In capitalism, the proletariat's lack of understanding of capitalism's nature and the erroneous belief that capitalism operates to workers' benefit; this exists when large numbers of people do not have a clear and correct sense of their true interests.

family: A group of two people or more (one of whom is the householder) related by birth, marriage, or adoption and residing together.

family household: A household consisting of two or more people who occupy a given domicile and are related by blood, marriage, or adoption.

fantasy city: A city in which great emphasis is placed on creating a spectacle, especially in the areas of consumption, leisure, tourism, and impressive buildings and other real estate developments.

felonies: Serious crimes punishable by a year or more in prison.

female proletarianization: The channeling of an increasing number of women into low-status, poorly paid manual work.

feminism: The belief that women are equal to men, especially socially, politically, and economically.

feminist theory: A set of ideas critical of the social situation confronting women and offering solutions for improving, if not revolutionizing, their situation.

feminization of labor: The rise of female labor participation in all sectors and the movement of women into jobs traditionally held by men.

feminization of poverty: The rise in the number of women falling below the poverty line.

fertility: People's reproductive behavior, especially the number of births.

field experiments: Research that occurs in natural situations but allows researchers to exert at least some control over who participates and what happens during the experiment.

financescapes: Landscapes that use various financial instruments to allow huge sums of money and other things of economic value to move into and across nations and around the world at great speed, almost instantaneously.

folkways: Norms that are relatively unimportant and, if violated, carry few if any sanctions.

food insecurity: Lack of sufficient access to safe and nutritious food.

Fordism: The ideas, principles, and systems created by Henry Ford (who is credited with the development of the modern mass production system) and his associates at the beginning of the twentieth century.

foreign aid: Economic assistance given by countries or global institutions to a foreign country in order to promote its development and social welfare.

front stage: The part of the social world where the social performance is idealized and designed to define the situation for those who observe it.

functions: Observable, positive consequences that help a system survive, adapt, or adjust.

fundamentalism: A strongly held belief in the fundamental or foundational precepts of any religion, or a rejection of the modern secular world.

game stage: Mead's second stage in the socialization process, in which a child develops a self in the full sense of the term, because it is then that the child begins to take on the role of a group of people simultaneously rather than the roles of discrete individuals.

gated communities: Communities in which gates, surveillance cameras, and guards provide the residents with a feeling of security from the problems (crime, panhandling) that they think they left behind in the city.

gemeinschaft societies: Traditional societies characterized by face-to-face relations.

gender: The physical, behavioral, and personality characteristics that are socially defined as appropriate for one's sex.

gender identity: A person's internal sense of gender.

gender role: The social presentation of gender, which includes clothing, hairstyle, and attitudinal and behavioral traits.

gender-swapping: An individual's representation of himself or herself online as a gender that is different from his or her offline gender; also called gender-switching.

general deterrence: The deterrence of the population as a whole from committing crimes, for fear that they will be punished or imprisoned for their actions.

generalized other: The attitude of the entire group or community taken by individuals in the process of developing their own behaviors and attitudes.

genocide: An active, systematic attempt to eliminate an entire group of people.

gentrification: The reinvestment of real estate capital in blighted inner-city areas in order to rebuild residences and create a new infrastructure for the well-to-do.

geopolitics: Political relationships that involve large geographic areas or the globe as a whole.

gesellschaft societies: Modern societies characterized by impersonal, distant, and limited social relationships.

gestures: Movements of one animal or human that elicit a mindless, automatic, and appropriate response from another animal or human.

global care chains: Series of personal relationships between people across the globe based on the paid or unpaid work of caring.

global cities: The cities, especially New York City, London, and Tokyo, with the world's leading industries and marketplaces.

global ethnography: A type of ethnography that is "grounded" in various parts of the world and that seeks to understand globalization as it exists in people's social lives.

globalization: The increasing fluidity of global flows and the structures that expedite and impede those flows.

group: A relatively small number of people who over time develop a patterned relationship based on interaction with one another.

group pluralism: The competition of society's various interest groups and organizations for access to political power in an attempt to further their interests.

habitus: An internalized set of preferences and dispositions that are learned through experience and social interactions in specific social contexts.

hate crimes: Crimes that stem from the fact that the victims are in various ways different from, and disesteemed by, the perpetrators.

hegemonic masculinity: The dominant form or most idealized vision of masculinity; taken for granted as natural and linked to the patriarchy.

hegemony: The subordination of one race (or other group) by another, more on the basis of dominant ideas, especially about cultural differences, than through material constraints.

heterosexism: The belief that heterosexuality is superior to other sexual orientations; individual and institutional discrimination against those with other orientations.

heterosexual double standard: A cultural belief system in which men are expected to desire and seek sex from whomever, whenever, while women are expected to be sexual only within committed, romantic relationships.

hidden curriculum: A school's unofficial norms, routines, and structures that transmit dominant cultural norms and values.

high-income economies: Economies in countries with the highest wealth and income in the world, defined by the World Bank in 2014 as having a gross national income per capita of at least $12,746.

historical-comparative research: A research methodology that contrasts how different historical events and conditions in various societies (or components of societies) lead to different societal outcomes.

homophobia: The fear of being, appearing, or seeming gay; fear of anyone or "anything" gay.

horizontal mobility: Movement within one's social class.

hyperconsumption: Consumption of more than one needs, really wants, and can afford.

hyperdebt: Borrowing more than one should, thereby owing more than one will be able to pay back.

hypodescent rule: A law or judicial ruling that classified persons with even one nonwhite ancestor, or a nonwhite ancestor within a certain number of generations, as black or colored.

"I": The immediate response of an individual to others; the part of the self that is incalculable, unpredictable, and creative.

ideal culture: Norms and values indicating what members of a society should believe in and do.

ideal type: An exaggeratedly rational model that is used to study real-world phenomena.

identity politics: The use of a minority group's power to strengthen the position of the cultural group with which it identifies.

ideology: A set of shared beliefs that explains the social world and guides people's actions.

ideoscapes: Landscapes that include images, largely political images, often in line with the ideologies of nation-states.

imagined communities: Communities that are socially constructed by those who see themselves as part of them.

imperialism: Control over geographic areas without the creation of colonies.

impression management: People's use of a variety of techniques to control the images of themselves that they want to project during their social performances.

income: The amount of money a person earns in a given year from a job, a business, or various types of assets and investments.

independent variable: In an experiment, a condition that can be independently manipulated by the researcher, with the goal of producing a change in some other variable.

individualized marriage: A model of marriage emphasizing the satisfaction of the individuals involved.

inequality: The condition whereby some positions in society yield a great deal of money, status, and power, while others yield little, if any, of these.

inferential statistics: Numerical data that allow researchers to use data from a small group to speculate with some level of certainty about a larger group.

informal organization: How an organization actually works as opposed to the way it is supposed to work.

informationalism: The processing of knowledge.

informed consent: Agreement by participants in social research that they understand and accept the true nature and purpose of the study and any sensitive or dangerous aspects of the research.

informed (or effective) sexual consent: Participants' understanding of and free consent to specific sexual activities in a mutually understandable way.

in-group: A group to which people belong and with which they identify, perhaps strongly.

innovators: Individuals who accept cultural goals but reject conventional means of achieving success.

institutional marriage: The predominant model of marriage in the early twentieth century; emphasizes maintenance of the institution of marriage itself.

institutional racism: Race-based discrimination that results from the day-to-day operation of social institutions and social structures and their rules, policies, and practices.

interaction: A social engagement that involves two or more individuals who perceive, and orient their actions to, one another.

interaction order: An area of interaction that is organized and orderly, but in which the order is created informally by those involved in the interaction rather than by some formal structure.

intergenerational mobility: The difference between the parents' social class position and the position achieved by their child(ren).

intersectionality: The confluence, or intersection, of various social statuses and the inequality and oppression associated with each in combination with others; the idea that members of any given minority group are affected by the nature of their position in other systems or other forms of social inequality.

intersex: A general term used for a variety of medical conditions in which a person is born with reproductive or sexual anatomy that does not seem to fit the typical definitions of male or female.

interviews: A research method in which information is sought from participants (respondents) who are asked a series of questions that have been spelled out, at least to some degree, before the research is conducted.

intimacy: A close and personal relationship that is built over time.

intimate relationship: A close, personal, and domestic relationship between partners.

intragenerational mobility: Movement up or down the stratification system in one's lifetime.

labeling theory: A theory contending that a deviant is someone to whom a deviant label has been successfully applied.

laboratory experiments: Research that occurs in a laboratory, giving the researcher great control over both the selection of the participants to be studied and the conditions to which they are exposed.

labor migrants: Those who migrate because they are driven by either "push" factors (a lack of work, low pay) in their homeland or "pull" factors (jobs and higher pay available elsewhere).

landscapes (scapes): Fluid, irregular, and variable global flows that produce different results throughout the world.

language: A set of meaningful symbols that makes possible the communication of culture as well as communication more generally within a given culture, and that calls out the same meaning in the person to whom an utterance is aimed as it does to the person making the utterance.

latent functions: Unintended positive consequences.

laws: Norms that have been codified, or written down, and are formally enforced through institutions such as the state.

legitimations: Systems of ideas generated by the social system to support its own existence.

leisure: A means of escape from the obligations associated with work and family, involving social activities that are uncoerced, relaxing, and perhaps informative and that are set apart in time and often in space.

liminal period: A special time set apart from ordinary reality.

local: Inward looking rather than outward looking.

looking-glass self: The self-image that reflects how others respond to a person, particularly as a child.

low-income economies: Economies in countries with the lowest levels of income in the world, defined by the World Bank as a gross national income per capita below $1,046.

macro: Macroscopic; used to describe large-scale social phenomena, such as groups, organizations, cultures, society, and the globe.

macrofinance: The globalization of money and finance.

majority group: A group in a dominant position along the dimensions of wealth, power, and prestige.

majority-minority population: A population in which more than 50 percent of the members are part of a minority group.

manifest functions: Positive consequences that are brought about consciously and purposely.

marriage: The socially acknowledged and approved and often legal union of two people, allowing them to live together and to have children by birth or adoption.

mass culture: Cultural elements that are administered by large organizations, lack spontaneity, and are phony.

mass production: Production characterized by large numbers of standardized products, highly specialized workers, interchangeable machine parts, precision tools, a high-volume mechanized production process, and the synchronization of the flow of materials used in production, with the entire process made as continuous as possible.

master status: A position that is more important than any others, both for the person in the position and for all others involved.

material culture: All the material objects that are reflections or manifestations of a culture.

McDonaldization: The process by which the rational principles of the fast-food restaurant are coming to dominate more and more sectors of society and more societies throughout the world.

"me": The organized set of others' attitudes assumed by the individual; involves the adoption by the individual of the generalized other.

mechanical solidarity: Cohesion among a group of people based on the fact that they all do essentially the same things.

mediascapes: Landscapes that include the electronic capability to produce and transmit information and images around the world.

mediated interaction: Social interaction in which technological devices come between the participants, unlike in face-to-face interaction.

medicalization: The process of labeling and defining aspects of life as medical problems that were not previously so labeled and defined.

medical sociology: A field concerned with the social causes and consequences of health and illness.

megachurches: Churches having at least 2,000 people in attendance at worship services each week.

megacities: Cities with populations greater than 10 million.

megalopolis: A cluster of highly populated cities that can stretch over great distances.

meritocracy: A system based on a dominant ideology involving the widely shared belief that all people have an equal chance of succeeding economically based on their hard work and skills.

metropolis: A large, powerful, and culturally influential urban area that contains a central city and surrounding communities that are economically and socially linked to the center.

micro: Microscopic; used to describe small-scale social phenomena, such as individuals and their thoughts and actions.

micro-macro continuum: The range of social entities from the individual, even the mind and self, to the interaction among individuals, the groups often formed by that interaction, formally structured organizations, societies, and increasingly the global domain.

middle-income economies: Economies in countries with income that is average for the world, defined by the World Bank in 2014 as having a gross national income per capita between $1,046 and $12,745.

migration: The movements of people and their impact on the sending and receiving locales.

mind: An internal conversation that arises in relation to, and is continuous with, interactions, especially conversations that one has with others in the social world.

minority group: A group in a subordinate position in terms of wealth, power, and prestige.

misdemeanors: Minor offenses punishable by imprisonment of less than a year.

modernization theory: A structural-functionalist theory that explains unequal economic distributions based on the structural (especially technological) and cultural differences between countries.

monogamy: Marriage between two individuals, whether one wife and one husband, two wives, or two husbands.

monopoly capitalism: A form of capitalism in which huge corporations monopolize the market.

moral entrepreneurs: Individuals or groups who come to define an act as a moral outrage, and who lead a campaign to have it defined as deviant and to have it made illegal and therefore subject to legal enforcement.

moral panic: A widespread and disproportionate reaction to a form of deviance.

mores: Important norms whose violation is likely to be met with severe sanctions.

mortality: Deaths and death rates within a population.

multiculturalism: The encouragement of cultural differences within a given environment, both by the state and by the majority group.

nation: A group of people who share similar cultural, religious, ethnic, linguistic, and territorial characteristics.

nation-state: The combination of a nation with a geographic and political structure; encompasses both the populations that define themselves as a nation with various shared characteristics and the organizational structure of the state.

natural experiments: Experiments that occur when researchers take advantage of a naturally occurring event to study its effect on one or more dependent variables.

neomodernization: A structural-functional theory that explains differences in the economic and social development of countries based on technological and cultural differences.

netnography: An online research method that takes into account observations and interactions that transpire online.

network organization: A new organizational form that is flat and horizontal, is intertwined with other organizations, is run and managed in very different ways from traditional organizations, uses more flexible production methods, and is composed of a series of interconnected nodes.

networks: "Interconnected nodes" that are open, capable of unlimited expansion, dynamic, and able to innovate without disrupting the system in which they exist.

new religious movements: Movements that attract zealous religious converts, follow charismatic leaders, appeal to an atypical portion of the population, have a tendency to differentiate between "us" and "them," are characterized by distrust of others, and are prone to rapid fundamental changes.

nonfamily household: A household consisting of a person who lives either alone or with nonrelatives.

nonparticipant observation: A research method in which the sociologist plays little or no role in what is being observed.

nonresident parents: Fathers and mothers who live apart from their children.

norms: Informal rules that guide what members of a culture do in given situations and how they live.

nuclear family: A family with two married adults and one or more children.

observation: A research method that involves systematically watching, listening to, and recording what takes place in a natural social setting over some (extended) period of time.

occupational mobility: Changes in people's work, either across or within generations.

offshore outsourcing: The transfer of work to organizations in other countries.

oligarchy: An organization with a small group of people at the top obtaining, and exercising, far more power than they are supposed to have.

organic solidarity: Cohesion among a group of people based on their differences.

organizations: Collectives purposely constructed to achieve particular ends.

organized crime: Crime that may involve various types of organizations but is most often associated with syndicated organized crime that uses violence (or its threat) and the corruption of public officials to profit from illegal activities.

Orientalism: A set of ideas and texts produced in the West that served as the basis for dominating, controlling, and exploiting the Orient (the East) and its many minority groups.

out-group: A group to which outsiders (at least from the perspective of the in-group) belong.

outsourcing: The transfer of activities once performed by one organization to another organization in exchange for money.

paradigm: A general model of the world that is accepted by most practitioners in a field.

parole: The supervised early release of a prisoner for such things as good behavior while in prison.

participant observation: A research method in which the researcher actually plays a role, even a minor one, in the group or setting being observed.

passionate love: A kind of love typified by sudden onset, strong sexual feelings, and idealization of the one who is loved.

play stage: Mead's first stage in the socialization process, in which children learn to take on the attitudes of specific others toward themselves.

pluralism: The coexistence of many groups without any of them losing their individual qualities.

political crimes: Crimes involving either illegal offenses against the state to affect its policies or offenses by the state, whether domestically or internationally.

politics: Societal competition through established governmental channels to determine which group's members get what, as well as when and how they get it.

polyandry: Marriage (of a wife) to multiple husbands.

polygamy: Marriage to multiple spouses.

polygyny: Marriage (of a husband) to multiple wives.

positive deviance: Actions that violate norms but are defined by society as having beneficial effects on it.

postcolonialism: The era in a once-colonized area after the colonizing power has departed, although postcolonial thinking and work could already be well underway before the colonizing power departs.

post-Fordism: A production environment associated with smaller production runs of more specialized products, especially those high in style and quality; more flexible machinery made possible by

advances in technology largely traceable to the computer; more skilled workers with greater flexibility and autonomy; less reliance on economies of scale; and more differentiated markets for those more specialized products.

postindustrial society: A society that was at one time industrial, but where the focus on the manufacture of goods has been replaced by an increase, at least initially, in service work—that is, work in which people are involved in providing services for one another rather than producing goods.

postmodernism: The emergence of new and different cultural forms in music, movies, art, architecture, and the like.

postmodernity: The state of having moved beyond the modern era analyzed by the classic social theorists and into a new postmodern epoch characterized by less rationality and more eclecticism.

postmodern theory: A set of ideas oriented in opposition to modern theory by, for example, rejecting or deconstructing the grand narratives of modern social theory.

poverty line: The threshold, in terms of income, below which a household is considered poor.

power: The ability to get others to do what you want them to do, even if it is against their will.

power elite theory: A theory holding that power is not dispersed throughout a stable society but is concentrated in a small number of people who control the major institutions of the state, the corporate economy, and the military.

prejudice: Negative attitudes, beliefs, and feelings toward minorities.

primary deviance: Early, nonpatterned acts of deviance, or an act here or there that is considered to be strange or out of the ordinary.

primary groups: Groups that are small, are close-knit, and have intimate face-to-face interaction.

primary socialization: The acquisition of language, identities, gender roles, cultural routines, norms, and values from parents and other family members at the earliest stages of an individual's life.

probation: A system by which those who are convicted of less serious crimes may

be released into the community, but under supervision and under certain conditions, such as being involved in and completing a substance abuse program.

profane: To Durkheim, what has not been defined as sacred, or what is ordinary and mundane.

profession: An occupation distinguished from other occupations mainly by its power and considerable autonomy.

proletariat: Workers as a group, or those in the capitalist system who own little or nothing except for their capacity for work (labor), which they must sell to the capitalists in order to survive.

property crimes: Crimes that do not involve injury or force, but rather the theft or destruction of property.

prosumer: A consumer who produces value in the process of consumption; one who combines the acts of consumption and production.

Protestant ethic: A belief in hard work, frugality, and good work as means to achieve both economic success and heavenly salvation.

pure relationship: A relationship that is entered into for what each partner can get from it, and in which those involved remain only as long as each derives enough satisfaction from it.

qualitative research: Research methods employed in natural settings that produce in-depth, descriptive information (e.g., in respondents' own words) about the social world.

quantitative research: Research methods that involve the analysis of numerical data, usually derived from surveys and experiments.

queer theory: A theory based on the idea that there are no fixed and stable identities (such as "heterosexual" or "homosexual") that determine who we are; a diverse group of ideas about how cultures develop gender and sexuality norms, notions of conformity, and power relations.

questionnaires: Self-administered, written sets of questions.

race: A social definition based on some real or presumed physical, biological characteristic of a person, such as skin color or hair texture, as well as a shared lineage.

racism: The act of defining a group as a race and attributing negative characteristics to that group.

random sample: A subset of a population in which every member of the group has an equal chance of being included.

rape: Penetration, no matter how slight, of the vagina or anus with any body part or object, or oral penetration with a sex organ of another person, without the consent of the victim.

rational choice theory: A set of ideas that sees people as rational and as acting purposively to achieve their goals.

rationalization: The process by which social structures are increasingly characterized by the most direct and efficient means to their ends.

rational-legal authority: Authority that is legitimated on the basis of legally enacted rules and the right of those with authority under those rules to issue commands.

real culture: What people actually think and do in their everyday lives.

rebels: Individuals who reject both traditional means and goals and instead substitute nontraditional goals and means to achieving those goals.

recidivism: The repetition of a criminal act by one who has been convicted of a prior offense.

reciprocity: The expectation that those involved in an interaction will give and receive rewards of roughly equal value.

reference groups: Groups that people take into consideration in evaluating themselves.

reflexivity: Reflection on what one does, which tends to affect what one thinks about oneself, and does, in the future.

refugees: Migrants who are forced to leave their homeland, or who leave involuntarily because they fear for their safety.

relative poverty: The state of being or feeling poor relative to others, irrespective of income.

reliability: The degree to which a given question (or another kind of measure) produces the same results time after time.

religion: A social phenomenon that consists of beliefs about the sacred; the experiences, practices, and rituals that reinforce those beliefs; and the communities that share similar beliefs and practices.

representative democracies: Political systems in which people, as a whole body, do not actually rule themselves but rather have some say in who will best represent them in the state.

resocialization: The unlearning of old behaviors, norms, and values and the learning of new ones.

resource mobilization theory: An approach to understanding social movements that focuses on what groups of people need to do to mobilize to bring about social change.

retreatists: Individuals who reject both cultural goals and the traditional routes to their attainment; they have completely given up on attaining success within the system.

reverse socialization: The socialization of those who normally do the socializing—for example, children socializing their parents.

riot: A temporary unruly collective behavior that causes damage to persons or property.

risk society: A society in which central issues involve risks and ways to protect oneself from them.

rites of passage: Events, usually rituals, that surround major transitions in life, such as birth, puberty, marriage, and death.

ritualists: Individuals who realize that they will not be able to achieve cultural goals, but who nonetheless continue to engage in the conventional behavior associated with such success.

rituals: Sets of regularly repeated, prescribed, and traditional behaviors that serve to symbolize some value or belief.

role: What is generally expected of a person who occupies a given status.

role conflict: Conflicting expectations associated with a given position or multiple positions.

role making: The ability of people to modify their roles, at least to some degree.

role overload: Confrontation with more expectations than a person can possibly handle.

rule creators: Individuals who devise society's rules, norms, and laws.

rule enforcers: Individuals who threaten to or actually enforce the rules.

sacred: To Durkheim, what is extraordinary, set aside, and of ultimate concern and leads to awe and reverence.

sample: A representative portion of the overall population.

sanctions: The application of rewards (positive sanctions) or punishments (negative sanctions) when norms are accepted or violated.

scapes: *See* landscapes (scapes).

scientific method: A structured way to find answers to questions about the world.

secondary data analysis: Reanalysis of data, often survey data, collected by others, including other sociologists.

secondary deviance: Deviant acts that persist, become more common, and eventually cause people to organize their lives and personal identities around their deviant status.

secondary groups: Generally large, impersonal groups in which ties are relatively weak and members do not know one another very well, and whose impact on members is typically not very powerful.

sect: A small group of people who have joined the group consciously and voluntarily to have a personal religious experience.

secularization: The declining significance of religion.

segregation: The physical and social separation of majority and minority groups.

self: The sense of oneself as an object.

separation of powers: The separation and counterbalancing of different branches of government so that no one branch of government can wield too much power.

sex: A biological term, expressed as *female* or *male*; typically reflected in chromosomes, gonads, genitalia, and hormones.

sex tourism: Activity that occurs when individuals travel to other countries for the purpose of buying sex from men, women, and sometimes children in those locations; sex is the primary or sole purpose of these trips.

sex trafficking: A commercial sex act that includes force, fraud, or coercion and transporting and obtaining a person for sex acts.

sexual assault: Sexual acts of domination, usually enacted by men against women, other men, and children.

sexual harassment: Unwanted sexual attention that takes place in the workplace or other settings.

sexual identity: An internal sense of one's sexual self.

sexuality: The ways in which people think about, and behave toward, themselves and others as sexual beings.

sexual orientation: Involves whom one desires (fantasies), with whom one wants to have sexual relations (behavior), and with whom one has a sense of connectedness (feelings).

sexual scripts: The culturally produced, shared, and reinforced social norms that serve as blueprints, or maps, to guide sexual and gender behavior.

significant symbol: A gesture that arouses in the individual the same kind of response, although it need not be identical, as it is supposed to elicit from those to whom the gesture is addressed.

simulation: An inauthentic or fake version of something.

social change: Variations over time in every aspect of the social world, ranging from changes affecting individuals to transformations having an impact on the globe as a whole.

social class: One's economic position in the stratification system, especially one's occupation, which strongly determines and reflects one's income and wealth.

social construction of reality: The continuous process of individual creation of structural realities and the constraint and coercion exercised by those structures.

social control: The process by which a group or society enforces conformity to its demands and expectations.

social control agents: Those who label a person as deviant.

social control theory: A theory that focuses on the reasons why people do not commit deviant acts and the stake people have in engaging in conformist behavior.

social facts: Macro-level phenomena—social structures and cultural norms and values—that stand apart from and impose themselves on people.

socialism: A historical stage following communism involving the effort by society to plan and organize production consciously and rationally so that all members of society benefit from it.

socialization: The process through which a person learns and generally comes to accept the ways of a group or of society as a whole.

social mobility: The ability or inability to change one's position in the social hierarchy.

social movement: A sustained and intentional collective effort, usually operating outside established institutional channels, either to bring about or to retard social change.

social processes: The dynamic and ever-changing aspects of the social world.

social reproduction: The systematic reproduction of class relations and the capitalist order.

social stratification: Hierarchical differences and inequalities in economic positions, as well as in other important areas, especially political power and status or social honor.

social structures: Enduring and regular social arrangements, such as the family and the state.

society: A complex pattern of social relationships that is bounded in space and persists over time.

sociological imagination: A unique perspective that gives sociologists a distinctive way of looking at data and reflecting on the world around them.

sociology: The systematic study of the ways in which people are affected by and affect the social structures and social processes that are associated with the groups, organizations, cultures, societies, and world in which they exist.

spaces of flows: Settings that are unlikely to have clear and defensible borders; they are likely to be quite fluid and more likely than spaces of places to be temporary in nature.

spaces of places: Settings that are more likely to have clear borders and to be able to limit flows of all kinds and even stop them from entering completely.

specific deterrence: Deterrence from criminal behavior based on the concept that the experience of punishment in general, and incarceration in particular, makes it less likely that an individual will commit crimes in the future.

state: A political body organized for government and civil rule.

statistics: The mathematical method used to analyze numerical data.

status: A dimension of the social stratification system that relates to the prestige attached to people's positions within society.

status consistency: The occupation of similar positions in the stratification system across the dimensions of class, status, and power; people with status consistency rank high, medium, or low on all three dimensions; also called *crystallization status.*

status inconsistency: The occupation of different positions on different dimensions of the stratification system.

stepfamily: A family in which two adults are married or cohabiting and at least one of them has a child or children from a previous marriage or cohabitation living with him or her.

stereotype: An exaggerated generalization about an entire category of people that is thought to apply to everyone in that category.

stigma: A person's characteristic that others find, define, and often label as unusual, unpleasant, or deviant.

strain theory: A theory based on the idea that the discrepancy between the larger structure of society and the means available to people to achieve what the society considers to be of value produces strain that may cause an individual to undertake deviant acts.

stratified sample: A sample created when a larger group is divided into a series of subgroups, and then random samples are taken within each of these groups.

structural-functionalism: A set of ideas focused on social structures as well as the functions and dysfunctions that such structures perform.

structuralism: A social theory interested in the social impact of hidden or underlying structures.

structural mobility: The effect of changes in the larger society on the position of individuals in the stratification system, especially the occupational structure.

subcultures: Groups of people who accept much of the dominant culture but are set apart from it by one or more culturally significant characteristics.

suburbanization: The process whereby large numbers of people move out of the city and into nearby, less densely populated environs.

suburbs: Communities that are adjacent to, but outside the political boundaries of, large central cities.

survey research: A research methodology that involves the collection of information from a population, or more usually a representative portion of a population, through the use of interviews and, more important, questionnaires.

sustainable development: Economic and environmental changes that meet the needs of the present, especially of the world's poor, without jeopardizing the ability to meet the needs of the future.

symbol: A word, gesture, or object that stands in for something or someone (a "label").

symbolic culture: Aspects of culture that exist in nonmaterial forms.

symbolic exchange: A process whereby people swap all sorts of things in a setting where the process of exchange is valued in itself and for the human relationships involved and not because of the economic gains—the money—that may be derived from it.

symbolic interaction: Interaction on the basis of not only gestures but also significant symbols.

symbolic interactionism: A sociological perspective focusing on the role of symbols and how their meanings are shared and understood by those involved in human interaction.

technology: The interplay of machines, tools, skills, and procedures for the accomplishment of tasks.

technoscapes: Landscapes that use mechanical and informational technologies as well as the material that moves quickly and freely through them.

telemedicine: Using technology to consult with doctors, such as an online video call, rather than going to a physical office.

terrorism: Acts of violence by nongovernmental actors that target noncombatants, property, or military personnel to influence politics.

theories: Sets of interrelated ideas that have a wide range of application, deal with centrally important issues, and have stood the test of time.

theories of colonialism: Systems of thought that address the causes and consequences of a powerful nation-state's control of a less powerful geographic area.

total institution: A closed, all-encompassing place of residence and work set off from the rest of society that meets all of the needs of those enclosed within it.

traditional authority: Authority based on a belief in long-running traditions.

transgender: An umbrella term for people whose gender identity and/or gender presentation differs from the gender assigned at birth or in infancy.

transnational capitalism: An economic system in which transnational economic practices predominate.

triad: A three-person group.

unanticipated consequences: Unexpected social effects, especially negative effects.

underemployment: Employment in jobs that are not consonant with one's training and ability, as a part-time worker when one is capable and desirous of full-time work, or in jobs that are not fully occupying.

undernutrition: A form of malnutrition involving an inadequate intake of nutrients, including calories, vitamins, and minerals.

undocumented immigrants: Immigrants residing in a receiving country without valid authorization.

unemployment: The state of being economically active and in the labor force, being able and willing to work, and seeking employment, but being unable to find a job.

urban: City dwelling; in the United States, to be considered urban, an area must have more than 50,000 inhabitants.

urbanism: The distinctive way of life (lifestyles, attitudes, social relationships) that emerges in, and is closely associated with, urban areas.

urbanization: The process by which an increasing percentage of a society's population comes to be located in relatively densely populated urban areas.

validity: The degree to which a question (or another kind of measure) gets an accurate response, or measures what it is supposed to measure.

values: General and abstract standards defining what a group or society as a whole considers good, desirable, right, or important—in short, its ideals.

vertical mobility: Both upward and downward mobility.

violent crime: Crime that involves the threat of injury or the threat or actual use of force, including murder, rape, robbery, and aggravated assault, as well as terrorism and, globally, war crimes.

vouchers: Government-issued certificates that allow students to use public tax dollars to pay tuition at private schools.

war: Armed conflict in which a nation uses its military to attempt to impose its will on others.

wealth: The total amount of a person's assets less the total of various kinds of debts.

welfare states: States that seek both to run their economic markets efficiently, as capitalism does, and to do so equitably, which capitalism does not do.

white-collar crimes: Crimes committed by responsible and (usually) high-social-status people in the course of their work.

white racial frame: An array of racist ideas, racial stereotypes, racialized stories and tales, racist images, powerful racial emotions, and various inclinations to discriminate against blacks.

world cities: Thirty cities that perform most of the same functions as global cities.

world-systems theory: A system of thought that focuses on the stratification of nation-states on a global scale.

xenophobia: Prejudices that cause people to reject, exclude, and vilify groups who are outsiders or foreigners to the dominant social group.

REFERENCES
Chapter-Opening Vignettes

CHAPTER 1

Fahim, Kareem. 2016. "Freed from Jail, Dissident Flees Bahrain." *New York Times,* June 12.

Ryan, Yasmine. 2011. "How Tunisia's Revolution Began." *Al Jazeera English,* January 26. Accessed May 5, 2011. http://english.aljazeera.net/indepth/features/2011/01/2011126121815985483.html.

"Tunisia Protests against Ben Ali Left 200 Dead, Says UN." 2011. *BBC News,* February 1. Accessed May 5, 2011. http://www.bbc.co.uk/news/world-africa-12335692.

Worth, Robert F. 2016. A Rage for Order: The Middle East in Turmoil, from Tahir Square to ISIS. New York: Farrar, Straus and Giroux.

CHAPTER 2

Berman, Russell. 2016. "What's the Answer to Political Polarization in the U.S.?" *The Atlantic*, March 8. Accessed July 20, 2017 (www.theatlantic.com/politics/archive/2016/03/whats-the-answer-to-political-polarization/470163/).

Geiger, Abigail. 2016. "16 Striking Findings from 2016," Pew Research Center, December 22. Accessed July 20, 2017 (www.pewresearch.org/fact-tank/2016/12/21/16-striking-findings-from-2016/).

CHAPTER 3

Freedman, Andrew. 2011. "Public Remains Confused about Global Warming, but Less So." *Washington Post,* June 14. Accessed June 15, 2011. http://www.washingtonpost.com/blogs/capital-weather-gang/post/public-remains-confused-about-global-warming-but-less-so/2011/06/13/AG04TaUH_blog.html.

Oreskes, Naomi. 2004. "Beyond the Ivory Tower: The Scientific Consensus on Climate Change." *Science* 306(5702): 1686. Accessed June 15, 2011. http://www.sciencemag.org/content/306/5702/1686.full.

CHAPTER 4

Carr, Ian. 1998. *Miles Davis: The Definitive Biography.* New York: Thunder Mouth Press.

Smith, Jeff, and Jean Wylie. 2004. "China's Youth Define 'Cool.'" *China Business Review,* July/August. Accessed June 17, 2011. http://www.chinabusinessreview.com/public/0407/smith.html.

Thompson, Robert Farris. 1973. "An Aesthetic of the Cool." *African Arts* 7(1). Accessed June 16, 2011. http://www.jstor.org/pss/3334749.

CHAPTER 5

Associated Press. 2017. "Transgender Boy Wins Texas Girls' Wrestling Title." February 25. Accessed March 1, 2017. https://www.nytimes.com/2017/02/25/sports/transgender-boys-matches-with-girls-leave-all-unsatisfied.html.

Domonoske, Camila. 2017. "17-Year Old Transgender Boy Wins Texas Girls' Wrestling Championship." *NPR,* February 27. Accessed March 1, 2017. http://www.npr.org/sections/thetwo-way/2017/02/27/517491492/17-year-old-transgender-boy-wins-texas-girls-wrestling-championship.

James, S. E., J. L. Herman, S. Rankin, M. Keisling, L. Mottet, and M. Anafi. 2016. *The Report of the 2015 U.S. Transgender Survey.* Washington, DC: National Center for Transgender Equality.

CHAPTER 6

Castle, Stephen. 2013. "Report of U.S. Spying Angers European Allies." *New York Times,* June 30. Accessed November 3, 2013. http://www.nytimes.com/2013/07/01/world/europe/europeans-angered-by-report-of-us-spying.html?pagewanted=all.

Neuman, William, and Randal C. Archibold. 2013. "U.S. Is Pressuring Latin Americans to Reject Snowden." *New York Times,* July 12. Accessed November 3, 2013. http://www.nytimes.com/2013/07/12/world/americas/us-is-pressing-latin-americans-to-reject-snowden.html?pagewanted=1&ref=todayspaper.

Sanger, David E. 2014. "New N.S.A. Chief Calls Damage from Snowden Leaks Manageable." *New York Times,* June 29.

Savage, Charlie, and Jonathan Weisman. 2015. "N.S.A. Collection of Bulk Call Data Is Ruled Illegal." *New York Times,* May 11.

CHAPTER 7

Ewing, Walter A., Daniel E. Martinez, and Ruben G. Rumbaut. 2015. *The Criminalization of Immigration in the United States.* Washington, DC: Washington Immigration Council. Accessed January 31, 2017. https://www.americanimmigrationcouncil.org/research/criminalization-immigration-united-states.

Fox, Vicente. 2017. Tweet, January 26. Accessed March 8, 2017. https://twitter.com/VicenteFoxQue/status/824619429728288770.

Mandell, Andrea. 2016. "Cheryl Burke Dumps Trump Too." *USA Today,* June 30.

Perez-Pena, Richard. 2017. "Migrants Less Likely to Commit Crime." *New York Times,* January 27.

Sampson, Robert J. 2008. "Rethinking Crime and Immigration." *Contexts* 7: 28–33.

CHAPTER 8

Brams, Rachel, and Jessica Silver-Greenberg. 2014. "Companies That Offer Help with Student Loans Are Often Predatory, Officials Say." *New York Times,* July 13.

"For-Profit Education Scams." 2012. *New York Times,* March 23.

Lewin, Tamar. 2010. "Report Finds Low Graduation Rates at For-Profit Colleges." *New York Times,* November 23.

Olson, Elizabeth. 2014. "Student Loan Debt Burdens More than Just the Young." *New York Times,* September 12.

CHAPTER 9

Alderman, Liz, and Steven Greenhouse. 2014. "Living Wages, Rarity for U.S. Fast-Food Workers, Served Up in Denmark." *New York Times,* October 27.

Allegretto, Sylvia, Marc Doussard, Dave Graham-Squire, Ken Jacobs, Dan Thomson, and Jeremy Thompson. 2013. *Fast Food, Poverty Wages: The Public Cost of Low-Wage Jobs in the Fast Food Industry.* Berkeley: University of California, Center for Labor Research and Education.

Ehrenreich, Barbara. 2001. *Nickel and Dimed: On (Not) Getting By in America.* New York: Henry Holt.

CHAPTER 10

"Profile: Bolivia's President Evo Morales." 2011. *BBC News,* January 12. Accessed October 21, 2011. http://www.bbc.co.uk/news/world -latin-america-12166905.

Romero, Simon. 2009. "In Bolivia, a Force for Change Endures." *New York Times,* December 5. Accessed October 21, 2011. http://www.nytimes.com/2009/12/06/world/ americas/06bolivia.html?ref=evomorales.

Webber, Jeffery R. 2011. From Rebellion to Reform in Bolivia: Class Struggle, Indigenous Liberation, and the Politics of Evo Morales. Chicago: Haymarket Books.

CHAPTER 11

Promundo Global. n.d. *MenCare Brazil* (video). Accessed April 22, 2015. http://promundo global.org/resources/mencare-brazil-film.

CHAPTER 12

"Lance Loud! A Death in an American Family." 2011. *PBS.* Accessed November 18, 2011. http://www.pbs.org/lanceloud/american.

Winer, Laurie. 2011. "Reality Replay." *New Yorker,* April 25. Accessed November 18, 2011. http://www.newyorker.com/talk/2011/ 04/25/110425ta_talk_winer.

CHAPTER 13

Armstrong, Elizabeth A., and Laura T. Hamilton. 2013. *Paying for the Party: How College Maintains Inequality.* Cambridge, MA: Harvard University Press.

CHAPTER 14

Ouroussoff, Nicholas. 2010. "New Look for Mecca: Gargantuan and Gaudy." *New York Times,* December 29.

Peer, Basharat. 2016. "Pilgrimage: A 21st-Century Journey to Mecca and Medina." *New York Times,* July 21.

Power, Carla. 2014. "Saudi Arabia Bulldozes over Its Heritage." *Time,* November 14. Accessed April 17, 2015. http://time.com/3584585/ saudi -arabia-bulldozes-over-its-heritage.

Sardar, Ziauddin. 2014. "The Destruction of Mecca." *New York Times,* October 1.

CHAPTER 15

Brinded, Lianna. 2017. "ING: Bad Brexit Deal for Britain Could Kick Europe Into Recession." *Business Insider,* April 4. Accessed July 20, 2017 (www.businessinsider.com/bad-brexit -deal-impact-on-european-and-uk-economy -trade-single-market-2017-4).

Frost, Wilfred. 2016. "Trump and Brexit: How They're Similar—and Different." CNBC, June 16. Accessed July 20, 2017 (www.cnbc .com/2016/06/15/trump-and-the-brexit -how-theyre-similar--and-different.html).

McGill, Andrew. 2016. "Who Voted for The Brexit?" *The Atlantic,* June 25. Accessed July 20 (www.theatlantic.com/international/ archive/2016/06/brexit-vote-statistics-united -kingdom-european-union/488780/).

CHAPTER 16

Bostwick, J. Michael. 2012. "Blurred Boundaries: The Therapeutics and Politics of Medical Marijuana." *Mayo Clinic Proceedings* 87: 172–186.

Hoffmann, Diane E., and Ellen Weber. 2010. "Medical Marijuana and the Law." *New England Journal of Medicine* 362: 1453–1457.

Kramer, Joan L. 2015. "Medical Marijuana for Cancer." *CA: A Cancer Journal for Clinicians* 65(2): 109–122.

Saint Louis, Catherine. 2014. "Politicians' Prescriptions for Marijuana Defy Doctors and Data." *New York Times,* June 26.

"A Sensible Bill on Medical Marijuana." 2015. *New York Times,* March 11.

CHAPTER 17

Coleman, Jasmine. 2011. "World's 'Seven Billionth Baby' Is Born." *The Guardian,* October 31. Accessed November 17, 2011. http://www .guardian.co.uk/world/2011/oct/31/ seven-bil lionth-baby-born-philippines.

"Don't Panic: A UN Study Sparks Fears of a Population Explosion. The Alarm Is Misplaced." 2014. *Economist,* September 24. Accessed April 22, 2015. http:// www.economist.com/news/international/ 21619986-un-study-sparks-fears-population -explosion-alarm-misplaced-dont-panic.

McQueeney, Kerry. 2011. "Welcome to a Very Full World, Danica: Was This the World's Seven Billionth Baby?" *Daily Mail,* October 30. Accessed November 17, 2011. http://www .dailymail.co.uk/news/article-2055419/ Danica-Camacho-Seven-billionth-baby -born-Philippines.html.

Newcomb, Alyssa. 2011. "7 Billion People: What Number Are You?" *ABC News,* October 30. Accessed November 17, 2011. http://abc news.go.com/blogs/headlines/2011/10/7-bil lion-people-what-number-are-you.

World Bank Development Data Group. 2011. "World Development Indicators." Accessed November 17, 2011. http://data.world bank .org/data-catalog/world-development-indi cators?cid=GPD_WDI.

CHAPTER 18

Forno, Francesca. 2013. "Consumer Movements." In *The Wiley-Blackwell Encyclopedia of Social and Political Movements,* 3 vols., edited by D. A. Snow, D. Della Porta, B. Klandermans, and D. McAdam, 253–256. Malden, MA: Wiley-Blackwell.

Glickman, Lawrence B. 2009. *Buying Power: A History of Consumer Activism in America.* Chicago: University of Chicago Press.

Holmes, Seth. 2013. Fresh Fruit, Broken Bodies: Migrant Farmworkers in the United States. Berkeley: University of California Press.

Tammelleo, Steve, and Louis Lombardi. 2014. "Consumer Social Responsibility?" *Business & Professional Ethics Journal* 33(1): 99–126.

Wiedenhoft Murphy, Wendy. 2017. "Boycotts, Buycotts, and Legislation: Tactical Lessons from Workers and Consumers during the Progressive Era." In *Shopping for Social Change: Consumer Activism and the Possibilities of Purchasing Power,* edited by Louis Hyman and Joseph Tohill. Ithaca, NY: Cornell University Press.

REFERENCES
Comprehensive List

Aas, Katja Franko. 2013. *Globalization and Crime.* London: Sage.

Abd-Allah, Umar F. 2005. "Mercy: The Stamp of Creation." Nawawi Foundation. Accessed March 28, 2012. http://www.nawawi.org/downloads/article1.pdf.

Abdul, Matin. 2015. "Relevance of Social Exclusion in Castellian Theory of Informationalism for South Asia." *Journal of Exclusion Studies* 5: 103–112.

Abella, Rudolfo. 2006. "An Analysis of the Academic Performance of Voucher Students in the Opportunity Scholarship Program." *Education and Urban Society* 38(40): 406–418.

Abercrombie, Sarah H., and Sarah L. Hastings. 2016. "Feminization of Poverty." In *Wiley-Blackwell Encyclopedia of Gender and Sexuality Studies*, edited by Nancy Naples. Malden, MA: Wiley-Blackwell (published online first).

Abrams, Rachel. 2016. "Barbie Ads Curvy and Tall to Body Shapes." *New York Times,* January 28.

Abrutyn, Seth. 2012. "Hinduism." In *The Wiley-Blackwell Encyclopedia of Globalization,* edited by George Ritzer, 932–937. Malden, MA: Wiley-Blackwell.

Acemoglu, Daron, and James A. Robinson. 2012. *Why Nations Fail: The Origins of Power, Prosperity, and Poverty.* New York: Crown Business.

Acemoglu, Daron, and Pierre Yared. 2010. "Political Limits to Globalization." Working Paper 15694, National Bureau of Economic Research, Cambridge, MA. Accessed March 28, 2012. http://www.nber.org/papers/w15694.

Acierno, Ron, Melba A. Hernandez, Ananda B. Amstadter, Heidi S. Resnick, Kenneth Steve, Wendy Muzzy, and Dean G. Kilpatrick. 2010. "Prevalence and Correlates of Emotional, Physical, Sexual, and Financial Abuse and Potential Neglect in the United States: The National Elder Mistreatment Study." *American Journal of Public Health* 100: 292–297.

Acker, Joan. 1990. "Hierarchies, Jobs, and Bodies: A Theory of Gendered Organizations." *Gender & Society* 4(2): 139–158.

Acker, Joan. 1992. "Gendered Institutions: From Sex Roles to Gendered Institutions." *Contemporary Sociology* 21: 565–569.

Acker, Joan. 2004. "Gender, Capitalism and Globalization." *Critical Sociology* 30(1): 17–41.

Acker, Joan. 2009. "From Glass Ceiling to Inequality Regimes." *Sociologie du Travail* 51(2): 199–217.

"Acquittal in Hoax Call That Led to Sex Assault." 2006. *NBC News*, October 31. Accessed April 24, 2015. http://www.nbcnews.com/id/15504125/#.VTqGqiFVhBd.

Adam, Barry D. 2006. "Relationship Innovation in Male Couples." *Sexualities* 9: 15–26.

Adams, Ann, Christopher D. Buckingham, Antje Lindenmeyer, John B. McKinlay, Carol Link, Lisa Marceau, and Sara Arber. 2008. "The Influence of Patient and Doctor Gender on Diagnosing Coronary Heart Disease." *Sociology of Health and Illness* 30(1): 1–18.

Adams, Josh. 2009. "Bodies of Change: A Comparative Analysis of Media Representations of Body Modification Practices." *Sociological Perspectives* 52: 103–129.

Adams, Margaret E., and Jacquelyn Campbell. 2012. "Being Undocumented and Intimate Partner Violence (IPV): Multiple Vulnerabilities through the Lens of Feminist Intersectionality." *Women's Health and Urban Life* 11(1): 15–34.

Addington, Lynn A., and Callie Marie Rennison. 2015. "Keeping the Barbarians Outside the Gate? Comparing Burglary Victimization in Gated and Non-gated Communities." *Justice Quarterly* 32(1): 168–192.

Adelman, Miriam, and Lennita Ruggi. 2015. "The Sociology of the Body." *Current Sociology* 64: 1–24. https://www.researchgate.net/publication/282835796_The_sociology_of_the_body.

Adler, Patricia A., and Peter Adler. 2011. *The Tender Cut: Inside the Hidden World of Self-Injury.* New York: New York University Press.

Adler, Patricia A., and Peter Adler. 2012. "Tales from the Field: Reflections on Four Decades of Ethnography." *Qualitative Sociology* 8: 10–32.

Adler, Paul S., et al., eds. 2016. *The Oxford Handbook of Sociology, Social Theory and Organization Studies: Contemporary Currents.* Oxford: Oxford University Press.

Agnew, Robert. 1992. "Foundation for a General Strain Theory of Crime and Delinquency." *Criminology* 30: 47–88.

Agrikoliansky, Eric. 2013. "Globalization and Movements." In *The Wiley-Blackwell Encyclopedia of Social and Political Movements*, 3 vols., edited by D. A. Snow, D. Della Porta, B. Klandermans, and D. McAdam, 528–531. Malden, MA: Wiley-Blackwell.

Aguirre, B. E., Manuel R. Torres, Kimberly B. Gill, and H. Lawrence Hotchkiss. 2011. "Normative Collective Behavior in the Station Building Fire." *Social Science Quarterly* 92: 100–118.

Ahituv, Avner, and Robert I. Lerman. 2007. "How Do Marital Status, Work Effort, and Wage Rates Interact?" *Demography* 44(3): 623–647.

Ahmed, Ishtiaq. 2013. "Muslim Immigrants in Europe: The Changing Realities." *India Quarterly* 69: 265–282.

Ahuvia, Aaron, and Elif Izberk-Bilgin. 2011. "Limits of the McDonaldization Thesis: EBayization and Ascendant Trends in Post-industrial Consumer Culture." *Consumption, Markets and Culture* 14: 361–364.

Ajrouch, Kristine A. 2007. "Reference Groups." In *The Blackwell Encyclopedia of Sociology,* edited by George Ritzer, 3828–3829. Malden, MA: Blackwell.

Akers, Donald S. 1967. "On Measuring the Marriage Squeeze." *Demography* 4: 907–924.

Alatas, Syed Farid. 2011. "Ibn Khaldun." In *The Wiley-Blackwell Companion to Major Social Theorists,* Vol. 1, *Classical Theorists*, edited by George Ritzer and Jeffrey Stepnisky, 12–29. Malden, MA: Wiley-Blackwell.

Alatas, Syed Farid. 2013. *Ibn Khaldun.* New York: Oxford University Press.

Alatas, Syed Farid. 2014. *Aplying Ibn Khaldun: The Recovery of a Lost Tradition in Sociology.* New York: Routledge.

Alazraki, Melly. 2010. "Global Pharmaceutical Sales Expected to Rise to $880 Billion in 2011." *DailyFinance*, October 7. Accessed January 25, 2012. http://www.dailyfinance.com/2010/10/07/global-pharmaceutical-sales-expected-to-rise-to-880-billion-in.

Alba, Richard. 2009. *Blurring the Color Line: The New Chance for a More Integrated America.* Cambridge, MA: Harvard University Press.

Albrow, Martin. 1996. *The Global Age.* Cambridge: Polity Press.

Alderman, Liz. 2016. "Smugglers Sense Opportunity as Borders Shut." *New York Times*, March 12.

Aleman, Ana M., and Katherine Link Wartman. 2008. *Online Social Networking on Campus: Understanding What Matters in Student Culture.* New York: Routledge.

Alesina, Alberto, and David Dollar. 2000. "Who Gives Foreign Aid to Whom and Why?" *Journal of Economic Growth* 5: 33–63.

Alexander, Bayarma, Dick Ettema, and Martin Dijst. 2010. "Fragmentation of Work Activity as a Multi-dimensional Construct and Its Association with ICT, Employment and Sociodemographic Characteristics." *Journal of Transport Geography* 18(1): 55–64.

Alexander, Douglas. 2010. "The Impact of the Economic Crisis on the World's Poorest Countries." *Global Policy* 1: 118–120.

Alexander, Karl, Doris Entwisle, and Linda Olson. 2007. "Lasting Consequences of the Summer Learning Gap." *American Sociological Review* 72: 167–180.

Alexander, Karl, Doris Entwisle, and Linda Olson. 2014. *The Long Shadow: Family Background, Disadvantaged Urban Youth, and the Transition to Adulthood.* New York: Russell Sage Foundation.

Alexander, M. Jacqui, and Chandra Talpade Mohanty, eds. 2013. *Feminist Genealogies, Colonial Legacies, Democratic Futures.* New York: Routledge.

Alexander, Michelle. 2012. *The New Jim Crow: Mass Incarceration in the Age of Colorblindness.* New York: New Press.

Alger, Janet M., and Steven F. Alger. 1997. "Beyond Mead: Symbolic Interaction between Humans and Felines." *Society and Animals* 5(1): 65–81.

Ali, S. Harris. 2012. "Diseases, Borderless." In *The Wiley-Blackwell Encyclopedia of Globalization,* edited by George Ritzer, 446–449. Malden, MA: Wiley-Blackwell.

Allan, Stuart. 2007. "Network Society." In *The Blackwell Encyclopedia of Sociology,* edited by George Ritzer, 3180–3182. Malden, MA: Blackwell.

Allegretto, Sylvia, Marc Doussard, Dave Graham-Squire, Ken Jacobs, Dan Thomson, and Jeremy Thompson. 2013. *Fast Food, Poverty Wages: The Public Cost of Low-Wage Jobs in the Fast Food Industry.* Berkeley: University of California, Center for Labor Research and Education.

Allen, Katherine R., and Ana L. Jaramillo-Sierra. 2015. "Feminist Theory and Research on Family Relationships: Pluralism and Complexity." *Sex Roles:* 73: 93–99.

Allison, Rachel, and Barbara J. Risman. 2013. "A Double Standard for 'Hooking Up': How Far Have We Come toward Gender Equality?" *Social Science Research* 42(5): 1191–1206.

Alon, Sigal, and Dafna Gelbgiser. 2011. "The Female Advantage in College Academic Achievements and Horizontal Sex Segregation." *Social Science Research* 40(1): 107–119.

Altbabbakh, Hanan, Susan Murray, Katie Grantham, and Siddharth Damle. 2013. "Variations in Risk Management Models: A Comparative Study of the Space Shuttle Challenger Disaster." *Engineering Management Journal* 25(2): 13–14.

Altman, Dennis. 2001. *Global Sex.* Chicago: University of Chicago Press.

Al-Tuwaijri, Sameera, Louis J. Currat, Sheila Davey, Andrés de Francisco, Abdul Ghaffar, Susan Jupp, and Christine Mauroux. 2003. *The 10/90 Report on Health Research 2003–2004.* Geneva: Global Forum for Health Research.

Alvarez, Lizette. 2011. "Pull of Family Reshapes U.S.–Cuban Relations." *New York Times,* November 22.

Alvesson, Mats, and Yvonne Due Billing. 2009. *Understanding Gender and Organizations.* 2nd ed. London: Sage.

Amankwah-Amoah, Joseph. 2015. "Solar Energy in Sub-Saharan Africa: The Challenges and Opportunities of Technological Leapfrogging." *Thunderbird International Business Review* 57: 15–31.

Amato, Paul R. 2004. "Tension between Institutional and Individual Views of Marriage." *Journal of Marriage and Family* 66: 959–965.

Amato, Paul R., Alan Booth, David A. Johnson, and Stacy J. Rogers. 2007. *Alone Together: How Marriage in America Is Changing.* Cambridge, MA: Harvard University Press.

Amato, Paul R., and Spencer James. 2010. "Divorce in Europe and the United States: Commonalities and Differences across Nations." *Family Science* 1: 2–13.

Amin, Ash, ed. 1994. *Post-Fordism.* Oxford: Blackwell.

Anaïs, Seantel, and Sean P. Hier. 2012. "Risk Society and *Current Sociology.*" *Current Sociology* 60(4): 1–3.

Anastasia, Désiré. 2010. "Living Marked: Tattooed Women and Perceptions of Beauty and Femininity." *Advances in Gender Research* 14: 11–33.

Anderson, Allan Heaton. 2013. *An Introduction to Pentecostalism: Global Charismatic Christianity.* Cambridge: Cambridge University Press.

Anderson, Benedict. 1991. *Imagined Communities: Reflections on the Origin and Spread of Nationalism.* 2nd ed. London: Verso Books.

Anderson, Chris. 2009. *Free: The Future of a Radical Price.* New York: Hyperion.

Anderson, David M., and Neil Carrier. 2006. "'Flower of Paradise' or 'Polluting the Nation': Contested Narratives of Khat Consumption." In *Consuming Cultures, Global Perspectives: Historical Trajectories, Transnational Exchanges,* edited by J. Brewer and F. Trentmann, 145–166. Oxford: Berg.

Anderson, Elijah. 1999. *Code of the Street: Decency, Violence, and the Moral Life of the Inner City.* New York: Norton.

Anderson, Elijah. 2011. *The Cosmopolitan Canopy: Race and Civility in Everyday Life.* New York: W. W. Norton & Company.

Anderson, Eric. 2005. "Orthodox and Inclusive Masculinity: Competing Masculinities among Heterosexual Men in a Feminized Terrain." *Sociological Perspectives* 48(3): 337–355.

Anderson, Monica, and Paul Hitlin. 2016. "Social Media Conversations About Race." Pew Research Center, August 15. Accessed January 27, 2017. http://www.pewinternet .org/2016/08/15/social-media-conversa tions-about-race.

Andreas, Peter. 2015. "International Politics and the Illicit Global Economy." *Perspectives on Politics* 13: 782–788.

Andreas, Peter, and Ethan Nadelmann. 2006. *Policing the Globe: Criminalization and Crime Control in International Relations.* New York: Oxford University Press.

Andrejevic, Mark. 2009. *Spy: Surveillance and Power in the Interactive Era.* Lawrence: University of Kansas Press.

Andrews, David L., and Ron L. Mower. 2012. "Spectres of Jordan." *Ethnic and Racial Studies* 35: 1059–1077.

Andrews, Kenneth T. 2013. "Civil Rights Movement." In *The Wiley-Blackwell Encyclopedia of Social and Political Movements,* 3 vols., edited by D. A. Snow, D. Della Porta, B. Klandermans, and D. McAdam 193–199. Malden, MA: Wiley-Blackwell.

Aneesh, A. 2012. "Negotiating Globalization: Men and Women of India's Call Centers." *Journal of Social Issues* 68: 514–533.

Angel, Jacqueline, Jennifer Montez, and Ronald Angel. 2010. "Work, Marriage, and Women's Retirement Security: The Significance of Race and Mexican Origin." Paper presented at the annual meeting of the American Sociological Association, Atlanta, GA.

Anspach, Renee, and Nissim Mizrachi. 2006. "The Field Worker's Fields: Ethics, Ethnography and Medical Sociology." *Sociology of Health and Illness* 28(6): 713–731.

Antonio, Robert J. 2011. "Karl Marx." In *The Wiley-Blackwell Companion to Major Social Theorists,* Vol. 1, *Classical Theorists,* edited by George Ritzer and Jeffrey Stepnisky, 115–164. Malden, MA: Wiley-Blackwell.

Antonio, Robert J. 2014. "Piketty's Nightmare Capitalism: The Return of Rentier Society and De-democratization." *Contemporary Sociology* 43: 783–790.

Antonio, Robert J., and Robert J. Brulle. 2012. "Ecological Problems." In *The Wiley-Blackwell Companion to Sociology,* edited by George Ritzer, 476–484. Malden, MA: Wiley-Blackwell.

Anyon, Jean. 2011. *Marx and Education.* New York: Routledge.

Apel, Robert S., and Daniel Nagin. 2011. "General Deterrence: A Review of Recent Literature." In *Crime and Public Policy,* edited by J. Q. Wilson and J. Petersilia, 411–436. Oxford: Oxford University Press.

Apesoa-Varano, Ester Carolina. 2007. "Educated Caring: The Emergence of Professional Identity among Nurses." *Qualitative Sociology* 30: 249–274.

Appadurai, Arjun. 1986. *The Social Life of Things: Commodities in Cultural Perspective.* Cambridge: Cambridge University Press.

Appadurai, Arjun. 1996. *Modernity at Large: Cultural Dimensions of Globalization.* Minneapolis: University of Minnesota Press.

Appelbaum, Binyamin. 2014. "The Vanishing Male Worker, Waiting It Out." *New York Times,* December 12.

Arbabzadah, Nushin. 2011. "Girls Will Be Boys in Afghanistan." *The Guardian,* November 30. Accessed April 18, 2015. http://www .theguardian.com/global/2011/nov/30/ afghanistan-girls-dressing-as-boys.

Archibold, Randal C. 2014. "As Child Migrants Flood to the Border, U.S. Presses Latin America to Act." *New York Times,* June 20.

Archibold, Randal C. 2015. "Mexico Officially Declares Missing Students Dead." *New York Times,* January 28.

Aries, Phillipe. 1978. "La Famille et La Ville." *Esprit* 1: 3–12.

Arminen, Ilkka. 2012. "Ethnomethodology in the Analysis of Discourse and Interaction." In *The Encyclopedia of Applied Linguistics,* edited by C. A. Chapelle, 2051–2056. Malden, MA: Wiley-Blackwell.

Armstrong, Elizabeth A. and Suzanna M. Crage. 2006. "Movements and Memory: The

Making of the Stonewall Myth." *American Sociological Review* 71(5): 724–751.

Armstrong, Elizabeth A. and Suzanna M. Crage. 2013. "Stonewall Riots." In *The Wiley-Blackwell Encyclopedia of Social and Political Movements,* 3 vols., edited by D. A. Snow, D. Della Porta, B. Klandermans, and D. McAdam, 1251–1253. Malden, MA: Wiley-Blackwell.

Armstrong, Elizabeth A., Paula England, and Alison C. K. Fogarty. 2012. "Accounting for Women's Orgasm and Sexual Enjoyment in College Hookups and Relationships." *American Sociological Review* 77(3): 435–462.

Armstrong, Elizabeth, and Laura Hamilton. 2013. *Paying for the Party: How College Maintains Inequality.* Cambridge, MA: Harvard University Press.

Aronson, Jay D., and Simon A. Cole. 2009. "Science and the Death Penalty: DNA, Innocence, and the Debate over Capital Punishment in the United States." *Law and Social Inquiry* 34: 603–633.

Arriola, Elvia. 2006–2007. "Accountability for Murder in the Maquiladoras: Linking Corporate Indifference in Gender Violence at the U.S.–Mexico Border." *Seattle Journal of Social Justice* 5: 603–659.

Arthur, Mikaila, and Mariel Lemonik. 2007a. "Race." In *The Blackwell Encyclopedia of Sociology,* edited by George Ritzer, 3731–3734. Malden, MA: Blackwell.

Arthur, Mikaila, and Mariel Lemonik. 2007b. "Racism, Structural and Institutional." In *The Blackwell Encyclopedia of Sociology,* edited by George Ritzer 3765–3767. Malden, MA: Blackwell.

Arthur, Mikaila, and Mariel Lemonik. 2013. "Emergent Norm Theory." In *The Wiley-Blackwell Encyclopedia of Social and Political Movements,* 3 vols., edited by D. A. Snow, D. Della Porta, B. Klandermans, and D. McAdam, 397–399. Malden, MA: Wiley-Blackwell.

Arvidsson, Adam. 2012. "Brands." In *The Wiley-Blackwell Encyclopedia of Globalization,* edited by George Ritzer, 135–138. Malden, MA: Wiley-Blackwell.

Asayama, Shinichiro. 2015. "Catastrophism toward "Opening Up' or 'Closing Down'? Going beyond the Apocalyptic Future and Geoengineering." *Current Sociology* 63(1): 89–93.

Asch, Solomon E. 1952. *Social Psychology.* New York: Prentice Hall.

Asch, Solomon E. 1955. "Opinions and Social Pressure." *Scientific American,* November, 31–35.

Ashwin, Sarah, and Olga Isupova. 2014. "'Behind Every Great Man . . .': The Male Marriage Wage Premium Examined Qualitatively." *Journal of Marriage and Family* 76(1): 37–55.

Aspers, Patrik, and Nigel Dodd, eds. 2015. *Re-Imagining Economic Sociology.* New York: Oxford University Press.

Associated Press. 2014. "10 Injured as Migrants Storm Spanish Border Fence." *New York Times,* October 15.

Associated Press. 2015. "Thousands Spend Night Outdoors as Death Toll Rises in Nepal." *New York Times,* May 12.

Associated Press. 2016. "Thousands of Migrants Are Rescued off the Libyan Coast." *New York Times,* August 29.

Atkinson, Lucy, Michelle R. Nelson, and Mark A. Rademacher. 2015. "A Humanistic Approach to Understanding Child Consumer Socialization in US Homes." *Journal of Children and Media* 9(1): 95–112.

Atkinson, Michael. 2003. *Tattooed: The Sociogenesis of a Body Art.* Toronto: University of Toronto Press.

Atkinson, Rowland. 2014. *Shades of Deviance: A Primer on Crime, Deviance, and Social Harm.* New York: Routledge.

Atkinson, Rowland, and Sarah Blandy. 2005. "Introduction: International Perspectives on the New Enclavism and the Rise of Gated Communities." *Housing Studies* 20: 177–186.

Atsushi, Miura. 2014. *The Rise of Sharing: Fourth-Stage Consumer Society in Japan.* Tokyo: International House of Japan.

Attanapola, Chamila T. 2006. "Were They Ever 'in Place'? Sense of Place and Self-Identities among Migrant Female Export-Processing Zone Workers in Sri Lanka." *Norwegian Journal of Geography* 60(3): 217–226.

Au, Wayne. 2013. "Hiding behind High-Stakes Testing: Meritocracy, Objectivity and Inequality in U.S. Education." *International Educational Journal: Comparative Perspectives* 12: 7–19.

Aud, Susan, and Gretchen Hannes, eds. 2011. *The Condition of Education 2011 in Brief* (NCES 2011-034). Washington, DC: U.S. Department of Education, National Center for Education Statistics.

Auster, Carol J. 2016. "Gender Neutral" In *The Wiley Blackwell Encyclopedia of Gender and Sexuality Studies,* edited by Nancy Naples. Published online.

Austin, Scott, Chris Canipe, and Sarah Slobin. 2015. "The Billion Dollar Startup Club." *Wall Street Journal,* February 18. http://graphics .wsj.com/billion-dollar-club.

Auyero, Javier, and Timothy Patrick Moran. 2007. "The Dynamics of Collective Violence: Dissecting Food Riots in Contemporary Argentina." *Social Forces* 85(3): 1341–1367.

Aveline, David. 2006. "'Did I Have Blinders On or What?' Retrospective Sense Making by Parents of Gay Sons Recalling Their Sons' Earlier Years." *Journal of Family Issues* 27(6): 777–802.

Avishai, Orit. 2007. "Managing the Lactating Body: The Breast-Feeding Project and the Privileged Mother." *Qualitative Sociology* 30: 135–142.

Ayanian, John Z., and Arnold M. Epstein. 1991. "Differences in the Use of Procedures between Men and Women Hospitalized for Coronary Heart Disease." *New England Journal of Medicine* 325(1): 221–225.

Ayres, Jeffrey M. 2014. "Framing Collective Action Against Neo-liberalism: The Case of the Anti-Globalization Movement." *Journal of World-Systems Research* 10: 11-34.

Ayres, Tammy C., and James Treadwell. 2012. "Bars, Drugs and Football Thugs: Alcohol, Cocaine Use and Violence in the Night Time Economy among English Football Firms." *Criminology and Criminal Justice* 12: 83–100.

Babb, Sarah. 2005. "The Social Consequences of Structural Adjustment: Recent Evidence and Current Debates." *Annual Review of Sociology* 31: 199–222.

Babson Survey Research Group. 2015. "Survey of Online Learning. Grade Level: Tracking Online Education in the United States, 2014." *Online Learning Consortium.* https:// onlinelearningconsortium.org/read/survey-reports-2014.

Baehr, Peter, and Daniel Gordon. 2012. "Unmasking and Disclosure as Sociological Practices: Contrasting Modes for Understanding Religious and Other Beliefs." *Journal of Sociology* 48: 380–396.

Bair, Jennifer, and Gary Gereffi. 2013. "Better Work in Central America: Assessing the Opportunities for Upgrading in Nicaragua's Apparel Sector." Working Paper 17, *Capturing the Gains,* University of Manchester. Accessed April 19, 2015. http://www.capturing thegains.org/pdf/ctg-wp-2013-17.pdf.

Bajaj, Vikas. 2011. "Philippines Replaces India as Companies Seek American English." *New York Times,* November 26, B1, B4.

Baker, Carolyn. 1997. "Ethnomethodological Studies of Talk in Educational Settings." In *Encyclopedia of Language and Education,* Vol. 3, *Oral Discourse and Education,* edited by B. Davies and D. Corson, 43–52. Netherlands: Kluwer.

Baker, David Mc.A. 2015. "Tourism and the Health Effects of Infectious Diseases: Are There Potential Risks for Tourists?" *International Journal of Safety and Security in Tourism and Hospitality* 1.12: 1–17.

Baker, Peter. 2010. "Book Says Afghanistan Divided White House." *New York Times,* September 22.

Ball, Derek, and Peter Kivisto. 2006. "Couples Facing Divorce." In *Couples, Kids, and Family Life,* edited by J. F. Gubrium and J. A. Holstein, 145–161. New York: Oxford University Press.

Bancroft, Angus. 2005. *Roma and Gypsy—Travellers in Europe: Modernity, Race, Space, and Exclusion.* Burlington, VT: Ashgate.

Bancroft, Kim. 2009. "To Have and to Have Not: The Socioeconomics of Charter Schools." *Education and Urban Society* 41(2): 248–279.

Bandura, Albert, Claudio Barbaranelli, Gian Vittorio Caprara, and Concetta Pastorelli. 1996. "Mechanisms of Moral Disengagement in the Exercise of Moral Agency." *Journal of Personality and Social Psychology* 71: 364–374.

Bannon, Lisa, and Bob Davis. 2009. "Spendthrift to Penny Pincher: A Vision of the New Consumer." *Wall Street Journal,* December 17.

Baran, Paul A., and Paul M. Sweezy. 1966. *Monopoly Capital: An Essay on American Economic and Social Order.* New York: Modern Reader.

Barbaro, Michael, and Steve Eder. 2016. "Former Trump University Workers Call the School a 'Lie' and a 'Scheme' in Testimony." *New York Times,* May 31

Barber, Benjamin R. 2007. *Consumed: How Markets Corrupt Children, Infantilize Adults, and Swallow Citizens Whole.* New York: MTM.

Barker, Dean, Mikael Quennerstedt, and Claes Annerstedt, 2015. "Learning Through Group

Work in Physical Education: A Symbolic Interactionist Approach." *Sport, Education and Society* 20: 604-623.

Barker, Eileen. 2007. "New Religious Movements." In *The Blackwell Encyclopedia of Sociology*, edited by George Ritzer, 3201–3206. Malden, MA: Blackwell.

Barmaki, Reza. 2016. "On the Origin of the Concept of Deviant Subculture in Criminology: W. I. Thomas and the Chicago School of Sociology." *Deviant Behavior* 37: 795–810.

Barnard, Anne. 2016. "Muslims Stung By Indifference to Their Losses." *New York Times*, July 6: A1, A7.

Barr, Rebecca, and Robert Dreeben. 1983. *How Schools Work*. Chicago: University of Chicago Press.

Barrett, Donald C., and Lance M. Pollack. 2011. "Testing a Typology of Adaptations to Same-Sex Sexual Orientation among Men." *Sociological Perspectives* 54: 619–640.

Barro, Josh. 2015. "A $15 Minimum Wage: But Why Just for Fast-Food Workers?" *New York Times*, July 28.

Barron, James. 1995. "A Church's Chief Executive Seeks the Target Audience." *New York Times*, April 18.

Barry, Ellen. 2017. "'There are No Homes Left': Rohingya Tell of Rape, Fire and Death in Myanmar." *New York Times*, January 10.

Barstow, David. 2010. "Tea Party Lights Fuse for Rebellion on the Right." *New York Times*, February 16.

Bartfeld, Judith, Craig Gundersen, Timothy M. Smeeding, and James P. Ziliak, eds. 2016. *SNAP Matters: How Food Stamps Affect Health and Well-Being*. Stanford, CA: Stanford University Press.

Bartky, Sandra. 1990. *Femininity and Domination*. New York: Routledge.

Barton, Bernadette. 2012. *Pray the Gay Away: The Extraordinary Lives of Bible Belt Gays*. New York: New York University Press.

Basu, Amrita, ed. 2010. *Women's Movements in the Global Era: The Power of Local Feminisms*. Boulder, CO: Westview Press.

Baudrillard, Jean. [1968] 1996. *The System of Objects*. London: Verso Books.

Baudrillard, Jean. [1970] 1998. *The Consumer Society*. London: Sage.

Baudrillard, Jean. [1976] 1993. *Symbolic Exchange and Death*. London: Sage.

Baudrillard, Jean. [1983] 1990. *Fatal Strategies*. New York: Semiotext(e).

Bauman, Kurt, and Camille Ryan. 2015. "Women Now at the Head of the Class, Lead Men in College Attainment." *Random Samplings: The Official Blog of the U.S. Census Bureau*. October 7. Accessed February 1, 2017. http://blogs.census.gov/2015/10/07/women-now-at-the-head-of-the-class-lead-men-in-college-attainment/?cid=RS23.

Bauman, Zygmunt. 1989. *Modernity and the Holocaust*. Ithaca, NY: Cornell University Press.

Bauman, Zygmunt. 1992. *Intimations of Postmodernity*. London: Routledge.

Bauman, Zygmunt. 1997. *Postmodernity and Its Discontents*. Cambridge: Polity Press.

Bauman, Zygmunt. 1999. "The Self in Consumer Society." *Hedgehog Review* 1(1): 35–40.

Bauman, Zygmunt. 2000. *Liquid Modernity*. Cambridge: Polity Press.

Bauman, Zygmunt. 2003. *Liquid Love*. Cambridge: Polity Press.

Bauman, Zygmunt. 2005. *Liquid Life*. Cambridge: Polity Press.

Bauman, Zygmunt. 2006. *Liquid Fear*. Cambridge: Polity Press.

Bauman, Zygmunt. 2007. *Liquid Times: Living in an Age of Uncertainty*. Cambridge: Polity Press.

Bauman, Zygmunt, and David Lyon. 2012. *Liquid Surveillance: A Conversation*. London: Polity Press.

Baumgardner, Jennifer. 2011. *F'em: Goo Goo, Gaga, and Some Thoughts on Balls*. Berkeley, CA: Seal Press.

Bazelon, Emily. 2016. "Oppression or Profession?" *New York Times Magazine*, May 8, 34–43, 55–57.

Bearak, 2014. "The New Bazaar: In India, Online Stores Catch on with Buyers." *New York Times*, July 29.

Beccaria, Cesare. [1764] 1986. *On Crimes and Punishments*. Indianapolis: Hackett.

Beck, Colin, and Emily Minor. 2013. "Who Gets Designated a Terrorist and Why?" *Social Forces* 91: 837–872.

Beck, Ulrich. [1986] 1992. *Risk Society: Towards a New Modernity*. London: Sage.

Beck, Ulrich. 2007. "Cosmopolitanism: A Critical Theory for the Twenty-First Century." In *The Blackwell Companion to Globalization*, edited by George Ritzer, 162–176. Malden, MA: Blackwell.

Beck, Ulrich, and Elisabeth Beck-Gernsheim. 2002. *Individualization: Institutionalized Individualism and Its Social and Political Consequences*. London: Sage.

Beck, Ulrich, and Elisabeth Beck-Gernsheim. 2012. "Families." In *The Wiley-Blackwell Encyclopedia of Globalization*, edited by George Ritzer, 637–639. Malden, MA: Wiley-Blackwell.

Becker, Howard S. 1963. *Outsiders: Studies in the Sociology of Deviance*. New York: Free Press.

Becker, Howard S., and Blanche Geer. 1958. "The Fate of Idealism in Medical School." *American Sociological Review* 23: 50–56.

Becker, Penny Edgell, and Phyllis Moen. 1999. "Scaling Back: Dual Earner Couples' Work-Family Strategies." *Journal of Marriage and the Family* 61: 995–1007.

Beer, Todd. 2012. "Global Warming." In *The Wiley-Blackwell Companion to Sociology*, edited by George Ritzer, 841–844. Malden, MA: Wiley-Blackwell.

Behbehanian, Laleh, and Michael Burawoy. 2014. "Appendix: Global Pedagogy in a Digital Age." *Current Sociology* 62(2): 285–291.

Beilharz, Peter. 2012. "Liquidity." In *The Wiley-Blackwell Encyclopedia of Globalization*, edited by George Ritzer, 1299–1230. Malden, MA: Wiley-Blackwell.

Belk, Russell W. 1987. "A Child's Christmas in America: Santa Claus as Deity, Consumption as Religion." *Journal of American Culture* 10(1): 87–100.

Belk, Russell W. 2007. "Consumption, Mass Consumption, and Consumer Culture." In *The Blackwell Encyclopedia of Sociology*, edited by George Ritzer, 737–746. Malden, MA: Blackwell.

Belk, Russell. 2013. "The Sacred in Consumer Culture." In *Consumption and Spirituality*, edited by D. Rinallo, L. Scott, and P. Maclaren, 69–80. New York: Routledge.

Belk, Russell. 2014. "Sharing vs. Pseudo-Sharing in Web 2.0." *Anthropologist* 18: 7–23.

Bell, Ann V., Barret Michalec, and Christine Arenson. 2014. "The (Stalled) Progress of Interprofessional Collaboration: The Role of Gender." *Journal of Interprofessional Care* 28: 98–102.

Bell, Daniel. 1973. *The Coming of Post-industrial Society: A Venture in Social Forecasting*. New York: Basic Books.

Bell, David. 2007. "Sexualities, Cities and." In *The Blackwell Encyclopedia of Sociology*, edited by George Ritzer, 4254–4256. Malden, MA: Blackwell.

Bell, Kerryn. 2009. "Gender and Gangs: A Quantitative Comparison." *Crime and Delinquency* 55: 363–387.

Bell, Robert R. 1971. *Social Deviance: A Substantive Analysis*. Homewood, IL: Dorsey.

Bell, Sheri. 2011. "Through a Foucauldian Lens: A Genealogy of Child Abuse." *Journal of Family Violence* 26: 101–108.

Bellafante, Ginia. 2015. "The Dark Side of 'Broken Windows' Policing." *New York Times*, January 16.

Bellah, Robert N. 1967. "Civil Religion in America." *Daedalus*, Winter.

Bellah, Robert. 1975. *The Broken Covenant: American Civil Religion in Time of Trial*. New York: Seabury.

Belluck, Pam. 2016. "Patch of Miami is Ground Zero for the Zika Virus." *New York Times*, August 8.

Belson, Ken. 2014. "Brain Trauma to Affect One in Three Players, NFL Agrees." *New York Times*, September 12.

Belson, Ken. 2016. "Pop Warner is Facing a Class-Action Lawsuit Over Concussions." *New York Times*, September 1.

Bendix, Reinhard, and Seymour Martin Lipset, eds. 1966. *Class, Status, and Power: Social Stratification in Comparative Perspective*. 2nd rev. ed. New York: Free Press.

Bengali, Shashank. 2016. "For Hindus Far from Home, Online Religious Services Can Be a Valued Connection." *Los Angeles Times*, May 1.

Benjamin, Walter. 1999. *The Arcades Project*. Cambridge, MA: Belknap.

Benko, Jessica. 2016. "He Survived Ebola. Now He's Fighting to Keep it From Spreading." *New York Times Magazine*, May 26.

Bennett, Jessica. 2016. "Paula Broadwell, David Petraeus and the Afterlife of a Scandal." *New York Times*, May 28.

Bennett, M. D., and M. W. Fraser. 2000. "Urban Violence among African American Males: Integrating Family, Neighborhood, and Peer Perspectives." *Journal of Sociology and Social Welfare* 27: 93–117.

Bennett, Tony, Mike Savage, Elizabeth Silva, Alan Warde, Modesto Gayo-Cal, and David Wright. 2009. *Culture, Class, Distinction*. London: Routledge.

Ben-Yehuda, Nachman. 1980. "The European Witch Craze of the 14th to 17th Centuries:

A Sociologist's Perspective." *American Journal of Sociology* 86(1): 1–31.

Ben-Yehuda, Nachman. 1985. *Deviance and Moral Boundaries.* Chicago: University of Chicago Press.

Ben-Yehuda, Nachman. 2012. "Deviance: A Sociology of Unconventionalities." In *The Wiley-Blackwell Companion to Sociology,* edited by George Ritzer, 197–211. Malden, MA: Wiley-Blackwell.

Benzaquen, Adriana. 2006. *Encounters with Wild Children: Temptation and Disappointment in the Study of Human Nature.* Montreal: McGill-Queen's University Press.

Berard, T. J. 2007. "Deviant Subcultures." In *The Blackwell Encyclopedia of Sociology,* edited by George Ritzer, 4872–4877. Malden, MA: Blackwell.

Berends, Mark. 2015. "Sociology and School Choice: What We Know After Two Decades of School Choice." *Annual Review of Sociology* 41: 159-180.

Berger, Arthur Asa. 2015. *Ads, Fads & Consumer Culture.* Lanham, MD: Rowman & Littlefield.

Berger, Peter L. 1963. *Invitation to Sociology.* New York: Doubleday.

Berger, Peter L. 1969. *The Sacred Canopy: Elements of a Sociological Theory of Religion.* New York: Doubleday.

Berger, Peter L., and Thomas Luckmann. 1967. *The Social Construction of Reality: A Treatise in the Sociology of Knowledge.* New York: Anchor Books.

Berger, Ronald. 2012. *The Holocaust, Religion, and the Politics of Collective Memory: Beyond Sociology.* New Brunswick, NJ: Transaction.

Bergquist, Magnus. 2003. "Open-Source Software Development as Gift Culture: Work and Identity Formation in an Internet Community." In *New Technologies at Work: People, Screens, and Social Virtuality,* edited by C. Garsten and H. Wulff. New York: Berg.

Berkovitch, Nitza. 1999. *From Motherhood to Citizenship: Women's Rights and International Organizations.* Baltimore: Johns Hopkins University Press.

Berkovitch, Nitza. 2012. "Women's Movement(s), Transnational." In *The Wiley-Blackwell Encyclopedia of Globalization,* edited by George Ritzer, 2233–2242. Malden, MA: Wiley-Blackwell.

Bernhardt, Annette, Martina Morris, Mark S. Handcock, and Marc A. Scott. 2001. *Divergent Paths: Economic Mobility in the New American Labor Market.* New York: Russell Sage Foundation.

Berrone, Pascual, Joan Enric Ricart Costa, and Ana Isabel Duch T-Figueras. 2016. *Cities and the Environment: The Challenge of Becoming Green and Sustainable.* CreateSpace Independent Publishing Platform.

Berry, David M. 2014. *Critical Theory and the Digital.* New York: Bloomsbury.

Bertrand, Marianne, and Sendhil Mullainathan. 2004. "Are Emily and Greg More Employable than Lakisha and Jamal? A Field Experiment on Labor Market Discrimination." *American Economic Review* 94(4): 991–1013.

Bérubé, Allan. 2010. *Coming Out under Fire: The History of Gay Men and Women in World War II.* Chapel Hill: University of North Carolina Press.

Best, Amy L. 2007. "Consumption, Girls' Culture and." In *The Blackwell Encyclopedia of Sociology,* edited by George Ritzer, 724–727. Malden, MA: Blackwell.

Betegeri, Aarti. 2011. "Cricket World Cup Final: You May Not Care, but India Sure Does." *Christian Science Monitor,* March 29. Accessed March 29, 2012. http://www.csmonitor.com/World/Global-News/2011/0329/Cricket-World-Cup-final-You-may-not-care-but-India-sure-does.

Bethmann, Dirk, and Michael Kvasnicka. 2013. "World War II, Missing Men and Out of Wedlock Childbearing." *Economic Journal* 123: 162–194.

Beyer, Peter. 2006. *Religion and Globalization.* London: Sage.

Beynon, Huw. 2016. "Beyond Fordism." In *The Sage Handbook of the Sociology of Work and Employment,* edited by Stephen Edgell, Heidi Gottfried, and Edward Granter, 306–328. London: Sage.

Beynon, Huw, and Theo Nichol, eds. 2006. *The Fordism of Ford and Modern Management: Fordism and Post-Fordism.* Cheltenham, UK: Elgar.

BeyondMarriage.org. 2006. "Beyond Same-Sex Marriage: A New Strategic Vision for All Our Families and Relationships." July 16. Accessed May 23, 2015. http://www.beyondmarriage.org/full_statement.html.

Bhambra, Gurminder K. 2007. "Sociology and Postcolonialism: Another 'Missing' Revolution?" *Sociology* 41: 871–884.

Bhatnagar, Rashmi, Renu Dube, and Reena Dube. 2006. *Female Infanticide in India: A Feminist Cultural History.* Albany: State University of New York Press.

Bhatty, Ayesha. 2010. "Haiti Devastation Exposes Shoddy Construction." *BBC News,* January 15. Accessed March 31, 2012. http://news.bbc.co.uk/2/hi/8460042.stm.

Bhaumik, Subir. 2010. "India to Deploy 36,000 Extra Troops on Chinese Border." *BBC News,* November 23. Accessed May 26, 2011. http://www.bbc.co.uk/news/world-south-asia-11818840.

Bian, Y. J. 1997. "Bringing Strong Ties Back In: Indirect Ties, Network Bridges, and Job Searches in China." *American Sociological Review* 62: 366–385.

Bianchi, Suzanne M., and Melissa A. Milkie. 2010. "Work and Family Research in the First Decade of the 21st Century." *Journal of Marriage and Family* 72: 705–725.

Bianchi, Suzanne M., John R. Robinson, and Melissa A. Milkie. 2006. *Changing Rhythms of American Family Life.* New York: Russell Sage Foundation.

Bianchi, Suzanne M., and Vanessa Wight. 2012. "Population." In *The Wiley-Blackwell Companion to Sociology,* edited by George Ritzer, 470–487. Malden, MA: Wiley-Blackwell.

Biblarz, Timothy J., and Judith Stacey. 2010. "How Does the Gender of Parents Matter?" *Journal of Marriage and Family* 72(1): 3–22.

Bielby, Rob, Julie Renee Posselt, Ozan Jaquette, and Michael N. Bastedo. 2014. "Why Are Women Underrepresented in Elite Colleges and Universities? A Non-linear Decomposition Analysis." *Research in Higher Education* 55: 735–760.

Bilefsky, Dan. 2008. "Albanian Custom Fades: Woman as Family Man." *New York Times,* June 25. Accessed April 18, 2015. http://www.nytimes.com/2008/06/25/world/europe/25virgins.html.

Bilefsky, Dan. 2010. "Dark Film on Teenagers Echoes from Mall to Church." *New York Times,* March 4.

Bills, David. 2007. "Educational Attainment." In *The Blackwell Encyclopedia of Sociology,* edited by George Ritzer, 1333–1336. Malden, MA: Blackwell.

Bills, David B. 2013. "Comments from the Editor: The Sociology of Failure and Rejection." *Sociology of Education* 86: 270–271.

Binkley, Sam. 2007. "Counterculture." In *The Blackwell Encyclopedia of Sociology,* edited by George Ritzer, 809–810. Malden, MA: Blackwell.

Binnie, Jon. 2004. *The Globalization of Sexuality.* London: Sage.

Bitler, Marianne, and Hilary Hoynes. 2015. "Living Arrangements, Doubling Up, and the Great Recession: Was This Time Different?" *American Economic Review* 105: 166–170.

Black, Donald. 2013. "On the Almost Inconceivable Misunderstandings Concerning the Subject of Value-Free Social Science." *British Journal of Sociology* 64: 763–780.

Black, Jeremy. 2016. *Geopolitics and the Quest for Dominance.* Bloomington: Indiana University Press

Blair-Loy, Mary. 2003. *Competing Devotions.* Cambridge, MA: Harvard University Press.

Blakely, Edward J., and M. G. Snyder. 1997. *Fortress America: Gated Communities in the United States.* Washington, DC: Brookings Institution Press.

Blaschke, Steffen, Dennis Schoeneborn, and David Seidl. 2012. "Organizations as Networks of Communication Episodes: Turning the Network Perspective Inside Out." *Organization Studies* 33: 879–906.

Blatt, Jessica. 2007. "Scientific Racism." In *The Blackwell Encyclopedia of Sociology,* edited by George Ritzer, 4113–4115. Malden, MA: Blackwell.

Blau, Francine D., Peter Brummund, and Albert Yung-Hsu Liu. 2012. "Trends in Occupational Segregation by Gender 1970–2009: Adjusting for the Impact of Changes in the Occupational Coding System." Discussion Paper 6490, Institute for the Study of Labor (Bonn, Germany). Accessed April 18, 2015. http://ftp.iza.org/dp6490.pdf.

Blau, Peter. 1963. *The Dynamics of Bureaucracy.* Chicago: University of Chicago Press.

Blau, Peter, and Otis Dudley Duncan. 1967. *The American Occupational Structure.* New York: Wiley.

Blee, Kathleen. 2002. *Inside Organized Racism.* Berkeley: University of California Press.

Blewitt, John. 2014. *Understanding Sustainable Development.* New York: Routledge.

Blight, James G., and Janet M. Lang. 2005. *The Fog of War: Lessons from the Life of Robert S. McNamara.* Lanham, MD: Rowman & Littlefield.

Blommaert, Lieselotte, and Marcel Coenders, 2014. "Discrimination of Arabic-Named Applicants in the Netherlands: An Internet-Based Field Experiment Examining Different Phases in Online Recruitment Procedures." *Social Forces* 92: 957–982.

Bloom, Barbara, Lindsey I. Jones, and Gulnur Freeman. 2013. "Summary Health Statistics for U.S. Children: National Health Interview Survey, 2012." *Vital Health Statistics* 10(258). Accessed April 22, 2015. http://www.cdc .gov/nchs/data/series/sr_10/sr10_258.pdf.

Bloom, Harold. 1992. *The American Religion: The Emergence of a Post-Christian Nation.* New York: Simon & Schuster.

Bluestein, Adam. 2014. "DDP Yoga Is Everywhere, but Does It Deliver?" *Men's Journal,* June. Accessed April 18, 2015. http://www .mensjournal.com/health-fitness/exercise/ddp-yoga-is-everywhere-but-does-it-deliver-20140609.

Bluestone, Barry, and Bennett Harrison. 1984. *The Deindustrialization of America: Plant Closings, Community Abandonment, and the Dismantling of Basic Industry.* New York: Basic Books.

Blum, Linda. 2000. *At the Breast: Ideologies of Breastfeeding and Motherhood in the Contemporary United States.* Boston: Beacon Press.

Boas, Morten. 2012. "Failed States." In *The Wiley-Blackwell Encyclopedia of Globalization,* edited by George Ritzer, 633–635. Malden, MA: Wiley-Blackwell.

Bocian, Debbie Gruenstein, Wei Li, and Keith S. Ernst. 2010. *Foreclosures by Race and Ethnicity: The Demographics of a Crisis.* Durham, NC: Center for Responsible Lending.

Bodinger-deUriarte, Cristina. 1992. *Hate Crime Sourcebook for Schools.* Philadelphia: RBS.

Boesler, Matthew. 2013. "Here's How America's Minimum Wage Stacks Up against Countries Like India, Russia, Greece, and France." *Business Insider,* August 19. Accessed May 7, 2015. http://www.businessinsider.com/a-look-at-minimum-wages-around-the-world-2013-8.

Bogle, Kathleen. 2008. *Hooking Up: Sex, Dating, and Relationships on Campus.* New York: New York University Press.

Bolkan, Joshua. 2013. "Report: Students Taking Online Courses Jumps 96 Percent over 5 Years." *Campus Technology,* June 24. Accessed April 22, 2015. http://campustechnology.com/articles/2013/06/24/report-students-taking-online-courses-jumps-96-percent-over-5-years.aspx.

Bolton, Kenneth, and Joe R. Feagin. 2004. *Black in Blue: African American Police Officers and Racism.* New York: Routledge.

Bonanno, Alessandro. 2012. "Fordism post Fordism." In *The Wiley-Blackwell Encyclopedia of Globalization,* edited by George Ritzer, 680–682. Malden, MA: Wiley-Blackwell.

Bond, Matthew. 2012. "The Bases of Elite Social Behaviour: Patterns of Club Affiliation among Members of the House of Lords." *Sociology* 46: 613–632.

Bonilla-Silva, Eduardo. 1997. "Rethinking Racism: Toward a Structural Interpretation." *American Sociological Review* 62: 465–480.

Bonilla-Silva, Eduardo. 2009. *Racism without Racists: Color-Blind Racism and the Persistence of Racial Inequality in the United States.* Lanham, MD: Rowman & Littlefield.

Bonilla-Silva, Eduardo. 2015. "The Structure of Racism in Color-Blind, "Post–Racial" America." *American Behavioral Scientist* 59: 1358–1376.

Bontje, Marco, and Joachim Burdack. 2005. "Edge Cities, European-Style: Examples from Paris and the Randstad." *Cities* 22(4): 317–330.

Bordo, Susan. 1993. *Unbearable Weight: Feminism, Western Culture, and the Body.* Berkeley: University of California Press.

Boris, Eileen. 2012. "Feminist Currents." *Frontiers: A Journal of Women Studies* 33: 101–105.

Bornstein, Kate. 1994. *Gender Outlaw: On Men, Women, and the Rest of Us.* New York: Routledge.

Boswell, A. Ayres, and Joan Z. Spade. 1996. "Fraternities and Collegiate Rape Culture: Why Are Some Fraternities More Dangerous Places for Women?" *Gender & Society* 10(2): 133–147.

Botz-Bornstein, Thorsten. 2013. "From the Stigmatized Tattoo to the Graffitied Body: Femininity in the Tattoo Renaissance." *Gender, Place and Culture* 20(2): 236–252.

Boudette, Neal, and Mike Isaac. 2016. "Head of Fiat Chrysler Sees Self-Driving Cars in Five Years, Not 20." *New York Times,* May 6.

Bourdieu, Pierre. 1984. *Distinction: A Social Critique of the Judgment of Taste.* Cambridge, MA: Harvard University Press.

Bourdieu, Pierre. 1992. *The Logic of Practice.* Palo Alto, CA: Stanford University Press.

Bourdieu, Pierre, and Jean-Claude Passeron. 1977. *Reproduction in Education, Society, and Culture.* Beverly Hills, CA: Sage.

Bourgeois, Phillippe. 2003. *In Search of Respect: Selling Crack in El Barrio.* Cambridge: Cambridge University Press.

Boushey, Heather. 2008. "Motherhood Penalty and Women's Earnings, Opting Out? The Effect of Children on Women's Employment in the United States." *Feminist Economics* 14(1): 1–36.

Boustan, Leah P., and Robert A. Margo. 2013. "A Silver Lining to White Flight? White Suburbanization and African-American Homeownership, 1940–1980." *Journal of Urban Economics* 78: 71–80.

Bowen, Ted Smalley. 2001. "English Could Snowball on Net." *Technology Research News,* November 21. Accessed January 3, 2012. http://www .trnmag.com/Stories/2001/112101/English_could_snowball_on_Net_112101.html.

Bowler, Kate, and Wen Reagan. 2014. "Bigger, Better, Louder: The Prosperity Gospel's Impact on Contemporary Christian Worship." *Religion & American Culture* 24: 186–230.

Bowles, Samuel, and Herbert Gintis. 1976. *Schooling in Capitalist America: Educational Reform and the Contradictions of Economic Life.* New York: Basic Books.

Bowling, Ben, and James W. E. Sheptycki. 2012. *Global Policing.* London: Sage.

Bowman, John R., and Alyson Cole. 2009. "Do Working Mothers Oppress Other Women? The Swedish 'Maid Debate' and the Welfare State Politics of Gender Equality." *Signs* 35(1): 157–184.

Bowring, Finn. 2016. "The Individual and Society in Durkheim: Unpicking the Contradictions." *European Journal of Social Theory* 19: 21–38.

Boyd, Danah. 2014. *It's Complicated: The Social Lives of Networked Teens.* New Haven: Yale University Press.

Boykoff, Jules, and Eulalie Laschever. 2011. "The Tea Party Movement, Framing, and the U.S. Media." *Social Movement Studies* 10: 341–366.

Brady, David, and Denise Kall. 2008. "Nearly Universal, but Somewhat Distinct: The Feminization of Poverty in Affluent Western Democracies, 1969–2000." *Social Science Research* 37(3): 976–1007.

Braga, Anthony A., and David L. Weisburd. 2012. "The Effects of Focused Deterrence Strategies on Crime: A Systematic Review and Meta-analysis of the Empirical Evidence." *Journal of Research in Crime and Delinquency* 49(3): 323–358.

Braithwaite, John. 2010. "Diagnostics of White-Collar Crime Prevention." *Criminology and Public Policy* 9: 621–626.

Branch, John. 2013. "The X Games, Driven by Risk, Have First Death." *New York Times,* January 31.

Brandle, Gaspar, and J. Michael Ryan. 2012. "Consumption." In *The Wiley-Blackwell Encyclopedia of Globalization,* edited by George Ritzer, 289–295. Malden, MA: Wiley-Blackwell.

Brass, Kevin. 2015. "House Hunting in Singapore." *New York Times,* December 30.

Bratton, William J. 2011. "Reducing Crime through Prevention Not Incarceration." *Criminology and Public Policy* 10: 63–68.

Braun, Virginia. 2010. "Female Genital Cosmetic Surgery: A Critical Review of Current Knowledge and Contemporary Debates." *Journal of Women's Health* 19: 1393–1407.

Braveman, P. A., C. Cubbin, S. Egerter, S. Chideya, K. S. Marchi, M. Metzler, and S. Posner. 2005. "Socioeconomic Status in Health Research: One Size Does Not Fit All." *Journal of the American Medical Association* 294(22): 2879–2888.

Braw, Elisabeth. 2014. "The Three Letter Word Driving a Gender Revolution." *Newsweek,* September 29. Accessed April 17, 2015. http://www.newsweek.com/2014/10/03/three-letter-word-driving-gender-revolution-272654.html.

Breeden, Aurelien. 2015. "A Furor in France over Resting Place for a Roma Child." *New York Times,* January 6.

Breetzke, Gregory D., Karina Landman, and Ellen G. Cohn. 2014. "Is It Safer behind the Gates? Crime and Gated Communities in South Africa." *Journal of Housing and the Built Environment* 29: 123–139.

Brennan, Bridget. 2013. "The Real Reason Women Shop More than Men." *Forbes,* March 6. Accessed April 17, 2015. http://www.forbes .com/sites/bridgetbrennan/2013/03/06/the-real-reason-women-shop-more-than-men.

Brennan, Denise. 2002. "Selling Sex for Visas: Sex Tourism as a Stepping-Stone to International Migration." In *Global Woman: Nannies, Maids, and Sex Workers in the New Economy,* edited by B. Ehrenreich and A. R. Hochschild. New York: Henry Holt.

Brennan, Denise. 2004. *What's Love Got to Do with It? Transnational Desires and Sex Tourism in* the Dominican Republic. Durham: NC: Duke University Press.

Brennan, John, Niccolo Durazzi, and Tanguy Séné. 2013. "Things We Know and Don't Know about the Wider Benefits of Higher Education: A Review of the Recent Literature." BIS Research Paper, URN BIS/13/1244. Department for Business, Innovation and Skills, London.

Brewer, John, and Frank Trentmann. 2006. "Introduction: Space, Time and Value in Consuming Cultures." In Consuming Cultures, Global Perspectives: Historical Trajectories, Transnational Exchanges, edited by J. Brewer and F. Trentmann, 1–17. Oxford: Berg.

Brewster, Zachary W., and Sarah Nell Rusche. 2012. "Quantitative Evidence of the Continuing Significance of Race: Tableside Racism in Full-Service Restaurants." Journal of Black Studies 43: 359–384.

Briggs, Laura. 2012. Somebody's Children: The Politics of Transracial and Transnational Adoption. Durham, NC: Duke University Press.

Brim, Orville. 1968. "Adult Socialization." In Socialization and Society, edited by J. A. Clausen, 182–226. Boston: Little, Brown.

Brimeyer, T. M., J. Miller, and R. Perrucci. 2006. "Social Class Sentiments in Formation: Influence of Class Socialization, College Socialization, and Class Aspirations." Sociological Quarterly 47: 471–495.

Brinded, Lianna. 2014. "JPMorgan CEO Jamie Dimon Cries That $13bn Mortgage Scandal Fines Were 'Unfair.'" International Business Times, January 23. Accessed April 28, 2015. http://www.ibtimes.co.uk/jpmorgan-ceo-jamie-dimon-cries-that-13bn-mortgage-scandal-fines-were-unfair-1433525.

Britannica. 2012. "Religion: Year in Review 2010." In Britannica Book of the Year. Accessed May 29, 2012. http://www.britannica.com/EBchecked/topic/1731588/religion-Year-In-Review-2010.

Brody, Jane E. 2009. "Buyer Beware of Home DNA Tests." New York Times, September 1.

Brody, Jane E. 2016. "No Such Thing as a Healthy Smoker." New York Times, June 20.

Bromley, David G. 2016. "Categorizing Religious Organizations: In Search of a Theoretically Meaningful Strategy." In New Religious Social Movements, Vol. 2, edited by James R. Lewis and Inga B. Tollefson, eds., 17–24. New York: Oxford University Press.

Bronfenbrenner, Kate, ed. 2007. Global Unions: Challenging Transnational Capital through Cross-Border Campaigns. Ithaca, NY: Cornell University Press.

Bronner, Ethan. 2011. "Virtual Bridge Allows Strangers in Mideast to Seem Less Strange." New York Times, July 10. Accessed March 29, 2012. http://www.nytimes.com/2011/07/10/world/middleeast/10mideast.html.

Brooks, Robert A. 2011. Cheaper by the Hour: Temporary Lawyers and the Deprofessionalization of the Law. Philadelphia: Temple University Press.

Brosdahl, Deborah J. C., and Jason M. Carpenter. 2012. "U.S. Male Generational Cohorts: Retail Format Preferences, Desired Retail Attributes, Satisfaction and Loyalty."

Journal of Retailing & Consumer Services 19(6): 545–552.

Brouwer, Steve, Paul Gifford, and Susan D. Rose. 2013. Exporting the American Gospel: Global Christian Fundamentalism. New York: Routledge.

Brown, David. 2007. "As Temperature Rise, Health Could Decline." Washington Post, December 17.

Brown, Keith. 2013. Buying into Fair Trade: Culture, Morality, Consumption. New York: NYU Press.

Brown, Philip, Sally Power, Gerbrand Tholen, and Annabelle Allouch. 2014. "Credentials, Talent and Cultural Capital: A Comparative Study of Educational Elites in England and France." British Journal of Sociology of Education, August 8 (published online). doi: 10.1080/01425692.2014.920247.

Brown, Stephen E. 2007a. "Criminology." In The Blackwell Encyclopedia of Sociology, edited by George Ritzer, 856–860. Malden, MA: Blackwell.

Brown, Stephen E. 2007b. "Ethnocentrism." In The Blackwell Encyclopedia of Sociology, edited by George Ritzer, 1478–1479. Malden, MA: Blackwell.

Brown, Susan L., Wendy D. Manning, and Krista K. Payne, 2015a. "Family Structure and Children's Economic Well-Being: Incorporating Same-Sex Cohabitating Mother Families." Population Research and Policy Review 35(1): 1–21.

Brown, Timothy C., William B. Bankston, and Craig Forsyth. 2013. "'A Service Town': An Examination of the Offshore Oil Industry, Local Entrepreneurs, and the Civic Community Thesis." Sociological Spectrum 33: 1–15.

Brownmiller, Susan. 1975. Against Our Will: Men, Women, and Rape. New York: Simon & Schuster.

Brubaker, Ralph, Robert W. Lawless, and Charles J. Tabb. 2012. A Debtor World: Interdisciplinary Perspectives on Debt. Oxford: Oxford University Press.

Bruce, Steve. 2002. God Is Dead: Secularization in the West. Malden, MA: Wiley-Blackwell.

Bruce, Steve. 2013. Secularization: In Defense of an Unfashionable Theory. New York: Oxford University Press.

Brumberg, Joan Jacobs. 1998. The Body Project: An Intimate History of American Girls. New York: Vintage.

Bryant, Melanie, and Vaughan Higgins. 2010. "Self-Confessed Troublemakers: An Interactionist View of Deviance during Organizational Change." Human Relations 63: 249–277.

Bryk, Anthony, Valerie Lee, and Peter Holland. 1993. Catholic Schools and the Common Good. Cambridge, MA: Harvard University Press.

Bryman, A. 2004. The Disneyization of Society. London: Sage.

Buchmann, Claudia, and Thomas DiPrete. 2006. "The Growing Female Advantage in College Completion: The Role of Family Background and Academic Achievement." American Sociological Review 71(4): 515–541.

Buchmann, Claudia, and Emily Hannum. 2001. "Education and Stratification in Developing Countries: A Review of Theories and

Research." Annual Review of Sociology 27: 77–102.

Buck, Brad. 2014. "Process Converts Human Waste into Rocket Fuel." University of Florida News Center, November 25. Accessed May 22, 2015. http://news.ufl.edu/archive/2014/11/process-converts-human-waste-into-rocket-fuel.html.

Buckingham, David, ed. 2008. Youth, Identity and Digital Media. Cambridge, MA: MIT Press.

Budig, Michelle J., Joya Misra, and Irene Boeckman. 2012. "The Motherhood Penalty in Cross-National Perspective: The Importance of Work–Family Policies and Cultural Attitudes." Social Politics 19: 163–193.

Budig, Michelle J., Joya Misra, and Irene Boeckman. 2016. "Work-Family Policy Tradeoffs for Mothers? Unpacking the Cross-National Variations in Motherhood Earnings Penalties." Work and Occupations 43: 119–177.

Buie, Lisa. 2014. "Judge Sets March 2 as Tentative Trial Date in Movie Theater Shooting Case." Tampa Bay Times, September 10. Accessed April 27, 2015. http://www.tampabay.com/news/courts/civil/judge-sets-march-2-as-tentative-trial-date-in-movie-theater-shooting-case/2197007.

Bukowski, William M., Melisa Castellanos, Frank Vitaro, and Mara Brendgen. 2015. "Socialization and Experiences with Peers." In Handbook of Socialization: Theory and Research, 2nd ed., edited by Joan E. Grusec and Paul D. Hastings, 228–250. New York: Guilford Press.

Bulut, Elif. 2016. "Pride and Prejudice: The Context for Reception of Muslims in the United States." Contemporary Social Science May 16 (published online).

Burawoy, Michael. 2000. "Introduction: Reaching for the Global." In Global Ethnography: Forces, Connections, and Imaginations in a Postmodern World, edited by M. Burawoy, J. A. Blum, S. George, Z. Gille, T. Gowan, L. Haney, M. Klawiter, S. H. Lopez, S. Ó Riain, and M. Thayer, 1–40. Berkeley: University of California Press.

Burgess, Ernest W., and Harvey J. Locke. 1945. The Family: From Institution to Companionship. New York: American Book.

Burke, Kelsey. 2016. Christians Under Covers: Evangelicals and Sexual Pleasure on the Internet. Berkeley: University of California Press.

Burnett, Victoria. 2016. "Bathroom Debate Complicates A Town's Acceptance of a Third Gender." New York Times, June 22.

Burns, Diane, Paula Hyde, and Anne Killett, 2013. "Wicked Problems or Wicked People? Reconceptualizing Institutional Abuse." Sociology of Health and Illness 35: 514–528.

Burns, Thomas J. 2012. "Marine Pollution." In The Wiley-Blackwell Companion to Sociology, edited by George Ritzer, 1324–1325. Malden, MA: Wiley-Blackwell.

Bursell, Moa. 2014. "The Multiple Burdens of Foreign-Named Men: Evidence from a Field Experiment on Gendered Ethnic Hiring Discrimination in Sweden." European Sociological Review 30(3): 399–409.

Burton, Thomas. 1993. Serpent-Handling Believers. Knoxville: University of Tennessee Press.

Buss, Paulo, and Jose Roberto Ferreira. 2010. "Developing Global Public Health Links." *UN Chronicle* 47(2). Accessed March 29, 2012. http://www.un.org/wcm/content/site/chronicle/cache/bypass/home/archive/issues2010/achieving_global_health/developing publichealthlinks?ctnscroll_articleContainerList=1_0&ctnlistpagination_articleContainerList=true.

Butler, Judith. 1990. *Gender Trouble: Feminism and the Subversion of Identity*. New York: Routledge.

Buzinde, Christine N., and Careen Yarnal. 2012. "Therapeutic Landscapes and Postcolonial Theory: A Theoretical Approach to Medical Tourism." *Social Science & Medicine* 74: 783–787.

Cable, Sherry, Thomas E. Shriver, and Tamara L. Mix. 2008. "Risk Society and Contested Illness: The Case of Nuclear Weapons Workers." *American Sociological Review* 73: 380–401.

Cabrera, Nolan L. 2014. "Beyond Black and White: How White, Male, College Students See Their Asian Peers." *Equity and Excellence in Education* 47: 133–151.

Cagatay, Nilufer and Sule Ozler. 1995. "Feminization of the Labor Force: The Effect of Long Term Development and Structural Adjustment." *World Development* 23(11): 1827–1836.

Cahill, Spencer E., William Distler, Cynthia Lachowetz, Andrea Meaney, Robyn Tarallo, and Teena Willard. 1985. "Meanwhile Backstage: Public Bathrooms and the Interaction Order." *Journal of Contemporary Ethnography* 14: 33–58.

Caird, Jeff K., Kate A. Johnston, Chelsea R. Willness, Mark Asbridge, and Piers Steel. 2014. "A Meta-analysis of the Effects of Texting on Driving." *Accident Analysis & Prevention* 71: 311–318.

Calasanti, Toni and Kathleen Slevin. 2001. *Gender, Social Inequality, and Aging*. Walnut Creek, CA: AltaMira Press.

Caldwell, Christopher. 2009. *Reflections on the Revolution in Europe: Immigration, Islam, and the West*. New York: Doubleday.

Calhoun, Craig, Mark Juergensmeyer, and Jonathan VanAntwerpen, eds. 2011. *Rethinking Secularism*. New York: Oxford University Press.

Camera, Lauren. 2016. "Achievement Gap Between White and Black Students Still Gaping." *U.S. News & World Report*, January 13. www.usnews.com/news/blogs/data-mine/2016/01/13/achievement-gap-between-white-and-black-students-still-gaping.

Cameron, Abigail. 2015. "How I Learned to Stop Worrying and Love the IRB." *Contexts* 14: 72–74.

Campbell, Colin. 1987. *The Romantic Ethic and the Spirit of Modern Consumerism*. Oxford: Blackwell.

Campbell, Colin. 2007. *The Easternization of the West: A Thematic Account of Cultural Change in the Modern Era*. Boulder, CO: Paradigm Press.

Campbell, Nnenia M. 2010. "Coil Conscious: African American Women's Development of Internet-Based Alternative Hair Communities." Paper presented at the annual meeting of the American Sociological Association, Atlanta, GA.

Caniglia, Beth. 2012. "Environmental Protection Movement." In *The Wiley-Blackwell Encyclopedia of Globalization*, edited by George Ritzer, 536–541. Malden, MA: Wiley-Blackwell.

Cannato, Vincent J. 2009. *American Passage: The History of Ellis Island*. New York: Harper.

Cannon, Lou. 1997. "Scars Remain Five Years after Los Angeles Riots." *Washington Post*, April 28. Accessed March 28, 2012. http://www.washingtonpost.com/wp-srv/national/longterm/lariots/lariots.htm.

Caprile, Maria, and Amparo Serrano Pascual. 2011. "The Move Towards the Knowledge-Based Society: A Gender Approach." *Work and Organization* 18: 48–72.

Capron, Christiane, and Michel Duyme. 1989. "Assessment of the Effects of Socioeconomic Status on IQ in a Full Cross-Fostering Study." *Nature* 340: 552–554.

Cara, Daniel H., Kai S. Cortina, and Jacquelynn S. Eccles. 2014. "Socioeconomic Background, Education and Labor Force Outcomes: Evidence from a U.S. Regional Sample." *British Journal of Sociology of Education*, January 10 (published online). doi: 10.1080/01425692.2013.868784.

Carbonaro, William. 2005. "Tracking, Student Effort, and Academic Achievement." *Sociology of Education* 78: 27–49.

Carbonaro, William, and Elizabeth Covay. 2010. "School Sector and Student Achievement in the Era of Standards Based Reforms." *Sociology of Education* 83: 160–182.

Carey, Kevin. 2016. "Donald Trump Isn't Alone in Exploiting the Word 'University.'" *New York Times*, March 21.

Carey, Stephen. 2011. *A Beginner's Guide to Scientific Method*. Boston: Wadsworth.

Carmichael, Stokely, and Charles V. Hamilton. 1967. *Black Power: The Politics of Liberation*. New York: Vintage Books.

Carmody, Dianne Cyr. 2007. "Domestic Violence." In *The Blackwell Encyclopedia of Sociology*, edited by George Ritzer, 1219–1220. Malden, MA: Blackwell.

Carnevale, Anthony P., Stephen J. Rose, and Ban Cheah. 2009. "The College Payoff: Education, Occupations, Lifetime Earnings." Georgetown University Center on Education and the Workforce. Accessed March 29, 2012. https://www2.ed.gov/policy/highered/reg/hearulemaking/2011/collegepayoff.pdf.

Carpenter, Laura M. 2005. *Virginity Lost: An Intimate Portrait of First Sexual Experiences*. New York: New York University Press.

Carpenter, Laura M. 2011. "Like a Virgin . . . Again? Secondary Virginity as an Ongoing Gendered Social Construction." *Sexuality & Culture* 15(2): 115–140.

Carrillo, Héctor, and Jorge Fontdevila. 2014. "Border Crossings and Shifting Sexualities among Mexican Gay Immigrant Men: Beyond Monolithic Conceptions." *Sexualities* 17(8): 919–938.

Carroll, Aengus. 2016. *State-Sponsored Homophobia, A World Survey of Sexual Orientation Laws: Criminalisation, Protection and Recognition*. 11th ed. International Lesbian, Gay, Bisexual, Trans and Intersex Association, October. Accessed February 15, 2017. http://ilga.org/downloads/02_ILGA_State_Sponsored_Homophobia_2016_ENG_WEB_150516.pdf.

Carson, Rachel. 1962. *Silent Spring*. New York: Houghton Mifflin.

Carter, Bill, and Tanzia Vega. 2011. "In Shift, Ads Try to Entice Over-55 Set." *New York Times*, May 13.

Carter, Bob and Steve Fenton. 2010. "Not Thinking Ethnicity: A Critique of the Ethnicity Paradigm in an Over-ethnicised Sociology." *Journal for the Theory of Social Behaviour* 40: 1–18.

Carty, Victoria. 2013. "Internet and Social Movements." In *The Wiley-Blackwell Encyclopedia of Social and Political Movements*, 3 vols., edited by D. A. Snow, D. Della Porta, B. Klandermans, and D. McAdam, 620–623. Malden, MA: Wiley-Blackwell.

Casey, Emma. 2015. "Gender and Consumer Culture." In Daniel Thomas Cook and J. Michael Ryan, eds. *The Wiley Blackwell Encyclopedia of Consumption and Consumer Studies*. Malden, MA: Wiley-Blackwell: 316–321.

Casey, Nicholas. 2016. "Colombia and FARC Reach Deal to End the Americas' Longest War." *New York Times*, August 24.

Casper, Lynne M. 2007. "Family Demography." In *The Blackwell Encyclopedia of Sociology*, edited by George Ritzer, 1583–1589. Malden, MA: Blackwell.

Castells, Manuel. 1996. *The Information Age: Economy, Society and Culture, Vol. 1, The Rise of the Network Society*. Oxford: Blackwell.

Castells, Manuel. 1997. *The Information Age: Economy, Society and Culture, Vol. 2, The Power of Identity*. Oxford: Blackwell.

Castells, Manuel. 1998. *The Information Age: Economy, Society and Culture, Vol. 3, End of Millennium*. Oxford: Blackwell.

Castells, Manuel. 2010. *The Rise of the Network Society. The Information Age: Economy, Society and Culture, Vol. 1*. Malden, MA: Wiley-Blackwell.

Castells, Manuel. 2015. *Networks of Outrage and Hope: Social Movements in the Internet Age*. 2nd ed. Cambridge: Polity Press.

Castle, Stephen. 2010. "France Faces European Action after Expulsions." *New York Times*, September 29.

Castles, Stephen. 2013. "The Forces Driving Global Migration." *Journal of Intercultural Studies* 34: 122–140.

Cave, Damien. 2011. "Mexico Turns to Social Media for Information and Survival." *New York Times*, September 25.

Center for Research on Education Outcomes, Stanford University. 2013. "National Charter School Study 2013." Accessed May 18, 2015. http://credo.stanford.edu/documents/NCSS%202013%20Final%20Draft.pdf.

Centers for Disease Control and Prevention. 2012. "Child Abuse and Neglect Cost the United States $124 Billion." Press release, February 1. Accessed May 13, 2015. www.cdc.gov/media/releases/2012/p0201_child_abuse.html.

Centers for Disease Control and Prevention. 2014. "Summary Health Statistics: National Health Interview Survey, 2014." Accessed May 16, 2017. http://ftp.cdc.gov/pub/Health_Statistics/NCHS/NHIS/SHS/2014_SHS_Table_C-3.pdf.

Centers for Disease Control and Prevention. 2016a. "Changes in Life Expectancy by Race and Hispanic Origin in the United States, 2013–2014." https://www.cdc.gov/nchs/products/databriefs/db244.htm.

Centers for Disease Control and Prevention. 2016b. "Unmarried Childbearing." Accessed March 9, 2017. https://www.cdc.gov/nchs/fastats/unmarried-childbearing.htm.

Centers for Disease Control and Prevention. 2017. "Births: Final Data for 2015." *National Vital Statistics Report* 66(1). Accessed February 22, 2017. https://www.cdc.gov/nchs/data/nvsr/nvsr66/nvsr66_01.pdf.

Centers for Medicare and Medicaid Services. 2015. "National Health Expenditures 2015Highlights2015." Accessed February 11, 2017. https://www.cms.gov/Research-Statistics-Data-and-Systems/Statistics-Trends-and-Reports/NationalHealthExpendData/downloads/highlights.pdf.

Central Intelligence Agency. 2015. "Country Comparison: Life Expectancy at Birth." *World Factbook.* Accessed May 20, 2015. https://www.cia.gov/library/publications/the-world-factbook/rankorder/2102rank.html.

Central Intelligence Agency. 2016. *The World Factbook.* Accessed March 9, 2017. https://www.cia.gov/library/publications/the-world-factbook.

Cerkez, Aida. 2010. "UN Official: Bosnia War Rapes Must Be Prosecuted." *Washington Post,* November 26.

Cerny, Phillip G. 2007. "Nation-State." In *Encyclopedia of Globalization,* edited by J. A. Scholte and R. Robertson. New York: MTM.

Cha, Youngjoo. 2013. "Overwork and the Persistence of Gender Segregation in Occupations." *Gender & Society* 27: 158–184.

Cha, Youngjoo and Kim A. Weeden. 2014. "Overwork and the Slow Convergence in the Gender Gap in Wages." *American Sociological Review* 79: 457–484.

Chae, Haesook. 2014. "Marx on the Family and Class Consciousness." *Rethinking Marxism* 26: 262–277.

Chae, Jiyoung. 2015. "Am I a Better Mother Than You?" *Communication Research* 42: 503–525.

Chakravarti, Arjun, Tanya Menon, and Christopher Winship. 2014. "Contact and Group Structure: A Natural Experiment of Interracial College Roommate Groups." *Organization Science* 25(4): 1216–1233.

Chambers, Erve. 2010. *Native Tours: The Anthropology of Travel and Tourism.* Prospect Heights, IL: Waveland Press.

Chambliss, William J. 1964. "A Sociological Analysis of the Law of Vagrancy." *Social Problems* 12: 67–77.

Chan, Sewell. 2016. "Migration to Greece From Turkey By Sea Has Plummeted, U.N. Says." *New York Times* July 9.

Chanda, Nayan. 2007. *Bound Together: How Traders, Preachers, Adventurers, and Warriors Shaped Globalization.* New Haven, CT: Yale University Press.

Charles, Maria and Karen Bradley. 2009. "Indulging Our Gendered Selves: Sex Segregation by Field of Study in 44 Countries." *American Journal of Sociology* 114: 924–976.

Cheal, David. 2007. "Family Theory." In *The Blackwell Encyclopedia of Sociology,* edited by George Ritzer, 1630–1634. Malden, MA: Blackwell.

Chen, Chih-Chin, and George Ritzer, 2015. "Globalization and Consumption." In *The Wiley-Blackwell Encyclopedia of Consumption and Consumer Studies,* edited by Daniel Thomas Cook and J. Michael Ryan, 333–338. Malden, MA: Wiley-Blackwell.

Chen, James K. C., and Dulamjav Zorigt. 2013. "Managing Occupational Health and Safety in the Mining Industry." *Journal of Business Research* 66: 2321–2331.

Chen, Katherine. 2009. *Enabling Creative Chaos: The Organization behind the Burning Man Event.* Chicago: University of Chicago Press.

Chen, Zihong, Ying Ge, Huiwen Lai, and Chi Wan. 2013. "Globalization and Gender Wage Inequality in China." *World Development* 44: 256–266.

Cherlin, Andrew J. 1978. "Remarriage as an Incomplete Institution." *American Journal of Sociology* 84: 634–650.

Cherlin, Andrew J. 2004. "The Deinstitutionalization of American Marriage." *Journal of Marriage and Family* 66: 848–861.

Cherlin, Andrew J. 2009. *The Marriage-Go-Round: The State of Marriage and the Family in America Today.* New York: Knopf.

Cherlin, Andrew J. 2010. "The Housewife Anomaly." *New York Times,* January 24.

Chernilo, Daniel. 2012. "Nation." In *The Wiley-Blackwell Encyclopedia of Globalization,* edited by George Ritzer, 1485–1492. Malden, MA: Wiley-Blackwell.

Chesnut, Andrew. 2015. "Spirited Competition: Pentecostal Success in Latin America's New Religious Marketplace." In *Spirit and Power: The Growth and Global Influence of Pentecostalism,* edited by Donald E. Miller, Kimon H. Sargeant and Richard Foley, 65–82. New York: Oxford University Press.

Chetty, Raj, Nathaniel Hendren, Patrick Kline, Emmanuel Saez, and Nicholas Turner. 2014. "Is the United States Still a Land of Opportunity? Recent Trends in Intergenerational Mobility." *American Economic Review* 104: 141–147.

Childress, C. Clayton, and Alison Gerber, 2015. "The MFA in Creative Writing: The Uses of a 'Useless' Credential." *Professions and Professionalism* 5: 1–16.

Chilton, Roland, and Ruth Triplett. 2007a. "Class and Crime." In *The Blackwell Encyclopedia of Sociology,* edited by George Ritzer, 542–545. Malden, MA: Blackwell.

Chilton, Roland, and Ruth Triplett. 2007b. "Race and Crime." In *The Blackwell Encyclopedia of Sociology,* edited by George Ritzer, 3734–3737. Malden, MA: Blackwell.

Chin, Elizabeth. 2007. "Consumption, African Americans." In *The Blackwell Encyclopedia of Sociology,* edited by George Ritzer, 706–709. Malden, MA: Blackwell.

Chishti, Muzaffar, Faye Hipsman, and Bonnie Bui. 2014. "The Stalemate over Unaccompanied Minors Holds Far-Reaching Implications for Broader U.S. Immigration Debates." Migration Policy Institute, August 15. Accessed April 18, 2015. http://www.migrationpolicy.org/article/stalemate-over-unaccompanied-minors-holds-far-reaching-implications-broader-us-immigration.

Chokshi, Niraj. 2016. "Snowden and Wikileaks Clash Over How to Disclose Secrets." *New York Times,* July 29.

Chokshi, Niraj. 2017. "Boys Scouts Reversing Century-Old Stance, Will Allow Transgender Boys." *New York Times,* January 30.

Chomsky, Noam. 1985. *Turning the Tide: U.S. Intervention in Central America and the Struggle for Peace.* Boston: South End Press.

Chriqui, James F., Rosalie Liccardo Pacula, Duane C. McBride, Deborah A. Reichmann, Curtis J. Vanderwaal, and Yvonne Terry-McElrath. 2002. *Illicit Drug Policies: Selected Laws from the 50 States.* Princeton, NJ: Robert Wood Johnson Foundation.

Chriss, James J. 2007. "Networks." In *The Blackwell Encyclopedia of Sociology,* edited by George Ritzer, 3182–3185. Malden, MA: Blackwell.

Cicero, Theodore J., Matthew S. Ellis, Hilary L. Surratt, and Steven P. Kurtz. 2014. "The Changing Face of Heroin Use in the United States: A Retrospective Analysis of the Past 50 Years." *JAMA Psychiatry* 71: 821–826.

Clancy, Michael. 2012. "Cruise Tourism." In *The Wiley-Blackwell Encyclopedia of Globalization,* edited by George Ritzer, 360–362. Malden, MA: Wiley-Blackwell.

Clapson, Mark, and Ray Hutchison, eds. 2010. *Suburbanization in Global Society.* Bingley, UK: Emerald.

Clark, Jocalyn. 2014. "Medicalization of Global Health 2: The Medicalization of Global Mental Health." *Global Health Action* 7: 24000. Accessed April 18, 2015. http://dx.doi.org/10.3402/gha.v7.24000.

Clegg, Stewart. 2007. "Ideal Type." In *The Blackwell Encyclopedia of Sociology,* edited by George Ritzer, 2201–2202. Malden. MA: Blackwell.

Clegg, Stewart, and Michael Lounsbury. 2009. "Sintering the Iron Cage: Translation, Domination and Rationalization." In *The Oxford Handbook of Sociology and Organization Studies: Classical Foundations,* edited by P. S. Adler, 118–145. Oxford: Oxford University Press.

Clogher, R. 1981. "Weaving Spiders Come Not Here: Bohemian Grove: Inside the Secret Retreat of the Power Elite." *Mother Jones,* August, 28–35.

Clotfelter, Charles T. 2010. *American Universities in a Global Market.* Chicago: University of Chicago Press.

Clough, Patricia Ticineto. 2013. "The Digital, Labor, and Measure beyond Biopolitics." In *Digital Labor: The Internet as Playground and Factory,* edited by T. Scholz, 112–126. New York: Routledge.

Clougherty, Jane E., Kerry Souza, and Mark R. Cullen. 2010. "Work and Its Role in Shaping the Social Gradients in Health." *Annals of the New York Academy of Sciences* 1186: 102–124.

Coakley, Jay. 2007. "Socialization and Sport." In *The Blackwell Encyclopedia of Sociology,* edited by George Ritzer, 4576–4579. Malden, MA: Blackwell.

Cockerham, William C. 2007. "Medical Sociology." In *The Blackwell Encyclopedia of Sociology,* edited by George Ritzer, 2932–2936. Malden, MA: Blackwell.

Cockerham, William. 2012. "Current Directions in Medical Sociology." In *The Wiley-Blackwell Companion to Sociology,* edited by George Ritzer, 385–401. Malden, MA: Wiley-Blackwell.]

Cockerham, William. 2016. "Current Directions in Medical Sociology." In *The Wiley-Blackwell Companion to Sociology,* edited by George Ritzer, 385–401. Malden, MA: Wiley-Blackwell.

Cockerham, William C., and Brian P. Hinote. 2015. "PAs in a Changing Society: A Sociologic Perspective." *Journal of the American Academy of Physicians Assistants* 28: 18–20.

Cohen, Noam. 2011. "Define Gender Gap? Look Up Wikipedia's Contributor List." *New York Times,* January 30. Accessed December 3, 2011. http://www.nytimes.com/2011/01/31/business/media/31link.html.

Cohen, Patricia. 2010. "'Culture of Poverty' Makes a Comeback." *New York Times,* October 17. Accessed March 29, 2012. http://www.nytimes.com/2010/10/18/us/18poverty.html.

Cohen, Patricia, and Chad Bray. 2016. "University of Phoenix Owner, Apollo Education Group, Will Be Taken Private." *New York Times,* February 8. https://www.nytimes.com/2016/02/09/business/dealbook/apollo-education-group-university-of-phoenix-owner-to-be-taken-private.html?_r=0.

Cohen, Patricia. 2015. "Study Finds Global Wealth Is Flowing to the Richest." *New York Times,* January 19.

Cohen, Philip. 2014. *The Family: Diversity, Inequality and Social Change.* New York: Norton.

Cohen, Rina. 2015. "Transnational Motherhood: Constructing Intergenerational Relations between Filipina Migrant Workers and Their Children." In *Engendering Transnational Voices,* edited by Guina Man and Rina Cohen, 155–171. Waterloo, Canada: Wilfred Laurier Press.

Cohen, Robin. 1997. *Global Diasporas: An Introduction.* London: Routledge.

Cohen, Roger. 2016. "The Arab Withering." *New York Times,* May 12.

Cohen-Cole, Ethan, Steven Durlauf, Jeffrey Fagan, and Daniel Nagin. 2009. "Model Uncertainty and the Deterrent Effect of Capital Punishment." *American Law and Economics Review* 11: 335–369.

Colby, Sandra L., and Jennifer M. Ortman, 2015. *Projections of the Size and Composition of the U.S. Population: 2014–2060.* Washington, DC: United States Census Bureau.

Cole, Ellen, and Jessica Henderson Daniel. 2005. *Featuring Females: Feminist Analyses of Media.* Washington, DC: American Psychological Association.

Coleman, David, and Robert Rowthorn. 2011. "Who's Afraid of Population Decline? A Critical Examination of Its Consequences." *Population and Development Review* 37: 217–248.

Coleman, James. 1966. *Equality of Educational Opportunity.* Washington, DC: U.S. Department of Health, Education, and Welfare.

Coleman, James. 1990. *Foundations of Social Theory.* Cambridge, MA: Belknap Press.

Coleman, Marilyn, and Lawrence H. Ganong. 2007a. "Stepfamilies." In *The Blackwell Encyclopedia of Sociology,* edited by George Ritzer, 4765–4768. Malden, MA: Blackwell.

Coleman, Marilyn, and Lawrence H. Ganong. 2007b. "Stepmothering." In *The Blackwell Encyclopedia of Sociology,* edited by George Ritzer, 4770–4772. Malden, MA: Blackwell.

Coleman, Marilyn, Lawrence H. Ganong, and Ashton Chapman. Forthcoming. "Stepmothering." In *Encyclopedia of Sociology,* 2nd ed., edited by George Ritzer. Malden, MA: Wiley-Blackwell.

Coleman, Marilyn, Lawrence H. Ganong, and Luke T. Russell. 2013. "Resilience in Stepfamilies." In *Handbook of Family Resilience,* edited by D. S. Becvar, 85–103. New York: Springer.

Coll, Sami. 2012. "The Social Dynamics of Secrecy: Rethinking Information and Privacy through Georg Simmel." *International Review of Information Ethics* 17: 15–20.

Collet, Francois. 2009. "Does Habitus Matter? A Comparative Review of Bourdieu's Habitus and Simon's Bounded Rationality with Some Implications for Economic Sociology." *Sociological Theory* 27: 419–434.

Collier, Paul. 2007. *The Bottom Billion: Why the Poorest Countries Are Failing and What Can Be Done about It.* New York: Oxford University Press.

Collier, Paul. 2012. "The Bottom Billion." In *The Wiley-Blackwell Encyclopedia of Globalization,* edited by George Ritzer, 126–130. Malden, MA: Wiley-Blackwell.

Collier, Paul. 2013. ""Migration Hurts the Homeland." *New York Times,* November 29.

Collier, Paul. Forthcoming. "The Bottom Billion: Why the Poorest Countries Are Failing and What Can Be Done about It." In *The Blackwell Encyclopedia of Sociology,* 2nd ed., edited by George Ritzer. Malden, MA: Blackwell.

Collins, Jane L. 2003. *Threads: Gender, Labor, and Power in the Global Apparel Industry.* Chicago: University of Chicago Press.

Collins, Patricia Hill. 1990. *Black Feminist Thought: Knowledge, Consciousness, and the Politics of Empowerment.* Boston: Unwin Hyman.

Collins, Patricia Hill. 2000. *Black Feminist Thought: Knowledge, Consciousness, and the Politics of Empowerment.* 2nd ed. New York: Routledge.

Collins, Patricia Hill. 2004. *Black Sexual Politics: African Americans, Gender and the New Racism.* New York: Routledge.

Collins, Patricia Hill. 2009. *Another Kind of Public Education: Race, the Media, Schools, and Democratic Possibilities.* Boston: Beacon Press.

Collins, Patricia Hill. 2012. "Looking Back, Moving Ahead: Scholarship in Service to Social Justice." *Gender & Society* 26: 14–22.

Collins, Patricia Hill, and Sirma Bilge, 2016. *Intersectionality.* Cambridge: Polity.

Collins, Patricia Hill, and Valerie Chepp. 2013. "Intersectionality." In *Oxford Handbook of Gender and Politics,* edited by Georgina Waylen et al. Oxford: Oxford University Press.

Collins, Randall. 1975. *Conflict Society: Toward an Explanatory Science.* New York: Academic Press.

Collins, Randall. 1979. *The Credential Society: An Historical Sociology of Education and Stratification.* New York: Academic Press.

Collins, Randall. 2008. *Violence: A Micro-sociological Theory.* Princeton, NJ: Princeton University Press.

Collins, Randall. 2009. "Micro and Macro Causes of Violence." *International Journal of Conflict and Violence* 3: 9–22.

Collins, Randall. 2012. "C-Escalation and D-Escalation: A Theory of the Time-Dynamics of Conflict." *American Sociological Review* 77: 1–20.

Collins, Randall. 2013. "Entering and Leaving the Tunnel of Violence: Micro-sociological Dynamics of Emotional Entrainment in Violent Interactions." *Current Sociology* 61(2): 132–151.

Colosi, Rachel. 2010. *Dirty Dancing? An Ethnography of Lap-Dancing.* Abingdon, UK: William.

Comaroff, John L., and Jean Comaroff. 2009. *Ethnicity, Inc.* Chicago: University of Chicago Press.

Comella, Lynn. 2013. "Fifty Shades of Erotic Stimulus." *Feminist Media Studies* 13(3): 563–566.

Common Sense Media. 2013. "Zero to Eight: Children's Media Use in America 2013." Fall. Accessed April 22, 2015. https://www.commonsensemedia.org/research/zero-to-eight-childrens-media-use-in-america-2013.

Common Sense Media. 2015. *The Common Sense Census: Media Use by Teens and Tweens.* San Francisco: Author. https://www.commonsensemedia.org/sites/default/files/uploads/research/census_executivesummary.pdf.

Compton, D'Lane, and Tristan Bridges. 2014. "Power, Pomp, and Plaid: Lumbersexuals and White, Heteromasculine Pageantry." *Society Pages,* December 25. Accessed April 18, 2015. http://thesocietypages.org/feminist/2014/12/25/power-pomp-and-plaid-lumbersexuals-and-white-heteromasculine-pageantry.

Comstock, George, and Erica Scharrer. 2007. *Media and the American Child.* Burlington, MA: Academic Press.

Conca, Ken. 2006. *Governing Water: Contentious Transnational Political and Global Institution Building.* Cambridge, MA: MIT Press.

Conca, Ken. 2007. "Water." In *Encyclopedia of Globalization,* edited by J. A. Scholte and R. Robertson. New York: MTM.

Condron, Dennis J., Daniel Tope, Christina R. Steidl, and Kendralin J. Freeman. 2013. "Racial Segregation and the Black/White Achievement Gap, 1992 to 2009." *Sociological Quarterly* 54(1): 130–157.

Conley, Dalton, and Brian J. McCabe. 2011. "Body Mass Index and Physical Attractiveness: Evidence from a Combination of Image-Alteration/List Experiment." *Sociological Methods and Research* 40: 6–31.

Conley, Dean, and Benjamin Dominique. 2016. "The Bell Curve Revisited: Testing Controversial Hypotheses with Molecular Genetic Data." *Sociological Science* 3: 520-539.

Connell, Raewyn. 2009. *Gender.* Cambridge: Polity Press.

Connell, Robert W. 1987. *Gender and Power: Society, the Person and Sexual Politics.* Palo Alto, CA: Stanford University Press.

Connell, Robert W. 1997. "Hegemonic Masculinity and Emphasized Femininity." In *Feminist Frontiers IV,* edited by L. Richardson, V. Taylor, and N. Whittier, 22–25. New York: McGraw-Hill.

Connellan, Kathleen. Forthcoming. "Cult of Domesticity." In *The Wiley-Blackwell Encyclopedia of Gender and Sexuality Studies,* edited by Nancy Naples.

Connor, Phillip. 2012. *Faith on the Move: The Religious Affiliation of International Migrants.* Washington, DC: Pew Research Center.

Conrad, Peter. 1986. "Problems in Health Care." In *Social Problems,* 2nd ed., edited by George Ritzer, 415–450. New York: Random House.

Conrad, Peter, Thomas Mackie, and Ateev Mehrota. 2010. "Estimating the Costs of Medicalization." *Social Science & Medicine* 70: 1943–1947.

Conrad, Peter, and Joseph W. Schneider. 1980. *Deviance and Medicalization: From Badness to Sickness.* St. Louis, MO: Mosby.

Considine, Austin. 2012. "Gay Marriage Victory Still Shadowed by AIDS." *New York Times,* January 1.

Contreras, Randol. 2017. *The Stickup Kids: Race, Drugs, Violence, and the American Dream.* Berkeley: University of California Press.

Cook, Alison, and Christy Glass. 2014. "Women and Top Leadership Positions: Towards an Institutional Analysis." *Gender, Work & Organization* 21(1): 91–103.

Cook, Daniel Thomas 2004. *The Commodification of Childhood: The Children's Clothing Industry and the Rise of the Child Consumer.* Durham, NC: Duke University Press.

Cook, Daniel Thomas. 2007. "Consumer Culture, Children's." In *The Blackwell Encyclopedia of Sociology,* edited by George Ritzer, 693–697. Malden, MA: Blackwell.

Cook, Daniel Thomas, and J. Michael Ryan, eds. 2015. *The Wiley-Blackwell Encyclopedia of Consumption and Consumer Studies.* Malden, MA: Wiley-Blackwell.

Cook, John, Dana Nuccitelli, Sarah A. Green, Mark Richardson, Bärbel Winkler, Rob Painting, Robert Way, Peter Jacobs, and Andrew Skuce. 2013. "Quantifying the Consensus on Anthropogenic Global Warming in the Scientific Literature." *Environmental Research Letters* 8(2): 024024. Accessed April 18, 2015. http://iopscience.iop.org/1748-9326/8/2/024024.

Cook, Karen S., Richard M. Emerson, Mary B. Gilmore, and Toshio Yamagishi. 1983. "The Distribution of Power in Exchange Networks: Theory and Experimental Results." *American Journal of Sociology* 89: 275–305.

Cooksey, Elizabeth. 2007. "Fertility: Adolescent." In *The Blackwell Encyclopedia of Sociology,* edited by George Ritzer, 1725–1729. Malden, MA: Blackwell.

Cooley, Charles Horton. 1909. *Social Organization: A Study of the Larger Mind.* New York: Scribner.

Coontz, Stephanie. 2013. "Why Gender Equality Stalled." *New York Times Sunday Review,* February 17, SR1.

Cooper, Cary L., Alankrita Pandey, and James Quick Campbell, eds. 2012. *Downsizing: Is Less Still More?* Cambridge: Cambridge University Press.

Cooper, Helene. 2016. "U.S. Drops Snark in Favor of Emotion to Undercut Extremists." *New York Times,* July 28.

Copes, Heith, and Crystal Null. 2007. "Property Crime." In *The Blackwell Encyclopedia of Sociology,* edited by George Ritzer, 3675–3676. Malden, MA: Blackwell.

Corak, Miles. 2013. "Income Inequality, Equality of Opportunity, and Intergenerational Mobility." *Journal of Economic Perspectives* 27: 79–102.

Corak, Miles, Matthew J. Lindquist, and Bhashkar Mazumder. 2014. "A Comparison of Upward and Downward Intergenerational Mobility in Canada, Sweden and the United States." *Labour Economics* 30: 185–200.

Corbett, Steven. 2014. "Challenging the Commodification of Public Spheres: The Hacker Work Ethic in a Free Media Lab." *First Monday* 19(12). Accessed April 18, 2015. http://firstmonday.org/ojs/index.php/fm/article/view/3555.

Corder, Mike. 2014. "Dutch Marijuana Laws Rollback Provides Lessons for Legalization in U.S. States." *World Post,* March 7. Accessed April 18, 2015. http://www.huffingtonpost.com/2014/03/07/dutch-marijuana-laws-us-states_n_4918305.html.

Corprew, Charles S., III, and Avery D. Mitchell. 2014. "Keeping It Frat: Exploring the Interaction among Fraternity Membership, Disinhibition, and Hypermasculinity on Sexually Aggressive Attitudes in College-Aged Males." *Journal of College Student Development* 55(6): 548–562.

Correll, Shelley J. 2001. "Gender and the Career Choice Process: The Role of Biased Self-Assessments." *American Journal of Sociology* 106(6): 1691–1730.

Correll, Shelley J. 2004. "Constraints into Preferences: Gender, Status, and Emerging Career Aspirations." *American Sociological Review* 69(1): 93–113.

Correll, Shelley J., Stephen Benard, and In Paik. 2007. "Getting a Job: Is There a Motherhood Penalty?" *American Journal of Sociology* 112(5): 1297–1338.

Corwin, Zoe Blumberg, and William G. Tierney. 2007. "Institutional Review Boards and Sociological Research." In *The Blackwell Encyclopedia of Sociology,* edited by George Ritzer, 2345–2351. Malden, MA: Blackwell.

Coser, Lewis. 1956. *The Functions of Social Conflict.* New York: Free Press.

Costalli, Stefano. 2016. "Expulsion." In *The Wiley-Blackwell Encyclopedia of Race, Ethnicity and Nationalism,* edited by John Stone, Rutledge M. Dennis, Polly Rizova, Anthony D. Smith, and Xiaoshuo Hou. Malden, MA: Wiley-Blackwell.

Cousins, Mel. 2005. *European Welfare States: Comparative Perspectives.* London: Sage.

Coventry, Martha. 2006. "Tyranny of the Esthetic: Surgery's Most Intimate Violation." In *Reconstructing Gender: A Multicultural Anthology,* edited by E. Disch, 203–211. New York: McGraw-Hill.

Covey, Herbert C. 2015. *Crips and Bloods: A Guide to An American Subculture.* Santa Barbara, CA: Greenwood.

Coward, Martin. 2012. "Urban." In *The Wiley-Blackwell Encyclopedia of Globalization,* edited by George Ritzer, 2130–2134. Malden, MA: Wiley-Blackwell.

Cox, Lloyd. 2007. "Socialism." In *The Blackwell Encyclopedia of Sociology,* edited by George Ritzer, 4549–4554. Malden, MA: Blackwell.

Creswell, John. 2008. *Research Design: Qualitative, Quantitative, and Mixed Methods Approaches.* Thousand Oaks, CA: Sage.

Croll, Paul R. 2013. "Explanations for Racial Disadvantage: Beliefs about Both Sides of Inequality in America." *Ethnic and Racial Studies* 36(1): 47–74.

Cross, Remy, and David Snow. 2012. "Social Movements." In *The Wiley-Blackwell Companion to Sociology,* edited by George Ritzer, 522–544. Malden, MA: Wiley-Blackwell.

Crossley, Alison Dahl, and Heather McKee Hurwitz. 2013. "Women's Movements." In *The Wiley-Blackwell Encyclopedia of Social and Political Movements,* 3 vols., edited by D. A. Snow, D. Della Porta, B. Klandermans, and D. McAdam, 1402–1408. Malden, MA: Wiley-Blackwell.

Crothers, Charles. 2011. "Robert K. Merton." In *Wiley-Blackwell Companion to Major Social Theorists,* Vol. 2, *Contemporary Social Theorists,* edited by George Ritzer and Jeffrey Stepnisky, 65–88. West Sussex, UK: Wiley-Blackwell.

Crothers, Lane. 2010. *Globalization and American Popular Culture.* 2nd ed. Lanham, MD: Rowman & Littlefield.

Croucher, Sheila. 2009. *The Other Side of the Fence: American Migrants in Mexico.* Austin: University of Texas Press.

Crowder, Kyle, and Liam Downey. 2010. "Interneighborhood Migration, Race, and Environmental Hazards: Modeling Microlevel Processes of Environmental Inequality." *American Journal of Sociology* 115(4): 1110–1149.

Crowder, Kyle, and Matthew Hall. 2007. "Migration, Internal." In *The Blackwell Encyclopedia of Sociology,* edited by George Ritzer, 3014–3019. Malden, MA: Blackwell.

Crowley, Gregory J. 2007. "Urban Renewal and Development." In *The Blackwell Encyclopedia of Sociology,* edited by George Ritzer, 5128–5132. Malden, MA: Blackwell.

Crump, Jeff. 2007. "Exurbia." In *The Blackwell Encyclopedia of Sociology,* edited by George Ritzer, 1549–1551. Malden, MA: Blackwell.

Crutsinger, Martin. 2010. "G20 Leaders Facing Worries about Rising Deficits." *Bloomberg Businessweek,* June 24. Accessed March 29, 2012. http://www.businessweek.com/ap/financialnews/D9GHNNI81.htm.

Cuaresma, Jesus Crespo, Wolfgang Lutz, and Warren Sanderson. 2014. "Is the Demographic Dividend an Education Dividend?" *Demography* 51: 299–315.

Cullen, Francis T., Cheryl Lero Jonson, and Daniel S. Nagin. 2011. "Prisons Do Not Reduce Recidivism: The High Cost of Ignoring Science." *Prison Journal* 91: 48S–65S.

Culver, Leigh. 2007. "Criminal Justice System." In *The Blackwell Encyclopedia of Sociology,* edited by George Ritzer, 851–856. Malden, MA: Blackwell.

Cumming-Bruce, Nick. 2015. "United Nations Investigators Accuse ISIS of Genocide over Attacks on Yazidis." *New York Times,* March 19.

Cumming-Bruce, Nick. 2016. "Mass Rape, a Weapon of War, Traumatizes South Sudan." *New York Times,* March 11.

Cunningham, Carolyn, ed. 2013. *Social Networking and Impression Management: Self-Presentation in the Digital Age.* Lanham, MD: Lexington Books.

CursedByTheDiceGods. n.d. "Wal-Mart." *Imgflip.* Accessed February 27, 2017. https://i.img flip.com/4vml7.jpg.

Curtiss, Susan. 1977. *Genie: A Psycholinguistic Study of a Modern-Day "Wild Child."* New York: Academic Press.

Cyert, Richard Michael, and James G. March. 1963. *A Behavioral Theory of the Firm.* Englewood Cliffs, NJ: Prentice Hall.

Dahlberg, Lincoln. 2010. "Cyber-Libertarianism 2.0: A Discourse Theory/Critical Political Economy Examination." *Cultural Politics* 6: 331–356.

Dahrendorf, Ralf. 1959. *Class and Class Conflict in Industrial Society.* Stanford, CA: Stanford University Press.

Daipha, Phaedra. 2012. "Weathering Risk: Uncertainty, Weather Forecasting, and Expertise." *Sociological Compass* 6: 15–25.

Daley, Suzanne. 2011. "N.Y.U., in the U.A.E." *New York Times,* April 15.

Damer, Sean. 1974. "Wine Alley: The Sociology of a Dreadful Enclosure." *Sociological Review* 22: 221–248.

Dandaneau, Steven P. 2007. "Norms." In *The Blackwell Encyclopedia of Sociology,* edited by George Ritzer, 3229–3232. Malden, MA: Blackwell.

Dandaneau, Steven P. 2012. "Deindustrialization." In *The Wiley-Blackwell Encyclopedia of Globalization,* edited by George Ritzer, 385–387. Malden, MA: Wiley-Blackwell.

Daniels, Jessie. 2009. *Cyber Racism: White Supremacy Online and the New Attack on Civil Rights.* Lanham, MD: Rowman & Littlefield.

Dant, Tim. 2007. "Material Culture." In *The Blackwell Encyclopedia of Sociology,* edited by George Ritzer, 2835. Malden, MA: Blackwell.

Dargent, Fanny. 2014. "Scarifications Rituelles = Ritual Scarifications." *Revue Adolescence* 32: 47–56.

Da Silva, Julia. 2015. "Children and Electronic Media: How Much is Too Much?" *In the Public Interest Newsletter,* June. Washington, DC: American Psychological Association. www.apa.org/pi/about/newsletter/2015/06/electronic-media.aspx.

Datar, Srikant, David A. Garvin, and Patrick G. Cullen. 2010. *Rethinking the MBA: Business Education at a Crossroads.* Cambridge, MA: Harvard Business Review Press.

Davenport, Christian. 2015. *How Social Movements Die: Repression and Demobilization of the Republic of New Africa.* Cambridge: Cambridge University Press.

Davenport, Coral, and Campbell Robertson. 2016. "Resettling the First American 'Climate Refugees.'" *New York Times,* May 2.

David, Matthew, and Peter Millwood. 2012. "Football's Coming Home? Digital Reterritorialization, Contradictions in the Transnational Coverage of Sport and the Sociology of Alternative Football Broadcasts." *British Journal of Sociology* 63: 349–369.

David, Richard J., and James W. Collins. 2014. "Layers of Inequality: Power, Policy, and Health." *American Journal of Public Health,* suppl. 104(S1): S8–S10.

Davidson, Alexander, Sally Slavinski, Kendra Komoto, Jennifer Rakeman, and Don Weiss. 2016. "Suspected Female-to-Male Sexual Transmission of Zika Virus—New York City, 2016." *Centers for Disease Control and Prevention* 65.

Davie, Grace. 2013. *The Sociology of Religion: A Critical Agenda.* Thousand Oaks, CA: Sage.

Davis, Deborah, and Sara Friedman, eds. 2014. *Wives, Husbands and Lovers: Marriage and Sexuality in Hong Kong, Taiwan and Urban China.* Redwood, CA: Stanford University Press.

Davis, F. James. 1991. *Who Is Black? One Nation's Definition.* Philadelphia: Penn State University Press. Accessed January 27, 2012. http://www.pbs.org/wgbh/pages/frontline/shows/jefferson/mixed/onedrop.html.

Davis, Flora. [1991] 1999. *Moving the Mountain: The Women's Movement in America since 1960.* New York: Simon & Schuster.

Davis, Kingsley. 1940. "Extreme Social Isolation of a Child." *American Journal of Sociology* 45(4): 554–565.

Davis, Kingsley. 1945. "The World Demographic Transition." *Annals of the American Academy of Political and Social Science* 237: 1–110.

Davis, Kingsley. 1947. "Final Note on a Case of Extreme Isolation." *American Journal of Sociology* 50: 432–437.

Davis, Kingsley, and Wilbert E. Moore. 1945. "Some Principles of Stratification." *American Sociological Review* 10(2): 242–249.

Davis, Mike. 2002. *Late Victorian Holocausts: El Niño Famines and the Making of the Third World.* New York: Verso Books.

Davis, Mike. 2007. *Planet of Slums.* London: Verso Books.

Davis-Blake, Allison, and Joseph P. Broschak. 2009. "Outsourcing and the Changing Nature of Work." *Annual Review of Sociology* 35: 321–340.

Dean, Cornelia. 2007. "Experts Discuss Engineering Feats, Like Space Mirror, to Slow Climate Change." *New York Times,* November 10.

Death Penalty Information Center. 2016. "Executions and Death Sentences Around the World." http://www.deathpenaltyinfo.org/death-penalty-international-perspective#interexec.

Debas, Haile T. 2010. "Global Health: Priority Agenda for the 21st Century." *UN Chronicle* 47(2). Accessed March 29, 2012. http://www.un.org/wcm/content/site/chronicle/cache/bypass/home/archive/issues2010/achieving_global_health/globalhealth_priorityagendaforthe21stcentury?ctnscroll_articleContainerList=1_0&ctnlistpagination_articleContainerList=true.

de Beauvoir, Simone. [1952] 1973. *The Second Sex,* translated by H. M. Parshley. New York: Vintage Books.

Decker, Scott H., and G. David Curry. 2000. "Addressing Key Features of Gang Membership: Measuring the Involvement of Young Members." *Journal of Criminal Justice* 28: 473–482.

Decuir-Gunby, Jessica T., and Jocelyn D. Taliaferro. 2013. "The Impact of School Resegregation on the Racial Identity Development of African American Students: The Example of Wake County." In *The Resegregation of Schools: Education and Race in the Twenty-First Century,* edited by J. K. Donnor and A. D. Dixson, 139–163. New York: Routledge.

Deeming, Chris, and David Hayes. 2012. "Worlds of Welfare Capitalism and Wellbeing: A Multilevel Analysis." *Journal of Social Policy* 41(4): 811–829.

de Graaf, Paul M. 2007. "Stratification: Functional and Conflict Theories." In *The Blackwell Encyclopedia of Sociology,* edited by George Ritzer, 4797–4799. Malden, MA: Blackwell.

de Kerckhove, Derrick Tupper, Charles Kenneth Minns, and Chu, Cindy. 2015. "Estimating Fish Exploitation and Aquatic Habitat Loss across Diffuse Inland Recreational Fisheries." *PLoS ONE* 10(4).

De Laat, Kim, and Shyon Baumann, 2016. "Caring Consumption as Marketing Schema: Representations of Motherhood in an Era of Hyperconsumption." *Journal of Gender Studies* 25: 183–199.

DeLamater, John. 2012. "Sexual Expression in Later Life: A Review and Synthesis." *Journal of Sex Research* 49(2–3): 125–141.

Delaney, Tim. 2012. "Georg Simmel's Flirting and Secrecy and Its Application to the Facebook Relationship Status—'It's Complicated.'" *Journalism and Mass Communication* 2: 637–647.

De Lissovoy, Noah, and José García. 2013. "Doing School Time: The Hidden Curriculum Goes to Prison." *Journal of Critical Education Policy Studies* 11(4): 49–68.

Della Porta, Donatella, and Mario Diani, eds. 2015. *The Oxford Handbook of Social Movements.* Oxford: Oxford University Press.

DeLuzio Chasin, C. J. 2011. "Theoretical Issues in the Study of Asexuality." *Archives of Sexual Behavior* 40(4): 713–723.

D'Emilio, John. 1983. *Sexual Politics, Sexual Communities.* Chicago: University of Chicago Press.

DeNavas-Walt, Carmen, and Bernadette Proctor. 2015. *Income and Poverty in the United States: 2014.* Washington, DC: U.S. Census Bureau. https://www.census.gov/content/dam/Census/library/publications/2015/demo/p60-252.pdf.

DeNavas-Walt, Carmen, Bernadette D. Proctor, and Jessica C. Smith. 2012. *Income, Poverty, and Health Insurance Coverage in the United States: 2011.* Current Population Reports P60-243. Washington, DC: U.S. Census Bureau, September. Accessed March 29, 2012. https://www.census.gov/prod/2012pubs/p60-243.pdf.

Denegri-Knott, Janice, and Detlev Zwick. 2012. "Tracking Prosumption Work on eBay: Reproduction of Desire and the Challenge of Slow Re-McDonaldization." *American Behavioral Scientist* 56: 439–458.

Dentler, Robert A., and Kai T. Erikson. 1959. "The Function of Deviance in Small Groups." *Social Problems* 7: 98–107.

Denyer, Simon. 2016. "China's Scary Lesson to the World: Censoring the Internet Works." *The Washington Post,* March 23.

Denzin, Norman K., and Yvonna S. Lincoln. 2011. "Introduction: The Discipline and Practice of Qualitative Research." In *The SAGE Handbook of Qualitative Research,* 4th ed., edited by Norman K. Denzin and Yvonna S. Lincoln, 1–20. Thousand Oaks, CA: Sage.

DeParle, Jason, Robert Gebeloff, and Sabrina Tavernise. 2011. "Older, Suburban and Struggling." *New York Times,* November 19.

de Regt, Marina. 2009. "Preferences and Prejudices: Employers' Views on Domestic Workers in the Republic of Yemen." *Signs* 34(3): 559–581.

Desai, Sonalde. 2010. "The Other Half of the Demographic Dividend." *Economic and Political Weekly* 45(40): 12–14.

De Silva, Dakshina G., Robert P. McComb, Young-Kyu Moh, Anita R. Schiller, and Andres J. Vargas. 2010. "The Effect of Migration on Wages: Evidence from a Natural Experiment." *American Economic Review: Papers and Proceedings* 100(May): 321–326.

DeSilver, Drew. 2013. "U.S. Income Inequality, on Rise for Decades, Is Now Highest since 1928." Pew Research Center, December 5. Accessed April 29, 2015. http://www.pewresearch.org/fact-tank/2013/12/05/u-s-income-inequality-on-rise-for-decades-is-now-highest-since-1928.

Desmond, Matthew. 2010. *Eviction and the Reproduction of Poverty.* PhD dissertation, University of Wisconsin.

Desmond, Matthew. 2016. *Evicted: Poverty and Profit in the American City.* NY: Crown.

Deutsch, Kevin. 2014. *The Triangle: A Year on the Ground with New York's Bloods and Crips.* Guilford, CT: Lyons Press.

Deutsch, Nancy L., and Eleni Theodorou. 2010. "Aspiring, Consuming, Becoming: Youth Identity in a Culture of Consumption." *Youth & Society* 42(2): 229–254.

DeVault, Marjorie. 1991. *Feeding the Family: The Social Organization of Caring as Gendered Work.* Chicago: University of Chicago Press.

Dewey, Susan. 2015. "Sex Work." In *Handbook of the Sociology of Sexualities,* edited by J. DeLamater and R. F. Plante. Dordrecht, Netherlands: Springer.

Dey, Eric L. 1997. "Undergraduate Political Attitudes: Peer Influence in Changing Social Contexts." *Journal of Higher Education* 68: 398–416.

Diamond, Jared. 2006. *Collapse: How Societies Choose to Fail or Succeed.* New York: Penguin.

Dicke, Thomas S. 1992. *Franchising in America: The Development of a Business Method, 1840–1980.* Chapel Hill: University of North Carolina Press.

Dickson, Lynda, Richard Dukes, Hilary Smith, and Noel Strapko. 2014. "Stigma of Ink: Tattoo Attitudes among College Students." *Social Science Journal* 51(2): 268–276.

Dikötter, Frank. 2008. "The Racialization of the Globe: An Interactive Interpretation." *Ethnic and Racial Studies* 31(8): 1478–1496.

Dill, Janette S., Kim Price-Glynn, and Carter Rakovski. 2016. "Does the 'Glass Escalator' Compensate for the Devaluation of Care Work Occupations?: The Careers of Men in Low- and Middle-Skill Health Care Jobs," *Gender & Society* 0(2): 334–360.

DiMaggio, Paul J., and Walter W. Powell. 1983. "The Iron Cage Revisited: Institutional Isomorphism and Collective Rationality in Organizational Fields." *American Sociological Review* 48: 147–160.

Diotallevi, Luca. 2007. "Church." In *The Blackwell Encyclopedia of Sociology,* edited by George Ritzer, 483–489. Malden, MA: Blackwell.

DiPrete, Thomas A., Gregory M. Eirich, Karen S. Cook, and Douglas S. Massey. 2006. "Cumulative Advantage as a Mechanism for Inequality: A Review of Theoretical and Empirical Developments." *Annual Review of Sociology* 32: 271–297.

Directorate-General for Employment, Industrial Relations and Social Affairs. 1998. "Sexual Harassment at the Workplace in the European Union." Brussels, European Commission.

DiTomaso, Nancy. 2013. *The American Non-dilemma: Racial Inequality without Racism.* New York: Russell Sage Foundation.

Dobbelaere, Karel. 2007. "Secularization." In *The Blackwell Encyclopedia of Sociology,* edited by George Ritzer, 4140–4148. Malden, MA: Blackwell.

Dodd, Nigel. 2012. "Money." In *The Wiley-Blackwell Encyclopedia of Globalization,* edited by George Ritzer, 1444–1448. Malden, MA: Wiley-Blackwell.

Doherty, Carroll. 2013. "For African Americans, Discrimination Is Not Dead." Pew Research Center, *Fact Tank,* June 28. Accessed May 7, 2015. http://www.pewresearch.org/fact-tank/2013/06/28/for-african-americans-discrimina tion-is-not-dead.

Dolan, Kerry A., and Luisa Kroll. 2014. "Inside the 2014 Forbes 400: Facts and Figures about America's Wealthiest." *NBC News,* September 29. Accessed April 18, 2015. http://www.nbcnews.com/business/economy/rich-get-richer-bill-gates-tops-forbes-400-list-richest-n214196.

Dolata, Ulrich, and Jan-Felix Schrape, 2016. "Masses, Crowds, Communities, Movement: Collective Action in the Internet Age." *Social Movement Studies* 15: 1–18.

Dombrink, John, and Daniel Hillyard. 2007. *Sin No More: From Abortion to Stem Cells, Understanding Crime, Law, and Morality in America.* New York: New York University Press.

Dombrowski, Stefan C., Karen L. Gischlar, and Martin Mrazik. 2011. "Feral Children." In *Assessing and Treating Low Incidence/High Severity Psychological Disorders of Childhood,* 81–93. New York: Springer.

Domhoff, G. William. 1974. *The Bohemian Grove and Other Retreats: A Study in Ruling-Class Cohesiveness.* New York: Harper & Row.

Domhoff, G. William. 2013. *Who Rules America? The Triumph of Corporate Rich.* New York: McGraw-Hill.

Dominguez, Sylvia, and Amy Lubitow. 2008. "Transnational Ties, Poverty, and Identity: Latin American Immigrant Women in Public Housing." *Family Relations* 57: 419–430.

Dooley, David, and JoAnn Prause. 2009. *The Social Costs of Underemployment: Inadequate Employment as Disguised Unemployment.* Cambridge: Cambridge University Press.

Dorius, Shawn, and Glenn Firebaugh. 2010. "Trends in Global Gender Inequality." *Social Forces* 88(5): 1941–1968.

Dotter, Daniel L., and Julian B. Roebuck. 1988. "The Labeling Approach Re-examined: Interactionism and the Components of Deviance." *Deviant Behavior* 9(1): 19–32.

Douglas, Susan J., and Meredith W. Michaels. 2006. "The New Momism." In *Reconstructing Gender: A Multicultural Anthology,* edited by E. Disch, 226–238. New York: McGraw-Hill.

Douglas-Gabriel, Danielle. 2016. "The Surprising Growth of Graduate Enrollment at For-Profit Colleges." *Washington Post,* December 1.

Dow, Dawn Marie. 2016. "The Deadly Challenges of Raising African American Boys. *Gender & Society* 30: 161–188.

Downes, David, Paul Rock, and Eugene McLaughlin. 2016. *Understanding Deviance: A Guide to the Sociology of Crime and Rule-Breaking.* Oxford: Oxford University Press.

Downey, Douglas B., and Dennis J. Condron. 2016. "Fifty Years Since the Coleman Report: Rethinking the Relationship between Schools and Inequality." *Sociology of Education* 89: 207–220.

Downey, Douglas B., Paul T. von Hippel, and Beckett A. Broh. 2004. "Are Schools the Great Equalizer? Cognitive Inequality during the Summer Months and the School Year." *American Sociological Review* 69: 613–635.

Doyle, Thomas P. 2003. "Roman Catholic Clericalism, Religious Duress, and Clergy Sexual Abuse." *Pastoral Psychology* 51(3): 189–231.

Drache, D. (with M. D. Froese). 2008. *Defiant Publics: The Unprecedented Reach of the Global Citizen.* Cambridge: Polity Press.

Drake, Bruce. 2014. "Polls Show Strong Support for Minimum Wage Hike." Pew Research Center, *Fact Tank,* March 4. Accessed April 29, 2015. http://www.pewresearch.org/fact-tank/2014/03/04/polls-show-strong-support-for-minimum-wage-hike.

Drane, John. 2008. *After McDonaldization: Mission, Ministry, and Christian Discipleship in an Age of Uncertainty.* Grand Rapids, MI: Baker.

Drane, John. 2012. *The McDonaldization of the Church: Consumer Culture and the Church's Future.* Macon, GA: Smith and Helwys.

Dreeben, Robert. 1968. *On What Is Learned in School.* Reading, MA: Addison-Wesley.

Dreher, Axel, Jan-Egbert Sturm, and James Raymond Vreeland. 2009. "Global Horse Trading: IMF Loans for Votes in the United Nations Security Council." *European Economic Review* 53: 742–757.

Drori, Gili. 2006. *Global E-litism: Digital Technology, Social Inequality and Transnationality.* New York: Worth.

Drori, Gili S. 2012. "Digital Divide." In *The Wiley-Blackwell Encyclopedia of Globalization,* edited by George Ritzer, 435–438. Malden, MA: Wiley-Blackwell.

Duany, Andrés, and Elizabeth Plater-Zyberk. 1990. "Projects of Villages, Towns and Cities, Territories, and Codes." In *Towns and*

Town-Making Principles, edited by A. Krieger and W. Lennertz. New York: Rizzoli.

Duany, Andrés, Elizabeth Plater-Zyberk, and Jeff Speck. 2010. Suburban Nation: The Rise of Sprawl and the Decline of the American Dream. 10th anniversary ed. New York: North Point Press.

Duany, Andrés, and Emily Talen, eds. 2013. Landscape Urbanism and its Discontents: Dissimulating the Sustainable City. Gabriola Island, BC: New Society.

Duberman, Martin B. 1994. Stonewall. New York: Plume.

Du Bois, W. E. B. [1899] 1996. The Philadelphia Negro: A Social Study. Philadelphia: University of Pennsylvania Press.

Du Bois, W. E. B. [1903] 1966. The Souls of Black Folk. New York: Modern Library.

Duckworth, Angela L., and Stephanie M. Carlson. 2013. "Self-Regulation and School Success." In Self-Regulation and Autonomy: Social and Developmental Dimensions of Human Conduct, edited by B. W. Sokol, F. M. E. Grouzet, and U. Müller, 208–230. New York: Cambridge University Press.

Duckworth, Angela L., and Martin E. P. Seligman. 2005. "Self-Discipline Outdoes IQ in Predicting Academic Performance of Adolescents." Psychological Science 16: 939–944.

Duhigg, Charles. 2017. "Business Government." New York Times, January 19.

Duhigg, Charles, and Keith Bradsher. 2012. "How the U.S. Lost Out on iPhone Work." New York Times, January 22.

Dujarier, Marie-Anne. 2014. "The Three Sociological Types of Consumer Work." Journal of Consumer Culture, April 9 (published online). doi: 10.1177/1469540514528198.

Dukes, Richard L., and Judith A. Stein. 2011. "Ink and Holes: Correlates and Predictive Associations of Body Modification among Adolescents." Youth & Society 43: 1547–1569.

Dumazadier, Joffre. 1967. Toward a Society of Leisure. New York: Free Press.

Duncan, Greg J., Kathleen M. Ziol-Guest, and Ariel Kalil. 2010. "Early-Childhood Poverty and Adult Attainment, Behavior, and Health." Child Development 81: 306–325.

Duncan, Simon. 2014. "Women's Agency in Living Apart Together: Constraint, Strategy, and Vulnerability." Sociological Review, September 5 (published online). doi: 10.1111/1467-954X.12184.

Duneier, Mitchell. 1999. Sidewalk. New York: Farrar, Straus and Giroux.

Dunham, Lena. 2014. Not That Kind of Girl: A Young Woman Tells You What She's Learned. New York: Random House.

Dunlap, Eloise, Bruce D. Johnson, Joseph A. Kotarba, and Jennifer L. Fackler. 2010. "Macro-level Social Forces and Micro-level Consequences: Poverty, Alternate Occupations, and Drug Dealing." Journal of Ethnicity in Substance Abuse 9(2): 115–127.

Dunlap, Riley E., and William R. Catton Jr. 2002. "Which Functions of the Environment Do We Study? A Comparison of Environmental and Natural Resource Sociology." Society and Natural Resources 15: 239–249.

Dunlap, Riley E., and Andrew K. Jorgenson. 2012. "Environmental Problems." In The Wiley-Blackwell Companion to Sociology, edited by George Ritzer, 529–536. Malden, MA: Wiley-Blackwell.

Dunn, Gregory. 2013. "Water Wars." Harvard International Review 35: 46–49.

Dunn, Jennifer L. 2005. "'Victims' and 'Survivors': Emerging Vocabularies of Motive for 'Battered Women Who Stay.'" Sociological Inquiry 75: 1–30.

Dunning, Eric, Patrick Murphy, and John Williams. 1988. The Roots of Football Hooliganism. London: Routledge & Kegan Paul.

Durkheim, Émile. [1893] 1964. The Division of Labor in Society. New York: Free Press.

Durkheim, Émile. [1897] 1951. Suicide. New York: Free Press.

Durkheim, Émile. [1912] 1965. The Elementary Forms of the Religious Life. New York: Free Press.

Durkheim, Émile. [1912] 1972. Émile Durkheim: Selected Writings, edited by A. Giddens. Cambridge: Cambridge University Press.

Durkheim, Émile. [1922] 1956. Education and Society. Glencoe, IL: Free Press.

Durkheim, Émile. [1925] 1973. Moral Education. New York: Free Press.

Durkheim, Émile, and Marcel Mauss. [1903] 1963. Primitive Classification, translated by R. Needham. Chicago: University of Chicago Press.

Duster, Troy. 2003. Backdoor to Eugenics. New York: Routledge.

Dustin, Donna. 2007. The McDonaldization of Social Work. Burlington, VT: Ashgate.

Dutton, Donald G., and Katherine R. White. 2013. "Male Victims of Domestic Violence." New Male Studies 2: 5–17.

Dworkin, Andrea. 1974. Woman Hating. New York: E. P. Dutton.

Earl, Jennifer. 2007. "Social Movements, Repression of." In The Blackwell Encyclopedia of Sociology, edited by George Ritzer, 4475–4479. Malden, MA: Blackwell.

Easterly, William and Tobias Pfutze. 2008. "Where Does the Money Go? Best and Worst Practices in Foreign Aid." Journal of Economic Perspectives 22: 1–35.

"Ebola: Mapping the Outbreak." 2014. BBC News, November 28.

Eckenwiler, Lisa. 2014. "Care Worker Migration, Global Health Equity, and Ethical Place-Making." Women's Studies International Forum 47: 213–222.

Eckert, Penelope, and Sally McConnell-Ginet. 2013. Language and Gender. 2nd ed. New York: Cambridge University Press.

Eder, Steve. 2014. "Points for Product Placement: N.C.A.A. Cashes In, but Not the Players." New York Times, April 5.

Eder, Steve. 2016. "Donald Trump Agrees to Pay $25 Million In Trump University Settlement." New York Times, November 18.

Edin, Kathryn, and Laura Lein. 1997. Making Ends Meet: How Single Mothers Survive Welfare and Low-Wage Work. New York: Russell Sage Foundation.

Edin, Kathryn J., and H. Luke Schaefer, 2015. $2 a Day: Living on Almost Nothing in America. New York: Houghton, Mifflin, Harcourt.

Edmonds, Alex. 2010. Pretty Modern: Beauty, Sex, and Plastic Surgery in Brazil. Durham, NC: Duke University Press.

Edwards, Bob, and Patrick F. Gillham. 2013. "Resource Mobilization Theory." In The Wiley-Blackwell Encyclopedia of Social and Political Movements, 3 vols., edited by D. A. Snow, D. Della Porta, B. Klandermans, and D. McAdam, 1096–1101. Malden, MA: Wiley-Blackwell.

Edwards, Rosalind. Forthcoming. "Stepfathering." In Encyclopedia of Sociology, 2nd ed., edited by George Ritzer. Malden, MA: Wiley-Blackwell.

Edwards, Rosalind, and Lucy Hadfield. 2007. "Stepfathering." In The Blackwell Encyclopedia of Sociology, edited by George Ritzer, 4768–4770. Malden, MA: Blackwell.

Ehrenreich, Barbara. 2001. Nickel and Dimed: On (Not) Getting By in America. New York: Henry Holt.

Ehrenreich, Barbara. 2002. "Maid to Order." In Global Woman: Nannies, Maids, and Sex Workers in the New Economy, edited by B. Ehrenreich and A. R. Hochschild. New York: Henry Holt.

Ehrenreich, Barbara, and Arlie Russell Hochschild. 2002. "Introduction." In Global Woman: Nannies, Maids, and Sex Workers in the New Economy, edited by B. Ehrenreich and A. R. Hochschild, 1–14. New York: Henry Holt.

Ehrlich, Paul. 1968. The Population Bomb. New York: Ballantine.

Eisenhower, Dwight D. 1961. "Farewell address by President Dwight D. Eisenhower, January 17, 1961." Speech Series, Papers of Dwight D. Eisenhower as President, 1953–61, Eisenhower Library; National Archives and Records Administration.

Ekland-Olson, Sheldon. 2012. Who Lives, Who Dies, Who Decides. New York: Routledge.

Elborgh-Woytek, Katrina, Monique Newiak, Kalpana Kochhar, Stefania Fabrizo, Kangi Kpodar, Philippe Wingender, Benedict Clements, and Gerd Schwartz. 2016. Women, Work, and the Economy: Macroeconomic Gains from Gender Equity. Washington, DC: International Monetary Fund.

Elder, Todd, and Christopher Jepsen. 2014. "Are Catholic Primary Schools More Effective than Public Primary Schools?" Journal of Urban Economics 80: 28–38.

Elgin, Duane. 2010. Voluntary Simplicity: Toward a Way of Life That Is Outwardly Simple, Inwardly Rich. 2nd ed. New York: Quill.

Elias, Sean, and Joe R. Feagin. 2016. Racial Theories in Social Science: A Systemic Racism Critique. New York: Routledge.

Elias, Vicky L., Andrew S. Fullerton, and Joseph M. Simpson. 2015. "Long-Term Changes in Attitudes toward Premarital Sex in the United States: Reexamining the Role of Cohort Replacement." Journal of Sex Research 52(2): 129–139.

Eligon, John. 2016. "A Question of Environmental Racism in Flint." New York Times January 22.

Ellin, Abby. 2016. "With Coercive Control, the Abuse Is Psychological." New York Times, July 11.

Elliott, Anthony, and John Urry. 2010. Mobile Lives. London: Routledge.

Elliott, David L. 2012. "Urbanism." In *The Wiley-Blackwell Encyclopedia of Globalization,* edited by George Ritzer, 2134–2136. Malden, MA: Wiley-Blackwell.

Elliott, Diana B., Rebekah Young, and Jane Lawler Dye. 2011. "Variation in the Formation of Complex Family Households during the Recession." SEHSD Working Paper 2011-32. Paper presented at the 73rd Annual Conference of the National Council on Family Relations, Orlando, FL, November 16–19.

Ellis, Allison M., Talya N. Bauer, and Berrin Erdogan. 2015. "New-Employee Organizational Socialization: Adjusting to New Roles, Colleagues, and Organizations." In *Handbook of Socialization: Theory and Research,* 2nd ed., edited by Joan E. Grusec and Paul D. Hastings, 301–324. New York: Guilford Press.

Ellison, Christopher G. 1999. "Introduction to Symposium: Religion, Health, Well-Being." *Journal for the Scientific Study of Religion* 37: 692–693.

Ellison, Katherine. 2015. "A.D.H.D. Rates Rise Around the Globe, but Sympathy Often Lags." *New York Times,* November 9.

Elo, Irma T. 2007. "Mortality: Transitions and Measures." In *The Blackwell Encyclopedia of Sociology,* edited by George Ritzer, 3096–3102. Malden, MA: Blackwell.

Elo, Irma T. 2009. "Social Class Differentials in Health and Mortality: Patterns and Explanations in Comparative Perspective." *Annual Review of Sociology* 35: 553–572.

Ember, Sydney. 2014. "On To-Do List: Deposit Cash in Bitcoin ATM." *New York Times,* August 25.

Emerson, Robert M., ed. 2001. *Contemporary Field Research: Perspectives and Formulations.* 2nd ed. Long Grove, IL: Waveland Press.

Ender, Morton. 2002. *Military Brats and Other Global Nomads: Growing Up in Organization Families.* Westport, CT: Praeger.

Engels, Friedrich. [1884] 1970. *The Origins of the Family, Private Property and the State.* New York: International Publishers.

England, Paula. 2010. "The Gender Revolution: Uneven and Stalled." *Gender & Society* 24(2): 149–166.

England, Paula, and Kathryn Edin. 2009. "Briefing Paper: Unmarried Couples with Children: Why Don't They Marry? How Can Policy-Makers Promote More Stable Relationships?" In *Families as They Really Are,* edited by B. J. Risman, 307–312. New York: Norton.

English, Beth. 2013. "Global Women's Work: Historical Perspectives on the Textile and Garment Industries." *Journal of International Affairs* 67(1): 67–82.

EnglishEnglish.com. n.d. "The English Language: Facts and Figures." Accessed January 3, 2012. http://www.englishenglish.com/english_facts_8.htm.

Entwhistle, Joanne. 2015. *The Aesthetic Economy of Fashion: Markets and Value in Clothing and Modelling.* New York: Berg.

Entwisle, Doris, Karl Alexander, and Linda Olson. 1998. *Children, Schools, and Inequality.* Boulder, CO: Westview Press.

Epstein, Cynthia Fuchs. 1988. *Deceptive Distinctions: Sex, Gender, and the Social Order.* New Haven, CT: Yale University Press.

Epstein, Richard A. 2014. "Big Law and Big Med: The Deprofessionalization of Legal and Medical Services." *International Review of Law and Economics* 38: 64–76.

Epstein, Steve. 2009. *Inclusion: The Politics of Difference in Medical Research.* Chicago: University of Chicago Press.

Erikson, Erik. 1994. *Identity and the Life Cycle.* New York: Norton.

Erikson, Kai T. 1964. "Notes on the Sociology of Deviance." In *The Other Side: Perspectives on Deviance,* edited by H. S. Becker. New York: Free Press.

Erikson, Kai T. 1976. *Everything in Its Path: Destruction of Community in the Buffalo Creek Flood.* New York: Simon & Schuster.

Erlanger, Steven. 2008. "Tense Rivalries Threaten a Melting-Pot District." *New York Times,* September 24.

Erlanger, Steven. 2010a. "Expulsion of Roma Raises Questions in France." *New York Times,* August 19.

Erlanger, Steven. 2010b. "A French Castle Built of Stone and Dreams." *New York Times,* August 1.

Erlanger, Steven. 2014. "In West ISIS Finds Women Eager to Enlist." *New York Times,* October 23.

Esping-Anderson, Gosta. 1990. *The Three Worlds of Welfare Capitalism.* Princeton, NJ: Princeton University Press.

Etezadazdeh, Chirine. 2016. *Smart City—Future City? Smart City 2.0 as a Livable City and Future Market.* Neu-Isenburg: Springer.

Etzioni, Amitai, ed. 1969. *The Semi-professions and Their Organization: Teachers, Nurses, and Social Workers.* New York: Free Press.

Fabricant, Michael, and Michelle Fine. 2012. *Charter Schools and the Corporate Makeover of Public Education.* New York: Teachers College Press.

Fackler, Martin. 2011. "Severed from the World, Villagers Survive on Tight Bonds and To-Do Lists." *New York Times,* March 23. Accessed March 29, 2012. http://www.nytimes.com/2011/03/24/world/asia/24isolated.html?adxnnl=1&adxnnlx=1332612166-pPLwIe5h gFAW4cQM2m4bWQ.

Faderman, Lillian. 1991. *Odd Girls and Twilight Lovers: A History of Lesbian Life in Twentieth-Century America.* New York: Penguin.

Fadiman, Anne. 2012. *The Spirit Catches You and You Fall Down: A Hmong Child, Her American Doctors, and the Collision of Two Cultures.* Rev. ed. New York: Farrar, Straus and Giroux.

Fahim, Kareem. 2010. "Away from Home, Fleeing Domestic Life: Immigrant Maids Suffer Abuse in Kuwait." *New York Times,* August 2.

Fair Trade International. 2015. *Global Change, Local Leadership.* Accessed March 8, 2017. https://www.fairtrade.net/new/latest-news/single-view/article/global-change-local-leadership-new-ideas-and-new-markets-drive-increased-benefits-for-farmers-and.html.

Faist, Thomas. 2012. "Migration." In *The Wiley-Blackwell Encyclopedia of Globalization,* edited by George Ritzer, 1384–1388. Malden, MA: Wiley-Blackwell.

Faist, Thomas, Margit Fauser, and Eveline Reisenauer. 2013. *Transnational Migration.* Cambridge: Polity Press.

Fallon, James. 2013. *The Psychopath Inside: A Neuroscientist's Personal Journey into the Dark Side of the Brain.* New York: Penguin.

Fantasia, Rick. 1992. "The Assault on American Labor." In *Social Problems,* edited by C. Calhoun and G. Ritzer. New York: McGraw-Hill.

Fantasia, Rick, and Kim Voss. 2007. "Labor Movement." In *The Blackwell Encyclopedia of Sociology,* edited by George Ritzer, 2518–2521. Malden, MA: Blackwell.

Fantasia, Rick, Kim Voss, and Barry Eidlin. 2013. "Labor Movement." In *The Wiley-Blackwell Encyclopedia of Social and Political Movements,* 3 vols., edited by D. A. Snow, D. Della Porta, B. Klandermans, and D. McAdam, 665–671. Malden, MA: Wiley-Blackwell.

Farber, Henry. 2011. "Job Loss in the Great Recession: Historical Perspective from Displaced Workers Survey, 1984–2010." Paper presented at a Federal Reserve Conference, San Francisco, May.

Farber, Henry S. 2015 *Job loss in the Great Recession and Its Aftermath: U.S. Evidence from the Displaced Workers Survey.* Cambridge, MA: National Bureau of Economic Research.

Farley, John E. 2007. "Metropolitan Statistical Area." In *The Blackwell Encyclopedia of Sociology,* edited by George Ritzer, 2993–2996. Malden, MA: Blackwell.

Farley, John E. 2011. *Majority–Minority Relations.* 6th ed., Census Update. Upper Saddle River, NJ: Prentice Hall.

Farr, Kathryn. 2005. *Sex Trafficking: The Global Market in Women and Children.* New York: Worth.

Farrell, Betty, Alicia VandeVusse, and Abigail Ocobock. 2012. "Family Change and the State of Family Sociology." *Current Sociology* 60(3): 283–301.

Farrell, Caitlin, Priscilla Wolhstetter, and Joanna Smith. 2012. "Charter Management Organizations: An Emerging Approach to Scaling Up What Works." *Educational Policy* 26(4): 499–532.

Farrell, Dan, and James C. Peterson. 2010. "The Growth of Internet Research Methods and the Reluctant Sociologist." *Sociological Inquiry* 80: 114–125.

Fassmann, Heinz, and Rainer Munz. 1992. "Patterns and Trends of International Migration in Western Europe." *Population and Development Review* 18: 457–480.

Fausto-Sterling, A. 1999. "The Five Sexes: Why Female and Male Are Not Enough." *The Sciences,* March/April, 20–24.

Feagin, Joe R. 2006. *Systemic Racism: A Theory of Oppression.* New York: Routledge.

Feagin, Joe R. 2010. *The White Racial Frame: Centuries of Racial Framing and Counter-framing.* New York: Routledge.

Feagin, Joe R. 2012. *White Party, White Government: Race, Class, and U.S. Politics.* New York: Routledge.

Feagin, Joe R. 2013. *The White Racial Frame: Centuries of Racial Framing and Counter-framing.* 2nd ed. New York: Routledge.

Feagin, Joe R., and Jose A. Cobas. 2014. *Latinos Facing Racism: Discrimination, Resistance, and Endurance.* New York: Paradigm Publishers.

Federal Bureau of Investigation. 2014. "Frequently Asked Questions about the Change in the UCR Definition of Rape." December 11. Accessed April 19, 2015. http://www.fbi .gov/about-us/cjis/ucr/recent-program-up dates/new-rape-definition-frequently-asked-questions.

Ferguson, Ann Arnett. 2001. *Bad Boys: Public Schools in the Making of Black Masculinity.* Ann Arbor: University of Michigan Press.

Fernandes, Leela. 2013. *Transnational Feminism in the United States: Knowledge, Ethics, Power.* New York: New York University Press.

Fernandez, Bina. 2010. "Cheap and Disposable? The Impact of the Global Economic Crisis on the Migration of Ethiopian Women Domestic Workers to the Gulf." *Gender and Development* 8(2): 249–262.

Fernandez, Manny. 2015. "A Global Community's College." *New York Times,* October 30. www .nytimes.com/2015/11/01/education/edlife/ houston-community-college-international-students.html?_r=1.

Fernandez, Manny, Richard Perez-Pena, and Jonah Engel Bromwich, 2016. "Five Dallas Police Officers Were Killed as Payback, Police Chief Says." *New York Times,* July 8.

Fernyhough, Charles. 2014. "Do Deaf People Hear an Inner Voice?" *Psychology Today,* Voices Within blog, January 24. Accessed April 27, 2015. https//:www.psychologytoday.com/ blog/the-voices-within/201401/do-deaf-people-hear-inner-voice.

Ferrara, Antonio. 2015. "Beyond Genocide and Ethnic Cleansing: Demographic Surgery as a New Way to Understand Mass Violence." *Journal of Genocide Research* 17: 1–20.

Ferrarini, Tommy, and Kenneth Nelson. 2016. "Social Tranfers and Poverty in Middle- and High-Income Countries—A Global Perspective." *Global Social Policy* 16: 22–46.

Ferraro, Emilia. 2011. "Trueque: An Ethnographic Account of Barter, Trade and Money in Andean Ecuador." *Journal of Latin American and Caribbean Anthropology* 16: 168–184.

Ferraro, Kenneth F., and Seoyoun Kim. 2014. "Health Benefits of Religion among Black and White Older Adults? Race, Religiosity, and C-Reactive Protein." *Social Science & Medicine* 120: 92–99.

Ferree, Myra Marx, and Aili Mari Tripp. 2006. "Preface." In *Global Feminism: Transnational Women's Activism, Organizing, and Human Rights,* edited by M. M. Ferree and A. M. Tripp, vii–ix. New York: New York University Press.

Ferreira, Vitor Sérgio. 2014. "Becoming a Heavily Tattooed Young Body: From a Bodily Experience to a Body Project." *Youth & Society* 46(3): 303–337.

Fetscherin, Marc, and Renee-Marie Stephano, 2016. "The Medical Tourism Index: Scale Development and Validation." *Tourism Management* 52: 539-556.

Few-Demo, April L., and David H. Demo, 2016. "Family Diversity." In *The Wiley-Blackwell Encyclopedia of Race, Ethnicity and Nationalism,* edited by John Stone, Rutledge M. Dennis, Polly Rizova, Anthony D. Smith, and Xiaoshuo Hou. Malden, MA: Wiley-Blackwell.

Fiddian-Qasmiyeh, Elena. 2012. "Diaspora." In *The Wiley-Blackwell Encyclopedia of Globalization,* edited by George Ritzer, 430–433. Malden, MA: Wiley-Blackwell.

Fielding, A. J. 1989. "Migration and Urbanization in Western Europe since 1950." *Geographical Journal* 155: 60–69.

Fields, Jessica, Martha Copp, and Sherryl Kleinman. 2007. "Symbolic Interactionism, Inequality, and Emotions." In *Handbook of the Sociology of Emotions,* edited by J. E. Stets and J. H. Turner, 155–178. New York: Springer.

Figlio, David, and Cassandra M. Hart. 2014. "Competitive Effects of Means-Tested of School Vouchers." *American Economic Journal: Applied Economics* 6: 133–156.

Figueiredo, Zenólia Christina Campos, Janaína Esfalsini Figueira, Sandra Soares Della Fonte, and Francisco Eduardo Caparróz. 2016. "Between the Prescribed and the Lived in Physical Education lessons." *Sport, Education and Society* 21: 945–962.

Filkins, Dexter. 2016. "The End of Ice: Exploring a Himalayan Glacier." *New Yorker,* April 4.

Fillipi, Veronique, Carine Ronsman, Oona M. R. Campbell, Wendy J. Graham, Anne Mills, Jo Borghi, Marjorie Koblinsky, and David Osrin. 2006. "Maternal Health in Poor Countries: The Broader Context and a Call for Action." *The Lancet* 368: 1525–1541.

Fine, Gary Alan. 1987. *With the Boys: Little League Baseball and Preadolescent Culture.* Chicago: University of Chicago.

Fine, Gary Alan. 2008. *Kitchens: The Culture of Restaurant Work.* Berkeley: University of California Press.

Fine, Gary Alan. 2010. *Authors of the Storm: Meteorologists and the Culture of Prediction.* Chicago: University of Chicago Press.

Fine, Gary Alan. 2012. "Group Culture and the Interaction Order: Local Sociology on the Meso-Level." *Annual Review of Sociology* 38: 159–179.

Fine, Gary Alan. 2015. *Players and Pawns: How Chess Builds Community and Culture.* Chicago: University of Chicago Press.

Fink, Sheri. 2014. "Treating those Treating Ebola in Liberia." *New York Times,* November 3.

Finke, Roger and Rodney Stark. 2005. *The Churching of America, 1776–2005: Winners and Losers in Our Religious Economy.* New Brunswick, NJ: Rutgers University Press.

Firebaugh, Glenn, and Brian Goesling. 2007. "Globalization and Global Inequalities: Recent Trends." In *The Blackwell Companion to Globalization,* edited by George Ritzer, 549–564. Malden, MA: Blackwell.

Fischer, Claude S., Michael Hout, Martin Sanchez Jankowski, and Samuel R. Lucas, eds. 1996. *Inequality by Design: Cracking the Bell Curve Myth.* Princeton, NJ: Princeton University Press.

Fisher, Dana. 2012. "Environmental Activism." In *The Wiley-Blackwell Encyclopedia of Globalization,* edited by George Ritzer, 517–519. Malden, MA: Wiley-Blackwell.

Fisher, Max. 2016. "Attack in Nice, France, Represents Terrorism's New Reality." *New York Times,* July 15.

Fitzsimmons, Emma G. 2016. "Subways in Northeast Showing Their Age. That Isn't the Only Problem." *New York Times,* May 27.

Flack, William F., Jr., Kimberly A. Daubman, Marcia L. Caron, Jenica A. Asadorian, Nicole R. D'Aureli, Shannon N. Gigliotti, et al. 2007. "Risk Factors and Consequences of Unwanted Sex among University Students: Hooking Up, Alcohol, and Stress Response." *Journal of Interpersonal Violence* 22(2): 139–157.

Flavin, Jeanne. 2008. *Our Bodies, Our Crimes.* New York: New York University Press.

Fleming, Crystal M., and Aldon Morris. 2015. "Theorizing Ethnic and Racial Movements in the Global Age: Lessons from the Civil Rights Movement." *Sociology of Race and Ethnicity* 1: 105–126.

Flodgren, Gerd, Antoine Rachas, Andrew Farmer, Marco Inzitiari, and Sasha Shepperd. 2015. "Interactive Telemedicine: Effects on Professional Practice and Healthcare Outcomes." *Cochrane Database of Systemic Reviews,* Issue 9.

Floyd, Larry A., Feng Xu, Ryan Atkins, and Cam Caldwell. 2013. "Ethical Outcomes and Business Ethics: Toward Improving Business Ethics Education." *Journal of Business Ethics* 117(4): 753–776.

Flynn, James R. 2007. *What Is Intelligence? Beyond the Flynn Effect.* Cambridge: Cambridge University Press.

Flynn, Nicole. 2007. "Deindustrialization." In *The Blackwell Encyclopedia of Sociology,* edited by George Ritzer, 992–994. Malden, MA: Blackwell.

Flynn, Sean. 2011. "The Sex Trade." In *Deviant Globalization: Black Market Economy in the 21st Century,* edited by N. Gilman, J. Goldhammer, and S. Weber, 41–66. London: Continuum.

Fontana, Andrea. 2007. "Interviewing, Structured, Unstructured, and Postmodern." In *The Blackwell Encyclopedia of Sociology,* edited by George Ritzer, 2407–2411. Malden, MA: Blackwell.

Ford, Martin. 2015. *Rise of the Robots: Technology and the Threat of a Jobless Future.* New York: Basic Books.

Forno, Francesca. 2013. "Consumer Movements." In *The Wiley-Blackwell Encyclopedia of Social and Political Movements,* 3 vols., edited by D. A. Snow, D. Della Porta, B. Klandermans, and D. McAdam, 253–256. Malden, MA: Wiley-Blackwell.

Forsyth, Craig J., and Heath Copes, eds. 2014. *Encyclopedia of Social Deviance.* Thousand Oaks, CA: Sage.

Fothergill, Alice, and Lori Peek. 2015. *Children of Katrina.* Austin: University of Texas Press.

Foucault, Michel. 1975. *The Birth of the Clinic: An Archaeology of Medical Perception.* New York: Vintage Books.

Foucault, Michel. [1975] 1979. *Discipline and Punish: The Birth of the Prison.* New York: Vintage Books.

Foucault, Michel. 1978. *The History of Sexuality,* Vol. 1, *An Introduction.* New York: Vintage Books.

Fountain, Henry. 2015. "Panel Urges Research on Geoengineering as a Tool against Climate Change." *New York Times,* February 10.

Fourcade, Marion. 2009. *Economists and Societies: Discipline and Profession in the United States, Britain, and France, 1890s to 1990s.* Princeton, NJ: Princeton University Press.

Fourcade-Gourinchas, Marion. 2007. "Culture, Economy and." In *The Blackwell Encyclopedia of Sociology,* edited by George Ritzer, 932–936. Malden, MA: Blackwell.

Fournier, Marcel. 2013. *Émile Durkheim: A Biography.* Cambridge: Polity Press.

Fox, Jesse, and Wai Yen Tang. 2014. "Sexism in Online Video Games: The Role of Conformity to Masculine Norms and Social Dominance Orientation." *Computers in Human Behavior* 33: 314–320.

Frakt, Austin. 2016. You Mean I Don't Have to Show Up? The Promise of Telemedicine. *The New York Times,* May 16.

France, Anatole. [1894] 2011. *The Red Lily.* Kindle ed.

Francis, Mark. 2011. "Herbert Spencer." In *The Wiley-Blackwell Companion to Major Social Theorists,* Vol. 1, *Classical Theorists,* edited by George Ritzer and Jeffrey Stepnisky, 165–184. Malden, MA: Wiley-Blackwell.

Frank, David John. 2012. "Global Sex." In *The Wiley-Blackwell Encyclopedia of Globalization,* edited by George Ritzer. Malden, MA: Wiley-Blackwell.

Frank, Katherine. 2015. "Observational Methods in Sexuality Research." In *Handbook of the Sociology of Sexualities,* edited by John DeLemater and Rebecca F. Plante. Switzerland: Springer.

Frank, Robert H. 2011. *The Darwin Economy: Liberty, Competition, and the Common Good.* Princeton, NJ: Princeton University Press.

Frank, Robert H. 2013. *Falling Behind: How Rising Inequality Harms the Middle Class.* Berkeley: University of California Press.

Frank, Robert. 2014. "Another Widening Gap: The Haves vs. the Have-Mores." *New York Times,* November 15. Accessed April 19, 2015. http://www.nytimes.com/2014/11/16/business/another-widening-gap-the-haves-vs-the-have-mores.html?_r=0.

Frank, Robert H. 2016. *Success and Luck: Good Fortune and the Myth of Meritocracy.* Princeton, NJ: Princeton University Press.

Frank, Robert H., and Philip J. Cook. 1995. *The Winner-Take-All Society.* New York: Penguin.

Frank, Robert H., and Philip J. Cook. 2013. "Winner-Take-All Markets." *Studies in Microeconomics* 1: 131–154.

Fransen, Marieke L., Peeter W. J. Verlegh, Anna Kirmani, and Edith G. Smit. 2015. "A Typology of Consumer Strategies for Resisting Advertising, and a Review of Mechanisms for Countering Them." *International Journal of Advertising: The Review of Marketing Communications* 34(1), published online. doi: 10.1080/02650487.2014.995284.

Freedman, Russell. 2009. *Freedom Walkers: The Story of the Montgomery Bus Boycott.* New York: Holiday House.

Freedman, Samuel G. 2016. "North Dakota Mosque a Symbol of Muslims' Long Ties in America." *New York Times,* May 27.

Freeman, Richard B., and James L. Medoff. 1984. *What Do Unions Do?* New York: Basic Books.

Freudenheim, Milt. 2009. "Tool in Cystic Fibrosis Fight: A Registry." *New York Times,* December 22.

Friedan, Betty. 1963. *The Feminine Mystique.* New York: Dell.

Friedkin, N. E. 2001. "Norm Formation in Social Influence Networks." *Social Networks* 23(3): 167–189.

Friedman, Debra, and Michael Hechter. 1988. "The Contribution of Rational Choice Theory to Macrosociological Research." *Sociological Theory* 6: 201–218.

Friedman, Judith J. 2007. "Suburbs." In *The Blackwell Encyclopedia of Sociology,* edited by George Ritzer, 4878–4881. Malden, MA: Blackwell.

Friedman, Thomas. 2005. *The World Is Flat: A Brief History of the Twenty-First Century.* New York: Farrar, Straus and Giroux.

Friedmann, John. 1986. "The World City Hypothesis." *Development and Change* 17(1): 69–83.

Friedmann, Naama, and Dana Rusou, 2015. "Critical Period for First Language: The Crucial Role of Language Input During the First Year of Life." *Current Opinion in Neurobiology* 35: 27–34.

Friedrichs, David O. 2007. "Organizational Deviance." In *The Blackwell Encyclopedia of Sociology,* edited by George Ritzer, 3303–3306. Malden, MA: Blackwell.

Friedrichs, Robert. 1970. *A Sociology of Sociology.* New York: Free Press.

Frieze, Irene Hanson. 2007. "Love and Commitment." In *The Blackwell Encyclopedia of Sociology,* edited by George Ritzer, 2671–2674. Malden, MA: Blackwell.

Fritsch, Jane. 2001. "A Day of Terror: The Response; Rescue Workers Rush In, and Many Do Not Return." *New York Times,* September 12. Accessed March 29, 2012. http://www.nytimes.com/2001/09/12/us/a-day-of-terror-the-response-rescue-workers-rush-in-and-many-do-not-return.html?ref=sept112001.

Frohlick, Susan. 2013. *Sexuality, Women, and Tourism: Cross-Border Desires through Contemporary Travel.* New York: Routledge.

Fulbrook, Julian. 2007. "Tobacco." In *Encyclopedia of Globalization,* edited by J. A. Scholte and R. Robertson 1146–1149. New York: MTM.

Fuller, Gillian. 2014. "Queue." In *The Routledge Handbook of Mobilities,* edited by P. Adey, D. Bissell, K. Hannam, P. Merriman, and M. Sheller, 205–213. New York: Routledge.

Fuller, Thomas, and Joe Cochran. 2015. "Rohingya Migrants from Myanmar, Shunned by Malaysia, Are Spotted Adrift in Andaman Sea." *New York Times,* May 14.

Fung, Archon. 2004. *Empowered Participation: Reinventing Urban Democracy.* Princeton, NJ: Princeton University Press.

Funk, Laura M., and Karen M. Kobayashi. 2016. "From Motivations to Accounts: An Interpretive Analysis of 'Living Apart Together' Relations in Mid- to Later-Life Couples." *Journal of Family Issues* 37: 1101–1122.

Furneaux, Craig. 2013. "Outsourcing and Subcontracting." In *Sociology of Work: An Encyclopedia,* edited by V. Smith, 669–673. Thousand Oaks, CA: Sage.

Gabaccia, Donna R. Forthcoming. "The Feminization of Migration." In *The Wiley-Blackwell Encyclopedia of Gender and Sexuality Studies,* edited by Nancy Naples.

Gabriel, Yiannis, Marek Korczynski, and Kirsten Rieder, 2015. "Organizations and Their Consumers: Bridging Work and Consumers." *Organization* 22: 629–643.

Gagnon, John, and William H. Simon. 1973. *Sexual Conduct: The Social Sources of Human Sexuality.* Chicago: Aldine.

Galston, William A., Steven Kull, and Clay Ramsay. 2009. *Battleground or Common Ground? American Public Opinion on Health Care Reform.* Washington, DC: Brookings Institution.

Gambino, Matthew. 2013. "Erving Goffman's *Asylums* and Institutional Culture in the Mid-Twentieth-Century United States." *Harvard Review of Psychiatry* 21: 52–57.

Gamoran, Adam, and Daniel A. Long. 2006. "Equality of Educational Opportunity: A 40-Year Retrospective." WCER Working Paper 2006-9, Wisconsin Center for Education Research, Madison. Accessed July 13, 2013. http://www.wcer.wisc.edu.

Gamoran, Adam, and Robert D. Mare. 1989. "Secondary School Tracking and Educational Inequality: Compensation, Reinforcement, or Neutrality?" *American Journal of Sociology* 94: 1146–1183.

Gamoran, Adam, Martin Nystrand, Mark Berends, and Paul C. LePore. 1995. "An Organizational Analysis of the Effects of Ability Grouping." *American Educational Research Journal* 32: 687–715.

Gangl, Markus. 2007. "Welfare State." In *The Blackwell Encyclopedia of Sociology,* edited by George Ritzer, 5242–5246. Malden, MA: Blackwell.

Ganong, Lawrence, and Marilyn Coleman, eds. 2017. *Stepfamily Relationships: Development, Dynamics and Intervention.* 2nd ed. New York: Springer.

Gans, Herbert J. 1979. *Deciding What's News.* New York: Pantheon.

Gans, Herbert J. 2009. "First Generation Decline: Downward Mobility among Refugees and Immigrants." *Ethnic and Racial Studies* 32: 1658–1670.

Gansky, Lisa. 2010. *The Mesh: Why the Future of Business Is Sharing.* New York: Penguin.

Garcia, David. 2008. "The Impact of School Choice on Racial Segregation in Charter Schools." *Educational Policy* 22(6): 805–829.

Garcia, Lorena. 2012. *Respect Yourself, Protect Yourself: Latina Girls and Sexual Identity.* New York: New York University Press.

Gardner, Margo, and Laurence Steinberg. 2005. "Peer Influence on Risk Taking, Risk Preference, and Risky Decision Making in Adolescence and Adulthood: An Experimental Study." *Developmental Psychology* 41: 625–635.

Garfield, Bob. 1991. "How I Spent (and Spent and Spent) My Disney Vacation." *Washington Post,* July 7.

Garfinkel, Harold. 1967. *Studies in Ethnomethodology.* Malden, MA: Blackwell.

Garlick, Steve. 2014. "The Biopolitics of Masturbation: Masculinity, Complexity, and Security." *Body & Society* 20: 44–67.

Garon, Sheldon. 2006. "Japan's Post-war 'Consumer Revolution,' or Striking a 'Balance' between Consumption and Saving." In *Consuming Cultures, Global Perspectives: Historical*

Trajectories, Transnational Exchanges, edited by J. Brewer and F. Trentmann. Oxford: Berg.

Garreau, Joel. 1991. *Edge City: Life on the New Frontier.* New York: Doubleday.

Garrett, William R. 2007. "Christianity." In *Encyclopedia of Globalization,* edited by J. A. Scholte and R. Robertson, 139–144. New York: MTM.

Gartner, Rosemary. 2007. "Violent Crime." In *The Blackwell Encyclopedia of Sociology,* edited by George Ritzer, 5206–5208. Malden, MA: Blackwell.

Gates, Robert M. 2014. *Duty: Memoirs of a Secretary at War.* New York: Knopf.

Gauchat, Gordon, Maura Kelly, and Michael Wallace. 2012. "Occupational Gender Segregation, Globalization, and Gender Earnings Inequality in U.S. Metropolitan Areas." *Gender & Society* 26: 718–747.

Gautier, Pieter A., Michael Svarer, and Coen N. Teulings. 2010. "Marriage and the City: Search Frictions and Sorting of Singles." *Journal of Urban Economics* 67: 206–218.

Gawande, Atul. 2011. "The Hot Spotters." *New Yorker,* January 24.

Gawley, Tim. 2008. "University Administrators as Information Tacticians: Understanding Transparency as Selective Concealment and Instrumental Disclosure." *Symbolic Interaction* 31(2): 183–204.

Gee, Laura K., Jason Jones, and Moira Burke. Forthcoming. "Social Networks and Labor Markets: How Strong Ties Relate to Job Finding on Facebook's Social Network." *Journal of Labor Economics.*

Geertz, Clifford. 1973. *The Interpretation of Cultures.* New York: Basic Books.

Gehlert, S., I. H. Song, C. H. Chang, and S. A. Hartlage. 2009. "The Prevalence of Premenstrual Dysphoric Disorder in a Randomly Selected Group of Urban and Rural Women." *Psychological Medicine* 39: 129–136.

Geis, Gilbert. 2007a. "Crime, Corporate." In *The Blackwell Encyclopedia of Sociology,* edited by George Ritzer, 826–828. Malden, MA: Blackwell.

Geis, Gilbert. 2007b. "Crime, White-Collar." In *The Blackwell Encyclopedia of Sociology,* edited by George Ritzer, 850–851. Malden, MA: Blackwell.

Gentina, Elodie, and Isabelle Muratore. 2012. "Environmentalism at Home: The Process of Ecological Resocialization by Teenagers." *Journal of Consumer Behaviour* 11: 162–169.

Gentry, Caron, and Laura Sjoberg. 2015. "Terrorism and Political Violence." In *Gender Matters in Global Politics: A Feminist Introduction to International Relations,* 2nd ed., edited by L. J. Shepherd, 120–130. New York: Routledge.

George, Kimberly. 2007. "Woman's Movements." In *Encyclopedia of Globalization,* edited by J. A. Scholte and R. Robertson, 1257–1260. New York: MTM.

George, Sheba. 2000. "'Dirty Nurses' and 'Men Who Play': Gender and Class in Transnational Migration." In *Global Ethnography: Forces, Connections, and Imaginations in a Postmodern World,* edited by M. Burawoy, J. A. Blum, S. George, Z. Gille, T. Gowan, L. Haney,

M. Klawiter, S. H. Lopez, S. Ó Riain, and M. Thayer, 144–174. Berkeley: University of California Press.

Gerami, Shahin, and Melodye Lehnerer. 2007. "Gendered Aspects of War and International Violence." In *The Blackwell Encyclopedia of Sociology,* edited by George Ritzer, 1885–1888. Malden, MA: Blackwell.

Gereffi, Gary. 2005. "The Global Economy: Organization, Governance, and Development." In *Handbook of Economic Sociology,* edited by N. Smelser and R. Swedberg. Princeton, NJ: Princeton University Press.

Gereffi, Gary. 2012. "Value Chains." In *The Wiley-Blackwell Encyclopedia of Globalization,* edited by George Ritzer, 2144–2147. Malden, MA: Wiley-Blackwell.

Gerhardt, H. Carl, and Franz Huber. 2002. *Acoustic Communication in Insects and Anurans: Common Problems and Diverse Solutions.* Chicago: University of Chicago Press.

Gerland, Patrick, Adrian E. Raftery, Hana Ševčíková, Nan Li, Danan Gu, Thomas Spoorenberg, Leontine Alkema, Bailey K. Fosdick, Jennifer Chunn, Nevena Lalic, Guiomar Bay, Thomas Buettner, Gerhard K. Heilig, and John Wilmoth. 2014. "World Population Stabilization Unlikely This Century." *Science* 346(6206): 234–237.

Gerson, Kathleen. 2011. *The Unfinished Revolution: Coming of Age in a New Era of Gender, Work, and Family.* Oxford: Oxford University Press.

Gervais, Sarah J., Arianne M. Holland, and Michael D. Dodd. 2013. "My Eyes Are Up Here: The Nature of the Objectifying Gaze toward Women." *Sex Roles* 69: 557–570.

Gesselamn, Amanda N., Gregory D. Webster, and Justin R. Garcia, 2016. "Has Virginity Lost Its Virtue? Relationship Stigma Associated With Being a Sexually Inexperienced Adult." *Journal of Sex Research,* March 2016 (published online).

Gettleman, Jeffrey. 2011. "Congo Study Sets Estimate for Rapes Much Higher." *New York Times,* May 11.

Gettleman, Jeffrey. 2014. "Ebola Ravages Economies in West Africa." *New York Times,* December 20.

Ghaziani, Amin, Verta Taylor, and Amy Stone. 2016. "Cycles of Sameness and Difference in LGBT Social Movements." *Annual Review of Sociology* 42: 165–183.

Ghumman, Sonia, and Ann Maries Ryan. 2013. "Not Welcome Here: Discrimination towards Women Who Wear the Muslim Headscarf." *Human Relations* 66: 671–698.

Giacalone, Robert A., and Mark D. Promislo. 2013. "Broken When Entering: The Stigmatization of Goodness and Business Ethics Education." *Academy of Management Learning & Education* 12: 86–101.

Gibson, Campbell J., and Emily Lennon. 1999. *Historical Census Statistics on the Foreign-Born Population of the United States: 1850 to 1990.* Working Paper 29, U.S. Census Bureau. Washington, DC: Government Printing Office.

Giddens, Anthony 1984. *The Constitution of Society: Outline of the Theory of Structuration.* Berkeley: University of California Press.

Giddens, Anthony. 1992. *The Transformation of Intimacy: Sexuality, Love and Eroticism in Modern Societies.* Stanford, CA: Stanford University Press.

Gilbert, Dennis L. 2011. *The American Class Structure in an Age of Growing Inequality.* 8th ed. Thousand Oaks, CA: Pine Forge Press.

Gilbert, Dennis L. 2015. *The American Class Structure in an Age of Growing Inequality.* 9th ed. Thousand Oaks, CA: Sage.

Gilbert, Dennis L., and Joseph A. Kahl. 1993. *The American Class Structure: A New Synthesis.* Belmont, CA: Wadsworth.

Gillespie-Lynch, Kristen, Patricia M. Greenfield, Yunping Feng, Sue Savage-Rumbaugh, and Heidi Lyn. 2013. "A Cross-Species Study of Gesture and Its Role in Symbolic Development: Implications for the Gestural Theory of Language Development." *Frontiers in Psychology* 4.

Gillis, Justin. 2015. "Climate Accord is a Healing Step, if Not a Cure." *New York Times,* December 12.

Gillis, Justin. 2016. "Flooding of Coast, Caused by Global Warming, Has Already Begun." *New York Times,* September 3.

Gilman, Nils, Jesse Goldhammer, and Steven Weber, eds. 2011. *Deviant Globalization: Black Market Economy in the 21st Century.* London: Continuum.

Gilroy, Paul. 1993. *The Black Atlantic: Modernity and Double Consciousness.* London: Verso Books.

Gimlin, Debra. 2007. "Accounting for Cosmetic Surgery in the USA and Great Britain: A Cross-Cultural Analysis of Women's Narratives." *Body and Society* 13: 41–60.

Giordano, Peggy C., Angela M. Kaufman, Wendy D. Manning, and Monica A. Longmore. 2015. "Teen Dating Violence: The Influence of Friendships and School Context." *Sociological Focus* 48: 150–171.

Giridharadas, Anand. 2010. "Getting in (and out of) Line." *New York Times,* August 8. Accessed November 9, 2011. http://www.nytimes.com/2010/08/07/world/asia/07iht-currents.html.

Giroux, Henry A. 2012. *Education and the Crisis of Public Values: Challenging the Assault on Teachers, Students, and Public Education.* New York: Peter Lang.

Giroux, Henry A., and David E. Purpel, eds. 1983. *The Hidden Curriculum and Moral Education.* Berkeley, CA: McCutchan.

Gitlin, Todd. 1993. *The Sixties: Years of Hope, Days of Rage.* New York: Bantam.

Givoni, Michal. 2016. "Between Micro Mappers and Missing Maps: Digital Humanitarianism and the Politics of Material Participation in Disaster Response." *Environment and Planning D: Society and Space* 34(6): 1025–1043.

Gladstone, Rick. 2014. "Global Piracy Hits Lowest Level Since 2007, Report Says." *New York Times,* January 15.

Gladstone, Rick. 2015. "Report Details New Atrocities in Darfur by Sudanese Forces." *New York Times,* September 9.

Gladstone, Rick. 2016a. "New Ebola Case Confirmed in Liberia; Guinea Tries a Vaccine." *New York Times,* April 1.

Glantz, Michael H., ed. 1977. *Desertification: Environmental Degradation in and around Arid Lands.* Boulder, CO: Westview Press.

Glenn, Evelyn Nakano. 2002. *Unequal Freedom: How Race and Gender Shaped American Citizenship and Labor.* Cambridge, MA: Harvard University Press.

Glenny, Misha. 2008. *McMafia: A Journey through the Global Criminal Underworld.* New York: Knopf.

Glenny, Misha. 2015. "The Refugee Crisis Has Produced One Winner: Organized Crime." *New York Times,* September 20.

Global Nonviolent Action Database, Swarthmore College. 2011. "East Los Angeles Students Walkout for Educational Reform (East L.A. Blowouts), 1968." Accessed May 8, 2015. http://nvdatabase.swarthmore.edu/content/east-los-angeles-students-walkout-educational-reform-east-la-blowouts-1968.

Global Nutrition Report. 2016. *From Promise to Impact: Ending Malnutrition by 2030.* Washington, DC: International Food Policy Research Institute.

Gloor, Peter, and Scott Cooper. 2007. *Coolhunting: Chasing Down the Next Big Thing.* New York: AMACOM.

Gmelch, Sharon Bohn, ed. 2010. *Tourists and Tourism: A Reader.* Prospect Heights, IL: Waveland Press.

Godlee, Fiona, Neil Pakenham-Walsh, Dan Ncayiyana, Barbara Cohen, and Abel Packer. 2004. "Can We Achieve Health Information for All by 2015?" *The Lancet* 364: 295–300.

Godwyn, Mary, and Jody Hoffer Gittell, eds. 2011. *Sociology of Organizations: Structures and Relationships.* Thousand Oaks, CA: Pine Forge Press.

Goffman, Alice. 2014. *On the Run: Fugitive Life in an American City.* Chicago: University of Chicago Press.

Goffman, Erving. 1959. *The Presentation of Self in Everyday Life.* Garden City, NY: Anchor Books.

Goffman, Erving. 1961a. *Asylums: Essays on the Social Situation of Mental Patients and Other Inmates.* Garden City, NY: Anchor Books.

Goffman, Erving. 1961b. *Encounters.* Indianapolis: Bobbs-Merrill.

Goffman, Erving. 1963. *Stigma: Notes on the Management of Spoiled Identity.* Englewood Cliffs, NJ: Prentice Hall/Spectrum.

Goffman, Erving. 2000. *Exploring the Interaction Order.* Cambridge: Polity Press.

Goldberg, David Theo. 2009. "Racial Comparisons, Relational Racisms: Some Thoughts on Method." *Ethnic and Racial Studies* 32: 1271–1282.

Goldberg, Gertrude Schaffner, ed. 2010. *Poor Women in Rich Countries: The Feminization of Poverty over the Life Course.* New York: Oxford University Press.

Goldberg, Harvey E. 2007. "Judaism." In *Encyclopedia of Globalization,* edited by J. A. Scholte and R. Robertson, 690–693. New York: MTM.

Goldburg, Rebecca J. 2008. "Aquaculture, Trade, and Fisheries Linkages: Unexpected Synergies." *Globalization* 5(2): 143–150.

Goldenberg, Suzanne. 2005. "Why Women Are Poor at Science, by Harvard President." *The Guardian,* January 18. Accessed April 19, 2015. http://www.theguardian.com/science/2005/jan/18/educationsgendergap.genderissues.

Goldfield, Michael. 1987. *The Decline of Organized Labor.* Chicago: University of Chicago Press.

Goldfield, Michael, and Amy Bromsen. 2013. "The Changing Landscape of U.S. Unions in Historical and Theoretical Perspective." *Annual Review of Political Science* 16: 231–257.

Goldfrank, Walter. 2005. "Fresh Demand: The Consumption of Chilean Produce in the United States." In *The Cultural Politics of Food and Eating: A Reader,* edited by J. L. Watson & M. L. Caldwell, 42–53. Malden, MA: Blackwell.

Goldin, Claudia, Lawrence F. Katz, and Ilyana Kuziemko. 2006. "The Homecoming of American College Women: The Reversal of the College Gender Gap." *Journal of Economic Perspectives* 20: 133–156.

Goldman, Liran, Howard Giles, and Michael A. Hogg. 2014. "Going to Extremes: Social Identity and Communication Processes Associated with Gang Membership." *Group Processes & Intergroup Relations* 17: 813–832.

Goldman, Robert, and Stephen Papson. 1998. *Nike Culture.* London: Sage.

Goldscheider, Calvin. 2012. "Judaism." In *The Wiley-Blackwell Encyclopedia of Globalization,* edited by George Ritzer, 1225–1234. Malden, MA: Wiley-Blackwell.

Goldschmied, Nadav, and Jason Kowalczyk. 2016. "Gender Performance in the NCAA Rifle Championship: Where Is the Gap?" *Sex Roles* 74: 310–322.

Goldstein, Joseph, and Nate Schweber, 2014. "Man's Death after Chokehold Raises Old Issue for Police." *New York Times,* July 18.

Goldstein, Warren. 2009. "Secularization Patterns in the Old Paradigm." *Sociology of Religion* 70: 157–178.

Goldstone, Jack. 1991. *Revolution and Rebellion in the Early Modern World.* Berkeley: University of California Press.

Goli, Srinivas, Riddhi Doshi, and Arokiasamy Perianayagam. 2013. "Pathways of Economic Inequalities in Maternal and Child Health in Urban India: A Decomposition Analysis." *PLoS ONE* 8(3): e58573. Accessed April 19, 2015. http://www.plosone.org/article/info%3Adoi%2F10.1371%2Fjournal.pone.0058573#pone-0058573-g001.

Gonzalez, Michelle A. 2010. *Shopping.* Minneapolis: Fortress Press.

Gooch, Liz. 2012. "With Opening Near, Yale Defends Singapore Venture." *New York Times,* August 27. Accessed July 5, 2013. http://www.nytimes.com/2012/08/27/world/asia.

Goode, Erich. 2002. "Sexual Involvement and Social Research in a Fat Civil Rights Organization." *Qualitative Sociology* 25(4): 501–534.

Goode, Erich. 2007a. "Deviance." In *The Blackwell Encyclopedia of Sociology,* edited by George Ritzer, 1075–1082. Malden, MA: Blackwell.

Goode, Erich. 2007b. "Deviance: Explanatory Theories of." In *The Blackwell Encyclopedia of Sociology,* edited by George Ritzer, 1100–1107. Malden, MA: Blackwell.

Goode, Erich. 2014. "Labeling Theory." In *Encyclopedia of Criminology and Criminal Justice,* edited by G. Bruinsma and D. Weisburd, 2807–2814. New York: Springer.

Goode, Erich, and Nachman Ben-Yehuda. 1994. *Moral Panics: The Social Construction of Deviance.* Oxford: Blackwell.

Goode, Erich, and Alex Thio. 2007. "Deviance, Crime and." In *The Blackwell Encyclopedia of Sociology,* edited by George Ritzer, 1092–1095. Malden, MA: Blackwell.

Goode, William J. 1963. *World Revolution and Family Patterns.* New York: Free Press.

Goodlin, Wendi E., and Christopher S. Dunn. 2011. "Three Patterns of Domestic Violence in Households: Single Victimization, Repeat Victimization, and Co-occurring Victimization." *Journal of Family Violence* 26: 101–108.

Goodman, David M. 2016. "The McDonaldization of Psychotherapy: Processed foods, Processed Therapies, and Economic Class." *Theory and Psychology* 26: 77–95.

Goodnough, Abby. 2010. "Doctors Point to Caffeinated Alcoholic Drinks' Dangers." *New York Times,* October 27.

Goodwin, Jennifer. 2011. "U.S. Rates of Autism, ADHD Continue to Rise: Report." *U.S. News & World Report,* May 23. Accessed May 25, 2011. http://health.usnews.com/health-news/family-health/brain-and-behavior/articles/2011/05/23/us-rates-of-autism-adhd-continue-to-rise-report.

Gopal, Prashant. 2014. "Brooklyn Worst in U.S. for Home Affordability." *Bloomberg Business,* December 3. Accessed April 19, 2015. http://www.bloomberg.com/news/articles/2014-12-04/brooklyn-worst-in-u-s-for-home-affordability.

Gorman, Elizabeth H., and Julie A. Kmec. 2009. "Hierarchical Rank and Women's Organizational Mobility: Glass Ceilings in Corporate Law Firms." *American Journal of Sociology* 114: 1428–1474.

Gorski, Philip S. 2011. "Barack Obama and Civil Religion." In *Rethinking Obama,* edited by J. Go. Bingley, 179–214. Bingley, UK: Emerald.

Gorski, Philip S., David Kyuman Kim, John Torpey, and Jonathan VanAntwerpen, eds. 2012. *The Post-secular Question: Religion in Contemporary Society.* New York: New York University Press and the Social Science Research Council.

Gotham, Kevin Fox. 2007. "Megalopolis." In *The Blackwell Encyclopedia of Sociology,* edited by George Ritzer, 2942–2944. Malden, MA: Blackwell.

Gotham, Kevin Fox. 2012. "Urbanization." In *The Wiley-Blackwell Companion to Sociology,* edited by George Ritzer, 488–503. Malden, MA: Wiley-Blackwell.

Gotham, Kevin Fox. 2015. "Tourism." In *The Wiley-Blackwell Encyclopedia of Consumption and Consumer Studies,* edited by Daniel Thomas Cook and J. Michael Ryan, 549–551. Malden, MA: Wiley-Blackwell.

Gottfredson, Michael R., and Travis Hirschi. 1990. *A General Theory of Crime.* Stanford, CA: Stanford University Press.

Gottman, Jean. 1961. *Megalopolis: The Urbanized Northeastern Seaboard of the United States.* New York: Twentieth Century Fund.

Gottman, John M., Tames Coan, Sybil Carrere, and Catherine Swanson. 1998. "Predicting Marital Happiness and Stability from Newlywed Interactions." *Journal of Marriage and the Family* 60: 5–22.

Gottschalk, Simon. 2010. "The Presentation of Avatars in Second Life: Self and Interaction in Social Virtual Spaces." *Symbolic Interaction* 33(4): 501–525.

Gough, Brendan. Forthcoming. "Hegemonic Masculinities." In *The Wiley Blackwell Encyclopedia of Gender and Sexuality Studies,* edited by Nancy Naples.

Gould, Kenneth, David N. Pellow, and Allan Schnaiberg. 2008. *The Treadmill of Production: Injustice and Unsustainability in the Global Economy.* Boulder, CO: Paradigm.

Gould, Stephen Jay. 1981. *The Mismeasure of Man.* New York: Norton.

Gouldner, Alvin W. 1960. "The Norm of Reciprocity: A Preliminary Statement." *American Sociological Review* 25(2): 161–178.

Gouldner, Alvin W. 1962. "Anti-Minotaur: The Myth of a Value-Free Sociology." *Social Problems* 9(3): 199–213.

Gove, Walter R. 1980. *The Labelling of Deviance.* Beverly Hills, CA: Sage.

Gove, Walter R., and Michael Hughes. 1979. "Possible Causes of the Apparent Sex Differences in Physical Health: An Empirical Investigation." *American Sociological Review* 44: 126–146.

Gozdecka, Dorota A., Slen A. Ercan, and Magdalena Kmak. 2014. "From Multiculturalism to Post-multiculturalism: Trends and Paradoxes." *Journal of Sociology* 50: 51–64.

Grace, Anthony R., and Janet E. Palmer. 2015. "The Homogeneity of Society: The Role of Franchising in the Health and Food Sectors." *Sociology and Anthropology* 3: 661–664.

Grady, Denise. 2015. "Measles: Perilous but Preventable." *New York Times,* February 2.

Graff, Kaitlin A., Sarah K. Murnen, and Anna K. Krause. 2013. "Low-Cut Shirts and High-Heeled Shoes: Increased Sexualization Across Time in Magazine Depictions of Girls." *Sex Roles* 69: 571–582.

Grandin, Greg. 2010. *Fordlandia: The Rise and Fall of Henry Ford's Forgotten Jungle City.* New York: Picador.

Grandin, Temple. 2000. "My Experiences with Visual Thinking Sensory Problems and Communication Difficulties." Autism Research Institute. Accessed April 27, 2015. http://www.autism.com/advocacy_grandin_visual%20thinking.

Granfield, Robert. 1992. *Making Elite Lawyers: Visions of Law at Harvard and Beyond.* New York: Routledge, Chapman and Hall.

Granovetter, Mark. 1973. "The Strength of Weak Ties." *American Journal of Sociology* 78(6): 1360–1380.

Granovetter, Mark. 1974. *Getting a Job: A Study of Contacts and Careers.* Cambridge, MA: Harvard University Press.

Granovetter, Mark, and Richard Swedberg, eds. 2011. *The Sociology of Economic Life.* 3rd ed. Boulder, CO: Westview Press.

Granville, Kevin. 2016. "The Trans-Pacific Partnership Trade Accord Explained." *New York Times,* July 26.

Gray, Clark, and Valerie Mueller. 2012. "Drought and Population Mobility in Rural Ethiopia." *World Development* 40(1): 134–145.

Greeley, Andrew. 1989. *Religious Change in America.* Cambridge, MA: Harvard University Press.

Greenebaum, Jessica, and Clinton R. Sanders. Forthcoming. "Human-Animal Interaction." In *The Wiley-Blackwell Encyclopedia of Sociology,* 2nd ed., edited by George Ritzer. Malden, MA: Wiley-Blackwell.

Greenfield, Lauren [Director]. 2012. *Queen of Versailles.* Documentary. Magnolia Pictures.

Greenhouse, Steven. 2011. "Union Membership in U.S. Fell to a 70-Year Low Last Year." *New York Times,* January 21.

Greenhouse, Steven. 2015. "The Mystery of the Vanishing Pay Raise." *New York Times,* October 31.

Greenwald, Glenn. 2014. *No Place to Hide: Edward Snowden, the NSA, and the U.S. Surveillance State.* New York: Metropolitan Books.

Gressman, Eugene. 2005. "Judgments Judged and Wrongs Remembered: Examining the Japanese American Civil Liberties Cases on Their Sixtieth Anniversary." *Law and Contemporary Problems* 68: 15–27.

Grice, Elizabeth. 2006. "Cry of an Enfant Sauvage." *Daily Telegraph,* July 17.

Griffin, Christine, Isabelle Szmigin, Andrew Bengry-Howell, Chris Hackley, and Willm Mistral. 2012. "Inhabiting the Contradictions: Hypersexual Femininity and the Culture of Intoxication among Young Women in the UK." *Feminism & Psychology* 23(2): 184–206.

Griffin, Lauren N., Gregory Pavela, and Julia Arroyo. 2015. "Tourism and the Treadmill of Production: A Cross-National Analysis." *Environmental Sociology:* 127–138.

Griffin, Sean Patrick. 2007. "Crime, Organized." In *The Blackwell Encyclopedia of Sociology,* edited by George Ritzer, 833–834. Malden, MA: Blackwell.

Grigsby, Mary. 2004. *Buying Time and Getting By: The Voluntary Simplicity Movement.* Albany: State University of New York Press.

Griswold, Alison. 2014. "Are Smartphones Ruining the Restaurant Experience?" *Slate,* July 16. Accessed April 22, 2015. http://www.slate.com/articles/business/moneybox/2014/07/viral_craigslist_post_on_smartphones_in_restaurants_is_tech_ruining_the.html.

Gronow, Jukka. 2007. "Taste, Sociology of." In *The Blackwell Encyclopedia of Sociology,* edited by George Ritzer, 4930–4935. Malden, MA: Blackwell.

Gu, Dongfeng, Tanika N. Kelly, Xigui Wu, Jing Chen, Jonathan M. Samet, Jian-feng Huang, Manlu Zhu, Ji-chun Chen, Chung-shiuan Chen, Xiufang Duan, Michael J. Klag, and Jiang He. 2009. "Mortality Attributable to Smoking in China." *New England Journal of Medicine* 360: 150–159.

Gubrium, Jaber F., James A. Holstein, Amir B. Marvasti, and Karyn D. McKinney, eds. 2012. *The SAGE Handbook of Interview Research: The Complexity of the Craft.* 2nd ed. Thousand Oaks, CA: Sage.

Guetterman, Tomothy C., Michael D. Fetters, and John W. Creswell. 2015. "Integrating Quantitative and Qualitative Results in Health Science Mixed Methods Research Through Joint Displays." *Annals of Family Medicine* 13: 554–561.

Guhathakurta, Subhrajit, David Jacobson, and Nicholas C. DelSordi. 2007. "The End of Globalization? The Implications of Migration for State, Society and Economy." In *The Blackwell Companion to Globalization,* edited by George Ritzer, 201–215. Malden, MA: Blackwell.

Gulati, Ranjay, and Phanish Puranam. 2009. "Renewal through Reorganization: The Value of Inconsistencies between Formal and Informal Organization." *Organization Science* 20: 422–440.

Gulmohamad, Zana Khasraw. 2014. "The Rise and Fall of the Islamic State of Iraq and Al-Sham (Levant) ISIS." *Global Security Studies* 5(2).

Gündüz, Zuhal Yesilyurt. 2013. "The Feminization of Migration: Care and the New Emotional Imperialism." *Monthly Review* 65(7): 32–43.

Guo, Guang, Yilan Fu, Hedwig Lee, Tianji Cai, Kathleen Mullan Harris, and Yi Li. 2014. "Genetic Bio-Ancestry and Social Construction of Racial Classification in Social Surveys in the Contemporary United States." *Demography* 51: 141–172.

Guo, Guang, Michael E. Roettger, and Tianji Cai. 2008. "The Integration of Genetic Propensities into Social-Control Models of Delinquency and Violence among Male Youths." *American Sociological Review* 73(4): 543–568.

Guo, Shibao. 2013. "Economic Integration of Recent Chinese Immigrants in Canada's Second-Tier Cities: The Triple Glass Effect and Immigrants' Downward Social Mobility." *Canadian Ethnic Studies* 45: 95–115.

Gupta, Akhil. 2012. *Red Tape: Bureaucracy, Structural Violence and Poverty in India.* Durham, NC: Duke University Press.

Gylling, Michael, et al. 2015. "Making Decisions on Offshore Outsourcing and Backsourcing: A Case Study in the Bicycle Industry." *International Journal of Production Economics* 162: 925100

Habermas, Jürgen. 1975. *Legitimation Crisis.* Boston: Beacon Press.

Hacker, Jacob S., and Paul Pierson. 2010. *Winner-Take-All Politics: How Washington Made the Rich Richer—and Turned Its Back on the Middle Class.* New York: Simon & Schuster.

Haddad, Emma. 2003. "The Refugee: The Individual between Sovereigns." *Global Society* 17(3): 297–322.

Haddad, Nick M., Lars A. Brudvig, Jean Clobert, Kendi F. Davies, Andrew Gonzalez, Robert D. Holt, Thomas E. Lovejoy, Joseph O. Sexton, Mike P. Austin, Cathy D. Collins, William M. Cook, Ellen I. Damschen, Robert M. Ewers, Bryan L. Foster, Clinton N. Jenkins, Andrew J. King, William F. Laurance, Douglas J. Levey, Chris R. Margules, Brett A. Melbourne, A. O. Nicholls, John L. Orrock, Dan-Xia Song, and John R. Townshend. 2015. "Habitat Fragmentation and Its Lasting Impact on Earth's Ecosystems." *Science Advances* 1: 1–9.

Hadid, Diaa, and Majd al Waheidi. 2016. "As Hamas Tunnels Back Into Israel; Palestinians are, Afraid, Too." *New York Times,* May 20.

Hadjicostandi, Joanna. 2007. "Migration: Undocumented/Illegal." In *The Blackwell Encyclopedia of Sociology,* edited by George Ritzer, 3031–3034. Malden, MA: Blackwell.

Hafferty, Frederic W. 2009. "Professionalism and the Socialization of Medical Students." In *Teaching Medical Professionalism,* edited by R. L. Cruess, S. R. Cruess, and Y. Steinert, 53–69. New York: Cambridge University Press.

Hafferty, Frederic W., and Brian Castellani. 2011. "Two Cultures: Two Ships: The Rise of a Professionalism Movement within Modern Medicine and Medical Sociology's Disappearance from the Professionalism Debate." In *Handbook of the Sociology of Health, Illness, and Healing: A Blueprint for the 21st Century,* edited by B. A. Pescosolido, J. K. Martin, J. D. McLeod, and A. Rogers, 201–220. Dordrecht, Netherlands: Springer.

Hage, Jerald, and Charles H. Powers. 1992. *Post-industrial Lives: Roles and Relationships in the 21st Century.* Newbury Park, CA: Sage.

"Haiti, Unfinished and Forsaken." 2014. *New York Times,* January 10.

Hakim, Catherine. 2011. *Erotic Capital: The Power of Attraction in the Boardroom and the Bedroom.* New York: Basic Books.

Hall, Elaine J., and Marnie Salupo Rodriguez. 2003. "The Myth of Postfeminism." *Gender & Society* 17(6): 878–902.

Hall, Peter, and David Soskice, eds. 2001. *Varieties of Capitalism: The Institutional Foundations of Comparative Advantage.* New York: Oxford University Press.

Hamermesh, Daniel S. 2011. *Beauty Pays: Why Attractive People Are More Successful.* Princeton, NJ: Princeton University Press.

Hamilton, Laura, and Elizabeth A. Armstrong. 2009. "Gendered Sexuality in Young Adulthood: Double Binds and Flawed Options." *Gender & Society* 23(5): 589–616.

Hamilton Project. 2013. "Multimedia: Charts: U.S. Personal Saving Rate, 1970–2012." March 14. Accessed May 13, 2015. http://www.hamiltonproject.org/multimedia/charts/u.s._personal_saving_rate_1970-2012.

Hammersley, Martyn. 2007. "Ethnography." In *The Blackwell Encyclopedia of Sociology,* edited by George Ritzer, 1479–1483. Malden, MA: Blackwell.

Hamouda, Manel, and Abderrazak Gharbi. 2013. "The Postmodern Consumer: An Identity Constructor?" *International Journal of Marketing Studies* 5(2): 41–49.

Handelman, Jay M., and Robert V. Kozinets. 2007. "Culture Jamming." In *The Blackwell Encyclopedia of Sociology,* edited by George Ritzer, 945–946. Malden, MA: Blackwell.

Haner, Josh. 2016. "Climate Refuges: Bolivia." *New York Times,* July 7.

Hankin, Janet R., and Eric R. Wright. 2010. "Reflections on Fifty Years of Medical Sociology." *Journal of Health and Social Behavior* 51: S10–S14.

Hannigan, John. 1998. *Fantasy City: Pleasure and Profit in the Postmodern Metropolis.* London: Routledge.

Hannigan, John. 2007. "Fantasy City." In *The Blackwell Encyclopedia of Sociology,* edited by George Ritzer, 1641–1644. Malden, MA: Blackwell.

Hannigan, John. 2014. *Environmental Sociology.* 3rd ed. New York: Routledge.

Hanson, Andrew, and Zackary Hawley. 2010. "Do Landlords Discriminate in the Rental Housing Market? Evidence from an Internet Field Experiment in US Cities." *Journal of Urban Economics* 70: 99–14.

Hanushek, Eric, and Steven Rivkin. 2006. "School Quality and the Black–White Achievement Gap." Working Paper 12651, National Bureau of Economic Research, Cambridge, MA.

Haraway, Donna. 1991. "A Cyborg Manifesto: Science, Technology, and Socialist-Feminism in the Late Twentieth Century." In *Simians, Cyborgs and Women: The Reinvention of Nature,* 149–181. New York: Routledge.

Harcourt, Bernard E., and Jens Ludwig. 2006. "Broken Windows: New Evidence from New York City and a Five-City Social Experiment." *University of Chicago Law Review* 73: 271–320.

Harding, David. 2010. *Living the Drama: Community, Conflict, and Culture among Inner-City Boys.* Chicago: University of Chicago Press.

Hardoon, Deborah. 2015. "Wealth: Having It All and Wanting More." Oxfam International, January. Accessed April 17, 2015. https://www.oxfam.org/sites/www.oxfam.org/files/file_attachments/ib-wealth-having-all-wanting-more-190115-en.pdf.

Hargrove, Barbara. 1989. *Sociology of Religion: Classical and Contemporary Approaches.* 2nd ed. Arlington Heights, IL: Harlan Davidson.

Harmon, Corinne, Glenda Carne, Kristina Lizardy-Hajbi, and Eugene Wilkerson. 2010. "Access to Higher Education for Undocumented Students: 'Outlaws' of Social Justice, Equity, and Equality." *Journal of Praxis in Multicultural Education* 5(1): 67–82.

Harris, Douglas N., Carolyn D. Herrington, and Amy Albee. 2007. "The Future of Vouchers: Lessons from the Adoption, Design, and Court Challenges of Florida's Three Voucher Programs." *Educational Policy* 21(1): 215–244.

Harris, Gardiner, and Edward Wong. 2013. "Where China Meets India in a High-Altitude Desert, Push Comes to Shove." *New York Times,* May 2.

Harris Interactive. 2016. "Doctor Tops List of Prestigious Occupations." Press release, March 29. Accessed January 23, 2016. http://media.theharrispoll.com/documents/Prestigious+Occupations_Data+Tables.pdf.

Harrison, Bennett. 1994. *Lean and Mean: The Changing Landscape of Corporate Power in the Age of Flexibility.* New York: Basic Books.

Hart, Betty, and Todd Risley. 1995. *Meaningful Differences in the Everyday Experience of Young American Children.* Baltimore: Paul H. Brookes.

Hart, Jeni. 2016. "Dissecting a Gendered Organization: Implications for Career Trajectories for Mid-Career Faculty Women in STEM." *Journal of Higher Education* 87(5):605–634.

Hartigan, John. 2014. "Whiteness, Class and the Legacies of Empire: On Home Ground." *Ethnic and Racial Studies* 37(10): 1941–1944.

Hartmann, Christopher D. 2013. "Garbage, Health, and Well-Being in Managua." *NACLA Report on the Americas* 46(4): 62–65.

Hartmann, Heidi. 1979. "Capitalism, Patriarchy and Job Segregation by Sex." In *Capitalist Patriarchy and the Case for Socialist Feminism,* edited by Z. Eisenstein, 206–247. New York: Monthly Review Press.

Harvey, Adia Wingfield. 2009. "Racializing the Glass Escalator: Reconsidering Men's Experiences with Women's Work." *Gender & Society* 23(1): 5–26.

Harvey, David. 2005. *A Brief History of Neoliberalism.* Oxford: Oxford University Press.

Harvey, David. 2007. "Poverty and Disrepute." In *The Blackwell Encyclopedia of Sociology,* edited by George Ritzer, 3589–3594. Malden, MA: Blackwell.

Hashemian, Farnoosh, and Derek Yach. 2007. "Public Health in a Globalizing World: Challenges and Opportunities." In *The Blackwell Companion to Globalization,* edited by George Ritzer, 516–538. Malden, MA: Blackwell.

Hatch, Anthony. 2009. *The Politics of Metabolism: The Metabolic Syndrome and the Reproduction of Race and Racism in the United States.* PhD dissertation, University of Maryland.

Hatch, Anthony. 2016. *Blood Sugar: Racial Pharmacology and Food Justice in Black America.* Minneapolis: University of Minnesota Press.

Hatfield, Elaine, Lisamarie Bensman, and Richard L. Rapson. 2012. "A Brief History of Social Scientists' Attempts to Measure Passionate Love." *Journal of Social and Personal Relationships* 29: 143–164.

Hatton, Erin, and Mary Nell Trautner. 2011. "Equal Opportunity Objectification? The Sexualization of Men and Women on the Cover of *Rolling Stone.*" *Sexuality & Culture* 15: 256–278.

Haub, Carl. 2013. "Rising Trend of Births Outside Marriage." Population Reference Bureau, April. Accessed April 20, 2015. http://www.prb.org/Publications/Articles/2013/nonmarital-births.aspx.

Hauskeller, Christine, Steve Sturdy, and Richard Tutton. 2013. "Genetics and the Sociology of Identity." *Sociology* 47: 875–886.

Hausmann, Ricardo, Ina Ganguli, and Martina Viarengo. 2009. "The Dynamics of the Gender Gap: How Do Countries Rank in Terms of Making Marriage and Motherhood Compatible with Work?" In *Global Gender Gap Report,* edited by R. Hausmann, L. D. Tyson, and S. Zahidi, 27–29 Geneva: World Economic Forum.

Hawkesworth, Mary. 2006. *Globalization and Feminist Activism.* Lanham, MD: Rowman & Littlefield.

Hawkins, Alan J., Brian J. Willoughby, and William J. Doherty, 2012. "Reasons for Divorce and Openness to Marital Reconciliation." *Journal of Divorce and Remarriage* 53: 563-463.

Hay, Harry. 2012. "Birth of a Consciousness." *Gay & Lesbian Review Worldwide* 19: 15–18.

Hayes, Dennis, ed. 2017. *Beyond McDonaldization: Visions of Higher Education.* London: Routledge.

Hayes, Dennis, and Robin Wynyard, eds. 2002. *The McDonaldization of Higher Education.* Westport, CT: Bergin and Garvey.

Haynie, L. 2001. "Delinquent Peers Revisited: Does Network Structure Matter?" *American Journal of Sociology* 106: 1013–1057.

Hays, Sharon. 1998. *The Cultural Contradictions of Motherhood.* New Haven, CT: Yale University Press.

"Head Injuries in Football." 2010. *New York Times,* October 21. Accessed March 30, 2012. topics.nytimes.com/top/reference/timestopics/subjects/f/football/head_injuries/index.html.

Healy, Jack. 2016. "Fitful Recovery in Las Vegas Fuels Voter Anger." *New York Times,* August 3.

Heaphy, Brian. 2007a. "Lesbian and Gay Families." In *The Blackwell Encyclopedia of Sociology,* edited by George Ritzer, 2606–2609. Malden, MA: Blackwell.

Heaphy, Brian. 2007b. "Same-Sex Marriage/Civil Unions." In *The Blackwell Encyclopedia of Sociology,* edited by George Ritzer, 3995–3998. Malden, MA: Blackwell.

Heckart, Druann Maria, and Daniel Alex Heckart, 2015. "Positive Deviance." In *The Handbook of Deviance,* edited by Erich Goode, 80–100. Malden, MA: Wiley-Blackwell.

Heckman, James. 2006. "Skill Formation and the Economics of Investing in Disadvantaged Children." *Science* 312: 1900–1902.

Heckman, James J., Seong Hyeok Moon, Rodrigo Pinto, Peter A. Savelyev, and Adam Yavitz. 2010. "The Rate of Return to the HighScope Perry Preschool Program." *Journal of Public Economics* 94: 114–128.

Hedgecoe, Adam. 2016. "Reputational Risk, Academic Freedom and Research Ethics Review." *Sociology* 50: 486–501.

Heintz, James. 2006. "Globalization, Economic Policy and Employment: Poverty and Gender Implications." Employment Strategy Unit, International Labour Organization. Accessed November 4, 2013. http://www.ilo.org/wcmsp5/groups/pub lic/@ed_emp/@emp_elm/documents/publica tion/wcms_114024.pdf.

Helle, Horst. 2015. *The Social Thought of Georg Simmel.* Thousand Oaks, CA: Sage.

Heller, Joseph. 1961. *Catch-22.* New York: Simon & Schuster.

Heller, Nathan. 2013. "Laptop U." *New Yorker,* May 20, 80ff.

Helliwell, Christine. 2000. "'It's Only a Penis': Rape, Feminism, and Difference." *Signs* 25(3): 789–816.

Helweg-Larsen, Marie, and Barbara L. LoMonaco. 2008. "Queuing among U2 Fans: Reactions to Social Norm Violations." *Journal of Applied Social Psychology* 38(9): 2378–2393.

Hendershott, Anne. 2002. *The Politics of Deviance.* San Francisco: Encounter Books.

Henningsen, David Dryden. 2004. "Flirting with Meaning: An Examination of Miscommunication in Flirting Interactions." *Sex Roles* 50: 481–489.

Henry, Stuart. 2007. "Deviance, Constructionist Perspectives." In *The Blackwell Encyclopedia of Sociology,* edited by George Ritzer, 1086–1092. Malden, MA: Blackwell.

Hepburn, Stephanie, and Rita J. Simon. 2013. *Human Trafficking around the World: Hidden in Plain Sight.* New York: Columbia University Press.

Herbert, Bob. 2011. "Losing Our Way." *New York Times,* March 25. Accessed March 30, 3012. http://www.nytimes.com/2011/03/26/opinion/26herbert.html.

Heritage, John, and Tanya Stivers. 2012. "Conversation Analysis and Sociology." In *The Handbook of Conversation Analysis,* edited by J. Sidnell and T. Stivers, 659–673. Malden, MA: Wiley Blackwell.

Herod, Andrew. 2009. *Geographies of Globalization: A Critical Introduction.* Malden, MA: Wiley-Blackwell.

Herper, Matthew, and Peter Kang. 2006. "The World's Ten Best-Selling Drugs." *Forbes,* March 22. Accessed January 25, 2012. http://www.forbes.com/2006/03/21/pfizer-merck-amgen-cx_mh_pk_0321topdrugs.html.

Herrnstein, Richard J., and Charles Murray. 1994. *The Bell Curve: Intelligence and Class Structure in American Life.* New York: Free Press.

Hershkovitz, Shay. 2012. "Nation-State." In *The Wiley-Blackwell Encyclopedia of Globalization,* edited by George Ritzer, 1492–1496. Malden, MA: Wiley-Blackwell.

Herzog, Lawrence A. 2015. *Global Suburbs: Urban Sprawl from the Rio Grande to Rio de Janeiro.* New York: Routledge.

Heslin, Peter A., Myrtle P. Bell, and Pinar O. Fletcher. 2012. "The Devil Without and Within: A Conceptual Model of Social Cognitive Processes Whereby Discrimination Leads Stigmatized Minorities to Become Discouraged Workers." *Journal of Organizational Behavior* 33: 840–862.

Hesse-Biber, Sharlene. 1996. *Am I Thin Enough Yet? The Cult of Thinness and Commercialization of Identity.* London: Oxford University Press.

Hetherington, E. M. 2003. "Intimate Pathways: Changing Patterns in Close Personal Relationships across Time." *Family Relations* 52: 183–206.

Heywood, Andrew. 2014. *Global Politics.* 2nd ed. New York: Palgrave Macmillian.

Higgins, Andrew. 2016. "Russia's Troll Army Retaliates Against an Effort to Expose It." *New York Times,* May 31.

Higgins, Andrew, and Dan Bilefsky. 2015. "French Police Storm Hostage Sites Killing Gunmen." *New York Times,* January 9.

Higley, John, and Michael Burton. 2006. *Elite Foundations of Liberal Democracy.* Lanham, MD: Rowman & Littlefield.

Hildebrandt, Achim. 2014. "Routes to Decriminalization: A Comparative Analysis of the Legalization of Same-Sex Sexual Acts." *Sexualities* 17: 230–253.

Hill, Jessica, and Pranee Liamputtong. 2011. "Being the Mother of a Child with Asperger's Syndrome: Women's Experiences of Stigma." *Health Care for Women International* 32: 708–722.

Hill, Nancy E., and Joshua B. Marion. 2016. *Introduction to Cybercrime.* Santa Barbara, CA: Praeger.

Hillyard, Daniel. 2007. "Deviance, Criminalization of." In *The Blackwell Encyclopedia of Sociology,* edited by George Ritzer, 1095–1100. Malden, MA: Blackwell.

Himanen, Pekka. 2001. *The Hacker Ethic, and the Spirit of the Information Age.* New York: Random House.

Hindin, Michelle J. 2007. "Role Theory." In *The Blackwell Encyclopedia of Sociology,* edited by George Ritzer, 3951–3954. Malden, MA: Blackwell.

Hinze, Susan W., and Dawn Aliberti. 2007. "Feminization of Poverty." In *The Blackwell Encyclopedia of Sociology,* edited by George Ritzer, 1718–1725. Malden, MA: Blackwell.

Hirschi, Travis. 1969. *The Causes of Delinquency.* Berkeley: University of California Press.

Hirschi, Travis. 2004. "Self-Control and Crime." In *Handbook of Self-Regulation: Research, Theory and Application,* edited by R. F. Baumeister and K. D. Vohs, 537–552. New York: Guilford.

Hirth, Kenneth, and Joanne Pillsbury. 2013. "Redistribution and Markets in Andean South America." *Current Anthropology* 54: 642–647.

Hoang, Kimberly Kay. 2015. *Dealing in Desire: Asian Ascendancy, Western Decline, and the Hidden Currencies of Global Sex Work.* Berkeley: University of California Press.

Hobsbawm, E. J., and Chris Wrigley. 1999. *Industry and Empire: The Birth of the Industrial Revolution.* New York: New Press.

Hochschild, Adam. 2011. "Explaining Congo's Endless Civil War." *New York Times Book Review,* April 1. Accessed January 29, 2012. http://www.nytimes.com/2011/04/03/books/review/book-review-dancing-in-the-glory-of-monsters-the-collapse-of-the-congo-and-the-great-war-of-africa-by-jason-k-stearns.html?pagewanted=all.

Hochschild, Arlie Russell (with Anne Machung). 1989. *The Second Shift.* New York: Viking.

Hochschild, Arlie Russell. 2000. "Global Care Chains and Emotional Surplus Value." In *On the Edge: Living with Global Capitalism,* edited by W. Hutton and A. Giddens. London: Jonathan Cape.

Hochschild, Arlie Russell (with Anne Machung). 2012. *The Second Shift.* Updated ed. New York: Penguin.

Hochschild, Arlie Russell. 2016. *Strangers in Their Own Land: Anger and Mourning on the American Right.* New York: The New Press.

Hodge, David. 2008. "Sexual Trafficking in the US: A Domestic Problem with Transnational Dimensions." *Social Work* 53(2): 143–152.

Hodkinson, Paul. 2015. "Bedrooms and Beyond: Youth, Identity and Privacy on Social Network Sites." *New Media and Society* 10.

Hoecker-Drysdale, Susan. 2011. "Harriet Martineau." In *The Wiley-Blackwell Companion to Major Social Theorists,* Vol. 1, *Classical Theorists,* edited by George Ritzer and Jeffrey Stepnisky, 61–95. Malden, MA: Wiley-Blackwell.

Hoefer, Michael, Nancy Rytina, and Bryan C. Baker. 2010. "Estimates of the Unauthorized Immigrant Population Residing in the United States: January 2009." U.S. Department of Homeland Security. Accessed February 28, 2012. http://www.dhs.gov/xlibrary/assets/statistics/publications/ois_ill_pe_2009.pdf.

Hoekstra, Arjen J. 2012. "Water." In *The Wiley-Blackwell Companion to Sociology,* edited by George Ritzer, 2202–2210. Malden, MA: Wiley-Blackwell.

Hoffman, Jan. 2016. "Estimate of the U.S. Transgender Population Doubles." *New York Times,* July 1.

Hoffman, Lily M., Susan S. Fainstein, and Dennis R. Judd, eds. 2003. *Cities and Visitors: Regulating People, Markets, and City Space.* New York: Blackwell.

Hoffman, Steve. 2013. "Who Needs a General Theory of Social Reality?" *Contemporary Sociology* 42: 51–55.

Hoffnung, Michele, and Michelle A. Williams. 2013. "Balancing Act: Career and Family during College-Educated Women's 30s." *Sex Roles* 68(5–6): 321–334.

Hokayem, Charles, and Misty L. Heggeness. 2014. *Living in Near Poverty in the United States: 1966–2012.* Current Population Reports P60-248. Washington, DC: U.S. Census Bureau, May. Accessed April 19, 2015. https://www.census.gov/prod/2014pubs/p60-248.pdf.

Holdstock, Nick. 2014. "What We Talk about When We Talk about 'the Uyghurs.'" *Dissent* 61: 65–69.

Holland, Samantha. 2013. "Three Generations of Women's Leisure: Changes, Challenges, and Continuities." *Journal of Gender Studies* 22: 309–319.

Hollifield, James E., and David Jacobson. 2012. "Migration and the State." In *The Wiley-Blackwell Encyclopedia of Globalization,* edited by George Ritzer, 1390–1400. Malden, MA: Wiley-Blackwell.

Hollister, Geoff. 2008. *Out of Nowhere: The Inside Story of How Nike Marketed the Culture of Running.* Maidenhead, UK: Meyer and Meyer Sport.

Holmes, Seth. 2013. *Fresh Fruit, Broken Bodies: Migrant Farmworkers in the United States.* Berkeley: University of California Press.

Holt, Douglas B. 2004. *How Brands Become Icons: Principles of Cultural Branding.* Cambridge, MA: Harvard Business School Press.

Holt, Douglas B. 2007. "Distinction." In *The Blackwell Encyclopedia of Sociology,* edited by George Ritzer, 1189–1191. Malden, MA: Blackwell.

Holt, John, and Pat Farenga. 2003. *Teach Your Own: The John Holt Book of Homeschooling.* Cambridge, MA: Da Capa Press.

Holt, Justin. 2015. *The Social Thought of Karl Marx.* Thousand Oaks, CA: Sage.

Holton, Robert J. 2011. *Globalization and the Nation State.* 2nd ed. New York: Palgrave Macmillan.

Homans, George. 1961. *Social Behavior: Its Elementary Forms.* New York: Harcourt, Brace, and World.

Hondagneu-Sotelo, Pierette. 2000. *Doméstica: Immigrant Workers Cleaning and Caring in the Shadows of Affluence.* Berkeley: University of California Press.

Hondagneu-Sotelo, Pierette, and Ernestine Avila. 2005. "'I'm Here, but I'm There': The Meanings of Latina Transnational Motherhood." In *Gender through a Prism of Difference,* edited by M. B. Zinn, P. Hondagneu-Sotelo, and M. Messner. New York: Oxford University Press.

Honwana, Alcinda. 2007. *The Child Soldiers in Africa.* Philadelphia: University of Pennsylvania Press.

Hood, Roger, and Carolyn Hoyle. 2015. *The Death Penalty: A Worldwide Perspective.* 5th ed. Oxford: Oxford University Press.

hooks, bell. 2000. *Feminist Thought: From Margin to Center.* Cambridge, MA: South End Press.

Horkheimer, Max, and Theodor W. Adorno. [1944] 1997. *Dialectic of Enlightenment,* translated by J. Cumming. London: Verso Books.

Horrey, William J., and Christopher D. Wickens. 2006. "Examining the Impact of Cell Phone Conversations on Driving Using Meta-analytic Techniques." *Human Factors* 48: 196–205.

Horrigan, John. 2008. "Online Shopping." *Pew Internet and American Life Project,* February 13. Accessed April 19, 2015. http://www.pewinternet.org/2008/02/13/online-shopping.

Horton, Alicia D. 2013. "Flesh Hook Pulling: Motivations and Meaning-Making from the 'Body Side' of Life." *Deviant Behavior* 34: 115–134.

Horton, Richard. 2000. "North and South: Bridging the Information Gap." *The Lancet* 355: 2231–2236.

Houck, Davis W., and David E. Dixon, eds. 2011. *Women and the Civil Rights Movement, 1954–1965.* Jackson: University of Mississippi Press.

Hout, Michael. 2015. "A Summary of What We Know About Social Mobility." *The Annals* 657: 27-36.

"How America Shops Now." 2014. *Consumer Reports,* November: 27–33.

Howard, Vicki. 2015. *From Main Street to Mall: The Rise and Fall of the American Department Store.* Philadelphia: University of Pennsylvania Press.

Hu, Winnie. 2017. "An Endangered Call of the New York Wild: Taxi!" *New York Times,* January 16.

Huaco, George. 1966. "The Functionalist Theory of Stratification: Two Decades of Controversy." *Inquiry* 9: 215–240.

Huang, Penelope M., Pamela J. Smock, Wendy D. Manning, and Cara A. Bergstrom-Lynch. 2011. "He Says, She Says: Gender and Cohabitation." *Journal of Family Issues* 32: 876–905.

Hubbard, Phil, Andrew Gormley-Murray, and Catherine J. Nash. 2015. "Cities and Sexualities." In *Handbook of the Sociology of Sexualities,* edited by John DeLamater and Rebecca F. Plante, 287–303. New York: Springer.

Huddleston, Gabriel S., Julie C. Garlen, and Jennifer A. Sandlin. 2016. "The New Dimension of Disney Magic." In *Disney, Culture and Curriculum,* edited by Jennifer A. Sandlin and Julie C. Garlen, 220–232. New York: Routledge.

Huesemann, Michael, and Joyce Huesemann. 2011. *Techno-fix: Why Technology Won't Save Us or the Environment.* Gabriola Island, BC: New Society.

Hughes, Donna M. 2000. "Welcome to the Rape Camp: Sexual Exploitation and the Internet in Cambodia." *Journal of Sexual Aggression* 6: 1–23.

Hughey, Mathew W., and W. Carson Byrd. 2015. "Beautiful Melodies Telling Me Terrible Things: The Future of Race and Genetics for Scholars and Policy-Makers." *The Annals* 661: 238-258.

Hull, Kathleen E., Ann Meier, and Timothy Ortyl. 2010. "The Changing Landscape of Love and Marriage." *Contexts* 9: 32–37.

Human Rights Watch. 2015. "UN: Sexual Violence as a 'Tactic of War.'" Accessed March 8, 2017. https://www.hrw.org/news/2015/04/14/un-sexual-violence-tactic-war.

Humphreys, Laud. 1970. *Tearoom Trade: A Study of Homosexual Encounters in Public Places.* Chicago: Aldine.

Hunt, Stephen. 2007. "Social Structure." In *The Blackwell Encyclopedia of Sociology,* edited by George Ritzer, 4524–4526. Malden, MA: Blackwell.

Hunter, James Davison. 1992. *Culture Wars: The Struggle to Control the Family, Art, Education, Law, and Politics in America.* New York: Basic Books.

Huntington, Samuel P. 1996. *The Clash of Civilizations and the Remaking of the World Order.* New York: Simon & Schuster.

Hurdle, Jon. 2014. "A Casino Shuts Down amid Tears and Questions about a City's Direction." *New York Times,* September 1.

Hussain, Zaheer, and Mark Griffiths. 2008. "Gender Swapping and Socializing in Cyberspace: An Exploratory Study." *CyberPsychology & Behavior* 11(1): 47–53.

Hutson, Brittany. 2010. "Overcoming Gender Differences." *Black Enterprise* 40(8): 56–57.

Hutson, David J. 2016. "Training Bodies, Building Status: Negotiating Age and Gender Differences in the U.S. Fitness Industry." *Qualitative Sociology* 39: 49–70.

Hwang, Jinyoung, and Jong Ha Lee. 2014. "Women's Education and the Timing and Level of Fertility." *International Journal of Social Economics* 41: 862–874.

Iceland, John. 2007. "Poverty." In *The Blackwell Encyclopedia of Sociology,* edited by George Ritzer, 3587–3588. Malden, MA: Blackwell.

Iceland, John. 2013. *Poverty in America: A Handbook.* Updated ed. Berkeley: University of California Press.

Imtiaz, Saba, and Declan Walsh. 2015. "Pakistan Raids Offices of Fake Diploma Company." *New York Times,* May 20.

Inda, Jonathan Xavier. 2012. "Flows." In *The Wiley-Blackwell Encyclopedia of Globalization,* edited by George Ritzer, 668–670. Malden, MA: Wiley-Blackwell.

Inda, Jonathan Xavier, and Renato Rosaldo, eds. 2008. *The Anthropology of Globalization: A Reader.* 2nd ed. Malden, MA: Blackwell.

Inglehart, Ronald, and Wayne E. Baker. 2000. "Modernization, Cultural Change, and the Persistence of Traditional Values." *American Sociological Review* 65: 19–51.

Inglehart, Ronald, Roberto Foa, Christopher Peterson, and Christian Welzel. 2008. "Development, Freedom, and Rising Happiness: A Global Perspective (1981–2007)." *Perspectives on Psychological Science* 3(4): 264–285.

Inglis, David. 2016. "Globalization and Food." In *The Routledge International Handbook of Global Studies,* 2nd ed., edited by Bryan S. Turner and Robert S. Holton, 469–489. New York: Routledge.

Ingoldsby, Bron B., and Suzanna D. Smith, eds. 2006. *Families in Global and Multicultural Perspective.* 2nd ed. Thousand Oaks, CA: Sage.

Innis, Michelle. 2016. "Climate-Related Death of Coral Around the World Alarms Scientists." *New York Times,* April 9.

Inoue, Keiko, and Gili S. Drori. 2006. "The Global Institutionalization of Health as a Social Concern." *International Sociology* 21(1): 199–219.

Insch, Gary S., Nancy McIntyre, and Nancy C. Napier. 2008. "The Expatriate Glass Ceiling: The Second Layer of Glass." *Journal of Business Ethics* 83: 19–28.

Intergovernmental Panel on Climate Change. 2007. "Summary for Policymakers." In *Climate Change 2007: The Physical Science Basis,* edited by S. Solomon, D. Qin, M. Manning, Z. Chen, M. Marquis, K. B. Averyt, M. Tignor, and H. L. Miller. Contribution of Working Group I to the Fourth Assessment Report of the Intergovernmental Panel on Climate Change. Cambridge: Cambridge University Press.

Interlandi, Jeneen. 2010. "Why the Palace Fell: Lessons Learned from the Destruction of Haiti's Presidential Home." *Newsweek,* January 20. Accessed March 31, 2012. http://www.thedailybeast.com/news-week/2010/01/20/why-the-palace-fell.html.

International Centre for Prison Studies. 2011. "World Prison Brief." Accessed April 27, 2015. http://www.prisonstudies.org/world-prison-brief.

International Labour Organization. 2017. "Forced Labour, Modern Slavery and Human Trafficking." http://www.ilo.org/global/top-ics/forced-labour/lang--en/index.htm.

International Monetary Fund. 2011. "WEO Data: April 2011 Edition." Accessed May 26, 2011. http://www.imf.org/external/pubs/ft/weo/2011/01/weodata/WEOApr2011all.xls.

International Organization for Migration. 2005. "World Migration 2005: Costs and Benefits of International Migration." Accessed March 30, 2012. http://www.iom.int/jahia/Jahia/cache/offonce/pid/1674?entryId=932.

Intersex Society of North America. 2008. "FAQ: What Is Intersex?" Accessed May 15, 2015. http://www.isna.org/faq/what_is_intersex.

Intravia, Jonathan, Shayne Jones, and Alex R. Piquero. 2012. "The Roles of Social Bonds, Personality, and Perceived Costs: An Empirical Investigation of Hirschi's 'New' Social Control Theory." *International Journal of Offender Therapy and Comparative Criminology* 56: 1182–1200.

Introvigne, Masimo. 2007. "New Age." In *The Blackwell Encyclopedia of Sociology,* edited by George Ritzer, 3189–3192. Malden, MA: Blackwell.

Irvine, Leslie. 2004. "A Model of Animal Selfhood: Expanding Interactionist Possibilities." *Symbolic Interaction* 27: 3–21.

Irwin, Neil. 2016. "Rich People are Living Longer: That's Tilting Social Security in Their Favor." *New York Times,* April 22.

Ives, Mike. 2016. "A Remote Pacific Nation, Threatened by Rising Seas." *New York Times,* July 2.

Jackson, Michelle and D.R. Cox. 2013. "Principles of Experiment al Design and their Application to Sociology." *Annual Review of Sociology* 39: 27-49.

Jackson, Shirley A. 2007. "Majorities." In *The Blackwell Encyclopedia of Sociology,* edited by George Ritzer, 2701–2702. Malden, MA: Blackwell.

Jackson, Tim. 2014. "Sustainable Consumption." In *Handbook of Sustainable* Development, 2nd ed., edited by Giles Atkinson et al., 279–290. Northampton, MA: Edward Elgar.

Jackson-Jacobs, Curtis. 2005. "Hard Drugs in a Soft Context: Managing Trouble and Crack Use on a College Campus." *Sociological Quarterly* 45(4): 835–856.

Jacobs, Andrew. 2013. "Uighurs in China Say Bias is Growing." *New York Times,* October 8.

Jacobs, Harrison. 2014. "We Ranked YouTube's Biggest Stars by How Much Money They Make." *Business Insider,* March 10. Accessed April 22, 2015. http://www.businessinsider.com/richest-youtube-stars-2014-3?op=1.

Jacobs, Jerry. 1996. "Gender Inequality and Higher Education." *Annual Review of Sociology* 22: 153–185.

Jacobs, Mark D. 2007. "Interaction Order." In *The Blackwell Encyclopedia of Sociology,* edited by George Ritzer, 2365–2366. Malden, MA: Blackwell.

Jacobs, Nicholas. 2013. "Racial, Economic, and Linguistic Segregation: Analyzing Market Supports in the District of Columbia's Public Charter Schools." *Education and Urban Society* 45(1): 120–141.

Jacobsen, Joannes. 2015. "Revisiting the Modernization Hypothesis: Longevity and Democracy." *World Development* 67: 174–185.

Jacobsen, Linda A., Mark Mather, and Genevieve Dupuis. 2012. "Household Change in the United States." *Population Bulletin* 67: 1.

Jacobsen, Michael Hviid, and Soren Kristiansen. 2015. *The Social Thought of Erving Goffman.* Thousand Oaks, CA: Sage.

Jacques, Martin. 2009. *When China Rules the World: The End of the Western World and the Birth of a New Global Order.* London: Penguin.

Jakobi, Anja P. 2012. "Human Trafficking." In *The Wiley-Blackwell Encyclopedia of Globalization,* edited by George Ritzer, 953–956. Malden, MA: Wiley-Blackwell.

Jamal, Ahmad, Lisa Penaloza, and Michel LaRouche, eds. 2015. *The Routledge Companion to Ethnic Marketing.* New York: Routledge.

James, Nalita. 2016. "Using Email Interviews in Qualitative Research: Creating Space to Think and Time to Talk." *International Journal of Qualitative Studies in Education* 29: 150–163.

James, William. [1902] 1960. *The Varieties of Religious Experience.* New York: Random House.

Jamieson, Lynn. 1998. *Intimacy: Personal Relationships in Modern Societies.* Cambridge: Polity Press.

Jamieson, Lynn. 2007. "Intimacy." In *The Blackwell Encyclopedia of Sociology,* edited by George Ritzer, 2411–2414. Malden, MA: Blackwell.

Jamieson, Lynn. 2011. "Intimacy as a Concept: Explaining Social Change in the Context of Globalisation of Another Form of Ethnocentrism?" *Sociological Research Online* 16(4). Accessed April 19, 2015. http://www.socre sonline.org.uk/16/4/15.html.

Jamieson, Lynn. 2012. "Intimacy as a Concept: Explaining Social Change in the Context of Globalisation or Another Form of Ethnocentricism?" *The Clarion* 1(1): 133–147.

Janoski, Thomas. 2015. "The New Division of Labor as Lean Production." *International Journal of Sociology* 45: 85–94.

Janoski, Thomas, and Darina Lepadatu. 2013. *Dominant Divisions of Labor: Models of Production That Have Transformed the World of Work.* New York: Palgrave Pivot.

Jansen, Jim. 2010. "Online Product Research." Pew Research Center, September 29. Accessed May 27, 2011. http://www.pewinternet.org/~/media//Files/Reports/2010/PIP%20Online%20Product%20Research%20final.pdf.

Jay, Karla. 1999. *Tales of the Lavender Menace: A Memoir of Liberation.* New York: Basic Books.

Jay, Martin. 1973. *The Dialectical Imagination.* Boston: Little Brown.

Jean-Charles, Régine Michelle. 2010. "Cracks of Gender Inequality: Haitian Women after the Earthquake." Social Science Research Council. Accessed March 30, 2012. http://www.ssrc.org/features/pages/haiti-now-and-next/1338/1428.

Jefferson, Gail. 1979. "A Technique for Inviting Laughter and Its Subsequent Acceptance Declination." In *Everyday Language: Studies in Ethnomethodology,* edited by G. Psathas, 79–96. New York: Irvington.

Jeffreys, Sheila. 2005. *Beauty and Misogyny: Harmful Cultural Practices in the West.* New York: Routledge.

Jemielniak, Dariusz. 2016. "Breaking the Glass Ceiling on Wikipedia." *Feminist Review* 1: 103–108.

Jenkins, J. C. 1983. "Resource Mobilization Theory and the Study of Social Movements." *Annual Review of Sociology* 9: 248–267.

Jenness, Valerie. 2004. "Explaining Criminalization: From Demography and Status Politics to Globalization and Modernization." *Annual Review of Sociology* 30: 141–171.

Jensen, Gary F. 1988. "Functional Perspectives on Deviance: A Critical Assessment and Guide for the Future." *Deviant Behavior* 9: 1–17.

Jerolmack, Colin. 2009. "Humans, Animals, and Play: Theorizing Interaction When Inter-subjectivity Is Problematic." *Sociological Theory* 27(4): 371–389.

Jerolmack, Colin. 2013. *The Global Pigeon.* Chicago: University of Chicago Press.

Johns, Nicole, Krycia Cowling, and Emmanuela Gakidou. 2013. "The Wealth (and Health) of Nations: A Cross-Country Analysis of the Relation between Wealth and Inequality in Disease Burden Estimation." *The Lancet* 381: S66.

Johnson, Allan. 2005. *The Gender Knot: Unraveling Our Patriarchal Legacy.* Philadelphia: Temple University Press.

Johnson, C., R. Ford, and J. Kaufman. 2000. "Emotional Reactions to Conflict: Do Dependence and Legitimacy Matter?" *Social Forces* 79(1): 107–137.

Johnson, David. 2011. "Households Doubling Up." U.S. Census Bureau. Accessed March 8, 2017. http://blogs.census.gov/2011/09/13/households-doubling-up.

Johnson, David K. 2004. *The Lavender Scare: The Cold War Persecution of Gays and Lesbians in the Federal Government.* Chicago: University of Chicago Press.

Johnson, Kirk. 2011. "At 84 Square Feet, Home Takes Tiny House Movement Tinier." *New York Times,* December 2. Accessed May 13, 2015. http://www.nytimes.com/2011/12/03/us/at-84-square-feet-home-takes-tiny-house-movement-tinier.html?_r=0.

Johnson, Naomi. 2010. "Consuming Desires: Consumption, Romance, and Sexuality in Best-Selling Teen Romance Novels." *Women's Studies in Communication* 33: 54–73.

Johnston, Lloyd D., Patrick M. O'Malley, Jerald G. Bachman, John E. Schulenberg, and Richard A. Miech. 2014. *Monitoring the Future National Survey Results on Drug Use, 1975–2013,* Vol. 2, *College Students and Adults Ages 19–55.* Ann Arbor: Institute for Social Research, University of Michigan. Accessed April 24, 2015. http://monitoringthefuture.org/pubs/monographs/mtf-vol2_2013.pdf.

Jolly, David. 2012. "Amsterdam Shops Selling Marijuana to Stay Open." *New York Times,* November 1.

Jolly, David. 2014. "Heat Waves in Europe Will Increase Study Finds. *New York Times,* December 9.

Jones, Adele. 2008. "A Silent but Mighty River: The Costs of Women's Economic Migration." *Signs* 33(4): 761–769.

Jones, Nicholas, and Jungmiwha Bullock. 2013. "Understanding Who Reported Multiple Races in the U.S. Decennial Census: From Census 2000 and the 2010 Census." *Family Relations* 62: 5–16.

Jones, Richard G. 2015. "Queering the Body Politic: Intersectional Reflexivity in the Body Narratives of Queer Men." *Qualitative Inquiry* 21: 766–775.

Jones, Steven T. 2011. *The Tribes of Burning Man: How an Experiment in the Desert Is Shaping the New American Counterculture.* San Francisco: Consortium of Collective Consciousness.

Joppke, Christian. 2009. *Veil: Mirror of Identity.* Cambridge: Polity Press.

Jordan, Mary. 2007. "The New Face of Global Mormonism: Tech-Savvy Missionary Church Thrives as Far Afield as Africa." *Washington Post,* November 19.

Jorgenson, Andrew, and Jennifer Givens. 2012. "Pollution, Water." In *The Wiley-Blackwell Companion to Sociology,* edited by George Ritzer, 1674. Malden, MA: Wiley-Blackwell.

Jose, Paul E., Kerstin Kramar, and Yubo Hou. 2014. "Does Brooding Rumination Moderate the Stress to Depression Relationship Similarly for Chinese and New Zealand Adolescents?" *Journal of Educational and Developmental Psychology* 4(1): 114–127.

Joy, Annamma, John F. Sherry Jr., Alladi Venkatesh, Jeff Wang, and Ricky Chan. 2012. "Fast Fashion, Sustainability, and the Ethical Appeal of Luxury Brands." *Fashion Theory* 16: 273–295.

Joyner, Chris. 2010. "Miss. Prom Canceled after Lesbian's Date Request." *USA Today,* March 11. Accessed March 30, 2012. http://www.usatoday.com/news/nation/2010-03-10-noprom_N.htm.

Juergensmeyer, Mark. 2003. *Terror in the Mind of God: The Global Rise of Religious Violence.* Berkeley: University of California Press.

Juergensmeyer, Mark. 2009. *Global Rebellion: Religious Challenges to the Secular State, from Christian Militias to al Qaeda.* Berkeley: University of California Press.

Jula, Megan, and Julia Preston. 2016. "Delayed Care Faulted in Immigrants' Deaths at Detention Centers." *The New York Times,* July 7.

Jung, Jaehee, Gordon Forbes, and Priscilla Chan. 2010. "Global Body and Muscle Satisfaction among College Men in the United States and Hong Kong–China." *Sex Roles* 63(1/2): 104–117.

Jung, Moon-Kie, João H. Costa Vargas, and Eduardo Bonilla-Silva, eds. 2011. *State of White Supremacy: Racism, Governance, and the United States.* Stanford CA: Stanford University Press.

Jurgenson, Nathan. 2012. "When Atoms Meet Bits: Social Media, the Mobile Web and Augmented Revolution." *Future Internet* 4: 83–91.

Juris, Jeffrey S. 2005. "The New Digital Media and Activist Networking within Anti-corporate Globalization Movements." *Annals of the American Academy of Political and Social Science* 597(January): 189–208.

Kaarbo, Juliet, and James Ray. 2010. *Global Politics.* Boston: Cengage.

Kabeer, Naila, Ratna Sudarshan, and Kristi Milward. 2013. *Organizing Women Workers in the Informal Economy: Beyond the Weapons of the Weak.* London: Zed Books.

Kadushin, Charles. 2012. *Understanding Social Networks: Theories, Concepts, and Findings.* New York: Oxford University Press.

Kaeble, Danielle, Laura M. Maruschak, and Thomas P. Bonczar. 2015. "Probation and Parole in the United States U.S. Department of Justice, Bureau of Justice Statistics. Accessed January 25, 2017. https://www.bjs.gov/content/pub/pdf/ppus14.pdf.

Kahlenberg, Richard D., ed. 2010. *Affirmative Action for the Rich: Legacy Preferences in College Admissions.* Washington, DC: Brookings Institution Press.

Kahlenberg, Susan G., and Michelle M. Hein. 2010. "Progression on Nickelodeon? Gender-Role Stereotypes in Toy Commercials." *Sex Roles* 62(11–12): 830–847.

Kahn, Richard, and Douglas Kellner. 2007. "Resisting Globalization." In *The Blackwell Companion to Globalization,* edited by George Ritzer, 662–674. Malden, MA: Blackwell.

Kaiser Family Foundation. 2015a. "Population Distribution by Gender." Accessed January 25, 2017. http://kff.org/other/state-indicator/distribution-by-gender/?currentTimeframe=0&sortModel=%7B%22colId%22:%22Location%22,%22sort%22:%22asc%22%7D.

Kaiser Family Foundation. 2015b. "Poverty Rate by Race/Ethnicity." Accessed January 26, 2017. http://kff.org/other/state-indicator/poverty-rate-by-raceethnicity/?currentTimeframe=0&sortModel=%7B%22colId%22:%22Location%22,%22sort%22:%22asc%22%7D.

Kalberg, Stephen. 1980. "Max Weber's Types of Rationality: Cornerstones for the Analysis of Rationalization Processes in History." *American Journal of Sociology* 85(5): 1145–1179.

Kalberg, Stephen. 2011. "Max Weber." In *The Wiley-Blackwell Companion to Major Social Theorists,* Vol. 1, *Classical Theorists,* edited by George Ritzer and Jeffrey Stepnisky, 305–372. Malden, MA: Wiley-Blackwell.

Kalberg, Stephen. 2017. *The Social Thought of Max Weber.* Thousand Oaks, CA: Sage.

Kalev, Alexandra. 2009. "Cracking the Glass Cages? Restructuring and Ascriptive Inequality at Work." *American Journal of Sociology* 114: 1591–1643.

Kaminer, Ariel, and Sean O'Driscoll. 2014. "Workers at N.Y.U.'s Abu Dhabi Site Faced Harsh Conditions." *New York Times,* May 18.

Kane, Emily W. 2006. "'No Way My Boys Are Going to Be Like That!' Parents' Responses to Children's Gender Nonconformity." *Gender & Society* 20(2): 149–176.

Kane, Emily W. 2012. *The Gender Trap: Parents and the Pitfalls of Raising Boys and Girls.* New York: New York University Press.

Kang, Cecilia. 2016. "Court Backs Ruling Treating Internet as a Utility, Not Luxury." *New York Times,* June 14.

Kang, J. 2000. "Cyber-race." *Harvard Law Review* 113: 1130–1208.

Kang, Miliann, and Katherine Jones. 2007. "Why Do People Get Tattoos?" *Contexts* 6(1): 42–47.

Kangas, Olli E. 2007. "Welfare State, Retrenchment of." In *The Blackwell Encyclopedia of Sociology,* edited by George Ritzer, 5247–5249. Malden, MA: Blackwell.

Kanter, James, and Sewell Chan. 2016. "Europe, Reeling from Strain, Tells Economic Migrants: Don't Bother." *New York Times,* March 3.

Kanter, Rosabeth Moss. 1993. *Men and Women of the Corporation.* New York: Basic Books.

Kaplan, Fred. 2016. *Dark Territory: The Secret History of Cyber War.* New York: Simon and Schuster.

Kaoma, Kapya. 2014. "The Paradox and Tension of Moral Claims: Evangelical Christianity, the Politicization and Globalization of Sexual Politics in Sub-Saharan Africa." *Critical Research on Religion* 2(3): 227–245.

Karlson, Kristian Berndt. 2015. "Expectations on Track? High School Tracking and Adolescent Educational Expectations." *Social Forces* 94: 115–141.

Karraker, Meg Wilkes. 2013. *Global Families.* 2nd Edition. Boston: Pearson.

Karstedt, Susanne. 2007. "Genocide." In *The Blackwell Encyclopedia of Sociology,* edited by George Ritzer, 1909–1913. Malden, MA: Blackwell.

Karstedt, Suzanne. 2012. "Genocide." In *The Wiley-Blackwell Encyclopedia of Globalization,* edited by George Ritzer, 793–797. Malden, MA: Wiley-Blackwell.

Karstedt, Suzanne. 2016. "Genocide." In *The Wiley-Blackwell Encyclopedia of Race, Ethnicity and Nationalism,* edited by John Stone, Rutledge M. Dennis, Polly Rizova, Anthony D. Smith, and Xiaoshuo Hou. Malden, MA: Wiley-Blackwell.

Kasarda, John D. 2016. "Welcome to Aerotropolis, The City of The Future." *The World Post*, May 1. Accessed March 13, 2017. http://www.huffingtonpost.com/john-d-kasarda/aerotropolis-city-future_b_7269152.html.

Kasarda, John D., and Greg Lindsay. 2011. *Aerotropolis: The Way We'll Live Next.* New York: Farrar, Straus and Giroux.

Kasten, Erich. 2004. *Properties of Culture, Culture as Property: Pathways to Reform in Post-Soviet Siberia.* Berlin: Reimer.

Katsulis, Yasmina. 2010. "'Living Like a King': Conspicuous Consumption, Virtual Communities, and the Social Construction of Paid Sexual Encounters by U.S. Sex Tourists." *Men and Masculinities* 27: 1–18.

Katz, Jonathan Ned. 2004. "'Homosexual' and 'Heterosexual': Questioning the Terms." In *Sexualities: Identities, Behaviors, and Society,* edited by M. S. Kimmel and R. F. Plante, 44–46. New York: Oxford University Press.

Katz-Gerro, Tally, and Mads Meier Jaeger. 2013. "Top of the Pops, Ascend of the Omnivores, Defeat of the Couch Potatoes: Cultural Consumption Profiles in Denmark 1975–2004." *European Sociological Review* 29(2): 243–260.

Kaufman, Dan. 2016. "Which Side Are You On, Hillary?" *New York Times*, March 12.

Kaufman, Jason, and Orlando Patterson. 2005. "Cross-National Cultural Diffusion: The Global Spread of Cricket." *American Sociological Review* 70: 82–110.

Kaufman-Scarbrough, Carol. 2006. "Time Use and the Impact of Technology: Examining Workspaces in the Home." *Time and Society* 15(1): 57–80.

Kauppinen, Ilkka. 2013. "Academic Capitalism and the Informational Fraction of the Transnational Capitalist Class." *Globalisation, Societies and Education* 11: 1–22.

Keane, John. 2003. *Global Civil Society.* Cambridge: Cambridge University Press.

Kefalas, Maria J., Frank F. Furstenberg, Patrick J. Carr, and Laura Napolitano. 2011. "'Marriage Is More Than Being Together': The Meaning of Marriage for Young Adults." *Journal of Family Issues* 32: 845–875.

Keller, Bill. 1990. "Of Famous Arches, Been Meks and Rubles." *New York Times*, January 28.

Kellerhals, Jean. 2007. "Family Conflict." In *The Blackwell Encyclopedia of Sociology,* edited by George Ritzer, 1580–1583. Malden, MA: Blackwell.

Kellerhals, Jean, and Eric D. Widmer. Forthcoming. In George Ritzer, ed. *Encyclopedia of Sociology,* 2nd ed. Malden, MA: Wiley-Blackwell.

Kellezi, Blerina, and Stephen Reicher. 2014. "The Double Insult: Explaining Gender Differences in the Psychological Consequences of War." *Peace & Conflict* 20(4): 491–504.

Kellner, Douglas. 2008. *Guys and Guns Amok.* NY: Routledge.

Kellner, Douglas. 2011. "Jean Baudrillard." In *The Wiley-Blackwell Companion to Major Social Theorists,* Vol. 1, *Classical Theorists,* edited by George Ritzer and Jeffrey Stepnisky, 310–339. Malden, MA: Wiley-Blackwell.

Kellner, Douglas and Tyson E. Lewis. 2007. "Cultural Critique." In *The Blackwell Encyclopedia of Sociology,* edited by George Ritzer, 896–898. Malden, MA: Blackwell.

Kelly, Sean. 2004. "Are Teachers Tracked? On What Basis and with What Consequences?" *Social Psychology of Education* 7: 55–72.

Kempadoo, Kamala. 1996–1997. "'Sandoms' and Other Exotic Women: Prostitution and Race in the Caribbean." *Race and Reason* 1(3): 48–53.

Kennedy, M. Alexis, Carolin Klein, Jessica T. K. Bristowe, Barry S. Cooper, and John C. Yuille. 2007. "Routes of Recruitment: Pimps' Techniques and Other Circumstances that Lead to Street Prostitution." *Journal of Aggression, Maltreatment and Trauma* 15(2):1–19.

Kennedy, Peter G. 2013. "Clinical Features, Diagnosis, and Treatment of Human African Trypanosomiasis (Sleeping Sickness)." *The Lancet Neurology* 12(2): 186–194.

Kennedy, Randall. 2013. *For Discrimination: Race, Affirmative Action, and the Law.* New York: Vintage.

Kerber, Linda K. 1988. "Separate Spheres, Female Worlds, Woman's Place: The Rhetoric of Women's History." *Journal of American History* 75(1): 9–39.

Kern, Soeren. 2014. "The Islamization of Belgium and the Netherlands in 2013." Gatestone Institute, International Policy Council, January 13. Accessed April 27, 2015. http://www.gatestoneinstitute.org/4129/islamization-bel gium-netherlands.

Kershaw, Sarah. 2008. "Starving Themselves, Cocktail in Hand." *New York Times,* March 2. Accessed January 1, 2012. http://www.nytimes.com/2008/03/02/fashion/02drunk.html.

Kershner, Isabel. 2015. "Netanyahu Urges 'Mass Immigration' of Jews from Europe." *New York Times,* April 15.

Kestnbaum, Meyer. 2012. "Organized Coercion and Political Authority: Armed Conflict in a World of States." In *The Wiley-Blackwell Companion to Sociology,* edited by George Ritzer, 588–608. Malden, MA: Wiley-Blackwell.

Khan, Shamus Rahman. 2011. *Privilege: The Making of an Adolescent Elite at St. Paul's School.* Princeton, NJ: Princeton University Press.

Khanna, Nikki, and Cherise A. Harris. 2015. "Discovering Race in a 'Post-racial' World: Teaching Race through Primetime Television." *Teaching Sociology* 43: 39–45.

Khanna, Parag. 2016. "A New Map for America." *New York Times,* April 15.

Kharif, Olga. 2014. "Not Just for Libertarians and Anarchists Anymore." *Bloomberg,* October 9.

Khatchadourian, Raffi. 2007. "Neptune's Navy." *New Yorker,* November 5.

Khrais, Reema. 2013. "Showing Off Shopping Sprees, Fashion 'Haulers' Cash In Online." *NPR,* March 14. Accessed April 19, 2015. http://www.npr.org/2013/03/14/174305909/showing-off-shopping-sprees-fashion-haulers-cash-in-online.

Kiaye, Risper Enid, and Anesh Maniraj Singh. 2013. "The Glass Ceiling: A Perspective of Women Working in Durban." *Gender in Management* 28: 28–42.

Kidder, Jeffrey L. 2012. "Parkour, the Affective Appropriation of Urban Space, and the Real/Virtual Dialectic." *City and Community* 11: 229–253.

Kimmel, Michael S. 2012. *The Gendered Society.* 5th ed. New York: Oxford University Press.

Kimmel, Michael, ed. 2014. *Sexualities, Identities and Behaviors.* 2nd ed. New York: Oxford University Press.

Kimmelman, Michael. 2016. "The Vertical Frontier." *New York Times Magazine,* June 5.

King, Anthony. 2004. *The Structure of Social Theory.* London: Routledge.

King, Keith A,. and Rebecca A. Vidourek. 2013. "Getting Inked: Tattoo and Risky Behavioral Involvement among University Students." *Social Science Journal* 50: 540–546.

King, Martin Luther, Jr. [1958] 2010. *Stride toward Freedom: The Montgomery Story.* Boston: Beacon Press.

Kinney, William J. 2007. "Asch Experiments." In *The Blackwell Encyclopedia of Sociology,* edited by George Ritzer, 189–191. Malden, MA: Blackwell.

Kirk, Roger E. 2007. "Experimental Design." In *The Blackwell Encyclopedia of Sociology,* edited by George Ritzer, 1533–1537. Malden, MA: Blackwell.

Kivisto, Peter. 2012a. "Fundamentalism." In *The Wiley-Blackwell Encyclopedia of Globalization,* edited by George Ritzer, 709–713. Malden, MA: Wiley-Blackwell.

Kivisto, Peter. 2012b. "Refugees." In *The Wiley-Blackwell Encyclopedia of Globalization,* edited by George Ritzer, 1761–1765. Malden, MA: Wiley-Blackwell.

Kivisto, Peter, and Paul R. Croll. 2012. *Race and Ethnicity: The Basics.* New York: Routledge.

Kivisto, Peter, and Thomas Faist. 2007. *Citizenship: Discourse, Theory, and Transnational Prospects.* Malden, MA: Blackwell.

Kivisto, Peter, and Thomas Faist. 2010. *Beyond a Border: The Causes and Consequences of Contemporary Immigration.* Thousand Oaks, CA: Pine Forge Press.

Klaasen, Marleen J. E., and Jochen Peter. 2015. "Gender (In)equality in Internet Pornography: A Content Analysis of Popular Pornographic Internet Videos." *The Journal of Sex Research* 52: 721–735.

Klein, Alan. 1993. *Little Big Men: Bodybuilding Subculture and Gender Construction.* Albany: State University of New York Press.

Klein, Kate, Alix Holtby, Katie Cook, and Rob Travers. 2015. "Complicating the Coming Out Narrative: Becoming Oneself in a Heterosexist and Cissexist World." *Journal of Homosexuality* 62(3): 297–326.

Klein, Markus. 2016. "Educational Expansion, Occupational Closure and the Relation between Educational Attainment and Occupational Prestige Over Time." *Sociology* 50: 3–23.

Klein, Naomi. [2000] 2010. *No Logo: Taking Aim at the Brand Bullies.* Toronto: Vintage.

Klein, Naomi. 2014. *This Changes Everything: Capitalism vs. the Climate.* New York: Simon and Scuster.

Kleinman, Daniel Lee, and Robert Osley-Thomas. 2016. "Codes of Commerce and Codes of

Citizenship: A Historical Look at Students as Consumers with US Higher Education." In *The University Under Pressure,* edited by Elisabeth Popp Berman and Catherine Paradeise, 197–220. Bingley, UK: Emerald Publishing Ltd.

Kleinplatz, Peggy. 1992. "The Erotic Experience and the Intent to Arouse." *Canadian Journal of Sexuality* 1(3): 133–139.

Klinenberg, Eric. 2012. *Going Solo: The Extraordinary Rise and Surprising Appeal of Living Alone.* New York: Penguin.

Klinenberg, Eric. 2015. *Heat Wave: A Social Autopsy of Disaster in Chicago.* Chicago: University of Chicago Press.

Knoblauch, Hubert, and Rene Wilke, 2016. "The Common Denominator: The Reception and Impact of Berger and Luckman's *The Social Construction of Reality.*" *Human Studies* 39: 51–69.

Knorr Cetina, Karin. 2012. "Financial Markets." In *The Encyclopedia of Globalization,* edited by George Ritzer, 653–664. Malden, MA: Wiley-Blackwell.

Koblin, John, Emily Steel, and Jim Rutenberg, 2016. "Roger Ailes Leaves Fox News, and Rupert Murdoch Steps In." *New York Times,* July 21.

Koch, Jerome R., Alden E. Roberts, Myrna L. Armstrong, and Donna C. Owen. 2010. "Body Art, Deviance, and American College Students." *Social Science Journal* 47: 151–161.

Kohler, Kristopher. 2012. "World Social Forum." In *The Wiley-Blackwell Encyclopedia of Globalization,* edited by George Ritzer, 2325–2327. Malden, MA: Wiley-Blackwell.

Kohrmann, M. 2008. "Smoking among Doctors: Governmentality, Embodiment, and the Diversion of Blame in Contemporary China." *Medical Anthropology* 27(1): 9–42.

Koistinen, David. 2013. *Confronting Decline: The Political Economy of Deindustrialization in Twentieth-Century New England.* Gainesville: University Press of Florida.

Koivusalo, Meri and Eeva Ollila. 2014. "Global Health Policies." In *Understanding Global Social Policy,* edited by N. Yeates, 159–186. Cambridge: Polity Press.

Kolata, Gina. 1999. *The Flu: The Story of the Great Influenza Pandemic of 1918 and the Search for the Virus That Caused It.* New York: Touchstone.

Kolata, Gina. 2016. "A Cautionary Tale of 'Stem Cell Tourism.'" *New York Times,* June 22.

Köllen, Thomas. 2013. "Bisexuality and Diversity Management: Addressing the *B* in LGBT as a Relevant 'Sexual Orientation' in the Workplace." *Journal of Bisexuality* 13(1): 122–137.

Kollmeyer, Christopher. 2009. "Explaining Deindustrialization: How Affluence, Productivity Growth, and Globalization Diminish Manufacturing Employment." *American Journal of Sociology* 114: 1644–1674.

Kollmeyer, Christopher, and Florian Pichler. 2013. "Is Deindustrialization Causing High Unemployment in Affluent Countries? Evidence from 16 OECD Countries, 1970–2003." *Social Forces* 91: 785–812.

Kolodny, Andrew, David T. Courtwright, Catherine S. Hwang, Peter Kreiner, John L. Eadie, Thomas W. Clark, and G. Caleb Alexander. 2015. "The Prescription Opioid and Heroin Crisis: A Public Health Approach to an Epidemic of Addiction." *Annual Review of Public Health* 36: 449–574.

Kong, Travis. 2010. *Chinese Male Homosexualities.* London: Routledge.

Konrad, Waleca. 2009. "Seeking the Best Medical Care Prices." *New York Times,* November 28.

Koopmans, Ruud. 2015. "Religious Fundamentalism and Hostility against Out-Groups: A Comparison of Muslims and Christians in Western Europe." *Journal of Ethnic and Migration Studies* 41: 33–57.

Korda, Andrew. 2006. "The Nazi Medical Experiments." *ADF Health* 7(April): 33–37.

Korkki, Phyllis. 2012. "When the H.R. Office Leaves the Building." *New York Times,* December 12.

Kosic, Ankica, Arie W. Kruglanski, Antonio Pierro, and Lucia Mannetti. 2004. "The Social Cognition of Immigrants' Acculturation: Effects of the Need for Closure and the Reference Group at Entry." *Journal of Personality and Social Psychology* 86: 796–813.

Kotarba, Joseph A. 2007. "Socialization, Adult." In *The Blackwell Encyclopedia of Sociology,* edited by George Ritzer, 4563–4566. Malden, MA: Blackwell.

Kotarba, Joseph A., Andrea Salvini, and Bryce Merrill, eds. 2012. *The Present and Future of Symbolic Interactionism: Proceedings of the International Symposium, Pisa 2010.* Pisa: Franco Angeli.

Kovacs, Zoltan, and Gábor Hegedus. 2014. "Gated Communities as New Forms of Segregation in Post-socialist Budapest." *Cities* 36: 200–209.

Kozinets, Robert. 2015. *Netnography Redefined.* London: Sage.

Krass, Frauke, ed. 2012. *Megacities: Our Global Urban Future.* New York: Springer.

Krass, P. 1990. "The Dollars and Sense of Outsourcing." *Information Week,* February 26, 26–31.

Kraus, Michael W., Shai Davidai, and A. David Nussbaum. 2015. "American Dream? Or Mirage?" *New York Times,* May 3.

Krauss, Clifford. 2004. "Internet Drug Exporters Feel Pressure in Canada." *New York Times,* December 11. Accessed March 30, 2012. http://query.nytimes.com/gst/fullpage.html?res=9F04EED81131F932A25751C1A9629C8B63&&scp=4&sq=pharmaceutical%20purchase%20over%20inter net&st=cse.

Kreager, Derek. 2007. "Unnecessary Roughness? School Sports, Peer Networks, and Male Adolescent Violence." *American Sociological Review* 72(5): 705–724.

Krinsky, Charles, ed. 2013. *The Ashgate Research Companion to Moral Panics.* Burlington, VT: Ashgate.

Kritz, Mary M. 2007. "Migration, International." In *The Blackwell Encyclopedia of Sociology,* edited by George Ritzer, 3019–3025. Malden, MA: Blackwell.

Kritz, Mary M. 2008. "International Migration." In *The Blackwell Encyclopedia of Sociology Online,* edited by George Ritzer. Malden, MA: Blackwell.

Kritz, Mary M., Lin Lean Lim, and Hania Zlotnik, eds. 1992. *International Migration Systems: A Global Approach.* Oxford: Oxford University Press.

Kroeger, Rhiannon A., and Pamela J. Smock. 2014. "Cohabitation." In *The Wiley-Blackwell Companion to Sociology of Families,* edited by J. Treas, J. Scott, and M. Richards. Malden, MA: Wiley-Blackwell.

Kroen, Sheryl. 2006. "Negotiations with the American Way: The Consumer and the Social Contract in Post-war Europe." In *Consuming Cultures, Global Perspectives: Historical Trajectories, Transnational Exchanges,* edited by J. Brewer and F. Trentmann, 251–278. Oxford: Berg.

Krogstad, Jens Manuel. 2015a. "Social Media Preferences Vary by Race and Ethnicity." Pew Research Center, February. 3. Accessed January 27, 2017. http://www.pewresearch.org/fact-tank/2015/02/03/social-media-preferences-vary-by-race-and-ethnicity.

Krogstad, Jens Manuel. 2015b. "What LGBT Americans Think of Same-Sex Marriage." Pew Research Center, *Fact Tank,* January 27. Accessed May 23, 2015. http://www.pewresearch.org/fact-tank/2015/01/27/what-lgbt-americans-think-of-same-sex-marriage.

Krogstad, Jens Manual, Jeffrey S. Passel, and D'Vera Cohn. 2016. "5 Facts about Illegal Immigration in the U.S." Pew Research Center, November 3.

Kroneberg, Clemens, and Frank Kalter. 2012. "Rational Choice Theory and Empirical Research: Methodological and Theoretical Contributions in Europe." *Annual Review of Sociology* 38: 73–92.

Kuehn, Kathleen. 2015. "Culture Jamming." In Daniel Thomas Cook and Michael Ryan, eds. *Encyclopedia of Consumption and Consumer Studies* Malden, MA: Wiley-Blackwell, 2015: 236–238.

Kuhn, Thomas. [1962] 1970. *The Structure of Scientific Revolutions.* 2nd ed. Chicago: University of Chicago Press.

Kuisel, Richard. 1993. *Seducing the French: The Dilemma of Americanization.* Berkeley: University of California Press.

Kulish, Nicholas. 2007. "Europe Fears That Meth Foothold is Expanding." *New York Times,* November 23.

Kumar, Hari. 2015. "Indian and Pakistani Guards Trade Fire on Disputed Border." *New York Times,* January 3.

Kunzman, Robert, and Milton Gaither. 2013. "Homeschooling: A Comprehensive Survey of the Research." *Other Education* 2: 4–59.

Kuo, Janet Chen-Lan, and R. Kelly Raley, 2016. "Diverging Patterns of Union Transition Among Cohabitors by Race/Ethnicity and Education: Trends and Marital Intentions in the United States." *Demography* June 15 (published online first).

Kuperberg, Arielle, and Jospeh E. Padgett, 2015. "The Role of Culture in Explaining College Students' Selection into Hookups, Dates and Long-term Romantic Relationships." *Journal of Social and Personal Relationships:* 1–27.

Kupfer, Antonia. 2012. "A Theoretical Concept of Educational Upward Mobility." *International Studies in Sociology of Education* 22: 57–72.

Kurtz, Annalyn. 2014. "Americans Still Hesitant to Spend More." *CNN Money*, June 26. Accessed April 22, 2015. http://money.cnn.com/2014/06/26/news/economy/americans-not-spend.

Kurtz, Lester R. 2005. "From Heresies to Holy Wars: Toward a Theory of Religious Conflict." *Ahimsa Nonviolence* 1(March–April): 143–157.

Kurtz, Lester R. 2016. *Gods in the Global Village.* 4th ed. Thousand Oaks, CA: Sage.

Kurzban. 2006. "Post-Sept. 11, 2001." In *Immigration Law Sourcebook*, 10th ed., xxi–xxiii. Washington, DC: American Immigration Law Foundation.

Kushkush, Isma'il. 2015. "President of Sudan Is Re-elected with 94 Percent of Vote." *New York Times,* April 27.

Kwan, Samantha, and Mary Nell Trautner. 2011. "Judging Books by Their Covers: Teaching about Physical Attractiveness Biases." *Teaching Sociology* 39: 16–26.

Lacey, Marc. 2011. "Rift in Arizona as Latino Class Is Found Illegal." *New York Times,* January 7. Accessed March 30, 2012. http://www.nytimes.com/2011/01/08/us/08ethnic.html.

Lachance-Grzela, Mylene and Genevieve Bouchard. 2010. "Why Do Women Do the Lion's Share of Housework? A Decade of Research." *Sex Roles* 63(11–12): 767–780.

Lacity, Mary Cecelia, and R. A. Hirschheim. 1993. *Information Systems Outsourcing: Myths, Metaphors and Realities.* New York: Wiley.

Lacy, Karyn. 2016. "The Sociology of Suburbs: A Research Agenda for Analysis of Emerging Trends." *Annual Review of Sociology* 42: 369–384.

Lahelma, Eero. 2007. "Health and Social Class." In *The Blackwell Encyclopedia of Sociology,* edited by George Ritzer, 2086–2091. Malden, MA: Blackwell.

Lahelma, Eero. Forthcoming. "Health and Social Class." In *The Wiley-Blackwell Encyclopedia of Sociology,* 2nd ed., edited by George Ritzer. Malden, MA: Wiley-Blackwell.

Laible, Deborah, Ross A. Thompson, and Jill Froimson. 2015. "Early Socialization: The Influence of Close Relationships." In *Handbook of Socialization: Theory and Research,* 2nd ed., edited by Joan E. Grusec and Paul D. Hastings, 35–59. New York: Guilford Press.

Lakoff, Andrew. 2008. "Diagnostic Liquidity: Mental Illness and the Global Trade in DNA." In *The Anthropology of Globalization: A Reader,* 2nd ed., edited by J. X. Inda and R. Rosaldo, 277–300. Malden, MA: Blackwell.

Lal, Dinesh. 2008. *Indo-Tibet-China Conflict.* Delhi: Kalpaz.

Landler, Mark. 2008. "Credit Cards Tighten Grip Outside US." *New York Times,* August 30.

Landry, Bart. 1988. *The New Black Middle Class.* Berkeley: University of California Press.

Landry, Bart and Kris Marsh. 2011. "The Evolution of the New Black Middle Class." *Annual Review of Sociology* 37: 373–394.

Landstedt, Evelina, and Katja Gillander Gådin. 2012. "Seventeen and Stressed: Do Gender and Class Matter?" *Health Sociology Review* 21: 82–98.

Lane, Harlan. 1975. *The Wild Boy of Aveyron.* Cambridge, MA: Harvard University Press.

Lara-Millán, Armando. 2014. "Public Emergency Room Overcrowding in the Era of Mass Imprisonment." *American Sociological Review* 79: 866–887.

Lareau, Annette. 2015. "Cultural Knowledge and Social Inequality." *American Sociological Review* 80: 1–27.

Larsen, Gretchen, Maurice Patterson, and Lucy Markham. 2014. "A Deviant Art: Tattoo-Related Stigma in an Era of Commodification." *Psychology & Marketing* 31: 670–681.

Lash, Scott, and Celia Lury. 2007. *Global Culture Industry.* Cambridge: Polity Press.

Lasn, Kalle. 2000. *Culture Jam: How to Reverse America's Suicidal Consumer Binge—and Why We Must.* New York: Quill.

Lasn, Kalle. 2012. *Meme Wars.* New York: Seven Stories Press.

Lasswell, Harold D. 2012. *Politics: Who Gets What, When, How.* Whitefish, MT: Literary Licensing.

Lauderdale, Pat. 2007. "Deviance, Moral Boundaries and." In *The Blackwell Encyclopedia of Sociology,* edited by George Ritzer, 1114–1116. Malden, MA: Blackwell.

Lauer, Sean, and Carrie Yodanis. 2010. "The Deinstitutionalization of Marriage Revisited: A New Institutional Approach to Marriage." *Journal of Family Theory and Review* 2: 58–72.

Lauer, Sean, and Carrie Yodanis. 2011. "Individualized Marriage and the Integration of Resources." *Journal of Marriage and Family* 73: 669–683.

Laurie, Nina, Claire Dwyer, Sarah Holloway, and Fiona Smith. 1999. *Geographies of New Femininities.* London: Longman.

LaViollete, Alyce D., and Ola W. Barnett. 2014. *Why Battered Women Stay: It Could Happen to Anyone.* Thousand Oaks, CA: Sage.

Lavorgna, Anita. 2015. "The Online Trade in Counterfeit Pharmaceuticals: New Criminal Opportunities, Trends and Challenges." *European Journal of Criminology* 12(2): 226–241.

Law, Ian. 2007. "Discrimination." In *The Blackwell Encyclopedia of Sociology,* edited by George Ritzer, 1182–1184. Malden, MA: Blackwell.

Law, Ian. 2010. *Racism and Ethnicity: Global Debates, Dilemmas.* London: Pearson.

Law, Ian. 2012a. "Race." In *The Wiley-Blackwell Encyclopedia of Globalization,* edited by George Ritzer, 1737–1743. Malden, MA: Wiley-Blackwell.

Law, Ian. 2012b. "Racism." In *The Wiley-Blackwell Encyclopedia of Globalization,* edited by George Ritzer, 1743–1746. Malden, MA: Wiley-Blackwell.

Law, John, and John Hassard, eds. 1999. *Actor Network Theory and After.* Oxford: Blackwell.

Layte, Richard, and Christopher T. Whelan. 2009. "Explaining Social Class Inequalities in Smoking: The Role of Education, Self-Efficacy, and Deprivation." *European Sociological Review* 25: 399–410.

Lazer, David. Forthcoming. "General Introduction to Big Data." *Annual Review of Sociology.*

Leaper, Campbell, and Timeas Farkas. 2015. "The Socialization of Gender During Childhood and Adolescence." In *Handbook of Socialization: Theory and Research,* 2nd ed., edited by Joan E. Grusec and Paul D. Hastings, 541–565. New York: Guilford Press.

Lechner, Frank J. 1993. "Global Fundamentalism." In *A Future for Religion?,* edited by W. H. Swatos. Thousand Oaks, CA: Sage.

Lechner, Frank J. 2008. *The Netherlands: Globalization and National Identity.* New York: Routledge.

Lechner, Frank J., and John Boli. 2005. *World Culture: Origins and Consequences.* Oxford: Blackwell.

Ledbetter, James. 2011. *Unwarranted Influence: Dwight D. Eisenhower and the Military-Industrial Complex.* New Haven, CT: Yale University Press.

Lee, Jacqueline G. C., Ray Paternoster, and Zachary Rowan. 2016. "Death Penalty and Race." In *The Wiley Encyclopedia of Race, Ethnicity and Nationalism,* edited by John Stone, Rutledge M. Dennis, Polly Rizova, Anthony D. Smith, and Xiaoshuo Hou. Malden, MA Wiley Blackwell.

Lee, Jaekyung. 2012. "Educational Equity and Adequacy for Disadvantaged Minority Students: School and Teacher Resource Gaps toward National Mathematics Proficiency Standard." *Journal of Educational Research* 105: 64–75.

Lee, Julie. 2012. "The Relationship between Appearance-Related Stress and Internalizing Problems in South Korean Adolescent Girls." *Women's Studies International Journal* 40: 903–918.

Lee, Ronald D. 2007. *Global Population Aging and Its Economic Consequences.* Washington, DC: American Enterprise Institute Press.

Lee, Susan Hagood. 2012. "Sex Trafficking." In *The Wiley-Blackwell Encyclopedia of Globalization,* edited by George Ritzer. Malden, MA: Wiley-Blackwell.

Lee, Teresa Y. 2013. "Top 10 Trends of the Next Generation of Travel: The Millennials." *HVS Global Hospitality Services,* April. Accessed April 22, 2015. http://www.hospitalitynet.org/file/152005087.pdf.

Lees, Loretta, Tom Slater, and Elvin Wyly, eds. 2010. *The Gentrification Reader.* New York: Routledge.

Le Gales, Patrick. 2007. "Cities in Europe." In *The Blackwell Encyclopedia of Sociology,* edited by George Ritzer, 493–497. Malden, MA: Blackwell.

Legerski, Elizabeth Miklya. 2012. "The Cost of Instability: The Effects of Family, Work, and Welfare Change on Low-Income Women's Health Insurance Status." *Sociological Forum* 27: 641–657.

Leicht, Kevin, and Scott Fitzgerald. 2006. *Postindustrial Peasants: The Illusion of Middle-Class Prosperity.* New York: Worth.

Leidner, Robin. 1993. *Fast Food, Fast Talk.* Berkeley: University of California Press.

Lemert, Charles, and Anthony Elliott. 2006. *Deadly Worlds: The Emotional Costs of Globalization.* Lanham, MD: Rowman & Littlefield.

Lemert, Edwin. [1951] 2012. *Social Pathology: A Systematic Approach to the Theory of Sociopathic Behavior.* Whitefish, MT: Literary Licensing.

Lengermann, Patricia Madoo, and Gillian Niebrugge-Brantley. 2014. "Feminist Theory." In *Sociological Theory,* 9th ed., edited by George Ritzer and Jeffrey Stepnisky, 440–485. New York: McGraw-Hill.

Lenski, Gerhard. 1954. "Status Crystallization: A Non-vertical Dimension of Stratification." *American Sociological Review* 19: 405–413.

Leonhardt, David. 2017. "O'Reilly Ousted." *New York Times,* April 20.

Lerum, Kari, and Barbara G. Brents, 2016. "Sociological Perspectives on Sex Work and Human Trafficking." *Sociological Perspectives* 59: 17–26.

Lessenich, Stephan. Forthcoming. "Welfare Regimes." In *The Wiley-Blackwell Encyclopedia of Sociology,* 2nd ed., edited by George Ritzer. Malden, MA: Wiley-Blackwell.

Lesthaeghe, Ron J. 2007. "Second Demographic." In *The Blackwell Encyclopedia of Sociology,* edited by George Ritzer, 4123–4127. Malden, MA: Blackwell.

Lesthaeghe, Ron J. 2010. "The Unfolding Story of the Second Demographic Transition." *Population and Development Review* 36: 211–251.

Lesthaeghe, Ron. 2014. "The Second Demographic Transition: A Concise Overview of its Development." *Proceedings of the National Academy of the United States.* 111: 18112–18115.

Lesthaeghe, Ron J., and D. J. van de Kaa. 1986. "Twee Demografische Transities?" In *Bevolking: Groei en Krimp, Mens en Maatschappij* (book supplement), edited by R. Lesthaeghe and D. J. van de Kaa, 9–24. Deventer, Netherlands: Van Loghum, Slaterus.

Leventoglu, Bahar. 2014. "Social Mobility, Middle Class, and Political Transitions." *Journal of Conflict Resolution* 58: 825–864.

Levin, Jack. 2007. "Hate Crimes." In *The Blackwell Encyclopedia of Sociology,* edited by George Ritzer, 2048–2050. Malden, MA: Blackwell.

Levitt, Peggy. 2001. *The Transnational Villagers.* Berkeley: University of California Press.

Levitt, Steven D., and Stephen J. Dubner. 2005. *Freakonomics: A Rogue Economist Explores the Hidden Side of Everything.* New York: HarperCollins.

Levitt, Steven D., and S. A. Venkatesh. 2000. "An Economic Analysis of a Drug-Selling Gang's Finances." *Quarterly Journal of Economics* 115(3): 755–789.

Levy, Frank. 1987. *Dollars and Dreams: Changing American Income Distribution.* New York: Russell Sage Foundation.

Levy, Frank. 1999. *The New Dollars and Dreams: American Incomes and Economic Change.* New York: Russell Sage Foundation.

Levy, Steven. 2010. *Hackers: Heroes of the Computer Revolution.* 25th anniversary ed. Sebastopol, CA: O'Reilly Media.

Lewin, Tamar. 2008a. "Oil Money Cultivates a Mideast Ivy League." *New York Times,* February 11.

Lewin, Tamar. 2008b. "Universities Rush to Set Up Outposts Abroad." *New York Times,* February 10.

Lewin, Tamar. 2008c. "U.S. Universities Join Saudis in Partnerships." *New York Times,* March 6.

Lewin, Tamar. 2012. "College of Future Could Be Come One, Come All." *New York Times,* November 19.

Lewin, Tamar. 2013. "Students Rush to Web Classes, but Profits May Be Much Later." *New York Times,* January 7.

Lewin, Tamar. 2014. "After Setbacks, Online Courses Are Rethought." *New York Times,* December 10.

Lewin, Tamar. 2016. "Millenials' No. 1 Roommates Are Their Parents." *New York Times,* May 25.

Lewis, James R., and Inga B. Tollefson, eds. 2016. *New Religious Social Movements,* Vol. 2. New York: Oxford University Press, 2016.

Lewis, Melissa A., Hollie Granato, Jessica A. Blayney, Ty W. Lostutter, and Jason R. Kilmer. 2012. "Predictors of Hooking Up Sexual Behaviors and Emotional Reactions among U.S. College Students." *Archives of Sexual Behavior* 41(5): 1219–1229.

Lewis, Nathaniel. 2014. "Moving 'Out,' Moving On: Gay Men's Migrations through the Life Course." *Annals of the Association of American Geographers* 104(2): 225–233.

Lewis-Kraus, Gideon. 2016. "The Trials of Alice Goffman." *New York Times Magazine,* January 12. www.nytimes.com/2016/01/17/magazine/the-trials-of-alice-goffman.html?_r=0.

Li, Yi, Hexuan Liu, and Guang Guo. 2015. "Does Marriage Moderate Genetic Effects on Delinquency and Violence." *Journal of Marriage and the Family* 77: 1217–1233.

Liana, Sara Miller. 2007. "Wealth Gospel Propels Poor Guatemalans." *Christian Science Monitor,* December 17.

Liaw, Karen Ron-Li, and Aron Janssen. 2014. "Not by Convention: Working with People on the Sexual and Gender Continuum." In *Massachusetts General Hospital Textbook on Diversity and Cultural Sensitivity in Mental Health,* edited by R. Parekh, 89–117. New York: Springer.

Liberman, Akiva M., David S. Kirk, and Kideuk Kim. 2014. "Labeling Effects of First Juvenile Arrest: Secondary Deviance and Secondary Sanctioning." *Criminology* 52: 345–370.

Lichter, Daniel T. 2007. "Family Structure and Poverty." In *The Blackwell Encyclopedia of Sociology,* edited by George Ritzer, 1463–1465. Malden, MA: Blackwell.

Lichter, Daniel T. 2013. "Integration or Fragmentation: Racial Diversity and the American Future." *Demography* 50: 359–391.

Lidskog, Rolf, Arthur P. J. Mol, and Peter Oosterveeer. 2015. "Towards Global Environmental Sociology? Legacies, Trends and Future Directions." *Current Sociology* 63: 339–368.

Liebling-Kalifani, Helen, Ruth Ojiambo-Ochieng, Angela Marshall, Juliet Were-Oguttu, Seggane Musisi, and Eugene Kinyanda. 2013. "Violence against Women in Northern Uganda: The Neglected Health Consequences of War." *Journal of International Women's Studies* 9(3): 174–192.

Liebow, Elliot. 1967. *Tally's Corner: A Study of Negro Streetcorner Men.* New York: Little, Brown.

Liftin, Karen T. 2007. "Ozone Depletion." In *Encyclopedia of Globalization,* edited by J. A. Scholte and R. Robertson, 927–930. New York: MTM.

Limoncelli, Stephanie A. Forthcoming. "Informal Economy." In Nancy Naples, ed. *The Wiley Blackwell Encyclopedia of Gender and Sexuality Studies.*

Lin, Jan. 2012. "World Cities." In *The Wiley-Blackwell Encyclopedia of Globalization,* edited by George Ritzer, 2254–2262. Malden, MA: Wiley-Blackwell.

Lin, Nan. 1999. "Social Networks and Status Attainment." *Annual Review of Sociology* 25: 467–487.

Lin, Nan, and Yanjie Bian. 1991. "Getting Ahead in Urban China." *American Journal of Sociology* 97: 657–688.

Lin, Nan, Walter M. Ensel, and John C. Vaughn. 1981. "Social Resources and Strength of Ties: Structural Factors in Occupational Status Attainment." *American Sociological Review* 46: 393–403.

Lind, Amy. 2007. "Femininities/Masculinities." In *The Blackwell Encyclopedia of Sociology,* edited by George Ritzer, 1662–1666. Malden, MA: Blackwell.

Linn, James G., and Debra Rose Wilson. 2012. "Health." In *The Wiley-Blackwell Encyclopedia of Globalization,* edited by George Ritzer, 910–923. Malden, MA: Wiley-Blackwell.

Lipovetsky, Gilles. [1987] 2002. *The Empire of Fashion: Dressing Modern Democracy.* Princeton, NJ: Princeton University Press.

Lipovetsky, Gilles. 2005. *Hypermodern Times.* Cambridge: Polity Press.

Lipset, Seymour M. 1981. *Political Man.* Expanded ed. Baltimore: Johns Hopkins University Press.

Lipton, Eric, David E. Sanger, and Scott Shane, 2016. "The Perfect Weapon: How Russian Cyberpower Invaded the U.S." *New York Times,* December 13.

Lipton, Eric, and Scott Shane. 2016. "Democratic House Candidates Were Also Targets of Russian Hacking." *New York Times,* December 13.

Liss, Miriam. 2014. "Inequality in the Division of Household Labor and Childcare." In *Women, Work, and Family: How Companies Thrive with a 21st-Century Multicultural Workforce,* edited by M. A. Paludi, 23–40. Santa Barbara, CA: ABC-CLIO.

Little, Craig B. 2007. "Deviance, Absolutist Definitions of." In *The Blackwell Encyclopedia of Sociology,* edited by George Ritzer, 1082–1084. Malden, MA: Blackwell.

Liu, Yu Cheng. 2012. "Ethnomethodology Reconsidered: The Practical Logic of Social Systems Theory." *Current Sociology* 60: 581–598.

Livermore, Michelle, Rebecca S. Powers, Belinda Creel Davis, and Younghee Lim. 2011. "Failing to Make Ends Meet: Dubious Financial Success among Employed Former Welfare to Work Program Participants." *Journal of Family Economic Issues* 32: 73–83.

Lloréns, Hilda. 2013. "Latina Bodies in the Era of Elective Aesthetic Surgery." *Latino Studies* 11(4): 547–569.

Logan, John, Richard Alba, and Wenquan Zhang. 2002. "Immigrant Enclaves and Ethnic Communities in New York and Los Angeles." *American Sociological Review* 67(2): 299–322.

Logan, John R., Elisabeta Minca, and Sinem Adar. 2012. "The Geography of Inequality: Why Separate Means Unequal in American Public Schools." *Sociology of Education* 85(3): 287–301.

Lois, Jennifer. 2013. *Home Is Where the School Is: The Logic of Homeschooling and the Emotional Labor of Mothering.* New York: New York University Press.

Looney, Adam, and Kevin B. Moore, 2016. "Changes in the Distribution of After-Tax Wealth in the U.S.: Has Income Policy Increased Wealth Inequality?" *Fiscal Studies* 37: 77–104.

Lopez, Ian Haney. 2015. *Dog Whistle Politics.* New York: Oxford University Press.

Lopez, Steven H., Randy Hodson, and Vincent J. Roscigno. 2009. "Power, Status, and Abuse at Work: General and Sexual Harassment Compared." *Sociological Quarterly* 50: 3–27.

Lorber, Judith. 1967. "Deviance as Performance: The Case of Illness." *Social Problems* 14: 302–310.

Lorber, Judith. 2000. "Using Gender to Undo Gender: A Feminist Degendering Movement." *Feminist Theory* 1(1): 79–95.

Lorber, Judith, and Lisa Jean Moore. 2002. *Gender and the Social Construction of Illness.* 2nd ed. Walnut Creek, CA: AltaMira Press.

Lorenz, Edward. 1995. *The Essence of Chaos.* Seattle: University of Washington Press.

"Louisiana Oil Rig Explosion: Underwater Machines Attempt to Plug Leak." 2010. *Telegraph,* April 26. Accessed March 31, 2012. http://www.telegraph.co.uk/finance/newsbysector/energy/oilandgas/7633286/Louisiana-oil-rig-explosion-Underwater-machines-attempt-to-plug -leak.html.

Love, Brad, Charee M. Thompson, and Jessica Knapp. 2014. "The Need to Be Superman: The Psychosocial Support Challenges of Young Men Affected by Cancer." *Oncology Nursing Forum* 41(1): E21–E27.

Lovell, David W. 2007. "Communism." In *The Blackwell Encyclopedia of Sociology,* edited by George Ritzer, 612–617. Malden, MA: Blackwell.

Low, Setha. 2003. *Behind the Gates: Life, Security, and the Pursuit of Happiness in Fortress America.* New York: Routledge.

Lowe, Brian. 2002. "Hearts and Minds and Morality: Analyzing Moral Vocabularies in Qualitative Studies." *Qualitative Sociology* 25(1): 105–112.

Lowrey, Annie. 2014. "Even among the Richest of the Rich, Fortunes Diverge." *New York Times,* February 10.

Loyal, Steve. 2007. "Refugees." In *The Blackwell Encyclopedia of Sociology,* edited by George Ritzer, 3837–3838. Malden, MA: Blackwell.

Lubbers, Marcel, Eva Jaspers, and Wout Ultee. 2009. "Primary and Secondary Socialization Impacts on Support for Same-Sex Marriage after Legalization in the Netherlands." *Journal of Family Issues* 30: 1714–1745.

Lubienski, Christopher. 2006. "School Sector and Academic Achievement: A Multilevel Analysis of NAEP Mathematics Data." *American Educational Research Journal* 43: 651–698.

Lucas, Jeffrey W., Corina Graif, and Michael J. Lovaglia. 2008. "Prosecutorial Misconduct in Serious Cases: Theory and Design of a Laboratory Experiment: Can You Study a Legal System in a Laboratory?" In *Experiments in Criminology and Law: A Research Revolution,* edited by C. Horne and M. J. Lovaglia, 119–136. Lanham, MD: Rowman & Littlefield.

Lui, Li. 2014. "A Comparative Study of Intergenerational Mobility." *Russian Social Science Review* 55(4): 4–15.

Lukacs, George. [1922] 1968. *History and Class Consciousness.* Cambridge, MA: MIT Press.

Luker, Kristin. 1984. *Abortion and the Politics of Motherhood.* Berkeley: University of California Press.

Lunneborg, Clifford E. 2007. "Convenience Sample." In *The Blackwell Encyclopedia of Sociology,* edited by George Ritzer, 788–790. Malden, MA: Blackwell.

Luo, Wei. 2013. "Aching for the Altered Body: Beauty Economy and Chinese Women's Consumption of Cosmetic Surgery." *Women's Studies International Forum* 38: 1–10.

Luo, Weixang, and Xie Yu. 2015. "Has Smoking Really Declined in China? *Chinese Journal of Sociology* 1: 165–176.

Lupton, Deborah. 2007. "Health Risk Behavior." In *The Blackwell Encyclopedia of Sociology,* edited by George Ritzer, 2083–2085. Malden, MA: Blackwell.

Lutfey, K., and J. Mortimer. 2006. "Development and Socialization through the Adult Life Course." In *Handbook of Social Psychology,* edited by J. DeLamater. New York: Kluwer Academic/Plenum.

Lutz, Helma, and Ewa Palenga-Mollenbeck. 2016. "Global Care Chains." In *Routledge Handbook of Immigration and Refugee Studies,* edited by Anna Triandafillidou. New York: Routledge:

Luxton, David D., Jennifer D. June, and Julie T. Kinn. 2011. "Technology-Based Suicide Prevention: Current Applications and Future Directions." *Telemedicine and e-Health* 17(1): 50–54.

Lyall, Sarah. 2013. "A Slice of London So Exclusive Even the Owners Are Visitors." *New York Times,* April 1.

Lydaki, Anna. 2012. "Gypsies." In *The Wiley-Blackwell Encyclopedia of Sociology Online,* edited by George Ritzer. Malden, MA: Wiley-Blackwell.

Lyman, Rick. 2015a. "Bulgaria Puts Up a New Wall, but This One Keeps People Out." *New York Times,* April 5.

Lyman, Rick. 2015b. "Hungary Seals Border With Croatia in Migrant Crackdown." *New York Times,* October 16.

Lynch, Marc. 2013. *The Arab Uprising: The Unfinished Revolutions of the New Middle East.* New York: PublicAffairs.

Lynch, Michael Patrick. 2016. *The Internet of Us: Knowing More and Understanding Less in the Age of Big Data.* New York: Liveright.

Lynch, Marc, Deen Freelon, and Sean Aday. 2014. "Syria in the Arab Spring: The Integration of Syria's Conflict with the Arab Uprisings, 2011–2013." *Research & Politics* 1(3), published online. doi: 10.1177/2053168014549091.

Lynn, Richard. 2013. "Who Discovered the Flynn Effect? A Review of Early Studies of the Secular Increase in Intelligence." *Intelligence* 41: 765–769.

Lyon, David. 2015a. "The Snowden Stakes: Challenges for Understanding Surveillance Today." *Surveillance and Society* 13: 139–152.

Lyon, David. 2015b. *Surveillance after Snowden.* Cambridge: Polity.

Lyotard, Jean-François. [1979] 1984. *The Postmodern Condition: A Report on Knowledge.* Minneapolis: University of Minnesota Press.

Ma, Xiulian, and Michael Timberlake. 2013. "World City Typologies and National City System Deterritorialism: USA, China, and Japan." *Urban Studies* 50(2): 255–275.

Macdonald, Neil. 2010. "The Tea Party's Freak Show." *CBC News,* September 27. Accessed March 31, 2012. http://www.cbc.ca/news/world/story/2010/09/24/f-rfa-macdonald.html.

Machida, Satoshi. 2012. "Does Globalization Render People More Ethnocentric? Globalization and People's Views on Cultures." *American Journal of Economics and Sociology* 71: 436–469.

Mackay, Richard. 2014. *The Atlas of Endangered Species.* New York: Routledge.

Maclean, Mairi, Charles Harvey, and Robert Chia. 2010. "Dominant Corporate Agents and the Power Elite in France and Britain." *Organization Studies* 31: 327–348.

Madan, T. N. 2007. "Hinduism." In *Encyclopedia of Globalization,* edited by J. A. Scholte and R. Robertson, 571–573. New York: MTM.

Madhok, Diksha. 2014. "For All Those Jibes about Shopping, Indian Men Buy More Clothes than Women." *Quartz,* September 4. Accessed April 20, 2015. http://qz.com/259305/for-all-those-jibes-about-shopping-indian-men-buy-more-clothes-than-women.

Maginn, Paul J., and Christine Steinmetz. 2015. "Spatial and Regulatory Contours of the (Sub)Urban Sexscape." In *(Sub)Urban Sexscapes: Geographies and Regulation of the Sex Industry,* edited by P. J. Maginn and C. Steinmetz, 1–17. London: Routledge.

Maguire, Jennifer Smith, and Kim Stanway. 2008. "Looking Good: Consumption and the Problems of Self-Production." *European Journal of Cultural Studies* 11(1): 63–81.

Maguire, Mike, Rob Morgan, and Robert Reiner, eds. 2012. *The Oxford Handbook of Criminology.* 5th ed. New York: Oxford University Press.

Mahoney, James, and Dietrich Rueschemeyer. 2003. *Comparative Historical Analysis in the Social Sciences.* Cambridge: Cambridge University Press.

Mahoney, James, and Kathleen Thelen, eds, 2015. *Advances in Comparative-Historical Analysis.* Cambridge: Cambridge University Press.

Maiba, Herman. 2005. "Grassroots Transnational Social Movement Activism: The Case of People's Global Action." *Sociological Focus* 38(1): 41–63.

Maines, Rachel. 2001. *The Technology of Orgasm: "Hysteria," the Vibrator, and Women's Sexual Satisfaction.* Baltimore: Johns Hopkins University Press.

Majora Carter Group. 2009. "Majora Carter Group." Accessed February 28, 2012. http://www.majoracartergroup.com.

Mak, Athena H. N., Margaret Lumbers, and Anita Eves. 2012. "Globalisation and Food Consumption in Tourism." *Annals of Tourism Research* 39: 171–196.

Malesevic, Sinisa. 2010. *The Sociology of War and Violence.* Cambridge: Cambridge University Press.

Maliepaard, Mieke, and Richard Alba, 2016. "Cultural Integration in the Muslim Second Generation in the Netherlands: The Case of Gender Ideology." *International Migration Review* 50: 70–94.

Malik, Anand. 2014. "Thomas Kuhn and Changing Paradigm in Geography: Critical Review." *Asian Journal of Multiple Disciplinary Studies* 4: 41–46.

Malik, Ved. 2011. "Too Close for Comfort." *Hindustan Times,* April 7. Accessed May 26, 2011. http://www.hindustantimes.com/News-Feed/columnsothers/Too-close-for-comfort/Article1-682474.aspx.

Mamo, Laura. 2007. *Queering Reproduction: Achieving Pregnancy in the Age of Technoscience.* Durham, NC: Duke University Press.

Mandel, Hadas. 2012. "Occupational Mobility of American Women: Compositional and Structural Changes, 1980–2007." *Research in Social Stratification and Mobility* 30: 5–16.

Mandery, Evan. 2014. "End College Legacy Preferences." *New York Times,* April 24.

Manjoo, Farhad. 2014. "The Future Could Work, If We Let It." *New York Times,* August 28.

Mannheim, Karl. [1931] 1936. *Ideology and Utopia.* New York: Harcourt, Brace, and World.

Manning, Jimmie. 2015. "Communicating Sexual Identities: A Typology of Coming Out." *Sexuality & Culture* 19(1): 122–138.

Manning, Peter. 2005. "Impression Management." In *The Encyclopedia of Social Theory,* edited by George Ritzer, 397–399. Thousand Oaks, CA: Sage.

Manning, Peter. 2007. "Dramaturgy." In *The Blackwell Encyclopedia of Sociology,* edited by George Ritzer, 1226–1229. Malden, MA: Blackwell.

Manning, Robert D. 2001. *Credit Card Nation: The Consequences of America's Addiction to Debt.* New York: Basic Books.

Manning, Wendy D. 2013. "Trends in Cohabitation: Over Twenty Years of Change, 1987–2010." In *National Family Profiles.* Bowling Green, OH: National Center for Family and Marriage Research.

Manning, Wendy D., and Jessica A. Cohen. 2012. "Premarital Cohabitation and Marital Dissolution: An Examination of Recent Marriages." *Journal of Marriage and Family* 74: 377–387.

Manning, Wendy D., and Jessica A. Cohen. 2015. "Teenage Cohabitation, Marriage and Childbearing." *Population Research and Policy Review* 34: 161–177.

Manning, Wendy D., Peggy Giordano, and Monica Longmore. 2006. "Hooking Up: The Relationship Contexts of 'Non-relationship' Sex." *Journal of Adolescent Research* 21: 459–483.

Manzo, John. 2010. "Coffee, Connoisseurship, and an Ethnomethodologically Informed Sociology of Taste." *Human Studies* 33(2): 141–155.

Ma'oz, Moshe. 2014. "The Arab Spring in Syria: Domestic and Regional Developments." *Dynamics of Asymmetric Conflict* 7(1): 49–57.

Marginson, Simon. 2016. "The Worldwide Trend to High Participation Higher Education: Dynamics of Social Stratification in Inclusive Systems." *Higher Education* (published online first).

Margolin, Leslie. 1994. *Goodness Personified: The Emergence of Gifted Children.* New York: Aldine de Gruyter.

Margono, Belinda Arunarwati, Peter V. Potapov, Svetlana Turubanova, Fred Stolle, and Matthew C. Hansen. 2014. "Primary Forest Cover Loss in Indonesia over 2000–2012." *Nature Climate Change* 4: 730–735.

Marmor, Michael. 2005. *The Status Syndrome: How Social Standing Affects Our Health and Longevity.* New York: Holt.

Marre, Diana, and Laura Briggs. 2009. *International Adoption: Global Inequalities and the Circulation of Children.* New York: New York University Press.

Marron, Donncha. 2009. *Consumer Credit in the United States: A Sociological Perspective from the 19th Century to the Present.* New York: Palgrave Macmillan.

Marsden, Peter V., and Elizabeth H. Gorman. 2001. "Social Networks, Job Changes, and Recruitment." In *Sourcebook on Labor Markets: Evolving Structures and Processes,* edited by I. Berg and A. L. Kalleberg, 467–502. New York: Kluwer Academic/Plenum.

Marsh, Robert M. 2012. "Musical Taste and Social Structure in Taiwan." *Comparative Sociology* 11: 493–525.

Marshall, Catherine, and Gretchen Rossman. 2010. *Designing Qualitative Research.* Thousand Oaks, CA: Sage.

Martey, Rosa Mikeal, Jennifer Stromer-Galley, Jaime Banks, Jingsi Wu, and Mia Consalvo. 2014. "The Strategic Female: Gender-Switching and Player Behavior in Online Games." *Information, Communication & Society* 17(3): 286–300.

Martin, Andrew. 2008. "Mideast Facing Difficult Choice, Crops or Water." *New York Times,* July 21.

Martin, Edward J. 2015. "Oligarchy, Anarchy, and Social Justice." *Contemporary Justice Review* 18.

Martin, Jonathan. 2017. "Angry Democrats Study the Tea Party's Playbook." *New York Times* January 23.

Martin, Karin A. 2005. "William Wants a Doll. Can He Have One? Feminists, Child Care Advisors, and Gender-Neutral Child Rearing." *Gender & Society* 19: 456–479.

Martinez, Daniel, and Jeremy Slack. 2013. "What Part of 'Illegal' Don't You Understand? The Social Consequences of Criminalizing Unauthorized Mexican Migrants in the United States." *Social & Legal Studies* 22: 535–551.

Martin-Uzzi, Michelle, and Denise Duval-Tsioles. 2013. "The Experience of Remarried Couples in Blended Families." *Journal of Divorce and Remarriage* 54: 43–57.

Marx, Karl. [1843] 1970. "A Contribution to the Critique of Hegel's Philosophy of Right." In *Marx/Engels Collected Works,* Vol. 3, 3–129. New York: International Publishers.

Marx, Karl. [1857–1858] 1964. *Pre-capitalist Economic Formations.* New York: International Publishers.

Marx, Karl. [1859] 1970. *A Contribution to the Critique of Political Economy.* New York: International Publishers.

Marx, Karl, and Friedrich Engels. 1848. *The Communist Manifesto.* London: Communist League.

Mason, Brandon, and Martha Smithey. 2012. "The Effects of Academic and Interpersonal Stress on Dating Violence among College Students." *Journal of Interpersonal Violence* 27: 974–986.

Mashal, Mujib. 2016. "Clash of Values Emerges After Afghan Child Bride Burns to Death." *New York Times,* July 18.

Massaro, Vanessa A., and Emma Gaalaas Mullaney. 2011. "Philly's 'Flash Mob Riots' and the Banality of Post-9/11 Securitization." *City* 15: 591–604.

Massey, Douglas. 2003. *Beyond Smoke and Mirrors: Mexican Immigration in an Era of Economic Integration.* New York: Russell Sage Foundation.

Massey, Douglas. 2008. *Categorically Unequal: The American Stratification System.* New York: Russell Sage Foundation.

Massey, Douglas. 2015. "The Legacy of the 1968 Fair Housing Act." *Sociological Forum* 51: 571–588.

Massey, Douglas. 2016. "Residential Segregation is the Linchpin of Racial Stratification." *City and Community* 15: 4–7.

Massey, Douglas, and Karen Pren. 2012. "Unintended Consequences of US Immigration Policy: Explaining the Post-1965 Surge from Latin America." *Population and Development Review* 38(1): 1–29.

Massey, Douglas, Jacob S. Rugh, Justin P. Steil, and Len Albright. 2016. "Riding the Stagecoach to Hell: A Qualitative Analysis of Racial Discrimination in Mortgage Lending." *Community and Society* 15: 118–136.

Massey, Garth. 2016. *Ways of Social Change: Making Sense of Modern Times,* 2nd ed. Thousand Oaks, CA: Sage.

Mather, Mark. 2009. *Reports on America: Children in Immigrant Families Chart New Path.* Washington, DC: Population Reference Bureau.

Mathews, Russell A., Doan E. Winkel, and Julie Holiday Wayne. 2014. "A Longitudinal Examination of Role Overload and Work-Family Conflict: The Mediating Role of Interdomain Transfers." *Journal of Organizational Behavior* 35: 72–91.

Matza, David. 1966. "The Disreputable Poor." In *Class, Status, and Power: Social Stratification in Comparative Perspective,* 2nd rev. ed., edited by R. Bendix and S. M. Lipset, 289–302. New York: Free Press.

Mawathe, Anne. 2010. "Haunted by Congo Rape Dilemma." *BBC News*, May 15. Accessed January 29, 2012. http://news.bbc.co.uk/2/hi/africa/8677637.stm.

Maynard, Douglas W., and Courtney L. Marlaire. 1992. "Good Reasons for Bad Testing Performance: The Interactional Substrate of Educational Exams." *Qualitative Sociology* 15(2): 177–202.

Mazelis, Joan Maya, 2015. "'I Got to Try to Give Back': How Reciprocity Norms in a Poor Peoples' Organization Influence Members' Social Capital." *Journal of Poverty* 19: 109–131.

McAdams, Dan P., Michelle Albaugh, Emily Farber, Jennifer Daniels, Regina L. Logan, and Brad Olson. 2008. "Family Metaphors and Moral Intuitions: How Conservatives and Liberals Narrate Their Lives." *Journal of Personality and Social Psychology* 95: 978–990.

McAuley, Paul. 2016. "France Busses 1,600 Migrants out of Notorious 'Jungle' Camp in Calais." *Washington Post*, October 24.

McCaghy, Charles H., Timothy A. Capron, J. D. Jamieson, and Sandra Harley H. Carey. 2016. *Deviant Behavior: Crime, Conflict and Interest Groups*. 8th ed. New York: Routledge.

McCann, Eugene, and Kevin Ward, eds. 2011. *Mobile Urbanism: Cities and Policymaking in the Global Age*. Minneapolis: University of Minnesota Press.

McCarthy, Justin. 2014. "Same-Sex Marriage Support Reaches New High at 55%." Gallup, May 21. Accessed April 28, 2015. http://www.gallup.com/poll/169640/sex-marriage-support-reaches-new-high.aspx.

McClelland, Robert, Shannon Mok, and Kevin Pierce. 2014. "Labor Force Participation Elasticities of Women and Secondary Earners within Married Couples." Working Paper 2014-06, Congressional Budget Office, September. Accessed April 20, 2015. https://www.cbo.gov/sites/default/files/cbofiles/attachments/49433-LaborForce.pdf.

McCombs, Brady. 2013. "LDS Church Membership Hits 15 Million as Mormon Women Question Gender Inequality." *Huffington Post*, October 5. Accessed April 20, 2015. http://www.huffingtonpost.com/2013/10/05/lds-membership-numbers_n_4051539.html.

McCormick, Ken. 2011. "Thorstein Veblen." In *The Wiley-Blackwell Companion to Major Social Theorists*, Vol. 1, *Classical Theorists*, edited by George Ritzer and Jeffrey Stepnisky, 185–204. Malden, MA: Wiley-Blackwell.

McEvily, Bill, Giuseppe Soda, and Marco Tortoriello, 2014. "More Formally: Rediscovering the Missing Link between Formal Organization and Informal Social Structure." *The Academy of Management Annals* 8: 299–345.

McGrew, Ken. 2011. "A Review of Class-Based Theories of Student Resistance in Education." *Review of Educational Research* 81: 234–266.

McGuffey, Shawn. 2008. "'Saving Masculinity': Gender Reaffirmation, Sexuality, Race, and Parental Responses to Male Child Sexual Abuse." *Social Problems* 55(2): 216–237.

McHale, Susan, Ann C. Crouter, and Shawn D. Whiteman. 2003. "The Family Contexts of Gender Development in Childhood and Adolescence Social Development." *Social Development* 12: 125–148.

McHugh, Maureen C., and Joan C. Chrisler, eds. 2015. *The Wrong Prescription for Women*. Santa Barbara, CA: ABC-CLIO.

McIntosh, Peggy. 2010. "White Privilege: Unpacking the Invisible Knapsack." In *Race, Class and Gender in the United States*, 8th ed., edited by P. S. Rothenberg, 172–177. New York: Worth.

McLanahan, Sara S. 1999. "Father Absence and the Welfare of Children." In *Coping with Divorce, Single Parenting, and Remarriage: A Risk and Resiliency Perspective*, edited by E. M. Hetherington. Mahwah, NJ: Lawrence Erlbaum.

McLanahan, Sara S., and Erin L. Kelly. 1999. "The Feminization of Poverty: Past and Future." In *Handbook of the Sociology of Gender*, edited by J. S. Chafetz, 127–145. New York: Kluwer Academic/Plenum.

McLaughlin, Caitlin, and Jessica Vitak. 2011. "Norm Evolution and Violation on Facebook." *New Media & Society* 14(2) 299-315.

McMichael, Anthony J. 2013. "Globalization, Climate Change, and Human Health." *New England Journal of Medicine* 368: 1335–1343.

McMichael, Philip. 2011. *Development and Social Change: A Global Perspective*. 5th ed. Thousand Oaks, CA: Sage.

McNair, Brian. 2002. *Striptease Culture: Sex, Media and the Democratization of Desire*. London: Routledge.

McNeil, Donald G., Jr. 2009. "New Web Site Seeks to Fight Myths about Circumcision and H.I.V." *New York Times*, March 3.

McNeil, Donald G., Jr. 2016. "Malnutrition and Obesity Coexist in Many Countries, Report Finds." *New York Times*, June 13.

McNichol, Tom. 2011. "Mint That Kills: The Curious Life of Menthol Cigarettes." *Atlantic Monthly*, March 25.

McPhail, Clark. 2007. "Crowd Behavior." In *The Blackwell Encyclopedia of Sociology*, edited by George Ritzer, 880–883. Malden, MA: Blackwell.

McPhate, Mike. 2016. "Ashley Madison Faces F.T.C. Inquiry Amid Rebranding." *New York Times*, July 6.

McShane, Marilyn D., and Frank P. Williams. 2007. "Beccaria, Cesare (1738–94)." In *The Blackwell Encyclopedia of Sociology*, Vol. 1, edited by George Ritzer, 255–256. Malden, MA: Blackwell.

Mead, George Herbert. [1934] 1962. *Mind, Self, and Society: From the Standpoint of a Social Behaviorist*. Chicago: University of Chicago Press.

Medina, Jennifer. 2012. "Mexicali Tour, from Tummy Tuck to Root Canal." *New York Times*, June 27. Accessed November 5, 2013. http://www.nytimes.com/2012/06/28/health/mexicali-lures-american-tourists-with-medical-care.html?pagewanted%253Dall&_r=0.

Medina, Martin. 2007. *The World's Scavengers: Salvaging for Sustainable Consumption and Production*. Walnut Creek, CA: AltaMira Press.

Meier, Barry. 2013. "More Emergency Visits Linked to Energy Drinks." *New York Times*, January 11.

Meier, Robert F. 2007a. "Deviance, Normative Definitions of." In *The Blackwell Encyclopedia of Sociology*, edited by George Ritzer, 1116–1117. Malden, MA: Blackwell.

Meier, Robert F. 2007b. "Deviance, Positivist Theories of." In *The Blackwell Encyclopedia of Sociology*, edited by George Ritzer, 1117–1121. Malden, MA: Blackwell.

Meier, Robert F. 2015. "Explanatory Paradigms in the Study of Deviance." In *The Handbook of Deviance*, edited by Erich Goode, 225–235. Malden, MA: Wiley-Blackwell.

Meister, Sandra. 2012. *Brand Communities for Fast-Moving Consumer Goods*. Wiesbaden, Germany: Gabler.

Melde, Chris, Terrance J. Taylor, and Finn Aage Esbensen. 2009. "'I Got Your Back': An Examination of the Protective Function of Gang Membership in Adolescence." *Criminology* 47(2): 565–594.

Melnick, Merrill L., and Daniel L. Wann. 2011. "An Examination of Sport Fandom in Australia: Socialization, Team Identification, and Fan Behavior." *International Review for the Sociology of Sport* 46: 456–470.

Meloni, Maurizio. 2014. "Biology without Biologism: Social Theory in a Postgenomic Age." *Sociology* 48: 731–746.

Menkes, Suzy. 2008. "Is Fast Fashion Going out of Fashion?" *New York Times*, September 21.

Merluzzi, Thomas V., Errol J. Philip, Zhiyong Zhang, and Courtney Sullivan. 2014. "Perceived Discrimination, Coping, and Quality of Life for African-American and Caucasian Persons with Cancer." *Cultural Diversity and Ethnic Minority Psychology*, August 4 (published online). doi: 10.1037/a0037543.

Merrick, Amy. 2014. "Are Malls Over?" *New Yorker*, March 11.

Merton, Robert K. [1949] 1968. *Social Theory and Social Structure*. 3rd ed. New York: Free Press.

Merton, Robert K. 1957. *Social Theory and Social Structure*. Rev. ed. Glencoe, IL: Free Press.

Merton, Robert, and Alice S. Kitt. 1950. "Contributions to the Theory of Reference Group Behavior." In *Continuities in Social Research*, edited by R. K. Merton and P. F. Lazarsfeld. Glencoe, IL: Free Press.

Messinger, Adam M. 2014. "Marking 35 Years of Research on Same-Sex Intimate Partner Violence: Lessons and New Directions." In *Handbook of LGBT Communities, Crime, and Justice*, edited by D. Peterson and V. R. Panfil, 65–85. New York: Springer.

Messner, Stephen F., and Richard Rosenfeld. 1997. "Political Restraint of the Market and Levels of Criminal Homicide: A Cross-National Application of Institutional-Anomie Theory." *Social Forces* 75: 1393–1416.

Mészáros, István. 2006. *Marx's Theory of Alienation*. 5th ed. London: Merlin Press.

Mettler, Suzanne. 2014. *Degrees of Inequality: How the Politics of Education Sabotaged the American Dream*. New York: Basic Books.

Meuleman, Roza, and Marcel Lubbers. 2016. "Parental Socialization and the Consumption of Domestic Films, Books and Music. *Journal of Consumer Culture*. May 16 (published online).

Meyer, Hans-Dieter, and Aaron Benavot, eds. 2013. *PISA, Power and Policy: The Emergence of Global Educational Governance.* Oxford: Symposium Books.

Meyer, John, J. Boli, and F. Ramirez. 1997. "World Society and the Nation State." *American Journal of Sociology* 103: 144–181.

Michels, Robert. [1915] 1962. *Political Parties.* New York: Collier Books.

Miles, Andrew, Mike Savage, and Felix Bühlmann. 2011. "Telling a Modest Story: Accounts of Men's Upward Mobility from the National Child Development Study." *British Journal of Sociology* 62: 418–441.

Milgram, Stanley. 1974. *Obedience to Authority: An Experimental View.* New York: Harper & Row.

Milibrandt, Tara, and Frank Pearce. 2011. "Émile Durkheim." In *The Wiley-Blackwell Companion to Major Social Theorists,* Vol. 1., *Classical Theorists,* edited by George Ritzer and Jeffrey Stepnisky, 236–282. Malden, MA: Wiley-Blackwell.

Milkie, Melissa A. 1999. "Social Comparisons, Reflected Appraisals, and Mass Media: The Impact of Pervasive Beauty Images on Black and White Girls' Self-Concepts." *Social Psychology Quarterly* 62: 190–210.

Miller, Amanda, and Sharon Sassler. 2010. "Stability and Change in the Division of Labor among Cohabiting Couples." *Sociological Forum* 25(4): 677–702.

Miller, Claire Cain. 2015. "Extreme Study Abroad: The World is Their Campus." *New York Times,* October 30.

Miller, Claire Cain. 2016. "Why Women Still Get the Short End of the Dollar." *New York Times,* March 3: 1, 5.

Miller, Daniel. 1998. *A Theory of Shopping.* Ithaca, NY: Cornell University Press.

Miller, Daniel, and Donald Slater. 2000. *The Internet: An Ethnographic Approach.* London: Berg.

Miller, Donald E., Kimon H. Sargeant and Richard Foley, eds. 2013. *Spirit and Power: The Growth and Global Influence of Pentecostalism.* New York: Oxford University Press.

Miller, Donald E., and Tetsunao Yamamori. 2007. *Global Pentecostalism: The New Face of Christian Social Engagement.* Berkeley: University of California Press.

Miller, Robert. 2001. "The Industrial Context of Occupational Mobility: Change in Structure." *Research in Social Stratification and Mobility* 18: 313–353.

Mills, C. Wright. 1951. *White Collar.* New York: Oxford University Press.

Mills, C. Wright. 1956. *The Power Elite.* New York: Oxford University Press.

Mills, C. Wright. 1959. *The Sociological Imagination.* New York: Oxford University Press.

Mintel. 2015. "Online Shopping - US - June 2015." http://store.mintel.com/online-shopping-us-june-2015.

Mirza, Heidi Safia. 2013. "Embodying the Veil: Muslim Women and Gendered Islamophobia in 'New Times.'" In *Gender, Religion and Education in a Chaotic Postmodern World,* edited by Z. Gross, L. Davies, and A.-K. Diab, 303–316. Dordrecht, Netherlands: Springer.

Mishel, Lawrence, and Josh Bivens. 2011. "Occupy Wall Streeters Are Right about Skewed Economic Rewards in the United States." Briefing Paper 331. Economic Policy Institute, October 26. Accessed March 31, 2012. http://www.epi.org/files/2011/BriefingPaper331.pdf.

Misra, Joya, and Eiko Strader. 2013. "Gender Pay Equity in Advanced Countries: The Role of Parenthood and Policies." *Journal of International Affairs* 67(1): 27–41.

MIT Technology Review Custom. 2016. "Smart City Living Transforms the Urban Landscape." July 19. Accessed March 9, 2017. https://www.technologyreview.com/s/601928/smart-city-living-transforms-the-urban-landscape.

Mitchell, Gregory. 2011. "TurboConsumers in Paradise: Tourism, Civil Rights, and Brazil's Gay Sex Industry." *American Ethnologist* 38: 666–682.

Mitchell, Ojmarrh, and Michael S. Caudy, 2015. "Examining Racial Disparities in Drug Arrests." *Justice Quarterly* 32: 288–313.

Moberg, Mark. 2015. "Can Shopping Change the World? Fair Trade Social Premiums and Neoliberal Development in the Global Recession." In *Beyond Free Trade,* edited by Kate Ervine and Gavin Fridell. New York: Palgrave Macmillan.

Modood, Tariq. 2007. "Multiculturalism." In *The Blackwell Encyclopedia of Sociology,* edited by George Ritzer, 3105–3108. Malden, MA: Blackwell.

Moghadam, Valentine M. 1999. "Gender and Globalization: Female Labor and Women's Mobilization." *Journal of World-Systems Research* 5: 301–314.

Moisio, Risto, and Mariam Beruchashvili. 2014. "Mancaves and Masculinity." *Journal of Consumer Culture,* October 8 (published online). doi: 10.1177/1469540514553712.

Molaei, Hamideh. 2015. "Discursive Opportunity Structure and the Contribution of Social Media to the Success of Social Movements in Indonesia." *Information, Communication and Society* 18: 94–108.

Molla, Rani, and Shira Ovide. 2016. "The Wars on the Internet." *BloombergGadfly,* March 23. Accessed January 26, 2017. http://www.bloomberg.com/gadfly/articles/2016-03-23/google-and-media-titans-clash-in-a-war-on-internet-piracy.

Mollard, Elizabeth K. 2014. "A Qualitative Meta-synthesis and Theory of Postpartum Depression." *Issues in Mental Health Nursing* 35(9): 656–663.

Molm, Linda D. 2007. "Power-Dependence Theory." In *The Blackwell Encyclopedia of Sociology,* edited by George Ritzer, 3598–3602. Oxford: Blackwell.

Molm, Linda D. 2010. "The Structure of Reciprocity." *Social Psychology Quarterly* 73: 119–131.

Molm, Linda D., and Karen S. Cook. 1995. "Social Exchange and Exchange Networks." In *Sociological Perspective on Social Psychology,* edited by K. S. Cook, G. A. Fine, and J. S. House, 209–235. Boston: Allyn & Bacon.

Molm, Linda D., Monica M. Whithama, and David Melameda. 2012. "Forms of Exchange and Integrative Bonds: Effects of History and Embeddedness." *American Sociological Review* 77: 141–165.

Molotch, Harvey. 2003. *Where Stuff Comes From.* New York: Routledge.

Monaghan, Jeffrey, and Kevin Walby. 2012. "Making Up 'Terror Identities': Security Intelligence, Canada's Integrated Threat Assessment Centre and Social Movement Suppression." *Policing & Society* 22: 133–151.

Monte, Andrew A., Richard D. Zane, and Kennon J. Heard. 2015. "The Implications of Marijuana legalization in Colorado." *Journal of the American Medical Association* 313: 241–242.

Montoya, I. D. 2005. "Effect of Peers on Employment and Implications for Drug Treatment." *American Journal of Drug and Alcohol Abuse* 31: 657–668.

Montt, Guillermo. 2011. "Cross-National Differences in Educational Inequality." *Sociology of Education* 84: 49–68.

Moore, Dahlia. 1995. "Role Conflict: Not Only for Women? A Comparative Analysis of 5 Nations." *International Journal of Comparative Sociology* 36(1–2): 17–35.

Moore, Mignon R., and Michael Stambolis-Ruhstorfer. 2013. "LGBT Sexuality and Families at the Start of the Twenty-First Century." *Annual Review of Sociology* 39: 491–507.

Moore, R. Laurence. 1997. *Selling God: American Religion in the Marketplace of Culture.* Oxford: Oxford University Press.

Moraga, Cherrie, and Gloria Anzaldua, eds. 2015. *This Bridge Called My Back: Writings by Radical Women of Color.* 4th ed. Albany: SUNY Press.

Moran, Mary, Javier Guzman, Anne-Laure Ropars, Alina McDonald, Nicole Jameson, Brenda Omune, Sam Ryan, and Lindsey Wu. 2009. "Neglected Disease Research and Development: How Much Are We Really Spending?" *PLoS Med* 6(2): e1000030.

Morgan, George, and Scott Poynting, eds. 2012. *Global Islamaphobia: Muslims and the Moral Panic in the West.* New York: Routledge.

Morgan, Stephen G. 2007. "Direct-to-Consumer Advertising and Expenditures on Prescription Drugs: A Comparison of Experiences in the United States and Canada." *Open Medicine* 1(1): e37–e45.

Morris, Aldon. 1984. *The Origins of the Civil Rights Movement: Black Communities Organizing for Change.* New York: Free Press.

Morris, Aldon. 2007. "Civil Rights Movement." In *The Blackwell Encyclopedia of Sociology,* edited by George Ritzer, 507–512. Malden, MA: Blackwell.

Morris, Aldon. 2015. *The Scholar Denied: W. E. B. Du Bois and the Birth of Modern Sociology.* Oakland: University of California Press.

Morris, Betsy. 2013. "More Consumers Prefer Online Shopping." *Wall Street Journal,* June 3.

Morris, J. Glenn, Lynn M. Grattan, Brian M. Mayer, and Jason K. Blackburn. 2013. "Psychological Responses and Resilience of People and Communities Impacted by the Deepwater Horizon Oil Spill." *Transactions of the American Clinical and Climatological Association* 124: 191–201.

Mortimer, Gary. 2013. "Rolling in the Aisles: A Comparative Study of Male and Female Grocery Shopper Typologies." *International Review of Retail, Distribution and Consumer Research* 23(1): 1–30.

Moses, Jonathon W. 2006. *International Migration: Globalization's Last Frontier.* London: Zed Books.

Mosley, Philip E. 2009. "Bigorexia: Bodybuilding and Muscle Dysmorphia." *European Eating Disorders Review* 17: 191–198.

Moss, Dana M. 2013. "Arab Spring." In *The Wiley-Blackwell Encyclopedia of Social and Political Movements*, 3 vols., edited by D. A. Snow, D. Della Porta, B. Klandermans, and D. McAdam, 118–125. Malden, MA: Wiley-Blackwell.

Mount, Ian. 2014. "Shopping in Europe: The New 'Grand Tour.'" *Fortune*, July 2. Accessed April 22, 2015. http://fortune.com/2014/07/02/europe-global-shopping-tourism.

Mucherah, Winnie, and Andrea Dawn Frazier. 2013. "How Deep Is Skin-Deep? The Relationship between Skin Color Satisfaction, Estimation of Body Image, and Self-Esteem among Women of African Descent." *Journal of Applied Social Psychology* 43: 1177–1184.

Mui, Chunka. 2013. "Google's Trillion-Dollar Driverless Car—Part 2: The Ripple Effects." *Forbes*, January 24. Accessed April 22, 2015. http://www.forbes.com/sites/chunkamui/2013/01/24/googles-trillion-dollar-driverless-car-part-2-the-ripple-effects.

Mundy, Liza. 2012. *The Richer Sex: How the New Majority of Female Breadwinners Is Transforming Our Culture.* New York: Free Press.

Munford, Monty. 2010. "India Digs a Tunnel at the Top of the World as China Bides Its Time." *Telegraph*, August 11. Accessed May 26, 2011. http://blogs.telegraph.co.uk/news/montymunford1/100050206/india-digs-a-tunnel-at-the-top-of-the-world-as-china-bides-its-time.

Muniz, Albert M., Jr. 2007. "Brands and Branding." In *The Blackwell Encyclopedia of Sociology*, edited by George Ritzer, 357–360. Malden, MA: Blackwell.

Muniz, Albert M., Jr., and Thomas C. O'Guinn. 2001. "Brand Community." *Journal of Consumer Research* 27: 412–432.

Muniz, Ana. 2014. "Maintaining Racial Boundaries: Criminalization, Neighborhood Context, and the Origins of Gang Injunctions." *Social Problems* 61(2): 216–236.

Munro, Ealasaid. 2013. "Feminism: A Fourth Wave?" *Political Insight* 4: 22–25.

Munton, Don, and Ken Wilkening. 2007. "Acid Rain." In *Encyclopedia of Globalization*, edited by J. A. Scholte and R. Robertson. New York: MTM.

Murphy, Susan, and Patrick Paul Walsh. 2014. "Social Protection beyond the Bottom Billion." *Economic and Social Review* 45(2): 261–284.

Murray, Charles. 2013. *Coming Apart: The State of White America, 1960–2010.* New York: Crown Forum.

Musick, Kelly. 2007. "Fertility: Nonmarital." In *The Blackwell Encyclopedia of Sociology*, edited by George Ritzer, 1734–1737. Malden, MA: Blackwell.

Myers, Daniel J. 2007. "Riots." In *The Blackwell Encyclopedia of Sociology*, edited by George Ritzer, 3921–3926. Malden, MA: Blackwell.

Myers, Daniel J. 2013. "Riots." In *The Wiley-Blackwell Encyclopedia of Social and Political Movements*, 3 vols., edited by D. A. Snow, D. Della Porta, B. Klandermans, and D. McAdam, 1124–1129. Malden, MA: Wiley-Blackwell.

Nagourney, Adam. 2013. "Unfinished Luxury Tower Is Stark Reminder of Las Vegas's Economic Reversal." *New York Times*, January 22.

Nagourney, Adam. 2015. "The Debate over California's Drought Crisis." *New York Times*, April 15.

Naheem, Mohammed Ahmad. 2015. "AML Compliance—A Banking Nightmare? The HSBC Case Study." *International Journal of Disclosure and Governance* 12: 300–310.

Naples, Nancy A., and Manisha Desai. 2002. "Women's Local and Transnational Responses: An Introduction to the Volume." In *Women's Activism and Globalization: Linking Local Struggles and Transnational Politics*, edited by N. A. Naples and M. Desai. New York: Routledge.

Naples, Nancy A., and Barbara Gurr. 2012. "Genders and Sexualities in Global Context: An Intersectional Assessment of Contemporary Scholarship." In *The Wiley-Blackwell Companion to Sociology*, edited by George Ritzer, 304–332. Malden, MA: Wiley-Blackwell.

Napoli, Lisa. 1999. "Dispensing of Drugs on Internet Stirs Debate." *New York Times*, April 6. Accessed March 31, 2012. http://query.nytimes.com/gst/fullpage.html?res=9B02E1D61139F935A35757C0A96F958260&scp=8&sq=pharmaceutical%20purchase%20over%20internet&st=cse.

Naquin, Charles E., Terri R. Kurtzberg, and Liuba Y. Belkin. 2008. "E-mail Communication and Group Cooperation in Mixed Motive Contexts." *Social Justice Research* 21: 470–489.

Nardi, Peter M., David Sanders, and Judd Marmor. 1994. *Growing Up before Stonewall: Life Stories of Some Gay Men.* London: Routledge.

Nash, Catherine J., and Andrew Gorman-Murray. 2014. "LGBT Neighbourhoods and 'New Mobilities': Towards Understanding Transformations in Sexual and Gendered Urban Landscapes." *International Journal of Urban & Regional Research* 38(3): 756–772.

National Coalition of Anti-Violence Programs. 2014. "National Report on Hate Violence against Lesbian, Gay, Bisexual, Transgender, Queer and HIV-Affected Communities Released Today." Press release, May 29. Accessed April 17, 2015. http://www.avp.org/storage/documents/2013_mr_ncavp_hvreport.pdf.

National Geographic Channel. 2014. "About Inside: Undercover in North Korea." Accessed April 24, 2015. http://www.natgeotv.com/asia/inside-undercover-in-north-korea/about.

Nayyer, Deepak. 2010. "China, India, Brazil, and South Africa in the World Economy: Engines of Growth?" In *Southern Engines of Global Growth*, edited by A. U. Santos-Paulino and G. Wan. New York: Oxford University Press.

Nederveen Pieterse, Jan. 2015. *Globalization and Culture: Global Melange.* 2nd ed. Lanham, MD: Rowman & Littlefield.

Negri, Stefania. 2016. "Transplant Ethics and the International Crime of Organ Trafficking." *International Criminal Law Review* 16: 287–303.

Negrusa, Sebastian, and Brighita Negrusa. 2014. "Home Front: Post-deployment Mental Health and Divorces." *Demography* 51: 895–916.

Negrusa, Sebastian, Brighita Negrusa, and James Hosek. 2014. "Gone to War: Have Deployments Increased Divorces?" *Journal of Population Economics* 27: 473–496.

Neuendorf, Kimberly A., Thomas D. Gore, Amy Dalessandro, Patricie Janstova, and Sharon Snyder-Suh. 2009. "Shaken and Stirred: A Content Analysis of Women's Portrayals in James Bond Films." *Sex Roles* 62: 747–776.

Neuman, William. 2015. "Americans May See Appeal of Medical Tourism in Cuba." *New York Times*, February 17.

Newell, Peter, and J. Timmons Roberts, eds. 2017. *The Globalization and Environment Reader.* Malden, MA: Wiley-Blackwell.

Newton, David E. 2009. *Gay and Lesbian Rights: A Reference Handbook.* Santa Barbara, CA: ABC-CLIO.

Newton, Isaac (with Stephen Hawking). [1687] 2005. *Principia (On the Shoulders of Giants).* Philadelphia: Running Press.

Newton, Michael. 2002. *Savage Girls and Wild Boys: A History of Feral Children.* London: Faber and Faber.

New York Times Editorial Board. 2014. "China and the Toll of Smoking." *New York Times*, April 17. https://www.nytimes.com/2014/04/18/opinion/china-and-the-toll-of-smoking.html.

New York Times Editorial Board. 2015. "France's War on the Roma." *New York Times*, September 4.

New York Times Editorial Board. 2016a. "Doctors Will Play a Critical Role in the Opioid Epidemic." *New York Times*, August 30.

New York Times Editorial Board. 2016b. "Rethinking the Global War on Drugs." April 25.

Nguyen, Tina. 2017. "Are Democrats Having Their Tea Party Moment?" *Vanity Fair* February 10.

Nguyen, Tomson H., and Henry N. Pontell. 2011. "Fraud and Inequality in the Subprime Mortgage Crisis." In *Economic Crisis and Crime*, edited by M. Deflem, 3–24. Bingley, UK: Emerald.

Nichols, Brian J. 2012. "Buddhism." In *The Wiley-Blackwell Encyclopedia of Globalization*, edited by George Ritzer, 142–145. Malden, MA: Wiley-Blackwell.

Nicholson, Linda. 2008. *Identity before Identity Politics.* Cambridge: Cambridge University Press.

Niebuhr, Gustav. 1995. "Where Shopping-Mall Culture Gets a Big Dose of Religion." *New York Times*, April 16.

Niebuhr, H. Richard. 1929. *The Social Sources of Denominationalism.* New York: Holt.

Noble, David F. 2011. *Forces of Production: A Social History of Industrial Automation.* New Brunswick, NJ: Transaction.

Nobles, Jenna. 2011. "Parenting from Abroad: Migration, Nonresident Father Involvement, and Children's Education in Mexico." *Journal of Marriage and Family* 73: 729–746.

Noller, Patricia, and Gery C. Karantzas. 2012. "Conflict in Family Relationships." In *The Wiley-Blackwell Handbook of Couples and Family Relationships,* edited by P. Noller and G. C. Karantzas, 129–143. Malden, MA: Wiley-Blackwell.

Noppers, Ernst H., Kees Keizer, Jan Willem Bolderdijk, and Linda Steg. 2014. "The Adoption of Sustainable Innovations: Driven by Symbolic and Environmental Motives." *Global Environmental Change:* 1–11.

Nordberg, Jenny. 2014. *The Underground Girls of Kabul: In Search of a Hidden Resistance in Afghanistan.* New York: Crown Group.

Nordenmark, Mikael. 2007. "Unemployment." In *The Blackwell Encyclopedia of Sociology,* edited by George Ritzer, 5090–5091. Malden, MA: Blackwell.

Nordgren, Johan. 2013. "The Moral Entrepreneurship of Anti-khat Campaigners in Sweden: A Critical Discourse Analysis." *Drugs and Alcohol Today* 13(1): 20–27.

Norris, Dawn. 2011. "Interactions That Trigger Self-Labeling: The Case of Older Undergraduates." *Symbolic Interaction* 34: 173–197.

Norris, Trevor. 2011a. *Consuming Schools: Commercialism and the End of Politics.* Toronto: University of Toronto Press.

Norris, Trevor. 2011b. "Response to David Waddington's Review of Consuming Schools: Commercialization and the End of Politics." *Studies in the Philosophy of Education* 30: 93–96.

"North Korea Country Profile—Overview." 2015. *BBC News,* April 30. Accessed May 18, 2015. http://www.bbc.com/news/world-asia -pacific-15256929.

Norton, Michael I., and Dan Ariely. 2011. "Building a Better America—One Wealth Quintile at a Time." *Perspectives on Psychological Science* 6(1): 9–12.

Nossiter, Adam. 2014. "Ebola is Taking a Second Toll, On Economies." *New York Times,* September 5.

Nunn, Samuel. 2007. "Cybercrime." In *The Blackwell Encyclopedia of Sociology,* edited by George Ritzer, 960–961. Malden, MA: Blackwell.

Nuru-Jeter, Amani, Tyan Parker Dominguez, Wizdom Powell Hammond, Janxin Leu, Marilyn Skaff, Susan Egerter, Camara P. Jones, and Paula Braveman. 2009. "'It's the Skin You're In': African-American Women Talk about Their Experiences of Racism. An Exploratory Study to Develop Measures of Racism for Birth Outcome Studies." *Maternal Child Health Journal* 13(1): 29–39.

Nwachukwu, Saviour L., and Rajiv P. Dant. 2014. "Consumer Culture in Developing Economies: Is It Really So Different?"

Proceedings of the Academy of Marketing Science 2015, November 25, 35–40.

Nynäs, Peter, Mika Lassander, and Terhi Utriainen, eds. 2012. *Post-secular Society.* New Brunswick, NJ: Transaction.

Obara-Minnitt, Mika. 2014. "Alternative Globalizations: An Integrative Approach to Studying Dissident Knowledge in the Global Justice Movement." *Journal of Contemporary European Studies* 22: 222–223.

Oberschall, Anthony. 2012. "Ethnic Cleansing." In *The Wiley-Blackwell Encyclopedia of Globalization,* edited by George Ritzer, 547–551. Malden, MA: Wiley-Blackwell.

O'Brien, Elizabeth. 2013. "Why Concierge Medicine Will Get Bigger." *Market Watch,* January 17.

O'Brien, Jodi. 2016. "Seeing Agnes: Notes on a Transgender Biocultural Ethnomethodology." *Symbolic Interaction* 39: 306–329.

O'Brien, Timothy L., and Shiri Noy, 2015. "Traditional, Modern and Post-Secular Perspectives on Science and Religion in the United States." *American Sociological Review* 80: 92–115.

Ochiai, Emiko. 2014. "The Meaning of the Second Demographic Transition and the Establishment of a Mature Society." *European Societies* 16: 343–346.

Ocloo, Josephine Enyonam. 2010. "Harmed Patients Gaining Voice: Challenging Dominant Perspectives in the Construction of Medical Harm and Patient Safety Reforms." *Social Science & Medicine* 71: 510–516.

O'Connor, Brendan, and Martin Griffiths. 2005. *The Rise of Anti-Americanism.* London: Routledge.

Ogas, Ogi, and Sai Gaddam. 2012. *A Billion Wicked Thoughts: What the Internet Tells Us about Sexual Relationships.* New York: Plume.

O'Grady, Siobhan. 2014. "Colonial Lines Drawn Again for Ebola Aid." *Foreign Policy,* September 22.

O'Guinn, Thomas C., and Russell W. Belk. 1989. "Heaven on Earth: Consumption at Heritage Village, USA." *Journal of Consumer Research* 16: 227–238.

Ohlsson-Wijk, Sofi. 2011. "Sweden's Marriage Revival: An Analysis of the New-Millennium Switch from Long-Term Decline to Increasing Popularity." *Population Studies* 65: 183–200.

Oliver, Pamela. 2013. "Collective Action (Collective Behavior)." In *The Wiley-Blackwell Encyclopedia of Social and Political Movements,* 3 vols., edited by D. A. Snow, D. Della Porta, B. Klandermans, and D. McAdam, 210–215. Malden, MA: Wiley-Blackwell.

Olivier, Jos G. J., Greet Janssens-Maenhout, and Jeroen A. H. W. Peters. 2012. *Trends in Global CO_2 Emissions: 2012 Report.* The Hague: PBL Netherlands Environmental Assessment Agency. Accessed April 17, 2015. http://www.pbl.nl/en/publications/2012/trends-in-global-co2-emissions-2012 -report.

O'Loughlin, Deirdre M., Isabelle Szmigin, Morven G McEachern, Belem Barbosa, Kalipso Karantinou, and María Eugenia Fernández-Moya. 2016. "Man Thous Art Dust: Rites of Passage in Austere Times." *Sociology* March 15 (published online).

Olson, Lynn. 2002. *Freedom's Daughters: The Unsung Heroines of the Civil Rights Movements from 1830 to 1970.* New York: Scribner.

Omi, Michael, and Howard Winant. 1994. *Racial Formation in the United States: From the 1960s to the 1990s.* New York: Routledge.

Ong, Paul. 2007. "Bovine Spongiform Encephalopathy." In *Encyclopedia of Globalization,* edited by J. A. Scholte and R. Robertson, 102–106. New York: MTM.

Opsal, Tara D. 2011. "Women Disrupting a Marginalized Identity: Subverting the Parolee Identity through Narrative." *Journal of Contemporary Ethnography* 40(2): 135–167.

Orfield, Gary. 2001. *Schools More Separate: Consequences of a Decade of Resegregation.* Cambridge, MA: Harvard University, Civil Rights Project. Accessed July 8, 2013. http://www.civilrightsproject.harvard.edu/research/deseg/Schools_More_Separate.pdf.

Orfield, Gary, and Erica Frankenberg. 2013. *Educational Delusions? Why Choice Can Deepen Inequality and How to Make Schools Fair.* Berkeley: University of California Press.

Organisation for Economic Co-operation and Development. 2016. "Development Aid Rises Again in 2015, Spending on Refugees Doubles." www.oecd.org/dac/development-aid-rises-again-in-2015-spending-on-refugees-doubles.htm.

Orlikowski, Wanda J. 2010. "Technology and Organization: Contingency All the Way Down." In *Technology and Organization: Essays in Honour of Joan Woodward,* edited by N. Phillips, G. Sewell, and D. Griffiths, 239–246. Bingley, UK: Emerald.

Orr, Martin. 2012. "Great Recession." In *The Encyclopedia of Globalization,* edited by George Ritzer, 890–891. Malden, MA: Wiley-Blackwell.

Ortiz, Susan Y., and Vincent J. Roscigno. 2009. "Discrimination, Women, and Work: Processes and Variations by Race and Class." *Sociological Quarterly* 50(2): 336–359.

Ortmeyer, David L., and Michael A. Quinn. 2012. "Coyotes, Migration Duration, and Remittances." *Journal of Developing Areas* 46: 185–203.

Orum, Anthony M. 2007. "Urbanization." In *Blackwell Encyclopedia of Sociology,* edited by George Ritzer, 5151–5154. Malden, MA: Blackwell.

Orwell, George. 1949. *Nineteen Eighty-Four.* London: Secker and Warburg.

Oshri, Ilan, Julia Kotlarsky, and Leslie Willcocks. 2009. *The Handbook of Global Outsourcing and Offshoring.* Basingstoke, UK: Palgrave Macmillan.

Osman, Suleiman. 2011. *The Invention of Brownstone Brooklyn: Gentrification and the Search for Authenticity in Postwar New York.* New York: Oxford University Press.

Ostergaard, Per, James Fitchett, and Christian Jantzen. 2013. "A Critique of the Ontology of Consumer Enchantment." *Journal of Consumer Behaviour* 12: 337–344.

Otnes, Cele C., and Mary Ann McGrath. 2001. "Perceptions and Realities of Male Shopping Behavior." *Journal of Retailing* 77: 111–137.

Otnes, Cele C., and Linda Tuncay Zayre, eds. 2012. *Gender, Culture, and Consumer Behavior.* New York: Routledge.

Otto, Rudolph. 1923. *The Idea of the Holy.* Oxford: Oxford University Press.

Ousey, Graham C., and Matthew R. Lee. 2008. "Racial Disparity in Formal Social Control: An Investigation of Alternative Explanations of Arrest Rate Inequality." *Research in Crime and Delinquency* 45: 322–355.

Outlaw, Lucius T. 2010. "Toward a Critical Theory of 'Race.'" In *Arguing about Science,* edited by A. Bird and J. Ladyman, 140–159. New York: Routledge.

Ovaska, Tomi, and Ryo Takashima. 2010. "Does a Rising Tide Lift All the Boats? Explaining the National Inequality of Happiness." *Journal of Economic Issues* 44(1): 205–223.

Oyogoa, Francisca. 2016. "Cruise Ships: Continuity and Change in the World System." *Journal of World-Systems Research* 22: 32–37.

Pace, Julie. 2010. "Obama Takes on Election-Year Fears over Big Debt." *CBS News,* September 19. Accessed March 31, 2012. http://www.cbsnews.com/stories/2010/09/19/national/main6881308.shtml.

Packer, George. 2016. "The Theorist in the Palace." *New Yorker,* July 4: 32–41.

Padilla, Mark. 2007. *Caribbean Pleasure Industry: Tourism, Sexuality, and AIDS in the Dominican Republic.* Chicago: University of Chicago Press.

Pager, Devah. 2009. *Marked: Race, Crime, and Finding Work in an Era of Mass Incarceration.* Chicago: University of Chicago.

Pager, Devah, and Hana Shepherd. 2008. "The Sociology of Discrimination: Racial Discrimination in Employment, Housing, Credit, and Consumer Markets." *Annual Review of Sociology* 34: 181–209.

Pager, Devah, and Bruce Western. 2012. "Identifying Discrimination at Work: The Use of Field Experiments." *Journal of Social Issues* 68: 221–237.

Pager, Devah, Bruce Western, and Bart Bonikowski. 2009. "Discrimination in a Low-Wage Labor Market: A Field Experiment." *American Sociological Review* 74(5): 777–799.

Paine, Crispin. 2016. "Religious Theme Parks." *Journal of Material Religion* 12: 402–403.

Pakulski, Jan. 2014. "Confusions about Multiculturalism." *Journal of Sociology* 50: 23–36.

Palfrey, John, and Urs Gasser. 2008. *Born Digital: Understanding the First Generation of Digital Natives.* New York: Basic Books.

Panitch, Leo. 2009. "Thoroughly Modern Marx." *Foreign Policy,* April 15.

Pantaleo, Katherine. 2010. "Gendered Violence: An Analysis of the Maquiladora Murders." *International Criminal Justice Review* 20: 349–365.

Pantzar, Mike, and Elizabeth Shove. 2010. "Understanding Innovation in Practice: A Discussion of the Production and Re-production of Nordic Walking." *Technology Analysis and Strategic Management* 22: 447–461.

Park, Haeyoun, and Iaryna Mykhyalyshyn, 2016. "Hate Crimes Now Directed at L.G.B.T. People the Most." *New York Times,* June 18.

Park, Julie, and Dowell Myers. 2010. "Intergenerational Mobility in the Post-1965 Immigration Era: Estimates by an Immigrant Generation Cohort Method." *Demography* 47: 369–392.

Parker, Pamela. 2012. "Study: Mobile and Video Are Key Drivers of Apparel Purchases." *Marketing Land,* August 14. Accessed April 20, 2015. http://marketingland.com/study-mobile-and-video-are-key-drivers-of-apparel-purchases-18927.

Parker, Richard, Jonathan Garcia, and Robert M. Buffington. 2014. "Sexuality and the Contemporary World: Globalization and Sexual Rights." In *A Global History of Sexuality: The Modern Era,* edited by R. M. Buffington, E. Luibheid, and D. J. Guy, 221–260. Chichester, UK: Wiley.

Parker, R. Stephen, Christina S. Simmers, and Allen D. Schaefer. 2014. "An Exploratory Study: Gen Y Males and Their Attitudes toward Fashion." *Academy of Marketing Studies Journal* 18(2): 79–89.

Parker, Stanley. 1971. *The Future of Work and Leisure.* London: MacGibbon & Kee.

Parkinson, Cyril Northcote. 1955. "Parkinson's Law." *Economist,* November 19.

Parlapiano, Alicia, Robert Gebeloff, and Shan Carter. 2015. "The Shrinking American Middle Class." *New York Times,* January 26.

Parreñas, Rhacel Salazar. 2001. *Servants of Globalization: Women, Migration, and Domestic Work.* Stanford, CA: Stanford University Press.

Parrillo, Vincent N. 2007. "Urban." In *The Blackwell Encyclopedia of Sociology,* edited by George Ritzer, 5101–5104. Malden, MA: Blackwell.

Parry, Marc. 2013. "A Star MOOC Professor Defects—at Least for Now." *Chronicle of Higher Education,* September 3.

Parsons, Talcott. 1951. *The Social System.* Glencoe, IL: Free Press.

Parsons, Talcott. 1966. *Societies.* Englewood Cliffs, NJ: Prentice Hall.

Pascoe, C. J. 2012. *Dude, You're a Fag: Masculinity and Sexuality in High School.* Berkeley: University of California Press.

Pascoe, John M., David L. Wood, James H. Duffee, and Alice Kuo. 2016. "Mediators and Adverse Effects of Child Poverty in the United States." *Pediatrics* 37: e1–e17

Passel, Jeffrey. 2010. "Race and the Census: The 'Negro' Controversy." Pew Research Center, January 21. Accessed January 16, 2012. http://www.pewsocialtrends.org/2010/01/21/race-and-the-census-the-%E2%80%9Cnegro%E2%80%9D-controversy.

Patch, Jason, and Neil Brenner. 2007. "Gentrification." In *The Blackwell Encyclopedia of Sociology,* edited by George Ritzer, 1917–1920. Malden, MA: Blackwell.

Patchin, Justin W., and Sameer Hinduja. 2010. "Trends in Online Social Networking: Adolescent Use of MySpace over Time." *New Media and Society* 12: 197–216.

Patchin, Justin W., and Sameer Hinduja. 2011. "Traditional and Nontraditional Bullying among Youth: A Test of General Strain Theory." *Youth & Society* 43: 727–751.

Patel, Jugal K. 2017. "How 2016 Became Earth's Hottest Year on Record." *New York Times,* January 18.

Patel, Reena. 2010. *Working the Night Shift: Women in India's Call Centers.* Palo Alto, CA: Stanford University Press.

Paternoster, Ray. 2007. "Capital Punishment." In *The Blackwell Encyclopedia of Sociology,* edited by George Ritzer, 385–388. Malden, MA: Blackwell.

Paternoster, Raymond, Robert Brame, and Sarah Bacon. 2007. *The Death Penalty: America's Experience with Capital Punishment.* Oxford: Oxford University Press.

Patterson, Charlotte J., Rachel H. Farr, and Paul D. Hastings. 2015. "Socialization in the Context of Family Diversity." In *Handbook of Socialization: Theory and Research,* 2nd ed., edited by Joan E. Grusec and Paul D. Hastings, 202–227. New York: Guilford Press.

Patterson, Maurice, and Jonathan Schroeder. 2010. "Borderlines: Skin, Tattoos and Consumer Culture Theory." *Marketing Theory* 10: 253–267.

Patterson, Orlando, and Ethan Fosse, eds. 2015. *The Cultural Matrix: Understanding Black Youth.* Cambridge, MA: Harvard University Press.

Patton, Elizabeth, and Mimi Choi, eds. 2014. *Home Sweat Home: Perspectives on Housework and Modern Relationships.* Lanham, MD: Rowman & Littlefield.

Paulson, Michael. 2014. "Latin America Losing Bond to Catholicism, Study Says." *New York Times,* November 15.

Pavalko, Eliza K., and Glen H. Elder Jr. 1990. "World War II and Divorce: A Life-Course Perspective." *American Journal of Sociology* 95: 1213–1234.

Payne, Elizabeth, and Melissa Smith. 2014. "The Big Freak Out: Educator Fear in Response to the Presence of Transgender Elementary School Students." *Journal of Homosexuality* 61(3): 399–418.

Payton, Andrew, and Peggy A. Thoits. 2011. "Medicalization, Direct-to-Consumer Advertising, and Mental Illness Stigma." *Society and Mental Health* 1: 55–70.

PBS. 2010. *Frontline: Digital Nation.* Accessed May 25, 2011. http://www.pbs.org/wgbh/pages/frontline/digitalnation/view.

Pear, Robert. 2016. "Obama Offers Ways to Improve His Health Care Law." *New York Times,* July 11.

Pearce, Diane. 1978. "The Feminization of Poverty: Women, Work, and Welfare." *Urban and Social Change Review* 11: 28–36.

Pearlin, Leonard I. 1989. "The Sociological Study of Stress." *Journal of Health and Social Behavior* 30: 241–256.

Pellow, David N., and Hollie Nyseth Brehm, 2013. "An Environmental Sociology for the Twenty-first century." *Annual Review of Sociology* 39: 229-250.

Peñaloza, Lisa. 2000. "Have We Come a Long Way, Baby? Negotiating a More Multicultural Feminism in the Marketing Academy in the USA." In *Marketing and Feminism: Current Issues and Research,* edited by M. Catterall, P. Maclaran, and L. Stevens, 39–56. London: Routledge.

Penn, Roger. Forthcoming. "Marital Endogamy, Friendship Homogamy, and Ethnic/Nationality Group." *Journal of Marriage and Family.*

Pennington, Bill. 2015a. "Brady Receives a 4-Game Ban." *New York Times,* May 12.

Pennington, Bill. 2015b. "In a Man's Game: Mark Herzlich is Standing Up for Women." *New York Times,* October 24.

Pennington, Jon C. 2003. "It's Not a Revolution but It Sure Looks Like One: A Statistical Accounting of the Post-sixties Sexual Revolution." *Radical Statistics* 83: 104–116.

Peoples, Clayton D. 2012. "Welfare State." In *The Encyclopedia of Globalization,* edited by George Ritzer, 2218–2221. Malden, MA: Wiley-Blackwell.

Perelli-Harris, Brienna, and Nora Sanchez Gassen. 2012. "How Similar Are Cohabitation and Marriage? Legal Approaches to Cohabitation across Western Europe." *Population and Development Review* 38: 435–467.

Perez-Agote, Alfonso. 2014. "The Notion of Secularization: Drawing the Boundaries of Its Contemporary Scientific Validity." *Current Sociology,* May 30 (published online). doi: 10.1177/0011392114533333.

Perez-Felkner, Lara. 2013. "Socialization in Childhood and Adolescence." In *Handbook of Social Psychology,* 2nd ed., edited by J. DeLamater and A. Ward, 119–149. Dordrecht, Netherlands: Springer.

Perloff, Richard M., Bette Bonder, George B. Ray, Eileen Berlin Ray, and Laura A Siminoff. 2006. "Doctor–Patient Communication, Cultural Competence, and Minority Health: Theoretical and Empirical Perspectives." *American Behavioral Scientist* 49(6): 835–852.

Perlroth, Nicole. 2014. "Reporting from the Debt's Underbelly." *New York Times,* February 16.

Perlroth, Nicole. 2015. "Online Attacks on Infrastructure Are Increasing at a Worrying Rate." *New York Times* October 14.

Perna, Laura W. 2006. "Studying College Access and Choice: A Proposed Conceptual Model." In *Higher Education: Handbook of Theory and Research,* Vol. 21, edited by J. Smart, 99–157. Dordrecht, Netherlands: Springer.

Perrin, Robin D. 2007. "Deviant Beliefs/Cognitive Deviance." In *The Blackwell Encyclopedia of Sociology,* edited by George Ritzer, 1140–1142. Malden, MA: Blackwell.

Perrow, Charles. 1999. *Normal Accidents.* Princeton, NJ: Princeton University Press.

Peter, Lawrence J. and Raymond Hull. 1969. *The Peter Principle: Why Things Always Go Wrong.* New York: Morrow.

Peters, Jeremy W. 2014. "After Immigration Action, a Blast of Energy for the Tea Party." *New York Times,* November 25.

Peterson, Helen. 2016. "Is managing academics 'women's work'? Exploring the glass cliff: in higher education management." *Educational Management Administration and Leadership* 44: 112–127.

Peterson, Richard A., and Roger M. Kern. 1996. "Changing Highbrow Taste: From Snob to Omnivore." *American Sociological Review* 61: 900–907.

Pettijohn, Terry F., Erik Frazier, Elizabeth Rieser, Nicholas Vaughn, and Bobbi Hupp-Wilds.2015. "Classroom Texting in College Students." *College Student Journal* 49: 513–516.

Pew Research Center. 2009. "Public More Optimistic about the Economy, but Still Reluctant to Spend." Press release, June 19. Accessed April 17, 2015. http://pewresearch.org/pubs/1260/more-optimistic-about-economy-but-reluctant- to-spend.

Pew Research Center. 2013. "A Survey of LGBT Americans: Attitudes, Experiences and Values in Changing Times." June 13. Accessed April 17, 2015. http://www.pewsocialtrends.org/2013/06/13/a-survey-of-lgbt-americans.

Pfeffer, Max J. – and Pilar A. Parra. 2009. "Strong Ties, Weak Ties, and Human Capital: Latino Immigrant Employment outside the Enclave." *Rural Sociology* 74(2): 241–269.

Pfeffer, Naomi. 2011. "Eggs-ploiting Women: A Critical Feminist Analysis of the Different Principles in Transplant and Fertility Tourism." *Reproductive Biomedicine Online* 23: 634–641. doi: 10.1016/j.rbmo.2011.08.005.

Phelan, Jo C., Bruce G. Link, Ana Diez-Roux, Ichiro Kawachi, and Bruce Levin. 2004. "'Fundamental Causes' of Social Inequalities in Mortality: A Test of the Theory." *Journal of Health and Social Behavior* 45: 265–285.

Phelan, Jo C., Bruce G. Link, and Parisa Tehranifar. 2010. "Social Conditions as Fundamental Causes of Health Inequalities: Theory, Evidence, and Policy Implications." *Journal of Health and Social Behavior* 51: S28–S40.

Phelps, Michelle S. 2011. "Rehabilitation in the Punitive Era: The Gap between Rhetoric and Reality in U.S. Prison Programs." *Law and Society Review* 45: 33–68.

Phelps, Nicholas A., and Andrew M. Wood. 2011. "The New Post-suburban Politics?" *Urban Studies* 48: 2591–2610.

Phelps, Nicholas, and Fulong Wu, eds. 2011. *International Perspectives on Suburbanization: A Post-Suburban World?* New York: Palgrave-Macmillan.

Philips, Bernard, ed. 2016. *Understanding Terrorism.* New York: Routledge.

Phillips, Leigh, Kate Connolly, and Lizzy Davies. 2010. "EU Turning Blind Eye to Discrimination against Roma, Say Human Rights Groups." *The Guardian,* July 30. Accessed November 29, 2011. http://www.guardian.co.uk/world/2010/jul/30/europe-an-union- roma-human-rights.

Piarroux, Renaud. 2016. "The U.N.'s Responsibility in Haiti's Cholera Crisis." *New York Times,* September 7.

Picca, Leslie Houts and Joe R. Feagin. 2007. *Two-Faced Racism: Whites in the Backstage and Frontstage.* New York: Routledge.

Pick, James B., and Aviit Sarkar.2015. *The Global Digital Divides: Explaining Change.* Dordrecht, Netherlands: Springer.

Pickering, Mary. 2011. "Auguste Comte." In *The Wiley-Blackwell Companion to Major Social Theorists,* Vol. 1, *Classical Theorists,* edited by George Ritzer and Jeffrey Stepnisky, 30–60. Malden, MA: Wiley-Blackwell.

Pickett, Kate, and Richard Wilkinson. 2011. *The Spirit Level: Why Greater Equality Makes Societies Stronger.* New York: Bloomsbury Press.

Pickren, Graham. 2015. "Making Connections Between Global Production Networks for Used Goods and the Realm of Production: A Case Study on E-Waste Governance." *Global Networks,* Vol. 15, 4: 40--423.

Piketty, Thomas. 2014. *Capital in the Twenty-First Century.* Cambridge, MA: Belknap Press.

Pilcher, Jane. 2013. "'Small but Very Determined': A Novel Theorization of Children's Consumption of Culture." *Cultural Sociology* 7: 86–100.

Pinker, Steven. 2011. *The Better Angels of Our Nature: Why Violence Has Declined.* New York: Viking Press.

Piquero, Alex R., Raymond Paternoster, Greg Pogarsky, and Thomas Loughran. 2011. "Elaborating the Individual Difference Component in Deterrence Theory." *Annual Review of Law and Social Science* 7: 335–360.

Piquero, Nicole Leeper. 2010. "Causes and Prevention of Intellectual Property Crime." In *Cybercrime: An Introduction to an Emerging Phenomenon,* edited by George Higgins, 88–109. Boston: McGraw Hill.

Pitts, Victoria. 2003. *In the Flesh: The Cultural Politics of Body Modification.* New York: Palgrave Macmillan.

Plante, Rebecca F. 2014. "Sexuality." In *Investigating Social Problems,* edited by A. J. Treviño, 108–133. Thousand Oaks, CA: Sage.

Plante, Rebecca F. 2015. *Sexualities in Context: A Social Perspective.* 2nd ed. New York: Routledge.

Plante, Rebecca F., and Andrew P. Smiler. 2014. "Time for a Sexual-Climate Change." *Chronicle of Higher Education,* November 26. Accessed April 17, 2015. http://chronicle.com/blogs/conversation/2014/11/26/time-for-a-sexual-climate-change.

Pleyers, Geoffrey. 2010. *Alter-Globalization: Becoming Actors in the Global Age.* Cambridge: Polity Press.

Plummer, Ken. 1975. *Sexual Stigma: An Interactionist Account.* London: Routledge.

Plummer, Ken. 1995. *Telling Sexual Stories: Power, Change and Social Worlds.* London: Routledge.

Plummer, Ken. 2007a. "Sexual Identities." In *The Blackwell Encyclopedia of Sociology,* edited by George Ritzer, 4238–4242. Malden, MA: Blackwell.

Plummer, Ken. 2007b. "Sexual Markets, Commodification, and Consumption." In *The Blackwell Encyclopedia of Sociology,* edited by George Ritzer, 4242–4244. Malden, MA: Blackwell.

Plummer, Ken. 2012. "Critical Sexuality Studies." In *The Wiley-Blackwell Companion to Sociology,* edited by George Ritzer, 243–268. Malden, MA: Wiley-Blackwell.

Poff, Deborah. 2010. "Ethical Leadership and Global Citizenship: Considerations for a Just and Sustainable Future." *Journal of Business Ethics* 93: 9–14.

Pogash, Carol. 2015. "Gentrification Spreads an Upheaval in San Francisco's Mission District." *New York Times,* May 22.

Pogue, David. 2014. "Smart Sharing." *Scientific American,* June.

Polgreen, Linnea A. and Nicole B. Simpson. 2011. "Happiness and International Migration." *Journal of Happiness Studies* 12(3): 819–840.

Polgreen, Lydia. 2010. "India Digs under the Top of the World to Match a Rival." *New York*

Times, August 1. Accessed May 26, 2011. http://www.nytimes.com/2010/08/01/world/asia/01pass.html.

"Police Discover Five Children 'Hidden from Society in Squalid Home and Raised without Schooling or Healthcare.'" 2010. *Daily Mail,* November 30. Accessed May 25, 2015. http://www.dailymail.co.uk/news/article-1334132/Police-discover-5-children-hidden-society-squalid-home.html.

Polonko, Karen. 2007. "Child Abuse." In *The Blackwell Encyclopedia of Sociology,* edited by George Ritzer, 448–451. Malden, MA: Blackwell.

Pontell, Henry L. 2007. "Deviance, Reactivist Definitions of." In *The Blackwell Encyclopedia of Sociology,* edited by George Ritzer, 1123–1126. Malden, MA: Blackwell.

Popenoe, David. 1987. "Beyond the Nuclear Family: A Statistical Portrait of the Changing Family in Sweden." *Journal of Marriage and the Family* 49: 173–183.

Popenoe, David. 1993. "American Family Decline, 1960–1990: A Review and Appraisal." *Journal of Marriage and the Family* 55: 527–542.

Popenoe, David. 2009. "Cohabitation, Marriage, and Child Wellbeing: A Cross-National Perspective." *Society* 46: 429–436.

Popham, James and Sirotnik, Kenneth. 1973. *Educational Statistics: Use and Interpretation.* New York: Harper & Row.

Popper, Nathaniel. 2015. *Digital Gold.* New York: Harper.

Population Reference Bureau. 2010. "World Population Data Sheet." Accessed October 28, 2010. http://www.prb.org/Publications/Datasheets/2010/2010wpds.aspx.

Porter, Eduardo. 2016a. "The Crumbling Case for a Mexican Border Wall." *New York Times,* September 6.

Porter, Eduardo. 2016b. "Moving on From Farm and Factory." *New York Times,* April 27.

Portes, Alejandro, and Min Zhou 1993. "The New Second Generation: Segmented Assimilation and Its Variants." *Annals of the American Academy of Political and Social Science* 530: 75–96.

Poster, Winnifred. 2007. "Who's on the Line? Indian Call Center Agents Pose as Americans for U.S.-Outsourced Firms." *Industrial Relations* 46(2): 271–304.

Postmes, Tom, and Russell Spears. 1998. "Deindividuation and Antinormative Behavior: A Meta-analysis." *Psychological Bulletin* 123(3): 238–259.

Powell, Brian, Catherine Bolzendahl, Claudia Geist, and Lala Carr Steelman. 2010. *Counted Out: Same-Sex Relations and Americans' Definitions of Family.* New York: Russell Sage Foundation.

Powell, Jason L. 2012. "Internet." In *The Wiley-Blackwell Encyclopedia of Globalization,* edited by George Ritzer, 1188–1190. Malden, MA: Wiley-Blackwell.

Powell, Joe, and Karen Branden. 2007. "Family, Sociology of." In *The Blackwell Encyclopedia of Sociology,* edited by George Ritzer, 1614–1618. Malden, MA: Blackwell.

Pramuk, Jacob. 2015. "There Are Now More Uber Cars Than Yellow Taxis in NYC." *CNBC,* March 18.

Prechel, Harlan. 2007. "Taylorism." In *The Blackwell Encyclopedia of Sociology,* edited by George Ritzer, 4939–4940. Malden, MA: Blackwell.

Preisendorfer, Peter, and Andreas Diekmann. 2007. "Ecological Problems." In *The Blackwell Encyclopedia of Sociology,* edited by George Ritzer, 1281–1286. Malden, MA: Blackwell.

Prell, C., M. Reed, L. Racin, and K. Hubacek. 2010. "Competing Structure, Competing Views: The Role of Formal and Informal Social Structures in Shaping Stakeholder Perceptions." *Ecology and Society* 15(4): 34.

Premack, David. 2007. "Human and Animal Cognition: Continuity and Discontinuity." *Proceedings of the National Academy of Sciences* 104: 13861–13867.

Presser, Harriet B. 2005. *Working in a 24/7 Economy.* New York: Russell Sage Foundation.

Preves, Sharon E., and Jeylan T. Mortimer. 2013. "Socialization for Primary, Intimate and Work Relationships in the Adult Life Course." In *Handbook of Social Psychology,* 2nd ed., edited by J. DeLamater and A. Ward, 151–187. Dordrecht, Netherlands: Springer.

Prideaux, Bruce, and Petra Glover. 2014. "'Santa Claus Is Coming to Town': Christmas Holidays in a Tropical Destination." *Asia Pacific Journal of Tourism Research,* September 29 (published online). doi: 10.1080/10941665.2014.951061.

Prince, Julie. 2004. "Queer History, This: An American Synthesis." *Journal of GLBT Family Studies* 3: 60–63.

Prior, Nick. 2011. "Critique and Renewal in the Sociology of Music: Bourdieu and Beyond." *Cultural Sociology* 5: 121–138.

Pritchard, Mary, and Brooke Cramblitt. 2014. "Media Influence on Drive for Thinness and Drive for Muscularity." *Sex Roles* 71: 208–218.

Proctor, Bernadette D., Jessica L. Semega, and Melissa A. Kollar. 2016. "Income and Poverty in the United States: 2015." Current Population Reports, P60-256(RV). September. Accessed January 26, 2017. http://www.census.gov/content/dam/Census/library/publications/2016/demo/p60-256.pdf.

Prot, Sara, Craig A. Anderson, Douglas A. Gentile, Wayne Warburton, Muniba Saleem, Christopher L. Groves, and Stephanie C. Brown. 2015. "Media as Agents of Socialization." In *Handbook of Socialization: Theory and Research,* 2nd ed., edited by Joan E. Grusec and Paul D. Hastings, 276–300. New York: Guilford Press.

Prus, Robert. 2011. "Examining Community Life 'in the Making': Émile Durkheim's Moral Education." *American Sociologist* 42(1): 56–111.

Pudrovska, Tetyana and Amelia Karraker. 2014. "Gender, Job Authority, and Depression." *Journal of Health and Social Behavior* 55: 424–441.

Pugh, Allison. 2009. *Longing and Belonging: Parents, Children, and Consumer Culture.* Berkeley: University of California Press.

Pugh, Allison. 2015. *The Tumbleweed Society: Working and Caring in an Age of Insecurity.* New York: Oxford University Press.

Pugh, Derek S., David Hickson, C. R. Hinings, and C. Turner. 1968. "The Context of Organizational Structures." *Administrative Science Quarterly* 14: 91–114.

Pullum, Amanda. 2013. "Tea Party Movement (United States)." In *The Wiley-Blackwell Encyclopedia of Social and Political Movements,* 3 vols., edited by D. A. Snow, D. Della Porta, B. Klandermans, and D. McAdam, 1327–1328. Malden, MA: Wiley-Blackwell.

Pun, Nagi. 1995. "Theoretical Discussions on the Impact of Industrial Restructuring in Asia." In *Silk and Steel: Asia Women Workers Confront Challenges of Industrial Restructuring,* edited by H. O'Sullivan. Hong Kong: Committee for Asian Women.

Putnam, Robert. 2001. *Bowling Alone: The Collapse and Revival of American Community.* New York: Simon & Schuster.

Purdam, Kingsley, Elisabeth A. Garratt, and Aneez Esmail, 2015. "Hungry? Food Insecurity, Social Stigma, and Embarrassment in the UK." *Sociology* (published online first).

Qian, Zhenchao, and Daniel T. Lichter. 2011. "Changing Patterns of Interracial Marriage in a Multiracial Society." *Journal of Marriage and Family* 73: 1065–1084.

Qin, Amy. 2014. "Smoking Prevalence Steady in China, but Numbers Rise." *New York Times,* Sinosphere blog, January 9. Accessed April 28, 2015. http://sinosphere.blogs.nytimes.com/2014/01/09/smoking-prevalence-steady-in-china-but-numbers-rise.

Quach, Thu, Amani Nuru-Jeter, Pagan Morris, Laura Allen, Sarah J. Shema, June K. Winters, Gem M. Le, and Scarlett Lin Gomez. 2012. "Experiences and Perceptions of Medical Discrimination among a Multiethnic Sample of Breast Cancer Patients in the Greater San Francisco Bay Area, California." *American Journal of Public Health* 102: 1027–1034.

Quadagno, Jill, and Deana Rohlinger. 2009. "Religious Conservatives in U.S. Welfare State Politics." In *The Western Welfare State and Its Religious Roots,* edited by K. van Kersbergen and P. Manow, 236–266. New York: Cambridge University Press.

Quealy, Kevin, and Margaret Sanger-Katz. 2016. "The U.S. Is a World Apart in Gun Death Rates." *New York Times,* June 14.

Quinones, Sam. 2015. "Serving All Your Heroin Needs." *New York Times,* April 17.

Rabin, Roni Caryn. 2009. "Tool to Offer ReFast Help for H.I.V. Exposure." *New York Times,* September 8.

Raby, C. R., D. M. Alexis, A. Dickenson, and N. S. Clayton. 2007. "Planning for the Future by Western Scrub-Jays." *Nature* 445: 919–921.

"Racial Disparity in Marijuana Arrests: Black Americans Are Nearly 4 Times More Likely than Whites to Be Arrested for Possession of Pot." 2013. *Huffington Post,* June 3. Accessed April 28, 2015. http://www.huffington post.com/2013/06/03/racial-disparity-in-marijuana-arrests_n_3381725.html.

Radesky, Jenny S., Caroline J. Kistin, Barry Zuckerman, Katie Nitzberg, Jamie Gross, Margot Kaplan-Sanoff, Marilyn Augustyn, and Michael Silverstein. 2014. "Patterns of Mobile Device Use by Caregivers and

Children during Meals in Fast Food Restaurants." *Pediatrics,* March 10 (published online). doi: 10.1542/peds.2013-3703.

Ragin, Charles. 2014. *The Comparative Method: Moving beyond Qualitative and Quantitative Strategies.* Rev. ed. Berkeley: University of California Press.

Ram, Uri. 2007. *The Globalization of Israel: McWorld in Tel Aviv, Jihad in Jerusalem.* London: Routledge.

Ramella, Francesco. 2007. "Political Economy." In *The Blackwell Encyclopedia of Sociology,* edited by George Ritzer, 3433–3436. Malden, MA: Blackwell.

Ramirez, Francisco O., Yasemin Soysal, and Suzanne Shanahan. 1997. "The Changing Logic of Political Citizenship: Cross-National Acquisition of Women's Suffrage Rights, 1890–1990." *American Sociological Review* 62: 735–745.

Rank, Mark R. 2014. "Challenging the Conventional Understanding of American Poverty." In *Race and Social Problems,* edited by Ralph Bangs and Larry E. Davis, 93–104. New York: Springer.

Rao, Smriti, and Christina Presenti. 2012. "Understanding Human Trafficking Origin: A Cross-Country Empirical Analysis." *Feminist Economics* 18: 231–263.

Rape, Abuse, and Incest National Network. n.d. "Victims of Sexual Violence: Statistics." Accessed March 8, 2017. https://www.rainn .org/statistics/victims-sexual-violence.

Rappeport, Alan, and Maggie Haberman, 2016. "How Donald Trump Keeps Changing His Mind on Abortion, Torture and Banning Muslims." *New York Times,* June 29.

Ratha, Dilip, and Sanket Mohapatra. 2012. "Remittances and Development." In *The Wiley-Blackwell Encyclopedia of Globalization,* edited by George Ritzer, 1782–1792. Malden, MA: Wiley-Blackwell.

Rauer, Amy J., Gregory S. Pettit, Jennifer E. Lansford, John E. Bates, and Kenneth A. Dodge. 2013. "Romantic Relationship Patterns in Young Adulthood and Their Developmental Antecedents." *Developmental Psychology* 49: 2159–2171.

Ravitch, Diane. 2011. *The Death and Life of the Great American School System: How Testing and Choice Are Undermining Education.* New York: Basic Books.

Ravitch, Diane. 2012. "Schools We Can Envy." *New York Review of Books,* March 8, 19–20.

Rawls, Anne. 2011. "Harold Garfinkel." In *The Wiley-Blackwell Companion to Major Social Theorists,* Vol. 2, *Contemporary Sociological Theorists,* edited by George Ritzer and Jeffrey Stepnisky, 89–124. Malden, MA: Wiley-Blackwell.

Rawls, Ann. 2015. "Interaction Order: The Making of Social Facts." In *Order on the Edge of Chaos,* edited by Edward J. Lawler, Shane R. Thye, and Jeongkoo Yoon, 227–247. New York: Cambridge University Press.

Ray, Larry. 2007. "Civil Society." In *The Blackwell Encyclopedia of Sociology,* edited by George Ritzer, 512–513. Malden, MA: Blackwell.

Raynolds, Laura, and Elizabeth Bennett, Eds. 2015. *Handbook of Research on Fair Trade.* Northampton, MA: Edward Elgar Publishing.

Reader, Ian. 2013. "Murder on the Tokyo Subway: Nerve Centres, Religion and Violence." *Space & Polity* 17: 377–392.

Reardon, Sean F., and Claudia Galindo. 2008. "The Hispanic–White Achievement Gap in Math and Reading in the Elementary Grades." Working Paper 2008-01, Institute for Research on Education Policy & Practice, Stanford University.

Reay, Barry. 2014. "Promiscuous Intimacies: Rethinking the History of American Casual Sex." *Journal of Historical Sociology* 27: 1–24.

Recording Industry Association of America. 2015. "IFPI Digital Music Report: Charting the Path to Sustainable Growth." Accessed January 26, 2017. http://www.riaa.com/ wp-content/uploads/2015/09/Digital-Music-Report-2015.pdf.

Reczek, Ciorinne. 2016. "Ambivalence in Gay and Lesbian Family Relationships." *Journal of Marriage and the Family* 78: 644–659.

Reed, Mark S., and Lindsay C. Stringer. 2016. *Land Degradation, Desertification and Climate Change: Anticipating, Assessing and Adapting to Future Change.* New York: Routledge.

Reed College. 2015. "Sexual Assault Prevention and Response at Reed." Accessed March 28, 2015. http://www.reed.edu/sexual_assault/ definitions/consent.html.

Rees, Karen L. 2013. "The Role of Reflective Practices in Enabling Final Year Nursing Students to Respond to the Distressing Emotional Challenges of Nursing Work." *Nurse Education in Practice* 13: 48–52.

Reger, Jo. 2007. "Feminism, First, Second, and Third Waves." In *The Blackwell Encyclopedia of Sociology,* edited by George Ritzer, 1672–1681. Malden, MA: Blackwell.

Regnerus, Mark, and Jeremy Uecker. 2011. *Premarital Sex in America: How Young Americans Meet, Mate, and Think about Marrying.* Oxford: Oxford University Press.

Reid, Charles J. 2014. "The Journey to Seneca Falls: Mary Wollstonecraft, Elizabeth Cady Stanton and the Legal Emancipation of Women." *University of St. Thomas Law Journal* 10(4), art. 9.

Reid, Colleen. 2004. "Advancing Women's Social Justice Agendas: A Feminist Action Research Framework." *International Journal of Qualitative Methods* 3(3): 1–15.

Reid, Julie A., Sinikka Elliott, and Gretchen R. Webber. 2011. "Casual Hookups to Formal Dates: Refining the Boundaries of the Sexual Double Standard." *Gender & Society* 25(5): 545–568.

Reiman, Jeffrey H., and Paul Leighton. 2012. *The Rich Get Richer and the Poor Get Prison: Ideology, Class, and Criminal Justice.* 10th ed. Boston: Prentice Hall.

Ren, Ping. 2007. "Church or Sect? Exploring a Chuirch of New Chinese Immigrants in Southern California." *Marburg Journal of Religion* 12: 1–25.

Reskin, Barbara. 1993. "Sex Segregation in the Workplace." *Annual Review of Sociology* 19: 241–270.

Restivo, Emily, and Mark M. Lanier. 2015. "Measuring the Contextual Effects and Mitigating Factors of Labeling Theory." *Justice Quarterly* 32(1): 116–141.

"Return Visit to Communist Cuba Finds New Hope Amid Change." 2015. *New York Times,* February 18.

Reuters. 2016a. "Child Hunger Here to Stay Unless World 'Dramatically Changes Course': Charity." *New York Times,* August 5.

Reuters, 2016b. "Indonesia Wages War on Drugs But Cuts Funding for Rehabilitation." *New York Times* August 1.

Reuters. 2017. "Cyber Attack Hits 200,000 in at least 150 Countries: Europol." *New York Times,* May 14.

Reuveny, Rafael, and William R. Thompson. 2001. "Leading Sectors, Lead Economies and Economic Growth." *Review of International Political Economy* 8(4): 689–719.

Reverby, Susan. 2009. *Examining Tuskegee: The Infamous Syphilis Study and Its Legacy.* Chapel Hill: University of North Carolina Press.

Rich, Motoko. 2015. "Homeschooling: More Pupils, Less Regulation." *New York Times,* January 4.

Rideout, Victoria J., Ulla G. Foehr, and Donald F. Roberts. 2010. *Generation M2: Media in the Lives of 8- to 18-Year-Olds.* Menlo Park, CA: Kaiser Family Foundation.

Ridgeway, Cecilia L., and Shelley L. Correll. 2004. "Unpacking the Gender System: A Theoretical Perspective on Gender Beliefs and Social Relations." *Gender & Society* 18(4): 510–553.

Rieger, Jon H. 2007. "Key Informant." In *The Blackwell Encyclopedia of Sociology,* edited by George Ritzer, 2457–2458. Malden, MA: Blackwell.

Rieker, Patricia R., and Chloe E. Bird. 2000. "Sociological Explanations of Gender Differences in Mental and Physical Health." In *Handbook of Medical Sociology,* edited by C. E. Bird, P. Conrad, and A. Freemont. New York: Prentice Hall.

Riera-Crichton, Daniel. 2012. "Euro Crisis." In *The Encyclopedia of Globalization,* edited by George Ritzer, 566–570. Malden, MA: Wiley-Blackwell.

Riffkin, Rebecca. 2014. "New Record Highs in Moral Acceptability." Gallup, May 30. Accessed April 17, 2015. http://www.gallup .com/poll/170789/new-record-highs-moral-acceptability.aspx.

Rifkin, Jeremy. 1995. *The End of Work.* New York: Putnam.

Riger, Stefanie. 1992. "Epistemological Debates, Feminist Voices: Science, Social Values, and the Study of Women." *American Psychologist* 47(6): 730–740.

Riis, Ole. 2012. "Combining Quantitative and Qualitative Methods in the Sociology of Religion." In *Annual Review of the Sociology of Religion: New Methods in Sociology of Religion,* edited by L. Berzano and O. Riis, 91–116. Leiden, Netherlands: Brill.

Rinaldo, Lindsay, and Kenneth Ferraro. 2012. "Inequality, Health." In *The Wiley-Blackwell Encyclopedia of Globalization,* edited by George Ritzer, 1034–1037. Malden, MA: Wiley-Blackwell.

Rindermann, Heiner, and Antonia E. E. Baumeister. 2015. "Parents' SES vs. Parental Educational Behavior and Children's Development: A Reanalysis of the Hart and Risley Study." *Learning and Individual Differences* 37: 133–138.

Ringrose, Jessica, and Laurie Harvey. 2015. "Boobs, Back-Off, Six Packs, and Bits: Mediated Body Parts, Gendered Reward and Sexual Shame in Teens' Sexting Images." *Continuum* 29: 207–215.

Rippeyoug, Phyllis L. F., and Mary C. Noonan. 2012. "Is Breastfeeding Truly Cost Free? Income Consequences of Breastfeeding for Women." *American Sociological Review* 77: 244–267.

Riska, Elianne. 2007. "Health Professions and Occupations." In *The Blackwell Encyclopedia of Sociology,* edited by George Ritzer, 2075–2078. Malden, MA: Blackwell.

Ristau, Carolyn A. 1983. "Language, Cognition, and Awareness in Animals." *Annals of the New York Academy of Sciences* 406: 170–186.

Ritzer, George. 1975. *Sociology: A Multiple Paradigm Science.* Boston: Allyn & Bacon.

Ritzer, George. 1993. *The McDonaldization of Society.* Newbury Park, CA: Sage.

Ritzer, George. 1995. *Expressing America: A Critique of the Global Credit Card Society.* Thousand Oaks, CA: Pine Forge Press.

Ritzer, George. 2001. *Explorations in the Sociology of Consumption: Fast Food, Credit Cards, and Casinos.* London: Sage.

Ritzer, George, ed. 2007a. *The Blackwell Encyclopedia of Sociology.* Malden, MA: Blackwell.

Ritzer, George. 2007b. *The Globalization of Nothing.* Thousand Oaks, CA: Pine Forge Press.

Ritzer, George. 2010a. "Cathedrals of Consumption: Rationalization, Enchantment, and Disenchantment." In *McDonaldization: The Reader,* 3rd ed., edited by George Ritzer, 234–239. Thousands Oaks, CA: Pine Forge Press.

Ritzer, George. 2010b. *Enchanting a Disenchanted World: Continuity and Change in the Cathedrals of Consumption.* Thousand Oaks, CA: Sage.

Ritzer, George, ed. 2010c. *The McDonaldization of Society: The Reader.* 3rd ed. Thousand Oaks, CA: Pine Forge Press.

Ritzer, George. 2012a. "'Hyperconsumption' and 'Hyperdebt': A 'Hypercritical' Analysis." In *A Debtor World: Interdisciplinary Perspective on Debt,* edited by Ralph Brubaker, Robert W. Lawless, and Charles J. Tabb, 60–80. New York: Oxford University Press.

Ritzer, George, ed. 2012b. *The Wiley-Blackwell Encyclopedia of Globalization.* Malden, MA: Wiley-Blackwell.

Ritzer, George. 2013. "The 'New' Prosumer: Collaboration on the Digital and Material 'New Means of Prosumption.'" Paper presented at the annual meeting of the Eastern Sociological Society, Boston, March.

Ritzer, George. 2015a. *The McDonaldization of Society.* 8th ed. Thousand Oaks, CA: Sage.

Ritzer, George. 2015b. "Prosumer Capitalism." *Sociological Quarterly* 56: 413–445.

Ritzer, George. 2016. "Deglobalization? Not a Chance." November 24. Accessed March 13,2017. https://georgeritzer.wordpress.com/2016/11/24/deglobalization-not-a-chance.

Ritzer, George. 2017. "Woefully Little 'Sharing' in the Neo-Liberal Sharing Economy." January 10. https://georgeritzer.wordpress.com/2017/01/19/woefully-little-sharing-in-the-neo-liberal-ride-hailing-industry.

Ritzer, George. Forthcoming. *The McDonaldization of Society.* 9th ed. Thousand Oaks, CA: Sage.

Ritzer, George, and Paul Dean. 2015. *Globalization: A Basic Text.* 2nd ed. Malden, MA: Wiley-Blackwell.

Ritzer, George, Paul Dean, and Nathan Jurgenson. 2012. "The Coming of Age of the Prosumer." *American Behavioral Scientist* 56(4): 379–398.

Ritzer, George, Douglas Goodman, and Wendy Wiedenhoft. 2001. "Theories of Consumption." In *Handbook of Social Theory,* edited by George Ritzer and B. Smart, 410–427. London: Sage.

Ritzer, George and Nathan Jurgenson. 2010. "Production, Consumption, Prosumption: The Nature of Capitalism in the Age of the Digital 'Prosumer.'" *Journal of Consumer Culture* 10(1): 13–36.

Ritzer, George, and Craig Lair. 2007. "Outsourcing: Globalization and Beyond." In *The Blackwell Companion to Globalization,* edited by George Ritzer, 307–329. Malden, MA: Blackwell.

Ritzer, George, and Jeffrey Stepnisky, eds. 2017. *Sociological Theory.* 10th ed. Thousand Oaks, CA: Sage.

Rivoli, Pietra. 2015. *The Travels of a T-Shirt in the Global Economy: An Economist Examines the Markets, Power, and Politics of World Trade.* 2nd ed. Hoboken, NJ: Wiley.

Rizvi, Fazal. 2012. "Bollywood." In *The Wiley-Blackwell Encyclopedia of Globalization,* edited by George Ritzer, 120–121. Malden, MA: Wiley-Blackwell.

Robeck, Cecil M. Jr. 2013. "Launching a Glonbal Movement: The Role of Azusa Street in Pentecosttalism's Growth and Expansion." In *Spirit and Power: The Growth and Global Influence of Pentecostalism,* edited by Donald E. Miller, Kimon H. Sargeant, and Richard Foley, 42–65. New York: Oxford University Press.

Roberts, Sam. 2008. "Study Foresees the Fall of an Immigration Record That Has Lasted a Century." *New York Times,* February 12.

Roberts, Sam. 2009. "In 2025, India to Pass China in Population, U.S. Estimates." *New York Times,* December 16.

Roberts, Sam. 2010. "More Men Marrying Wealthy Women." *New York Times,* January 19.

Robertson, Craig. 2010. *The Passport in America: The History of a Document.* New York: Oxford University Press.

Rochon, T. R. 1990. "The West European Peace Movements and the Theory of Social Movements." In *Challenging the Political Order,* edited by R. Dalton and M. Kuchler. Cambridge: Polity Press.

Roda, Allison, and Amy Stuart Wells. 2013. "School Choice Policies and Racial Segregation: Where White Parents' Good Intentions, Anxiety, and Privilege Collide." *American Journal of Education* 119: 261–293.

Rodriguez-Franco, Diana. 2016. "Internal Wars, Taxation, and State Building." *American Sociological Review.* (81)1: 190–213.

Roehling, Patricia, Loma Hernandez Jarvis, and Heather Swope. 2005. "Variations in Negative Work–Family Spillover among White, Black, and Hispanic American Men and Women." *Journal of Family Issues* 26(6): 840–865.

Rogin, Josh. 2016. "Congress Wary of National Security Implications of Chinese Deal for Chicago Stock Exchange," *Chicago Tribune,* February 17. Accessed March 8, 2017. http://www.chicagotribune.com/business/ct-congress-chicago-stock-exchange-sale-20160217-story.html.

Rohlinger, Deana A. 2007. "Socialization, Gender." In *The Blackwell Encyclopedia of Sociology,* edited by George Ritzer, 4571–4574. Malden, MA: Blackwell.

Rojas, Rene, and Jeff Goodwin. 2013. "Revolutions." In *The Wiley-Blackwell Encyclopedia of Social and Political Movements,* 3 vols., edited by D. A. Snow, D. Della Porta, B. Klandermans, and D. McAdam, 1102–1110. Malden, MA: Wiley-Blackwell.

Rojek, Chris. 2005. *Leisure Theory: Principles and Practice.* New York: Palgrave Macmillan.

Rojek, Chris. 2007. *The Labour of Leisure: The Culture of Free Time.* London: Sage.

Roof, Wade Clark. 2001. *Spiritual Marketplace: Baby Boomers and the Remaking of American Religion.* Princeton, NJ: Princeton University Press.

Room, Graham. 2011. "Social Mobility and Complexity Theory: Towards a Critique of the Sociological Mainstream." *Policy Studies* 32(2): 109–126.

Rootes, Christopher, ed. 1999. *Environmental Movements: Local, National and Global.* London: Routledge.

Roscigno, Vincent J., and M. Keith Kimble. 1995. "Elite Power, Race, and the Persistence of Low Unionization in the South." *Work and Occupations* 22(3): 271–300.

Roscoe, Will. 1998. *Changing Ones: Third and Fourth Genders in Native North America.* New York: Palgrave/St. Martin's Press.

Rose, Arnold. 1967. *The Power Structure.* New York: Oxford University Press.

Rose, Claire. 2010. *Making, Selling, and Wearing Boys' Clothes in Late-Victorian England.* Burlington, VT: Ashgate.

Rosenbaum, James. 2001. *Beyond College for all: Career Paths for the Forgotten Half.* New York: Russell Sage Foundation.

Rosenbaum, James. 2011. "The Complexities of College for All: Beyond Fairy-Tale Dreams." *Sociology of Education* 84: 113–117.

Rosenberg, Matthew. 2016. "Pentagon Removes Barrier for Transgender People." *New York Times,* July 1.

Rosenberg, Morris. 1979. *Conceiving the Self.* New York: Basic Books.

Rosenfield, Richard. 2011. "The Big Picture: 2010 Presidential Address to the American Society of Criminology." *Criminology* 49: 1–26.

Rosenstein, Judith E. 2008. "Individual Threat, Group Threat, and Racial Policy: Exploring the Relationship between Threat and Racial Attitudes." *Social Science Research* 37: 1130–1146.

Rosenthal, Elisabeth. 2007. "W.H.O. Urges Effort to Fight Fast-Spreading Disease." *New York Times,* August 27.

Rosenthal, Lisa, and Marci Lobel, 2016. "Stereotypes of Black American Women Related to Sexuality and Motherhood," *Psychology of Women Quarterly* 40: 414–427.

Rosewarne, Laruen. 2016. *Intimacy on the Internet.* New York: Routledge

Rossi, Alice. 1983. "Gender and Parenthood." *American Sociological Review* 49: 1–19.

Rostow, Walt. 1960. *The Stages of Economic Growth: A Non-Communist Manifesto.* Cambridge: Cambridge University Press.

Rostow, Walt. 1978. *The World Economy: History and Prospect.* Austin: University of Texas Press.

Roszak, Theodore. [1968] 1995. *The Making of a Counter Culture: Reflections on the Technocratic Society and Its Youthful Opposition.* Berkeley: University of California Press.

Roth, Benita. 2004. *Separate Roads to Feminism: Black, Chicana and White Feminist Movements in America's Second Wave.* Cambridge: Cambridge University Press.

Roth, Julius A. 1963. *Timetables: Structuring the Passage of Time in Hospital Treatment and Other Careers.* Indianapolis: Bobbs-Merrill.

Roth, Silke. 2007. "Social Movements, Biographical Consequences of." In *The Blackwell Encyclopedia of Sociology,* edited by George Ritzer, 4451–4453. Malden, MA: Blackwell.

Roudometof, Victor. 2012. "Imagined Communities." In *The Wiley-Blackwell Encyclopedia of Globalization,* edited by George Ritzer, 996–998. Malden, MA: Wiley-Blackwell.

Rousseau, Nicole. 2011. *Black Women's Burden: Commodifying Black Reproduction.* New York: Palgrave Macmillan.

Roxburgh, S. 2004. "There Just Aren't Enough Hours in the Day: The Mental Health Consequences of Time Pressures." *Journal of Health and Social Behavior* 45: 115–131.

Rozdeba, Suzanne. 2011. "Firefighters Recall Spirit of 9/11 Hero." *New York Times,* East Village Local, January 10. Accessed March 31, 2012. http://eastvillage.thelocal.nytimes.com/2011/01/10/firefighters-recall-spirit-of-911-hero/?scp=3&sq=9/11%20heroism&st=cse.

Rubin, Alissa J. 2016. "From Bikinis to Burkinis, Regulating What Women Wear." *New York Times,* August 27.

Rubington, Earl, and Martin Weinberg, eds. 2016. *Deviance: The Interactionist Approach.* 10th ed. New York: Routledge.

Rudrappa, Sharmila. 2012. "Rape." In *The Wiley-Blackwell Encyclopedia of Globalization,* edited by George Ritzer, 1748–1751. Malden, MA: Wiley-Blackwell.

Rueschemeyer, Dietrich, Evelyne Stephens, and John Stephens. 1992. *Capitalist Development and Democracy.* Chicago: University of Chicago Press.

Ruiz, Ariel G., Jie Zong, and Jeanne Batalova. 2015. "Immigrant Women in the United States." Migration Policy Institute, March 20. Accessed May 11, 2015. http://www.migrationpolicy.org/article/immigrant-women-united-states.

Runyon, Anne Sisson. 2012. "Gender." In *The Wiley-Blackwell Encyclopedia of Globalization,* edited by George Ritzer, 725–734. Malden, MA: Wiley-Blackwell.

Rupp, Leila J. 1997. *Worlds of Women: The Making of an International Women's Movement.* Princeton, NJ: Princeton University Press.

Rupp, Leila, and Verta Taylor. 1999. "Forging Feminist Identity in an International Movement: A Collective Identity Approach to Twentieth-Century Feminism." *Signs* 24(2): 363–386.

Rutherford, Alexandra, Kelli Vaughn-Blount, and Laura C. Ball. 2010. "Responsible, Disruptive Voices: Science, Social Change, and the History of Feminist Psychology." *Psychology of Women Quarterly* 34(4): 460–473.

Rutherford, Paul. 2007. *The World Made Sexy: Freud to Madonna.* Toronto: University of Toronto Press.

Rutledge, Leigh W. 1992. *The Gay Decades: From Stonewall to the Present.* New York: Plume.

Ryan, Barbara. 2007. "Sex and Gender." In *The Blackwell Encyclopedia of Sociology,* edited by George Ritzer, 4196–4198. Malden, MA: Blackwell.

Ryan, Camille. 2013. "Language Use in the United States: 2011." American Community Survey Reports ACS-22. U.S. Census Bureau, August. Accessed April 24, 2015. http://www.census.gov/prod/2013pubs/acs-22.pdf.

Ryan, Kevin. 1994. "Technicians and Interpreters in Moral Crusades: The Case of the Drug Courier Profile." *Deviant Behavior* 15: 217–240.

Ryan, M. K., and S. A. Haslam. 2005. "The Glass Cliff: Evidence That Women Are Over-represented in Precarious Leadership Positions." *British Journal of Management* 16: 81–90.

Ryan, William. 1976. *Blaming the Victim.* New York: Pantheon.

Ryave, A. Lincoln, and James N. Schenkein. 1974. "Notes on the Art of Walking." In *Ethnomethodology: Selected Readings,* edited by R. Turner, 265–275. Harmondsworth, UK: Penguin.

Rysst, Mari. 2008. *"I Want to Be Me. I Want to Be Kul": An Anthropological Study of Norwegian Preteen Girls in the Light of a Presumed "Disappearance" of Childhood.* PhD dissertation, University of Oslo.

Sabo, Don. 1998. "Masculinities and Men's Health: Moving Towards Post-Superman Era Prevention." In *Men's Lives,* edited by M. Kimmel and M. Messner. Needham Heights, MA: Allyn & Bacon.

Sacchi, Agnese, and Simone Salotti. 2014. "The Effects of Fiscal Decentralization on Household Income Inequality: Some Empirical Evidence." *Spatial Economic Analysis* 9: 202–222.

Sack, Kevin. 2009. "Despite Recession, Personalized Health Care Remains in Demand." *New York Times,* May 11.

Sadker, Myra, and David Sadker. 1994. *Failing at Fairness: How Our Schools Cheat Girls.* New York: Simon & Schuster.

Saez, Emmanuel, and Gabriel Zucman. 2014. "The Explosion in U.S. Wealth Inequality Has Been Fuelled by Stagnant Wages, Increasing Debt, and a Collapse in Asset Values for the Middle Classes." London School of Economics and Political Science. Accessed April 20, 2015. http://bit.ly/1pXQ3Or.

Sagi-Schwartz, Abraham. 2008. "The Well Being of Children Living in War Zones: The Palestinian–Israeli Case." *International Journal of Behavioral Development* 32(4): 322–336.

Sahlberg, Pasi. 2011. *Finnish Lessons: What Can the World Learn from Educational Change in Finland?* New York: Teachers College Press.

Said, Edward W. [1979] 1994. *Orientalism.* New York: Knopf.

Salinas, Rebecca. 2014. "Corpus Christi 'Mantique' Store Equips the Man Cave." *San Antonio Express-News,* My San Antonio blog, July 28. Accessed April 21, 2015. http://www.mysanantonio.com/news/local/article/Corpus-Christi-man-opens-mantique-store-5651705.php.

Salkind, Neil. 2004. *Statistics for People Who (Think They) Hate Statistics.* Thousand Oaks, CA: Sage.

Sallaz, Jeffrey. 2010. "Talking Race, Marketing Culture: The Racial Habitus in and out of Apartheid." *Social Problems* 57(2): 294–314.

Saltmarsh, Matthew. 2010. "Sarkozy Toughens on Illegal Roma." *New York Times,* July 29.

Salzman, Todd. 2000. "'Rape Camps,' Forced Impregnation, and Ethnic Cleansing: Religious, Cultural, and Ethical Responses to Rape Victims in the Former Yugoslavia." In *War's Dirty Secret: Rape, Prostitution, and Other Crimes against Women,* edited by A. L. Barstow, 63–92. Ohio: Pilgrim Press.

Sampson, Robert J., and John H. Laub. 1993. *Crime in the Making: Pathways and Turning Points through Life.* Cambridge, MA: Harvard University Press.

Sampson, Robert J., and John H. Laub. 2005. "A General Age-Graded Theory of Crime: Lessons Learned and the Future of Life-Course Criminology." In *Integrated Developmental and Life-Course Theories of Offending,* edited by D. P. Farrington, 165–182. New Brunswick, NJ: Transaction.

Samuels, Robert. 2015. "Walker's Anti-union Law Has Labor Reeling in Wisconsin." *New York Times,* February 22.

Sander, Ake, and Clemen Cavallin. 2015. "Hinduism Meets the Global Order: The 'Easternization of the West'" In *The Changing World Religion Map,* edited by Stanley D. Brunn, 1743–1763. New York: Springer.

Sanders, George. 2014. "Religious Non-places: Corporate Megachurches and Their Contributions to Consumer Capitalism." *Critical Sociology,* July 7 (published online). doi: 10.1177/0896920514531605.

Sanders, Teela. 2013. *Sex Work.* London: Routledge.

Sanger, David E., and Nicole Perlroth. 2016. "As Democrats Gather, a Russian Subplot Raises Intrigue." *New York Times,* July 24.

Sanger, David, and Scott Shane. 2016. "Russian Hackers Acted to Aid Trump in Election, U.S. Says." *New York Times,* December 9.

Sanger-Katz, Margot. 2016."Obamacare Seems to be Reducing Peoples' Medical Debt." *New York Times,* April 20.

Sanneh, Kelefa. 2015. "Don't Be Like That: Does Black Culture Need to Be Reformed?" *New Yorker,* February 9, 62–69.

Santoro, Wayne A. 2015. "Was the Civil Rights Movement Successful? Tracking and Understanding Black Views." *Sociological Forum* 30: 627–647.

Santoro, Wayne A., and Lisa Broidy. 2014. "Gendered Rioting: A General Strain Theoretical Approach." *Social Forces* 93(1): 329–354.

Santos, Fernanda, and Motoko Rich. 2013. "With Vouchers, States Shift Aid for Schools to Families." *New York Times,* March 27.

Santos, Xuan. 2009. "The Chicana Canvas: Doing Class, Gender, Race, and Sexuality through Tattooing in East Los Angeles." *NWSA Journal* 21: 91–120.

Sarwal, Amit. 2012. "A Journey through Places: Politics of Spatial Location in the Stories of South Asian Diaspora in Australia." *South Asian Diaspora* 4: 195–213.

Sassatelli, Monica. 2010. "European Identity between Flows and Places: Insights from Emerging European Landscape Policies." *Sociology* 44: 67–83.

Sassatelli, Roberta. 2007. Consumer Culture: History, Theory and Politics. London: Sage.

Sassen, Saskia. 1991. *The Global City: New York, London, Tokyo.* Princeton, NJ: Princeton University Press.

Sassen, Saskia. 2004. "Local Actors in Global Politics." *Current Sociology* 52(4): 649–670.

Sassen, Saskia. 2012. "Cities." In *The Wiley-Blackwell Encyclopedia of Globalization,* edited by George Ritzer, 187–202. Malden, MA: Wiley- Blackwell.

Sassler, Sharon. 2010. "Partnering across the Life Course: Sex, Relationships, and Mate Selection." *Journal of Marriage and Family* 72: 557–575.

Sassler, Sharon, and Amanda J. Miller. 2011. "Class Differences in Cohabitation Processes." *Family Relations* 60: 163–177.

Sattar, Maher. 2017. "Rohingya Refugees in Bangladesh to be Relocated to Remote Island." *New York Times,* January 31.

Saul, Stephanie. 2016. "Recruiting Students Overseas to Fill Seats, Not to Meet Standards." *New York Times,* April 10.

Saussure, Ferdinand de. [1916] 1966. *Course in General Linguistics.* New York: McGraw-Hill.

Sauter, Mike, Thomas C. Frohlich, and Alexander E. M. Hess. 2013. "Fast-Food Chains Costing Taxpayers the Most Money." *Yahoo! Finance,* October 23. Accessed April 21, 2015. http://finance.yahoo.com/news/fast-food-chains-costing-taxpayers-173510741.html.

Savage, Charlie. 2016. "Rights Groups, Riding Films Publicity, Urge Pardon for Edward Snowden" *New York Times,* September 14.

Savage, Charlie, and Cheryl Gay Stolberg. 2011. "In Shift, U.S. Says Marriage Act Blocks Gay Rights." *New York Times,* February 23. Accessed December 20, 2011. http://www.nytimes.com/2011/02/24/us/24marriage.html.

Saxon, Wolfgang. 2003. "Adm. Richard E. Bennis, a Hero of 9/11, Dies at 52." *New York Times,* August 9. Accessed March 31, 2012. http://www.nytimes.com/2003/08/09/nyregion/adm-richard-e-bennis-a-hero-of-9-11-dies-at-52.html.

Sayyid, Salman. 2012. "Political Islam." In *The Wiley-Blackwell Encyclopedia of Globalization,* edited by George Ritzer, 1202–1204. Malden, MA: Wiley-Blackwell.

Scaff, Lawrence A. 2011. "Georg Simmel." In *The Wiley-Blackwell Companion to Major Social Theorists,* Vol. 1, *Classical Theorists,* edited by George Ritzer and Jeffrey Stepnisky, 205–235. Malden, MA: Wiley-Blackwell.

Scambler, Graham, and Frederique Paoli. 2008. "Health Work, Female Sex Workers and HIV/AIDS: Global and Local Dimensions of Stigma and Deviance as Barriers to Effective Interventions." *Social Science & Medicine* 66: 1848–1862.

Schaller, Jessamyn. 2013. "For Richer, If Not for Poorer? Marriage and Divorce over the Business Cycle." *Journal of Population Economics* 26: 1007–1033.

Scheffer, David. 2008. "Rape as Genocide in Darfur." *Los Angeles Times,* November 13.

Schemo, Diana Jean. 2003. "Rate of Rape at Academy Is Put at 12% in Survey." *New York Times,* August 23. Accessed December 3, 2011. http://www.nytimes.com/2003/08/29/national/29ACAD.html?th.

Schenker, Marc. 2015. "Former MySpace CEO Explains Why MySpace Lost Out to Facebook so Badly." *Digital Trends,* March 12. Accessed March 8, 2017. http://www.digitaltrends.com/social-media/former-myspace-ceo-reveals-what-facebook-did-right-to-dominate-social-media.

Scheper-Hughes, Nancy. 2001. "Commodity Fetishism in Organs Trafficking." *Body and Society* 7: 31–62.

Scherschel, Karin. 2007. "Migration, Ethnic Conflicts, and Racism." In *The Blackwell Encyclopedia of Sociology,* edited by George Ritzer, 3011–3014. Malden, MA: Blackwell.

Schilt, Kristen. 2010. *Just One of the Guys? Transgender Men and the Persistence of Inequality.* Chicago: University of Chicago Press.

Schlossberg, Tatiana. 2016. "Storms in Succession." *New York Times—Science Times,* September 13.

Schlueter, E., and P. Scheepers. 2010. "The Relationship between Outgroup Size and Anti-outgroup Attitudes: A Theoretical Synthesis and Empirical Test of Group Threat and Intergroup Contact Theory." *Social Science Research* 39(2): 285–295.

Schmidt, John, Kris Warner, and Sarika Gupta. 2010. *The High Budgetary Cost of Incarceration.* Washington, DC: Center for Economic and Policy Research.

Schmidt, Susanne, Ulrike Roesler, Talin Kusserow, and Renate Rau. 2014. "Uncertainty in the Workplace: Examining Role Ambiguity and Role Conflict, and Their Link to Depression—A Meta-analysis." *European Journal of Work and Organizational Psychology* 23(1): 91–106.

Schmitt, Vanessa, and Julia Fischer. 2009. "Inferential Reasoning and Modality Dependent Discrimination Learning in Olive Baboons (*Papio hamadryas anubis*)." *Journal of Comparative Psychology* 123(3): 316–325.

Schneider, Barbara, and David Stevenson. 1999. *The Ambitious Generation: America's Teenagers, Motivated but Directionless.* New Haven, CT: Yale University Press.

Schneider, S. L. 2008. "Anti-immigrant Attitudes in Europe: Outgroup Size and Perceived Ethnic Threat." *European Sociological Review* 24(1): 53–67.

Schoch, Deborah, and Rong-Gong Lin II. 2007. "15 Years after L.A. Riots, Tension Still High." *Los Angeles Times,* April 29. Accessed March 31, 2012. http://articles.latimes.com/2007/apr/29/local/me-riots29.

Schock, Kurt. 2013. "Anticolonial Movements." In *The Wiley-Blackwell Encyclopedia of Social and Political Movements,* 3 vols., edited by D. A. Snow, D. Della Porta, B. Klandermans, and D. McAdam, 66–70. Malden, MA: Wiley-Blackwell.

Scholz, Trebor, ed. 2013. *Digital Labor: The Internet as Playground and Factory.* New York: Routledge.

Schor, Juliet. 1993. *The Overworked American: The Unexpected Decline of Leisure.* New York: Basic Books.

Schor, Juliet. 1998. *The Overspent American: Why We Want What We Don't Need.* New York: Basic Books.

Schor, Juliet. 2005. *Born to Buy: The Commercialized Child and the New Consumer Culture.* New York: Scribner.

Schor, Juliet. 2015. "Conspicuous Consumption." In *Encyclopedia of Consumption and Consumer Studies,* edited by Daniel Thomas Cook and Michael Ryan, 101–105. Malden, MA: Wiley-Blackwell.

Schorzman, Cindy M., Melanie A. Gold, Julie S. Downs, and Pamela J. Murray. 2007. "Body Art: Attitudes and Practices regarding Body Piercing among Urban Undergraduates." *Journal of the American Osteopathic Association* 107: 432–438.

Schroeder, Jonathan E. 2007. "Brand Culture." In *The Blackwell Encyclopedia of Sociology,* edited by George Ritzer, 351–353. Malden, MA: Blackwell.

Schroeder, Jonathan E. 2015. "Brands and Branding." In Daniel Thomas Cook and J. Michael Ryan, eds. *The Wiley-Blackwell Encyclopedia of Consumption and Consumer Studies.* Malden, MA: Wiley-Blackwell: 59–63.

Schroyer, Trent. 1970. "Toward a Critical Theory of Advanced Industrial Society." In *Recent Sociology: No. 2,* edited by H. P. Dreitzel, 210–234. New York: Macmillan.

Schudson, Michael. 1987. *Advertising, the Uneasy Persuasion: Its Dubious Impact on American Society.* New York: Basic Books.

Schuman, Michael. 2016. "Is China Stealing Jobs? It May be Losing Them, Instead." *New York Times,* July 22.

Schuster, Liza. 2012a. "Asylum-Seekers." In *The Wiley-Blackwell Encyclopedia of Globalization,* edited by George Ritzer, 89–92. Malden, MA: Wiley-Blackwell.

Schuster, Liza. 2012b. "Migration Controls." In *The Wiley-Blackwell Encyclopedia of Globalization,* edited by George Ritzer, 1388–1390. Malden, MA: Wiley-Blackwell.

Schutt, Russell K. 2007. "Secondary Data Analysis." In *The Blackwell Encyclopedia of Sociology,* edited by George Ritzer, 4127–4129. Malden. MA: Blackwell.

Schwalbe, Michael, Sandra Godwin, Daphne Holden, Douglas Schrock, Shealy Thompson, and Michele Wolkomir. 2000.

"Generic Processes in the Reproduction of Inequality: An Interactionist Analysis." *Social Forces* 79: 419–452.

Schwartz, Nelson D. 2016a. "Good Jobs, Goodbye." *New York Times—Sunday Business,* March 20.

Schwartz, Nelson D. 2016b. "In an Age of Privilege, Not Everyone is in the Same Boat." *New York Times,* April 23.

Schwartzman, Kathleen C. 2013. *The Chicken Trail: Following Workers, Migrants and Corporations across the Americas.* Ithaca: Cornell University Press.

Schweinhart, Lawrence J. W., Steven Barnett, and Clive R. Belfield. 2005. *Lifetime Effects: The High/Scope Perry Preschool Study through Age 40.* Ypsilanti, MI: High/Scope Press.

Scott, Amy. 2011. "Pumping Up the Pomp: An Exploration of Femininity and Female Bodybuilding." *Explorations in Anthropology* 11: 70–88.

Scott, Austin. 1982. "The Media's Treatment of Blacks: A Story of Distortion." *Los Angeles Times,* September 5.

Scott, Barbara Marliene, and Mary Ann A. Schwartz. 2008. *Sociology: Making Sense of the Social World.* New York: Allyn & Bacon.

Scott, John, and Ann Nilsen, eds. 2013. *C. Wright Mills and the Sociological Imagination: Contemporary Perspectives.* Cheltenham: Edward Elgar.

Scott, W. Richard. 2014. *Institutions and Organizations: Ideas and Interests.* 4th ed. Thousand Oaks, CA: Sage.

Scraton, Sheila. 2007. "Leisure." In *The Blackwell Encyclopedia of Sociology,* edited by George Ritzer, 2588–2592. Malden, MA: Blackwell.

Searcey, Dionne. 2016. "Nigeria is Freeing Children from Boko Haram, Then Locking them Up." *New York Times,* August 18.

Searcey, Dionne, and Robert Gebeloff. 2015. "Middle Class Shrinks Further as More Fall Out Instead of Climbing Up." *New York Times,* January 25.

Seidman, Steven. 2003. *The Social Construction of Sexuality.* New York: Norton.

Sekulic, Dusko. 2007a. "Ethic Cleansing." In *The Blackwell Encyclopedia of Sociology,* edited by George Ritzer, 1450–1452. Malden, MA: Blackwell.

Sekulic, Dusko. 2007b. "Social Change." In *The Blackwell Encyclopedia of Sociology,* edited by George Ritzer, 4360–4364. Malden, MA: Blackwell.

Sekulic, Dusko. 2007c. "Values, Global." In *The Blackwell Encyclopedia of Sociology,* edited by George Ritzer, 5172–5176. Malden, MA: Blackwell.

Sekulic, Dusko. 2016. "Ethnic Cleansing and Ethnic Swamping." In *The Wiley-Blackwell Encyclopedia of Race, Ethnicity and Nationalism,* edited by John Stone, Rutledge M. Dennis, Polly Rizova, Anthony D. Smith, and Xiaoshuo Hou. Malden, MA: Wiley-Blackwell.

Seligmann, Linda J. 2013. *Broken Links, Enduring Ties: American Adoption Across Race, Class and Nation.* Stanford, CA: Stanford University Press.

Selingo, Jeffrey. J. 2014. "Demystifying the MOOC." *New York Times,* October 29.

Semple, Kirk. 2016. "Defending Their Nation's Honor on Social Media: #PanamaIsMoreThanPapers." *New York Times,* May 4.

Semple, Kirk, Azam Ahmed, and Eric Lipton, 2016. "Panama Papers Leak Casts Light on a Law Firm Founded on Secrecy." *New York Times,* April 6.

Sen, Amartya. 2011. "Quality of Life: India vs. China." *New York Review of Books,* May 12. Accessed June 5, 2011. http://www.nybooks .com/articles/archives/2011/may/12/quality -life-india-vs-china.

Sen, Jai, Anita Anand, Arturo Escobar, and Peter Waterman, eds. 2004. *World Social Forum: Challenging Empires.* New Delhi: Viveka Foundation.

Serra-Majem, Luis and Joy Ngo. 2012. "Undernutrition." In *The Wiley-Blackwell Encyclopedia of Globalization,* edited by George Ritzer, 2055–2058. Malden, MA: Wiley-Blackwell.

Seto, Karen C., Burak Güneralp, and Lucy R. Hutyra. 2012. "Global Forecasts of Urban Expansion to 2030 and Direct Impacts on Biodiversity and Carbon Pools." *Proceedings of the National Academy of Sciences of the United States of America* 109(40): 16083–16088.

Settle, Jaime E., Christopher T. Dawes, Nicholas A. Christakis, and James H. Fowler. 2010. "Friendships Moderate an Association between a Dopamine Gene Variant and Political Ideology." *Journal of Politics* 72: 1189–1198.

Shamir, Ronen. 2005. "Without Borders? Notes on Globalization as a Mobility Regime." *Sociological Theory* 23(2): 197–217.

Shane, Scott, and Michael Gordon. 2008. "Dissident's Tale of Epic Escape from Iran's Vise." *New York Times,* July 13.

Shane, Scott, and Ben Hubbard. 2014. "ISIS Displaying a Deft Command of Varied Media." *New York Times,* August 30.

Sharp, Gwen. 2012. "Gender in the Hidden Curriculum (Update)." *Society Pages,* November 16. Accessed April 11, 2013. http://www.the societypages.org/socimages/2012/11/16/ gender-in-the-hidden-curriculum.

Shattuck, Roger. 1980. *The Forbidden Experiment: The Story of the Wild Boy.* New York: Kodansha Globe.

Shaw, Susan M., and Janet Lee. 2009. *Women's Voices, Feminist Visions.* New York: McGraw-Hill.

Shear, Michael D. 2013. "Obama Calls for 'Moral Courage' at Naval Academy Graduation." *New York Times,* May 24.

Shear, Michael D. 2014. "Obama, Daring Congress, Acts to Overhaul Immigration." *New York Times,* November 20.

Shehan, Constance, and Susan Cody. 2007. "Inequalities in Marriage." In *The Blackwell Encyclopedia of Sociology,* edited by George Ritzer, 2301–2304. Malden, MA: Blackwell.

Sheldon, Jane P. 2004. "Gender Stereotypes in Educational Software for Young Children." *Sex Roles* 51(7/8): 433–444.

Sheller, Mimi. 2014. "The New Mobilities Paradigm for a Live Sociology." *Current Sociology* 62: 789–811.

Sheller, Mimi, and John Urry, 2016. "Mobilizing the New Mobilities Paradigm." *Applied Mobilities* 1: 10-25.

Shelley, Louise, John Picarelli, and Chris Corpora. 2011. "Global Crime Inc." In *Beyond Sovereignty: Issues for a Global Agenda,* 4th ed., edited by M. C. Love, 141–169. Boston: Wadsworth, Cengage Learning.

Shen, Lucinda. 2016. "For-Profit Colleges Account for a Third of all Federal Student Loan Defaults." *Fortune,* September 29.

Shepard, Gary. 2007. "Cults: Social Psychological Concepts." In *The Blackwell Encyclopedia of Sociology,* edited by George Ritzer, 884–887. Malden, MA: Blackwell.

Shepherd, Dawn. 2016. *Building Relationships.* Lanham MD,: Lexington Books.

Sherif, Muzafer, O. J. Harvey, William R. Hood, Carolyn W. Sherif, and Jack White. [1954] 1961. *Intergroup Conflict and Cooperation: The Robbers Cave Experiment.* Norman: University of Oklahoma Book Exchange.

Shevchenko, Olga. 2012. "Socialism." In *The Wiley-Blackwell Encyclopedia of Globalization,* edited by George Ritzer, 1882–1886. Malden, MA: Wiley-Blackwell.

Shildrick, Tracy, and Robert MacDonald. 2013. "Poverty Talk: How People Experiencing Poverty Deny Their Poverty and Why They Blame the Poor." *Sociological Review* 61: 285–303.

Shinberg, Diane S. 2007. "Women's Health." In *The Blackwell Encyclopedia of Sociology,* edited by George Ritzer, 5275–5279. Malden, MA: Blackwell.

Shosie, Luz. 2011. "Learning to Trust." *Unschoolers Unlimited,* September 11. Accessed June 28, 2013. http://www.unschoolersunmlimited .blog spot.com.

Shroedel, Jean Reith, and Pamela Fiber. 2000. "Lesbian and Gay Policy Priorities: Commonality and Difference." In *The Politics of Gay Rights,* edited by C. A. Rimmerman, K. D. Wald, and C. Wilcox, 97–118. Chicago: University of Chicago Press.

Shullenberger, Geoff. 2014. "The Rise of the Voluntariat." *Jacobin,* May 15. Accessed April 23, 2015. https://www.jacobinmag .com/2014/05/the-rise-of-the-voluntariat.

Siebold, G. L. 2007. "The Essence of Military Cohesion." *Armed Forces and Society* 33(2): 286–295.

Siegel, Larry J. 2014. *Criminology: The Core.* Stamford, CT: Cengage.

Siegel, Larry J., and John L. Worrall. 2014. *Essentials of Criminal Justice.* 9th ed. Stamford, CT: Cengage.

Silva, Eric Orion. 2014. "Neutralizing Problematic Frames in the Culture Wars: Anti-evolutionists Grapple with Religion." *Symbolic Interaction* 37: 226–245.

Silver, Hilary. 2007. "Disasters." In *The Blackwell Encyclopedia of Sociology,* edited by George Ritzer, 1174–1176. Malden, MA: Blackwell.

Silver, Hilary. 2015. "Editorial: The Urban Sociology of Detroit." *City and Community* 14: 97–101.

Silverman, David, ed. 2016. *Qualitative Research.* 4th ed. London: Sage.

Silvernail, David L., and Amy F. Johnson. 2014. "The Impacts of Public Charter Schools on

Students and Traditional Public Schools: What Does the Empirical Evidence Tell Us?" Maine Education Policy Research Institute, University of Southern Maine, January. Accessed April 17, 2015. https://usm.maine.edu/sites/default/files/cepare/PublicCharterSchoolsWeb.pdf.

Simi, Pete. 2013. "9 Cycles of Right-Wing Terror in the US." In *Right-Wing Radicalism Today: Perspectives from Europe and the US*, edited by S. von Mering and T. W. McCarty, 144–160. New York: Routledge.

Simmel, Georg. [1903] 1971. "The Metropolis and Mental Life." In *Georg Simmel: On Individuality and Social Forms*, edited by D. Levine. Chicago: University of Chicago Press.

Simmel, Georg. [1904] 1971. "Fashion." In *Georg Simmel: On Individuality and Social Forms*, edited by D. Levine, 294–323. Chicago: University of Chicago Press.

Simmel, Georg. [1906] 1950. "The Secret and the Secret Society." In *The Sociology of Georg Simmel*, edited by K. H. Wolff, 307–376. New York: Free Press.

Simmel, Georg. [1907] 1978. *The Philosophy of Money*, edited and translated by T. Bottomore and D. Frisby. London: Routledge & Kegan Paul.

Simmel, Georg. [1908] 1971a. "Domination." In *Georg Simmel: On Individuality and Social Forms*, edited by D. Levine, 96–120. Chicago: University of Chicago Press.

Simmel, Georg. [1908] 1971b. "The Stranger." In *Georg Simmel: On Individuality and Social Forms*, edited by D. Levine, 143–149. Chicago: University of Chicago Press.

Simmel, Georg. 1950. *The Sociology of Georg Simmel*, edited and translated by K. Wolff. New York: Free Press.

Simon, Bryant. 2009. *Everything but the Coffee: Learning about America from Starbucks*. Berkeley: University of California Press.

Simon, David R. 2012. *Elite Deviance*. 10th ed. Boston: Pearson/Allyn & Bacon.

Simon, Herbert A. [1945] 1976. *Administrative Behavior*. New York: Macmillan.

Simone, Alina. 2015. "How My Mom Got Hacked." *New York Times*, January 2. Accessed April 27, 2015. http://www.nytimes.com/2015/01/04/opinion/sunday/how-my-mom-got-hacked.html?_r=0.

Simons, Marlise. 2010a. "France: Roma Policy Challenged." *New York Times*, August 28.

Simons, Marlise. 2010b. "Rights Panel Criticizes France over Roma Policy." *New York Times*, August 27.

Simooya, Oscar O. 2016. "Editorial: HIV Infection and AIDS in Africa: Issues, Lessons Learnt, and Next Steps." *Open AIDS Journal* 10: 14–15.

Simpson, George Eaton, and J. Milton Yinger. 1985. *Racial and Cultural Minorities: An Analysis of Prejudice and Discrimination*. 5th ed. New York: Plenum Press.

Simpson, Sally S. 2002. *Corporate Crime, Law, and Social Control*. New York: Cambridge University Press.

Simpson, Sally S. 2013. "White-Collar Crime: A Review of Recent Developments and Promising Directions for Future Research." *Annual Review of Sociology* 39: 309–331.

Simpson, Sally S., and David Weisburd, eds. 2009. *The Criminology of White-Collar Crime*. New York: Springer.

Singer, Natasha. 2009. "Lawmakers Seek to Curb Drug Commercials." *New York Times*, July 27.

Singer, Natasha. 2010. "The Financial Time Bomb of Longer Lives." *New York Times*, October 16.

Singer, Natasha. 2011. "On Campus, It's One Big Commercial." *New York Times*, September 10, 2011.

Singh, Devendra, and Dorian Singh. 2011. "Shape and Significance of Feminine Beauty: An Evolutionary Perspective." *Sex Roles* 64: 723–731.

Singh, Gopal K., and Mohammad Siahpush. 2014. "Widening Rural–Urban Disparities in Life Expectancy, U.S., 1969–2009." *American Journal of Preventive Medicine* 46: e19–e29.

Sirkin, Monroe G., Rosemarie Hirsch, William Mosher, Chris Moriarty, and Nancy Sonnenfeld. 2011. "Changing Methods of NCHS Surveys: 1960–2010 and Beyond." *Morbidity and Mortality Weekly Report*, suppl. 60(7): 42–48.

Sitton, John F., ed. 2010. *Marx Today: Selected Works and Recent Debates*. New York: Palgrave Macmillan.

Sivalingam, G. 1994. *The Economic and Social Impact of Export Processing Zones: The Case of Malaysia*. Geneva: International Labour Organization.

Skinner, Quentin, ed. 1985. *The Return of Grand Theories in the Human Sciences*. Cambridge: Cambridge University Press.

Sklair, Leslie. 2002. *Globalization: Capitalism and Its Alternatives*. Oxford: Oxford University Press.

Skloot, Rebecca. 2011. *The Immortal Life of Henrietta Lacks*. New York: Crown.

Skocpol, Theda, and Vanessa Williamson. 2016. *The Tea Party and the Remaking of Republican Conservatism*. Updated Edition. Oxford: Oxford University Press.

Skoog, Therese, Emma Sobring, and Margareta Bohlin. 2015. "Facebook as a Means to Make New Peers among Early Maturing Girls." *Computers in Human Behavior* 48: 500–505.

Slater, Don. 2015. "Consumer Culture." In *Encyclopedia of Consumption and Consumer Studies*, edited by Daniel Thomas Cook and Michael Ryan, 112–118. Malden, MA: Wiley-Blackwell.

Slatton, Brittany Chevon, and Joe R. Feagin. 2012. "Racial and Ethnic Issues: Critical Race Approaches in the United States." In *The Wiley-Blackwell Companion to Sociology*, edited by George Ritzer, 287–303. Malden, MA: Wiley-Blackwell.

Smangs, Mattias. 2016. "Doing Violence, Making Race: Southern Lynching and White Racial Group Formation." *American Journal of Sociology* 121: 1329–1374.

Smart, Barry, ed. 2011. *Post-industrial Society*. London: Sage.

Smelser, Neil. 1994. *Sociology*. Cambridge, MA: Blackwell.

Smith, Aaron. 2016. "15% of American Adults Have Used Online Dating Site or Mobile Dating Apps." Pew Research Center, February 11. Accessed February 2, 2016. http://www.pewinternet.org/2016/02/11/15-percent-of-american-adults-have-used-on-line-dating-sites-or-mobile-dating-apps.

Smith, David Norman, Brock Ternes, James P. Ordner, Russell Schloemer, Gabriela Moran, Chris Goode, Joshua Homan, Anna Kern, Lucas Keefer, Nathan Moser, Kevin McCannon, Kaela Byers, Daniel Sullivan, and Rachel Craft. 2011. "Mapping the Great Recession: A Reader's Guide to the First Crisis of 21st Century Capitalism." *New Political Science* 33(4): 577–601.

Smith, Gavin. 2015. *Opening the Black Box: The Work of Watching*. London: Routledge.

Smith, Jackie. 2008. *Social Movements for Global Democracy*. Baltimore: Johns Hopkins University Press.

Smith, Jessi L., and Meghan Huntoon. 2014. "Women's Bragging Rights: Overcoming Modesty Norms to Facilitate Women's Self-Promotion." *Psychology of Women Quarterly* 38: 447–459.

Smith, Paula. 2007. "Recidivism." In *The Blackwell Encyclopedia of Sociology*, edited by George Ritzer, 3818–3819. Malden, MA: Blackwell.

Smith, Robert Courtney. 2006. *Mexican New York: Transnational Lives of New Immigrants*. Berkeley: University of California Press.

Smith, William C., Emily Anderson, Daniel Salinas, Renata Horvatek, and David P. Baker. 2015. "A Meta-analysis of Education Effects on Chronic Disease: The Causal Dynamics of the Population Education Transition Curve." *Social Science & Medicine* 127: 29–40.

Smock, Pamela L., and Wendy Manning. 2004. "Living Together Unmarried in the United States: Demographic Perspectives and Implications for Family Policy." *Law and Policy* 26(1): 87–117.

Smyth, Bruce. 2007. "Non-resident Parents." In *The Blackwell Encyclopedia of Sociology*, edited by George Ritzer, 3223–3227. Malden, MA: Blackwell.

Snow, David A. 2013a. "Grievances, Individual and Mobilizing." In *The Wiley-Blackwell Encyclopedia of Social and Political Movements*, 3 vols., edited by D. A. Snow, D. Della Porta, B. Klandermans, and D. McAdam, 540–542. Malden, MA: Wiley-Blackwell.

Snow, David A. 2013b. "Social Movements." In *The Wiley-Blackwell Encyclopedia of Social and Political Movements*, 3 vols., edited by D. A. Snow, D. Della Porta, B. Klandermans, and D. McAdam, 1200–1204. Malden, MA: Wiley-Blackwell.

Snow, David A., D. Della Porta, B. Klandermans, and D. McAdam, eds. 2013. *The Wiley-Blackwell Encyclopedia of Social and Political Movements*. 3 vols. Malden, MA: Wiley-Blackwell.

Snow, David A., and Peter B. Owens. 2013. "Crowds (Gatherings) and Collective Behavior (Action)." In *The Wiley-Blackwell Encyclopedia of Social and Political Movements*, 3 vols., edited by D. A. Snow, D. Della Porta, B. Klandermans, and D. McAdam, 289–296. Malden, MA: Wiley-Blackwell.

Snow, David A., Sarah A. Soule, and Daniel M. Cress. 2005. "Identifying the Precipitants of

Homeless Protest across 17 U.S. Cities, 1980 to 1990." *Social Forces* 83: 1183–1210.

Snyder, Kieran. 2014. "The Abrasiveness Trap: High-Achieving Men and Women Are Described Differently in Reviews." *Fortune,* August 26. Accessed May 12, 2015. http://fortune.com/2014/08/26/performance-review-gender-bias.

Snyder, Patricia. 2007. "Survey Research." In *The Blackwell Encyclopedia of Sociology,* edited by George Ritzer, 4898–4900. Malden, MA: Blackwell.

Sollee, Kristen. 2015. "6 Things to Know About 4th Wave Feminism." *Bustle,* October 30. Accessed March 9, 2017. https://www.bustle.com/articles/119524-6-things-to-know-about-4th-wave-feminism.

Sommellier, Estelle, Mark Price, and Ellis Wazater, 2016. *Income Inequality in the U.S. by State, Metropolitan Area and County.* Washington DC: Economic Policy Institute, 2016.

Song, Haeyeop and Jaemin Jung. 2015. "Antecedent and Consequences of Gender Swapping in Online Games." *Journal of Computer-Mediated Communication* 20: 434–449.

Song, Miri. 2007. "Racial Hierarchy." In *The Blackwell Encyclopedia of Sociology,* edited by George Ritzer, 3360–3364. Malden, MA: Blackwell.

Sontag, Deborah. 2012. "Rebuilding in Haiti Lags after Billions in Post-quake Aid." *New York Times,* December 23.

Sontag, Deborah. 2015. "'Every Day I Struggle': Transgender Inmate Cites Attacks and Abuse in Men's Prison." *New York Times,* April 6.

Soysal, Yasemin Nuhoglu. 2012. "Citizenship, Immigration, and the European Social Project: Rights and Obligations of Individuality." *British Journal of Sociology* 63: 1–21.

Spade, Joan Z., and Catherine G. Valentine. 2011. *The Kaleidoscope of Gender: Prisms, Patterns, and Possibilities.* Thousand Oaks, CA: Pine Forge Press.

Sparman, Anna. 2015. "Children' Consumer Culture." In *Encyclopedia of Consumption and Consumer Studies,* edited by Daniel Thomas Cook and Michael Ryan, 75–77. Malden, MA: Wiley-Blackwell, 2015.

Spencer, Herbert. 1851. *Social Statics.* London: Chapman.

Spencer, James H. 2004. "Los Angeles since 1992: How Did the Economic Base of Riot-Torn Neighborhoods Fare after the Unrest?" *Race, Gender and Class* 11(1): 94–115.

Spitz, Vivien. 2005. *Doctors from Hell: The Horrific Account of Nazi Experiments on Humans.* Boulder, CO: Sentient.

Spotts, Greg, and Robert Greenwald. 2005. *Wal-Mart: The High Cost of Low Price.* New York: Disinformation Press.

Spröber, Nina et al. 2014. "Child Sexual Abuse in Religiously Affiliated and Secular Institutions: A Retrospective Descriptive Analysis of Data Provided by Victims in a Government-Sponsored Reappraisal Program in Germany." *BMC Public Health* 14, published online. doi:10.1186/1471-2458-14-282.

Stacey, Clare L., and Lindsey L. Ayers. 2012. "Caught between Love and Money: The Experiences of Paid Family Caregivers." *Qualitative Sociology* 35: 47–64.

Stacey, Judith. 1998. *Brave New Families.* Berkeley: University of California Press.

Stack, Carol B. 1974. *All Our Kin: Strategies for Survival in a Black Community.* New York: Harper & Row.

Standing, Guy. 1989. "Global Feminization through Flexible Labor: A Theme Revisited." *World Development* 27(3): 583–602.

Staples, Brent. 1986. "Black Men and Public Space." *Harper's Magazine,* December, 19.

Stark, Rodney, and William Sims Bainbridge. 1979. "Of Churches, Sects, and Cults: Preliminary Concepts for a Theory of Religious Movements." *Journal for the Scientific Study of Religion* 18(2): 117–131.

Statista. 2015. "Statistics and Facts about the Pharmaceutical Industry Worldwide." Accessed May 19, 2015. www.statista.com/topics/1764/global-pharmaceutical-industry.

Stausberg, Michael. 2011. *Religion and Tourism: Crossroads, Destinations, and Encounters.* New York: Routledge.

Stearns, Cindy A. 2009. "The Work of Breastfeeding." *Women's Studies Quarterly* 37: 63–80.

Stearns, Cindy A. 2011. "Cautionary Tale about Extended Breastfeeding and Weaning." *Health Care for Women International* 32: 538–554.

Stebbins, Robert A. 1977. "The Meaning of Academic Performance: How Teachers Define a Classroom Situation." In *School Experience,* edited by P. Woods and M. Hammersley. New York: St. Martin's Press.

Stebbins, Robert A. 2007. "Leisure, Popular Culture and." In *The Blackwell Encyclopedia of Sociology,* edited by George Ritzer, 2596–2600. Malden, MA: Blackwell.

Steele, Valerie. 2011. "The Homogenization Effect." *New York Times,* August 21.

Stein, Joel. 2015. "Baby, You Can Drive My Car, and Do My Errands, and Rent My Stuff . . ." *Time,* February 9, 34–40.

Steinberg, L., and K. C. Monahan. 2007. "Age Differences in Resistance to Peer Influence." *Developmental Psychology* 43: 1531–1543.

Steinfatt, Thomas. 2011. "Sex Trafficking in Cambodia: Fabricated Numbers versus Empirical Evidence." *Crime, Law and Social Change* 56: 443–462.

Steinmetz, George. 2012. "Geopolitics." In *The Wiley-Blackwell Encyclopedia of Globalization,* edited by George Ritzer, 800–823. Malden, MA: Wiley-Blackwell.

Steinmetz, George. 2014. "The Sociology of Empires, Colonies and Postcolonialism." *Annual Review of Sociology* 40: 77–103.

Steinmetz, Katy. 2014. "The Transgender Tipping Point." *Time,* May 29. Accessed April 21, 2015. http://time.com/135480/transgender-tipping-point.

Steinmetz, Suzanne K. 1987. "Family Violence." In *Handbook of Marriage and the Family,* edited by M. B. Sussman and S. K. Steinmetz. New York: Plenum Press.

Steketee, Gail, and Randy Frost. 2011. *Stuff: Compulsive Hoarding and the Meaning of Things.* Boston: Mariner Books.

Stepan-Norris, Judith, and Caleb Southworth. 2007. "Churches as Organizational Resources: A Case Study in the Geography of Religion and Political Voting in Postwar Detroit." *Social Science History* 31(3): 343–380.

Stepfamily Foundation. n.d. "Stepfamily Statistics." www.stepfamily.org/stepfamily-statistics.html.

Sterling, Toby. 2016. "U.S. Blocks Philips' $3.3 Billion Sale of Lumileds to Asian Buyers," *Reuters,* January 22. Accessed March 8, 2017. http://www.reuters.com/article/us-philips-lumileds-sale-idUSKCN0V02D4.

Stermer, S. Paul, and Melissa Burkley. 2015. "SeX-Box: Exposure to Sexist Video Games Predicts Benevolent Sexism." *Psychology of Popular Media Culture* 4(1): 47–55.

Stevens, Mitchell L. 2001. *Kingdom of Children: Culture and Controversy in the Home Schooling Movement.* Princeton, NJ: Princeton University Press.

Stevens, Mitchell L. 2007. "Schooling, Home." In *The Blackwell Encyclopedia of Sociology,* edited by George Ritzer, 4032–4034. Malden, MA: Blackwell.

Stevenson, Howard. 2016. "Challenging School Reform from Below: Is Leadership the Missing Link in Mobilization Theory?" *Leadership and Policy in Schools* 15: 67–90.

Stevis, Dimitris. 2005. "The Globalization of Environment." *Globalizations* 2(3): 323–333.

Stewart, Heather. 2013. "Eurozone Bailouts: Which Countries Remain?" *The Guardian,* December 13.

Stewart, Katherine. 2016. "Betsy DeVos and God's Plan for Schools." *New York Times,* December 13.

Stewart, Susan D. 1999. "Disneyland Dads, Disneyland Moms: How Non-Resident Parents Spend Time with Absent Children." *Journal of Family Issues* 20: 539–556.

St. Fleur, Nicholas. 2015. "Deforestation May Threaten Majority of Amazon Tree Species, Study Finds." *New York Times,* November 20.

Stillerman, Joel. 2015. *The Sociology of Consumption: A Global Approach.* London: Polity.

Stockdill, Brett C. 2013. "ACT UP (AIDS Coalition to Unleash Power)." In *The Wiley-Blackwell Encyclopedia of Social and Political Movements,* 3 vols., edited by D. A. Snow, D. Della Porta, B. Klandermans, and D. McAdam, 5–9. Malden, MA: Wiley-Blackwell.

Stockemer, Daniel, and Rodrigo Praino, 2015. "Blinded by Beauty? Physical Attractiveness and Candidate Selection in the U.S. House of Representatives." *Social Science Quarterly* 96: 430–443.

Stokes, Allyson. 2015. "The Glass Runway: How Gender and Sexuality Shape the Spotlight in Fashion Design." *Gender and Society* 29: 219–243.

Stokoe, Elizabeth. 2006. "On Ethnomethodology, Feminism, and the Analysis of Categorical Reference to Gender in Talk-in-Interaction." *Sociological Review* 54(3): 467–494.

Stolow, Jeremy. 2004. "Transnationalism and the New Religio-politics: Reflections on a Jewish Orthodox Case." *Theory, Culture and Society* 21(2): 109–137.

Stone, Amy, and Jill Weinberg. 2015. "Sexualities and Social Movements: Three Decades of Sex and Social Change." In *Handbook of the Sociology of Sexualities*, edited by J. DeLamater and R. F. Plante. Dordrecht, Netherlands: Springer.

Stoolmiller, Michael. 1999. "Implications of the Restricted Range of Family Environments for Estimates of Heritability and Nonshared Environments in Behavior-Genetic Adoption Studies." *Psychological Bulletin* 125: 392–409.

Story, Louise, and Stephanie Saul. 2015. "Stream of Foreign Wealth Flows to Elite New York Real Estate." *New York Times*, February 7.

"Story of Cricket Part V: India and Pakistan." 2004. *BBC News*, February 3. Accessed March 29, 2012. http://news.bbc.co.uk/sport2/hi/cricket/3447829.stm.

Stouffer, S. A., E. A. Suchman, L. C. DeVinney, S. A. Star, and R. M. Williams. 1949. *The American Soldier: Adjustment during Army Life*. Vol. 1. Princeton, NJ: Princeton University Press.

Strandbu, Ase, and Ingela Lundin Kvalem. 2014. "Body Talk and Body Ideals among Adolescent Boys and Girls: A Mixed-Gender Focus Group Study." *Youth & Society* 46(5): 623–641.

Stratton, Greg, and Jeremy Northcote. 2014. "When Totems Beget Clans: The Brand Symbol as the Defining Marker of Brand Communities." *Journal of Consumer Culture*, April 4 (published online). doi: 10.1177/1469540514528194.

Straus, Murray A. 1980. "Victims and Aggressors in Marital Violence." *American Behavioral Scientist* 23: 681–704.

Streitfeld, David. 2014. "Airbnb Listings Mostly Illegal, State Contends." *New York Times*, October 16.

Strobel, Frederick R. 1993. *Upward Dreams, Downward Mobility: The Economic Decline of the American Middle Class*. Lanham, MD: Rowman & Littlefield.

Stromquist, Nelly P. 2012. "The Educational Experience of Hispanic Immigrants in the United States: Integration through Marginalization." *Race, Ethnicity & Education* 15: 195–221.

Struck, Doug. 2007. "Warming Will Exacerbate Global Water Conflicts." *Washington Post*, October 22.

Stryker, Sheldon. 1959. "Symbolic Interaction as an Approach to Family Research." *Marriage and Family Living* 21(2): 111–119.

Stryker, Sheldon, and Anne Statham Macke. 1978. "Status Inconsistency and Role Conflict." *Annual Review of Sociology* 4: 57–90.

Suárez-Orozco, Carola, Jean Rhodes, and Michael Milburn. 2009. "Unraveling the Immigrant Paradox: Academic Engagement and Disengagement among Recently Arrived Immigrant Youth." *Youth & Society* 41(2): 151–185.

Subramaniam, Mangala, David Whitlock, and Beth Williford. 2012. "Water Crisis." In *The Wiley-Blackwell Encyclopedia of Globalization*, edited by George Ritzer, 2210–2212. Malden, MA: Wiley-Blackwell.

Subramanian, Ramesh. 2012. "Computer Viruses." In *The Wiley-Blackwell Encyclopedia of Globalization*, edited by George Ritzer, 220–274. Malden, MA: Wiley-Blackwell.

Subramanian, Ramesh, and Eddan Katz, eds. 2011. *The Global Flow of Information: Legal, Social, and Cultural Perspectives*. New York: New York University Press.

Sullivan, Gail. 2014. "United Kingdom's First 'Poo Bus' Runs on Human Waste." *Washington Post*, November 21. Accessed April 21, 2015. http://www.washingtonpost.com/news/morning-mix/wp/2014/11/21/united-kingdoms-first-poo-bus-runs-on-human-waste.

Sullivan, John P. 2010. "Attacks on Journalists and 'New Media' in Mexico's Drug War: A Power and Counter Power Assessment." *Small Wars Journal*. Accessed March 31, 2012. http://smallwarsjournal.com/jrnl/art/attacks-on-journalists-and-new-media-in-mexicos-drug-war.

Sumner, Colin. 1994. *The Sociology of Deviance: An Obituary*. New York: Continuum.

Sumner, William Graham. [1906] 1940. *Folkways: A Study of the Sociological Implications of Usages, Manners, Customs, Mores and Morals*. Boston: Ginn.

Sundarajan, Arun. 2016. *The Sharing Economy: The End of Employment and the Rise of Crowd-Based Capitalism*. Cambridge, MA: MIT Press.

Surk, Barbara. 2015. "Slovenia Builds Border Fence to Stem Flow of Migrants." *New York Times*, November 11.

Suroor, Hasan. 2011. "U.K. to Raise Diplomatic Profile in India, China." *The Hindu*, May 11. Accessed May 26, 2011. http://www.thehindu.com/news/article2009518.ece.

Surowiecki, James. 2015. "The Rise and Fall of For-Profit Schools." *New Yorker*, November 2.

Surtees, Nicola. 2008. "Teachers Following Children? Heteronormative Responses within a Discourse of Child-Centredness and the Emergent Curriculum." *Australian Journal of Early Childhood* 33(3): 10–17.

Sutherland, Edwin H. 1924. *Criminology*. Chicago: University of Chicago Press.

Sutton, Susan Buck. 2014. "On the Ground Overseas: How the International Engagement of US Institutions of Higher Learning Prepares Students for a Global Future." Accessed April 21, 2015. http://www.wm.edu/offices/revescenter/internationalization/papers%20and%20presentations/bucksutton.pdf.

Swami, Viren, Amy Henry, Nicola Peacock, Ahkin Roberts-Dunn, and Alan Porter. 2013. "'Mirror, Mirror . . .': A Preliminary Investigation of Skin Tone Dissatisfaction and Its Impact among British Adults." *Cultural Diversity and Ethnic Minority Psychology* 19(4): 468–476.

Swanson, Jen. 2012. "At a Busy Gurgaon Call Center, Putting the Phones on Hold for 'Family Day.'" *New York Times*, December 14.

Swatos, William H., Jr. 2007. "Sect." In *The Blackwell Encyclopedia of Sociology*, edited by George Ritzer, 4135–4140. Malden, MA: Blackwell.

Swatos, William H., Jr. n.d. "Church-Sect Theory." In *Encyclopedia of Religion and Society*, edited by W. H. Swatos Jr. Accessed January 25, 2012. http://hirr.hartsem.edu/ency/cstheory.htm.

Swedberg, Richard. 2007. *Principles of Economic Sociology*. Princeton, NJ: Princeton University Press.

Sykes, Gresham. [1958] 2007. *The Society of Captives: A Study of a Maximum Security Prison*. Princeton, NJ: Princeton University Press.

Sylvia Rivera Law Project. 2015. "Who Was Sylvia Rivera?" Accessed March 17, 2015. http://srlp.org/about/who-was-sylvia-rivera.

Sztompka, Piotr. 1993. *The Sociology of Social Change*. West Sussex, UK: Wiley-Blackwell.

Tabassum, Nafeesa, and Mohammed Tanvir Zubair Ahmed. 2014. "The Long Reign of the United States Is Over; the 21st Century Belongs to China." *International Affairs and Global Strategy* 21: 57–62.

Tammelleo, Steve, and Louis Lombardi. 2014. "Consumer Social Responsibility?" *Business & Professional Ethics Journal* 33(1): 99–126.

Tan, Celine. 2007. "Liberalization." In *Encyclopedia of Globalization*, edited by J. A. Scholte and R. Robertson, 735–739. New York: MTM.

Tansey, Oisín. 2006. "Process Tracing and Elite Interviewing." Paper presented at the annual meeting of the American Political Science Association, Philadelphia, August 31.

Taplin, Jonathan. 2016. "Do You Love Music? Silicon Valley Doesn't." *New York Times*, May 26.

Tatangelo, Gemma L., and Lina A. Ricciardelli. 2013. "A Qualitative Study of Preadolescent Boys' and Girls' Body Image: Gendered Ideals and Sociocultural Influences." *Body Image* 10: 591–598.

Taub, Amanda. 2016. "A Lesson from Brexit: On Immigration, Feelings Trump Facts." *New York Times*, June 26.

Tavernise, Sabrina. 2016. "Life Spans of the Rich Leave the Poor Behind." *New York Times*, February 13.

Tavernise, Sabrina, and Robert Gabeloff. 2016. "Immigrants and Minorities Gain Insurance." *New York Times*, April 18.

Tavernise, Sabrina, and Denise Grady, 2016. "An Infection Raises the Specter of Superbugs Resistant to All Antibiotics." *New York Times*, A12, A15.

Taylor, Charles. 2007. *A Secular Age*. Cambridge, MA: Belknap Press.

Taylor, J. L. 2007. "Buddhism." In *Encyclopedia of Globalization*, edited by J. A. Scholte and R. Robertson, 108–113. New York: MTM.

Taylor, Laura E., and Patrick T. Hurley, eds. 2016. *Exurbia, Planning Environmental Management, and Landscape Change*. Springer.

Taylor, Paul C. 2011. "William Edward Burghardt Du Bois." In *The Wiley-Blackwell Companion to Major Social Theorists*, Vol. 1, *Classical Theorists*, edited by George Ritzer and Jeffrey Stepnisky, 426–447. Malden, MA: Wiley-Blackwell.

Taylor, Paul, Cary Funk, and April Clark. 2007. "From 1997 to 2007, Fewer Mothers Prefer Full-Time Work." Pew Research Center, July 12. Accessed April 21, 2015. http://www.pewsocialtrends.org/files/2010/10/WomenWorking.pdf.

Taylor, Yvette. 2007. "Sexualities and Consumption." In *The Blackwell Encyclopedia of Sociology*, edited by George Ritzer, 4256–4260. Malden, MA: Blackwell.

Teivainen, Teivo. 2007. "World Social Forum." In *Encyclopedia of Globalization*, edited by

J. A. Scholte and R. Robertson, 1302–1304. New York: MTM.

Terranova, Tiziana. 2013. "Free Labor." In *Digital Labor: The Internet as Playground and Factory,* edited by T. Scholz, 33–57. New York: Routledge.

Terrill, Robert E. 2015. *Double-Consciousess and the Rhetoric of Barack Obama; The Price and Promise of Citizenship.* Columbia, South Carolina: University of South Carolina Press.

Tescione, Sara. 2013. "Civil Disobedience." In *The Wiley-Blackwell Encyclopedia of Social and Political Movements,* 3 vols., edited by D. A. Snow, D. Della Porta, B. Klandermans, and D. McAdam, 191–193. Malden, MA: Wiley-Blackwell.

Tetrault, Lisa. 2014. *The Myth of Seneca Falls: Memory and the Women's Suffrage Movement, 1848–1898.* Chapel Hill: University of North Carolina Press.

Thai, Hung Cam. 2014. *Insufficient Funds: The Culture of Money in Low-Wage Transnational Families.* Stanford University Press.

Thébaud, Sarah. 2016. "Passing Up the Job: The Role of Gendered Organizations and Families in the Entrepreneurial Career Process." *Entrepreneurship: Theory and Practice* 40(2): 269–287.

Thebaud, Sarah, and David S. Pedulla, 2016. "Masculinity and the Stalled Revolution: How Gender Ideologies and Norms Shape Young Men's Responses to Work-Family Policies." *Gender & Society* 30: 590–617.

Thoits, Peggy A. 1985. "Self-Labeling Processes in Mental Illness: The Role of Emotional Deviance." *American Journal of Sociology* 91(2): 221–249.

Thoits, Peggy A. 2011. "Perceived Social Support and the Voluntary, Mixed, or Pressured Use of Mental Health Services." *Society and Mental Health* 1: 4–19.

Tholen, Gerbrand. Forthcoming. "Symbolic Closure: Towards a Renewed Sociological Perspective on the Relationship between Higher Education, Credentials and the Graduate Labour Market." *Sociology.*

Thomas, George. 2012. "Christianity." In *The Wiley-Blackwell Encyclopedia of Globalization,* edited by George Ritzer, 179–187. Malden, MA: Wiley-Blackwell.

Thomas, Jeremy N., Lauren Crosby, and Jessica Milford, 2015. "Gender Differences among Self-Reported Genital Piercing Stories." *Deviant Behavior* 36: 441–462.

Thomas, William I., and Dorothy S. Thomas. 1928. *The Child in America: Behavior Problems and Programs.* New York: Knopf.

Thompson, Beverly Yuen. 2015. *Covered in Ink: Tattoos, Women, and the Politics of the Body.* New York: New York University Press.

Thorn, Elizabeth. 2007. "Gender, Work, and Family." In *The Blackwell Encyclopedia of Sociology,* edited by George Ritzer, 1880–1885. Malden, MA: Blackwell.

Thorne, Barrie. 1993. *Gender Play: Girls and Boys in School.* New Brunswick, NJ: Rutgers University Press.

Thornton, Alex, and Katherine McAuliffe. 2006. "Teaching in Wild Meerkats." *Science* 313(5784): 227–229.

Thornton, Arland, William Axinn, and Y. Xie. 2007. *Marriage and Cohabitation.* Chicago: University of Chicago Press.

Thorpe, Holly, and Nida Ahmad, 2015. "Youth Action Sports and Political Agency in the Middle East: Lessons from a Grassroots Parkour Group in Gaza." *International Review for the Sociology of Sport* 50: 678–704.

Tierney, John. 2013. "Prison Population Can Shrink When Police Crowd Streets." *New York Times,* January 26.

Timasheff, Nicholas S. 1965. *War and Revolution.* New York: Sheed and Ward.

Timberlake, Michael, and Xiulian Ma. 2007. "Cities and Globalization." In *The Blackwell Companion to Globalization,* edited by George Ritzer, 254–271. Malden, MA: Blackwell.

Timberlake, Michael, Yehua Dennis Wei, Xiulian Ma, and Jianmei Hao. 2014. "Global Cities with Chinese Characteristics." *Cities* 41: 162–170.

Timmermans, Stefan, and Hyeyoung Oh. 2010. "The Continued Social Transformation of the Medical Profession." *Journal of Health and Social Behavior* 51: S94–S106.

Timms, Jill. 2012. "Labor Movements." In *The Encyclopedia of Globalization,* edited by George Ritzer, 1259–1261. Malden, MA: Wiley-Blackwell.

Tiryakian, Edward. 1991. "Modernization: Exhumateur in Pace (Rethinking Macrosociology in the 1990s)." *International Sociology* 6(2): 165–180.

Tocqueville, Alexis de. [1835–1840] 1969. *Democracy in America.* Garden City, NY: Doubleday.

Toennies, Ferdinand. [1887] 1957. *Community and Society.* New York: Harper Torchbooks.

Tolbert, Pamela. 2013. "The Iron Law of Oligarchy." In *The Wiley-Blackwell Encyclopedia of Social and Political Movements,* 3 vols., edited by D. A. Snow, D. Della Porta, B. Klandermans, and D. McAdam, 637–639. Malden, MA: Wiley-Blackwell.

Tomlinson, John. 1999. *Globalization and Culture.* Chicago: University of Chicago Press.

Tomlinson, John. 2000. "Globalization and Cultural Identity." In *The Global Transformations Reader,* edited by D. Held and A. McGrew, 269–277. Cambridge: Polity Press.

Tomlinson, John. 2012. "Cultural Imperialism." In *The Wiley-Blackwell Encyclopedia of Globalization,* edited by George Ritzer, 371–374. Malden, MA: Wiley-Blackwell.

Tong, Rosemarie. 2009. *Feminist Thought: A More Comprehensive Introduction.* 3rd ed. Boulder, CO: Westview Press.

Torpey, John C. 2000. *The Invention of the Passport: Citizenship, Surveillance, and the State.* New York: Cambridge University Press.

Torpey, John C. 2012. "Passports." In *The Wiley-Blackwell Encyclopedia of Globalization,* edited by George Ritzer, 1644–1647. Malden, MA: Wiley-Blackwell.

Townsend, Peter. 2010. "The Meaning of Poverty." *British Journal of Sociology* 61: 85–102.

Trans Murder Monitoring Project. 2016. Accessed January 30, 2016. http://transrespect.org/en/research/trans-murder-monitoring.

Tranter, Bruce, and Dallas Hanson. 2015. "The Social Bases of Cosmetic Surgery in Australia." *Journal of Sociology* 51: 189–206.

Trask, Bahira Sherif. 2010. *Globalization and Families: Accelerated Systemic Social Change.* New York: Springer.

Treas, Judith, Jonathan Lui, and Zoya Gubernskaya. 2014. "Attitudes on Marriage and New Relationships: Cross-National Evidence on the Deinstitutionalization of Marriage." *Demographic Research* 30: 1495–1526.

Trebay, Guy. 2008. "Tattoos Gain Even More Visibility." *New York Times,* September 24. Accessed December 20, 2011. http://www.nytimes.com/2008/09/25/fashion/25tattoo.html?scp=1&sq=September%2025,%202008%20tattoo&st=cse.

Treiman, Donald J. 2007. "Occupational Mobility." In *The Blackwell Encyclopedia of Sociology,* edited by George Ritzer, 3240–3244. Malden, MA: Blackwell.

Treitler, Vilna Bashi. 2016. "Racialization and Its Paradigms: From Ireland to North America." *Current Sociology* 64: 213–227.

Tremblay, Manon, David Paternotte, and Carol Johnson, eds. 2013. *The Lesbian and Gay Movement and the State: Comparative Insights into a Transformed Relationship.* Farnham, UK: Ashgate.

Trentmann, Frank. 2016. *Empire of Things: How We Became a World of Consumers, from the Fifteenth Century to the Twenty-First.* New York: Harper.

Trepagnier, Barbara. 2010. *Silent Racism: How Well-Meaning People Perpetuate the Racial Divide.* Boulder, CO: Paradigm.

Troeltsch, Ernst. 1932. *The Social Teaching of the Christian Churches,* translated by O. Wyon. New York: Macmillan.

Tsuda, Takeyuki. 2014. "'I'm American, Not Japanese!': The Struggle for Racial Citizenship among Later-Generation Japanese Americans." *Ethnic and Racial Studies* 37(3): 405–424.

Tsuda, Takeyuki, Maria Tapias, and Xavier Escandell. 2014. "Locating the Global in Transnational Ethnography." *Journal of Contemporary Ethnography* 43: 123–147.

Tsutsui, Kiyoteru, and Christine Min Wotipka. 2004. "Global Civil Society and the International Human Rights Movement: Citizen Participation in Human Rights International Nongovernmental Organizations." *Social Forces* 83(2): 587–620:

Tumber, Howard, and Frank Webster. 2006. *Journalists under Fire: Information War and Journalistic Practices.* London: Sage.

Tumin, Melvin E. 1953. "Some Principles of Stratification: A Critical Analysis." *American Sociological Review* 18: 387–394.

Tunnell, Kenneth D. 2007. "Crime, Political." In *The Blackwell Encyclopedia of Sociology,* edited by George Ritzer, 835–836. Malden, MA: Blackwell.

Turkle, Sherry. 2011. *Alone Together: Why We Expect More from Technology and Less from Each Other.* New York: Basic Books.

Turner, Bryan S. 2007a. "Body and Cultural Sociology." In *The Blackwell Encyclopedia of Sociology,* edited by George Ritzer, 324–328. Malden, MA: Blackwell.

Turner, Bryan S. 2007b. "Body and Society." In *The Blackwell Encyclopedia of Sociology,* edited by George Ritzer, 335–38. Malden, MA: Blackwell.

Turner, Bryan S. 2008. *The Body and Society: Explorations in Social Theory.* 3rd ed. London: Sage.

Turner, Bryan S. 2011. *Religion and Modern Society: Citizenship, Secularisation and the State.* Cambridge: Cambridge University Press.

Turner, Bryan, ed. 2012. *Routledge Handbook of Body Studies.* New York: Routledge.

Turner, Bryan S. 2014. "Religion and Contemporary Sociological Theories." *Current Sociology* 62: 771–788.

Turner, Fred. 2008. *From Counterculture to Cyberculture: Stewart Brand, the Whole Earth Network, and the Rise of Digital Utopianism.* Chicago: University of Chicago Press.

Turner, Jonathan. 2005. "A New Approach for Theoretically Integrating Micro and Macro Analysis." In *The Sage Handbook of Sociology,* edited by C. Calhoun, C. Rojek, and B. Turner, 403–422. London: Sage.

Turner, Leigh. 2007. "'First World Health Care at Third World Prices': Globalization, Bioethics and Medical Tourism." *BioSocieties* 2: 303–325.

Turner, Margery Austin, Rob Santos, Diane K. Levy, Doug Wissoker, Claudia Aranda, and Rob Pitingolo. 2013. *Housing Discrimination against Racial and Ethnic Minorities 2012.* Washington, DC: Urban Institute.

Turner, Ralph H. 1978. "The Role and the Person." *American Journal of Sociology* 84: 1–23.

Turner, Ralph H., and Lewis M. Killian. 1987. *Collective Behavior.* 3rd ed. Englewood Cliffs, NJ: Prentice Hall.

Turner, Victor. 1967. *The Forest of Symbols: Aspects of Ndembu Ritual.* Ithaca, NY: Cornell University Press.

Tweedy, Damon. 2015. "The Case for Black Doctors." *New York Times,* May 15.

Tyler, Meagan, and Kaye Quek, 2016. "Conceptualizing Pornographication: A Lack of Clarity and Problems for Feminist Analysis." *Sexualization, Media & Society* 2(2).

Tynes, Brendesha, Joshua Schuschke, and Safiya Umoja Noble. 2016. "Digital Intersectionality Theory and the #BlackLivesMatter Movment." In *The Intersectional Internet,* edited by Safiya Umoja Noble and Brendesah Tynes, 21–40.

Uchitelle, Louis. 2010. "Another Shifting Industry." *New York Times,* January 19.

Ultee, Wout. 2007a. "Mobility, Horizontal and Vertical." In *The Blackwell Encyclopedia of Sociology,* edited by George Ritzer, 3060–3061. Malden, MA: Blackwell.

Ultee, Wout. 2007b. "Mobility, Intergenerational and Intragenerational." In *The Blackwell Encyclopedia of Sociology,* edited by George Ritzer, 3061–3062. Malden, MA: Blackwell.

United Nations. 2006. "Ending Violence against Women: From Words to Action Study of the Secretary-General, Fact Sheet." Accessed March 31, 2012. http://www.un.org/women-watch/daw/vaw/launch/english/v.a.w-exeE-use.pdf.

United Nations. 2014. "World Urbanization Prospects." Revised Edition. Accessed February 22, 2017. https://esa.un.org/unpd/wup/publications/files/wup2014-highlights.Pdf.

United Nations. 2016. "The World's Cities in 2016." http://www.un.org/en/development/desa/population/publications/pdf/urbanization/the_worlds_cities_in_2016_data_booklet.pdf.

United Nations Department of Economic and Social Affairs. 2015a. "International Migrant Stock, Total." Accessed March 19, 2015. http://esa.un.org/unmigration/TIMSA2013/migrant stocks2013.htm.

United Nations Department of Economic and Social Affairs. 2015b. "Probabilistic Population Projections Based on the *World Population Prospects: The 2012 Revision.*" Accessed March 19, 2015. http://esa.un.org/unpd/ppp/Data-Output/UN_PPP2012_output-data.htm.

United Nations Development Programme. 2014. "Gender and Poverty Reduction." Accessed April 21, 2015. http://www.undp.org/content/undp/en/home/ourwork/povertyreduction/focus_areas/focus_gender_and_poverty.

United Nations General Assembly. 2006. *In-Depth Study on All Forms of Violence against Women: Report of the Secretary-General.* A/61/122/Add.1. New York: Author.

United Nations Human Settlements Programme. 2016. "World's Cities Report 2016." Accessed March 9, 2017. http://wcr.unhabitat.org.

United Nations Population Fund. 2015. "Migration." Accessed March 19, 2015. http://www.unfpa.org/migration.

United States Department of State. *Trafficking in Persons Report 2016.* Accessed January 31, 2017. https://www.state.gov/j/tip/rls/tiprpt/2016.

United States Elections Project. 2016. *November General Election Turnout Rates.* www.electproject.org/2016g.

UN Women. 2014. "Facts and Figures: Ending Violence against Women." October. Accessed April 18, 2015. http://www.unwomen.org/en/what-we-do/ending-violence-against-women/facts-and-figures#sthash.5L0ZPGBH.dpuf.

Uriely, Natan, and Yaniv Belhassen. 2005. "Drugs and Tourists' Experiences." *Journal of Travel Research* 43(3): 238–246.

Urry, John. 2000. *Sociology beyond Societies: Mobilities for the Twenty-first Century.* London: Routledge.

Urry, John. 2007. *Mobilities.* Cambridge: Polity Press.

U.S. Census Bureau. 2012. "Population." 2011 Statistical Abstract. Accessed March 31, 2012. http://www.census.gov/compendia/statab/cats/population.html.

U.S. Census Bureau. 2013. "Trade in Goods with China." Accessed February 14, 2013. http://www.census.gov/foreign-trade/balance/c5700.html.

U.S. Census Bureau. 2014a. *Current Population Survey, 2014 Annual Social and Economic (ASEC) Supplement* (machine-readable data file). Accessed April 23, 2015. ftp://ftp2.census.gov/programs-surveys/cps/techdocs/cpsmar14.pdf.

U.S. Census Bureau. 2014b. "Income, Poverty and Health Insurance Coverage in the United States, 2013." Press release CB14-169,

September 16. Accessed April 29, 2015. http://www.census.gov/newsroom/press-releases/2014/cb14-169.html.

U.S. Census Bureau. 2015. "Income: Frequently Asked Questions." Accessed February 19, 2015. https://www.census.gov/hhes/www/income/about/faqs.html.

U.S. Department of Commerce, Economics and Statistics Administration; Executive Office of the President, Office of Management and Budget; and White House Council on Women and Girls. 2011. "Women in America: Indicators of Economic and Social Well-Being." Accessed May 25, 2011. http://www.whitehouse.gov/sites/default/files/rss_viewer/Women_in_America.pdf.

U.S. Department of Education, National Center for Education Statistics. 2014. "Fast Facts: Homeschooling." Accessed May 14, 2015. http://nces.ed.gov/fastfacts/display.asp?id=91.

U.S. Department of Health and Human Services. 2014. "HHS Disparities Action Plan." Accessed April 21, 2015. http://minorityhealth.hhs.gov/omh/browse.aspx?lvl=2&lvlid=10.

U.S. Department of Health and Human Services, Assistant Secretary for Planning and Evaluation. 2017. "2017 Poverty Guidelines." Accessed February 13, 2017. https://aspe.hhs.gov/poverty-guidelines.

U.S. Department of Health and Human Services, National Institutes of Health. 2011. "Human Genome Project." Accessed April 15, 2011. http://report.nih.gov/NIHfactsheets/ViewFactSheet.aspx?csid=45&key=H#H.

U.S. Department of Labor, Bureau of Labor Statistics. 2009. "Ranks of Discouraged Workers and Others Marginally Attached to the Labor Force Rise during Recession." *Issues in Labor Statistics,* April.

U.S. Department of Labor, Bureau of Labor Statistics. 2013. "Earnings and Unemployment Rates by Educational Attainment." Accessed June 26, 2013. http://www.bls.gov/emp/ep_chart_001.htm.

U.S. Department of State. 2007. *Trafficking in Persons Report 2007.* Washington, DC: Author. Accessed May 15, 2015. http://www.state.gov/j/tip/rls/tiprpt/2007/index.htm.

Useem, Elizabeth L. 1992. "Middle Schools and Math Groups: Parents' Involvement in Children's Placement." *Sociology of Education* 65: 263–279.

U.S. Equal Employment Opportunity Commission. 2015. "Charges Alleging Sexual Harassment, FY 2010–FY 2015." Accessed March 8, 2016. https://www.eeoc.gov/eeoc/statistics/enforcement/sexual_harassment_new.cfm.

Vaidhyanathan, Siva. 2011. *The Googlization of Everything (and Why We Should Worry).* Berkeley: University of California Press.

Vail, D. Angus. 1999. "Tattoos Are Like Potato Chips . . . You Can't Have Just One: The Process of Becoming and Being a Collector." *Deviant Behavior* 20: 253–273.

Vail, D. Angus. 2007. "Body Modification." In *The Blackwell Encyclopedia of Sociology,* edited by George Ritzer, 328–330. Malden. MA: Blackwell.

Valocchi, Stephen. 2007. "Gay and Lesbian Movement." In *The Blackwell Encyclopedia of Sociology*, edited by George Ritzer, 1833–1838. Malden, MA: Blackwell.

Valocchi, Stephen. 2013. "Gay and Lesbian Movement." In *The Wiley-Blackwell Encyclopedia of Social and Political Movements*, 3 vols., edited by D. A. Snow, D. Della Porta, B. Klandermans, and D. McAdam, 498–503. Malden, MA: Wiley-Blackwell.

Van de Poel, Ellen, Ahmad Reza Hosseinpoor, Niko Speybroeck, Tom Van Ourti, and Jeanette Vega. 2008. "Socioeconomic Inequality in Malnutrition in Developing Countries." *Bulletin of the World Health Organization* 86(4): 241–320.

van der Lippe, Tanja, Vincent Frey, and Milena Tsvetkova. 2012. "Outsourcing of Domestic Tasks: A Matter of Preferences?" *Journal of Family Issues* 34(12): 1574–1597.

Van de Werfhorst, Herman G., and Jonathan J. B. Mij. 2010. "Achievement Inequality and the Institutional Structure of Educational Systems: A Comparative Perspective." *Annual Review of Sociology* 36: 407–428.

Van Dijk, Jan A. G. M. 2012. *The Network Society.* 3rd ed. Thousand Oaks, CA: Sage.

van Dyke, Nella, and David S. Meyer, eds. 2014. *Understanding the Tea Party Movement.* Farnham, UK: Ashgate.

van Eeden, Jeanne. 2006. "Shopping for Gender." In *Sex, Gender, Becoming: Post-apartheid Reflections*, edited by K. van Marle, 61–92. Pretoria: Pretoria University Law Press.

Vanek, Joann, Martha Chen, Ralf Hussmanns, and Francoise Carre. 2014. *Women and Men in the Informal Economy: A Statistical Picture.* 2nd ed. Geneva: International Labour Organization.

van Gennep, Arnold. 1961. *The Rites of Passage.* Chicago: University of Chicago Press.

Van Kessel, Ineke. 2013. "Antiapartheid Movements (South Africa)." In *The Wiley-Blackwell Encyclopedia of Social and Political Movements*, 3 vols., edited by D. A. Snow, D. Della Porta, B. Klandermans, and D. McAdam, 60–66. Malden, MA: Wiley-Blackwell.

van Leeuwen, Marco H. D., and Ineke Maas. 2010. "Historical Studies of Social Mobility and Stratification." *Annual Review of Sociology* 36: 429–451.

Van Maanen, John. 1983. "The Moral Fix: On the Ethics of Field Work." In *Contemporary Field Research: Perspectives and Formulations*, edited by R. M. Emerson. Longrove, IL: Waveland Press.

Van Slyke, Shanna R., Michael L. Benson, and Francis T. Cullen, eds. 2016. *The Oxford Handbook of White-Collar Crime.* New York: Oxford University Press.

Van Valen, L. 1974. "Brain Size and Intelligence in Man." *American Journal of Physical Anthropology* 40: 417–423.

Varcoe, Ian. 2007. "Historical and Comparative Methods." In *The Blackwell Encyclopedia of Sociology*, edited by George Ritzer, 2133–2136. Malden, MA: Blackwell.

Vaughan, Diane. 1996. *The Challenger Launch Decision: Risky Technology, Culture, and Deviance at NASA.* Chicago: University of Chicago Press.

Veblen, Thorstein. [1899] 1994. *The Theory of the Leisure Class.* New York: Penguin.

Veldkamp, Ted I. E., Yoshihide Wada, Hans de Moel, Matti Kummu, Jeroen C. J. H. Aerts, and Philip J. War. 2014. "Impact of Socio-economic Trends and Climate Variability on the Occurrence and Severity of Blue Water Shortage and Stress Events at the Global Scale." *EGU General Assembly Conference Abstracts* 16. Accessed April 21, 2015. http://meetingorganizer.copernicus.org/EGU2014/EGU2014-2146.pdf.

Venkatesh, Alladi. 2007. "Postmodern Consumption." In *The Blackwell Encyclopedia of Sociology*, edited by George Ritzer, 3552–3556. Malden, MA: Blackwell.

Venkatesh, Alladi. 2015. "Consumption, Postmodern." In *The Wiley-Blackwell Encyclopedia of Consumption and Consumer Studies*, edited by Daniel Thomas Cook and J. Michael Ryan, 183–187. Malden, MA: Wiley-Blackwell.

Venkatesh, Sudhir. 1994. "Learnin' the Trade: Conversations with a Gangsta." *Public Culture* 6: 319–341.

Venkatesh, Sudhir. 2002. "'Doin' the Hustle': Constructing the Ethnographer in the American Ghetto." *Ethnography* 3: 91–111.

Venkatesh, Sudhir. 2008. *Gang Leader for a Day: A Rogue Sociologist Takes to the Streets.* New York: Penguin.

Venkatesh, Sudhir. 2014. *Floating City: A Rogue Sociologist Lost and Found in New York's Underground Economy.* New York: Penguin.

Verde Group. 2007. "He Buys, She Shops: A Study of Gender Differences in the Retail Experience." Executive summary. Accessed April 18, 2015. http://www.wharton.upenn.edu/bakerretail/files/He_Buys_She_Shops_fall_2007_exec_summary.pdf.

Verkaik, Robert. 2006. "Sex Harassment in Armed Forces Is Rife, Say Women." *Independent*, May 26. Accessed December 3, 2011. http://www.independent.co.uk/news/uk/crime/sex-harassment-in-armed-forces-is-rife-say-women-479769.html.

Vertigans, Stephen. 2011. *The Sociology of Terrorism: People, Place and Processes.* New York: Routledge.

Vespa, Jonathan, Jamie M. Lewis, and Rose M. Kreider, 2013. *America's Families and Living Arrangements: 2012.* Washington, DC: US Census Bureau.

Vidal, Matt. 2016. "Fordism and the Golden Age of Capitalism." In *The Sage Handbook of the Sociology of Work and Employment*, edited by Stephen Edgell, Heidi Gottfried, and Edward Granter, 283–305. London: Sage.

Vidal, Matt, Paul Adler, and Rick Delbridge. 2015. "When Organization Studies Turns to Societal Problems: The Contribution of Marxist Grand Theory." *Organization Studies* 36: 405–422.

Viladrich, Anahi, and Rita Baron-Faust. 2014. "Medical Tourism in Tango Paradise: The Internet Branding of Cosmetic Surgery in Argentina." *Annals of Tourism Research* 45: 116–131.

Villareal, Andres, and Wei-hsin Yu. 2007. "Economic Globalization and Women's Employment: The Case of Manufacturing in Mexico." *American Sociological Review* 72(3): 365–389.

Vlase, Ionela, and Ma'lina Voicu. 2014. "Romanian Roma Migration: The Interplay between Structures and Agency." *Ethnic and Racial Studies* 37(13): 2418–2437.

Vlasic, Bill. 2013. "Lawyer Outlines Challenges in New Job Fixing Detroit." *New York Times*, March 25.

Voas, David, and Mark Chaves. 2016. "Is the United States a Counterexample to the Secularization Thesis."*American Journal of Sociology* 121: 1517–1556.

Voas, David, and Fenella Fleischmann. 2012. "Islam Moves West: Religious Change in the First and Second Generations." *Annual Review of Sociology* 38: 525–545.

Vogel, Ezra F. 2011. *Deng Xiaoping and the Transformation of China.* Cambridge, MA: Belknap Press.

Vogli, Roberto De, Anne Kouvonen, Marko Elovainio, and Michael Marmot. 2014. "Economic Globalization, Inequality and Body Mass Index: A Cross-National Analysis of 127 Countries." *Critical Public Health* 24(1): 7–21.

Vogt, Kristoffer Chelsom. 2016. "The Post-Industrial Society: From Utopia to Ideology." *Work, Employment and Society* 30: 366–376.

Vohs, Kathleen D., Jaideep Sengupta, and Darren W. Dahl. 2014. "The Price Had Better Be Right: Women's Reactions to Sexual Stimuli Vary with Market Factors." *Psychological Science* 25(1): 278–283.

vom Lehn, Dirk. 2007. "Interaction." In *The Blackwell Encyclopedia of Sociology*, edited by George Ritzer, 2361–2365. Malden, MA: Blackwell.

von Grebmer, Klaus, Derek Headey, Tolulope Olo Nbiyi, Doris Wiesmann, Heidi Fritschel, Sandra Yin, and Yisehac Yohannes. 2013. *2013 Global Hunger Index.* Washington, DC: International Food Policy Research Institute.

von Sivers, Isabella, Anne Templeton, Gerta Köster, John Drury, and Andrew Philippides. 2014. "Humans Do Not Always Act Selfishly: Social Identity and Helping in Emergency Evacuation Simulation." *Transportation Research Procedia* 2: 585–593.

Vos, Jeroen, and Leonith Hinojosa, 2016. "Virtual Water Trade and the Contestation of Hydrosocial Territories." *Water International* 41: 37–53.

Waddington, David. 2015. "Riots." In *The Oxford Handbook of Social Movements*, edited by Donatella Della Porta and Mario Diani, 423–439. Oxford: Oxford University Press.

Waddington, Ivan. 2007. "Health and Sport." In *The Blackwell Encyclopedia of Sociology*, edited by George Ritzer, 2091–2095. Malden, MA: Blackwell.

Wade, Lisa. 2017. *American Hookup: The New Culture of Sex on Campus.* New York: Norton.

Wajcman, Judy. 2010. "Feminist Theories of Technology." *Cambridge Journal of Economics* 34: 143–152.

Wakefield, Kelly. 2013. "Global Digital Divide: Inequality and Internet Access." *Geography Review* 26: 10–13.

Walder, Andrew. 2009. "Political Sociology and Social Movements." *Annual Review of Sociology* 35: 393–412.

Waldmeir, Patti. [1997] 2001. *Anatomy of a Miracle: The End of Apartheid and the Birth of a New South Africa.* New Brunswick, NJ: Rutgers University Press.

Walker, Henry A., and David Willer. 2007. "Experimental Methods." In *The Blackwell Encyclopedia of Sociology,* edited by George Ritzer, 1537–1541. Malden. MA: Blackwell.

Wallerstein, Immanuel. 1974. *The Modern World-System.* New York: Academic Press.

Wallerstein, James S., and Clement J. Wyle. 1947. "Our Law-Abiding Law-Breakers." *Federal Probation* 25: 107–112.

Walsh, Anthony. 1990. "Twice Labeled: The Effect of Psychiatric Labeling on the Sentencing of Sex Offenders." *Social Problems* 37: 375–389.

Walsh, Declan. 2015. "Fake Diplomas, Real Cash: A Net of Made-Up Schools." *New York Times,* May 18.

Walsh, Declan. 2017. "Trump Targets Muslim Areas in Refugee Ban." *New York Times,* January 28.

Walters, G. D. 2003. "Changes in Criminal Thinking and Identity in Novice and Experienced Inmates: Prisonization Revisited." *Criminal Justice and Behavior* 30(4): 399–421.

Wang, Lin, Glen H. Elder Jr., and Naomi J. Spence. 2012. "Status Configurations, Military Service and Higher Education." *Social Forces* 91: 397–422.

Wang, Shanshan, and Eric Pfanner. 2013. "China's One-Day Shopping Spree Sets Record in Online Sales." *New York Times,* November 11.

Wang, Wendy, Kim Parker, and Paul Taylor. 2013. "Breadwinner Moms." Pew Research Center, Pew Social and Demographic Trends, May 29. Accessed February 27, 2017. http://www.pewsocialtrends.org/files/2013/05/Breadwinner_moms_final.pdf.

Ward, James D., and Mario A. Rivera. 2014. *Institutional Racism, Organizations & Public Policy.* New York: Peter Lang.

Ward, Kathryn. 1990. "Introduction and Overview." In *Women Workers and Global Restructuring,* edited by K. Ward, 1–24. Ithaca, NY: ILR Press.

Warner, R. Steven. 1993. "Work in Progress toward a New Paradigm for the Sociological Study of Religion in the United States." *American Journal of Sociology* 98: 1044–1093.

Warren, Cortney S. 2014. "Body Area Dissatisfaction in White, Black and Latina Female College Students in the USA: An Examination of Racially Salient Appearance Areas and Ethnic Identity." *Ethnic and Racial Studies* 37: 537–556.

Warren, John Robert, and Elaine M. Hernandez. 2007. "Did Socioeconomic Inequalities in Morbidity and Mortality Change in the United States over the Course of the Twentieth Century?" *Journal of Health and Social Behavior* 48: 335–351.

Waskul, Dennis. 2015. "Sex and the Internet." In Patricia Whelehan and Anne Bolin, eds. *The International Encyclopedia of Human Sexuality.* Malden, MA: Wiley-Blackwell.

Wasserman, J., M. A. Flannery, and J. M. Clair. 2007. "Raising the Ivory Tower: The Production of Knowledge and Distrust of Medicine among African Americans." *Journal of Medical Ethics* 33(3): 177–180.

Wasserman, Varda, and Michal Frenkel. 2015. "Spatial Work In Between Glass Ceiling and Glass Walls: Gender-Class Intersectionality and Organizational Aesthetics." *Organization Studies* 36: 1485–1505.

Wasson, Leslie. 2007. "Identity Politics/Relational Politics." In *The Blackwell Encyclopedia of Sociology,* edited by George Ritzer, 2214–2215. Malden, MA: Blackwell.

Watkins, S. Craig. 2009. *The Young and the Digital: What the Migration to Social Network Sites, Games, and Anytime, Anywhere Media Means for Our Future.* Boston: Beacon Press.

Watkins, Steven Mark. 2014. *An Analysis of the Creation Museum: Hermeneutics, Language, and Information Theory.* PhD dissertation, University of Louisville.

Watson, Ivan. 2013. "China: The Electronic Wastebasket of the World." *CNN,* May 30.

Wax, Emily. 2007. "An Ancient Indian Craft Left in Tatters." *Washington Post,* June 6.

Way, Sandra. 2007. "School Discipline." In *The Blackwell Encyclopedia of Sociology,* edited by George Ritzer, 4019–4023. Malden, MA: Blackwell.

Wayne, Leslie. 2009. "Dubious Claims for H1N1 Cures Are Rife Online." *New York Times,* November 6.

Weaver, Adam. 2012. "Tourism." In *The Wiley-Blackwell Encyclopedia of Globalization,* edited by George Ritzer, 1980–1983. Malden, MA: Wiley-Blackwell.

Webb, Haley J., Melanie J. Zimmer-Gembeck, and Caroline L. Donovan. 2014. "The Appearance Culture between Friends and Adolescent Appearance-Based Rejection Sensitivity." *Journal of Adolescence* 37: 347–358.

Weber, Jonetta D., and Robert M. Carini. 2012. "Where Are the Female Athletes in *Sports Illustrated*? A Content Analysis of Covers." *International Review for the Sociology of Sport,* January 30.

Weber, Max. [1903–1917] 1949. *The Methodology of the Social Sciences.* New York: Free Press.

Weber, Max. [1904–1905] 1958. *The Protestant Ethic and the Spirit of Capitalism.* New York: Scribner.

Weber, Max. [1919] 1958. "Politics as a Vocation." In *From Max Weber: Essays in Sociology,* edited by H. Gerth and C. Wright Mills. New York: Oxford University Press.

Weber, Max. [1920] 1963. *The Sociology of Religion,* translated by E. Fischoff. Boston: Beacon Press.

Weber, Max. [1921] 1968. *Economy and Society: An Outline of Interpretive Sociology,* edited by G. Roth and C. Wittich. Totowa, NJ: Bedminster Press.

Weber, Samuel R., and Kenneth I. Pargament. 2014. "The Role of Religion and Spirituality in Mental Health." *Current Opinion in Psychiatry* 27: 358–363.

Webster, Murray, and Jane Sell. 2012. "Groups and Institutions, Structures and Processes." In *The Wiley-Blackwell Companion to Sociology,* edited by George Ritzer, 139–163. Malden, MA: Wiley-Blackwell.

Weeks, John R. 2007. "Demographic Transition Theory." In *The Blackwell Encyclopedia of Sociology,* edited by George Ritzer, 1033–1038. Malden, MA: Blackwell.

Weeks, John R. 2011. *Population: An Introduction to Concepts and Issues.* 11th ed. Belmont, CA: Wadsworth.

Wegener, B. 1991. "Job Mobility and Social Ties: Social Resources, Prior Job, and Status Attainment." *American Sociological Review* 56: 60–71.

Weigel, Moira. 2016. *Labor of Love: The Invention of Dating.* New York: Farrar, Straus and Giroux.

Weiler, Bernd. 2007. "Cultural Relativism." In *The Blackwell Encyclopedia of Sociology,* edited by George Ritzer, 908–910. Malden, MA: Blackwell.

Weinstein, Jay. 2010. *Social Change.* 3rd ed. Lanham, MD: Rowman & Littlefield.

Weinstein, Mary. 2013. "How Many People Shop Online?" *Ecommerce,* August 9. Accessed April 27, 2015. http://www.cpcstrategy.com/blog/2013/08/ecommerce-infographic.

Weisenthal, Joe. 2013. "Here's the New Ranking of Top Countries in Reading, Science, and Math." *Business Insider,* December 3. Accessed May 17, 2015. http://www.businessinsider.com/pisa-rankings-2013-12#ixzz3SokWhusf.

Weisman, Jonathan. 2016. "The Nazi Tweets of 'Trump God Emperor.'" *New York Times Sunday Review,* May 26.

Weiss, Gregory L., and Lynne E. Lonnquist. 2009. *Sociology of Health, Healing, and Illness.* Upper Saddle River, NJ: Pearson/Prentice Hall.

Weitz, Rose. 2010. *The Sociology of Health, Illness, and Health Care: A Critical Approach.* 5th ed. Boston: Wadsworth Cengage.

Weitz, Rose. 2013. *The Sociology of Health, Illness, and Health Care: A Critical Approach.* 6th ed. Belmont, CA: Thompson Wadsworth.

Weitzer, Ronald. 2009. "Sociology of Sex Work." *Annual Review of Sociology* 35: 213–234.

Weitzer, Ronald. 2012. *Legalizing Prostitution: From Illicit Vice to Lawful Business.* New York: New York University Press.

Weitzer, Ronald. 2014. "New Directions in Research on Human Trafficking." *Annals of the American Academy of Political and Social Science* 653(1): 6–24.

Weitzer, Ronald. 2015. "Human Trafficking and Contemporary Slavery." *Annual Review of Sociology* 41: 223–242.

Weitzman, Abigail, and Julia Andrea Behrman. 2016. "Disaster, Disruption to Family Life, and Intimate Partner Violence: The Case of the 2010 Earthquake in Haiti." *Sociological Science* 3: 167–189.

"Welcome to Our Shrinking Jungle." 2008. *Economist,* June 5. Accessed March 9, 2012. http://www.economist.com/node/11496950.

Wellard, Ian. 2012. "Body-Reflexive Pleasures: Exploring Bodily Experiences within the Context of Sport and Physical Activity." *Sport, Education and Society* 17: 21–33.

Wellford, Charles. 2012. "Criminology." In *The Wiley-Blackwell Companion to Sociology,* edited by George Ritzer, 229–242. Malden, MA: Wiley-Blackwell.

Wellings, Kaye, Martine Collumbien, Emma Slaymaker, Susheela Singh, Zoe Hodges, Dhavai Patel, and Nathalie Bajos. 2009. "Sexual Behavior in Context: A Global Perspective." *The Lancet* 368: 349–358.

Wellman, Elizabeth. 2004. *The Road to Seneca Falls: Elizabeth Cady Stanton and the First Woman's Rights Convention*. Champaign: University of Illinois Press.

Welter, Barbara. 1966. "The Cult of True Womanhood: 1820–1860." *American Quarterly* 18(2, pt. 1): 151–174.

Welzel, Christian, and Ronald Inglehart. 2009. "Mass Beliefs and Democratization." In *Democratization*, edited by C. W. Haerpfer, P. Bernhagen, R. F. Inglehart, and C. Welzel. New York: Oxford University Press.

Wessel, Anika, and Erich Kasten. 2014. "Body Piercing and Self-Mutilation: A Multifaceted Relationship." *American Journal of Applied Psychology* 3(4): 104–109.

West, Candace, and Don Zimmerman. 1987. "Doing Gender." *Gender & Society* 1: 125–151.

Westergaard, Ryan P., Mary Catherine Beach, Somnath Saha, and Elizabeth A. Jacobs. 2014. "Racial/Ethnic Differences in Trust in Health Care: HIV Conspiracy Beliefs and Vaccine Research Participation." *Journal of General Internal Medicine* 29(1): 140–146.

Western, Bruce, and Jake Rosenfeld. 2012. "Workers of the World Divide: The Decline of Labor and the Future of the Middle Class." *Foreign Affairs*, May/June.

Whaley, Floyd. 2012. "A Youthful Populace Helps Make the Philippines an Economic Bright Spot in Asia." *New York Times*, August 27.

Wharton, Amy S., and Mary Blair-Loy. 2006. "Long Work Hours and Family Life: A Cross-National Study of Employees' Concerns." *Journal of Family Issues* 27(3): 415–436.

White, James M. 2013. "The Current Status of Theorizing about Families." In *Handbook of Marriage and the Family*, 3rd ed., edited by G. W. Peterson and K. R. Bush, 11–38. New York: Springer.

Whitehead, John T. 2007. "Crime." In *The Blackwell Encyclopedia of Sociology*, edited by George Ritzer, 818–822. Malden, MA: Blackwell.

Whiteside, Alan. 2008. *A Very Short Introduction to HIV/AIDS*. Oxford: Oxford University Press.

Whiteside, Alan. 2012. "AIDS." In *The Wiley-Blackwell Encyclopedia of Globalization*, edited by George Ritzer, 45–49. Malden, MA: Wiley-Blackwell.

Whittier, Nancy. 2016. "Where Are the Children? Theorizing the Missing Piece in Gendered Sexual Violence." *Gender & Society* 30: 95–108.

Whitton, Sarah W., Scott M. Stanley, Howard J. Markman, and Christine A. Johnson. 2013. "Attitudes Toward Divorce, Commitment and Divorce Proneness in First Marriages and Remarriages." *Journal of Marriage and the Family* 75: 276–287.

Whyte, William Foote. 1943. *Street Corner Society: The Social Structure of an Italian Slum*. Chicago: University of Chicago.

Wiedenhoft Murphy, Wendy. 2017a. "Boycotts, Buycotts, and Legislation: Tactical Lessons from Workers and Consumers during the Progressive Era." In *Shopping for Social Change: Consumer Activism and the Possibilities of Purchasing Power*, edited by Louis Hyman and Joseph Tohill. Ithaca, NY: Cornell University Press.

Wiedenhoft Murphy, Wendy. 2017b. *Consumer Culture and Society*. Thousand Oaks, CA: Sage.

Wiederman, Michael W. 2015. "Sexual Script Theory: Past, Present and Future." In *Handbook of the Sociology of Sexualities*, edited by John DeLemater and Rebecca F. Plante, 7–22. New York: Springer:.

Wiegner, Lilian, Dominique Hange, Cecilia Björkelund, and Gunnar Ahlborg Jr. 2015. "Prevalence of Perceived Stress and Associations to Symptoms of Exhaustion, Depression and Anxiety in a Working Age Population Seeking Primary Care—An Observational Study." *BMC Family Practice* 16.

Wieringa, Saskia and Horacio Sívori. 2013. "Sexual Politics in the Global South: Framing the Discourse." In *The Sexual History of the Global South*, edited by S. Wieringa and H. Sívori, 1–21. New York: Zed Books.

Wight, Vanessa R. 2007. "Demography." In *The Blackwell Encyclopedia of Sociology*, edited by George Ritzer, 1038–1045. Malden, MA: Blackwell.

Wiklund, Maria, Carita Bengs, Eva-Britt Malmgren-Olsson, and Ann Öhman. 2010. "Young Women Facing Multiple and Intersecting Stressors of Modernity, Gender Orders and Youth." *Social Science Medicine* 71(9): 1567–1575.

Wilk, Kenneth Aarskaug, Eva Bernhardt, and Turid Noack. 2010. "Love or Money? Marriage Intentions among Young Cohabitors in Norway and Sweden." *Acta Sociologica* 53: 269–287.

Williams, Christine L. 1995. *Still a Man's World*. Berkeley: University of California Press.

Williams, Christine L. 2006. *Inside Toyland: Working, Shopping, and Social Inequality*. Berkeley: University of California Press.

Williams, Christine L. 2013. "The Glass Escalator, Revisited: Gender Inequality in Neoliberal Times." *Gender & Society* 27: 609–629.

Williams, Christine L., Chandra Muller, and Kristine Kilanski. 2012. "Gendered Organizations in the New Economy." *Gender & Society* 26: 549–573.

Williams, Christine L., and Laura Sauceda. 2007. "Gender, Consumption and." In *The Blackwell Encyclopedia of Sociology*, edited by George Ritzer, 1848–1852. Malden, MA: Blackwell.

Williams, David R. 1999. "Race, Socioeconomic Status, and Health: The Added Effects of Racism and Discrimination." *Annals of the New York Academy of Sciences* 896: 173–188.

Williams, Frank P., and Marilyn D. McShane. 2007. "Lombroso, Cesare (1835–1909)." In *The Blackwell Encyclopedia of Sociology*, edited by George Ritzer, 2662–2663. Malden, MA: Blackwell.

Williams, Glyn, Paula Meth, and Katie Willis. 2014. *Geographies of Developing Areas: The Global South in a Changing World*. 2nd ed. New York: Routledge.

Williams, Joan. 2001. *Unbending Gender: Why Family and Work Conflict and What to Do about It*. New York: Oxford University Press.

Williams, Patrick, and Laura Chrisman, eds. 1994. *Colonial Discourse and Post-colonial Theory: A Reader*. New York: Columbia University Press.

Williams, Rosalind. [1982] 1991. *Dream Worlds: Mass Consumption in Late Nineteenth-Century France*. Berkeley: University of California Press.

Williams, Simon J. 2012. "Health and Medicine in the Information Age: Castells, Informationalism and the Network Society." In *Contemporary Theorists for Medical Sociology*, edited by G. Scambler, 167–192. London: Routledge.

Williams, Stacy J., Laura Pecenco, and Mary Blair-Loy. 2013. "Medical Professions: The Status of Women and Men." Center for Research on Gender in the Professions, University of California, San Diego. Accessed April 21, 2015. http://crgp.ucsd.edu/documents/GenderinMedicalProfessionsCaseStudy.pdf.

Williams, Timothy. 2016. "One Robber's 3 Life Sentences: '90s Legacy Fills Prisons Today." *New York Times*, July 4.

Williams, Victoria. 2014. "Foreign Aid." In *Encyclopedia Britannica*. Accessed April 21, 2015. http://www.britannica.com/EBchecked/topic/213344/foreign-aid.

Williamson, Oliver E. 1975. *Markets and Hierarchies: Analysis and Antitrust Implications*. New York: Free Press.

Williamson, Oliver E. 1985. *The Economic Institutions of Capitalism*. New York: Free Press.

Williamson, Vanessa, Theda Skocpol, and John Coggin. 2011. "The Tea Party and the Remaking of Republican Conservativism." *Perspectives on Politics* 9: 25–43.

Willis, Paul. 1977. *Learning to Labor: How Working Class Kids Get Working Class Jobs*. New York: Teachers College Press.

Willyard, Cassandra. 2014. "Malaria Vaccine, Destined for Africa, Seeks OK from Europe." *Nature Medicine* 20: 968–969.

Wilper, Andrew P., Steffie Woolhandler, Karen E. Lasser, Danny McCormick, David H. Bor, and David U. Himmelstein. 2009. "Health Insurance and Mortality in US Adults." *American Journal of Public Health* 99(12): 2289–2295.

Wilson, Bryan R. 1966. *Religion and Secular Society*. London: Watts.

Wilson, George, Vincent J. Roscigno, and Matt L. Huffman. 2013. "Public Sector Transformation, Racial Inequality, and Downward Occupational Mobility." *Social Forces* 91: 975–1006.

Wilson, James Q., and George Kelling. 1982. "The Police and Neighborhood Safety: Broken Windows." *Atlantic Monthly*, March, 29–38.

Wilson, Midge, and Kathy Russell. 1996. *Divided Sisters: Bridging the Gap between Black and White Women*. New York: Anchor Books.

Wilson, Stephen R. 1984. "Becoming a Yogi: Resocialization and Deconditioning as Conversion Processes." *Sociological Analysis* 45(4): 301–314.

Wilson, William Julius. 1978. *The Declining Significance of Race: Blacks and Changing American Institutions.* Chicago: University of Chicago Press.

Wilson, William Julius. 1997. *When Work Disappears: The World of the New Urban Poor.* New York: Vintage.

Wilterdink, Nico. 2007. "Inequality, Wealth." In *The Blackwell Encyclopedia of Sociology,* edited by George Ritzer, 2310–2313. Malden, MA: Blackwell.

Wimmer, Andreas. 2013. *Ethnic Boundary Making: Institutions, Power, Networks.* New York: Oxford University Press.

Winant, Howard. 2001. *The World Is a Ghetto: Race and Democracy since World War II.* New York: Basic Books.

Winchester, M. S., R. BeLue, T. Oni, U. Wittwer-Backofen, D. Deobagkar, H. Onya, T. A. Samuels, S. A. Matthews, C. Stone, and C. Airhihenbuwa. 2016. "The Pan-University Network for Global Health: Framework for Collaboration and Review of Global Health Needs." *Globalization and Health* 12. Accessed February 7, 2017. https://globalizationandhealth.biomedcentral.com/articles/10.1186/s12992-016-0151-2.

Wines, Michael. 2011. "Picking Brand Names in China Is a Business Itself." *New York Times,* November 11. Accessed April 1, 2012. http://www.nytimes.com/2011/11/12/world/asia/picking-brand-names-in-china-is-a-business-itself.html.

Wingfield, Nick. 2014a. "Feminist Critics of Video Games Facing Threats in 'Gamergate.'" *New York Times,* October 15.

Wingfield, Nick. 2014b. "In Games Like Minecraft, Tech Giants See More than Fun." *New York Times,* September 11.

Wingfield, Nick. 2014c. "Virtual Games Draw Real Crowds and Big Money." *New York Times,* August 31.

Wisman, Jon D. 2013. "Wage Stagnation, Rising Inequality, and the Financial Crisis of 2008." *Cambridge Journal of Economics* 37: 921–945.

Wolf, Naomi. [1991] 2002. *The Beauty Myth: How Images of Beauty Are Used against Women.* New York: Harper & Row.

Wolfers, Justin. 2015. "We Can't Blame a Few Rich People for Global Poverty." *New York Times,* January 28.

Wolff, Kristina. 2007. "Content Analysis." In *The Blackwell Encyclopedia of Sociology,* edited by George Ritzer, 776–779. Malden, MA: Blackwell.

Wood, Elizabeth Jean, and Dara Kay Cohen. 2015. "How to Counter Rape During War." *New York Times,* October 28.

Wood, Robert T. 2006. *Straightedge Youth: Complexity and Contradictions of a Subculture.* Syracuse, NY: Syracuse University Press.

Wood, Wendy, and Alice H. Eagly. 2015. "Two Traditions on Research on Gender Identity." *Sex Roles* 73: 461–473.

Woodruff, G., and David Premack. 1979. "Intentional Communication in the Chimpanzee: The Development of Deception." *Cognition* 7: 333–362.

Woodward, Bob. 2010. *Obama's Wars.* New York: Simon & Schuster.

Woolf, Steven H., and Laudan Y. Aron. 2013. "The US Health Disadvantage Relative to Other High-Income Countries: Findings from a National Research Council/Institute of Medicine Report." *Journal of the American Medical Association* 309(8): 771–772.

World Bank. 2015a. "Country and Lending Groups." Accessed January 31, 2017. https://datahelpdesk.worldbank.org/knowledgebase/articles/906519-world-bank-country-and-lending-groups.

World Bank. 2015b. "Urban Population (% of Total)." Accessed February 12, 2017. http://data.worldbank.org/indicator/SP.URB.TOTL.IN.ZS.

World Bank. 2016. "Health Expenditure, Total (% of GDP), 1995–2014." Accessed February 13, 2017. http://data.worldbank.org/indicator/SH.XPD.TOTL.ZS.

World Bank. n.d. "Fertility Rate, Total (Births per Woman)." data.worldbank.org/indicator/SP.DYN.TFRT.IN

World Economic Forum. 2016. *The Global Gender Gap Report 2015.* Geneva: Author.

World Health Organization. 2003. *World Health Report: Shaping the Future.* Geneva: Author.

World Health Organization. 2010a. "Tobacco Free Initiative: China Releases Its Global Adult Tobacco Survey Data." Accessed April 1, 2012. http://www.who.int/tobacco/surveillance/gats_china/en/index.html.

World Health Organization. 2010b. "World Health Report: Health Systems Financing: The Path to Universal Coverage." Accessed April 1, 2012. http://whqlibdoc.who.int/whr/2010/9789241564021_eng.pdf.

World Health Organization, 2014. "Adolescent Pregnancy: Fact Sheet," September. Accessed February 14, 2017. http://www.who.int/mediacentre/factsheets/fs364/en.

World Health Organization. 2015a. "Global Health Observatory (GHO) Data: Tuberculosis (TB)." http://www.who.int/gho/tb/epidemic/cases_deaths/en.

World Health Organization. 2015b. "Life Expectancy." Accessed March 9, 2017. http://www.who.int/gho/mortality_burden_disease/life_tables/situation_trends_text/en.

World Health Organization. 2015c. "Water Sanitation and Health." Accessed March 19, 2015. http://www.who.int/water_sanitation_health/mdg1/en.

World Health Organization. 2016. "Life Expectancy Increased by 5 Years Since 2000, but Health Inequalities Persist," May 19. Accessed March 8, 2017. http://www.who.int/mediacentre/news/releases/2016/health-inequalities-persist/en.

World Health Organization. 2017. "Tobacco Fact Sheet." www.who.int/mediacentre/factsheets/fs339/en.

Worldometers. 2015. "Current World Population." Accessed March 19, 2015. http://www.worldometers.info/world-population.

Worth, Robert F. 2016. *A Rage for Order: The Middle East in Turmoil, From Tahrir Square to ISIS.* New York: Farrar, Straus and Giroux.

Wortham, Jenna. 2013. "A Growing App Lets You See It, Then You Don't." *New York Times,* February 9.

Wortmann, Susan L. 2007. "Sex Tourism." In *The Blackwell Encyclopedia of Sociology,* edited by George Ritzer, 4200–4203. Malden, MA: Blackwell.

Wren, Anne. 2013. *The Political Economy of the Service Transition.* New York: Oxford University Press.

Wright, Katherine Fairfax, and Malika Zouhali-Worrall [directors]. 2012. *Call Me Kuchu.* Cinedigm and Docuramafilms.

Wright, Lawrence. 2013. *Going Clear: Scientology, Hollywood, and the Prison of Belief.* New York: Knopf.

Wu, Caiwei, Yongping Wei, and Mark Y. Wang. 2014. "Planned Gated Communities in Urban China." In *Transforming Chinese Cities,* edited by M. Y. Wang, P. Kee, and J. Gao, 189–201. New York: Routledge.

Wunder, Delores F. 2007. "Agents, Socialization of." In *The Blackwell Encyclopedia of Sociology,* edited by George Ritzer, 4566–4568. Malden, MA: Blackwell.

Wysocki, Diane Kholos, and Cheryl D. Childers. 2011. "'Let My Fingers Do the Talking': Sexting and Infidelity in Cyberspace." *Sexuality & Culture* 15: 217–239.

Yamamoto, Ryoko. 2012. "Undocumented Immigrants." In *The Wiley-Blackwell Encyclopedia of Globalization,* edited by George Ritzer, 1005–1008. Malden, MA: Wiley-Blackwell.

Yamane, David. 2007. "Civil Religion." In *The Blackwell Encyclopedia of Sociology,* edited by George Ritzer, 506–507. Malden, MA: Blackwell.

Yancy, George. 2008. *Black Bodies, White Gazes: The Continuing Significance of Race.* Lanham, MD: Rowman & Littlefield.

Yardley, Jim. 2010. "Soaring above India's Poverty, a 27-Story Single-Family Home." *New York Times,* October 29.

Yassky, David. 2016. "Unlocking the Truth About the Clinton Crime Bill." *New York Times,* April 10.

Yearley, Steve. 2007. "Globalization and the Environment." In *The Blackwell Companion to Globalization,* edited by George Ritzer, 239–253. Malden, MA: Blackwell.

Yeates, Nicola. 2009. *Globalizing Care Economies and Migrant Workers: Explorations in Global Care Chains.* New York: Palgrave Macmillan.

Yeates, Nicola. 2012. "Global Care Chains: A State-of-the-Art Review and Future Directions in Care Transnational Research." *Global Networks* 12(2): 135–154.

Yeginsu, Ceylan, and Anemona Hartocollis, 2015. "Amid Perilous Mediterranean Crossings, Migrants Find a Relatively Easy Path to Greece." *New York Times,* August 16.

Yeh, Kuang-Hui, Chin-Chun Yi, Wei-Chun Tsao, and Po-San Wan. 2013. "Filial Piety in Contemporary Chinese Societies: A Comparative Study of Taiwan, Hong Kong, and China." *International Sociology* 28: 277–296.

Yetman, Norman R., ed. 1991. *Majority and Minority: The Dynamics of Race and Ethnicity in American Life.* 5th ed. Boston: Allyn & Bacon.

Yeung, Wei-Jun J., and Kathryn M. Pfeiffer. 2009. "The Black–White Test Score Gap and Early Home Environment." *Social Science Research* 38: 412–437.

Yip, Jeaney, and Susan Ainsworth. 2014. "'We Aim to Provide Excellent Service to Everyone Who Comes to Church!': Marketing Megachurches in Singapore." *Social Compass* 60: 503–516.

Yodanis, Carrie, and Sean Lauer. 2014. "Is Marriage Individualized? What Couples Actually Do." *Journal of Family Theory and Review* 6: 184–197.

York, Richard, and Eugene A. Rosa. 2007. "Environment and Urbanization." In *The Blackwell Encyclopedia of Sociology,* edited by George Ritzer, 1423–1426. Malden. MA: Blackwell.

Yoshihara, Susan, and Douglas A. Sylva, eds. 2011. *Population Decline and the Remaking of Great Power Politics.* Washington, DC: Potomac Books.

Young, Michael, and Johan Muller, eds. 2014. *Knowledge Expertise and the Professions.* New York: Routledge.

Young, Robert L., and Carol Y. Thompson. 2013. "The Selves of Other Animals: Reconsidering Mead in Light of Multidisciplinary Evidence." *Studies in Symbolic Interaction* 40: 467–483.

Yuval-Davis, Nira. 2006. "Human/Women's Rights and Feminist Transversal Politics." In *Global Feminism: Transnational Women's Activism, Organizing, and Human Rights,* edited by M. M. Ferree and A. M. Tripp. New York: New York University Press.

Zafirovski, Milan. 2013. "Beneath Rational Choice: Elements of 'Irrational Choice Theory.'" *Current Sociology* 61: 3–21.

Zammuel, Elnat, Orna Sasson-Levy, and Guy Ben-Porat. 2014. "Voluntary Simplifiers as Political Consumers: Individuals Practicing Politics through Reduced Consumption." *Journal of Consumer Culture* 14: 199–217.

Zeiler, Kristin, and Annette Wickstrom. 2009. "Why Do 'We' Perform Surgery on Newborn Intersexed Children? The Phenomenology of the Parental Experience of Having a Child with Intersex Anatomies." *Feminist Theory* 10: 359–377.

Zellner, William W. 1995. *Counterculture: A Sociological Analysis.* New York: St. Martin's Press.

Zeni, Jane. 2007. "Ethics, Fieldwork." In *The Blackwell Encyclopedia of Sociology,* edited by George Ritzer, 1442–1447. Malden. MA: Blackwell.

Zepp, Ira G., Jr. 1997. *The New Religious Image of Urban America: The Shopping Mall as Ceremonial Center.* 2nd ed. Niwot: University Press of Colorado.

Zerelli, Sal. 2007. "Socialization." In *The Blackwell Encyclopedia of Sociology,* edited by George Ritzer, 4558–4563. Malden, MA: Blackwell.

Zhang, Yang, and Michael John Hitchcock. 2014. "The Chinese Female Tourist Gaze: A Netnography of Young Women's Blogs on Macao." *Current Issues in Tourism,* June 9 (published online). doi: 10.1080/13683500.2014.904845.

Zhou, Min. 2009. *Contemporary Chinese America: Immigration, Ethnicity, and Community Transformation.* Philadelphia: Temple University Press.

Zhou, Min. 2014. "Segmented Assimilation and Socio-economic Integration of Chinese Immigrant Children in the USA." *Ethnic and Racial Studies* 37: 1172–1183.

Zhou, Yanqui Rachel, and William D. Coleman. 2016. "Accelerated Contagion and Response: Understanding the Relationship Among Globalization, Time and Disease" *Globalizations* 13: 285–299.

Zhuge, Ying, Joyce Kaufman, Diane M. Simeone, Herbert Chen, and Omaida C. Velazquez. 2011. "Is There Still a Glass Ceiling for Women in Academic Surgery?" *Annals of Surgery* 253: 637–643.

Ziemke, Jen. 2012. "Crisis Mapping: The Construction of a New Interdisciplinary Field?" *Journal of Map and Geography Libraries* 8: 191–117.

Zilberfarb, Ben-Zion. 2005. "From Socialism to Free Market: The Israeli Economy, 1948–2003." *Israel Affairs* 11: 12–22.

Zimbardo, Philip. 1973. "On the Ethics of Intervention in Human Psychological Research: With Special Reference to the Stanford Prison Experiment." *Cognition* 2: 243–256.

Zimmer, Ron, and Richard Buddin. 2009. "Is Charter School Competition in California Improving the Performance of Traditional Public Schools?" *Public Administration Review* 69(5): 831–845.

Zimmerman, Don H. 1988. "On Conversation: The Conversation Analytic Perspective." In *Communication Yearbook 11,* edited by James A. Anderson, 406–432. Newbury Park, CA: Sage.

Zimring, Franklin E. 2011. *The City That Became Safe: New York's Lessons for Urban Crime and Its Control.* New York: Oxford University Press.

Zinn, Maxine Baca. 2012. "Patricia Hill Collins: Past and Future Innovations." *Gender & Society* 26: 28–32.

Zippel, Kathrin. 2007. "Sexual Harassment." In *The Blackwell Encyclopedia of Sociology,* edited by George Ritzer, 4233–4234. Malden, MA: Blackwell.

Ziyanak, Sebahattin, and James L. Williams. 2014. "Functionalist Perspectives on Deviance." *International Journal of Human Sciences* 11: 1–9.

Zuberi, An. 2013. *Cleaning Up: How Hospital Outsourcing Is Hurting Workers and Endangering Patients.* Ithaca, NY: Cornell University Press.

Zuev, Dennis. 2015. "The Internet and Consumption." In *Encyclopedia of Consumption and Consumer Studies,* edited by Daniel Thomas Cook and Michael Ryan, 368–372. Malden, MA: Wiley-Blackwell.

Zukin, Sharon. 1982. *Loft Living: Culture and Capital in Urban Change.* Baltimore: Johns Hopkins University Press.

Zukin, Sharon. 2004. *Point of Purchase: How Shopping Changed American Culture.* New York: Routledge.

INDEX

Deforestation, 494–495
Deindustrialization, 424–427
Deinstitutionalization of marriage, 326–328
Democracy, 410–411
Democracy in America (Tocqueville), 88
Demographers, 472
Demographic transition theory, 476–478
Demography, 472
Denmark, 233–234
Dependent variable, 69
Deprofessionalization of health care, 450–451
Descriptive statistics, 61
Descriptive survey, 67
Desertification, 496
Desmond, Matthew, 226
Deviance:
  broken windows theory, 181–182
  conflict/critical theories, 183–184
  conformists, 179
  constructionist theories of, 178
  consumption and, 174–177
  criminalization process, 172
  defined, 172–174
  discreditable stigma, 188
  discredited stigma, 188
  drug use, 173–174, 175, 176, 177 (figure), 186
  economic inequality and, 174–175, 183–184
  elite and, 184
  explanatory theories of, 177–178
  folk devil, 187
  global context, 173, 174, 176
  homosexuality as, 173, 174, 178
  innovators, 179
  inter/actionist theories, 184–188
  labeling theory, 185–186
  media portrayal, 173, 179, 188
  moral panic, 186–187
  positive deviance, 188
  primary deviance, 186
  rebels, 179
  retreatists, 179
  ritualists, 179
  rule creators, 186
  rule enforcers, 186
  secondary deviance, 186
  self-control, 182
  social control, 186
  social control agents, 185
  social control theory, 180–181
  stigma, 187–188
  strain theory, 178–180
  structural/functional theories, 178–182
  study guide, 171, 199–200
  symbols, 185
  theoretical perspectives, 177–188
DeVinney, L. C., 65
DeVos, Betsy, 427

Diagnostic and Statistical Manual of Mental Disorders (DSM), 515
Diaspora, 282, 417
Dictatorship, 411–412
Differential association theory, 189
Digital divide, 237–239
Digital Millennium Copyright Act (1998), 196
Digital native, 130
Digital piracy, 196
Digital technology:
  Bitcoin, 164, 207
  collective action role, 523–524
  copyleft movement, 108
  crime impact, 196
  crisis mapping, 523
  cultural aspects of, 95–96, 106, 108, 109
  cyberactivism, 528–531
  cyberattack, 16
  cyberbullying, 109
  cybercrime, 195
  cyberculture, 108
  cyberfeminism, 511–512
  digital native, 130
  digital piracy, 196
  education impact, 362
  family impact, 333, 336
  free labor, 4, 46
  gender and sexuality, 295, 304
  gender-swapping, 295
  global information economy, 156, 157
  in global relationships, 161, 162, 164, 167
  hackers, 95–96, 159, 412
  hacking, 412
  health care impact, 453, 458–459
  information age, 3–4
  massive open online courses (MOOCs), 362
  netnography, 64
  new language development, 91
  online dating, 333
  open-source software, 97, 108
  organizational impact, 141–142, 148, 152, 153 (photo), 154, 156, 157
  political impact, 412
  racial cyberspace, 269
  self-development role, 121, 123
  sexuality impact, 311
  sharing economy, 213
  smart cities, 500
  social change impact, 528–531
  social interaction impact, 130, 134
  social isolation of, 121
  socialization impact, 126–127
  social movement impact, 511–512, 521
  social stratification, global, 237–239, 241, 242
  social stratification, United States, 207, 213

  in sociological research, 64, 67, 70
  sociological study of, 5, 13–15
  telemedicine, 453
  virtual faith, 389
  viruses, 164, 528
  voluntariat, 46
  See also Internet; Internet resources; Social networking sites; *specific platform/technology*
Dimon, Jamie, 186
Direct democracies, 410
Disasters, 524–526
Discouraged workers, 429–430
Discreditable stigma, 188
Discredited stigma, 188
Discrimination, 267–268, 284
Disease, 239, 240–241, 441 (figure), 460, 462–465
Disney World, 433
Distinction, 228
Divergent (2014), 119
Division of Labor in Society, The (Durkheim), 34–35
Divorce, 345–346
DNA testing, 459
Domestic violence, 343–344, 345
Domestic workers (Kuwait), 246
Domination, 144
Double consciousness, 37–38
Downward mobility, 220
Dramaturgy, 119
Dreeben, Robert, 356
Drugs:
  arrests by race (1980–2009), 177 (figure)
  crime and, 198–199
  deviance and, 173–174, 175, 176, 177 (figure), 186
  drug dealers, 179
  global context, 176, 197, 198–199
  medical marijuana, 439–440
  See also *specific drug*
Du Bois, W. E. B.:
  literature, 36, 37, 62, 65
  photo, 36
  sociological theory of, 36–38
Dude, You're a Fag (Pascoe), 308
Duke, David, 47
Duncan, Dan, 214
Duneier, Mitch, 362
Dunham, Lena, 85–86
Durkheim, Émile:
  on education, 355–356
  photo, 33
  on religion, 382–383, 395–396
  sociological theory of, 33 (photo), 34–35, 178
Duty (Gates), 148
Dyad relationship, 133
Dysfunctions, 40